W9-BCK-996

Encyclopedia of Small Business

THIRD EDITION

Encyclopedia of Small Business

THIRD EDITION

VOLUME II
J–Z

Arsen J. Darnay
Monique D. Magee

EDITORS

Detroit • New York • San Francisco • New Haven, Conn. • Waterville, Maine • London

THOMSON

GALE

Encyclopedia of Small Business, Third Edition

Arsen J. Darnay and Monique D. Magee, Editors

Project Editor
Virgil L. Burton III

Editorial
Julie Gough
Sonya D. Hill
Kristen Peltonen

Composition and Electronic Prepress
Evi Seoud

Manufacturing
Rita Wimberley

For permission to use material from this product, submit your request via Web at http://www.gale-edit.com/permissions, or you may download our Permissions Request form and submit your request by fax or mail to:

Permissions Department
Thomson Gale
27500 Drake Rd.
Farmington Hills, MI 48331-3535

Permissions Hotline:
248-699-8006 or 800-877-4253, ext. 8006
Fax: 248-699-8074 or 800-762-4058

Since this page cannot legibly accommodate all copyright notices, the acknowledgments constitute and extension of the copyright notice.

While every effort has been made to ensure the reliability of the information presented in this publication, Thomson Gale does not guarantee the accuracy of the data contained herein. Thomson Gale accepts no payment for listing; and inclusion in the publication of any organization, agency, institution, publication, service, or individual does not imply endorsement of the editors or publisher. Errors brought to the attention of the publisher and verified to the satisfaction of the publisher will be corrected in future editions.

LIBRARY OF CONGRESS CATALOGING-IN-PUBLICATION DATA

Encyclopedia of small business / Arsen J. Darnay, Monique D. Magee, editors. -- 3rd ed.
p. cm.
Rev. ed. of: Encyclopedia of small business / Kevin Hillstrom, Laurie Collier Hillstrom. 2nd ed. © 2002
Includes bibliographical references and index.
ISBN-13: 978-0-7876-9112-7 (set hardcover : alk. paper) --
ISBN-10: 0-7876-9112-7 (set hardcover : alk. paper) --
ISBN-13: 978-0-7876-9113-4 (vol. 1 hardcover : alk. paper) --
ISBN-10: 0-7876-9113-5 (vol. 1 hardcover : alk. paper) --
[etc.]
1. Small business--Management--Encyclopedias. 2. Small business--Finance--Encyclopedias.
I. Darnay, Arsen. II. Magee, Monique D. III. Hillstrom, Kevin, 1963– .

HD62.7.H553 2007
658.02'2--dc22   2006022623

ISBN-13:
978-0-7876-9112-7 (set)
978-0-7876-9113-4 (vol. 1)
978-0-7876-9114-1 (vol. 2)

ISBN-10:
0-7876-9112-7 (set)
0-7876-9113-5 (vol. 1)
0-7876-9114-3 (vol. 2)

This title is also available as an e-book
ISBN-13: 978-1-4144-1040-1, ISBN-10: 1-4144-1040-9
Contact your Thomson Gale sales representative for ordering information.
Printed in the United States of America

10 9 8 7 6 5 4 3 2

Contents

VOLUME 1, A–I

Absenteeism 1
Accelerated Cost Recovery System
  (ACRS) 3
Accounting 4
Accounting Methods 8
Accounts Payable 9
Accounts Receivable 11
Activity-Based Costing 12
Advertising Agencies 14
Advertising Budget 17
Advertising, Evaluation of Results 20
Advertising Media—Audio 22
Advertising Media—Infomercials 23
Advertising Media—Internet 24
Advertising Media—Print 25
Advertising Media—Video 27
Advertising Strategy 28
Affirmative Action 29
Age Discrimination 32
Age Discrimination in Employment Act 35
AIDS in the Workplace 37
Alien Employees 38
Alternative Dispute Resolution (ADR) 41
Americans with Disabilities Act (ADA) 43
Amortization 46
"Angel" Investors 47
Annual Percentage Rate (APR) 48
Annual Reports 49
Annuities 52
Application Service Providers 55
Apprenticeship Programs 56
Articles of Incorporation 57

Assembly Line Methods 58
Assets 59
Assumptions 61
Audits, External 62
Audits, Internal 65
Automated Guided Vehicle (AGV) 70
Automated Storage and Retrieval Systems (AS/RS) . . 71
Automation 72
Automobile Leasing 75
Baby Bonds 77
Balance Sheet 78
Bankruptcy 79
Banks and Banking 82
Banner Advertisements 84
Bar Coding 86
Barriers to Market Entry 87
Bartering 88
Benchmarking 89
Best Practices 90
Better Business Bureaus (BBBs) 92
Biometrics 93
Blue Chip 95
Board of Directors 96
Bonds 98
Bookkeeping 99
Boundaryless 100
Brainstorming 101
Brand Equity 102
Brands and Brand Names 103
Break-Even Analysis 105
Budget Deficit 106
Budget Surplus 107
Budgets and Budgeting 108

Business Appraisers. 110
Business Associations 111
Business Brokers. 112
Business Cycles 114
Business Education. 117
Business Ethics. 118
Business Expansion. 120
Business Failure and Dissolution 122
Business Hours. 124
Business Incubators 125
Business Information Sources 127
Business Insurance 129
Business Interruption Insurance 133
Business Name. 134
Business Plan. 135
Business Planning. 137
Business Proposals 139
Business Travel 141
Business-to-Business 143
Business-to-Business Marketing 145
Business-to-Consumer. 148
Buying an Existing Business 150
C Corporation 155
Capital 158
Capital Gain/Loss. 160
Capital Structure 161
Career and Family 162
Career Planning and Changing 165
Cash Conversion Cycle. 167
Cash Flow Statement 168
Cash Management 170
Casual Business Attire. 171
Census Data 173
Certified Lenders 175
Certified Public Accountants. 175
Chambers of Commerce 177
Charitable Giving. 178
Child Care. 180
Children's Online Privacy Protection
    Act (COPPA) 183
Choosing a Small Business 185
Clean Air Act. 187
Clean Water Act 189
Closely Held Corporations 190
Clusters. 191
Code of Ethics. 194
Collateral. 196
Collegiate Entrepreneurial
    Organizations 197
Communication Systems. 198
Community Development
    Corporations 202
Community Relations. 203

Comp Time. 205
Competitive Analysis 206
Competitive Bids 207
Comprehensive Environmental
    Response Cleanup and
    Liability Act (CERCLA) 209
Computer Applications. 211
Computer Crimes 214
Computer-Aided Design (CAD)
    and Computer-Aided
    Manufacturing (CAM) 217
Computers and Computer Systems 219
Consolidated Omnibus Budget
    Reconciliation Act (COBRA). 222
Construction 225
Constructive Discharge 226
Consultants 228
Consulting. 231
Consumer Advocacy. 234
Consumer Price Index (CPI). 235
Consumer Product Safety Commission
    (CPSC) 236
Contracts. 237
Cooperative Advertising 239
Cooperatives 241
Copyright 243
Corporate Culture 247
Corporate Image 249
Corporate Logo 251
Corporate Sponsorship 252
Cost Control and Reduction 254
Cost Sharing 257
Cost-Benefit Analysis 258
Costs. 260
Coupons 263
Credit 264
Credit Bureaus. 268
Credit Card Financing 270
Credit Evaluation and Approval. 271
Credit History 274
Crisis Management. 275
Cross-Cultural/International
    Communication 278
Cross-Functional Teams 281
Cross-Training. 285
Customer Retention 287
Customer Service 288
Data Encryption. 291
Database Administration. 293
Day Trading 296
Debt Collection 298
Debt Financing 300
Decision Making 303
Decision Support Systems. 306
Delegation. 308

Delivery Services 311
Demographics 312
Depreciation 313
Desktop Publishing 315
Difficult Customers 318
Difficult Employees 320
Direct Mail 322
Direct Marketing 325
Direct Public Offerings. 329
Disability Insurance 331
Disabled Customers 333
Disaster Assistance Loans 335
Disaster Planning 337
Discount Sales 339
Discounted Cash Flow 342
Discretionary Income 344
Distribution Channels. 345
Distributorships and Dealerships 347
Diversification 350
Dividends 352
Dot-coms 353
Double Taxation 355
Downloading Issues 356
Drug Testing 359
Due Diligence 361
Economic Order Quantity (EOQ) 363
Economies of Scale. 364
Economies of Scope 366
8(a) Program 367
Elasticity 370
Eldercare 371
Electronic Bulletin Boards. 373
Electronic Data Interchange 374
Electronic Mail 376
Electronic Tax Filing 378
Emerging Markets 379
Employee Assistance Programs. 381
Employee Benefits 384
Employee Compensation. 386
Employee Hiring 388
Employee Leasing Programs 392
Employee Manuals. 394
Employee Motivation 395
Employee Performance Appraisals 397
Employee Privacy. 400
Employee References 402
Employee Registration Procedures 403
Employee Reinstatement. 404
Employee Retention 405
Employee Retirement Income
   Security Act (ERISA). 406
Employee Reward and Recognition
   Systems 407
Employee Rights 410

Employee Screening Programs. 412
Employee Stock Ownership
   Plans (ESOPs) 413
Employee Strikes 415
Employee Suggestion Systems 417
Employee Termination 419
Employee Theft 422
Employer Identification Number
   (EIN). 423
Employment Applications 424
Employment Contracts. 425
Employment Interviews. 427
Employment of Minors. 429
Employment Practices Liability
   Insurance 432
Empowerment Zones 433
Endorsements and Testimonials. 435
Enterprise Resource Planning (ERP) 437
Entrepreneurial Couples 440
Entrepreneurial Networks 442
Entrepreneurship 444
Environmental Audit 447
Environmental Law and Business. 449
Environmental Protection
   Agency (EPA). 451
Equal Employment Opportunity
   Commission 453
Equipment Leasing. 454
Equity Financing 456
Ergonomics 458
Estate Tax 460
European Union (EU) 462
Expense Accounts. 464
Export-Import Bank. 465
Exporting 467
Exporting—Financing and Pricing. 470
Facility Layout and Design 473
Facility Management 475
Factoring 478
Family Limited Partnership. 480
Family and Medical Leave Act. 483
Family-Owned Businesses 485
Feasibility Study. 489
Federal Trade Commission (FTC). 490
FICA Taxes 492
Fiduciary Duty. 493
Finance Companies 495
Finance and Financial Management 496
Financial Analysis. 497
Financial Planners 499
Financial Ratios 501
Financial Statements. 504
Firewalls 507
Fiscal Year 509

Fixed and Variable Expenses 510
Flexible Benefit Plans 511
Flexible Spending Account (FSA). 513
Flexible Work Arrangements 514
Flow Charts. 517
Focus Groups 518
Forecasting 521
Fortune 500. 523
401(k) Plans 524
Franchising 526
Free-lance Employment/
    Independent Contractors 531
Gender Discrimination 533
Global Business 536
Globalization 539
Goodwill. 542
Government Procurement 543
Graphical User Interface 546
Green Marketing 546
Green Production. 549
Grievance Procedures 551
Groupthink 552
Groupware. 554
Health Insurance Options 557
Health Maintenance Organizations and
    Preferred Provider Organizations 561
Health Promotion Programs 563
High-Tech Business 564
Home Offices 566
Home-Based Business. 569
Hoteling 572
HTML 573
HUBZone Empowerment Contracting
    Program. 575
Human Resource Management 576
Human Resource Policies 580
Human Resources Management and
    the Law 582
Income Statements 585
Incorporation. 588
Individual Retirement Accounts (IRAs) 592
Industrial Safety 594
Industry Analysis 596
Industry Life Cycle. 598
Information Brokers 600
Initial Public Offerings 601
Innovation. 605
Insurance Pooling. 606
Intellectual Property 608
Intercultural Communication 609
Interest Rates. 611
Internal Revenue Service (IRS) 613
International Exchange Rate 615

Internet Domain Names. 616
Internet Payment Systems 617
Internet Security. 620
Internet Service Providers (ISPs) 622
Internships. 625
Interpersonal Communication 627
Intranet 629
Intrapreneurship. 632
Inventions and Patents 633
Inventory. 637
Inventory Control Systems 640
Investor Presentations 642
Investor Relations and Reporting. 644
IRS Audits. 646
ISO 9000 647

VOLUME 2, J–Z

Job Description 651
Job Sharing 653
Job Shop. 655
Joint Ventures 656
Keogh Plan 659
Labor Surplus Area. 661
Labor Unions. 662
Labor Unions and Small Business 666
Layoffs, Downsizing, and Outsourcing 669
Learning Curves. 671
Leasing Property. 672
Legal Services. 675
Letter of Intent 677
Leveraged Buyouts 678
Liabilities. 681
Licensing. 682
Licensing Agreements 684
Life Insurance 685
Limited Liability Company 687
Liquidation and Liquidation Values 689
Loan Proposals. 691
Loans 693
Local Area Networks (LANs). 696
Loss Leader Pricing. 699
Mailing Lists 701
Mail-Order Business. 703
Management Information Systems
    (MIS). 706
Management by Objectives 708
Manager Recruitment 710
Managing Organizational Change 711
Manufacturers' Agents 713
Market Analysis 715
Market Questionnaires 716
Market Research. 717
Market Segmentation 720

Market Share 723
Marketing 723
Markup 727
Material Requirements Planning
    (MRP) 728
Medicare and Medicaid 730
Meetings 732
Mentoring 735
Merchandise Displays 737
Mergers and Acquisitions 738
Metropolitan Statistical Area (MSA) 740
Mezzanine Financing 741
Minimum Wage 743
Minority Business Development
    Agency 744
Minority-Owned Businesses 745
Mission Statement 748
Mobile Office 749
Modem 751
Money Market Instruments 752
Multicultural Work Force 753
Multilevel Marketing 756
Multiple Employer Trust 757
Multitasking 758
Myers-Briggs Type Indicator (MBTI) 759
Mystery Shopping 760
National Association of Small Business
    Investment Companies (NASBIC) 763
National Association of Women
    Business Owners 764
National Business Incubation
    Association (NBIA) 765
National Labor Relations Board
    (NLRB) 766
National Venture Capital Association
    (NVCA) 767
Negotiation 768
Nepotism 770
Net Income 772
Net Worth 773
Networking 773
New Economy 775
Newsgroups and Blogs 776
Non-Competition Agreements 778
Nonprofit Organizations 780
Nonprofit Organizations, and Human
    Resources Management 785
Nonprofit Organizations, and Taxes 788
Nonqualified Deferred Compensation
    Plans 791
Nontraditional Financing Sources 793
Nonverbal Communication 795
North American Free Trade
    Agreement (NAFTA) 795

North American Industry Classification
    System (NAICS) 798
Occupational Safety and Health
    Administration (OSHA) 803
Office Automation 807
Office Romance 809
Office Security 811
Office Supplies 815
Online Auctions 815
Operations Management 819
Opportunity Cost 821
Optimal Firm Size 822
Oral Communication 823
Organization Chart 824
Organization Theory 826
Organizational Behavior 829
Organizational Development 830
Organizational Growth 833
Organizational Life Cycle 834
Organizational Structure 836
Original Equipment
    Manufacturer (OEM) 838
Outsourcing 839
Overhead Expense 841
Overtime 842
Packaging 845
Partnership 847
Partnership Agreement 850
Part-Time Business 851
Part-Time Employees 853
Patent and Trademark Office (PTO) 855
Payroll Taxes 856
Penetration Pricing 859
Pension Plans 860
Per Diem Allowances 862
Personal Selling 863
Physical Distribution 865
Point-of-Sale Systems 867
Portability of Benefits 868
Postal Costs 869
Pregnancy in the Workplace 871
Present Value 873
Press Kits 874
Press Releases 875
Price/Earnings (P/E) Ratio 876
Pricing 877
Private Labeling 880
Private Placement of Securities 882
Privatization 883
Pro Forma Statements 885
Probationary Employment Periods 889
Product Costing 890
Product Development 891
Product Liability 894

Product Life Cycle 896
Product Positioning 898
Productivity 900
Professional Corporations 902
Profit Center 904
Profit Impact of Market Strategies
    (PIMS) 905
Profit Margin 906
Profit Sharing 907
Program Evaluation and Review
    Technique (PERT) 909
Promissory Notes 910
Proprietary Information 911
Prototype 912
Proxy Statements 914
Public Relations 914
Purchasing 918
Quality Circles 923
Quality Control 925
Racial Discrimination 929
Rebates 932
Reciprocal Marketing 933
Record Retention 934
Recruiting 936
Recycling 938
Reengineering 940
Refinancing 942
Regulation D 943
Regulatory Flexibility Act 944
Relocation 946
Remanufacturing 948
Renovation 950
Request for Proposal 951
Research and Development 953
Résumés 956
Retail Trade 958
Retirement Planning 959
Return on Assets (ROA) 963
Return on Investment (ROI) 964
Return Policies 965
Revenue Streams 967
Right-to-Know (RTK) Laws 968
Risk Management 971
Risk and Return 973
Robotics 975
Royalties 977
Royalty Financing 981
Rural Businesses 982
S Corporation 985
Sales Commissions 987
Sales Contracts 989
Sales Force 990
Sales Forecasts 991
Sales Management 993

Sales Promotion 996
Sarbanes-Oxley 1000
Scalability 1003
Search Engines 1004
Seasonal Businesses 1006
SEC Disclosure Laws and Regulations 1008
Securities and Exchange
    Commission (SEC) 1011
Seed Money 1012
Self-Assessment 1014
Self-Employment 1015
Self-Employment Contributions Act
    (SECA) 1017
Selling a Business 1019
Seniority 1022
Service Businesses 1024
Service Corps of Retired Executives
    (SCORE) 1026
Sexual Harassment 1026
Shared Services 1030
Shoplifting 1031
Sick Leave and Personal Days 1032
Simplified Employee Pension (SEP)
    Plans 1034
Site Selection 1036
Small Business 1038
Small Business Administration 1041
Small Business Consortia 1045
Small Business Development Centers
    (SBDC) 1046
Small Business Innovation Research
    (SBIR) Program 1046
Small Business Investment Companies
    (SBIC) 1048
Small Business Job Protection Act 1050
Small Business/Large Business
    Relationships 1051
Small Business Technology Transfer
    (STTR) Program 1053
Small Business-Dominated Industries 1054
Small Claims Court 1056
Smoke Free Environment 1058
Sole Proprietorship 1060
Spam 1062
Span of Control 1064
Standard Mileage Rate 1066
Stocks 1067
Strategy 1071
Subcontracting 1073
Substance Abuse 1075
Succession Plans 1077
Supplier Relations 1079
Supply and Demand 1082
Sustainable Growth 1083

Syndicated Loans 1084
Target Markets. 1087
Tariffs. 1088
Tax Deductible Business Expenses 1089
Tax Planning 1093
Tax Preparation Software 1096
Tax Returns. 1097
Tax Withholding 1099
Telecommuting 1100
Telemarketing 1102
Temporary Employment Services. 1106
Testing Laboratories 1107
Toll-Free Telephone Numbers. 1110
Total Preventive Maintenance 1111
Total Quality Management (TQM). 1112
Trade Shows 1114
Trademarks 1117
Training and Development 1120
Transaction Processing 1124
Transportation. 1125
Transportation of Exports. 1127
Tuition Assistance Programs 1129
Undercapitalization. 1131
Underwriters Laboratories (UL). 1132
Uniform Commercial Code (UCC) 1133
U.S. Chamber of Commerce 1135
U.S. Department of Commerce. 1135

U.S. Small Business Administration
    Guaranteed Loans 1136
Valuation. 1141
Value-Added Tax 1144
Variable Pay. 1145
Variance 1146
Venture Capital 1147
Venture Capital Networks. 1150
Vertical Marketing System 1152
Virtual Private Networks. 1152
Virus. 1155
Warranties 1157
Web Site Design 1159
Wholesaling. 1161
Wide Area Networks (WANs) 1163
Women Entrepreneurs 1164
Work for Hire 1165
Workers' Compensation 1166
Workplace Anger 1168
Workplace Safety 1171
Workplace Violence 1174
Workstation. 1176
Written Communication. 1178
Young Entrepreneurs' Organization
    (YEO) 1181
Zoning Ordinances. 1183

Index 1185

J

JOB DESCRIPTION

A job description is the official written account of an employment position. It is a structured and factual statement of a job's functions and objectives, and should give the boundaries of the position holder's authority. This account usually lists the typical tasks to be performed by the position holder, the training, education, and experience required to do the work, and it includes a description of the essential functions to be performed. Job descriptions also include information about salary ranges and any benefits that are offered to employees in the position. In many cases a job description also outlines how the position fits into a larger organizational whole. The term job specification is often used as a synonym for job description.

Recruiters and personnel managers rely on clear and concise job descriptions to streamline the application and interviewing process and to judge work performance after a person has been hired. Job descriptions and specifications usually include, in addition to the basic items listed above, details about:

- The position's travel obligations
- Normal work schedule
- Physical location where duties will be carried out
- Union status, if any
- Supervisory relationships
- Bonuses that may be earned and how they may be earned

In essence, effective job descriptions let employees know what is expected of them. If a person is to perform her assigned task she needs to know what it is, how to do it, and how to measure the results. All of these directives should be discernable from the job description.

Job descriptions can be useful in organizing and assessing the work being done at all levels of an organization. They are not useful only in the recruiting process. As the authors of a Charters Management Institute article explain, apart from giving the job holder and immediate line manager a clear overall view of a position, job descriptions can serve as the basis upon which to carry out performance appraisals and job evaluations. They can also help to identify any duplication or absence of particular functions or activities within an organization.

JOB DESCRIPTIONS AND COMPANY CULTURE

The level of detail utilized in the creation of job descriptions and the monitoring of employee execution of the duties articulated therein can vary tremendously from organization to organization. A multinational corporation, for example, may have job descriptions that are far more formal and detailed in their contents than those used by a small local business. Companies in different industries tend to approach the issue of job descriptions differently as well (tool and die manufacturers, for example, are more likely to institute job definitions for various positions than are fishing charter services). And, finally, some business owners and management teams simply institute and nourish different company cultures that may have dramatically different conceptions of job descriptions and their utility. For example, companies that operate in a flexible working environment, one in which employee roles are fluid and expectations change, may find the quest to define various job parameters to be daunting. The essence of the problem is how to reconcile clear directives with flexible work systems. One approach to solving this problem is for a manager to write a theoretical job description for how he or she sees the work being done. Then, those involved in actually doing this work can edit the description as needed in order to fine tune the description to the realities of the work environment.

But researchers note that on the whole, larger organizations will often, out of either real or imagined necessity, institute more formalized job description/monitoring procedures. Still, in many companies with detailed plans in this area, job descriptions are often thought of as necessary for only the lower-level people within the organization. Managerial positions usually come with what are called 'mission statements' and while this sounds very good, mission statements made a very poor gauge against which to actually measure anything. Most human resource experts suggest that all positions within a company should include a job description. These documents can help business enterprises maintain their focus at all job levels, including top management and ownership positions. Owners of family establishments or very small business enterprises, meanwhile, may simply decide that formal job descriptions are unnecessary. Ultimately, each small business owner needs to consider the unique aspects of his or her own business situation when deciding how to define and monitor the responsibilities of each work position.

JOB DESCRIPTIONS AND PERFORMANCE APPRAISALS

The many advantages of having formal job descriptions for all positions within a company should not blind business owners to the need for consistency between what is stated in a job description and what is stated in the personnel policies of the company. The existence, for example, in a job description of details about how overtime pay will be handled must mirror the overtime descriptions in the personnel policy if a company is to avoid the potential for legal troubles.

Performance Reviews Annual or semi-annual performance reviews are fixtures in most establishments, and they are useful to both employee and employer for many reasons. But employers should know that they can also run into trouble here if they give an employee poor marks for their work on tasks that are not delineated in

their official job description. A company may be at legal risk if it holds employees responsible for work that has not been defined in writing. This problem is most likely to crop up in situations where a reorganization or attrition has prompted a reallocation of responsibilities within the organization. Of course, bestowing praise on an individual who takes on responsibilities not mentioned within his or her job description is unlikely to have unwanted repercussions. The key is to avoid linking negative outcomes (such as discipline or denial of a raise) to duties that are not included on the job description or to unduly focus on those duties at the expense of those responsibilities that are specifically mentioned.

Overtime As most employers are aware, federal law differentiates between employees who are owed overtime pay (non-exempt employees) and those who are not owed overtime pay (exempt employees). Exempt positions are excluded from minimum wage, overtime regulations, and other rights and protections afforded under the provisions of the Fair Labor Standards Act (FLSA). Employers must pay a salary rather than an hourly wage for a position for it to be exempt. Non-exempt positions are those that are not exempt from FLSA requirements. Employees who fall within this category must be paid at least the federal minimum wage for each hour worked and are paid overtime pay of not less than one and a half times their hourly rate for any hours worked beyond 40 each week.

What many employers do not know is that overtime liability can be linked to an employee's duties *as they are described in his or her job description,* not according to what tasks the employee actually performs. For example, suppose you decide that one of your managers' should occupy and office closer to the production department. If that manager comes in to pack or move boxes over the weekend, the employer may be liable for overtime—even if the employee is exempt—because packing and moving are not part of the employee's usual job activities. This principle applies to any tasks not normally performed by the employee, or to tasks that are not directly related to his or her normal job. The important issue to consider isn't whether the activity is a one-time event, but whether the task relates to the employee's usual job duties.

Employee Dismissals Small business owners that decide to terminate an employee for poor performance have to make sure that they are doing so because of their dissatisfaction with the targeted employee's work on tasks that are discussed in the job description. Otherwise, the employ may have some legal basis upon which to challenge the dismissal.

USING AND MAINTAINING JOB DESCRIPTIONS

Job descriptions can be valuable business resources when used correctly. But many companies do not take full advantage of these documents, either because they are ignorant of their possibilities or because of company-wide perceptions that they are of limited use. There are several factors that can limit the effectiveness of these documents:

- Managers unfamiliar with purpose and usage of job descriptions.

- Vague, inaccurate, outdated, or incomplete job descriptions.

- Managers not motivated to utilize job descriptions.

- Job descriptions arranged in format that is not standardized or friendly to managers or employees.

- Job in question "escapes definition" because of fluidity, variety of tasks, etc.

Entrepreneurs and managers, then, need to attend to all of these potential pitfalls when creating job descriptions for their workforce. In addition, human resource management experts hasten to point out that job descriptions are only effective if they are subject to continuous review and revision.

1. Continuous updating—Each employee's job description should be amended as his or her duties change. One commonly overlooked aspect of this requirement is that employers should react quickly when an employee quits or is terminated. In such instances, each task formerly carried out by the ex-employee should be formally reassigned in writing to another person's job description.

2. Proper classification—Employers who remain cognizant of job descriptions and classifications when assigning various tasks are far less likely to get tripped up on overtime hassles than businesses that are careless about such issues.

3. Communication—In addition to regularly scheduled performance reviews, employers should make sure that employees who find their duties and responsibilities undergoing change have the opportunity to ask questions--and even raise objections.

SEE ALSO *Employee Hiring; Human Resource Management; Organizational Chart*

BIBLIOGRAPHY
Kleiman, Carol. "Job Descriptions Too Often Fail Seeker and Hirer." *Chicago Tribune.* 24 January 2006.

"Preparing and Using Job Descriptions." *Chartered Management Institute: Checklists: Small Business.* October 2005.

"Reality Doesn't Have a Job Description." *Workforce.* December 1999.

Sutton, Gart. "Job Descriptions Keep Employees Focused." *Powersports Business.* 15 August 2005.

Willis, Ron. "Job Descriptions." *Masonry Construction.* November-December 2005.

Hillstrom, Northern Lights
updated by Magee, ECDI

JOB SHARING

Job sharing is a flexible work option in which two or possibly more employees share a single job. For example, one person may work in a certain position Monday and Tuesday, and a second person may occupy that same position Thursday and Friday. The two people may both work on Wednesday and use that time to update each other on the current status of the various projects on which they collaborate. A variety of other arrangements are possible as well.

Job sharing is a somewhat controversial alternative to telecommuting, flexible working hours, compressed work weeks, and other arrangements used by businesses to offer their employees more flexibility in terms of work schedules without increasing costs and while maintaining productivity. Job sharing is an option for employees who wish to work somewhat shorter hours. In many cases, a job sharing position doe require that the individuals involved are willing to be contacted during the work week even on days they do not work so that questions may be answered and the coordination between the two or more individuals sharing a position is maximized.

According to an article in the *Managing Benefits Plans* magazine, "Job sharing peaked in 2001 when 26 percent of companies offered it as a flexible work option, according to a recent report by the Society for Human Resource Management. The number of companies that permit job sharing dropped to 17 percent in 2004, and stood at 19 percent in 2005, the SHRM survey reported."

Job sharing offers small businesses a chance to retain valued employees who are either approaching retirement or starting families and would consider leaving if more flexible options were not made available. Job sharing can also help eliminate the need to train new employees if a valued employee were to leave the company. Job sharing can seem intimidating to managers, who may fear that it could lead to confusion, more paperwork, and a host of other hassles. If a proper plan is in place and each job sharer is held accountable for his or her duties, however, these issues can be avoided.

PLANNING A JOB SHARING POSITION

In order for a job-sharing program to succeed, a solid plan must be put in place to ensure that the work gets done properly. Managers must pay close attention to how the system is working. Solid communication between work partners and management, as well as other employees who are not in the job-sharing program, is a must. Done properly, job sharing can lead to a high level of productivity—perhaps even higher than the level contributed by a single, traditional employee.

The first step in implementing a job-sharing program is to decide whether the job can be shared and if there are likely candidates with whom to share it. Most often, these candidates already exist within the company, although potential job sharers can be recruited from the outside workforce. Jobs with clearly defined individual tasks are the best to consider for job-sharing. Those that are more complex have a tendency of failing under this type of arrangement. Above all, management has to be committed to the job-sharing program, as do the employees who are participating in it.

Several specific issues should be dealt with in advance of starting a job-sharing program. These include:

- Clarify how the salary for a position will be divided between the job sharers and how the hours will be covered.

- Determining how vacation and sick days will be divided between the participants.

- Establishing a division of employment benefits that provide both parties some coverage but does not cost the company twice the cost that it would bear for a single employee.

- Iron out the details about who will have responsibility for what elements of the work.

- Define how employment evaluation will be handled in advance so that the job sharers know how much of their evaluation will be based on the work product of the other job sharer.

Because of the need to work very closely with one another, job sharers should have a hand in deciding with whom they wish to share a job. According to the authors of the Managing Benefits Plans article, "Job sharers should find their own partners. It is up to the prospective job sharer, not the employer, to find a coworker who wants to share a job." They go one to explain that employers will need to be involved in this decision so that they can make sure that the job partners are at the same career level and are compatible. Finally, the job-sharing situation must benefit the company as well as the employees involved.

JOB SHARING AND EMPLOYEES

It is important to find partners in a job sharing position that have work styles, habits, preferences, quality standards, and communications skills that are compatible and closely matched. Many times, it can be advantageous if the employees select their own partners to ensure that these conditions are met. Most often it is important for employers to find job-sharing partners with comparable skill levels, but there are still possible benefits if they do not. For instance, a more experienced worker can train an up-and-coming employee in a job-sharing situation. When this happens, the employer can cut back on the time and money it would normally take to train the new employee, while also paying them a lower salary than the veteran worker during this time.

Employees who participate in job sharing divide their responsibilities in several different ways. They can share the job evenly or separate it into individual tasks that better suit each individual. If the job has unrelated tasks, those can also be divided. The work week can be split in half and shifts can be alternated so one employee works three days one week and two the next. Job sharing employees must be able to coordinate their schedules to make sure someone is always on the job when they are required to be.

THE ADVANTAGES OF JOB SHARING

It would seem that the one who benefits most from job sharing is the employee. This type of arrangement allows the employee to work part-time in order to spend more time with their families, attend school, or pursue other personal interests. New mothers find that it is a way to continue their careers while not having to deal with the stress and guilt that comes with putting their child in full-time day care. Experienced senior workers who wish to cut back a bit while still continuing their careers also benefit from job sharing, as do employees who wish to pursue more than one career opportunity at the same time. In addition, job sharing employees often find that this type of arrangement helps them to cut down on work-related stress and burnout.

Despite its often intimidating nature and the possibility for confusion, job sharing can also be seen as advantageous and desirable to small business owners and managers. First, there is the simple theory that two or more individual employees can bring a greater variety of abilities to the job than a single employee can. In some instances, job sharing can also lead to extended work days and therefore more productivity without having to pay employees overtime. Employers can also ask job sharers to work more during busy times, therefore eliminating the hassles of having to hire and train temporary employees.

HOW TO KEEP A SHARED JOB RUNNING SMOOTHLY

Employees who share a job have an arsenal of resources at their disposal to communicate with each other and ensure that the job is getting done. These resources include e-mail, phone and fax messages, checklists, and daily logs.

It is probably in the best interest of small business owners to conduct performance reviews of employees involved in a job-sharing program to ensure that things are going smoothly. These reviews can either be individual evaluations of each worker or take the form of a team review. If one person is carrying the weight of the team and the other is not doing his or her fair share, it is up to management to decide if this is just an isolated problem with that particular team or if the job-sharing program is just not a successful one for their business.

If a meeting that is pertinent to the job comes up, the employees and management must decide if both employees should attend or just one. It often helps if the job sharing employees who work on the same days are able to overlap their schedules in order to interact and keep things running as smoothly as possible.

Benefits for employees who participate in job-sharing can be handled in a variety of different ways. Full or partial benefits can be given to the job sharer according to the specific situation. Benefits such as insurance and pension plans are easier to negotiate and are often prorated. Vacation-time, personal and sick days, and even salary can also be prorated to the amount of time each employee spends on the job. As stated above, these issues should all be decided upon and agreed to by all parties before the job-sharing program is implemented. A guide or formal contract is suggested to make sure everyone involved understands these issues. Usually job sharing results in a slight increase in benefit costs, mainly in covered statutory benefits like Social Security and employment taxes. Small business owners must decide if the assumed increase in productivity is enough to offset these costs. Since job sharers work fewer hours then do typical employees, overtime pay is rarely an issue in these types of situations.

SEE ALSO *Flexible Work Arrangements*

BIBLIOGRAPHY
Arndt, Michael. "The Family That Flips Together..." *Business Week.* 17 April 2006.

Hirschman, Carolyn. "Share and Share Alike: Job sharing can boost productivity and help retain vital workers, but it can't work effectively without help from HR." *HRMagazine.* September 2005.

"Job Sharing: One Way to Hold on to Valued Employees." *Managing Benefits Plans.* January 2006.

Hillstrom, Northern Lights
updated by Magee, ECDI

JOB SHOP

A job shop is a type of manufacturing process in which small batches of a variety of custom products are made. In the job shop process flow, most of the products produced require a unique set-up and sequencing of process steps. Job shops are usually businesses that perform custom parts manufacturing for other businesses. However, examples of job shops include a wide range of businesses—a machine tool shop, a machining center, a paint shop, a commercial printing shop, and other manufacturers that make custom products in small lot sizes. These businesses deal in customization and relatively small production runs, not volume and standardization.

CHARACTERISTICS OF A JOB SHOP

Layout In the job shop, similar equipment or functions are grouped together, such as all drill presses in one area and grinding machines in another in a process layout. The layout is designed to minimize material handling, cost, and work in process inventories. Job shops use general purpose equipment rather than specialty, dedicated product-specific equipment. Digital numerically controlled equipment is often used to give job shops the flexibility to change set-ups on the various machines very quickly. Because economies of scale are usually not a part of a job shop's competitive edge, they compete on factors other than price. They compete on quality, speed of product delivery, customization, and new product introduction.

Routing When an order arrives in the job shop, the part being worked on travels throughout the various areas according to a sequence of operations. Not all jobs will use every machine in the plant. Jobs often travel in a jumbled routing and may return to the same machine for processing several times. This type of layout is also seen in services like department stores or hospitals, where areas are dedicated to one particular product (men's clothing) or one type of service (maternity ward).

Employees Employees in a job shop are typically highly skilled craft employees who can operate several different classes of machinery. These workers are paid higher wages for their skill levels. Due to their high skill level, job shop employees need less supervision. Workers may be paid a standard hourly wage or by an incentive system. The role of management is to bid on jobs and to establish prices for customer orders. The key activity in a job shop is processing information.

Information Information is the most critical aspect of a job shop. Information is needed to quote a price, bid on a job, route an order through the shop, and specify the exact work to be done. Information begins with quoting, then a job sheet and blueprint are prepared before the job is released to the floor. Once on the production floor, employees complete job sheets and time cards for labor cost calculations and to update records for quoting future jobs when variances are present.

While it is often easy to bid on jobs the shop has manufactured before, new jobs require accurate costing of labor, materials, and equipment as well as accurate assigning of overhead to the job. Tickets follow each job through the shop, where time and activities are recorded. Because the job shop makes specialty, custom items, it competes on quality and customer service and not on price. The job shop has little if any raw materials inventory because customers bring in the parts and materials to be worked on. The job shop has work-in-process inventory while jobs are being completed, but typically the customer is waiting on the order and expects prompt delivery, so there is no finished goods inventory in this make-to-order environment. Some job shops, like many small businesses, thrive on managing cash flow. They may work on small jobs to complete them by the end of the month so they can bill customers for the work.

Scheduling A job is characterized by its route, its processing requirements, and its priority. In a job shop the mix of products is a key issue in deciding how and when to schedule jobs. Jobs may not be completed based on their arrival pattern in order to minimize costly machine set-ups and change-overs. Work may also be scheduled based on processing time, from shortest to longest.

Capacity is difficult to measure in the job shop and depends on lot sizes, the complexity of jobs, the mix of jobs already scheduled, the ability to schedule work well, the number of machines and their condition, the quantity and quality of labor input, and any process improvements.

JOB SHOPS AS AN EARLY FORM OF MANUFACTURING ORGANIZATION

Most manufacturers today began as job shops and grew into the other manufacturing processes as volume allowed. The job shop allows entrepreneurs the most flexibility in making a variety of products to meet cus-

tomer quality and service standards. As customers request repeat jobs and as volumes grow, the job shop may group machines into work cells to process batches of like jobs.

Job shops are one of the first structures for a manufacturer in the process life cycle. As volume increases and manufacturers reduce or standardize their product offerings, structures change from the job shop to a batch flow to an assembly line and then to a continuous flow. Over the life cycle, flexibility decreases due to high volume and standardization, but unit costs decrease. The job shop is organized by process, where assembly lines or continuous flow operations are organized in a product layout. In the latter layout, equipment or work processes are arranged according to the exact steps in which the product is made and the path for each part resembles a straight line.

BIBLIOGRAPHY

Chass, R. B., N. J. Aquilamo, and F. R. Jacobs. *Operations Management for Competitive Advantage.* Nineth Edition. McGraw-Hill Irwin, 2001.

Framinan, Jose M. "Efficient Heuristic Approaches to Transform Job Shops into Flow Shops." *IIE Transactions.* May 2005.

Schmenner, Roger W. *Plant and Service Tours in Operations Management.* Prentice Hall, 1998.

"Software Suits Job Shops and Manufacturers." *Product News Network.* 20 September 2004.

Hillstrom, Northern Lights
updated by Magee, ECDI

JOINT VENTURES

A joint venture is a business enterprise undertaken by two or more persons or organizations to share the expense and (hopefully) profit of a particular business project. A joint venture is not a business organization in the sense of a proprietorship, partnership, or corporation. It is an agreement between parties for a particular purpose and usually a defined timeframe. Joint ventures may be very informal, such as a handshake and an agreement for two firms to share a booth at a trade show. Other arrangements may be extremely complex, such as a consortium of major electronics firms joining to develop new microchips. The key factor in a joint venture partnership is its single, definable objective. Joint ventures have grown in popularity in recent years, despite the relatively high failure rate of such efforts for one reason or another. Creative small business owners have been able to use this business strategy to good advantage over the years, although the practice remains one primarily associated with larger corporations.

Most joint ventures are formed for the ultimate purpose of saving money. This is as true of small neighborhood stores that agree to advertise jointly in the weekly paper as it is of international oil companies that agree to work together for purposes of oil and gas exploration or extraction. Joint ventures are attractive because they enable companies to share both risks and costs.

LEGAL STRUCTURE OF JOINT VENTURES

Joint ventures are governed entirely by the legal agreements that brought them into existence.

Some joint venture partners may wish to formalize the venture by creating a new joint venture company. Joint venture companies can be very flexible entities in which partners each own shares and agree on how they will be managed. More common are joint venture agreements that do not include the formation of a new entity. Instead, the venture is operated through the existing legal status of the venture partners, or co-venturers. Since the joint venture is not a legal entity, it does not enter into contracts, hire employees, or have its own tax liabilities. These activities and obligations are handled through the co-venturers directly and are governed by contract law. Corporate law, partnership law, and the law of sole proprietorship do not govern joint ventures. Finally, since the venture ends at the conclusion of a specific project, there is no need to address issues of continuity of life and free transferability, unless a joint venture company has been created.

WHY JOINT VENTURES FAIL

Many small business consultants counsel clients to approach joint ventures cautiously. They acknowledge that such partnerships can be most valuable in nourishing a company's growth and stability, but also point out that smaller businesses usually have far less margin for error than do multinational corporations, or even mid-sized companies. Some experts recommend that business owners considering a joint venture with another establishment (or establishments) launch a small joint venture first. Such small projects allow companies to test the relationship without committing large amounts of money. This is especially true when companies with different structures, corporate cultures, and strategic plans work together. These sorts of differences often make it difficult to work together smoothly. So, going through a period of "courtship" before committing to the marriage is usually a wise move.

In addition to a period of courtship, a small business should investigate the prospective partner thoroughly including interviews with prior joint venture partners, suppliers, and customers. This is especially true for a small company considering a joint venture agreement with a larger firm. Joint ventures can benefit all parties to the agreement greatly, and often do. But when they go wrong, the pattern is often a familiar one, explains Gabriel Berg, a partner in the New York City Law firm of Berg & Androphy, a firm that handles many claims of idea theft. Ms. Berg is quoted in an *Entrepreneur* article that highlights difficulties that often arise when a small firm wishing to market or advance a new product idea enters or attempts to enter a joint venture agreement with a large corporation.

Berg outlines the pattern she has seen in countless lawsuits arising from failed joint ventures this way. Early on, the small company will try to protect itself through the use of nondisclosure agreements and by withholding key information. Over time it may feel pressure to share proprietary information too early in the process because it needs the larger company's resources—capital or market distribution network. By divulging this information too early and before contracts exist to strictly define the terms under which the parties will develop the joint venture project, the small firm puts itself in a vulnerable position. "It's easy to think nondisclosure agreements are enough, but most leave room for either party to claim that nothing new has been invented.... [and] both sides have room to come back later and say, 'Oh, we always knew how to do that.' "

People sitting down to discuss a joint venture partnership are usually in an optimistic mood and want to trust their potential partners. So far so good. However, if the optimism causes the partners to proceed before their relationship is thoroughly documented in the form of contracts, then trouble may follow. It is crucial that contracts exist that clearly define how the costs and benefits of the joint venture will be shared by each partner. Otherwise, a small business owner may wake up to the nightmare scenario described by Berg this way. "A large company calls, promising the moon, and you end up out of business, watching your ideas go to market without you." Lawsuits are very costly and they take time. Although many small firms may win lawsuits resulting from failed joint ventures they are often described as hollow victories because they cost so much to litigate and often cause the company to fail in the process. It is, of course, far better to avoid such litigation if at all possible.

Managing a joint venture partnership is another area that often causes friction in the partnership. The managers of one company may be more adept and/or decisive with their decision making than their counterparts at the other company. This can lead to tension and a lack of cooperation. Projects are made more difficult if they lack a well-defined decision making process that is predicated on mutually recognized goals and strategies.

BENEFITS OF JOINT VENTURES

Among the most significant benefits derived from joint ventures is that parties to the venture save money and reduce their risks through capital and resource sharing. Joint ventures also give smaller companies the chance to work with larger ones to develop, manufacture, and market new products. They also give companies of all sizes the opportunity to increase sales, gain access to wider markets, and enhance technological capabilities through research and development underwritten by more than one party. Until relatively recently, U.S. companies were often reluctant to engage in research and development partnerships, and government agencies tried not to become involved in business development. However, with the emergence of countries that feature technologically advanced industries (such as electronics or computer microchips) supported extensively by government funding, American companies have become more willing to participate in joint ventures in these areas. In addition, both federal and state agencies have become more generous with their financial support in these areas. Government's increased involvement in the private business environment has created more opportunities for companies to engage in domestic and international joint ventures.

SEE ALSO *Cooperative Advertising; Cooperatives*

BIBLIOGRAPHY

Choi, Cheng-Bum, and Paul W. Beamish. "Split Management Control and International Joint Venture Performance." *Journal of International Business Studies.* May 2004.

Johnson, Howard E. "Reducing the Risks in Joint Ventures." *CMA Management.* December 2000.

Moeller, Bud. "Becoming a Corporate 'Partner of Choice.' " *Corporate Board.* November 2000.

Penttila, Chris. "Stop, Thief! A Joint Venture with a Big Company Sounds Like a Dream—Until the Company Backs Out, Takes Your Idea With it and Leaves You in the Dust." *Entrepreneur.* June 2005.

Hillstrom, Northern Lights
updated by Magee, ECDI

K

KEOGH PLAN

A Keogh Plan is an employer-funded, tax-deferred retirement plan designed for unincorporated businesses or self-employed persons, including those who earn only part of their income from self-employment. Covered under Section 401(c) of the tax code, Keogh plans are named after Eugene Keogh, the congressman who first came up with the idea. Keogh plans feature relatively high allowable contributions—$42,000 annually as of 2006—which makes them popular among sole proprietors and small businesses with high incomes. In general, however, Keoghs are more costly to set up and administer than similar retirement programs, such as Simplified Employee Pension (SEP) plans, because they require annual preparation and filing of IRS Form 5500. This long and complicated document usually requires a small business to obtain the services of an accountant or financial advisor. In addition, financial information becomes available to the public under Keogh Plans.

As is the case with other common types of retirement programs, Keogh contributions made on employees' behalf are tax-deductible for the employer, and the funds are allowed to grow tax-deferred until the employee withdraws them upon retirement. The funds held in a Keogh may be invested in certificates of deposit, mutual funds, stocks, bonds, annuities, or some combination thereof. Withdrawals are not permitted until after the employee has reached age 59 ½, or else the amount withdrawn is subject to a 10 percent penalty in addition to regular income taxes. Usually only the employer may contribute to a Keogh plan. In addition, the employer can establish a vesting schedule through which employees gradually gain full rights to the funds in their accounts over a number of years. Keogh accounts must be opened by December 31 in order to qualify for tax deductions in a given year, but funds can be contributed until the company's tax deadline.

TYPES OF KEOGH PLANS

Keogh plans can be structured in a number of ways. Although it is possible to design a Keogh as a defined benefit plan (which determines a fixed amount of benefit to be paid upon retirement, then uses an actuarial formula to calculate the annual contribution required to provide that benefit), most Keoghs take the form of a defined contribution plan (which determines an amount of annual contribution without regard to the total benefit that will be available upon retirement). The two most common types of Keoghs are profit-sharing and money purchase plans—each of which fall under the category of defined contribution plans.

Profit-sharing Keoghs are the most flexible, allowing the employer to make larger contributions in good financial years and skip contributions in lean years. In contrast, money purchase Keoghs are highly restrictive, requiring the employer to make a mandatory annual contribution of a predetermined percentage of compensation. For this reason, many smaller businesses or those with variable levels of income shy away from this type of plan. In 2006, maximum contributions to Keogh plans, whether profit-sharing or money purchase plans, enabled the employer to contribute a maximum of $42,000, or 100 percent of compensation, whichever is small, to each employees account.

Although Keoghs give small business owners valuable tax deductions and enable them to provide a valuable benefit to their employees, the plans also have some disadvantages. Business owners who employ other people are required to fund a retirement program for non-owner employees if they establish one for themselves. But because the owner's contributions to his or her own plan are based upon the net income of the business—from which self-employment taxes and contributions to employees' retirement accounts have already been deducted—the owner's allowable contributions are reduced.

For small business owners interested in establishing additional retirement savings, tax law changes that took effect in 2002 created a new personal retirement plan option for business owners that has become very popular. This retirement savings option is only open to business owners who do not have full time employees. It is called the Self-Employed 401(k). Advantages that the Self-Employed 401(k) plan has over the Keogh plan include easier administration of the plan; higher contribution limits; provisions for "catch-up salary deferral contributions for those over the age of 50, and loan options that allow the account holder to borrow from his or her own account.

For small business owners with full time employees, the benefits of Keogh plans may still be one of the best retirement savings options. Other plans to consider include Simplified Employee Pension Plans (SEPs), Simple IRAs, and Simple 401(k)s. Small businesses that offer such plans can use them to attract potential employees and deter current employees from leaving the company to work for a larger competitor. With their high allowable contribution levels, Keogh plans also give the business owner a good opportunity to achieve a financially secure retirement.

SEE ALSO *Employee Benefits; Retirement Planning*

BIBLIOGRAPHY

Reeves, Scott. "A Small Business Retirement Plan." *Forbes.com.* 12 September 2005.

Sifleet, Jean D. *Beyond 401(k)s for Small Business Owners : A Practical Guide to Incentive, Deferred Compensation, and Retirement Plans.* Wiley, 2003.

Tuckey, Steve. "Regulation Blizzard: Legislation out of Washington, often with temporary changes, is keeping small business retirement plans in flux." *National Underwriter Life & Health.* 1 August 2005.

U.S. Department of Labor. Employee Benefits Security Administration. "Easy Retirement Solutions for Small Business." Available from http://www.dol.gov/ebsa/publications/easy_retirement_solutions.html. Retrieved on 12 April 2006.

Hillstrom, Northern Lights
updated by Magee, ECDI

L

LABOR SURPLUS AREA

Labor surplus areas (LSAs) are government-designated towns and counties that have experienced severe unemployment. These area are designated by the government in a yearly survey. Such a designation is then linked to federal procurement policies aimed at reducing unemployment.

Technically speaking, and as defined by the U.S. Department of Labor (DOL), an area is first defined as a "civil jurisdictions" and such a jurisdiction has a surplus of labor "when its average unemployment rate is at least 20 percent above the average unemployment rate for all states (including the District of Columbia and Puerto Rico) during the previous two calendar years. During periods of high national unemployment, the 20 percent ratio is disregarded and an area is classified as a labor surplus are a if its unemployment rate during the previous two calendar years was 10 percent or more." In turn, for purposes of this definition, "civil jurisdictions" are defined as cities with a population of at least 25,000; all counties also fall under the definition. In four states (Michigan, New Jersey, New York, and Pennsylvania) townships also qualify if they have 25,000 people or more. Finally, in Connecticut, Massachusetts, Puerto Rico, and Rhode Island "towns" are included because counties have little or no governmental functions. DOL points out that data are collected based on the narrower definition of "city" or "town" rather than metropolitan area. This permits more precise targeting of preference. Thus a large metro area with a poor core and rich suburbs would have its inner city designated—not its opulent "burbs."

DOL issues an annual list of such areas; the list is published in the Federal Register. For FY 2006 (the most recent), the period under consideration was January 2003 through December 2004. In that period the national average unemployment rate was 5.8 percent. Jurisdictions with 7 percent unemployment or higher (5.8 times 1.2) therefore qualified.

Two federal executive orders make use of these designations. One is Executive Order 12073, Federal Procurement in Labor Surplus Areas, the second is Executive Order 10582, Implementing the Buy American Act. Both create preferences for employers located in such areas when the employers bid for federal contracts. Typically state governments further publicize the "labor surplus areas designated in their states, alerting employers there to the opportunities now available, minimally for one year, usually for longer periods—because economic conditions in these areas rarely just bounce back.

Other federal programs also use the designation to modify the distribution of their services in such areas. For example, food stamp distribution rules are eased in LSAs so that food stamps are available for longer periods under U.S. Department of Agriculture rules than in other areas.

The term itself predates its use as a governmental designation and meant precisely what the three words signify, but without the official numerical qualifications—namely that an area has more labor, with the implied proviso of "appropriately qualified," than it needs. Another implication of the phrase is that an employer will find it easier and more economical to staff a new operation in such an area than in another one. The wider use of the term has lost its currency in recent decades in part because it has been preempted by government usage. A search of business literature turns up only a few articles—and all of these narrowly focused on the DOL program.

Instead, business usage has evolved in another direction, namely to express (and to complain about) the opposite condition by talking about a "tight labor market," indicating *low* unemployment in a market with high-skilled employees—and in consequence high salary or wage demands and difficulty staffing. In the modern employment climate, specialization of the workforce, including its educational qualifications and exposure to new technology, has become primary. States and localities, therefore, in pursuing new business, stress an "educated, skilled workforce," not simply the availability of lots of bodies—which the old term still carries as a connotation.

BIBLIOGRAPHY

"Labor Surplus Area Classification Under Executive Orders 12073 and 10582; Notice." *Federal Register.* 11 January 2006.

U.S. Deparment of Labor. "FY 2006 Labor Surplus Area List." Available from http://www.doleta.gov/programs/lsa.cfm. Retrieved on 29 March 2006.

Darnay, ECDI

LABOR UNIONS

A labor union is an organization of wage earners or salary workers established for the purpose of protecting their collective interests when dealing with employers. Although unions are prevalent in most industrialized countries, union representation of workers has generally declined in most countries over the past 30 to 40 years. In the United States, unions represented about one-third of all workers in the 1950s. In 2005 unions represented less than 12.5 percent of the labor force—7.8 percent of the labor force in the private sector; unions represented between 36.5 percent of public-sector workers.

TYPES OF UNIONS

Unions can be categorized by ideology and organizational form. A distinction is often made between political unionism and business unionism. The goals and objectives of these types may overlap, political unions are related to some larger working-class movement. Most political unions have some formal association with a working-class political party; these types of unions are more prevalent in Europe than they are in the United States. Contemporary American labor unions are best

viewed as business unions. Business unions generally accept the capitalist economy and focus their attention on protecting and enhancing workers' economic welfare by collective bargaining. U.S. law entitles unions to bargain with employers over wages, hours, and working conditions.

But while most American unions are classified as business rather than political unions, U.S. business unions are also involved in politics. Most lobby and participate in electoral activities to support their economic goals. For example, many unions campaigned against passage of the North American Free Trade Agreement (NAFTA). The labor movement feared that NAFTA would undercut jobs of union workers and weaken unions' ability to negotiate favorable contracts with employers.

The earliest unions in the United States were known as craft unions. They represented employees in a single occupation or group of closely related occupations. Members of craft unions are generally highly skilled workers, in construction, for example, carpenters, plumbers, and electrical workers. Craft unions are most common in occupations in which employees frequently switch employers. A construction worker is usually hired to complete work at a specific job site and then moves on to work elsewhere (often for another employer). In addition to collective bargaining, craft unions often serve as a placement service for members. Employers contact the union's hiring hall and union members currently out of work are referred to the job.

Closely related to craft unions, though distinct in many respects, are professional unions. A professional is generally understood to be an employee with advanced and highly specialized skills, often requiring some credentials, such as a college degree and/or a license. Professional unions are much more recent than craft unions and are most common in the public sector. Teacher's unions are one of the most visible examples of this kind of union.

Most unionized workers in the United States belong to industrial unions. An industrial union represents workers across a wide range of occupations within one or more industries. A good example of a typical industrial union is the United Automobile Workers (UAW). It represents skilled craft workers, assembly-line workers, and unskilled workers in all of the major American automobile companies. The UAW negotiates separate contracts for workers in each of these companies. Although most industrial unions began by organizing workers in a single industry or group of related industries, most have diversified over the past 30 to 40 years. For example, the UAW also represents workers in the tractor and earth-moving equipment industry (e.g.,

Caterpillar and John Deere) and in the aerospace industry (e.g., Boeing), and in the late 1990s it added such disparate groups as the Graphics Artists Guild (3,000 members), the National Writers Union (5,000 members), and various service, technical, and graduate student employees at more than 20 colleges and universities across the country. In addition, the UAW and other national unions have increasingly sought to expand their influence into emerging high-tech sectors of the economy.

Another organizational form is the general union. General unions organize workers across all occupations and industries. Although some highly diversified unions, such as the Teamsters, may appear to be general unions at first glance, this form of organization does not really exist in the United States. Because they are typically politically oriented, general unions are more common in Europe and developing countries.

Open Shop and Closed Shop The term "open shop" refers to a company policy that does not restrict the business's employee work force to union members. "Closed shop," on the other hand, refers to a company that hires only union members. Under this latter arrangement, employees are required to join the existing union within a specified time after they have been hired.

UNION GROWTH AND DECLINE

Union membership in the United States has varied considerably throughout the country's history. Although unions have been in existence in some form in the United States for nearly 200 years, they did not attain any meaningful level of power and influence until the 1930s, when several factors combined to spur a dramatic rise in union growth (the unionization rate went from about 12 percent of the labor force in 1935 to between 32 percent and 35 percent in the mid-1950s):

1. The American economy shifted from an agricultural to an industrial base; industrial workers, who were concentrated in urban areas and increasingly shared the same language (English), were thus able to create a common culture that was absent among earlier generations of workers.

2. The Depression created a backlash against big business entities, who were viewed as the chief culprits for the country's economic difficulties.

3. Changing political dynamics also played an important role. Active support for organized labor was an integral part of Roosevelt's New Deal, and the passage of the National Labor Relations Act (NLRA) in 1935 was a potent new weapon for union organizers. The NLRA provided a means for official recognition of labor unions. Once recognized, an employer was legally bound to bargain with the union, enforceable by government action.

4. Economic growth during World War II and in the post-war era was an important facilitator of union growth.

By the mid-1950s, the most union-prone sectors of the American economy had largely been organized, and millions of workers saw improvements in their living standards as a direct result of union activity. Many economists observed that this rise in union fortunes helped non-union workers as well. "Collective bargaining has significantly improved the wages and working conditions of unionized and nonunionized workers," contended Levitan, Carlson, and Shapiro in *Protecting American Workers.* "Other benefits of union representation include increased leisure, better medical coverage, and more secure pensions.... Finally, unions have helped nonunion workers by lobbying for legislation that grants all workers such protections as equal employment, safe and healthy workplaces, and secure pensions."

Unions maintained their strength at just under one-third of the labor force until about 1960. Union membership declined gradually, decreasing to about 25 percent of the labor force in the mid-1970s. The rate of decline was much sharper in the 1980s, and by the year 2005 private sector union membership had declined to less than 8 percent of the total.

Factors often cited for the decline in union membership include the following:

• Changing nature of the global economy. International competition has increased significantly over the past few generations, especially in sectors of the economy that were heavily unionized (e.g., automobiles, steel, and textiles). As these industries became more competitive globally, employer resistance to unions often increased. In addition, it became feasible for employers to relocate production facilities to areas of the country which have traditionally been less supportive of unionism (such as the southern and Mountain states) or overseas to less developed countries that have low wages and few unions. Finally, employment in traditionally nonunion industries expanded, while employment in heavily unionized sectors declined.

• Shifting demographics of the labor force. In the 1930s, "blue collar" workers represented a large proportion of the labor force. Now "white collar" workers (i.e., managers, professionals, and clericals) are a very large component of the labor force. Historically, white collar workers have been more difficult to organize (except in the public sector).

- Changing attitudes of government. As early as 1947, amendments were added to the NLRA that significantly expanded employer rights and limited the rights of unions. The best-known of these laws was the Taft-Hartley Act. Moreover, appointees to the National Labor Relations Board, which enforces the NLRA, became more pro-management in outlook during the 1970s and early 1980s.

- Growing public and management perceptions that some union demands and attitudes were unreasonable.

- Ineffective union organization efforts, despite continued belief in the legitimacy of labor unions among the American workforce. "Labor leaders are partly to blame for the disconnect between pro-union sentiment and dwindling membership," charged *Business Week*. "For decades, they have focused on preserving jobs rather than organizing the fastest-growing parts of the economy, such as services and high tech."

By the mid-1990s, however, there were indications that America's leading unions had adopted more proactive measures in order to shore up existing membership and expand the presence of unions into high-tech "New Economy" sectors and other areas. But this revival of organized labor, since then, has not translated into growing union membership.

INDUSTRIES FEATURING STRONG UNION PRESENCE

Unions have traditionally been strong in four sectors of the American economy: manufacturing, mining, construction, and transportation. They have lost substantial ground in all four of these sectors in the last few decades, however. In the transportation sector, an important factor has been deregulation, particularly in the trucking and airline industries. Substantial increases in competition in those industries have made it difficult for unions to negotiate favorable contracts or organize new units. In construction, the growth of nonunion contractors, able to hire qualified workers outside of the union hall hiring system, undercut union contractors. At one time, more than 80 percent of all commercial construction in the United States had been unionized; today, however, the percentage of workers engaged in construction that belong to unions is a fraction of that. Foreign competition, technological change, and played-out mines, meanwhile, have all weakened mining unions. In manufacturing, the whole range of factors previously discussed has been responsible for union decline. The only sector of the economy where unions have gained strength in recent years has been public employment. In the mid-2000s, almost more than 36 percent of public

employees at all levels of government—local, state, and federal—were unionized.

INTERNAL STRUCTURE AND ADMINISTRATION

Labor unions are complex and vary considerably with respect to internal structure and administrative processes. It is easiest to differentiate among three distinct levels within the labor movement: local unions, national unions, and federations.

Local Unions Local unions are the building blocks of the labor movement. Although there are some free-standing local unions, the vast majority of locals are in some way affiliated with a national or international union. Most craft unions began as local unions, which then joined together to form national organizations. Some major industrial unions also began as amalgamations of local unions, though it was generally more common for national organizations to be formed first, with locals to be established later.

The duties of a local union almost always include the administration of a union contract, which means assuring that the employer is honoring all of the provisions of the contract at the local level. In some instances, local unions might also negotiate contracts, although unions vary considerably in terms of the degree to which the parent union is involved in the negotiation process.

Another important function of the local union is servicing the needs of those represented by the union. If a worker represented by the union believes his or her rights under the union contract have been violated, then the union may intervene on that person's behalf. Examples of such situations include the discharge of an employee, failure to promote an employee according to a contract seniority clause, or failure to pay an employee for overtime. Virtually any provision of a contract can become a source of contention. The local union may try to settle the issue informally. If that effort is not successful, the union may file what is known as a *grievance*. This is a formal statement of the dispute with the employer; most contracts set forth a grievance procedure. In general, grievance procedures involve several different steps, with higher levels of management entering at each step. If the grievance cannot be settled through this mechanism, then the union may, if the contract allows, request a hearing before a neutral arbitrator, whose decision is final and binding.

Most craft unions have *apprenticeship programs* to train new workers in the craft. The local union, usually in cooperation with an employers' association, will be responsible for managing the apprenticeship program.

In addition, local unions with hiring halls are responsible for making job referrals.

The jurisdiction of a local union depends to a large extent on the organizational form of the parent organization. Locals of industrial unions most often represent workers within a single plant or facility of a company (and thus are termed *plant locals*.) For example, in the case of the UAW, each factory or production facility of each automobile manufacturer has a separate local union. In some instances, a factory may be so big that it requires more than a single local, but this is not usually the case.

In contrast to plant locals, local craft unions (as well as some industrial unions) are best described as *area locals*. An area local represents all of a union's members in a particular geographical region and may deal with many different employers. Area locals are typically formed for one of two reasons. First, members may in the course of a year work for a number of different employers, as in the case of craft unions. Consequently, it would be difficult, if not impossible, to establish and maintain a separate local in each work location. Second, members may work continuously for a single employer, but each employer or location may be too small to justify a separate local union. The latter case is more typical of some industrial unions. The size of the region served by a local union depends on the number of members available. In large metropolitan areas, an area local might serve only members in a particular city. In less densely populated regions, an area local may have a jurisdiction that covers an entire state.

Internal structures and administrative procedures differ between plant and area locals. In almost all local unions, the membership meeting represents the apex of power, as the officers of the union are accountable to the members much as the officers of a corporation are accountable to stockholders. However, in practice, membership participation in union affairs may be quite limited. In such instances, local union officers often enjoy considerable power.

Plant locals have a number of elected officials—usually a president, vice president, secretary, and treasurer. In almost all cases, the officers are full-time employees of the company the union represents, and the contract generally allows some release time for union affairs. In addition to the principal officers of the local, there are also a number of *stewards*. Stewards may be elected or appointed, depending upon the union. The steward serves as the everyday contact between the union and its rank-and-file members. If members have concerns about the affairs of the union, these may be voiced to the steward. The steward's most important responsibility is handling grievances. Should a worker represented by the union have a dispute with the employer over his or her rights under the contract, the steward has the initial responsibility of representing the worker. Usually the steward will discuss the matter with the employee's supervisor to see if the dispute can be resolved. If not, then a formal grievance may be filed, and it then proceeds through the grievance system. At higher levels in the grievance system the employee may be represented by a chief steward or union officers.

Area locals typically have more complex internal structures than plant locals. This is usually because of the large geographical region under the local's jurisdiction, along with the greater dispersion of members within the region. As in the case of plant locals, area locals hold periodic meetings in which the officials of the union are accountable to members. There are also elected officers in area locals, as well as stewards for the various work sites in the local's jurisdiction. The principal difference between a plant local and an area local is that the latter typically employs one or more full-time staff members to handle the affairs of the union on a daily basis. These staff members are usually called *business agents*. Given the dispersion of members over a large geographical area and the possibility that the local may be responsible for administering many different contracts, it is the business agent's responsibility to visit work sites regularly and deal with problems that may arise. The business agent may also be responsible for managing any apprenticeship programs and the union's hiring hall. Contracts are often negotiated directly by local unions and the business agents are usually responsible for these negotiations. In some unions, elected officers may serve as business agents, but normally business agents are separate staff members. Depending on the size of the local union, there may be a number of assistant business agents.

National Unions National unions are composed of the various local unions that they have chartered. Some unions have locals in Canada and therefore call themselves *international* unions. However, the terms *international union* and *national union* are generally used interchangeably.

As with local unions, the administrative structures of national unions vary considerably in complexity. One important factor is the size of the union: larger unions are structurally more complex. Structural complexity also differs between craft and industrial unions. Craft unions tend be smaller organizations that feature a decentralized decision-making structure. With craft unions, contracts usually have a limited geographical scope and are negotiated by local unions. The parent union can be of significant assistance, however. The national union pools the resources of local unions, thus helping out with things such as strike funds, and it may also provide research services and serve as the local union's voice in political matters at the national and state levels. In general, there are few intermediate units between the national office and the local craft unions. National officers, elected periodically, generally work on a full-time basis for the union. Such unions also hold national conventions, most often every couple of years. The officers of the national union are accountable to the convention, much as the officers of a local are accountable to membership meetings.

National industrial unions are typically more complex. They tend to be larger and have a more heterogeneous membership than craft unions (both in terms of skills and demographic traits). Although there are exceptions, contracts in industrial unions tend to be negotiated primarily by staff members from the national office. In many cases, the bargaining unit will include all locals from a particular company (across the entire country). Even if contracts are negotiated by locals, representatives from the national union will often participate in talks to assure that the contract conforms to patterns established by the national organization.

As with craft unions, national unions have periodic conventions and national officers. Depending on the union, the national officers may be elected directly by rank-and-file members or by some other body (such as convention delegates). National unions generally have a substantial paid staff who provide a variety of different services (e.g., research, legal representation, organizing new members, negotiating contracts, and servicing locals). National unions may also have one or more layers of hierarchy between the local unions and the national offices. For example, in the case of the UAW, there are different divisions responsible for the major industries in which that union represents workers. Within the automobile industry, there are divisions that correspond to each of the major manufacturers. There are other divisions that deal with the needs of special groups within the union (such as minority workers and skilled craft workers). Consequently, the structures of large industrial unions are often as complex as the companies with which they deal.

Federations A federation is an association of unions. It is not a union in the usual sense of the term. Rather, it provides a range of services to affiliated unions, much as an organization such as the National Association of Manufacturers provides services to its member firms.

BIBLIOGRAPHY

"All's Not Fair in Labor Wars." *Business Week.* 19 July 1999.

Lawler, J.J. *Unionization and Deunionization: Strategy, Tactics, and Outcomes.* University of South Carolina Press, 1990.

Levitan, Sar A., Peter E. Carlson, and Isaac Shapiro. *Protecting American Workers: An Assessment of Government Programs.* Bureau of National Affairs, 1986.

Powell, Adam Lee. "The Future of Our Profession Depends on Unions, This Nurse Asserts." *RN.* December 2005.

Strope, Leigh. "Union Seeks Net Increase: Web site used in bid to attract new members." *The Houston Chronicle.* 23 June 2004.

Trombly, Maria, and Kathleen Ohlson. "Unions Take Aim at High-Tech Workers." *Computerworld.* 14 August 2000.

Troy, Leo. "Beyond Unions and Collective Bargaining." *WorkingUSA.* January/February 2000.

U.S. Department of Labor. "Table 3. Union Affiliation of Employed Wage and Salary Workers by Occupation and Industry." Available from http://www.bls.gov/news.release/union2.t03.htm. Retrieved on 30 March 2006.

Hillstrom, Northern Lights
updated by Magee, ECDI

LABOR UNIONS AND SMALL BUSINESS

The labor movement had its origins in the rise of the industrial revolution beginning around 1750—whereas small business is ancient, its twin origins being family farms and craftsmen's shops of ancient times. Craft guilds, which formed during medieval times and were central to the bourgeoisie of early market towns, in part later also inspired labor associations. Although later the interest of small business and unions diverged, ironically the first strike in America took place in New York City in 1741 when bakers rebelled against price-setting by the municipal authorities and stopped baking to make their point. Union time-lines cite the 1741 Bakers' Strike but scholarly opinion is divided—precisely because the Bakers' Strike was by small business owners against "the public sector" (not then called that, of course) rather than by labor against capital.

Careless use of language by many pundits and observers classifies small business as just another battalion in the army of capitalism, although the monumental work of the French scholar, Fernand Braudel, *Civilization and Capitalism* (Harper & Row, 1979) draws distinctions which leave small business out. Small businesses, of course, sometimes behave in typical capitalist ways (one thinks of highly exploitive sweat-shops) but in the overwhelming majority of small business enterprises the relationship between owners and workers is close, sometimes the two are members of the same family; the scale is such that blatant exploitation is not even a temptation. Small businesses are also much more vulnerable;

an extended strike against them will put them out of business. Primarily for these reasons, the labor unions and small businesses have had little effective contact. To be sure, some small businesses are unionized, but they represent (as best as one can discover) a tiny minority of such enterprises.

The history of unionized labor shows that severe down-turns in economic activity have hurt labor temporarily; coincidentally long periods of expansion have caused labor unions to go into decline. Union membership stood at a peak of 19.4 million members in 1972 but had declined to 8.25 million by 2005. Membership as a percent of the work force stood at 29.8 percent in 1962 but had declined to 12.5 percent by 2005. As membership has declined, the percentage of unionized labor working for the public sector has increased, private sector unionized labor has decreased in share. In 1983 more than two-thirds of union members were in the private sector (67.2 percent). By 2004, the private sector's share was down to just over a half (52.6 percent)—47.4 percent of unionized labor worked for government or other public sector agencies (e.g., public schools).

In 2005, the highest rates of unionization (24 percent) were in the transportation and utilities industries. Finance and related services had the lowest rate (2.3 percent). Thirteen percent of construction and manufacturing labor was unionized. In wholesale and retail (where the highest proportion of small businesses operate) the rate was 5.2 percent. In professional and business services, another important small business sector, the rate was 2.7 percent. These percentages do not tell the whole story. For cost/benefit reasons unions have tended in the past to target large operations—unless unusual grievances caused unusual organizing activity. In practice this means that small businesses have gotten a pass from the union movement—unless, as it were, they drew unwelcome attention to themselves by aggressive moves and harsh practices. In the mid-2000s there were some rumblings that this may be changing, but little evidence.

LABOR LAW

The six most important pieces of legislation governing business-labor relations are the National Labor Relations Act of 1935 (NLRA), the Labor Management Relations Act of 1947 (LMRA), the Fair Labor Standards Act of 1938 (FLSA), the Labor-Management Reporting and Disclosure Act of 1959 (LMRDA), the Civil Rights Act of 1964, and the Occupational Safety and Health Act of 1970.

The National Labor Relations Act, which created the National Labor Relations Board (NLRB), gives employees the right to organize and bargain collectively with their employers—in essence, it gives them the right to

unionize. It also confers legal protection on employees who try to organize their fellow workers into a union—but also protects nonunion employees from being forced or otherwise coerced into joining a labor organization or engaging in collective bargaining. The act ensures that employees can choose their own representatives for the purpose of collective bargaining, establishes procedures for secret-ballot elections, and defines unfair labor practices, to which both employers and unions are subject. This law is also known as the Wagner Act in honor of New York Senator Robert Wagner.

The Labor Management Relations Act, known as the Taft-Hartley Act, amended the NLRB in ways that are generally thought to benefit business owners and management. It forbade businesses from launching unwarranted or sudden lockouts of union employees but also imposed restrictions on some union activities in the areas of organizing, picketing, striking, and other activities. It also outlawed the "closed shop" (which required that employers hire only union members) and gave the government the power to obtain injunctions against strikes that "will imperil the national health or safety" if they take place or continue.

The Fair Labor Standards Act, also known as the Wage-Hour Act, established the minimum wage for hourly employees and mandatory overtime pay for work in excess of 40 hours a week. This is the law that created the "exempt" and "non-exempt" employee categories, the former being salaried employees who are *not subject* to FLSA and are therefore "exempt" and hourly workers who *are* subject to the law and therefore "non-exempt." All states also have minimum wage rules; where the state minimum wage is higher than the federal, employers must pay the state-set rate.

The Labor-Management Reporting and Disclosure Act, also known as the Landrum-Griffin Act, was in large measure shaped to regulate the internal affairs of unions and to provide additional safeguards to ensure that the rules laid out in the Labor Management Relations Act of 1947 were adhered to.

The Civil Rights Act of 1964 prohibited employers from discriminating in their hiring practices on the basis of race, religious beliefs, gender, or natural origin—later also by age.

The Occupational Safety and Health Act of 1970 created the Occupational Safety and Health Administration (OSHA). It established guidelines and regulations to make workplaces safer and healthier for employees. "Each employer shall furnish to each of his employees employment and a place of employment which are free from recognized hazards that are causing or are likely to cause death or serious physical harm to his [or her] employees," read one portion of the Act.

ORGANIZING EFFORTS AND THE SMALL BUSINESS OWNER

Joshua Kurlantzik, writing in *Entrepreneur* has pointed out that unions are turning organizing activities toward white-collar and service employees in the mid-2000s: these jobs are more difficult to export to foreign countries; at the same time, employees have been frightened by waves of layoffs and outsourcings and now are more prone to seek security. Evidence of such activities is anecdotal, on the whole, and it is difficult to determine whether it constitutes a trend toward (re-)unionization or a rear-guard action by labor as it continues to lose membership. Nonetheless, small businesses of the larger size, anyway, may in fact encounter organizing efforts. At the first sign of such activity in the community, the owner owes it to him- or herself to become familiar with the duties and rights involved. Early defensive action is important.

For example, a business may ban union literature in the work place, restrict internal efforts to convince employees to sign union authorization cards, and expressly forbid outside organizers from any activity on company property. But such rules must be in place before any organizational activity begins. If the rules are published after activities have already been launched, the business is subject to charges of unlawful retaliation.

Under current rules, a union must initially garner sufficient interest from a business's employees (30 percent of the work force is a rule of thumb), before it can petition the National Labor Relations Board for an election by secret ballot to determine whether the work force will join the union in question; if the interest level is 50 percent or higher, union recognition may be granted without an election.

During an organizing campaign, the owner must safeguard him- or herself from engaging in activities normally held to be unfair practices contrary to workers' rights to organize. These include, among others:

- Polling employees about their attitudes toward the proposed union.

- Suggesting that a union victory will spell a loss of employment or benefits.

- Once an election agreement has been reached, withholding employees' names and addresses from union organizers.

- Lobbying against the union in visits to employees' homes.

- Setting uneven rules for solicitation at the company for those for and against unionizations.

- Favoritism toward antiunion employees.

- Discrimination against prounion workers.

Dealing with Election Outcomes Once the NLRB-supervised election has been held, the small business owner is confronted with one of two outcomes. The business may carry the day but then will face disappointed employees who had hoped for unionization. And it may not be over. The union may apply for a nullification of the results (based on allegations of unfair labor practices, etc.) or simply regroup and make another attempt down the line.

If the union wins the vote, the small business owner has four choices. He or she can—

- Charge the union with unfair labor practices and attempt to have the election results annulled.

- Sell the business and leave the problems to the new owner.

- Go out of business.

- Recognize the union and enter into collective bargaining arrangements in good faith.

The collective bargaining agreement is basically a contract between the business and the union that explicitly states how workplace issues between management and employees will be handled.

LIVING WITH THE UNION

Small businesses do not necessarily suffer from living with a union. As Sarah Klein put it, writing for *Crain's Chicago Business,* "A union is supposed to be bad for business. Conventional wisdom holds that unions drive up costs and create a more contentious workplace. But labor relations are just another business problem; look hard enough and you'll find entrepreneurs who've figured a way to make it work in their favor." Klein offers four cases of successful "cohabitation." In the first case a restaurant experienced a 12 percent increase in the base pay of wait staff but discovered that its turn-over rate significantly declined. In a second case a printing shop became unionized and saw its costs rise in consequence— but then discovered a new business serving insurance and money-management firms that required the "union label" on all of their printed goods. In the third case, a unionized parking operation found that an increase in hourly pay of $2 dollars also purchased management help from the union in the form of employee training, reduced pilferage, and lobbying help in keeping down parking garage taxes. In the final case, a specialized cleaning company discovered that unionization (it cost between $20 and $50 per hour more) resulted in incentives for workers to get better training which the company translated into higher sales.

SEE ALSO *Employee Strikes; Grievance Procedures; National Labor Relations Board*

BIBLIOGRAPHY

Dannin, Ellen, and Terry Wagar. "Impasse and Implementation: How to Subvert the National Labor Relations Act." *Working USA.* Fall 2000.

Hartley, Roger C. "The Framework of Democracy in Union Government." *Catholic University Law Review.* Available from http://www.thelaborers.net/HISTORY/framework_of_democracy_in_union.htm. Retrieved on 30 March 2006.

Klein, Sarah A. "Union, Yes: Smart entrepreneurs make union labor work." *Crain's Chicago Business.* 14 February 2005.

Kurlantzick, Joshua. "United We Fall? Workers interest in unions may threaten your business. How will you respond?" *Entrepreneur.* March 2003.

U.S. Department of Labor. "Table 3. Union Affiliation of employed wage and salary workers by occupation and industry." Available from http://www.bls.gov/news.release/union2.t03.htm. Retrieved on 30 March 2006.

Hillstrom, Northern Lights
updated by Magee, ECDI

LAYOFFS, DOWNSIZING, AND OUTSOURCING

A "layoff" is an action by an employer to terminate employees for lack of work. The term connotes that the termination is temporary—but it may well become permanent. A "downsizing" simply means releasing employees because the operation no longer needs them; reorganization or restructuring of the institution has eliminated jobs. The euphemistic "right-sizing" is sometimes substituted—to flatter management, one assumes. An "RIF," which stands for "reduction in force," is an old and rather straightforward term, its most likely source being governmental and military changes in employment: both actually take place from time to time. The newest addition to this lugubrious terminology (at least from the employees' point of view) is "outsourcing" or "off-shoring," meaning that the work is being transferred to another organization either domestically or overseas.

The layoff is a necessary corollary to seasonal or intermittent employment common in some industries, for example in construction, where building activity typically slows or stops in the winter months and resumes in spring. Industries that manufacture goods sold for winter use often have high levels of production (including lots of overtime) in the summer. The inverse of that takes place when spring and summer goods are made in winter. Industries highly linked with the tourist season typically have layoffs. People employed in these types of activities adapt to the layoffs by having alternative forms of employment in the "off-season." Layoffs also take place in times of economic down-turn because overall demand declines. Producers will cut back from three shifts to two or one or release some employees even when only operating one shift. But economy-driven layoffs are not permanent, and workers are "called back" when things pick up again. Based on statistics collected by the U.S. Department of Labor (DOL), extended mass layoffs have affected on average 1.3 million employees in the period 1996 through 2003—at higher rates during the recessionary period that began in 2000, at lower levels in the booming 1990s.

The laid-off worker has no guarantee of being called back to work; similarly, the employer may not be able to hire back labor if contracts don't renew or the business does not pick up. In the last decade or so the layoff itself has become a euphemism for force reduction. It is a telling sign of the times that DOL began collecting data on layoffs in April 1995 for the first time and has since published such data monthly. Even more revealing is the fact that DOL later added categories such as layoffs due to "overseas relocation" and "import competition"—the last category indicating jobs lost because work in-house has been replaced by imports. All this suggests that the term "layoff" shades imperceptibly into the "downsizing" category.

Downsizing typically has multiple causes of which one may well be increased productivity. According to the DOL productivity in manufacturing (output per hour) increased on average 4.4 percent *a year* from 1995 to 2005 and 2.3 percent a year in business as a whole. If demand for goods and services is steady, this means that each year fewer workers are needed to supply the economy. The second factor behind downsizing is declining revenue due either to a poor economy or increased foreign competition. Finally, if labor is available at lower costs overseas and the work can be transferred, business will relocate jobs to reduce costs.

The stream of business news over at least the 1990s and the mid-2000s seems to suggest that these factors are very much present, indeed that corporate well-being and layoffs are inversely proportional—as a sampling of headlines shows: **Compaq Stock Rises 8% on Sales and Job Forecast** (The New York Times, October 9, 1992; the article cites the elimination of 1,000 jobs); **Stock Rises on News of Possible, Bigger Layoffs** (Annex News Watch, September 29, 2004, regarding EDS); and **Ford Slashes Jobs, Stocks Rise** (CBS News, January 24, 2006). Many more stories carry the same message in the body—if not in the headline. To be sure, stocks rise on any news that a company—especially a troubled company—is cutting costs. Notable in the present context is that so many companies shed jobs as a way of cutting costs.

SMALL BUSINESS IS NOT EXEMPT

Small business is also subject to seasonal patterns and therefore lays off employees as needed, calling them back at a later time. More painfully, however, the small business must also respond to economic and market pressures and therefore must occasionally reduce its employment because the revenues are just not there. Every owner, therefore, should have plans and policies for reducing employment permanently. Such managerial techniques involve 1) conformity with law, 2) appropriate communications, and 3) employee assistance, sometimes called "outplacement" in human resources jargon.

In common parlance the first issue is based on fairness but fairness is enforced by employment and civil rights statues. When downsizing the workforce, the owner must base his or her actions on the requirements of the business and lean over backwards to avoid even the suggestion of bias against protected minorities: women, the disabled, racial minorities, workers over the age of forty, and veterans. In most cases job terminations will be based on functions that can no longer be supported; if these have to be reduced rather than eliminated, a neutral criterion like job tenure may be used, with the most junior employees terminated first. Such a rule would also apply if an across-the-board reduction, based on a percentage of all employees, is adopted. The rules being applied should be made public so that their fairness is visible to all involved, whether they stay or leave.

Communications are important both to maintain the morale of employees retained and to hold the good will of those discharged. They may be back again. The practice of announcing a downsizing late on Friday or the day before Christmas reflects very adversely on the owner's courage and tact, of course. Employees may have to leave, but they appreciate a clear statement of the reason why they're being terminated and like to have as much notice as possible. Some owners feel that they may lose the effective labor of those laid off by announcing early; but in almost all such situations, employees have long anticipated problems; therefore early notice may actually improve productivity during this period by removing uncertainty. If the selection rules are obviously fair and impartial, all employees will react favorably toward the company. And this will be doubly true if the announcement includes information about help the employer intends to provide to those leaving.

Providing outplacement help involves extra work on the owner's part but invariably has a favorable effect. Such help may involve getting assistance from one or more employment agencies, providing information on how to file for unemployment benefits, counseling by the owner or a third party, helping to prepare good resumes, providing leads and contacts, and preparing letters of recommendation.

Many owners, quite naturally, feel the need to downsize as a sign of personal failure—and this despite a good track record of long and successful employment of lots of people. Experience, however, teaches that business does have its downs as well as ups—and also teaches that the owner will benefit from minimizing his or her own frustrations. A good way to do that is trying to help those affected.

ALTERNATIVES TO DOWNSIZING

A few companies have had, and continue to have, "no-layoff" policies or, more realistically, a "no-layoff" philosophy. Julia King, writing in *Computerworld,* described two such companies, Lincoln Electric Co. and FedEx Corp. "The employment practices go by different names," King wrote, "but the spirit and business strategies behind them are the same. By shunning downsizing as a matter of corporate values, both companies are looking to create a fiercely loyal and productive workforce, which in turn generates high customer satisfaction ratings and bottom-line results. And so far, it's a strategy that seems to work well, in both good economic times and bad."

Elizabeth Smith Barnes, writing in *Workforce Management* described the no-layoff policy of Hypertherm, Inc. Barnes provided a telling quote from the company's founder, Dick Couch, revealing the mindset behind such policies. "I was at a conference on entrepreneurship at Dartmouth," Barnes quotes Couch saying. "The guy next to me was a young, very bright venture capitalist who believed that the purpose of business is to maximize shareholder equity. I say that the purpose of business is to satisfy the customer and to focus on the development and well-being of your associates, from which good things will happen—including the 'accidental' benefit to shareholders. It seems some corporate folks are never going to understand the value of no layoffs because their fundamental philosophy about what we're in business for is very different."

No-layoff policies are not realistic for many small businesses, but the practices of leaders suggest ways and means both of avoiding layoffs and dealing with cost problems creatively. Techniques mentioned include very careful hiring, cross-training of employees so that many are able to shift from job to job, intense employee involvement in the business through suggesting programs and innovations, and, in the extreme case, pay reductions or reduced work hours so that all employees stay—and share the hardship in common.

SEE ALSO *Constructive Discharge; Employee Termination*

BIBLIOGRAPHY

Barnes, Elizabeth Smith. "No-Layoff Policy." *Workforce Management.* July 2003.

Chappell, Lindsay. "Nissan Sizes Up Detroit Job Seekers." *Automotive News.* 13 March 2006.

Crew, Vince. "Layoffs Only As a Last Resort." *Home Care Magazine.* 1 March 2006.

King, Julia. "Jobs for Life." *Computerworld.* 14 January 2002.

Langreth, Robert, and Matthew Herper. "Storm Warnings." *Forbes.* 13 March 2006.

"PA Examines Merger-Related Job Losses." *TelecomWeb News Digest.* 17 March 2006.

"Recent Layoffs In the Mortgage Industry." *Origination News.* March 2006.

Sheff, Harry. "Weekly News Briefs; Back-Pay, Unions, and Layoffs—Oh My! Brief accounts of call center news from Tucson to Dubai." *CommWeb.* 9 March 2006.

Tobin, Bill. "Last in the lifeboat: Being a loyal employee doesn't preclude preparing to be RIF'd. It's in your best interest to be prepared for any eventuality." *Modern Plastics Worldwide.* March 2006.

U.S. Department of Labor. "Mass Layoff Statistics." Available from http://www.bls.gov/mls/home.htm. Retrieved on 30 March 2006.

U.S. Department of Labor. "Productivity and Costs." Available from http://www.bls.gov/lpc/home.htm#overview. Retrieved on 31 March 2006.

Darnay, ECDI

LEARNING CURVES

Learning curves graphically portray the costs and benefits of experience when performing routine or repetitive tasks. Also known as experience curves, cost curves, efficiency curves, and productivity curves, they illustrate how the cost per unit of output decreases over time as the result of accumulated workforce learning and experience. That is, as cumulative output increases, learning and experience cause the cost per unit to decrease. Experience and learning curves are used by businesses in production planning, cost forecasting, and setting delivery schedules, among other applications.

Learning curves are geometric curves that can be graphed on the basis of a formula. Typically the X (horizontal) axis measures cumulative output, and the Y (vertical) axis measures the cost per unit. The curve starts with a high cost per unit at the beginning of output, decreases quickly at first, then levels out as cumulative output increases. The slope of the learning curve is an indication of the rate at which learning becomes transformed into cost savings.

An 80 percent learning curve is standard for many activities and is sometimes used as an average in cost forecasting and production planning. An 80 percent learning curve means that, for every doubling of output, the cost of new output is 80 percent of prior output. As output doubles from one unit to two units to four units, etc., the learning curve descends quite sharply as costs decrease dramatically. As output increases, it takes longer to double previous output, and the learning curve flattens out. Thus, costs decrease at a slower pace when cumulative output is higher.

One can explain the shape of learning curves another way. When a new task or production operation begins, a person or system learns quickly, and the learning curve is steep. With each additional repetition, less learning occurs and the curve flattens out. At the beginning of production or learning, individuals or systems are said to be "high" on the learning curve. That means that costs per unit are high, and cumulative output is low. Individuals and systems "move down" the experience or learning curve by learning to complete repetitive tasks more efficiently, eliminating hesitation and mistakes, automating certain tasks, and making adjustments to procedures or systems.

Some theorists believe that learning curves are not actually curves, but more like jagged lines that follow a curving pattern. They assert that learning occurs in brief spurts of progress, followed by small fallbacks to previous levels, rather than in a smooth progressive curve. Such a model of learning, however, does not affect the usefulness of learning curves in business and production applications.

The phrase, of course, has spread from management science to business and other activities generally. In the broader frame "learning curve" has come to mean that every new activity requires the acquisition of knowledge and skill. It takes time (and therefore money) to master new jobs and new fields, but later knowledge provides efficiency and leverage.

BIBLIOGRAPHY

Chambers, Stuart, and Robert Johnston. "Experience Curves in Services: Macro and Micro Level Approaches." *International Journal of Operations and Production Management.* July 2000.

Das, Gurcharan. "Education: A Learning Curve; What's behind India's success in the global knowledge economy? One key is a boom in private schools for all." *Newsweek International.* 6 March 2006.

Lapre, Michael A., Amit Shankar Mukherjee, and Luk N. Van Wassenhove. "Behind the Learning Curve: Linking Learning Activities to Waste Reduction." *Management Science.* May 2000.

Stock, Howard J. "Learning Curve: How one rep who wasn't afraid to ask (and pay) for help has found it is boosting his production." *Bank Investment Consultant.* February 2006.

Waterworth, Christopher J. "Relearning the Learning Curve: A Review of the Derivation and Applications of Learning-Curve Theory." *Project Management Journal.* March 2000.

Hillstrom, Northern Lights
updated by Magee, ECDI

LEASING PROPERTY

A lease is a contract between an owner and a user of property. In business lease agreements, the owner (lessor) receives financial compensation and in exchange, the tenant (lessee) is given the right to operate his or her business on the property. There are many different types of property lease arrangements and many different considerations that business owners should weigh before entering into such a contract. But leasing is very popular with small business owners: such arrangements allow new or financially-strapped businesses to divert their capital to other business needs. Indeed, many small businesses operate in leased facilities for their entire existence. Leasing property, of course, may itself be a small business activity.

TYPES OF PROPERTY LEASES

Full-Service Lease This type of lease is used primarily in multi-tenant office buildings. In essence, lessees who agree to such arrangements pay a single lump sum for a wide range of supplementary services in addition to the lease payment. Under the terms of full-service leases, the landlord is responsible for providing a number of different services for his or her tenants, including security, maintenance, janitorial, and various utilities (water, electricity, air conditioning, heat).

Gross Lease Under the terms of a gross lease contract, the lessee pays the lessor a gross amount for rent (as well as sales tax when applicable). Property costs such as property taxes, insurance, and maintenance are the landlord's responsibility; the tenant is responsible for utilities. Sometimes the lease contract will include provisions that require the tenant to cover property costs that go over a certain specified level.

Variations of this basic lease arrangement include the flat lease and the step lease. The flat lease is the most basic type of agreement and generally the most popular with small businesses. It calls for the lessee to pay a flat set price for a specific period of time. The step lease, on the other hand, calls for a gradual escalation of the base rent payment over time in recognition of the likely rise in owner expenses in such areas as taxes, insurance premi-

ums, and maintenance. A related lease contract, usually known as the cost-of-living lease, includes rent increases based on general inflation figures rather than increases in specific expenses.

Net Lease The net lease is the most ubiquitous of the various lease contract types. Under the terms of a net lease, the tenant pays the landlord a base rent plus an additional sum that covers the tenant's share of property taxes. When taxes increase, it is the tenant's responsibility to cover those costs. The obligations of each tenant are figured by determining what percentage of the total facility is occupied by each tenant; thus a tenant occupying 20 percent of the facility pays 20 percent of the increase.

Variations of the basic net lease include the "double-net" and "triple-net" lease. Under a double-net lease, the tenant is responsible for picking up added insurance premiums as well as tax increases; under triple-net leases, tenants are responsible for covering insurance premiums, tax increases, *and* costs associated with maintenance and/ or repairs of the building, the parking lot, and other areas used by the lessee. The triple-net lease is popular with landlords for obvious reasons; small business owners should note that such arrangements sometimes make landlords less attentive to upkeep in these areas than they might be if they had to foot the bill themselves.

Percentage Lease This arrangement calls for tenants to pay a base rent and/or a percentage of the lessee's gross revenue. This percentage, which can run as high as 10-12 percent in some contracts, is paid on an annual, semi-annual, or quarterly basis (some malls and shopping centers, however, call for even more frequent payments). This arrangement is a favorite of lessors with property in coveted retail areas; tenants are less favorably inclined, but the laws of supply and demand often make it possible for owners of desirable property to insist on it. Small business owners should fully understand what the contract defines as "gross revenue." "Be specific in how you define gross sales," wrote Fred Steingold in *Legal Guide for Starting & Running a Small Business*. "Depending on your type of business, certain items should be deducted from gross sales before the percentage rent is determined. Here are some possibilities:

- returned merchandise
- charges you make for delivery and installation
- sales from vending machines
- refundable deposits
- catalog or mail-order sales
- sales tax

In short, make sure your lease excludes all items that overstate your sales from the location you're renting."

ADVANTAGES AND DISADVANTAGES OF LEASING

The Small Business Administration (SBA) counsels small business owners to consider a variety of factors when weighing whether to lease or buy property. These considerations include:

- Operating requirements—if the business's operating requirements are expected to change significantly over the next several years, leasing would probably be preferable, since it allows businesses to move more easily.

- Capital supply and capital needs—leasing frees up a greater percentage of a small business's capital for other operating needs (advertising, production, equipment, payroll, etc.). If the business does not have a lot of extra cash on hand (and few small businesses do), then leasing may be the more sensible choice. This is probably the biggest reason why small companies lease.

- Financing and payment flexibility—It is generally easier to secure financing to lease rather than purchase a property. In addition, leases can be spread out over longer periods than loans and can be structured to compensate for cash flow variations (the latter can be an important factor for seasonal businesses).

- Resale value—Is the value of the property likely to increase? If so, how much? Many small business owners choose to purchase rather than lease—even if they have to accrue significant debt—if they decide that the asset is a worthwhile long-term investment.

- Equipment—Many lease agreements include stipulations that provide lessees with increased flexibility in terms of upgrading and/or maintaining equipment.

- Taxes—Property owners enjoy tax benefits such as depreciation and investment tax credits that are not open to tenants.

OTHER LEASE TERMS

In addition, there are other elements of a lease agreement that can weigh heavily on a contract's overall acceptability. Details of lease contracts can vary enormously. "In theory," noted Steingold, "all terms of a lease are negotiable. Just how far you can negotiate, however, depends on economic conditions. If desirable properties are close to full occupancy in your city, landlords may not be willing to negotiate with you over price or other major lease terms. On the

other hand, in many parts of the country where commercial space has been over-built, landlords are eager to bargain with small businesses to fill empty units."

Leasehold Improvements Leases typically cover any remodeling that needs to be done to the property and specify who will pay for it. Most such work falls under the category of "leasehold improvements": carpeting, insulation, plumbing and electrical wiring, lighting, windows, ceiling tiles, sprinkler and security systems, and heating and air conditioning systems. The lease should specify each improvement and when they will be made— ideally before move-in. A landlord will be more willing to make such improvements if the lease duration is long and/or the space taken is substantial, and the improvements are general in nature. However, as Steingold noted, "if you [the small business owner] have specialized needs—for example, you're running a photo lab or a dance studio—and your darkroom or hardwood floor would be of limited value to most future tenants, don't expect the landlord to willingly pick up the costs of the improvements. The landlord may even want to charge you something to cover the cost of remodeling the space after you leave." Some leases provide tenants with the option of making improvements themselves provided that they adhere to certain guidelines and restrictions.

Length of Lease Negotiations between tenants and landlords often snag on the question of lease length unless the small business owner has a clear picture of the future. Lessors normally want long leases, lessees short leases with rights of renewal. Generally, small business owners try to secure leases with mid-range lengths. Leases of less than a year can leave them more vulnerable than they would like, but multi-year terms can be dangerous as well, especially if the business is new and unproven. A common compromise is to include an "option clause" in the contract so that the lessee can stay if he or she wishes at the conclusion of the original lease period.

Exclusivity Many small business owners quite reasonably insist that any lease agreement they sign contain what is commonly known as an "exclusivity clause." This clause provides the tenant with an exclusive right to sell his or her product or service on the property, obliging the lessor to prevent such sales by other tenants.

Insurance Landlords often ask lessees to secure insurance in the event that 1) the tenant damages the leased property, or 2) customers or others suffer injuries on the premises. Such clauses may be absent if the space rented is strictly for office use. When insurance is required by the tenant, the landlord frequently sets the amount.

Use of Premises Shopping center/strip mall landlords typically include language in the lease contract providing specific details on approved uses of the premises that are being rented. Such stipulations often serve to protect the businesses of other tenants. For example, the owner of a cafe in a strip mall may be quite unhappy if his neighbor, who formerly ran a quiet sports memorabilia shop, decides to change gears and launch a tattoo parlor.

In addition, lease contracts provide stipulations and regulations on many other issues of interest to both lessors and lessees. These include:

- Signage (regulates the size, style, and brightness of tenant advertising signs)

- Compliance with various zoning laws, permits, and restrictions on use of space

- Compliance with other local, state, and federal laws

- Subletting or assigning the lease

- Definition of the space being leased

- Security deposit

- Landlord's right to enter leased space

- Relocation (wherein the landlord relocates a tenant to another space because of remodeling or expansion by a neighboring tenant)

- Default provisions

- Hours of operation

- Incidents of damage or destruction from natural causes

- Repairs

- Indemnification provisions

- Abandonment (by the tenant, either through outright abandonment, diminished hours of operation, etc.)

- Condemnation (cases where all or part of the property is taken by city, county, state, or federal government for other use, such as road, right-of-way, or utility easement)

- Bailout clauses (in the event of catastrophic developments—tornadoes, riots, wars, floods, droughts, etc.)

- Cotenancy clauses (allows the business owner to break the lease if an anchor store closes or moves)

- Recapture clauses (also known as a cancellation clause, this allows landlords to evict tenants for breach of contract if the tenant is unable to meet minimum rent requirements)

CHOOSING BETWEEN EXISTING AND PLANNED BUILDINGS

Most start-up businesses move into already existing facilities. Many small business owners with the means to do so choose new facilities for the features or the prestige and take out leases while the facility is still in its planning stages. The savvy small business owner will consider the potential benefits and drawbacks of both choices before deciding. "Leasing in an existing building provides the Lessee … with more [knowledge about the place] at the time new space is occupied than any other facility option," said Wadman Daly in *Relocating Your Workplace*. "More so than in any other circumstances, the [lessee] is in a position to closely inspect both the facility and the terms of proposed leases in a number of competing locations. However, the nature of the lease in an existing building signifies minimum tenant control over the potential variables in either lease or facility. Rental rates, maintenance and escalation costs, utilities and building features are fixed or relatively non-negotiable. Landlords may vary in their abatements and finish-to-suit clauses, however their basic price structure, like that of the building and mechanical systems, remains unchanged. Of course, there are no investor implications with this option."

But Daly cautions that leasing in a planned building contains its own mix of attractive features and uncertainties: "Building features [in a planned building] will be new, up-to-date and, to a certain minimal extent, capable of adjustment to tenant need. If your lease is important enough to the developer, you may receive some attention when it comes to special requests for identification, parking, security, a prime location in the building, etc." Nonetheless, small business owners should be cautious when approaching such leases, for both the final appearance and utility of the building—as well as its costs—remain unseen and untested when the building is in its planning stages. "Proposed rental rates must be examined in the light of comparable projects with similar advantages," Daly wrote. "Descriptions of less obvious features like parking, air handling systems, security, maintenance, etc., should be clear and complete. The track record of the developer making the offer should be inspected carefully. Is there a history of quality construction at the rental rate asked, or one of build for quick re-sale? Is there a reputation for good maintenance or benign neglect? Regardless [of] the size of the lease or the duration of the proposed tenancy, these and related questions should be probed."

PROPERTY LEASING AS A BUSINESS

Buying, holding, and leasing property is also a common small business practice. It may begin modestly when a couple has difficulty selling a residence and chooses instead to rent it out. Then, with experience gained, they expand the activity business by buying, restoring, and leasing other properties. The small business owner, now a lessor, will be guided by those principles which favor the lessor, already indicated above. Leasing commercial property is sometimes the start and sometimes the culmination of such ventures. While most of the fundamentals of leasing are well-established and traditional, innovation is still possible in marketing such properties. An example is reported by Brandice Armstrong, writing in the *Journal Record* (Oklahoma City). Armstrong writes about the success of an Oklahoma City couple engaged in home and commercial leasing in leasing a commercial building. The owners hit upon the idea to hold an "open house," virtually unknown in the commercial field. They offered refreshments and door prizes. They immediately garnered 14 meaningful leads.

BIBLIOGRAPHY

Armstrong, Brandice J. "Couple Takes Unique Approach to Commercial Property Leasing." *Journal Record.* 18 January 2006.

Daly, Wadman. *Relocating Your Workplace: A User's Guide to Acquiring & Preparing Business Facilities.* Crisp Publications, 1994.

"Free Kit Offers Help to Commercial Tenants." *Business First-Columbus.* 26 May 2000.

Kahn, Jeremy. "Disownership is Everything." *Fortune.* 30 March 1998.

Sivaraman, Aarthi. "Leasing Requires Care at Several Key Phases." *Los Angeles Business Journal.* 13 June 2005.

Steingold, Fred S. *Legal Guide for Starting & Running a Small Business.* Nolo Press, 1997.

Hillstrom, Northern Lights
updated by Magee, ECDI

LEGAL SERVICES

Legal services are an important consideration for any business owner, but especially for small business owners, who often face a number of legal hurdles. Protecting the owner's personal assets from lawsuits against the business, ensuring protection for the business against lawsuits charging discrimination, wrongful termination, and sexual harassment, and handling employee contracts, copyright claims, and incorporation are just a few of the legal issues that commonly face small business owners.

The high costs of retaining a lawyer often make it seem as if competent legal services are out of reach of most small business owners. In addition, experts emphasize the dangers of entering into legal agreements without first obtaining advice from a qualified attorney. But there are reasonably priced methods of obtaining such services, like pre-paid plans and legal software. In many cases, this attempt to cut corners can turn small problems into big ones for small business owners. "Perhaps your tax structure is not to your best advantage, or you are not adequately protected from liability," Charles Poling noted in the *New Mexico Business Journal.* "If you're in a regulated business, you might run afoul of the law simply because you haven't gotten educated by your lawyer. Failing to consult with a securities or financial lawyer when you're raising capital can cause serious problems."

The type of legal services a small business should obtain varies with the size and age of the business. "Exactly what type of lawyer you need depends on what business you're in, and what stage it's at," Poling wrote. "A general business lawyer can help you as day-to-day questions come up, reviewing contracts and tax questions. But for more complicated matters, you might need a specialist. . . . Just starting up? Find someone who specializes in forming corporations or partnerships. Going public? Find a securities lawyer. Other specialties include environmental law, banking, patenting, copyrighting, medicine, nonprofit corporations, employment law, and so on."

According to Michael Barrier in *Success,* the best way to find a good attorney is by getting referrals from people you trust, especially those with similar legal needs. Before signing a retainer, small business owners should inquire about the attorney's experience, charges, and potential conflicts of interest. It may also be helpful to check your insurance policy, because certain litigation expenses may be covered.

PRE-PAID LEGAL SERVICES

Perhaps the most cost-effective way for small business owners to obtain legal advice is through a pre-paid legal services plan. These plans provide companies with affordable access to legal advice and attorney's services for one low, monthly fee.

Caldwell Legal, U.S.A. pioneered the concept in 1967 and remains one of the largest pre-paid firms serving small business. It offers Caldwell's Business Protector Program, available in all 50 states. At each Caldwell field office, attorneys provide telephone consultation, document review, letter writting, and other services, all for $37 per month. The plan includes unlimited hours of toll-free telephone consultation. The fee is indeed modest—based on Caldwell's own research which shows that 73 percent of legal problems can be solved with a single phone call. If more extensive services are needed, additional fees are applied as they are accrued. Caldwell charges hourly fees, if necessary, at the rate of $85 per hour ($125 per hour in New York).

Pre-Paid Legal Services is another company specializing in family and employee legal plans and may have solutions for the family-based small business and for businesses that wish to provide legal coverage for their employees (in the same way as they might provide health insurance). A family plan will range from around $16 to $36 a month for basic services—or higher if certain add-ons are selected.

ADVANTAGES OF PRE-PAID SERVICES

The primary advantage associated with pre-paid legal services is savings. For example, a typical pre-paid plan might charge $85 to $125 per hour for attorney's fees, plus the monthly premium, which can range up to $100 per month. Without the plan, the attorney's fees begin at around $200 per hour with a retainer fee of several thousand dollars often demanded up front.

Quality service is another promise of most pre-paid plans. For example, one plan requires its attorneys to have a minimum of 15 years of service, experience in business law, a favorable rating from Martindale-Hubbell (the rating service of the American Bar Association), and a clean record that shows no indication of ethical or malpractice claims against the attorney. Of course, these services vary in quality, just as attorneys vary in quality. Small business owners should do their research before signing up with a service. There are new ones joining the industry each year.

Another benefit of pre-paid plans is their size. Because they pool hundreds of small businesses, they instantly become one of the largest clients of whatever firm handles the plan's account. This is a huge benefit for small business owners. One owner on his or her own will be a very small part of any law firm's business. As one business owner in Ohio said of his former legal firm, "I felt I wasn't important enough to them." As part of the pre-paid plan, however, the small business becomes one part of a very important client that the law firm wants to keep happy to ensure continued business. Like HMOs, pre-paid plans offer collective bargaining power, as lawyers find it worth their while to offer low-cost services to plan members because of the high volume of business that is generated.

Pre-paid plans also make it easier for small businesses to practice preventive law instead of reacting to crises. Without the plan, a business owner is more likely to take his or her chances in any given situation and hope that no legal problems arise. This is because asking for legal advice can be so expensive. The plan, however, makes advice readily available and encourages owners to make use of it so that small problems do not become big problems.

HOW TO SELECT THE PLAN THAT IS RIGHT FOR YOU

The most important thing to look for is the number and type of services offered at a reduced rate as part of the plan. The number of services might be lower than you expect, so make sure the plan has what you need. Also find out what the plan charges for services that are not covered as part of the basic plan. A set fee for additional work may be cheaper in the long run than receiving a discount on the firm's "usual fee" for such services.

Additional steps to take include:

- Deciding whether you would prefer to work with just one lawyer over the years, or whether the service can provide a different lawyer for each legal matter.

- Do your homework. Obtain a list of clients and ask them if they have been satisfied with the quality of the legal work they have received.

- Ask how the law firm handles conflicts of interest when the person or business with a case against you uses the same pre-paid plan.

LEGAL SOFTWARE AND ONLINE ADVICE

Small business owners can also gain expertise and reduce risks and costs by utilizing one of the legal software packages that are designed just for small businesses. McGraw-Hill offers the *Small Business Lawyer,* a CD-ROM that contains more than 320 customized legal forms and agreements that cover such things as power of attorney, partnerships, loans, real estate, leases, and the sale of business assets. Once the software is installed, the business owner enters information about his business just once, after which all of the forms can be generated using that information.

A CD-ROM from Nolo Press called *Quicken Legal Business Pro 2006* includes the full text of five books published by Nolo, each targeted at the small business owner. The books, which are fully searchable, address hundreds of legal situations that are common to small businesses. The disc includes 140 forms and sample contracts and other useful legal documents.

Another potential source of legal forms and advice is the Internet. A number of Web sites exist that provide directories of attorneys, sources for legal research, samples of various types of forms and documents, and even free legal advice in chat rooms. For example, the American Bar Association site provides the addresses of state and local bar associations and lawyer referral services at http://www.abanet.org/legalservices/lris/directory.html. Martindale-Hubbell also sponsors an online "lawyer locator" at http://www.martindale.com/. The Web site www.uslaw.com offers overviews of the law as it affects small business and also provides a directory of affiliated lawyers.

But according to Carol Ebbinghouse in *Searcher,* small business owners should approach online legal services with caution. Obtaining legal advice online makes it difficult to establish a recognized attorney-client relationship, which may leave a small business without the protection of confidentiality and with no recourse in cases of malpractice or conflict of interest. Another potential pitfall is that online attorneys may not be licensed in the business owner's state. They may even be law students or otherwise lack the necessary experience or qualifications to provide good advice. For those who do use online legal services, Ebbinghouse recommends making sure the site is in compliance with Internet privacy and security protocols, reviewing all disclaimers and conditions, and double-checking the advice received.

BIBLIOGRAPHY

Barrier, Michael. "The Maw of the Law." *Success.* October 2000.

Britton, Akissi. "Do You Need Legal Insurance?" Essence. December 2002.

Bell, David M.M. "Ethics and the Internet: In a Chaotic Dot-Com World, Internet Use Presents Many Practical, Ethical, and Regulatory Questions for Lawyers." *California Bar Journal.* July 2000.

Ebbinghouse, Carol. "Medical and Legal Misinformation on the Internet." *Searcher.* October 2000.

Mogharabi, Shabnam. "Justice for All: Small businesses sometimes can't afford full-time lawyers. Prepaid legal plans might help ease your legal fees." *Pool & Spa News.* 8 August 2005.

Poling, Charles. "Is Your Lawyer Doing Right for You?" *New Mexico Business Journal.* March 1997.

Prizinsky, David. "Alliance specializes in counsel for cost-conscious companies." *Crain's Cleveland Business.* 6 February 2006.

Shottenkirk, Jerry. "Ada-based Pre-Paid Legal continues to prosper." *Journal Record.* 23 March 2006.

Hillstrom, Northern Lights
updated by Magee, ECDI

LETTER OF INTENT

A letter of intent is a document in which one or more parties signify an intention to do or to refrain from doing one or several things. Letters of intent (LOIs) are controversial under law being viewed ambiguously, as both binding and not binding. In *Corbin on Contracts,* a highly respected 14-volume law book updated twice yearly, the late Arthur Corbin commented on a letter of intent in the following terms: ". . . a letter of intent is not a useless document, but it is not, in principle, a contract except perhaps a contract to continue bargaining in good faith." Based on Merriam-Webster's dictionary definition, the term evidently arose in the context of government purchases in times of war when time was insufficient for executing contracts. The ambiguity inherent in the concept (is it or isn't it an agreement?) continues to be litigated.

The chief utility of letters of intent appears to be 1) to obtain a preliminary agreement on a matter before full details are worked out, 2) to establish confidentiality of elements being negotiated, and 3) to agree on how negotiations shall proceed. The general outlines of the deal may be included in the form of intentions, but not as binding until a final contract is negotiated. Thus LOIs have psychological value in somewhat committing both parties *early;* in other words, an agreement has been reached in principle. If made public, a letter of intent also serves as a signal to other interested or potential competing or hostile parties that the "deal is made." Signers of LOIs, however, continue occasionally to back out of deals—which leads to litigation. Courts are then required to settle which parts of LOIs are and are not binding.

CHARACTERIZATIONS

Gregory Gosfield, writing for the American Bar Association's *Business Law Today,* suggests that LOIs can be put into four groups arranged from least to most binding. The first type openly disclaims any contractual force to the letter, but as Gosfield points out, the letter will have "contractual effect as to the disclaimer." He places letters that deal only with rules for negotiation into the second group and views this type as the best use of LOIs. The third involves letters of intent that clearly spell out elements of the agreement in such a manner "as to permit a competent drafter to complete final documentation without a tremendous amount of additional negotiation." Letters of this type will specify a condition, left to the future, which will make the agreement legal, e.g., approval by a board of directors or signature by a specified officer. The last and fourth type of LOI Gosfield labels "letters of intent that have failed." In fact they *are* contracts. Gosfield suggests that "To reduce the risk of litigation, the single most important provision of the letter of intent is to disclaim contractual effect as to all but specifically preserved terms, a key one being the disclaimer itself."

Vasilios Kalogredis, writing for *Physician's News Digest,* provides categories typically listed as binding. He includes 1) confidentiality agreements relating to mutual information sharing, 2) non-disclosure of information to third parties, 3) "no-shop" clauses under which, for instance, a seller is prohibited from dealing with others during the negotiation, 4) setting of break-up fees in advance should the deal collapse, 5) termination dates and conditions to limit the negotiations, and 6) allocation of expenses to each party. Kalogredis suggests that non-binding aspects would deal with terms of the transaction itself. Finally, he indicates that closing conditions are often included in LOIs. These would include financing contingencies such as loan approvals, third-party approvals if needed, etc.

PROS AND CONS

In complex negotiations such as, for instance, the purchase or sale of a business, multiple contracts between buyers and sellers usually take place, many things are discussed, many things are said. The process may also take substantial amounts of time. Oral transactions of this type are subject to misinterpretation later, and oral agreements also have contractual force. In such situations a letter of intent written at the proper time—before final closing and drafting of actual language—can fix the main issues under discussion in written form and also clearly lay down rules which may be hampering negotiations, such as confidentiality of information. One may also have tactical advantages in having an LOI, especially in cases where multiple buyers are competing for one property. Writing the LOI serves to focus issues and to identify neglected matters. The LOI may also assure an insecure seller that the buyer is serious—and vice versa. LOIs also sometimes produce momentum and clarity and hence speed up a process that both wish to conclude. Finally, a well-written LOI is of substantial help to those charged with drafting the final contract.

On the negative side, LOIs take time to prepare and may turn into final negotiations which are supposed to *follow* the LOI. This can happen because parties may feel that even non-binding terms will become non-negotiable later, so why not negotiate them now? Thus time delays may be introduced. An LOI opens up channels of information for at least one of the parties—which may harm the other party if the deal ultimately fails. Letters of intent, by nature ambiguous, may become public (at least internally) and produce expectations or anxieties on the parts of employees, vendors, and customers. Kalogredis in addition points to "no-shop" clauses which may prevent a seller from discussing alternative deals, thus losing time, if in final negotiations an impasse arises.

TO SIGN OR NOT TO SIGN

Judith Silver, writing for *Intellectual Property Law Server,* headlines her story saying: "Letters of Intent: Why Business People Love 'Em and Lawyers Hate 'Em." Business people love them because they help to move negotiations along,

provide protections along the way, and occasionally garner positive press and upticks in stock values. As for lawyers, Silver says: "Letters of Intent, legally, are the worst of all worlds. In law, you either have a contract or you don't. LOIs are the legal equivalent of 'almost pregnant.' Letters of Intent emphatically state that they are not formal agreements and then often proceed to set forth agreed terms of the proposed transaction. Given this paradox, *if the deal goes sour,* one party can argue that those agreed-upon points were, in fact, agreed upon—or, in fact, a binding contract and, in some cases, furthermore, that the party relied on the LOI and has monetary damages based on such reliance." The emphasized phrase in the quote (the emphasis is ours) tells the whole story—and further underlines the difficulties: because, in advance, no one can be certain that the deal will *not* go sour. When all goes well . . . all goes well. But when not, and the LOI is poorly written, that is not likely to be the end of the story. Fortunately, in the overwhelming majority of small business transactions, good faith negotiation to a finished contract is very often achievable without letters of intent. If not, the letter should be written with the same care as the contract—and reviewed by a lawyer, however much he or she may hate the job.

BIBLIOGRAPHY

Corbin, Arthur L. (the late), Joseph M. Perillo (editor of Revised Edition), John A. Murray, Jr. (supplement author), and contributing authors. *Corbin on Contracts.* Matthew Bender, 2006.

Evanson, David R., and Art Beroff. "Write Soon." *Entrepreneur.* October 2001.

Gosfield, Gregory. "It's a Question of What's Binding." *Business Law Today.* July/August 2004.

Kalogredis, Vasilios J., J.D. "Should You Sign a Letter of Intent?". *Physician's News Digest.* September 2002.

Schiffman, Dana I., and Ben Hirasawa. "Use of Letters of Intent in Retail Leasing: When is a Non-Binding Letter of Intent Really Binding?" *Real Estate Issues.* Winter 2003/2004.

Silver, Judith. "Letter of Intent: Why Lawyers Hate 'Em and Business People Love 'Em." Intellectual Property Law Server. 26 July 2004. Available from http://www.intelproplaw.com/Articles/cgi/download.cgi?v=1090895569. Retrieved on 2 April 2006.

Darnay, ECDI

LEVERAGED BUYOUTS

A leveraged buyout (LBO) is the acquisition of a company in which the buyer puts up only a small amount of money and borrows the rest. The buyer's own equity thus "leverages" a lot more money from others. The buyer can achieve this desirable result because the targeted acquisition is profitable and throws off ample cash used to repay the debt. Such transactions are also known as "bootstraps" or HLTs, i.e., "highly leveraged transactions." Since they first appeared in the 1960s and took hold in the 1970s, LBOs have had mixed reviews from business people and other observers. Some see them as tools to streamline corporate structures, to rationalize meaninglessly diversified companies, and to reward neglected stockholders. Others see the LBO as a destructive force destroying economic and social values, the activity motivated by greed-driven predation.

TYPES OF LBOs

LBOs are typically used for three purposes, each in the category of corporate acquisitions generally. These are 1) taking a public company private, 2) financing spin-offs, and 3) carrying out private property transfers frequently related to ownership changes in small business.

Public to Private The first situation arises when an investor (or investment group) buys all of the outstanding stock of a publicly traded company and thus turns the company into a privately-held enterprise ("taking private" in reverse of "going public"). These deals may be friendly or hostile, the two terms related to management's point of view. Friendly cases typically involve the management buying the company for itself with plans to operate it thereafter as a privately-held entity. Hostile cases involve an investor or investor group intent on buying, reorganizing, and then reselling the company again to realize a high return. The sale of the company may be to another company or may be to the public in a stock offering. In the last case the situation actually amounts to a transaction more aptly labeled *public-to-private-to-public.* There are other variants in the disposition or in the payback of a third-party investor, although they tend to be rare, such as very high dividend payments and recapitalization by other groups.

Spin-Offs Public or private companies often wish to sell off elements of their business to get cash. In some cases the seller may itself have been bought in an LBO and is spinning off assets to pay the investors back. In such situations the spun-off element's management may itself be the buyer or may be passive in the transaction. An LBO is used to purchase the subsidiary or division in question. The fundamental financial logic of such deals, however, remains the same.

Private Deals The last situation concerns cases where a privately held operation is bought by an investor group.

Such cases often arise when a small businesses owner, having reached retirement age, wishes to divest him- or herself of the company and either cannot find a corporate buyer or does not wish to sell to a company. The buying group itself may be the company's employees or individuals associated in some way with the owner. These people organize an LBO because they only have limited equity.

FINANCING AND PAYBACK

The target of an LBO must, almost by definition, be profitable, growing, and produce a suitably large cash flow. In acquisitions jargon this is often abbreviated as EBITDA, meaning earnings before interest, taxes, depreciation, and amortization—the component elements of cash flow as ordinarily defined. Why cash flow? Because repayment of the large, leveraged debt is *from* future cash flows of the company. Other assets, of course, are also taken into consideration. If cash flow cannot keep pace with repayment, it is desirable that the company has saleable components (e.g., potential spin-offs) or liquid assets. Third party investors cannot be persuaded to put up cash unless the numbers look good, the elements of the company seem easily saleable, the company has lots of cash on its books, or all of the above are present.

The leveraged portion of the LBO may be as high as 90 percent of the deal but can be lower. In periods of unusual frenzy, the percent has even climbed above 90 percent. The rest is in the form of equity. Multiple "layers" of financing are involved: senior debt, senior subordinated debt, subordinated debt, mezzanine debt, bridge financing, and finally purchaser's own equity. The instruments described here are listed in increasing order of risk. In the case of a default, those holding senior debt will be paid first, owners of equity last (if at all); these security relationships are contractually built into the instruments themselves. Mezzanine financing is a hybrid between straight equity and debt, structured so that "mezzanine" holders are just barely paid something in an extreme case where equity holders lose everything. Bridge loans are short-term loans intended to be repaid either from the acquired company's cash holdings or from rapid disposition of company assets. Debt, of course, may be in the form of high-yield and therefore high-risk "junk" bonds.

LBO risks are high because payback depends entirely on the company's future performance. If the economy falters—or some event halts the purchased company in its tracks (a major lawsuit, the loss of a major account)—or if the high re-payments actually hamper the company by starving it of capital, investors may see their money turn into thin air. Healthy, growing, cash-rich companies purchased by an LBO therefore may lose their flexibility by losing their cash and simultaneously acquiring a huge load of debt: small shocks in the past become large shocks in the present. For these reasons investors expect returns above 20 percent per annum.

FOR AND AGAINST

Philosophical views of business go far in explaining positive and negative views of LBOs as well—and LBOs particularly (among merger and acquisition methods) because users of LBOs are predominantly interested in *changing* companies in order to extract benefits in the process. Those who see corporations predominantly in capitalist terms favor a business model in which stockholder equity is always maximized regardless of any other consideration. Those who view corporations as economic and social institutions with a wide penumbra of other interests also involved—stakeholders including employees, distributors, customers, vendors, etc.—view this method of acquisition, especially if used in hostile takeovers aimed at dismembering the corporation, slashing its employment, and taking it public again as disruptive and predatory.

In more mechanical terminology, proponents of such acquisitions claim multiple benefits. One of these is a more optimal debt-to-capital ratio. High debt and low capital mean lower taxes: interest costs are deductible. Reduced ability to invest in capital good increases the company's efficiency by reducing over-capacity. Companies using their profits for growth rather than dividends short-change the stockholder. Highly diversified companies in many unrelated businesses have much higher overheads—unnecessary if badly fitting parts are spun off. These motives translate into leaner and more profitable ventures producing higher return on investment—all of which favors ownership interests. Opponents, on the contrary, favor control and predictability through diversification, market share gains, flexibility in production and in ability to respond—all of which favors management, employees, and other stakeholders. Ultimately both sides have legitimate points to make, and the controversy, therefore, is likely to continue.

LBO TRENDS

The first LBOs were made in the 1960s; their use took hold in the 1970s and began to boom in the 1980s. LBOs in the first half of the 1980s were very successful, leading to a boom mentality in the second half of the 1980s with extraordinarily high rates of leverage, leading to many bankruptcies and failures in the early 1990s. A legislative reaction at the state level (states control incorporation and rules related to them) went through several cycles. States tightened rules against hostile takeovers;

the Supreme Court curbed such activities in a 1982 judgment; states then revised their rules to get around the high court's ruling—and these work-arounds were later approved in another Supreme Court case in the late 1980s. The upshot was to make hostile takeover more difficult, requiring buyers to acquire a higher percent of stock in order to take control. LBO deals diminished in the 1990s but began to heat up again in the new century, reaching another boom in the mid-2000s.

In general, LBOs are highly dependent on the availability of investment funds—money chasing opportunity. When money is tight and less risky ventures pay high returns, LBOs diminish and/or the degree of leverage used declines—buyers having to put up more of their own equity. When the economy is flush with cash, the number of deals and their magnitudes increase, purchase prices balloon, and investors also begin "reaching down" to purchase smaller companies ("microcaps" in the jargon of investment). Second, leveraged deals depend on healthy companies with high and predictable future cash flows—without which investors are difficult to attract to a deal. Hostile LBOs also require publicly traded companies so that the buyer can reach stockholders and persuade them to give the buyer control. As the 2000s roll along, conditions very much favor LBOs. Enormous trade deficits have produced a strong influx of foreign investments and the economy is flush with money. The future will undoubtedly bring a correction as the mid-2000s' exuberance brings a flurry of bankruptcies—echoing the crashes in the 1980s.

SEE ALSO *Mergers and Acquisitions*

BIBLIOGRAPHY

Burrough, Bryan, and John Heylar. *Barbarians at the Gate: The Fall of RJR Nabisco.* Collins; Reprint edition, 1 June 2003.

deBrauwere, Dan. "Six Major Catalysts of the M&A Market." *Westchester County Business Journal.* 23 January 2006.

Henry, David. "Why Junk Bonds Are Getting Junked; Leveraged loans offer better terms, but their floating rates could spell trouble." *Business Week.* 13 February 2006.

"Leverage Buyouts: A Brief History." Marshall Capital Corporation. Available from http://www.marshallcapital.com/AS6.asp. Retrieved on 4 April 2006.

Peters, Andy, and Michael Moline. "U.S. Deals Broke $1 Trillion Mark in 2005." *Fulton County Daily Report.* 15 February 2006.

Sherefkin, Robert. "Ross on Running Up Debt: Forget it." *Automotive News.* 19 December 2005.

Stires, David. "LBO Kings Go 'Clubbin'." *Fortune.* 3 April 2006.

Tully, Kathryn. "Could More Mean Worse? The biggest LBO club deals of 2005 will soon be surpassed." *Euromoney.* February 2006.

Turner, Shawn A. "Riverside Execs Anticipate Another Big Year: Microcap acquisitions fuel momentum." *Crain's Cleveland Business.* 13 February 2006.

Darnay, ECDI

LIABILITIES

A liability is a debt assumed by a business entity as a result of its borrowing activities or other financial obligations (such as funding pension plans for its employees). Liabilities are paid off under either short-term or long-term arrangements. The amount of time allotted to pay off the liability is typically determined by the size of the debt; large amounts of money usually are borrowed under long-term plans.

Payment of a liability generally involves payment of the total sum of the amount borrowed. In addition, the business entity that provides the money to the borrowing institution typically charges interest, figured as a percentage of the amount that has been lent.

A company's liabilities are critical factors in understanding its financial status. The company's liability status also enters into every transaction related to obtaining loans or leases on equipment.

TYPES OF LIABILITIES

Current Liabilities Current liabilities are short-term financial obligations paid off within one year or one current operating cycle, whichever is longer. (A normal operating cycle, while it varies from industry to industry, is the time from a company's initial investment in inventory to the time of collection of cash from sales of that inventory or of products created from that inventory.) Typical current liabilities include such accrued expenses as wages, taxes, and interest payments not yet paid; accounts payable; short-term notes; cash dividends; and revenues collected in advance of actual delivery of goods or services.

Economists, creditors, investors, and other members of the financial community all regard a business entity's current liabilities as an important indicator of its overall financial health. One indicator associated with liabilities often studied is working capital. The term refers to the dollar difference between a business's total current liabilities and its total current assets. Another barometer is the current ratio. Creditors and others compute the current ratio by dividing total current assets by total current liabilities, which provides the company's ratio of assets to liabilities. For example, a company with $1.5 million in current assets and $500,000 in current liabilities would have a three-to-one ratio of assets to liabilities.

Long-Term Liabilities Liabilities not paid off within a year (or within a business's operating cycle) are known as long-term or noncurrent liabilities. These often involve large sums of money necessary to undertake opening of a business, major expansion of a business, replace assets, or make a purchase of significant assets. Such debt typically requires a longer period of time to pay off. Examples of long-term liabilities include notes, mortgages, lease obligations, deferred income taxes payable, and pensions and other post-retirement benefits.

When debt classified as long-term is paid off within the next year, the amount of that paid-off liability should be reported by the company as a current liability in order to reflect the expected drain on current assets. An exception to this rule comes into effect if a company decides to pay off the liability through the transfer of noncurrent assets that have been previously accumulated for that very purpose.

Contingent Liabilities A third kind of liability accrued by companies is known as a contingent liability. The term refers to instances in which a company reports that there is a possible liability for an event, transaction, or incident that has already taken place; the company, however, does not yet know whether a financial drain on its resources will result. It also is often uncertain of the size of the financial obligation or the exact time that the obligation might have to be paid.

Contingent liabilities often come into play when a lawsuit or other legal measure has been taken against a company. An as yet unresolved lawsuit concerning a business's products or service, for example, would qualify as a contingent liability. Environmental cleanup and/or protection responsibility sometimes falls under this classification as well if the monetary impact of new regulations or penalties on a company is uncertain.

Companies are legally bound to report contingent liabilities. These are typically recorded in notes attached to a company's financial statement rather than as an actual part of the financial statement. If a loss due to a contingent liability is seen as probable, however, it must be included as part of the company's financial statement.

SEE ALSO *Assets*

BIBLIOGRAPHY
Pinson, Linda. *Keeping the Books: Basic Record Keeping and Accounting for the Successful Small Business.* Kaplan Business, 1 February 2004.

Stimpson, Jeff. "Small-Business Accounting Programs: Profiting by helping users is a valuable revenue source, well supported by the software suppliers." *The Practical Accountant.* March 2006.

Wirken, Jim. "Commentary: Accounts Payable: Keeping track is staying on track." *Daily Record.* 7 September 2005.

Wirken, Jim. "Commentary: Keep an eye on your firm's operating expenses." *Daily Record.* 26 October 2005.

Hillstrom, Northern Lights
updated by Magee, ECDI

LICENSING

A license is simply the right to do or to use something. The word, from Latin, means "permission," thus implying that a license is given by a party who controls something to another. Licenses divide into three basic forms: 1) the right or permission to carry out an activity otherwise regulated or prohibited by government; 2) the right to use a name, image, or representation (including a brand) in packaging, promotion, signage, marketing, and similar contexts; and 3) the right to use and apply proprietary know-how, whether patented or not, for any legal purpose, including its integral embodiment in products. Licensing activity comes in two forms: Licensors*give* licenses *to* others; licensees *receive* licenses *from* others.

Terminology The word itself, licensing, does not cover all forms and instances of the underlying relationship. For example, users of other people's patents are typically "licensed" to do so, but users of other people's copyrights are said to have "permission" to do so. In municipal government, many activities require "permits." These are functionally identical to licenses in that the permit holder must qualify in some way and is subject to rules. In commercial relationships a franchise is said to be "held" ("franchise holder"), but to franchise someone is equivalent to two forms of licensing (image and know-how). "Certification" is a widely used alternative, as in "Certified Public Accountant"; the CPA, however, is typically *licensed* by the state. "Certification" connotes something more advanced or refined than "licensing," hence is used in relation to professional permits—but professions well known to be of a high order of skill disdain from using the term. It is impossible to find a "certified physician" or "certified attorney" even though they are all licensed by the state. Conversely, when in ordinary speech someone is referred to as a "certified idiot," we know that the idiocy is of a high order.

GOVERNMENT LICENSING

The most common form of licensing is the governmental kind. After all, most adults are licensed drivers. But state government, in addition, licenses many skilled and professional occupations, including those that form the core of many small business activities. Small business, therefore, is most likely to be touched by this form of licensing. Municipal government issues all kinds of permits, equivalent to licenses. In Miami-Dade County, Florida, for instance, the county requires that all businesses have "occupational" licenses—but here in the sense of occupying a store.

A surprisingly large number of occupations are subject to license. In the state of Rhode Island, for example (picked at random), the state licenses 149 occupations. Thirty-two of those 149 occupations are architects and attorneys; barbers, but also beekeepers and boxers; chiropractors; dieticians, also dentists, and anyone associated with dog racing; electricians as well as professional engineers; funeral directors and buyers of fur at wholesale; hairdressers, cosmetologists, estheticians, and manicurists; investment advisers; occupations associated with the sport Jai Alai; lottery agents and livestock dealers; massage therapists; every kind of professional level nurse and midwife; occupational therapists and opticians; plumbers and physicians; real estate brokers; speech-language pathologists and many school-related occupations; travel agents and tattoo artists; veterinarians; wildlife rehabilitators; and even professional wrestlers.

The rationale behind licensing of occupations is obviously varied and based on the enforcement of health, safety, commercial, and other laws. One rationale behind Rhode Island's licensing of beekeepers, for instance, is to control importation of bee hives from another state, on which a fee is levied. In 2002, the state issued 160 such licenses, managed by its Division of Agriculture and Resource Marketing. Licensing of Jai Alai occupations is evidently part of enforcing gambling rules by the state's Division of Racing and Athletics; in 2002, the state issued 319 such licenses. In professional categories educational requirements must be met. A nurse-midwife, for example, must have completed "an approved educational program in midwifery that is accredited by the American College of Nurse-Midwives." The licensing is handled by Rhode Island's Office of Health Professions Regulation, part of its Department of Health. In 2002, 69 licenses were issued; Jai Alai wins by a wide margin.

Most businesses affected by licensing rules learn of these requirements in the course of qualifications or startup. Information on rules is, however, widely and easily available. The small business owner wishing to check on his or her need for such licensing might begin at the Web site of America's Career/InfoNet (see references) where access is provided to every state's occupational licensing requirements.

IMAGE LICENSING

Marketing of goods and services relies, in the first place, on capturing a potential customer's attention and then holding it by inducing a favorable reaction. Famous icons—be they celebrities, cartoon figures like Mickey Mouse, or widely recognized symbols like the letters NFL, GM, IBM or the five interlocking rings of the Olympics—have a function in attracting attention and in passing on the values that they represent to objects or messages to which they are attached. Icons are created in commerce by arduous performance and promotion, in which case they are brand identities; they are also "borrowed" or "recruited" by associating famous names with products. For purposes of brevity, all of these recognizable symbols may be summed up as "images." Images are licensed for the purpose of helping people market goods.

Underlying such licensing is law which protects brands, logos, and other trade-marked symbols from use by others; individuals also have the right to permit or to restrict their names from commercial exploitation by others. Thus, for instance, a newspaper may use the name Schwarzenegger in a headline but cannot label its paper as "The paper Schwarzenegger reads each day" without the California Governor's express permission. Should such permission be forthcoming, the paper would be*licensed* to use the name.

According to Stuart Elliott in *The New York Times,* citing The Licensing Letter published by EPM Communications, retail sales of licensed products in North America were $70.5 billion in 2004; based on the phrasing the number includes Canadian sales. But if all these sales had taken place in the U.S., they would have represented a mere 1.8 percent of total retail sales of $3,850 billion in 2004—thus a quite negligible portion of the total. Elliott also reports that such sales were down 1.3 percent from 2003. Amy Johannes, writing for *Promo* put worldwide retails sales at $175.3 billion in the same year, citing License! magazine. (Johannes' *headline* mistakenly shows $1.75 billion.) These two numbers indicate that image licensing affects a tiny proportion of sales at retail and therefore represents a sometimes-used marketing tactic.

KNOW-HOW OR TECHNOLOGY LICENSING

Many inventors and technology companies use patented methods and closely-held practices as the basis of licensing activity. Under a know-how or technology license, the licensee is enabled to deploy a design or use a patented process in his or her own manufacturing activities. The practice is as old as patent law and is present in all of the modern arts of production. Wherever the focus of invention is most intense, there new technologies

spring up and are spread by licensing. In the mid-2000s these techniques were mushrooming in electronics, pharmaceuticals, genetic manipulation, alternative energy, and exotic materials technologies, while, at the same time, continuing in traditional fields like mechanics and chemical and petrochemical processing.

Whereas image licensing is likely to be extremely rare in small business, virtually every small business engages in licensing some know-how—although the vast majority would be surprised to learn this. So would the vast public engaged in the same activity: the use of computer software takes place under a license that comes with the software itself. The licensing agreement explicitly prohibits using a purchased package on more than one machine. Such practices are extremely common and also difficult to police. In the international field piracy is a constant refrain. Confusion appears to reign domestically. As *Computer Trade Shopper* reported, "SMEs are failing to recognize the implications of not meeting licensing requirements, with only 56 per cent having a formal licensing policy. According to research by PC World Business (PCWB), 58 percent did not keep records of the software they owned or file license certificates, but 87 percent believed they were compliant." (SMEs are "small to medium enterprises.") At the same time, as Ed Foster reported in *InfoWorld,* pressures are mounting to bring small business into compliance. "Under the name of the Business Software Alliance (BSA)," Foster wrote, "Microsoft and its allies continue to bombard small businesses with anti-piracy mailings demanding that customers audit their licensing compliance; it is becoming pretty obvious who the real buccaneers are in search of plunder." The message in these developments for the small business owner is that he or she *is* engaged in licensing, knowingly or not, and that it might require a closer look.

LICENSING IN, LICENSING OUT

Using software purchased from others—or operating a proprietary process under a license—is to be "licensing *in.*" But the small business may also have an opportunity to "license *out*" if it has made a useful invention which may be of interest to others. In most cases the activity of licensing others is a new business in its own rights with unique activities and problems, of which the first may be patenting the invention itself to secure all rights to the new art. The activity is relatively easy if the company experiences positive demand for its invention and buyers are calling or visiting. When not, help from an experienced patent attorney may be the best first step in examining the feasibility of turning invention into profit.

SEE ALSO *Brand Equity; Inventions and Patents; Licensing Agreements; Royalties*

BIBLIOGRAPHY

"Branding News: Danger Mouse in clothing range." *Marketing.* 18 January 2006.

"Davy Process Technology (London, UK) has secured a second Chinese licensee in a month for its ethyl acetate technology, the only such technology to be based on bioethanol as feedstock." *Chemistry and Industry.* 6 February 2006.

Elliott, Stuart. "The Media Business: Advertising — Addenda; Licensed Products Fall 1.3% in Sales." *The New York Times.* 10 January 2005.

Foster, Ed. "The Gripe Line: BSA's truce campaigns – So-called anti-piracy truce campaigns leave customers feeling more like the distrusted enemy than a valued partner." *InfoWorld.* 27 August 2001.

Henricks, Mark. "License to Thrive: How you can profit from big companies' tech ideas." *Entrepreneur.* October 2005.

Johannes, Amy. "Live from Licensing International: 2004 Sales Reach $1.75 B." *Promo.* 6 October 2005.

"Licensed Occupations." America's Career/InfoNet. Available from http://www.acinet.org/acinet/licensedoccupations/lois_agency.asp. Retrieved on 4 April 2006.

Murphy, Terry. "The Licensing Handbook: How to make money in licensed products and stay out of trouble." *Impressions.* March 2006.

Rhode Island Department of Labor and Training. "Rhode Island Licensed Occupations." Available from http://www.dlt.ri.gov/lmi/jobseeker/license.htm. Retrieved on 5 April 2006.

Rivkin, Victoria. "Licensing Gets Bag Designer in Gear: Deal gives Yasmena manufacturing chops to expand its market; preserving its options." *Crain's New York Business.* 5 December 2005.

"SMEs Confused Over Licensing Needs." *Computer Trade Shopper.* 12 October 2005.

Darnay, ECDI

LICENSING AGREEMENTS

A licensing agreement is a legal contract between two parties, known as the licensor and the licensee. In a typical licensing agreement, the licensor grants the licensee the right to produce and sell goods, apply a brand name or trademark, or use patented technology owned by the licensor. In exchange, the licensee usually submits to a series of conditions regarding the use of the licensor's property and agrees to make payments known as royalties.

Licensing agreements cover a wide range of well-known situations. For example, a retailer might reach agreement with a professional sports team to develop, produce, and sell merchandise bearing the sports team's logo. Or a small manufacturer might license a proprietary production technology from a larger firm to gain a competitive edge rather than expending the time and money trying to develop its own technology. Or a greeting card company might reach agreement with a movie distributor to produce a line of greeting cards bearing the image of a popular animated character.

ELEMENTS OF A TYPICAL LICENSING AGREEMENT

Because of the legal ground they must cover, some licensing agreements are fairly lengthy and complex documents. But most such agreements cover the same basic points. These include the scope of the agreement, including exclusivity or territorial restrictions; financial aspects including required advances, royalty rates, and how royalties are calculated; guarantees of minimum sales; time schedules involving "to market" dates, length of contract, and renewal options; the lessor's rights of monitoring and quality control, including procedures to be followed; minimum inventories required to be maintained; finally, returns and allowances.

One of the most important elements of a licensing agreement covers the financial arrangement. Payments from the licensee to the licensor usually take the form of guaranteed minimum payments and royalties on sales. Royalties typically range from 6 to 10 percent, depending on the specific property involved and the licensee's level of experience and sophistication. Not all licensors require guarantees, although some experts recommend that licensors get as much compensation up front as possible. In some cases, licensors use guarantees as the basis for renewing a licensing agreement. If the licensee meets the minimum sales figures, the contract is renewed; otherwise, the licensor has the option of discontinuing the relationship.

Another important element of a licensing agreement establishes the time frame of the deal. Many licensors insist upon a strict market release date for products licensed to outside manufacturers. After all, it is not in the licensor's best interest to grant a license to a company that never markets the product. The licensing agreement will also include provisions about the length of the contract, renewal options, and termination conditions.

Most licensing agreements also address the issue of quality. For example, the licensor may insert conditions in the contract requiring the licensee to provide prototypes of the product, mockups of the packaging, and even occasional samples throughout the term of the contract. Of course, the best form of quality control is usually achieved before the fact—by carefully checking the reputation of the licensee. Another common quality-related provision in licensing agreements involves the method for disposal of unsold merchandise. If items remaining in inventory are sold as cheap knockoffs, it can hurt the reputation of the licensor in the marketplace.

Another common element of licensing agreements covers which party maintains control of copyrights, patents, or trademarks. Many contracts also include a provision about territorial rights, or who manages distribution in various parts of the country or the world. In addition to the various clauses inserted into agreements to protect the licensor, some licensees may add their own requirements. They may insist on a guarantee that the licensor owns the rights to the property, for example, or they may insert a clause prohibiting the licensor from competing directly with the licensed property in certain markets.

SEE ALSO *Licensing*

BIBLIOGRAPHY
Christian, Glynna K. "Joint Ventures: Understanding licensing issues." *The Licensing Journal.* October 2005.

Frost, Charles. "Good Business Means Protecting Your Intellectual Property." *Pipeline & Gas Journal.* May 2005.

Truesdell, Mark. "Structuring Licensing Agreements." *Association Management.* April 2005.

"What You Need to Know About Licensing." *Cabinet Maker.* 1 April 2005.

Wilcox, Deborah A. and Rosanne T. Yang. "Character Licensing." *The Licensing Journal.* January 2006.

Hillstrom, Northern Lights
updated by Magee, ECDI

LIFE INSURANCE

In general, life insurance is a type of coverage that pays benefits upon a person's death or disability. In exchange for relatively small premiums paid in the present, the policy holder receives the assurance that a larger amount of money will be available in the future to help his or her beneficiaries pay debts and funeral expenses. Some forms of life insurance can also be used as a tax-deferred investment to provide funds during a person's lifetime for retirement or everyday living expenses.

A small business might provide life insurance to its workers as a tax-deductible employee benefit—like health insurance and retirement programs—in order to compete with larger companies in attracting and retaining qualified employees. In addition, there are a number of specialized life insurance plans that allow small business owners to reduce the impact of estate taxes on their heirs and protect their businesses against the loss of a key employee, partner, or stockholder. Group life insurance is generally inexpensive and is often packaged with health insurance for a small additional fee. Companies that provide life insurance for their employees can deduct the cost of the policies for tax purposes, except when the company itself is named as the beneficiary.

Life insurance is important for individuals as well, particularly those who—like many entrepreneurs—are not covered by a company's group plan. Experts recommend that every adult purchase a minimum amount of life insurance, at least enough to cover their debts and burial expenses so that these costs do not fall upon their family members. The insurance industry uses a standard of five times annual income in estimating how much coverage an individual should purchase. The individual can also use a "backwards" calculation to establish what survivors will need to cope: current debt, two years of income for the spouse to find work, college funds for children, balance on the house, and estimated funeral expenses.

The cost of life insurance policies depends upon the type of policy, the age and gender of the applicant, and the presence or absence of dangerous life-style habits. Insurance company actuaries use these statistics to determine an individual's mortality rate, or estimated number of years that person can be expected to live. Policies for women usually cost less than those for men, because women tend to live longer on average. This means that the insurance company will receive premiums and earn interest on them longer before it has to make a payment. Experts recommend that companies or individuals seeking life insurance coverage choose an insurance agent with a rating of A or better, and compare the costs of various options before settling on a policy.

TYPES OF LIFE INSURANCE POLICIES

Term Insurance Term life insurance is the simplest and least expensive type, as it pays benefits only upon the policy holder's death. With annual renewable term insurance, the policy holder pays a low premium at first, which increases annually as he or she gets older. With level term insurance, the premium amount is set for a certain number of years, then increases at the end of each time period. Experts recommend that people who select term insurance make sure that their policies are convertible, so they can switch to a cash-value plan later if needed. They also should purchase a guaranteed renewable policy, so that their coverage cannot be terminated if they have health problems. Term insurance typically works best for younger people with children and limited funds who are not covered through an employer. This type of policy enables such a person's heirs to cover mortgage and college costs, estate taxes, and funeral expenses upon his or her death.

Whole Life Insurance With whole life insurance, the policy holder pays a level premium on an annual basis. The policy usually covers until the end of the person's life—age 90 or 100. In most cases, the policy holder is overcharged for the premium, and the extra amount goes into an interest-bearing dividend account known as a cash value account. The individual can use the money in this account to pay future premiums, or can withdraw it or borrow against it to cover living expenses. With a variable whole life policy, the individual controls the investments made with his or her cash value account. Selecting certain types of investments, such as mutual funds, may allow the policy holder to increase the balance in the account significantly. Regardless of the performance of the investments, however, the amount of the insurance benefit can never drop below its original value. When choosing a whole life policy, it is important to analyze the fund's past performance and inquire about commissions and hidden costs. Although whole life insurance can provide added security upon retirement, it should not be considered a replacement for retirement savings. Ordinary investment approaches are meant to provide for the future, life insurance, above all else, is meant to handle the contingency of death.

Universal Life Insurance Universal life insurance was introduced in the 1980s as a higher-interest alternative to whole life insurance. Universal life premiums are based not only on the cost of the insurance, but also on the interest rate offered on investments. Still, they are usually less expensive than whole life policies. Universal life policies provide individuals with a wider array of investment choices and higher projected interest rates. They are essentially similar to a term policy with a fixed rate of interest guaranteed for a year at a time.

Current Assumption Life Insurance Current assumption life insurance features a fixed annual premium for the duration of the plan. This type of policy pays a set interest rate on premiums received, less the actual cost of the insurance. They can be useful as a tax-deferred investment vehicle, since they usually pay 2 to 4 percent more than banks. Policy holders may elect to overpay their premiums early in the plan period to accumulate cash value. They can withdraw or borrow from the funds later for any purpose, including retirement income, or can use the cash value to pay the premiums for the remainder of the plan period.

Riders and Options Most types of life insurance policies give individuals the opportunity to add optional coverage, or riders. One popular option is accelerated benefits (also called living benefits), which pays up to 25 percent of the policy value to the holder prior to his or her death if he or she is struck by a serious illness. Another option, known as a waiver of premium, allows an individual to continue coverage without paying premiums if he or she becomes disabled. Many policies also provide an accidental death and dismemberment option, which pays twice the amount of the policy if the insured dies or loses the use of limbs as a result of an accident.

KEY PERSON PROTECTION

Small businesses tend to depend on a few key people, some of whom are likely to be owners or partners, to keep operations running smoothly. Even though it is unpleasant to think about the possibility of a key employee becoming disabled or dying, it is important to prepare so that the business may survive and the tax implications may be minimized. In the case of a partnership, the business is formally dissolved when one partner dies. In the case of a corporation, the death of a major stockholder can throw the business into disarray. In the absence of a specific agreement, the person's estate or heirs may choose to vote the shares or sell them. This uncertainty could undermine the company's management, impair its credit, cause the flight of customers, and damage employee morale.

Life insurance can help small businesses protect themselves against the loss of a key person by providing a source of income to keep business running in his or her absence. Partnership insurance basically involves each partner acting as beneficiary of a life insurance policy taken on the other partner. In this way, the surviving partner is protected against a financial loss when the business ends. Similarly, corporate plans can ensure the continuity of the business under the same management, and possibly fund a repurchase of stock, if a major stockholder dies. Although life insurance is not tax deductible when the business is named as beneficiary, the business may deduct premium costs if a partner or owner is the beneficiary.

BIBLIOGRAPHY

Bougue, Jeff. "Life Insurance Basics." *National Fisherman.* November 2003.

Fried, Julie. "Details Count When Employers Shift to New Group Life Plans." *National Underwriter Life & Health.* 28 November 2005.

"In Brief: Variable Life Policy Eyes Small Business." *American Banker.* 23 February 2006.

Koco, Linda. "Life By the Numbers." *National Underwriter Life & Health.* 6 March 2006.

Shuntich, Louis S. *The Life Insurance Handbook.* Marketplace Books, 25 July 2003.

"Tax Planning: The Meaning of Life Insurance." *Money Marketing.* 30 March 2006.

Zultowski, Walter H. "High-Net-Worth Business Owners Need Retirement Planning Help." *National Underwriter Life & Health.* 17 October 2005.

Hillstrom, Northern Lights
updated by Magee, ECDI

LIMITED LIABILITY COMPANY

The Limited Liability Company (LLC), a hybrid of the partnership and the corporation, has become a popular legal alternative for business owners. Now available in almost all states, the LLC combines the benefits of limited liability and pass-through taxation, much like an S corporation. But the LLC's legal structure is much looser, allowing many companies that find S corporation status too restrictive to take advantage of its benefits. Small business owners are taking advantage of the LLC because it is easier to set up and maintain than a corporation.

Because the LLC is a fairly new option in the United States (it first became available in Wyoming in 1977, but most other states did not follow suit until the 1990s), the laws governing this business form are largely uninterpreted by court cases. In addition, each state has its own statutes concerning LLCs. Therefore, learning and keeping up with the laws that govern LLCs, which are still being fine-tuned, can be a tricky business. When considering the LLC option, consulting knowledgeable and up-to-date legal and tax advisors is a must.

ADVANTAGES OF FORMING AN LLC

Limited Liability Like corporations, LLCs provide their members (owners) with protection from personal responsibility for the company's debt. Members are only liable to the extent of their investments in the company. If a customer slips and is injured on company property, a law suit may still bankrupt the business, but it cannot touch the personal assets of the LLC's members. This limited liability, then, is a great advantage over partnerships. In general partnerships, all members are liable for the company's debts and in a limited partnership, at least one member must still be liable.

Avoiding Double Taxation Like S corporations, LLCs enjoy exemption from the double taxation required of C corporations. In other words, the LLC's profits pass through to the company's members who report their share of the profits on personal federal tax returns. The company itself does not pay a federal tax before the money is distributed to the members, as in the case of C corporations. But state and local taxes may still be levied against the LLC.

Flexibility of Income Distribution According to some observers, one of the biggest benefits that small businesses enjoy when choosing LLC status is that allocation of profits and losses for tax purposes is easier under this form. Whereas the amount of profits the S corporation's shareholders report on their federal tax returns must be proportional to their share of stock, an LLC's members can determine amongst themselves how to divide their income as long as they follow the Internal Revenue Service's rules on partnership income distribution.

Simplicity Another great advantage of LLCs over corporations is the ease of setting up and running them. Whereas incorporation can be an involved and costly process, all that is required to start an LLC is the filing of an Articles of Organization and the drafting of an Operating Agreement defining the company's policies and procedures (a filing fee, however, will still be required of LLCs). And whereas a corporation requires a board of directors, officers, and regular shareholders' and directors' meetings, an LLC is not required to observe such formalities in its operation. An LLC can be run from day to day essentially as if it were a partnership.

No Ownership Restrictions The biggest drawback of forming an S corporation—the restrictions on the type and number of shareholders the corporation may have—is avoided by forming an LLC. The members of an LLC may be foreign nationals or other companies, both of which are prohibited from owning stock in an S corporation. In addition, there is no limit on the number of members an LLC may have, as there is with an S corporation.

Member Involvement in the Company One problem with limited partnerships is that those partners who wish to protect themselves with limited liability (which may be all but one of the members) are prohibited from direct involvement in running the company. These partners may have only a financial investment in the firm. All members of an LLC may be directly involved in the company's management without jeopardizing their limited liability.

Attractive to Foreign Investors Because LLCs have been in existence in Europe and Latin America for over a century, investors from those parts of the world are particularly knowledgeable about this business form. According to *The Essential Limited Liability Handbook,*

"LLCs often prove to be the most familiar and least imposing business structure for foreign entrepreneurs who wish to enter the American market."

DRAWBACKS OF FORMING AN LLC

Newness LLCs are still a very new option in most states (only Wyoming and Florida had LLC statutes on the books prior to the 1990s). This means that the statutes governing the establishment of LLCs are still evolving. And there is virtually no case history in the courts to indicate how these laws will be interpreted. The Internal Revenue Service is also still working out its position concerning LLCs, so it will be imperative for small business owners to solicit legal and tax advice on the current laws before making a decision about whether or not to form an LLC. And because the laws may change while the LLC is in existence, it will be important to keep on top of the developments in LLC statutes to determine whether it remains in the company's best interests to operate as an LLC.

Interstate Business More Complicated Laws governing LLCs can vary widely from state to state, complicating the conduct of business across state lines. There are, as of yet, no uniform laws concerning LLCs, so an even greater knowledge of the state laws will be required of the company that does business in more than one state.

No Perpetual Existence Most states require that an LLC's Operating Agreement set a limit to the company's existence (usually 30 years). And in the absence of a clause in the Operating Agreement providing for the continuance of the LLC in the event of the death or withdrawal of a member, the LLC will cease to exist when such events occur. The transfer of ownership is also more restricted for an LLC (like a partnership) than for a corporation.

Exclusions A few types of entities cannot be organized as LLCs. These include banks, insurance companies, and non-profit organizations. The situation may change in the future. Banking groups are pressuring the IRS for rule changes which would permit them to form such entities, particularly newly constituted banks.

CREATING AN LLC

It is important that the organizer(s) of a prospective LLC follow the "enabling statutes" or formation laws of the state in which the company will be formed in order to be designated as an LLC. Without this designation, the company will lack the protection of limited liability and will be treated as a general partnership. Therefore, the first step in creating an LLC is to find out your state's specific enabling statutes.

The organizer does not have to be one of the company's members. The organizer's function is to file the articles of organization, a task which can be accomplished by a lawyer, a hired agent from a service company specializing in such business, or a manager of the prospective company.

Naming an LLC Before forming an LLC, the company name must be reserved with the secretary of state or its equivalent. Most states require that the words "Limited Liability Company" or the abbreviation "LLC" be included in the name of the company. In some states, "Limited Company" or "LC" is the preferred designation. In all states, however, the name of the LLC must not resemble the name of any other corporation, LLC, partnership, or sole proprietorship that is registered with the state.

The Articles of Organization This form, called the articles of organization or certificate of formation, must be obtained from the secretary of state's office or its equivalent, filled out by the organizer(s), and filed with the same office. A filing fee, which varies from state to state, will also be charged. This simple document requires, at minimum, the company name and address, a description of the business to be conducted, the name and address of the registered agent (the contact to whom notices of lawsuit or other official matters can be served), the names of the company's members and managers (usually the members themselves), and the dissolution date. Other information may be required, depending on which state the articles of organization are filed in. It is important that the articles describe the business in a way that will allow the Internal Revenue Service to designate the company a partnership for tax purposes, and not a corporation. In order for the IRS to do so, the articles must show that the company possesses no more than two of the following four characteristics (which describe a corporation):

- Perpetual existence.
- Centralized management.
- Free transferability of ownership interest.
- Limited liability.

One of the easiest ways to show that the LLC is not a corporation is to limit its existence. In fact, most states require that a dissolution date be determined in the articles of organization. On this date the LLC's assets will be liquidated and its business will cease (occurrences such as the mutual written agreement of the members or the death or retirement of a member may also terminate the LLC's existence before the dissolution date). If no date is specified, a default period of usually 30 years will be enacted. However, the members may decide to continue the LLC's existence at a later date.

Fees Filing fees vary from state to state, from $50 to $500. In addition, some states require the LLC to publish an announcement of its creation to the public in a generally circulated newspaper. This latter requirement can be very expensive, ranging from $500 to $2,000.

The Operating Agreement At the first meeting of the members, called the organizational meeting, an operating agreement should be drafted. Although each state has laws governing how LLC's should be operated, the members should create their own operating agreement to document that all members agree on how the company should be run. It should be carefully constructed with an eye to preventing future disagreements and deadlocks. Most basically, the agreement should address the division of profits, members' voting rights, and company management. A good operating agreement will address the following issues:

- Who the members are and how they will be elected in the future.

- Grounds on which members may be terminated, and procedures to execute such terminations.

- Stipulations regarding allocation of business shares after the death of a member.

- If a member becomes disabled, how will the company provide for him/her (with disability insurance or out of its own funds)?

- How managers will be selected and what their duties, salaries, and grounds for dismissal will be.

- How major decisions will be made. (Which decisions will require unanimous approval of the members and which a simple majority vote? Which decisions can be delegated to the manager in charge of daily affairs?)

- How often meetings will be held and how much notice members must receive.

- Who will keep records and how they will be kept.

- How members will invest in the LLC: will only cash contributions be allowed, or can members contribute services as well? If so, which services will be accepted and how will they be valued?

- How profits and losses will be allocated to members.

- How compensation (salary) for actively participating members will be determined.

- How new capital should be acquired should the company need it.

- What procedures must be followed to transfer interests in the company.

- What banking procedures should be followed.

- Penalties, if any, if members or managers fail to act in accordance with the operating agreement.

BIBLIOGRAPHY

Bennett, Elizabeth. "Federal Tax Advantages Help LLCs Gain Favor in Delaware." *Delaware Law Weekly.* 29 March 2006.

Fink, Philip R. "Limited Liability Companies: Tax and Business Law." *The Tax Adviser.* June 2005.

Krebsbach, Karen. "Community Banks Press IRS Change: De novo and startup banks are eager to consider LLC status. But to be truly worthwhile, an IRS rule change is needed to make the switch more tax advantageous. So what's the holdup?" *US Banker.* October 2005.

Schnee, Edward J. "Debt Allocation and LLCs." *Journal of Accountancy.* September 2004.

Thompson, Margaret Gallagher. "Where We Were and Where We Are in Family Limited Partnerships." *The Legal Intelligencer.* 1 August 2005.

U.S, Department of the Treasury. Internal Revenue Service. "Publications – Limited Liability Company (LLC)." Available from http://www.irs.gov/businesses/small/article/0, id=98277,00.html. Retrieved on 4 April 2006.

Hillstrom, Northern Lights
updated by Magee, ECDI

LIQUIDATION AND LIQUIDATION VALUES

Liquidation means turning fixed assets into liquid assets, namely into cash. Thus an owner selling his or her business for cash as a going concern is technically liquidating it—but in usual parlance the term is applied only to a situation where a business is closed and all of its assets are sold. This may happen voluntarily or involuntarily; the owner may simply decide to stop doing business, puts a "Closed" sign on the shop or a message to that effect on his or her answering service, and proceeds to sell everything; alternatively the owner finds him- or herself forced into liquidation to pay off a foreclosed loan or, alternatively, assets are insufficient to cover debt and Chapter 7 bankruptcy liquidation is necessary.

It is a truism of business that a going concern is always worth more than its parts. It's a good rule unless the business is actually losing money and cannot be turned around. There is no particular magic involved in this valuation. The assets of a running business include its clients and their purchases. Machinery, equipment, shelving, and communications systems arranged complexly for a purpose are more valuable as a group than taken individually. The assets of a business may fetch as little as 20 cents on the dollar, possibly even less, all depending on the nature of the business and its inventory. A jewelry shop, the assets of which are mostly unsold diamonds and gold, will do much better than a machine shop with most tools 30 years old or older.

A liquidation tends to be a painful time in business life. Many liquidations follow months, occasionally years of anxiety and agony as a business gradually fails, and liquidation is *still* painful. It is, furthermore, as painful for a manager liquidating a subsidiary or a division for a large company as for an owner liquidating his or her business. While it is happening, those involved do not appreciate that they will gain valuable experience from the process—as people no less than as business persons. And to liquidate a business effectively is itself a business skill. It can be done well or poorly.

THE LIQUIDATION PROCESS

Deciding to Liquidate Good timing and sober judgment are important aspects of "success" in times of failure. The earlier the owner realizes that liquidation cannot be avoided, the more resources will be present to liquidate with least pain. Human nature and reason tend to conflict in such situations, as owners hang on for dear life in the face of clearest evidence and lottery-like odds. Almost always the tantalizing possibility of being saved is out there in the form of a big bid, a potential buyer, or some hoped-for event. Setting clear, hard deadlines and proceeding in a business-like manner toward a closing is the best policy. A business liquidating voluntarily and in an orderly fashion will almost always discover that its creditors, customers, and vendors will be cooperative. The sense of control will remain. If in the midst of such a process the miraculous turn-around event actually takes place, reversing course will also be easier.

Preparations Once a decision to liquidate has been reached, the business needs to be closed, employees discharged, and company assets must be secured and inventoried. In larger operations, the owner will require help in managing the liquidation. Therefore selecting one or more trusted employees to participate in the process is essential before lay-offs are announced and implemented as rapidly as possible. Effective actions in good time are important. Business closures sometimes produce unusual behavior in employees; they may feel cheated; the atmosphere of a free-for-all sometimes develops and caution is indicated to avoid wholesale theft and sabotage. Arrangements must be made to have locks changed and

valuable goods safely stored. This is sometimes difficult to do and requires early arrangements. Vendors and customers must be notified after the layoffs are accomplished. This, too, will require early planning. Finally, the owner should take his or her own inventory before third parties become involved.

Participants People entering the twilight zone of liquidation will discover it is populated by an entire industry little suspected to exist. There are professional appraisal firms whose routine business it is to value business assets. They appraise all manner of inventories and equipment daily and have an enormous depth of expertise. The owner facing such an appraisal, however, must brace him- or herself because prices named will seem extraordinarily low. If an experienced firm has been engaged, it will *not* be low-balling the assets but accurately valuing them in the current market. Alongside appraisers are liquidators specializing in selling inventory and equipment; a variety of selling techniques are used, including auctions. Unusual venues may be common. For example, all the inventory may be moved to an empty warehouse and laid out for a sale that might extend over several days. Some liquidators have added Internet outlets to their marketing and therefore a photographer may be taking digital shots of selected items as part of inventory.

The owner usually can and sometimes does set aside equipment to be held indefinitely or for sale by him- or herself. By the nature of their contacts, owners may have ideal clients for certain kinds of equipment. The owner can then assign the remainder to a specialist who will sell everything else and dispose as waste or scrap what cannot be moved.

VOLUNTARY AND INVOLUNTARY LIQUIDATIONS

In a bankruptcy liquidation under Chapter 7 of the bankruptcy law a court-appointed trustee will oversee the process and make crucial decisions. However distressed the owner might be—and the distress will be much greater if liquidation is forced by a foreclosure—he or she should refrain from letting things "get ugly." Such liquidations are termed "hostile." The owner then resists liquidation by neglecting orderly preparations, refusing to cooperate, delaying or denying necessary papers, and engaging in various kinds of disruption. Such situations can lead to further legal action and ultimately to much higher costs.

Voluntary liquidations take two forms. The best of these takes place when the owner decides to go out of business while still solvent and able, after liquidation, to pay off all outstanding debt. The second form involves an agreement with one or more creditors to liquidate but without a formal process. In the latter case, which tends to be rather rare, the owner will work in close cooperation with one or more agents of creditors, all parties endeavoring to get the highest possible yield for all assets.

ALTERNATIVES TO LIQUIDATION

If an owner feels that he or she must stop operating the business, the only real alternative to liquidation is to sell the business. This will be possible only if the decision is reached early enough, i.e., before the business actually fails. Sales may have been slipping; profits may have disappeared; but if there is still "life" in the business, it may well be possible to sell it—and at a price higher than liquidation will guarantee. For details on selling a business, see the entry *Selling a Business* in this volume. Many options are available. For a failing business the route most likely to be successful will involve letting the new owner pay off the acquisition price over time—with the current owner continuing to share the risk with the new owner up to a point.

SEE ALSO *Bankruptcy; Business Failure and Dissolution; Selling a Business*

BIBLIOGRAPHY

Hood, Doug. "Hard Sell – Managing liquidation of assets." *Entrepreneur.* November 2000.

Kupetz, David. "A Graceful Strategy for Liquidating a Business." *San Diego Business Journal.* 2 April 2001.

Kruger, Jennifer Barr. "When it Doesn't Make Sense to Go On: If you're looking at closing your store, you're not alone." *Photo Marketing.* January 2005.

Robbins, Steven. "Exit Strategies for Your Business." *Entrepreneur.* 27 July 2005.

Woolmore, John. "More Tips on Ensuring That You Get Paid." *Contract Flooring Journal.* January 2006.

Darnay, ECDI

LOAN PROPOSALS

Small businesses can obtain modest lines of credit by applying for credit cards—most of which will issue on the basis of a mere credit check by the issuing agency. Significant loans for the purchase of real estate, equipment, raw materials, or purchased components—and serious lines of credit—will require documentation of a correspondingly serious nature. Getting large loans is functionally identical to getting start-up financing in that the same kind of preparation, planning, care, and documents are necessary. A loan proposal will minimally consist of the proposal itself, a business plan, and financial data. Comprehensive presentations fare better than brief, skinny, and minimal packages—all other things

equal. The miraculous also sometimes happens—namely a large loan approved on the basis of a conversation with your bosom buddy, the local banker, but that sort of arrangement usually only happens after decades of dealings, not in the ordinary case.

A focused and professional approach is stressed by experts as a crucial element in getting funded. Kenneth DeWitt, for example, writing in *Commercial Carrier Journal,* cited the New Hampshire Commercial Financial Group (NHGC) as follows: "The vast majority of all business-financing proposals are eventually turned down. Key reasons for decline include (1) inadequate cash flow, collateral or security, and (2) proposing financing that is not compatible with a reasonable assessment of risk. *But another reason is a submission that is either unprofessional or insufficient.*" [Emphasis added.] DeWitt added that most business owners start with two strikes against them. "They are unaware of and unprepared for the standards they will be expected to meet in order to obtain financing."

PREPARATIONS AND RECONNAISSANCE

Most lenders give more attention to loan proposals prepared specifically for them and therefore tend to give lower rank to "one size fits all" submissions obviously aimed at multiple lending agencies. But in order to personalize a loan proposal, the business owner must get to know the lender and internalize the lender's needs and biases. It is, of course, best to select a bank in the first place with a view of using it later as a lender. In that process the owner begins his or her own "look at the landscape" before a loan is ever discussed. Later, as the need for a loan makes itself felt, financial advisors to small business (the Small Business Administration in the lead, but echoed by virtually every one else) recommend preliminary discussion to get a feel for the lender's criteria, qualification rules, the kinds of proposals the lender expects to receive, and the process of review to follow. As a minimum the owner ought to know smallest and largest amounts available, kinds of collateral expected, types of loans offered (line of credit? real estate only? lease financing?). Some banks have policy-based restrictions which may involve geography or type of business. If the lender is a poor match, the owner is well-advised to go elsewhere—and possibly open a second account at (or move the account to) the bank which looks most promising. Lenders tend to favor their own customers, again, all else equal.

It is generally desirable to have preliminary contact with the lending officer before a proposal is actually submitted. In smaller banks and when substantial loans are involved, this person may well be the bank's president. The business owner researching the loan application process and potential lender can indicate the size and nature of the loan in broad outline and thus get a feel if a proposal is likely to be welcomed. Many banks handle unusually large numbers of transactions, the evaluation of which is automated by using so-called loan origination software (LOS). In attempting to talk to people, the owner can determine in advance the amount and kind of attention the loan proposal is likely to receive and either adapt to the procedures or go elsewhere.

ELEMENTS OF THE PROPOSAL

The loan proposal may be broken into four elements: 1) the loan itself, 2) description of the business subdivided into several categories, 3) financial data, and 4) references. In addition the owner will typically write a concise cover letter which briefly highlights the proposal; and the proposal may have appendices as well, if appropriate, such as photographs, testimonials, possibly even samples. It is well to keep the objective in mind: the loan proposal is a document intended to communicate facts and projections, the latter documented as well as possible, and to persuade the lender of the merits of a case. Everything helpful to achieve this objective should be present.

Loan Description The first element should describe the loan—why it is sought; the benefits anticipated; how much is being borrowed; anticipated repayment schedule; how repayment will be accomplished and from what sources of money; and the collateral being offered to secure the loan. Many banks require that this portion of the loan proposal be put on forms that they provide. If the forms are unsuitable for communicating some piece of vital information, additional sheets may be added to amplify the presentation.

Business Description This part of the proposal should include information on the company's history and projected future path; its management, including resumes of key individuals; and an assessment of the business's market, including its general features and trends, competitors of the business, and key vendors and customers. If the company is relatively new, this information is sometimes supplied in the form of a business plan—typically an updated version of the plan used to obtain initial financing. If the company has been in operation for some time and it prepares an annual plan, that plan itself may be usable or adaptable for this purpose.

Financial Documents The business should submit at least three years' of financials—balance sheets and income statements. These should be year-end data for

the past and the last month of data for the current year. Federal income tax returns for the same period should be included. Projections of operations should be made out for one year at least by month. A separate cash flow projection should accompany this part of the proposal—vital because ability to repay the loan is based on net cash flow. If finances are audited, the audit report will be included, of course. In some situation it will be also necessary for the owner(s) to submit personal financial statement(s) as well. Details on important liabilities should be provided up front—other loans, lines of credit, leases etc., the providing agency's or agencies' names, terms, maturities, etc.

References Included in this section will be contacts with knowledge of the business, including its outside accountant, if any, a payroll service, the law firm, and occasionally major suppliers able to comment on the company's bill-payment performance and clients who can testify about future intentions to buy from the company.

REVIEW AND SUBMISSION

The business owner should anticipate presenting and defending the loan proposal to the lender. The best preparation for this will be careful review of the proposal, looking at it as if from the lender's perspective. Thinking through the questions that are likely to be asked and preparing thorough answers to those questions in advance is also very helpful.

Successful businesspeople come in every conceivable variety, from detail-oriented number crunchers to charismatic, high-flying salesmen barely able to multiply 12 by 3. The lender, of course, will be oriented toward numbers and facts, will want to talk about them, and will expect the owner to interact effectively on the details. For most owners this is not a problem, although a little homework will help. Those unskilled at this sort of thing and relying on a financial officer to herd the numbers is well advised to take that officer with him or her to the presentation.

In the real world all aspects of the loan process are vital—the initial reconnaissance and lender qualification, the proposal itself not only in its comprehensiveness but also in the rationality of its internal strategy, and finally the presentation to the lender. When all these aspects are handled effectively, the loan may still be turned down. If so, the final step, careful follow-up to discover the reasons for the turn-down, will get the owner ready for the next assault on Money Mountain.

BIBLIOGRAPHY
Chautin, Jerry K. "How To Make A Winning Loan Proposal." The Entrepreneur Network. Available from http://tenonline. org/sref/jc1.html. Retrieved on 9 April 2006.

"Credit Cards Only Useful for Short-Term Fix, Warns Recovery Expert." Financial Adviser. 21 July 2005.

DeWitt, Kenneth. "Financing Process Gets Tougher: Troubleshoot your own proposal—before it's too late." *Commercial Carrier Journal.* September 2002.

Green, Charles. *The SBA Loan Book.* Adams Media Corporation, July 2005.

"Make Preparations Before Approaching Bank for Your Loan." *Memphis Business Journal.* 3 November 2000.

"SBA Loans." Business.gov. Available from http://www.business.gov/topics/finances/sba_loans/index.html. Retrieved on 9 April 2006.

"Writing a Business Loan Proposal: Suggested Contents." Arkansas Small Business Development Center. Available from http://asbdc.ualr.edu/bizfacts/515.asp. 7 December 2005.

Darnay, ECDI

LOANS

Businesses are financed either by equity or debt, usually by both. Equity, of course, is the capital paid into the business by its owner and other investors who buy shares. This money can be recovered only by selling the shares or by selling the company, and investors are at risk for the total of their investment. Debt is based on contractual arrangements under which both repayment of the principal and payment of interest are specified, although certain forms of debt bear no interest: an example is trade credit under which a buyer may have up to 90 days to satisfy a bill. All forms of credit, in effect, represent loans from one party to another. Thus leasing of rental space or of equipment may be viewed as loans of real estate or of equipment, with rents and lease payments representing interest. All such transactions are recorded on a company's books as liabilities. A company's debt-equity ratio (liabilities divided by equity) represents the degree to which it is said to be "leveraged." The ratio is one of the measures lenders use to make judgments on whether to lend or not or, alternatively, on how much to lend. The old-fashioned, traditional view is that debt should be avoided; progressive thought holds that a good balance between debt and equity gives a company optimum flexibility for growth; speculative views favor maximum leverage in order to achieve the highest possible return for stockholders.

CHARACTERISTICS OF LOAN TRANSACTIONS

Lending and borrowing transactions are characterized by time factors, costs, and risk considerations; all three are closely related.

Time Factors. Term loans are classified by the length of time for which money is lent. Loans come in short-term, intermediate-, and long-term forms. Revolving credit and perpetual debt, however, have no fixed retirement dates. Revolving credit, better known as a "line of credit," provides a sum of money which the borrower draws down and then pays back, borrowing again when funds are needed again. Interest is paid only when funds are being used. Brokerage houses that extend margin credit for customers on certain securities work the same way. The holder of a perpetual loan, usually issued through a registered offering, only pays interest on the money and decides in his or her own time when to retire the principal.

Repayment Schedules match the type of loan obtained and also affect the costs of the borrowing. Payment terms available either call for combined payments of principal and interest at regular intervals or require interest payments only with the principal repaid as a single sum at the end of the contract. In the first case interest is charged only on the remaining balance of principal so that the interest portion declines over time. Under some types of leases, the lessor gradually acquires the real estate or the equipment being leased. In these cases the lease payment remains the same but the lessor's costs decline because he or she is able to claim a portion of the property as depreciation against taxes.

Cost. The cost of a loan is the interest charged. Interest may be fixed for the term of the loan or may be variable. If the rates are variable, they may be adjusted daily, annually, or at intervals of years (3, 5, and 10). Such rates (called floating rates) are tied to some index such as the prime federal lending rate. As a general rule interest costs are based on the current cost of money and the relative risk of the loan, so that collateralized debt costs less than unsecured debt.

Security. Assets pledged as security against the loss of the loan are known as collateral. Credit backed by collateral is secured. In many cases, the asset purchased by the loan often serves as the only collateral, but in other cases the borrower puts other assets, including cash, aside as collateral. Real estate or land collateralize mortgages. Unsecured debt relies on the earning power of the borrower.

COMMON TYPES OF LOANS

Consumers and small businesses obtain loans with varying maturities in order to fund purchases of real estate, transportation and production equipment, raw materials, parts, and other needs. The source of such funding may be friends and relatives, banks, credit unions, finance companies, insurance companies, leasing companies, and trade credit. State and federal governments sponsor a number of loan programs to support small businesses.

Short-Term Loans A special commitment loan is a single-purpose loan with a maturity of less than one year. Its purpose is to cover cash shortages resulting from a one-time increase in current assets, such as a special inventory purchase, an unexpected increase in accounts payable, or a need for interim financing. Trade credit is also a kind of short-term loan extended to the business by a vendor who allows the purchaser up to three months to settle a bill. In the past it was common practice for vendors to discount trade bills by one or two percentage points as an incentive for quick payment.

A seasonal line of credit of less than one year may be used to finance inventory purchases or production. The successful sale of inventory repays the line of credit. A permanent working capital loan provides a business with financing from one to five years during times when cash flow from earnings does not coincide with the timing or volume of expenditures. Such loans are common in seasonal businesses where, for instance, goods are manufactured in summer for winter sale or vice versa. In all such cases, creditors expect future earnings to be sufficient to retire the loan.

Intermediate-Term Loans Term loans finance the purchase of furniture, fixtures, vehicles, and plant and office equipment. Maturity generally runs more than one year but less than five. Consumer loans for autos, boats, and home repairs and remodeling are analogous intermediate loans.

Long-Term Loans Mortgage loans are used to purchase real estate and are secured by the asset itself. Mortgages generally run between ten and forty years. A bond is a contract held in trust with the obligation of repayment. An indenture is a legal document specifying the terms of a bond issue, including the principal, maturity date, interest rates, any qualifications and duties of the trustees, and the rights and obligations of the issuers and holders. Corporations and government entities issue bonds in a form attractive to both public and private investors. A debenture bond is unsecured, while a mortgage bond holds specific property in lien. A bond may contain safety measures to provide for repayment.

MIXED MOTIVES

In virtually all lending/borrowing situations the motives of the parties involved are in some conflict, at least on the margins. The business borrower's primary motive is to obtain the necessary financing to run the business at the least possible cost. His or her ideal source of funding is paid-in capital, but such equity is put at risk, and the owner feels this risk particularly if it is his or her own money. At the same time, if the money comes from investors, they will own shares of the company, and the more is owned by outsiders the less control the owner has. Even the most persuasive owner, able to get equity funding from others easily, will be constrained at some point—lest he or she lose control of the business. In this balancing act debt becomes an attractive alternative source of money. The owner's motive will be to get as much unsecured financing of this type as necessary at the lowest possible rates of interest and to obtain secured loans only if there is no other way. The owner will try to avoid debt because servicing it costs money—and it has to happen from cash flow. The less debt the business has to carry, the more rapidly his or her own equity will grow.

Independent investors in the business (if any) have yet another set of motives: they want to pay as little as possible for each share and see the value of that share grow. Investors like to "leverage" their investment by seeing it matched by borrowing. Since the borrowed money is used on their behalf, the more borrowing they can leverage the better. But, here too, constraints set it. Under current law the creditors of a business are first in line when the business fails. If the company is highly leveraged, investors are likely to lose their entire investment. Thus leverage is good—but it must be kept in line.

The lender, finally, is moved by a desire to earn money by lending it safely. Sources of large amounts of cash (banks, credit unions, insurance companies) are typically restrained by law and prudence from speculative investment of the money they hold in trust for others. They are conservative by their very structure and aim at predictable earnings by the safest possible means. Lenders ideally want secured loans at high interest rates, the latter kept low by competitive forces. They prefer to lend to the financially strongest possible borrowers; if competitive pressures force them to lend to weaker customers, they hedge the risks by charging more. From the lender's point of view, a financially strong borrower is one who has invested much and therefore has a great stake in the business's success; the business will also have a long, successful, and steady history of operations, and will offer ample collateral.

A small start-up with a brief history of mild success is thus in a relatively weak bargaining position and must make a very strong case before a favorable action by a potential lender is assured.

QUALIFYING FOR A LOAN

The three main factors that will help the small business qualify for a loan—aside from a successful track record—are good cash flow, a favorable debt-equity ratio, and carefully prepared documentation.

Net Cash Flow to Debt The lender first looks at a loan-applicant's cash flow because it is the source of loan repayment. Cash flow is often different from the profitability or assets of a business because sales booked appear on the books immediately but may show up as cash only later (when payment is received) and purchases made are immediately shown as costs but may only require cash later (when payments are actually made). The lender will initially calculate the amount of cash available to service the current portions of any new debt. If this amount is minimally 1.25 times the debt service required, the business is at least in the ballpark to receive a loan. A company with a net cash flow of $5,000 a month and a future debt with a $1,750 monthly payment, has a ratio of cash to debt of 2.86—plenty, in other words. To be sure, the lender will look for a *history* of such cash flows: a two-month history will not be enough. The higher this ratio and the longer the history, the more inclined the lender will be to lend. If the cash flow is lower, the battle is almost certainly lost—for now.

Debt-Equity Ratio This ratio is calculated by taking a company's liabilities and dividing them by the company's equity. A ratio of 1 means that for every dollar in equity the company has 1 dollar of debt. A company with no debt at all will have a debt-equity ratio of 0. Using data provided by MSN Money, in 2006 the combined debt-equity ratios of all companies part of the S&P 500 Stock Index was 1.04, suggesting that debt was just a hair greater than equity in these leading companies. But this ratio varies industry to industry. In capital-intensive industries the ratio will be significantly higher; in others much lower. In 2006 Microsoft's ratio was 4 cents to each dollar of investment; General Motors, struggling to stay solvent, had a ratio of nearly $20 in debt for each $1 of equity; General Electric's ratio was $1.94 to $1.

The ratio will tell the lender the commitment investors have made in the company, and the higher this commitment is in relation to borrowing, the more confidence the lender will have in being repaid.

Documentation In addition to favorable financial ratios, the lender will be looking at the company's performance over time. The borrower should anticipate providing the lender a loan proposal justifying the loan. Parts of that proposal will be a business plan, financial statements, and details on other debts and liabilities. Sometimes unfavorable ratios can be overcome by a consistent history of profitable performance and high growth—and even innovative plans with high potential

for success will carry weight. But the wise business owner will not bet on that.

The New Automation In the modern lending environment, computers and the Internet have amplified (and sometimes even usurped) the role of lending officers at financial institutions. One such development is loan origination software (LOS) offered by a number of companies over the Internet to banks, credit unions, and other financing agencies. These packages automate judgment on loan applications by calculating ratios, using averages for industrial categories, weighting experience factors, and even obtaining credit ratings automatically. One such package is LiquidCredit Bank2Business offered by Fair Isaac Corporation, a leading company in the field—but there are a number of others. These packages "score" loan applications and thus give loan officers confirmation for their own judgment—or give them pause. Downsizing in the banking sector, as reported by Mike Byfield in *Alberta Report* has caused an increase in caseloads and thus reliance on such services. So much for the bad news. The good news is that capital markets in the mid-2000s were flush with money. Conditions continuously change and cycle, to be sure, but the well-prepared business owner with good justification can still prevail and get his or her loan. That, of course, is just the beginning of getting on with the program.

BIBLIOGRAPHY

Anderson, Tom. "Choosing a Corporate Bank for Business Loan, Partnership." *Memphis Business Journal.* 3 November 2000.

Booth, James R. and Lena Chua Booth. "Loan Collateral Decisions and Corporate Borrowing Costs." *Journal of Money, Credit & Banking.* February 2006.

Byfield, Mike. "Small Business Borrowing Gets Trickier." *Alberta Report.* 3 January 2000.

Green, Charles. *The SBA Loan Book.* Adams Media Corporation, July 2005.

Jepsom, Kevin. "Solution To Scoring Biz Loans." *Credit Union Journal.* 27 February 2006.

"LiquidCredit Bank2Business." Fair Isaac Corporation. Available from http://www.fairisaac.com/fairisaac/. Retrieved on 7 April 2006.

"Make Preparations Before Approaching Bank for Your Loan." *Memphis Business Journal.* 3 November 2000.

MSN Money. Available from http://moneycentral.msn.com/home.asp. Retrieved on 6 April 2006.

Zhai, David. "Comment: Lenders, Beware Pitfalls In Loan Scoring Systems." *American Banker.* 30 May 2000.

Hillstrom, Northern Lights
updated by Magee, ECDI

LOCAL AREA NETWORKS (LANs)

In the modern office environment, each worker is equipped with a personal computer with its own processor and multiple disk drives. The computer may be free-standing (very much the exception these days) or it may be connected to a network, minimally to the Internet. In many small operations, like a doctor's office, a single computer may be used—but linked to the Internet. In most typical office situations, the computers of the organization are interconnected to each other as well by way of a local area network (LAN), typically by means of a single dedicated computer known as the "server," short for "file server." The linkage may be by wire or by a special radio frequency. The server used may also provide each "node" in the network with Internet service; and interoffice communications between computers are by e-mail. As the name suggests, such networks are *local* and shielded from external influences except as these are mediated by the network server, which is itself protected by so-called "firewalls" from unauthorized interference. In larger organizations local networks may be connected to one another. This extended arrangement is then referred to as a wide area network or WAN. Communications between LANs may be over proprietary communications lines (wired, wireless, or a combination) or may use the Internet.

One of the benefits of a LAN is that it may be installed simply and incrementally, upgraded or expanded with little difficulty, and moved or rearranged with little disruption. LANs are also useful because they can transmit data quickly. Use of such networks is becoming ever easier because new employees almost always bring computer skills and Internet experience easily adapted to the local customs.

HISTORY

The advent of personal computers (PCs) changed the type of information sent over office computer networks. Before their rapid spread in the 1970s, employees communicated with mainframe and mini-computers by means of so-called "dumb" terminals. All the processing took place on the main computer that all individuals used simultaneously. When use was heavy, the system's performance slowed. The PCs took over processing tasks at the desk and thus speeded things up substantially. With massive computing power no longer needed, smaller and simpler "file servers" could be substituted. Computerization thus opened up to even quite tiny operations.

LANs developed simultaneously to connect free-standing computers in offices that, until LANs came, exchanged data by passing diskettes around, and in operations using dumb terminals, such terminals first being replaced by PCs and, later, the connection to mainframes severed with the PCs now connected either to each other or to a server; using servers became by far the most common LAN configuration.

Developments in LANs proceeded along two fronts in the 1990s: competing networking software systems developed and changes in wiring took place to provide ever-faster communications speeds. Wireless transmission appeared in the mid-1990s and had become the leading edge of LAN technology by the mid-2000s using a new radio-communications standard known as 802.11, issued by the Institute of Electrical and Electronics Engineers, Inc. With the foundation of Wi-Fi Alliance in 1998 as a certification agency, "Wi-Fi" has come to mean wireless communications. The abbreviation stands for *Wireless Fidelity*. Wireless LANs are referred to as WLANs and sometimes as LAWNs.

During the 1990s, as well, global networking brought about by the explosive development of the Internet has played an enhancing role—enhancing the intimate *local* aspects of LANs by giving such networks national, indeed international, access too. LAN technology, in fact, has migrated from businesses to homes. In many residences multiple computers are linked by network connections, some connected by wire and some by radio links.

PHYSICAL COMPONENTS OF LANs

The physical properties of a LAN include network access units (or interfaces) that connect the personal computer to the network. These units are actually interface cards installed on computer motherboards. Their job is to provide a connection, monitor availability of access to the LAN, set or buffer the data transmission speed, ensure against transmission errors and collisions, and assemble data from the LAN into usable form for the computer.

Network cards may communicate with the network either by wire or by radio signal. Wiring remains the most common form in the mid-2000s but may change over time. Where wiring is used, it determines transmission speeds. The first LANs were connected with coaxial cable, the same type used to deliver cable television. These facilities are relatively inexpensive and simple to attach. More importantly, they provide great bandwidth (the system's rate of data transfer), enabling transmission speeds initially up to 20 megabits per second.

Another type of wiring, developed in the 1980s, used ordinary twisted wire pair (commonly used for telephones). The primary advantages of twisted wire pair are low cost and simplicity. The downside is a more limited bandwidth.

A yet more recent development in LAN wiring was optical fiber cable. This type of wiring uses thin strands of glass to transmit pulses of light between terminals. It provides tremendous bandwidth, allowing very high transmission speeds and (because it is optical rather than electronic) it is impervious to electromagnetic interference. Still, splicing it can be difficult and requires a high degree of skill. The primary application of fiber is not between computers, but between LAN buses (terminals) located on different floors. As a result, fiber-distributed data interface is used mainly in building risers. Within individual floors, LAN facilities remain coaxial or twisted wire pair.

Wireless communication is between radio devices which are themselves cards or specialized modems. Advantages are avoidance of wiring costs and hassle; disadvantages are distance limitations and interference. Unless a wireless system is properly configured to use signal encryption, the problem of the "evil twin" appears—a phrase used to label a device that appears to participate in communications because it inadvertently interferes with a poorly configured network.

WIRED LAN TOPOLOGIES

LANs are designed in several different physical arrangements of node computers, known as topologies. These patterns can range from straight lines to a ring. Each terminal on the LAN contends with other terminals for access to the system. When it has secured access, it broadcasts its message to all the terminals at once. The message is picked up by the terminal for which it is intended—or multiples of these. The branching tree topology is an extension of the bus, providing a link between two or more buses.

A third topology, the star network, also works like a bus in terms of contention and broadcast. But in the star, stations are connected to a single, central node (individual computer) that administers access. Several of these nodes may be connected to one another. For example, a bus serving six stations may be connected to another bus serving 10 stations and a third bus connecting 12 stations. The star topology is most often used where the connecting facilities are coaxial or twisted wire pair.

The ring topology connects each station to its own node, and these nodes are connected in a circular fashion. Node 1 is connected to node 2, which is connected to node 3, and so on, and the final node is connected back to node 1. Messages sent over the LAN are regenerated by each node, but retained only by the addressees. Eventually, the message circulates back to the sending node, which removes it from the stream.

TRANSMISSION METHODS USED BY LANs

LANs function because their transmission capacity is greater than any single terminal on the system. As a result, each station terminal can be offered a certain amount of time on the LAN, like a time-sharing arrangement. To economize on this small window of opportunity, stations organize their messages into compact packets that can be quickly distributed. When two messages are sent simultaneously, they could collide on the LAN causing the system to be temporarily disrupted. Busier LANs usually utilize special software that virtually eliminates the problem of collisions by providing orderly, non-contention access.

The transmission methods used on LANs are either baseband or broadband. The baseband medium uses a high-speed digital signal consisting of square wave DC voltage. While it is fast, it can accommodate only one message at a time. As a result, it is suitable for smaller networks where contention is low. It also is very simple to use, requiring no tuning or frequency discretion circuits. This transmission medium may be connected directly to the network access unit and is suitable for use over twisted wire pair facilities.

By contrast, the broadband medium tunes signals to special frequencies, much like cable television. Stations are instructed by signaling information to tune to a specific channel to receive information. The information within each channel on a broadband medium may also be digital, but they are separated from other messages by frequency. As a result, the medium generally requires higher capacity facilities, such as coaxial cable. Suited for busier LANs, broadband systems require the use of tuning devices in the network access unit that can filter out all but the single channel it needs.

THE FILE SERVER

The administrative software of the LAN resides either in a dedicated file server; in a smaller, less busy LAN; or in a personal computer that acts as a file server. In addition to performing as a kind of traffic controller, the file server holds files for shared use in its hard drives, administers applications such as the operating system, and allocates functions.

When a single computer is used as both a workstation and a file server, response times may lag because its processors are forced to perform several duties at once. This system will store certain files on different computers on the LAN. As a result, if one machine is down, the entire system may be crippled. If the system were to crash due to undercapacity, some data may be lost or corrupted.

The addition of a dedicated file server may be costly, but it provides several advantages over a distributed system. In addition to ensuring access even when some machines are down, its only duties are to hold files and provide access.

OTHER LAN EQUIPMENT

LANs are generally limited in size because of the physical properties of the network including distance, impedance, and load. Some equipment, such as repeaters, can extend the range of a LAN. Repeaters have no processing ability, but simply regenerate signals that are weakened by impedance. Other types of LAN equipment with processing ability include gateways, which enable LANs operating dissimilar protocols to pass information by translating it into a simpler code, such as ASCII. A bridge works like a gateway, but instead of using an intermediate code, it translates one protocol directly into another. A router performs essentially the same function as a bridge, except that it administers communications over alternate paths. Gateways, bridges, and routers can act as repeaters, boosting signals over greater distances. They also enable separate LANs located in different buildings to communicate with each other.

The connection of two or more LANs over any distance is referred to as a wide area network (WAN). WANs require the use of special software programs in the operating system to enable dial-up connections that may be performed by telephone lines or radio waves. In some cases, separate LANs located in different cities—and even separate countries—may be linked over the public network.

LAN DIFFICULTIES

LANs are susceptible to many kinds of transmission errors. Electromagnetic interference from motors, power lines, and sources of static, as well as shorts from corrosion, can corrupt data. Software bugs and hardware failures can also introduce errors, as can irregularities in wiring and connections. LANs generally compensate for these errors by working off an uninterruptable power source, such as batteries, and using backup software to recall most recent activity and hold unsaved material. Some systems may be designed for redundancy, such as keeping two file servers and alternate wiring to route around failures.

Security problems can also be an issue with LANs. They can be difficult to manage and access because the data they use is often distributed between many different networked sources. In addition, many times these data are stored on several different workstations and servers. Most companies have specific LAN administrators who deal with these issues and are responsible for the use of LAN software. They also work to backup files and recover lost files.

PURCHASING A LAN

When considering if a LAN is suitable for a business, several things must be considered. The costs involved and the administrative support needed often far exceed reasonable predictions. A complete accounting of potential costs should include such factors as purchase price of equipment, spare parts, and taxes, installation costs, labor and building modifications, and permits. Operating costs include forecasted public network traffic, diagnostics, and routine maintenance. In addition, the buyer should seek a schedule of potential costs associated with upgrades and expansion and engineering studies.

The vendor should agree to a contract expressly detailing the degree of support that will be provided in installing and tuning up the system. In addition, the vendor should provide a maintenance contract that binds the company to make immediate, free repairs when performance of the system exceeds prescribed standards. All of these factors should be addressed in the buyer's request for proposal that is distributed to potential vendors.

LANs can also be purchased for home use. Initially, these kits were expensive and slow and transmitted data via the phone lines in the home. New products have emerged that are faster, more affordable and use wireless technology to allow multiple computers to share printers and perform other LAN functions. This technology allows phone lines, cable connections, and LANs to be used simultaneously and is perfect for a small business owner who works out of his or her home.

SEE ALSO *Wide Area Networks*

BIBLIOGRAPHY
"The Basics of 802.11 Wireless LANs." *Communications News.* October 2005.

"Ethernet Essentials." *CommWeb.* 25 April 2002.

Flinders, Karl. "Small Firms Seek Big Functionality." *Computer Trade Shopper.* 11 May 2005.

Johnston, Randolph P. "High Tech for the Small Office: Hardware and software to improve your efficiency." *Journal of Accountancy.* December 2005.

Muff, Carol Ann. "How To Set Up a Wi-Fi Network — New Opportunities are in the air, literally." *VARbusiness.* 6 March 2006.

Murawski, Frank. "Fiber Soon to Overtake Copper in LAN Deployments." *Cabling Installation & Maintenance.* August 2005.

Hillstrom, Northern Lights
updated by Magee, ECDI

LOSS LEADER PRICING

Loss leader pricing is an aggressive pricing strategy in which a store sells selected goods below cost in order to attract customers who will, according to the loss leader philosophy, make up for the losses on highlighted products with additional purchases of profitable goods. Loss leader pricing is employed by retail businesses; a somewhat similar strategy sometimes employed by manufacturers is known as penetration pricing. Loss leader pricing is, in essence, a bid to lure customer traffic away from the businesses of retail competitors. Retail stores employing this pricing strategy know that they will not make a profit on those goods that are earmarked as loss leaders. But such businesses reason that the use of such pricing mechanisms can sometimes attract large numbers of consumers who would otherwise make their purchases elsewhere. In the world of e-commerce, loss leader strategies are intended to draw consumer traffic to an online retailer's Web site. The technique is also used for product introduction—thus several free copies of a magazine to induce purchase of a subscription, low rates for cable services, and other "introductory" pricing which, if not always priced at a loss, function in the same way.

In recent years, loss leader pricing has been practiced with considerable success, especially by large national discount retailers. The strategy is not without its critics, however. Indeed, many states have passed laws that severely limit—or explicitly forbid—selling products below cost. Very similar trends have emerged in Europe as well, with a ban on loss lead pricing in Irish groceries being a case in point. Lawsuits alleging that some loss leader pricing strategies amount to illegal business practices have also increased, although plaintiffs have not always been victorious. Opponents of such pricing practices argue that the strategy is basically predatory in nature, designed to ultimately force competitors out of business.

Defenders of the practice contend that loss leader pricing is simply one of many measures that retail establishments take to increase in-store traffic and, ultimately, their financial well-being. They note that U.S. antitrust and trade regulation statutes are designed to protect competition, not individual competitors, and that legitimate marketplace competition inevitably results in economic winners and losers. The furor over the practice is not expected to subside any time soon, however, because many small businesses, with strong support in many state legislatures, have been economically damaged over the past several years by larger competitors willing to take losses or razor-thin profit margins on some products in order to expand their customer bases.

Business experts note that suppliers sometimes object to loss leader pricing as well, despite the greater volume of sales that the practice often spurs within a given store. These increases may be offset by drops in sales at other stores where the brand is still priced high. Such developments can strain relations between supplier and customer, and in worst case scenarios, bring pressure on the supplier to lower its price for the good(s) in question. The practice is most debated among retailers. Some see loss leader pricing potentially inducing downward spirals of pricing which hurt everyone—except the chuckling consumer carrying 10 cans of peanut butter or instant coffee out to the car at 7:05 in the morning, five minutes after the store's opening.

Indeed, in recent years, retail industries have acknowledged a side effect of loss leader pricing. It's known as "cherry picking." This is a practice wherein customers move from store to store, making purchases only on those products that are priced near or below acquisition cost. Such purchasing patterns effectively foil the strategy underlying loss leader pricing—to lure customers who will also buy products with healthier profit margins—but to date the practice is not deemed to be sufficiently widespread as to be of concern.

SEE ALSO *Pricing*

BIBLIOGRAPHY

Garvey, Anthony. "Ireland's Below-Cost Ban Could Still Be Abolished." *Grocer.* 7 May 2005.

Hirschman, Celia. "Decoding Retailer's Disk Mojo." *Daily Variety.* 5 January 2006.

Hamilton, David P. "The Price Isn't Right: Internet Pricing Has Turned Out to Be a Lot Trickier Than Retailers Expected." *Wall Street Journal.* 12 February 2001.

Turen, Richard. "Loss Leader is No Loss." *Travel Weekly.* 13 December 2001.

Zettelmeyer, Florian. "Expanding to the Internet: Pricing and Communications Strategies When Firms Compete on Multiple Channels." *Journal of Marketing Research.* August 2000.

Hillstrom, Northern Lights
updated by Magee, ECDI

M

MAILING LISTS

Advertising is all about reaching the right people with the right message, and direct mail is one of many other advertising media used to deliver that message. Direct mail is thought to be a powerful tool precisely because it can be directed at pre-selected audiences, including sub-groups of those proven to respond to direct mail. This targeting of the message is accomplished by creating and using mailing lists for many different profiles of potential buyers. A business can gradually build up its own mailing list by directly soliciting the addresses of its customers in its outlets and/or by using print advertising. Alternatively it can rent mailing lists from compilers. It may even choose to sell its own list to others.

Based on data published in the 2006 *Statistical Abstract of the United States,* citing Universal McCann of New York, expenditures on direct mail in 2004 were $52.2 billion, 19.8 percent of total advertising expenditures. In the 1990 to 2004 period, total advertising expenditures increased 203 percent but direct mail expenditures grew 224 percent. Thus direct mail was outpacing advertising as a whole. During this same period, a new type of direct mail solicitation also came of age—electronic solicitation over the Internet. This mode of contact, by the nature of its very low costs, rapidly aroused spirited consumer opposition and came to be regulated under the CAN-SPAM Act of 2003.

MAILING LISTS IN CONTEXT

Mailing lists are compiled using various categories likely to appeal to a prospective mailing list buyer and thus represent virtually a catalog of any and all kinds of interests and profiles. Important classes are lists based on 1) income and demographics, 2) political, religious, and charitable characteristics—based on donations and memberships in organizations, 3) occupations and professional society memberships, 4) avocational and other interests as drawn from subscription lists to magazines, 5) past purchases of classes of products, 6) public lists available to list builders from government and regulatory agencies, 7) stockholders in companies, and 8) geographical lists compiled from telephone directories. The great variety of lists available for purchase ensures that most businesses looking for potential clients will be able to get a suitable list, whether their criteria are general ("the super rich") or very specific ("kayakers in Colorado").

Mailing lists are costly to assemble and to maintain. People are constantly in motion both physically and in other ways (they get divorced, go bankrupt, they sell their stock, they pick up other hobbies, change political affiliations, recover from ailments, etc.). Even if they remain on a list, they may no longer *belong* on a list. As a consequence of this dynamism, mailing lists are never completely up to date and tend to vary in quality based on the effort expended on purging and requalifying lists by the vendor; list vendors rarely expend the same intense efforts on *all* their lists. The upshot of this is that the list buyer will always also buy some "waste." He or she may be able to recover the cost of these names from the vendor but not the money spent on mailing to useless addresses.

Although people speak of "buying" mailing lists—and selling these to list vendors *does* take place routinely—the typical user of a mailing list actually *rents* the list for a one-time use. List vendors include addresses in every list intended to monitor what their customers send out. If a business rents a lists for a single mailing and then uses the list several times instead of only once, the vendor will know about this and send a new bill for second and subsequent uses—with proof in hand that the list has been reused.

Response rates to mailings tend to be very low. The best rates are achieved by the very costly mass mailings of sweepstakes marketeers ("You May Have Already Won!"—"Winner Notification Certificate Inside!"): these occasionally achieve return rates above 10 percent. Many direct mail users routinely get returns of less than 1 percent—and only a portion of these translate into sales. Direct mail is a medium like any other, not a silver bullet. List vendors typically require a minimum purchase (rental) of 5,000 names at rates between 8 and 25 cents per name. Minimum postage for pre-sorted mail in large quantities begins at 17 cents for non-profits, 18 cents for commercial users but may go as high as 24 cents if less sorting is done or quantities are relatively low. Production costs of the mailed piece will average 40 cents an item on a print run of 25,000 copies according to David Yates of *ControlBeaters*—not including costs of professional writers and artists, if employed. To achieve appropriate address formatting and sorting acceptable to the Post Office the business may have to employ a letter shop specializing in stuffing, addressing, sealing, stamping, and bagging the mail, labeling the bag, and getting the bags to the post office at between 2 to 3 cents per item. Assuming a somewhat minimal 25,000 item mailing, the business may be looking at a $17,000 cost, the material all written in house and creative costs *not* included. This estimate assumes the *lowest* range of costs throughout and average item cost (40 cents) for the mailing piece itself. This may, if the package is attractive enough, produce 250 leads at a cost of $68 a piece. If two-thirds of these leads translate into sales (165 items), each will have to absorb $103 in marketing expense. Obviously the item being sold has to be able to absorb such a surcharge or, in the long run, result in additional sales at much lower expense so that, ultimately, total sales will make the mailing worth while.

TYPES OF LISTS

Mailing lists are classified by the method of compilation. *Response lists* consist of names and addresses of individuals who have responded to an offer of some kind (by mail, telephone, billing inserts, etc.). The addresses provided may be that of a business or a home. Because these people are known responders, their names are generally priced higher than those in lists compiled by other means. But individuals on response lists may have responded to solicitation other than direct mail (e.g., a

phone call) and may not even open their "junk mail." Thus it is important for the small business owner to know what percentage of a list was direct-mail compiled. And always, the business owner's most valuable response list is the "house list" of current and past customers.

Compiled lists contain names and addresses of individuals gleaned from the White Pages and Yellow Pages, often enhanced with information gathered from public records (e.g., auto registrations, birth announcements, business start-ups). A very popular method of list compilation is through magazine subscriptions, since lists of readers provide an excellent means of targeting individuals in specific industries (e.g., *Institutional Investor,*) or within distinct areas of interest (e.g., *Field and Stream.*) Lists may also be compiled based on zip code when the small business owner seeks to reach consumers in a particular geographic area or income level. The average income of a zip code area is determinable from the decennial population census and thus can be used to classify such lists fairly precisely by level of wealth. Credit card lists are also an effective means of list compilation.

Membership lists come from all manner of associations and organizations with permanent members. Selling such lists is a source of income for the associations and groups involved. To be sure, this category itself is a compilation, but with the special character that members of such grouping are self-selecting and have specific profiles and associate income and interest patterns.

LIST SELLERS AND SERVICERS

Direct mail is an industry of $52.2 billion in sales, it is populated by a large number of list sellers. The base of the pyramid is represented by *list owners* who may be businesses with customer lists, banks with credit card customers, publishers of periodicals with subscription lists—anyone, in fact, with a list of names he or she is entitled to rent or sell to others. *List compilers* rent or purchase such lists for retail to final users and frequently combine and create their own composite lists. Compilers, being specialists in the management of lists, typically employ staffs for the purpose of qualifying, analyzing, purging, and otherwise engineering mailing lists. They are in the business of renting lists directly to end users and supplying list brokers. The *list broker* is a marketing expert specializing in direct mail; his or her job is to know what lists are available and which can be deployed for the purposes of a client. Brokers work with list owners or compilers and are paid a commission for list rentals (around 20 percent of the transaction). They typically represent the final user and are thus technically "buyers." The industry also has a specialized seller, known as the *list manager.* Managers represent owners and promote lists to ultimate users, compilers, and brokers.

Service bureaus have emerged in this industry. They specialize in the physical management of lists on behalf of owners and compilers. These operations are computationally advanced businesses which perform data mining, enhancement, and the more routine maintenance steps of merging and purging huge lists, eliminating duplicates, and "normalizing" variant forms of the same names and addresses.

Letter shops, already mentioned, service the ultimate list user by minimally performing mailing operations as already outlined. Many also offer data processing services to ensure that the addresses used conform to U.S. Postal service regulations and that the sorting is done to achieve lowest possible postage costs.

E-Mailings and Spam With the dramatic rise in Internet communications, e-mail rapidly came to be used for commercial solicitation. Here the mailing list transforms into a list of e-mail addresses which Web sites can capture from visitors mechanically and build into databases with a little programming effort. The volume of this new kind of mail grew so rapidly that it acquired the derogatory label of "spam." It was used and abused by organizations sending out millions of unsolicited e-mail messages selling anything from drugs to insurance to pornography. E-mail solicitation continues but has been curbed somewhat by Internet gateway providers that filter it out. E-mail solicitation has also come under government regulation.

This took the form of legislation awkwardly by cutely titled Controlling the Assault of Non-Solicited Pornography and Marketing Act—which just happens to abbreviate to the CAN-SPAM Act of 2003 (Public Law 108-197). The law was signed in December of 2003 and took effect on January 1, 2004. It requires that senders of unsolicited commercial e-mail label their messages, but Congress did not require a standard labeling language. Such messages must carry instructions on how to opt-out of receiving such mail; the sender must also provide its actual physical address. Misleading headers and titles are prohibited. Congress authorized the Federal Trade Commissioned to establish a "do-not-mail" registry but did not *require* the FTC do so. CAN-SPAM also has preemptive features: it prohibits states from outlawing commercial e-mail or to require their own labeling. Since 2003 other bills have been proposed but have not been enacted. Congress clearly hesitated straddling a fence: on the one hand consumer protection, on the other the free-wheeling market in virtual space.

Paper Spam? Curiously the "opt-out" feature required by U.S. law in electronic transmission is also available to people who receive unwanted sexually-oriented material by snail-mail. A person can obtain a Post Office form, entitled "Application for Listing and/or Prohibitory Order." It is available over the Internet (see citations). Using this form, the unhappy recipient of such mail can stop receiving such mail or gain the right to sue the sender. As for the rest of the junk mail, it will keep on coming.

SEE ALSO *Direct Mail*

BIBLIOGRAPHY
"AccuZip Inc.: AccuZIP6." *Quick Printing.* November 2005.

Davies, Kent R. "Little Black Book: How to buy and keep mailing lists." *Aftermarket Business.* November 2005.

"Direct News: New mailing list data in decline." *Marketing.* 20 April 2005.

Federal Trade Commission. "The Can-SPAM Act: Requirements for Commercial E-mailers." Available on http://www.ftc.gov/bcp/conline/pubs/buspubs/canspam.htm. Retrieved on 28 February 2006.

Goldberg, Laurence. "Get the Word Out With List Servers." *Learning & Leading with Technology.* February 2006.

Levey, Richard H. "Data by Design." *Direct.* 15 May 2005.

"Most E-Retailers Comply with Can-SPAM: FTC." *Promo.* 11 August 2005.

U.S. Postal Services. "Application for Listing and/or Prohibitory Order." Available from http://www.usps.com/forms/_pdf/ps1500.pdf. Retrieved on 10 April 2006.

Yale, David R. "Direct Marketing Beginners: What You Need to Know." ControlBeaters. Available from http://www.controlbeaters.com/L5.html. Retrieved on 10 April 2006.

Darnay, EDCI

MAIL-ORDER BUSINESS

A mail-order business is one that receives and fulfills orders for merchandise through the mail. The terms "mail-order," "direct mail," and "direct marketing" are sometimes used interchangeably; in fact the mail-order category is a subset of the two other categories which include any and all kinds of solicitation by mail, be it of sales or contributions to causes. Prior to the introduction to the official North American Industrial Classification System (NAICS), the Bureau of the Census classified mail-order as "Catalog and Mail-Order Houses" with the Standard Industrial Classification (SIC) code of 5961. As a sign of the times, beginning in 1997 the Bureau began using NAICS code 45411 and calling these businesses "Electronic Shopping and Mail-Order Houses." Since that time both in governmental classification as well as in common reference, "catalog sales" are treated as a single category regardless of what form the catalog takes. Within the industry as well, many participating companies use both print and electronic catalogs to sell their products.

BY THE NUMBERS

Sales Data from the Bureau of the Census for 2003 (the most current in 2006), indicated an industry with sales of $131,173 million that year. Of this total $90,794 million were traditional catalog sales (using printed media) and $40,379 million were e-commerce distribution (30.8 percent). The industry as a whole increased its sales by 7 percent over 2002, the print folks by 1.2 percent, the electronics people by 20.6 percent. Similar patterns of difference—e-commerce growing dramatically, traditional sales less energetically—were observable for retail sales as a whole. The chief difference was that in 2003 total electronic retail was around 2 percent of total retail but in the catalog category the e-share was ten times higher. This indicates that the "catalog shopping" mindset is more easily satisfied online than the "shopping" mindset generally.

Companies In 2003 the industry had 15,172 participating companies. The industry was predominantly populated by small businesses. Firms with 1 to 99 employees numbered 12,688, and the majority of these had 5 employees or fewer (9,324). To these must be added 1,856 companies without any employees at all, the owners doing all the work—for a total small business participation of 14,544 companies.

Employment The industry employed just under 265,000 people. Average earnings of employees were $24,800 in firms with 1-4 employees, $27,700 in firms with 5-9, $30,300 in firms with 10-19, and $33,000 in firms with 20-99 employees. The earnings of owners without employees were $77,000 per company. The largest employer category (2,500 employees or more) paid its employees $44,100 a year.

Products In the catalog business as a whole, the top-ranking product category was drugs, health, and beauty aids ($27.2 billion). In rank order the next four categories were computer hardware ($23.7 billion), clothing and accessories, including footwear ($15.1 billion), furniture and home furnishings ($8.3 billion), and office equipment and supplies ($6.96 billion). In the electronic component of this business rankings were slightly different and the volume, of course, lower. Top rank went to computer hardware ($6.7 billion) followed by clothing and related ($5.5 billion), office and related ($3.47 billion), the furniture category ($3.4 billion), and electronics and appliances ($2.9 billion).

PERENNIAL MOTIVE: CONVENIENCE

Mail-order businesses date back to pre-Revolutionary War days when gardeners and farmers ordered seeds through catalogs. Early catalog sales of general merchandise drew their support from a predominantly rural population for which shopping usually meant a day-long absence from the farm; but the retail stores the isolated farmers visited in nearby towns usually stocked only necessities/commodities with but a rare item of luxury now and then. In the 19th century catalog sales filled a vacuum, the catalogs always at hand, Montgomery Ward being the early dominant merchant, soon yielding market share to Sears Roebuck and Company. Until the late 20th century and the rise of the Internet, catalogs were always on paper but transformed themselves by using color photography. Both the solicitation and the ordering were at first by mail but, as telephone service became universal, telephone ordering from a printed catalog became an alternative. Since the 1990s, catalogs have appeared on the Web. The same catalog may be accessible both in printed and in online formats. And ordering in the mid-2000s took place by mail, by phone, and by the mouse-click.

The driving force behind "distance sales," as this field is sometimes characterized, has always been convenience—in rural times isolation made the catalog handy; in modern times very busy lifestyles (not least high and increasing female work-force participation), have motivated shoppers. Catalog shopping has always shown peaks in busy holiday seasons. In addition to the perennial motivation of convenience, catalog sales have always also offered customers a greater variety of choices than those available in brick-and-mortar establishments—as evidenced by catalog sales counters inside large department stores.

A VARIETY OF CATALOGS

Catalogs come in three major categories: business-to-business, consumer catalogs, and catalog showrooms. Business-to-business catalogs provide merchandise to be used in the course of business, including everything from office supplies to computers. In industrial settings, business-to-business catalogs are used to sell everything from heavy machinery to hand tools. Business-to-business catalogs are mailed to individuals at their place of business, with most purchases being made on behalf of the business.

Consumer catalogs are mailed to consumers at home and come in a variety of forms: independent catalog houses sell only from a catalog; retailers use catalog to generate store traffic, to sell goods directly, and catalogs intended to do both. Manufacturers' catalogs feature only products by a single producer. Catalogs distributed by museums or in the context of a major exhibition are a variant. Some catalogs are used by credit card companies to stimulate credit purchasing.

Catalog showrooms combine retail and with catalog marketing. A catalog showroom is essentially a retail outlet. The catalog, usually quite large, serves primarily to build traffic in the showroom. The trend in catalog showrooms has been to de-emphasize the mail order aspect of the catalog and present the showroom as a retail outlet with the added benefit of being able to place catalog orders from the showroom.

ISSUES OF STARTING A CATALOG BUSINESS

It might be said of mail-order and catalog sales is that "the product is the message," but paradoxically, the reverse is true as well: "the message is the product." In other words a catalog business must be some kind of innovative fusion between uniqueness of the products offered and the manner in which they are presented. Quite successful catalog ventures have been launched largely on message alone: the catalog has a mode of presentation that a segment of the buying public finds irresistible. Many gardening and seed catalogs, many clothing catalogs, have such an aura. The pleasure of using the catalog and contemplating what it offers is part of the experience. It draws the prospective buyer in. Prolonged attention to the catalog produces sales. Conversely, if the product line is genuinely unique featuring desirable but hard-to-get items, the presentation is much less important. A good example of such products are difficult-to-find electronic components or out-of-print and rare books. Uniqueness is sometimes achieved by having an incredible variety of all manner of products: the sheer wealth draws people in and holds the attention. In other cases the uniqueness arises from the source of the products or their unusual context—a feature of museum catalogs.

Another important consideration before startup is the cost of this particular channel of distribution. Catalogs are quite expensive to print and mail. A careful study of the costs and mechanics of mail- or web-based marketing should be undertaken. Aside from high catalog costs, catalog sales are a form of direct marketing which require the acquisition of mailing lists (usually priced for one-time use only), purchasing mailing services from letter shops, and the payment of postage based on weight. Response rates tend to be low (around 1 percent) and/or are proportional to the cost of the item sent out. A

catalog likely to be studied for an hour because it is very attractive will produce a higher response—but will also cost a good deal more to make. The business may need sufficient funding to survive quite some time while the sales build.

The prospective mail-order business may wish to sell its own product or be a merchant for others. In the latter case the business should make every effort to purchase the goods directly from the manufacturers themselves in order to avoid intermediate transfer commissions. But experts note that in some instances—such as scenarios where an offered product dramatically exceeds estimated sales—it may be necessary to deal with secondary sources in order to meet customer orders.

Some mail-order businesses arrange for their suppliers to ship the goods themselves. Under this system, mail-order outfits accept paid orders on behalf of the manufacturer then pay the manufacturer to mail the product directly to the customer. Some mail-order houses shy from this arrangement; such systems eliminate most inventory costs, they also compromise the independence of the mail-order house and its ability to ensure quality service. If a manufacturer proves incompetent or engages in questionable business tactics—such as using the addresses supplied by the mail-order business to compile its own mailing list, thus cutting the mail-order house out of the action down the road—a mail-order enterprise can find its very existence threatened.

REGULATIONS

A mail-order or other type of catalog business must comply with the regulations of the Federal Trade Commission (FTC) and the U.S. Postal Service (USPS). The business may also be subject to applicable state laws, especially concerning the collection of sales tax.

The FTC has issued several directives, guidelines, and advisory opinions concerning mail-order businesses. These and other relevant regulations are published in the Code of Federal Regulations (CFR), Title 16, Chapters 1 and 2, which is available in most large libraries or directly from the FTC. Among the most important of these FTC rules is the Mail-Order Merchandise Rule. This regulation, also known as the 30-Day Rule, is designed to protect consumers from unexpected delays in receiving merchandise ordered through the mail. It allows the customer to cancel any order not received within the time period advertised or, if none is stated, 30 days of order. According to the rule, in those instances in which shipment of goods is delayed, a customer must be notified within 15 days of placing his or her order. Moreover, if shipment is delayed past the agreed-upon delivery date (or 30 days), then the business must send a postage-paid return notice notifying the buyer that he or she may terminate the order for a full refund, which must be received within seven business days.

Another FTC rule requires all mail-order advertising to indicate the country of origin of the product being advertised if the product has a fabric as part of its content. This rule was designed to protect domestic textile and wool producers. Mail-order businesses are also subject to FTC guidelines concerning product guarantees and warranties that apply to all businesses.

Mail-order advertising frequently contains endorsements or testimonials. Under FTC guidelines, any endorsement must reflect the views of the endorser, and must not be reworded or taken out of context. In addition, the endorser must be a genuine user of the product. If the endorser has been paid, the ad must disclose that fact, unless they are celebrities or experts. Additional FTC rules apply specifically to endorsements by average consumers and expert endorsements.

The FTC has also issued guidelines to curb deceptive pricing by some mail-order businesses. These rules affect two-for-one offers, price comparisons, and other issues. The practice of advertising products that have yet to be manufactured, while legal, is subject to FTC requirements as well. FTC regulations call for this advertising practice, also called dry testing, to clearly state that sale of the product is only planned and that it is possible that consumers who order the product may not receive it. In addition, if the product is not manufactured, consumers who ordered it must be notified within four months of the original ad or mailing, and they must be given the opportunity to cancel their order without obligation.

In addition to FTC regulations, mail-order businesses must also be aware of USPS regulations. Lotteries, for example, are illegal under USPS regulations. As defined by the USPS, a lottery includes the element of chance, consideration—a term that means that one must make a purchase to enter—and a prize. In recognition of this definition, mail-order businesses instead organize sweepstakes that do not require any consideration, payment, or purchase on the part of the consumer. While sweepstakes have proved to be an effective method of advertising mail-order merchandise, many states have laws affecting their use.

Post office operations can impact on a mail-order enterprise in other ways as well. A mail-order house that presorts direct mailings by zip code can sometimes lower its postage costs, for example, while business-reply cards are subject to the approval of your postmaster. For complete information on postal rates, regulations, and requirements that could potentially impact a mail-order (or any other) business, contact your local post office or the Customer Programs Division of the U.S. Postal Service, Washington, DC 20260.

BIBLIOGRAPHY

Caplan, Jeremy. "Paper War: Environmentalists Take on Victoria's Secret for Mailing More than 1 Million Catalogs a Day." *Time.* 19 December 2005.

Entrepreneur Magazine. *Start Your Own Mail Order Business.* Entrepreneur Press, 1 December 2003.

Magill, Ken. "How to Boost Online Catalog Sales." *Direct.* 1 November 2005.

Retzlaff, Heather. "Cleaning Up Catalog Spoilage." *Multichannel Merchant.* 1 April 2006.

Schmidt, Jack. *Creating a Profitable Catalog: Everything You Need to Know to Create a Catalog That Sells.* McGraw-Hill, 1 April 2000.

Schultz, Ray. "For Catalogers, Print Rules." *Direct.* 1 July 2005.

Sloan, Carole. "Direct Retailing Outpaces Other Channels." *Textiles Today.* 20 January 2006.

Tierney, Jim. "The Paper Chase." *Multichannel Merchant.* 1 March 2006.

U.S. Bureau of the Census. *2003 Annual Retail Trade Survey.* Available from http://www.census.gov/svsd/retlann/pdf/artse-comml.pdf. Retrieved on 13 April 2006.

Hillstrom, Northern Lights
updated by Magee, ECDI

MANAGEMENT INFORMATION SYSTEMS (MIS)

A management information system (MIS) is a computerized database of financial information organized and programmed in such a way that it produces regular reports on operations for every level of management in a company. It is usually also possible to obtain special reports from the system easily. The main purpose of the MIS is to give managers feedback about their own performance; top management can monitor the company as a whole. Information displayed by the MIS typically shows "actual" data over against "planned" results and results from a year before; thus it measures progress against goals. The MIS receives data from company units and functions. Some of the data are collected automatically from computer-linked check-out counters; others are keyed in at periodic intervals. Routine reports are preprogrammed and run at intervals or on demand while others are obtained using built-in query languages; display functions built into the system are used by managers to check on status at desk-side computers connected to the MIS by networks. Many sophisticated systems also monitor and display the performance of the company's stock.

ORIGINS AND EVOLUTION

The MIS represents the electronic automation of several different kinds of counting, tallying, record-keeping, and accounting techniques of which the by far oldest, of course, was the ledger on which the business owner kept track of his or her business. Automation emerged in the 1880s in the form of tabulating cards which could be sorted and counted. These were the punch-cards still remembered by many: they captured elements of information keyed in on punch-card machines; the cards were then processed by other machines some of which could print out results of tallies. Each card was the equivalent of what today would be called a database record, with different areas on the card treated as fields. World-famous IBM had its start in 1911; it was then called Computing-Tabulating-Recording Company. Before IBM there was C-T-R. Punch cards were used to keep time records and to record weights at scales. The U.S. Census used such cards to record and to manipulate its data as well. When the first computers emerged after World War II punch-card systems were used both as their front end (feeding them data and programs) and as their output (computers cut cards and other machines printed from these). Card systems did not entirely disappear until the 1970s. They were ultimately replaced by magnetic storage media (tape and disks). Computers using such storage media speeded up tallying; the computer introduced calculating functions. MIS developed as the most crucial accounting functions became computerized.

Waves of innovation spread the fundamental virtues of coherent information systems across all corporate functions and to all sizes of businesses in the 1970s, 80s, and 90s. Within companies major functional areas developed their own MIS capabilities; often these were not yet connected: engineering, manufacturing, and inventory systems developed side by side sometimes running on specialized hardware. Personal computers ("micros," PCs) appeared in the 70s and spread widely in the 80s. Some of these were used as free-standing "seeds" of MIS systems serving sales, marketing, and personnel systems, with summarized data from them transferred to the "mainframe." In the 1980s networked PCs appeared and developed into powerful systems in their own right in the 1990s in many companies displacing midsized and small computers. Equipped with powerful database engines, such networks were in turn organized for MIS purposes. Simultaneously, in the 90s, the World Wide Web came of age, morphed into the Internet with a visual interface, connecting all sorts of systems to one another.

Midway through the first decade of the 21st century the narrowly conceived idea of the MIS has become somewhat fuzzy. Management information systems, of course, are still doing their jobs, but their function is now one among many others that feed information to people in business to help them manage. Systems are

available for computer assisted design and manufacturing (CAD-CAM); computers supervise industrial processes in power, chemicals, petrochemicals, pipelines, transport systems, etc. Systems manage and transfer money worldwide and communicate world-wide. Virtually all major administrative functions are supported by automated system. Many people now file their taxes over the Internet and have their refunds credited (or money owning deducted) from bank accounts automatically. MIS was thus the *first* major system of the Information Age. At present the initials IT are coming into universal use. "Information Technology" is now the category to designate any and all software-hardware-communications structures that today work like a virtual nervous system of society at all levels.

MIS AND SMALL BUSINESS

If MIS is defined as a computer-based coherent arrangement of information aiding the management function, a small business running even a single computer appropriately equipped and connected is operating a management information system. The term used to be restricted to large systems running on mainframes, but that dated concept is no longer meaningful. A medical practice with a single doctor running software for billing customers, scheduling appointments, connected by the Internet to a network of insurance companies, cross-linked to accounting software capable of cutting checks is de facto an MIS. In the same vein a small manufacturer's rep organization with three principals on the road and an administrative manager at the home office has an MIS system, that system becomes the link between all the parts. It can link to the inventory systems, handle accounting, and serves as the base of communications with each rep, each one carrying a laptop. Virtually all small businesses engaged in consulting, marketing, sales, research, communications, and other service industries have large computer networks on which they deploy substantial databases. MIS has come of age and has become an integral part of small business.

But while virtually every company now uses computers, not all have as yet undertaken the kind of integration described above. To take the last step, however, has become much easier—provided that good reasons are present for doing so. The motivation for organizing information better usually comes from disorder—ordering again what has already been ordered, and sitting in boxes somewhere, because the company controls its inventory poorly. Motivation may arise also from hearing about others who are exploiting some resource, like a customer list, while the owner's own list is in sixteen pieces all over the place. There are sometimes also reasons for *not* automating things too much: in modern times a business can grind to a dead halt because "the network is down."

Upgrading the information system usually begins by identifying some kind of a problem and then seeking a solution. In that process a knowledgeable resource-person brought in from the outside can provide a great deal of help. If the problem is over-stocking, for example, solving that problem will often become the starting point for a new information system touching on many other aspects of the business. The first question a consultant is likely to ask will concern how things are managed now. In the description of the process, the discovery of potential solutions will begin. It is usually a good idea to call on two or three service firms for initial consultations; these rarely cost any money. Once the owner feels comfortable with one of these vendors, the process can then be deepened.

The business owner has the option of buying various software packages for various problems and then gradually linking them into a system with the help of a value-added reseller (VAR) or a systems integrator. This solution is probably best for the small business with fewer than 50 employees. Larger companies may in addition also want to explore options offered by application services providers or management service providers (ASPs and MSPs respectively, collectively referred to as xSPs) in installing ERP systems and providing Web services. ASPs deliver high-end business applications to a user from a central web site. MSPs offer on-site or Web-based systems management services to a company. ERP stands for "enterprise resource planning," a class of systems that integrate manufacturing, purchasing, inventory management, and financial data into a single system with or without Web capabilities. ERPs are very popular with larger and midsized firms but were increasingly penetrating the small business sector as well in the mid-2000s.

SEE ALSO *Automation*

BIBLIOGRAPHY

"History of IBM—1910s." IBM. Available from http://www03.ibm.com/ibm/history/history/decade_1910.html. Retrieved on 15 April 2006.

Laudon, Kenneth C., and Jane Price Laudon. *Management Information Systems: Managing the Digital Firm.* Prentice Hall, 2005.

"Learning Zone – MIS: Time to plunge into automated systems." *Printing World.* 6 April 2006.

Shim, Jae K. and Joel F. Siegel. *The Vest Pocket Guide to Information Technology.* John Wiley & Sons, 2005.

Torode, Christina. "xSPs Rethink Business Models." *Computer Reseller News.* 15 July 2002.

Darnay, ECDI

MANAGEMENT BY OBJECTIVES

Management by objectives is a technique applied primarily to personnel management. In its essence it requires deliberate goal formulation for periods of time (like the next calendar or business year); goals are recorded and then monitored. The management guru Peter Drucker (1909-2005) first taught and then described the technique in a 1954 book (*The Practice of Management*). In Drucker's formulation the technique was called "management by objectives and self-control," and Drucker saw it as one of the forms of "managing managers." It became popular in the 1960s, by then abbreviated as MBO, the "self-control" parts more or less neglected, at least in talking about the subject. It experienced both an upward and downward drift: it came to be applied to the organization as a whole and to employees below the managerial level as well so that in many corporations many employees labored and still labor, at least once yearly, in formulating objectives. It was and remains an activity practiced predominantly in large corporations, although it spread in the 1970s and 80s to midsized organizations, commercial and other. In the mid-2000s it is viewed in many circles as a somewhat dated technique not well adapted to the rapid changes and uncertainties of a dynamic Information Age. However, it continues to have committed and enthusiastic supporters. In current practice it has also undergone changes and refinements.

MBO BASICS

Planning is the central concept supporting MBO in the sense that individuals and organizations do better by formulating goals than just by working or living alone—simply responding to crises and events. If an organization has clear objectives and managers and employees have set themselves objectives which support and harmonize with the company goals, then a coordination and orchestration of conscious motives will be driving the corporate activity. Thus management by objectives moves corporate planning downward so that it becomes translated into personal goals. But MBO was always articulated as a collective and supervised activity rather than as a personal discipline—precisely so that objectives could be coordinated. Goal setting is an annual exercise. The employee is asked to set five to ten personal goals; ideally these should be measurable in some way. Goals are discussed with the supervisor one level up. If the objectives are too vague or too easy, the employee must try again. Goals are next fixed in writing. Finally, periodic reviews of accomplishments against goals are carried out, the manager evaluating the employee. Reward systems are built around achieving the objectives.

MBO came of age in a time of change and ferment in U.S. management history, with corporations then responding to the dramatic rise of Japanese industry and Japan's commercial invasion—most visibly of the automobile market. To be sure Japanese business culture had different roots than the American; it had its origins in tribal associations and featured a very loyal work force, the latter no doubt supported by Japan's practice of lifetime employment. Meanwhile the American system, based on the creative energy of the entrepreneur, had evolved into very large and bureaucratic organizations. In this environment Japanese techniques were admired and imitated—under the leadership of MBA programs in business schools. "Quality Circles" sprang up and corporations were adopting numerical quality control—a Japanese technique the Japanese had learned from an American, Dr. W. Edwards Deming, and then perfected. Along with these methods came the promotion of other innovations all based on the conviction that loyalty could be trained and commitment induced: catch-phrases like the "learning organization," "total quality control," "team management," "matrix management," "reengineering," and "empowerment" arose in this environment with battalions of consultants and gurus in business to teach the way.

Pros and Cons The fundamental concept underlying management by objectives is based on wisdom: "If you don't know where you're going, you're certainly not going to get there." In any kind of complex activity, planning is good—be it a wedding or a new product introduction. Highly motivated individuals have conscious goals, pursue them with concentration, and do not rest until their aims are met. Effective individuals have to-do lists—on slips of paper, on personal digital assistants (PDAs), or in the head. In a sense MBO is simply the extension of the to-do list to a longer period with a few additional refinement: goals should be precise and measurable in some way. Discovering a measure in itself leads to closer attention to the goal. If the goal is broad and vague ("Greater Customer Satisfaction") looking for a measurement might refine it into ("Reduce Product Returns by 80 percent")—which goal will then more correctly focus attention on a company's quality problems or poor packaging. Focused, goal driven activity produces all sorts of benefits, not least more effective use of resources, saved time, and also higher morale. Conversely, companies and individuals that simply "go with the flow" may find themselves "swept away." One might say that effective managers and employees practice MBO knowingly or not.

The negative aspects of MBO have been due primarily to the more or less thoughtless and mechanical—and wholesale—application of the technique. MBO was and still is typically introduced as an exercise from the top and then administered by the numbers. Frequently employees with relatively narrow and straight-forward job descriptions (not just managers) are required to scratch their heads and come up with a precisely fixed number of goals. If the technique does not fit job descriptions well—if the only reasonable goals employees can come up with are restatements of tasks they ought to do in any case—the exercise becomes a ritual. Groups of people instinctively know when a technique is pro-forma. For this reason, in many organizations, the exercises resulted in detailed objectives recorded on paper and filed in notebooks to be routinely forgotten. Experience has shown that MBO works reasonably well where management leads and actively promotes goal achievement. But in such situations it is difficult to know whether it was the MBO program or *leadership* which actually achieved the results.

Rodney Brim, CEO of Performance Solutions Technology, LLC, and a critic of MBO, identified four reasons for the weakness of the MBO technique. He believed that the method went into decline in the market turn-down of the early 1990s when "downsizing," "right sizing," and other coping mechanisms captured management attention. "With the upturn of the market and the start of the Internet gold rush," Brim wrote, "management by objectives slipped further into the past. The term 'management' itself seemed to lose a sense of compelling interest. Riches were made based upon technology, upon acquisitions, upon something new, upon association with the WEB, not (for heaven's sake) management of work effectiveness." Brim's tally of weaknesses includes the following points:

1. Emphasis on goal setting rather than on working a plan.

2. Underestimation of environmental factors, including resources available or absent and the crucial role of management participation (already referred to above).

3. Inadequate attention to unforeseeable contingencies and shocks—which sometimes make objectives irrelevant.

4. Finally, a neglect of human nature.

Concerning the last point, Brim wrote: "People, the world over, set goals every year but don't follow them through to completion. One can surmise that this is the standard goal follow through behavior." Brim points out that business is well aware of this tendency, one reason why "work-out clubs... predictably sell more memberships at the first of the year than they plan on supporting through the year. The problematic assumption is that if you manage by goals and objectives, direct reports and team members will organize their work around what you are managing by, e.g. those same goals and objectives."

MBO AND SMALL BUSINESS

The small business owner who has a vague feeling that his or her business may be adrift might wish to look into management by objectives as a way of reviving focus. The owner will probably benefit from reading one or two books on the subject, including Drucker's own work, available in paperback—and then trying the method on him or herself. MBO was originally conceptualized as a management tool for managers—the managers presumed to be inherently motivated. MBO works well when its principles are *internalized*. It tends to fail when it is imposed. Its great benefits lie in the planning that it requires. In the case of the small business, corporate plans and the owner's personal plans often coincide, thus giving MBO ideal scope. The requirement of formulating *measurable* objectives is a good discipline. And "working the plan" with "self-control" applied, may produce quite tangible benefits. Experience with this technique, more than 50 years old and counting, indicates that committed management involvement is vital for success. If the MBO works well for the owner, the owner's own enthusiasm may act infectiously on other managers in the business. Use of the technique beyond a few key managers is more problematical.

BIBLIOGRAPHY

Batten, Joe D. *Beyond Management by Objectives: A Management Classic.* Resource Publications, December 2003.

Brim, Rodney. "A Management by Objectives History and Evolution." Performance Solutions Technology, LLC. Available from http://www.performancesolutionstech.com/FromMBOtoPM.pdf. 2004.

Drucker, Peter F. *The Practice of Management.* Reissue Edition. Collins, 26 May 1993.

Weihrich, Heinz. "A New Approach to MBO." *Management World.* January 2003.

Darnay, ECDI

MANAGER RECRUITMENT

The hiring of managers may take on a special dimension in a small business based on its history—and the owner's personal experience. Problems are likely to be few in cases where the business was launched by an experienced executives who had recruited perhaps dozens of managers during an extensive career before heading out to start a business of his or her own. Similarly, the owner may have bought the business with an effective management already in place. In yet other enterprises the owners began it as a partnership and share the management roles from the start; thus adding another manager is not a big deal. Problems may arise in family businesses where successive generations have been running a business, with top leadership passing from fathers or mothers to sons or daughters—until a time comes when an "outsider" must be hired. The issue of management hiring may also be unusually difficult in those situations where a founder has been the very soul and center of the business, having seen the business grow up, having made all the big decisions for many decades. Then, suddenly, it is time to share command with someone new because business is growing too big to manage alone any longer.

As these cases illustrate, adding management to small business can be or can develop into a problematical situation unless the owner consciously faces the issue long before it arises and prepares for it mentally and in practical ways. In part, the issue belongs in the category of forward planning. An owner seeing the business grow must put some conscious thought into expansion and anticipate the shock of having to share control. Depending on the person's experience, confidence, and temperament, different routes are available. An obvious approach is to hire a future manager early and then to coach this person gradually until he or she can assume the role in the course of time. Another is to set a milestone and, on reaching it, simply begin recruiting the right person with the qualifications long since outlined. In part the issue belongs in the category of succession. If the business is stable but not growing unusually fast—and the owner is nearing retirement—he or she is well advised to put in place the person who will run the business later.

In the case of a family business special considerations apply. If two or more members of a family are all working in the business as managers, integration of a new manager not related to the family requires considerable discussion so that the newcomer will feel welcome and a member of the team. This may be relatively easy to achieve if the business can offer the new manager a share in the company some time in the future if everything works out. If not, the family members, as a minimum, should all reach a consensus that the newcomer will require active involvement in decision processes so that no "we" vs. "they" feelings develop.

A consciously-developed, open, and professional human resources policy, especially if it is of long standing and well-understood by all the employees, can eliminate problems of this sort from the start. To institute and to implement such a policy may be something of a burden for the hard-driving, self-starting owner accustomed to making all the decisions. But if management *must* be hired, organizing or re-organizing the business to fit the new style will be much less burdensome than would be years in the course of which one new manager after the other departs in a huff because he or she is not given room and scope in which to work.

Some of the problems described above are, of course, not unique to small business but also appear in larger organizations in which divisions, departments, and branch offices frequently operate more or less autonomously under long-establishment managements and develop "family" or "tribal" traits. Such traits, paradoxically, can be very good for a business because the participants feel loyalty and commitment—and become problematical only when disturbed by change. For the small business manager, finding the right balance is the chief task when a smoothly running and coherent enterprise needs new talent. Finding the right solution is itself part of the entrepreneurial requirement. It requires management attention, planning, preparation, and careful watching. Aside from this requirement, management recruiting, of course, still leaves the more important part: finding the right person for the job.

SEE ALSO *Span of Control; Succession Planning*

BIBLIOGRAPHY
Angus, Jeff. "'Leadership' Myth Hides Need for Solid Managers." *CioInsight.* 6 July 2005.

"Fast-Track Recruitment." *Commercial Motor.* 23 February 2006.

Field, Katherine. "Multigenerational Retail: Both teens and seniors have a place in the labor pool." *Chain Store Age.* January 2006.

Hymowitz, Carol. "Managers Can't Limit Hiring To Clones of Themselves." *The Wall Street Journal Online.* Available from http://www.careerjournal.com/columnists/inthelead/20041013-inthelead.html. Retrieved on 16 April 2006.

Smith, Tony. "We Reap What We Recruit." *Journal of Property Management.* July-August 2005.

Yate, Martin. *Hiring the Best: Manager's Guide to Effective Interviewing and Recruiting.* Adams Media Corporation, December 2005.

Darnay, ECDI

MANAGING ORGANIZATIONAL CHANGE

Organizational change occurs when a company makes a transition from its current state to some desired future state. Managing organizational change is the process of planning and implementing change in organizations in such a way as to minimize employee resistance and cost to the organization while simultaneously maximizing the effectiveness of the change effort.

Today's business environment requires companies to undergo changes almost constantly if they are to remain competitive. Factors such as globalization of markets and rapidly evolving technology force businesses to respond in order to survive. Such changes may be relatively minor—as in the case of installing a new software program—or quite major—as in the case of refocusing an overall marketing strategy, fighting off a hostile takeover, or transforming a company in the face of persistent foreign competition.

Organizational change initiatives often arise out of problems faced by a company. In some cases, however, companies change under the impetus of enlightened leaders who first recognize and then exploit new potentials dormant in the organization or its circumstances. Some observers, more soberly, label this a "performance gap" which able management is inspired to close.

But organizational change is also resisted and—in the opinion of its promoters—fails. The failure may be due to the manner in which change has been visualized, announced, and implemented or because internal resistance to it builds. Employees, in other words, sabotage those changes they view as antithetical to their own interests.

AREAS OF ORGANIZATIONAL CHANGE

Students of organizational change identify areas of change in order to analyze them. Daniel Wischnevsky and Fariborz Daman, for example, writing in *Journal of Managerial Issues*, single out strategy, structure, and organizational power. Others add technology or the corporate population ("people"). All of these areas, of course, are related; companies often must institute changes in all areas when they attempt to make changes in one. The first area, strategic change, can take place on a large scale—for example, when a company shifts its resources to enter a new line of business—or on a small scale—for example, when a company makes productivity improvements in order to reduce costs. There are three basic stages for a company making a strategic change: 1) realizing that the current strategy is no longer suitable for the company's situation; 2) establishing a vision for the company's future direction; and 3) implementing the change and setting up new systems to support it.

Technological changes are often introduced as components of larger strategic changes, although they sometimes take place on their own. An important aspect of changing technology is determining who in the organization will be threatened by the change. To be successful, a technology change must be incorporated into the company's overall systems, and a management structure must be created to support it. Structural changes can also occur due to strategic changes—as in the case where a company decides to acquire another business and must integrate it—as well as due to operational changes or changes in managerial style. For example, a company that wished to implement more participative decision making might need to change its hierarchical structure.

People changes can become necessary due to other changes, or sometimes companies simply seek to change workers' attitudes and behaviors in order to increase their effectiveness or to stimulate individual or team creativeness. Almost always people changes are the most difficult and important part of the overall change process. The science of organization development was created to deal with changing people on the job through techniques such as education and training, team building, and career planning.

RESISTANCE TO CHANGE

A manager trying to implement a change, no matter how small, should expect to encounter some resistance from within the organization. Resistance to change is normal; people cling to habits and to the status quo. To be sure, managerial actions can minimize or arouse resistance. People must be motivated to shake off old habits. This must take place in stages rather than abruptly so that "managed change" takes on the character of "natural change." In addition to normal inertia, organization change introduces anxieties about the future. If the future after the change comes to be perceived positively, resistance will be less.

Education and communication are therefore key ingredients in minimizing negative reactions. Employees can be informed about both the nature of the change and the logic behind it before it takes place through reports, memos, group presentations, or individual discussions. Another important component of overcoming resistance is inviting employee participation and involvement in both the design and implementation phases of the change effort. Organized forms of facilitation and support can be deployed. Managers can ensure that employees will have the resources to bring the change about; managers can make themselves available to provide explanations and to minimize stress arising in many scores of situations.

Some companies manage to overcome resistance to change through negotiation and rewards. They offer employees concrete incentives to ensure their cooperation. Other companies resort to manipulation, or using subtle tactics such as giving a resistance leader a prominent position in the change effort. A final option is coercion, which involves punishing people who resist or using force to ensure their cooperation. Although this method can be useful when speed is of the essence, it can have lingering negative effects on the company. Of course, no method is appropriate to every situation, and a number of different methods may be combined as needed.

TECHNIQUES FOR MANAGING CHANGE EFFECTIVELY

Managing change effectively requires moving the organization from its current state to a future desired state at minimal cost to the organization. Key steps in that process are:

1. Understanding the current state of the organization. This involves identifying problems the company faces, assigning a level of importance to each one, and assessing the kinds of changes needed to solve the problems.

2. Competently envisioning and laying out the desired future state of the organization. This involves picturing the ideal situation for the company after the change is implemented, conveying this vision clearly to everyone involved in the change effort, and designing a means of transition to the new state. An important part of the transition should be maintaining some sort of stability; some things--such as the company's overall mission or key personnel--should remain constant in the midst of turmoil to help reduce people's anxiety.

3. Implementing the change in an orderly manner. This involves managing the transition effectively. It might be helpful to draw up a plan, allocate resources, and appoint a key person to take charge of the change process. The company's leaders should try to generate enthusiasm for the change by sharing their goals and vision and acting as role models. In some cases, it may be useful to try for small victories first in order to pave the way for later successes.

Change is natural, of course. Proactive management of change to optimize future adaptability is invariably a more creative way of dealing with the dynamisms of industrial transformation than letting them happen willy-nilly. That process will succeed better with the help of the the company's human resources than without.

SEE ALSO *Organizational Growth*

BIBLIOGRAPHY
Gilley, Ann. *The Manager as Change Leader.* Praeger, 2005.

"The Industry Isn't Changing. It Has Changed!" *Beef.* 13 March 2006.

Lawler III, Edward E. and Christopher G. Worley. "Winning Support for Organizational Change: Designing employee reward system that keep on working." *Ivey Business Journal Online*. March-April 2006.

Murray, Art and Kent Greenes. "The Enterprise of the Future." *KMWorld*. March 2006.

Schneider, Dan. "It's a Leader's Duty to Manage Change." *Business Record (Des Moines)*. 20 February 2006.

Schraeder, Mike, Paul M. Swamidass, and Rodger Morrison. "Employee Involvement, Attitudes and Reactions to Technology Changes." *Journal of Leadership & Organizational Studies*. Spring 2006.

Wallington, Patricia M. "Making Change." *CIO*. 1 April 2000.

Wischenvsky, J. Daniel and Fariborz Damanpour. "Organizational Transformation and Performance: An examination of three perspectives." *Journal of Managerial Issues*. Spring 2006.

Hillstrom, Northern Lights
updated by Magee, ECDI

MANUFACTURERS' AGENTS

Manufacturers' agents or representatives are independent contractors who work on commission to sell products for more than one manufacturer. They are not under the immediate supervision of the manufacturers—typically called principals—that they sell for, so their relationship generally falls into client-customer patterns.

Manufacturers' agent firms range from businesses operated by a sole entrepreneur to considerably more extensive organizations armed with numerous salespeople covering specific territories. Based on data from the U.S. Department of Labor, approximately 1.9 million individuals work as manufacturers' and wholesalers' representatives, but those working in independent organizations are a smaller number, around 150,000 based on estimates provided by the Manufacturers' Agents National Association (MANA). Kellysearch, a long-established supplier and service organization cataloger, listed 950 companies engaged in that business; total so-called "rep organizations" are much more numerous. These firms, tend to be concentrated in major metropolitan areas but are found in every state selling every conceivable product line, including goods produced in the automotive, plastics, electronics, food and beverage processing, apparel, lumber and wood, paper, chemical, and metals industries. Virtually any product that is made and sold can be handled by a manufacturers' agent.

Manufacturers' agents generally represent several different companies that offer compatible—but not competing—products to the same industry. This approach reduces the cost of sales by spreading the agent's costs over the different products that he or she represents. Consequently, manufacturers' agents view themselves as a cost-effective alternative to full-time salaried sales forces; reps' self-evaluation that is shared by thousands of small- and medium-sized manufacturers in the United States. Indeed, manufacturers' agents are particularly popular among companies that do not have the financial resources to launch their own sales team. In addition, since manufacturers' agents are generally paid by commission, the small manufacturer incurs no cost until a sale is made.

SMALL BUSINESSES AND MANUFACTURERS' AGENTS

Advantages In addition to the above-mentioned financial benefits that manufacturers' agents offer to small business owners, they also provide relocating or start-up firms with immediate front-line information on marketplace trends and demographics. By contracting with a manufacturers' agent, a company gains instant access to industry expertise or knowledge of a particular country or region.

There are other distinct advantages as well. For manufacturers with a narrow product line, agencies offer one of the best ways to access the market. Because they normally sell compatible products to a single market, the manufacturers' agent firms are usually well-connected with the manufacturers' principal market targets. This offers manufacturers immediate entry to markets that may be hard to reach with a direct sales force. In addition, rep firms can provide new businesses with ideas about where to advertise, comment on what the competition is doing, and give estimates of a given territory's potential.

Disadvantages Consultants and business owners note, however, that while using manufacturers' agents may make a lot of sense to the small company that needs to allocate its financial resources carefully and learn about the marketplace quickly, there are drawbacks associated with the practice as well. Lack of control over the agent is easily the most frequently mentioned complaint that business owners cite when discussing rep firms. Since the manufacturers' agent is not an employee of the company, the company's ownership cannot dictate how he or she goes about business. Certainly, the small business owner can negotiate for certain things in his or her business dealings with the agent, just as any client can do with any vendor. But in the final analysis, the agent has far greater freedom to operate as he or she feels fit than do salespeople that are actual employees of the company.

Some critics also claim that since manufacturers' agents conduct business on behalf of more than one manufacturer, they are not always able to devote the necessary time to one single product line. Finally, some agents also may be reluctant or unable to provide service beyond the point of sale. Fundamental elements of customer service, such as start-up assistance and follow-up service, often must be supplied by the manufacturer even if the goods were sold through a manufacturers' agent.

Another concern frequently raised about manufacturers' agents is that they add to the cost of sales by acting as another layer in the distribution process. But the sales function must be carried out, and costs incurred in engaging a rep will show up as in-house costs if that alternative is avoided. Rep firms in effect represent an instance of outsourcing of the sales function.

SELECTING AN AGENT

Manufacturers have many factors to consider when going through the process of selecting a manufacturers' representative. Small business owners should look for someone who shows an ability and a willingness to become knowledgeable about their products and applications, as well as someone who will respond quickly to calls and present the product in terms of how it will meet customer needs. A good agent will also represent the various product lines he or she markets in a just fashion, giving each line the attention it deserves, regardless of how much income it accounts for (this latter concern is especially acute for small and start-up businesses).

The best rule of thumb for manufacturers is to be patient and do plenty of preliminary research. After all, the choice is going to be the primary link between the company and its target audience. A poor selection can ruin a company; conversely, a good choice can help launch a new manufacturer to long-term financial stability. Given the stakes involved in this choice, then, MANA suggested in the print version of *Directory of Manufacturers' Sales Agencies* (it has since been automated) that business owners consider doing the following when weighing their choices.

- Create a profile of the ideal agency—Make the profile clear, but also be flexible and realistic. Perfect agencies are nonexistent, but there are many that will do a good job if given the opportunity.

- Create a profile of the manufacturing firm— Manufacturers are encouraged to compile a profile of their target customers, a rundown of the business's needs, and a summary of the governing philosophy of the business. Many agencies can be selective in terms of who they will add to their client list, so it makes sense to inform them about the business and its goals and prospects. The profile should be honest

and touch on growth plans, real advantages of the product(s) it manufacturers, and previous history.

- Secure referrals from other agencies— Manufacturers' representatives are a close-knit fraternity in the United States, and many can provide the names of several agencies that would be a good fit for the line.

- Get referrals from other manufacturers—Companies in the same area that sell similar but noncompetitive products can be a good source of information in locating potential representatives. Some may even recommend their own agencies, although others may be reluctant to have their agents take on additional product lines and responsibilities.

- Be patient—While manufacturers do not have the luxury of waiting forever when filling rep openings, doing preliminary research usually is a good idea. Many manufacturers who have been burned in this regard later admit that they did not devote sufficient time to exploring their options and learning about the agent they did select. It is better to take the needed time to select the right prospect than to rush into a bad situation and have to rectify it later.

- Be flexible in setting up territories—Agents must have exclusive rights within a territory, but rather than assign arbitrary territories based on geography, it is often preferable to select the agents that best fit your line and let their coverage determine the territories.

Finding the right agent to represent a business is not unlike hiring a trusted employee. A good match, not least good chemistry and shared values, is essential because the rep is an independent agent and the inherent distance created by that relationship can introduce problems unless both sides feel that they are part of one team. To be sure, nothing succeeds like success—so that a good product line will move if in the right hands; and the rep will sell it enthusiastically if it fits his or her usual clientele.

DEALING WITH AGENTS

Manufacturers must remember that their rep firms are independent sales agencies that are not employees of any of its principals, but business partners with each of them. As such, the manufacturers cannot have the same type of direct control as they do over their own personnel. From a legal standpoint, it is important to remember that the manufacturers pay nothing to a rep until a sale is made. They also pay no withholding taxes or Social Security. Using manufacturers' agents also means that some of the manufacturer's bookkeeping needs will be taken care of by non-employees. This is an important distinction for the Internal Revenue Service, which frowns mightily upon arrangements in which companies disguise employees under the veil of independent agencies or contractors. When judging this, the IRS typically uses as one of its tests the amount of direct control exercised over sales reps. If regular reports are demanded of independent agents, the IRS can declare the rep an employee and require the various withholding taxes that apply.

Communication remains an integral part of the relationship between agents and their clients. Both parties need to keep the other appraised about their operations. Agents should let their principals know what they are doing for them in the field, regardless of the level of sales at that particular moment, while agents need updated information on matters such as product specifications and pricing. Ultimately, both parties simply need to recognize that a cohesive working relationship is in their shared best interests. In their dealings with representatives, manufacturers expect: loyalty; knowledge of the territory and/or industry; knowledge of product lines after a reasonable amount of exposure; quick response to suggestions; regular follow-up; and a fair share of the agent's time. Agents, meanwhile, have every right to expect: a fair contract that recognizes performance and rewards success and longevity; access to customer service, training, and technical back-up; a quality product; timely delivery; and a true commitment to build business in their territory.

BIBLIOGRAPHY

Darlington, Hank. "How to Make Manufacturers Reps More Valuable to Your Business: Create a job description for your repos." *Supply House Times*. December 2005.

Friedman, Ira. "Reps Get Bad Rap." *Residential Systems*. 1 April 2005.

"How to Work Successfully with Manufacturers' Agencies." Manufacturers' Agents National Association, 1994.

Liescheidt, Steven G. "What to Look for in a Manufacturer's Representative." *Snips*. January 2006.

"Manufacturers' Agents or Representatives – US". Kellysearch. Available from http://www.kellysearch.com/us-product-58616.html. Retrieved on 11 April 2006.

Hillstrom, Northern Lights
updated by Magee, ECDI

MARKET ANALYSIS

"Market analysis" is sometimes used to describe what is more broadly termed "market research" and sometimes with an emphasis on "analysis." "Market research," in a broad context, is described under that heading elsewhere in this volume. Here the emphasis will be on analytical techniques. In such a context two elements of the research are pictured side by side. On one side are all kinds of data and other information collected during the first part of the investigation. On the other are mental and mechanical tools ready to make sense out of the data. These two aspects, of course, are in practice intimately linked. Market research is almost always undertaken for a good reason. It is triggered by some event and the research is meant to accomplish some purpose.

The event itself might be the start-up of a picture-framing shop (cutely named "You're Framed") by a couple experienced in the business. One of them is a photographer. During preliminary discussions with potential investors, it became obvious that the company needed a business plan; the plan needs a market assessment. Alternatively, perhaps, a small mechanical service firm ("J&J Machining") wishes to buy a milling center to be used on behalf of a single customer in the gas compressor business. The loan package requires a business assessment of the compressor market.

YOU'RE FRAMED

These two different contexts will require quite different analytical approaches. The data collected for You're Framed involves the location of all framing shops in a cluster of five suburbs divided from a larger urban mass by a freeway. The couple have also gathered census data which show the income levels in their market area by census tract. They have three different potential locations identified for their own store. Both have surveyed a neighborhood of similar size to theirs "across the freeway," have similar income data, and an inventory of frame shops over there. Finally, the photographer has visited all of the competing frame shops and developed estimates of their floor space. The other member has some good estimates on the sales of three shops, one in which she has actually worked.

The analytical approach in this case will involve estimating total volume in the chosen suburban area by calculating ratios of income per square footage for the three known stores and applying this ratio to all the stores. The same is next done for the neighborhood across the way. In both cases, frame-shop sales will be correlated to income and population in both areas. Data then show that the chosen cluster is under-served in comparison with the other neighborhood, indicating a good opportunity. Next, analysis will become geographical, each competing store being plotted on a map. Based on this plot and an analysis of traffic patterns, the couple identify the ideal location for their shop and estimate the drive- and walk-by traffic. Finally, the analysis will pinpoint the fact that the photographer, being the only professional portrait and wedding photographer in the cluster, can generate walk-in traffic to the frame shop by moving his studio to the new location, giving You're Framed a unique profile, drawing power, and synergies in marketing.

J&J MACHINING

J&J's market analysis is motivated very differently. They have to prove to the bank that their gas compressor client will be in good shape for some years to come—time enough to repay the milling center loan. The client's future in turn will depend on the future of natural gas transmission in the U.S. The data collected for this purpose include a great deal of information on the compressor company (publicly traded) and two of its competitors, energy statistics with emphasis on natural gas, and data on gas pipeline capacities, expansions, and maintenance histories. J&J also has some data and some looser estimates of parts pricing by its own competitors using similar milling centers.

Here the analysis will center on the compressor company. Using market share data it is shown to be the second largest producer of such machinery but growing more rapidly than its senior competitor particularly in the export market supplying expanding Russian pipeline capacity. The future of nature gas consumption is analyzed next and shown to be promising—because gas reserves are projected to last at least a decade longer than oil reserves. J&J's own history with the compressor company is excellent, its pricing competitive with that of others—and likely to be more competitive with the new milling center.

ANALYTICAL ELEMENTS

Notice that here two small businesses both engaged in analytical activities. But in one case local data only were employed whereas in the other not only national but international trends were drawn into the analysis. Both, however, addressed a fundamental point. In the first case this was the viability of the entire business, in the other the low risk of lending money on a single project. Neither analysis, of course, is quite complete but intended merely to illustrate some points.

Good analysis requires certain elements:

1. Data presented must be complete; if pricing is mentioned, costs must be mentioned as well.

2. Data must have context; a product may be growing at 20 percent a year, but that is not terribly impressive if the class of products of which it is a part is growing at 28 percent.

3. Data must be relevant to the issue under discussion and in the same ballpark; a web site with animated cartoon figures cannot be justified by statistics of the popularity of video games—unless some video-game characters appear in the animation.

4. Negative data should be presented alongside positive findings; if sales are soaring but margins are hairthin, the latter must be mentioned.

5. Projections must be justified; if they are not extensions of established trend lines, the reasons for deviations must be documented.

6. Sources of data must be fully explained with appropriate weights; three favorable comments by travelling salespeople are not a "survey."

7. The mathematical basis of the analysis should be transparent; in practice this means that tabular data should be presented alongside graphics and sufficient detail should be provided to the user so that he or she can trace the logic; this includes explicitly stating the methodology used, e.g., regression analysis or compounded growth calculation.

8. Data should be graphed on a log scale so that growth curves can be compared from one chart to the next regardless of the magnitudes presented.

9. Finally, conclusions based on judgmental factors need sufficient documentation so that the user can judge for him- or herself how much weight to give them.

SEE ALSO *Advertising Strategy; Market Research*

BIBLIOGRAPHY
Alfano, Hayden. "Know Thy Market: A step-by-step crash course in market analysis." *Remodeling.* January 2006.

Clegg, Alicia. "Market Research: Through the looking glass." *Marketing Week.* 16 March 2006.

"How to Choose a Niche?" *Accounting Technology.* March 2006.

Rymer, John. "How Well Do You Know Your Competitor?." *Professional Builder.* 1 October 2005.

Vincour, M. Richard. "When Your Customer Speaks, Listen." *American Printer.* 1 April 2006.

Zarembski, Mike. "Tech Talk: The Trend(line) is Your Friend!." *Futures.* March 2006.

Darnay, ECDI

MARKET QUESTIONNAIRES

Market questionnaires are a form of quantitative, primary market research that can provide small business owners with specific information about their customers' needs. Whether conducted over the telephone, through the mail, over the Internet, or in person, market questionnaires are designed to survey a sample group of respondents whose opinions reflect those of the business's target customers.

Like other forms of market research, questionnaires are designed to connect marketers to consumers through information gathering and evaluation. Market research is commonly used to identify marketing problems and opportunities, as well as to develop and evaluate the effectiveness of marketing strategies. Small business owners, because of their usually limited financial resources, have a particular need for adequate, accurate, and current information to aid them in making decisions. Market research can help entrepreneurs evaluate the feasibility of a start-up venture before investing a great deal of time and capital, for example, as well as assist them in effectively marketing their goods and services.

Questionnaire design requires a great deal of thought and skill, and mistakes are easy. Jodie Monger, for instance, writing for *Call Center,* pointed out a number of common errors which she labels, not quite tongue-in-cheek, as "survey malpractice." Her list includes, among other issues, measuring too many things or not measuring enough, using an unreliable scale, e.g. using words like "excellent" and "fair" without defining them, "measuring the wrong thing or the right things wrong," relying on people's memories after these have degraded, and poorly qualifying the people answering the questionnaire.

In general, a good market questionnaire will consist of a screening or qualifying question, an introduction, demographic questions, closed-ended questions, and open-ended questions. Each of these elements serves a particular purpose. The screening question, which should usually be posed first, makes sure that the respondent is a member of the target group and thus is qualified to participate in the survey. For example, a home remodeling and repair company might ask whether the person has had any work done in the previous six months. The introduction then informs qualified respondents what company is conducting the survey and why, and explains the benefits answering might have on their future business relationship with that company. Demographic questions—which cover such basic information as age, gender, marital status, education level, income level, etc.—allow the business to categorize responses. Since some respondents may be hesitant to answer such personal questions, demographics should usually be addressed near the end of the questionnaire.

Closed-ended questions ask respondents to select from a limited set of answers. This enables businesses to collate responses and analyze results more easily. Closed-ended questions may require a "yes" or "no," or "true" or "false" answer. They may also be set up as a multiple-choice question, so that respondents choose one possible answer from a list. Finally, closed-ended questions may involve a scaled response, such as rating a product or service on a scale of one to ten or on the basis of categories such as "strongly like," "like," "neither like nor dislike," etc. In contrast, open-ended questions enable respondents to provide a more lengthy response in their own words. Although open-ended questions can provide valuable information, the results can also be difficult for companies to analyze and categorize.

Good rules to follow—at least until experience has been gained—may be summed up under five points: 1) The survey should be as short as possible and collect only necessary information. 2) Questions should be clearly worded and concise, without excessive technical jargon. 3) Questions should be framed so that they don't imply a correct answer. 4) Questions should be limited so that they only seek one piece of information and answers fall into distinct categories. Finally, 5) Questionnaires should be arranged so that they begin with easier questions and progress into more difficult ones after a measure of trust has been achieved. It may be helpful to test a market questionnaire on a small group and then make any necessary refinements before using it in a large-scale market research effort.

BIBLIOGRAPHY

Monger, Jodie. "Are You Guilty of Survey Malpractice?" *Call Center.* 1 April 2006.

Hayes, Lallie. "Questionnaire Design, Printing, and Distribution." *Technical Communications.* November 2000.

Hillstrom, Northern Lights
updated by Magee, ECDI

MARKET RESEARCH

If the "market" is viewed as the totality of all environmental factors that bear down on a business, market research may be defined as a disciplined investigation aimed at discovering what is going on and, most importantly, on what is *changing* in the environment. The object is to discover opportunities and threats—and to assess how some intended action might play itself out. The research may be designed broadly or narrowly, but even limited studies must have sufficient scope to give the investigation context.

GENERAL ASPECTS

Market research answers questions along the following lines: How big is the market and how does it divide?—into product lines or services or geographically? Who are the buyers and why do they buy? Who is the competition and what methods are they using? What's on the horizon that will change this market? How will we benefit or suffer if these changes take place?

Managements undertake such research for some motive; thus market research always has a context. The context may be negative (declining profitability or sales) or positive (new technology, rapid growth); it may be brought about by forces outside the company's control such as legislative events, the economy as a whole, a new entrant to the market. Most start-ups that need front-end funding begin their careers by doing a comprehensive market study in order to put the results into a business plan.

Company size is itself a context, and while, in general, business is business at any scale, problems and opportunities manifest differently. Managements in large organizations, for example, are inevitably at a much greater distance from the actual interface where customers and products meet—where the action is. Small business owners are closer to the market but rarely have vast resources at their command. Distance from the market and the extent of it that must be surveyed influences the techniques deployed. Market research may take the simple form of driving around and talking to a lot of people—or just parking someplace and counting the number of cement trucks a competitor sends out. At the other extreme, it may cost hundreds of thousands of dollars and may even involve undertaking test marketing in several cities.

A general rule of market research is that costs vary inversely with level of detail and currency. A business can get a broad view of a market by finding free materials at the library. Expert studies on a national or global market cost between $150 to $700 (depending on the subject). But a business wishing to have detailed information at the county level on some cluster of products is looking at minimally $3,000 for a commissioned study—and more likely four times that. Baseline economic data are collected by the U.S. Bureau of the Census. These are better at the aggregate than at the detailed level. Good data on specific products are simply not there, but data on physical products are better than on services. The Bureau collects fewer data on service sectors and these at a rougher granularity. The future auto dealer, in other words, has an easier job plotting the future than the future independent midwife. Government data are invariable three-or-more years old when they become available. Collecting current, real-time data is very costly. Grocery chains collect such data digital at the check-out counter, but access to it runs into hundreds of thousands of dollars.

Useful market research has a time element. It will present a history of developments and include a projection of future events. A manager wants to make decisions about what to do next and therefore needs a look at the future. Projecting data forward requires special but somewhat opposing skills: statistical expertise on the one hand and an inspired, open, and yet sober sort of gaze. Market research that merely confirms management's prejudices, hopes, or fears is worth little—but the findings, of course, may do just that. Managements often *do* see the future accurately.

MAJOR COMPONENTS

Market Size and Structure Market size is an important aspect of orientation in business: it tells the owner how he or she is doing. Measuring market size at the national level is easy, at the local level difficult and costly. The government collects data at the county level in a series called the County Business Patterns, but the CPB only reports establishments, employment, and payroll. Product detail is not available. Nonetheless, CBP data are the most objective look at what is happening locally. Data from the CBP, combined with averages on shipments or revenues at the national level, can produce an estimate of the market size for broad industry categories locally. Where an activity is visible (e.g., picture framing shops), market size can be approximated by looking at telephone directories and using an average sales volume. Federal data for framing shops will *not* be available because the activity is "too detailed." Therefore alternative approaches are necessary. Where only factories are visible, local sales are very difficult to estimate, but the "production market" may be estimated similarly.

At the local level the structure of the market—its divisions into products, its channels of distribution, its concentration—are also subject more to guesswork than study. Telephone surveying is the method most likely to yield reasonable results, but such work is very expensive.

Not surprisingly, most small businesses develop a sense of their market in the course of day-to-day operations—rather than by spending thousands of dollars on studies. They talk with vendors, customers, and competitors. They listen to the gossip and translate bits and pieces of information into rough numbers. This process is rarely—but *can* be—formalized. A small business owner and his and her key managers can sit down with notepads and work out the market size and structure. Sometimes this is useful for planning or for justifying loan applications. At the local level, disciplined recording and analysis of such information yields results comparable to very expensive studies at the larger scale—and looking at CBP data can produce rough confirmation.

Market Share and Competition An important aspect of every market is its concentration, measured by creating a list of participants, sorting them by sales, and then adding up the market shares of the top layer—the top five, the top three. If the top three have most of the market, the industry is highly concentrated; if the top five have around 15 to 20 percent, concentration is low. Most market share listings have an "All Other" category. Small businesses are invariably hidden in that line. The sales volumes of small operations are rarely available publicly, but "work arounds" are available to infer their size. Important measures are employment and square footage. A "typical" small business can calculate its own sales per square foot in retail, for instance—or its sales per employee—and can then proceed to develop approximate company size estimates for its competitors by applying the same unit measures to them after counting their people and eyeballing their floor space. There are all kinds of other "proxy" measures available. A ready-mix concrete supplier knows his/her revenues per truck—and can count competitors' trucks. Economic forces tend always to produce the same averages across an industry.

Competitive strategies are also accessible to the small business. The method of detecting such strategies will depend, of course, on the relative visibility of the competitor. Retail stores advertise; the frequency of their sales and the items they use as loss leaders indicate strategy. They can be visited. Vendors are a useful source of information on less visible competitors' strategies—as are observations of such companies at trade shows. The alert small business owner will constantly watch his or her competitors and note when they enlarge their leases, build, or pave their parking lots—or when their inventories overflow *to* the parking lots. Problems that they encounter also leave tell-tale signs. When such observation becomes routine—and when the owner collects ads, news stories, and records observation in notes—doing a market share and competitive analysis for a plan will be relatively easy.

Products Research and Consumer Surveys A small business intending to test products before launching them to the market will expose them to employees, friends, customers, relatives, vendors, suppliers—anyone at all with a likely opinion—and will thus gradually discover what seems to be the best design, positioning, packaging, name, and even marketing slogan. The more systematic this type of exposure is—and the more effectively informants' opinions are recorded and analyzed—the more it will resemble the practices of large organizations who deploy sophisticated methodologies like focus groups and consumer surveys.

In general "sophistication" translates into disciplined planning of tests and the application of specialized expertise in that planning. Focus groups and customer surveys frequently employ psychologists before a trial (preparing settings, choosing respondents, framing questionnaires, etc.), during a trial (observing reactions), and after the trial (analyzing results). But, in effect, a high level of sophistication is simply an attempt to formalize and then to apply mechanically what is nothing other than good entrepreneurial "feel" and "instinct." Many a very successful product was launched because the entrepreneur simply *liked* it—and so did the people around him or her.

Small businesses generally lack the resources for massive, costly trials and surveys and, instead, rely on innovative ways to obtain consumer feedback. A store, for instance, may mount two very different product displays and then instruct the clerks to note which one the customers spend more time examining. Surveys can be conducted at very modest costs by simply asking every customer a question at checkout time—and then recording the answer. Such approaches may lack the "scientific" halo of big studies but will produce actionable and reliable results if properly done.

Keeping record of informal events is another low-cost method to accomplish in a small business what large companies spend huge amounts achieving. Customers complain. Customers make complimentary comments. Customers criticize products or comment on them. To jot down such comments with appropriate annotations, to collect them in one place, periodically to review them can be a source of intelligence on customer satisfaction.

Other Market Influences An important component of all market research is identification and assessment of forces external to the market itself—but likely to influence it. A classical example of government action for a small business might be the routing of a freeway; it could isolate the business from major parts of its clientele or massively increase its traffic. External influences include *government,* as already mentioned, which can by its enactments increase pay (up minimum wage) or returns (accelerate depreciation), impose costs by regulation, modify interest rates, stimulate or inhibit exports, and do hundreds of other things. Changes in *demographic patterns* were underway in the mid-2000s as the baby boom generation marched toward retirement, eroding some markets, swelling others. *International events* may have great influence by disturbing raw material or energy availability or stimulating competition (outsourcing). *Technological change* of a massive character impacted communications and distribution by means of the Internet—but less visible changes, like improvements in materials or equipment have sometimes dramatic impacts of a particular business too.

In most industries, insiders watch certain indicators vital to the industry: interest rates in residential construction are an example; housing starts, in turn, send signals to a large number of suppliers, e.g., producers of appliances. Publishers of references watch budgetary trends in libraries. Hotels and resorts watch gas prices and air travel costs. And so on. The small business doing market research may find it more difficult to find precise indicators that serve as signal for its operations. One way to identify them is to spend some time with trade publications which like to track and publicize changes in relevant second- and third-order influences on the market.

RESEARCH TOOLS AND TECHNIQUES

Most formalized market research techniques are used by large corporations to "see" a market difficult to track by its very diversity and size. Major categories are 1) audience research, 2) product research, 3) brand analysis, 4) psychological profiling, 5) scanner research, 6) database research, also called database "mining," and 7) post-sale or consumer satisfaction research. When these techniques involve people, researchers use questionnaires administered in written form or person-to-person, either by personal or telephone interview; questionnaires may be closed-end or open-ended; the first type provides users choices to a question ("excellent," "good," "fair") whereas open-ended surveys solicit spontaneous reactions and capture these as given. Focus groups are a kind of opinion-solicitation but without a questionnaire; people interact with products, messages, or images and discuss them. Observers evaluate what they hear.

Some major techniques are intimately linked with targeting marketing efforts or designing messages. Audience research is aimed at discovering who is listening, watching, or reading radio, TV, and print media respectively. Such studies in part profile the audience and in part determine the popularity of the medium or portions of it. Brand research has similar profiling features ("Who uses this brand?") and also aims at identifying the reasons for brand loyalty or fickleness. Psychological profiling aims at construction profiles of customers by temperament, lifestyle, income, and other factors and tying such types to consumption patterns and media patronage.

Scanner research uses checkout counter scans of transactions to develop patterns for all manner of end uses, including stocking, of course. From a marketing point of view, scans can also help users track the success of coupons and to establish linkages between products. Database mining attempts to exploit all kinds of data on hand on customers—which frequently have other revealing aspects. Purchase records, for example, can reveal the buying habits of different income groups—the income classification of accounts taking place by census tract

matching. Data on average income by census tract can be obtained from the Bureau of the Census.

Product tests, of course, directly relate to use of the product. Good examples are tasting tests used to pick the most popular flavors—and consumer tests of vehicle or device prototypes to uncover problematical features or designs.

Post-consumer surveys are familiar to many consumers from telephone calls that follow having a car serviced or calling help-lines for computer- or Internet-related problems. In part such surveys are intended to determine if the customer was satisfied. In part this additional attention is intended also to build good will and word-of-mouth advertising for the service provider.

SEE ALSO *Focus Groups*

BIBLIOGRAPHY

Clegg, Alicia. "Market Research: Through the looking glass." *Marketing Week.* 16 March 2006.

Lury, Giles. "Market Research Cannot Cover for the 'Vision Thing.'" *Marketing.* 9 November 2000.

Mariampolski, Hy. *Qualitative Market Research: A Comprehensive Guide.* Sage Publications, 21 August 2001.

"Market Research Is Accessible, Rewarding to Small Retailers." *Knight-Ridder/Tribune Business News.* 19 January 2000.

McQuarrie, Edward F. *The Market Research Toolbox: A Concise Guide for Beginners.* Sage Publications, 15 June 2005.

Vincour, M. Richard. "When Your Customer Speaks, Listen." *American Printer.* 1 April 2006.

Darnay, ECDI

MARKET SEGMENTATION

Market segmentation is the science of dividing an overall market into customer subsets or segments, whose in segment sharing similar characteristics and needs. Segmentation typically involves significant market research and can thus be costly. It is practiced especially in major companies with highly differentiated product lines or serving large markets. The small business tends to discover the segment it serves best by the trial and error of dealing with customers and stocking products more and more suitable to its particular clientele.

Segmentation lies somewhere near the middle of a continuum of marketing strategies that range from mass marketing—in which a single product is offered to all customers in a market—to one-to-one marketing—in which a different product is specifically designed for each individual customer (e.g., plastic surgery). Most businesses realize that since no two people are exactly alike, it is unlikely that they will be able to please all customers in a market with a single product. They also realize that it is rarely feasible to create a distinct product for every customer. Instead, most businesses attempt to improve their odds of attracting a significant base of customers by dividing the overall market into segments, then trying to match their product and marketing mix more closely to the needs of one or more segments. A number of customer characteristics, known as segmentation bases, can be used to define market segments. Some commonly used bases include age, gender, income, geographical area, and buying behavior.

MARKETING STRATEGIES

Although mass marketing (also known as market aggregation or undifferentiated marketing) cannot fully satisfy every customer in a market, many companies still employ this strategy. It is commonly used in the marketing of standardized goods and services—including sugar, gasoline, rubber bands, or dry cleaning services—when large numbers of people have similar needs and they perceive the product or service as largely the same regardless of the provider. Mass marketing offers some advantages to businesses, such as reduced production and marketing costs. Due to the efficiency of large production runs and a single marketing program, businesses that mass market their goods or services may be able to provide consumers with more value for their money.

Some producers of mass market goods employ a marketing strategy known as product differentiation to make their offering seem distinct from that of competitors, even though the products are largely the same. For example, a producer of bath towels might embroider its brand name on its towels and sell them only through upscale department stores as a form of product differentiation. Consumers might tend to perceive these towels as somehow better than other brands, and thus worthy of a premium price. But changing consumer perceptions in this way can be very expensive in terms of promotion and packaging. A product differentiation strategy is most likely to be effective when consumers care about the product and there are identifiable differences between brands.

Despite the cost advantages mass marketing offers to businesses, this strategy has drawbacks. A single product offering cannot fully satisfy the diverse needs of all consumers in a market, and consumers with unsatisfied needs expose businesses to challenges by competitors who are able to identify and fulfill consumer needs more precisely. In fact, markets for new products typically begin with one competitor offering a single product, then gradually splinter into segments as competitors enter the market with products and marketing messages targeted at groups of consumers the original producer may have missed. These new competitors are able to enter a market ostensibly controlled by an established competitor because they can identify and meet the needs of unsatisfied customer segments. In recent times, the proliferation of computerized customer databases has worked to drive marketing toward ever-more-narrowly focused market segments.

Applying a market segmentation strategy is most effective when an overall market consists of many smaller segments whose members have certain characteristics or needs in common. Through segmentation, businesses can divide such a market into several homogeneous groups and develop a separate product and marketing program to more exactly fit the needs of one or more segments. Though this approach can provide significant benefits to consumers and a profitable sales volume (rather than a maximum sales volume) to businesses, it can be costly to implement. For example, identifying homogeneous market segments requires significant amounts of market research, which can be expensive. Also, businesses may experience a rise in production costs as they forfeit the efficiency of mass production in favor of smaller production runs that meet the needs of a subset of the market. Finally, a company may find that sales of a product developed for one segment encroach upon the sales of another product intended for another segment. Nonetheless, market segmentation is vital to success in many industries where consumers have diverse and specific needs, such as homebuilding, furniture upholstery, and tailoring.

SEGMENTATION BASES

In order successfully to implement a market segmentation strategy, a business must employ market research techniques to find patterns of similarity among customer preferences in a market. Ideally, customer preferences will fall into distinct clusters based upon identifiable population characteristics. This means that if customer requirements were plotted on a graph using certain characteristics, or segmentation bases, along the axes, the points would tend to form clusters.

In marketing jargon, customer segments must be measurable by clear characteristics; they must be large enough to constitute a market; reaching them should be predictably easy (they all watch *American Idol,* for example, or subscribe to one of four magazines); they must be predictably responsive to marketing; the segment must be stable over time and not a one-time aggregation.

Determining how to segment a market is one of the most important questions a marketer must face. Creative and effective market segmentation can lead to the development of popular new products; unsuccessful segmentation can consume a lot of dollars and yield nothing. There are three main types of segmentation bases for businesses to consider—descriptive, behavioral, and benefit bases—each of which breaks down into numerous potential customer traits.

Descriptive bases for market segmentation include a variety of factors that describe the demographic and geographic situations of the customers in a market. They are the most commonly used segmentation bases because they are easy to measure, and because they often serve as strong indicators of consumer needs and preferences. Some of the demographic variables that are used as descriptive bases in market segmentation might include age, gender, religion, income, and family size, while some of the geographic variables might include region of the country, climate, and population of the surrounding area.

Behavioral bases for market segmentation are generally more difficult to measure than descriptive bases, but they are often considered to be more powerful determinants of consumer purchases. They include those underlying factors that help motivate consumers to make certain buying decisions, such as personality, lifestyle, and social class. Behavioral bases also include factors that are directly related to consumer purchases of certain goods, such as their degree of brand loyalty, the rate at which they use the product and need to replace it, and their readiness to buy at a particular time.

Businesses that segment a market based on benefits hope to identify the primary benefit that consumers seek in buying a certain product, then supply a product that provides that benefit. This segmentation approach is based upon the idea that market segments exist primarily because consumers seek different benefits from products, rather than because of various other differences between consumers. One potential pitfall to this approach is that consumers do not always know or cannot always identify a single benefit that influences them to make a purchase decision. Many marketers use a combination of bases that seem most appropriate when segmenting a market. Using a single variable is undoubtedly easier, but it often turns out to be less precise.

THE SEGMENTATION PROCESS

The process itself begins with narrowing the universe to be studied into a specific market now served by the company and obtaining basic information on competing products or services now on offer. Once this step has been completed, variables to be used are identified, reviewed, and tested. At the most basic level such variables, for example, might involve income and demographic characteristics of the consumers.

With these preparations completed, actual market research is organized to collect and to analyze data on the selected broad body of consumers. Analysis of the data will begin to cluster the consumers into distinct groupings based on the variables. Additional analysis, possibly involving more research, will next be conducted to develop detailed profiles of each segment already identified.

If the right variables were chosen at the outset and the market research was competently done, the resulting groupings will have characteristics distinct enough, and documented well enough, to permit the company to select one or more segments which will be easiest or more profitable to serve. The company's own strategy will play a role. Its aim, for example, may be use its capacity more fully and the company will therefore select a segment which will purchase the largest volume; alternative the company's aim may be low production levels with high profits, leading to a focus on another segment.

The last stage of the segmentation process will be the development of product and marketing plans based on the segment(s) most closely matching the company's "ideal" situation.

In general, customers are willing to pay a premium for a product that meets their needs more specifically than does a competing product. Thus marketers who successfully segment the overall market and adapt their products to the needs of one or more smaller segments stand to gain in terms of increased profit margins and reduced competitive pressures. Small businesses, in particular, may find market segmentation to be a key in enabling them to compete with larger firms. Many management consulting firms offer assistance with market segmentation to small businesses. But the potential gains offered by market segmentation must be measured against the costs, which—in addition to the market research required to segment a market—may include increased production and marketing expenses.

SEE ALSO *Demographics; Target Market*

BIBLIOGRAPHY

Eliya, Susan A. "No Sweat: Segmentation continues to create opportunities for growth." *Household & Personal Products.* March 2006

"Hidden Identity: Retailers still struggle to know their customers." *Chain Store Age.* January 2006.

"Market Segmentation Pays Off in Big Way in Mexico." *MMR.* 12 December 2005.

Millier, Paul. "Intuition Can Help in Segmenting Industrial Markets." *Industrial Marketing Management.* March 2000.

Simon, Karen. "Stay Ahead of Your Customers." *Apply.* 1 February 2006.

Hillstrom, Northern Lights
updated by Magee, ECDI

MARKET SHARE

A company's market share is the percentage of all products in a category that that company sells. Thus market share is calculated by dividing a company's sales by the total sales in a category. If the company sells all the product in a market, it will have a 100 percent share—and it will have a monopoly. Market share is typically measured at fixed intervals like once a quarter or once a year.

CALCULATING MARKET SHARE

All companies with reasonable record-keeping practices know what their own sales in a particular product or services category are during any selected period of time. The difficulty arises in knowing what *total sales* are. Unless data on total sales are collected by the government in its economic census activities every four years (years ending in 2 and 7)—and by sampling surveys in the years in between—or unless sales data are cumulated by an industry association or by regulatory agencies (e.g., electrical power generation) total sales may be impossible to determine—and so will a company's market share.

The granularity of data on product sales tends to be rather coarse, meaning that data on canned vegetables may be available but data on canned artichoke hearts will be very difficult to get. If a product moves in different size categories, detail on packaging size categories is rarely available. For this reason major durable goods categories like autos or aircraft are easier to track than custom jewelry or specific clothing items. Services are even more difficult to measure. It is possible to get a count of open-heart surgeries, but data on home-care delivery will forever be rather approximate.

Indirect measures are often employed to get at total sales. Examples of this are tracking "installed capacity" in such industries as cement, paper, oil refining, and power generation. Data on capacity must, of course, be refined by gathering information on whether on capacity utilization. If utilization is running at 40 percent, total capacity must be discounted. Hotels have a determinable number of rooms—but occupancy is what counts.

These measurement problems serve as a general indicator concerning the nature of the "market share" measure. It is almost always a very rough measure—and in most categories the underlying factual basis is equal parts data and guesswork.

HOW MARKET SHARES ARE USED

Companies attempt to calculate their own shares of the market in attempts at self-evaluation. They also try to obtain share information on their competitors. Market share, of course, is a measure of relative strength. And, as it changes over time, it is an indicator of progress or regress. Companies "gaining share" are reassured—unless competitors are gaining shares faster; a company that is "losing share" is getting a strong hint that something is amiss. In most large corporations where formal annual planning is practiced, managers routinely assemble market share data on their competitors and calculate their own as part of planning. A long and persistent loss of market share has been the sad accompaniment of the decline of domestic auto makers.

Market share being a measure of strength, such data are used in economic analysis to evaluate industries as a whole. One such measure is concentration. Industry concentration is calculated by ranking all major competitors on the basis of market share. The shares of the top companies are summed. These may be the top three, five, or more companies. If the total share of the leaders is high, the industry is said to be concentrated. Where concentration is very high, e.g., where the top three have 60 percent or more of the market, entry industry is difficult, competition is low, and pricing will be high. If the two ten companies have less than 10 percent share in the aggregate, entry will be easy. Concentration is, of course, also an indicator of capital intensity or monopoly over some production art available through control of patents. Market share measurements are thus used in government evaluation of mergers and acquisitions in order to determine whether or not antitrust laws would be violated by proposed combinations.

SHARE AND SMALL BUSINESS

Market share is rarely used as a measure in small business for the simple reason that the data necessary to obtain reasonably precise share data on competitors are rarely available. Small businesses tend to use other and more indirect ways of tracking how they're doing. They watch the competition and collect data from vendors and customers.

BIBLIOGRAPHY

Lazich, Robert S. ed. *Market Share Reporter.* Thomson Gale, 2006.

"Market Report: Present Perfect?." *In-Store.* 10 April 2006.

McCloughan, Patrick and Patrick Abounoori. "How to Estimate Market Concentration Given Grouped Data." *Applied Economics.* 20 May 2003.

"The Top 25 by Sector." *Forbes Global.* 17 April 2006.

Darnay, ECDI

MARKETING

"Marketing" is a term used to describe the various activities involved in transferring goods and services from producers to consumers. In addition to the functions commonly associated with it, such as advertising and sales promotion, marketing also encompasses product development, packaging, distribution channels, pricing, and many other functions. Modern marketing is often presented as an effort to discover and satisfy customer *needs*. It is often also a method of inventing products and services and *creating a demand* for them by artful persuasion.

In most large organizations the selling function is divided into distinct marketing and sales functions. In organizations where symbolic product presentation is all-important and buying decisions tend to be emotional, marketing is given much higher rank and emphasis. Such is the case typically with mature products that have over time achieved a commodity status and therefore persuasion to buy *this brand* is the central focus. In organizations where the product performance as such remains the chief selling feature, sales activity is dominant. Business-to-business distribution tends to have this character, with the selling burden carried by experts (e.g. in finance), sales engineers, and skilled product-savvy sales people. In some industries, e.g., in Pharmaceuticals, emphasis is evenly divided, with the public bombarded by marketing messages ("Ask your doctor...") while "detail men" (and women) are doing technical selling at the doctor's office.

BACKGROUND

"Marketing" used to mean going to the market—either to sell or to buy. The modern concept emerged in the wake of the industrial revolution in the 19th and 20th centuries. During that period, the proliferation of goods and services, increased worker specialization, and technological advances in transportation, refrigeration, and other factors that facilitated the transfer of goods over long distances resulted in the need for more advanced market mechanisms and selling techniques. But it was not until the 1930s that companies began to place a greater emphasis on advertising and promoting their products and began striving to tailor goods to please specific consumer groups. By the 1950s, and the rise of television as a communications medium, many large companies had developed marketing departments charged with devising and implementing strategies that would complement, and later direct, overall sales operations.

MACRO- AND MICRO-MARKETING

Macro-marketing refers to the overall economic/communications process that directs the flow of goods and services from producer to consumer. It includes 1) the buyer's behavior in seeking and judging goods and services; 2) the seller's efforts to draw and to persuade customers to buy; 3) the physical distribution of goods including warehousing and storage at intermediate stages; 3) product-related activities like standardization, grading, and sorting; 4) the financing of distribution at all stages, not least consumer credit; and 5) the communications processes supporting all of these activities.

Micro-marketing refers to the activities of the individual providers operating within this system. Organizations or businesses use various marketing techniques to accomplish objectives related to profits, market share, cash flow, and other economic factors that can enhance their well being and position in the marketplace. The micro-marketing function within an entity is commonly referred to as marketing management. Marketing managers strive to match products to customers; in this process they are equally interested in getting products customers will want to buy and influencing consumers to buy the products the company wishes to sell.

THE TARGET MARKETING CONCEPT

Micro-marketing encompasses a number of related activities and responsibilities. Marketing managers must carefully design their marketing plans to ensure that they complement related production, distribution, and financial constraints. They must also allow for constant adaptation to changing markets and economic conditions. Perhaps the core function of a marketing manager, however, is to identify a specific market, or group of consumers, and then deliver products and promotions that ultimately maximize the profit potential of that targeted market. This is particularly important for small businesses, which more than likely lack the resources to target large aggregate markets. Often, it is only by carefully selecting and wooing a specific group that a small firm can attain profit margins sufficient to allow it to continue to compete in the marketplace.

For instance, a manufacturer of fishing equipment would not randomly market its product to the entire U.S. population. Instead, it would likely conduct market research—using such tools as demographic reports, market surveys, or focus groups—to determine which customers would be most likely to purchase its offerings. It could then more efficiently spend its limited resources in an effort to persuade members of its target group(s) to buy its products. Perhaps it would target males in the Midwest between the ages of 18 and 35. The company may even strive to further maximize the profitability of its target market through market segmentation, whereby the group is further broken down by age, income, zip code, or other factors indicative of buying patterns. Advertisements and promotions could then be tailored for each segment of the target market.

There are many ways to address the wants and needs of a target market. For example, product packaging can be designed in different sizes and colors, or the product itself can be altered to appeal to different personality types or age groups. Producers can also change the warranty or durability of the good or provide different levels of follow-up service. Other influences, such as distribution and sales methods, licensing strategies, and advertising media also play an important role. It is the responsibility of the marketing manager to take all of these factors into account and to devise a cohesive marketing program that will appeal to the target customer.

THE FOUR PS

The different elements of a company's marketing mix can be divided into four basic decision areas—known as the "four Ps": product, place, promotion, and price—which marketing managers can use to devise an overall marketing strategy for a product or group of goods. These four decision groups represent all of the variables that a company can control. But those decisions must be made within the context of outside variables that are not entirely under the control of the company, such as competition, economic and technological changes, the political and legal environment, and cultural and social factors.

Marketing decisions related to the product (or service) involve creating the right product for the selected target group. This typically encompasses research and data analysis, as well as the use of tools such as focus groups, to determine how well the product meets the wants and needs of the target group. Numerous determinants factor into the final choice of a product and its presentation. A completely new product, for example, will entail much higher promotional costs to raise consumer awareness, whereas a product that is simply an improved version of an existing item likely will make use of its predecessor's image. A pivotal consideration in product planning and development is branding, whereby the good or service is positioned in the market according to its brand name. Other important elements of the complex product planning and management process may include selection of features, warranty, related product lines, and post-sale service levels.

Considerations about place, the second major decision group, relate to actually getting the good or service to the target market at the right time and in the proper quantity. Strategies related to place may utilize middlemen and facilitators with expertise in joining buyers and sellers, and they may also encompass various distribution channels, including retail, wholesale, catalog, and others. Marketing managers must also devise a means of transporting the goods to the selected sales channels, and they may need to maintain an inventory of items to meet demand. Decisions related to place typically play an important role in determining the degree of vertical integration in a company, or how many activities in the distribution chain are owned and operated by the manufacturer. For example, some larger companies elect to own their trucks, the stores in which their goods are sold, and perhaps even the raw resources used to manufacture their goods.

Decisions about promotion, the third marketing mix decision area, relate to sales, advertising, public relations, and other activities that communicate information intended to influence consumer behavior. Often promotions are also necessary to influence the behavior of retailers and others who resell or distribute the product. Three major types of promotion typically integrated into a market strategy are personal selling, mass selling, and sales promotions. Personal selling, which refers to face-to-face or telephone sales, usually provides immediate feedback for the company about the product and instills greater confidence in customers. Mass selling encompasses advertising on mass media, such as television, radio, direct mail, and newspapers, and is beneficial because of its broad scope. A relatively new means of promotion involves the Internet, which combines features of mass media with a unique opportunity for interactive communication with customers. Publicity entails the use of free media, such as feature articles about a company or product in a magazine or related interviews on television talk shows, to spread the word to the target audience. Finally, sales promotion efforts include free samples, coupons, contests, rebates, and other miscellaneous marketing tactics.

Determination of price, the fourth major activity related to target marketing, entails the use of discounts and long-term pricing goals, as well as the consideration of demographic and geographic influences. The price of a product or service generally must at least meet some minimum level that will cover a company's cost of producing and delivering its offering. Also a firm would logically price a product at the level that would maximize profits. The price that a company selects for its products, however, will vary according to its long-term marketing strategy. For example, a company may under price its product in the hopes of increasing market share and ensuring its competitive presence, or simply to generate a desired level of cash flow. Another producer may price a good extremely high in the hopes of eventually conveying to the consumer that it is a premium product. Another reason a firm might offer a product at a very high price is to discount the good slowly in an effort to maximize the dollars available from consumers willing to pay different prices for the good. In any case, price is used as a tool to achieve comprehensive marketing goals.

COMPETITIVE STRATEGIES

Decisions about product, place, promotion, and price will often be dictated by the competitive stance that a firm assumes in its target market. Common strategies are to be the low-cost supplier, to be highly differentiated, or to satisfy a niche market.

Companies that adopt a low-cost supplier strategy are usually characterized by a vigorous pursuit of efficiency and cost controls. A company that manufactures a low-tech or commodity product, such as wood paneling, would likely adopt this approach. Such firms compete by offering a better value than their competitors, accumulating market share, and focusing on high-volume and fast inventory turnover.

Companies that adhere to a differentiation strategy achieve market success by offering a unique product or service. They often rely on brand loyalty, specialized distribution channels or service offerings, or patent protection to insulate them from competitors. Because of their uniqueness, they are able to achieve higher-than-average profit margins, making them less reliant on high sales volume and extreme efficiency. For example, a company that markets proprietary medical devices would likely assume a differentiation strategy.

Firms that pursue a niche market strategy succeed by focusing all of their efforts on a very narrow segment of an overall target market. They strive to prosper by dominating their selected niche. Such companies are able to overcome competition by aggressively protecting market share and by orienting every action and decision toward the service of its select group. An example of a company that might employ a niche strategy would be a firm that produced floor coverings only for extremely upscale commercial applications.

BUSINESS VERSUS CONSUMER MARKETS

An important micro-marketing delineation is that between industrial and consumer markets. Selling to business is often very different than selling to the consumer. The industrial buyer is almost never moved by fancies and emotions and buys on price and technical specifications. To be sure, in many consumer markets the same rules apply as well; where they do, the situation is, of course, the same. Examples are elderly couples buying retirement packages and do-it-yourselfers buying tools. Buyers in the middle levels of distribution, such as wholesalers, think in terms of *their customers,* the retailers. Retailers, in turn, will view products from the consumer's

point of view. Both of these levels, of course, will be very interested in price and performance issues as well.

Technical know-how and deep product knowledge is more valued in selling business-to-business. The industrial buyers will use components or machinery and will wish to satisfy him- or herself on their suitability to a particular end-use of operation. Distribution channel buyers will see the products as items they will have to explain to others or service in-house.

INTERNET MARKETING

A discussion of marketing would not be complete without mentioning the emerging field of Internet marketing. Increasingly, small businesses have sought to take advantage of the global reach of the World Wide Web and the huge number of potential customers available online. Although it may seem like a completely new field, Internet marketing actually combines many of the basic elements of traditional marketing. "Internet marketing employs the same methods and theory as traditional public relations and integrated marketing—the basic tools for any campaign," Maria Duggan and John Deveney wrote in *Communication World.*

In their article, Duggan and Deveney outline five steps for marketing managers to follow in putting together an Internet marketing campaign. Whether the campaign is intended to increase awareness of an existing brand, draw visitors to a Web site, or promote a new product offering, the first step involves identifying the target market. As is the case with any other type of marketing campaign, the small business must conduct market research in order to define the target audience for the campaign, and then use the information gathered to determine how best to reach them.

The next step is to develop a strategy for the campaign. This involves setting concrete and measurable goals and tying the campaign into the organization's traditional marketing efforts. The third step is to present the strategy to key decision-makers in the small business. It is important at this stage to develop a timeline and budget, and also to be prepared to encounter resistance among colleagues not familiar with cyberspace. The fourth step is to implement the Internet marketing campaign. The final step, evaluation, should be conducted throughout the process. Online surveys of customers are one source of potential feedback.

MARKETING FOR SMALL BUSINESSES

In the early stages of forming a small business, a business plan is a vital tool to help an entrepreneur chart the future direction of the enterprise. A good plan will have a marketing component and demonstrate the owner's understanding of how to advertise and promote his or her product or service line. The more the business is narrowly focused on selling, the more important this element will be. Some businesses, of course, will be engaged in activities barely touched by marketing in the modern sense—but will always have a sales component.

As a small business grows, it may be helpful to create a separate marketing plan. While similar in format to the general business plan, a marketing plan will focus on expanding a certain product line or service rather than on the overall business. Such plans will be especially valuable in obtaining financing for ventures relying upon persuading buyers to try novel products not already on the market.

A number of resources are available to assist small businesses in marketing their products and services. It may be prudent to seek legal advice before implementing a marketing plan, for example. A firm with experience in consumer law could review the small business's product, packaging, labeling, advertising, sales agreements, and price policies to be sure that they meet all relevant regulations to prevent problems from arising later. In addition, many advertising agencies and market research firms offer a variety of means of testing the individual elements of marketing programs. Although such testing can be expensive, it can significantly increase the effectiveness of a company's marketing efforts.

BIBLIOGRAPHY

Duggan, Maria, and John Deveney. "How to Make Internet Marketing Simple." *Communication World.* April 2000.

"Office Depot Helps Small Business Hitch a Ride with Nascar." *Brandweek.* 13 March 2006.

"Picture Your Business with a Logo; Logoworks.com creates affordable logos and identities for small businesses." *Business Week Online.* 4 April 2006.

Schaller, Marcus. "Analyze the Basics When Evaluating Marketing." *San Diego Business Journal.* 13 March 2006.

Scharich, Joanne. "Learn to Take Small Business Global." *Crain's Detroit Business.* 10 April 2006.

Simkin, Lyndon. "Marketing Is Marketing—Maybe!" *Marketing Intelligence and Planning.* March 2000.

Stephenson, James. *Ultimate Small Business Marketing Guide: Over 1500 Great Marketing Tricks That Will Drive Your Business Through the Roof.* Entrepreneur Press, 2003.

Tracy, Joe. *Web Marketing Applied: Web Marketing Strategies for the New Millennium.* Advanstar Communications, 2000.

Zyman, Sergio. "Put the Petal to the Metal: Marketing and the Internet." *Brandweek.* 2 October 2000.

Hillstrom, Northern Lights
updated by Magee, ECDI

MARKUP

Markup is the amount that a seller of goods or services charges over and above the total cost of delivering its product or service in order to make a desired profit. For example, if the total cost of a manufacturer's product is $20, but its selling price is $29, then the extra $9 is understood to be the "markup." Markup is utilized by wholesalers, retailers, and manufacturers alike.

For entrepreneurs in the process of starting a business, establishing markup is one of the most important parts of pricing strategy. Markups must be sizable enough to cover all anticipated business expenses and reductions (markdowns, stock shortages, employee and customer discounts) and still provide the business with a good profit. The informed small business owner, then, is far more likely to arrive at a good markup price than the business owner who has a flawed understanding of the company's likely sales, its total operating expenses—including material, labor, and overhead costs—and its place in larger economic trends.

Entrepreneurs should also recognize that a flat markup percentage should not be blindly stamped on all of the company's products or services regardless of the frequency with which customers purchase those goods or services. As the Small Business Administration noted in its brochure *Pricing Your Products,* small business owners "should seriously consider different markup figures when some lines have very different characteristics. For instance, a clothing retailer might logically have different initial markup figures for suits, shirts, pants, and accessories. [The small business owner] may want those items with the highest turnover rates to carry the lowest initial markup."

Indeed, a small business may be able to realize a hefty profit even when it attaches a considerably smaller markup to one line of products, provided that the sales volume for that product line is high. For example, if company A and company B are selling the same $5 product, but company A insists on attaching a $4 markup on the product while company B limits itself to a $2 markup, the disparity in retail price may allow company B to register sales three or four times greater than the sales posted by company A. Company B thus realizes greater profits from the product than company A, even though the latter business had a higher markup.

Markups in Specific Industries Markups vary enormously from industry to industry. In some industries, the markup is only a small percentage of the total cost of the product or service. Companies in other industries, however, are able to attach a far higher markup. Small appliance manufacturers can sometimes assign markups of 30 percent or more, while clothing is often marked up by as much as 100 percent. Even within industries, markups can vary widely. The automotive industry, for example, is usually limited to a 5-10 percent markup on new cars, but it realizes a far higher profit in the hugely popular sports utility vehicle market, where markups of 25 percent or more are not uncommon.

SEE ALSO *Pricing*

BIBLIOGRAPHY

Henke, John W. "Strategic Selling in the Age of Modules and Systems." *Industrial Marketing Management.* May 2000.

Hogan, John and Tom Lucke. "Driving Growth with New Products: Common pricing traps to avoid." *Journal of Business Strategy.* January-February 2006.

Southall, Brooke. "Advisers Lower Fees to Capture Assets: Many firms have decided they will compete on price." *Investment News.* 16 January 2006.

Walkup, Carolyn. "Restaurateurs Enjoy Higher Sales with Lower Markups on Bottled Wine." *Nation's Restaurant News.* 21 November 2005.

U.S. Small Business Administration. *Pricing Your Products.* Available from http://www.sba.gov/library/pubs/fm-13.doc. Retrieved on 11 April 2006.

Hillstrom, Northern Lights
updated by Magee, ECDI

MATERIAL REQUIREMENTS PLANNING (MRP)

Material requirements planning (MRP) is a computer-based inventory management system designed to assist production managers in scheduling and placing orders for items of dependent demand. Dependent demand items are components of finished goods—such as raw materials, component parts, and subassemblies—for which the amount of inventory needed depends on the level of production of the final product. For example, in a plant that manufactured bicycles, dependent demand inventory items might include aluminum, tires, seats, and bike chains.

The first MRP systems of inventory management evolved in the 1940s and 1950s. They used mainframe computers to explode information from a bill of materials for a certain finished product into a production and purchasing plan for components. Before long, MRP was expanded to include information feedback loops so that production personnel could change and update the inputs into the system as needed. The next generation of MRP, known as manufacturing resources planning or MRP II, also incorporated marketing, finance, accounting, engineering, and human resources aspects into the planning process. A related concept that expands on MRP is enterprise resources planning (ERP), which uses computer technology to link the various functional areas across an entire business enterprise.

MRP works backward from a production plan for finished goods to develop requirements for components and raw materials. MRP begins with a schedule for finished goods that is converted into a schedule of requirements for the subassemblies, the component parts, and the raw materials needed to produce the final product within the established schedule. MRP is designed to answer three questions: *what* is needed? *how much* is needed? and *when* is it needed?"

MRP breaks down inventory requirements into planning periods so that production can be completed in a timely manner while inventory levels—and related carrying costs—are kept to a minimum. Implemented and used properly, it can help production managers plan for capacity needs and allocate production time. But MRP systems can be time consuming and costly to implement, which may put them out of range for some small businesses. In addition, the information that comes out of an MRP system is only as good as the information that goes into it. Companies must maintain current and accurate bills of materials, part numbers, and inventory records if they are to realize the potential benefits of MRP.

MRP INPUTS

The information input into MRP systems comes from three main sources: a bill of materials, a master schedule, and an inventory records file. The bill of materials is a listing of all the raw materials, component parts, subassemblies, and assemblies required to produce one unit of a specific finished product. Each different product made by a given manufacturer will have its own separate bill of materials. The bill of materials is arranged in a hierarchy, so that managers can see what materials are needed to complete each level of production. MRP uses the bill of materials to determine the quantity of each component that is needed to produce a certain number of finished products. From this quantity, the system subtracts the quantity of that item already in inventory to determine order requirements.

The master schedule outlines the anticipated production activities of the plant. Developed using both internal forecasts and external orders, it states the quantity of each product that will be manufactured and the time frame in which they will be needed. The master schedule separates the planning horizon into time "buckets," which are usually calendar weeks. The schedule must cover a time frame long enough to produce the final product. This total production time is equal to the sum of the lead times of all the related fabrication and assembly operations. It is important to note that master schedules are often generated according to demand and without regard to capacity. An MRP system cannot tell in advance if a schedule is not feasible, so managers may have to run several possibilities through the system before they find one that works.

The inventory records file provides an accounting of how much inventory is already on hand or on order, and thus should be subtracted from the material requirements. The inventory records file is used to track information on the status of each item by time period. This includes gross requirements, scheduled receipts, and the expected amount on hand. It includes other details for each item as well, like the supplier, the lead-time, and the lot size.

MRP PROCESSING

Using information culled from the bill of materials, master schedule, and inventory records file, an MRP system determines the net requirements for raw materials, component parts, and subassemblies for each period on the planning horizon. MRP processing first determines gross material requirements, then subtracts out the inventory on hand and adds back in the safety stock in order to compute the net requirements.

The main outputs from MRP include three primary reports and three secondary reports. The primary reports consist of: planned order schedules, which outline the quantity and timing of future material orders; order releases, which authorize orders to be made; and changes to planned orders, which might include cancellations or revisions of the quantity or time frame. The secondary reports generated by MRP include: performance control reports, which are used to track problems like missed delivery dates and stock outs in order to evaluate system performance; planning reports, which can be used in forecasting future inventory requirements; and exception reports, which call managers' attention to major problems like late orders or excessive scrap rates.

Although working backward from the production plan for a finished product to determine the requirements for components may seem like a simple process, it can actually be extremely complicated, especially when some raw materials or parts are used in a number of different products. Frequent changes in product design, order quantities, or production schedule also complicate matters. The importance of computer power is evident when one considers the number of materials schedules that must be tracked.

BENEFITS AND DRAWBACKS OF MRP

MRP systems offer a number of potential benefits to manufacturing firms. Some of the main benefits include helping production managers to minimize inventory levels and the associated carrying costs, track material requirements, determine the most economical lot sizes for orders, compute quantities needed as safety stock, allocate production time among various products, and plan for future capacity needs. The information generated by MRP systems is useful in other areas as well. There is a large range of people in a manufacturing company that may find the use of information provided by an MRP system very helpful. Production planners are obvious users of MRP, as are production managers, who must balance workloads across departments and make decisions about scheduling work. Plant foremen, responsible for issuing work orders and maintaining production schedules, also rely heavily on MRP output. Other users include customer service representatives, who need to be able to provide projected delivery dates, purchasing managers, and inventory managers.

MRP systems also have several potential drawbacks. First, MRP relies upon accurate input information. If a small business has not maintained good inventory records or has not updated its bills of materials with all relevant changes, it may encounter serious problems with the outputs of its MRP system. The problems could range from missing parts and excessive order quantities to schedule delays and missed delivery dates. At a minimum, an MRP system must have an accurate master production schedule, good lead-time estimates, and current inventory records in order to function effectively and produce useful information.

Another potential drawback associated with MRP is that the systems can be difficult, time consuming, and costly to implement. Many businesses encounter resistance from employees when they try to implement MRP. For example, employees who once got by with sloppy record keeping may resent the discipline MRP requires. Or departments that became accustomed to hoarding parts in case of inventory shortages might find it difficult to trust the system and let go of that habit.

The key to making MRP implementation work is to provide training and education for all affected employees. It is important early on to identify the key personnel whose power base will be affected by a new MRP system. These people must be among the first to be convinced of the merits of the new system so that they may buy into the plan. Key personnel must be convinced that they personally will be better served by the new system than by any alternate system. One way to improve employee acceptance of MRP systems is to adjust reward systems to reflect production and inventory management goals.

MRP II

In the 1980s, MRP technology was expanded to create a new approach called manufacturing resources planning, or MRP II. "The techniques developed in MRP to provide valid production schedules proved so successful that organizations became aware that with valid schedules other resources could be better planned and controlled," Gordon Minty noted in his book *Production Planning and Controlling.* "The areas of marketing, finance, and personnel were affected by the improvement in customer delivery commitments, cash flow projections, and personnel management projections."

Minty went on to explain that MRP II "has not replaced MRP, nor is it an improved version of it. Rather, it represents an effort to expand the scope of production resource planning and to involve other functional areas of the firm in the planning process," such as marketing, finance, engineering, purchasing, and human resources. MRP II differs from MRP in that all of these functional areas have input into the master production schedule. From that point, MRP is used to generate material requirements and help production managers plan capacity. MRP II systems often include simulation capabilities so managers can evaluate various options.

SEE ALSO *Enterprise Resource Planning; Inventory Control Systems*

BIBLIOGRAPHY
Hasin, M. Ahsan A., and P.C. Pandey. "MRP II: Should Its Simplicity Remain Unchanged?" *Industrial Management.* May-June 1996.

Minty, Gordon. *Production Planning and Controlling.* Goodheart-Willcox, 1998.

Stevenson, William J. *Production/Operations Management.* Seventh Edition. McGraw-Hill, 2002.

"Why SMEs Should Embrace MRP/ERP. " *Manufacturers' Monthly.* 16 March 2005.

Hillstrom, Northern Lights
updated by Magee, ECDI

MEDICARE AND MEDICAID

Medicare and Medicaid are health insurance programs sponsored by the federal government that cover medical expenses for elderly, disabled, and low-income Americans. Both programs took effect in 1965 and are administered by the Health Care Finance Administration (HCFA) which is part of the Department of Health and Human Services. The U.S. Government provides health care coverage to a variety of groups—including federal employees, military personnel, veterans, and Native Americans—but the Medicare and Medicaid programs

account for the largest proportion of the federal government's health care expenditures.

The cost of administering the programs has increased dramatically over the years with the rapid escalation in health care costs. In fact, the portion of overall federal government spending that was spent to support Medicare and Medicaid increased from 5 percent in 1970 to 20 percent in 2005 and is expected to continue to rise, exceeding 25 percent by 2010. When the estimated costs of a new Medicare prescription drug program that will become effective in 2006 are added to this total, the already high price tag rises even more sharply. As a result, many experts predict that Americans will not be able to depend upon these programs for their long-term health care needs in the future. For self-employed persons and small business owners, who are less likely to be covered by an employer's health insurance program, these statistics highlight the need to plan on obtaining private health insurance coverage to supplement Medicare.

MEDICARE
Medicare is the nation's largest health insurance program, providing coverage in 2003 for 41 million Americans who were at least age 65 or who had a disability. Medicare coverage consists of four parts, labeled Parts A – D.

Part A of Medicare is financed largely through Social Security taxes. It provides for the following services:

- Inpatient hospital services up to 90 days per "spell of illness"
- Skilled nursing facility services for up to 100 days per "spell of illness" following a 3+ day hospital stay
- Home health care up to 100 visits per "spell of illness" following a 3+ day hospital stay
- Hospice care
- Inpatient psychiatric care, for up to 190 days during a beneficiary's lifetime
- Blood (after the beneficiary pays for the first 3 pints per year)

Part B is financed through premiums paid by those who choose to enroll in the program and pay an extra fee for its services, and provides:

- Physicians' services, including office visits and a one-time physical examination for new beneficiaries
- Durable medical equipment (e.g., wheelchairs, oxygen) and supplies
- Outpatient hospital services
- Outpatient mental health services

- Clinical laboratory (e.g., blood tests, some screening tests, etc.) and diagnostic tests

- Outpatient occupational, physical, and speech therapy

- Home health care not preceded by a hospital stay and visits over the 100-day Part A limit

- Some preventive services (e.g., mammograms, diabetes screening)

- Blood (after the beneficiary pays for the first 3 pints per year)

Part C refers to the Medicare Advantage program (formerly known as Medicare+Choice), under which private plans provide Medicare benefits to enrollees.

Part D is a new prescription drug program available as of January 2006 to everyone eligible for Medicare regardless of income and resources, health status, or current prescription drug expenses. There are two ways to get Medicare prescription drug coverage. One is to join a Medicare prescription drug plan, the other is to join a Medicare Advantage Plan or other Medicare Health Plans that offer drug coverage. Whichever is chosen, the plan is designed to help participants cover the cost of both brand-name and generic drugs.

Participants in the new program are required to pay a monthly premium, an annual deductible, and a percentage of the cost of the drugs they acquire (a copayment). The program does offer some assistance for participants who can prove that they have limited incomes. The program is a complicated patchwork of private and competing insurance company policies, each with a list of covered medications and each with a different premium structure. Critics of the plan focus on these complications in addition to its overall high cost as well as the fact that it does nothing to negotiate on the part of all participants for lower prices with pharmaceutical companies. Once the program has been operating for a period of time, assessments of its efficacy will likely be made and amendments to the program may be anticipated.

Qualified people can enroll in the Medicare program by completing an application at their local Social Security Administration office. It is important to note that, once an employee becomes eligible for Medicare, a small business owner is no longer required to offer him or her health insurance continuation coverage under the provisions of the Consolidated Omnibus Budget Reconciliation Act (COBRA). Since Medicare does not cover all of an elderly or disabled person's health care costs, many insurance companies offer Medicare Supplemental Insurance (also known as Medigap coverage) to fill in the gaps. Medigap policies commonly take care of co-payments and over-limit expenses, for example, in exchange for a small premium. Due to past problems with disreputable Medigap providers, experts recommend that individuals shop carefully for this type of coverage.

MEDICAID

As the nation's second-largest health insurance program, Medicaid provided medical assistance to 52 million low-income Americans in 2004. It was established through Title XIX of the Social Security Act of 1965 to pay the health care costs for members of society who otherwise could not afford treatment. The program is jointly funded by the federal government and the state governments, but is administered separately by each state within broad federal guidelines. Medicaid recipients include adults, children, and families, as well as elderly, blind, and disabled persons, who have low or no income and receive other forms of public assistance. Medicaid also covers the "medically needy," or those whose incomes are significantly reduced by large medical expenses.

Medicaid covers the full cost of a wide range of medical services, including inpatient and outpatient hospital care, doctor visits, lab tests, X-rays, nursing home and home health care, family planning services, and preventative medicine. A large proportion of the Medicaid population is elderly or disabled, and thus also qualifies for Medicare. In these cases, Medicaid usually pays for Medicare premiums, deductibles, and co-payments, in addition to some non-covered services.

THE FUTURE

Although many Americans plan to rely on Medicare to meet their health insurance needs later in life, the program as it stood in 2000 actually covered only half of an average elderly person's medical costs, according to the American Association of Retired Persons (AARP). Medicare does not provide funds for dental, vision, or hearing care, for example, and 97 percent of the time it does not cover nursing home care. And the program faces significant challenges in the coming years as the baby-boom generation reaches retirement age.

The United State's Congressional Budget Office (CBO) projects that the Medicare program will run a $5.8 trillion cumulative deficit during the period 2003–2026 when the transfers that the trust fund receives from the general fund are excluded. This means that the revenues coming into the system will be far short of the funds the system will need to pay out. The CBO summarizes the situation this way in its report *The Impact of Social Security and Medicare on the Federal Budget.* "The looming fiscal strains are not a temporary phenomenon caused by the retirement of post-World

War II baby boomers over the next few decades. They reflect a growing imbalance driven by currently prescribed entitlements as well as long-lasting and powerful demographic trends that could have major unfavorable consequences for the economy. Enacting changes to the Social Security and Medicare programs sooner is better than enacting them later because future beneficiaries would have longer to prepare, because the revisions could be less drastic, and because the changes could enhance economic growth."

The question is not whether or not changes will be made but when will they be made and how will they effect future retirees. All Americans need to include some form of contingency planning for post retirement health care coverage as a part of their retirement planning. And the same advice that the CBO offers our legislature in terms of the benefits of taking action early applies to individuals. The sooner one takes action to plan for the future, the longer one will have to prepare and the less dramatic the process may be.

BIBLIOGRAPHY

Caplan, Craig. "What Share of Beneficiaries' Total Health Care Costs Does Medicare Pay?" American Association of Retired Persons (AARP). Available from http://www.aarp.org/research/medicare/outofpocket/aresearch-import-657-DD78.html September 2002.

Connolly, Ceci. "OMB Says Medicare Drug Law Could Cost Still More." *Washington Post.* 19 September 2004.

"Medicare Requires Serious Help." *Business Insurance.* 11 September 2000.

Shapiro, Joseph P. "Medicare's Drug Woes." *U.S. News & World Report.* 21 February 2000.

"Trend: U.S. health spending projections for 2004-2014." *Medical Benefits.* 30 March 2005.

U.S. Congressional Budget Office. "The Impact of Social Security and Medicare on the Federal Budget." Available from http://www.cbo.gov/showdoc.cfm?index=3982&sequence=0. 14 November 2002.

U.S. Government Printing Office. GPOAccess.gov. "Budget of the United States Government." Available from http://www.gpoaccess.gov/usbudget/browse.html. Retrieved on 18 April 2006.

U.S. Social Security Administration. "Status of the Social Security and Medicare Programs." Available from http://www.ssa.gov/OACT/TRSUM/trsummary.html. 23 March 2005.

Wolosky, Howard W. "The Growing Medical Care Component of Retirement Planning: Planners must deal with rapidly rising costs, a confusing Medicare prescription drug program, and a decrease in employer-paid benefits." *The Practical Accountant.* March 2006.

Hillstrom, Northern Lights
updated by Magee, ECDI

MEETINGS

Meetings, while disliked by many, are an essential part of many business operations. They are often the best venue in which communications can take place, for issues to be discussed, for priorities to be set, and for decisions to be made in various realms of business management. Because it is more common for responsibility to be spread out across an organization these days, and because cross-functional efforts are common at almost every business, meetings are the best method for achieving organizational participation.

Calling a meeting is not, however, enough. Holding successful meetings is essential. Poorly run meetings waste time and fail to generate ideas, and unfortunately, far too high a percentage of business meetings are characterized by ineffective processes. Indeed, some analysts estimate that up to 50 percent of meeting time is wasted. Entrepreneurs and small business managers should thus take the appropriate steps to ensure that the meetings that they call and lead are productive.

PLANNING A SUCCESSFUL BUSINESS MEETING

The most important step in holding a successful meeting is planning. This includes determining who should attend, who will run the meeting, and what will be discussed. Before the meeting, finalize a list of attendees. This is especially important for meetings where a quorum is needed to conduct official business. Without a quorum, it is usually best to simply postpone the meeting until more group members can attend.

When determining who should be included in a meeting, there are several criteria to be weighed. Charlie Hawkins pointed out in *Public Relations Quarterly* that the most important personnel to invite are those people who can best achieve the objective of the meeting. This can be people who are affected by a problem, those who will be most affected by the outcome of the meeting, experts on the subject at hand, or people who are known to be good problem-solvers or idea generators. Inviting people solely for political reasons should be avoided, although experts recognize that this may not always be possible. Avoid inviting disruptive people unless they absolutely have to be there. Finally, some meeting topics may benefit from the inclusion of an informed outsider who has no stake in the issue; sometimes a fresh, objective perspective can be most beneficial.

Once the meeting's moderator has determined who needs to be in attendance, he or she should develop an agenda and circulate it in advance of the meeting. There are two schools of thought on how to order the agenda. One school recommends starting the agenda with less-important items that can be handled quickly and easily.

The theory is that this helps to build a positive atmosphere and makes it easier to move on to tougher issues later in the meeting. The other school of thought, however, feels that this is a waste of time and that the agenda should be prioritized, with the most important items coming first. This means jumping right into the most significant issue. Regularly scheduled meetings, such as staff meetings, lend themselves to the "most important first" style.

Many consultants, managers, and business owners contend that the traditional agenda model of "old minutes/old business/new business/adjournment" does not really work anymore. Agendas need to be more fluid and dynamic, yet still need to be structured and effective. Adhering to the following tips can help ensure that the meeting agenda can be addressed effectively:

- State the purpose of the meeting and write it clearly at the top of the agenda. If no clear goal or topic comes to mind, then perhaps the meeting is not even necessary. Consider using a memo, e-mail, conference call, or series of one-to-one meetings to canvas participants about meeting topics prior to creating the agenda.

- Set priorities. Reading the minutes from a past meeting is a colossal waste of time. It is ok to hand out the minutes from the previous meeting, but reading them is just not needed.

- Less is more. One of the fundamental meeting mistakes is tackling too many issues. Keep the agenda focused on a few key items.

If other group members are to play a role at the meeting, call or visit them once the agenda is established so that they clearly understand their role. Assign a time limit to each of the agenda items. Having time limits helps keep a meeting on track and prevents rambling discussions. Never include the agenda item "Any Other Business." It encourages time-wasting at the end of the meeting and also serves as a method for a savvy (or sneaky) meeting participant to exploit the meeting by bringing up an item that is of importance to him or her alone.

Once an agenda has been established, many consultants recommend the appointment of a meeting facilitator in advance of the meeting itself. It is the facilitator's job to keep the meeting focused and on-schedule. He or she must remain "issue neutral" and encourage the free exchange of ideas without taking sides. The best facilitators are good listeners and communicators who successfully blend assertiveness with tact and discipline with humor, set a cooperative tone, and are achievement-oriented. The facilitator should remain focused and not allow side issues to distract from the agenda. Appointing

a separate time-keeper who alerts the facilitator when agreed-upon time limits are approaching is recommended. Some professional meeting planners recommend using co-facilitators—this keeps one facilitator from falling in love with his or her own ideas. For small companies, this idea may not be feasible. However, if the company does hold a lot of meetings, perhaps several company members can be sent for formal training in meeting facilitation. This would make it easier to appoint co-facilitators.

For small companies, perhaps facilitators are not needed at every meeting. Indeed, small business owners often serve as facilitator, key information source, and chief strategist all in one. But some small businesses have successfully instituted systems in which meeting planning and leadership responsibilities are rotated among staff members.

CONDUCTING A SUCCESSFUL MEETING

Once the planning has been concluded, it is time to hold the meeting. Adhering to several simple rules can dramatically increase the likelihood that your meeting will be a productive one.

1. If you are facilitating the meeting, arrive early and be prepared. No exceptions to this rule are allowed. A late facilitator dampens the mood and gets the meeting off on the wrong foot because it makes it impossible for the meeting to start on time. Indeed, provided the facilitator is present, the meeting should begin at the time scheduled, even if other scheduled participants have not yet arrived. Waiting for latecomers rewards them for their behavior and implies that you value their time more than you value the time of those who showed up on time. If one of the latecomers is essential to the first agenda item, be flexible and move on to a later agenda item to keep things moving.

2. Facilitators interested in making certain that the meeting proceeds effectively should set the appropriate tone from the outset. Chit-chat should be kept to a minimum, especially at the start of the meeting. Do not be a dictator--social interaction is an important part of building a cohesive team--but do not let valuable meeting time be wasted either. "Nothing saps the spirit like watching, powerless, as a meeting wanders into oblivion," observed Phaedra Hise in *Inc.*

3. Be sure to stick to the timed meeting agenda that was developed at the planning stage. This builds consensus for tabling discussions that are going nowhere. It also makes it easier to agree to send problems back

to committees, and it keeps one long-winded group member from dominating the meeting. Using a phrase such as "We would like to hear what you have to say, but in order for the group to be out on time we have to move on," is a very successful tactic.

4. If some members of the group are not participating, actively seek out their opinion. Groups tend to be dominated by the most outgoing or opinionated members, but the quiet members often have great ideas of their own. Do not let one person or group dominate the floor.

5. Stay focused on the purpose of the meeting. If the group that is meeting is a large board that is primarily responsible for delegating tasks to smaller committees, make sure the larger group does not make the mistake of doing the work for the smaller groups instead of passing it on.

6. Schedule meetings for times that are likely to encourage concentrate on agenda items. For example, facilitators may want to consider holding short meetings before lunch and quitting time, when staff are less likely to dawdle over non-work related subjects. Conversely, many analysts believe that meetings that are held immediately after lunch, when people are often at their least energetic, are apt to be less effective.

7. Stand-up meetings are often touted as a great way to ensure that meeting participants stay focused. Another way to stay focused is to use what Hawkins termed the "parking lot" strategy. During the course of one discussion, it is not unusual for important ideas or concerns to arise that are not related to the topic at hand. When that happens, the facilitator can call "time out," identify the issue, and place it in a so-called "parking lot" so that it can be addressed at a later time. The group can then get back to the main focus of the meeting without losing topics or ideas that may be of importance to the firm.

8. Try to establish a consensus on business decisions that are arrived at in meetings. "Building consensus does not mean caving in to conform with what the boss wants," said Hawkins. "It does mean examining the plus and minus aspects of possible alternatives, and picking the one(s) that best meet the defined goals. The normal way of deciding--by voting--inevitably produces a win-lose situation. Those who are in the minority are liable to undermine the decision. Even if a voting process is used to pick the winners, a consensus process is recommended to isolate the concerns and address them. When this is done, the solution is refined to the point where everyone in the group can live with the recommendation and support it. A group that builds consensus in a constructive atmosphere is most likely a highly effective team."

9. Ensure that decisions that are made in meetings are adequately disseminated, especially to staff members who are personally impacted by the decision. Make sure that company resources are appropriately redistributed to enable execution of decisions.

MEETING PITFALLS

Despite the best efforts and the strongest facilitator, meetings can quickly spin out of control. Following are some common pitfalls that beset meetings, launching them into downward spirals of inaction and/or flawed decision making:

- The facilitator puts aside the meeting agenda for his or her own personal agenda

- The facilitator allows interruptions such as telephone calls, etc.

- Loud group members are allowed to dominate the meeting

- Decisions are made based on generalizations, exaggeration, guesswork, and assumptions

- Discussions consistently wander off the topic

- Key members of the group are not present

- Overly ambitious agendas

- Meetings that exceed previously agreed-upon time limits

- Minutes that are inaccurate or biased

- Too many participants

- Waiting for latecomers to arrive

- An unclear, or inappropriate, decision-making process. For example, taking a vote when leadership and unilateral action by a company's CEO is clearly needed.

MEETINGS IN A FAMILY-OWNED BUSINESS

Many small businesses are family-owned. While it might seem that a family-operated business might not need to worry about holding successful meetings, that is not true. Family meetings can be an important means of keeping the business fresh, generating new ideas, and keeping grievances to a minimum.

Family meetings, when run properly, can help ensure business success and its continued survival into the next generation. The meetings do not need to be formal, but they should be structured and should be held on a regular basis. Because a family business affects all family members—not just those who are an active part of the business—some analysts contend that everyone in the family should be invited to the meetings. If everyone takes the meeting seriously and is willing to participate, the meeting can lead to greater cohesion, communication, and long-range planning.

Business experts say that the agenda for such a meeting can combine business and pleasure. Serious topics—creating a mission statement, strategy planning, setting a clear path of succession, professional growth and development, market analysis, and estate planning are some examples—typically need to be addressed during these meetings, but the agenda should also reflect a recognition of the family environment in which it is taking place. Meetings that include a meal (dinner, picnic, etc.) as a centerpiece are among the most popular options.

As with any other meeting, the family meeting should have a facilitator. An outside facilitator can be brought in if family members are concerned that objectivity might otherwise be hard to achieve, but be forewarned that hiring a facilitator can be expensive. It is possible to use a family member as a facilitator as long as that person is able to remain unbiased in the face of emotional discussions. Steering clear of long-time family conflicts is also a must if the facilitator is to succeed at his or her job, although admittedly this can sometimes be difficult. "Facilitating one's own family meeting can seem daunting because of the potential emotional intensity of family discussions," wrote John Ward and Sharon Krone in *Nation's Business*. "To be effective, a family member acting as a facilitator must overcome emotional barriers, dispel longtime family stereotypes, and curtail long-standing conflicts among family members. All are tough to do."

Ward and Krone provided several other tips for holding successful family meetings, including the following:

- Consider using co-facilitators as a safeguard to prevent one family member from wielding undue influence over the meeting's direction and tone.

- The facilitator must keep others involved. Assign jobs—keeping notes, creating charts or overheads, keying and distributing minutes, or chairing committees—and avoid the impression that one person is dominating the meeting.

- Provide formal training for the facilitator. While the person selected may have strong interpersonal and leadership skills, formal training in communications, conflict resolution, active listening, decision making, and group management can prove invaluable.

- Each person attending the meeting should reflect on his or her own strengths and weaknesses and personality style.

- Recognize when professional help *is* needed. Intense conflicts and domination by one person or a small group of people are examples of when it might be time to bring in a professional facilitator.

- Avoid surprises. Distribute agendas and notes in advance if possible.

- Set ground rules for the meeting.

- Have fun. Even if the business at hand is very serious, set aside some time for relaxation or fun.

- Use a well-lit meeting room with comfortable furniture. Make sure refreshments are provided and provide ample breaks.

- Do not rush things, and do not overload the agenda with too many heavy topics if at all possible.

BIBLIOGRAPHY

Hawkins, Charlie. "First Aid for Meetings." *Public Relations Quarterly.* Fall 1997.

Hise, Phaedra. "Keeping Meetings Brief." *Inc.* September 1994.

Koh, Peter. "A Complete Waste of Time." *Euromanagement.* October 2005.

Krone, Sharon P., and John L. Ward. "Do-It-Yourself Family Meetings." *Nation's Business.* November 1997.

McManus, Kevin. "Too Many Meetings." *Industrial Engineer.* August 2005.

Miers, John. "The Natural: Are your presentations engaging or enraging? By treating them like conversations, rather than dictations, your management meetings can come to life." *CMA Management.* December 2004.

Williams, Kelly. "No More Boring Meetings." *Office Solutions.* February 2001.

Hillstrom, Northern Lights
updated by Magee, ECDI

MENTORING

Mentoring denotes a relationship between a more experienced person—the mentor—and a less experienced person—the protégé. The mentor's role is to guide, instruct, encourage, and correct the protégé. The protégé should be willing to listen to instruction and constructive criticism, and should also feel as though the mentor is concerned with his/her welfare. Mentor/protégé relationships are less structured and more personal than traditional teacher/student situations.

HOW MENTORING WORKS IN SMALL BUSINESSES

In many large corporations, formal systems of mentoring have been established in recent years. They are designed to quickly involve new employees in the work at hand, and to strengthen the work force in much the same way that other teambuilding strategies are designed to do. These systems pair experienced workers exhibiting strong leadership skills with new employees not yet acquainted with the nuances of the corporation, the work at hand, or their potential within the framework of the company.

But while mentoring is perhaps most closely associated with large corporate settings, the practice can be effectively utilized by small businesses as well. In fact, in many small businesses, an informal mentor/protégé relationship develops naturally as manager and business owners work closely with a small staff.

Small business owners themselves can become involved in mentoring relationships, on either the mentor or the protégé side. Entrepreneurs may seek out business owners or executives with more experience in certain areas, and approach them about establishing a mentoring relationship. Because this kind of approach acknowledges success, experience, and market savvy, a potential mentor will likely be flattered and appreciate the drive and initiative of the potential protégé. In other instances, more experienced small business owners may wish to initiate mentor/protégé relationships from the mentor angle, spurred by philanthropic instincts or a wish to strengthen the skills and knowledge of other people within his or her organization. These mentoring systems can be loosely or formally structured, either determined by the owner or simply encouraged by the owner and initiated by employees. A mentoring program may even prove to be a useful part of a succession plan.

Protégés and mentors should feel relatively comfortable together, as the relationship ideally is one of trust and mutual growth. Mentors should not be expected to become drill sergeants. The mentor relationship is not intended to be one of management exerting its will over young or inexperienced employees. Rather, the relationship should reduce anxiety by clearly defining goals and boundaries, and should increase productivity as a result.

Small business owners seeking mentors have several structured alternatives to choose from. For example, the Small Business Administration can put potential protégés into contact with some groups. In addition, the Service Corps of Retired Executives (SCORE) includes mentoring among its various offerings.

BENEFITS OF MENTORING

Mentoring relationships can be beneficial to all parties. Any mentoring situation requires an investment of time, experience, and trust. But these investments will be rewarded in a strong tie between colleagues and the deepened experience of not just the protégé, but also the mentor.

Benefits for the Mentor Mentors may receive great satisfaction from their experience with protégés. They feel respected and appreciated for their knowledge and skill. And mentors can become more invested in their work as a result: they have personal relationships to foster in the business setting, and they feel that the owner trusts and respects their judgment and talents. In their position of role models, mentors may even more closely evaluate their own performances and become more productive in their own business dealings and duties.

Benefits for the Protégé The protégé, whether a new employee of a business or a new entrepreneur, will benefit from the transfer of knowledge and know-how that can be passed on by a mentor of greater experience. Perhaps the greatest benefit is being able to learn from other people's mistakes. A mentor can warn of pitfalls as yet unforeseen by the protégé, saving the time and the pain of having to make those mistakes.

An employee who is a protégé also benefits by having a mentor trained in the management of a business, who can pass along the true meanings behind policy decisions, and the unwritten rules of the workplace. The mentoring relationship can make the transition into productive, comfortable employee a much smoother one. Protégés will quickly learn what is expected of them, their place within the framework of the business, and the responsibilities of other departments and personnel within the workplace. Career opportunities and areas of improvement can both be sensitively illustrated by a mentor, and transitions within the company and changes of business practice can be made less stressful with suitable guidance.

Benefits For the Business Owner The business owner benefits from the mentor/protégé relationship within his or her business in some very real ways. New employees can be thoroughly trained in technical aspects of the work by a mentor, resulting in employees who move quickly through the learning curve and into productive work. Mentoring relationships have also been shown to promote employee satisfaction, leading to decreased turnover in the workforce and higher production rates.

SEE ALSO *Apprenticeship Programs; Cross-Functional Teams; Cross-Training*

BIBLIOGRAPHY

Benabou, Charles, and Raphael Banabou. "Establishing a Formal Mentoring Program for Organizational Success." *National Productivity Review.* Autumn 2000.

Dortch, Thomas W., Jr. *The Miracles of Mentoring: The Joy of Investing in Our Future.* Cahners Publishing, 2000.

Eddy, Sandra E. "Computer Ease: Virtual Mentors." *Entrepreneur Online.* November 1997.

Graham, Anne. "A Mentoring Mindset." *Folio.* September 2000.

Kennedy, Danielle. "Guiding Light." *Entrepreneur.* July 1997.

Kremer, Dennis B. "Learn from Experience—Find a Mentor." *Westchester County Business Journal.* 22 August 2005.

Martin, Anya. "Mentoring Within." *Atlanta Business Chronicle.* 4 August 2000.

Roberts, Lee. "Mentoring May Develop Both Loyalty and Retention." *Minneapolis-St. Paul Business.* 4 August 2000.

Hillstrom, Northern Lights
updated by Magee, ECDI

MERCHANDISE DISPLAYS

Merchandise displays are special presentations of a store's products used to attract and entice the buying public. The nature of these displays may vary somewhat from industry to industry, but all merchandise displays are predicated on basic principles designed to increase product purchases. Indeed, merchandise displays are an integral element of the overall merchandising concept, which seeks to promote product sales by coordinating marketing, advertising, and sales strategies.

Many business consultants believe that small business owners are among the leaders in innovative merchandise display strategies. W. Rae Cowan noted in *Chain Store Age Executive,* for example, that "in many instances, smaller specialty chains are leading the way in store ambience supporting their overall marketing strategy in a broad range of categories from fashion through hardware and housewares and building supplies areas. By their very nature, specialty stores depend on their fixturing to generate a differentiation or niche in the marketplace. And being physically smaller in some cases allows for faster response to market trends and conditions.... Successful retailers today are using their fixturing to productively dispense their merchandise and communicate an appropriate environment on the retail floor."

Merchandise displays generally take one of several basic forms:

- Storefront Window Displays—These typically open on to a street or shopping mall walk or courtyard and are intended to attract passerby that might not otherwise enter the store.

- Showcase Displays—These typically feature items that 1) are deemed to be too valuable for display in storefront set-ups, or 2) are niche items of high interest to the business's primary clientele. These display centers are usually located in high traffic areas and typically feature multiple tiers for product display and a sliding door on the clerk's side for access.

- "Found-Space" Displays—This term refers to product presentations that utilize small but nonetheless usable areas of the store, such as the tops of product carousels or available wall space.

Storefront window displays and "found space" displays are particularly popular tools for publicizing and selling sale items.

KEYS TO SUCCESSFUL MERCHANDISE DISPLAY

Trudy Ralston and Eric Foster, authors of *How to Display It: A Practical Guide to Professional Merchandise Display,* cited several key components of successful merchandise display that are particularly relevant for small business owners. First, displays should be economical, utilizing only space, materials, and products that are already available. Second, displays should be versatile, able to "fit almost anywhere, exhibit almost any merchandise, and convey almost any message. Finally, displays have to be effective. The ideal display, said Ralston and Foster, "is readily visible to any passer-by and [should be arranged so that] there is no time or space lag between when a potential buyer sees the design and when he or she can react to it. [The ideal display] also shows the customer what the product actually looks like, not some flat and intangible picture of it. Few other forms of promotion can give such a vivid presentation of both the merchandise and character of a store."

The effectiveness of these cornerstones of merchandising display strategy can be increased by remembering several other tips as well, including the following:

- Allocate merchandise display space and expenditures appropriately in recognition of customer demographics. If the bulk of your business's customers are males between the ages of 20 and 40, the bulk of your displays should probably be shaped to catch their interest.

- Be careful of pursuing merchandise display designs that sacrifice effectiveness for the sake of originality.

- Make certain that the cleanliness and neatness of the display is maintained.

- Do not overcrowd a display. Customers tend to pass over messy, busy-looking displays. Instead, Ralston and Foster affirm that "a display should feature a single item or point of interest....Every primary article [in a display] must interact with every other so that they all come together as a group. If they don't it will look as if there is not one design, but several.

- Combine products that are used together in displays. For example, pairing ski goggles with other outdoor apparel is apt to be more effective than placing it alone or with some other product that is only tangentially related to skiing.

- Small items should be displayed so that would-be customers can get a good look at them without having to solicit the help of a member of the staff.

- Pay attention to details when constructing and arranging display backgrounds. For example, Foster and Ralston counsel business owners to "avoid dark backgrounds when customers will be looking through a window, since this makes the glass behave as a giant mirror."

- Merchandise displays can sometimes be utilized to educate customers. A well-conceived display could, for example, illustrate a product use that may not have occurred to most customers. "In addition to selling actual merchandise, display can be used to introduce a new product, a fashion trend, and a new 'look' or idea," explained Martin Pegler in *Visual Merchandising and Display.* "Display can be used to educate the consumer concerning what the new item is, how it can be worn or used, and how it can be accessorized. The display may also supply pertinent information, the price, and other special features."

All of these considerations need to be weighed when putting together a merchandise display. But ultimately, the final barometer of a display's worthiness is its ability to sell products. As Martin Pegler bluntly stated, "The test of a good display today is: *Does it sell?*"

BIBLIOGRAPHY

Cowan, W. Rae. "Store Fixturing and Display—Retailer's Strategic Tool for Product Positioning and Productivity in the '90s." *Chain Store Age Executive.* December 1993.

Edelson, Sharon. "Mass Stores Go Class: Upgrading Apparel Areas to Attract New Shoppers." *WWD.* 13 June 2005.

"Merchandise Displays." *Do-It-Yourself Retailing.* December 2005.

Pegler, Martin M. *Visual Merchandising and Display.* Fairchild Publications, 1983.

Ralston, Trudy, and Eric Foster. *How to Display It: A Practical Guide to Professional Merchandise Display.* Art Direction Book Co., 1985.

Stickland, Allison M. "Out With the Old." *Pet Product News.* January 2006.

Strong-Michas, Jennifer. "Show Off Your Company: Tips for a better trade show booth: What to know when you are an exhibitor." *Alaska Business Monthly.* February 2006.

Hillstrom, Northern Lights
updated by Magee, ECDI

MERGERS AND ACQUISITIONS

Mergers and acquisitions (M&As) is a phrase used to describe a host of financial activities in which companies are bought and sold. In an *acquisition* one party buys another by acquiring all of its assets. The acquired entity ceases to exist as a corporate body, but the buyer sometimes retains the name of the acquired company, indeed may use it as its own name. In a *merger* a new entity is created from the assets of two companies; new stock is issued. Mergers are more common when the parties have similar size and power. Sometimes acquisitions are labeled "mergers" because "being acquired" carries a negative connotation (like "being eaten"); a merger suggests mutuality. M&A activity involves both privately held and publicly traded companies; acquisitions may be friendly (both entities are willing) or may be hostile (the buyer is opposed by the management of the acquisition target).

WHY M&A?

M&A activity is invariably explained as creating greater stockholder value. Stockholder interests are, indeed, central, because these transactions must have the approval of a majority of stockholders, and stockholders are unlikely to vote their shares in favor of a sale, purchase, or merger unless they believe that they will benefit. The real motivation behind M&A activity, however, is almost always a mixture in which financial, structural, institutional, and even personal aims are present. Companies make acquisitions to grow more rapidly, to gain control over their raw materials, to obtain new technology, to pump up their stock, to take advantage of weaknesses in others, to diversify, etc.

A major element of M&A activity in hostile acquisitions is resistance to being acquired. It is motivated by the management's fear of losing control, distrust of the buyer's motivation, disagreement with the buyer's methods and strategy, etc. Frequently management resists an acquisition although their stockholders would clearly benefit; thus they try to persuade the stockholders that "in the long run" the stockholders will suffer. Resisting managements are frequently correct—but often lose because stockholders look at the bird in the hand.

Motivations for selling a company are equally complex. Retiring founders of small businesses sell companies to realize the business's cash value after a life-time of work. Companies projecting failure sell before the failure is actually knocking on the door. Companies reach the limit of their resources, financial or technical, and see great benefit in joining a larger company able to fund growth and to enhance their own art by major engineering inputs. In the first two cases the motives are liquidity and fear of bankruptcy respectively. The third case is mixed, with structural, institutional, and opportunistic motives leading to a sale. In periods of M&A frenzy (common in expansionary periods) a company may also face an offer it just can't refuse.

TYPES OF ACQUISITIONS

Acquisitions are classified by their structural effects, the attitudes of the parties, and by the mechanisms of the transaction. The classifications are not mutually exclusive, just different ways of looking at M&A.

Acquisitions can be horizontal, vertical, or conglomerative. The first case involves a company that simply expands by purchasing another company in its own field: two real-estate firms merging or one buying the other. The second case, the vertical, involves a company buying another which heretofore supplied it: a construction company buying a lumber yard or a brick yard. In a conglomerative acquisition the buyer's business has nothing to do with that of the purchased company's: a steel mill buying a chain of clothing stores. The building of vast conglomerates by acquisition is a cyclic corporate fad, viewed as a way of diversifying, justified by the notion that management is fundamentally a financial enterprise.

Acquisitions are classified as "friendly" or "hostile" depending on the attitudes of the managements on either side. In a friendly merger or acquisition both parties are willing participants and negotiate in that spirit. Hostile acquisitions tend to be launched by dissident stockholder groups (or raiders who first buy in to have a share); the targeted company may have a large amount of cash, may be paying thin dividends, may (in the opinion of the hostile bidder) be favoring growth over stockholder return, etc. In friendly acquisitions management teams cooperate in communicating with stockholders; in hostile takeovers, the acquiring group solicits the votes of the target's stockholders in order to obtain enough votes to prevail.

Classification by mechanism involves how the buyer pays for the seller. Payment may take the form of cash, stock, or a combination. Cash-for-stock is the simplest method but more costly for the stockholder: the transaction is taxable, the stockholder having to pay capital gains taxes. The stock-for-stock method is the most popular because it is tax free; the seller's stockholders receive stock in the buyer's company; if the action is a merger, stock in the new entity is issued in payment instead. If the deal is a combination, the cash portion of the deal is taxable.

VALUING THE CANDIDATE

What is a company worth? The balance sheet provides a partial answer. The company's assets less its liabilities produce the company's net worth. Very few companies, however, are willing to sell for net worth. It represents a static value, a snapshot in time. A company is a dynamic entity expected to produce earnings in the future.

A common measure used for valuation is the price-earnings ratio (P/E Ratio) in which the price of a share of stock is divided by the company's after-tax earning per share. A $100 share earning $10 per share a year, is said to have a 10:1 ratio. The market, in other words, is willing to pay $10 for every $1 of earnings. A company with an annual after-tax earnings of $500,000 and a P/E Ratio of 7 would thus be valued at $3.5 million.

Another ratio used is the enterprise value to sales ratio (EV/Sales Ratio). Enterprise value is calculated by taking the company's outstanding stock, adding its debt, and deducting its cash or cash-equivalent assets. This value is then divided by the company's sales (not earnings) to arrive at an EV/Sales Ratio. The concept here is to treat both stock and debt as values that need to be paid back with sales. If the ratio is low, the value of the company is high. If the company has a lot of cash, the ratio may be negative, indicating that the target can be bought using its own cash.

The most common method of valuation used in M&A is discounted cash flow (DCF) analysis. The method is described in detail in this volume (see *Discounted Cash Flow*). It involves projecting the financial performance of the company over some period, typically ten years, and then calculating net cash flow for every year. The analyst then discounts (reduces) future earnings using the purchaser's actual rate of return on capital. The logic here is that capital invested now would earn the buyer interest in future years. That same interest is deducted from the projected cash flows. The sum of discounted cash flows is then viewed as the acquisition target's current value. The analyst usually assumes that the company will be sold in the 11th year for a conservative multiple of earnings; this residual is also discounted and added. The drawback of DCF is its complexity—above all the need to project all of the complex financial flows into the future. Its benefits are greater detail which typically requires a very full understanding of the candidate.

In virtually all valuations of companies, the prospective buyer also factors in so-called synergies which will help it increases in market share and sales, lower costs, and increased profitability. Projected synergy gains are then used as part of the valuation. Following many acquisitions, large layoffs are announced because the merger of functions eliminates duplications. Such layoffs are an example of a "synergy"; often the announcement lifts the stock.

SUCCESS AND FAILURE

Are mergers and acquisitions a success or a failure? The answer is that results are mixed. Many smaller companies are successfully sold to larger operation and, transformed (often beyond recognition), continue to operate and grow. Larger deals are evidently less successful. Investopedia.com, in its article regarding M&A states: "Historical trends show that roughly two thirds of big mergers will disappoint on their own terms, which means that they will lose value on the stock market. The motivations that drive mergers can be flawed and efficiencies from economies of scale may prove elusive. In many cases the problems associated with trying to make merged companies work are all too concrete."

Results for stockholders depend on which side of the deal they are on. There is substantial empirical evidence that the shareholders in acquired firms benefit substantially. Gains for this group typically amount to 20 percent in mergers and 30 percent in tender offers above the market prices prevailing a month prior to the merger announcement. Most small company owners realize substantial gains when selling successful, privately-held corporations to a public buyer. The gains of stockholders of acquiring firms are difficult to measure, but the best evidence suggests that shareholders in bidding firms gain little. Losses in value subsequent to merger announcements are not unusual. In post-acquisition periods, managements are often distracted with cost cutting and integration processes and spend less time on the business, sometimes with unfavorable results. This seems to suggest that overvaluation by bidding firms is common. Managers may also have incentives to increase firm size at the potential expense of shareholder wealth. If so, merger activity may very often happen for structural, "legacy," and other reasons as already indicated above.

SEE ALSO *Discounted Cash Flow; Leveraged Buyout*

BIBLIOGRAPHY
Burt, Erin. "Five Money Rules for Moving in Together." *Kiplinger's Starting Out Web Column.* 6 April 2006.

Davenport, Todd. "Pent-up M&A Demand, But Pricey Supply." *American Banker.* 20 March 2006.

Hoover, Kent. "Bill Would Aid Mergers of Small Businesses." *Sacramento Business Journal.* 21 July 2000.

"Hospital Mergers Result in Price Hikes and Drops in Quality: Study." *Healthcare Financial Management.* April 2006.

Kilpatrick, Christine. "More Owners Put Small Businesses on the Sale Block." *San Francisco Business Times.* 9 June 2000.

"Mergers and Acquisitions: Introduction." *Investopedia.com.* Available from http://www.investopedia.com/university/mergers/. Retrieved on 21 April 2006.

Miller, Karen Lowry. "Deals That Work: With the world caught up in merger mania again, studies suggest fewer tie-ups will fail, this time." *Newsweek International.* 24 April 2006.

Pablo, Amy L. and Mansour Javidan. *Mergers and Acquisitions: Creating Integrative Knowledge.* Blackwell Publishing Ltd., 2004.

Darnay, ECDI

METROPOLITAN STATISTICAL AREA (MSA)

A Metropolitan Statistical Area (MSA) is a designation the U.S. government uses to refer to a region that, broadly speaking, consists of a city and its suburbs, plus any surrounding communities that are closely linked to the city because of social and/or economical factors. MSAs are, emphatically, *statistical* definitions and not *administrative* subdivisions. Thus, for instance, a reference in a report to "the Detroit MSA" refers to a geographical area of which the official City of Detroit is just a part. No one is actually administratively responsible for the MSA itself.

Defining urban areas has been the responsibility of the Office of Management and Budget (OMB), an element of the White House except in the period 1977 to 1981, during which time the Office of Federal Statistical Policy and Standards, in the Department of Commerce, did the job. The first such definition was issued in 1949 by OMB's predecessor, the Bureau of the Budget. Since then urban area definitions have been modified in 1958, 1971, 1975, 1980, 1990, and most recently in 2000. The purpose of these definitions has been to give a uniform basis for identifying urbanization in the context of the population census. The designations are widely used in government and industrial reference.

TERMINOLOGY

If many geese are a gaggle, many lions a pride, and many fish a school, one could refer to many designations of statistical areas as "a confusion" of names—because urban statistical designations have a history of being just that—confusing. The categories used before the 2000 redefinition were, in hierarchical order, free-standing MSAs, PMSAs (p from "primary") which were parts of a larger aggregate, and CMSAs (consolidated metropolitan statistical areas) which held multiple PMSAs. Now it would be nice if we could say, "Forget these old designations!" but we cannot. They still appear in reports issued before 2000. Therefore the analyst must remember the old abbreviations along with the new ones.

The new ones, still in hierarchical order by size, are Micropolitan Statistical Areas (no acronym yet, but in this essay we'll abbreviate them as MICROs), Metropolitan Statistical Areas (MSAs), and Combined Statistical Areas (CSAs, holding two or more MICROs or MSAs). Further complicating matters, MICROs and MSAs are collectively referred to as Core-Based Statistical Areas or CBSAs. To justify the "confusing" tag, the terminology also includes NECTAs, which are New England City and Town Areas—because in the New England states cities and towns are used as the basis of building up larger aggregates rather than counties—as in the rest of the U.S. and in Puerto Rico.

DEFINITIONS

Units definitions are based on population and population is measured by county except in the New England states where city and town populations are used for designation purposes instead.

Core-Based Statistical Area. A CBSA is one or more counties with an urbanized cluster of at least 10,000 people. The area as a whole is defined by the interaction between the core and the outlying areas. This interaction, measured by commuting, means that at least 25 percent of people in outlying areas are working in the core. The CBSA is a generic definition of MICROs and MSAs, the difference being core population size.

Micropolitan Statistical Areas. A MICRO is simply a small CBSA, i.e., a county or counties with an urbanized core of 10,000 but fewer than 50,000 in population. Outlying areas included are, again, defined by commuting patterns. As of November 2004, according to the Census Bureau, there were 575 MICROs in the U.S. and five in Puerto Rico.

Metropolitan Statistical Areas. An MSA has an urbanized core of minimally 50,000 population and includes outlying areas determined by commuting measures. In 2004, the U.S. had 361 MSAs and Puerto Rico eight.

Combined Statistical Areas. CSAs are two or more adjacent CBSAs in which there is at least a 15 employment interchange (measured by commuting) between cores. If this exchange is 25 percent or higher between a pair of CBSAs, they are combined into a CSA automatically; if the measure is at least 15 percent but below 25,

local opinion in both areas is used to decide on combination. The U.S. had 116 CSAs in 2004.

Metropolitan Divisions. Metropolitan divisions are used to further subdivide major metropolitan areas into divisions with minimally 2.5 million core populations. Thus, for instance, the Boston area is subdivided into four, the Chicago Area into three, Detroit into two, the New York area into five such divisions. All told there were 29 divisions in the 10 largest metro areas: Boston, Chicago, Dallas, Los Angeles, Miami, New York, Philadelphia, San Francisco, Seattle, and Washington, D.C.

NAMING CONVENTIONS

Statistical areas are named after the city the OMB defines as the "principal city," namely the administrative entity which forms the largest urban core. "Atlantic City, NJ MSA" is a typical MSA name. The area includes a single county, Atlantic County, NJ. Under OMB rules, however, additional cities may also qualify for the "principle" designation based on population and employment size measures. The names of up to the top three principal cities are included in the name of the MSA including the state abbreviations in which the cities and component counties are located. An example is "Philadelphia-Camden-Wilmington, PA-NJ-DE-MD MSA." The three principle cities shown are in Pennsylvania, New Jersey, and Delaware, but the state of MD is shown as well because Cecil County, MD is part of this metro region. This particular MSA is also divided into three Metropolitan Divisions, namely Camden, NJ, Philadelphia, PA, and Wilmington, DE-MD-NJ. Thus the divisions are named after "principal cities." Sometimes, however, division names are based on county rather than on principal city names.

BIBLIOGRAPHY

"Standards for Defining Metropolitan and Micropolitan Statistical Areas; Notice." Office of Management and Budget. *Federal Register.* 27 December 2000.

U.S. Bureau of the Census. "Metropolitan and Micropolitan Statistical Area Definitions." 19 January 2006. Available from http://www.census.gov/population/www/estimates/metrodef.html. Retrieved on 17 April 2006.

Hillstrom, Northern Lights
updated by Magee, ECDI

MEZZANINE FINANCING

Mezzanine financing is a hybrid between debt and equity. In a multi-tiered financing of an operation, for instances, the sources of money will be senior debt, senior subordinated debt, subordinated debt, *mezzanine debt*, and finally the owner's own equity. In other words, the mezzanine lender is very close to being *last* to get paid if something goes wrong.

Mezzanine financing is a loan to the owner with terms that subordinate the loan both to different levels of senior debt as well as to secured junior debt. But the mezzanine lender typically has a warrant (meaning a legal right fixed in writing) enabling him or her to convert the security into equity at a predetermined price per share if the loan is not paid on time or in full. Many variants exist, of course, the most common being that a portion of the money is paid back *as equity*. Being unsecured and highly subordinated, mezzanine financing is very expensive, with lenders looking for 20 percent returns and up. Unless a market is very flush with money and "irrational exuberance" reigns (to use a phrase coined by the retired chairman of the Federal Reserve, Alan Greenspan), the mezzanine lender will be reluctant to lend unless the company has a high cash flow, a good history of earnings and growth, and stature within its industry. Mezzanine is decidedly *not* a source of start-up funding. Major sources of mezzanine financing include private investors, insurance companies, mutual funds, pension funds, and banks.

MEZZANINE MECHANICS

Financing programs or acquisitions by this mechanism typically involve some combination of lending by the source of money and provision of equity by the borrower. The narrowest case is one in which the lender lends cash and gets a warrant to convert the loan, or portions of it, to stock either any time at the lender's option or in the case of partial or complete default. More usually the following conditions prevail: A sum of money changes hands. Most of it is lent to the borrower at an interest rate but a portion of it is in the form of a favorable sale of equity. In addition there may also be a warrant for the lender and restrictive covenants under which the lender is further protected. The loan will typically fetch an interest rate well above the prime rate and will be for a period of four to eight years.

In the ideal case, the mezzanine financier anticipates earning a high interest on the loan and rapid appreciation of the equity he or she has acquired (or can acquire at a low price with the warrant). Mezzanine financing is typically used in acquisitions based on leveraged buyouts in which all of the investors, not least the mezzanine financier, anticipate cashing out by taking the business public again and refinancing it after the acquisition. Thus the equity can be turned into cash with a substantial gain on the capital. In the event of a failure, the mezzanine lender has little recourse except to influence the company's

turnaround by using its stock acquired by means of the warrant.

The borrower turns to mezzanine lenders because he or she cannot acquire capital by other means for lack of collateral or because its finances cannot attract less expensive lending. The price of the money, of course, is high due to high rates of interest, but the owner is betting on being able to repay the loan without yielding too much control.

THE PROS AND CONS

Advantages

1. The owner rarely loses outright control of the company or its direction. Provided the company continues to grow and prosper, its owners are unlikely to encounter any interference from the mezzanine lender.

2. The method offers a lot of flexibility in shaping amortization schedules and the rules of the borrowing itself, not least specifying special conditions for repayment.

3. Lenders willing to enter into the world of mezzanine financing tend to be long-term investors rather than people looking to make a quick killing.

4. Mezzanine lenders can provide valuable strategic assistance.

5. Mezzanine financing increases the value of stock held by existing shareholders although mezzanine equity will dilute the value of the stock.

6. Most importantly, mezzanine financing provides business owners with the capital they need to acquire another business or expand into another production or market area.

Disadvantages

1. Mezzanine financing may involve loss of control over the business particularly if projections do not work out as envision or if the equity portion of the borrowing is high enough to give the mezzanine lender a larger share.

2. Subordinated debt agreements may include restrictive covenants. Mezzanine lenders frequently insist on restrictive covenants; these may include requirements that the borrower is not to borrow more money, refinance senior debt from traditional loans, or create additional security interests in the company's assets; covenants may also force the borrower to meet certain financial ratios—e.g., cash flow to equity.

3. Similarly, business owners who agree to mezzanine financing may be forced to accept restrictions in how they spend their money in certain areas, such as compensation of important personnel (in such instances, a business owner may not be able to offer above-market packages to current or prospective employees). In some cases, business owners have even been asked to take pay cuts themselves and/or limit dividend payouts.

4. Mezzanine financing is more expensive than traditional or senior debt arrangements.

5. Arranging for mezzanine financing can be an arduous, lengthy process. Most mezzanine deals will take at least three months to arrange, and many will take twice that long to complete.

SEE ALSO *Initial Public Offering; Leveraged Buyouts*

BIBLIOGRAPHY

"Are Hedge Funds Squeezing Out the Mezzanines?." *Private Equity Week.* 5 December 2005.

Boadmer, David. "Make Way for Mezzanine." *Retail Traffic.* 1 January 2006.

deBrauwere, Dan. "Six Major Catalysts of the M&A Market." *Westchester County Business Journal.* 23 January 2006.

Hoogesterger, John. "Economic Trends Boost the Fortunes of Mezzanine Funds." *Minneapolis-St. Paul CityBusiness.* 25 August 2000.

"Leverage Buyouts: A Brief History." Marshall Capital Corporation. Available from http://www.marshallcapital.com/AS6.asp. Retrieved on 4 April 2006.

"Mezzanine Financing." Investopedia.com. Available from http://www.investopedia.com/terms/m/mezzaninefinancing.asp. Retrieved on 18 April 2006.

Miller, Alan. "The Difference Between Mortgage and Mezzanine." *Money Management.* 9 March 2006.

Sinnenberg, John. "Making Sense of Mezzanine Financing." *Financial Executive.* December 2005.

Hillstrom, Northern Lights
updated by Magee, ECDI

MINIMUM WAGE

The Fair Labor Standards Act of 1938 (FLSA) is in a sense the basic law controlling employment and compensation issues in the United States. FLSA mandates that a minimum wage be paid, but the act classifies employees into two broad classes: those who are covered by the law because they are paid by the hour and those who are exempted because they are paid a salary. From this provision of the law we have the concept of "exempt" and "non-exempt"

employees. All matters pertaining to the minimum wage are applicable only to "non-exempt" employees, i.e. those *covered* by the legislation. In addition to the federal minimum wage, state minimum wage rates are also in place.

RATES AND COVERAGE

The last upward revision of the federal rate took place in October 1996 as part of the Small Business Job Protection Act (SBJA) of 1996. The act increased the rate from $4.75 an hour to $5.15 per hour. The rate has not changed since. In early 2006, six states (Alabama, Arizona, Louisiana, Mississippi, South Carolina, and Tennessee) had no minimum wage. Fifteen states had higher minimum wages than the U.S. as a whole: Alaska, California, Connecticut, Delaware, Florida, Hawaii, Illinois, Maine, Massachusetts, Minnesota, New Jersey, New York, Oregon, Washington, and Wisconsin. The highest wage was in Oregon, $7.63 an hour; in 2006 Connecticut had a $7.40 per hour minimum wage to be raised to $7.65 in 2007. The rest of the states had the same minimum wage as the national rate. Under the federal rules, a non-exempt worker is entitled to receive the highest minimum wage available in the place where he or she works. Changes in state law are monitored by the U.S. Department of Labor and may be consulted at http://www.dol.gov/esa/minwage/america.htm.

Exemptions Estimates of the number of people earning the minimum wage are difficult to establish in part because exemptions to the law exist for certain classes of worker—some of whose earnings may actually be higher than the minimum wage although, officially, they make less. For example, family members of the employer may be paid less than the minimum wage. Also exempted are employers of the disabled if the disability affects the person's ability to work. Such individuals are often employed in sheltered workshops and environments. Full time students are not covered; students and apprentices part of whose work is learning need not be paid the minimum wage. Finally and most importantly, employees earning tips are exempted under the presumption that tips will make up the difference.

Statistics Reporting on data for 2004 from the *Current Population Survey,* the Bureau of Labor Statistics (BLS) found that 73.9 million Americans earned hourly pay, representing 59.8 percent of all workers earning wages and salaries. Of this total 520,000 earned exactly $5.15 an hour—but some 1.483 million other hourly workers reported earning less. The two categories combined (2 million) were 2.7 percent of hourly workers.

BLS pointed out that about 350,000 of those in the "under minimum" category reported earning exactly

$5.00 an hour, which may have reflected mere rounding down from $5.15 by survey respondents. If so, the total number earning less would have been around 1.13 million people in 2004. The number tallies reasonably well with other BLS data which show that the largest category of those earning less than minimum wage (1.04 million individuals) worked in food preparation and serving occupations. The second largest such category were people working in sales and office occupations (104,000). Taking the "at minimum or below" category, the leading industrial category was "leisure and hospitality," employing 62 percent of all such employees. Of all those earning minimum wage or below, 51 percent were between 16 and 24 years of age, and nearly half of those were between 16 and 19. Part-time workers represented 62 percent of the total.

The data thus show that minimum wage workers are heavily skewed toward youth, part time work, and the restaurant/food, service/hotel sectors; in the aggregate they represent a small portion of the hourly work force.

BIBLIOGRAPHY

"Debating the Minimum Wage." *Economist*. 3 February 2001.

"Minimum Wage: A Hike Won't Hurt." *Business Week*. 9 October 2000.

Ramey, Joanna, and Dana Lenetz. "Democrats Promise Extensive Battle for Minimum Wage Hike." *Footwear News*. 19 February 2001.

U.S. Department of Labor. "Characteristics of Minimum Wage Workers: 2004." Available on http://www.bls.gov/cps/minwage2004.htm#1. Retrieved on 18 April 2006.

U.S. Department of Labor. "Minimum Wage Laws in the States – March 1, 2006" Available on http://www.dol.gov/esa/minwage/america.htm. Retrieved on 18 April 2006.

Darnay, ECDI

MINORITY BUSINESS DEVELOPMENT AGENCY

Established in 1969 by executive order, the Minority Business Development Agency (MBDA) works to foster the creation, growth, and expansion of minority-owned businesses in the United States as a part of the Department of Commerce. The agency was originally called the Office of Minority Business Enterprise (OMBE), but its name was changed to its current incarnation in 1979.

The MBDA describes its mission as one of several facets, including: 1) coordination of federal government plans, programs, and operations that affect minority business enterprises; 2) promotion and coordination of activities of government and private organizations that help minority businesses grow; 3) collection and dissemination of information that will help those interested in establishing or expanding a successful minority-owned firm; and 4) funding organizations to provide management and technical assistance to minority entrepreneurs. A wide range of individuals are eligible for MBDA assistance, including Hispanic Americans, Asian and Pacific Island Americans, Alaska Natives and Native Americans, African Americans, and Hasidic Jews.

The Minority Business Development Agency's primary headquarters are located in Washington, D.C., but it also maintains five regional offices (in Atlanta, Chicago, Dallas, New York, and San Francisco) and four district offices (in Miami, Boston, Philadelphia, and Los Angeles), as well as a group of local community-based outreach centers across the country. The centers are generally ensconced in regions that feature a large concentration of minority populations and large numbers of minority-owned businesses. These facilities include Minority Business Development Centers (MBDC), Native American Business Development Centers (NABDC), Business Resource Centers (BRC), and Minority Business Opportunity Committees (MBOC) that offer a variety of programs to assist minority entrepreneurs, including providing one-on-one assistance in writing business plans, marketing, management assistance, technical assistance, financial planning, and securing financing for business ventures. While these centers provide minority entrepreneurs with help in locating sources of financing and preparing loan proposals, they do not have any authority to make grants, loans, or loan guarantees to any qualified businessperson who wishes to purchase, start, or expand a small business. These centers are operated by private firms, government agencies (both state and local), educational institutions, and Native American tribes.

The MBDA has also shown an increased emphasis on making certain that minority entrepreneurs are able to compete in the international marketplace. In 1992, for instance, it entered into an agreement with the International Trade Administration (ITA) to assist American minority entrepreneurs in their efforts to negotiate exporting hurdles and compete in foreign markets. Shortly after consummating this agreement, the MBDA launched its International Trade Initiative, which attempts to close the information gap for minority-owned firms that have little direct knowledge or experience of exporting. The Agency's service initiatives provide basic data about export marketing plans, potential markets, and trade leads to assist minority-owned firms in becoming 'export-ready' and to profit from the export assistance services provided by the U.S. Commercial

Service. In addition, the MBDA has organized several "development matchmaker" delegations of minority business owners to foreign destinations. Minority-owned firms participating in the trade delegations represent a wide range of industries, from medical supplies and waste management to retail, clothing manufacturing, engineering, and architecture sectors. In addition to practical information on how best to do business overseas, the program puts participants in development matchmaker programs in direct contact with prospective business partners, prescreened by the Commerce Department's overseas commercial staff. Matchmakers are extremely cost effective and offer an excellent way to develop contacts with others in the minority business community. The synergies created by being part of a matchmaker delegation make the program an ideal vehicle for companies to exchange information about business opportunities in the United States, as well as other overseas markets of interest.

For more information on MBDA programs, minority entrepreneurs can contact the agency at its headquarters at 64 New York Avenue, NE, Washington, DC 20230; 202-671-1552 or via the Internet at their Web site www.mbda.gov.

BIBLIOGRAPHY

Cooper, Steve. "Minority Matters: Pick a resource and get all the help you need to overcome your obstacles." *Entrepreneur.* January 2003.

Hoover, Kent. "Study: Lack of Capital Hurts Minorities, Economy." *The Business Journal.* 29 September 2000.

Langston, Ronald M. "Bullish on Minority Business: MBDA director sees better days ahead." *Black Enterprise.* March 2002.

U.S. Department of Commerce. Minority Business Development Agency. "Welcome to the MBDA FAQ Center." Available from http://www.mbda.gov/index.php?action=faq. 2005.

Hillstrom, Northern Lights
updated by Magee, ECDI

MINORITY-OWNED BUSINESSES

Minority-owned businesses are on the rise. Over the past twenty years the United States has seen steady growth in the number of businesses owned by minorities of all sorts. The African-American, Hispanic, Asian, and Native American communities all saw significant surges in small business start-ups and growth during this period. This success has been attributed both to generally positive economic trends and to advances in the realms of education and access to capital.

Most observers agree, however, that minority entrepreneurs—like women entrepreneurs of all races—still face challenges that their white male counterparts are able to avoid more easily. Racism remains a sad reality in some communities, industries, and corporate environments. In addition, many minority entrepreneurs believe that affirmative action programs and "set-asides," which became a subject of considerable debate in the 1990s, remain important factors in the success of many minority-owned businesses.

COUNTING MINORITY-OWNED BUSINESSES

Despite lingering racism and the uncertainty surrounding affirmative action, minority entrepreneurs have carved out significant business niches for themselves across the nation. The U.S. Census Bureau is charged with collecting data on Americans. The Census Bureau performs surveys of businesses as one of their many data collection efforts and the most recent surveys included data on the minority status of the business owners. To qualify as a minority-owned business, the Census Bureau explained, 51 percent or more of the stock or equity of the business must be owned by a person or persons of the minority group being measured. The following figures on minority-owned businesses in the United States, as of 2002, are from Census Bureau data and reports.

African-American-Owned Businesses. In 2002, there were 1.2 million firms owned by African-Americans in the U.S., employing more than 756,000 people. The 1.2 million black-owned firms generated nearly $89 billion in revenues and accounted for 5.2 percent of all U.S. nonfarm businesses.

When the data on African-American-owned businesses for 2002 are compared with the data from 1997, interesting trends appear. The number of black-owned firms has grown by 45.4 percent over the period, a rate that was substantially higher than the national average for all businesses (10.3 percent). However, the number of black-owned firms with paid employees has grown by only 1.5 percent, a rate of growth under the national average of 4.3 percent. This suggests that a lot of African-Americans have gone into business for themselves and are self-employed but that far fewer have created businesses that are in need of, or can support, employees. Only 7.9 percent of African-American-owned businesses in 2002 had paid employees other than the owner. For this measure, the average for all businesses was 24.1 percent.

The areas in which black business ownership is highest are in the retail trades and in health care and social assistance. Of the revenue generated by black-owned retail businesses, 54 percent was from businesses in the industry classified as "motor vehicle and parts dealers."

Hispanic-Owned Businesses Hispanics owned 1.6 million nonfarm businesses in the United States in 2002. These businesses employed 1.5 million people and generated $222.0 billion in business revenues. These Hispanic-owned firms accounted for 6.8 percent of all nonfarm businesses in 2002. Of all Hispanic-owned businesses, 187.3 percent had no paid employees in 2002.

When the data on Hispanic-owned businesses for 2002 are compared with the data from 1997, a trend similar to that seen with black business ownership is seen. The number of Hispanic-owned businesses has grown at a faster rate than the rate for all business (31.1 percent versus 10.3 percent respectively) but the number of Hispanic-owned businesses with employees actually dropped between 1997 and 2002. In 1997 Hispanic-owned businesses with paid employees represented 4 percent of all firms with paid employees but in 2002 they were only 3.6 percent. So, again we see a case in which the number of self-employed Hispanics is growing but the number of Hispanic-owned businesses with paid employees fell by 5.8 percent between 1997 and 2002.

Hispanic-owned businesses are diversified but many, 29 percent, operated in construction and other services, such as personal services, and repair and maintenance. In fact, Hispanic-owned businesses owned 8.5 percent of all such businesses in the U.S. Retail and wholesale trade accounted for 35.9 percent of Hispanic-owned business revenue. Again, as with the African-American-owned businesses, a large part of the retail trade revenue (80 percent) was concentrated in the automobile industry, and motor vehicle and parts dealers.

Asian-Owned Businesses The 2002 business ownership data show that there were 1.1 million Asian-owned nonfarm businesses in the U.S., employing over 2.2 million persons and generating more than $326 billion in business revenues. Asian-owned firms accounted for 4.8 percent of all U.S. nonfarm businesses.

The number of Asian-owned businesses grew by 23.6 percent between 1997 and 2002. The number of Asian-owned businesses with paid employees also grew, 11.3 percent, a rate more than twice that of the national average for all businesses with paid employees (4.3 percent). Asian-owned businesses with paid employees account for almost a third (29 percent), a higher level than for either black-owned or Hispanic-owned businesses, and higher than the average for all businesses in the U.S. in 2002 (24.1).

The single industrial area in which the greatest number of Asian-owned businesses operate is wholesale trade. Retail trade and the services also rank high in terms of areas of concentration for Asian-owned firms.

Women-Owned Businesses In 2002, there were 6.5 million firms owned by women in the U.S., employing 7.1 million people and generating $940.8 billion in business revenues. These women-owned firms accounted for nearly one-third (28.2 percent) of all nonfarm businesses. Of all women-owned business in 2002, 85.8 percent had no paid employees other than the owner.

When the data on women-owned businesses for 2002 are compared with the data from 1997, increases are seen across all categories. The number of women-owned firms has grown by 19.8 percent over the period, compared to the national average for all businesses (10.3 percent). Similarly, the number of women-owned firms with paid employees grew by only 8.3 percent between 1997 and 2002, a rate of growth nearly twice as great as the national average of 4.3 percent. Women-owned businesses are, thus, growing at a faster rate than all businesses.

Thirty-two percent of women-owned firms operated in health care and social assistance, and other services (such as personal services, and repair and maintenance), where they owned 43.7 percent of all such businesses in the U.S. Wholesale and retail trade accounted for 38.3 percent of women-owned business revenue.

Other Minority-Owned Businesses The Census Bureau has not done detailed studies of the sort done for businesses owned by African-Americans, Hispanics, Asians, and Women so reliable data of the same sort are not currently available for other minority groups. The trends seen in all four of the studied categories show growth in the number of businesses in each group and this suggests that growth in minority-owned businesses of all sorts is occurring in the United States. In 1982 the Census Bureau reported a total of 750,000 minority-owned businesses and over the next 20 years that figure rose by more than 500 percent.

FACTORS IN MINORITY BUSINESS GROWTH

Analysts cite several reasons for the explosive growth in minority-owned businesses in the United States over the past two decades. Certainly, a shifting population demographic has been a major contributor to this shift in business ownership dynamics. Also contributing to the growth of minority-owned businesses has been affirmative action programs and general economic growth trends. But observers also cite several other factors, including community support, increased networking, efforts to revitalize inner cities, increased levels of education and business experience, and improved access to capital.

- Community Support—Many entrepreneurial ethnic minorities benefit by instituting businesses within their communities that meet needs of that community. When these businesses succeed, the individual communities gain a greater measure of autonomy and financial health, thus laying the groundwork for additional businesses. Community banks have been among the most visible supporters of minority entrepreneurs seeking to revitalize moribund neighborhoods and business districts. Finally, many immigrant groups have done a laudable job of supporting entrepreneurs within their communities.

- Increased Networking—As the number of minority entrepreneurs has grown, so too has the number of organizations, associations, and other groups that have formed to provide assistance and information to minority-owned businesses. In addition, minority entrepreneurs have become adept at taking advantage of established business practices such as networking to assist them in opening their own firms. Networking—interactions among business people for the purpose of discussing mutual problems, solutions, and opportunities—is extremely important to minority business owners.

- Programs—In addition to federal set-aside programs, a variety of local, state, and federal agencies have extended help—whether in the form of legal expertise, grants, loans, or some other type of assistance—to encourage the establishment of minority-owned businesses.

- Corporate Acceptance—Observers point to increased corporate acceptance of minority-owned businesses as a key factor in the successes that minority-owned enterprises have registered over the past two decades. Corporations and large firms are buying from minority businesses in greater and greater numbers.

- Urban Revitalization—Many minority entrepreneurs have established themselves as business owners in urban areas at a time when several large cities have experienced heartening signs of rebirth. Moreover, state and federal agencies have shown increased willingness to provide greater assistance to business owners and others who are intent on reversing declines in urban areas, which typically contain large minority populations.

- Higher Levels of Education and Business Experience—Modern-day minority-owned businesses are significantly stronger than they used to be in several important respects, most of which have to do with being better, more experienced, and better financed entrepreneurs.

- Access to Financing—Minority-owned businesses have benefited from several economic trends. Perhaps most importantly, black, Hispanic, Arab, Asian and other minority businesspeople have benefited from the financial community's belated recognition that small businesses are powering much of the nation's current economic growth, and that small companies will likely become an even more important component of the U.S. economy in the coming years. Moreover, the emergence of alternative financing sources friendly to minority entrepreneurs has made it easier for minority-owned businesses to secure funds for start-up costs or expansions. Finally, agencies such as the Small Business Administration (SBA) have increased the volume of loans to minorities (in fiscal year 1994, for example, the SBA increased the amount it loaned to minority business owners by nearly 60 percent over the previous year).

- Expansion Into Emerging Industries—Traditionally, minority business owners have been primarily involved in small-scale retailing and service industries such as restaurants, beauty parlors, dry cleaners, laundromats, grocery stores, etc. But increasing numbers of minority entrepreneurs have successfully ventured out into realms where minority owners had previously been less commonplace, such as manufacturing and high-technology industries.

AFFIRMATIVE ACTION AND "SET-ASIDE" PROGRAMS

Affirmative Action and "set-aside" programs—which were first instituted more than 20 years ago to help minority-owned businesses survive in an economic world that was all too often colored by racial prejudice—have become subjects of fierce, sometimes impassioned debate across much of the United States over the past several years.

Set-asides were first created in 1953, when the U.S. government passed a law that set aside five percent of all procurement contracts for small businesses owned by socially and economically disadvantaged people. The SBA has defined and redefined the term "socially and economically disadvantaged" many times since then by adding different groups and deleting others. The core group under the original law included Black Americans,

Hispanic Americans, Native Americans, Asian Pacific Americans, and other minorities.

By the early 1970s, the U.S. government passed a series of regulations and laws designed to ensure that private contractors with lucrative government contracts set aside a small percentage of their work for assignment to subcontractors owned by individuals from "socially and economically disadvantaged" backgrounds. Regulations in some government agencies were written specifically in an attempt to assist minorities requiring a specific percentage of participation by these minorities. The theory behind these laws was that when public money was being spent, all citizens should have an equal right to compete for contracts, and that minority- and women-owned companies needed special assistance to compensate disadvantage and secure reasonable opportunities to bid successfully. In ensuing years, it became clear that such programs were a tremendous boon to many minority-owned businesses.

By the 1980s and 1990s, though, critics of affirmative action and set-aside policies argued that minority-owned businesses were coming of age and could compete in the mainstream economy. In fact, they said, "set-asides" impede minority-owned businesses' chances of success, because companies came to depend on them to the detriment of seeking contracts through competition. Finally, some critics contended that such policies discriminated against white business owners. Although once these policies were seen as a way to redress past discrimination, many now characterize affirmative action programs as reverse discrimination.

Many researchers and minority entrepreneurs reject these arguments, however. They point out that revenues of minority-owned businesses still fall short of those found in comparable white-owned firms. Finally, many supporters of affirmative action programs contend that "public policy drives private behavior," and that any government decision to tear down programs designed to help minority-owned businesses would serve as a sort of tacit approval for companies to return to discriminatory behaviors in which they engaged in the past.

SOURCES OF ASSISTANCE

Minority entrepreneurs have several sources of assistance that they can pursue in building and expanding their businesses. The U.S. Small Business Administration is a source of many programs designed especially for minority entrepreneurs, programs designed to aid small businesses with everything from finding startup funding to bidding on government contracts and learning how to write a business plan. The SCORE program—which stands for service corps of retired executives—is another program overseen by the SBA and designed especially for small

businesses, among them, minority-owned small businesses.

Several organizations have also been developed to help minorities in the world of business. They include:

National Black Chamber of Commerce (1350 Connecticut Ave. NW, Suite 405, Washington, DC 20036, phone 202-466-6888),

U.S. Pan Asian American Chamber of Commerce (1329 18th St. NW, Washington, DC 20036, phone 202-296-5221)

U.S. Hispanic Chamber of Commerce (2175 K Street, Suite 100, Washington, DC 20037, phone 202-842-1212),

National Indian Business Association (1730 Rhode Island Ave., NW, Suite 1008, Washington, DC 20036, phone 202-223-3766),

National Association of Minority Contractors (666 11 Street NW, Suite 520, Washington, DC 20001, phone 202-347-8259),

National Minority Supplier Development Council (1040 Avenue of the Americas, Second Floor, New York, NY 10018, phone 212-944-2430)

National Association of Women Business Owners (8405 Greensboro Drive, Suite 800, McLean VA, 22102, phone 800-556-2926).

BIBLIOGRAPHY

Griffin, Cynthia E. "Where's the Dollar? Funding for Minority Owned Business Enterprises." *Entrepreneur.* February 1999.

National Directory of Minority-Owned Business Firms. Twelfth Edition. Gale Group, 2002.

Romell, Rick. "Minority-Owned Businesses Growing Fast in Wisconsin." *The Milwaukee Journal Sentinel.* 29 August 2005.

U.S. Census Bureau. "2002 Survey of Business Owners." Available from http://www.census.gov/csd/sbo/. 16 May 2006.

U.S. Small Business Administration. "Minority Enterprise Development – Hotlist." Available from http://www.sba.gov/hotlist/minor.html. Retrieved on 8 June 2006.

Hillstrom, Northern Lights
updated by Magee, ECDI

MISSION STATEMENT

Mission statements are documents intended to serve as a summary of a business's goals and values. Their contents often reflect the fact that they are used both to enhance performance and to serve a public relations purpose. Secondary purposes aside, mission statements are usually intended as a means by which a business's ownership or management attempt to attach meaning to an organization's operations beyond profit and loss statements.

The value of the mission statement is also sometimes thought to increase with the size of an organization. *Fortune* contributor Andrew Serwer, for instance, contended that entrepreneurial companies of relatively small size can sometimes thrive without a mission statement or an explicit guiding principle: the business owner/leader can communicate personally with each staff member. Expansion, however, can make it more difficult for entrepreneurs to communicate efficiently with individual staff members about their future plans, their vision of the company's goals, and the values that will guide the company's operation. "A mission statement not only provides that information, but it's also the foundation for any performance-enhancement initiative," wrote Karen Adler and Paul Swiercz in *Training & Development.*

When produced in a thoughtful and careful manner, mission statements can be good vehicles for communicating the importance of an organization's activities and the reasons why employees should value their work there. Unfortunately, *InfoWorld's* Bob Lewis echoed a widespread sentiment with his contention that many of today's mission statements are produced in a formulaic, jargon-heavy manner that renders them bereft of vitality and meaning. Lewis and others argue that all too often, businesses of all shapes and sizes attach far greater weight to the mission statement's public relations function than to its value as a potential touchstone that can help the business maintain a steady course through the many obstacles and challenges of the modern business world.

Characteristics of Effective Mission Statements Small business owners, consultants, and researchers all agree that effective mission statements generally feature most of the following characteristics:

1. Simple, declarative statements—Mission statements that are cluttered with trendy buzz words and jargon rather than basic declarations of organizational goals and values tend to fall flat. Conversely, a mission that can be easily articulated is more likely to be remembered and to have resonance.

2. Honest and realistic—Observers agree that it is pointless--or worse, that it can actually turn into a negative—for a business enterprise to create and publicize a mission statement if it is at odds with its known operating philosophy. A company may espouse an abiding concern for the environment in its statement of mission, but if its everyday operations reflect a callous disregard for or outright hostility to established environmental protections, the statement may merely engender or deepen employee

cynicism about management and generate negative public response. In short, hypocrisy often attracts greater attention than silence.

3. Communicates Expectations and Ethics—As Sharon Nelton noted in *Nation's Business,* a thoughtfully rendered mission statement can define not only what a company's business goals are but also the methodologies it chooses to get there. A good mission statement often includes general principles to which a business's workers are expected to adhere, and in return, includes declarations of the business's obligations to its employees, its customers, and the community in which it operates.

4. Periodically Updated—Just like other business documents, mission statements can lose their vitality and relevance over time if they are not reexamined on a regular basis. Mission statements should undergo continual review and refinement to ensure that they remain fresh and useful.

BIBLIOGRAPHY

Adler, Karen, and Paul Swiercz. "Taming the Performance Bell Curve." *Training & Development.* October 1997.

Carlino, Bill. "'Mission' accomplished?" *Accounting Today.* 27 February 2006.

Jenkins, Maureen. "What's Our Business? Why every employee needs to know the company's mission statement." *Black Enterprise.* October 2005.

Lewis, Bob. "Mission Statements: Don't Write a Word Until Your Ideas are Clear to All." *InfoWorld.* 29 January 1996.

Nelton, Sharon. "Put Your Purpose in Writing." *Nation's Business.* February 1994.

O'Hallaron, Richard, and David O'Hallaron. *The Mission Primer: Four Steps to an Effective Mission Statement.* Mission Inc., 2000.

Serwer, Andrew. "Lessons from America's Fastest Growing Companies." *Fortune.* 8 August 1994.

Stewart, Bruce A. "A New IT Vision and Mission." Computerworld. 9 January 2006.

Wordsworth, Dot. "Mind Your Language." *Spectator.* 22 October 2005.

Hillstrom, Northern Lights
updated by Magee, ECDI

MOBILE OFFICE

Advances in communication technology, entrepreneurial creativity, and the ever-more-hectic pace of modern life have all combined to encourage the development and refinement of mobile business offices. Indeed, entrepreneurs have been a driving force in the creation of computers, telephones, and other office equipment that are both effective and portable. Broadband networks and wireless communication devices have made it possible for office work of most types to be done from almost anywhere given the appropriate equipment. These advances have provided many benefits, many challenges, and they continue to alter the ways in which we communicate and work in the information age.

MOBILE BUSINESSES

Some businesses lend themselves more easily to mobility than do others. A manufacturing facility, for example, may benefit from the same technologies that make a mobile office possible—wireless communication devices like smartphones, laptops, and personal digital assistants (PDAs) as well as scanners and digital imaging devices—but they can hardly be considered mobile. The sales and marketing arms of manufacturing operations, however, are very likely to become more and more mobile as are service industry businesses generally.

Mobility of both people and data is implied in the term mobile office. Data mobility and the ease with which data may be accessed are both important aspects of making the mobile office a reality. Many businesspeople rely on portable office equipment primarily during transitional periods, such as at the airport or in a hotel room during a business trips. But observers have noted that mobile office technology has also become an essential performance tool for sales representatives, business planners, and busy entrepreneurs. Moreover, some enterprising small business owners have learned to synthesize communication technology with today's system of roadways to create truly mobile businesses that do not rely on a central office. In fact, equipment one may not expect to come ready for mobile office use is now being offered with equipment preinstalled. In late 2005, the Ford Motor Company announced that its 2006 line of full-size trucks would be offered with an optional mobile office preinstalled.

ADVANTAGES OF MOBILITY

Entrepreneurs with mobile businesses point to several major advantages associated with such arrangements. Mobile businesses do not have the expense of maintaining a store, which—with rent, furniture, utilities, and other costs—can be a very expensive part of operations. In addition, owners of mobile businesses report that they register savings because of reduced rates of theft and insurance. Finally, these business owners contend that by going to the customer's home or business, they 1) immediately establish their interest in satisfying the client, and 2) create a dynamic wherein both the businessperson and the customer can concentrate on one another rather than peripheral distractions such as other customers. Business consultants warn, however, that mobile

businesses need to adhere to a very high standard of professionalism to calm possible customer fears about legitimacy and quality.

DISADVANTAGES OF MOBILE EQUIPMENT

As the variety of mobile computing and communications devices increases, so do the risks of data theft and malicious viruses. Cell phones and PDAs are relatively small devices that are easily lost or stolen. And data are at risk of interception once they leave the relative safety of the corporate network. Unlike the wired infrastructures present in most companies, which tend to include safeguards against data theft, explains Scott Totzke, director of government technology at Research In Motion, in an article that appeared in *Computer Reseller News,* mobile devices are often managed with less rigid management policies leaving them more susceptible to data theft, and more vulnerable to hackers and viruses. Advances are being made but for the time being, most mobile communications devices provide far less data security than do older, wired systems. According to Paul Bray, author of the *Computer Reseller News* article, "Mobile security is likely to be the next big thing in IT security, as users continue to rely heavily on their devices and wake up to the real threat that faces all of us who fail to secure our laptops, PDAs, and phones."

SEE ALSO *Hoteling*

BIBLIOGRAPHY

Baker, Dean. "Desks on Wheels." *Oregon Business.* September 1997.

Berg, Katherine C. "Office Updates Bring Efficiency to the Workplace." *Dallas Business Journal.* 26 January 2001.

Bray, Paul. "Analysis – Keeping Things Safe Outside the Office. Mobile computing devices are big business offering a host of networking options to users who work outside the office." *Computer Reseller News.* 23 January 2006.

Brouillard, Sarah. "Hoteling Adapts to Mobile Workers." *Minneapolis—St. Paul City Business.* 16 February 2001.

"Ford's Mobile Office System." *Electrical Contracting Products.* December 2005.

Gilligan, Eugene. "Flex Time: Corporations bring back hoteling to improve efficiency." *Commercial Property News.* 1 February 2006.

McCollum, Tim, and Albert G. Holzinger. "Making a Move to Portability." *Nation's Business.* September 1997.

O'Brien, Kathleen. "Taking Advantage of the Mobile Office: Homeward Bound." *New York Times.* 5 April, 2000.

Hillstrom, Northern Lights
updated by Magee, ECDI

MODEM

Modem, an acronym for modulator/demodulator, is a device that allows one computer to "talk" with another over a standard telephone line. Modems act as a kind of interpreter between a computer and the telephone line. Computers transmit digital data, expressed as electrical impulses, whereas telephones transmit voice frequencies as analog signals. To transmit digital data, the sending modem must first *modulate,* or encode, a computer's digital signal into an analog signal that can travel over the phone line. The receiving modem must then *demodulate,* or decode, the analog signal back into a digital signal recognizable to a computer. A modem transmits data in bits per second (bps), with the fastest modems transmitting at 56K (kilobits per second). An *internal* modem is housed within the computer itself, while an *external* modem is a separate device connected to the computer by cable.

A variety of protocols (standards, rules) govern the conversion of data to and from digital and analog. These also govern error correction and data compression. Error correction is necessary to detect and correct data that may have become lost or garbled as the result of a poor telephone connection. Data compression speeds the data transfer by eliminating any redundant data sent between two modems, which the receiving modem then restores to its original form. Individual modems vary in the types of protocols they support, depending on such factors as manufacturer and age.

Communications software enables a modem to perform the many tasks necessary to complete a session of sending and receiving data. To initiate a modem session, the user issues the command appropriate to the software being used; the software then takes over and begins the complicated process of opening the session, transferring the data, and closing the session.

To open the session, the software dials the receiving modem and waits for an answering signal. Once the two modem have established a connection, they engage in a process called "handshaking": they exchange information about the types of protocols each uses, ultimately agreeing to use a set common to both. For example, if one modem supports a more recent set of protocols then does the other, the first will agree to use the earlier set so that each is sending data at the same rate, with error correction and data compression appropriate to those protocols. The handshaking process itself is governed by its own protocol.

In addition to transmitting and receiving data, the communications software may also automate other tasks for the user, such as dialing, answering, redialing, and logging onto an online service.

ALTERNATIVES TO THE TRADITIONAL MODEM

The functionality provided by a traditional dial-up modem—the ability to send and receive information electronically—is also offered in other technologies that offer faster transmission speeds, although each is not without its disadvantages. Integrated Services Digital Network (ISDN), Asymmetric Digital Subscriber Lines (ADSL), and Digital Subscriber Lines (DSL) all use more capacity of the existing phone to provide services.

At 128K, ISDN is more than twice as fast as a dialup modem, but not nearly as fast as ADSL or DSL. ADSL can deliver data at 8 mbps, but is available only in selected urban areas. DSL transmits at a high rate of speed, but to ensure reliable service, the user must be located near the phone company's central office or outlying transmitters. In addition, a DSL connection is always "on" and thus makes a computer more vulnerable to attacks from hackers. To secure a DSL connection, a user must install either a software package called a firewall or a piece of hardware called a router. With either of these in place, the DSL connection cannot be detected by outsiders.

Cable modems do not use phone lines. Instead, they utilize the same line that provides cable TV services to consumers. Offered by cable television companies, cable modems are about 50 times faster than a dialup modem, but transmission speed is dependent on the number of subscribers using the service at the same time. Because the service uses a shared connection, its speed decreases as the number of users increases. Satellite, or wireless, services are faster than a 56K modem, but slower than a DSL. In addition, the initial satellite installation is expensive. However, for users in rural areas who do not have access to other services, wireless service may be a viable option.

MODEMS AND THE WORKPLACE

As Bonnie Lund states in *Business Communication That Really Works!,* "the speed with which we can exchange documents has revolutionized business communications," which in turn has enabled business to be done "faster, cheaper, and more efficiently." Modems, along with the related technologies, facilitate this rapid transfer of information between colleagues or customers, regardless of their location. Communications that, in the past, may have taken several days or even weeks to complete, can now be accomplished in a fraction of the time. For example, during a typical work day, an employee could use a modem to facilitate sending an email message to a customer, transmitting a spreadsheet containing the annual budget to a manager for review, or downloading a file from the Internet. On a busy day this will take place dozens of times.

Lund also notes that "modems are changing the work style of corporate America" by enabling workers to *telecommute* or *telework*. As Amy Joyce reported in the *Washington Post*, citing data from the Telework Association and Council (ITAC), "the number of employed Americans who performed any kind of work from home, from as little as one day a year to full time, grew from 41.3 million in 2003 to 44.4 million in 2004, a 7.5 percent growth rate." A related development is the "distributed office," used in many small businesses involved in consulting, software development, publishing, and similar industries were members of the company work from home communicating by e-mail and using a common network server available to each by one of the faster modes of telecommunications.

BIBLIOGRAPHY

"Gateway Enables Remote Site Management." *Product News Network.* 18 April 2006.

Joyce, Amy. "Getting the Job Done at Home: Telecommuting Can Save Money and Boost Productivity." *Washington Post.* 26 June 2005.

Lund, Bonnie. *Business Communication That Really Works!* Affinity Publishing, Inc. 1995.

Poor, Alfred. "Phone as Modem?." *Computer Shopper.* April 2006.

Rae-Dupree, Janet. "Surfing the Web at Warp Speed with Minimal Expense." *U.S. News & World Report.* 19 June 2000.

Hillstrom, Northern Lights
updated by Magee, ECDI

MONEY MARKET INSTRUMENTS

The money market is the arena in which financial institutions make available to a broad range of borrowers and investors the opportunity to buy and sell various forms of short-term securities. There is no physical "money market." Instead it is an informal network of banks and traders linked by telephones, fax machines, and computers. Money markets exist both in the United States and abroad.

The short-term debts and securities sold on the money markets—which are known as money market instruments—have maturities ranging from one day to one year and are extremely liquid. Treasury bills, federal agency notes, certificates of deposit (CDs), eurodollar deposits, commercial paper, bankers' acceptances, and repurchase agreements are examples of instruments. The suppliers of funds for money market instruments are institutions and individuals with a preference for the highest liquidity and the lowest risk.

The money market is important for businesses because it allows companies with a temporary cash surplus to invest in short-term securities; conversely, companies with a temporary cash shortfall can sell securities or borrow funds on a short-term basis. In essence the market acts as a repository for short-term funds. Large corporations generally handle their own short-term financial transactions; they participate in the market through dealers. Small businesses, on the other hand, often choose to invest in money-market funds, which are professionally managed mutual funds consisting only of short-term securities.

Although securities purchased on the money market carry less risk than long-term debt, they are still not entirely risk free. After all, banks do sometimes fail, and the fortunes of companies can change rather rapidly. The low risk is associated with lender selectivity. The lender who offers funds with almost instant maturities ("tomorrow") cannot spend too much time qualifying borrowers and thus selects only blue-chip borrowers. Repayment therefore is assured (unless you caught Enron just before it suddenly nose-dived). Borrowers with fewer credentials, of course, have difficult getting money from this market unless it is through well-established funds.

TYPES OF MONEY MARKET INSTRUMENTS

Treasury Bills Treasury bills (T-bills) are short-term notes issued by the U.S. government. They come in three different lengths to maturity: 90, 180, and 360 days. The two shorter types are auctioned on a weekly basis, while the annual types are auctioned monthly. T-bills can be purchased directly through the auctions or indirectly through the secondary market. Purchasers of T-bills at auction can enter a competitive bid (although this method entails a risk that the bills may not be made available at the bid price) or a noncompetitive bid. T-bills for noncompetitive bids are supplied at the average price of all successful competitive bids.

Federal Agency Notes Some agencies of the federal government issue both short-term and long-term obligations, including the loan agencies Fannie Mae and Sallie Mae. These obligations are not generally backed by the government, so they offer a slightly higher yield than T-bills, but the risk of default is still very small. Agency securities are actively traded, but are not quite as marketable as T-bills. Corporations are major purchasers of this type of money market instrument.

Short-Term Tax Exempts These instruments are short-term notes issued by state and municipal governments. Although they carry somewhat more risk than T-bills and tend to be less negotiable, they feature the added benefit that the interest is not subject to federal income tax. For this reason, corporations find that the lower yield is worthwhile on this type of short-term investment.

Certificates of Deposit Certificates of deposit (CDs) are certificates issued by a federally chartered bank against deposited funds that earn a specified return for a definite period of time. They are one of several types of interest-bearing "time deposits" offered by banks. An individual or company lends the bank a certain amount of money for a fixed period of time, and in exchange the bank agrees to repay the money with specified interest at the end of the time period. The certificate constitutes the bank's agreement to repay the loan. The maturity rates on CDs range from 30 days to six months or longer, and the amount of the face value can vary greatly as well. There is usually a penalty for early withdrawal of funds, but some types of CDs can be sold to another investor if the original purchaser needs access to the money before the maturity date.

Large denomination (jumbo) CDs of $100,000 or more are generally negotiable and pay higher interest rates than smaller denominations. However, such certificates are only insured by the FDIC up to $100,000. There are also eurodollar CDs; they are negotiable certificates issued against U.S. dollar obligations in a foreign branch of a domestic bank. Brokerage firms have a nationwide pool of bank CDs and receive a fee for selling them. Since brokers deal in large sums, brokered CDs generally pay higher interest rates and offer greater liquidity than CDs purchased directly from a bank.

Commercial Paper Commercial paper refers to unsecured short-term promissory notes issued by financial and nonfinancial corporations. Commercial paper has maturities of up to 270 days (the maximum allowed without SEC registration requirement). Dollar volume for commercial paper exceeds the amount of any money market instrument other than T-bills. It is typically issued by large, credit-worthy corporations with unused lines of bank credit and therefore carries low default risk.

Standard and Poor's and Moody's provide ratings of commercial paper. The highest ratings are A1 and P1, respectively. A2 and P2 paper is considered high quality, but usually indicates that the issuing corporation is smaller or more debt burdened than A1 and P1 companies. Issuers earning the lowest ratings find few willing investors.

Unlike some other types of money-market instruments, in which banks act as intermediaries between buyers and sellers, commercial paper is issued directly by well-established companies, as well as by financial institutions. Banks may act as agents in the transaction, but they assume no principal position and are in no way obligated with respect to repayment of the commercial paper. Companies may also sell commercial paper through dealers who charge a fee and arrange for the transfer of the funds from the lender to the borrower.

Bankers' Acceptances A banker's acceptance is an instruments produced by a nonfinancial corporation but in the name of a bank. It is document indicating that such-and-such bank shall pay the face amount of the instrument at some future time. The bank accepts this instrument, in effect acting as a guarantor. To be sure the bank does so because it considers the writer to be credit-worthy. Bankers' acceptances are generally used to finance foreign trade, although they also arise when companies purchase goods on credit or need to finance inventory. The maturity of acceptances ranges from one to six months.

Repurchase Agreements Repurchase agreements—also known as repos or buybacks—are Treasury securities that are purchased from a dealer with the agreement that they will be sold back at a future date for a higher price. These agreements are the most liquid of all money market investments, ranging from 24 hours to several months. In fact, they are very similar to bank deposit accounts, and many corporations arrange for their banks to transfer excess cash to such funds automatically.

BIBLIOGRAPHY

Fabozzi, Frank J., Steven V. Mann, and Moorad Choudhry. *The Global Money Markets.* John Wiley and Sons, 2002.

Levinson, Marc. *Guide to Financial Markets.* Bloomberg Press, 2003.

Madura, Jeff. *Financial Markets and Instruments.* Thomson South-Western, 2006.

Hillstrom, Northern Lights
updated by Magee, ECDI

MULTICULTURAL WORK FORCE

A multicultural work force is one made up of men and women from a variety of different cultural and racial backgrounds. The labor force of any country is a reflection of the population from which it is drawn, despite some distortions that may be caused by discrimination or cultural bias in hiring. In the United States, the population has continued to grow more racially and ethnically diverse in the last decades and this diversity is now reflected in the work place. Managing this diversity in such a way that the benefits are maximized and the challenges minimized is an important aspect of managing any business today.

GROWTH IN DIVERSITY

Data from the U.S. Census Bureau on the racial and ethnic breakdown of the population in 2000 (the most recent decennial census data) show that those self identified as White represented 75.1 percent of the population, down from 85.9 percent in 1980. Those listing themselves as Black in 2000, represented 12.3 percent of the population, up slightly from 11.8 in 1980. Hispanics, who may be White or Black, accounted for 12.5 percent of the population in 2000, up substantially from 6.6 percent in 1980. Asian Americans in 2000 were 3.6 percent of the population, up from 1.7 percent in 1980. In some regions of the country, these race and ethnicity concentrations are even more striking. In California, for example, the Hispanic population in 2000 represented 32.4 percent of the population while in Georgia, 28.7 percent of the population was African American. These statistical data alone do not tell the whole story, although the colorful picture they paint is clear.

A great deal of diversity within the racial and ethnic divisions measured by the Census Bureau also exists— Italian Americans, for example, are likely to have very different cultural habits than do immigrants from Russia or from any one of the countries in the Middle East. Hispanics from Argentina are also likely to differ quite a lot in cultural habits from Hispanics whose origin is Puerto Rico. But these additional levels of diversity only add complexity to the picture. The overall trend is clearly towards greater racial, ethnic, religious, and cultural diversity in both the general population **and** the work force.

CHANGING THE WORK PLACE

These work force demographic trends are significant and when combined with an ever more globally focused business community they create a new emphasis on managing diversity. In this environment business leaders must think more and more about how best to manage a multicultural work force, sell to an increasingly diverse customer base, and deal with suppliers who represent a variety of world views. These tasks are not always easy since diversity is a two edged sword. On the one hand, with diversity come things like an increased numbers of world perspectives and new ways of looking at and attempting to solve problems. If fact, when properly encouraged, a diversity of views can serve to prevent the negative and myopic results of "group think." On the other hand, cultural differences often lead to difficulties with communications and a rise in the friction that can develop as

people with different expectations and habits interact. It is important, consequently, for an organization to create an environment in which the positives of diversity are harnessed and the negatives are minimized as much as possible.

Implementing change is always a challenge. People generally find change disconcerting and work to avoid it. In addition, not everyone within an organization values diversity and some may even find it threatening. Given such realities, companies need to go beyond simple recognition of cultural diversity to active diversity management. Managing diversity is a comprehensive process for developing an environment that works for all employees. Diversity management is an inclusive process and should not be viewed as an us/them kind of problem to be solved. Rather, it should be viewed and presented as a valuable resource to be fostered and used. Incorporating a positive and welcoming attitude towards diverse opinions and outlooks usually means making changes to existing practices and habits. But these changes can be explained in such a way as to highlight their value to the organization as a whole and to the ability of staff members to expand their roles.

In many ways, cultural diversity in the work place mirrors many of the same issues at play in the realm of international business. In international business interactions, people who have learned differing conceptions of normative behavior are forced to suspend judgment of one another. Cultural norms shift relative to language, technological expectations, social organization, face-saving, authority conception, nonverbal behavior and the perception of time.

EFFECTIVE MANAGEMENT OF A MULTICULTURAL WORK FORCE

A company that wishes to encourage diversity and a multiplicity of view points should start by restating the common goals and objectives of the company. This may seem contradictory but it is not. Establishing a well-defined sphere in which diverse ideas and view points may be freely expressed in the pursuit of a common goal is an essential part of encouraging a free flow of ideas.

Once this groundwork is laid, the following items provides a checklist for implementing policies that will foster and encourage a harmonious, multicultural work force.

- Start at the top—A commitment to the idea of an open and receptive work place must be seen from the owners and managers of a company early on, preferably before official policies are announced.

- Communicate in writing—Company policies that explicitly forbid prejudice and discriminatory behavior should be included in employee manuals, mission statements, and other written communications. This has been referred to by some as a way of broadcasting the diversity message internally in order to create a common language for all members of the organization.

- Training programs—Training programs designed to engender appreciation and knowledge of the characteristics and benefits of multicultural work forces have become ubiquitous in recent years. Two types of training are most popular: awareness and skill-building. The former introduces the topic of managing diversity and generally includes information on work force demographics, the meaning of diversity, and exercises to get participants thinking about relevant issues and raising their own self-awareness. The skill-building training provides more specific information on cultural norms of different groups and how they may affect communications and behavior. New employee orientation programs are also ideal for introducing workers to the company's expectations regarding treatment of fellow workers, whatever their cultural or ethnic background.

- Recognize individual differences—Do not make the mistake of assuming that differences are always 'cultural.' There are several sources of difference. Some relate personality, aptitude, or competence. Too many managers tend to fall back on the easy 'explanation' that individual behavior or performance can be attributed to the fact that someone is 'Hispanic' or 'Jewish' or 'a woman.' This sort of conclusion is more likely to reflect bias and intellectual laziness than it does culturally sensitive managers.

- Actively seek input from minority groups—Soliciting the opinions and involvement of minority groups on important work committees, etc., is beneficial not only because of the contributions that they can make, but also because such overtures confirm that they are valued by the company. Serving on relevant committees and task forces can increase their feelings of belonging to the organization. Conversely, relegating minority members to superfluous committees or projects can trigger a downward spiral in relations between different cultural groups.

- Revamp reward systems—An organization's performance appraisal and reward systems should reinforce the importance of effective diversity management. This includes assuring that minorities are provided with adequate opportunities for career development.

- Make room for social events—Company-sponsored social events—picnics, softball games, volleyball leagues, bowling leagues, Christmas parties, etc.—can be tremendously useful in getting members of different ethnic and cultural backgrounds together and providing them with opportunities to learn about one another.

- Flexible work environment—Flexible work environments may have particularly beneficial results with people from nontraditional cultural backgrounds because their approaches to problems are more likely to be different from past norms.

- Don't assume similar values and opinions—In the absence of reliable information there is a well-documented tendency for individuals to assume that other people are 'like them.' This is almost always an inappropriate assumption; for those who manage diverse work forces this tendency towards cultural assumptions can prove particularly damaging.

- Continuous monitoring—Experts recommend that business owners and managers establish and maintain systems that can continually monitor the organization's policies and practices to ensure that it continues to be a good environment for all employees. Be flexible and apply the lessons learned as new situations arise and are managed.

Increased diversity may present a challenge to business leaders who must work to maximize the opportunities that diversity provides while minimizing its costs. The organization that achieves this objective will create an environment in which all employees are able to contribute to their fullest potential, and in which the 'value in diversity' can be fully realized.

BIBLIOGRAPHY

Berta, Dina. "MFHA Confab: Straight Talk on Workplace Diversity." *Nation's Restaurant News.* 17 October 2005.

Connerley, Mary L., and Paul Pedersen. *Leadership In A Diverse and Multicultural Environment.* Sage Publications, Inc., March 2005.

Gemus, Jim. "Pleasing a Diverse Workforce." *National Underwriter Life & Health.* 9 August 2004.

Golden, Timothy, and John F. Veiga. "Spanning Boundaries and Borders: Toward understanding the cultural dimensions of team boundary spanning." *Journal of Managerial Issues.* Summer 2005.

Jonson, Karsten, and Martha Maznevski. "The Value of Different Perspectives A Diverse Workforce Leads to Innovative Solutions When Dealing with Uncertainty." *The Financial Times.* 24 March 2006.

Overell, Stephen. "An Issue That is Not Black and White: Corporate Diversity: Is there really a business case for having a diverse workforce?" *The Financial Times.* 21 February 2005.

Parhizgar, Kamal Dean. *Multicultural Behavior and Global Business Environments.* Haworth Press, 2001.

Simons, George. *Working Together: Succeeding in a Multicultural Organization.* Thomson Crisp Learning, 2002.

Stockdale, Margaret S., and Faye J. Crosby. *The Psychology and Management of Workplace Diversity.* Blackwell Publishing, 2003.

U.S. Bureau of the Census. Grieco, Elizabeth M, and Rachel C. Cassidy. *Overview of Race and Hispanic Origin, Census 2000 Brief.* March 2001.

U.S. Bureau of the Census. Perry, Marc J., and Paul J. Mackun. *Population Change and Distribution, Census 2000 Brief.* April 2001.

Hillstrom, Northern Lights
updated by Magee, ECDI

MULTILEVEL MARKETING

In his book, *According to Kotler,* Paul Kotler defined this subject as follows: "Multilevel marketing (also called network marketing), describes systems in which companies contract with individuals to sell a set of products door to door or office to office. It is called multilevel because a contractor can also invite others to work and earn money on their performance." The sales representative thus has incentives to enlarge the sales force and to earn added commissions on the sales of his or her recruits.

Multilevel marketing (MLM) is, strictly speaking, not marketing at all but a form of direct sales with special features, of which recruiting is fundamental. A person, recruited by the company to sell a product, earns commissions; if that person recruits others, this second layer is called the person's "downline." The person earns a cut on the sales of people in the downline, called an "override." But those in the second level may *also* recruit others and create their *own* "downlines." The first person in the chain gets an "override" from every level, however many there may be, although always less the farther removed the source is. Often recruits are required to purchase an initial "starting inventory" of the product. In many cases the MLM company will not repurchase this inventory or will do so at a very reduced price. These characteristics have caused MLM to be associated with pyramid schemes; and some technically *are* such schemes. Not surprisingly, reputable direct marketing companies and the associations to which they belong are continuously engaged in policing the field and in advocating legislation aimed at setting clear and unambiguous rules. The term "network marketing" is in part used because "multi-level" marketing has at best an ambiguous reputation.

Andrew Sherman has reported (in his book *Franchising & Licensing*) that six states explicitly regulate MLM: Georgia, Maryland, New York, New Mexico, Wyoming, and Louisiana. So does Puerto Rico. Laws regulating MLM typically 1) require that MLM companies explicitly permit their agents to cancel their agreements and to agree to repurchase inventories at not less than 90 percent of the original transfer price; 2) prohibit inducements under which the agent is told that he or she will earn a specific amount of money; 3) prohibit the purchase of a minimum inventory; and 4) prohibit operations under which agents are only paid for recruiting others. Many states without MLM regulation nevertheless have laws prohibiting pyramid schemes under which they attempt to police MLM companies that overstep the line.

In a strictly functional sense, MLM is a way to exploit natural networks of acquaintances, with participants (predominantly women), first selling/recruiting others in their circle; these latter, in turn, do the same, and so (in the hopes of the MLM company) *ad infinitum..* Many individuals participating in these networks do so part time. In due time they've sold all of their friends; success begins to fade. For this reason MLM companies are frequently tempted to make all sales final in the early stages so that inventories don't come trickling back.

In the hands of effective sales companies with appropriately chosen products, MLM has produced some very successful organizations. Among them are Amway, Mary Kay Cosmetics, Pampered Chef, and Longaberger Baskets, to name a few.

MLM businesses appeal to people who want to work part-time and need a flexible schedule, like students and mothers of young children. The Direct Selling Association has concluded from its studies that 90 percent of MLM sales representatives work fewer than 30 hours per week, and 50 percent work fewer than 10 hours per week. In addition, MLM businesses usually do not require a long-term commitment from their sales representatives.

An agent can enter an MLM business on very little capital (around $100)—and yet will feel as if in business for him of for herself. Jeffrey Gitomer, writing in the *Business Journal,* noted that many people value the opportunity to be their own boss and control their own destiny. "The secret to successful network marketing is you—the messenger—and your willingness to dedicate and focus on preparation," he wrote. "Your willingness to become a salesperson who believes in your own ability to succeed. Everyone wants success, but very few are willing to do what it takes to be successful."

Of course, like any other entrepreneurial venture, reaching significant success requires much more than a bit of selling here, a bit there. Only a tiny proportion of people entering this form of direct sales stay in it and make a good living. They do so because they work the job like any other successful sales agent operating between a customer and a producer.

BIBLIOGRAPHY

"Federal Legislation Will Differentiate Legitimate Multilevel Marketing Businesses from Illegal Pyramid Schemes." Press Release. Direct Selling Association. 14 April 2003.

Gitomer, Jeffrey. "Financial Freedom through Network Marketing." *Business Journal.* 14 April 2000.

Kotler, Paul. *According to Kotler: The World's Foremost Authority on Marketing Answers Your Questions.* AMACOM, 2005.

"Multi-Level Marketing." World Federation of Direct Selling Associations. Available from http://www.wfdsa.org/legal_reg/multimarketing.asp. Retrieved on 20 April 2006.

Sherman, Andrew J. *Franchising & Licensing: Two Powerful Ways to Grow Your Business in Any Economy.* AMACOM, 2004.

Hillstrom, Northern Lights
updated by Magee, ECDI

MULTIPLE EMPLOYER TRUST

A Multiple Employer Trust (MET) is a group of ten or more employers who form a trust in order to minimize the tax implications of providing certain types of benefits for their employees, particularly life insurance. The U.S. Congress authorized the formation of METs in 1984 under Section 419(A) of the Internal Revenue Code. The rules set forth for METs are stringent and require that no single employer contribute more than 10 percent of total funding for the benefit plan purchased by the MET. In addition, the MET must be an indivisible entity, with all participating employers sharing equally in the benefits forfeited by other members of the group. The employees of each participating employer are viewed as if they worked for a single company and are subject to the same requirements

A similar arrangement to a MET is a Multiple Employer Welfare Arrangement (MEWA). MEWAs include plans established by two or more employers to provide welfare benefits to their employees, including health care and pensions. The main difference between a MET and a MEWA is that a MEWA is generally subject to the requirements of the Employee Retirement Income Security Act of 1974 (ERISA), which regulates pension plans of businesses with more than 25 employees and imposes penalties on employers for breaches of fiduciary duty.

The main purpose of a MET is to give entrepreneurs and small business owners a tax-friendly way to provide life insurance benefits for themselves and their key employees. Under ordinary circumstances, life insurance is tax deductible for the employer in the current year, but any amounts that could be considered "bonus" life insurance must be reported as taxable income by the employee. Larger businesses are often able to get around this problem by funding life insurance benefits as part of a qualified retirement or profit-sharing plan. Although the benefits provided through such plans are usually tax free, there are a number of restrictions and complicated paperwork requirements associated with them that reduce the attractiveness of life insurance for smaller businesses. For example, the government requires companies that set up qualified plans to establish eligibility and vesting rules and then offer the benefits to all employees who meet them.

THE IMPORTANCE OF LIFE INSURANCE

It may seem odd for small businesses to go to the trouble of forming a MET just for the sake of providing life insurance for employees. But life insurance has a variety of uses that make it a very attractive benefit, particularly for key employees. A small business might need to provide life insurance to its workers in order to compete with larger companies in attracting and retaining qualified employees. For example, in addition to providing benefits upon the death or disability of the insured, some forms of life insurance can be used as a tax-deferred investment to provide funds during a person's lifetime for retirement or everyday living expenses. There are also a number of specialized life insurance plans that allow small business owners to reduce the impact of estate taxes on their heirs and protect their businesses against the loss of a key employee, partner, or stockholder.

Small businesses tend to depend on a few key people, some of whom are likely to be owners or partners, to keep operations running smoothly. Even though it is unpleasant to think about the possibility of a key employee becoming disabled or dying, it is important to prepare so that the business may survive and the tax implications may be minimized. In the case of a partnership, the business is formally dissolved when one partner dies. In the case of a corporation, the death of a major stockholder can throw the business into disarray. In the absence of a specific agreement, the person's estate or heirs may choose to vote the shares or sell them. This uncertainty could undermine the company's management, impair its credit, cause the flight of customers, and damage employee morale.

Life insurance can help small businesses protect themselves against the loss of a key person by providing a source of income to keep business running in his or her absence. Partnership insurance basically involves each partner acting as beneficiary of a life insurance policy taken on the other partner. In this way, the surviving partner is protected against a financial loss when the business ends. Similarly, corporate plans can ensure the continuity of the business under the same management, and possibly fund a repurchase of stock, if a major stockholder dies. Although life insurance is not tax deductible when the business is named as beneficiary, the business may deduct premium costs if a partner or owner is the beneficiary.

MET REQUIREMENTS

Participating in a MET enables a small business to provide life insurance to its key employees without subjecting them to negative tax implications. It does this by allowing tax-deductible contributions to a life insurance plan, made by the employer on behalf of employees, to be used for severance benefits. Basically, the cash value of the life insurance is available for severance benefits, while the mortality portion of the life insurance is payable to the beneficiary named by insured. A MET must be structured properly in order to comply with the tax laws, but the rules are significantly less extensive than with qualified pension and profit-sharing plans.

The rules that a MET must follow in order to gain tax benefits are laid out in IRS Notice 95-34. This notice states that severance benefits can only be paid when the termination of employment is beyond an employee's control. Otherwise, if the severance arrangements appear to be providing deferred compensation benefits to an employee, the employer's tax deduction will be denied. The notice also states that the deduction will not be allowed for "nondeductible prepaid expenses," which may include contributions to the plan that are made as lump sums or using accelerated funding techniques.

BIBLIOGRAPHY

Budihas, John S. "METs can provide tax deductible life insurance." *National Underwriter Life & Health.* 5 August 2002.

Fletcher, Meg. "NAIC scrutinizing MEWA regulation; Plan aims to curb fraud." *Business Insurance.* 14 February 2005.

U.S. Department of Labor. "Multiple Employer Welfare Arrangements under ERISA: A Guide to Federal and State Regulation." Available from http://www.dol.gov/ebsa/Publications/mewas.html. Retrieved on 19 April 2006.

U.S. Small Business Administration. Anastasio, Susan. *Small Business Insurance and Risk Management Guide.* n.d.

Hillstrom, Northern Lights
updated by Magee, ECDI

MULTITASKING

Multitasking refers to the ability of an individual or machine to perform more than one task at the same time. In the field of human resources, multitasking is a popular term that is often used to describe how busy managers or business practitioners are able to accomplish ever more in the same amount of time. The term was popularized in the late 1990s with the increasing move to a 24-hours-per-day, seven-days-per-week work and service culture. As globalization has continued to expand the number of time zones in which a business may operate, the need to be available around the clock has also expanded. Many use the term "24-7-365" as a shorthand for a growing reality for many businesses that feel they must be accessible around the clock and every day of the year. To keep up, people often feel that they must multitask. In fact, the term multitasking is now used regularly to describe what we do not only while at work but also in our roles as parents, friends, family members, and any number of other roles we perform as we try to balance our business lives and our personal lives.

MULTITASKING IN THE WORKPLACE

According to an article in *Manufacturing Engineering,* in the world of project teams and multitasking, professionals often find relationships blurring as to the difference between activities inside and outside the organization. The multitasking abilities of both individuals and teams are important as companies stay connected with customers, suppliers, and partners, and as new products and services are continually developed. Multitasking is becoming the norm as the amount of information a manager or professional feels he or she needs to process increases at a staggering rate.

Technological developments are emphasizing the trend towards multitasking as they make it possible, for example, to receive and reply to e-mail messages while attending an awards banquet or student concert. The demands we place on the machines we use are also growing as a part of this trend. For example, computers can now commonly perform or execute several programs at the same time, which is a form of multitasking or multiprocessing. In the computer arena, multiprocessing sometimes implies that more than one central processing unit (CPU) is involved. When only one CPU is involved, the computer may switch from one program to another quickly enough to give the appearance of simultaneous execution.

In another example of multitasking machines, people are demanding multitasking gasoline pumps. In addition to dispensing gasoline, new gas pumps are also giving travel directions, current weather reports, and stock quotes via an Internet link. Some pumps even let customers order food from neighborhood restaurants. Given the technologically complex and competitively intense environment in today's business world, the trend toward multitasking is expected to continue, for both individuals and machines.

THE DOWNSIDE OF MULTITASKING

Many experienced multitaskers have experienced an unexpected thing when, for example, their e-mail service was disabled for a period of time. They discovered that they were actually **more** productive during that period of time. What causes this increased productivity? The neurologist Richard Restak explains it this way in his book "The New Brain: How the Modern Age is Rewiring Your Mind," The human brain works most efficiently "on a single task and for sustained rather than intermittent or alternating periods of time.... This doesn't mean that we can't perform a certain amount of multitasking but we do so at a decreased efficiency and accuracy." Very similar results have been found in other well publicized studies—one carried out at the University of Michigan and another by scientists at Carnegie Mellon—namely that as the number of tasks undertaken simultaneously increases, the efficiency and accuracy with which each is done declines.

Most people these days are so accustomed to multitasking that they don't even realize they are doing it. However, a conscious effort to cut back on multitasking may actually help us to get more work done and done more efficiently. New ways of more efficiently managing the many business tasks that must be done regularly will be developed. In the meantime, it is worth noting that reducing one's own multitasking habits may help increase one's productivity and reduce one's sense of overload.

BIBLIOGRAPHY

Brown, Arnold. "The All Purpose Employee." *Across the Board.* May 2000.

Henig, Robin Marantz. "Driving? Maybe You Shouldn't Be Reading This." *The New York Times.* 13 July 2004.

Koucky, Sherri, and Stephan Mraz. "Multitasking Gas Pump." *Machine Design.* 3 August 2000.

Restak, Richard. *The New Brain: How the Modern Age Is Rewiring Your Mind.* Rodale Books, August 2003.

"Surviving in the New World." *Manufacturing Engineering.* December 1999.

Wallis, Claudia. "The Multitasking Generation." *Time.* 27 March 2006.

Hillstrom, Northern Lights
updated by Magee, ECDI

MYERS-BRIGGS TYPE INDICATOR (MBTI)

The Myers-Briggs Type Indicator (MBTI) is an instrument designed to evaluate people and provide descriptive profiles of their personality types. Based on the theories of psychologist Carl Jung, it is widely used in the fields of business, education, and psychology.

MBTI was developed by Isabel Briggs Myers and her mother, Katharine Cook Briggs, during World War II. The two women were acquainted with Jung's theories and sought to apply them to help civilians choose wartime jobs well-suited to their personality preferences. Myers and Briggs felt that this would make people happier and more productive in their work. Consulting Psychologists, Inc. (www.cpp-db.com) bought the rights to MBTI in 1975. The company estimates that it administers MBTI testing to 2 million people per year worldwide.

The MBTI system begins with a test in which participants respond to questions that provide clues about their basic outlook or personal preferences. These responses are scored to see where participants' preferences lie within four sets of attributes: extroversion/introversion; sensing/intuiting; thinking/feeling; and judging/perceiving.

The attributes extroversion (E) and introversion (I) are designed to indicate whether a participant derives his or her mental energy primarily from other people or from within. Similarly, the attributes sensing (S) and intuiting (N) explain whether a participant absorbs information best through data and details or through general patterns. The attributes thinking (T) and feeling (F) show whether a participant tends to make decisions based on logic and objective criteria or based on emotional intelligence. Finally, the attributes judging (J) and perceiving (P) indicate whether a participant makes decisions quickly or prefers to take a more casual approach and leave his or her options open.

The MBTI system organizes the four sets of attributes into a matrix of 16 different personality types. Each type is indicated by a four-letter code. For example, ESTJ would designate a person whose primary attributes were extroversion, sensing, thinking, and judging. For each personality type, the MBTI system includes a profile which describes the characteristics common to people who fit into that category.

For example, an article in the *Harvard Business Review* noted that people who fit into the category ISTP (introverted-sensing-thinking-perceiving) tend to be "cool onlookers—quiet, reserved, and analytical; usually interested in impersonal principles, how and why mechanical things work; flashes of original humor," while people of type ENFJ (extroverted-intuiting-feeling-judging) are "sociable, popular; sensitive to praise and criticism; responsive and responsible; generally feel real concern for what others think or want."

MBTI is a popular evaluative tool. Many colleges and universities use it in career counseling to help guide students into appropriate fields for their personality types. In the business world, companies use it to make hiring decisions, identify leadership potential among employees, design training for specific employee needs, facilitate team building, and help resolve conflicts between employees. By giving people an increased understanding of their behavior and preferences, MBTI is said to help them increase their productivity, build relationships, and make life choices.

Proponents of MBTI see the testing system as a valuable aid to personal development and growth. But critics of MBTI argue that its personality profiles are so broad and ambiguous that they can be interpreted to fit almost anyone. Some also worry that, once a university career counselor or employer knows a person's "type," that person might tend to be pigeonholed or pushed in a certain direction regardless of his or her desires. Criticism based on "confirmation bias," namely that people tend to behave in ways that are predicted for them, has been offered but runs counter to experience. This critique asserts that a person who learns that he or she is "outgoing," according to MBTI, will be more likely to behave that way. Temperaments, however, are not that easily influenced by "hear-say": shy people labeled outgoing won't take fire; and schmoozers labeled shy will just continue to babble and hug on.

BIBLIOGRAPHY

Hirsh, Sandra Krebs, and Jean M. Kummerow. *Introduction to Type in Organizations.* Consulting Psychologists Press, 2000.

"Identifying How We Think: The Myers-Briggs Type Indicator and the Hermann Brain Dominance Instrument." *Harvard Business Review.* July-August 1997.

Kahn, Alan R. and Kris Austen Radclifee. *Mind Shapes: Understanding the differences in thinking and communication.* Paragon House, 2005.

Quenk, Naomi L. *Essentials of Myers-Briggs Type Indicator Assessment.* John Wiley, 1999.

"Training and Development." *HRMagazine.* January 2006.

Hillstrom, Northern Lights
updated by Magee, ECDI

MYSTERY SHOPPING

Mystery shopping is a term that describes a field-based research technique of using independent auditors posing as customers to gather information about product quality and service delivery by a retail firm. The "mystery shopper" poses as a customer in order to objectively gather information on the business being studied. Getting a customer's view of one's business is a widely recognized tool in both the marketing and customer service arenas. When mystery shoppers are dispatched to visit a business, they use criteria developed by the client to evaluate the business and focus primarily on service delivery and the sales skills of employees. Their reports, usually written, are forwarded to the client and can be used in a number of ways. Mystery shoppers can also objectively evaluate competitors and their service delivery and product mix for comparisons and benchmarking.

The use of mystery shoppers is one way for a business to create a competitive edge. It may also serve retailers in developing and evaluating strategies to retain current customers. The first step in mystery shopping is to identify your firm's important customer service characteristics and objectives—often flowing from your strategy and overall goals and objectives. Next a firm uses these variables to develop a mystery shopping questionnaire, either alone or with the help or a consultant or mystery shopping firm. The survey can include a mix of narrative and check-off questions. Typical areas of assessment are customer service, suggestive selling and up-selling techniques, teamwork, employee and management activities, headcount, store appearance and organization, merchandise displays and stock, cleanliness of the location, signage and advertising compliance, time in line and time elapsed for service, product quality, order accuracy, customer's preferences, cash handling, and return policies. After pre-testing the questionnaire, mystery shoppers are hired to do an assessment. Assessments can be on-site or via the telephone or even the Internet. A sample size as well as a period of time for the mystery shopping program is determined and results are used for feedback.

USE OF MYSTERY SHOPPING RESULTS

Managers can use the reports from mystery shoppers to evaluate their locations, and the results can be used to provide employee recognition and other positive reinforcements of loyalty and morale through incentive programs. Many restaurants, banks, supermarkets, and clothing retailers have used the techniques, along with hotels, furniture stores, grocery stores, gas stations, movie theaters, automotive repair shops, bars, athletic clubs, bowling alleys, and almost any business where customer service is important. As the service sector of the economy has increased, so has the demand for mystery shoppers.

Some retailers are large enough to have their own in-house program in place. Other smaller companies who do not have the resources to develop a quality mystery shopping program in-house use mystery shopping contractors. These contractors directly hire and train the mystery shoppers. The association representing such contractors, the Mystery Shopping Providers Association (MSPA), operates in North and South America, Europe, and Asia/Pacific and has a membership of 150 companies; thus finding a contractor should be relatively easy.

The reports from mystery shoppers can measure training and levels of customer service pre- and post-training. Mystery shopping allows managers to determine if the services employees are providing are appropriate. Shopping reports can assess promotional campaigns and even verify employees' honesty in handling cash and charges.

The use of mystery shopping is just one part of a company-wide program to develop and augment employee performance. The idea is to learn from a consumer's point of view which areas of service and product quality are most important and what areas need improvement. In many cases, this allows a company to address problem areas more quickly than they might have otherwise. Most professional in the field advise that the results should be used for developmental and reward purposes and not for punishment.

Mystery shopping is a valuable tool to businesses and is especially helpful for small, start-up businesses that need accurate and fast information to assess their employees and compare their products and services to the competition.

BIBLIOGRAPHY

"Londis Mystery Shopper Aims to Boost Store Sales." *Grocer.* 18 February 2006.

"Mystery Shopper: Aberdeen." *Carpet/Flooring/Retail.* 7 April 2006.

Mystery Shopping Providers Association (MSPA). "What is the MSPA." Available from http://www.mysteryshop.org/. Retrieved on 15 April 2006.

"No Mystery Here: Courtesy Counts." *Convenience Store News.* 27 March 2006.

"Opinion: Reaction to mystery shopper." *Chemist & Druggist.* 18 March 2006.

Hillstrom, Northern Lights
updated by Magee, ECDI

N

NATIONAL ASSOCIATION OF SMALL BUSINESS INVESTMENT COMPANIES (NASBIC)

Small Business Investment Companies are privately organized and managed venture capital firms licensed by the U.S. Small Business Administration (SBA) to make equity capital or long-term loans available to small companies. The Small Business Investment Act of 1958 provided the legal basis upon which this program has been developed and outlines the licensing procedures used by the SBA to register SBICs. The National Association of Small Business Investment Companies (NASBIC) is the association that unites these independent SBICs. The primary concern of the NASBIC is providing representation before government on behalf of the SBIC industry. The association is located at 666 11th St., NW, Suite 750, Washington, DC 20001; 202-628-5055. The association's Web site is www.nasbic.org.

According to NASBIC, the several thousand SBICs operating in the United States and Puerto Rico are privately organized and managed financial institutions that invest capital in small independent businesses. They differ from venture capital firms in that they are licensed by the Small Business Administration. In exchange for investing only in small businesses, the SBA helps SBICs qualify for government-insured long-term loans. SBICs have complete control over their own lending policies and investment choices and are not bound by government regulation to make capital available to any particular type of business or business owner. Among the companies that began with funding from an SBIC are Apple Computer, Federal Express, Outback Steakhouse, America Online, and Intel. According to the NASBIC, since its inception in 1958, the SBIC program has provided $46 billion in long-term debt and equity growth capita to nearly 100,000 small U.S. companies.

SSBICs, or Special Small Business Investment Companies, are identical to SBICs except in the respect that they tend to concentrate their lending in the area of socially and economically disadvantage entrepreneurs. However, all SBICs may consider applicants from all backgrounds.

FACTORS IN APPROACHING AN SBIC

NASBIC reports that small business owners contemplating a pitch to an SBIC should be mindful of the following considerations.

1. Loan size—Consider the amount of capital your business will need when choosing a particular SBIC as their policies differ and many have a defined range within which they are willing to lend.

2. Loan type—Decide in advance whether your business will be better served by a straight loan, an equity investment, or another kind of financing is useful. Different SBICs offer different options.

3. Industry—Some SBICs choose to lend only to businesses in a particular industrial sector, due to the expertise of the SBIC's officers or directors.

4. Geography—Although SBICs may operate regionally or even nationally, it is wise to look into the

closest suitable SBIC, because they tend to lend to businesses in their general locale.

Seekers of financing should also note that SBICs may consider working in conjunction with one another to provide pooled capital if a special case merits a departure from standard policy, so no one company should be immediately ruled out.

Requirements Your business qualifies as a "small business" according to NASBIC parameters if it has a net worth under 18 million dollars and average after-tax earnings of less than $6 million for the past two years. If your business fails these tests, it may qualify under employment or annual sales parameters.

When presenting your business to an SBIC for consideration, business owners must provide a business plan that includes information on every aspect of your operation, including detailed descriptions of the product or service and the facilities; an explanation of your customer base and distribution system; a description of your business's competition; an account of all key personnel and their qualifications; and financial statements, such as balance sheets and revenue projections. The ultimate acceptance or denial process will take a few weeks, although an indication will be made immediately of general interest or lack thereof.

When considering all sources of funding, a small business owner should weigh the appropriateness of each source with his or her needs. The wide variety of funding options provide many choices, with only a small number, perhaps, that will be suitable. Small Business Investment Companies provide a unique offering in that they have the security of the government behind them, but the flexibility of a private firm.

BIBLIOGRAPHY

Anderson, Mark. "Investors Say Reform May Threaten SBA Venture Capital Funds." *Finance and Commerce Daily Newspaper, Minnesota.* 27 March 2004.

Barlas, Stephen. "Something Ventured." *Entrepreneur.* July 2000.

Gillis, Tom S. *Guts & Borrowed Money: Straight Talk for Starting & Growing Your Small Business.* Bard Press, 1997.

Janecke, Ron. "The National Association of Small Business Investment Companies." *St. Louis Business Journal.* 1 November 1999.

O'Hara, Patrick D. *SBA Loans, A Step-by-Step Guide.* John Wiley & Sons, Inc., May 2002.

The Small Business Investment Company (SBIC) Program. Available from http://www.nasbic.org/ Retrieved on 14 April 2006.

Hillstrom, Northern Lights
updated by Magee, ECDI

NATIONAL ASSOCIATION OF WOMEN BUSINESS OWNERS

As of 2002, there were 6.5 million majority women-owned businesses in the United States, employing 7.1 million persons according to the U.S. Bureau of the Census. The number of privately held women-owned businesses in U.S. exceeds 10 million if one counts partially women-owned businesses as well. As the number of women-owned businesses grows, representation and support for female entrepreneurs and business owners becomes more and more visible. The National Association of Women Business Owners (NAWBO), based in Washington D.C., provides women-owned businesses with a resource for such support and representation. Covering the many faceted interests of women entrepreneurs in all areas of business, the NAWBO has chapters all across the United States and maintains affiliate chapters around the world. Membership is available through annual dues paid to both the national organization and to a local chapter.

The NAWBO began as a small group of Washington, D.C., businesswomen who started meeting in 1974. They began as a networking group, meeting to discuss mutual experiences, exchange information, and help develop business skills for group members. They incorporated as the NAWBO on December 19, 1974. The first members in the newly formed organization were recruited in 1976, and in 1978, the first national chapters were formed. Today, its headquarters are located at 8405 Greenboro Drive, Suite 800, McLean, VA, 22102; 800-556-2926. It also maintains an informative Web site at www.nawbo.org.

The NAWBO's vision and mission statement states that the organization hopes to propel women entrepreneurs into "economic, social and political spheres of power worldwide." Principle aims of the organization, as articulated in their mission statement, include:

1. Strengthen the wealth-creating capacity of members and promote economic development

2. Create innovative and effective changes in the business culture

3. Build strategic alliances, coalitions, and affiliations

4. Transform public policy and influence opinion makers

In addition, the NAWBO provides women entrepreneurs with assistance in gaining access to financial opportunities. For instance, the organization offers special loans, discount prices on certain equipment and services, and other opportunities which may translate into substantial savings on the start-up costs of business. The NAWBO also provides educational experiences and leadership training, and sponsors a wide range of special conferences, workshops, seminars, and counseling services. Finally, the organization's local, regional, national and international contacts provide networking opportunities that may be otherwise unavailable to small businesses.

In addition to its position as "helping hand," the NAWBO has established a strong political presence, emerging as a strong voice of advocacy for small women-owned businesses. For example, the group was instrumental in supporting and helping to pass the 1988 Women's Business Ownership Act, which expanded women entrepreneurs' access to credit markets; instituted a three-year, $10 million training and technical support initiative for women business owners; and created a National Women's Business Council. A regular presence on Capitol Hill, members of the NAWBO work to make sure that the needs of women-owned businesses are represented.

Affiliations The NAWBO is the United States' representative in Les Femmes Chefs d'Entreprises Mondiales (FCEM, or The World Association of Women Entrepreneurs) with chapters in 40 countries, representing almost 30,000 businesses. This affiliation allows NAWBO members access to international business ideas and trends and provides networking opportunities throughout the world.

The National Foundation for Women Business Owners (NFWBO) is a nonprofit research and leadership development foundation established by NAWBO. This offshoot of the NAWBO gathers information about women-owned businesses and makes that information available to organizations around the globe.

NAWBO is also affiliated with the Small Business Technology Coalition (SBTC) and with the Women Business Owners Corporation (WBOC), which helps small women-owned businesses compete for government contracts. This organization helps women entrepreneurs and business owners to meet professional certification and training needs.

Finally, in 2003, NAWBO formed the NAWBO Institute for Entrepreneurial Development (IED). This 501(c)3 organization seeks to expand the educational opportunities for emerging and established women entrepreneurs. In 2006 NAWBO IED initiatives include the sponsorship of a tracks of educational programming at NAWBO's annual Women's Business Conferences. The program also supports the issuance of conference scholarships for emerging women entrepreneurs.

BIBLIOGRAPHY

"About NAWBO." National Association of Women Business Owners. Available from http://www.nawbo.org/about/index.php. Retrieved on 17 April 2006.

Fisher, Anne. "Which Women Get Big? When it comes to building large businesses, women lag far behind men—but that's changing fast." *Fortune Small Business.* 1 April 2006.

Gee, Sharon. "NAWBO Getting Serious About Women's Business." *Birmingham Business Journal.* 11 August 2000.

U. S. Bureau of the Census. *Survey of Business Owners – Women-Owned Firms: 2002.* Available from http://www.census.gov/csd/sbo/. 26 January 2006.

Vestil, Donna. "Businesses Owned by Women Fuel National Growth." *Kansas City Star.* 28 June 2005.

Hillstrom, Northern Lights
updated by Magee, ECDI

NATIONAL BUSINESS INCUBATION ASSOCIATION (NBIA)

The National Business Incubation Association (NBIA), founded in 1985, is a nonprofit organization comprised of business incubator developers and managers, corporate joint venture partners, venture capital investors, and economic development professionals. The association seeks to promote the growth of new business and educate the business and investor community about the benefits of incubators. NBIA offers information and training on how to form and manage incubators; conducts statistical research; provides a referral service; and publishes a newsletter, membership directory, various reports and monographs, and a state of the industry analysis. The NBIA also hosts an annual convention where it bestows a number of industry awards.

Business incubators are facilities that provide shared resources for young businesses, such as office space, consultants, and personnel. They may also provide access to financing and technical support. For new businesses, these services provide a more protected environment in which to grow before they becomes self-sustaining. The ultimate goal of any business incubator is to produce viable businesses, called "graduates" of the incubator. Today, there are an estimated 900 NBIA-affiliated business incubators in operation across the United States as well as affiliates in 40 countries.

A business qualifying for incubator assistance must meet certain criteria, in much the same way it would for a venture capital firm. Some incubators have diversified interests, accepting different types of start-ups into the fold, whereas others concentrate in one particular area or industry. For instance, some special interest incubators exclusively support women and minority-owned businesses and others choose to focus on innovative software or medical applications.

A variety of sponsors support incubators. Some incubators are supported by government and nonprofit bodies. These incubators' main goals are job creation, tax base expansion, and economic diversification. Other incubators are affiliated with universities and provide faculty, alumni, and related groups with research and business opportunities. In addition, a number of incubators are hybrids combining resources from both government and the private sector. For-profit incubators, meanwhile, surged in popularity during the 1990s. This growth was fed in general by the decade's explosive economic expansion, and specifically by the advent of e-commerce. These incubators are operated by various types of investment groups and maintained to provide returns on funds invested by the group. Their main focus is usually on innovative applications for new technology and the development of commercial real estate. But many for-profit incubators can provide only limited leadership, guidance, and financing. Indeed, the NBIA estimates that the majority of for-profit incubators fail within two years of opening. For this reason, the NBIA encourages entrepreneurs to carefully research incubators before committing to membership. The remainder of incubators are sponsored by a variety of non-traditional organizations, such as Indian tribes, chambers of commerce, church groups, and others.

Membership Membership in the NBIA conveys a variety of benefits. They include a subscription to the *NBIA Review*, the association's newsletter; access to BatorLink, the NBIA's Internet discussion group; research, documentation, and dissemination services; support from NBIA staff for information and referrals; legislative and government program updates; and discounts on publications, educational materials, Microsoft products, insurance products from Biddle Insurance Services, and Paychex payroll services. Contact the organization by mail or phone for information on how to apply for membership. The National Business Incubator Association's headquarters are at 20 East Circle Drive, Suite 37198, Athens, OH 45701; 740-593-4331. It also maintains a Web site at www.nbia.org/index.php.

BIBLIOGRAPHY
"Due Diligence Advised in Picking Business Incubator." *Business First-Columbus,* 1 September 2000.

Hayhow, Sally. *Business Incubation: Building Companies, Jobs and Wealth.* National Business Incubation Association, 1997.

Hayhow, Sally. *A Comprehensive Guide to Business Incubation.* National Business Incubation Association, 1996.

"Incubators Lay an Egg." *Business Week.* 9 October 2000.

Krizner, Ken. "Incubators: Help Startup Companies Get Off the Ground." *Expansion Management.* July 2005.

Rice, Mark P., and Jana Matthews. *Growing New Ventures, Creating New Jobs: Principles and Practices of Successful Business Incubation.* Quorum Books, 1995.

Hillstrom, Northern Lights
updated by Magee, ECDI

NATIONAL LABOR RELATIONS BOARD (NLRB)

The National Labor Relations Board (NLRB) is a federal organization that oversees the establishment and conduct of union organizations as well as the conduct of businesses involved with unions. Its national headquarters are located at 1099 14th St., Washington, DC 20570. The organization's phone number is 866-667-6572, and its Web site is located at www.nlrb.gov/nlrb/home/default.asp.

History and Purpose of the NLRB The NLRB was created in 1935 by Congress to administer the National Labor Relations Act (NLRA). The NLRA is the law that governs relations between labor unions and employers whose operations involve interstate commerce. Though there are other federal and state laws which also protect the rights of employees, such as the Fair Labor Standards Act (FLSA), the NLRA is the Act specifically tied to the NLRB and to union organization.

The Act itself gives employees the right to organize and bargain collectively with their employers, as well as the right not to organize. In short, employees may join a union or not, as they so choose. The laws covers only employees working for employers involved in interstate commerce with a few exceptions (airlines, railroads, agriculture, and government). The act ensures that employees can choose their own representatives for the purpose of collective bargaining, establishes procedures for secret-ballot elections, and defines unfair labor practices, to which both employers and unions are subject.

The NLRB conducts elections and prevents and remedies unfair labor practices. It is made up of two different branches. The Board is a group of five persons based in Washington, D.C., who act in a judicial capacity, though they are not judges. This group decides whether improper labor practices have actually occurred, either during an election campaign or during management-union bargaining sessions. The General Counsel is the prosecutorial side of the Board. It has offices throughout the country and is charged with the investigation and prosecution of those who engage in unfair labor practices. The NLRB is designed to be completely equitable, taking sides for neither management nor union, acting as a sort of "referee" in what is usually an emotionally charged action between employees and employers.

Impact on Business The employees of any business may seek representation by filing a petition with the NLRB requesting an election. The NLRA requires that representation must be by a "labor organization," as defined by the NLRA. The definition of a labor organization is fairly liberal, and entrepreneurs should always be familiar with both large and smaller unions that might seek to organize a business' employees. The larger ones, such as the AFL-CIO or the United Auto Workers (UAW), are well known, but there are many smaller organizations as well.

Once an election has been held and employees have determined that they want representation by a union for the purposes of collective bargaining, the employer is required by law to bargain with no other organization for the workers in that business. All workers are covered by the decision, whether they become members of the union or not. Generally, such employment concerns such as wages, hours, and working conditions are included in the collective bargaining agreement, which is set up during meetings between the employer and the union representatives.

Unfair Labor Practices The judicial arm of the NLRB becomes involved when there is a dispute about the conduct of the employer or the union during a union election campaign or during bargaining. The General Counsel investigates the charge to determine if it is valid and should be pursued. The charge can become a local level complaint at this stage, or can be dismissed. The great majority of charges filed with the NLRB are settled or withdrawn at the stage when investigation has been completed, before a complaint has been issued.

If a complaint is filed, the case is heard before an Administrative Law Judge, part of the judicial branch of the NLRB. The Administrative Law Judge's decision on the case is then adopted by the Board. If exceptions are made, the transcript, briefs, and other documentation of the case are all sent to the Board in Washington for a decision. The NLRB rarely hears oral arguments; it usually making decisions based on the documentation from the Administrative Law Judge.

The NLRB decisions do not have the impact of law because the NLRB is an administrative agency. Their decisions are, however, recommendations that carry a

great deal of weight in a court of law. If either the union or employer is unwilling to follow the guidelines set down in the decision, the NLRB files a petition in the Court of Appeals—the level directly below the Supreme Court—for the district where the case arose. If this decision is contested, the Board will request that the United States Supreme Court hear the case.

SEE ALSO *Labor Unions*

BIBLIOGRAPHY
The Developing Labor Law. BNA Books, January 2002.
Gould, William B, IV. *Labored Relations: Law, Politics, and the NLRB.* MIT Press, 2000.
How to Take a Case Before the NLRB. BNA Books, January 2000.
Lichtenstein, Nelson. *State of the Union: A Century of American Labor.* Princeton University Press, 28 August 2003.
U.S. National Labor Relation Board. "About the NLRB." Available from http://www.nlrb.gov/nlrb/about/default.asp. Retrieved on 17 April 2006.

Hillstrom, Northern Lights
updated by Magee, ECDI

NATIONAL VENTURE CAPITAL ASSOCIATION (NVCA)

The National Venture Capital Association (NVCA), founded in 1973, is an organization of venture capital firms, corporate backers, and individuals dedicated to professionally investing private capital in new companies. In their own words, they exist to "define, serve, and represent the interests of the venture capital and private equity industries" by, among other things, promoting the public policy interests of the venture capital and entrepreneurial communities.

The NVCA seeks to foster greater understanding of the necessity of investing in young companies and their role in the overall health of the United States economy. To that end, it works to stimulate the flow of risk equity capital to emerging and developing companies. It also aims to promote communication between venturing bodies throughout the United States and strives to improve the level of knowledge of the venturing process in government, universities, and the general business community. In support of these activities, the NVCA conducts research, hosts educational and networking programs, and serves as an information clearinghouse for its members. It makes available the results of its research in various publications, such as its *Annual Economic Impact of Venture Capital Study, Job Creation Survey, Expert*

Analysis of Legislative and Regulatory Issues, and other scholarly works. Specific information available through the NVCA includes industry statistics, venture capital news, and listings of venture capital firms. NVCA headquarters are located at 1655 North Fort Myer Drive, Suite 850, Arlington, VA 22209; 703-524-2549. The association also maintains a Web site at www.nvca.org.

According to a report published on the NVCA Web site, "Private Equity Fundraising Maintained Strong Momentum in First Quarter of 2006," private equity fundraising by venture capital firms started at a strong pace in 2006, following the very healthy showing during 2005. In 2005 the number of funds reported on in the report summed to 194 and accounted for just over $26 million in venture capital investments.

VENTURE CAPITAL

New business owners who lack the collateral and experience to garner traditional bank financing often must seek funds elsewhere. Many entrepreneurs seek "venture capital" informally, obtaining seed money from friends and family or wealthy individuals willing to risk an investment. Others, of course, seek funding by professional firms. In these cases, the new firm assesses any number of business plans to determine which holds the greatest potential for success and presents this plan to prospective venture capital firms. The venture capital firm which finances a new venture will have an ongoing relationship with the start-up, providing coaching, training, management expertise, and other services, and often holding a seat on the young company's board of directors. Should your business be accepted for funding by a venture capital firm, expect the organization to take an active part in shaping your business.

According to the NVCA, funds used by venture capital firms come from a variety of sources, including institutional investors such as pension funds, foundations and endowments, insurance companies, wealthy individuals, professional money managers, foreign investors, and the venture capitalists themselves.

NVCA MEMBERSHIP

The NVCA actively advocates public policies that are beneficial to the entrepreneurial and venture communities. The association also provides educational programs accessible throughout the United States to its membership. Programs are conducted by industry scholars, practitioners, and analysts. In addition, the NVCA offers a director and officer insurance program intended for both members and their portfolio companies that provides risk management and loss control protection.

The Regional Member Committee program, a network of liaison groups that represents members from across the United States, works with the NVCA Board of Directors and staff to design and enhance the programs offered by the association. The committees, which are composed of members from each of the six regions, include Education, Public Relations, Research, Tax Policy and others. Finally, the NVCA's affiliate organization, the American Entrepreneurs for Economic Growth (AEEG), seeks to "serve as a united voice on public policy issues for entrepreneurs." It represents thousands of small business owners and executives across the country.

NVCA has several requirements of potential members. Those seeking membership (by invitation) must be capital organizations, investment advisors, corporate investors, or buyout funds. Members need not be full time venture capitalists, but they must have as their primary business the deployment of venture capital. They also must represent capital funds and utilize a professional approach before and after they make an investment, including the maintenance of a continuing interest in companies they sponsor. The managers of the business must be American citizens or resident aliens and operate from an office located in the United States. In addition, members must invest from a dedicated U.S.-based venture capital pool of funds of at least one million dollars. Finally, the members' business must be subject to U.S. taxation and laws. Dues are scalable and depend on the amount of capital under management.

BIBLIOGRAPHY

Long, Mark H. *Financing the New Venture.* Adams Media, 2000.

Lundgren, Douglas A. *Venture Capital: An Authoritative Guide for Investors, Entrepreneurs, and Managers.* McGraw-Hill, 1998.

Mendell, Emily. *Private Equity Fundraising Maintained Strong Momentum in First Quarter of 2006.* NVCA and Thomson Venture Economics, April 2006.

"National Venture Capital Association and Dow Jones VentureOne Release First Ever Study on Differing Practices and Attitudes at Venture Capital-Backed Company Boards." *PR Newswire.* 10 April 2006.

Whitford, David. "We Can Fix Anything: Women can play the VC game and win big." *Fortune Small Business.* 1 April 2006.

Hillstrom, Northern Lights
updated by Magee, ECDI

NEGOTIATION

Negotiation describes any communication process between individuals that is intended to reach a compromise or agreement to the satisfaction of both parties. Negotiation involves examining the facts of a situation, exposing both the common and opposing interests of the parties involved, and bargaining to resolve as many issues as possible. Negotiation takes place every day in nearly every facet of life—from national governments negotiating border disputes, to companies negotiating work agreements with labor unions, to real estate agents negotiating the sale of property, to former spouses negotiating the terms of a divorce. Small business owners are likely to face negotiations on a daily basis when dealing with customers, suppliers, employees, investors, creditors, government agencies, and even family members. Many companies train members of their sales forces in negotiation techniques, and many others hire professional negotiators to represent them in business dealings. Good negotiation requires advance preparation, a knowledge of negotiating techniques, and practice.

Regardless of the type of negotiation, experts recommend entering into it with a cooperative rather than a competitive attitude. They stress that the point of negotiating is to reach agreement rather than to achieve victory. "Any method of negotiation may be fairly judged by three criteria," Roger Fisher and William Ury wrote in their book *Getting to Yes: Negotiating Agreement without Giving In.* "It should produce a wise agreement if agreement is possible. It should be efficient. And it should improve or at least not damage the relationship between the parties." When one of the parties uses "hard" negotiating techniques—or bullies and intimidates the other side in order to obtain a more favorable arrangement—it only creates resentment and poisons future negotiations. Instead, the idea should be to find a win/win solution that satisfies the needs and interests of both parties.

PREPARING FOR A NEGOTIATION

Four basic things are recommended for any party about to engage in discussions to arrive at a negotiated agreement. First, advance preparation. Second, an understanding of the underlying assumptions and needs to be satisfied on both sides. Third, a basic knowledge of human behavior. Fourth, mastery of a range of negotiating techniques, strategies, and tactics. In his classic book on the subject, *Fundamentals of Negotiating,* Gerard I. Nierenberg outlined a number of steps toward adequately preparing for a negotiation. The first step is to "do your homework" about the other side. In nearly every negotiation, this will entail research to uncover their underlying motivations. In negotiating a business property lease, for example, it may be useful to find out the cost to the landlord of keeping the building vacant. The next step is to assess your own side's needs and establish objectives for the negotiation. It is important that the objectives remain relatively fluid, however, so as not to

hinder progress with discussions and maintain maximum flexibility.

Another element of preparing for a negotiation involves deciding whether to use an individual or a team as your representative. This decision needs to be considered separately for every negotiation, and will always depend to some extent on what the other side is doing. A negotiating team offers a number of potential advantages. For example, it enables a small business to involve people with different areas of expertise in order to avoid misstatements of fact. Teams can also play into negotiating strategies and help gain concessions through consultation among team members. However, it is important to note that bringing extra people can be harmful to a negotiation when they do not have a distinct function. Using a single negotiator also offers some advantages. It prevents the weakening of positions that often occurs through differences of opinion within a team, and it also may help gain concessions through the negotiator's ability to make on-the-spot decisions.

The next step in preparing for a negotiation involves choosing a chief negotiator. Ideally, this person should have experience and training in negotiations, as well as a strong background in the area of the problem about which discussions are being held. Another important element of negotiation is selecting the meeting site. For a small business, holding the meeting on its own premises may provide a psychological advantage, plus will save on travel time and expense. It may also be helpful in enabling the negotiators to obtain approval from managers or use their own facilities to check facts and find additional information as needed. Holding a negotiation at the other side's offices, however, may help the negotiators to devote their full attention to the task at hand without distractions. It may also play into negotiating strategy by enabling the negotiators to temporarily withhold information by claiming a need to speak to higher level people or gather more information. A third alternative for a meeting site is a neutral location. Whatever site is chosen, it should be large enough to accommodate all parties and feature a telephone, comfortable chairs, visual aids, and available refreshments.

THE NEGOTIATION PROCESS

Fisher and Ury recommend conducting negotiations according to the process of "principled negotiation." Their method has four main tenets:

1. Separate the people from the problem. The idea should be for both sides to work together to attack a problem, rather than attacking each other. To achieve this goal, it is necessary to overcome emotional responses and set aside egos.

2. Focus on interests rather than positions. The natural tendency in many negotiations—for example, dickering over the price to be paid for an antique—is for both sides to state a position and then move toward middle ground. Fisher and Ury warn against confusing people's stated positions with their underlying interests, and claim that positions often tend to obscure what people truly hope to gain through negotiation.

3. Generate a variety of options before deciding what to do. The pressure involved in any type of negotiation tends to narrow people's vision and inhibit their creativity, making it difficult to find optimal solutions to problems. Instead, Fisher and Ury suggest developing a wide range of possible solutions as part of the negotiating process. These possible solutions should attempt to advance shared interests and reconcile differences.

4. Base the result on objective criteria. No one will be happy with the result of a negotiation if they feel that they have been taken advantage of. The solution is to find and apply some fair standard to the problem in order to guarantee a mutually beneficial result.

Fisher and Ury's principles provide a good overall guide for the actual negotiation process. In his book, Nierenberg offered a number of other tips and strategies that may be effective in promoting successful negotiations. For example, it may be helpful to ask questions in order to form a better understanding of the needs and interests of the other side. The questions must be phrased diplomatically and timed correctly in order to avoid an antagonistic response. The idea is to gain information and uncover basic assumptions without immediately taking positions. Nierenberg stressed the importance of listening carefully to the other side's responses, as well as studying their facial expressions and body language, in order to gain quality information.

Nierenberg noted that good negotiators tend to employ a variety of means to accomplish their objectives. Small business owners should be aware of some of the more common strategies and techniques that they may see others apply or may wish to apply themselves. One common strategy is forbearance, or "patience pays," which covers any sort of wait or delay in negotiations. If one side wishes to confer in private, or adjourn briefly, they are employing a strategy of forbearance. Another common strategy is to present a *fait accompli,* or come to a final offer and leave it up to the other side to decide whether to accept it. In a simple example, a small business owner may scratch out one provision in a contract that he or she finds unacceptable, then sign it and send it back. The other party to the contract then must decide whether to accept the revised agreement. Nierenberg warns that this strategy can be risky, and encourages those who employ it to carefully appraise the consequences first.

Another possible negotiating strategy is reversal, which involves taking a position that seems opposed to the original one. Similarly, feinting involves apparently moving in one direction in order to divert attention from the true goal. For example, a negotiator may give in on a point that is not very important in order to make the real objective more attainable. Another strategy involves setting limits on the negotiation, whether with regards to time, the people involved, or other factors. It is also possible to change the participation in the negotiation if it seems to be at an impasse. For example, a neutral third party may be enlisted to help, or one or two people from each side may be sent off to continue the negotiation separately. It may also be helpful to break down the problem into small pieces and tackle them one by one. Another strategy might be to trade sides for a short time and try to view the situation from each other's perspective. All of these techniques may be applied either to gain advantage or to push forward a negotiation that has apparently reached an impasse.

BIBLIOGRAPHY

Di Frances, John. "Use the Pro's Negotiation Strategies." *Selling.* December 2005.

Fisher, Roger, and William Ury. *Getting to Yes: Negotiating Agreement without Giving In.* Second Edition. Penguin, 2000.

Latz, Marty. "Are They Irrational or Are They Faking It? Negotiating a Business Deal with an Irrational Party." *Orlando Business Journal.* 5 January 2001.

Lauback, Christopher. *Mastering the Negotiation Process.* Health Administration Press, 2002.

Nierenberg, Gerard I. *Fundamentals of Negotiating.* Hawthorn Books, 1977.

Whitaker, Leslie, and Elizabeth Austin. *The Good Girl's Guide to Negotiating: How to Get What You Want at the Bargaining Table.* Little Brown, 2000.

Hillstrom, Northern Lights
updated by Magee, ECDI

NEPOTISM

In the business world, nepotism is the practice of showing favoritism toward one's family members or friends in economic or employment terms. For example, granting favors or jobs to friends and relatives, without regard to merit, is a form of nepotism. These practices can have damaging effects on businesses—such as eroding the support of non-favored employees or reducing the quality and creativity of management. In response, some larger companies have instituted "anti-nepotism" policies, which prevent relatives (by blood or marriage) from working in the same department or firm. But in many smaller, family-owned businesses, nepotism is viewed in more positive terms. Family members are trained in various aspects of management to ensure the continuity of the company when members of the earlier generation retire or die. In fact, in many small businesses nepotism is considered a synonym for "succession."

One of the most common arguments against nepotism is that the emotional ties between people who are related may negatively affect their decision making abilities and professional growth. In the past, many businesses sought to avoid even the appearance of nepotism by forbidding relatives from working closely together. This began to change as women entered the work force in ever greater numbers and began to rise to positions of prominence. Often, both the man and the woman in a married couple were too valuable for a company to lose. Instead of instituting strict anti-nepotism rules, many businesses decided that family members could be accommodated within a merit system, especially if there was no direct supervisory link between the positions of related employees.

NEPOTISM IN SMALL BUSINESSES

Even within small businesses where family members often work together concerns about how these nepotistic relationships may be viewed by others must be considered. Business owners have often feared that non-family employees would resent or even treat unkindly family members brought into the business. Newly hired family members may even be seen as roadblocks to advancement in a company by some non-family employees. A recent Inc.com poll reveled the extend to which this attitude prevails. In fact, nearly half of those polled (48 percent) believed that being the boss's son is the secret to getting ahead, while only a quarter agreed that success comes from doing good work.

This attitude suggests that family-owned businesses need to make serious efforts to establish an environment in which it is clear that employees will be rewarded based on merit. This does not necessarily mean that hiring a relative is a bad idea. What is necessary, however, are policies and actions that show clearly that all employees are rewarded fairly and equally for company success. The emotional bonds between family members can actually have a positive effect on individual performance and company results. In addition, hiring family members can fill staffing requirements with dedicated employees. And it should not be forgotten that preparing a family member to carry on a business is a perfectly legitimate enterprise for the owner of a family business.

But in order to avoid potential pitfalls and ensure that relatives work together effectively, the company should establish formal guidelines regarding hiring, responsibilities, reporting structure, training, and succession. These guidelines will be different depending on the family's size, culture, history, and line of business, in addition to other factors. "How strict or liberal the rules ... are is less important than clear communication of the rules before they are needed and fair application of the rules when timely," Craig E. Aronoff and John L. Ward wrote in *Nation's Business*. After all, most non-family employees recognize the legitimacy of preparing younger family members to assume the company's reins down the road. But experts agree that a widespread workforce perception that family members are not being held responsible for their performance can develop into a major morale problem.

Regarding hiring, Aronoff and Ward recommend in *Family Business Succession* that family members meet three qualifications before they are allowed to join the family business on a permanent basis: an appropriate educational background; three to five years' outside work experience; and an open, existing position in the firm that matches their background. Of these qualifications, Aronoff and Ward stress that outside work experience is the most important for both the business and the individual. They claim that it gives future managers a wider experience base that makes them better equipped to deal with challenges, lets them learn and make mistakes before coming under the watchful eye of the family, makes them realize what other options exist and thus appreciate the family firm, and provides them with an idea of their market value.

Aronoff and Ward also suggest that family members begin their association with the business by working part-time during their school years or participating in internships. In addition, they stress that companies who hire family members should make it clear to the individuals that they will be fired for illegal or unethical behavior, regardless of their family ties. Finally, they recommend that family businesses encourage their employees to maintain outside associations in order to avoid problems associated with a lack of creativity or accountability in management. For example, future managers could participate in industry or civic groups, enroll in night school classes or attend seminars, take responsibility for a division or profit center, and have their job performance reviewed by outside consultants or directors. Such steps can improve the employee's self-confidence and preparation for an eventual leadership role in the business.

SEE ALSO *Family-Owned Business*

BIBLIOGRAPHY

Aronoff, Craig E., and John L. Ward. *Family Business Succession: The Final Test of Greatness.* Business Owner Resources, 1992.

Aronoff and Ward. "Rules for Nepotism." *Nation's Business.* January 1993.

Bellow, Adam. *In Praise of Nepotism: A History of Family Enterprise from King David to George W. Bush.* Anchor Books, 2004.

Ferrazzi, Keith. "Nepotism Pays." *Inc.com.* Available from http://www.inc.com/resources/sales/articles/20040901/getahead.html Retrieved on 13 April 2006.

Lynn, Jacquelyn. "Lawfully Wedded Employees." *Entrepreneur.* April 2000.

Milazzo, Don. "All in the Family." *Birmingham Business Journal.* 11 August 2000.

Nelton, Sharon. "The Bright Sight of Nepotism." *Nation's Business.* May 1998.

Hillstrom, Northern Lights
updated by Magee, ECDI

NET INCOME

The net income of a company is its profit. The terminology is influenced by its source, which is the company's Income Statement. This statement shows Income at the top, namely the company's sales (also called revenues and, in British usage, turnover). All sorts of items are then deducted from this income—costs for raw materials, wages, supplies, purchased services, rents, lease payments, executive salaries, marketing expenses, management overhead, and depreciation. At each point the subtotals are less and less. At the very end, taxes are deducted. The last line of the income statement finally shows what is left over: Net Income. This, of course, is the company's profit, also called after-tax income. Wall Street calls this number "earnings after tax" or "earnings" for short. The designation is deceptive because most people think of earnings as their pay—and costs come after that. In corporate finance, earnings are "the bottom line."

Net income is typically tallied once a month for tracking purposes. In publicly traded companies it is published quarterly and annually. It can be negative, indicating that costs have exceeded revenues. It can be zero. In that case income and costs were exactly the same and the company has simply broken even.

While net income is the most important indicator of a company's profitability, it should not be confused with cash profit—unless the company accounts on a cash basis. Most companies use the accrual method of accounting. Under that system, income is "booked," i.e. recorded, at the time when a sale is made—not when payment is received. Similarly, costs are recorded when purchases are made—not when payments are sent out. Under certain circumstances, a company may show high profits and yet have no cash on hand. The timing differences between bookings and cash receipts may also work the other way: a company may have ample cash and be experiencing losses on the books. This difference between profitability and cash flow is important because in many situations, such as borrowing, getting a lease, or trying to sell a company, the lender, lessor, or buyer will be interested in cash flow above all.

Subcategories Most income statements will show four different income figures. The first is "operating income," common in companies that manufacture products. Operating income is what is left over from sales after production expenses have been subtracted but before overhead expenses have been applied. Next is "pretax income," the amount the company has left over after paying overhead but before deducting taxes. Reporting of this figure is optional under the accounting rules. The third is "income before extraordinary items," which is equal to ordinary revenues less ordinary expenses. Extraordinary items include any non-operating gains or losses that are unusual in nature and infrequent in occurrence. They are separated from ordinary income in order to avoid confusing the readers of income statements. Reporting of this figure is mandatory whenever there are extraordinary items to be included.

The fourth and final income figure shown on an income statement is net income. It is the difference between total revenues and total expenses for the period, including taxes and extraordinary items. Net income always appears as the last figure in the body of the income statement. Its reporting is mandatory. Corporations (but not sole proprietorships or partnerships) are also required to divide the net income figure by the number of shares of stock outstanding in order to report the earnings per share (EPS) for the period.

Ratios Net income is used in the calculation of various ratios that act as short-hand for evaluating a company's performance. Profit as a percent of sales is the most common measure. On average, profit is 5 percent of sales, and the business owner will watch this figure to see if he or she is "average." The measure is also called return on sales. Return on equity is also calculated by dividing the average share price by earnings-per-share—and the higher the better. To be sure, a high return will attract stock purchasers who, bidding up shares, will thus lower the return. Much used is the price-earnings (P/E) ratio, calculated by dividing share price by earnings-per-share. This produces a "multiple." If the shares are selling for $40 and earnings-per-share are $2.50, the P/E ratio is 16, suggesting that investors are willing to pay $16 for a dollar of earnings.

BIBLIOGRAPHY

Heintz, James A and Robert W. Parry. *College Accounting.* Thomson South-Western, 2005.

Pratt, Shannon P. Robert F. Reilly, and Robert P. Schweis. *Valuing a Business.* Fourth Edition. McGraw-Hill, 2000.

Warren, Carl S., Philip E. Fess, and James M. Reeve. *Accounting.* Thomson South-Western, 2004.

Darnay, ECDI

NET WORTH

The "net worth" of a business is the remainder after total liabilities are deducted from total assets. If total assets are $1 million and total liabilities $800,000, net worth will be $200,000. On a balance sheet Assets are typically shown in the left column, Liabilities in the right column. Beneath total liabilities in the right column will be listed the Net Worth. Thus liabilities ($800,000) plus net worth ($200,000), will equal assets ($1 million). Both columns will have $1 million on the last line, "Total Assets" on the left and "Liabilities and Net Worth" on the right. Let us now assume that the situation shown above is reversed: the company has $800,000 in assets and $1 million in liabilities. In that case, net worth will be -$200,000 so that this negative number, when added to liabilities, will produce $800,000 also. Again we have balance. But now, with a negative net worth, the company is insolvent. If that condition cannot be rapidly reversed, the company will fail.

In the usual case, Net Worth is made up of two figures. One is labeled "capital," "owner's equity," "partner's equity," or "shareholder equity." This line is the equivalent to the money initially received for shares sold in the company to all investors (or paid in by partners); in a privately held company it includes the owner's initial capital contributions along with that paid in by other investors. The second line is labeled "retained earnings." This represents profits (net income after tax) retained by the company for future investment or debt retirement after deducting dividends paid out (if any). Capital and retained earnings together are Net Worth.

A company has three different values, of which its net worth is just one. Every company has a "liquidation value," the money that its owners are likely to realize if the business stopped operating, all of its liabilities were satisfied, and all of its assets were sold off. The liquidation value will largely depend on the nature of the company's assets and what they will fetch when sold separately. Cash is worth exactly what it is, and the higher the cash, the higher the liquidation value. Land and buildings will normally sell above or at acquisition costs. Equipment, however, is rarely worth as much in separate pieces as it is when integrated into an up-and-running system of production. If the equipment is highly modified for a special purpose it will fetch least. Major machine tools transferable to another operation will fetch most. On furniture, fixtures, and excess inventories owners are likely to realize only pennies on the dollar.

The business also has a "market value." This is the amount of money a knowledgeable buyer of the company is likely to pay for it. Market value is based on a company's projected future earnings as an "on-going" business. A profitable company with low debt, a well-established history of steady earnings, and good cash flow will fetch the highest price. Other factors play a role, including its technological know-how, market share, and the presence or absence of competing buyers. In the case of a service business where the most important asset is represented by individuals with special skills and knowledge, the willingness of such people to continue on with the business will play a major role.

A company's liquidation value is almost always the lowest, its market value the highest, and its net worth represents a value between these two polarities. Net worth serves as an on-going measurement of the company's health, analogous to a blood-pressure measurement of a individual. Management and investors watch this figure closely. It is also of great interest to potential lenders to the company (along with other measures). Companies with high net worth relative to sales and good cash flow histories have the most success in attracting lenders.

BIBLIOGRAPHY

Heintz, James A., and Robert W. Parry. *College Accounting.* Thomson South-Western, 2005.

Pratt, Shannon P., Robert F. Reilly, and Robert P. Schweis. *Valuing a Business, 4th Edition.* McGraw-Hill, 2000.

Warren, Carl S., Philip E. Fess, and James M. Reeve. *Accounting.* Thomson South-Western, 2004.

Darnay, ECDI

NETWORKING

Gregarious people tend to have a wide circle of friends; they enjoy social contact, like to be with people, and have a knack for connecting with others and then staying in touch. When they need something they tend spontaneously to think of a person in their circle who might help or might know someone else who could. Similarly, if they hear of something that might interest a friend, they act. They make a quick call. . . . This type of temperament and way of behavior is as old as humanity. And successful use of contacts hasn't gone unnoticed either. There is a common saying to the effect that "it's not what you know but who you know"—which attempts to highlight the greater importance of social connectedness than that of abstract knowledge. A very popular bestseller by Dale Carnegie, the motivational teacher and author, was his 1936 title *How To Make Friends and Influence People*. It was probably not the first book attempting to teach what comes naturally to some. Around about the late 1970s and early 1980s, a time when the baby boom generation was moving into the workforce, the term "networking" appeared. Like Carnegie's method, it was intended to emulate gregarious behavior on purpose and with the goal of gaining benefits in business. Networking has always had an ambiguous character. When it is practiced openly, and the networker's desire to make useful business contacts is up front and visible, it is a kind of salesmanship. Quite a few people practice networking openly. Recipients of such attention are not offended; it is, in fact, slightly flattering to be considered important enough to be courted. When the contact-work is disguised as seeking social links or friendship, however, networking has a faintly calculating and exploitive connotation which, once it becomes known, will have the opposite effect from the one intended.

A rather benign form of networking is "social networking" that people engage in when they have problems finding a mate. This often takes the form of self-exposure in environments likely to have a fair supply of eligible partners. People start going to church again, take classes, or take up communal hobbies and sports. Very often others also participating in such activities are also seeking company. Interactions enable people to get to know each other and to test the water. Linkages are formed because of mutual attraction. Both business and social networking have been formalized, the latter in such interesting forms as "five-minute dating" services.

Business networking, certainly in its earlier stages of development, was viewed by many as a valuable new discovery, a kind of leverage with small inputs that have large consequences. But networking is equivalent to marketing a corporate identity, to "institutional advertising," in that nothing specific is being sold except the networker's existence—and this to one person at a time. Networking requires concentrated attention, record keeping, and the cultivation of the network—hence it costs time and money. If the networker, realizing the high costs, narrows the field of contacts to individuals deemed more likely to be helpful in the future, networking loses

one of its benefits, namely the discovery of unexpected and serendipitous helpers. The more narrowing is introduced, the more networking comes to resemble traditional forms of prospecting, selling, or simply acting in an entrepreneurial manner.

Networking has three basic components: 1) making contacts deliberately; 2) recording contacts made; and 3) cultivating the network. *Making contacts* means willingness to engage people in conversations (e.g., on airplanes, at parties, at concerts) and to expose oneself to others by visiting events, particularly those likely to yield good links. Showing interest in others, paying attention to them, and engaging in give-and-take are, of course, vital. Business conferences and expositions are a good venue for meeting potentially helpful people in a business context; the active networker will "work the booths" and get to know lots of people. *Keeping records* is central because relatively brief contacts will fade from the mind, but notes in a database will bring back the memories. The activity requires time and effort. Calling cards must be keyed in or annotated on the back. The use of keywords for contact retrieval is helpful. *Cultivating contacts* means to renew them from time to time. The more is known about the contact the easier it is to do this. The networker can send contacts clippings that may interest them or call them with some news of interest and thus maintain the linkage. Children's or the contact's birthdays afford opportunities. And so on. The key point regarding cultivation is that networking is a two-way process between any two nodes. The networker must strive to be of help to the contact in order to merit help, down the ways, if it should ever be needed. A natural part of doing this right is to observe the usual courtesies: people should neither be neglected nor smothered and badgered.

Networking in the Internet Age Not surprisingly, the greatest network of them all, the Internet, has been harnessed to the service of networking, both social and business. In the business networking category, for example, networking clubs have made an appearance. Among them are ItsNotWhatYouKnow (INWYK), LinkedIn, Ryze, and ZeroDegrees. According to Catherine Seda, writing in *Enterpreneur*, "It's simple to join, and most clubs are free or have a free level of access. Complete the registration form, invite your colleagues to join, and get on each other's 'connections' lists. The bigger your network, the greater your referral opportunities are, because members click on your contacts to see who you know."

Concerning networking in general, the last word on the subject ultimately belongs to George Ball, once Undersecretary of State in the Kennedy and Johnson

Administrations. Ball famously said: "Nothing propinques like propinquity."

BIBLIOGRAPHY

Horowitz, Alan S. "Social Software: Corporate and Web-based networking software helps people make critical business connections." *Computerworld.* 19 September 2005.

Kiehne, Thomas P. "Social Networking Systems: History, Critique, and Knowledge Management Potentials." University of Texas at Austin. 29 April 2004.

Lemaire, Barbara C. "52 Tips for Networking Success." New Mexico Business Journal. March 2006.

"Networking." *Chartered Management Institute: Checklists: Marketing Strategy.* October 2005.

"No Business in Social Networking." *eWeek.* 4 May 2004.

Pierce, Sarah. "Meet market." *Entrepreneur.* August 2005.

Seda, Catherine. "The Meet Market: Looking for new business leads? Networking clubs on the web make it easy." *Entrepreneur.* August 2004.

Shewmake, Brad. "Secrets of Successful Networking." *InfoWorld.* 3 July 2000.

Wright, Rob. "Before You Make That Next Hire . . .—Firm finds advisers in unlikely places." *VARbusiness.* 21 February 2005.

Darnay, ECDI

NEW ECONOMY

New economy is a term often used in the media to describe changes that have taken place in business since the widespread adoption of the Internet. The term has been applied to a wide range of situations and issues, most notably the rise and fall of high-tech and Internet startup companies. During the 1990s, as the United States experienced a long economic expansion and the stock market soared, many people started to think that basic economic principles no longer applied.

The basic idea behind the new economy was that computer and Internet technology had fundamentally changed the ways of doing business. Analysts and investors alike focused on technology adoption and stock price valuation rather than revenues and long-term business plans when evaluating companies. As a result, high-tech startup firms staged public stock offerings before they had turned a profit and still attracted huge numbers of eager investors. Employees gave up the stability of traditional firms to work long hours at dot-coms in hopes of achieving a windfall in stock options. The workplace at high-flying tech-companies evolved to include rooms full of toys and games to encourage employee creativity.

According to an article in *Business Week,* people made several assumptions about the new economy that ultimately proved to be false. First, they assumed that information technology was so important to business productivity that companies would always buy new systems and software, even in bad times. This belief caused big computer firms to give inflated earnings estimates which, when they were not met, contributed to the fall of the tech-heavy Nasdaq in 2000, signaling the dot-com bust. A popular assumption widespread in the 1990s was that economic growth had become so stable that investors would no longer require a risk premium for stocks over bonds. Some analysts predicted that stock market averages would continue to increase indefinitely. In actuality the tech driven expansion increased the risk and volatility of stocks.

Another assumption concerning the new economy was that companies would no longer lay off workers during downtimes because high-tech labor is so scarce. As a result, many people were lulled into believing that they had greater job security than they actually did. Employees gave up the stability of employment at traditional companies for the big signing bonuses and stock options offered at dot-coms. "It used to be that when you went to a startup, you were an individual with a very-high-risk tolerance and probably had an ideal you were trying to achieve," technology company president Christine Heckart told Paul Prince in *Tele.com.* "But a lot of people with very low risk tolerance left very good, secure jobs at the height of the frenzy to get rich quick in the world of startup-dom. And all of a sudden, before their dreams were achieved, the bubble burst."

When the Internet boom went bust and the U.S. economy slowed significantly in the early 2000s, many companies began laying off workers. As a result, employees began looking for jobs with more conservative companies once again. "Many [job seekers] are bent on finding a company with a future they can believe in, a dependable path to profitability, and a stable working environment where they won't be required to work around the clock for little more than stock options that may never pan out," Prince wrote. "Internet companies and technology startups in general must find a way to prove their stability and financial viability while giving employees some of what they gained in the new-economy environment. That includes room for creativity, as well as a sense of passion and ownership."

Some experts, even in the roaring 90s, claimed that the new economy was largely illusion. It was just the same old economy integrating technological breakthroughs. Supporters of the designation have been hanging in there, however. In an article for *Computerworld,* for instance, Don Tapscott argued that the Internet provides a new infrastructure that lowers transaction costs and encourages collaboration among firms. He said that it creates a new platform for strategic ventures. "Some claim that there isn't a New Economy. E-business and the Internet are a bust, and it's time to go back to tried-and-true principles that have guided commerce and investing for decades, if not centuries," Tapscott wrote. "But heeding such advice would be a stunning mistake. There is a New Economy, with the Internet at its heart. Spurn this notion, and your company's failure is assured."

Tapscott wrote this before the terrorist attacks, of 9/11/2001, in a very real sense changed both the economic as well as the political atmospherics. The recession, already underway, took hold in earnest. Later, the economy began recovering in a unique way, labeled the "job-less recovery." The new economy appeared to have two faces, one radiating electronic light, the other one darkened by staggering trade and budget deficits, layoffs, sluggish job growth, ambiguous globalization, and the displacement of jobs overseas. In the new environment characteristics of the mid-2000s, a reassessment was underway. Surviving dot-coms had consolidated their positions and e-trade was growing at a brisk pace. At the same time economic insecurity was wide spread. Some analysts were looking toward the "next economy" or focusing on the core of the last one: innovation. Whether or not the term will survive another decade remains to be seen.

SEE ALSO *Dot-Coms*

BIBLIOGRAPHY

Atkinson, Robert D. "Is the Next Economy Taking Shape? The United States needs to be preparing now for what it will do when the computer-driven new economy loses momentum." *Issues in Science and Technology.* Winter 2006.

Boatwright, Peter, Jonathan Cagan, and Craig M. Vogel. "Innovate or Else: The new imperative." Ivey Business Journal Online. January-February 2006.

Brock, Terry. "Old Principles, New Ideas Work in New Economy." *Atlanta Business Chronicle.* 3 November 2000.

Lofgren, Ovar, and Robert Willim, eds. *Magic, Culture and the New Economy.* Berg Publishers, 2005.

"The New Economy's New Reality." *Business Week.* 12 March 2001.

Paganetto, Luigi., ed. *Finance Markets, the New Economy and Growth.* Ashgate Publishing Co., 2005.

Prince, Paul. "Conventional Wisdom: Scarred by Dot-Bombs, Employees Are Fleeing New-Economy Flair for Traditional Nine-to-Fives." *Tele.com.* 16 April 2001.

Tapscott, Don. "Don't Doubt the Future of the New Economy." *Computerworld.* 19 February 2001.

Hillstrom, Northern Lights
updated by Darnay, ECDI

NEWSGROUPS AND BLOGS

Newsgroups are online discussion groups that deal with a variety of topics. A common analogy used to describe newsgroups is "online bulletin boards." All newsgroups were originally part of a worldwide network of discussion groups known as Usenet. No one organization "owns" or manages Usenet—it is a self-regulating community of an estimated 30,000 newsgroups, but the exact number is not known since these groups are not regulated by any single entity. Each newsgroup is comprised of a group of users who post public messages or articles to that group. These articles are then organized by subject category and tagged with a standard set of labels for the purpose of distribution from site to site. Each host site pays for its own transmission costs.

Newsgroups differ from discussion lists in that discussion lists are generated via e-mail while newsgroups require a special newsreader software in order to read and post messages. Like discussion lists, newsgroups can be active forums for the exchange of ideas and information, providing a small business with opportunities for networking, learning more about the industry and competition, and marketing and sales possibilities. Newsgroups also tend to be noncommercial (although commercial newsgroups do exist), so it is crucial that participants become aware of a group's purpose, makeup, and rules of etiquette.

Newsgroups are both moderated and unmoderated. A moderated newsgroup is monitored by an administrator who may screen posts to the group, on the basis of appropriateness of content. An unmoderated group is, obviously, not monitored. Articles posted by users appear "as is." Prior to joining or posting to a newsgroup, review its file of frequently asked questions, also known as an FAQ. In addition, some newsgroups will have a charter, which establishes the newsgroup's purpose and general rules. Both the FAQ and the charter can be helpful in selecting a newsgroup in which to participate.

Usenet does not allow commercial messages, and no advertising is allowed for most individual newsgroups. However, business newsgroups generally welcome and encourage commercial discussions, such as debate over products and services, and are useful for this purpose. Commercial information such as product announcements and price lists are commonplace here, providing a small business with the opportunity for free exposure without benefit of a Web site.

The entire archive of Usenet discussion groups dating back to 1995 is now available online from its new host, Google Groups which may be reached at the Web address: http://group.google.com.

HOW TO USE NEWSGROUPS

Participation in a newsgroup requires a special type of software known as a newsreader. For most Internet users, this is a part of a Web browser such as Netscape or Internet Explorer. If you do not have a Web browser, you may need to acquire a newsreader. Check with your Internet service provider (ISP) for more details.

Other computer basics, which may be helpful in using newsgroups, are the concepts of a signature file (.sig) and a plan file (.plan). A signature file is a small file of text which automatically appends to the bottom of all outgoing e-mail messages. At the minimum, a signature file should include an individual's name, company name, and contact information, including e-mail address and URL. The signature file can also be used as a brief advertisement for a company. The key is to keep it short and to the point in order to prompt the reader each time he or she reads your messages. The signature file will then be appended to any message you post on a newsgroup.

A plan file (also called .plan or dot plan, plan.txt, or .profile) is a small information file which is automatically sent to other Internet users in response to a utility command called a "finger." Usually, information sent in response to a finger is comprised of the account owner's name, login name, and some login details such as time of last login. You can provide a more detailed response to a finger by creating a plan file. Some ideas for inclusion in a plan file are the type of business, price and product information, and contact information. Contact your ISP or the maker of your Web browser for more details.

Before using any newsgroups, begin by determining those newsgroups which may be helpful to your business and to which your company or product may be of interest. To ensure the newsgroup to which you wish to post allows these types of posts, be sure to check the newsgroup's FAQ or file of frequently asked questions. Monitoring the newsgroup for a period of time prior to posting is also recommended, in order to ensure you are reaching the correct audience and not ruffling any feathers.

To identify appropriate newsgroups, use the domain or label found in the first part of the name. Business newsgroups are found under the *biz.* domain or label; for example, *biz.imports* might be a business newsgroup comprised of importers. Other newsgroups can serve as sources of information about computers and software (*comp.*), the Internet and networks (*news.*), and so on.

USING A NEWSGROUP FOR FUN AND PROFIT

Newsgroups can be an inexpensive method for a small business to learn more about its industry and competition, gain opportunities for networking, and generate marketing and sales possibilities.

Newsgroups can be a useful source of information about competitors. By reviewing postings and signatures and "fingering" plan files, a small business can determine who its competitors are and get a leg up on new product offerings. This information can also help a business to anticipate trends in the industry as well as to monitor related industries. According to Jill and Matthew Ellsworth, authors of *The New Internet Business Book*, newsgroups are "popular for postings of business networking opportunities, including opportunities to form business partnerships." For a small business looking to expand, newsgroups offer the kind of information distribution that normally only big money can buy.

The Ellsworths suggest that prior to posting a message with commercial content, a small business user should begin by participating in a discussion with well reasoned and to the point comments. This can secure a business's standing in the newsgroup and generate interest within in further posts. The unobtrusive use of a signature or *.sig* with each message provides an opportunity for other individuals and businesses to make contact with the small business, without including commercial content in the message.

Commercial posts to a newsgroup should be short and to the point. Use the subject line to clarify the topic of the post. This will allow other users of the newsgroup to determine if the post is of use to them. Phaedra Hise, author of *Growing Your Business Online*, recommends keeping language simple and without "sales" emphasis, such as "substantial business opportunity." As with most information online, recipients are not interested in wading through a lot of hyperbole to get to the facts. Hise also notes that it is important to be up front about being a company trying to sell a product, if that is your purpose, rather than posing as just another interested user. Her suggestion is to post a message asking if a specific commercial post would be acceptable to participants prior to posting the commercial article.

Using newsgroups can be a simple and rewarding method of finding out more about industry and competition. Used with sensitivity and purpose, they can also serve as an inexpensive path to marketing, sales, and business opportunities for a small business.

BLOGS

Another tool that may offer similar opportunities, again, if used with sensitivity and frankness, is the blog. The term blog is a truncated version of the earlier *weblog*. A blog is basically a journal that is published on the Web. The activity of updating a blog is called "blogging" and the person who keeps a blog is a "blogger." Blogs are typically updated frequently, if not daily, using software that allows people with little or no technical background to update and maintain the blog. Another key component of blogs is that they link to other sites and blogs. In this way, bloggers communicate with one another, establish online communities, and comment on topics and subject in the news.

In 1999, the first blogs appeared, still called weblogs at the time. There were, in 1999, a few hundred such sites but software came out that same year which made it much easier to create a blog and the number of blogs began to grow rapidly. Although nobody knows for sure how many blogs exist, all estimates place the number in the millions as of early 2006, 27 million according to Forrester Research. The community of bloggers, the blogosphere, is large and growing. This has tempted businesses to try and take advantage of this new community to reach out through it to potential customers.

Although blogs by their very nature occupy a noncommercial Web space, many believe that businesses may be able to use blogs to establish a communications avenue with customers and reach those who influence opinion through popular blogs. So far, there are few business blogs but that is changing quickly.

Through a blog a business can disseminate information about its products and services, gather opinions from customers and try to mold brand awareness through interaction with popular (well read) blogs. But, as Ben King explains in an article on the subject published in *The Financial Times,* making a weblog or blog is not simply a matter of sticking the word blog at the top of a column of chatty copy on a normal business Web site. Blogs are more complicated vehicles. "For the better corporate bloggers, the key to success has been to adopt the same software tools as the consumers they are imitating.... Of course, these tools do not guarantee a successful blogging project. No one will read a blog that is not interesting, and no software yet devised can guarantee that. The rapid spontaneous back and forth discourse of the blogosphere is not an easy fit with the slow, cautious approach favored by most corporate marketing departments." King recommends that any company wishing to open a serious dialogue with bloggers be ready to study the blogosphere, to be as open and frank about their objectives as possible, and to use standard software packages to develop the blog site.

Blogging is still relatively young. Whether it develops as a useful new tool for business entities has yet to be determined. Blogging is, however, something that entrepreneurs should follow as an interesting online development and one that may become useful in a business's effort to reach out to its clients. And, many companies are profiting from the blogosphere already, by teaching other companies how to use blogs. Forrester Research, for example, offers a two-day seminar on the subject. They explain the need to learn about blogs this way: "As customers increasingly tune out traditional advertising and turn to new communication channels to fill the void, companies must learn how to join in the conversation. Moreover, besides connecting companies and their customers, blogs are also becoming an invaluable collaboration tool within companies to facilitate knowledge management and cross-functional communications." The blogosphere appears to be a trend worth watching.

SEE ALSO *Electronic Bulletin Boards*

BIBLIOGRAPHY

Blood, Rabecca. *We've Got Blog: How Weblogs Are Changing Our Culture.* Perseus Books Group, 2002.

"Boot Camp—Blogging Fundamentals: Building a Business Strategy." *Forrester Research.* Available from http://www.forrester.com/Events/Overview/1,5158,1365,00.html. 11 May 2006.

Coates, James. "Hamstrung in Search? Give USENET a Try." *Chicago Tribune.* 20 July 2005.

Ellsworth, Jill H. and Matthew V. *The New Internet Business Book.* John Wiley & Sons, 1996.

Glossbrenner, Alfred, and John Rosenberg. *Online Resources for Business.* John Wiley & Sons, 1995.

Hise, Phaedra. *Growing Your Business Online.* Henry Holt and Co., 1996.

King, Ben. "A Company Voice True and Clear, Corporate Blogs." *The Financial Times.* 12 April 2006.

Pethokoukis, James M. "Chatting With Customers." *U.S. News & World Report.* 27 February 2006.

Whyte, Ellen. "Knowing and Joining Newsgroups." *Asia Africa Intelligence Wire.* 10 November 2005.

Hillstrom, Northern Lights
updated by Magee, ECDI

NON-COMPETITION AGREEMENTS

Non-competition agreements are restrictive contracts between employers and employees that 1) prohibit workers from revealing proprietary information about the company to competitors or other outsiders, or 2) forbid workers from themselves competing with their ex-employer for a certain period of time after leaving the company. Non-competition agreements often appear as clauses within a larger employment agreement. Such agreements are a tool that small business owners may use to try and ensure that key personnel do not walk off with company secrets or clients in order to start their own competing business or join an existing competitor in the area. Non-competition agreements have significant deterrent value in many situations, but they may also alienate some potential employees. It is important that their application within a firm is seen to be fair and equitable. Most firms that employ non-competition agreements do so to safeguard sensitive proprietary company information. Sensitive proprietary company information may cover any aspect of a business's operation, including production formulas, processes, and methods; business and marketing plans; pricing strategies; salary structure; customer lists, contracts; intellectual property; and computer systems.

These agreements are also called confidentiality or nondisclosure agreements or, simply, non-compete agreements, and they typically define confidential information, identify ownership rights, and detail employee obligations to ensure that confidentiality is maintained. But there are definite limits on the scope and duration of such covenants. Employers generally cannot use non-compete agreements to keep employees from practicing their trade or profession indefinitely. This is particularly true if the former employees were experienced in the specified occupation before they were hired. But while employees generally have every right to make use of skills and experiences gained in one company when they set off on the next stage of their lives, it is illegal for them to make off with trade secrets of their former place of employment.

Nonetheless, business owners do not always win court cases against ex-employees who pilfer in this area. In some cases, they lose for the simple reason that the business owner never identified the company's confidential or trade secret information. An ex-employee does not have the right to steal company confidential information or trade secrets that are identified as such. However, the ownership of information developed through company procedures must clearly differentiate between what belongs to the employee and what belongs to the company.

More often, however, courts throw out non-competition agreements out of concerns that such clauses constitute restraints of trade or that they force prospective employees to choose between signing or continuing their job search elsewhere. In deciding whether to enforce a non-compete agreement, courts generally focus on two things. First, whether the covenant is ancillary to a valid employment contract. Second, whether the agreement imposes reasonable restrictions in terms of time and geography.

Enforcing Non-Competition Agreements Non-competition covenants are usually enforced by the courts if they are reasonable with respect to time and place and do not unreasonably restrict the former employee's right to employment. Of course, different parties have different conceptions of what constitutes a "reasonable" restriction. Legal experts contend that the courts are far more likely to side with the business owner if he or she does not go overboard on imposing restrictions in the following areas:

- Nature of prohibition—Restrictive covenants often are shaped with an eye toward the type of position that was held by the employee. Companies are more likely to target high-level managers or executives for stringent non-compete measures than programmers, writers, architects or other staffers with specialized skills who have less overall knowledge of the company.

- Duration of agreement—Non-competition agreements are less likely to be enforced if they go beyond one year or so. In addition, according to Susan Gaylord Willis in an aricle in *HRMagazine,* businesses should consider establishing relatively short timeframes if the agreement stipulates a wide geographical scope "because the courts are unlikely to sustain a provision that leaves former employees with no way to earn a living in the field in which they are most experienced."

- Geographic area—It is generally recognized that small business owners have a right to request competition protection from ex-employees in the immediate area in which they operate. Agreements, however, that attempt to forbid ex-workers from setting up a similar business in some distant geographic area or region are likely to be overturned unless the company conducts business in a multi-state area or nationally.

- Restrictions on Solicitation—Who is the employee prohibited from soliciting? This is a question the answer to which should be covered. Is it customers whom the employee personally acquired or any of the company's customers? The narrower the restriction, the more likely a court will enforce it.

- Restrictions on contacting other employees—The courts generally consider it unfair competition for one company to induce employees of another company who have acquired unique technical skills and secret knowledge during their employment to terminate their employment and use their skills and knowledge for the benefit of the competing firm. In such a case the plaintiff company could seek an injunction to prevent its former employees and the competing company from using the proprietary information.

Business owners should keep in mind, however, that attitudes toward non-competition agreements vary considerably from jurisdiction to jurisdiction. No federal statutes exist to regulate these types of agreements with former employees, unless the restrictions violate existing anti-discrimination laws. Instead, each state has its own unique state contract laws. Some courts adhere to a "blue pencil" rule, meaning that they have the authority to edit unduly restrictive agreements so that the scope and/or duration of the agreement is lessened without throwing out the entire contract. Jurisdictions without such options in place, however, typically uphold the agreement in its entirety or strike it down entirely, leaving the employee free to pursue any course he/she wants. Consequently, it is important, when drawing up non-compete agreements, to be sure and investigate the related laws prevalent in the state (or states) in which the company conducts its business.

One way in which the business owner can minimize the danger of having a non-compete agreement overturned in court is to create unique non-competition agreements for each employee affected. A company that performs services locally, such as a diaper service or a carpet cleaning company, may need protection against pirating of customers in its area of operation. In that case, the company would want a covenant that would be of long duration, maybe two years, but limited geographically to the city, county, or metropolitan area. On the other hand, a company in a fast-moving field that sells nationally or internationally, like a software publisher, may prefer a worldwide non-compete of shorter duration. With fast-moving businesses, the chances are the any proprietary information gleaned from the employer would be public knowledge and/or obsolete within six months, and its disclosure after that would no longer pose a threat.

POTENTIAL NEGATIVES

Although a useful tool in securing trade secrets, the non-compete agreement or clause may also complicate the development of loyalty with key employees. Many, when asked to sign such an agreement will feel like the less affluent partner in a couple planning to marry when the richer partner brings up the subject of a prenuptial agreement. Very small businesses have few employees and it is important that each one feel that he or she is a part of the whole, and that the loyalty that they offer is reciprocated.

As Jeffrey Gitomer explains rather colorfully in an article he wrote for *Long Island Business News,* "This single clause alienates and threatens every single salesperson in a manner that they begin their term of employment with a negative feeling toward the employer. 'This guy doesn't trust me and I haven't even stepped foot inside his building.' This feeling of animosity deepens when some form of employment termination occurs. Other lawyers begin huddling as to the enforceability of the non-compete clause and business once again reduces itself to the low-life challenge, 'My lawyer can beat up your lawyer.'"

Small business owners must judge for themselves, and on a case-by-case basis, the value that having non-compete agreements has for their operations.

SEE ALSO *Employment Contracts*

BIBLIOGRAPHY

Fellman, David. "Non-Compete Agreements: Can protect your business." *Wide-Format Imaging.* November, 2005.

Gitomer, Jeffrey. "When You Leave, Hands Off Former Employers Clients." *Long Island Business News.* 11 April 2003.

Orr, Joel N. "The Employment Contract." *Computer-Aided Engineering.* May 2000.

Sidime, Aissitou. "Non-Compete Agreements Are Not Ironclad." *San Antonio Express-News.* 21 November 2005.

Willis, Susan Gaylord. "Protect Your Firm Against Former Employees' Actions." *HRMagazine.* August 1997.

Hillstrom, Northern Lights
updated by Magee, ECDI

NONPROFIT ORGANIZATIONS

Nonprofit organizations are institutions that conduct their affairs for the purpose of assisting other individuals, groups, or causes rather than garnering profits for themselves. Nonprofit groups have no shareholders; do not distribute profits in a way that benefits members, directors, or other individuals in their private capacity; and (often) receive exemption from various taxes in recognition of their contributions to bettering the general social fabric of the community.

Nonprofit groups "are as diverse as the National Football League, Harvard University, and Fannie Mae. A third of these organizations are churches," Roz Ayres-Williams wrote in *Black Enterprise.* "Because nonprofits cover so many fields of interest—charity, religion, health, science, literature, wildlife protection, the arts, even sports—it's easy to find a niche, whatever your calling."

Nonprofit organizations are far more important to the overall U.S. economy than is generally recognized. Indeed, some sources indicate that the sum total of nonprofit groups comprise a third sector of the American economy, along with the private (business) and public (government) sectors. According to a report published by the National Center for Charitable Statistics there were just shy of 1.4 million nonprofit organizations active in the U.S. in 2004, 59 percent were public charities, and 41 percent private foundations.

TYPES OF NONPROFIT ORGANIZATIONS

A wide range of charitable and other institutions are classified as nonprofit organizations under the Internal Revenue Code. Many of these qualify under the definition provided in Section 501(c)(3) of the Code, which stipulates that all of the following qualify for tax-exempt status: "Corporations, and any community chest, fund or foundation, organized and operated exclusively for religious, charitable, scientific, testing for public safety, literary or educational purposes, to foster certain national or international amateur sports competition, or for the prevention of cruelty to children or animals," provided that the institutions adhere to basic standards of behavior and requirements of net earnings allocation.

Charitable Organizations Charitable institutions comprise the bulk of America's nonprofit organizations. These include a wide variety of institutions involved in the realms of poverty assistance (soup kitchens, counseling centers, homeless shelters, etc.); religion (churches and their ancillary possessions, such as cemeteries, radio stations, etc.); science (independent research institutions, universities); health (hospitals, clinics, nursing homes, treatment centers); education (libraries, museums, schools, universities, and other institutions); promotion of social welfare; preservation of natural resources; and promotion of theatre, music, and other fine arts.

Advocacy Organizations "These groups attempt to influence the legislative process and/or the political process, or otherwise champion particular positions," explained Bruce R. Hopkins in The Law of Tax-Exempt Organizations. "They may call themselves 'social welfare organizations' or perhaps 'political action committees.' Not all advocacy is lobbying and not all political activity is political campaign activity. Some of this type of program can be accomplished through a charitable organization, but that outcome is rare where advocacy is the organization's primary undertaking."

Membership Groups This kind of nonprofit organization includes business associations, veterans' groups, and fraternal organizations.

Social/Recreational Organizations Country clubs, hobby and garden clubs, college and university fraternity and sorority organizations, and sports tournament organizations all can qualify as nonprofit organizations, provided that they adhere to basic guidelines of net earnings distribution, etc. Unlike other tax-exempt organizations, however, their investment income is taxable.

"Satellite" Organizations Hopkins pointed out that "some nonprofit organizations are deliberately organized as auxiliaries or subsidiaries of other organizations." Such organizations include cooperatives, retirement and other employee benefit funds, and title-holding companies.

Employee Benefit Funds Some profit-sharing and retirement programs can qualify for tax-exempt status.

ADVANTAGES AND DISADVANTAGES OF INCORPORATING

All nonprofit organizations are faced with the decision of whether or not to incorporate. As Ted Nicholas noted in *The Complete Guide to Nonprofit Corporations,* there are many benefits associated with incorporating: "Some are the same as those commonly enjoyed by *for-profit* business corporations. Others are unique to the nonprofit corporation. Perhaps the greatest advantages of all— granted exclusively to organizations with bona fide nonprofit status—is exemption from taxes at federal, state, and local levels." In addition to tax exemption, Nicholas cited the following as principal advantages of forming a nonprofit corporation:

- Permission to solicit funds—Many nonprofit organizations depend on their ability to solicit funds (in the form of gifts, donations, bequests, etc.) for their very existence. Nicholas noted that whereas some states bestow a fund-raising privilege on nonprofit corporations as soon as their articles of incorporation are filed, other states require groups to fulfill additional obligations before granting permission to solicit funds.

- Low postage rates—Many nonprofit corporations are able to use the U.S. mail system at considerably lower rates than private individuals or for-profit businesses. To secure these lower rates, nonprofits must apply to the Postal Service for a permit, but this is generally not a major hurdle, provided that the nonprofit group has its affairs in order. "The importance of the mailing rate advantage is directly proportional to the volume of mail the nonprofit corporation generates in the course of its business," said Nicholas. "Membership solicitations are usually mailed third class. Nonprofit corporations that rely on membership income can use the mail even more extensively to service their members. So potential savings from a special mailing permit are considerable."

- Exemption from labor rules—Nonprofit organizations enjoy exemption from the various rules and guidelines of union collective bargaining, even if their work force is represented by a union.

- Immunity from tort liability—This advantage is not available in all states, but Nicholas observed that some states still provide nonprofit charitable organizations with immunity to tort liability. "It is important to recognize, however, that where it exists, the immunity protects only the nonprofit corporation—not the agent or employee where negligence injures someone."

In addition, nonprofit corporations enjoy certain advantages that are also bestowed on for-profit corporations. These include legal life (nonprofit corporations are guaranteed the same rights and powers of individuals), limited personal liability, continued existence beyond the involvement of original founders, increased public recognition, readily available information on operations, ability to establish employee benefits programs, and flexibility in financial recordkeeping.

But there are also certain disadvantages associated with incorporating. Nicholas cited the following as principal drawbacks:

- Costs associated with incorporation—Although these costs are usually not too excessive, especially for organizations of any size, incorporation does generally involve some extra costs.

- Additional bureaucracy—"An unincorporated nonprofit organization can be structured so informally that its operators could keep whatever records they chose on the backs of envelopes or as scribbled notes on paper napkins," said Nicholas. "Not so in a nonprofit corporation. As a legal entity, the corporation is subject to some specific recordkeeping obligations set down by the state in which it is incorporated." In addition, there are certain activity guidelines to which incorporated organizations must adhere.

- Sacrifice of personal control—Depending on where incorporation takes place, the organization may have to appoint a board of directors to oversee operations (although founders of nonprofit groups can often exercise considerable control in influencing the composition of the board and the flavor of corporate bylaws and articles of incorporation). Founders and directors of unincorporated groups are under no such obligation.

"Generally, the advantages far outweigh the disadvantages," summarized Hopkins. "The disadvantages stem from the fact that incorporation entails an affirmative act of the state government: It 'charters' the entity. In exchange for the grant of corporate status, the state usually expects certain forms of compliance by the organization, such as adherence to rules of operation, an initial filing fee, annual reports, and annual fees. However, these costs are frequently nominal and the reporting requirements are usually not extensive."

ORGANIZING A NONPROFIT ORGANIZATION

"Being enthusiastic, imaginative, and creative about establishing a nonprofit organization is one thing," observed Hopkins. "Actually forming the entity and making it operational is another. For better or worse, the exercise is much like establishing one's own business. It is a big and important undertaking, and it should be done carefully and properly. The label 'nonprofit' does not mean 'no planning.' Forming a nonprofit organization is as serious as starting up a new company." He recommended that individuals interested in forming a nonprofit organization begin by determining the organization's main purpose and functions. The next step involves choosing a category of tax-exempt status to match its functions. From there, would-be founders need to study a wide range of issues, many of which are also basic considerations for small business owners and other individuals involved in for-profit endeavors. Often, the counsel of a good attorney and/or accountant can be valuable at this stage. Primary actions include the following:

- Decide what legal form the organization will take (public charity or private foundation, incorporated or unincorporated, etc.)

- If incorporating, take necessary legal steps to make that decision a reality (devise bylaws, submit articles of incorporation, etc.)

- Investigate options and decide on principal organization programs and emphases

- Determine the leadership of the organization (directors, officers, primary staff positions)

- Define compensation for such positions

- Find a physical location for the organization (factors here can range from variations in state law to availability of reasonable office space)

- Put together a strategic plan for achieving organization goals at both community and larger levels

- Decide how to go about funding those goals (gifts, grants, unrelated income, etc.?)

- Determine which media avenues will be best for publicizing the organization's goals and securing volunteers

- Devise an ongoing business plan that 1) serves as a blueprint for institution goals and development, and 2) can be periodically reviewed and adjusted as appropriate.

FUNDRAISING

Nonprofit institutions can turn to several different methodologies to raise funds designed to support their mission. This is especially true for nonprofits that have tax-exempt status, because it permits donors to deduct their gifts from their own personal income tax liability. Major avenues of fundraising used by nonprofit organizations include the following: fundraising events (dinners, dances, charity auctions, etc.); direct mail solicitation; foundation grant solicitation; in-person solicitation (door-to-door canvassing, etc.); telemarketing; and planned giving (this includes bequests, which are given to the organization after the donor's death, and gifts made during the donor's lifetime through trusts or other agreements).

Effective Solicitation and Revenue Management In order to prosper, nonprofit institutions not only need to know where the sources of funding are, they also need to know how to solicit those funds and how to effectively manage that revenue when it comes into their possession.

Certainly, solicitation of donors (whether they take the form of individuals, corporations, or foundations) is a vital component of many organizations' operations. After all, most activities can only be executed with funding. But many nonprofit institutions are not accomplished in this area, either because they do not allocate adequate resources or because of problems with execution. Writing in *Fund Raising Management,* Robert Hartsook listed the following as common solicitation errors that nonprofit groups make:

- Not listening to donor expectations

- Unwarranted assumption of a donor's willingness to contribute

- Lack of follow-up after initial contact

- Inadequate research on potential donors and their ability to contribute

- Inability to close presentation with donor commitment

- Neglecting to establish rapport with potential donors prior to solicitation

- Framing solicitation as "begging" rather than as a reasonable request for help with a worthy cause

- Neglecting to tailor solicitation to individual donors

- Approaching potential donors without knowledge of how donations impact them in the realms of tax deductions, etc.

Of course, even the most effective solicitation campaigns will wither if the organization proves unable to allocate its financial and other resources wisely. Fundraising begins by determining exactly what financial and human resources are needed to accomplish the organization's mission. In the short run, fundraising may be successful based on the organization's vision and the promises it makes to help its clients and community. In the longer run, contributors will want to see results. Performance is what counts. Indeed, an organization may be devoted to addressing a perfectly worthwhile cause, and its membership may be enthusiastic and dedicated, but most nonprofit organizations—and especially charitable ones—rely on funds from outside sources. And poorly run nonprofits will find that their revenue streams will dry up quickly if they do not leverage their funds wisely.

TRENDS IN THE NONPROFIT WORLD

Observers have pointed to several trends in the nonprofit community that are expected to continue or develop in the next few years. These range from changes in fundraising targets to expanded competition between nonprofit organizations to regulatory developments. The following is a listing of some issues that nonprofit organizations will be tracking in the coming years:

1. Increased emphasis on retaining donors—According to Robert F. Hartsook of *Fund Raising Management,* "Non-profit organizations will focus on the renewal of donors rather than on the acquisition of new ones. As our country's population growth begins to plateau, it will be necessary for non-profits to more keenly target their marketing efforts."

2. Corporate giving—Corporate giving to philanthropic causes has emerged as a major marketing tool for corporations in recent years, and this source of funds is expected to assume even greater importance as federal and state governments pare back their spending on various social programs.

3. Increased reliance on volunteerism—Reduced government expenditures on social programs is also expected to spur increased demand for volunteers

who can meet the expected growth in organization activity. This need will be especially acute for non-profit organizations primarily involved in charitable activities.

4. Competition with for-profit enterprises—Many analysts believe that this issue could have tremendous implications for nonprofit organizations in the future. Spurred by representatives of the for-profit small business community, regulatory agencies have undertaken more extensive reviews of ways in which some activities of tax-exempt groups allegedly damage the fortunes of for-profit businesses (who, of course, are subject to local, state, and federal taxes). Much of the controversy in this area centers around the definition and treatment of unrelated business income (income generated by tax-exempt organizations from ventures that are unrelated to their primary mission). "There is a potential that all of this will lead to nothing," wrote Hopkins, "or it could bring an in-depth inquiry into the federal and state law distinctions between for-profit and non-profit organizations, the rationale for the tax exemption of certain types of nonprofit organizations, and whether some existing tax exemptions are outmoded and some new forms of tax exemption are required."

5. Continued emphasis on planned giving— "Nonprofit organizations will enjoy a significant increase in realized bequests," said Hartsook. "This will happen as a result of planned giving programs put in place 10 to 15 years ago. With the evidence at hand of how successful planned giving can be, many institutions will increase their dependence on this methodology."

6. Continued dominance of women in the nonprofit community—According to *Fund Raising Management,* women occupied approximately two-thirds of all staff positions in nonprofit organizations in the mid-1990s, a percentage that may increase in the coming years.

7. Increase in government regulation among nonprofits—Government oversight of fundraising activities may continue to increase at both the state and federal levels, at least in part because of the solicitation practices of some "fringe philanthropic groups," said Hartsook. "Unfortunately, telemarketing for non-profit organizations has received a bad name because of fringe philanthropic organizations that solicit and collect large sums of money—while dedicating most of those funds to the costs of fund raising and salaries." According to Hopkins, this increase in government regulation may be especially evident at the state level: "States that have formerly foregone the desire for a fund-raising law have suddenly

decided that their citizens now need one. States with fund-raising regulation laws are making them tougher. Those who administer these laws—the state regulators—are applying them with new vigor."

8. Growth in self-regulation within the nonprofit community—Self-regulation within various sectors of nonprofit operation underwent a noticeable increase in the late 1980s and early 1990s, and this trend is expected to continue with the introduction of new certification systems, codes of ethics, and watchdog groups.

9. Major donors will maximize benefits from contributions—According to Hartsook, major donors will increasingly incorporate aspects of planned giving into their philanthropic efforts in order to maximize their tax deductions. "Significant gift giving will incorporate an aspect of planned gifts in order to afford the donor maximum tax deductions," he stated. "As the level of tax recognition diminishes, major donors will turn to this methodology in order to maximize tax advantages."

BIBLIOGRAPHY

Ayres-Williams, Roz. "The Changing Face of Nonprofits." *Black Enterprise.* May 1998.

Bray, Ilona M. *Effective Fundraising For Nonprofits: Real World Strategies That Work.* Nolo, March 2005.

Drucker, Peter F. *Managing the Non-profit Organization: Principles and Practices.* Harper Business, 1990.

Hartsook, Robert F. "Predictions for 1997." *Fund Raising Management.* January 1997.

Hartsook, Robert F. "Top Ten Solicitation Mistakes." *Fund Raising Management.* March 1997.

Hopkins, Bruce R. *The Law of Tax-Exempt Organizations.* Eighth Edition. John Wiley & Sons, 2003

Hopkins, Bruce R. *A Legal Guide to Starting and Managing a Nonprofit Organization.* Second Edition. John Wiley & Sons, 1993.

Mancuso, Anthony. *How to Form a Nonprofit Corporation.* Seventh Edition. Nolo, July 2005.

Nicholas, Ted. *The Complete Guide to Nonprofit Corporations.* Enterprise Dearborn, 1993.

Schoenhals, G. Roger. *On My Way in Planned Giving.* Planned Giving Today, 1995.

"U.S. and State Profiles." National Center For Charitable Statistics. Available from http://nccsdataweb.urban.org/PubApps/profileStateList.htm. Retrieved on 2 May 2006.

Warwick, Mal. "Outsider-In Marketing: A New Way to Look at Marketing for Nonprofits." *Nonprofit World.* 1997.

Hillstrom, Northern Lights
updated by Magee, ECDI

NONPROFIT ORGANIZATIONS, AND HUMAN RESOURCES MANAGEMENT

Staffing decisions are among the most important decisions that nonprofit organizations make. Just as businesses and organizations of all sizes and areas of operation rely on their personnel to execute their strategies and advance their goals, so too do nonprofit groups. It follows, then, that nonprofit organizations need to attend to the same tasks as profit-seeking companies do when they turn to the challenges of establishing and maintaining a solid work force. To accomplish this, nonprofit organizations have to address the following six personnel issues, as delineated in the Small Business Administration publication *Human Resources Management:*

- Assessing personnel needs
- Recruiting personnel
- Screening personnel
- Selecting and hiring personnel
- Orienting new employees to the organization
- Deciding compensation issues

"An effective non-profit manager *must* try to get more out of the people he or she has," wrote Peter F. Drucker in *Managing the Non-Profit Organization.* "The yield from the human resource really determines the organization's performance. And that's decided by the basic people decisions: whom we hire and whom we fire; where we place people, and whom we promote. The quality of these human decisions largely determines whether the organization is being run seriously, whether its mission, its values, and its objectives are real and meaningful to people rather than just public relations and rhetoric."

ASSESSING ORGANIZATION NEEDS

A key component of any endeavor to build a quality core of personnel is an honest assessment of current and future internal needs and external influences. Leaders and managers of nonprofit organizations should study workload history, trends in the larger philanthropic community, pertinent changes in the environment in which they operate (layoffs, plant closings, introduction of a new organization with a similar mission, legislative developments, etc.), personnel demands associated with current and planned initiatives, operating budget and costs, and the quality and quantity of the area worker pool, both for volunteer and staff positions. Moreover, all of these factors need to be studied within the framework of the organization's overarching mission statement. As many

nonprofit leaders have noted, adherence to other general business principles (sound fiscal management, retention of good employees through good compensation packages, etc.) is of little solace if the organization loses sight of its mission—it's reason for being—in the process.

Writing in *Human Resources Management,* Gary Roberts, Carlotta Roberts, and Gary Seldon noted several fundamental business principles concerning assessment of personnel needs that apply to nonprofits as well. These principles include:

- Fill positions with people who are willing and able to take on the job.
- Providing accurate and realistic job and skill specifications for each position helps ensure that it will be filled by someone capable of handling the responsibilities associated with that position.
- Written job descriptions are essential to communicating job expectations.
- Employees who are chosen because they are the best available candidates are far more likely to have a positive impact than those who are chosen on the basis of friendship or expediency.
- Performance appraisals, when coupled with specific job expectations, help boost performance.

"The process of selecting a competent person for each position is best accomplished through a systematic definition of the requirements for each job, including the skills, knowledge and other qualifications that employees must possess to perform each task," the authors concluded. "To guarantee that personnel needs are adequately specified, 1) conduct a job analysis, 2) develop a written job description, and 3) prepare a job specification."

RECRUITING, SCREENING, AND SELECTING ORGANIZATION WORK FORCE

Recruiting For many nonprofit organizations, publicizing its very existence is the most important step that it can take in its efforts to recruit staff and volunteers alike. This is especially true if one wishes to encourage volunteers to become involved. Volunteers are the life-blood of countless nonprofit organizations, for they attend to the basic tasks that need performing, from paperwork to transportation of goods and/or services to maintenance. Writing in *Quality Management in the Nonprofit World,* Larry W. Kennedy noted that "they supply valuable human resources which, when properly engaged, can be worth tens of thousands of dollars in conserved personnel costs to even the smallest organizations."

Nonprofit groups rely on two basic avenues to publicize their work and their staffing needs: local media (newspapers, newsletters, radio advertising, billboards, etc.) and other community organizations (municipal governments, churches, civic groups, other nonprofit organizations, etc.) Many nonprofit groups have found that contact with some community organizations, particularly churches and civic groups, can be particularly rewarding since these organizations already have members that may be predisposed toward lending a hand.

Screening and Selection The interviewing process is another essential component of successful staffing for nonprofit groups. This holds true for volunteers as well as for officers, directors, and paid staff. Indeed, Larry W. Kennedy remarked in his book that "volunteers should be recruited and interviewed systematically the same way you would recruit paid staff. An orderly and professional approach to volunteer management will pay off handsomely for your organization. What you do in the recruitment phase of your work will set the standard for volunteer performance. If you are disciplined and well organized, you will often attract more qualified volunteers."

Managers of nonprofit organizations should make sure that they do the following when engaged in the process of staffing, screening and selection:

- Recognize that *all* personnel, whether they are heading up your organization's annual fundraising drive or lending a hand for a few hours every other Saturday, have an impact on the group's performance. Certainly, some positions are more important than others but countless nonprofit managers can attest to the fact that an underperforming, unethical, or unpleasant individual can have an enormously negative impact on organization morale and/or organization reputation in the community. This can be true of the occasional volunteer as well as the full-time staff member.

- Use an application form that covers all pertinent areas of the applicant's background.

- Ensure that your screening process provides information about an individual's skills, attitudes, and knowledge.

- Try to determine if the applicant or would-be volunteer is interested in the organization for legitimate reasons (professional development and/or advancement, genuine interest in your group's mission) or primarily for reasons that may not advance your organization's cause (loneliness, corporate burnout, etc.).

- Objectively evaluate prospective employees and volunteers based on criteria established in the organization's job specifications.

- Be realistic in putting together your volunteer work force. "Managers cause most of the problems with volunteers by making unreasonable assumptions about their intentions and capabilities," wrote Kennedy. An organization that sets the bar too high in its expectations of volunteers (in terms of services provided, hours volunteered, etc.) may find itself with a severe shortage of this potentially valuable resource.

- Recognizing that would-be volunteers and employees bring both assets and negative attributes to your organization, nonprofit groups should be flexible in accommodating those strengths and weaknesses. "If you want people to perform in an organization, you have to use their strengths—not emphasize their weaknesses," said Drucker.

Organizations that pay attention to these guidelines will be far more likely to enjoy positive and lasting relationships with their volunteers and staff than those who fill their human resource needs in haphazard fashion. As Kennedy said, "the time to begin evaluating the probable reliability of human resources is prior to their insertion into your internal structure."

ORIENTING STAFF AND VOLUNTEERS TO THE ORGANIZATION

Training is a vital component of successful nonprofit organization management. But many nonprofit managers fail to recognize that training initiatives should be built for all members of the organization, not just those who are salaried employees. "Specialized training should be designed for every person in the organization, including board members and volunteers," contended Kennedy. "The principles of quality management should be reinforced in each phase of training, with generous opportunities given to the trainees to talk about their questions and concerns.... If we select and train people with well-established and consistently implemented guidelines, we greatly increase the potential for team building. Beyond that, a common objective, a commitment to quality, a sincere concern for the team members, and a dedicated leader can cause wonderful things to happen. When those factors are not present, things can occur that are not so pleasant.... Volunteers who are shoddily intruded into an organization's processes or who are not well managed can create chaotic inconsistency in services. The additional, time, energy, and money needed to clean up well-intentioned but off-target volunteer efforts can quickly offset any gains provided by their services."

Poor Performers Many nonprofit organizations find that at one point or another, they must address poor performance by a member of the organization. When that person is a paid member of the staff, dealing with the issue is in many respects no different than it would be in the for-profit world. Organizations of all types have a right to assume certain standards of performance from paid employees, and if that standard is not met, they should by all means take the steps necessary to ensure that they receive the necessary level of performance from that position, even if that means firing a poor worker.

The situation becomes more complex when the person is a volunteer, however. The volunteer worker is an essential element of many nonprofit organizations, and the primary characteristics of volunteerism—selfless service—make it difficult to remove poor performers. In addition, insensitive handling of one volunteer can have a negative impact on other volunteers upon which your organization relies. Nonetheless, Kennedy stated that "volunteers should be held accountable just as though they were being paid top dollar to work. This does not mean that you can be careless about people's feelings. Even for-profit managers have learned that managing and supervising requires certain social graces and sensitivity to every individual. However, the reluctance of nonprofit managers to hold volunteers accountable to reasonable levels of performance or to terminate bad volunteer relationships can be their downfall."

Drucker noted that most nonprofits will, sooner or later, have to deal with people "who volunteer because they are profoundly lonely. When it works, these volunteers can do a great deal for the organization—and the organization, by giving them a community, gives even more back to them. But sometimes these people for psychological or emotional reasons simply cannot work with other people; they are noisy, intrusive, abrasive, rude. Non-profit executives have to face up to that reality." If all else fails, such disruptive volunteers should be asked to leave. Otherwise, other members of the organization, including the executive, will find that their capacity to contribute is diminished.

Drucker agreed that dismissing an under-performing or otherwise undesirable volunteer can be a difficult task. "The non-profit executive is always inclined to be reluctant to let a non-producer go. You feel he or she is a comrade-in-arms and make all kinds of excuses," he granted. He contended that nonprofit managers should adhere to a basic guideline in such instances: "If they try, they deserve another chance. If they don't try, make *sure* they leave.... An effective non-profit executive owes it to the organization to have a competent staff wherever performance is needed. To allow non-performers to stay on means letting down both the organization and the cause."

COMPENSATING THE ORGANIZATION'S EMPLOYEES AND VOLUNTEERS

Tangible Benefits As Ted Nicholas noted in *The Complete Guide to Nonprofit Corporations*, nonprofit corporations may establish fringe benefits programs for their employees. People that can be covered under these programs include not only staff personnel, but also directors and officers. "The benefits," wrote Nicholas, "can be as attractive as those provided by for-profit business corporations. In addition, the benefits can be far more economical for the corporation and beneficial to the employees than any program that could be offered by unincorporated organizations. The nonprofit corporation can establish an employee pension and retirement income plan. It can provide for sick pay and vacation pay. It may arrange for group life, accident and health insurance coverage for its officers and employees. It can elect to cover its employees' personal medical expenses that are not covered by the group insurance plans, provided that the corporation can pay all or part of the cost of the various employee benefits it sets up. It can require some contribution from the employees covered by the fringes."

Bruce Hopkins observed in his *Legal Guide to Starting and Managing a Nonprofit Organization* that "there is a tendency in our society to expect employees of nonprofit organizations to work for levels and types of compensation that are less than those paid to employees of for-profit organizations. Somehow, the nonprofit characteristics of the organization become transferred to the 'nonprofit' employee." Hopkins goes on to note that while this perception may indeed be a reality because of the budgetary constraints under which many nonprofit organizations operate, in other instances employees do not feel entitled to compensation levels that are offered to employees of for-profit businesses. In fact, some nonprofit groups feel no obligation whatsoever to provide comparable levels of compensation in terms of salary, benefits, etc., relying instead on the altruistic leanings of those who become involved. Organizations that operate under these assumptions are short sighted and run the risk of losing out on many talented people. Indeed, Hopkins pointed out that "many nonprofit organizations, particularly the larger ones (universities, hospitals, major charities, and trade associations), require sophisticated and talented employees. Because these individuals are not likely to want to be 'nonprofit' employees, nonprofit and for-profit organizations compete for the same pool of talented persons. This competition extends not only to salaries but also to benefits and retirement programs."

Experts indicate that although the compensation packages that are offered by nonprofit organizations are constrained by the so-called private inurement doctrine, which holds that the profits realized by a nonprofit organization can not be passed along to private individuals (as dividends are passed along to shareholders in a for-profit enterprise), they can still offer attractive compensation packages to employees provided that they are judged to be "reasonable." When weighing whether it considers compensation to be reasonable, the Internal Revenue Service studies whether compensation arrangements exceed a certain percentage of the organization's gross revenues. Excessive compensation can be penalized by imposition of additional taxes and fines, but the most damage to organizations who do this can often be found in the realm of reputation; few allegations are more damaging to a nonprofit organization's community standing than the charge that it is bestowing excessive compensation (in the form of salary, country club memberships, etc.) to top executives or others.

Intangible Benefits Successful managers of nonprofit organizations recognize that the people who compose their organizations' work force—volunteers, employees, officers, and directors alike—are often participating in the group at least in part for altruistic reasons. Indeed, Drucker noted that "although successful business executives have learned that workers are not entirely motivated by paychecks or promotions—they need more—the need is even greater in non-profit institutions. Even paid staff in these organizations need achievement, the satisfaction of service, or they become alienated and even hostile. After all, what's the point of working in a non-profit institution if one doesn't make a clear contribution?"

Leaders of nonprofit organizations, then, need to always be on the look out for ways in which they can show their paid staff, their volunteers, and their leadership how their involvement in the organization is making a difference, whether the group is involved with ministering to the economically disadvantaged or devoted to protecting a beloved natural resource. As Father Leo Bartel, Vicar for Social Ministry of the Catholic Diocese of Rockford, Illinois, told Drucker, "We give [volunteers] opportunities to deepen in themselves and in each other the sense of how important the things are that they are doing."

BIBLIOGRAPHY

Bray, Ilona M. *Effective Fundraising For Nonprofits: Real World Strategies That Work.* Nolo, March 2005.

Drucker, Peter F. *Managing the Non-profit Organization: Principles and Practices.* Reprint Edition. Collins, 1992.

Hartsook, Robert F. "Predictions for 1997." *Fund Raising Management.* January 1997.

Hopkins, Bruce R. *A Legal Guide to Starting and Managing a Nonprofit Organization.* Second Edition. John Wiley & Sons, 1993.

Kennedy, Larry W. *Quality Management in the Nonprofit World: Combining Compassion and Performance to Meet Client Needs and Improve Finances.* Jossey-Bass, 1991.

Mancuso, Anthony. *How to Form a Nonprofit Corporation.* Seventh Edition. Nolo, July 2005.

Nicholas, Ted. *The Complete Guide to Nonprofit Corporations.* Enterprise Dearborn, 1993.

Pakroo, Peri. *Starting and Building a Nonprofit: A Practical Guide.* Nolo, April 2005.

Roberts, Gary, Gary Seldon, and Carlotta Roberts. *Human Resources Management.* Small Business Administration, n.d.

Hillstrom, Northern Lights
updated by Magee, ECDI

NONPROFIT ORGANIZATIONS, AND TAXES

In recognition of the "public good"-oriented goals and objectives of nonprofit organizations, U.S. law grants these groups a number of special privileges. Of these, perhaps none is more valuable than the bestowal of tax-exempt status. Such status basically means that the organization's income and assets are not subject to federal taxes, and federal exemptions often (though not always) pave the way for state and local tax exemptions as well. For-profit enterprises, on the other hand, are subject to local, state, and federal taxation.

One of the main objectives of private enterprise is the pursuit of profit for the owners of the enterprise. Profits gained through private enterprise are taxable. Activities undertaken by tax-exempt organizations have as their objective obtaining profits for use in the continued provision of services for the public good. Profits earned by organizations as a result of their tax-exempt missions are not taxable. Nonprofit organizations can engage in virtually any business enterprise in the fulfillment of their mission objectives without jeopardizing their tax-exempt status. When these organizations undertake activities that are *unrelated* to their stated missions, than the profits generated from those activities are taxable. It should be noted, however, that complete exemption from federal taxation does not *automatically* mean that the organization avoids other kinds of taxation, such as state and/or local income taxes, sales taxes, and property taxes.

Bruce R. Hopkins noted in his *Legal Guide to Starting and Managing a Nonprofit Organization* that not all nonprofit organizations qualify as tax-exempt organizations: "Nearly every tax-exempt organization is a non-profit organization, but not all nonprofit organizations are eligible to be tax-exempt," he said. "The concept of a nonprofit organization is broader than that of a tax-exempt organization. Some types of non-profit organizations (such as mutual, self-help type entities) do not, as a matter of federal law, qualify for tax-exempt status." While the majority of nonprofit organizations are presumed to be tax-exempt in nature, there are exceptions to that premise. The terms *nonprofit* and *charitable* are not interchangeable. A nonprofit organization is not necessarily charitably motivated while an organization that is truly charitable in nature may well be a profit-making enterprise. Both types of organizations may be entitled to tax-exempt status from the IRS. For example, a religious and apostolic association, even if it is organized for profit, and a teacher's retirement fund association, which is operated to produce profits for its beneficiaries, are both eligible for tax exemptions.

DEVELOPMENT OF NONPROFIT TAX-EXEMPT STATUS

Until the end of the 19th century, all U.S. entities—whether they were private individuals or businesses—were exempt from taxation unless they were subject to a particular tax levy. The Tariff Act of 1894, however, changed that situation irrevocably. That legislation imposed a flat 2 percent tax rate on all U.S. corporations, but in recognition of the fundamentally different goals and objectives of for-profit businesses and charitable and educational groups, the bill exempted the latter organizations from the tax. The important aspect of this legislation is that organizations involved in activities and those whose profits would be used for altruistic purposes were specifically excluded from the requirement to share the profits of their work through taxation. The initial emphasis of tax exemption was to protect those organizations involved in charitable activities from taxation, and it has remained as the central function of tax-exempt law to this day.

In recent years, the United States has seen a dramatic increase in the number of tax-exempt organizations operating around the country. Indeed, the rise in the number of churches, nursing homes, hospitals, chambers of commerce, charitable organizations, and social service agencies in many communities has led some observers to voice concern about the tax-base stability of some areas. Some cities and towns find that a substantial portion of their entire lot of privately held real estate is owned by tax-exempt organizations. In such areas there may not be any revenue flowing into local tax coffers from a taxable base. This state of affairs has led some corporate and individual taxpayers to register complaints about the "free ride" that some exempt organizations enjoy. Even

the tax-exempt status of churches, protected from the very beginning of the tax code, has been questioned in recent years.

NONPROFITS AND PROFITABILITY

Many people operate under a fundamental misconception about nonprofit organizations and revenue. The word 'nonprofit' may carry with it an inference about profit that causes some people to think profitability by a nonprofit organization is illegal. This is not at all the case. Nonprofit, tax-exempt organizations are free to do anything a for-profit company might do in pursuit of their goals, *including making profits*. The law is designed to provide all the benefits of a free-market system plus the special favor of tax incentives for individuals and corporations who want to contribute financially to our efforts. Not only may nonprofit organizations operate enterprises profitably as tax-exempt organizations, they may also prosper through the patronage of others.

But there are significant stipulations in place concerning the *distribution* of those profits that must be met for an organization to claim tax-exempt status. These are delineated in Section 501 of the Internal Revenue Code:

1. The organization must be organized and operated exclusively for one or more of the following purposes: for religious, educational, charitable, scientific, or literary purposes; to test for public safety; to encourage amateur sports competition (either national or international); to prevent cruelty to children or animals; to lessen the burdens of government (through creation and/or maintenance of public buildings, monuments, parks, natural attractions, etc.); and to maintain public confidence in the legal system. Naturally, the organization may be involved in more than one of the above areas.

2. Net earnings garnered by the organization may not, under any circumstances, be distributed for the private benefit of individuals.

3. The organization may not participate in any way in any political campaigns, directly or indirectly (although it can use a political action committee or PAC to engage in political activities that are not political campaign activities).

4. The organization may not spend "excessive" time or energy on efforts to influence legislation. It is a common misconception that nonprofits may not engage in legislative activities, but as Hopkins stated, "a charity is permitted to engage in far more lobbying efforts than most people realize. Indeed, under some circumstances, a charitable organization can spend more than one-fifth of its funds for legislative ends."

FILING FOR TAX-EXEMPT STATUS

A wide variety of organizations are eligible for tax-exempt status because of their goals and activities. These include the following:

- Corporations organized under an Act of Congress (includes federal credit unions)
- Title-holding corporations for exempt organizations
- Religious organizations
- Educational organizations
- Charitable organizations
- Scientific organizations
- Literary organizations
- Public safety organizations
- Organizations devoted to national or international amateur sports competitions
- Organizations devoted to preventing cruelty to children
- Organizations devoted to preventing cruelty to animals
- Civic leagues
- Social welfare organizations
- Local associations
- Labor organizations
- Agricultural and horticultural organizations
- Business leagues, chambers of commerce, and real estate boards
- Social and recreational clubs
- Fraternal beneficiary societies and associations
- Voluntary employees' beneficiary associations
- Domestic fraternal societies and associations
- Teachers' retirement fund associations
- Benevolent life insurance associations
- Mutual irrigation or ditch companies
- Mutual or cooperative telephone companies
- Cemetery companies
- State-chartered credit unions and mutual reserve funds
- Mutual insurance companies or associations
- Cooperative agricultural organizations
- Supplemental unemployment benefit trusts
- Employee funded pension trusts (provided they were created prior to June 25, 1959)

- Organizations of past or present Armed Forces members
- Group legal services organizations
- Black lung benefit trusts
- Withdrawal liability payment funds
- Veteran's organizations (provided they were created prior to 1880)
- Religious and apostolic associations
- Cooperative hospital service organizations
- Cooperating service groups of operating educational organizations
- Farmer's cooperatives
- Political organizations (parties, committees, etc.)
- Homeowners' associations

Some organizations such as churches, associations of churches, and auxiliary agencies of churches—like mission societies and youth groups—are generally considered automatically tax-exempt. They are not required to request this status from the government taxing agencies. Virtually all other kinds of organizations that fit legal definitions of eligibility for tax-exempt status because of their special benevolent purposes and goals cannot make the same assumption. They must ask the Internal Revenue Service to officially recognize their tax-exempt status."

To do so, organizations have to file an application for tax exemption with the IRS (nonprofit organizations may also have to make separate applications to state and local tax agencies if they wish to secure exemptions from taxes imposed by those jurisdictions). In most instances, this filing step is a mere formality; approval of tax exemption is almost always based on the IRS's ruling on the organization's exemption application (the primary legal basis for all tax exemptions is Section 501 of the Internal Revenue Code of 1954). Organizations that have their exemption application approved, then, will often find that they are free from tax obligations at the local and state levels as well.

Experts note that while some nonprofit organizations are exempted from paying certain taxes, that does not mean that they have no filing obligations. "Despite the favoritism the law frequently bestows on nonprofit organizations, the reporting requirements are not one of them, particularly when the organization is tax-exempt," said Hopkins. "The annual information return that most tax-exempt organizations have to file with the IRS is far more extensive than the tax returns most commercial businesses must file. Then, there may be several state annual reports (if the organization is doing business in more than one state) and the state annual charitable solicitation act reports (perhaps over 40 of them)." Given this reality, most nonprofit organizations choose to use the services of professional attorneys and accountants in compiling and delivering these reports.

UNRELATED BUSINESS INCOME

United States law has long differentiated between the activities of tax-exempt organizations that are related to the performance of tax-exempt functions and those that are not. Income garnered from these latter activities is subject to taxation. For incorporated organizations, net revenue from unrelated activities is subject to federal corporate income tax law, while for organizations that are not incorporated, this revenue—commonly referred to as "unrelated business income"—is subject to the canon of federal tax law on individuals. "The objective of the unrelated business income tax is to prevent unfair competition between tax-exempt organizations and for-profit, commercial enterprises," explained Hopkins. "The rules are intended to place the unrelated business activities of an exempt organization on the same tax basis as those of a nonexempt business with which it competes.... An organization's tax exemption will be denied or revoked if an inappropriate portion of its activities is not promoting one or more of its exempt purposes."

This area of tax law, noted Hopkins, has been one marked by upheaval and change in recent years. "As tax-exempt organizations struggle to generate additional income in these days of declining governmental support, proposed adverse tax reform, more sophisticated management, and greater pressure for more services, [tax-exempt organizations] are increasingly drawn to service-provider activities, some of which may be unrelated to their exempt purposes. The growth of service-provider activities, the increasing tendencies of the courts to find activities unrelated because they are 'commercial,' and the unrest over 'unfair competition' between tax-exempt organizations and for-profit entities—all of these are clear evidence that this aspect of the law of tax-exempt organizations is constantly evolving and will be reshaped." One emerging issue involves use of the Internet by nonprofit organizations. Some experts have expressed concern that linking to non-exempt sites, soliciting contributions online, or disseminating protected information could put an entity's exempt status at risk.

BIBLIOGRAPHY

Anderson, Alice M., and Robert A. Wexler. "Making Use of the Internet—Issues for Tax-Exempt Organizations." *Journal of Taxation*. May 2000.

Baldas, Tresa. "Profiting at Nonprofits? The IRS gets tough on charities after reports of high pay for some nonprofit executives." *Corporate Counsel*. December 2004.

Hopkins, Bruce R. *The Law of Tax-Exempt Organizations.* Eighth Edition. John Wiley & Sons, April 2003

Hopkins, Bruce R. *A Legal Guide to Starting and Managing a Nonprofit Organization.* Second Edition. John Wiley & Sons, 1993.

Jacobs, Jerald A., and Karen L. Cipriani. "Establishing an Affiliated Organization." *Association Management.* June 2000.

Pakroo, Peri. *Starting and Building a Nonprofit.* Nolo, April 2005.

Schlesinger, Sanford J. "Unrelated Business Income and the Charitable Organization." *Estate Planning.* May 2000.

Wright, Carolyn D. "IRS Request for Comments on EO Web Activity: Good Start." *Tax Notes.* 23 October 2000.

Hillstrom, Northern Lights
updated by Magee, ECDI

NONQUALIFIED DEFERRED COMPENSATION PLANS

Nonqualified deferred compensation plans are used by businesses to supplement existing qualified plans and provide an extra benefit to key personnel and highly compensated employees. In small businesses, this usually includes the owner and founder. Broadly defined, a nonqualified deferred compensation plan (NDCP) is a contractual agreement in which a participant agrees to be paid in a future year for services rendered this year. Deferred compensation payments generally commence upon termination of employment (e.g., retirement) or pre-retirement death or disability. Nonqualified deferred compensation plans are often geared toward anticipated retirement in order to provide cash payments to the retiree and to defer taxation to a year when the recipient is in a lower tax bracket.

There are two broad categories of nonqualified deferred compensation plans: elective and non-elective. In an elective NDCP an employee chooses to receive less current salary and bonus compensation than he or she would otherwise receive, postponing the receipt of that compensation until a future tax year. Non-elective NDCPs are plans in which the employer funds the benefit and does not reduce current compensation in order to fund future payments. Such plans are, in essence, post-termination salary continuation plans. The argument behind such non-elective plans, funded by employers, is the retention of key employees.

One feature of nonqualified deferred compensation plans that has made them a very popular tool for use by large corporations and some small businesses, is the fact that they are not limited by the same non-discrimination rules imposed on qualified plans. NDCPs may be offered to a select group of employees only, unlike qualified plans to which all employees are eligible by definition. Consequently, the cost of this benefit is lower since it accrues to fewer people. Companies have recognized other advantages associated with nonqualified deferred compensation plans as well. Administrative costs, for example, are lower with a nonqualified plan than for similar qualified plans. Until December 31, 2004, NDCP plans had no need to report to the IRS and were only required to send a one-time letter to the U.S. Department of Labor stating that the plan is in place and reporting the number of participants it covered. With the passage of the American Jobs Creation Act of 2004, an additional reporting requirement was added. Companies with NDCPs now must also report to the IRS amounts deferred and earned under the plan on Form W-2 or 1099, even if these amounts are not included as taxable income.

There are two main types of nonqualified deferred compensation plans from which small business owners may choose: supplemental executive retirement plans (SERPs) and deferred savings plans. These two options share several common characteristics, but there are also important differences between the two. For example, eligibility for both plans may be based on the executive's salary, position, or both. But whereas deferred savings plans require employees to contribute their own earnings, executives that are placed in SERPs receive their compensation from their employers.

SUPPLEMENTAL EXECUTIVE RETIREMENT PLANS (SERPS)

SERPs generally are structured to mirror defined-benefit pension plans. They promise a stated benefit from the employer at retirement. SERP benefits, which can be allocated in conjunction with other benefit plans like qualified-plan savings and Social Security benefits, may be calculated in any number of ways. Employers may choose to pay their executives a flat dollar amount for an agreed-upon number of years; a percentage of their salary at retirement multiplied by their years with the company; or a fixed percentage of their salary at retirement for a given number of years. Companies also have the option of funding SERPs either through general assets (at the time of the employee's retirement) or via sinking funds or corporate-owned life insurance (COLI).

Sinking Funds Businesses that utilize the sinking fund method allocate money on an annual basis to a fund that will cover benefit payments as they come due. This money can be invested by the company as it sees fit, but it is nonetheless earmarked for retirement payments.

Corporate-Owned Life Insurance (COLI) Under the COLI funding method, businesses buy life insurance plans on those directors and executives that they wish to compensate. Each company pays the premiums on the purchased policies, and as each executive retires, the firm pays out his or her benefits from operating assets for a previously established period of time. The key benefit for the small business owner under the COLI arrangement is that his or her business is designated the sole beneficiary of the tax-free proceeds from the insurance policy. Upon the death of an executive for whom such a policy has been acquired, the company is reimbursed for some or all of the costs of the insurance plan—the actual benefits paid, the insurance premiums. Entrepreneurs should note, however, that their firm will not receive a tax deduction for its contributions to a SERP until the director or executive actually receives the benefit payments (businesses using qualified compensation plans, on the other hand, receive deductions in the current year).

DEFERRED SAVINGS PLANS

Deferred savings plans are similar to 401(k) plans in that affected employees are allowed to set aside a portion of their salary (usually up to 25 percent) and bonuses (as much as 100 percent) to put into the plan. This money is directly deducted from employee paychecks, and taxes are not levied on the money until the employee receives it. Plans are set up to cover obligations in one of two ways. First, the company simply guarantees a fixed rate of return on the deferred contributions, which come from its general operating assets at the time of payout. Second, the company ties each executive's savings to the performance of a particular mutual fund which the executive selects from among several offered by your plan. Companies that set up a fixed rate of return on the deferrals may invest the monies in question however they wish, provided they ultimately meet their payout obligations. In addition, consultants note that some small businesses (and large ones as well) have established a policy wherein they will offer matching funds on employee deferrals or add profit-sharing or incentive-based contributions.

Executives with deferred savings plans have a variety of payout options to choose from, although the number of options was reduced with the passage of the American Jobs Creation Act of 2004. Distribution of plan funds is allowed in the following ways under the American Jobs Creation Act: separation of service; disability; a specific time under the plan that is defined in the plan documentation; a change in company ownership or control of the corporation, and unforeseen emergency (as defined in the statute); or death. If an executive enrolled in this type of plan dies or is fired from the company prior to retirement, he or she (or their family) receives a lump-sum payout of their benefits. It should be noted, however, that nonqualified deferred compensation plans will not be protected from creditors if the company that created them files for bankruptcy.

PLANS FOR TAX-EXEMPT ORGANIZATIONS

Nonqualified deferred compensation plans may also be utilized by tax-exempt organizations, but managers of these entities should be aware that for tax-exempt organizations, such plans are subject to considerably more stringent Internal Revenue Service (IRS) regulations. Nonetheless, by subjecting employer-paid, tax-deferred compensation to risk of forfeiture or by paying the required taxes for these plans, tax-exempt organizations are able to develop workable alternatives for funding nonqualified deferred compensation plans.

Funding Options Tax-exempt organizations seeking to fund employer-paid deferred compensation plans can choose from a number of options:

1. Unfunded benefits that vest at retirement. Under this strategy, employers provide supplemental retirement benefit plans with assets that are not dedicated to funding the plan. If the employer runs into financial trouble before the employee or employees covered under the plan retire, it can use those assets to pay off its creditors.

2. Unfunded benefits that vest during employment. Vesting occurs according to plan objectives as defined by the employer. As vesting occurs, the employer provides a cash distribution to cover taxes. The ultimate benefit at retirement is reduced to reflect the annual distribution of a portion of the benefit to pay taxes.

3. Benefits funded with deferred annuities. Under this arrangement, the small business owner would acquire deferred annuities in the name of participating employees. The employer that takes this track usually provides cash distributions to cover the tax on both the contribution and the cash distribution, since contributions to the annuity are regarded by the IRS as taxable income.

Similarly, organizations looking to fund voluntary nonqualified deferred compensation plans may pursue the following funding alternatives:

1. Traditional deferred compensation plans with non-compete clauses. These do not pay out money until the end of a specified period of time. If an employee

who is part of the plan leaves the company to join a competing business before that specified period of time elapses, then the employee forfeits the contributions. Analysts note, however, that this choice is often not a palatable one for employers, since employees will likely resent efforts to impose such restrictions.

2. Deferred annuities. Under this alternative, employees purchase deferred annuities with after-tax income, and they do not owe taxes on annuity earnings until payout.

3. Deferral using after-tax dollars. Under this plan, employees are immediately vested and taxed on the deferred compensation. After-tax compensation is subsequently placed in a mutual fund by the employer, but it is maintained for the benefit of the employee.

SEE ALSO *Employee Benefits; Employee Compensation; Recruiting; Retirement Planning*

BIBLIOGRAPHY

"The 401(k) Paper Chase." *Business Week.* 27 March 2000.

Altieri, Mark P. "Nonqualified Deferred Compensation Plans." *The CPA Journal.* February 2005.

Madsen, Dawilla, and Dominick Pizzano. "The 401(k) Gamble." *Strategic Finance.* December 1999.

Olson, John. "A Powerful Weapon in the War for Talent." *National Underwriter Life & Health-Financial Services Edition.* 23 June 2003.

Postal, Arthur D. "New Tax Bill Changes Rules on Nonqualified Deferred Comp Plans." *National Underwriter Life & Health.* 18 October 2004.

U.S. Department of the Treasury. Internal Revenue Service. "Nonqualified Deferred Compensation Audit Techniques Guide." Available from http://www.irs.gov/businesses/corporations/article/0,,id=134878,00.html. 10 January 2005.

Van Dyke, George. "Examining Your 401 K." *Business Credit.* January 2000.

Hillstrom, Northern Lights
updated by Magee, ECDI

NONTRADITIONAL FINANCING SOURCES

Entrepreneurs can turn to a variety of sources to finance the establishment or expansion of their businesses. Common sources of business capital include personal savings, loans from friends and relatives, loans from financial institutions such as banks or credit unions, loans from commercial finance companies, assistance from venture capital firms or investment clubs, loans from the Small Business Administration and other government agencies, and personal or corporate credit cards. But for some businesspeople, these sources of financing are either unavailable, or available with restrictions or provisions that are either impossible for the company to meet or deemed excessive by the business owner. In such instances, the capital-hungry entrepreneur has the option of pursuing a number of nontraditional financing sources to secure the money that his or her company needs. Some of the more common nontraditional financing sources include selling assets, borrowing against the cash value of a life insurance policy, and taking out a second mortgage on a home or other property.

Selling Assets Some entrepreneurs choose to sell some of their personal or business assets in order to finance the opening or continued existence of their enterprises. Generally, business owners who have already established the viability of their firms and are looking to expand their operations do not have to take this sometimes dramatic course of action, since their records will often allow them to secure capital from other sources, either private or public. Whether selling personal or business assets, the small business owner should take a rational approach. Some entrepreneurs, desperate to secure money, end up selling business assets that are important to basic business operations. In such instances, the entrepreneur may end up accelerating rather than halting the demise of his or her business. Only nonessential equipment and inventory should be sold. Similarly, care should be taken in the selling of personal assets. Items like boats, antiques, etc. can fetch a decent price. But before embarking on this course of action, the entrepreneur should objectively study whether the resulting income will be sufficient, or whether the enterprise's financial straits are an indication of fundamental flaws.

Borrowing Against the Cash Value of Your Life Insurance Entrepreneurs who have a whole life policy have the option of borrowing against the policy (this is not an option for holders of term insurance). This can be an effective means of securing capital provided that the owner has held the policy for several years, thus giving it some cash value. Insurers may let policyholders borrow as much as 90 percent of the value of the policy. As long as the policyholder continues to meet his or her premium payment obligations, the policy will remain intact. Interest rates on such loans are generally not outrageous, but if the policyholder dies during the period in which he or she has a loan on the policy, benefits are usually dramatically reduced.

Second Mortgage Some entrepreneurs secure financing by taking out a second mortgage on their home. This risky alternative does provide the homeowner with a couple of advantages: interest on the mortgage is tax deductible and is usually lower than what he or she would pay with a credit card or an unsecured loan. But if the business ultimately fails, this method of financing could result in the loss of your home. Using a second mortgage as a vehicle for financing a company is very risky and is best for people who want to borrow all the money they need at one time and secure fixed, equal payments.

Other Possible Sources of Financing Some entrepreneurs obtain financing for growth and expansion through franchising or licensing. Basically, they get money by selling the rights to a unique business or product to other companies. Other small business owners are able to form alliances or partnerships with other firms that have a vested interest in their success, such as customers, suppliers, or distributors. These business owners may obtain funds from their partners through cooperative work agreements, barter arrangements, or trade credit. The Internet provides another potential source of leads for loans from nontraditional sources. For example, America's Business Funding Directory, at http://www.businessfinance.com, includes a searchable database of nontraditional funding sources.

Experts recommend using nontraditional financing to start a business or provide funds during periods of rapid growth, but emphasize that small business owners should consider it a temporary arrangement. The use of nontraditional financing is a last resort move and a business owner should make every effort possible to limit the time frame during which such financing is used.

SEE ALSO *Financial Planning*

BIBLIOGRAPHY

Caracciolo, Daniel, and Christian Fuccinos. "Non-Traditional Financing Alternatives and Their Tax Incentives." *International Tax Review.* December 2004.

"Creative Financing." *Phoenix Business Journal.* 29 September 2000.

"Despite Higher Interest Rates, More Fast Growth CEOs Report New Bank Loans and Increased Credit Lines: Many more considering non-traditional financing in next 12 months." *Business Credit.* February 2005.

U.S. Small Business Administration. Press Release. "Woman Business Owner Uses Non-traditional Financing for Non-traditional Career." 14 September 2005.

Vanac, Mary. "Alternative Financing Helps Small Businesses Bridge the Lending Gap." *Business News.* 15 August 1999.

Hillstrom, Northern Lights
updated by Magee, ECDI

NONVERBAL COMMUNICATION

Nonverbal communication—such as facial expressions, gestures, posture, and tone of voice—is an important component of most human communications, including, of course, business communications. Most people use nonverbal signals when communicating. Even the blind use nonverbal communications to aid in both sending and receiving messages since nonverbal techniques includes such things as tone of voice and physical proximity. Understanding nonverbal communication techniques can help a small business owner to get a message across or successfully interpret a message received from another person. On the other hand, nonverbal communication can also send signals that interfere with the effective presentation or reception of messages. "Sometimes nonverbal messages contradict the verbal; often they express true feelings more accurately than the spoken or written language," Herta A. Murphy and Herbert W. Hildebrandt noted in their book *Effective Business Communications.* In fact, studies have shown that between 60 and 90 percent of a message's effect may come from nonverbal clues. Therefore, it is important for small business owners and managers to be aware of the nonverbal messages they send and to develop the skill of reading the nonverbal messages contained in the behavior of others. There are three main elements of nonverbal communication: appearance, body language, and sounds.

Appearance In oral forms of communication, the appearance of both the speaker and the surroundings are vital to the successful conveyance of a message. "Whether you are speaking to one person face to face or to a group in a meeting, personal appearance and the appearance of the surroundings convey nonverbal stimuli that affect attitudes—even emotions—toward the spoken words," according to Murphy and Hildebrandt. For example, a speaker's clothing, hairstyle, use of cosmetics, neatness, and stature may cause a listener to form impressions about her occupation, socioeconomic level, competence, etc. Similarly, such details of the surroundings as room size, furnishings, decorations, lighting, and windows can affect a listener's attitudes toward the speaker and the message being presented. The importance of nonverbal clues in surroundings can be seen in the desire of business managers to have a corner office with a view rather than a cubicle in a crowded work area.

Body Language Body language, and particularly facial expressions, can provide important information that may not be contained in the verbal portion of the communication. Facial expressions are especially helpful as they may show hidden emotions that contradict verbal statements. For example, an employee may deny having knowledge of a problem, but also have a fearful expression and glance around guiltily. Other forms of body language that may provide communication clues include posture and gestures. For example, a manager who puts his feet up on the desk may convey an impression of status and confidence, while an employee who leans forward to listen may convey interest. Gestures can add emphasis and improve understanding when used sparingly, but the continual use of gestures can distract listeners and convey nervousness.

Sounds Finally, the tone, rate, and volume of a speaker's voice can convey different meanings, as can sounds like laughing, throat clearing, or humming. It is also important to note that perfume or other odors contribute to a listener's impressions, as does physical contact between the speaker and the listener. Silence, or the lack of sound, is a form of nonverbal communication as well. Silence can communicate a lack of understanding or even hard feelings in a face-to-face discussion.

BIBLIOGRAPHY

Irwin, David. *Effective Business Communications.* Thorogood Publishing, 2001.

Mintzberg, Henry. *Managers Not MBAs: A Hard Look at the Soft Practice of Managing and Management Development.* Berrett-Koehler Publishers, May 2004.

Murphy, Herta A., and Herbert W. Hildebrandt. *Effective Business Communications.* Seventh Edition. McGraw-Hill, 1997.

"The Silent Factor." *Denver Business Journal.* 18 August 2000.

Strugatch, Warren. "More Than Words Can Say." *LI Business News.* 26 May 2000.

Hillstrom, Northern Lights
updated by Magee, ECDI

NORTH AMERICAN FREE TRADE AGREEMENT (NAFTA)

The North American Free Trade Agreement (NAFTA) is a treaty entered into by the United States, Canada, and Mexico; it went into effect on January 1, 1994. (Free trade had existed between the U.S. and Canada since 1989; NAFTA broadened that arrangement.) On that day, the three countries became the largest free market in the world—the combined economies of the three nations at that time measured $6 trillion and directly affected more than 365 million people. NAFTA was created to eliminate tariff barriers to agricultural, manufacturing, and services; to remove investment restrictions; and to protect intellectual property rights. This was to be done while also addressing environmental and labor concerns (although many observers charge that the three governments have been lax in ensuring environmental and labor safeguards since the agreement went into effect). Small businesses were among those that were expected to benefit the most from the lowering of trade barriers since it would make doing business in Mexico and Canada less expensive and would reduce the red tape needed to import or export goods.

Highlights of NAFTA included:

- Tariff elimination for qualifying products. Before NAFTA, tariffs of 30 percent or higher on export goods to Mexico were common, as were long delays caused by paperwork. Additionally, Mexican tariffs on U.S.-made products were, on average, 250 percent higher than U.S. duties on Mexican products. NAFTA addressed this imbalance by phasing out tariffs over 15 years. Approximately 50 percent of the tariffs were abolished immediately when the agreement took effect, and the remaining tariffs were targeted for gradual elimination. Among the areas specifically covered by NAFTA are construction, engineering, accounting, advertising, consulting/management, architecture, health-care management, commercial education, and tourism.

- Elimination of nontariff barriers by 2008. This includes opening the border and interior of Mexico to U.S. truckers and streamlining border processing and licensing requirements. Nontariff barriers were the biggest obstacle to conducting business in Mexico that small exporters faced.

- Establishment of standards. The three NAFTA countries agreed to toughen health, safety, and industrial standards to the highest existing standards among the three countries (which were always U.S. or Canadian). Also, national standards could no longer be used as a barrier to free trade. The speed of export-product inspections and certifications was also improved.

- Supplemental agreements. To ease concerns that Mexico's low wage scale would cause U.S. companies to shift production to that country, and to ensure that Mexico's increasing industrialization would not lead to rampant pollution, special side agreements were included in NAFTA. Under those agreements, the three countries agreed to establish commissions to handle labor and environmental issues. The commissions have the power to impose steep fines against any of the three governments that failed to impose its laws consistently. Environmental and

labor groups from both the United States and Canada, however, have repeatedly charged that the regulations and guidelines detailed in these supplemental agreements have not been enforced.

- Tariff reduction for motor vehicles and auto parts and automobile rules of origin.

- Expanded telecommunications trade.

- Reduced textile and apparel barriers.

- More free trade in agriculture. Mexican import licenses were immediately abolished, with most additional tariffs phased out over a 10-year period.

- Expanded trade in financial services.

- Opening of insurance markets.

- Increased investment opportunities.

- Liberalized regulation of land transportation.

- Increased protection of intellectual property rights. NAFTA stipulated that, for the first time, Mexico had to provide a very high level of protection for intellectual property rights. This is especially helpful in fields such as computer software and chemical production. Mexican firms will no longer be able to steal intellectual property from companies and create a "Mexican" version of a product.

- Expanded the rights of American firms to make bids on Mexican and Canadian government procurement contracts.

One of the key provisions of NAFTA provided "national goods" status to products imported from other NAFTA countries. No state, provincial, or local governments could impose taxes or tariffs on those goods. In addition, customs duties were either eliminated at the time of the agreement or scheduled to be phased out in 5 or 10 equal stages. The one exception to the phase out was specified sensitive items, for which the phase-out period would be 15 years.

Supporters championed NAFTA because it opened up Mexican markets to U.S. companies like never before. The Mexican market is growing rapidly, which promises more export opportunities, which in turn means more jobs. Supporters, though, had a difficult time convincing the American public that NAFTA would do more good than harm. Their main effort centered on convincing people that all consumers benefit from the widest possible choice of products at the lowest possible price—which means that consumers would be the biggest beneficiaries of lowered trade barriers. The U.S. Chamber of Commerce, which represents the interests of small businesses, was one of the most active supporters of NAFTA, organizing the owners and employees of small and mid-size businesses to support the agreement.

This support was key in countering the efforts of organized labor to stop the agreement.

NAFTA AND SMALL BUSINESS

Analysts agree that NAFTA has opened up new opportunities for small and mid-size businesses. Mexican consumers spend more each year on U.S. products than their counterparts in Japan and Europe, so the stakes for business owners are high. (Most of the studies of NAFTA concentrate on the effects of U.S. business with Mexico. Trade with Canada has also been enhanced, but the passage of the trade agreement did not have as great an impact on the already liberal trade practices that America and its northern neighbor abided by.)

Some small businesses were affected directly by NAFTA. In the past, larger firms always had an advantage over small ones because the large companies could afford to build and maintain offices and/or manufacturing plants in Mexico, thereby avoiding many of the old trade restrictions on exports. In addition, pre-NAFTA laws stipulated that U.S. service providers that wanted to do business in Mexico had to establish a physical presence there, which was simply too expensive for small firms to do. Small firms were stuck—they could not afford to build, nor could they afford the export tariffs. NAFTA leveled the playing field by letting small firms export to Mexico at the same cost as the large firms and by eliminating the requirement that a business establish a physical presence in Mexico in order to do business there. The lifting of these restrictions meant that vast new markets were suddenly open to small businesses that had previously done business only in the United States. This was regarded as especially important for small businesses that produced goods or services that had matured in U.S. markets.

Still, small firms interested in conducting business in Mexico have to recognize that Mexican business regulations, hiring practices, employee benefit requirements, taxation schedules, and accounting principles all include features that are unique to that country. Small businesses, then, should familiarize themselves with Mexico's foundation of business rules and traditions—not to mention the demographics culture of the marketplace—before committing resources to this region.

OPPOSITION TO NAFTA

Much organized opposition to NAFTA centered on the fear that the abolishment of trade barriers would spur U.S. firms to pack up and move to Mexico to take advantage of cheap labor. This concern grew during the early years of the 2000s as the economy went through a recession and the recover that followed turned out to be a "jobless recovery." Opposition to NAFTA was also strong among

environmental groups, who contended that the treaty's anti-pollution elements were woefully inadequate. This criticism has not abated since NAFTA's implementation. Indeed, both Mexico and Canada have been repeatedly cited for environmental malfeasance.

Controversy over the treaty's environmental enforcement provisions remained strong in the late 1990s. In fact, North American business interests have sought to weaken a key NAFTA side accord on environmental protections and enforcement. This accord—one of the few provisions welcomed by environmental groups—allows groups and ordinary citizens to accuse member nations of failing to enforce their own environmental laws. A tri-national Commission for Environmental Cooperation is charged with investigating these allegations and issuing public reports. "That process is slow, but the embarrassment factor has proven surprisingly high," noted *Business Week*. As of 2005, the U.S. government has expressed opposition to revisions in the NAFTA agreement. But the Canadian government and many businesses in all three countries continue to work to change this accord.

THE EFFECTS OF NAFTA

Since NAFTA's passage, American business interests have often expressed great satisfaction with the agreement. Trade has grown sharply between the three nations who are parties to NAFTA but that increase of trade activity has resulted in rising trade deficits for the U.S. with both Canada and Mexico—the U.S. imports more from Mexico and Canada than it exports to these trading partners. Critics of the agreement argue that NAFTA has been at least partially responsible for these trade deficits as well as the striking loss of manufacturing jobs experienced in the U.S. over the last decade. But, manufacturing jobs began to decline before the NAFTA agreement. The debate about NAFTA continues.

Isolating the effects of NAFTA within the larger economy is impossible. It is difficult, for example, to say with certainty what percentage of the current U.S. trade deficit—which stood at a record $65,677 million at the end of 2005—is directly attributable to NAFTA. It is also difficult to say what percentage of the 3.3 million manufacturing jobs lost in the U.S. between 1998 and 2004 are the result of NAFTA and what percent would have occurred without this trade agreement. It is not even possible to say with certainly that the increased trade activity among the NAFTA nations is entirely the result of the trade agreement. Those who favor the agreement usually claim credit for NAFTA for the increased trade activity and reject the idea that the agreement resulted in job losses or the rising trade deficit with Canada and Mexico, ($8,039 million and $4,263 million respectively in

December 2005). Those who are critical of the agreement usually link it to these deficits and to job losses as well.

What is clear is that NAFTA remains a lightening rod for political opinions about globalization and free trade generally. Opposition to NAFTA has grown and has made it far more difficult, politically, to pass other similar free trade agreements. This was demonstrated clearly in the summer of 2005 when the Central American Free Trade Agreement (CAFTA) was stalled in Congress for lack of support. Two journalists, Dawn Gilbertson and Jonathan J. Higuera, writing in the *Arizona Republic* at the ten year anniversary of NAFTA, summed things up this way: "The Reality of NAFTA at 10 is this: a still-developing story of winners and losers, split largely by where you work and what you make." The same may be said about the effects of NAFTA on small businesses. For some it has been an opportunity to grow and for others a challenge to be met.

SEE ALSO *Globalization*

BIBLIOGRAPHY

Barreto, Hector V. "New Trade Opportunities a Boon to Small Biz." *San Diego Business Journal.* 13 June 2005.

Gilbertson, Dawn, and Jonathan J. Higuera. "Decade of NAFTA Brings Pains, Gains." *The Arizona Republic.* 18 June 2003.

"A Green Thumb in NAFTA's Eye?" *Business Week.* 12 June 2000.

Hagenbaugh, Barbara. "U.S. Manufacturing Jobs Fading Away Fast." *USA Today* 12 December 2002.

Jette, Julie. "NAFTA at Ten: Did It Work?" *Harvard Business School Working Knowledge.* 12 April 2004.

Rowe, Claudia. "Ten Years Later, A Look at NAFTA's Promise, Flaws." *Seattle Post-Intelligencer.* 6 January 2004.

U.S. Department of Commerce. Bureau of the Census, Foreign Trade Statistics. "New 2005 Data Updates." Available from http://www.census.gov/foreign-trade/statistics/. Retrieved on 17 April 2006.

U. S. Federal Reserve Bank of Dallas. Canas, Jesus, and Roberto Coronado. "U.S.—Mexico Trade: Are We Still Connected?" Available from http://www.dallasfed.org/research/busfront/bus0403a.html. Retrieved on 18 April 2006.

Hillstrom, Northern Lights
updated by Magee, ECDI

NORTH AMERICAN INDUSTRY CLASSIFICATION SYSTEM (NAICS)

The North American Industry Classification System (NAICS) is an industry coding system designed to facilitate the collection, analysis, and presentation of economic data in the United States, Canada, and Mexico, all member nations of the North American Free Trade Agreement (NAFTA). First implemented in 1997, the NAICS is the successor to the Standard Industrial Classification (SIC) system, which had been used by U.S. agencies to compile and track national business data, and economic activity data generally, for more than six decades.

Collecting information about and reporting on something as large as the U.S. economy is an enormous task. Organizing this task by creating a hierarchical classification for the incoming data is an essential part of tackling the job. NAICS is the newest industry classification system being used to do this job in the U.S. Experienced business analysts, journalists, and economists are all familiar with both the SIC and NAICS systems. They are also frequent users of the wealth of data that U.S. federal government agencies collect and publish regularly. When those data are economic in nature—for example, average labor unit cost for bicycle manufacturing, annual output by the financial services industry, or number of gas stations in a metropolitan area—they are organized by NAICS codes. The easiest way to access these data sources is to use the classification system used to organize them, the NAICS.

The U.S. Census Bureau touts the NAICS as "a unique, all-new system for classifying business establishments. It is the first economic classification system to be constructed based on a single economic concept. Economic units that use like processes to produce goods or services are grouped together. This 'production-oriented' system means that statistical agencies in the United States will produce data that can be used for measuring productivity, unit labor costs, and the capital intensity of production; constructing input-output relationships; and estimating employment-output relationships and other such statistics that require that inputs and outputs be used together.... NAICS is forward looking and flexible, anticipating increasing globalization and providing enhanced industry comparability among the NAFTA trading partners while recognizing important national industries and providing for periodic updates through three-country review [the United States, Canada, and Mexico]. NAICS recognizes the structural and technological changes occurring in the economies of the three North American countries and provides the means to measure these changes well into the next millennium."

THE SIC SYSTEM

The predecessor to the NAICS—the Standard Industrial Classification system—was the first comprehensive classification system used by American government agencies to organize economic statistics.

The SIC system was an establishment-based industry classification system that classified each establishment (defined as a single physical location at which economic activity occurs) according to its primary activity. For each of these recognized industries, the government kept detailed statistics in such areas as employment, payroll, receipts, profits, and capital investment.

After its unveiling in 1937, the SIC system's universe of economic data became a heavily utilized tool for conducting business research and tracking economic trends. Government agencies, nongovernmental organizations, and private businesses alike made extensive use of the data. But despite periodic updates and revisions to the SIC classification system, its inadequacies became more glaring with the passage of time.

The fundamental problem was that the SIC system was based on concepts developed in an era of American history—the 1930s and 1940s—when manufacturing was the dominant economic engine. Many service activities were not separately identified, and as service-oriented businesses became more important, SIC revisions did not keep pace. The economic statistics contained in the SIC system thus became progressively more incomplete as newly technologies and areas of endeavor were not covered. This under representation of important economic sectors was further exacerbated by the SIC's framework, which gathered unrelated industries together into similar categories.

Despite its imperfections, however, the Standard Industrial Classification system continued to be widely used by business marketers through the 1990s. The SIC data did provide them with a method for classifying organizational customers and gauging industry trends (especially in manufacturing sectors), and it remained the only source of these important economic statistics. In addition, the 1987 revision added approximately 20 new service industries and tweaked several manufacturing industry classifications to reflect changing technological realities. Ultimately, however, the SIC system remained an outmoded one. For example, of the 1004 industries recognized in the 1987 Standard Industrial Classification program, nearly half (459) represented manufacturing, even though manufacturing's share of the U.S. Gross Domestic Product (GDP) has shrunk to less than 20 percent of the nation's total. "The SIC did a superb job of describing and detailing the structure of the footwear industry in the United States, but failed to recognize and account for the information age in which we live and work," summarized Carole Ambler in *Business America*. "The SIC scattered the production of high-tech products such as computers, semiconductors, and communications equipment in groupings of industrial machinery and electrical equipment, and included the reproduction of shrink-wrapped software in the same industry with software publishing."

The various inadequacies of the SIC system finally prompted America's public and private sectors to unite and call for a new industry classification system that would be based on the reality of today's service-based, Internet-driven, technology-powered global economy. The ultimate shape and character of this new system was dramatically influenced by the implementation of the North American Free Trade Agreement between the United States, Canada, and Mexico in 1994. This major trade treaty highlighted the need to develop a new industry classification system that would take into consideration the increased flow of goods, services, and capital between the three North American nations. Moreover, it emphasized the need for a system that could provide users with country-to-country comparability of statistical information.

CREATION OF THE NAICS

The North American Industrial Classification System was a cooperative effort that required the active involvement of U.S., Canadian, and Mexican government agencies. The primary U.S. body involved in NAICS creation and implementation was the Economic Classification Policy Committee (ECPC) of the Office of Management and Budget, but the Bureau of Economic Analysis, the Bureau of Labor Statistics, and the Census Bureau all contributed to the initiative. Statistics Canada and Mexico's Instituto Nacional de Estadistica, Geografia e Informatica (INEGI), meanwhile, worked with the ECPC to ensure that the new system would be able to provide comparable statistics for industries in place in all three countries, while simultaneously providing flexibility so that each country could accommodate industries unique to its own economy.

In 1997 the Office of Management and Budget (OMB) announced its decision to adopt the new NAICS as the industry classification system used by statistical agencies of the United States. During this same period, the nuts and bolts of the NAICS were unveiled to largely positive reviews. "NAICS recognizes new, emerging, and advanced technology industries; NAICS acknowledges the information age in which Americans live and work; NAICS considers over 150 new service industries; NAICS provides for comparability of data with other NAFTA trading partners; and NAICS is based on a production-oriented conceptual framework," observed *Energy Conservation News*. Marketing professionals were particularly pleased with the new proposed system. "NAICS is based on an entirely different concept than SIC," stated Suzanne Sabrosk in *Searcher*. "Its goals were not only to identify new industries but to acknowledge a more consistent economic principle—namely types of production activities performed, rather than the mix of production and market-based categories in the SIC. This process orientation, as opposed to an approach stressing supply and demand, accounts for the presentation of more detail in the service sector. NAICS classifies industries based on what the industries do, rather than whom the industries serve. For example, NAICS classifies bakeries that bake and sell on the premises under manufacturing, instead of as retailers, because of the way in which the bakeries produce their baked goods."

FRAMEWORK OF THE NAICS

The North American Industry Classification System defines a total of 1,170 industries in the United States. Nearly 360 of these industries are delineated for the first time (many in high-tech fields such as fiber optic cable manufacturing and satellite communications), while 565 are service-based. These industries are grouped in 20 industrial sectors that are progressively subdivided into three-digit subsectors, four-digit industry groups, and five-digit industries. The definition of most five-digit industries is the same in all three countries (the United States, Mexico, and Canada) so that they can produce comparable data, but some U.S. industries feature a sixth digit. The old SIC system was based on a four-digit code that did not have any linkages between the NAFTA-member economies. "NAICS allows each country to recognize activities that are important in the respective countries, but may not be large enough or important enough to recognize in all three countries. The sixth digit is reserved for this purpose," explained the Census Bureau.

The base two-digit NAICS Industry Sectors are as follows:

11	Agriculture, Forestry, Fishing and Hunting
21	Mining
22	Utilities
23	Construction
31-33	Manufacturing
42	Wholesale Trade
44-45	Retail Trade
48-49	Transportation and Warehousing
51	Information
52	Finance and Insurance
53	Real Estate and Rental and Leasing
54	Professional, Scientific, and Technical Services
55	Management of Companies and Enterprises
56	Administrative and Support and Waste Management and Remediation Services
61	Education Services
62	Health Care and Social Assistance
71	Arts, Entertainment, and Recreation
72	Accommodation and Food Services
81	Other Services (Except Publish Administration
92	Public Administration

Of these base sectors, five of them are primarily goods-producing (manufacturing) in nature, while the remaining 15 are services-oriented. This is a dramatic departure from the manufacturing-oriented perspective of the old Standard Industrial Classification system. Complete NAICS listings are available on the Census Bureau Web site at www.census.gov/naics.

Many of the NAICS sectors feature combinations of old SIC divisions, while others are long-neglected economic sectors. For instance, the NAICS has an information sector that includes all establishments that create, disseminate, or provide the means to distribute information. "So everything from data-processing services to motion pictures, broadcasting, and sound recording industries ended up here, as did newspaper, book, and periodical publishers, previously classified as manufacturing, and software publishers, previously included in SIC services," explained Sabrosk. "There are 34 industries in this sector, of which, 20 are new, such as paging, cellular, wireless, and satellite communications. In NAICS, publishing—including reporting, writing, and editing—appears as a major economic activity in its own right, whereas printing remains in NAICS manufacturing. Software publishing goes here because creating a copyrighted product and brining it to market equates to the creative process for other types of intellectual products." This sector's creation will enable the U.S. government and business (and other governments and business enterprises for that matter) to track the tremendous impact of information-based industries on the U.S., Canadian, and Mexican economies for the very first time.

Other important new or overhauled sectors in the North American Industry Classification System include:

Professional/scientific/technical services—This grouping consists of businesses whose major input is "human capital," such as physicians and attorneys.

Health care/social assistance—The number of industries classified in this sector nearly doubled from those listed under the old SIC system. Among the 27 new industries included in this sector, particularly notable ones include health maintenance organizations (HMOs), organ banks, and continuing care retirement facilities.

Computer and electronics manufacturing (including software reproduction, compact disc reproduction, and printed circuit assembly).

Arts, entertainment and recreation—This new sector includes a variety of ascendant industries that reflect our changing lifestyles, such as fitness and recreational sports centers, casinos, skiing facilities, and outfitting companies.

Insurance and real estate—the parameters of these important economic sectors have been expanded and extensively reshaped to reflect current realities.

Wholesale and retail trade—"The distinction between retail and wholesale trade is now based on how the establishment conducts its business rather than on the class of customer that it serves," wrote Ambler in *Business America*. "Those businesses that operate from a store-front, advertise to the general public, and provide retail-type services are considered retailers in NAICS regardless of whether they sell primarily to businesses or consumers. This new definition reflects the changing structure of retail trade."

DIFFERENCES BETWEEN NAICS AND SIC SYSTEMS

Analysts have pointed out a number of significant differences between the new NAICS system and the Standard Industrial Classification arrangement that it replaces. Key areas in which the two systems differ include:

Focus—The NAICS focused on services industries and new industries driven by advanced technology, whereas the SIC system was heavily weighted toward manufacturing. In addition, the NAICS benefits from a unified, production-oriented conceptual framework. "Businesses that use similar production processes to produce a good or service are grouped together," explained Ambler. "This single conceptual framework ensures that the classification system will produce data for improved analysis of input/output patterns, productivity, unit labor costs, and industrial performance. There was no consistent conceptual framework for the SIC." However, analysts note that the differing definitions that exist between the NAICS and the SIC will make historical trend analysis a difficult undertaking in many instances. "Comparative statistics and bridge tables may help at the 2-digit SIC and 3-digit NAICS level of activity," noted Robert Haas and Thomas Wotruba in *Agency Sales Magazine*. "[But] more detailed comparisons and links with past data may require what the Census Bureau calls 'synthetic estimates.' These involve applying proportions or trends from details making up one data set to the totals in a related data set or category."

Nomenclature—Groupings within NAICS are known by different names than those in the SIC system. For example, the SIC called the highest level of aggregation in its system a "division," whereas the NAICS calls it a "sector." The SIC's next highest level of aggregation, meanwhile, was designated "major group," but in the NAICS it is known as a "subsector."

Update-friendly—NAICS codes will be reviewed and updated on a regular five-year cycle by NAFTA member countries to make the system as useful and relevant as possible. The old SIC system, on the other hand, was only revised every 10 or 15 years.

Comparability—The Four-digit SIC system was not linked to the economic data tracking systems of Canada or Mexico in any way. The NAICS system, on the other hand, enables analysts to directly compare industrial production statistics collected and published by all three NAFTA members. In addition, NAICS provides for increased compatibility with the International Standard Industrial Classification System, developed and maintained by the United Nations and widely used in Europe.

The ECPC published a revision to the original NAICS structure in 2002 as part of a planned five year update cycle. The next update is scheduled for release in 2007.

The North American Industry Classification System is regarded as a welcome development by most heavy users of economic statistics, despite the choppy conditions that may prevail during the transition away from the old SIC framework. "The SIC system was dated and badly in need of revision," stated Haas and Watruba. "The new system should provide much more detailed information on a wider spectrum of industries, which in the long run should prove more beneficial to all concerned. In addition, its application to Canadian and Mexican markets and its compatibility with the ISIC system should greatly facilitate more effective global marketing by U.S. marketers. Once NAICS has been adopted and implemented over an extended time period, the short-run problems may well be forgotten because of the long-run benefits of the new system."

BIBLIOGRAPHY

Ambler, Carole A. "NAICS: The 'S' Doesn't Stand for Services (But It Could)." *Business America*. April 1998.

"Good Bye to SIC, Hello to NAICS!" *Energy Conservation News*. March 2000.

Haas, Robert W., and Thomas R. Wotruba. "From SIC to NAICS—What Does It Mean for Business Marketers?" *Agency Sales Magazine*. January 1998.

"The History of NAICS." NAICS Association. Available from http://www.naics.com/info.htm. Retrieved on 18 April 2006.

Ojala, Marydee. "SIC Those NAICS on Me: Industry Classification Codes for Business Research." *Online.* January-February 2005.

Sabrosk, Suzanne. "NAICS Codes: A New Classification System for a New Economy." *Searcher.* November 2000.

Saunders, Norman C. "The North American Industry Classification System: Change on the Horizon." *Occupational Outlook Quarterly.* Fall 1999.

"SIC Codes Get Revamped." *Quality.* December 1998.

U.S. Department of Commerce. Bureau of the Census. "North American Industrial Classification System (NAICS)" Available from http://www.census.gov/epcd/www/naics.html. Retrieved on 18 April 2006.

Hillstrom, Northern Lights
updated by Magee, ECDI

O

OCCUPATIONAL SAFETY AND HEALTH ADMINISTRATION (OSHA)

The Occupational Safety and Health Administration (OSHA) was established by the Williams-Steiger Occupational Safety and Health Act (OSH Act) of 1970, which took effect in 1971. OSHA's mission is to ensure that every working man and woman in the nation is employed under safe and healthful working conditions. Nearly every employee in the United States comes under OSHA's jurisdiction. The only exceptions are people who are self-employed, workers in mining and transportation industries (who are covered by other agencies), and most public employees. Thus, nearly every private employer in the United States needs to be cognizant of OSHA rules and regulations. OSHA is an administrative agency within the United States Department of Labor and is therefore administered by an assistant secretary of labor.

OSHA OBJECTIVES AND STANDARDS

OSHA seeks to make workplaces safer and healthier by making and enforcing regulations called standards in the OSH Act. The Act itself establishes only one workplace standard, which is called the "general duty standard." The general duty standard states: "Each employer shall furnish to each of his employees employment and a place of employment which are free from recognized hazards that are causing or are likely to cause death or serious physical harm to his employees." In the OSH Act, Congress delegated authority to OSHA to make rules further implementing the general duty standard.

Standards made by OSHA are published in the *Code of Federal Regulations* (*CFR*). The three types of regulations are called interim, temporary emergency, and permanent. Interim standards were applicable for two years after OSH Act was passed. For this purpose, OSHA was authorized to use the standards of any nationally recognized "standards setting" organization such as those of professional engineering groups. Such privately developed standards are called "national consensus standards." Temporary emergency standards last only six months and are designed to protect workers while OSHA goes through the processes required by law to develop a permanent standard. Permanent standards are made through the same processes as the regulations made by other federal administrative agencies.

As OSHA drafts a proposal for a permanent standard, it consults with representatives of industry and labor and collects whatever scientific, medical, and engineering data is necessary to ensure that the standard adequately reflects workplace realities. Proposed standards are published in the *Federal Register*. A comment period is then held, during which input is received from interested parties including, but not limited to, representatives of industry and labor. At the close of the comment period, the proposal may be withdrawn and set aside, withdrawn and re-proposed with modifications, or approved as a final standard that is legally enforceable. All standards that become legally binding are first published in the *Federal Register* and then compiled and published in the *Code of Federal Regulations*. Many of OSHA's permanent standards originated as national consensus standards developed by private professional organizations such as the National Fire Protection Association and the American National Standards Institute. Examples of permanent OSHA standards include limits for exposure of employees to hazardous substances such as asbestos, benzene, vinyl chloride, and cotton dust. See the OSHA Web site at www.osha.gov/SLTC/index.html for more information.

National Institute of Occupational Safety and Health
The OSH Act of 1970 also established a research institute called the National Institute of Occupational Safety and Health (NIOSH). Since 1973, NIOSH has been a division of the U.S. government's Centers for Disease Control (CDC). The purpose of NIOSH is to gather data documenting incidences of occupational exposure, injury, illness and death in the United States. This information, which is highly valued by OSHA, is gathered from a wide variety of sources, ranging from industry groups to labor unions, as well as independent organizations.

OSHA RECORD-KEEPING REQUIREMENTS

OSHA requires all companies subject to its workplace standards to abide by a variety of occupational regulations. One of OSHA's major requirements is that companies keep records on facets of their operations relevant to employee health and safety. All employers covered by the OSH Act are required to keep four kinds of records:

- Records regarding enforcement of OSHA standards

- Research records

- Job-related injury, illness, and death records

- Job hazard records

OSHA ENFORCEMENT OF STANDARDS

OSHA inspectors conduct planned or surprise inspections of work sites covered by the OSH Act to verify compliance with the OSH Act and standards promulgated by OSHA. The OSH Act allows the employer *and* an employee representative to accompany OSHA's representative during the inspection. In 1978, in *Marshall v. Barlow*, the United States Supreme Court declared that in most industries, employers have a right to bar an OSHA inspector from his/her premises if the inspector has not first obtained a search warrant.

If violations are found during an inspection, an OSHA citation may be issued in which alleged violations are listed, notices of penalties for each violation are given, and an abatement period is established. The abatement period is the amount of time the employer has to correct any violation(s). Penalties for a violation can be civil or criminal and vary depending on the nature of the violation (minor or serious, willful or non-willful, first offense of repeat offense). Penalties are naturally more severe for serious, repeated, willful violations. Since OSHA must refer cases to the United States Justice Department for criminal enforcement. OSHA has not made extensive use of criminal prosecution as an enforcement mechanism preferring instead to rely on the deterrent effect of civil penalties.

An employer has 15 days to contest an OSHA citation, and any challenge is heard by an Administrative Law Judge (ALJ) within OSHA. The ALJ receives oral and written evidence, decides issues of fact and law, and enters an order. If the employer is dissatisfied with that order, it can be appealed to the Occupational Safety and Health Review Commission, which will, in turn, enter an order. Finally, within 30 days of the issuance of that order, the employer or the Secretary of Labor can take the case to the United States federal court system by filing an appeal with a United States court of appeals.

OSHA AND ITS STATE COUNTERPARTS

Pursuant to the OSH Act, an individual state can pass its own worker health and safety laws and standards. Indeed, the 1970 legislation encouraged individual states to develop and operate their own job safety and health programs. If the state can show that its job safety and health standards are "at least as effective as" comparable federal standards, the state can be certified to assume OSH Act administration and enforcement in that state. OSHA approves and monitors state plans, and provides up to 50 percent of operating costs for approved plans.

To gain OSHA approval for a "developmental plan," the first step in the process of instituting a state plan for job safety and health, the applying state must first assure OSHA that it will, within three years, have in place all the structural elements necessary for an effective occupational safety and health program. These elements include: 1) appropriate legislation; 2) regulations and procedures for standards setting, enforcement, appeal of citations, and penalties; 3) adequate resources (both in number and qualifications of inspectors and other personnel) for enforcement of standards.

Once a state has completed and documented all its developmental requirements, it is eligible for certification. Certification is basically an acknowledgment that the state has put together a complete plan. Once the state has reached a point where it is deemed capable of independently enforcing job safety and health standards, OSHA may enter into an 'operational status' agreement with the state. Once this occurs, OSHA in effect steps aside and allows the state to enforce its laws.

The ultimate accreditation of a state plan is known as "final approval." When OSHA grants final approval, it relinquishes its authority to cover occupational safety and health matters that are addressed by the state's rules and regulations. Final approval can not be given until at least one year after certification, and it is predicated on OSHA's judgment that worker protection is at least as effective under the state's standards as it is under the federal program. The state must meet all required staffing levels and agree to participate in OSHA's computerized inspection data system before being allowed to operate without OSHA supervision.

HISTORY OF THE RELATIONSHIP BETWEEN OSHA AND BUSINESS

OSHA has traditionally used "command and control" kinds of regulation to protect workers. "Command and control" regulations are those which set requirements for job safety (such as requirements for guard rails on stairs) or limits on exposure to a hazardous substance (such as a given number of fibers of asbestos per cubic milliliter of air breathed per hour). They are enforced through citations issued to violators.

In 1984 OSHA promulgated the Hazard Communication Standard (HCS), which was viewed as a new kind of regulation differing from "command and control." The HCS gives workers access to information about long-term health risks resulting from workplace exposure to toxic or hazardous substances, and requires manufacturers, importers, and distributors to provide employers with evaluations of all toxic or hazardous materials sold or distributed to those employers. This information is compiled in a form known as a Material Safety Data Sheet (MSDS). The MSDS describes the chemical's physical hazards such as ignitability and reactivity, gives associated health hazards, and states the exposure limits established by OSHA. In turn, the employer must make these documents available to employees, and requires employers to establish hazard communication education programs. The employer must also label all containers with the identities of hazardous substances and appropriate warnings. Worker "Right-to-Know," as implemented on the federal level through the HCS, is designed to give workers access to information so that they can make informed decisions about their exposure to toxic chemicals.

OSHA has been criticized by businesses and industry groups throughout its history. In the 1970s, it was criticized for making job-safety regulations that businesses considered to be vague or unnecessarily costly. For example, a 1977 OSHA regulation contained detailed specifications regarding irregularities in western hemlock trees used to construct ladders. In the Appropriations Act of 1977, Congress directed OSHA to get rid of certain standards that it described as "trivial." As a result, in 1978 OSHA revoked 928 job-safety standards and increased its efforts to deal with health hazards.

On the other hand, OSHA has also been criticized by unions and other pro-worker groups throughout its history for doing too little to protect employees. Throughout its existence, OSHA has been criticized for issuing too few new standards, for failing to protect workers who report violations, for failing to adequately protect workers involved in the clean up of toxic-waste sites, and for failing to enforce existing standards. The latter charge has been a particularly frustrating one for OSHA. Funding for enforcement has dwindled in recent years, and over the last 20 years, both Congress and various presidential administrations have publicly supported efforts to keep OSHA and other agencies "off the backs" of business.

OSHA REFORMS

OSHA is criticized from both sides, for being too arbitrary with employers and for being too lax on employers. A 2000 survey of members of the National Association of Manufacturers cited OSHA as the nation's most intrusive federal agency (34 percent of responding manufacturers cited OSHA, while 18 percent pointed to the Environmental Protection Agency, the second-highest vote-getter; another 11 percent said no federal agency significantly impeded their efficiency). The most frequent complaint leveled against OSHA is that American workplace safety and health regulations are excessively burdensome on businesses of all shapes and sizes. Critics call for fundamental changes in OSHA's regulatory environment, insisting that changes should be made to encourage voluntary industry compliance on worker safety issues and reductions of penalties for nonserious violators of standards. OSHA itself has acknowledged that "in the public's view, OSHA has been driven too often by numbers and rules, not by smart enforcement and results. Business complains about over-zealous enforcement and burdensome rules.... And too often, a "one-size-fits-all" regulatory approach has treated conscientious employers no differently from those who put workers needlessly at risk." Worker advocates and others, however, point out that OSHA standards have been an important factor in the dramatic decline of injury and illness rates in many industries over the past few decades, and they express concern that reforms could put workers in a variety of businesses at greater risk.

OSHA's recent reform initiatives have sought to address those issues raised by its critics while simultaneously ensuring that American workers receive adequate health and safety protection in the workplace. In 1995 OSHA announced a new emphasis on treating employers with aggressive health and safety programs differently from employers who lack such programs. "At its core," said OSHA, "this new approach seeks to encourage the development of worksite health and safety programs." The features that OSHA will be looking for are:

- Management commitment

- Meaningful participation of employees

- a systematic effort to find safety and health hazards whether they are covered by existing standards or not

- Documentation that the identified hazards are fixed

- Training for employees and supervisors

- A reduction in injuries and illnesses

Those firms equipped with good safety programs will receive special recognition that will include: the lowest priority for enforcement inspections, the highest priority for assistance, appropriate regulatory relief, and major penalty reductions. Businesses that do not adequately provide for their workers' health and safety, however, will be subject to "strong and traditional OSHA enforcement procedures.... In short, for those who have a history of endangering their employees and are unwilling to change, OSHA will rigorously enforce the law without compromise to assure that there are serious consequences for serious violators."

OSHA also announced its plans to make more tightly focused inspections on companies that have effective safety and health programs. If a company with a strong record meets selected safety/health criteria, the OSHA inspector will conduct an abbreviated inspection. Conversely, in situations where a safety and health program is nonexistent or inadequate, a complete site inspection, including full citations, will be undertaken.

OSHA and business interests clashed repeatedly during the late 1990s over proposed new regulations designed to identify and address workplace injuries and illnesses traced to the issue of ergonomics. "OSHA would require companies to implement permanent engineering controls and employ interim personal protective equipment," noted *Purchasing*. "Examples of engineering controls involve changing, modifying, or redesigning the following: workstations, tools, facilities, equipment, materials, and processes.... Many businesses have already adopted ergonomic design tools and workstations that reduce strain where repetitive motions, sitting for long periods, or reaching are required. It's not clear yet what companies will be required to do in the way of changes in processes and materials used."

OSHA AND SMALL BUSINESS

In recognition of the special challenges that often face small businesses—and the limited financial resources that they often have—the Occupational Safety and Health Administration administers a number of special programs specifically designed to help entrepreneurs and small business owners provide a productive yet safe environment for their employees.

Among the special programs that OSHA has instituted for small businesses are the following:

- Penalty Reduction—OSHA may grant reductions of 60 percent for employers with 25 employees or fewer; 40 percent if the employer has 26-100 employees; and 20 percent if the employer has 101-250 employees.

- Penalty Reductions for Good Faith—OSHA has the option of granting a 25 percent penalty reduction if a small business has instituted an effective safety and health program for its employees.

- Flexible Requirements—OSHA gives smaller firms greater flexibility in certain safety areas in recognition of their limited resources (i.e., lead in construction, emergency evacuation plans, process safety management).

- Reduced Paperwork Requirements— OSHA has fewer recordkeeping requirements for very small business. Employers with 10 or fewer employees are exempt from most OSHA recordkeeping requirements for recording and reporting occupational injuries and illnesses.

- Consultation Program—While not limited to small businesses, OSHA on-site consultation program has been particularly helpful to smaller companies (small firms accounted for about 40 percent of the program during the mid-1990s). This service, which is run by state agencies, provides businesses with the option of requesting a free on-site consultation with a state representative who helps them identify potential workplace hazards and improve or implement effective workplace safety and health programs.

- Training Grants—OSHA awards grant money to non-profit groups for the development of programs designed to help entrepreneurs and small business owners establish safety and health guidelines for their companies.

806

- Mentoring—OSHA and the Voluntary Protection Programs Participants Association (VPPA) operate a mentoring program to help small firms applying for entry into VPP refine their health and safety programs. The VPP is an OSHA program that is intended to recognize a firm's safety and health achievements. This mentoring program matches applicants with VPP members (often in the same or a related industry) who can help by sharing their experience with and knowledge about workplace safety and health programs.

In addition to these federal level programs, many states have their own federally approved safety and health standards and these states often provide additional programs of assistance to small businesses.

The Value of Consultation Programs OSHA and business consultants alike encourage small business owners to take advantage of available consultation programs. A comprehensive consultation can provide small business owners with a wide variety of information that can help ensure that they are in compliance with regulatory requirements.

Consultations will typically include appraisal of all mechanical and environmental hazards and physical work practices; appraisal of the firm's present job safety and health program; conference with management on findings; written report of recommendations and agreements; and training and assistance with implementing recommendations. "The consultant will then review detailed findings with you in a closing conference," noted OSHA. "You [the business owner] will learn not only what you need to improve, but also what you are doing right. At that time you can discuss problems, possible solutions and abatement periods to eliminate or control any serious hazards identified during the walk-through. . . . The consultant can help you establish or strengthen an employee safety and health program, making safety and health activities routine considerations rather than crisis-oriented responses."

BIBLIOGRAPHY

"Ergonomics, S&H Rules on OSHA's Front Burner." *Purchasing.* 22 April 1999.

Fletcher, Meg. "Workplace Rule Governs Whistleblower Practices: Sarbanes-Oxley expands OSHA investigations." *Business Insurance.* 13 June 2004.

Martin, William, and James Walters. *Safety and Health Essentials: OSHA Compliance for Small Businesses.* Elsevier, September 2001.

"OSHA Most Intrusive Agency." *Products Finishing.* June 2000.

U. S. Department of Labor. Occupational Safety and Health Administration. "OSHA Benefits for Small Business."

Available from http://www.osha.gov/dcsp/smallbusiness/benefits.html. Retrieved on 18 April 2006.

Hillstrom, Northern Lights
updated by Magee, ECDI

OFFICE AUTOMATION

Office automation refers to the integration of office functions usually related to managing information. There are many tools used to automate office functions and the spread of electronic processors inside computers as well as inside copiers and printers is at the center of most recent advances in office automation. Raw data storage, electronic data transfer, and the management of electronic business information comprise the basic activities of an office automation system.

The modern history of office automation began with the typewriter and the copy machine, which mechanized previously manual tasks. Today, however, office automation is increasingly understood as a term that refers not just to the mechanization of tasks but to the conversion of information to electronic form as well. The advent of the personal computer revolutionized office automation, and today, popular operating systems and user interfaces dominate office computer systems. This revolution has been so complete, and has infiltrated so many areas of business, that almost all businesses use at least one commercial computer business application in the course of daily activity. Even the smallest companies commonly utilize computer technology to maintain financial records, inventory information, payroll records, and other pertinent business information. "Workplace technology that started as handy (but still optional) business tools in the 1980s evolved into a high-priority requirement in the 1990s," summarized Stanley Zarowin in *Journal of Accountancy.* "As we enter the new millennium, it has taken another quantum leap, going from a priority to a prerequisite for doing business."

THE BASICS OF OFFICE AUTOMATION

Generally, there are three basic activities of an office automation system: storage of information, data exchange, and data management. Within each broad application area, hardware and software combine to fulfill basic functions.

Information Storage The first area within office automation is information storage which is usually considered to include office records and other primary office forms and documents. Data applications involve the capture and editing of files, images, or spreadsheets. Word processing and desktop presentation packages accommodate raw textual and graphical data, while spreadsheet applications provide users with the capacity to engage in the easy manipulation and output of numbers. Image applications allow the capture and editing of visual images.

Text handling software and systems cover the whole field of word processing and desktop publishing. Word processing, the most basic and common office automation activity, is the inputting (usually via keyboard) and manipulation of text on a computer. Today's commercial word processing applications provide users with a sophisticated set of commands to format, edit, and print text documents. One of the more popular features of word processing packages is its preformatted document templates. Templates automatically set up such things as font size, paragraph styles, headers and footers, and page numbers so that the user does not have to reset document characteristics every time he or she creates a new record.

Desktop publishing adds another dimension to text manipulation. By combining the features of a word processor with advanced page design and layout features, desktop publishing packages have emerged as valuable tools in the creation of newsletters, brochures, and other documents that combine text and photographs, charts, drawings and other graphic images.

Image handling software and systems are another facet of office automation. Examples of visual information include pictures of documents, photographs, and graphics such as tables and charts. These images are converted into digital files, which cannot be edited the same way that text files can. In a word processor or desktop publishing application, each word or character is treated individually. In an imaging system, the entire picture or document is treated as one whole object. One of the most popular uses of computerized images is in corporate presentations or speeches. Presentation software packages simplify the creation of multimedia presentations that use computer video, images, sound, and text in an integrated information package.

Spreadsheet programs allow the manipulation of numeric data. Early popular spreadsheet programs such as VisiCalc and Lotus 123 greatly simplified common business financial recordkeeping. Particularly useful among the many spreadsheet options is the ability to use variables in pro-forma statements. The pro-forma option allows the user to change a variable and have a complex formula automatically recalculated based on the new numbers. Many businesses use spreadsheets for financial management, financial projection, and accounting.

Data Exchange While data storage and manipulation is one component of an office automation system, the exchange of that information is another equally important component. Electronic transfer is a general application area that highlights the exchange of information among multiple users. Electronic mail, voice mail, and facsimile are examples of electronic transfer applications. Systems that allow instantaneous or "real time" transfer of information (i.e., online conversations via computer or audio exchange with video capture) are considered electronic sharing systems. Electronic sharing software illustrates the collaborative nature of many office automation systems.

Office automation systems that include the ability to electronically share information between more than one user simultaneously are sometimes referred to as groupware systems. One type of groupware is an electronic meeting system. Electronic meeting systems allow geographically dispersed participants to exchange information in real time. Participants in such electronic meetings may be within the same office or building, or thousands of miles apart. Long-distance electronic sharing systems usually use a telephone line connection to transfer data, while sharing in the same often involves just a local area network of computers (no outside phone line is needed). The functional effectiveness of such electronic sharing systems has been one factor in the growth of telecommuting as an option for workers. Telecommuters work at home, maintaining their ties to the office via computer.

Electronic transfer software and systems allow for electronic transmission of office information. Electronic mail uses computer-based storage and a common set of network communication protocols to forward electronic messages from one user to another. Most of these systems allow users to relay electronic mail to more than one recipient, although they refer to this in an old-fashioned way as carbon copying or "ccing." Electronic mail, or e-mail systems, provide security features, automatic messaging, and mail management systems like electronic folders or notebooks. Voice mail offers essentially the same applications, but for telephones, not computers.

Other traditional office machines continue to undergo changes that improve their data exchange capacities as well. Digital copiers, for example, are increasingly multifunctional (with copying, printing, faxing, and scanning capabilities) and connectable to computer networks. Laptops, Personal Digital Assistants (PDAs), and Blackberries (wireless cell phone and PDA units) use wireless data transfer technologies to provide users with almost instant access to information stored on a company's computer networks and servers from just about anywhere within reach of a cell phone tower or wireless Internet transmitter. That means just about anywhere within an urban area of the United States these days.

Data Management Office automation systems are also often used to track both short-term and long-term data in the realms of financial plans, workforce allocation plans, marketing expenditures, inventory purchases, and other aspects of business. Task management or scheduling systems monitor and control various projects and activities within the office. Electronic management systems monitor and control office activities and tasks through timelines, resource equations, and electronic scheduling.

OFFICE AUTOMATION CONSIDERATIONS: PEOPLE, TOOLS, AND THE WORKPLACE

Businesses engaged in launching or upgrading office automation systems must consider a wide variety of factors that can influence the effectiveness of those systems. These factors include budgetary and physical space considerations, and changes in communication infrastructure, among others. But two other factors that must be considered are employee training and proliferating office automation choices:

- Training—People involved with office automation basically include all users of the automation and all providers of the automation systems and tools. A wide range of people—including software and hardware engineers, management information scientists, executives, mid-level workers, and secretaries—are just a few of the people that use office automation on a daily basis. As a result, training of personnel on these office automation systems has become an essential part of many companies' planning. After all, the office automation system is only as good as the people who make it and use it, and smart business owners and managers recognize that workplace resistance to these systems can dramatically lessen their benefits. "It's true that as technology matures the need for special training will decline—because tomorrow's software and hardware will be much more intuitive and loaded with built-in teaching drills—that time is not here yet," wrote Zarowin. "Training is still essential."

- Choice—A dizzying array of office automation alternatives are available to businesses of all shapes, sizes, and subject areas. Such systems typically involve a sizable investment of funds, so it is wise for managers and business owners to undertake a careful course of study before making a purchase. Primary factors that should be considered include: cost of the system, length of time involved in introducing the system, physical condition of the facility into which the system will be introduced, level of technical support, compatibility with other systems,

complexity of system (a key factor in determining allocations of time and money for training), and compatibility of the system with the business area in which the company is involved.

As the high-tech economy, information age economy, or new economy continues to evolve, business experts warn small businesses not to fall too far behind. Some small businesses remain resistant to change and thus fall ever further behind in utilizing office automation technology, despite the plethora of evidence that it constitutes the wave of the future. The entrepreneurs and managers who lead these enterprises typically defend their inaction by noting that they remain able to accomplish their basic business requirements without such investments, or by claiming that new innovations in technology and automation are too expensive or challenging to master. But according to Zarowin, "those rationalizations don't acknowledge what many recent converts to technology are discovering: the longer one delays, the larger the gap and the harder it is to catch up. And though many businesses still can function adequately with paper and pencil, their customers—and their competition—are not sitting on their hands."

BIBLIOGRAPHY

Bauroth, Nan. "Selling Upper Management on New Equipment." *OfficeSolutions.* April 2000.

Douglas, Heather. "Extracting More Hours from Your Day: Could you do with an extra pair of hands, but without the hassle of putting staff on the payroll?" *NZ Business.* September 2005.

McKeller, Hugh. "Capture: Past, Present and Future." *KMWorld.* June 2005.

Lewers, Christine. "A Keystroke Away." *Indiana Business Magazine.* September 1999.

Rosenzweig, Stan. "Your New Technology is Dead. Live With It." *Fairfield County Business Journal.* 19 July 2004.

"Workshare Solution Reduces Metadata Risk." *Information Management Journal.* January-February 2005.

Zarowin, Stanley. "Technology for the New Millennium." *Journal of Accountancy.* April 2000.

Hillstrom, Northern Lights
updated by Magee, ECDI

OFFICE ROMANCE

Office romances—romantic relationships between two people employed by the same employer—are as common now as they have been throughout history. The long hours many people spend at work make for a situation in which those with whom we work are for many not only colleagues but our primary source of social contact. Therefore, romantic relationships are bound to develop. In fact, according to an article on the *Discovery Health Channel* Web site, 4 out of 10 people now meet their spouses at the office and more than half of those partaking in a survey reported to having had at least one office romance. Many office romances end happily, but not all. For businesses, workplace romances carry with them the potential to complicate the work environment and cause difficulties of various types—lost productivity due to distraction; accusations of favoritism; jealousy among co-workers; the potential for an antagonistic mood should the relationship end poorly; and, in a worst-case scenario, allegations of sexual harassment in the event that one of the parties asserts that he or she was coerced. Because of these potential pitfalls, many firms have policies that were established to try and discourage or even prohibit such liaisons from forming. The question for the small business owner or manager becomes: how best is one to manage such relationships so that they do not have a negative impact on the company without infringing unduly on the privacy of employees?

DEALING WITH OFFICE ROMANCES

Most experts suggest that a company establish some sort of policy addressing this issue so that it is not put in a position of being reactionary when confronted with the first such romance. By planning ahead, incorporating guidelines on workplace romances into the employment policies, and publicizing these policies, a company can remove confusion and in most cases the concern about favoritism.

Small companies may be in a more difficult position than larger firms when it comes to managing workplace romances. In a large firm, an office romance may be more easily worked around. A large firm has multiple departments into which employees who are romantically involved may be transferred so that they do not work as closely together. Arlene Vernon, a human resource consultant with HRX, explained it this way in an interview with journalist Janice Rhoshalle Littlejohn, in a *Pool & Spa News* article, "It becomes an issue for a smaller organization because everyone's watching and wondering if this one's going to last. It becomes this whole saga. You might as well turn it into a sitcom.... I think it is actually harder for the smaller organizations than the larger ones. It can be more invisible in the larger ones."

Knowing what to include in a workplace policy on dating or romantic relationships is not easy. Banning dating among employees may not be a reasonable solution, although exceptions can certainly be made in instances where one of the principals involved has a supervisory role over the other. One concern with a newly forming romance in the workplace is that it will

be accompanied by inappropriate displays of affection in the office. This, in turn, can cause an uncomfortable environment for others and certainly presents a less than professional image. A company may address this concern by establishing an on-the-job code of conduct that specifically addresses a professional work environment and prohibits "public displays of affection."

As a minimum, any policy designed to regulate dating or office romances should be designed to protect the company against sexual harassment liability and ensure a professional work environment. Actions to consider when preparing such a policy include:

1. State what is not acceptable—Define in the policy exactly what types of relationships will and will not be tolerated. Most human resource professionals recommend establishing policies that prohibit supervisors from dating a direct report. Policies may also note that staff members are expected to behave professionally and that romantic trysts should be kept out of the work environment.

2. Make penalties clear—Define what actions will be undertaken if the policies are violated—transfer, demotion, termination.

3. Address sexual harassment head on—State outright that any alleged sexual harassment will be handled in a legally proper manner. Managers must make employees aware that the company has a zero-tolerance policy on sexual harassment. Information should be provided about the consequences of such behavior. Companies may even require that their employees sign documentation indicating that they understand and will abide by the policy.

4. Reinforce policies on sexual harassment—Provide training for all supervisors/managers about sexual harassment in all its forms. Educate them on the various signs that an office romance is having a negative impact on the company's efficiency (these signs can range from increased workplace friction to unprofessional displays of affection, anger, or other emotions).

5. Show respect for privacy—Do not overstep boundaries of employee privacy. A company needs to make it abundantly clear that workplace performance is its primary concern.

6. Encourage open communications—Consider requesting employees to disclose a relationship if it becomes romantic. This may be a difficult task for employees if the penalties for such a relationship are severe. If, on the other hand, the company is willing to work with the couple then it is more likely that they will communicate their involvement in an appropriate manner.

Do not flinch from intervening promptly in situations where a workplace relationship is having a detrimental effect on business productivity. In cases of sexual harassment claims, more often than not, court decisions on liability have little to do with whether a company had a dating policy in place and everything to do with how a company responded when a complaint was lodged. Prompt response to workplace issues that arise from an office romance gone sour can go far toward addressing the problem.

DISTINGUISHING BETWEEN FLIRTING AND SEXUAL HARASSMENT

Given the increase in sexual harassment lawsuits that have exposed an ongoing problem in many businesses, it is not surprising that small business owners have expressed concern about the sometimes blurry boundaries between office flirtations—which may lead to full-fledged office romances—and ugly instances of sexual harassment. While businesses can take certain steps to define inappropriate office conduct, many of them quite effective, stopping sexual harassment is often a more complicated issue if the two people involved were formerly romantically involved. Indeed, some people resort to harassment in the wake of a breakup, while others have been known to level false harassment charges after being jilted. If an office relationship degenerates to such a point, it is important for the business owner to maintain an impartial stance and make sure that decisions are made on the basis of the evidence at hand.

DISPARATE VIEWS OF OFFICE ROMANCE

Assessments of the dangers of office romance vary dramatically. Some observers view it as a wholly undesirable condition that should be avoided by business owners and managers if at all possible, while others view it as a potential positive development, provided that the relationship lies within certain parameters. But what happens when a philanderer dates and discards casually within a company, leaving angry, litigation-prone employees in his/her wake? Reasons for dating policies to address supervisors, subordinates, and clients, not to mention patients and vendors, are understandable.

The risks that a deteriorating romance pose for a company that employes both parties are undeniable. Perhaps, however, the benefits of happily partnered employees is another possible outcome to an office romance. Famous cases abound: Microsoft's founder Bill Gates and opera impresario Luciano Pavarotti both married employees of their organizations. Obviously, businesses create dating policies to try and manage the negative aspects of office romances, and those that crash

and burn. But, since perfectly happy relationships may result from office romances, policies that are clear and specific about exactly what they prohibit are best.

SEE ALSO *Employee Privacy; Human Resource Policies; Nepotism*

BIBLIOGRAPHY

"The Downside of Office Romance." *OfficeSolutions.* March-April 2006.

Feeney, Sheila Anne. "Love Hurts: Romance may be in the air at your company, but passion can have its price." *Workforce Management.* 1 February 2004.

Greenwald, Judy. "Office Romances May Court Trouble." *Business Insurance.* 14 February 2000.

Gurchiek, Kathy. "Be Ready for Slings, Arrows of Cupid in the Cubicles." *HRMagazine.* March 2005.

Littlejohn, Jancie Rhoshalle. "Risky Business: In the first installment of this two-part series on office romance, we explore ways employers can deal with workplace dating and avoid potential liabilities." *Pool & Spa News.* 7 May 2004.

Moses, Jeffrey. "Office Romance in the New Millennium." National Federation of Independent Business. Available from http://www.nfib.com/object/IO_22940.html. 21 June 2005.

Penttila, Chris. "In the Hot Seat: One person's promotion is another's harassment claim." *Entrepreneur.* January 2006.

Weiss, Donald H. *Fair, Square, and Legal.* AMACOM, 1 April 2004.

*Hillstrom, Northern Lights
updated by Magee, ECDI*

OFFICE SECURITY

Office security can be broken down into two main areas: 1) protecting your office and employees from vandalism, theft, and personal attacks; and 2) protecting your office from corporate sabotage, both from inside the company and out. The first area deals more with the actual office itself—its layout, the use of security guards, alarm systems, and so on. The second area is primarily concerned with protecting a firm's intellectual property through the introduction and utilization of such measures as shredders, computer security, and employee surveillance.

PHYSICAL SECURITY: PROTECTING THE OFFICE AND EMPLOYEES

Office security is an issue for every business, no matter the size. There are many steps that can be taken to improve security, many of which require relatively inexpensive outlays. To find out what is best for his or her company, a small business owner should hire a security consultant to visit the business premises and conduct a thorough security analysis. This review can identify weak spots and provide a clear plan for upgrading security.

The best place to start when examining office security is the physical layout of the office itself, or the layout of the larger building of which the office is a part. Office design should stress wide, open areas with clear sight lines. Hallways and offices should be open and have no nooks or crannies where an intruder could hide in the shadows. All areas should be well lit, especially after hours when employees might be working alone or in small groups. Mirrors in stairwells and inside and outside of elevators allow employees to see around corners or past obstructions.

Doors and windows are the most obvious access points to an office and should be secure. Avoid double doors because they are easily hinged open. Ideally, entranceway doors—particularly those used for deliveries, etc.—should be steel, or steel-sheathed. This helps with security and also aids in fire prevention. Door hinges should face inward whenever possible; use non-removable pins and screws if it is not possible. Simply upgrading hinges and door locks is one of the cheapest and most effective security steps a business can take. Deadbolt locks are best, whether they are electronically controlled or manual in nature. Combination locks on washrooms and other common areas are also an excellent option. Employees don't have to carry keys and the combination can be changed frequently. All windows should use key locks, and windows near the ground level or fire escapes should have steel bars or lockable gates that meet local fire codes.

INCREASED USE OF ELECTRONICS

Improvements in electronics, computers, and other high-tech security features have given business owners new tools to fight crime in recent years. Perhaps the most common electronic tools are closed-circuit surveillance systems and access-control systems.

Closed-circuit surveillance systems use television cameras to monitor specific areas of a company's workspace. Signals from the cameras are fed back to a central monitoring post, where a security guard or company employee watches for signs of abnormal activity. These systems are effective both during business hours and after hours. But while video technologies can be an effective deterrent and investigative tool, a closed-circuit system only works as well as the people monitoring it. The guard or employee must give the video monitors his or her complete attention.

Access-control systems start with establishing "point of control" access over an office. That means that all tenants and guests are routed through a control area before admittance is authorized. The control point can be as low-tech as a sign-in sheet or as high-tech as an elaborate system to scan the fingerprints or retinas of visitors (most security experts understandably cite the former as an inadequate measure, in and of itself). Most common is the use of access cards, or "swipe" cards. These cards are electronic "keys"—the user passes a part of the card through an electronic reader stationed outside a door, and, if the person is authorized to enter, the door is unlocked. Newer versions of the swipe cards include video imaging. A central computer stores a photo of the employee and as much pertinent information as the company desires, including work hours, emergency contact numbers, license plate numbers and make of car, and other information. Electronic cards are preferable to metal keys because an electronic key can be deactivated at a moment's notice if an employee is fired or deemed a security risk. If metal keys are used, every lock in the building has to be replaced if a security breach is suspected.

Other electronic systems that are being used by security-conscious firms include tiny hidden cameras, panic buttons that summon security when pressed, and electronic door chimes that make it easy to tell when someone has entered a workspace. The tiny cameras are perhaps the most popular innovation. They are small enough to be hidden in a clock face or a heating vent, yet provide a powerful tool for monitoring employees in areas where employee theft is suspected. Use of the cameras only works if their existence is kept a secret from the employees that are under suspicion.

Finally, identification tag systems are an increasingly popular tool in many businesses. Laminated photo identification cards are inexpensive to produce and update, and they can instantly identify employees and the department from which they hail. These photo ID cards can be particularly useful for larger, diversified enterprises in which employees may not know or interact with every other member of the workforce.

ALARM SYSTEMS

Alarm systems are another popular office security tool. There are two primary types of alarm systems: those that sound a loud siren or other noise when a break-in is detected, and those that send a silent alarm directly to a security company or to the police, who then respond to the alarm. The type of alarm chosen depends in large part on where the business is located. Loud alarms work well in small towns or in low-crime areas, but businesses located in urban or high-crime areas have found that nearby residents have often become so used to alarms going off that they ignore them. In that case, a silent system linked directly to the police may be preferable.

Systems can range in complexity and price. However, any alarm system must cover all the doors and windows into a business to be effective. Most common are motion sensors that detect movement where it is not supposed to be occurring, or window glass bugs that are activated when glass is broken. Examples of advanced systems include combined audio and video alert systems that are triggered by noise. When the sounds of a break-in are detected, the security company is alerted and can listen in to what is occurring at the site. The security company can then activate video monitors to see what is happening at the site, or the cameras can be set up to begin recording automatically when the first sound is detected.

As with the closed-circuit television systems, the key to a good alarm system is that it must be monitored at all times. If an alarm goes off and no one is there to notice, or if it is ignored, then office security has not been enhanced at all. In fact, the alarm may have provided a false sense of security that kept a company from pursuing other security measures.

SECURITY GUARDS

Using security guards is an increasingly popular form of office security. Guards can be used in two ways: to monitor the front desk of a company or building (the access control point); or, to patrol the grounds of a larger company or office complex.

The old image of the security guard—an elderly gentleman who slept as much as he monitored the grounds—is a thing of the past. Today's guards, especially those who monitor building access, should have good communication skills and be able to handle many roles. Guards often act as concierges and goodwill ambassadors, greeting the public as they come into a company and answering questions and providing directions. Ideally, they should present a positive public image for the company and/or building that employs them. With this in mind, traditional uniforms have given way to a casual but professional wardrobe of blazers and trousers at many security firms. Guards are almost never armed—the practice has come to be regarded as just too dangerous—and they are primarily expected to do four things at all times: deter, detect, observe, and report. Today's guards can also be expected to help out by arranging for building maintenance or even assisting in life-threatening situations.

The other type of security guard—the type that patrols the grounds of a larger company or an office park—receive conflicting marks from security experts. Some feel that simply driving or walking by each part of an office complex every hour or half-hour does little to prevent crime because such measures still leave large windows of time for criminal activity to occur. Others argue the very presence of the guards is enough to deter all but the most professional or determined criminals. The question of whether to use such guards is one that each company will have to answer for itself.

Small business owners should know that using security guards is not cheap. Round-the-clock coverage by a team of guards can cost upwards of $100,000 annually. Additionally, theft by the guards themselves has been a definite problem for some businesses. Many security firms pay minimum wage, so turnover is high, and background checks are not always thorough. To ensure that you are really hiring the best firm possible, screen prospective choices carefully. Look for firms that perform thorough background checks, pay better than minimum wage, and have low turnover. Fellow members of the local business community can be a valuable resource in this regard.

THE ROLE OF EMPLOYEES

It is common knowledge that a security system is only as secure as its weakest link. In many cases, that weak link is the company's employees. Untrained in security measures and prone to the attitude that "it can't happen to me," many employees are their own worst enemies when it comes to security. When a company installs a new security system, it should take the time to bring in a security consultant to speak to employees about what they can do to increase their own safety and improve the company's security. Among the measures the consultant will advise are:

- Do not leave valuables unattended.
- Lock doors after hours.
- Do not go into poorly lighted areas after dark.
- Bolt down or secure equipment if possible.
- Engrave identification numbers on office equipment and keep a list of serial numbers to give to the police and insurance companies in case of theft.
- Provide each employee with a drawer that locks.
- Verify identification and purpose of visit before letting non-employees into office space.
- Deposit checks and cash daily.
- Never leave visitors unsupervised.
- Try to leave with at least one other employee if working late.
- Do not advertise vacation plans.
- Keep emergency numbers posted at every phone.
- Make sure confidential files are secured when the office is closed.

CORPORATE SABOTAGE AND PROTECTING INTELLECTUAL PROPERTY

As computers have become an everyday part of almost every business, companies have found it harder and harder to protect their proprietary information and their money. (Only failed attempts at espionage lead to arrests and quantifying the problem is difficult.) According to the Federal Bureau of Investigation, espionage and espionage-related matters cost the nation an estimated $100 billion per year. This does not include the estimated $250 billion American companies lose to copyright piracy annually. Much of that theft occurs electronically.

Unfortunately for most companies, the greatest risk of theft or sabotage (conventional or computer), often comes from the firm's employees themselves. In fact, many experts believe that a significant percentage of small business failures are directly related to internal theft of money, property, information, and time. Few occurrences are as potentially destructive to a business as employee theft, embezzlement, or misappropriation of company funds.

Business security experts warn that employee theft can take many forms. Examples include:

- Forgery of company checks for personal gain.

- Using a "ghost payroll," which occurs when one or more employees create "phantom" employees, submit time cards for those employees, and then cash their paychecks themselves.

- Outright theft of cash from a register drawer.

- "Sweethearting," at the cash register, which can mean granting a friend or other person a discount at the register when they pay, undercharging them, or ringing up fewer items than the person has actually bought.

Internal computer theft has become one of the most common forms of employee theft now that computers have become more common in nearly every industry sector. Indeed, employees often are more computer literate than their supervisors, which may strengthen the temptation to abscond with proprietary information or otherwise engage in illicit activities. Computer theft can take many forms, including false data entry, which is almost impossible to track; slicing off small amounts of data or money that add up over time; superzapping, which occurs when a computer network security bypass code falls into the wrong hands; and scanning, or using a high-speed computer to locate data that would be impossible to find by hand, then using that data for illegal purposes.

Sabotage, which can also cost millions, almost always involves disgruntled current or former employees and can take almost any form, from defacing company property to deleting or altering important company data. As mentioned above, using access-control cards for employees that can be easily deactivated makes it easier to keep ex-employees out of the workplace and track the activities of current employees.

Because employee theft is so prevalent and so costly to businesses, a business owner needs to take every precaution and use every means possible to stop employee theft. Some of the steps that can be taken include:

- Making sure that security starts at the top. Executives must set a good and honest example. Establish a clear policy on theft and security and distribute it to all employees.

- Install a security program that meets your company's needs.

- Follow up on references provided by prospective new hires.

- Keep checkbooks locked up.

- Control cash flow and have good documentation on where money is spent.

- Do not leave bookkeeping to just one person without checks and balances.

- Audit internal financial documents frequently using independent auditors.

- Only allow a few people to have authority to sign checks.

- Check all invoices to make sure they match what was delivered.

SEE ALSO *Computer Crimes; Crisis Management; Firewall; Workplace Safety*

BIBLIOGRAPHY

Mackenzie, Kate. "Big Danger Lurks in Small Things Portable Memory Devices: Portable mass storage devices contain huge threats to security." *The Financial Times.* 9 November 2005.

Marshall, Jeffrey, and Ellen M. Heffes. "Small business: security issues rise as automation gains." *Financial Executive.* October 2005.

"Office Building Security Getting Smarter." *Access Control & Security Systems Integration.* 20 March 2006.

U.S. Department of Commerce. StopFakes.gov. "What's New In StopFakes." Available from http://www.stopfakes.gov/ Retrieved on 28 April 2006.

U.S. Department of Justice. Federal Bureau of Investigation. "FQA—Why do we so seldom hear about arrests for espionage?" Available from http://www.fbi.gov/aboutus/faqs/faqsone.htm. Retrieved on 28 April 2006.

Hillstrom, Northern Lights
updated by Magee, ECDI

OFFICE SUPPLIES

Office supplies encompass a wide range of materials that are used on a regular, daily basis by businesses of all sizes. The standard set of office supplies utilized by even the smallest company or home office includes pens; writing paper; notebooks; Post-It notes; scissors; erasers; staplers; computer diskettes and CDs; binders; file folders; labels; tape; basic reference materials (dictionaries, etc.); envelopes; toner cartridges; to mention but the most common. In addition, equipment that is used in most office environments—printers, copy machines, fax machines, etc.—is often included under this umbrella term.

Despite the growth of technologies that had promised us a future in which we would operate in "paperless offices," most offices today are still filled with paper and with all the accessories needed to keep paper organized. In fact, a paper shredder is a common item in offices these days. Although the cost of office supplies is relatively small when items are purchased separately, in the aggregate this cost can amount to a substantial quantity. Consequently, small business owners should make sure that they pay attention to office supply costs and keep all receipts of such purchases, since office supplies are a legitimate business deduction for tax purposes.

Entrepreneurs and business managers also need to take care to ensure that they get what they pay for. Most companies engaged in selling office supplies and equipment are scrupulous and reliable, but fraudulent suppliers do exist. For this reason, experts urge small businesses to proceed methodically, especially if dealing with a new supplier. "Prevent supplier swindles by adopting a written purchasing policy, which includes a list of your approved vendors," stated Scott Clark in *Pugent Sound Business Journal.* "A specific credit check procedure must be completed for a new vendor to be added to this list." Small business owners should also insist on written confirmation of all supplier claims and demand an opportunity to review sample goods before placing an order.

Procurement Options In recent years, office superstores and catalogue supply houses have emerged as the most efficient and inexpensive way to purchase various types of supplies. The average client of these superstores is the small- to medium-sized business, as well as the home office market. The convenience of being able to find virtually any office supply at one location is one of the primary reasons for the increased popularity of the superstores. In addition to convenience, these stores and catalogues offer merchandise that is very competitively priced since they are able to purchase their goods at bulk rates. Some of these savings are usually passed along to small business customers, especially if the stores are operating in a competitive environment.

The proliferation of Internet shopping has opened up a new avenue for office supply procurement as well. Most large office supply chains not offer online shopping sites through which a business may order supplier for pick-up or delivery.

Finally, many small (and large) businesses are choosing suppliers who offer materials made from recycled materials. This trend towards "green" procurement can be seen in all types of paper products (computer paper, envelopes, tablets, file folders, etc.) as well as big-ticket items like office furniture. In the latter case, remanufactured, refurbished or reused furniture has emerged as a particularly attractive option for cash-strapped start-ups and growing businesses because they are able to garner savings of 30-50 percent by pursuing used items. According to some experts, furniture recyclers now represent almost 10 percent of the $13.6 billion commercial furniture industry.

BIBLIOGRAPHY

Atkinson, William. "Buyer Demand for Green Office Products Blossoms." *Purchasing.* 13 July 2000.

Belyea, Kathryn. "Purchasing Exec Urges Peers to Embrace E-Buying." *Purchasing.* 13 July 2000.

Clark, Scott. "Don't Let Fraudulent Suppliers Rip You Off." *Puget Sound Business Journal.* 14 July 2000.

Cullen, Scott, and Ellen Gragg. "Top 20 Trends, Office Innovations, and Products of the Past 20 Years." *OfficeSolutions.* July-August 2004.

Jeffress, Charles N. "Ergonomics Standard Good for Business." *Business Insurance.* 23 October 2000.

"Quiet Revolution: The working environment will be revolutionized over the next decade and office products companies need to get their strategies in place if they are to survive." *Office Products International.* July 2004.

Hillstrom, Northern Lights
updated by Magee, ECDI

ONLINE AUCTIONS

Online auctions are sales transactions that result from a competitive bidding process conducted over the Internet. Whether the sales take place between individuals, between consumers and merchants, or between businesses, online auctions have enjoyed rapid growth with the spread of Internet access. The value of goods and services traded through online auctions is not tracked but is estimated to have grown rapidly in the last five years, from under $10 billion in 2000 to well over three times that figure in 2005. According to an *Entrepreneur* magazine article about online auction marketplace leader eBay, sales through that company's online auction space alone accounted for more than $32 billion in 2004.

The consumer online auction process has been described as being similar to a garage sale, with commonly offered items including collectibles, antiques, toys, clothing, art, cars, tickets, electronics, and even real estate. Online auctions appeal to individuals who enjoy the competitive bidding process and like to feel as if they are getting a bargain. Most Web sites that host auctions allow buyers and sellers to negotiate payment methods and shipping details. Auction-related costs are usually limited to a small percentage of the final sales price.

Auctions have been a means of economic transaction for centuries. By moving onto the Internet, auctions have become accessible to a much larger number of participants, increasing the size of the marketplace dramatically. Although transactions between individuals are an important driver of the online auction market, the business-to-consumer and business-to-business portions of the market are growing rapidly. Online auctions offer potential benefits to all types of businesses. For example, since 2000 the firm SalvageSales has been helping insurance companies and their clients sell damaged shipments of commercial and industrial goods. In the past these salvage sale operations would have been handled locally, but the online auction option offered by SalvageSales has increased the size of the marketplace that can be easily reached in salvage sales. The same increase in market size is being seen across the board for both used and new products. Another example of an online auction-based business is Cashco 1000, Inc., a business started by a stay-at-home mother who wanted to try something she could manage from home while raising her children. Founder and owner, Angle Cash expected her business to sell $500,000 worth of home-decorations on eBay in 2005.

"Many companies wonder when and why they should use online auctions as part of their business trading strategy," Lori Mitchell wrote in *InfoWorld*. "The short answer is, if you sell goods and services or if you purchase items to run your business, online auctions can work for you.... Companies of practically any size and within any industry can benefit from them."

Internet analysts note that online retailers who incorporate auctions into their sales activities tend to see a higher level of repeat visits, more frequent purchases, and increased promotional opportunities compared to other online retailers. Auctions also offer advantages for those businesses interested in selling to or buying from other businesses. Some businesses choose to host closed or private auctions for their existing business contacts. But online auction companies may be able to assist companies in enlarging the audience for auctions by analyzing the bidding patterns of previous auctions to identify potential new customers.

EBAY

By far the largest online auction host is eBay, a company founded in 1995 and through which an estimated 95 percent of all online auctions took place in 2005. Other online auctioneers include such companies as Amazon; Liquidity Services, Inc.; Overstock.com; uBid; and Yahoo to name just a few. But by far the largest online auction space belongs to eBay.

Small businesses may use eBay to boost sales in a number of ways. "Whether you're starting a brand-new business or just looking for ways to grow an existing operation, you can do it on eBay." This statement of introduction appears on an *Entrepreneur.com* Web site dedicated to providing guidance to those interested in setting up an eBay business. The site offers step-by-step guidelines for establishing an eBay account and creating a successful eBay vendor profile. The popularity and growth of eBay businesses can be seen clearly through a quick review of recently published books. There are more than 35 books that have been published since 2001 that deal specifically, in one form or another, with doing business through eBay. Many businesses have been formed based exclusively on the sale of products through eBay auctions and/or direct eBay sales and many others have taken existing retail businesses and expanded them by using eBay as a supplemental sales venue.

Starting Out Becoming familiar with the eBay way of doing business is an important first step in becoming involved in online auctions. Browsing the www.ebay.com site, watching auctions, taking the virtual tours offered on the site, are all ways to become familiar with the overall eBay experience. No registration is required to browse the site.

In order to buy on eBay one must be registered. The key element in registering on eBay, for which there is no fee, is the selection of a User ID. Jim Griffith, author of *The Official eBay Bible*, advises new users to take care in selecting a User ID since it will be the official "handle" for all eBay transactions by that person or the organization he or she represents. It is crucial that a small company picks a User ID that is well suited to the company, conveys some meaning, and does not include the name eBay for reasons of trademark protection.

Selling on eBay requires a seller's account, and a PayPal account. Setting up a seller's account is a simple process very similar to the registration process, and includes providing eBay with sufficient information to verify one's identity and preferred method of paying seller fees. The seller fees are nominal and vary by category of item being sold. A PayPal account is necessary because it is the most popular online payment method used by eBay buyers. The PayPal system is owned by eBay and there is no charge to open the account. The account is either used as a deposit account into which the account holder deposits and withdraws cash as necessary or it is linked to a credit card that may be debited or credited as needed. The seller on eBay may choose to accept payments by any method he or she prefers but PayPal is the most commonly used method on eBay and therefore, the simplest account through which to manage eBay transactions.

Selling on eBay Before attempting to sell on eBay it is recommended by most experienced eBay users that a person first try partaking in an auction and/or purchasing something offered on the site. There are many strategies used by buyers and sellers alike to try and get the best possible price. Entire books have been written offering advice on how to maximize the eBay auction experience. In summary, here are eleven areas that need attention when planning to sell through an eBay auction. This list provides a glimpse into the process.

- Fully use the "About Me" page—The "About Me" page is a free Web page offered to an eBay seller. This is a useful resource that any small business or individual seller should use and keep updated.

- Shop the competition—It is always a good idea to search for items already listed on eBay before preparing to list new items and set up auctions. A little competitive research will provide a new seller with important information about what category is most commonly used for an item, the price range for other similar objects, and the availability of supply of similar items currently listed.

- Choose a category—Items up for sale and auction on eBay are listed by category. Having one's items assigned to a category correctly is essential since customers looking for that perfect, customized swing set you have listed will never find it if it is erroneously listed as yard equipment.

- Write an informative and compelling description— Writing catchy and informative product descriptions is not a simple task. The auction title needs to catch a potential buyer's attention and compel him or her to click on the item. Because eBay's search engine uses the auction title to index items for sale, use this precious title real estate wisely and refrain from using cute words like "wow" or "L@@K!" Include as many terms as possible for the item you wish to sell, since people will refer to things in many ways—pants, jeans, dress slacks, trousers, suit pants, etc. . . Be as informative as possible

in the description. For an additional fee, there are other features that may be added to a listing. eBay offers several options for increasing visibility, like bold-face fonts and highlighting, but these come at a cost and their use should be weighed against the benefit added.

- Select a format—In addition to the classic auction format, there are other ways to sell on eBay. One can add a "Buy It Now" button to the auction, which permits a potential buyer to skip the auction process and purchase the item for the assigned price. Another option is to use a Dutch-style auction to sell multiple identical items in the same listing. This is popular among small businesses. Formats that tend to work best for some products may not be the optimum formats for others products. For example, a 'Buy it Now" bottom may work best for lower-priced, more impulse-buy items but may not help with higher priced or very unique items.

- Use photos to advantage—The use of photos in an auction is very important. Bidders do not have the opportunity to look at an item in person, so pictures factor heavily in their decisions about whether or not to bid and if so, how much to bid.

- Set the price—Setting a price can become complicated depending on the auction format chosen. One way that eBay makes it easy to list and sell is by allowing sellers to set a reserve price: a price below which the seller refuses to sell. Unless the bidding meets or exceeds the reserve, the item will not sell. Reserves make some buyers uncomfortable.

- Establish the auction length— Seven days is the default length, but there are reasons to select a different length. For example, many sellers want the bidding to conclude on a Sunday, a popular day for eBay bidding activity. Auctions may run for 1, 3, 5, 7, or 10 days.

- State payment methods acceptable—The seller decides what forms of payment will be acceptable. The more forms of payment accepted, the bigger the potential pool of bidders will be.

- Determine shipping costs and who will pay— Establishing from the outset who is responsible for shipping costs is the best policy. Most sellers require the buyer to pay for shipping costs, particularly as they are an unknown until the location of the buyer is revealed. Offering free shipping is, of course, one way to get a listing to stand out.

- Provide quality customer service—This may seem a self-evident recommendation, and, of course, it is sound advice for any business undertaking. When working with eBay, however, one's record of customer service and follow-through becomes a matter for public record. The eBay system has a built in mechanism for monitoring the actions of customers and sellers. It is called feedback and anyone active on eBay is encouraged to send feedback on the person or entity with whom he or she has had a transaction. These feedback comments and ratings are made a part of the recipient's eBay profile and are then used by future potential sellers and buyers in assessing the likely reliability of the trading partner.

EBAY BUSINESS PARTNER PROGRAMS

ProStores The eBay company provides a large number of software tools to its members, as eBay sellers and buyers are called. Among the more sophisticated of these is called eBay stores. An eBay store is a business and is designed to help a casual eBay seller become a viable business that sells merchandise through eBay on a steady and regular basis. It is recommended that anyone wishing to establish an eBay store first start out by becoming established on the site and getting to know the rhythm of an eBay business before opening a store. Sell at least 50 items a month, have a good source of merchandise, and prepare to be creative when it comes to servicing customers and accumulating a regular client base.

In early 2005, eBay brought to market a new service for businesses with an eBay store presence. It is called ProStores and is a suite of services that integrate with their existing stores. ProStores provide a new eBay business with its own e-commerce-enabled Web site. As Marsha Collier explains in her article "5 eBay Tools You Need to Have," the Web sites used by ProStores work in concert with a company's existing eBay auction activity. "In my eBay classes, I always teach that once you get the hang of eBay selling, you need to open an eBay store. Once you have your eBay store management mastered (and are running a successful enterprise), it's time for you to expand and open your own website. It's the website part that causes many sellers to stumble. eBay sellers aren't usually masters of HTML and the idea of running and setting up a website is a huge, daunting task. ProStores supplies you with practically everything you need to set up a website. If you want help you can always search eBay for ProStores support or website graphics and you'll find people who'll help you make it perfect. You won't find more reasonable website hosting, especially when you consider that it includes a shopping cart and e-commerce specialties. You can jump aboard with ProStores for as little as $6.95 a month."

Affiliates Online affiliate programs have become very popular among online retailers. These programs are arrangements in which a Web site carries a banner ad for a company in exchange for a small percentage of any sales that result from the referral. One of the most successful affiliate programs on the Web today is the one run by eBay. The success is usually attributed to two factors. The first is the sheer volume of traffic on the eBay site each day. The second is the high commission rates paid by eBay to its affiliates. Melissa Campanelli writes about the program in an article for *Entrepreneur,* and explains that "depending on monthly activity, affiliates can earn between $10 and $20 for each active registered user sent to eBay." An active registered user is defined by eBay as a user who registers with the company and bids on or buys an item within 30 days of the registration.

The affiliate program can be very lucrative. According to eBay, it has 10,000 such affiliates, the top 50 of whom make more than $1 million in commissions annually. In order to succeed in this program one must have marketing savvy and a Web presence that includes a substantial advertising budget. But for businesses in this position, becoming active in the eBay affiliates program may be a move that would help to leverage the investment already made in an online presence.

ISOLD IT ON EBAY

One final way in which an entrepreneur may be able to build upon the online auction trend in order to start a retail business is by becoming an iSold It franchisee. The iSold It franchise concept is to offer customers an easy and effortless way to sell their items online without ever going online themselves. Customers of an iSold It franchise simply stop by a store to drop off items they wish to sell, and iSold It takes care of the rest. The business provides the following services to its customers for a small set fee and a percentage of the sale price:

- Professionally photographs each item.

- Posts the item for sale online.

- Holds the item in inventory.

- Answers buyer questions.

- Packs and ships the item.

- Collects from the buyer.

Like any franchising opportunity, the iSold It franchise requires a considerable up-front investment but it also comes with a proven business model and all the tools necessary to put that business in place. And the iSold It franchise is all made possible because of the popularity and strength of the robust online auction market.

ONLINE CLASSIFIED ADS

Online auctions have changed the world for retailers and entrepreneurs by giving them a national and international venue from which to sell. But shipping and transportation costs are not an insignificant barrier to the sale of many large items. A move back to geographically centered trading, to the local marketplace, is being accomplished online through the use of online classified ad sites. Two such sites that have shown strong growth during 2004–2005 are Craigslist.org and LiveDeal. These online classified ad sites are another venue through which small businesses may wish to sell products generally, post an ad for a particularly large item, post job openings, or use as a sales outlet for their overstock items.

SEE ALSO *Internet Payment Systems*

BIBLIOGRAPHY

Campanelli, Melissa. "Sharing the Wealth: Want to get a piece of the eBay pie? Joining its affiliate program can be a good way to do just that." *Entrepreneur.* February 2005.

Collier, Marsha. "5 eBay Tools You Need to Have." *Entrepreneur.com.* 20 March 2006.

Conner, Nancy. *EBay: The Missing Manual.* O'Reilly, August 2005.

Griffith, Jim. *The Official eBay Bible.* Gotham, June 2003.

Lynn, Jacquelyn, and Chris Penttila. "Getting Started on eBay: Behind every eBay success story is a tale of trial and error. We'll help you skip straight ahead to the success part." *Entrepreneur.com* Available from http://www.entrepreneur.com/ebay. 1 October 2004.

Mitchell, Lori. "Sold! On Online Auctions." *InfoWorld.* August 7, 2000.

Nissanoff, Daniel. *FutureShop: How the New Auction Culture Will Revolutionize the Way We Buy, Sell, and Get the Things We Really Want.* The Penguin Press HC, January 2006.

Pofeldt, Elaine. "The Digital Dump." *FSB.* May 2006.

Schuman, Evan. "eBay Pushes to Be Everything to Its Sellers." *CIO Insight.* 26 June 2005.

Tessler, Joelle. "Online Auction Sites Create Vast Global Marketplaces." *Knight-Ridder/Tribune Business News.* 23 October 2000.

Hillstrom, Northern Lights
updated by Magee, ECDI

OPERATIONS MANAGEMENT

Operations management is a multi-disciplinary field that focuses on managing all aspects of an organization's operations. The typical company carries out various functions as a part of its operation. The dividing of a company's activities into functional categories occurs very early on, even in a company formed and operated by a single individual. Most companies make a product of some kind or produce a salable service. They must also carry out a sales and marketing function, an accounting function, and an administrative function to manage employees and the business as a whole. Operations management focuses on the function of providing the product or service. Their job is to assure the production of a quality good and/or service. They apply ideas and technologies to increase productivity and reduce costs, improve flexibility to meet rapidly changing customer needs, assure a safe workplace for all employees, and when possible assist in assuring high-quality customer service.

For the most part, the title "Operations Manager" is used in companies that produce a tangible good—manufacturers on the whole. In service-oriented businesses, the person responsible for the operations manager role is often called by another name, one that addresses the service being offered. Examples include project manager, consultant, lawyer, accountant, office manager, datacenter manager, etc.

KEY ISSUES IN OPERATIONS

As an organization develops plans and strategies to deal with the opportunities and challenges that arise in its particular operating environment, it should design a system that is capable of producing quality services and goods in the quantities demanded and in the time frames necessary to meet the businesses obligations.

Designing the System Designing the system begins with product development. Product development involves determining the characteristics and features of the product or service to be sold. It should begin with an assessment of customer needs and eventually grow into a detailed product design. The facilities and equipment used in production, as well as the information systems needed to monitor and control performance, are all a part of this system design process. In fact, manufacturing process decisions are integral to the ultimate success or failure of the system. Of all the structural decisions that the operations manager makes, the one likely to have the greatest impact on the operation's success is choice of the process technology. This decision answers the basic question: How will the product be made?

Product design is a critical task because it helps to determine the characteristics and features of the product, as well as how the product functions. Product design determines a product's cost and quality, as well as its features and performance. These are important factors on which customers make purchasing decisions. In recent years, new design models such as Design for Manufacturing and Assembly (DFMA) have been implemented to improve product quality and lower costs. DFMA focuses on operating issues during product design. This can be critical even though design costs are a small part of the total cost of a product, because, procedures that waste raw materials or duplicate effort can have a substantial negative impact on a business's operating profitability. Another innovation similar to DFMA in its emphasis on design is Quality Functional Deployment (QFD). QFD is a set of planning and communication routines that are used to improve product design by focusing design efforts on customer needs.

Process design describes how the product will be made. The process design decision has two major components: a technical (or engineering) component and a scale economy (or business) component. The technical component includes selecting equipment and selecting a sequence for various phases of operational production.

The scale economy or business component involves applying the proper amount of mechanization (tools and equipment) to make the organization's work force more productive. This includes determining: 1) If the demand for a product is large enough to justify mass production; 2) If there is sufficient variety in customer demand so that flexible production systems are required; and 3) If demand for a product is so small or seasonal that it cannot support a dedicated production facility.

Facility design involves determining the capacity, location, and layout for the production facility. Capacity is a measure of an company's ability to provide the demanded product in the quantity requested by the customer in a timely manner. Capacity planning involves estimating demand, determining the capacity of facilities, and deciding how to change the organization's capacity to respond to demand.

Facility location is the placement of a facility with respect to its customers and suppliers. Facility location is a strategic decision because it is a long-term commitment of resources that cannot easily or inexpensively be changed. When evaluating a location, management should consider customer convenience, initial investment necessary to secure land and facilities, government incentives, and operating transportation costs. In addition, qualitative factors such as quality of life for employees, transportation infrastructure, and labor environment should also be taken under consideration.

Facility layout is the arrangement of the workspace within a facility. It considers which departments or work areas should be adjacent to one another so that the flow of product, information, and people can move quickly and efficiently through the production system.

Implementation Once a product is developed and the manufacturing system is designed, it must be implemented, a task often more easily discussed than carried out. IF the system design function was done thoroughly, it will have rendered an implementation plan which will guide activities during implementation. Nonetheless, there will inevitably be changes needed. Decisions will have to be made throughout this implementation period about trade-offs. For example, the cost of the originally planned conveyor belt may have risen. This change will make it necessary to consider changing the specified conveyor belt for another model. This, of course, will impact upon other systems linked to the conveyor belt and the full implications of all these changes will have to be assessed and compared to the cost of the price increase on the original conveyor belt.

Planning and Forecasting Running an efficient production system requires a great deal of planning. Long-range decisions could include the number of facilities required to meet customer needs or studying how technological change might affect the methods used to produce services and goods. The time horizon for long-term planning varies with the industry and is dependent on both complexity and size of proposed changes. Typically, however, long-term planning may involve determining work force size, developing training programs, working with suppliers to improve product quality and improve delivery systems, and determining the amount of material to order on an aggregate basis. Short-term scheduling, on the other hand, is concerned with production planning for specific job orders (who will do the work, what equipment will be used, which materials will be consumed, when the work will begin and end, and what mode of transportation will be used to deliver the product when the order is completed).

Managing the System Managing the system involves working with people to encourage participation and improve organizational performance. Participative management and teamwork are an essential part of successful operations, as are leadership, training, and culture. In addition, material management and quality are two key areas of concern.

Material management includes decisions regarding the procurement, control, handling, storage, and distribution of materials. Material management is becoming more important because, in many organizations, the costs of purchased materials comprise more than 50 percent of the total production cost. Questions regarding quantities and timing of material orders need to be addressed here as well when companies weigh the qualities of various suppliers.

BUILDING SUCCESS WITH OPERATIONS

To understand operations and how they contribute to the success of an organization, it is important to understand the strategic nature of operations, the value-added nature of operations, the impact technology can have on performance, and the globally competitive marketplace.

Efficient organization operations are a vital tool in achieving competitive advantage in the daily contest for customers/clients. What factors influence buying decisions for these entities? For most services and goods, price, quality, product performance and features, product variety, and availability of the product are critical. All these factors are substantially influenced by actions taken in operations. For example, when productivity increases, product costs decline and product price can be reduced. Similarly, as better production methods are developed, quality and variety may increase.

By linking operations and operating strategies with the overall strategy of the organization (including engineering, financial, marketing, and information system strategy) synergy can result. Operations become a positive factor when facilities, equipment, and employee training are viewed as a means to achieve organizational objectives, rather than as narrowly focused departmental objectives. In recognition of this evolving viewpoint, the criteria for judging operations are changing from cost control (a narrowly defined operating objective) to global performance measurements in such areas as product performance and variety, product quality, delivery time, customer service, and operational flexibility.

In today's business environment, a key component of operational flexibility in many industries is technological knowledge. Advances in technology make it possible to build better products using fewer resources. As technology fundamentally changes a product, its performance and quality often increases dramatically, making it a more highly valued commodity in the marketplace. But the growth in high-tech business applications has created new competitors as well, making it important for businesses to try to register advantages in any and all areas of operations management.

Over time, operations management has grown in scope and increased in importance. Today, it has elements that are strategic, it relies on behavioral and engineering concepts, and it utilizes management science/operations research tools and techniques for systematic decision-making and problem-solving. As operations management continues to develop, it will increasingly interact with other functional areas within the organization to develop integrated answers to complex interdisciplinary problems. Indeed, such interaction is widely regarded as essential to long-term business success for small business establishments and multinational corporations alike.

BIBLIOGRAPHY

Dyson, Robert G. "Strategy, Performance and Operational Research." *Journal of the Operational Research Society.* January 2000.

Lester, Tom. "Why Manufacturers Must Take Advantage of Design Counsel Co-operation Between Managers and Designers Holds the Key to the Success of a Product and Even of the Company Behind It." *The Financial Times.* 27 February 2006.

Magnuson Coe, Thomas. *Electronic Supply Chain Collaboration for Small Job Shop Manufacturers.* Universal Publishers, March 2005.

Nie, Winter. "Waiting: Integrating Social and Psychological Perspectives in Operations Management." *Omega.* December 2000.

Ruffini, Frans A. J., Harry Boer, and Maarten J. Van Riemsdijk. "Organization Design in Operations Management." *International Journal of Operations and Production Management.* July 2000.

Sharma, Anand, and Patricia E. Moody. *The Perfect Engine: Driving Manufacturing Breakthroughs with the Global Production System.* Simon and Schuster, 2001.

Thrun, Walter. *Maximizing Profit: How to Measure the Financial Impact of Manufacturing Decisions.* Productivity Press, October 2002.

Hillstrom, Northern Lights
updated by Magee, ECDI

OPPORTUNITY COST

Simply stated, an opportunity cost is the cost of a missed opportunity. It is the opposite of the benefit that would have been gained had an action, not taken, been taken—the missed opportunity. This is a concept used in economics. Applied to a business decision, the opportunity cost might refer to the profit a company could have earned from its capital, equipment, and real estate if these assets had been used in a different way. The concept of opportunity cost may be applied to many different situations. It should be considered whenever circumstances are such that scarcity necessitates the election of one option over another. Opportunity cost is usually defined in terms of money, but it may also be considered in terms of time, person-hours, mechanical output, or any other finite resource.

Although opportunity costs are not generally considered by accountants—financial statements only include explicit costs, or actual outlays—they should be considered by managers. Most business owners do consider opportunity costs whenever they make a decision about which of two possible actions to take. Small businesses factor in opportunity costs when computing their operating expenses in order to provide a bid or estimate on the price of a job. For example, a landscaping firm may be bidding on two jobs each of which will use half of its equipment during a particular period of time. As a result, they will forgo other job opportunities some of which may be large and potentially profitable. Opportunity costs increase the cost of doing business, and thus should be recovered whenever possible as a portion of the overhead expense charged to every job.

EXAMPLES OF OPPORTUNITY COSTS

One way to demonstrate the concept of opportunity costs is through an example of investment capital. A private investor purchases $10,000 in a certain security, such as shares in a corporation, and after one year the investment has appreciated in value to $10,500. The investor's return is 5 percent. The investor considers other ways the $10,000 could have been invested, and discovers a bank certificate with an annual yield of 6 percent and a government bond that carries an annual yield of 7.5 percent. After a year, the bank certificate would have appreciated in value to $10,600, and the government bond would have appreciated to $10,750. The opportunity cost of purchasing shares is $100 relative to the bank certificate, and $250 relative to the government bond. The investor's decision to purchase shares with a 5 percent return comes at the cost of a lost opportunity to earn 6 or 7.5 percent.

Expressed in terms of time, consider a commuter who chooses to drive to work, rather than using public transportation. Because of heavy traffic and a lack of parking, it takes the commuter 90 minutes to get to work. If the same commute on public transportation would have taken only 40 minutes, the opportunity cost of driving would be 50 minutes. The commuter might naturally have chosen driving over public transportation because she had a use for the car after work or because she could not have anticipated traffic delays in driving. Experience can create a basis for future decisions, and the commuter may be less inclined to drive next time, knowing the consequences of traffic congestion.

In another example, a small business owns the building in which it operates, and thus pays no rent for office space. But this does not mean that the company's cost for office space is zero, even though an accountant might treat it that way. Instead, the small business owner must consider the opportunity cost associated with reserving the building for its current use. Perhaps the building could have been rented out to another company, with the business itself relocated to a location with a higher level of customer traffic. The foregone money from these alternative uses of the property is an opportunity cost of using the office space, and thus should be considered in calculations of the small business's expenses.

BIBLIOGRAPHY

Anderson, David Ray, Dennis J. Sweeney, and Thomas Arthur Williams. *Statistics for Business and Economics.* Thomson South-Western, 6 January 2004.

Blinder, Alan S., and William J. Baumol. *Microeconomics: Principles and Policy.* Thomson South-Western, June 2005.

Ernest, Robert Hall, and Marc Lieberman. *Microeconomics.* Thomson South-Western, 2004.

Vera-Munoz, Sandra C. "The Effects of Accounting Knowledge and Context on the Omission of Opportunity Costs in Resource Allocation Decisions." *Accounting Review.* January 1998.

Hillstrom, Northern Lights
updated by Magee, ECDI

OPTIMAL FIRM SIZE

Optimal firm size refers to the speed and extent of growth that is ideal for a specific small business. Optimal firm size is dependent on a variety of internal and external factors. For some home-based businesses, the optimal size may be the two founding partners—a husband and wife—if their primary operating goal is simply to bring in enough revenue for a comfortable standard of living, while leaving large blocks of time for family or travel. But most companies are intent on expanding their operations. Growth of some kind, either in revenues, profits, number of employees, or size of facilities, is essential for almost every business. For many companies competing in rapidly changing industries, expansion (of manufacturing capacity, geographic presence, market share, etc.) may be imperative for survival. But smart growth strategies can be elusive, as many entrepreneurs have learned to their chagrin. As James A. Schriner explained in *Industry Week,* "Growing a company is like blowing up a balloon. Your first few breaths, though difficult, produce immediate results. Subsequent breaths expand the balloon proportionally until it nears capacity. Stop too soon and the balloon never reaches its potential. Stop too late and it bursts."

Successful entrepreneurs and business experts agree that the key to finding the optimal firm size is to grow in a controlled way. In some cases, restraining growth is simply a matter of saying "no," or turning down new business. This is particularly true for service businesses that depend on the personal attention of the founder. When turning down business becomes necessary, the entrepreneur may wish to provide referrals in order to maintain good relations with potential customers. Another strategy in restraining growth involves hiring employees who like working in a small company atmosphere. These people tend to enjoy the diversity of challenges they encounter in a small business, and they often have a strong interest in the product and can provide their expertise to customers. It is important to note, however, that restraining growth does not mean refusing to change. Small businesses are not likely to remain in business long if they cannot be creative and adapt to changes in customer tastes and competitors' tactics.

Schriner noted that one factor influencing the optimal size of a business is the availability of workers and other resources in the surrounding community. In fact, he suggested that it is possible for businesses to outgrow the communities in which they operate, particularly when they are located in a remote area. In this case, it may be difficult to attract talented workers from outside the immediate area, forcing the company to pay sharply higher wages to compete for labor. In addition, some communities cannot afford to provide services to growing companies (or provide top schools, parks, and other quality of life elements that attract high-quality employees necessary for successful business expansion). Finally, Schriner claimed that being too integral a part of a community can make it difficult for a growing company to adapt to a changing business environment. Some factors that may indicate a company has outgrown its community include: employing more than 10 percent of the local work force; growing at a faster rate than the community's labor force; providing more than one-third of the local government's funding through taxes; and being responsible for the death of the community if the company should shut down.

SEE ALSO *Economies of Scale*

BIBLIOGRAPHY

Joaquin, Domingo Castelo, and Naveen Khanna. "Investment Timing Decisions Under Threat of Potential Competition: Why Firm Size Matters." *Quarterly Review of Economics and Finance.* Spring 2001.

Lawler, Edward E. III. "Rethinking Organization Size." *Organizational Dynamics.* Autumn 1997.

Koretz, Gene. "Little Guys Are Making Plans: Small Businesses Are Set to Expand." *Business Week.* 2 June 1997.

Orser, Barbara J., Sandy Hogarth-Scott, and Allan L. Riding. "Performance, Firm Size, and Management Problem Solving." *Journal of Small Business Management.* October 2000.

Rossi-Hansberg, Esteban, and Mark L.J. Wright. Academic Paper. "Firm Size Dynamics and the Aggregate Economy." Stanford University, 10 July 2004.

Schriner, James A. "How Big Is Too Big?" *Industry Week.* 6 May 1996.

Hillstrom, Northern Lights
updated by Magee, ECDI

ORAL COMMUNICATION

Oral communication describes any type of interaction that makes use of spoken words, and it is a vital, integral part of the business world, especially in an era dubbed the information age. "The ability to communicate effectively through speaking as well as in writing is highly valued, and demanded, in business," Herta A. Murphy, Herbert W. Hildebrandt, and Jane Thomas wrote in their book *Effective Business Communications.* "Knowing the content of the functional areas of business is important, but to give life to those ideas—in meetings or in solo presentations—demands an effective oral presentation." The types of oral communication commonly used within an organization include staff meetings, personal discussions, presentations, telephone discourse, and informal conversation. Oral communication with those outside of the organization might take the form of face-to-face meetings, telephone calls, speeches, teleconferences, or videoconferences.

Conversation management skills are essential for small business owners and managers who often shoulder much of the burden in such areas as client/customer presentations, employee interviews, and conducting meetings. For oral communication to be effective, it should be clear, relevant, tactful in phraseology and tone, concise, and informative. Presentations or conversations that bear these hallmarks can be an invaluable tool in ensuring business health and growth. Unclear, inaccurate, or inconsiderate business communication, on the other hand, can waste valuable time, alienate employees or customers, and destroy goodwill toward management or the overall business.

ORAL PRESENTATIONS

The public presentation is generally recognized as the most important of the various genres of oral business communication. As is true of all kinds of communication, the first step in preparing a public speech or remarks is to determine the essential purpose/goal of the communication. As Hildebrandt, Murphy, and Thomas note, business presentations tend to have one of three general purposes: to persuade, to inform or instruct, or to entertain. Out of the purpose will come the main ideas to be included in the presentation. These ideas should be researched thoroughly and adapted to the needs of the audience.

The ideas should then be organized to include an introduction, a main body or text, and a summary or conclusion. Or, as the old adage about giving speeches goes, "Tell them what you're going to tell them, tell them, and tell them what you told them." The introduction should grab the listener's interest and establish the theme of the remainder of the presentation. The main body should concentrate on points of emphasis. The conclusion should restate the key points and summarize the overarching message that is being conveyed.

Visual aids can be a useful component of some presentations. Whether they are projected from a PC, displayed on chalkboards, dry-erase boards, or flip charts visual aids should be meaningful, creative, and interesting in order to help the speaker get a message across. The key to successful use of visual aids is that they should support the theme of the presentation, aid in its transmittal but do so without detracting by being sloppy, complicated, or even too entertaining.

Once the presentation has been organized and the visual aids have been selected, the speaker should rehearse the presentation out loud and revise as needed to fit time constraints, and to assure thorough coverage of the main points. It may help to practice in front of a mirror or in front of a friend in order to gain confidence. A good oral presentation will include transitional phrases to help listeners move through the material, and will not be overly long or technical. It is also important for the speaker to anticipate questions the audience might have and either include that information in the presentation or be prepared to address them in a Q&A session at the end of the presentation. Professional and gracious presentation is another key to effective communication, whether the setting is a conference, a banquet, a holiday luncheon, or a management retreat. "Recognize that when you speak at a business event, you represent your company and your office in that company," stated Steve Kaye in *IIE Solutions*. "Use the event as an opportunity to promote good will. Avoid complaints, criticism, or controversy. These will alienate the audience and destroy your credibility quickly. Instead, talk about what the audience wants to hear. Praise your host, honor the occasion, and compliment the attendees. Radiate success and optimism."

Oral presentations can be delivered extemporaneously (from an outline or notes); by reading from a manuscript; or from memory. The extemporaneous approach is often touted as a method that allows the speaker to make eye contact and develop a rapport with the audience while simultaneously conveying pertinent information. Reading from a manuscript is more often utilized for longer and/or detailed communications that cover a lot of ground. Memorization, meanwhile, is usually only used for short and/or informal discussions.

The delivery of effective oral presentations requires a speaker to consider his or her vocal pitch, rate, and volume. It is important to incorporate changes in vocal pitch to add emphasis and avoid monotony. It is also helpful to vary the rate of speaking and incorporate pauses to allow the listener to reflect upon specific elements of the overall message. Finding the appropriate volume is crucial to the success of a presentation as well. Finally, speakers should be careful not to add extraneous words or sounds—such as "um," "you know," or "okay"—between words or sentences in a presentation.

Nonverbal elements such as posture, gestures, and facial expressions are also important factors in developing good oral communication skills. "Your outward appearance mirrors your inner mood," Hildebrandt, Murphy, and Thomas confirmed. "Thus good posture suggests poise and confidence; stand neither at rigid attention nor with sloppy casualness draped over the podium, but erect with your weight about equally distributed on each foot." Some movement may be helpful to hold listeners' attention or to increase emphasis, but constant shifting or pacing should be avoided. Likewise, hand and arm gestures can be used to point, describe, or emphasize, but they should be varied, carefully timed, and adapted to the audience. Finally, good speakers should make frequent eye contact with the audience, let their facial expression show their interest in the ideas they are presenting, and dress in a way that is appropriate for the occasion.

Small business owners reflect the general population in that their enthusiasm for public speaking varies considerably for individual to individual. Some entrepreneurs enjoy the limelight and thrive in settings that call for public presentations (formal or informal). Others are less adept at public speaking and avoid being placed in such situations. But business consultants urge entrepreneurs to treat public presentations and oral communication skills as a potentially invaluable tool in business growth. "You may consider hiring a presentation coach or attending a workshop on business presentations," counseled Kaye. "These services can show you how to maximize your impact while speaking. In fact, learning such skills serves as a long-term investment in your future as an effective leader."

BIBLIOGRAPHY

Hardingham, Alison. "Charged with Intent." *People Management.* 30 March 2000.

Holmes, Godfrey. "Tactical Blunder." *Accountancy.* June 2000.

Kaye, Steve. "Make an Impact with Style: Presentation Tips for Leaders." *IIE Solutions.* March 1999.

Murphy, Herta A., Herbert W. Hildebrandt, and Jane P. Thomas. *Effective Business Communications.* Seventh Edition. McGraw-Hill, 1997.

Rosenbaum, Bernard L., "Presentation Techniques." *American Salesman.* January 2005.

Hillstrom, Northern Lights
updated by Magee, ECDI

ORGANIZATION CHART

Organizational charts are detailed representations of organization structures and hierarchies. They are typically used to provide both employees and individuals outside the organization with a "snapshot" picture of its reporting relationships, divisions of work, and levels of management. Obviously, smaller firms—whether they consist of a single owner of a home-based business, a modest shop of a few employees, or a family-owned business with a few dozen workers—are less likely to need or to use organization charts. Small organizations can get along very well without them as long as everyone understands what he or she is to do and with whom to do it. But many consultants and small business owners contend that an organization chart can be a useful tool for growing firms.

Business owners endeavoring to allocate responsibilities, activities, and management authority to various employees also have to make certain that they coordinate the activities of those employees to avoid gaps and/or redundancies in operations and management. "It is helpful to think of organizational design elements as building blocks that can be used to create a structure to fulfill a particular purpose," stated Allan R. Cohen in *The Portable MBA in Management*. "A structure is built by defining the requirements of each individual job and then grouping the individual jobs into units. These units are grouped into larger and larger units and coordinating (or integrating) mechanisms are established for these units. In this way, the structure has been built to support organizational goals and achieve the key factors for success." Ideally, a detailed organizational chart will provide the business owner or manager with an accurate overview of the relationships of these units/responsibilities to one another and a reliable indication as to whether the firm is positioned to meet the business's fundamental goals.

ADVANTAGES AND DISADVANTAGES ASSOCIATED WITH ORGANIZATION CHARTS

While organizational charts are commonly used by mid- and large-sized companies, as well as by significant numbers of smaller businesses with varied operations and a substantial workforce, their usefulness has been a subject of some debate.

Advantages Supporters of organization charts claim that they are tools that can effectively delineate work responsibilities and reporting relationships. Managers of different organizational units may not fully understand how their work fits into the work of other units. An organization chart can provide this relationship guide and thus prevent the development of illogical and confusing relationships. In fact, the very process of charting the organization is a good test of the company's structure because any relationship that cannot be charted is likely to be confusing to those working in it.

Supporters also argue that "org charts" can be particularly useful as a navigational tool when small businesses expand their operations. Small firms that do rather well in the early stages of their development often begin to fail when the founders can no longer manage everything in their personal styles. The transition from small firm to successful large firm is impaired when employees are allowed to do jobs that fit their personality and unique skills rather than jobs necessary for organizational performance. The early adoption of an organization chart can help to identify the areas in which a small firm is lacking the supervisory role before this lack begins to have a more serious impact on the organization.

Disadvantages The above perspective is not universally accepted by business consultants, researchers, executives, and managers, however. Detractors point out that formal organization charts do not recognize informal lines of communication and influence that are quite vital in many business settings. Organization charts are often seen as narrow and static in perspective. They may exclude important relationship and reporting factors like leader behavior, the impact of the environment, informal relations, power distribution, etc.

Critics of organization charts also sometimes charge that the diagrams may paint a misleading picture of the importance and influence of various people within an organization. Charts are, out of necessity, somewhat streamlined representations that only provide so much detail to a user. In some instances, for example, an organization chart may depict two employees as being equal in power and influence, when in reality, one of the individuals is rapidly ascending through the ranks and has the ear of the firm's principal decision-makers, while the other may be regarded as steady but unremarkable (or even worse, an individual whose position has deteriorated from a higher level over the previous years).

Finally, observers suggest that organization charts may encourage individuals to take a very narrow view of their jobs and in this way the org chart may discourage the development of leadership skills in some employees. In these situations, the result is an organization that is not responsive to change and lacks flexibility. The organization chart and all the supporting documentation become substitutes for action and creative responses.

USING ORGANIZATION CHARTS TO STUDY ORGANIZATION STRUCTURE

As alluded to earlier, the process of constructing an organization chart is sometimes cited as a valuable means by which a company can test its structural soundness. Proponents say that charts can be used to ensure that no one individual's productivity is constrained by the organizational structure.

Researchers, consultants, and executives note that this benefit can be even more pronounced in today's business world, which has seen dramatic changes in operating philosophies and management direction over the past few decades. Indeed, corporations are increasingly implementing innovative organizational redesigns in efforts to increase their productivity. The growth in cross-functional teams and the increasing frequency of reorganizations increase the usefulness of organizational charts for keeping track of operational relationships and lines of authority. It is important, then, for businesses that do rely on organizational charts to continually examine and update those diagrams to ensure that they reflect current business realities. In fact, the changes in organizational structures have spurred innovative changes in the format of many organizational charts. Whereas traditional models have been formatted along general "up-down" lines, newer models sometimes utilize flattened or "spoke" frameworks.

BIBLIOGRAPHY

Cohen, Allan R. *The Portable MBA in Management.* Second Edition. John Wiley & Sons, 2002.

Doloff, Phyllis Gail. "Beyond the Org Chart." *Across the Board.* February 1999.

Dressler, Soeren. *Strategy, Organizational Effectiveness and Performance Management.* Universal Publishers, 2004.

Galbraith, Jay, Amy Kates, and Diane Downey. *Designing Dynamic Organizations.* AMACOM, 2001.

Longenecker, Justin G., Carlos W. Moore, J. William Petty, and Leslie E. Palich. *Small Business Management with Infotrac.* Thomson South-West, 2005.

LaZara, Vincent A. "Put the Customer on Top: Updating Your Organizational Chart." *Manage.* October 1999.

Hillstrom, Northern Lights
updated by Magee, ECDI

ORGANIZATION THEORY

An organization, by its most basic definition, is an assembly of people working together to achieve common objectives through a division of labor. An organization provides a means of using individual strengths within a group to achieve more than can be accomplished by the aggregate efforts of group members working individually. Business organizations are formed to deliver goods or services to consumers in such a manner that they can realize a profit at the conclusion of the transaction. Over the years, business analysts, economists, and academic researchers have pondered several theories that attempt to explain the dynamics of business organizations, including the ways in which they make decisions, distribute power and control, resolve conflict, and promote or resist organizational change. As Jeffrey Pfeffer summarized in *New Directions for Organization Theory*, organizational theory studies provide "an interdisciplinary focus on a) the effect of social organizations on the behavior and attitudes of individuals within them, b) the effects of individual characteristics and action on organization, ... c) the performance, success, and survival of organizations, d) the mutual effects of environments, including resource and task, political, and cultural environments on organizations and vice versa, and e) concerns with both the epistemology and methodology that undergird research on each of these topics."

Of the various organizational theories that have been studied in this realm, the open-systems theory has emerged as perhaps the most widely known, but others have their proponents as well. Indeed, some researchers into organizational theory propound a blending of various theories, arguing that an enterprise will embrace different organizational strategies in reaction to changes in its competitive circumstances, structural design, and experiences.

BACKGROUND

Modern organization theory is rooted in concepts developed during the beginnings of the Industrial Revolution in the late 1800s and early 1900s. Of considerable import during that period was the research done by of German sociologist Max Weber (1864-1920). Weber believed that bureaucracies, staffed by bureaucrats, represented the ideal organizational form. Weber based his model bureaucracy on legal and absolute authority, logic, and order. In Weber's idealized organizational structure, responsibilities for workers are clearly defined and behavior is tightly controlled by rules, policies, and procedures.

Weber's theories of organizations, like others of the period, reflected an impersonal attitude toward the people in the organization. Indeed, the work force, with its personal frailties and imperfections, was regarded as a potential detriment to the efficiency of any system. Although his theories are now considered mechanistic and outdated, Weber's views on bureaucracy provided important insight into the era's conceptions of process efficiency, division of labor, and authority.

Another important contributor to organization theory in the early 1900s was Henri Fayol. He is credited with identifying strategic planning, staff recruitment, employee motivation, and employee guidance (via policies and procedures) as important management functions in creating and nourishing a successful organization.

Weber's and Fayol's theories found broad application in the early and mid-1900s, in part because of the influence of Frederick W. Taylor (1856-1915). In a 1911 book entitled *Principles of Scientific Management*, Taylor outlined his theories and eventually implemented them on American factory floors. He is credited with helping to define the role of training, wage incentives, employee selection, and work standards in organizational performance.

Researchers began to adopt a less mechanical view of organizations and to pay more attention to human influences in the 1930s. This development was motivated by several studies that shed light on the function of human fulfillment in organizations. The best known of these was probably the so-called Hawthorn Studies. These studies, conducted primarily under the direction of Harvard University researcher Elton Mayo, were conducted in the mid-1920s and 1930s at a Western Electric Company plant known as the Hawthorn Works. The company wanted to determine the degree to which working conditions affected output.

Surprisingly, the studies failed to show any significant positive correlation between workplace conditions and productivity. In one study, for example, worker productivity escalated when lighting was increased, but it also increased when illumination was decreased. The results of the studies demonstrated that innate forces of human behavior may have a greater influence on organizations than do mechanistic incentive systems. The legacy of the Hawthorn studies and other organizational research efforts of that period was an emphasis on the importance of individual and group interaction, humanistic management skills, and social relationships in the workplace.

The focus on human influences in organizations was reflected most noticeably by the integration of Abraham Maslow's "hierarchy of human needs" into organization theory. Maslow's theories introduced two important implications into organization theory. The first was that people have different needs and therefore need to be motivated by different incentives to achieve organizational objectives. The second of Maslow's theories held that people's needs change over time, meaning that as the needs of people lower in the hierarchy are met, new needs arise. These assumptions led to the recognition, for example, that assembly-line workers could be more productive if more of their personal needs were met, whereas past theories suggested that monetary rewards were the sole, or primary, motivators.

Douglas McGregor contrasted the organization theory that emerged during the mid-1900s to previous views. In the 1950s, McGregor offered his renowned Theory X and Theory Y to explain the differences. Theory X encompassed the old view of workers, which held that employees preferred to be directed, wanted to avoid responsibility, and cherished financial security above all else.

McGregor believed that organizations that embraced Theory Y were generally more productive. This theory held that humans can learn to accept and seek responsibility; most people possess a high degree of imaginative and problem-solving ability; employees are capable of effective self-direction; and that self-actualization is among the most important rewards that organizations can provide their workers.

OPEN-SYSTEMS THEORY

Traditional theories regarded organizations as closed systems that were autonomous and isolated from the outside world. In the 1960s, however, more holistic and humanistic ideologies emerged. Recognizing that traditional theory had failed to take into account many environmental influences that impacted the efficiency of organizations, most theorists and researchers embraced an open-systems view of organizations.

The term "open systems" reflected the newfound belief that all organizations are unique—in part because of the unique environment in which they operate—and that they should be structured to accommodate unique problems and opportunities. For example, research during the 1960s indicated that traditional bureaucratic organizations generally failed to succeed in environments where technologies or markets were rapidly changing. They also failed to realize the importance of regional cultural influences in motivating workers.

Environmental influences that affect open systems can be described as either specific or general. The specific environment refers to the network of suppliers, distributors, government agencies, and competitors with which a business enterprise interacts. The general environment encompasses four influences that emanate from the geographic area in which the organization operates. These are:

- Cultural values, which shape views about ethics and determine the relative importance of various issues.

- Economic conditions, which include economic upswings, recessions, regional unemployment, and many other regional factors that affect a company's ability to grow and prosper. Economic influences may also partially dictate an organization's role in the economy.

- Legal/political environment, which effectively helps to allocate power within a society and to enforce laws. The legal and political systems in which an open system operates can play a key role in determining the long-term stability and security of the organization's future. These systems are responsible for creating a fertile environment for the business community, but they are also responsible for ensuring—via regulations pertaining to operation and taxation—that the needs of the larger community are addressed.

- Quality of education, which is an important factor in high technology and other industries that require an educated work force. Businesses will be better able to fill such positions if they operate in geographic regions that feature a strong education system.

The open-systems theory also assumes that all large organizations are comprised of multiple subsystems, each of which receives inputs from other subsystems and turns them into outputs for use by other subsystems. The subsystems are not necessarily represented by departments in an organization, but might instead resemble patterns of activity.

An important distinction between open-systems theory and more traditional organization theories is that the former assumes a subsystem hierarchy, meaning that not all of the subsystems are equally essential. Furthermore, a failure in one subsystem will not necessarily thwart the entire system. By contrast, traditional mechanistic theories implied that a malfunction in any part of a system would have an equally debilitating impact.

BASIC ORGANIZATIONAL CHARACTERISTICS

Organizations differ greatly in size, function, and makeup. Nevertheless, the operations of nearly all organizations—from the multinational corporation to a newly opened delicatessen—are based on a division of labor; a decision-making structure; and rules and policies. The degree of formality with which these aspects of business are approached vary tremendously within the business world, but these characteristics are inherent in any business enterprise that utilizes the talents of more than one person.

Organizations practice division of labor both vertically and horizontally. Vertical division includes three basic levels—top, middle, and bottom. The chief function of top managers, or executives, typically is to plan long-term strategy and oversee middle managers. Middle managers generally guide the day-to-day activities of the organization and administer top-level strategy. Low-level managers and laborers put strategy into action and perform the specific tasks necessary to keep the organization operating.

Organizations also divide labor horizontally by defining task groups, or departments, and assigning workers with applicable skills to those groups. Line units perform the basic functions of the business, while staff units support line units with expertise and services. In general, line units focus on supply, production, and distribution, while staff units deal mostly with internal operations and controls or public relations efforts.

Decision-making structures, the second basic organizational characteristic, are used to organize authority. These structures vary from operation to operation in their degree of centralization and decentralization. Centralized decision structures are referred to as "tall" organizations because important decisions usually emanate from a high level and are passed down through several channels until they reach the lower end of the hierarchy. Conversely, flat organizations, which have decentralized decision-making structures, employ only a few hierarchical levels. Such organizations are typically guided by a management philosophy that is favorably disposed toward some form of employee empowerment and individual autonomy.

A formalized system of rules and policies is the third standard organizational characteristic. Rules, policies, and procedures serve as templates of managerial guidance in all sectors of organizational production and behavior. They may document the most efficient means of accomplishing a task or provide standards for rewarding workers. Formalized rules provide managers with more time to spend on other problems and opportunities and help ensure that an organization's various subsystems are working in concert. Ill-conceived or poorly implemented rules, of course, can actually have a negative impact on business efforts to produce goods or services in a profitable or satisfactory manner.

Thus, organizations can be categorized as informal or formal, depending on the degree of formalization of rules within their structures. In formal organizations, say researchers, management has determined that a comparatively impersonal relationship between individuals and the company for which they work is viewed as the best environment for achieving organizational goals. Subordinates have less influence over the process in which they participate, with their duties more clearly defined.

Informal organizations, on the other hand, are less likely to adopt or adhere to a significant code of written rules or policies. Instead, individuals are more likely to adopt patterns of behavior that are influenced by a number of social and personal factors. Changes in the organization are less often the result of authoritative dictate and more often an outcome of collective agreement by members. Informal organizations tend to be more flexible and more reactive to outside influences. But some critics contend that such arrangements may also diminish the ability of top managers to effect rapid change.

ORGANIZATIONAL THEORY IN THE 1980S AND 1990S

By the 1980s several new organizational system theories received significant attention. These included Theory Z, a blending of American and Japanese management practices. This theory was a highly visible one, in part because of Japan's well-documented productivity improvements—and the United States' manufacturing difficulties—during that decade. Other theories, or adaptations of existing theories, emerged as well, which most observers saw as indicative of the ever-changing environment within business and industry.

The study of organizations and their management and production structures and philosophies continued to thrive throughout the 1990s. Indeed, an understanding of various organizational principles continues to be seen as vital to the success of all kinds of organizations—from government agencies to business—of all shapes and sizes, from conglomerates to small businesses. The study continues and although academics are far from a single theory of organization development each serious academic undertaking adds to the knowledge base on the subject. The changes in the ways in which we communicate and others brought about by advances in technology will likely create more opportunity for study. As our societies change, so to do the ways in which our organizations operate.

BIBLIOGRAPHY

Hatch, Mary Jo. *Organization Theory: Modern, Symbolic, and Postmodern Perspectives.* OUP-USA, 1997.

Nickelson, Jack A., and Todd R. Zenger. "Being Efficiently Fickle: A dynamic theory of organizational choice." *Organizational Science.* September-October 2002.

Pfeffer, Jeffrey. *New Directions for Organization Theory: Problems and Prospects.* Oxford University Press, 1997.

Putnam, Linda L., and Fredrick M. Jablin. *New Handbook of Organizational Communications: Advances in Theory, Research, and Methods.* Sage Publications Inc., December 2004.

Wagner-Tsukamoto, Sigmund. *Human Nature and Organization Theory.* Edward Elgar Publishing, 2003.

Hillstrom, Northern Lights
updated by Magee, ECDI

ORGANIZATIONAL BEHAVIOR

The study of organizational behavior is an academic discipline concerned with describing, understanding, predicting, and controlling human behavior in an organizational environment. Organizational behavior has evolved from early classical management theories into a complex school of thought—and it continues to change in response to the dynamic environment and proliferating corporate cultures in which today's businesses operate. Crafting an organization that functions as efficiently as possible is a difficult task. Understanding the behavior of a single person is a challenge. Understanding the behavior of a group of people, each one with a complex relationship with the others in the group is an even more difficult undertaking. It is, however a worthy undertaking because ultimately the work of an organization is done through the behavior driven actions of people, individually or collectively, on their own or in collaboration with technology. Therefore, a central part of the management task is the management of organizational behavior.

THE BEHAVIORAL SCIENCES

Organizational behavior scientists study four primary areas of behavioral science: individual behavior, group behavior, organizational structure, and organizational processes. They investigate many facets of these areas like personality and perception, attitudes and job satisfaction, group dynamics, politics and the role of leadership in the organization, job design, the impact of stress on work, decision-making processes, the communications chain, and company cultures and climates. They use a variety of techniques and approaches to evaluate each of these elements and its impact on individuals, groups, and organizational efficiency and effectiveness. The behavioral sciences have provided the basic framework and principles for the field of organizational behavior. Each behavioral science discipline provides a slightly different focus, analytical framework, and theme for helping managers answer questions about themselves, non-managers, and environmental forces.

In regard to individuals and groups, researchers try to determine why people behave the way they do. They have developed a variety of models designed to explain individuals' behavior. They investigate the factors that influence personality development, including genetic, situational, environmental, cultural, and social factors. Researchers also examine various personality types and their impact on business and other organizations. One of the primary tools utilized by organizational behavior researchers in these and other areas of study is the job satisfaction study. These tools are used not only to measure job satisfaction in such tangible areas as pay, benefits, promotional opportunities, and working conditions, but also to gauge how individual and group behavior patterns influence corporate culture, both positively and negatively.

ORGANIZATIONAL BEHAVIOR AND CORPORATE CULTURE

The terms "corporate culture" and "organizational behavior" are sometimes used interchangeably, but in reality, there are differences between the two. Corporate culture encompasses the shared values, attitudes, standards, and beliefs and other characteristics that define an organization's operating philosophy. Organizational behavior, meanwhile, can be understood in some ways as the academic *study* of corporate culture and its various elements, as well as other important components of behavior such as organization structure and organization processes. Organizational behavior is the field of study that draws on theory, methods, and principles from various disciplines to learn about *individual* perceptions, values, learning capacities, and actions while working in *groups* and within the total *organization;* analyzing the external environment's effect on the organization and its human resources, missions, objectives, and strategies. Therefore, managers need to develop diagnostic skills and be trained to identify conditions symptomatic of a problem requiring further attention. The problems to watch for include declining profits, declining quantity or quality of work, increases in absenteeism or tardiness, and negative employee attitudes. Each of these problems is an issue of organizational behavior.

BIBLIOGRAPHY

Allen, Stephanie. "Water Cooler Wisdom: How to make employees who share knowledge around the water cooler into a community of practice." *Training.* August 2005.

Connors, Roger, and Tom Smith. "Benchmarking Cultural Transition." *Journal of Business Strategy.* May 2000.

Greenberg, Jerald. *Organizational Behavior: The State of the Science.* Lawrence Erlbaum Associates, 2003.

Humphrey, Stephen. "Jam Science: Improvisation is essential for good jazz—and a great tool for effective teams." *CMA Management.* May 2004.

Karriker, Joy H. "Cyclical Group Development and Interaction-Based Leadership Emergence in Autonomous Teams: An integrated model." *Journal of Leadership and Organizational Studies.* Summer 2005.

Locke, Edwin A. *The Blackwell Handbook of Principles of Organizational Behavior.* Blackwell Publishing, 2002.

Miner, John B. *Organizational Behavior: Foundations, Theories, and Analyses.* Oxford University Press, 2002.

Punnett, Betty Jane. *International Perspectives on Organizational Behavior and Human Resource Management.* M.E. Sharpe, July 2004.

Willging, Paul R. "It's All About Leading and Managing People." *Nursing Homes.* March 2005.

Hillstrom, Northern Lights
updated by Magee, ECDI

ORGANIZATIONAL DEVELOPMENT

Organizational development (OD) encompasses the actions involved with applying the study of behavioral science to organizational change. It covers a wide array of theories, processes, and activities, all of which are oriented toward the goal of improving individual organizations. Generally speaking, however, OD differs from traditional organizational change techniques in that it typically embraces a more holistic approach that is aimed at transforming thought and behavior throughout an enterprise. Definitions of OD abound, but they are all predicated on the notion of improving organizational performance through proactive techniques and activities. It is also worth noting that organizational development, though concerned with improving workforce performance, should not be mistaken for human resource development. "Organization development is the planned process of developing an organization to be more effective in accomplishing its desired goals," wrote Rima Shaffer in *Principles of Organization Development.* "It is distinguished from human resource development in that HRD focuses on the personal growth of individuals within organizations, while OD focuses on developing the structures, systems, and processes within the organization to improve organizational effectiveness."

ORGANIZATIONAL DEVELOPMENT BASICS

Although the field of OD is broad, it can be differentiated from other systems of organizational change by its emphasis on process rather than problems. Indeed, traditional group change systems have focused on identifying problems in an organization and then trying to alter the behavior that creates the problem. OD initiatives focus on identifying the behavioral interactions and patterns that cause and sustain problems. Then, rather than simply changing isolated behaviors, the OD process aims at creating a behaviorally healthy organization that will naturally anticipate and prevent problems.

OD programs usually share several basic characteristics. First, they are considered long-term efforts of at least one to three years in most cases. Second, OD stresses collaborative management, whereby managers and employees at different levels of the hierarchy cooperate to solve problems. Third, OD recognizes that every organization is unique and that the same solutions cannot simply be applied at any company—this assumption is reflected in an OD focus on research and feedback. Fourth, OD programs emphasize the value of teamwork and small groups. In fact, most OD systems use small teams—or even individuals—as a vehicle to implement broad organizational changes.

The catalyst—whether a group or individual—that facilitates the OD process is known as the "change agent." Change agents are often outside consultants with experience managing OD programs, although companies sometimes utilize inside managers. The advantage of bringing in outside OD consultants is that they can provide a different perspective and have a less biased view of the organization's problems and needs. The primary drawback associated with outside change agents is that they may lack an in-depth understanding of key issues particular to the company. In addition, outside change agents may have trouble securing the trust and cooperation of key players in the organization. For these reasons, some companies employ an external-internal team approach, which seeks to combine the advantages of internal and external change agents while minimizing the drawbacks associated with the two approaches.

MANAGING CHANGE THROUGH ORGANIZATIONAL DEVELOPMENT

Organizational development initiatives do not automatically succeed. The benefits of effective OD programs are myriad, as many executives, managers, and business owners will attest. As with any undertaking, an OD intervention that is pursued in a sloppy, half-hearted, or otherwise faulty manner is far less likely to bring about meaningful change than one that is carried out with the full support of the people involved. The following list presents conditions that should be present in as a part of any OD intervention in order to maximize the likelihood of a successful outcome.

- All those involved in the process need to be genuinely and visibly committed to the effort.

- People involved in OD should be informed in advance of the nature of the intervention and the role they will be expected to play in the process.

- The OD effort has to be connected to other parts of the organization.

- The effort has to be directed by appropriate managers and guided by change agents (which, if used, must be competent).

- The intervention should be based on accurate diagnosis of organizational conditions.

- Owners and managers should show their commitment to OD at all stages of the effort, including the diagnosis, implementation, and evaluation.

- Evaluation is key to success, and should consist of more than asking people how they felt about the effort.

- Owners and managers need to show employees how the OD effort relates to the organization's goals and overriding mission.

IMPLEMENTING OD PROGRAMS

OD efforts basically entail two groups of activities: "action research" and "interventions." Action research is a process of systematically collecting data on a specific organization, feeding them back for action planning, and evaluating results. Data gathering techniques include everything from surveys and questionnaires to interviews, collages, drawings, and tests. The data are often evaluated and interpreted using advanced statistical analysis techniques.

OD interventions are plans or programs comprised of specific activities designed to effect change in some facet of an organization. Numerous interventions have been developed over the years to address different problems or create various results. However, they all are geared toward the goal of improving the entire organization through change. In general, organizations that wish to achieve a high degree of organizational change will employ a full range of interventions, including those designed to transform individual and group behavior and attitudes. Entities attempting smaller changes will stop short of those goals, applying interventions targeted primarily at operating policies, management structures, worker skills, or personnel policies. Typically, organizational development programs will simultaneously integrate more than one of these interventions. A few of the more popular interventions are briefly described below.

Interpersonal Interventions Interpersonal interventions in an OD program are designed to enhance individual skills, knowledge, and effectiveness. This type of program utilizes group dynamics by gathering individuals together in loosely structured meetings. Subject matter is determined by the group, within the context of basic goals stipulated by a facilitator. As group members try to exert structure on fellow members, group members gain a greater awareness of their own and other's feelings, motivations, and behaviors. Other types of interpersonal interventions include those designed to improve the performance review process, create better training programs, help workers identify their true wants and set complementary career goals, and resolve conflict.

Group Interventions OD group interventions are designed to help teams and groups within organizations become more effective. Such interventions usually assume that the most effective groups communicate well, facilitate a healthy balance between both personal and group needs, and function by consensus as opposed to autocracy or majority rule.

Group diagnostic interventions are simply meetings wherein members of a team analyze their unit's performance, ask questions about what the team needs to do to improve, and discuss potential solutions to problems. The benefit of such interventions is that members often communicate problems of which their co-workers were unaware. Ideally, such communication will spur problem-solving and improved group dynamics.

Role analysis technique (RAT) is used to help employees get a better grasp on their role in an organization. In the first step of a RAT intervention, people define their perception of their role and contribution to the overall company effort in front of a group of coworkers. Group members then provide feedback to more clearly define the role. In the second phase, the individual and the group examine ways in which the employee relies on others in the company, and how they define his or her expectations. RAT interventions help people to reduce role confusion, which can result in either conflict or the perception that some people are not doing their job. A popular intervention similar to RAT is responsibility charting, which utilizes a matrix system to assign decision and task responsibilities.

Inter-group Interventions Inter-group interventions are integrated into OD programs to facilitate cooperation and efficiency between different groups within an organization. For instance, departmental interaction often deteriorates in larger organizations as different units battle for limited resources or become detached from the needs of other units.

Conflict resolution meetings are one common inter-group intervention. First, different group leaders are brought together to secure their commitment to the intervention. Next, the teams meet separately to make a list of their feelings about the other group(s). Then the groups meet and share their lists. Finally, the teams meet to discuss the problems and to try to develop solutions that will help both parties. This type of intervention, say supporters, helps to gradually diffuse tension between groups that has arisen because of faulty communication.

OD joint activity interventions involve melding members of different groups to work together toward a common goal. Similarly, common enemy interventions achieve the same results by finding an adversary common to two or more groups and then getting members of the groups to work together to overcome the threat. Examples of common enemies targeted in such programs include competitors, government regulation, and economic conditions.

Comprehensive Interventions OD comprehensive interventions are used to directly create change throughout an entire organization, rather than focusing on organizational change through subgroup interventions. One of the most popular comprehensive interventions is survey feedback. This technique basically entails surveying employee attitudes at all levels of the company and then disseminating a report that details those findings. The employees then use the data in feedback sessions to create solutions to perceived problems. A number of questionnaires developed specifically for such interventions have been developed.

Structural change interventions are used by OD change agents to implement organizational alterations related to departmentalization, management hierarchy, work policies, compensation and benefit incentives programs, and other cornerstones of the business. Often, the implemented changes emanate from feedback from other interventions. One benefit of change interventions is that companies can often realize an immediate and very significant impact in productivity and profitability (provided the changes are warranted and implemented appropriately).

Sociotechnical system design interventions are similar to structural change techniques, but they typically emphasize the reorganization of work teams. The basic goal is to create independent groups throughout the company that supervise themselves. This administration may include such aspects as monitoring quality or disciplining team members. The theoretic benefit of sociotechnical system design interventions is that worker and group productivity and quality is increased because workers have more control over (and subsequent satisfaction from) the process in which they participate.

A fourth OD intervention that became extremely popular during the 1980s and early 1990s is total quality management (TQM). TQM interventions utilize established quality techniques and programs that emphasize quality processes, rather than achieving quality by inspecting products and services after processes have been completed. The important concept of continuous improvement embodied by TQM has carried over into other OD interventions.

BIBLIOGRAPHY

Allen, Stephanie. "Water Cooler Wisdom: How to make employees who share knowledge around the water cooler into a community of practice." *Training.* August 2005.

Dobrianski, John. "Critical Issues in Organizational Development." *Contract Management.* April 2005.

Golembiewski, Robert T. *Ironies in Organizational Development.* Marcel Dekker, 2002.

Greenberg, Jerald. *Organizational Behavior: The State of the Science.* Lawrence Erlbaum Associates, 2003.

Humphrey, Stephen. "Jam Science: Improvisation is essential for good jazz—and a great tool for effective teams." *CMA Management.* May 2004.

Karriker, Joy H. "Cyclical Group Development and Interaction-Based Leadership Emergence in Autonomous Teams: An integrated model." *Journal of Leadership and Organizational Studies.* Summer 2005.

Locke, Edwin A. *The Blackwell Handbook of Principles of Organizational Behavior.* Blackwell Publishing, 2002.

Miner, John B. *Organizational Behavior: Foundations, Theories, and Analyses.* Oxford University Press, 2002.

Punnett, Betty Jane. *International Perspectives on Organizational Behavior and Human Resource Management.* M.E. Sharpe, July 2004.

Recardo, Ronald J. "Best Practices in Organizations Experiencing Extensive and Rapid Change." *National Productivity Review.* Summer 2000.

Shaffer, Rima. *Principles of Organization Development.* American Society for Training and Development, 2000.

Willging, Paul R. "It's All About Leading and Managing People." *Nursing Homes.* March 2005.

Hillstrom, Northern Lights
updated by Magee, ECDI

ORGANIZATIONAL GROWTH

Growth is something for which most companies strive, regardless of their size. Small firms want to get big, big firms want to get bigger. Indeed, companies have to grow at least a bit every year in order to accommodate the increased expenses that develop over time. With the passage of time, salaries increase and the costs of employment benefits rise as well. Even if no other company expenses rise, these two cost areas almost always increase over time. It is not always possible to pass along these increased costs to customers and clients in the form of higher prices. Consequently, growth must occur if the business wishes to keep up.

Organizational growth has the potential to provide small businesses with a myriad of benefits, including things like greater efficiencies from economies of scale, increased power, a greater ability to withstand market fluctuations, an increased survival rate, greater profits, and increased prestige for organizational members. Many small firms desire growth because it is seen generally as a sign of success, progress. Organizational growth is, in fact, used as one indicator of effectiveness for small businesses and is a fundamental concern of many practicing managers.

Organizational growth, however, means different things to different organizations. There are many parameters a company may use to measure its growth. Since the ultimate goal of most companies is profitability, most companies will measure their growth in terms of net profit, revenue, and other financial data. Other business owners may use one of the following criteria for assessing their growth: sales, number of employees, physical expansion, success of a product line, or increased market share. Ultimately, success and growth will be gauged by how well a firm does relative to the goals it has set for itself.

WAYS IN WHICH ORGANIZATIONS ACHIEVE GROWTH

Many academic models have been created that depict possible growth stages/directions of a company. Six of the most commonly used methods for creating organizational growth within a small business are discussed below.

Joint Venture/Alliance—This strategy is particularly effective for smaller firms with limited resources. Such partnerships can help small business secure the resources they need to grapple with rapid changes in demand, supply, competition, and other factors. Forming joint ventures or alliances gives all companies involved the flexibility to move on to different projects upon completion of the first, or restructure agreements to continue working together. Subcontracting, which allows firms to concentrate on those aspects of their business that they do best, is sometimes defined as a type of alliance arrangement (albeit one in which the parties involved generally wield differing levels of power). Joint ventures and other business alliances can inject partners with new ideas, access to new technologies, new approaches, and new markets, all of which can help the involved businesses to grow. Indeed, establishing joint ventures with overseas firms has been hailed as one of the most potentially rewarding ways for companies to expand their operations. Finally, some firms realize growth by acquiring other companies.

Licensing—A firm may wish to expand and grow by licensing its most advanced technology. This course of action is often recommended to firms with their own proprietary technologies because competitors will likely copy whatever a company develops at some point. Licensing is one method that can be used to maximize the benefit that a firm can gain from its technology. It is also a way to gain the resource to fund future research and development efforts.

Sell Off Old Winners—Some organizations engaged in a concerted effort to grow divest themselves of mature "cash cow" operations to focus on new and innovative lines of products or services. This option may sound contradictory, but analysts note that businesses can command top prices for such tried and true assets. An addendum to this line of thinking is the divestment of older technology or products. Emerging markets in Latin America and Eastern Europe, for instance, have been favorite places for companies to sell products or technology that no longer attract high levels of interest in the United States. These markets may not yet be able to afford large quantities of state-of-the-art goods, but they can still benefit from older models.

New Markets—Some businesses are able to secure significant organizational growth by tapping into new markets. Creating additional demand for a firm's product or service, especially in a market where competition has yet to fully develop, can spur phenomenal growth for a small company, although the competitive vacuum will generally close very quickly in these instances. In the last ten years, many small firms have turned to an online marketing presence as a tool for reaching beyond their traditional markets. For those who do not yet market and sell online, this is one area that may be explored.

New Product Development—Creation of new products or services is a primary method by which companies grow. Indeed, new product development is the linchpin of most organizations' growth strategies.

Outside Financing—Many small companies turn to outside financing sources to fund their expansion. Smaller private firms search for capital from banks, private investors, government agencies, or venture capital firms.

PROBLEMS ENCOUNTERED WITH ORGANIZATIONAL GROWTH

Organizational growth has obvious upsides. It spurs job creation. It creates a stimulating and exciting environment within a firm. It creates opportunities for the business founder and others in the company to become wealthy. Organizational growth also has downsides. When growth is too rapid, chaos can prevail. In such a situation a company may see increased sales but a drop in profits. A business may outgrow the skills of its leader, its employees, and its advisers. All those involved are likely to become stressed out trying to keep up with the demands of expansion.

Small business owners seeking to guide their organizations through periods of growth—whether that growth is dramatic or incremental—must plan to deal with both the upsides and downsides of growth. When a firm is small in size, the entrepreneur who founded it and usually serves as its primary strategic and operational leaders can often easily direct and monitor the various aspects of daily business. In such an environment, the business owner and founder understands the personalities within the firm, the relationships that each has with others in the company, as well as with suppliers and customers. Organizational growth, however, brings with it an inevitable dilution of that "hands-on" capability, while the complexity of various organizational tasks simultaneously increases. As small organizations grow, so to do the complexities of managing the organization. There are ways of reducing the complexity by delegating responsibility and installing better date systems but there is no way of avoiding it altogether.

Most entrepreneurs who are fortunate enough to experience growth soon discover that success as a business owner doesn't mean you have arrived and can now sleep at night. Expanding a company doesn't just mean grappling with the same problems on a larger scale. It means understanding, adjusting to, and managing a whole new set of challenges. It often means building and managing a very

different sort of business. Organizational growth almost always produces a company that's much more complex— one that needs a much more sophisticated management team, and one that may well need a new infrastructure.

Organizational growth, then, may well require as much planning, effort, and work as did starting a company in the first place. Small business owners face a dizzying array of organizational elements that have to be revised during a period of growth. Maintaining effective methods of communications with and between employees and departments, for example, become ever more important as the firm grows. Similarly, good human resource management practices—from hiring to training to empowerment—have to be implemented and maintained. Establishing and improving standard practices is often a key element of organizational growth as well. Indeed, a small business that undergoes a significant burst of growth will find its operations transformed in any number of ways. And often, it will be the owner's advance planning and management skills that will determine whether that growth is sustained, or whether internal constraints rein in that growth prematurely.

BIBLIOGRAPHY

Boggs, Robert L. *Honored Feathers of Wisdom: Attributes for Personal and Organizational Growth.* iUniverse, 2004.

Coffman, Curt, and Gabriel Gonzalez-Molina. *Follow this Path: How the World's Greatest Organizations Drive Growth by Unleashing Human Potential.* Warner Business Books, 2002.

Conner, Daryl R. "How to Create a Nimble Organization." *National Productivity Review.* Autumn 2000.

Gould, Dwight. "Leading the Lead Generation Challenge With Online Marketing: Online lead generation can maximize organizational growth and profitability from the national to the local level." *Franchising World.* February 2006.

Lipton, Mark. *Guiding Growth: How Vision Keeps Companies on Course.* Harvard Business School Press, 2003.

Roberts, John. *The Modern Firm: Organizational Design for Performance and Growth.* Oxford University Press, 2004.

Treen, Doug. "Vanishing Walls." *Ivey Business Journal.* September 2000.

Hillstrom, Northern Lights
updated by Magee, ECDI

ORGANIZATIONAL LIFE CYCLE

Historians and academics have observed that organizations, like living organisms, have life cycles. They are born (established or formed), they grow and develop, they reach maturity, they begin to decline and age, and finally, in many cases, they die. Study of the organizational life cycle

(OLC) has resulted in various predictive models. These models, which have been a subject of considerable academic discussion, are linked to the study of organizational growth and development. Organizations at any stage of the life cycle are impacted by external environmental circumstances as well as internal factors. We're all aware of the rise and fall of organizations and entire industries. Products too have life cycles, a fact that has been long recognized by marketing and sales experts. It seems reasonable to conclude that organizations also have life cycles.

Students of this subject agree for the most part that predictable patterns can be seen when viewing the life span of a business organization. These patterns can be characterized by stages, often referred to as development stages. These development stages tend to be sequential, occur as a hierarchical progression that is not easily reversed, and involve a broad range of organizational activities and structures. The number of life cycle stages identified by any particular researcher will vary with the finds of other researchers depending on the granularity of his or her study. Some analysts have delineated as many as ten different stages of an organizational life cycle, while others have flattened it down to as few as three stages. Most models, however, hold to a view that the organizational life cycle is comprised of four or five stages that can be summarized simply as start-up, growth, maturity, decline, and death (or revival).

TRENDS IN OLC STUDY

While a number of business and management theorists alluded to developmental stages in the early to mid-1900s, Mason Haire's 1959 work *Modern Organization Theory* is generally recognized as one of the first studies that used a biological model for organizational growth and argued that organizational growth and development followed a regular sequence. The study of organizational life cycles intensified, and by the 1970s and 1980s it was well-established as a key component of overall organizational growth.

Organizational life cycle is an important model because of its premise and its prescription. The model's premise is that requirements, opportunities, and threats both inside and outside the business firm will vary depending on the stage of development in which the firm finds itself. For example, threats in the start-up stage differ from those in the maturity stage. As the firm moves through the developmental stages, changes in the nature and number of requirements, opportunities, and threats exert pressure for change on the business.

Organizations move from one stage to another because the fit between the organization and its environment is so inadequate that either the organization's efficiency and/or effectiveness is seriously impaired or the organization's survival is threatened. The OLC model's prescription is that the firm's managers must change the goals, strategies, and strategy implementation devices to fit the new set of issues. Thus, different stages of the company's life cycle require alterations in the firm's objectives, strategies, managerial processes (planning, organizing, staffing, directing, controlling), technology, culture, and decision-making. Five growth stages are observable: birth, growth, maturity, decline, and revival. They traced changes in the organizational structure and managerial processes as the business proceeds through the growth stages. At birth, the firms exhibited a very simple organizational structure with authority centralized at the top of the hierarchy. As the firms grew, they adapted more sophisticated structures and decentralized authority to middle- and lower-level managers. At maturity, the firms demonstrated significantly more concern for internal efficiency and installed more control mechanisms and processes.

Growth Phases Most scholarly works focusing on organizational life cycles have been conceptual and hypothetical in content. Only a small minority have attempted to test empirically the organizational life cycle model. One widely-cited conceptual work, however, was published in the *Harvard Business Review* in 1972 by L. Greiner. He used five growth phases: growth through creativity; growth through direction; growth through delegation; growth through coordination; and growth through collaboration. Each growth stage encompassed an evolutionary phase ("prolonged periods of growth where no major upheaval occurs in organization practices"), and a revolutionary phase ("periods of substantial turmoil in organization life"). The evolutionary phases were hypothesized to be about four to eight years in length, while the revolutionary phases were characterized as the crisis phases. At the end of each one of the five growth stages listed above, Greiner hypothesized that an organizational crisis will occur, and that the business's ability to handle these crises will determine its future:

Phase 1—Growth through creativity eventually leads to a crisis of leadership. More sophisticated and more formalized management practices must be adopted. If the founders can't or won't take on this responsibility, they must hire someone who can, and give this person significant authority.

Phase 2—Growth through direction eventually leads to a crisis of autonomy. Lower level managers must be given more authority if the organization is to continue to grow. The crisis involves top-level managers' reluctance to delegate authority.

Phase 3—Growth through delegation eventually leads to a crisis of control. This occurs when autonomous employees who prefer to operate without interference from the rest of the organization clash with business owners and managers who perceive that they are losing control of a diversified company.

Phase 4—Growth through coordination eventually leads to a crisis of red tape. Coordination techniques like product groups, formal planning processes, and corporate staff become, over time, a bureaucratic system that causes delays in decision-making and a reduction in innovation.

Phase 5—Growth through collaboration, is characterized by the use of teams, a reduction in corporate staff, matrix-type structures, the simplification of formal systems, an increase in conferences and educational programs, and more sophisticated information systems. While Greiner did not formally delineate a crisis for this phase, he guessed that it might revolve around "the psychological saturation of employees who grow emotionally and physically exhausted by the intensity of team work and the heavy pressure for innovative solutions."

ORGANIZATION LIFE CYCLE AND THE SMALL BUSINESS OWNER

Entrepreneurs who are involved in the early stages of business creation are unlikely to become preoccupied with life cycle issues of decline and dissolution. Indeed, their concerns are apt to be in such areas as securing financing, establishing relationships with vendors and clients, preparing a physical location for business operations, and other aspects of business start-up that are integral to establishing and maintaining a viable firm. Basically, these firms are almost exclusively concerned with the very first stage of the organization life cycle. Small business enterprises that are well-established, on the other hand, may find OLC studies more relevant. Indeed, many recent examinations of organization life cycles have analyzed ways in which businesses can prolong desired stages (growth, maturity) and forestall negative stages (decline, death). Certainly, there exists no timeline that dictates that a company will begin to falter at a given point in time. "Because every company develops at its own pace, characteristics, more than age, define the stages of the cycle," explained Karen Adler and Paul Swiercz in *Training & Development.*

Small business owners and other organization leaders may explore a variety of options designed to influence the enterprise's life cycle—from new products to new markets to new management philosophies. After all, once a business begins to enter a decline phase, it is not inevitable that the company will continue to plummet into ultimate failure; many companies are able to reverse such slides (a development that is sometimes referred to as turning the OLC bell curve into an "S" curve). But entrepreneurs and managers should recognize that their business is always somewhere along the life cycle

continuum, and that business success is often predicated on recognizing where your business is situated along that measuring stick and adopting strategies best suited to that position in the cycle.

SEE ALSO *Business Cycles; Industry Life Cycle; Product Life Cycle*

BIBLIOGRAPHY

Adizes, Ichak. *Managing Corporate Lifecycles: Founding Principles in the Management of the Arts.* The Adizes Institute Publishing, December 2000.

Adler, Karen R., and Paul M. Swiercz. "Taming the Performance Bell Curve." *Training & Development.* October 1997.

Fletcher, Douglas A., and Ian M. Taplin. "Organizational Evolution: The American Life Cycle." *National Productivity Review.* Autumn 2000.

Greiner, L. "Evolution and Revolution as Organizations Grow." *Harvard Business Review.* July-August 1972.

Shulman, Joel M., and Thomas T. Stalkamp. *Getting Bigger by Growing Smaller: A New Growth Model for Corporate America.* Financial Times Prentice Hall, 2003.

Van Batenburg, Greg. "How Does Your Business Grow? Many shop owners scarcely notice that there are four stages to their business' growth." *Motor Age.* April 2003.

Hillstrom, Northern Lights
updated by Magee, ECDI

ORGANIZATIONAL STRUCTURE

An organizational structure defines the scope of acceptable behavior within an organization, its lines of authority and accountability, and to some extent the organization's relationship with its external environment. More specifically, it shows the pattern or arrangement of jobs and groups of jobs within an organization and yet it is more than an organizational chart. The organizational structure pertains to both reporting and operational relationships, provided they have some degree of permanence. The individual elements of an organizational structure typically include a variety of components that one may usefully see as building blocks: 1) departments or divisions; 2) management hierarchy; 3) rules, procedures, and goals; and 4) more temporary building blocks such as task forces or committees.

Ideally, organizational structures should be shaped and implemented for the primary purpose of facilitating the achievement of organizational goals in an efficient manner. Indeed, having a suitable organizational structure in place—one that recognizes and addresses the various human and business realities of the company in question—is a prerequisite for long-term success. Nonetheless, all too often organizational structures do not contribute positively to a company's performance. This is usually because the structure was allowed to grow somewhat organically and was not redesigned as the company grew so as to more efficiently guide the behavior of individuals and groups so that they would be maximally productive, efficient, flexible, and motivated. Small business owners seeking to establish a beneficial organizational structure need to recognize that the process may be complex since this task is often left until a start-up organization has already been established. By then, a de facto structure exists and changing it will need to be done carefully so as not to alienating or frustrating key players.

Even large corporations that attempt to restructure or reorganize and implement a new or changed organizational structure may discover that simply announcing a new structure does not immediately translate into actual change. Hierarchy is an important element of any organizational structure. The more levels of management are present in an organization, the more hierarchical it is. During the late 1990s and early 2000s it became fashionable to reduce the hierarchy in large corporations and the trend was dubbed flattening the corporate structure. But, as Eileen Shapiro, a management consultant and author told Patrick J. Kiger in his article "Hidden Hierarchies," things aren't always what they seem. "I've been inside a lot of companies that espouse flat organizational structures and self-management. But when you really start looking at how things actually work, you find that there is in fact a hierarchy—one that is not explicit." She explains that most firms, regardless of style, do actually have a hierarchy, whether explicit or not, and that trying to reflect the true, functional hierarchy in the organizational structure will help prevent the hidden hierarchy phenomenon. It also prevents the misunderstandings that can arise when the explicit organizational structure does not match the actual, functional structure.

KEYS TO ERECTING AN EFFECTIVE ORGANIZATIONAL STRUCTURE

All sorts of different organizational structures have been proven effective in contributing to business success. Some firms choose highly centralized, rigidly maintained structures, while others—perhaps even in the same industrial sector—develop decentralized, loose arrangements. Both of these organizational types can survive and even thrive. There is no one best way to design an organization or type of structure. Each depends upon the company involved, its needs and goals, and even the personalities of the individuals involved in the case of small businesses. The type of business in which an organization is involved

is also a factor in designing an effective organizational structure. Organizations operate in different environments with different products, strategies, constraints, and opportunities, each of which may influence the design of an ideal organizational structure.

But despite the wide variety of organizational structures that can be found in the business world, the successful ones tend to share certain characteristics. Indeed, business experts cite a number of characteristics that separate effective organizational structures from ineffective designs. Recognition of these factors is especially important for entrepreneurs and established small business owners, since these individuals play such a pivotal role in determining the final layout of their enterprises.

As small business owners weigh their various options in this realm, they should make sure that the following factors are taken into consideration:

- Relative strengths and weaknesses of various organizational forms.

- Legal advantages and disadvantages of organizational structure options.

- Advantages and drawbacks of departmentalization options.

- Likely growth patterns of the company.

- Reporting relationships that are currently in place.

- Reporting and authority relationships that you hope will be implemented in the future.

- Optimum ratios of supervisors/managers to subordinates.

- Suitable level of autonomy/empowerment to be granted to employees at various levels of the organization (while still recognizing individual capacities for independent work).

- Structures that will produce greatest worker satisfaction.

- Structures that will produce optimum operational efficiency.

Once all these factors have been objectively examined and blended into an effective organizational structure, the small business owner will then be in a position to pursue his/her business goals with a far greater likelihood of success.

BIBLIOGRAPHY

Day, George. "Aligning Organizational Structure to the Market." *Business Strategy Review*. Autumn 1999.

Kiger, Patrick J. "Hidden Hierarchies." *Workforce Management*. 27 February 2006.

Nickelson, Jack A., and Todd R. Zenger. "Being Efficiently Fickle: A dynamic theory of organizational choice." *Organizational Science.* September-October 2002.

"Thinking for a Living." *The Economist.* 21 January 2006.

Wagner-Tsukamoto, Sigmund. *Human Nature and Organization Theory.* Edward Elgar Publishing, 2003.

Hillstrom, Northern Lights
updated by Magee, ECDI

ORIGINAL EQUIPMENT MANUFACTURER (OEM)

An original equipment manufacturer (OEM) makes equipment or components that are then marketed by its client, another manufacturer or a reseller, usually under that reseller's own name. An OEM may make complete devices or just certain components, either of which can then be configured by the reseller. An example of this relationship would be a large automobile manufacturer that uses an OEM's components in the production of the cars it makes and sells. Originally OEM was an adjective only used to describe a company that produced items, usually hardware or component parts, to be marketed under another company's brand. Although this is still the norm, OEMs have begun in recent years to sell their products more widely and in some cases, directly to the public. Developments within the computer industry have played a role in this expansion. As people choose to upgrade their PCs with new parts, they often wish to do so by purchasing replacement parts that have been produced by the same manufacturer that made the originally installed item. The assumption in this case is that components and other processed items may work better or fit better if they come from the OEM. They are more likely to meet the original standards and product specifications established for the product. OEM parts can be contrasted to other replacement parts that may be referred to as "functionally equivalent" or "of like kind and quality."

OEMS TODAY

Today, component parts and processed items are becoming branded, and as such their names are becoming well-known by consumers. In the past, these components were processed from raw materials and became part of a finished product without the consumer ever becoming aware of who made the component. In most cases, consumers did not care as long as the product worked as expected. But times have changed. Consumers upgrading their computers today, for example, may specify a new processor made by an OEM company that they respect, like Intel, and may request the processing power of the OEM's latest release, like the Pentium 4.

Component parts, like a computer's processor, include items that go into the assembly of the final product. Other examples include CD-ROM drives included in personal computers, air bags in cars, and motors for appliances. Consumers are also becoming interested in the component materials specifications and manufacturers of such items as wire, paper, textiles, or cement.

In another example, General Motors recommends that consumers request Goodwrench parts when replacements are needed for a GM vehicle. In fact, the GM Web site says, "GM parts are the highest-quality products for your GM vehicle and the only ones specifically designed, made, and tested to keep it running at peak performance and appearance. Heck, they're the same ones it was born with. So, whether you're restoring an old favorite or personalizing your newest baby, you can count on GM parts to provide genuine dependability." To stress the exact standards of OEM parts, they state, "It's reassuring to know you have a partner like GM Parts behind you. We offer a full line of products, all designed and manufactured to exacting standards specifically for your GM vehicle. So you know whenever you use GM parts, the feeling is genuine."

SETTING STANDARDS

Manufacturers must determine the quality and specify standards for components that go into their products. Some assembled products are not manufactured but put together from a variety of purchased component parts, like Dell computers. Some components may be custom made, requiring much teamwork between the engineering departments of both the buyer and the seller as well as management involvement in negotiating prices and other terms.

Components are produced to accepted standards or specifications. Production personnel in the purchasing organization may specify quality. Because components become part of an organization's own product, quality is extremely important. The buyer's own name and entire marketing mix are at stake. Thus a buyer tries to buy from sources that help ensure a good product. In such a situation, a buyer may even find it attractive to develop a close partnership with a single supplier who is dedicated to the same objectives as the buyer and use this partner as a sole source supplier. As an example, Ford Motor Company forged a partnership with Firestone Tires. When the supplier's product was implicated in a series of accidents involving Ford sports utility vehicles, Ford took some responsibility for the problems and deaths that resulted.

If the co-branding and awareness of OEM manufacturers continues, more profitable replacement markets may develop for producers. Since component parts go into finished products, a replacement market often develops on its own. This after-market can be both large and very profitable. Car tires and batteries are two examples of components originally sold in the OEM market that become consumer products in the after-market. But because the target markets are different, different marketing and overall strategies may be necessary for selling OEM parts directly to final consumers.

BIBLIOGRAPHY

Brown, Michael. "The Winds of Change: Tracking major trends impacting OEM markets." *Adhesive Age.* December 2002.

Convey, Mary Christine. "CAPA Refines Generic Auto Parts Definitions." *National Underwriter.* 4 September 2000.

Rayner, Bruce. "Some Industry Terms Need to Be Changed." *Electronic Buyers' News* 27 November 2000.

Hillstrom, Northern Lights
updated by Magee, ECDI

OUTSOURCING

Outsourcing is the movement of a function inside a company to an entity outside it. Before the word came into widespread use, people talked about "farming" or "contracting" things out. The corresponding opposite to outsourcing is to "bring it in-house." When something is brought in-house, the implication is that it will now be done properly; the implication of outsourcing something is that now it will be done cheaply. The outsourcing of functions has never been popular (to make an understatement) with employees affected by the action inside a corporation. But the activity only achieved a strongly negative flavor in general when the outsourcing became "off-shoring," meaning the shipment of jobs overseas. Until then a job might be outsourced but remained part of the U.S. economy; in its off-shored form it signaled trade deficits and lost jobs. The domestic form of outsourcing has always tended to benefit small business: small business was and is, more often than not, the recipient of the jobs farmed out by the large corporations. The outsourcing of a function, in fact, has been and continues to be an opportunity for a group of employees to set themselves up in business.

Outsourcing is also widely practiced by small business but usually for slightly different reasons. Small companies do not have the scale to support full-fledged accounting, payroll, and computer systems staffs of their own—or, if their managers try to do these jobs as well, they have to work too many hours. These functions, therefore, are farmed out. So are, frequently, large but intermittent jobs.

The driving force behind outsourcing, narrowly viewed, has always been and continues to be the desire to lower costs—although it has additional benefits. In times of shrinking economic activity, it easier to buy less of something or to eliminate buying something altogether than it is to lay off employees and to close departments. It is easier to shop an activity around when higher quality or greater speed is the objective than to get an internal supplier to change its behavior. Any manager of a small division in a large corporation whose main supplier is another and larger division knows how unresponsive the internal vendor can be. The external supplier, which, presumably, also has other clients, can be the source of interesting innovation.

Outsourcing also has its disadvantages many of which are easily overlooked in the hurry of achieving the costs savings that appear to be possible. When a company simply stops making some product and begins to buy it from the outside—and, furthermore, the product is widely available—outsourcing is generally fairly advantageous. But if the outsourced "object" is some kind of function normally handled in-house by a company, problems can arise. First, a portion of the function must be retained inside to act as an interface with the supplier—and because of language and other issues, this interface may start to grow rather large. Second, control is lost by distance and the presence of an institutional barrier. Solving problems can become more costly and take more time. If the function is unique, the buyer is exposed to risk due to potential vendor failure; the vendor may grow surprisingly independent, find other clients, raise prices, and erase the cost benefits. As Roger Parloff reports in *Fortune,* some contract producers overseas may establish a "third shift" to produce the buyer's own product, but relabeled and rebranded, for sale in competition but at a lower price. Close observers of the outsourcing phenomenon like to emphasize reality: outsourcing is just the old contracting; when, in addition, an ocean and/or a linguistic and cultural barrier is interposed, the initial cost advantage may disappear. Not surprisingly, as *Business Week* reports, western companies are beginning to buy up overseas suppliers, thus "internalizing" again what they had "outsourced" before.

MAJOR CATEGORIES

Outsourcing, as already noted above, may be divided into "domestic" and "overseas" categories—not taking "oceans" too literally in this definition: "over-the-border" would be more accurate. Data on outsourcing are not specifically collected except in the context of mass layoff data published by the U.S. Bureau of Labor Statistics. BLS specifically reports separations caused by "domestic relocation" as well as "out-of-country" relocations every quarter. Under both categories, BLS breaks down separations further into two categories: relocation "within company" and to a "different company." When the separations are due to relocation to another domestic site but the jobs are relocated to a "different company," one might speak of genuine "outsourcing." In the other category, however, *any* relocation overseas could be classified as outsourcing, "out" in this case meaning out of the country. Using these definitions ("domestic/different company" and "out-of-country"), BLS data indicate that off-shoring is the much larger component. In the fourth quarter of 2005, mass layoffs caused by out-of-country relocations caused 2,047 separations; relocations domestically to a different company caused 401. But total domestic relocations (including the 401 above) were 4,224. These jobs may also have been relocated to reduce wages. Data for a year earlier, the fourth quarter of 2004, indicated 5,258 separations caused by relocating jobs offshore; domestic relocations caused 8,093 separations, but of these only 808 were relocated to another company.

Outsourcing can also be defined as the transfer of specialized functions and the relocation of complete operations. When a business owner hires a payroll service to avoid spending weekends preparing payroll, he or she is transferring a specialized function, payroll. When a large corporation hires a company in India to provide over-the-phone tech support for computer and software installation, again a function has been transferred. But when a producer of bedsprings closes its U.S. factory and opens a factory in China, it has outsourced a complete operation.

Broad statistics are not available to measure which of these categories is more prevalent. What is clear is that computerization generally and the Internet specifically have produced a significant opportunity for the outsourcing of functions that require skills in symbol manipulation (thus engineering and technical functions) and/or linguistic skills that can be deployed by telephone. Data keying was an early activity outsourced, typically, to India—where knowledge of English is widespread. Engineering and technical support have gained share overseas; software engineering is growing—despite equally energetic growth in information technology (IT) employment here; interpretation of medical and other lab results by distant experts is growing; and, most recently, legal research and brief preparation are gaining as an outsourced activity.

BROAD FORCES AND TRENDS

At any point in time, outsourcing will tend to be defined by prevailing conditions in the structure of an industry, the national economy, and, currently, the global economy.

Economies show a cyclic movement between centralization and decentralization driven by a mix of factors: resources, technology, stage of development, confidence, communications, etc.

The cycle can be illustrated at the micro level by a process in which an enterprising contractor begins to build homes by working closely with small companies that specialize in concrete, carpentry, electrical work, plumbing, roofing, and so on. Gradually, to get ever better control, the contractor acquires little companies, hires his own craftsmen, and becomes a major building company that does its work exclusively with its own people. Many years later, during a prolonged recession in construction, the company may begin spinning off its functions until it retains only a managerial core which, as at the beginning, works with independents.

During a centralization phase an enterprise favors vertical integration; during decentralization, it favors specialization. In the early 21st century, with outsourcing common, the economy appears to have a decentralizing tendency; this movement already manifested itself in the last quarter of the 20th century. Large corporations are specializing in finance and technology and shedding the labor-intensive execution functions. This is possible, first, because human and other resources are widely available and differentially priced across the globe. Labor costs are very high at the center of the developed world and relatively low in the growing economies. Second, communications and global financial systems have matured so that overall control is relatively easier. Third, until the sudden shadow of terrorism appeared, stability reigned across much of the globe.

Outsourcing as an attractive mechanism to achieve strategic aims will continue until wage rates equalize across the globe—assuming nothing else changes first. However, trends in energy, increasing international instability, and consequently rising anxieties may cause it to diminish in the future as popular reaction causes political action. Change, in any case, is certain.

BIBLIOGRAPHY

Goodwin, Bill. "Outsourcing Users Taken by Surprise." *Computer Weekly.* 18 April 2006.

"More U.S. Workers Have IT Jobs Than Ever Before." *InformationWeek.* 24 April 2006.

"New Spin on Telework: Call center shift could mean home is where the job is." *Employee Benefit News.* 1 May 2006.

"Off the Record: The hidden costs of offshoring – Saving money south of the border can be an expensive proposition." *InfoWorld.* 24 April 2006.

"Open Season On Outsources; More Western giants are snapping up Indian companies that specialize in back-office operations." *Business Week.* 17 April 2006.

Parloff, Roger. "Not Exactly Counterfeit." *Fortune.* 1 May 2006.

U.S. Department of Labor. Bureau of Labor Statistics. "Mass Layoff Statistics." Available fromhttp://www.bls.gov/mls/home.htm. Retrieved on 30 March 2006.

Wilson, Taylor H. "Outsourced Around the World in a Billable Hour." *Texas Lawyer.* 1 May 2006.

Zimmer, Matt. "Outsourcing: From soup to nuts or a la carte?" *Club Management.* December 2004.

Darnay, ECDI

OVERHEAD EXPENSE

Costs in a business are traditionally divided into operating and administrative categories. Both are necessary for the company, but operating costs are closely tied to specific products and services whereas administrative costs are incurred on behalf of the enterprise as a whole. This latter expense is sometimes referred to as "overhead."

The distinctions are most clearly visible in manufacturing operations where, for instance, the "factory" has its own warehouses and yards while the "headquarters" is located elsewhere. All of the costs associated with production itself, including engineering, warehousing, energy, maintenance, and the like—and not least labor and raw materials costs—are accounted for as operating expenses. Ideally the accounting systems are well-enough developed so that these costs can be subdivided by major product lines. Supposing that the company makes golf carts, 4-wheeled recreational vehicles, and boats. Factory costs associated with each should then be available and, indeed, assignable down to each unit produced.

At the headquarters of the company administrative expenses are incurred. These include executives and staff salaries and fringes. Accruing in addition will be the costs of the buildings' rents and maintenance, outside services, expenditures on advertising and sales promotion, personnel, health programs, executive travel costs, etc. Let us assume that the company has engineers at the factory but also engages two engineers to conduct research. The research function will be part of the administrative expense. Depreciation on all of the company's assets, all taxes paid, all insurance carried will be part of administration. And all of these expenses will be accounted for as overhead. The money spent on these items or activities support all three of the major product lines together, not separately.

Given this definition of overhead—as costs incurred to make something else possible—it is clear that different kinds of overhead will be incurred in a larger operation. The factory itself will have an overhead ("factory overhead"), namely the costs associated with factory management staffs and services. Sales office operations may have overhead costs associated with general supervision, etc.

The *general* overhead is that of the company's central management.

On a company's income statement, sales represent the incoming money and net profits after tax represent what is left over. Operating profit is an intermediate sum left over after production costs have been taken from sales. The difference between operating profit and net profit is another definition of overhead. It is the cost of "all else" after products are made and/or services have been delivered.

From this comes the concept of "overhead absorption" commonly used in service operations or in contracting. Where the chief cost of an operation is the salary of employees, companies often develop an "overhead rate" used as a multiplier of salaries. In bidding a job, managers first calculate costs based on the individuals who will do the work, the amount of time they will spend, travel expenses, and other necessary purchases. Then the managers apply an "overhead," usually by multiplying the initial estimate by some factor like 1.8. This means that every dollar of salaries paid to employees must absorb 80 cents of overhead. Overhead rates are typically developed once a year and used thereafter. The obvious implication of an "overhead rate" is that the operation must sell enough staff time to absorb all of the overhead. And only after that does the operation make a profit.

A somewhat analogous concept arises in charitable operations that spend money on fundraising. Here, ideally, as little of each collected dollar is deducted for the fundraising itself as possible—and as much as possible handed over for the actual charitable operation itself.

In successful companies and in good times there is a tendency for overhead to increase because the money is there and additional services provide better information, less stress, and more amenities. When the economy slows or a company runs into difficulties, it will first reduce its overhead by shedding nice-to-have but not-absolutely-necessary services. The public is often amazed that a company can keep on operating after letting so many people go. The hidden part of this process is that the public is unaware just how much "weight" the company had put on before forced to go on a diet.

SEE ALSO *Activity-Based Costing; Product Costing*

BIBLIOGRAPHY

Heintz, James A., and Robert W. Parry. *College Accounting.* Thomson South-Western, 2005.

Pratt, Shannon P., Robert F. Reilly, and Robert P. Schweis. *Valuing a Business, 4th Edition.* McGraw-Hill, 2000.

Warren, Carl S., Philip E. Fess, and James M. Reeve. *Accounting.* Thomson South-Western, 2004.

Darnay, ECDI

OVERTIME

Overtime is work done by hourly employees beyond the regular work hours per week. Any work over forty hours per week for an hourly worker is considered overtime. Overtime and overtime compensation are provided for under the federal Fair Labor Standards Act of 1938. It is required under the FLSA that employers pay time-and-a-half to employees working more than forty hours per week or 150 percent of the worker's salary for those hours exceeding the weekly average.

EXEMPT AND NON-EXEMPT EMPLOYEES

U.S. labor law distinguishes between "exempt" and "non-exempt" employees regarding overtime. Exempt employees do not have to be paid overtime if they work more than 40 hours a week. According to the FLSA, members of this class of employee include workers "employed in a bona fide executive, administrative, or professional capacity (including any employee employed in the capacity of academic administrative personnel or teacher in elementary or secondary schools) or in the capacity of outside [salesperson]." Any worker employed in the above categories who meets Department of Labor salary and duty tests is exempt from receiving overtime pay regardless of the number of hours he or she works.

In some businesses, employees attend to a wide variety of tasks that may include a blend of "exempt" and "non-exempt" duties. In these instances, their overtime status is dictated by their "primary duty" to their employer. Time spent on each task is an important but not decisive factor in determining exemption status. Instead, federal regulations dictate that the decisive factor is "the relative importance of the [exempt] duties as compared with other types of duties . . . and the relationship between [the employee's] salary and the wages paid other employees for the kind of nonexempt work performed." For instance, the Code of Federal Regulations notes that "in some departments, or subdivisions of an establishment, an employee has broad responsibilities similar to those of the owner or manager of the establishment, but generally spends more than 50 percent of his time in production or sales work. While engaged in such work he supervises other employees, directs the work of warehouse and deliverymen, approves advertising, orders merchandise, handles customer complaints, authorizes payment of bills, or performs other management duties as the day-to-day operations require. He will be considered to have management as his primary duty." The Code of Federal Regulations also includes tests that can be used to determine the primary duties of other "white-collar" workers, including executives, professionals, computer programmers, and administrative personnel.

On April 23, 2004, the U.S. Department of Labor introduced new regulations relating to exemptions. An article in *Healthcare Financial Management* offered the following summary and the rationale behind the rule change. "The new rule, effective August 23, 2004, updates the regulations defining exemptions for 'white collar' executive, administrative, and professional employees. One of the most significant changes included in the rule involves the minimum salary level requirements, last updated almost 30 years ago. According to the rule, overtime protection is guaranteed for all workers earning less than $455 per week ($23,660 annually). Under original FLSA regulations, the minimum salary level for exemption was $155 per week ($8,060 annually)."

DECIDING TO USE OVERTIME

Businesses with seasonal peaks, with quotas and deadlines, or with the possibility of rush orders, will at some point probably not be able to meet staffing needs with the regular hours worked by employees. It is at these crisis points that overtime becomes an invaluable tool for the employer.

Most business experts, however, counsel owners and managers to use overtime sparingly if possible. The ideal use of overtime is when employees are willing to work longer hours for increased pay, and the employer needs qualified, trained individuals who will not need excessive supervision while tackling an increased work load. An employer should not, however, rely on employees working many more hours per week to routinely make up for work not accomplished during the regular work week. If this is the case—if overtime becomes essential to the performance of a business, even during regular operating scenarios—there may be other factors, such as poor compensation, morale, or inadequate staffing levels, to be considered.

One serious consideration often cited in the routine use of overtime is the effect it can have on employees' regular production. Increased work hours during one period may lead to increased absenteeism during others, due to family commitments that were put off during "crunch" periods or to illness exacerbated by stress. Family conflicts are also a common consequence and manifest themselves in higher levels of stress, alcohol and drug use, and absenteeism. In addition, employee productivity during regular business hours often undergoes a major downturn after periods of extensive overtime.

All overtime should be authorized by a manager or supervisor, preferably in writing. Consideration should be given to tracking the work accomplished during overtime hours; this ensures that employees are continuing to be productive at the increased pay rate, even with the stress of longer hours and increased sales or other pressures.

Tracking what work is done on overtime will also aid the owner or manager of a business to better plan for staffing needs in the future.

ALTERNATIVES TO OVERTIME PAY

Because overtime can become very expensive, and can sometimes be draining for regular employees, some businesses have embraced alternate plans of human resource management.

Expanding workforce size. The first determination to be made is whether the amount of overtime used throughout the year is enough to justify the hiring of additional staff. This step should be very carefully considered, however, because while overtime is expensive, so are the costs (salary, payroll taxes, social security, benefits) associated with hiring additional employees.

Temps. Another alternative to overtime is to utilize temporary workers. This can be done independently by the owner or manager, or through a temporary employment agency. Depending on the task (and how much training and supervision is required), the temporary employee can save businesses significant overtime expenses. This alternative can be particularly attractive if increased staffing needs are seasonal and predictable, so that temporary employees can be hired in advance.

Stock options. Many employers have begun offering their workers stock options as compensation in lieu of actual overtime pay. In 1999 employer rights to offer stock options were codified into law with the passage and signing of the Worker Economic Opportunity Act. This act amends the Fair Labor Standards Act to exclude profits from stock options or purchase plans from the calculation of non-exempt employee's overtime if various requirements are met (such as full disclosure of terms and voluntary participation). Supporters of this new law contend that it will allow employers to offer stock options as incentives to hourly workers while safeguarding employees against businesses that might try to disseminate risky stock options in place of overtime pay.

EMPLOYEE REACTIONS
TO OVERTIME

Many employees welcome the opportunity to augment their regular salaries with overtime pay. Some businesses can effectively use overtime as a kind of voluntary bonus: if the employees are willing to put in the added hours, they will be rewarded with increased pay. Because of the strong positive feelings many employees have about the opportunity to earn overtime pay, employers should carefully weigh the pros and cons of hiring temporary help; regular employees will recognize the loss of overtime, and morale may suffer, particularly if overtime has become an integral part of the business cycle.

But the prevailing feeling among many business owners and executives is that employees are placing ever greater value on leisure/family time, and that they are willing to make some sacrifices in the realm of compensation in order to enjoy personal interests. In addition, analysts point out that families that have both parents in the work force may not value overtime as much as employees of the past. Employers should remain sensitive to employees' needs and responsibilities outside of the workplace, and should recognize that employees may not always be willing to volunteer for overtime.

Mandatory Overtime In the medical field especially, affecting nurses particularly owing to shortages in this healthcare specialization, mandatory overtime is often imposed on employees. Hospital like to staff 12-hour shifts with the consequence that work-day overtime (at minimum) becomes mandatory. Lonnie Golden and Barbara Wiens-Tuers, writing for *Labor Studies Journal*, pointed out that the requirement extends more widely beyond health care. Citing the 2002 General Social Survey (sponsored by the National Science Foundation) they reported that 28 percent of full time workers were exposed to and 21 percent were actually required to work overtime involuntarily. Golden and Wiens-Tuers pointed out that collective bargaining agreements have failed to curb mandatory overtime effectively enough—thus stimulating seven states to curb the phenomenon by law or regulation.

BIBLIOGRAPHY

de Graaf, John. *Take Back Your Time: Fighting Overwork and Time Poverty in America.* Berrett-Koehler, 2003.

"DOL Rule Enhances 'White Collar' Exemption Regulations." *Healthcare Financial Management.* June 2004.

Federal Register. Department of Labor. "Defining and Delimiting the Exemptions for Executive, Administrative, Professional, Outside Sales and Computer Employees; Final Rule." 23 April 2004.

Golden, Lonnie and Barbara Wiens-Tuers. "Mandatory Overtime Work in the United States: Who, Where, and What?." *Labor Studies Journal.* Spring 2005.

Hart, Robert. *The Economics of Overtime Working.* University of Cambridge, 2004.

Luna, Michael. "Bedside Nurses and Managers Speak Out on Mandatory Overtime." *RN.* January 2006.

Schiff, Lisa. "Two More States Say No to Mandatory Overtime." *RN.* April 2004.

U.S. Department of Labor. "Fair Pay." Available from http://www.dol.gov/esa/regs/compliance/whd/fairpay/main.htm. Retrieved on 25 May 2006.

Hillstrom, Northern Lights
updated by Magee, ECDI

P

PACKAGING

There is a saying in the packaging industry to the effect that "everybody thinks he is an expert on the subject." The implication of this judgment is that, of course, "they don't know the half of it." The public is intensely exposed to packaging, and its members will *of course* have an opinion, indeed an *informed* opinion. At the same time packaging is a vast subject extending deep in one direction to very hidden and sophisticated areas of materials science, in another into the protection of public health and welfare; it is the pillar supporting at least three major industries (paper and board, plastics, and glass); it is fought over by people who want to use its labels for disclosure and those who want "truth in advertising"; it is a very important branch of marketing and also of design activities; it is in itself a large and expensive industrial activity sometimes separate from production, placed at its end, sometimes integrated into the manufacturing process; it has its major subdivision of portion packaging, packaging, and outer packaging or packing; everything rides on its pallets; it is an important aspect of transportation, warehousing, and distribution generally; the word is used symbolically to mean "the artful presentation" of something, such as the "packaging" of a celebrity; finally, spent packaging is the bulk of solid waste and carelessly discarded packaging that is the litter of the U.S.A.

EVOLUTION

Packaging is nothing new and predates modern times, but the form it takes is a direct reflection of settlement patterns, the reach of the economy, food preservation technology, and the nature of the transportation system. Before the modern era took serious hold after World War I, only a few products were packaged. Canning dates back to the days of Napoleon, some of whose formations, marching into Russia, received canned goods in newly invented tin-lined metal cans. Other long-lasting products (what today we call long shelf-life products), like hard biscuits and cookies, were packaged; chocolates and candies came in fancy boxes as well. Perfumes were an early and highly visible packaged product. All of these, and others, from the very beginning, bore brand identifications. Many small products like buttons and needles were prepackaged. Packaging initially served the needs and convenience of the seller; the package itself became a container in the consumer's home. Urban settlement was dense. Refrigeration was not yet wide-spread. Food shopping took place daily. People took milk or oil cans to the store to have them filled; preserves came in glass that could be recycled; paper packaging was used, often made on the spot from sheets by the merchant; the "shopping basket" itself was the generic carrier of groceries. Long distance packing used to be in crates fashioned of wood. Of that technology today only the wood pallet survives.

Packaging technology saw intense development immediately before and during World War II in efforts to supply the fighting forces—and not just those of the U.S. Mass distribution of packaged products began and then continued thereafter. Sturdy Kraft paper, two outer layers reinforced by a corrugated inner layer (the corrugated box) took over bulk packaging. Milk began to transit from recyclable glass bottles to paper containers initially coated with wax and then, after the war, by hot melt plastics, a combination of wax and plastics. Plastics

845

saw an immense expansion in the 1950s and 60s; polyethylene became a staple of flexible packaging, polyvinyl chloride (PVC) became a standard form of transparent packaging, and polyurethane foam plastics came to dominate a field that had once belong to pressed paper pulp. Composite materials (laminates) became possible as a consequence of the emergence of high-performance adhesives. Packaging grew stronger, lighter, and easier to process by machine. Aluminum entered the beverage market as aluminum cans and also as easy-open closures for steel cans. As mass production developed in the underlying materials, and forming and packaging machinery became ever more affordable, many products not heretofore packaged were now "shrink-wrapped" onto sheets of cardboard, bagged, and boxed. In parallel with the physical development of packaging, companies exploited the surfaces of packaging to print their brand names and messages, a process aided by rapidly advancing printing technology and improved inks. The potential of using the package itself as a means of differentiation or a means of delivering convenience (the single-cup tea bag, the single-serving ketchup package) rapidly created a brand-new dimension in packaging. Packaging and marketing began to merge. Packaging grew in total volume to such an extent that by the 1970s it began to attract government attention as a new cost imposed on waste disposal systems. Discarded packaging—particularly after cans took over beer and soft drink distribution from recyclable bottles—produced deposit legislation aimed at curbing litter.

By the 1970s packaging had reached maturity and has since evolved less dramatically and visibly. However, the underlying materials sciences are still producing ever better and ever more specialized and differentiated packaging. As the early 2000s advance, the protective capacities of packaging are improving so that some heretofore refrigerated products are available on ordinary shelves and others will likely follow. New composites are announced every year. Competition between materials continues; costlier materials like metals, paper, and glass are everywhere pressed by plastics; this trend, however, may reverse if the price of oil (the source of plastics) keeps climbing. Strange and wonderful extensions of the packaging-marketing synthesis are being talked about, like imprinting fresh fruit with messages adhering to microscopically thin coatings....

The continuing evolution of packaging *at a technical level* serves as an indicator that, despite much hype about the package as a promotional vehicle, the predominant function of packaging in the economy is product protection first, convenience next. The consumer also values objective information. Functionally, the hype comes last.

PACKAGING BASICS

Packaging divides into bulk, product, and portion packaging. Bulk packaging takes the form of cardboard boxes (much more rarely crates) and the pallets that carry these; it is intended to protect and is rarely ever used to advertise (except the maker of the box itself); even automobiles have bulk packaging in the form of protective sheets attached to windshields and other external features. Product packaging typically has two roles: protection and communication. The communication may be promotional, a service to the user (menus, preparation instructions), or a labeling requirement. The chief purpose of portion packaging is to deliver convenience—although such packaging also carries a message.

The producer needs to balance various aspects of a packaging system. In roughly the following order of importance, these are product protection, good production fit, low cost, and exploitability for marketing. To be sure, the package itself, first of all, must meet whatever regulations apply. Product protection includes basic product integrity and includes as long a shelf life as possible. The producer will prefer a system that permits rapid and efficient production with the lowest packaging equipment and packaging material costs. When given a choice, the surfaces should display the producer's messages as attractively as possible.

From the consumer's point of view, the ideal package will be easy to store, to open, and to close. It should be safe. It should carry warnings. If the product requires assembly or instructions to use, information should be present, and it should be clear. Consumers, of course, use brand identifications to choose products, but their strongest interest is in objective information carried on the labels, one reason why Congress has moved, in response, to require such labeling. People want to know what they are buying: Is it wool or polyester? How long will this half-and-half last? Can I use this as a diabetic? All else equal, the consumer also will prefer a package that can be reused in some way.

PACKAGING AS A BUSINESS FUNCTION

It is clear from the discussion thus far that packaging, for the business owner, touches all aspects of the business. All depending on the product, of course, it may involve significant engineering work to ensure fit with the production process, satisfy legal requirements regarding safety, yet incorporate the aesthetics chosen for product promotion. Packaging often involves aggregation of multiple units into one package. The optimal package cost for the right aggregate has to be priced properly to achieve desired volume while fitting vendors' shelf space. Product aesthetics must accommodate legal labeling requirements. Different modes of packaging will deliver higher and lower out-of-pocket costs but may produce harder-to-predict sales volumes.

These problems tend to sort out reasonably well because a great variety of analogous cases exist in the market to suggest which general model to follow—or which edge of which envelope to push. Packaging is a large and sophisticated industry, and the small business owner will be able to identify both package designers and suppliers of packaging equipment easily enough. Designers typically know the equipment available; conversely, packaging equipment suppliers can recommend designers they work with routinely.

LABELING: CONSUMERS WANT IT

The Fair Packaging and Labeling Act of 1966 regulates packaging and labeling. The act requires that every product package specify on its "principal display label"—that part of the label most likely to be seen by consumers—the following information: 1) the product type; 2) the producer or processor's name and location; 3) the quantity (if applicable); and 4) the number and size of servings (if applicable). Furthermore, several restrictions apply to the way that the label is displayed. For example, mandatory copy required by the act must be in boldface type. Also, if the company is not listed in the telephone book, the manufacturer's or importer's street address must be displayed.

Foods, toys, drugs, cosmetics, furs, and textiles require special labeling. Under the act, the label for edible products, for example, must provide sodium content if other nutritional information is also shown. Labels must also show ingredients, in descending order from the one of highest quantity to the one of least quantity. Certain food items, such as beef, may also be required to display qualitative "grade labels" or inspection labels. Likewise, "informative labeling" may be required for products such as home appliances. Informative label requirements mandate information about use, care, performance capability, life expectancy, safety precautions, gas mileage, or other factors. Certain major home appliances, for example, must provide the estimated cost of running each make and model for one year at average utility rates.

Congress passed significant new labeling legislation, the Nutrition Labeling and Education Act of 1990; the act became effective in the mid-1990s. This act is intended primarily to discourage misleading labeling related to health benefits of food items. Specifically, many package labels subjectively claimed that their contents were "low-fat," "high-fiber," or possessed some other health virtue when the facts indicated otherwise. Basically, the new laws require most food labels to specify values such as calorie and cholesterol content, fat and saturated fat percentages, and sodium levels.

BIBLIOGRAPHY

"Generics: Injecting some color." *Community Pharmacy.* 7 April 2006.

Gordon, Stacey King. *Packaging Makeovers: Graphic Redesign for Market Change.* Rockport Publishers, 2005.

"Palletizer Handles Small Packages." *Product News Network.* 14 April 2006.

Reardon, Corey M. "Metalized Papers and Films: A New Focus for Global Growth." *Paper, Film & Foil Converter.* 19 April 2006.

Roth, Laszlo, and George L. Wybenga. *The Packaging Designer's Book of Patterns.* Wiley, 2000.

Ryuko, Kazutomo, ed. *Limited Edition: To buy or not to buy? It's all in the packaging design.* Gingko Press, 2005.

Selke, Susan E. M., John D. Culter, and Ruben J. Hernandez. *Plastics Packaging: Properties, Processing, Applications, and Regulations.* Hanser Gardner Publications, 2004.

Sook Kim, Queena. "This Potion's Power is in Its Packaging." *Wall Street Journal.* 21 December 2000.

Special Packaging Designs. Pepin Press, 2004.

U.S. Food and Drug Administration. "Fair Packaging and Labeling Act." Available from http://www.fda.gov/opacom/laws/fplact.htm. Retrieved on 24 April 2006.

Darnay, ECDI

PARTNERSHIP

MAJOR TYPES OF ORGANIZATIONS

Various forms of business organizations are differentiated by the tax and other liabilities borne by their investors. Three major forms in the mid-2000s were corporations, partnerships, and limited liability companies (LLCs).

In a *corporation* an investor only risks the value of his or her investments in the company in the case of failure and only owes taxes on dividend income received. The corporation is legally a "person" and pays its own taxes. It is also at liberty to pay or not to pay dividends, although it is technically governed by the will of a majority of stockholders. The stockholder, in effect, is taxed twice: first on the net income of the corporation that he or she owns (in part) and then on the dividends. The investor, of course, never sees the first tax but gets less in dividends because it is paid by the company.

In a *partnership* each partner is an equal co-owner of the entity, pays an equal share of taxes due, and, in case of failure, equally shares in all of the liabilities of the partnership. Thus, in a partnership, liabilities are shared but not limited. The benefit of partnerships is that general partners are only taxed once. The partnership itself pays no taxes.

In an *LLC* the structures of a corporation and of a partnership are combined. Participants are "exposed" only to the extent of their investment because the LLC is treated as a corporation for purposes of liability; at the same time, the taxes owed by the LLC are paid by the participants in proportion to their share in the revenues. They are taxed once, not twice, as in corporations. LLCs, described in more detail elsewhere in this volume, are a relatively recent form of organization and growing rapidly because of the advantages that they offer. Because LLCs are limited in various ways, their growth appears above all to impact partnerships—the form of organization described in this article.

WHAT PARTNERSHIPS ARE

In the words of the Uniform Partnership Act, a partnership is "an association of two or more persons to carry on as Co-owners of a business for profit." The essential characteristics of this business form, then, are the collaboration of two or more owners, the conduct of business for profit (a nonprofit cannot be designated as a partnership), and the sharing of profits, losses, and assets by the joint owners. A partnership is not a corporate or separate entity; rather it is viewed as an extension of its owners for legal and tax purposes, although a partnership may own property as a legal entity. While a partnership may be founded on a simple agreement, even a handshake between owners, a well-crafted and carefully worded partnership agreement is the best way to begin the business. In the absence of such an agreement, the Uniform Partnership Act, a set of laws pertaining to partnerships that has been adopted by most states, governs the business.

There are two types of partnerships:

General Partnerships In this standard form of partnership, all of the partners are equally responsible for the business's debts and liabilities. In addition, all partners are allowed to be involved in the management of the company. In fact, in the absence of a statement to the contrary in the partnership agreement, each partner has equal rights to control and manage the business. Therefore, unanimous consent of the partners is required for all major actions undertaken. It is well to note, however, that any obligation made by one partner is legally binding on all partners, whether or not they have been informed.

Limited Partnerships In a limited partnership, one or more partners are general partners, and one or more are limited partners. General partners are personally liable for the business's debts and judgments against the business; they can also be directly involved in the management. Limited partners are essentially investors (silent partners, so to speak) who do not participate in the company's management and who are also not liable beyond their investment in the business. State laws determine how involved limited partners can be in the day-to-day business of the firm without jeopardizing their limited liability. This business form is especially attractive to real estate investors, who benefit from the tax incentives available to limited partners, such as being able to write off depreciating values.

ADVANTAGES

Collaboration. As compared to a sole proprietorship, which is essentially the same business form but with only one owner, a partnership offers the advantage of allowing the owners to draw on the resources and expertise of the co-partners. Running a business on your own, while simpler, can also be a constant struggle. But with partners to share the responsibilities and lighten the workload, members of a partnership often find that they have more time for the other activities in their lives.

Tax advantages. The profits of a partnership pass through to its owners, who report their share on their individual tax returns. Therefore, the profits are only taxed once (at the personal level of its owners) rather than twice, as is the case with corporations, which are taxed at the corporate level and then again at the personal level when dividends are distributed to the shareholders. The benefits of single taxation can also be secured by forming an S corporation (although some ownership restrictions apply) or by forming a limited liability company (a new hybrid of corporations and partnerships that is still evolving).

Simple operating structure. A partnership, as opposed to a corporation, is fairly simple to establish and run. No forms need to be filed or formal agreements drafted (although it is advisable to write a partnership agreement in the event of future disagreements). The most that is ever required is perhaps filing a partnership certificate with a state office in order to register the business's name and securing a business license. As a result, the annual filing fees for corporations, which can sometimes be very expensive, are avoided when forming a partnership.

Flexibility. Because the owners of a partnership are usually its managers, especially in the case of a small business, the company is fairly easy to manage, and decisions can be made quickly without a lot of bureaucracy. This is not the case with corporations, which must have shareholders, directors, and officers, all of whom have some degree of responsibility for making major decisions.

Uniform laws. One of the drawbacks of owning a corporation or limited liability company is that the laws governing those business entities vary from state to state and are changing all the time. In contrast, the Uniform Partnership Act provides a consistent set of laws about forming and running partnerships that make it easy for small business owners to know the laws that affect them. And because these laws have been adopted in all states but Louisiana, interstate business is much easier for partnerships than it is for other forms of businesses.

Acquisition of capital. Partnerships generally have an easier time acquiring capital than corporations because partners, who apply for loans as individuals, can usually get loans on better terms. This is because partners guarantee loans with their personal assets as well as those of the business. As a result, loans for a partnership are subject to state usury laws, which govern loans for individuals. Banks also perceive partners to be less of a risk than corporations, which are only required to pledge the business's assets. In addition, by forming a limited partnership, the business can attract investors (who will not be actively involved in its management and who will enjoy limited liability) without having to form a corporation and sell stock.

DRAWBACKS

Conflict with partners. While collaborating with partners can be a great advantage to a small business owner, having to actually run a business from day to day with one or more partners can be a nightmare. First of all, you have to give up absolute control of the business and learn to compromise. And when big decisions have to be made, such as whether and how to expand the business, partners often disagree on the best course and are left with a potentially explosive situation. The best way to deal with such predicaments is to anticipate them by drawing up a partnership agreement that details how such disagreements will be dealt with.

Authority of partners. When one partner signs a contract, each of the other partners is legally bound to fulfill it. For example, if Anthony orders $10,000 of computer equipment, it is as if his partners, Susan and Jacob, had also placed the order. And if their business cannot afford to pay the bill, then the personal assets of Susan and Jacob are on the line as well as those of Anthony. And this is true whether the other partners are aware of the contract or not. Even if a clause in the partnership agreement dictates that each partner must inform the other partners before any such deals are made, all of the partners are still responsible if the other party in the contract (the computer company) was not aware of such a stipulation in the partnership agreement. The only recourse the other partners have is to sue.

The Uniform Partnership Act does specify some instances in which full consent of all partners is required:

- Selling the business's good will

- Decisions that would compromise the business's ability to function normally

- Assigning partnership property in trust for a creditor or to someone in exchange for the payment of the partnership's debts

- Admission of liability in a lawsuit

- Submission of a partnership claim or liability to arbitration

Unlimited liability. As the previous example illustrated, the personal assets of the partnership's members are vulnerable because there is no separation between the owners and the business. The primary reason many businesses choose to incorporate or form limited liability companies is to protect the owners from the unlimited liability that is the main drawback of partnerships or sole proprietorships. If an employee or customer is injured and decides to sue, or if the business runs up excessive debts, then the partners are personally responsible and in danger of losing all that they own. Therefore, if considering a partnership, determine which of your assets will be put at risk. If you possess substantial personal assets that you will not invest in the company and do not want to put in jeopardy, a corporation or limited liability company may be a better choice. But if you are investing most of what you own in the business, then you don't stand to lose any more than if you incorporated. Then if your business is successful, and you find at a later date that you now possess extensive personal assets that you would like to protect, you can consider changing the legal status of your business to secure limited liability.

Vulnerability to death or departure. Unlike corporations, which exist perpetually, regardless of ownership, general partnerships dissolve if one of the partners dies, retires, or withdraws. (In limited partnerships, the death or withdrawal of the limited partner does not affect the stability of the business.) Even though this is the law governing partnerships, the partnership agreement can contain provisions to continue the business. For example, a provision can be made allowing a buy-out of a partner's share if he or she wants to withdraw or if the partner dies.

Limitations on transfer of ownership. Unlike corporations, which exist independently of their owners, the existence of partnerships is dependent upon the owners. Therefore, the Uniform Partnership Act stipulates that ownership may not be transferred without the consent of all the other partners. (Once again, a limited partner is an exception: his or her interest in the company may be sold at will.)

FORMING A PARTNERSHIP

Reserving a Name The first step in creating a partnership is reserving a name, which must be done with the secretary of state's office or its equivalent. Most states require that the words "Company" or "Associates" be included in the name to show that more than one partner is involved in the business. In all states, though, the name of the partnership must not resemble the name of any other corporation, limited liability company, partnership, or sole proprietorship that is registered with the state.

The Partnership Agreement A partnership can be formed in essentially two ways: by verbal or written agreement. A partnership that is formed at will, or verbally, can also be dissolved at will. In the absence of a formal agreement, state laws (the Uniform Partnership Act, except in Louisiana) will govern the business. These laws specify that without an agreement, all partners share equally in the profits and losses of the partnership and that partners are not entitled to compensation for services. If you would like to structure your partnership differently, you will need to write a partnership agreement. The subject is covered more fully in this volume under *Partnership Agreement*.

RIGHTS AND RESPONSIBILITIES OF PARTNERS

The Uniform Partnership Act defines the basic rights and responsibilities of partners. Some of these can be changed by the partnership agreement, except, as a general rule, those laws that govern the partners' relationships with third parties. In the absence of a written agreement, then, the following rights and responsibilities apply:

Rights

- All partners have an equal share in the profits of the partnership and are equally responsible for its losses.

- Any partner who makes a payment for the partnership beyond its capital, or makes a loan to the partnership, is entitled to receive interest on that money.

- All partners have equal property rights for property held in the partnership's name. This means that the use of the property is equally available to all partners for the purpose of the partnership's business.

- All partners have an equal interest in the partnership, or share of its profits and assets.

- All partners have an equal right in the management and conduct of the business.

- All partners have a right to access the books and records of the partnership's accounts and activities at all times. (This does not apply to limited partners.)

- No partner may be added without the consent of all other partners.

Responsibilities

- Partners must report and turn over to the partnership any income they have derived from use of the partnership's property.

- Partners are not allowed to conduct business that competes with the partnership.

- Each partner is responsible for contributing his or her full time and energy to the success of the partnership.

- Any property that a partner acquires with the intention of it being the partnership's property must be turned over to the partnership.

- Any disputes shall be decided by a majority vote.

SEE ALSO *Limited Liability Company*

BIBLIOGRAPHY
Clifford, Denis, and Ralph E. Warner. *The Partnership Book: How to Write A Partnership Agreement.* Nolo, 2001.

Gage, David. *The Partnership Charter: How to Start Out Right With Your New Business Partnership.* Basic Books, 2004.

Mancuso, Anthony. *Form Your Own Limited Liability Company.* Nolo, 2005.

Thompson, Margaret Gallagher. "Where We Were and Where We Are in Family Limited Partnerships." *The Legal Intelligencer.* 1 August 2005.

Hillstrom, Northern Lights
updated by Magee, ECDI

PARTNERSHIP AGREEMENT

Partnership agreements are written documents that explicitly detail the relationship between the business partners and their individual obligations and contributions to the partnership. Since partnership agreements should cover all possible business situations that could arise during the partnership's life, the documents are often complex; legal counsel in drafting and reviewing the finished contract is generally recommended. If a partnership does not have a partnership agreement in place when it dissolves, the guidelines of the Uniform Partnership Act and various state laws will determine how the assets and debts of the partnership are distributed.

RECOMMENDED ELEMENTS OF THE PARTNERSHIP AGREEMENT

1. Name and address of partnership.

2. Duration of partnership—Partners can point to a specific termination date or include a general clause explaining that the partnership will exist until all partners agree to dissolve it or a partner dies.

3. Business purpose—Some consultants recommend that partners keep this section somewhat vague in case opportunities for expansion arise, while others emphasize clear-cut and unambiguous entrepreneurial goals.

4. Bank account information—This section should note which bank accounts are to be used for partnership purposes, and which partners have check-signing privileges.

5. Partners' contributions—Valuation of all contributions, whether in cash, property or services.

6. Partners' compensation—Determine in detail how and when profits (and salaries, if applicable) will be distributed.

7. Management authority—What are the operational responsibilities of each partner? Will partners be able to make some decisions on their own? Which decisions will require the unanimous consent of all partners? What are the voting rights of each partner? How will tie votes be resolved?

8. Circumstances under which new partners might be admitted into the partnership.

9. Work hours and vacation.

10. Kinds of outside business activities that will be allowed for partners.

11. Disposition of partnership's name if a partner leaves.

12. Dispute resolution—Stipulates what kinds of mediation or arbitration will be utilized in the case of disputes that cannot be resolved amongst the partners. This is a way to avoid costly litigation.

13. Miscellaneous provisions—This portion of the agreement might delineate the circumstances under which the agreement could be amended, for example.

14. Buy-Sell Agreement.

The Buy-Sell Agreement The buy-sell agreement is one of the most important elements of any partnership agreement. Lance Wallach summarized the problem in an article for *Accounting Today:* "Large problems can result from the death, incapacity, resignation, etc., of one of the owners," Wallach wrote. "How would the decedent's heirs liquidate the business interest to pay expenses and taxes? What would happen if an heir or an unknown outside buyer of the decedent's share decides to interfere with the business? Could the business or other owners afford to buy back the decedent's ownership interests?"

A buy-sell agreement is intended to forestall all such problems. In essence, it specifies the terms of a buyout in the event of death, divorce, disability, or retirement. The buy-sell agreement has become a "must" in many instances in which a partnership is seeking financing—a loan or a lease. Lenders want to see the agreement and study its provisions.

The two primary structures for buy/sell agreements are cross-purchase agreements, in which the remaining partnership owners buy the departing partner's stock or partnership interest, and the stock-redemption agreement, in which the company buys the stock of the departing owner. Life insurance policies are the more typical technique employed to ensure that funds are available for cross-purchase transactions. With two partners in a business, the solution is very straightforward but requires more ingenuity to set up with multiple shareholders. With stock redemption agreements, on the other hand, the insurance would be written in favor of the company. One of the benefits of a buy-sell agreement is that, with the partners able to reach agreement, more innovative methods of solving the problem can be worked out and codified.

BIBLIOGRAPHY

Bentley, Ross. "Live in Peace with Your Contract." *Caterer & Hotelkeeper.* 11 August 2005.

Blaydon, Colin, and Fred Wainwright. "Survey: GPs and LPs Support Idea for Model LP Agreement." *Venture Capital Journal.* 1 July 2004.

Dunn, Ross. "Ye of Little Faith." *People Management.* 27 April 2000.

Spandaccini, Michael. "The Legal Ins and Outs of Forming a Partnership." *Entrepreneur.* 2 June 2005.

Wallach, Lance. "Buy-Sell Agreements Can Help Protect Your Business." *Accounting Today.* 7 November 2005.

Weisz, Richard L. "Breakup of Business Partnership isn't Easy Thing to Do." *Business First-Columbus.* 1 December 2000.

Zaritsky, Howard M. Structuring Buy-Sell Agreements. Warren Gorham Lamont, 2005.

Hillstrom, Northern Lights
updated by Magee, ECDI

PART-TIME BUSINESS

Thousands of American entrepreneurs supplement their income by starting and maintaining part-time small businesses. The circumstances and goals of these owners run the gamut, but many enterprises are operated out of the home and used to supplement income derived from other sources (a full-time job, retirement benefits, etc.). But not all people start part-time enterprises from economic necessity. Statistics indicate that many individuals—and especially people with higher levels of education—launch part-time entrepreneurial ventures to make use of skills that may not be tapped in their full-time work. Finally, the ability and desire to launch a business on a part-time basis is often impacted by family considerations; in some instances, the cost of raising children may serve as an incentive to start a business on the side. In other cases, a parent may decide that the hours involved in looking after his or her children precludes the possibility of a part-time business. Many owners of part-time businesses, however, contend that if the desire is there, a part-time venture can be managed by most people.

Part-time businesses are also regarded by many entrepreneurs as a sensible option in situations where the ultimate success of the venture seems unclear. "Part-time entrepreneurs can… limit their risks compared with those taken by individuals who plunge in full-time," wrote David E. Gumpert in *Working Woman.* "For one thing, part-timers don't have the same pressure to produce cash flow, because they can hold down a job at the same time and operate out of their homes. For another, part-timers can go more slowly and learn the skills of running a business as they go along; they have the luxury of making errors and revising their business concept as they proceed."

KEYS TO ESTABLISHING A SUCCESSFUL PART-TIME BUSINESS

Experts point to several important factors in creating and maintaining a profitable and healthy part-time business venture:

Recognize importance of full-time job. It is vitally important for entrepreneurs who already have a full-time job to make sure that their part-time business does not interfere with their obligations to their employers. Moreover, it is important for part-time business owners to make sure that their employers do not begin to *perceive* that the side business is taking priority, for in the final analysis, your ability to meet the demands of both businesses is irrelevant if your employer begins to feel—fairly or not—that the arrangement is detracting from your job performance. For this reason, part-time business owners may want to weigh the likely reaction of their employers before even publicizing the existence of the part-time venture.

Type of business. The nature of a part-time venture is often an important factor in its long-term viability. Certain businesses can be more easily maintained without unduly complicating regular job obligations. "Service

businesses often allow for this kind of flexibility," explained Gumpert. "Men have for years carved out entrepreneurial opportunities as part-time plumbers, electricians, and carpenters. Women [are] discovering similar opportunities in such areas as consulting and teaching." Retail stores and manufacturing establishments, on the other hand, are far less conducive to part-time businesses.

Scheduling flexibility. The individual's full-time job is flexible enough to give him or her the time and resources to take care of the entrepreneurial business's needs during normal business hours or during particularly busy periods.

Realistic workloads. Entrepreneurs launching part-time business ventures should also be wary of overextending themselves. Many individuals tend to take on more part-time work than they can easily handle, especially during the first few months of operation, when they have less experience in estimating the time involved in executing various tasks. While finances are often a factor in establishing a part-time business, most part-time entrepreneurs do not begin a venture with the expressed intention of turning their life into a chaotic rush of impending deadlines. Complications associated with underestimating the amount of time a given project or assignment will take are also typically compounded if the entrepreneur in question has significant family obligations (child or elder care, for instance).

Scaling back existing businesses. Small business researchers also note that some of the most successful part-time businesses are those that were formerly full-time endeavors. Indeed, many full-time entrepreneurs choose to scale back their hours after a certain number of years. They may do this for any number of reasons; some simply reach retirement age and wish to relax a little more, others decide to start a family, and still others may decide that they wish to spend more of their time traveling or indulging other interests (including other promising entrepreneurial ventures). In many instances, switching a business from full-time status to part-time status can actually strengthen the enterprise's hourly productivity. For example, the entrepreneur who decides to turn his 50-hours-a-week venture into one that requires him to spend half that amount of time on the business each week will naturally do his best to maintain relations with his best clients, while letting less valuable or more problematic clients go. As many business owners will quickly attest, having greater freedom to pick and choose who you do business with can be a most valuable side benefit of going part time.

Public perception of business. Some customers, especially if they are other businesses, may be wary of contracting with part-timers. The most effective way to counter the perception held in some quarters that part-time business owners are less reliable and responsive (because of obligations to their full-time employer) than full-time entrepreneurs is simply not to advertise your part-time status. Of course, you also should not lie about it if the issue comes up.

TAX CONSIDERATIONS

Owners of part-time businesses should also consider the potential tax ramifications of their activities—important as soon as the business begins to make money. Unless the business owner looks at the implications of his or her own net income early, the tax consequences later may be very painful, and the better the business the greater the pain. The ideal way of dealing with unexpected expenses come April 15 of the year following, the owner should calculate roughly what he or she would owe in taxes if the business income was added to regular income from a job. The difference between regular withholdings at the job and the extra amount likely to be payable should be submitted to the state and federal governments in the form of estimated quarterly tax payments.

Part of minding the taxes is also minding permissible deductions from income. Owners should make sure that they take full advantage of such deductions. Gumpert noted that "part-timers get the same tax advantages [as full-time entrepreneurs], including deductions for travel, entertainment, home office, and related expenses, plus deductible retirement plans." How exactly home-based business tax deductions can vary depending on whether the business is a full- or part-time venture. The IRS requires that a home office be used 'exclusively and regularly as a place of business to meet or deal with patients, clients, or customers' in the normal course of the business. The word 'exclusively' is very important because it means any room or space designated as a home office must be used 100 percent for business in order to qualify for the deduction.

MAKING THE LEAP TO FULL-TIME

Many part-time entrepreneurial ventures eventually expand into full-time businesses. Indeed, business owners who nurture their side-businesses into enterprises that are capable of covering their living and business expenses often waste little time in giving their employer two weeks notice and devoting their full attention to further expansion of their own business. But experts caution small business owners not to leave their long-time employer prematurely. For example, *Entrepreneur* pointed out that would-be full-time business owners can schedule health exams and other routine medical procedures while they are still covered by corporate insurance, and that they can sometimes convert existing health coverage to post-job

use. In addition, entrepreneurs thinking about leaving their full-time jobs to devote their energies to their own businesses should first determine if they are enrolled in any benefit plans that will vest or increase in value in the near term.

Entrepreneurs are also urged to organize their credit situation to their greatest advantage before leaving the security of their job. "Pay off or pay down the balance on your credit cards while you're still generating a steady income," stated *Entrepreneur.* "This helps your credit rating and enables you to finance various start-up costs." Finally, many entrepreneurs take out a home equity line of credit before leaving their full-time job. According to *Entrepreneur,* "having a line of credit to draw upon is invaluable during the first two years you're in business, although you probably won't qualify for one once you leave your job until your business has been successful for more than two years."

BIBLIOGRAPHY

Fishman, Stephen. *Working for Yourself: Law & Taxes for Independent Contractors, Freelancers & Consultants.* Nolo, 2006.

Gumpert, David E. "Doing a Little Business on the Side: How Entrepreneurs Start Up a Business and Hold Down a Job." *Working Woman.* October 1986.

"Part Time Business Opportunities." Entrepreneur.com. Available from http://www.entrepreneur.com/parttimefranchises/0,3385,294407,00.html. Retrieved on 1 May 2006.

Pleshette, Lyve Alexis. "Balancing Part-Time Business with Full-Time Job." *PowerHomebiz.com.* 24 February 2003.

Tyson, Eric, and Jim Schell. *Small Business for Dummies.* Second Edition. For Dummies, 2003.

Hillstrom, Northern Lights
updated by Magee, ECDI

PART-TIME EMPLOYEES

Part-time employees typically work fewer hours in a day or during a work week than full-time employees; the latter are typically employed for 40 hours. Part-time workers may also be those who only work during certain parts of the year. Part-time work is treated for all practical purposes in the same way as full-time work under federal law, specifically, the Fair Labor Standards Act (FLSA) applies to both types of workers in the same way. Under the Employee Retirement Income Security Act (ERISA), an employee who works 1,000 hours or more for a company during a calendar year is treated exactly in the same way as a full-time employee for purposes of qualifying for retirement coverage. The U.S. Department of Labor uses a definition of 34 or fewer hours a week as part-time work, but this definition is only used to gather statistical information.

MOTIVATIONS AND RATIONALES

Employer Motivations Employers use part-time workers for many reasons, most of them voluntary. Work is seasonal in many industries or has sharp up-and-down fluctuations. The retail industry's busiest season is Christmas; the sector therefore staffs up heavily during the season to handle an increased volume; the Postal Service, similarly, has a large increase in volume and for the same reason. Businesses that cater to summer or winter vacation seasons (hotels, restaurants, entertainment providers, transportation firms) build staffs with part-time workers and then release them at the end of the season. Agriculture has a similar seasonality during the planting, growing, and harvesting seasons. Industries that support seasonal activities with products and equipment very often produce during the opposite season and shut down or cut back in the season itself; thus snowmobile producers build during the summer; boat producers build during the winter.

In many industries temporary work-surges produce the equivalent of "seasons" but are not tied to the calendar—such as massive data keying after survey mailings return, preparations for market launches, the processing of perishable goods, and so on.

Businesses hire part-time workers when work increases but not enough to justify a full-time hire or to establish a new department. They take advantage of the availability of skilled and familiar workers for catch-up work or to fill in for vacationing full-timers in the summer when students are on vacation. Part-time workers are sometimes highly skilled professionals hired on during a certain phase of business—or serve continuously but part-time in order to fulfill a high function that does not require their continuous presence; financial work, software development, sales consulting, and other specialties fall into this category. In times of labor shortage businesses must sometimes hire part-time people they would be glad to put on the full-time staff, but the individuals don't wish to work a full schedule because they are retired or wish to pursue other interests.

In the last decade of the 20th and into the 21st century a new trend has become visible: employers who preferentially hire part-time labor in order to avoid paying benefits such as vacation pay, holidays, personal days, health-care, and retirement benefits—all of which they offer to their full-time employees. Regarding compensation, FLSA's only mandate is that hourly labor be paid the minimum wage. And under other statutes, discrimination is prohibited. But FLSA rules require consistent treatment of all classes of employees. Full-time and part-time workers are distinct classes; sufficient differentiation exists to treat the two categories differently. From this arises the "work-without-benefits" aspect of part-time work. If ordinary benefits are costly, transitioning to this type of labor can save the business a lot of money. The move also has costs, of course, not least in public perception.

Employee Rationales Employees take part-time work because they can find no other or they choose to work part time for a variety of personal reasons. Many part-time workers are students; some work part time for family or personal reasons; some because they take care of children, have medical limitations, or wish to stay within certain income limits for tax reasons (e.g., Social Security recipients). Of those who worked part-time voluntarily in 2005, 69 percent were women; among those forced to work part-time, women represented 49 percent.

THE PREVALENCE OF PART-TIME WORK

Based on data collected by the Bureau of Labor Statistics (BLS) in its Current Population Survey (CPS), of 141.7 million employed people in 2005, 24.7 million, 17.4 percent, fell into the part-time category, i.e., they worked fewer than 34 hours a week. Part-time work was highest among whites (18 percent), lowest among African Americans (14.2 percent), and just a shade higher among Asian Americans (14.7 percent). Among all those who worked 34 hours or less, 61.8 percent were women and 38.2 percent were men.

Of all part-time workers, only 13.5 percent of employees were working such hours for economic reasons (i.e., involuntarily); 86.5 percent did so for non-economic reasons. Economic reasons, as already noted, involve the unavailability of more attractive work. Specifically reported non-economic reasons recorded in the CPS include (in descending order of importance) attendance at school, family and personal reasons, retirement and the related wish to limit income for tax purposes, medical limitations, and child care duties.

If we take nonagricultural industries and divide them into major occupational sectors, part-time work was most prevalent in Services (36.8 percent of workers). After that came, in descending order, Sales (28.9 percent), Office Work (26.7), Transportation and Materials Moving (20.7), Management, Professional, and Related Work (19.5), Construction and Extraction (18.0), Production (13.4) and Installation, Maintenance, and Repair (11.6 percent of workers). Conventional wisdom holds that part-time work is most common in the retail sector. These data indicate that that sector comes in as a fairly distant second.

Not surprisingly, median weekly earnings of part-time workers are substantially lower than those engaged in full-time work: averaging $200 a week in 2006 contrasted to $668 a week for full-time work. What is initially surprising is that women working part time consistently earned higher pay than men. In 2005 women earned $201 a week to men's $188; in 2006, men's earnings were flat at $188, women's earnings had increased to $208. In full-time work women trail men—and have as far back as one wishes to look, and at all occupational levels. The explanation for the higher female pay in part-time work must have its roots in higher participation of functionally higher-ranking women in that work arrangement. Many women *want* to work part time. As *GP* magazine headlined, "80% of GPs want to be part-time." If the ranks of part-time women include quite a few doctors, lawyers, managers, and other professionals, their labor will, of course, lift the averages for women.

TRENDS AND INDICATIONS

Trends in part-time work have been rather steady and unchanging in the 10-year period between 1996, a year of very strong economic growth, and 2005, a year of slow recovery. Part-time workers in 1996 represented 17.3 percent of employment, in 2005 17.4 percent. Part-time work grew at a fractionally slower rate than total employment, but part-time work undertaken for non-economic, i.e., voluntary, reasons grew three times as rapidly as work undertaken for economic reasons—suggesting that a small part of the workforce *wants* to have part-time work.

Overall trends are difficult to discern because motivations are difficult to sort. Cost pressures in industry favor it, but efficiency concerns counter this benefit. The large and still increasing participation of women in the work force, and women's desire for flexibility in when and how they work—not surprising in that women still shoulder the chief burden of running families—are here and there also impacting sectors by depriving them of professional skills. For this reason, in recent years, signs have appeared that part-time workers may here and there, selectively, get benefits heretofore available only to full-time workers. That not-yet-formed trend may, of course, make part-time work both more attractive to employees and less so for employers. The crystal ball remains full of smoke.

BIBLIOGRAPHY

"80% of Female GPs Want to Be Part-Time." *GP*. 8 July 2005.

Lang, Joan. "Partners in Time: Managing part-time workers can be a full-time job, but the rewards are sizeable." *Food Service Director*. 15 March 2005.

McCall, Kimberly L. "Split Decision: Is hiring part-time sales reps a good idea?" *Entrepreneur*. November 2005.

Miracle, Barbara. "Part-Time Professionals: Not every business can afford a CFO full time, but many need a CFO's services to help their businesses grow." *Florida Trend*. July 2005.

Uelmen, Amelia J. "The Evils of 'Elasticity': Reflections on the rhetoric of professionalism and the part-time paradox in large firm practice." *Fordham Urban Law Journal*. November 2005.

U.S. Bureau of Labor Statistics. "Labor Force Statistics from the Current Population Survey." Available from http://www.bls.gov/cps/#charemp. Retrieved on 26 April 2006.

Darnay, ECDI

PATENT AND TRADEMARK OFFICE (PTO)

The Patent and Trademark Office (PTO) is responsible for administering all laws relating to trademarks and patents in the United States. It has thus been an important agency for several generations of entrepreneurs and small business owners, as well as for larger corporations and universities. The PTO describes itself as follows: "Through the issuance of patents, we encourage technological advancement by providing incentives to invent, invest in, and disclose new technology worldwide. Through the registration of trademarks, we assist businesses in protecting their investments, promoting goods and services and safeguarding consumers against confusion and deception in the marketplace. By disseminating both patent and trademark information, we promote an understanding of intellectual property protection and facilitate the developments and sharing of new technologies world wide."

In addition to handling the nation's patents and trademarks, the PTO also has a notable advisory function. It serves as both a developer of intellectual property policy and an advisor to the White House on patent/trademark/copyright policies. In addition, the PTO provides information and guidance on intellectual property issues to international commerce offices such as the International Trade Commission and the Office of the U.S. Trade Representative. In 1999 the PTO was established as an agency within the Department of Commerce.

By nearly all accounts, the PTO has historically done a laudable job of protecting the intellectual property rights of businesses and individuals while simultaneously encouraging the growth of business. "Since its inception, the patent system has encouraged the genius of millions of inventors," wrote *Inventor's Desktop Companion* author Richard C. Levy. "It has protected these creative individuals by allowing them an opportunity to profit from their labors, and has benefited society by systematically recording new inventions and releasing them to the public once the inventors' limited rights have expired.... Under the patent system, American industry has flourished. New products have been invented, new uses for old ones discovered, and employment given to millions."

LEGAL UNDERPINNINGS OF THE PTO

The fundamental principles of the modern American patent system were first codified into law in 1790. Guided by Secretary of State Thomas Jefferson in its early years, the patent office grew quickly, and in 1849 the Department of the Interior was given responsibility for maintaining it. In 1870 the powers of the patent office were expanded dramatically; the commissioner of patents was given jurisdiction to register and regulate trademarks. The office thus came to be responsible for all American trademarks, even though the word "trademark" would not appear in its name for another 105 years (the Patent Office became the Patent and Trademark Office on January 2, 1975). In 1926 responsibility for the Patent Office was handed over to the Department of Commerce, where it remains today.

The PTO currently touts the following laws as the primary statutory authorities guiding its programs:

- 15 U.S.C. 1051-1127—Contains provisions of the Trademark Act of 1946, a law that governs the office's trademark administration

- 15 U.S.C. 1511—Establishes the PTO as a subordinate agency of the Department of Commerce

- 35 U.S.C.—Provides the PTO with its basic authority to administer patent laws

- 44 U.S.C. 1337-1338—Gives the PTO authority to print trademarks, patents, and other material relevant to the business of the Office

In 1991 the PTO underwent a significant change in operation. The Omnibus Budget Reconciliation Act (OBRA) of 1990 included provisions to make the Office a self-supporting government agency that would not receive federal funding. In order to provide the PTO with needed operating funds, Congress raised the PTO's patent application fees to cover operating costs and maintain services for inventors. The PTO has been funded solely by fees since 1993. In 1999 it was formally established as an agency within the Department of Commerce.

As part of its efforts to process its patent applications in a timely manner, the Patent and Trademark Office established and opened an electronic patent application filing system open to all inventors in October 2000. The PTO's web site (www.uspto.gov) now allows inventors to assemble all components of a patent application online, including calculating fees, validating content, and encrypting and transmitting the filing. At the same time, the PTO raised its patent fees to match current rates of inflation. This increase, the first since 1997, was needed to pay for the electronic system and other expenses associated with processing the huge volume of patent and trademark applications that pass through the PTO's doors every year (the Office experienced an annual 10 percent growth in patent applications during the 1990s, and in Calendar Year 2004, the PTO issued more than 181,000 patents; in Fiscal Year 2005, it registered more than 92,500 trademarks.

SEE ALSO *Inventions and Patents*

BIBLIOGRAPHY
Hoover, Kent. "Patent Office Opens Electronic Filing to All." *Sacramento Business Journal.* 3 November 2000.

Levy, Richard C. "The Patent and Trademark Office." *The Inventor's Desktop Companion.* Visible Ink, 1995.

United States Patent and Trademark Office. Available from http://www.uspto.gov/index.html. Retrieved on 28 April 2006.

Hillstrom, Northern Lights
updated by Magee, ECDI

PAYROLL TAXES

Payroll taxes are all taxes that are collected, by federal, state, and local governments, based on salaries and wages paid to employees. These taxes must be withheld from wages by all businesses that have employees. These taxes are remitted on a monthly or semi-weekly basis, depending on the quantity owed. Businesses are also required to make regularly scheduled reports to the Internal Revenue Service (IRS) and to state and local taxing agencies about the amount of taxes owed and paid. Businesses are not required to withhold payroll taxes on wages paid to independent contractors. Self-employed persons are responsible for paying their own payroll or income taxes directly to the appropriate taxing entity.

Many small businesses fall behind in paying these taxes or filing the associated reports at some time during their existence. Such an error is, however, very costly because significant interest and penalties apply for late payment or nonpayment of payroll taxes. In fact, the Trust Fund Recovery Penalty allows the IRS to hold a small business owner or accountant personally liable for 100 percent of the amount owed, even in cases where the business has gone bankrupt.

TYPES OF PAYROLL TAXES

Three main types of taxes fall under the category of payroll taxes:

1. The regular income tax that must be withheld from employees' paychecks. Employees can adjust their income tax withholding by filing Form W-4 with their employer and designating the number of withholding allowances they wish to claim. Ideally, the total income tax withheld should come close to equaling their overall tax liability at the end of the year. By adjusting their withholding allowances properly, employees can avoid owing large amounts in taxes or providing the government with an interest-free loan.

2. Federal Insurance Contribution Act (FICA) taxes. This tax includes contributions to two federal programs, Social Security and Medicare. The tax rate for FICA taxes does not often change but the earnings on which those taxes are applied changes from year to year. In 2006, full FICA taxes of 7.65 percent were due on the first $94,200 earned. Only the Medicare portion of the FICA tax, 1.45 percent, was due on earnings over $94,200. Employers are required to match the FICA amount withheld for every employee, so that the total FICA contribution is 15.3 percent on the first $94,200 earned. Self-employed persons are required to pay both the employer and employee portions of the FICA tax.

3. Federal Unemployment Tax (FUTA, the "a" stands for the word Act in the original name of the act). This tax is approximately 1 percent of the first $7,000 in wages paid to an employee and is paid in full by the employer. Technically, the federal unemployment insurance payroll tax is 6.2 percent of the first $7,000 of an employee's wages. However, employers in states with their own unemployment insurance tax programs receive a 5.4 percent credit toward their federal tax payment, reducing their tax rate to 0.8 percent. Since all states have federally approved programs, the effective FUTA rate is 0.8 percent.

4. State Unemployment Taxes. Unemployment Insurance (UI) is a federal-state program jointly financed through federal and state employer payroll taxes. The federal portion is the FUTA. The state unemployment tax differs from state to state, the rate being determined by each state separately and within the state for each employer separately. The UI program is based on experience-ratings. This means that within a given state, firms that lay off a higher percentage of workers and whose employees collect a higher amount of UI benefits pay higher tax rates than firms that lay off fewer workers. The national average state tax rate in 2003 was 2.1 percent. This rate was paid on the first $7,000 to $9,000 of earnings depending on the state. In 2004, the states had a range of **maximum** UI tax rates from 5.4 percent to almost 11 percent.

5. Local Payroll Taxes. Cities and municipalities may impose a payroll tax. These taxes are usually paid by both the employee and employer and vary in range widely.

PAYROLL TAX REMITTANCE AND REPORTING

In addition to withholding payroll taxes for employees, employers must remit these taxes to the IRS in a timely manner. The regular income taxes and the portion of the FICA taxes that are withheld from employees' wages must be remitted to the IRS monthly, along with a Federal Tax Deposit Coupon (Form 8109-B). If the total withheld is less than $500, however, the business is allowed to make the payments quarterly. In 1996, the IRS began requiring businesses that owed more than $47 million in payroll taxes annually to make their monthly payments via telephone or computer through the Electronic Federal Tax Payment System. The threshold for electronic filing was scheduled to drop to $50,000 in annual payroll taxes by January 1, 1997, but the deadline was pushed back to June 30, 1998. In addition, two bills were introduced in Congress that would make electronic payments of payroll taxes voluntary for small businesses with few employees.

Employers must also file four different reports regarding payroll taxes. The first report, Form 941, is the Employer's Quarterly Federal Tax Return. This report details the number of employees the business had, the amount of wages they were paid, and the amount of taxes that were withheld for the quarter. The other three reports are filed annually. Form W-2—the Annual Statement of Taxes Withheld—must be sent to all employees before January 31 of the following year. It details how much each employee received in wages and how much was withheld for taxes over the course of the year. Copies of the W-2 forms for all employees also must be sent to the Social Security Administration. The third report, Form W-3, must be sent to the IRS by February 28 of the following year. It provides a formal reconciliation of the quarterly tax payments made on Form 941 and the annual totals reported on Form W-2 for all employees. The final report is the Federal Unemployment Tax Return, Form 940, which outlines the total FUTA taxes owed and paid for the year.

Most states—as well as some large cities—have their own income tax that businesses must withhold from employees' wages and report to the appropriate authorities. States may also have other payroll taxes that must be collected from employees, as well as unemployment taxes that must be paid by the company. The payment schedules and reporting procedures for state and local payroll taxes are usually consistent with those applied to federal payroll taxes.

EXCEPTIONS TO PAYROLL TAX RULES

There are certain situations in which small businesses can avoid owing payroll taxes. For example, special rules apply to sole proprietorships and husband-and-wife partnerships that pay their minor (under 18) children for work performed in the business. These small businesses receive an exemption from withholding FICA taxes from their children's paychecks, and are also not required to pay the employer portion of the FICA taxes. In this way, the parent and child each save 7.65 percent, for a total of 15.3 percent. In addition, the child's wages can still be deducted from the parents' income taxes as a business expense. Children employed in small family businesses also usually qualify for an exemption from the FUTA tax until they reach age 21.

There is no limit on how much children can earn and still receive the FICA tax exemption. However, it is important that the wages paid to the child are reasonable for the job performed, and that the hours worked by the child are carefully documented, so it will be clear to the IRS that the child has not been paid for little or no real work performed. In addition, parents should note that their child's financial aid for college may be reduced if they earn more than $1,750 per year.

Small businesses also are not required to withhold payroll taxes for persons who are employed as independent contractors. Using independent contractors rather than hiring employees may be an attractive option for some small businesses. By avoiding responsibility for payroll taxes and all the associated paperwork, as well as avoiding the need to pay benefits, businesses may find that using an independent contractor costs between 20 and 30 percent less than hiring an employee. But misclassifying an employee as an independent contractor can lead to costly consequences for a small business. The IRS examines such relationships very carefully, and in cases where an independent contractor must be reclassified as an employee, the business may be liable for back taxes plus a special penalty of 12 to 35 percent of the total tax bill.

The IRS uses a 20-step test to determine whether someone is an employee or an independent contractor. True independent contractors, according to the IRS definition, are in business for themselves with the intention of making a profit and are not under the direct control of the client company. To protect their companies from potential problems, small business owners should make sure that independent contractors are paid by the job rather than by the hour, set their own hours and rules, work on their own premises using their own equipment, sign a specific contract for each project, and make themselves available to multiple clients. Rather than withholding taxes, small businesses simply file an annual informational return—Form 1099, Statement of Miscellaneous Income—detailing the total amount paid to each contractor. No reporting is required for contractors that were paid less than $600 over the course of a year.

TRUST FUND RECOVERY PENALTY

Small businesses often find themselves faced with a cash flow crisis, one they believe will ease in a matter of days or weeks. The business owner who, when faced with this cash flow problem, decides to pay vendors before paying for payroll tax obligations is making a grave error. A typical scenario may play out as follows. For short-term survival, the business owner or executive decides to meet current creditors' requirements and oblige the IRS to become a creditor. The hope is that in the medium term the business will be able to pay the IRS the delinquent taxes plus interest and penalties. Often, however, the business becomes insolvent and declares bankruptcy. In order to address this problem and avoid significant erosion of tax revenue, in 1954 Congress enacted a penalty—equal to the unpaid payroll taxes—against all responsible persons who willfully fail to collect and turn over the money.

This penalty for the failure to withhold or remit payroll taxes, known as the Trust Fund Recovery Penalty (TFRP), is included under Section 6672 of the Internal Revenue Code. It allows the IRS to hold individuals associated with a business personally liable for 100 percent of the unpaid amount when the business fails to meet its payroll tax obligations. The TFRP applies to employee funds that the employer holds in trust for the IRS—all of the regular income tax withheld and the employee half of the FICA tax—but not to the employer portions of payroll taxes. The penalty is particularly severe because the IRS considers an employer who fails to pay to be violating a trust. The TFRP can be applied in addition to civil and criminal penalties, including the seizure of business assets and forced closure of the business. And since it is a penalty rather than a tax, the TFRP is not erased by bankruptcy.

In order to apply the TFRP to an individual, the IRS must prove the person's responsibility (that he or she had the power to make the decision about whether or not to pay) and willfulness (that he or she knowingly failed to act rather than made an honest mistake) for the business's failure to remit payroll taxes. In making its determination about who to hold responsible, the IRS looks at who made the financial decisions in the business, who signed the checks, and who had the duty of tax reporting. Under these rules, a small business owner can be found personally liable even if a staff member or outside accountant was directly responsible for payroll tax compliance. In cases where both the business and the owner go bankrupt, the company's accountant may be tagged as the responsible party and held personally liable.

Because the law regarding payroll tax noncompliance is so sweeping, small business owners should pay particular attention to the trust fund taxes. It is vital to keep the taxes that are covered by the TFRP current, even when the business is experiencing cash flow problems. If it appears as if the small business is heading for bankruptcy, these taxes should be paid prior to filing, when management can still designate where the IRS should apply payments. After the company files for bankruptcy it loses this option, and the IRS will apply any payments elsewhere since they can collect the TFRP from individuals associated with the company. Not paying the IRS may solve a company's short-term cash flow problems but it will cause serious problems for the person or persons responsible in the long term.

SEE ALSO *Electronic Tax Filing; FICA Taxes; Tax Withholding*

BIBLIOGRAPHY
"Bad Health Will Not Excuse Penalty for Unpaid Payroll Tax." *The Kiplinger Tax Letter.* 10 March 2006.

Bieg, Bernard J. *Payroll Accounting 2005.* Thomson South-Western, November 2004.

Daily, Frederick W. *Tax Savvy for Small Business.* Nolo, November 2004.

Grassi, Carl. "Federal Withholding Rules Enforced with an Iron Fist." *Crain's Cleveland Business.* 12 June 2000.

U.S. Department of the Treasury. Internal Revenue Service. "What is the difference between a Form W-2 and a Form 1099-MISC?" Available from http://www.irs.gov/faqs/faq12-2.html. Retrieved on 1 May 2006.

Hillstrom, Northern Lights
updated by Magee, ECDI

PENETRATION PRICING

Penetration pricing is one of two contrasting but attention-grabbing techniques for introducing new products or services to a market. In penetration pricing, the price is set low in order to acquire a following and market share. Once the product/service is established, price may move to a higher level. In its article on the subject, Wikipedia, the online encyclopedia, lists the following key advantages of penetration pricing:

- Speed. The seller can achieve rapid penetration by pricing low and also surprise its competition.
- Goodwill. All-important early adopters will welcome the product and spread news of it by word of mouth.
- Cost control incentives. Having to price low, the introducer will feel pressure to be as efficient as possible—for long-term benefit.
- Barrier to others. Low pricing will discourage competitors from matching the offering.
- Channel benefits. The technique can produce rapid turnover of stock and thus gain a following among distributors and retailers.
- Marginal cost pricing can be used so that a predicted volume will cover fixed costs and extra units will only bear variable costs.

The technique is particularly applicable when demand for a product is very elastic, i.e., people will buy more when the price is low. Gasoline purchases are relatively inelastic, for example, because people cannot store much gasoline. They also have to buy gas at almost any price to get to work, alternatives being difficult to find and slow to develop. A new kind of candy, however, may be very elastic.

The technique has disadvantages as well. If the product is not very sharply differentiated from competitors' offerings (i.e., has "commodity" status), low prices may attract "switchers" while the price is low but won't build the desired brand loyalty: switchers will leave again. The low initial price may build price expectations and it may be difficult, later, to raise prices without causing a market reaction. If the low price becomes part of the brand image, changing price will disturb that image in the consumer's mind. To counter this problem, penetration pricing is sometimes used in a disguised form. The pricing intended to be used later is applied to the product in outlets, but coupons are distributed very widely and for a long period of time to let consumers acquire the product at its penetration price. The coupons may be actually part of the package so that no additional marketing steps are needed to get them to the consumer.

The other method of price-based product introduction is called skimming. It works in the opposite way. The product initially carries a very high price and is intended to gather a small, elite, but influential following. In the case of skimming, volume will, of course, be low but profits will be high. The technique is well-suited for technology-based categories expected ultimately to have wide use. By pricing high the company attracts "early adaptors" who are often leaders and/or "show-offs" and thus give the product free publicity. Thus, here, too, word of mouth has an effect. High pricing will discourage would-be imitators unless the latter are fully aware of the seller's very high margin.

Both techniques may be used in relatively inexpensive ranges of product (sodas, candy, textiles) as well as very expensive categories (appliances and the like). Penetration pricing is more likely at the lower end, skimming at the high. Neither technique—penetration or skim pricing—should be confused with periodic sales pricing of goods, either to clear inventories or to price products as loss leaders.

SEE ALSO *Pricing*

BIBLIOGRAPHY

Gitman, Lawrence J., and Carl McDaniel. *The Future of Business.* Thomson South-Western, 2005.

Kongenecker, Justin G., Carlos W. Moore, J. William Petty, and Leslie E. Palich. *Small Business Management: An Entrepreneurial Emphasis.* Thomson South-Western, 2006.

"Penetration Pricing." Wikipedia. Available from http://en.wikipedia.org/wiki/Penetration_pricing. Retrieved on 23 April 2006.

Troilo, Tad. "No Excuses: No matter the rationale, razor-thin margins usually become big fat profit failures." *Prosales.* August 2005.

Darnay, ECDI

PENSION PLANS

The term "pension plan" is now used to describe a variety of retirement programs that companies establish as a benefit for their employees—including 401(k) plans, profit-sharing plans, simplified employee pension (SEP) plans, and Keogh plans. In the past pension plans were differentiated from other types of retirement plans in that employers were committed to providing a certain monetary level of benefits to employees upon retirement. These "defined benefit" plans, which were common among large employers with a unionized work force, have fallen into disfavor in recent years.

Some individuals also choose to establish personal pension plans to supplement their retirement savings. Making sound decisions about retirement is particularly important for self-employed persons and small business owners. Unlike the ever declining numbers of employees of large companies, who can simply participate in the pension plans and investment programs offered by their employers, entrepreneurs must set up and administer their own plans for themselves and for their employees.

Though establishing and funding pension plans can be both time-consuming and costly for small businesses, such programs are worth the effort for a number of reasons. In most cases, for example, employer contributions to retirement plans are tax deductible expenses. In addition, offering employees a comprehensive retirement program can help small businesses attract and retain qualified people who might otherwise seek the security of working for a company that does offer such benefits.

The number of small firms establishing pension plans grew considerably during the 1990s, but small employers still lag far behind larger ones in offering this type of benefit to employees. According to a 2005 Small Business Administration report, fewer small companies (those with 500 or fewer employees) offer any sort of retirement benefits to their employees than do larger firms—35 percent versus 75 percent respectively in 2002. For firms with five employees or fewer, only 11 percent offer a retirement savings program, like a 401(k) or Simplified Employee Pension (SEP) plan.

PENSION PLAN OPTIONS FOR SMALL BUSINESSES

Small business owners can set up a wide variety of pension plans by filling out the necessary forms at any financial institution (a bank, mutual fund, insurance company, brokerage firm, etc.). The fees vary depending on the plan's complexity and the number of participants. Some employer-sponsored plans are required to file Form 5500 annually to disclose plan activities to the IRS. The preparation and filing of this complicated document can increase the administrative costs associated with a plan, as the business owner may require help from a tax advisor or plan administration professional. In addition, all the information reported on Form 5500 is open to public inspection.

A number of different types of pension plans are available. The most popular plans for small businesses all fall under the category of defined contribution plans. Defined contribution plans use an allocation formula to specify a percentage of compensation to be contributed by each participant. For example, an individual can voluntarily deduct a certain portion of his or her salary, in many cases before taxes, and place the money into a qualified retirement plan, where it will grow tax-deferred. Likewise, an employer can contribute a percentage of each employee's salary to the plan on their behalf, or match the contributions employees make.

In contrast to defined contribution plans are defined benefit plans. These plans calculate a desired level of benefits to be paid upon retirement—using a fixed monthly payment or a percentage of compensation—and then the employer contributes to the plan annually according to a formula so that the benefits will be available when needed. The amount of annual contributions is determined by an actuary, based upon the age, salary levels, and years of service of employees, as well as prevailing interest and inflation rates. In defined benefit plans, the employer bears the risk of providing a specified level of benefits to employees when they retire. This is the traditional idea of a pension plan that has often been used by large employers with a unionized work force.

In nearly every type of qualified pension plan, withdrawals made before the age of 59 ½ are subject to an IRS penalty in addition to ordinary income tax. The plans differ in terms of administrative costs, eligibility requirements, employee participation, degree of discretion in making contributions, and amount of allowable contributions. Free information on qualified retirement plans is available through the Department of Labor at 800-998-7542, or on the Internet at www.dol.gov.

The most important thing to remember is that a small business owner who wants to establish a qualified plan for him or herself must also include all other company employees who meet minimum participation standards. As an employer, the small business owner can establish pension plans like any other business. As an employee, the small business owner can then make contributions to the plan he or she has established in order to set aside tax-deferred funds for retirement, like any other employee. The difference is that a small business owner must include all nonowner employees in any company-sponsored pension plans and make equivalent contributions to their accounts. Unfortunately, this requirement has the effect of reducing the allowable contributions that the owner of a proprietorship or partnership can make on his or her own behalf.

For self-employed individuals, contributions to a qualified pension plan are based upon the net earnings of their business. The net earnings consist of the company's gross income less deductions for business expenses, salaries paid to nonowner employees, the employer's 50 percent of the Social Security tax, and—significantly—the employer's contribution to retirement plans on behalf of employees. Therefore, rather than receiving pre-tax contributions to the retirement account as a percentage of gross salary, like nonowner employees, the small business owner receives contributions as a smaller percentage of net earnings. Employing other people thus detracts from the owner's ability to build up a sizeable before-tax retirement account of his or her own. For this reason, some experts recommend that the owners of proprietorships and partnerships who sponsor pension plans for their employees supplement their own retirement funds through a personal after-tax savings plan.

PERSONAL PENSION PLANS FOR INDIVIDUALS

For self-employed persons and small business owners, the tax laws that limit the amount of annual contributions individuals can make to qualified retirement plans, may make these plans insufficient as a sole vehicle through which to save for retirement. A non-qualified plan can be used to supplement retirement savings plans for business owners. Broadly defined, a nonqualified deferred compensation plan (NDCP) is a contractual agreement in which a participant agrees to be paid in a future year for services rendered this year. Deferred compensation payments generally commence upon termination of employment (e.g., retirement) or pre-retirement death or disability.

There are two broad categories of nonqualified deferred compensation plans: elective and non-elective. In an elective NDCP an employee or business owner chooses to receive less current salary and bonus compensation than he or she would otherwise receive postponing the receipt of that compensation until a future tax year. Non-elective NDCPs are plans in which the employer funds the benefit and does not reduce current compensation in order to fund future payments. Such plans are, in essence, post-termination salary continuation plans.

Establishing such a plan can be done in a number of ways. A variable life insurance policy is one way to structure the plan. A company purchases a variable life insurance policy for each participant and paying premiums for the policy annually. The amount paid in is invested and allowed to grow tax-free. Both the premiums paid and the investment earnings can be accessed to provide the individual with an annual income upon retirement. The only catch is that, unlike qualified retirement plans, the annual payments made on a personal pension plan are not tax-deductible.

Although other types of insurance policies—such as whole life or universal life—can also be used for retirement savings, they tend to be less flexible in terms of investment choices. In contrast, most variable life insurance providers allow individuals to select from a variety of investment options and transfer funds from one account to another without penalty. Many policies also allow individuals to vary the amount of their annual contribution or even skip making a contribution in years when cash is tight. Another worthwhile provision in some policies pays the premium if the individual should become disabled. In addition, most policies have more liberal early withdrawal and loan provisions than qualified retirement plans. The size of the annual contributions allowed depends upon the size of the insurance policy purchased. The bigger the insurance policy, the higher the premiums will be, and the higher the contributions. The IRS does set a maximum annual contribution level for each size policy, based on the beneficiary's age, gender, and other factors.

Upon reaching retirement age, an individual can begin to use the personal pension plan as a source of annual income. Withdrawals—which are not subject to income or Social Security taxes—first come from the premiums paid and earnings accumulated. After the total withdrawn equals the total contributed, however, the individual can continue to draw income in the form of a loan against the plan's cash value. This amount is repaid upon the individual's death out of the death benefit of the insurance.

SEE ALSO *Employee Benefits; Employee Retirement Income Security Act; 401(k) Plans; Keogh Plan; Nonqualified Deferred Compensation Plans; Retirement Planning*

BIBLIOGRAPHY

Altieri, Mark P. "Nonqualified Deferred Compensation Plans." *The CPA Journal*. February 2005.

"Bad News for Employers Contemplating Cash-Balance Pension Plans." *The Kiplinger Letter*. 21 April 2006.

MacDonald, John. "'Traditional' Pension Assets Lost Dominance a Decade Ago, IRAs and 401(k)s Have Long Been Dominant." *Fast Facts from EBRI*. Employee Benefit Research Institute, 3 February 2006.

Reeves, Scott. "A Small Business Retirement Plan." *Forbes.com*. 12 September 2005.

"Retirement Planning: Squeeze on Retirement Savings." *The Practical Accountant*. February 2006.

Sifleet, Jean D. *Beyond 401(k)s for Small Business Owners*. John Wiley & Sons, 2003.

U.S. Department of Labor. Employee Benefits Security Administration. "Easy Retirement Solutions for Small Business." Available from http://www.dol.gov/ebsa/publications/easy_retirement_solutions.html. Retrieved on 12 April 2006.

U.S. Internal Revenue Service. "401(k) Resource Guide – Plan Participants – Limitations on Elective Deferrals." Available fromhttp://www.irs.gov/retirement/participant/article/0,id=151786,00.html. Retrieved on 9 March 2006.

U.S. Small Business Administration. SBA Office of Advocacy. Popkin, Joel. "Cost of Employee Benefits in Small and Large Businesses." August 2005.

Hillstrom, Northern Lights
updated by Magee, ECDI

PER DIEM ALLOWANCES

The term "per diem" means "daily." In a business setting, the term has come to mean the daily rates employees use for expenses incurred while traveling on business-related activities. These rates are likely to differ based on whether the employee travels in his or her home area, away from home, or internationally. The per diem allowance is the amount given to a traveler to cover expenses such as lodging, meals, and entertainment in connection with the performance of service duties for a company.

Typically the human resources department of an organization will establish per diem rates for employee travel expense reimbursement as well as policies for submitting travel expense forms and for documenting all approved expenses. Per diem amounts are normally set in advance. Employees typically may either claim actual expenses incurred or use established per diem rates or combine these methods. For example, the employee may claim a per diem amount for meals and claim actual costs for lodging, as long as lodging expenses do not exceed the per diem allowance for lodging.

SETTING PER DIEM RATES

Per diem rates are established for a number of areas, including domestic air travel, international air travel, lodging, rental cars, vans, and trucks, other transportation, meals and entertainment, telephone usage, miscellaneous reimbursable and non-reimbursable expenses, and travel insurance. Companies also may specify preferred travel agencies and programs and establish policies for payment of travel expenses and per diem rates.

Companies that do not set their own rates may use per diem amounts based on U.S. federal travel regulations. Per diem amounts vary by city. U.S. meal per diem rates are set every January. Foreign meal per diem rates are issued on a monthly basis. Organizations will normally pro-rate per diems for less than a full day's travel. IRS regulations and reporting requirements governing per diems vary. For employees, if the per diem requested exceeds the federal per diem rate for the given location and duration of the trip, the excess amount is considered reportable income and is added to the employee's W-2. For independent contractors, per diem payments made to such individuals are reportable income and will be reported on Form 1099M.

It is important for a company to establish clear per diem amounts and travel policies before employees are hired and begin to travel for the company. For example, a company must decide whether it will reimburse employees' personal phone calls while traveling, if it will reimburse employees for using airphones, etc. Other decisions include fees for currency conversion for international travel, ground transportation (taxi, bus, subway, etc.), hotel health club fees, laundry/dry cleaning/suit pressing, overnight delivery/postage, parking and tolls, tips, and visa/passport/consulate fees.

As a perk for employees, some firms consider paying for extra services to either reward, motivate, or retain employees in tight labor markets. Some per diem items to consider may include: airline club membership dues, annual fees for personal credit cards, hairdressers, clothing or toiletry items, country club dues, expenses related to vacation or personal days taken before, during, or after a business trip, golf fees, luggage and briefcases, magazines, books, newspapers, personal reading materials, mini-bar alcoholic refreshments, movies (including in-flight and hotel in-house movies), personal automobile routine maintenance/tune-ups, pet boarding, rental car upgrades, saunas, massages, shoe shines, or U.S. traveler's check fees.

PER DIEM EXAMPLES

The Per Diem, Travel and Transportation Allowance Committee exists to ensure that uniform travel and transportation regulations are issued for members of the seven branches of the U.S. military (Army, Navy, Air Force, Marine Corps, Coast Guard, National Oceanic and Atmospheric Administration, and Public Health Service). The objective of these regulations is fair and equitable reimbursement of uniformed members and civilian personnel.

The U.S. Government, through the U.S. Department of State, provides per diem allowance amounts for travel in foreign areas in lieu of reimbursement for actual subsistence expenses. The allowances are provided to employees and eligible dependents for daily expenses while on temporary travel status in the listed localities on official business away from an official post or assignment. The established rates are maximum amounts. Under travel regulations implemented by the General Services Administration and individual federal agencies, authorizing officials are required to reduce the maximum rates as needed to maintain a level of payment consistent with necessary travel expenses. Separate amounts are established for lodging and meals plus incidental travel expenses. The maximum lodging amount is intended to substantially cover the cost of lodging at adequate, suitable, and moderately priced facilities. The meals and incidental expenses portion is intended to substantially cover the cost of meals and incidental travel expenses such as laundry and dry cleaning.

SEE ALSO *Expense Accounts*

BIBLIOGRAPHY
"Final Update?" *Payroll Manager's Letter.* 7 May 2006.

Luecke, Randall, et. al. "Should Your Company Use Travel Per Diems?" *Journal of Compensation and Benefits.* March-April 1998.

Luecke, Randall, et. al. "Pros and Cons of Travel Per Diems." *Workforce.* March 1998.

Weaver, Peter. "The IRS's Menu for Per Diem Dining Expenses." *Nation's Business.* May 1999.

Hillstrom, Northern Lights
updated by Magee, ECDI

PERSONAL SELLING

In the language of sales and marketing, "personal selling" singles out those situations in which a real human being is trying to sell something to another face-to-face. One might well ask what other type of genuine selling there is. The answer is that personal selling has a functional equivalent. The modern differentiation between "personal" and other selling arises from the fact that a very substantial volume of ordinary purchasing of food, textiles, household goods, entertainment, travel, subscriptions, fuel, books, etc., takes place without the presence of a live facilitator. The only human contact is usually the check-out clerk; and corporations are laboring hard to replace even this humble functionary by machines that read barcodes and recognize credit cards. In the vast majority of these situations whatever persuasion has been applied to the shopper has been delivered by disembodied images on television, radio, in print, by coupons, by signage, and by packaging. Thus "impersonal selling" is by advertising, sales promotion and public relations.

THE BUYING-SELLING SITUATION

In personal life few people buy a house, a car, or a life insurance policy after reading an ad or looking at a flashy brochure left hanging on the door knob. Major work on the house is approved after personal selling has taken place—and so does the choice of a retirement village for a grandparent. These situations, first of all, are not routine occurrences; second, they are transactions of some magnitude; third, many choices are usually available; one might say that the situations have a high "information density." In these cases interacting with the seller's knowledgeable representative in a prolonged exploratory give-and-take is both necessary and reassuring. Indeed, arguably, personal selling is also helpful when making smaller purchases provided that the decision is difficult for the buyer, as in a bride-to-be selecting a wedding gown or a man purchasing jewelry for his wife's birthday. In certain categories of retail—luggage stores and furniture stores come to mind—sales people are usually provided by the business, and on busy days customers get fidgety when no one is there to help them.

In business-to-business buying and selling the same rules apply. A business will typically obtain its office supplies from catalogs, but most of its other purchases involve personal selling by the vendor even if buying the commodity or services later becomes routine; in the latter cases, periodic calls from the sales person will continue to maintain the relationship. Business purchases are very often "technical" in nature, not necessarily because the goods are mechanical or electronic but because they have specialized aspects.

Psychological Aspects The psychological aspects of the buying-selling situation are highlighted in the purchase of more expensive items. Buying something is a decision in which the buyer must decide between opposing tendencies. There is desire for the object and reasons lined up to support a Yes. There is a cost involved and reasons present why it should be avoided. The buyer must ultimately persuade him or herself to say Yes or No. The importance of personal selling lies in tilting the balance toward a Yes. Only an interactive situation gives the seller this opportunity. Its abuse leads to—

Negative Attitudes In ancient times people feared that they would be cheated in sales transactions, hence the Latin proverb, *caveat emptor,* meaning *let the buyer beware.* From pre-industrial times comes the admonition not to buy a "pig in a poke." Again the emphasis is on deception because a "poke" is archaic for "bag." The hidden pig might have defects. We say: "Don't look a gift horse in the mouth," implying that in a buying situation looking at the horse's mouth (to determine its age from its teeth) was highly recommended. The modern attitude toward direct sales, however, emphasizes aggression or bullying with phrases like "high-pressure sales" or "the hard sell." In the old days people only bought what they genuinely wanted. The range of products competing for buyers was limited; supplies were never very abundant—hence people tried to move defective goods by deception. In our time great surplus reigns; there is too much of everything. A good deal of psychological force is routinely deployed to persuade people to buy, on credit if necessary. The savings rate, consequently, has virtually disappeared; people are in debt; and selling has acquired a negative reputation—whether it is indirect like advertising or direct. In direct selling telephone or door-to-door *prospecting* is particularly disliked by the public.

CHARACTERISTICS OF SALESMANSHIP

The hard sell is unlikely to disappear until its cause does too, but experts on salesmanship are virtually unanimous in viewing it as negatively as the public. The job of the salesperson is to discover what the buyer wants, to present the goods that match the desire as closely as possible, to answer questions about the product (or service, or contract, etc.), to deal effectively with objections, and finally to close the sale. When this job is done correctly, the buyer will be well served even if he or she does not buy.

The sales work is a complex activity in which many characteristics must be simultaneously present, hence it is misleading to single out or rank particular traits. The starting assumption, however, is that the salesperson has

integrity and will not sell something he or she knows to be defective or inferior, will have character, honesty, and be emotionally stable. Beyond that, the salesperson must have deep product knowledge and good communications skills, must internalize the customer's point of view, and must remain both unobtrusive and yet accessible. He or she must have a good sense for all kinds of people and a good sense of timing; thus he or she will know when to attend and when to leave the customer alone, when to press and when to withdraw. Salesmanship thus calls for a balanced, well rounded, outgoing, and knowledgeable person. Some experts also emphasize physical strength and energy—because sales work often requires many hours of standing about, travel, and exertions of one sort or another. Other emphasize a straightforward and candid attitude. Problems with products or contract contingencies should be discussed frankly. Pricing discussions should not be hedged. Maintenance issues should be discussed with candor.

Selling and entrepreneurship have a good deal in common—indeed are the same fundamental activity at the core. Both require active engagement with the market environment. But while an entrepreneur is often a person whose motivation springs from some type of interest, body of knowledge, or cluster of skills, salesmanship often manifests as a more generalized interest in interaction with the customer, so that skilled sales people readily adapt to selling anything at all while some entrepreneurs are only comfortable in narrow areas.

The very qualities that make sales people effective—enthusiasm for working with people one-on-one—make some of them less effective in activities that require patience, working alone, meticulous attention to detail, and certain types of concentration. For this reason personal selling staffs frequently require backup to ensure good order, organization, and follow-through.

TYPES OF PERSONAL SELLING

Sales positions or their equivalents range between the sales clerk with minimal selling skills up to the chief executive officer in public and in private enterprises. At the bottom of the sales-pyramid the primary skill is taking an order and guiding customers to the product; at the top great ability to present complex, often controversial and abstract cases persuasively, usually as just a part of other functions, is required. Most personal selling takes place in the middle.

Sales positions are classified as "inside" and "outside." Inside sales above the clerk level involve telephone sales, mainstream retail sales in stores where product knowledge and presentation skills are required, and auto sales and similar equipment sales where customers visit the dealership. Inside sales may be combined with other functions such as scheduling and early information gathering for an outside agent.

Outside sales take place either at the prospective client's residence or place of business or in a third-party location: real estate sales have this form. Outside sales may be combined with estimating tasks as in the case of bidding on construction work; it may also be combined with product delivery. The driver-salesperson has a stocking function sometimes combined with sales responsibilities. A special category is the sales engineer highly skilled in some aspect of industrial operations and thus able both to understand requirements and to provide technical support.

In many types of financial, consulting, market research, engineering, construction, and equipment sales categories personal selling may be both inside and out. In the consulting industry the manager likely to oversee a contract is likely to be the leading salesperson for the job. In such situations buyers may call on the seller and vice-versa depending on the circumstances.

The Reps An important category of personal selling is provided by manufacturers' representatives, usually called rep organizations or selling agents. These individuals, sometimes working in groups, are independent sellers representing a manufacturer, usually in exclusive territories, compensated by commissions only. Hiring a rep firm allows a small business to avoid the cost of an in-house sales force. In addition, an established rep may provide the business instant access to an established sales territory. Agents are particularly helpful for businesses with seasonal sales; the rep is only paid when sales are made. The chief disadvantage of selling agents is that they usually work for several different firms and do not devote all of their time to one client.

TRENDS

A broad movement is discernible in modern commerce to replace personal selling in all areas except those in which the service is indispensable or pricing permits its continuance: because personal selling is expensive. Packaging, promotion, and lower-cost and lower-skill clerks are replacing the sales person even in technical fields. An example of this is the distribution of computers and software. More and more such products are sold in standard packaged forms, even in retail outlets; the sales function is reduced to clerking aimed to help customers find—not to understand—products. Servicing products (including their installation) is being transferred overseas to lower labor-cost markets; the service is provided by telephone. Private selling remains central in selling financial products, real estate, and major consumer durables (autos, appliances, boats, furniture, carpeting, etc.). It is also used in service categories like construction and maintenance. And personal selling continues to be present in up-scale retail where high prices not only justify but require attention to customer needs. It also survives in analogous distribution systems attempting to reach more modest income levels with high margin but hard-to-sell (because expensive) products. In business-to-business or business-to-institution sales personal selling remains the principal mode of selling capital goods, raw materials, and parts, as well as services.

Personal selling is thus used either where it cannot be avoided or where it is paid for as a service but as part of the product. The absence of attentive sales assistance itself constitutes a kind of hidden demand in the economy which some small businesses have learned effectively to exploit. But doing so requires products able to carry its costs. Paradoxically, one might say, selling itself has to be sold as part of an ambiance or shopping experience. But it can be a hard sell. The erosion of personal selling owes as much to the collusion of the consumer (who is willing to put up with impersonal sales environments in order to save a little money) as to the cost-avoidance reflex of those intent on maximizing profits.

BIBLIOGRAPHY

Freedman, David H. "Meet Your New Executives. They're every bit as clever as your old ones. The difference? They may not be human." *Inc. Magazine.* January 2006.

"Good Personal Selling." *American Salesman.* December 2004.

"The Importance of Personal Selling." *Dealernews.* January 2005.

Ingram, Thomas N. et al. *Sales Management; Analysis and decision making.* South-Western College Publication, 2006.

"Job Performance—Productivity—Effectives—Effort—Failure." *Journal of Personal Selling and Sales Management.* Winter 2005.

Marks, Ronald. *Personal Selling: A Relationship Approach.* Atomic Dog Publishing, 2005.

Darnay, ECDI

PHYSICAL DISTRIBUTION

Economists and business people talk about the movement of goods in and out of business operations as "physical distribution"; it has its counterpart in "materials management," the movement of materials through a plant during production. When these materials movements are considered as part of a system which is planned and managed by people, it is called "logistics." In the commercial sector logistics involves sourcing of materials and marketing of goods, managing the distribution system, and planning and rationalizing materials flow in production.

Physical distribution costs money. The cost of incoming transportation tends to be hidden in the price, but the business owner will feel the price directly if he or she has to ship product any distance or deliver it locally to the consumer. Jean-Paul Rodrique, Claude Comtois, and Brian Slack, in their book titled *The Geography of Transportation Systems,* estimated that logistics accounts for 10 to 15 percent of worldwide Gross Domestic Product.

MODES AND NODES

Physical distribution, narrowly considered, is based on modes of transport that connect important nodes where goods are temporarily held. The major modes are air, water, rail, and road; to these must be added the highly specialized mode of transporting oil and gas in pipelines. The nodes are warehouses situated in close proximity to major systems of distribution. In the pipeline industry tank farms serve the same role; in gas distribution pumping stations are needed to boost the pressure of gas being moved at intervals.

In pre-industrial times the only effective long-distance mode of transportation was by water; early on ships "coasted" ocean shores, keeping them always in sight until navigation developed and sailors discovered nearby lands either by exploration or by storm-tossed accident; later they crossed oceans; inland they followed rivers, and in part access to water almost determined where major communities were formed. Canals were dug all over the world as this mode developed; their traces are still around but used largely for recreational travel today. In America George Washington was involved in canal construction before making his name as a soldier and father of his country. In current times waterborne shipping carries all imaginable goods in bulk and container vessels; in inland river transportation barge traffic mainly carries commodities—grains, gravel, coal, cement.

The development of the steam engine in the 18th century first influenced water transportation by providing an engine for ships—and in the 19th century led to the almost explosive development of rail as a major mode of transportation. Rail captured the bulk of long-distance goods distribution, of which a very substantial part was coal, the black gold that fueled the industrial revolution. Well into the 20th century the U.S. landscape was overlaid by a system of rails not unlike a fairly tight hairnet. Rails reached most towns of any size—and towns formed along the rails as before they'd formed around waterways. Much of the 19th century rail system has since been abandoned. In 1876 the first practical internal combustion engine saw the light of day.

Long-distance land transportation today is dominated by trucking, made possible by that combustion engine (modified into the diesel engine), the extensive development of a highway network, itself suggested by national defense needs, and the development of a major new oil and gas sector which, these days, itself heavily relies on water transportation to bring us fuel. In many areas oil moves by pipeline. Tonnage moved by truck overtook tonnage moved by rail in the last quarter of the 20th century. Much as rivers and rails stimulated location of businesses and people, so did the development of the Interstate Highway System. Its important interchanges became locations of choice for warehousing nodes.

Air transportation was the last major mode to develop. It expanded after World War II in the second half of the 20th century as a people-transport system, which it largely remains, but air freight eventually emerged and has a small share of air tonnage. Air shipment is used for small packages and, occasionally, for larger products that must be delivered in a hurry.

With the maturing of transport systems came combined modes generally referred to as "intermodal" transportation. Typical examples of it are "container ships" that carry boxes which can be placed directly on semi tractor trailers and trucked to their final destinations. Within these boxes goods are packed on pallets ready for unloading by forklift trucks. These same containers can be transported by rail for long-distance hauls and then transferred to trucks for the final leg of the trip.

In terms of costs, the lowest cost is associated with water, then with rail, then with trucking, and finally with air transportation.

EVERYTHING IS RELATIVE

What Einstein held to be true for bodies moving in space and time is true for physical distribution generally. In pre-industrial times physical distribution could be understood by simply looking at such factors as price of product, its size, weight, and its distance from the buyer; using such factors the cost of "sourcing" products could be readily calculated. In early days, however, labor costs were largely the same everywhere and most goods moved were raw materials rather than highly processed or manufactured goods. Labor costs and technology have changed all that so that physical distribution is today greatly influenced by factors external to physical movement. It is quite possible, for instance, to buy a heavy cast-iron outdoor umbrella stand at a lower cost from China—the stand itself made from scrap metal shipped to China from Los Angeles—than a functionally identical product made somewhere in Louisiana or Ohio. The driving force is the production cost of the item moved—itself based on the producer's raw material, energy, and labor costs. If the product has a low production cost, it can "carry" a high transportation cost and arrive at our door more inexpensively than an item traveling a short distance but having a higher production cost.

FIGURING IT OUT

Physical distribution is sometimes a problem for the small business if it is located in outlying areas poorly served by modes. Until the 1970s, transportation was regulated by the federal government under the laudable principle that transportation was, in a sense, a utility which should serve all locations—with the most cost-effective points subsidizing service to distant and less profitable points. Deregulation began in 1977 across the board of all "utilities" and continues in the mid-2000s with energy distribution. Airlines were deregulated first. Most small business, however, is located in or near major hubs. And distribution, running at somewhere around 15 to 20 percent of GDP, is a very big industrial sector and fairly competitive. Discovering the right match of modes to serve a business's markets is, of course, part of initial business planning.

Small businesses rarely have the resources to become experts in physical distribution and therefore converge on typical modes of distribution used in their industry by discovering how others do the job. Occasionally the small business is required to come up with something new and innovative as the consequence of an unusual contract, a new product launch, or the appearance of a new customer. An alternative to doing heavy homework is to make use of transport brokerage, freight forwarding, and transport service organizations that specialize in designing optimal methods of getting the goods where they belong. A Google search with the words "freight forwarding" followed by the name of the state will typically produce a large number of hits or a directory from which the business can select companies to call for initial discussions.

SEE ALSO *Distribution Channels; Transportation*

BIBLIOGRAPHY

Rodrique, Jean-Paul, Claude Comtois, and Brian Slack. *The Geography of Transportation Systems.* Routledge, 2006.

Sparks, Leigh, and John Fernie, eds. *Logistics and Retail Management: Insight Into Current Practice from Leading Experts.* Kogan Page Limited, 2004.

Stroh, Michael B. *A Practical Guide to Transportation and Logistics.* Logistics Network, 2001.

Waters, Donald, ed. *Global Logistics and Distribution Planning: Strategies for Management.* Kogan Page Limited, 2003.

Darnay, ECDI

POINT-OF-SALE SYSTEMS

Point-of-sale systems (POS) represent the computerization of the cash register—and their linking to databases—thus providing businesses with more digital data and the ability to know themselves. POS systems give businesses the ability to retain and analyze a wide variety of inventory and transaction data on a continuous basis. They have been touted as valuable tools for a wide variety of business purposes, including refining target marketing strategies; tracking supplier purchases; determining customer purchasing patterns; analyzing sales (on a daily, monthly, or annual basis) of each inventory item, department, or supplier; and creating reports for use in making purchases, reorders, etc. Basic point-of-sale systems currently in use include stand alone electronic cash registers, also known as ECRs; ECR-based network systems; and controller-based systems. All of these function essentially as sales and cash management tools, but each has unique features.

Stand alone ECRs. These electronic registers operate independently of one another; they are thus the most limited of the three POS system types. They cannot provide their owners with storewide reporting or file sharing; they can merely report the business activity at that particular register. Given their limitations, ECRs are usually used by small independent retailers that feature a limited number of register sites. Indeed, these systems are often well-suited for small businesses because they are the least expensive of the POS options yet nonetheless provide many helpful features, including automatic sales and tax calculation ability; calculation of change owed to the customer; sales report generation capability; capacity to sort food stamps and trading stamps (through programming of function keys); and scanning.

Network Systems. Network or ECR-based point-of-sale systems feature multiple terminals arranged into a primary/secondary configuration. One ECR in the store, equipped with extra memory capacity, serves as the primary terminal and receives data from the secondary terminals. These systems give businesses the added capacity to manage storewide data and transmit data to mainframe or network server.

Controller-Based POS Systems. The top POS systems are controller-based systems in which each terminal is connected to a computer—the "controller" of the system; it receives and stores all sales, merchandise, and credit data. The controller manages the system, checks for errors, and formats data for the main computer used by the enterprise. It does its own sales analysis and does price look-up. Dual-control systems provide additional safety in case of failure. The use of scanners as the input element to these systems eliminates many errors in keyed alternatives. For this reason scanning has become accepted even in mid-sized retail operations as well.

Point-of-sale systems, like many other computer-based innovations, continue to change and develop at a rapid pace. In addition, the demand for POS systems has spawned many new manufacturers, each of which offers a dizzying array of standard and optional POS features to their customers. For example, some electronic POS systems now cover hand-held scanning devices, customer promotions, credit-card confirmations, counterfeit money checks, and staff scheduling. Given the expense involved and the proliferating number of POS software packages, small business owners should make sure that they adequately research both their current and future needs before making a purchase so that they are able to acquire a customized POS system that best fills their current operating requirements and can accommodate future changes in the business. Research will be somewhat daunting because new products are appearing with great frequency—but the choice of implementations which support the right peripherals for the business will often justify a higher price.

BIBLIOGRAPHY

Garry, Michael. "POS Plans Abound; Point-of-Sale Systems Topped Retailers' Priority Lists in this Year's Tech Report, Though Many Other Applications Competed for Attention." *Supermarket News.* 16 January 2006.

Kroll, Karen M. "The POS Connection." *Catalog Age.* 1 January 2005.

Lee, Mie-Yun. "Purchasing the Proper POS System Can Perk Up Efficiency and Profits." *Crain's Cleveland Business.* 10 October 2005.

"Microsoft's POS Move May Make It a Viable Retail Option." *ExtremeTech.com.* 5 October 2004.

"Point of Returns: POS technology allows operators to learn more about their businesses than ever before." *Restaurants & Institutions.* 15 January 2004.

Hillstrom, Northern Lights
updated by Magee, ECDI

PORTABILITY OF BENEFITS

The portability of benefits is a concept that is rapidly gathering support in the U.S. workforce. It refers to the idea that common job benefits—such as health insurance and pension plans—can be set up in such a way that they can travel with a worker as he or she moves from one job to the next. In many cases, these benefits would be paid for by the employee, which makes them attractive to employers. The portability factor would give the employee security that was never available in the past, which is attractive to the employee.

The current structure of employee benefits is not portable. In most employment sectors, each company offers a unique benefit plan that is established and administered by the company's human resources department. Most of the benefits are paid for by the company, and employees often have little, if any, choice about what benefits they receive and from whom they receive them. This is true mostly for pension and health plans, both of which are affected by numerous government regulations that make portability difficult. There are literally hundreds of pension and health plans for employers to choose from. Any given 100 employers in one geographic area may utilize 100 different plan providers, making portability practically impossible under such circumstances.

Portable benefits are gaining popularity in all segments of the business community, but two job sectors are leading the way—temporary work agencies and private, independent contractors. For temp agencies, portable benefits are an attractive way to offer a comprehensive benefit package for temporary employees. For temp workers, the thought of getting benefits that were previously unattainable is an extremely attractive proposition, even if they have to pay for part or all of the benefits. For independent contractors—specialized workers such as advertising designers or accountants who are hired to complete specific, time-bound, and/or goal- oriented projects—portable benefits would be a perfect tool to improve their financial security as they move from one project to the next.

Several steps could be taken that would make portable benefits more likely. If numerous employers in the same geographic region banded together to offer the same benefits, it would make it easier for workers to change jobs and keep the level of seniority and money that they had accrued in their previous jobs. Also, if a government agency was established to oversee and encourage portable benefits, companies would have greater incentive to participate. Finally, the establishment of a national health care system would greatly facilitate the development of a far more portable employment benefit system. This final option is, however, very unlikely in the near term. Instead, the trend appears to be towards the privatization of benefits, making them employee-funded and managed.

The most likely alternative, and one that is already happening at temp agencies and among independent contractors, is that employees would purchase their benefits themselves. They would pay for their own health insurance and make regular contributions to a pension plan that would travel with them from job to job. The government could offer tax credits that would provide workers with an incentive to participate in portable plans, which could help offset the cost. Tax savings would also help offset what workers might lose by participating in a portable plan instead of a more traditional plan, such as the higher rate of accrual and greater earnings that occur when large numbers of employees pool their resources together. The economies of scale of the large, traditional plans make them economically feasible for most employees to join. Without the reduced price gained by such economies, however, many employees could not afford to purchase benefits in the current work environment.

Even state governments are jumping on the portable benefits bandwagon. In the state of Michigan, for example, Governor John Engler spearheaded a move in 1997 to transition the state's pension plan for state workers from a traditional plan—which was organized, managed, and paid for by the state—to a portable plan that allowed workers to select from a number of private investment options and invest their own pension dollars. No matter what state job they took, the pension benefits traveled with the workers, gaining money at each stop along the way. "We have a defined contribution plan that empowers our employees to make critical investment decisions concerning their future," Engler told *Institutional Investor.* "They're also not tied to the state civil service, [as they were with] the old defined benefits, and that fits much more logically with the lifestyles we have today. This is a fully portable benefits plan that goes with them. And the rate of investment [return] over the long term is going to be far better for them than their state DB."

To many employment experts, the move to portable benefits is a positive one, and it is the wave of the future. As Frank Doyle, chairman of the Committee of Economic Development, said in *HR Magazine,* "Corporate America found it couldn't deliver on those guarantees [of lifetime employment] in a highly competitive world economy. Companies that had job guarantees had to withdraw them. The substitute for this old form of job security—and frankly a much better alternative—is the security of having portable benefits and strong employability skills. If we can achieve those things, then we will have established the requisite security for maintaining a productive workforce into the next century."

SEE ALSO *Employee Benefits*

BIBLIOGRAPHY

Bernhardt, Annette, and Thomas Bailey. "Improving Worker Welfare in the Age of Flexibility." *Challenge.* September-October 1998.

Benson, George P. "The Workplace Revolution." *Georgia Trend.* December 1999.

Cook, Christopher D. "Temps Demand a New Deal." *The Nation.* 27 March 2000.

"Cutting Edge Benefits for Growing Companies." *Inc.* February 1997.

Diaz, Scott. "Securing Prosperity—The American Labor Market: How It Has Changed and What to Do about It." *Government Finance Review.* June 2000.

Leonard, Bill. "The Economic State of the Union." *HR Magazine.* December 1996.

McNerney, Donald. "Life in the Jobless Economy." *HR Focus.* August 1996.

Mitchell, Olivia S. *Benefits for the Workplace of the Future.* University of Pennsylvania Press, 2003.

Rehfeld, Barry. "Michigan Redefines Public Pensions." *Institutional Investor.* 1 October 1998.

Rosen, Stephanie. "On Their Own: There's No Employer Match, But Self-Employed Individuals Do Have Access to a Host of Qualified Retirement Plans." *Bank Investment Marketing.* 1 June 1999.

Zabel, Gary. "A New Labor Movement in the Academy." *Dollars & Sense.* March 2000.

Hillstrom, Northern Lights
updated by Magee, ECDI

POSTAL COSTS

All business owners have postal costs, no matter how small or technologically savvy the business. From the occasional letter or invoice to large regular shipments, businesses continue to have paper-based interaction with the market and with government institutions, although electronic communications are increasing in various and ever more sophisticated forms. The U.S. Postal Service remains the primary institution which handles communications on paper and provides a variety of services for businesses and individuals—and is the low-cost service provider.

IN GENERAL

Postal Service pricing changes from time to time to reflect costs incurred by the service. The most recent change became effective January 8, 2006. Rates are classified as "retail" and as "discount." The first category usually applies to single-piece mailings and the second to mass mailings with various additional criteria potentially deepening the discount. The USPS rate structure is complex enough so that even representative examples require a lot of space to reproduce. A single first-class letter weight at or under an ounce costs 39 cents; parcel post weighing one pound or less costs $2.96 per package if it can be processed by machine or $4.58 if it must be hand-processed; both rates are for local delivery, higher if destined to other zones. Priority mail will minimally run $4.50 for a one-pound or lighter-weight item. And express-mail will minimally run $10.95 to $14.40 for the first half pound. These rates increase as the weight of packages increase. Mass mailings are discounted; for example, a letter of lowest weight, mailed as part of a commercial mailing, will cost 18 cents versus 39 cents (17 cents for nonprofits). In all cases, the USPS rates are lower than those charged by private delivery services. The USPS provides a 38-page rate book online (see references) and also provides an online, interactive method of determining mailing costs.

CATEGORIES

Express Mail Service. The Postal Service's most competitive alternative to other private delivery services, such as FedEx and UPS, is Express Mail. This service provides next-day delivery by 12 p.m. to most destinations, even on weekends and holidays. Express Mail costs several dollars less than those of the large private delivery services, making it the best option for frequent large shipments under 70 lbs., if cost is the only consideration. The cost for Express Mail is scaled up to 70 lbs., so business owners needing to send heavier packages for quick delivery should check with their local post office for details on larger shipments.

Priority Mail. Priority Mail is similar to Express Mail and , provides two-day service to most domestic destinations. If an item can wait for two days to be delivered, this is the least expensive option. Again, this alternative is less expensive than those offered by privately owned delivery companies. Both Priority Mail and Express Mail rates end at 70 lbs. and packages must measure 108 inches or less in combined length and girth.

Standard Mail (A) and First-Class. Standard Mail (A) is the primary option used by retailers, catalogers, and other advertisers to promote products and services. Items must weigh less than 1 lb. to qualify under this designation. Although the charge per ounce on the single-piece rate is the same as First-Class mail, Standard Mail (A) bulk mailings (i.e., not single pieces) can, if pre-sorted by ZIP Code, save money. Pre-sorting saves the post office some processing time and the payoff for the mailer is a reduced rate. However, if the bulk mailing contains errors, found by random-sample checking by the postal staff, the charge increases. Then the mailer has the option of correcting the errors or paying the additional fee. Standard Mail (B) is the same system but it is applied to packages weighing more than 1 lb.

First-Class, on the other hand, allows the mailer the option of simply dropping mail into any mail drop box, provided it already has the correct amount of postage on each piece. Also, First-Class mail is the generally used option for post cards, regular mail such as bills or letters, and similar single items.

Postage Meters. Personal postal metering has long been an option for businesses that make heavy use of the mail system. It allows the user to pre-stamp his/her mailings according to precise weight while still at their business location. The convenience of this item has made it perennially popular with many small business owners. According to many experts, however, electronic postal metering is the wave of the future. Electronic postal metering (sometimes referred to as E-postage) enables customers to download postage over the Internet.

SAVING ON POSTAL EXPENSES

Direct marketers, periodical publishers, and other companies that make heavy use of the postal service for basic business operations can reduce expenses significantly by sorting direct mail or packages by zip code, assembling mail into sorted and pre-labeled bags, and by delivering the mail to designated drop-off sites. So-called letter shops are in business to provide all types of mailing services to business, including stuffing and addressing letters from sorted address lists with zip coding in conformity with postal regulations. Methods of minimizing mailing costs include the following points cited by mailing advisors:

- Regularly update customer mailing address data to eliminate outdated information and reduce unproductive mailings.

- Take advantage of reduced rates for drop shipments. The U.S. Postal Service offers discounts for mail delivered to them further down its distribution pipeline. Destination discounts can be realized by dropping off mail at bulk mail centers (BMCs), sectional center facilities (SCFs), or destination delivery units (DDUs).

- Lighten weight of packages. All postage costs—for both domestic and international destinations—are based in part on weight. For bulk mailings, then, reductions in weight can produce big savings. Easy ways of doing so range from reducing the stock of letters and order forms that are being mailed to culling the number of pages in newsletters, correspondence, and other materials.

SEE ALSO *Mailing Lists*

BIBLIOGRAPHY

United States Postal Service. "Mailing & Shipping Guidelines for Business. Available from http://www.usps.com/business/mailingshippingguidelines/welcome.htm. Retrieved on 29 April 2006.

United States Postal Service. "Rates and Fees." Available from http://pe.usps.com/text/dmm300/ratesandfees.htm#wp5906266. Retrieved on 28 April 2006.

Hillstrom, Northern Lights
updated by Magee, ECDI

PREGNANCY IN THE WORKPLACE

Most small business owners that maintain a paid staff will, at one time or another, have a pregnant employee in the workplace. In fact, Bureau of Labor Statistics figures indicate that fully 80 percent of all working women will become pregnant at some point in their working lives. Historically, this news has not always been welcomed by employers, and while research and highly publicized episodes indicated that mid-sized and large companies have been more likely to behave in a discriminatory fashion against pregnant employees than small businesses, which on the whole are more likely to cultivate a more relaxed, family-friendly atmosphere, the latter have also been known to look unkindly on news of an employee's pregnancy. Indeed, researchers have observed that attitudes toward pregnant employees have tended to be predicated more on company culture than on the size of the firm. For example, a small business headed by a driven entrepreneur who is determined to meet or exceed an ambitious agenda of growth may greet the news that his or her top salesperson is pregnant with far less equanimity than the leadership of a larger company that places greater weight on the long-term value of the salesperson.

For the most part, companies of all sizes have adopted more enlightened views of workplace pregnancy issues in recent years. This change can be traced in part to their need to comply with legal protections that have been established on behalf of pregnant workers, but it can also be attributed to increased recognition of the vital importance of women in the workplace and increased awareness of the negative impact that discriminatory practices can have on other women employees and on bottom-line performance. Nonetheless, unfair treatment of pregnant employees persists in some quarters. Despite the laws designed to protect workers who become pregnant, the statistics collected by the Equal Employment Opportunity Commission on charges lodged with them alleging pregnancy discrimination show that these allegations have risen over the last ten years. In 1996, there were 3,743 cases brought before the EEOC. That same year, the commission resolved 4,186 cases. Ten years later, in 2005, the EEOC received 4,449 such charges of pregnancy discrimination and settled 4,321.

PREGNANCY DISCRIMINATION AND FEDERAL LAW

Over the past few decades, the United States has passed three major federal laws that provide legal protections to pregnant employees as well as employees who might become pregnant. These are Title VII of the 1964 Civil Rights Act, the Pregnancy Discrimination Act of 1978, and the Family and Medical Leave Act (FMLA) of 1993.

Title VII of the Civil Rights Act This legislation expressly forbids employers with 15 or more workers on their payroll from refusing to hire, discharge, or otherwise discriminate against any person in any way, shape, or form because of that person's gender. However, this law left a giant loophole for employers, because the Supreme Court ruled in a mid-1970s case that discrimination based on pregnancy was not the same as discrimination based on sex. In other words, a disability plan that provided benefits to both men and *non-pregnant* women was found to meet the criteria of Title VII. Such plans, said the Court, were simply insurance policies that covered some risks and not others. Pregnancy was ruled to be one of those risks that was not covered.

Pregnancy Discrimination Act of 1978 This law was drawn up to close the above-mentioned loophole. This legislation stipulated that all employers treat pregnant and non-pregnant employees in the same way, both in terms of benefits received and all other respects.

Family and Medical Leave Act of 1993 When it passed in 1993, the Family and Medical Leave Act (FMLA) was hailed as a ground-breaking law that provided important federal protections for both men and women faced with issues related to pregnancy, childbirth, adoption, placement for foster care, and family sickness. It was bitterly opposed by some segments of the business community, but family advocates ultimately prevailed. The FMLA stipulates that men and women may take as many as 12 weeks of unpaid leave annually for the birth or adoption of a child, care of a sick child, placement for foster care, or because of morning sickness or other illness (the illness does not have to be pregnancy-related). Employers and employees alike should note, however, that the FMLA does not impact businesses with fewer than 50 employees.

AVOIDING DISCRIMINATORY BEHAVIOR

There are a number of ways in which employers—either intentionally or unintentionally—can run afoul of the various anti-discrimination rules that have been erected to protect women employees who are or may become pregnant. Examples of the ways in which an employer can discriminate range from intentionally eliminating pregnant applicants from the labor pool to unintentionally discriminating against a pregnant woman because of an apparently sex-neutral insurance policy.

- Employers may not refuse to hire, refuse to promote, or fire a pregnant employee because of her pregnancy. Moreover, experts warn that the person's pregnancy can not be *any* factor in the action taken.

If the pregnancy was a consideration in any way, shape, or form, then the employer is liable.

- Employers have to provide the same benefits to all employees, whether or not they are pregnant, although they do not have to provide additional benefits to pregnant workers.

- Employers may not refuse to adjust workloads for a pregnant employee if they do so for a worker who is not pregnant but claims some other disability or mitigating circumstance.

- Employers may not discriminate against staff members just because they might get pregnant.

- Employers may not discriminate against employees who 1) have had an abortion, or 2) are considering having an abortion.

- Employers may not forbid a pregnant employee from continuing to work if she wants to and is physically capable of doing all tasks associated with the work.

- Employers may not evaluate pregnant and non-pregnant employees differently. This is especially true when the employer has chosen to reduce the employee's work load in response to the pregnancy.

- Employers have a responsibility to make sure that pregnant employees are not excluded from taking part in the normal office environment, since such exclusions can have a detrimental impact on the employee's cognizance of important work-related issues.

- Employers may not threaten to fire an employee because of her pregnancy or potential pregnancy.

- Employers are not allowed to reassign employees to lower-paying positions because of pregnancy. Similarly, employers may not change a worker's job description and then eliminate the new job via reorganization.

- Employers may not engage in discriminatory practices against men whose wives or partners become pregnant. It should be noted, however, that application of this law may vary from state to state, since states have different views of the rights of married and unmarried couples.

- Employers can not demand medical notes from a pregnant woman's doctor concerning her work status if they do not require similar documentation from doctors of other employees who have short-term disabilities.

The above guidelines add up to a very simple mandate for employers: Treat your pregnant employees no differently than you would any other employees.

MANAGING THE LOSS OF EMPLOYEES DURING PREGNANCY AND MATERNITY LEAVE

Obviously, pregnant employees should not have to endure discrimination from their employers. Indeed, many researchers, executives, and business owners contend that employers that are understanding and treat their pregnant employees fairly can often count on a heightened level of loyalty from that employee upon her return from maternity leave. But businesses also have to recognize that employee pregnancy means the loss—sometimes temporary, sometimes permanent—of workers, some of whom may be quite valuable to the firm's operation.

Businesses, then, have to figure out how to balance the needs of a pregnant employee with the operational imperatives of running a business. In order to effectively manage this issue one must look carefully at the job being done by the pregnant woman and plan for how this job will be handled while she is still working and during her maternity leave.

Not surprisingly, prior planning is often cited as an essential element of effectively managing the impact of pregnancies on business operations. Business owners and managers should study in advance how the pregnant person's responsibilities will be handled in her absence. Many experts encourage those owners and managers to talk openly with the pregnant employee about possible work dispersal options. The pregnant employee is often the person best equipped to make knowledgeable decisions about allocation of responsibilities. Moreover, opening and maintaining good communication with the pregnant employee can provide owners and managers with the information (anticipated length of maternity leave, restrictions on travel, etc.) they need to make informed decisions about business operations.

In addition, companies have to make sure that other employees that are impacted by a staffer's absence due to pregnancy are adequately compensated for the extra work that they take on. Employees that are asked to "cover" for a pregnant colleague for an extended period of time without receiving any parallel adjustment in compensation or recognition will quickly recognize that their employer is in essence trying to get something for nothing. Employers who do this may manage to keep all facets of the business running fairly smoothly, but it can also erode employee loyalty to the business and create needless friction between the pregnant employee and her coworkers.

SEE ALSO *Family and Medical Leave Act*

BIBLIOGRAPHY

Dessler, Gary. *Human Resource Management.* Prentice Hall, 2000.

Karla, Ritu. "Maternity Leave: Less Pay, More Time Off." *The Hartford Courant.* 14 October 2005.

Lindemann, Barbara. *American Discrimination in Employment Law.* January 2003.

Shellenbarger, Sue. "Pregnant Employees Worry About Effects of Workplace Stress." *Wall Street Journal.* 26 July 2000.

Sparrow, Stephanie. "Ways of Keeping Mum." *Personnel Today.* 17 January 2006.

U.S. Department of Justice. Equal Employment Opportunity Commission. "Pregnancy Discrimination Charges: EEOC & FEPAs Combined FY 1992 – FY 2005." 27 January 2006.

U.S. Department of Labor. "Compliance Guide to the Family and Medical Leave Act." Available from http://www.dol.gov/esa/whd/fmla// Retrieved on 2 May 2006.

Hillstrom, Northern Lights
updated by Magee, ECDI

PRESENT VALUE

Present value (PV) is an accounting term meaning the value today of some amount of money expected to be available one or more years in the future. The concept behind this is that money available in the future is worth less than the same amount in hand today. One hundred dollars invested for a year at a 10 percent rate of return per annum will earn $10, hence will be worth $110 next year. This relationship can be reversed. If I can get 10 percent interest on my money, then $100 paid me a year from now will only be worth $90.91 today, derived by dividing 100 by 1.1. This is known as the time value of the money. Just how high that value is depends on two variables: the amount of time and the interest rate.

The formula for calculating present value for any given year in the future is the following:

$$PV = FV \times (1 + dr) \char`\^ -n.$$

In this formula, PV stands for present value, namely right now, in the year of analysis. Future Value (FV) is the cash projected for one of the years in the future. dr is the discount rate. A discount rate of 16.7 percent would be entered as .167. The caret symbol stands for exponentiation; n is the number of years; the negative n is the negative value of the year. Thus year 1 is −1, year 2 is −2 and so on.

When present value is calculated for multiple years of projected income, for example, two numbers in the formula would change. FV might be different from year to year. And n would be different for each year. The sum of the PVs calculated would be the present value of the entire stream. Let us assume that we have three future earnings of $5,000, $5,500, and $8,750 in the years 2008, 2009, 2010. These values total to $19,250. Now let us assume a discount rate of 15 percent. Using a Microsoft Excel spreadsheet, we could calculate the PV as follows, assuming that the current year is 2007.

We would enter the years beginning with 2008 in column A, row 1 and the values of future earnings,

beginning with $5,000, in column B, row 1. Next, we would enter the following formula into column C, row 1:

$$= B1*(1 + 0.15)\char`\^(-(A1-2007))$$

This formula in column C would now produce the present value of the first year. Replicating this formula in rows 2 and 3 would produce all the new values: $4,348, $4,159, and $5,753. These sum to $14,260. Thus the present value of $19,250, using our 15 percent discount rate, is $14,260. Notice, incidentally, that the −n term (represented by the −A1-2007) would be 1 in the first, 2 in the second, and 3 in the third year because '2007' is deducted from the years we keyed in.

The technique described can, of course, also be applied to quarterly or monthly income streams. In those cases the n term would be smaller increments and the discount rate would be for the shorter period. Thus a 15 percent interest rate for a quarterly calculation would be 3.75 percent and shown as 0.0375.

USES OF PV

The present value calculation can be used to determine the value of a property today expected to earn at least the projected stream of cash flows in the future... or the amounts that must be invested today in order to reap desired sums at future dates.

A common use of present value calculations is to determine the value of a business an investor is thinking of acquiring. The investor is likely to have a certain fairly predictable return on his or her investments based on past experience. That value is used as the discount rate. The future cash earnings of the acquisition target are projected year by year, usually for a ten-year period and using various conservative assumptions based on the target's own history. A residual value for the 11th year is calculated, typically assuming that the business will be sold for five or six times its earnings. The resulting series of annual cash flows are then reduced to present value using the investor's own rate of return. The annual results are summed. If this value is greater than or equal to the asking price, the acquisition might be desirable. If the PV of cash flows is lower, the investor can make more money investing his or her cash in something else. In using such techniques, inflation may be accounted for separately or simply added into the discount rate.

SEE ALSO *Discounted Cash Flow*

BIBLIOGRAPHY
"Discounted Cash Flow." *Chartered Management Institute: Checklists: Managing Information and Finance.* October 2005.

Ross, Stephen A., Randolph W. Westerfield, and Bradford D. Jordan. *Fundamentals of Corporate Finance.* McGraw-Hill/Irwin, 2005.

"What Are You Worth? For sellers, it's back to the future, but for buyers it's here and now." *Financial Planning*. 1 May 2005.

Darnay, ECDI

PRESS KITS

A business will typically prepare a press kit in conjunction with some important announcement to be made in a public forum—at the company's headquarters, at a hotel, at a conference—to which members of the press have been invited or where members of the media may likely appear. At a trade conference, for instance, trade press will usually be present to cover the conference itself; a press room may be part of the conference—where the company's announcement can be posted.

Press kits, as the very phrase implies, go beyond press releases. They will contain narrative materials (the press release being one of these) along with other ancillary documentary items (statistics, resumes, handbooks, and the like) as well as photographs and other visual materials suitable for reproduction by a magazine or newspaper. Occasionally it may be possible to provide samples of a product or miniatures to draw and hold the attention of reporters. If a business goes to the effort of making a public announcement, it is only reasonable to put sufficient effort into a press kit to make it an effective communications tools conveying in its appearance, design, graphics, colors, and contents a composite message in tune with the company's own desired image.

In the Information Age, the Media Age, the "Age of the Image," everybody appears to bend over backwards to catch the eye of a generally bored and jaded press. *PR Week* caught the flavor of the thing in an article writing: "Look on any reporter's desk (or the floor, shelves, and trash bins around it), and you'll likely find more than one press kit. These staples of the PR world have evolved from single-sheet releases placed neatly into folders to major UPS deliveries with gifts, samples, and swag dressed up in sometimes clever, more often corny, packages." Small business is as adept at playing at this game as major companies—if the will is present. Whether a company wants to go all out or keep things modest and dignified will depend as much on the event as on the temperament and style of the company's ownership.

A small business, typically, will either be making announcements in an industry context or unveiling a new facility, operation, acquisition, or outlet in the local community. In the latter case coverage is almost certainly forthcoming from the local press (if notified) because the business is creating genuine news. If the announcement is directed at the trade itself, favorable treatment by the trade press is also reasonably assured if the announcement is not "manufactured news" of little value. Francis Solomon, writing in *Policy & Practice* offered good advice by counseling companies: "Don't lie, don't hide. Creating news rarely works; the business, however, should not be shying from contact with the press, even though much experience indicates that they'll probably get something wrong. But to err is human. If the business is not particularly gifted with individuals familiar with media relations or hype, the best approach to making a press kit is to play it straight but light: a sense of humor helps. Thus the package should be attractive, may even feature something novel and eye-catching, but its contents should be factual and designed to help the recipient write an accurate and complete story."

A press kit should be put together with the reporter's perspective in mind. "What would I need to write a story about this event if I knew nothing about it and fell asleep during the press conference?" Reporters are always looking for unusual facets to make an ordinary story interesting to their readers. Interesting background should therefore be featured. Some companies have fascinating start-up stories. The company's headquarters building may have historic importance not generally known. The product or service may have a colorful inventor. The product may have novel and unexpected uses. Reporters also like to write their stories quickly and avoid a series of follow-up calls to get facts of obvious importance never mentioned in the press kit because, inside the company, "everybody knows." No knowledge on the Media's part must be assumed. It is not only reasonable but sensible to give blatant emphasis to names people always spell wrong. So if the owner or the company is called Quigly, a bold reminder, all in caps that QUIGLLY is spelled with A DOUBLE LL is not out of place. Technical subjects need to be explained in layman's language and, ideally, accompanied by diagrams. Phrases like "torque-resistant topography" or "PostScript-generating package" may be English inside the company but may be Greek to the reporter. All else being equal, a carefully prepared, complete, factual, and interesting content will always win out over a clever package that is puzzling—especially some days after the event was held.

SEE ALSO *Press Release; Public Relations*

BIBLIOGRAPHY
Blacklock, Dana. "Press Kits—What you should know." *Canadian Musician*. January/February 2005.
"Brainfood: Business Manners – Handling the Media." *Management Today*. 2 December 2005.
DeMartine, Karen. "Managing Your Media Risk." *Risk Management*. 2 September 2005.

"PR Technique: Press Kits – Creating press kits with a purpose." *PR Week*. 16 May 2006.

Solomon, Francis. "Key in Dealing with Reporters: Don't lie, don't hide." *Policy & Practice*. June 2005.

Darnay, ECDI

PRESS RELEASES

Press releases—also known as news releases—are brief, printed statements that outline the major facts of a news story in journalistic style. As part of its overall public relations effort, a small business may need to prepare press releases in order to disseminate new information about its products, services, operations, or other activities. A steady flow of news helps to make a small business more visible to the public and creates favorable interest in its activities.

If a company's business is likely to benefit from press coverage—publicity may have little impact on the business, e.g., if it provides services to distant corporate clients—it can generate such publicity by noting newsworthy events and producing press releases to announce them. Examples are promotions, transfers, retirements, or hiring of personnel or the negotiation of a new labor contract. Building new facilities, planning a major expansion, installing new equipment, or offering a new product are other newsworthy events that might occur in a small business. In addition, human interest stories might arise from the unusual hobbies or avocations of employees, the success of company-sponsored sports teams or events, or the company's participation in charity or community activities. If a small business received an award or a visit from a celebrity, these events might provide impetus for a news story as well. In general, a newsworthy story should be timely, of general or human interest, and somewhat unusual.

PREPARING A NEWS RELEASE

In order to attract the attention of the media to anything but a vitally important story, a small business will probably have to prepare and send out a news release. Ideally, the news release will generate enough interest that the media will choose to cover the story themselves. A news release may also be useful as a handout to provide basic information to reporters who come to cover a story.

The release itself should obey standard journalistic practice. The first paragraph should signal the essence of the story: who, what, when, where, why, and how. The remainder of the news release should provide more detail-supporting information—such as facts and figures or quotes from people involved—in most-important to least-important order. Overall, a news release should be crisp and concise, never exceeding two pages in length, and similar to a newspaper article in content and style. It is important that a small business owner find someone to write the news release who has a good command of language, grammar, and punctuation.

News releases should be typed on company letterhead and include the name and address of the company, its trademark or logo, the name and telephone number of a contact person (usually the small business owner, even if the job of preparing the news release is delegated to another person), the date, and the words "News Release." The importance and scope of the story determines where it should be sent. In most cases, it would be appropriate to send it to the business editors of the local print media. Sometimes sending it to local radio and television contacts might be appropriate as well. A small business can create a mailing list of relevant addresses, which can be found in media and trade journals and some reference books, to simplify the process. Some publications have begun accepting press releases online. But small business owners should avoid the temptation to follow up a news release with a telephone call.

PRESS RELEASES IN THE AGE OF ELECTRONIC INFORMATION

The common press release has undergone several significant changes in recent years as the Internet has revolutionized the way news is delivered. The wide availability of online information allows average investors to receive business news at the same time as analysts and news services. While some investors have been able to use this instantaneous information to their advantage, it has also opened the door to some dubious practices. For example, many companies have been victimized by fake press releases issued by disgruntled former employees, unscrupulous investors, or competitors. Such "news" is usually intended to cause harm to the targeted company by convincing investors to sell its stock.

On the other hand, some companies have taken advantage of the technology to issue press releases of debatable merit, apparently with the intention of increasing their stock prices. "Once a relatively mundane communications device, a press release now has the might to dramatically drive the price of a stock," according to *Business Week*. "As a result, more companies are designing press releases with that goal in mind. But it's not just edgy or pushing-the-truth headlines from lesser-known companies that are designed to spike share prices. Stock analysts say established companies are also playing fast and loose with press-release language, especially those involving earnings reports. They may exclude entire unprofitable subsidiaries, or leave out key information—such as certain losses—in order to appear rosy to investors."

Some companies release information prematurely—for example, they might announce a planned merger or joint venture before the deal is completed—while others bombard the information highway with daily press releases in an attempt to keep their stocks in the minds of analysts and investors. "Apparently, some high-tech companies use press releases not only to inform the trade press but also to impress Wall Street analysts and business reporters and—through them—to impress investors who have no other way to get news because they don't read the trade press," Mark Ferelli noted in *Computer Technology Review*. In any case, the Securities and Exchange Commission (SEC) has begun taking notice of business news releases on the Internet. Experts recommend that investors look beyond companies' paid public relations efforts and review their filings with the SEC before making investment decisions.

SEE ALSO *Public Relations*

BIBLIOGRAPHY

"Beware the Press Release." *Business Week.* 24 April 2000.

"Brainfood: Business Manners – Handling the Media." *Management Today.* 2 December 2005.

Ferelli, Mark, and Hal Glatzer. "The Power of the Press Release: For Better or Worse ... Much Worse." *Computer Technology Review.* September 2000.

Hennes, Amy. "Chamber Tip: Press releases." *Detroiter.* December 2002.

Jensen, J.J. "PR Web Taking Marketing to the Masses: Ferndale firm hooking up small- and medium-sized businesses to the media using the Internet." *Bellingham Business Journal.* July 2005.

Pelham, Fran. "The Triple Crown of Public Relations: Pitch Letter, News Release, Feature Article." *Public Relations Quarterly.* Spring 2000.

Hillstrom, Northern Lights
updated by Magee, ECDI

PRICE/EARNINGS (P/E) RATIO

The price/earnings ratio (P/E ratio) is one of a number of measures used to assess the value of a company. The "price" component of the ratio is the stock price of the company. The "earnings" portion is the net income (income after tax) reported by the company per share. These two numbers are divided to get a ratio. For example, if a company's stock sold for $24 per share and the company reported earnings per share of $1.50, the company's P/E ratio would be 16.

This is also sometimes referred to as a "multiple," in the sense that the price is, in this case, 16 times earnings. The ratio also means that investors are willing to pay $24 for $1.50 in earnings. The higher the multiple the higher investor enthusiasm for the stock is, for whatever reason. A high price paid for low earnings is, obviously, a more risky investment, but the investor has faith in the company.

The P/E ratio is often taken as a "hard" measurement because the stock price is determined by open bidding in a free market by investors assumed to be well-informed—and the earnings are taken from the company's own books as reported to the public under the requirements of the securities laws. In reality, however, the price component of the ratio only partially reflects the actual value of the company. A certain and unmeasurable portion of that price is set by investor opinion and is therefore influenced by subjective perceptions based on information, lack of it, reputation, rumor, speculation, and the like. "High-flying" stocks, for instance, may have an exaggeratedly high P/E whereas very solid stocks may be "undervalued" and thus have relatively low P/Es. During the dot-com boom the former chief of the Federal Reserve, Alan Greenspan, spoke of "irrational exuberance" in the market—one source of investor motivation. With the dot-com bust, which came early in 2000, dot-com stock tumbled—and so did P/E ratios.

For these reason it is better to view the P/E ratio as at least in part a thermometer of *investor* confidence and *not* as a thermometer measuring a company's health. At the same time, the P/E ratio can directly affect the company's well-being too. With a high P/E a company has easier access to capital. A low multiple can deprive a company of investor support—indeed can expose it to hostile takeovers if its value is not fully reflected in stock value. An example will make this clear.

A diversified, large, profitable producer of industrial machinery, components, and supplies (lubricants or abrasives, for instance) may be trading at low multiples of earnings because it is serving a wide range of industries in the "traditional" categories of manufacturing. None of its product lines are "sexy" but all are producing high margins. The complexity and diversity of the company makes it difficult for stock analysts to overview or to value, and for this reason it is ignored and rarely makes anybody's "buy" list. The company's management has accumulated a lot of cash and is attempting to spend it on new properties, in part to make the company more "exciting" and thus to lift its stock. Stockholders are restless despite high dividends because the stock is not increasing in value proportional to the company's stellar performance. The management is deeply troubled by the company's P/E of 8, sometimes dipping to 7, even 6. Then the inevitable happens. Another company, quite able to see the real value of this one, mounts a hostile take-over. The stock is underpriced, the company has a lot of cash, and the stockholders are likely to side with the attacker.

Another company, with a similarly low P/E ratio, may be quite clearly visible to the investor community. Its low stock valuation, and consequently low multiple, may be due directly to its shrinking share of the market, outdated product, and several failed acquisitions. In this case the P/E accurately reflects value, in the other case not. What is true of low ratios can also be true of high ones: management may be manipulating the news in order to inflate stock value; it may be fraudulently overstating revenues or may simply dazzle stock analysts and investors based on perceived but unsubstantiated trends. Also, often, the reason for the high ratio is fully justified—in fact the high multiple may not even accurately reflect the stock's upward potential.

Not surprisingly, the literature on this subject is filled with analysis on what P/E means and how it should be read. The careful investor and analyst will look deeply into a company's operation and not simply at the tea leaves left over at the bottom of the cup. P/E is an excellent starting point for analyzing a company—or an industry, by comparing the ratios of its major participants. More needs to be known to discover a company's true value. Most acquisitions, for example, are based on discounted cash flow analysis, discussed elsewhere in this volume.

SEE ALSO *Discounted Cash Flow*

BIBLIOGRAPHY

Damodaran, Aswath. "This Stock Is So Cheap! The Low Price-Earnings Story." informit.com. 11 June 2004. Available from http://www.informit.com/articles/article.asp?p=170894. Retrieved on 26 April 2006.

Heintz, James A., and Robert W. Parry. *College Accounting.* Thomson South-Western, 2005.

Pratt, Shannon P., Robert F. Reilly, and Robert P. Schweis. *Valuing a Business.* Fourth Edition. McGraw-Hill, 2000.

Smith, Richard L., and Janet Kiholm Smith. *Entrepreneurial Finance.* John Wiley, 2000.

Warren, Carl S., Philip E. Fess, and James M. Reeve. *Accounting.* Thomson South-Western, 2004.

Darnay, ECDI

PRICING

The pricing of goods and services is almost always determined by demand, which creates the market or confirms an offering as legitimate, by competition, which lowers prices when present and increases them by its absence, and, finally, by the cost of producing the item or providing the service. A good deal of mythology and mystification surrounds the subject of pricing, but these fundamental relationships enable the business owner to price his or her goods correctly without either gouging or leaving too much on the table.

At the most fundamental level a sale is the consequence of an auction in which the price is set by bidding. If the highest bid is not high enough, the seller will not sell. If no one bids, there is no price. The rarer and the more valuable an object is (i.e., the higher the demand relative to supply) the higher the price. The more common the good and the more sluggish the demand for it, the lower the price—but objects will not be sold below the seller's cost except under unusual circumstances.

Bidding for every little thing in an open auction is, of course, very inefficient. For this reason pricing methods have evolved but still represent, as it were, a kind of ritualized and very slow-motion auction. Prices will rise or drop depending on demand. Demand will rise and fall depending on supply. But while this happens instantly in live-auctions, it takes place almost imperceptively in normal commerce.

PRICING A GOOD

The price of a good or of a service (hereafter we'll mean both by simply saying "product") is its total cost for the seller plus a profit margin over and above this cost the purpose of which is to keep the business in business. The cost will be the cost, of course. The profit margin will depend on the strength of the demand and the intensity of the competition. To be sure, pricing is dynamic. If a seller discovers that consumers like a product but will not pay the price, this often acts as feedback. The seller will attempt to reduce the cost as much as possible while attempting to maintain quality high enough still to command consumer interest. One modern technique of cost-reduction is to buy goods from regions where labor costs are low—and this strategy has created the discounting and outsourcing phenomena so prevalent in the mid-2000s.

Ideally the seller will select a location and an "ambiance" appropriate to the products sold. Ideally the seller will understand his or her turnover of goods well enough to know which lines sell sufficient quantities to maintain the store in business and which products, even if slower-moving, provide the extra margin of profitability. Ideally the seller will be sufficiently aware of the effective competition, namely that likely directly to compete with him or her, and the prices charged by that competition.

Common mistakes in pricing arise from careless tracking of overhead costs, product mix, changing consumer preference, and competitors' behavior. If the out-of-pocket costs of products sold have been declining and the merchant is in the habit of marking things up by a standard percentage, the new pricing may not absorb the total overhead, especially if overhead has been growing. The merchant may also overprice if costs have been rising; a standard mark-up will now produce more than overhead costs and the usual profit—but customers may no longer buy as readily. In service operations where bidding on jobs is common, careless and mechanical methods of estimation may sometimes result in seriously underbidding difficult jobs because the owner or salesperson didn't want to bother getting the ladder out and climbing a roof—or an analyst has failed to make five preliminary phone calls to *really* understand how easy or difficult it will be to get the information a customer wishes to have collected.

Good pricing behavior is therefore dependent on—

- Detailed and up-to-date knowledge of costs beyond the cost of the actual item, i.e., overhead cost and how it is changing. Increases in rent, salaries, benefits, utilities, and services must be noted immediately and a running overhead rate must be available monthly in updated format.

- Product knowledge including, in some categories, the "service" costs a product is likely to demand after its sale. Selling a computer installation may require a certain number of hours spent on the telephone after installation just in holding customers' hands. This cost must be known in advance.

- Careful and detailed estimating of technical and services sales, sometimes including quick studies and tests and/or visits and close inspections in order to understand jobs fully.

- Current knowledge of competitor pricing.

- A deep understanding of the product mix sold with special attention to that mix of products which carries the business. A specialty grocer may "carry" the store by selling dairy products, bread, cereals, soups, and fresh produce. The expensive meat counter with expert butchers may simply be paying for itself but may be the very reason why customers put up with the limited parking. The real profit may come from the company's extensive line of wines for which its customers are willing to pay a premium. For good pricing strategy, all this must be known.

- Close and detailed knowledge of vendors' offerings to identify unusual opportunities.

PRICING STRATEGIES

Pricing itself is a form of communication. Not surprisingly, many different kinds and flavors of pricing strategy exist. Major categories include the following.

Manufacturer's Suggested Retail Price Many small businesses prefer to price their goods in accordance with the manufacturer's suggested retail price. In some cases this is forced on the business because the price is prominently printed on the packaging. Going below it is possible, but going above it is almost impossible. Where such pricing is literally suggested, not printed, the business adopting this approach without analysis can make mistakes.

Price Bundling This is the practice of giving the customers the option of buying several items or services for a single price. A furniture retailer might offer customers a sofa and love seat combination at a price somewhat lower than the two goods would cost if bought separately. Similarly, a landscaper might lure customers by offering two free months of lawn maintenance with any major landscaping job. These approaches, all pricing approaches, depend on precise pricing, at least for internal purposes, of each item—and good ability to predict volume changes due to the strategy.

Multiple Pricing Similar to price bundling, multiple pricing is the practice of selling multiples of a unit for a single price—two for the price of one, $10 for 10, and endless combinations. This sort of pricing is used for moving low-cost items in that few people will buy three cars for the price of two—even if offered.

Cost-Plus Pricing This method is the standard method of pricing everything initially, as described above. It combines all direct costs, apportions overhead to each product, and then adds the necessary profit margin, the "plus." Cost-plus should be the foundation on which all else is based.

Competitive Pricing Some small business owners choose to base their own prices on the prices of their principal competitors. Business owners who choose to follow this course, however, should make sure that they look at competing businesses of similar size and strength. Competitive pricing among service-oriented businesses is more difficult to achieve, first because competitive pricing is difficult to discover and second because service jobs are more more variable than identical products spat out three a second by an automated system.

Pricing Above Competition Oddly enough this strategy is used both in very up-scale and in rather poor areas. In the first the high income of the population permits an upward bias and is in part justified by providing convenience and ambiance. In poor neighborhoods prices are frequently higher than in middle-class neighborhoods because accessible outlets are few, the population has less access to transportation, and the merchant can therefore use his or her presence alone as a wedge and leverage. "Ghetto" pricing tends often to be of this nature, alas.

Pricing Below Competition Pricing below competition is the practice of setting one's prices below those of its competitors. Commonly employed by major discount chains such as Wal-Mart—which can do so because its purchasing power enables it to save on its costs per unit—this strategy can also be effectively used by smaller businesses in some instances (though not when competing directly with Wal-Mart and its ilk), provided they keep their operating costs down and do not spark a price war. Indeed, the smaller profit margins associated with this pricing strategy make it a practical necessity for participating companies to: exercise tight control over inventory; keep labor costs down; keep major operational expenses such as facility leases and equipment rental under control; obtain good prices from suppliers; and make effective use of its pricing strategy in all advertising.

Price Lining Companies that engage in this practice are basically hoping to attract a specific segment of the community by only carrying products within a specified price range. Here, again, very high-end retail (Cartier, Furla, Tiffany & Company) and very low-end ("Dollar stores") ultimately use the same strategy. Advantages sometimes accrued through price lining practices include reduced inventory and storage costs, ease of merchandise selection, and enhanced status or large volume. Analysts note, however, that this strategy frequently limits the company's freedom to react to competitors' pricing strategies, and that it can leave businesses particularly vulnerable to economic trends.

Odd Pricing Odd pricing is used in nearly all segments of the business world today. It is the practice of pricing goods and services at prices such as $9.95 (rather than $10) or $79.99 (rather than $80) because of the conviction that consumers will often round the price down rather than up when weighing whether to make a purchase. This little morsel of pricing psychology has become so universally employed that many observers rightly question its value. Everybody rounds *up,* not down. But the practice remains widespread and is practiced worldwide.

Other commonly used pricing policies include penetration pricing and skimming pricing (for manufacturers) and loss leader pricing (for retailers). Both subjects are discussed in more detail elsewhere in this volume.

REAL PRICE AND NOMINAL PRICE

For national accounting purposes and to help all sectors of the economy calculate adjustments to pensions, changes in prices for the same goods or services are calculated by using the Consumer Price Index (CPI), prepared and published at monthly intervals by the U.S. Bureau of Labor Statistics. CPI is calculated by systematically pricing all manner of goods and services in the dollars of the day, the actual dollars charged. This is then labeled the "nominal price." The nominal price today is compared with prices for identical "shopping baskets" of goods and clusters of services (e.g., rents, education, fuels, etc.) in an earlier period. If one basket is priced in 2006 and another in 1996, the total price will be different yet will have purchased the same goods and services. CPI data, therefore, can be used to calculate inflation or deflation between two periods. If a dollar's worth of purchases in 1996 cost $1.27 in 2006 (the actual change between the years), the inflation rate has been 27 percent. Thus a couple who received $40,000 in pensions in 1996 would have to have $50,800 in 2006 to have the same standard of living. Using simple arithmetic, it is thus possible to express prices at any time in the past in dollars comparable to any other time. This is called "real price," i.e., price with inflation removed. *Real* dollars are always associated with a year. Thus when people speak of real 2000 dollars, they mean that all values are expressed in values of the dollar as it had in 2000. Because inflation is increasing, someone earning $75,000 in 2006 earned only $64,500 in 2000 dollars because of the inflation between the two years.

RAISING PRICES

Small business owners are often reluctant to raise prices once a good baseline price has been established. They worry that a price increase will alienate customers and drive them to the competition. "Faced with such resistance, a lot of businesspeople are tempted to forgo price increases altogether, or at least put them off for as long as possible. If you do either one, however, you're making a big mistake," Norm Brodsky wrote in *Inc.* "Your profit margins will be shrinking.... You're gradually undermining the perceived value of your services or products." Brodsky noted that many of a small business's costs— such as payroll, insurance, and utilities—tend to rise every year, slowly cutting into profit margins. In addition, customers tend to associate price with quality. A business that does not increase prices to keep up with the competition risks being regarded as the cheap alternative in the marketplace.

When price increases are implemented gradually and cautiously, small businesses may be able to keep their customers happy while also keeping their profit margins intact. Customers typically base their purchase decisions on more than just price. Other factors influencing the decision process include quality, features, guarantees, and personal desires. In addition, people will always pay more for good, reliable customer service. In order to make an effective price increase, the business owner should be ready to explain the increase to the customer if asked. The more straightforward and justified the answer, the more effective it will be to cause a customer to nod—not with pleasure, to be sure.

SURVIVING COMPETITORS' DISCOUNT PRICING STRATEGIES

Major discount stores such as Wal-Mart, Sam's Club, Target, Kmart, Office Depot, Staples, Best Buy, and Circuit City have gained control of large blocs of the American business world over the last several years on the strength of their one-stop shopping and discount prices, the latter a result of their ability to buy goods at bulk rates. Many small business owners have felt the impact of these stores—indeed, cautionary tales concerning the impact that such stores can have on formerly vibrant downtown shopping areas have proliferated in recent years.

Surviving such assaults may not always be possible for the small business. A fundamental rule of pricing is that no one who is sane continues to sell below cost. When the "Big Box" moves in next door, the small business can only survive by changing—and sometimes only by changing radically. Hopeful observers suggest that small businesses innovate their way out of such competitive difficulties. They should offer more personal service, develop a niche the "Big Box" has neglected, segment the market more effectively, and/or adopt similar strategies. Yes, change is possible—but difficult if the small business cannot extract the assets invested in the business or if it was not wildly profitable and thus doesn't have reserves of cash. The best defenses are alertness, anticipation, and action before the inevitable happens. On the first news of the "Invasion of the Boxes," the business owner should be dusting off contingency plans and getting ready to liquidate, to move, or to change the business into something very different. The big retailers greatly increase traffic in and around their operations. One possibility of radical response may be to put up something nearby to tempt the masses drawn by low prices produced by Chinese labor. An ice cream shop, perhaps? It's a big change from running a family lumberyard, but entrepreneurs are endlessly creative!

SEE ALSO *Loss Leader Pricing; Penetration Pricing*

BIBLIOGRAPHY

Baker, Michael. *The Marketing Book.* Butterworth-Heinemann, 2003.

Brodsky, Norm. "Street Smarts: Raising Prices." *Inc.* May 2000.

Campanelli, Melissa. "Price Point: Score with a pricing strategy that keeps customers coming back." *Entrepreneur.* November 2005.

Hitt, Lorin M., and Pei-yu Chen. "Bundling with Customer Self-Selection: Simple approach to bundling low-marginal-cost goods." *Management Science.* October 2005.

Perryman, Bruce. "Business Sense: Pricing Products for Profit." *Stitches Magazine.* 22 February 2006.

Plack, Harry J. "Price Hikes Not Always a Bad Thing." *Baltimore Business Journal.* 14 July 2000.

U.S. Bureau of Labor Statistics. "Consumer Price Indexes." Available from http://www.bls.gov/cpi/home.htm. Retrieved on 1 May 2006.

Hillstrom, Northern Lights
updated by Magee, ECDI

PRIVATE LABELING

Private labeling is the interesting story of a how a segment of products, originally introduced as low-price alternatives to high-priced brands, is gradually evolving a new brand identity in its own right—increasingly deployed to build loyalty to stores that have plenty of brand identity of their own (e.g., Kroger, CVS, Rite-Aid, and many others). Private-label products, often referred to as "store brands," are made by manufacturers for stores but carry the store's rather than the producer's label. Sometimes the manufacturer produces solely for the PL market, distributing the same product with unique labels for different retailers; sometimes the manufacturer has a well-known brand of its own but sells a portion of its production under private label. When all else is equal, e.g., the identical product is sold under an established brand *and* under one or more private labels, the only real difference between the two is that the branded product carries all the costs of brand promotion and the PL product carries no such costs at all. The two products, of course, will have slightly different packaging too, for differentiation. PL products, for this reason, initially emerged as a way of exploiting a cost differential. They are typically sold at prices below that of their brand-bearing counterparts. All manner of variations on this theme exist and have been present. Thus the PL product may be indistinguishable, somewhat inferior, and (of late) even superior to a branded equivalent. Packaging in the past has ranged from deliberately unattractive to deliberately eye-catching, including imitative of the leading brand with which it competes.

Private labeling emerged visibly in the 1980s and, in those days, ranged from versions carrying store labels to so-called "generics" which came in bland, usually white packaging—including canned goods bearing the product identification and labeling, but no brand whatsoever, on white wrappers. The recession of the late 1980s helped to establish this new category. It continued to thrive even as the economy rebounded in the 1990s and proceeded to finish the 20th century with a great spurt of growth.

The situation in the mid-2000s is summed up by *Private Label Buyer* succinctly as follows: "Store brands have evolved from merely the generic low-priced product to a wide selection of items that have a brand identity of their own. Today, a store brand can be a premium, high-quality item that competes with national brands on image. Consumers have changed into value seekers—even those at the higher end of the economic scale consider themselves savvy shoppers looking for the best value." Trade statistics bear out the fact. Store brands slightly out-pace the growth of branded products. This is not surprising in that PL products tend to be lower priced; but it testifies at least to the adequacy and possibly to the increasing quality of private-label goods.

Quality is important, but, as Jill Rivkin pointed out, also writing for *Private Label Buyer,* price remains the most important factor. "When asked to rank the private label attributes of price, quality and package design in order of importance," Rivkin wrote, "about 60 percent of primary grocery shoppers surveyed put quality in the top spot. But just moments later, when asked if they would purchase a private label item only if there is a significant price difference between it and the comparable national brand item, 64.7 percent agreed."

Although private labeling is widespread and can be found in most consumer categories (ranging quite widely from plastics sacks on up to lawnmowers), it tends to dominate in the grocery and in the drugs and sundries categories. Major retailers in these categories are most active in exploiting the possibilities of private label by fusing low-price store-branding and store-identity into a promotional approach intended to build store loyalty. Thus in advertising and in issuing coupons, higher discounts are offered for store-branded items in order to attract and to keep the clientele.

PL and Small Business Producing for the private label market has been a valued strategy by small business in the middling-size category, especially those that have established recognized brands of their own in grocery categories (e.g., preserves, sauces, condiments, etc.). Plant expansions can be rationalized by adding a substantial private-label production run. A certain size is necessary because private label distribution must satisfy a mass market. Distributing privately labeled product to many small stores, each requiring its own unique labeling and packaging—combined with the need for low pricing—makes the approach less than cost-effective.

Some small businesses look for opportunities exclusively to satisfy a large private-label market by producing

for it a regional supply of some product the specifications for which are set for all participating manufacturers by the buying retailer.

Private Labels and E-Commerce A still emerging trend in private labels is the rapid adoption of these brands by firms involved in Internet commerce. "While supermarkets and department stores in the brick-and-mortar world can take years before they venture into private label merchandise, e-tailers—in a development that echoes the rapid emergence of the medium itself—are developing private label programs as they approach the starting gate," Elaine Underwood wrote in *Brandweek*.

According to Underwood, some electronic retailers are attracted by the higher margins typically offered by private-label merchandise. Others see it as a way to offer unique merchandise that helps differentiate them from competitors. For example, the online toy retailer eToys sold special cabinets and stands for customers to display their collections of toys under their own brand name. Some experts claim that offering private-label merchandise gives substance to online brand names and reminds customers of e-commerce Web sites. Electronic retailers must be careful not to offend big name manufacturers by copying their products and packaging too closely, however, because they lack the leverage in the chain of distribution that is enjoyed by regular retail stores.

SEE ALSO *Brands and Brand Names*

BIBLIOGRAPHY
"Building Shopper Loyalty with Store Brands." *Private Label Buyer.* March 2006.

Murray, Barbara. "Private Labels Pushed as Solutions." *Supermarket News.* 14 February 2000.

"PL Continues to Expand Its Market Share." *Chain Drug Review.* 13 March 2006.

"Private Label. At Long Last, Respect: Price becomes less important as consumers reach for quality." *Stagnito Communications.* Available from http://www.stagnito.com/fbr_pl.asp. Retrieved on 2 May 2006.

Rivkin, Jill. "Price Is Still Priority: Consumer research shows a commitment to private label, as long as the price is right, and a continuing need for consumer education." *Private Label Buyer.* March 2006.

Rivkin, Jill. "Reevaluating the Competition: National brands are paying more attention to private label, now considered a 'threat'." *Private Label Buyer.* March 2006.

Underwood, Elaine. "Store Brands, Without the Store." *Brandweek.* 19 June 2000.

Walden, Geoff. "Drug Chains Aim to Make Category Their Own." *Chain Drug Review.* 27 March 2006.

Hillstrom, Northern Lights
updated by Magee, ECDI

PRIVATE PLACEMENT OF SECURITIES

Private placement occurs when a company makes an offering of securities to an individual or a small group of investors. Since such an offering does not qualify as a public sale of securities, it does not need to be registered with the Securities and Exchange Commission (SEC) and is exempt from the usual reporting requirements. Private placements are generally considered a cost-effective way for small businesses to raise capital without "going public" through an initial public offering (IPO).

ADVANTAGES AND DISADVANTAGES

Private placements offer small businesses a number of advantages over IPOs. Since private placements do not require the assistance of brokers or underwriters, they are considerably less expensive and time-consuming. In addition, private placements may be the only source of capital available to risky ventures or start-up firms.

A private placement may also enable a small business owner to hand-pick investors with compatible goals and interests. Since the investors are likely to be sophisticated business people, it may be possible for the company to structure more complex and confidential transactions. If the investors are themselves entrepreneurs, they may be able to offer valuable assistance to the company's management. Finally, unlike public stock offerings, private placements enable small businesses to maintain their private status.

Of course, there are also a few disadvantages associated with private placements of securities. Suitable investors may be difficult to locate, for example, and may have limited funds to invest. In addition, privately placed securities are often sold at a deep discount below their market value. Companies that undertake a private placement may also have to relinquish more equity, because investors want compensation for taking a greater risk and assuming an illiquid position. Finally, it can be difficult to arrange private placement offerings in multiple states.

RESTRICTIONS AFFECTING PRIVATE PLACEMENT

The SEC formerly placed many restrictions on private placement transactions. For example, such offerings could only be made to a limited number of investors, and the company was required to establish strict criteria for each investor to meet. Furthermore, the SEC required private placement of securities to be made only to "sophisticated" investors—those capable of evaluating the merits and understanding the risks associated with the investment. Finally, stock sold through private offerings could not be advertised to the public and could only be resold under certain circumstances.

In 1992, however, the SEC eliminated many of these restrictions in order to make it easier for small companies to raise capital through private placements of securities. The rules now allow companies to promote their private placement offerings more broadly and to sell the stock to a greater number of buyers. It is also easier for investors to resell such securities. Although the SEC restrictions on private placements were relaxed, it is nonetheless important for small business owners to understand the various federal and state laws affecting such transactions and to take the appropriate procedural steps. It may be helpful to assemble a team of qualified legal and accounting professionals before attempting to undertake a private placement.

Many of the rules affecting private placements are covered under Section 4(2) of the federal securities law. This section provides an exemption for companies wishing to sell up to $5 million in securities to a small number of accredited investors. Companies conducting an offering under Section 4(2) cannot solicit investors publicly, and the majority of investors are expected to be either insiders (company management) or sophisticated outsiders with a preexisting relationship with the company (professionals, suppliers, customers, etc.). At a minimum, the companies are expected to provide potential investors with recent financial statements, a list of risk factors associated with the investment, and an invitation to inspect their facilities. In most respects, the preparation and disclosure requirements for offerings under Section 4(2) are similar to Regulation D filings.

Regulation D—which was adopted in 1982 and has been revised several times since—consists of a set of rules numbered 501 through 508. Rules 504, 505, and 506 describe three different types of exempt offerings and set forth guidelines covering the amount of stock that can be sold and the number and type of investors that are allowed under each one. Rule 504 covers the Small Corporate Offering Registration, or SCOR. SCOR gives an exemption to private companies that raise no more than $1 million in any 12-month period through the sale of stock. There are no restrictions on the number or types of investors, and the stock may be freely traded. The SCOR process is easy enough for a small business owner to complete with the assistance of a knowledgeable accountant and attorney. It is available in all states except Delaware, Florida, Hawaii, and Nebraska.

Rule 505 enables a small business to sell up to $5 million in stock during a 12-month period to an unlimited number of investors, provided that no more than 35 of them are non-accredited. To be accredited, an investor must have sufficient assets or income to make such an investment. According to the SEC rules, individual investors must have either $1 million in assets (other than their home and car) or $200,000 in net annual personal income, while institutions must hold $5 million in assets. Finally, Rule 506 allows a company to sell unlimited securities to an unlimited number of investors, provided that no more than 35 of them are non-accredited. Under Rule 506, investors must be sophisticated. In both of these options, the securities cannot be freely traded.

DISCLOSURE

Although the 1992 SEC revisions eliminated the requirement for companies to prepare a Private Placement Memorandum for investors, experts suggest that it is still a good idea. The memorandum should describe the business, provide background information on management, discuss the terms of the offering (including the number of shares available, the price, and the intended use for the funds), outline the company's capital structure before and after the sale of securities, disclose the opportunities and risks involved in the investment, and provide copies of financial statements. Overall, the level of disclosure should be consistent with applicable state and federal securities laws, as well as with the sophistication of potential investors and the complexity of the terms of the offering.

A series of documents known as subscription materials should also be included with the information sent to potential investors in a private placement transaction. Subscription materials consist of two major documents that investors sign to indicate their desire to subscribe to purchase the securities offered. One of these documents is the offeree and purchaser questionnaire, which asks for background information about the investor to determine his or her level of sophistication. The second document is the subscription agreement, which is a contract showing that the investor has reviewed the offering information, is aware of the risks involved, and wants to invest.

SEE ALSO *Initial Public Offerings*

BIBLIOGRAPHY

Brown, Philip L. *GSI's Primer to SEC Research.* Global Securities Information, Inc., 2004.

Dresner, Steven. *PIPE: A Guide to Private Investments in Public Equity.* Bloomberg Press, 2003.

Juarez, Madeleine. "Drawing Investors as a Small Business Owner." *San Fernando Valley Business Journal.* 10 November 2003.

Lewis, Jakema. "2000: A See-Sawing Year for Private Deals." *Private Placement Letter.* 29 January 2001.

Sherman, Andrew J. *Raising Capital: Get the Money You Need to Grow Your Business.* AMACOM, 2005.

Sweeney, Paul. "As Public Markets Fell, Equity Private Placements Filled the Gap." *Investment Dealers' Digest.* 26 February 2001.

Sweeney, Paul. "Staying Upbeat: Story Credits, Mezzanine Financing Boost Lackluster Private." *Investment Dealers' Digest.* 21 August 2000.

Walter, Robert W. *Financing Your Small Business.* Barron's Educational Series, Inc., 2004.

Hillstrom, Northern Lights
updated by Magee, ECDI

PRIVATIZATION

Privatization is the transfer of some property or activity from public to private control. In the international context privatization typically refers to the denationalization of government-run industries. In the U.S. the term is used to denote activities of local government; the word, however, occasionally occurs in policy debates at the federal level as well. When a function has been performed or a service delivered by government employees and is then contracted out to the private sector, the result is partial privatization because government continues to control the activity. Most "privatized" municipal functions are, in fact, *performed* by private sector companies but *controlled* by the government. Environmental functions like garbage collection, sewage treatment, and drinking water provision are increasingly privatized in this sense. Outright transfer of ownership to the private sector has also taken place, usually in the context of toll roads.

Control is a fundamental aspect of ownership. Government control over activities and property tends to increase in troubled times and decrease in good times. During a war government frequently in effect takes over industries by regulatory control. After 9/11 government took over airport security, for instance, presently managed by the Transportation Security Administration. When private initiative does not spontaneously supply necessary functions, government will get involved and perform the function; later it may hand it over. Major sewer systems were built and operated by government; space exploration continues to be dominated by government enterprise although private sector ventures have appeared.

Privatization is thus one phase in a broader spectrum of control and its relaxation in response to external stimuli. Privatization is "kissing cousin" to deregulation, another instance of government relaxing its grip over functions. Government's exercise of control and its opposite are ultimately sanctioned by the public will brought to expression in politics. Government involvement must be paid for by taxes (or, in recent history, by borrowing).

The public is more-or-less willing to let go of some functions or services. Attempts to privatize Social Security, for instance, by the institution of "private accounts" have failed; so have initiatives to privatize public education by the mechanism of "vouchers." In other areas privatization has gone forward side-by-side with deregulations more or less continuously since the end of World War II. When such efforts falter or fail, re-regulation is immediately in the news. Direct government control is the extreme form of regulation.

Promoters of privatization (and of deregulation) base their position on the greater efficiency of free markets and competition. They hold up consumer choice as a high value. But current events and history show that the population, expressing itself by means of government, will exert its power when it doesn't like the outcome of free market choices. Thus in the mid-2000s, sharp hikes in gasoline prices immediately led to demands for government intervention to control prices at the pump.

AREAS OF PRIVATIZATION

Municipal Services Narrowly viewed, privatization has had its greatest impact at the local level as municipal services performed by city or township employees have been converted into operating contracts handled by the private sector. This activity has created opportunities for small business for many decades, primarily in solid waste collection and disposal, street repair, in recreational facility management like landscaping and groundskeeping services, and, in the 1990s and early 2000s, in the operation of water and sewer systems. Larger businesses have, of course, participated in this activity as well. They have taken on the operation of ports from port authorities, have purchased toll roads or taken on their management and maintenance, and taken over entire functions like the construction and operation of recreational centers and water systems.

As *Public Works* magazine has pointed out, privatization, reaching back decades, has not been without controversy. "Some cities proclaim major cost savings and efficiency improvements through private ownership and/or operation of [systems]," the magazine wrote. "Other agencies, citizen groups, and public employees are less convinced of the long-term benefits of turning over control of public services to private entities." Citing a survey of 125 municipal decision makers conducted for the Malcolm Pirnie organization, *Public Works* noted the following: "When asked about the challenges they face, 23 percent of drinking water utility participants said they needed to improve business practices to face the 'threat from the private sector.' As to the benefits of privatization, 28 percent mentioned increased efficiency and 23 percent cost savings. Disadvantages included loss of control (39 percent), private companies' profit motive (18 percent), and financial disadvantages (18 percent)."

Joshua Kurlantzick, writing for *Entrepreneur* (and highlighting opportunities for small business) provided reasons for privatization. "With state and local governments desperately short of revenue," he wrote, "the privatization of public services is likely to increase at a faster pace."

Areas of greatest opportunity for small business, Kurlantzick wrote, were drinking-water and wastewater management. "Many cities' water and wastewater systems are in dire straits, with pipes dating back 100 years.... Privatization allows city governments to have a contractor do the upgrade and manage the systems, often for far less, since private firms are given incentive-laden contracts that push them to work more cheaply, says Clay Landry, a principal at WestWater Research LLC, a water economics research firm in Laramie, Wyoming. 'The cities and states are in fiscal crisis, and the Bush administration's answer to them is to look to the private sector to handle services, so we'll see more of this,' Landry says. What's more, as water scarcity increasingly becomes an issue, privatization will become even more attractive, since handing water management to a private firm that can set market-oriented rates helps manage scarcity."

Looming Ahead: Education Education is the largest public employer in the U.S. and enjoys substantial public support. The public does not view education as a consumable commodity, and for this reason it has thus far resisted the pressure to privatize it—although some observers foresee the intrusions of the free market into this realm as well. Governmental responses, thus far, chiefly at the state level, where education is controlled, have been characterized by pressures to reduce costs, shifting the tax burden from property to general taxes, and gradually pushing up tuitions for higher education. The advocacy of voucher systems—which would, in effect, commodify public education by making it more portable—has thus far not won much support. The No Child Left Behind legislation at the federal level represents a pressure for measuring performance, seen by some as a preliminary step towards commercialization. Whether or not this sector will also yield to market forces is as yet difficult to discern. Advocates of making schools compete for students anticipate both reductions in costs and increases in educational achievement. However, all currently available models open for comparison, including very-high-achieving foreign systems, are publicly staffed and administered.

Private Privatization A curious aspect of the private-public debate is that a very large component of private industry, whether measured in dollars or employment, is called "public." These are, of course, the publicly traded corporations operating under the regulatory oversight of the Securities and Exchange Commission. When privately held corporations offer their stock for trade on open markets, they are "going public." When a group of investors buy up a sufficiently large portion of the publicly traded stock (the percentage varies based on state incorporation laws), they can "take the company private" as well—a form of privatization of the private sector. This normally happens as a stage in merger and acquisition activity in order to bring a company under control, transform it in various ways, e.g., by spinning off elements of it, prior to taking it public again. But the process is also becoming popular as a way of shielding corporations from federal oversight by the SEC, thus escaping many costly and administratively onerous reporting and accounting requirements, not least the requirements of the Sarbanes-Oxley Act passed by Congress to curb excesses revealed in the bankruptcy of Enron Corporation.

Privatization is a broad socio-economic phenomenon. As shown above, it can affect public bodies as well as those nominally in the private sector. Periods of privatization are followed by periods of regulation. As the old verse has it, "around and round she goes; and where she stops, nobody knows."

BIBLIOGRAPHY

Arndt, Michael, and Catherine Arndt. "Roads to Revenue." *Business Week.* 17 October 2005.

"Chicago May Privatize Midway." *Airline Industry Information.* 6 March 2006.

Davis, Kirby Lee. "Councilor Urges City of Tulsa to Privatize Golf Courses." *Journal Record.* 29 March 2006.

"Education Vouchers." *School Administrator.* April 2006.

Fung, Amanda. "Techs Seek Privacy; After Languishing as Public Companies, Many Dot-coms Eye Private Buyouts." *Crain's New York Business.* 29 August 2005.

Kurlantzick, Joshua. "Private Partners: Can the privatization trend help your company grow?" *Entrepreneur.* November 2003.

Lyall, Katharine C. and Kathleen R. Sell. *The True Genius of America at Risk.* Praeger Publishers, 2005.

Martin, James and Kames E. Samels. "Colleges, Companies Write a New Learning Chapter." *Boston Business Journal.* 25 May 2001.

Meckler, Laura. "Making Public Highways Private: More state, local governments consider handing toll roads to companies to aid budgets." *The Wall Street Journal Eastern Edition.* 18 April 2006.

Savas, E.S. *Privatization in the City: Successes, Failures, Lessons.* CQ Press, 2005.

Singh, Shruti Date. "Going Private Saves Firm a Cool $1 Million." *Crain's Chicago Business.* 19 September 2005.

Darnay, ECDI

PRO FORMA STATEMENTS

Pro forma, a Latin term meaning "as a matter of form," is applied to the process of presenting financial projections for a specific time period in a standardized format. Businesses use pro forma statements for decision-making in planning and control, and for external reporting to owners, investors, and creditors. Pro forma statements can be used as the basis of comparison and analysis to provide management, investment analysts, and credit officers with a feel for the particular nature of a business's financial structure under various conditions. Both the American Institute of Certified Public Accountants (AICPA) and the Securities and Exchange Commission (SEC) require standard formats for businesses in constructing and presenting pro forma statements; new SEC rules require that, to avoid misrepresentation, companies issuing pro forma statements must also show the most comparable statement on the company's finances, prepared using Generally Accepted Accounting Principles (GAAP), alongside the pro forma statement.

As a vital part of the planning process, pro forma statements can help minimize the risks associated with starting and running a new business. They can also help convince lenders and investors to provide financing for a start-up firm. But pro forma statements must be based upon objective and reliable information in order to create an accurate projection of a small business's profits and financial needs for its first year and beyond. After preparing initial pro forma statements and getting the business off the ground, the small business owner should update the projections monthly and annually.

USES OF PRO FORMA STATEMENTS

Business Planning A company uses pro forma statements in the process of business planning and control. Because pro forma statements are presented in a standardized, columnar format, management employs them to compare and contrast alternative business plans. By arranging the data for the operating and financial statements side-by-side, management analyzes the projected results of competing plans in order to decide which best serves the interests of the business.

In constructing pro forma statements, a company recognizes the uniqueness and distinct financial characteristics of each proposed plan or project. Pro forma statements allow management to:

- Identify the assumptions about the financial and operating characteristics that generate the scenarios.
- Develop the various sales and budget (revenue and expense) projections.

885

- Assemble the results in profit and loss projections.

- Translate these data into cash-flow projections.

- Compare the resulting balance sheets.

- Perform ratio analysis to compare projections against each other and against those of similar companies.

- Review proposed decisions in marketing, production, research and development, etc., and assess their impact on profitability and liquidity.

Simulating competing plans can be quite useful in evaluating the financial effects of the different alternatives under consideration. Based on different sets of assumptions, these plans propose various scenarios of sales, production costs, profitability, and viability. Pro forma statements for each plan provide important information about future expectations, including sales and earnings forecasts, cash flows, balance sheets, proposed capitalization, and income statements.

Management also uses this procedure in choosing among budget alternatives. Planners present sales revenues, production expenses, balance sheet and cash flow statements for competing plans with the underlying assumptions explained. Based on an analysis of these figures, management selects an annual budget. After choosing a course of action, it is common for management to examine variations within the plan.

If management considers a flexible budget most appropriate for its company, it would establish a range of possible outcomes generally categorized as *normal* (expected results), *above normal* (best case), and *below normal* (worst case). Management examines contingency plans for the possible outcomes at input/output levels specified within the operating range. Since these three budgets are projections appearing in a standardized, columnar format and for a specified time period, they are pro forma.

During the course of the fiscal period, management evaluates its performance by comparing actual results to the expectations of the accepted plan using a similar pro forma format. Management's appraisal consists of testing and re-testing the assumptions upon which management based its plans. In this way pro forma statements are indispensable to the control process.

Financial Modeling Pro forma statements provide data for calculating financial ratios and for performing other mathematical calculations. Financial models built on pro forma projections contribute to the achievement of corporate goals if they: 1) test the goals of the plans; 2) furnish findings that are readily understandable; and 3) provide time, quality, and cost advantages over other methods.

Financial modeling tests the assumptions and relationships of proposed plans by studying the impact of variables in the prices of labor, materials, and overhead; cost of goods sold; cost of borrowing money; sales volume; and inventory valuation on the company in question. Computer-assisted modeling has made assumption testing more efficient. The use of powerful processors permits online, real-time decision making through immediate calculations of alternative cash flow statements, balance sheets, and income statements.

Assessing the Impact of Changes A company prepares pro forma financial statements when it expects to experience or has just experienced significant financial changes. The pro forma financial statements present the impact of these changes on the company's financial position as depicted in the income statement, balance sheet, and the cash-flow statement. For example, management might prepare pro forma statements to gauge the effects of a potential merger or joint venture. It also might prepare pro forma statements to evaluate the consequences of refinancing debt through issuance of preferred stock, common stock, or other debt.

External Reporting Businesses also use pro forma statements in external reports prepared for owners (stockholders), creditors, and potential investors. For companies listed on the stock exchanges, the SEC requires pro forma statements with any filing, registration statements, or proxy statements. The SEC and organizations governing accounting practices require companies to prepare pro forma statements when essential changes in the character of a business's financial statements have occurred or will occur. Financial statements may change because of:

- Changes in accounting principles due to adoption of a generally accepted accounting principle different from one used previously for financial accounting.

- A change in accounting estimates dealing with the estimated economic life and net residual value of assets.

- A change in the business entity resulting from the acquisition or disposition of an asset or investment, and/or the pooling of interests of two or more existing businesses.

- A correction of an error made in a report or filing of a previous period.

Management's decision to change accounting principles may be based on the issuance of a new accounting principle by the Financial Accounting Standards Board (FASB); internal considerations taking advantage of revised valuations or tax codes; or the accounting needs of a new business combination. By changing its accounting practices, a business might significantly affect the presentation of its financial position and the results of its operations. The change also might distort the earnings trend reported in the income statements for earlier years. Some examples of changes in accounting principles might include valuation of inventory via a first-in, first-out (FIFO) method or a last-in, first-out method (LIFO), or recording of depreciation via a straight-line method or an accelerated method.

When a company changes an accounting method, it uses pro forma financial statements to report the cumulative effect of the change for the period during which the change occurred. To enable comparison of the pro forma financial statements with previous financial statements, the company would present the financial statements for prior periods as originally reported, show the cumulative effect of the change on net income and retained earnings, and show net income on a pro forma basis as if the newly adopted accounting principle had been used in prior periods.

A change in accounting estimates may be required as new events occur and as better information becomes available about the probable outcome of future events. For example, an increase in the percentage used to estimate doubtful accounts, a major write-down of inventories, a change in the economic lives of plant assets, and a revision in the estimated liability for outstanding product warranties would require pro forma statements.

THE SEC FORMAT

The SEC prescribes the form and content of pro forma statements for companies subject to its jurisdiction in circumstances such as the above. Some of the form and content requirements are:

1. An introductory paragraph describing the proposed transaction, the entities involved, the periods covered by the pro forma information, and what the pro forma information shows.

2. A pro forma condensed balance sheet and a pro forma condensed income statement, in columnar form, showing the condensed historical amounts, the pro forma adjustments, and the pro forma amounts. Footnotes provide justification for the pro forma adjustments and explain other details pertinent to the changes.

3. The pro forma adjustments, directly attributable to the proposed change or transaction, which are expected to have a continuing impact on the financial statements. Explanatory notes provide the factual basis for adjustments.

With the passage of the Sarbanes-Oxley Act of 2002, modifying accounting and disclosure statements, the SEC has begun issuing new requirements related to pro forma statements. Most specifically, the SEC has found that pro forma statements, which are not required to follow Generally Accepted Accounting Principles (GAAP), may give a false impression of the company's actual financial status. For this reason, SEC requires that all pro forma statements be accompanied with forms that *do* conform to GAAP, the company required to select those versions of formal statements most closely resembling the pro forma.

Pro Forma Statements for Changes in Entity and for Business Combinations The FASB, the AICPA, and the SEC have provided significant directives to the form, content, and necessity of pro forma financial statements in situations where there has been a change in the form of a business entity. Such a change in form may occur due to changes in financial structure resulting from the disposition of a long-term liability or asset, or due to a combination of two or more businesses.

The purpose of pro forma financial statements is to facilitate comparisons of historic data and projections of future performance. In these circumstances users of financial statements need to evaluate a new or proposed business entity on a basis comparable to the predecessor business in order to understand the impact of the change on cash flow, income, and financial position. *Pro forma adjustments* to accounting principles and accounting estimates reformat the statements of the new entity and the acquired business to conform with those of the predecessor.

Occasionally, a partnership or sole proprietorship will sell all or part of the business interest. Sometimes it is necessary, especially if the business is "going public," to reorganize into a corporation. The financial statements of a corporation with a very short history are not helpful in a thoughtful analysis of future potential. Similarly, because of the differences in federal income tax liabilities, a restatement of the predecessor business in historical terms only confuses the picture. Since the financial statements of the predecessor business do not contain some of the expense items applicable to a corporation, the pro forma financial statements make adjustments to restate certain expenses on a corporate basis. In particular these would include:

- Stating the owners' salaries in terms of officers' salaries.

- Calculating the applicable federal taxes on the predecessor business as though it were a corporation.

- Including corporate state franchise taxes.

- Adding the balance of the partners' capital to contributed capital in the combined company rather than to retained earnings for partnerships acquired through the pooling of interests.

Subchapter S corporations exercise the tax-option of the shareholders to individually assume the tax liability rather than have it assumed by the corporation as a whole. If the shareholders choose to go public or change their qualifications, the corporation loses the tax-option. Therefore, in addition to the pro forma statement showing historical earnings, the new company will make pro forma provision for the taxes that it would have paid had it been a regular corporation in the past. When acquisition of a Subchapter S corporation is accomplished through the pooling of interests, the pro forma financial statement may not include any of the retained earnings of the Subchapter S corporation in the pooled retained earnings.

When presenting the historical operations of a business previously operated as a partnership, the financial information is adjusted to bring the statement in line with the acquiring corporation. Historical data listed in these instances includes net sales; cost of sales; gross profit on sales; selling, general, and administrative expenses; other income; other deductions; and income before taxes on income. Pro forma adjustments would restate partnership operations on a corporate basis, including estimated partnership salaries as officers and estimated federal and state taxes on income, as well as pro forma net income and pro forma net income per share. Accountants make similar adjustments to pro forma statements for businesses previously operated as sole proprietorships and Subchapter S corporations.

Acquisition or Disposal of Part of a Business For a company that decided to acquire part of a new business or dispose of part of its existing business, a meaningful pro forma statement should adjust the historical figures to demonstrate how the acquired part would have fared had it been a corporation. Pro forma statements should also set forth conventional financial statements of the acquiring company, and pro forma financial statements of the business to be acquired. Notes to the pro forma statements explain the adjustments reflected in the statements.

A pro forma income statement combines the historical income statement of the acquiring company and a pro forma income statement of the business to be acquired for the previous five years, if possible. Pro forma adjustments exclude overhead costs not applicable to the new business entity, such as division and head office expenses.

The purchase of a sole proprietorship, partnership, Sub-Chapter S corporation, or business segment requires pro forma statements for a series of years in order to reflect adjustments for such items as owners' or partners' salaries and income taxes. In this way, each year reflects the results of operations of a business organization comparable with that of the acquiring corporation. However, the pro forma statements giving effect to the business combination should be limited to the current and immediately preceding periods.

SUMMARY

Pro forma statements are an integral part of business planning and control. Managers use them in the decision-making process when constructing an annual budget, developing long-range plans, and choosing among capital expenditures. Pro forma statements are also valuable in external reporting. Public accounting firms find pro forma statements indispensable in assisting users of financial statements in understanding the impact on the financial structure of a business due to changes in the business entity, or in accounting principles or accounting estimates.

Although pro forma statements have a wide variety of applications for ongoing, mature businesses, they are also important for small businesses and start-up firms, which often lack the track record required for preparing conventional financial statements. As a planning tool, pro forma statements help small business owners minimize the risks associated with starting and running a new business. The data contained in pro forma statements can also help convince lenders and investors to provide financing for a start-up firm.

BIBLIOGRAPHY

Bygrave, William D., and Andrew Zacharakis. *The Portable MBA in Entrepreneurship.* John Wiley & Sons, 2004.

Pinson, Linda. *Keeping the Books: Basic Record Keeping and Accounting for the Successful Small Business.* Dearborn Trade Publishing, 2004.

Ruland, William, and Ping Zhou. "Pro Forma Financial Statements for Loan Evaluation." *Commercial Lending Review.* July 2004.

Smith, Richard L., and Janet Kilholm Smith. *Entrepreneurial Finance.* John Wiley, 2000.

U.S. Securities and Exchange Commission. "Proposed Rule: Conditions for Use of Non-GAAP Financial Measures." 17 CFR Parts 228, 229, 244 and 249. Available from http://www.sec.gov/rules/proposed/33-8145.htm. Retrieved on 9 May 2006.

Hillstrom, Northern Lights
updated by Magee, ECDI

PROBATIONARY EMPLOYMENT PERIODS

When hiring new employees, many employers use probationary employment periods to ascertain whether the new workers will be able to handle the duties and challenges associated with their new job. Such periods are intended to provide employers time to evaluate employees before making the job permanent.

Many consultants to small business owners believe that probationary employment periods—also sometimes known as trial periods—can be quite useful to both entrepreneurs hoping to get a start-up off the ground and established small business owners seeking to maintain or increase their current level of success. As countless small business owners and researchers will attest, the quality of a small company's work force can mean the difference between business success and failure. Indeed, personnel costs (wages, benefits, training, etc.) are among the most expensive elements of business operations; this cost becomes multiplied if your business is saddled with a poor worker. Probationary periods, which can range from two weeks to ninety days in length, are simply meant to give the small business owner the best possible chance of securing and retaining quality employees—and releasing substandard employees without legal penalty.

Analysts do note, however, that companies that terminate probationary employees do not enjoy total protection from lawsuits. These terminated employees do have fewer legal rights than established workers, but they are not without recourse in certain situations. For example, the employment "at-will" doctrine that characterizes probationary periods is not a valid legal defense for employers if it can be proven that the work arrangement suggested that termination would only be made for cause. Business owners should consult with an attorney to minimize their exposure in this regard.

ELEMENTS OF AN EFFECTIVE PROBATIONARY PERIOD

Business experts state that small business owners should take the following steps when implementing a probationary period with a new hire:

- Make sure that the specifics of the probationary period (length of probation, for instance) are explicitly stated in company guidelines.

- Make certain that the new employee is aware that he or she will be "on probation" for the specified period.

- Monitor how well the new employee executes assigned tasks, using quantitative measurements whenever possible.

- Monitor the new employee's work habits; for example, a new worker who is consistently tardy in arriving at work or returning from lunch may well be a cause for concern.

- Monitor how well the new employee gets along with supervisors/managers.

- Monitor how well the new employee gets along with fellow staff.

- Determine whether the new hire is a "self-starter," or one who needs continued guidance.

- Provide the new hire with feedback that will help him or her shape performance to business expectations; this will not only improve the likelihood of securing a good worker, but also provide the employer with possible legal protection in the event of an unfair dismissal legal action (documentation indicating a pattern of poor performance carries significant legal weight).

Of course, not every employee will be a superior one, and shortcomings in one (or even more) of the above areas does not necessarily mean that the employee should be let go. Factors such as availability of other workers, performance in critical areas, etc., usually have to be considered, and few companies are fortunate enough to be staffed entirely by workers of superior skills, excellent work habits, and healthy ambition.

But analysts indicate that new employees who perform poorly during probationary periods are rarely able to dramatically improve their performance after the trial period has ended. After all, if the worker did a bad job during a probationary period, when all parties were aware that performance would be monitored, why should the small business owner believe that the worker's performance would improve at the conclusion of that trial period, when pressure to "be on one's best behavior" would presumably be relieved somewhat. Ultimately, each business owner has to decide for him or herself whether the employee's performance during the trial period warrants continued employment.

BIBLIOGRAPHY

Cann, Steven J. *Administrative Law.* Sage Publications, 2002.

Covington, Robert, and Kurt H. Decker. *Employment Law in a Nutshell.* West Group Publishing, 2002.

Moye, John E. *The Law of Business Organizations.* Thomson Delmar Learning, 2005.

"Trial Periods: What's your probation period for new employees?" *Remodeling.* March 2005.

Hillstrom, Northern Lights
updated by Magee, ECDI

PRODUCT COSTING

Product costing is a methodology associated with managerial accounting, i.e., accounting intended to serve management in an operational context rather than to measure corporate performance as such, although, of course, any kind of cost accounting, including product costing, contributes to overall results. More specifically product costing is intended accurately to determine the cost of a unit of production (or of a service delivered) by study of every resource used in its creation. The activity is only in part motivated by obtaining an accurate final cost that incorporates all contributing streams. In part it is a way of identifying cost components that can be addressed specifically in order to take cost out of the product by purchasing, redesign, reengineering, retooling, packaging, and other interventions by management at whatever stage.

Product costing evolved in an environment of mass production in the second half of the 20th century as ever more managerial attention was focused on optimizing the production function. Traditional financial accounting approaches have been—and continue to be—based on measurements of fairly rough granularity. For determining corporate profitability, it is sufficient generally to track raw materials, labor, tooling, and energy inputs and to sum these into production costs. Pricing of different products, of course, necessitated finer distinctions so that costs associated with classes of products would be available as a basis for differential pricing. Closer attention to the costs of, for instance, low-, medium-, and high-end models of a vehicle or a device then proliferated "downward." The costing of composite products required costing of their components. In turn operations on each component might vary. Some might require more or less strength and hence heavier forgings; these in turn might need more or less additional machining. Some components could be attached mechanically, others had to be welded. These operations could be measured in time, time in dollars. A systematic analysis of how a product came to be, the inputs costed as received and then the operations performed on them individually estimated, produced the final cost of production from which receipts from sale of scrap would be deducted to get a net cost. Product costing evolved further from this point by assigning an appropriate percentage of total overhead and also measuring additional costs upstream—such as packaging, warehousing, and delivery to the ultimate buyer.

The analytical resources made available by such detailed information have made product costing a routine aspect of most significantly-sized manufacturing operations. Product costing data act as feedback to designers, are used in manufacturing management to identify ideal workflow, influence the purchase of tooling, and are used in precise pricing of goods. Product costing is used in most routine production activities, including service occupations, although the level of detail sought is variable and usually determined by the size of the operation. Even in quite small businesses, some level of product costing is practiced in that managements usually know the costs associated with important functions identified with different products.

In recent years product costing has given rise to Activity Based Costing (ABC). The subject is covered in more detail elsewhere in this volume. ABC is based on the notion that costs arise in various *activities*. The concept is well-summarized by John Stark Associates, a management consulting group, as follows: "The Activity Based Costing paradigm is based on the principle that it is not the products that a company produces that generate costs, but rather the activities that are performed in planning, procuring and producing the products. It is the resources that are necessary to support the activities performed during the course of business that result in costs being incurred. Product costs should therefore be calculated by determining the extent to which each product makes use of the activities being performed. Products 'consume' activities and activities 'consume' costs." ABC may be a more refined method for precisely capturing inputs that, in many operations, are associated with overhead functions, such as engineering and design.

PROBLEMS OF MEASUREMENT

In product costing much emphasis is placed on capturing *all* costs, even those that do not immediately spring to mind, one of the reasons why ABC is growing in popularity: it begins with activities and thus by definition encompasses all of a corporation's many involvements. In the production process, measurement is relatively easy even if complex. A complexity arises, for instance, in assigning the capital costs of equipment to individual products that pass through it—and including the costs of cooling liquids and lubricants used in machining. But raw materials purchasing, for instance, including the costs of developing good relations with suppliers, is difficult to measure in relation to individual products. Warranty service is yet another area that does not immediately spring to mind: it is typically handled long after a sale is completed.

Just how detailed product costing should be will naturally arise in the course of operations—motivated by the types of analysis a business requires to solve its problems or to adjust its pricing. Very detailed product costing has a cost of its own—the justification for which will be the use to which such data are put.

PRODUCT COSTING IN SERVICE OPERATIONS

The "product" of a sales consultancy may be a printed report to a client accompanied by a Microsoft Power-Point presentation at the client's headquarters. Here the real cost of the product will have little relationship to the costs of the tangible "deliverables." The business is actually selling information and judgments acquired by interviews, focus groups, data searches, reading, analysis, discussions, and consultations some of which may have required extensive travel. In another operation, engaged in evaluating sites for the presence of hazardous waste dumped in the past, the deliverables may again be a report, but the work may have required extensive groundwater sampling based on geological maps of the site and extensive searches of old real estate transactions. In yet a third operation, specializing in carpet cleaning operations, the product is a visit in the course of which equipment is used and labor applied.

In most such situations, product costing takes place in advance of all work actually accomplished. And, typically, good estimating is the difference between turning a profit or booking a loss. But the principles that apply are identical. Both in the services and in the manufacturing environments, accurate costing (hence pricing) will depend on subdividing the work carefully into its many categories, measuring time and purchased materials and services. As in manufacturing some products are rejected for faults, so in service work there is wasted time, false starts, and other experiential factors that must be factored in. In both cases, overhead must be known accurately and applied in proportion to the value of the service bid and supplied.

The chief difference is that service activities almost never repeat exactly. Therefore discoveries made in comparing estimates to actual costs can rarely be applied to future jobs with the same precision and expectation of exact results.

When all is said and done, the message conveyed by product costing translates into the sage words routinely murmured by the skilled carpenter: "Measure twice, cut once."

SEE ALSO *Activity-Based Costing; Overhead Costs*

BIBLIOGRAPHY

"A Few Words About Activity Based Costing." John Stark Associates. Available from http://www.johnstark.com/fwabc.html. Retrieved on 9 May 2006.

Baxendale, Sidney J. "Activity-based Costing for the Small Business: A Primer." *Business Horizons.* January 2001.

Hansen, Don R. *Management Accounting.* Thomson South-Western, 2005.

Jackson, Steve, Roby Sawyers, and Greg Jenkins. *Managerial Accounting: A Focus on Decision Making.* Thomson South-Western, 2006.

Smith, Richard L., and Janet Kilholm Smith. *Entrepreneurial Finance.* John Wiley, 2000.

Darnay, ECDI

PRODUCT DEVELOPMENT

Product development may be understood generically as all the things that happen from the initial conception or invention of a product to the point when a product is launched into the market. It can also be understood as a method, a discipline, and a formal process followed by a company as it does the same thing. In the modern business literature, the authors typically mean the latter, a "corporate process," and they are typically talking about the undertakings of large corporations in which equally massive teams are involved. As a formalized process with distinct aspects, product development can be disassembled for analysis, discussion, and comment. In actual experience, and especially in the small business environment, product development tends to be many other things; the process is likely to be more creative and hence also chaotic; the activity may be carried by a single individual or a small team. Small businesses rarely have new product managers or departments, and this activity is closer to invention than to engineering and more likely to be led by a charismatic figure—Thomas Edison comes to mind in technical invention or Gabrielle "Coco" Chanel in fashion design.

CONTEXT AND HISTORY

Product development is closely tied to creativity, invention, and insight—and follows the flash of an idea. Thus what we nowadays call a knife was the consequence of some prehistoric human's insight that a flat stone with one sharp edge could cut: the rest was product development.

According to Michael McGrath (in *Next Generation Product Development*) conscious focus on the *development* process began late in the 19th century. McGrath divides the time since then into "generations" of product development emphasis. In the first, ending in the 1950s, the focus was on commercialization of inventions; in the second, formalization of product development as a process began, and this emphasis lasted until the 1980s. In the third "generation" of product development, corporate management focused on getting product to market faster.

In the 21st century, according to McGrath, emphasis had shifted to R&D-based development.

McGrath, of course, was talking about trends and emphases as taking place in big-corporation culture and as illustrated by waves of products reaching the market—the vast majority of which were modified or adapted products rather than radical inventions. But the most dramatic and revolutionary product introduction of the latter-half of the 20th century did not obey the rules. It was the personal computer, slapped together by an inspired technical man, Steve Wozniak, and sold by a visionary entrepreneur, Steve Jobs. The product was the Apple computer, and the product development process consisted of the two Steves agonizing together in a garage. They didn't even intend to sell computers—just mother boards. They "evolved" the product by trial and error.

The many other inventions that burst on the market as the U.S. and then the world embraced small computers again illustrated (if proof was needed) the unruly nature of the creative process. It cannot be reduced to a recipe, algorithm, or bureaucratic procedure. All types of approaches to product development continue to exist side-by-side. As in gambling, no "system" guarantees success.

BASIC ELEMENTS

Product development is an iterative fusion of different disciplines in order to meet a specific goal. The disciplines are design, engineering, manufacturing, distribution, market positioning, marketing, distribution, and sales. A company developing a product must envision every stage of the process from the final perspective, that of the ultimate buyer, backward, and then from the design forward. Thus the process can readily become repetitive.

For example, initial estimates are made using prototypes; the prototypes are used to envision manufacturing processes and to establish a price range based on estimated production cost. But exposure of the prototypes to customers may elicit suggestions for improvement and negative reactions to features; sometimes suggestions come from dealers or retailers. Market research will often unearth reactions to competing products—or even their unsuspected presence. After this early exposure, flaws must be removed, advantages exploited, competitive challenges met. Redesign, reengineering, and new production estimates may be required. Iteration can also come later as problems are encountered. Some element of the product may be too costly to produce and the problem can only be overcome by changing the product. If the change is substantial enough, talking to customers becomes necessary again.

How much iteration is sensible? The answer depends on the ultimate size of the market and the projected product life. The resources of the company are also an issue. Most small businesses can only afford limited market research. The natural substitute is to consult the intuitive reactions of family and friends—in effect to use a much smaller sample than a global company would.

Product development is typically led by a product manager assisted by a small team representing basic specialties: engineering, manufacturing, marketing, and finance. It is the responsibility of the team to interact effectively with their counterpart in the company in order to obtain services, estimates, and feedback.

PLANNING VERSUS CREATIVITY

In product development, there tends to be a see-saw movement between formality and process and openness and innovation. This is illustrated by comments from two books on the subject. The first comes from a book by Edward K. Bower entitled *Specification-Driven Product Development*. Bower said: "Small companies typically conduct their development programs in an informal, hit-or-miss fashion, intuitively managing the process on a day-by-day basis. After agreement has been reached on the general nature of the desired new product, its design begins. The detailed features of the product evolve as side effects of implementation decisions. As market considerations are discovered, changes are made to the product's goals, leading to redesign. This unpredictable process leads to schedule and budget overruns, and produces products whose structure wasn't coherently planned, but evolved as requirements changed."

The second comments come from David M. Anderson's book, *Design for Manufacturability & Concurrent Engineering*. Anderson wrote: "For creative product development, start with a creative, open-minded, receptive team that is stimulated by the challenge. The team should be diverse in knowledge as well as cultural and thinking styles. The team should be fired up.... Creativity is enhanced when people *really want* to invent something.... Do *not* start creative product development discussing administrative issues.... This will immediately stifle creativity and shift attention to meeting deadlines and budgets."

The two quotes, although seemingly emphasizing opposite tendencies, actually both quite accurately highlight important aspects of product development. It requires the right mix of disciplined implementation and yet adaptive openness. Existing systems must be used to create a new product. This must happen as rapidly and as inexpensively as possible. Concentrated attention to process and detail and openness to possibilities are both necessary for success.

NEW PRODUCT DEVELOPMENT FOR SMALL COMPANIES

As business experts, analysts, executives, and entrepreneurs all know, there is no one way to organize a company for effective new product development. Nonetheless, analysts point to several factors fairly universal in determining whether a business will enjoy measurable success in new product development efforts. These include comprehensive market and cost analysis, top management commitment, enthusiasm among workers, clear lines of authority, and past experience. Concentration, funding, and leadership are key legs that hold up the structure.

Concentration. First, a small business needs to focus on its goals. Limited time and resources mean that hard decisions must be made and a strategic plan needs to be developed. Companies should "do the right things right" by using the best information available to choose the right technologies and decide on what new products to invest in. Growing companies are easily tempted to do too many things at once and finish none. Companies needing diversification are tempted to repeat the customary and therefore never establish that "second front" they need. Concentration on the goal will help keep the focus clearly on a well-thought out plan.

Funding. Another key to new product development for small businesses is to secure the resources and skills needed to create and market the new product. Small companies may lack the in-house resources needed to create a new product, making it seem out of reach, but analysts note that small business owners have other avenues that they can often pursue. If the product idea is good enough, the company may decide to look outside its own walls for partnership and outsourcing opportunities. Sometimes "funding" takes the form of assigning a highly talented person who knows the company well to the "new venture" though he or she will be sorely missed in his or her leadership position.

Leadership. The third and final pillar for building new products is to find the leadership needed to bring a new product from the idea stage to completed product. This leader will often take the form of a "product champion" who can bring both expertise and enthusiasm to the project. (In small business environments, this product champion will often be the entrepreneur/owner himself.) A strong product champion will be able to balance all the issues associated with a product—economic factors, performance requirements, regulatory issues, management issues, and more—and create a winning new product.

The product champion has to guide the project through a predetermined series of viability tests—checkpoints in the development process at which a company evaluates a new product to determine if the product should proceed to the next development stage. If it is determined that the market has shifted, or technology has changed, or the project has become too expensive, then the product must be killed, no matter how much money has already been poured into it. This is where a strong product champion makes the difference—he or she has to have the honesty and authority to make the call to kill the product and convey the reasons for that decision to the product development team. If goals were clearly defined, resources properly allocated, and leadership was strong, then the decision to kill a project should not be a difficult one.

LAUNCHING A NEW PRODUCT

Once the product-line architecture has been established and a new product is being developed, it is time for a company to think about how to successfully launch the product in its target market. This is the stage where an advertising or public relations agency can come into play, especially for small businesses without the internal resources to handle such a job themselves. When using an outside agency to launch a product, a company should:

- Have a well-defined product concept (which is where product-line architecture comes into play).

- Provide the agency with background information on its products and goals.

- Conduct necessary patent research, applying for new patents as needed.

- Have the manufacturing process in place and ready to go, either internally or via outsourcing.

- Have a formal business plan in place that defines funding of the project.

- Determine who will approve the marketing or advertising plan that the agency creates (the fewer people communicating with the agency, the better).

- Determine the proper timing for the launch.

SPEED-TO-MARKET AND PRODUCT DEVELOPMENT

In today's technology-fueled business environment, the always-important speed-to-market factor has become perhaps the most critical factor in new product development. Today, however, speed-to-market is perhaps the most crucial part of product development. Improved communication (especially the Internet), increased globalization, and rapid changes in technology have put tremendous pressure on companies to get their product to market first. To improve speed-to-market, a company should first make sure that it is making the best possible use of available technology. If it is, then there are other steps that can be taken to speed product development through efficient, market-oriented product planning that takes the customer into account:

SERVICE COMPANIES AND NEW PRODUCTS

Service companies should take a disciplined, analytical approach to developing new services, relying on targeted customer input just as companies outside the service sector do. Companies in the service industry know that they are competing for customers based on perceived value as much as actual price. If a customer feels he or she is getting better treatment, or more service options, or more "free" services as part of his or her purchase, he or she is more likely to remain a client of that company. If, however, a company stops innovating and adding new services to its core business, then the service becomes a commodity and clients look at only one thing—price—when deciding on what company to choose.

Service companies should routinely ask themselves a series of questions:

- Could current services be presented in a different way?

- Could they be offered to new customer groups?

- Are there little things that can be tweaked to freshen or update a service?

- Could services be improved or changed?

Because by their very nature services are easy to copy (no materials or product knowledge is needed), service companies actually face more pressure to innovate and develop new products than manufacturers. By continually asking the above questions and by following the same models manufacturing companies follow when pursuing product development, service companies can stay ahead of their competitors and make their services clearly identifiable to consumers.

PITFALLS TO PRODUCT DEVELOPMENT

Finally, when embarking on the product development process, try to remember in advance what the obstacles to success are. These pitfalls are many and varied, and can include:

- Inadequate market analysis.

- Inadequate cost analysis.

- Strong competitor reaction.

- Undue infatuation with your company's own technology and expertise.

- Overreaching to make products beyond your company's financial and knowledge grasp.

- Technical staff too attached to a project and too proud to admit defeat, even when a project can not be justified according to pre-established criteria.

- Problems with patent, license, or copyright issues.

- No real criteria for deciding if a project is good or bad.

- Changes in strategy at the corporate level are not conveyed to the product development team.

- Low product awareness.

- Money and staff allocated to a project are hidden in the budget of another project.

- Company decision-makers blinded by the charisma or charm of the person presenting the new product idea.

- Project accepted on the basis of who gets it first.

SEE ALSO *Prototypes*

BIBLIOGRAPHY

Anderson, David M. *Design for Manufacturability & Concurrent Engineering.* CIM Press, 2004.

Bower, Edward K. *Specification-Driven Product Development.* iUniverse, 2003.

Brandt, John R. "Our New-Product Plan: Keep Out: Involving customers and others is a pain. So is worrying about manufacturability and marketing." *Industry Week.* January 2006.

Kanellos, Michael. "The 64-bit Question: Why is no one buying?" *Computer Shopper.* May 2006.

McGrath, Michael. *Next Generation Product Development.* McGraw-Hill, 2004.

Teresko, John. "New Products Faster." *Industry Week.* January 2004.

"Who's Who: The Eco-Guide." *Time.* Summer 2006.

"The World's Most Innovative Companies: Their creativity goes beyond products to rewiring themselves." *Business Week.* 24 April 2006.

Hillstrom, Northern Lights
updated by Magee, ECDI

PRODUCT LIABILITY

Product liability comprises a number of laws and court rulings that apply to any business that makes or sells a product. Businesses that make or sell products are responsible for ensuring that those products are safe and do not pose a hazard to the public. Such businesses can be held liable for any damage or harm their products might cause.

According to Section 102(2) of the Uniform Product Liability Act, product liability includes "all claims or action brought for personal injury, death, or property damage caused by the manufacture, design, formula, preparation, assembly, installation, testing, warnings, instructions, marketing, packaging, or labeling of any product." Product liability issues have become increasingly important to manufacturers and marketing managers, due to the spread of the doctrine of strict liability and the adoption of new theories that permit recovery in so-called "delayed manifestation" cases.

Because of their limited resources, small businesses must be particularly aware of their responsibilities under product liability laws. In addition to making safe products, this responsibility extends to prominently displaying warnings of any potential hazards on products and packaging. Experts recommend that small business owners consult with legal counsel experienced in the product liability field. An attorney can help the small business owner sift through the numerous federal and state laws that apply to different types of products. Small businesses are also encouraged to purchase product liability insurance. Unfortunately, the increasing number of lawsuits and large damage awards in this area have made such insurance very expensive and reduced the amount of coverage available. In fact, the expense of insuring against product liability has prevented small manufacturers from competing in certain product areas.

DEVELOPMENT OF PRODUCT LIABILITY LAWS

Product liability began to have meaning in the mid-1800s, when the American courts increasingly found that sellers of goods had a "duty" to use reasonable care in the production of those goods. Sellers were held liable to third parties for negligence in the manufacture or sale of goods "inherently dangerous" (the danger of injury arises from the product itself, rather than from a defect in the product) to human safety, ranging from food and beverages to drugs, firearms, and explosives. In the early 1960s, tort principles were first applied to product liability. During this time, the concept of "inherently dangerous" goods was still held to be significant, but there was a shift to negligence (tort) principles that held that producers of goods were required to apply "due care" in the marketing of goods to users.

Since that time, businesses have operated under an understanding that because they knowingly market products which affect the interests of consumers, they owe a legal duty of caution and prudence to consumers. Since manufacturers may foresee potentially harmful product effects, they are responsible for attempting to minimize harm. Establishing this legal duty between the manufacturer and the consumer made it possible for plaintiffs to argue the negligent breach of that duty. These principles are now accepted throughout the country and followed by all American courts. Eventually, the concept of "inherently dangerous" products fell into disuse and the concept of negligence was expanded beyond production to include labeling, installation, inspection, and design.

Relief for Small Business? From time to time Congress has attempted to pass legislation to protect small business from heavy exposure to product liability suits and to ease their costs of product liability insurance. The most recent such attempt was The Small Business Liability Reform Act of 2001 sponsored by Representatives Asa Hutchinson (R-AR) and Tim Holden (D-PA) and Senators Mitch McConnel (R-KY) and Joseph Lieberman (D-CT). As reported by *Refrigerated Transporter* magazine, the legislation sought "to limit punitive damages against small business, to ensure that small business owners are only held liable for damages in proportion to their actual fault, and to reform the current product liability system to improve protection of companies that sell or lease products, but do not manufacture them." The legislation had not passed as of Spring 2006. Earlier attempts in this direction were the Product Liability Fairness Act of 1991 and the Product Liability Reform Act of 1998. No changes, however, have been enacted.

ELEMENTS OF PRODUCT LIABILITY

Four elements must be present for a product liability case to be considered under the negligent tort principles:

- The particular defendant owes a duty to the particular plaintiff to act as a reasonably prudent person under the same or similar circumstances.

- There is a breach of such a duty by the defendant— that is, a failure to act reasonably.

- There is an injury, including personal injury or property damage.

- There is a causal link between defendant's breach of duty and injuries sustained by the plaintiff.

The concept of negligence is applicable to every activity preceding a product's availability in the market. This encompasses everything from product design, the inspection and testing of materials, and the manufacture and assembly of the product to the packaging, the accompanying instructions and warnings, and the inspection and testing of the final product are all susceptible to negligence. Negligence can result from omission as well as commission—failure to discover a flaw is as negligent as creating one. Similarly, failing to provide adequate warnings about potential dangers in the use of a product is a violation of duty.

Still, it is often difficult to prove negligence in product liability cases. Defendants only must meet the general standards of reasonable behavior as judged against the behavior of a reasonably careful competitor who demonstrates the standard skills and expertise of the industry. In reality, a manufacturer must only show that "ordinary care under the circumstances" was applied to avoid liability for negligence. This is easy compared to the task of consumers showing evidence to the contrary.

Many products, even the most ordinary, pose some level of risk, and the law recognizes that it is often not possible to design a totally safe product. However, manufacturers are legally obligated to warn consumers about known dangers. Manufacturers may be found negligent if:

- They fail to warn users about recognized risk
- The warning is too vague to be adequate
- The warning is not brought to the user's attention

There is no duty to warn against misuse that is so rare or unusual that it cannot be foreseen. The obligation to warn consumers of potential dangers poses a unique difficulty for manufacturers who must not only provide warnings, but must communicate them such that a reasonable person will find and understand them. In some cases a warning buried in a product's instructions may be judged inadequate; in other situations, a warning sticker on the product itself may be considered sufficient.

STRICT PRODUCT LIABILITY

The most recent evolution in tort law, strict liability, has transformed the very nature of product liability because it eliminates the entire question of negligence. Strict liability only requires a plaintiff to demonstrate that a product caused an injury because it was defective; the reason for the defect is irrelevant. The product itself, not the defendant's use, is under investigation.

Under strict liability, the manufacturer is held liable for allowing a defective product to enter the marketplace. The issue is a matter of public policy, not the manufacturer's unreasonable or negligent conduct. The introduction of a defective product into the marketplace brings each member of the product's distribution channel into liability for negligence. The theory of strict liability holds that manufacturers: have the greatest control over the quality of their products; can distribute their costs by raising prices; and have special responsibilities in their role as sellers.

The tort of negligence at least provided the responsible person a standard by which to measure negligence, although it imposed the added burden of proving that the defendant was negligent. Although strict liability eases those burdens for the plaintiff and improves chances of recovery, it does not provide a universally accepted standard for measuring failure. Instead, it relies on what has become known as the "consumer-expectation" test: one who sells any product in a defective condition unreasonably dangerous to the user is subject to liability for physical harm caused to the user if: 1) the seller is engaged in the business of selling such a product, and 2) the product is expected to and does reach the user without substantial change in the condition in which it is used. "Unreasonably dangerous" is defined as dangerous beyond the expectations of the ordinary consumer who purchases it. Despite its great influence, this definition has not been universally accepted.

Tort law does recognize that some products beneficial to society cannot be made entirely safe. Prescription drugs and vaccines are notorious examples. Such products are not considered defective simply because of their inevitable hazards; something else must be wrong with them as well. Therefore, drug companies are not held strictly liable for a properly manufactured product accompanied by appropriate directions and warnings. In sum, design defects are not the same as manufacturing defects.

One defense manufacturers have employed with controversy is called "state of the art." This means that manufacturers should be held accountable only for information available to them at the time of manufacture. Flaws or defects which arose due to unavailable knowledge are not considered in questions of liability. The problem interpreting this defense concerns the variation of knowledge and its applications across the country.

BIBLIOGRAPHY

"APSA Supports Liability Reform Legislation." *Refrigerated Transporter.* 1 July 2001.

Greenberg, Lisa. "Federal—Punitive Damages." *Automotive Body Repair News.* August 2001.

Hart, Christine, and Mark Kinzie. *Product Liability for the Professional.* Thomson Leaning, 2002.

Miller, Roger LeRoy, and Gaylord A. Jentz. *Fundamentals of Business Law.* Thomson South-Western, 2005.

Hillstrom, Northern Lights
updated by Magee, ECDI

PRODUCT LIFE CYCLE

The theory of a product life cycle was first introduced in the 1950s to explain the expected life cycle of a typical product from design to obsolescence, a period divided into the phases of product introduction, product growth, maturity, and decline. The goal of managing a product's life cycle is to maximize its value and profitability at each stage. Life cycle is primarily associated with marketing theory.

INTRODUCTION

This is the stage where a product is conceptualized and first brought to market. The goal of any new product introduction is to meet consumers' needs with a quality product at the lowest possible cost in order to return the highest level of profit. The introduction of a new product can be broken down into five distinct parts:

- Idea validation, which is when a company studies a market, looks for areas where needs are not being met by current products, and tries to think of new products that could meet that need. The company's marketing department is responsible for identifying market opportunities and defining who will buy the product, what the primary benefits of the product will be, and how the product will be used.

- Conceptual design occurs when an idea has been approved and begins to take shape. The company has studied available materials, technology, and manufacturing capability and determined that the new product can be created. Once that is done, more thorough specifications are developed, including price and style. Marketing is responsible for minimum and maximum sales estimates, competition review, and market share estimates.

- Specification and design is when the product is nearing release. Final design questions are answered and final product specs are determined so that a prototype can be created.

- Prototype and testing occur when the first version of a product is created and tested by engineers and by customers. A pilot production run might be made to ensure that engineering decisions made earlier in the process were correct, and to establish quality control. The marketing department is extremely important at this point. It is responsible for developing packaging for the product, conducting the consumer tests through focus groups and other feedback methods, and tracking customer responses to the product.

- Manufacturing ramp-up is the final stage of new product introduction. This is also known as commercialization. This is when the product goes into full production for release to the market. Final checks are made on product reliability and variability.

In the introduction phase, sales may be slow as the company builds awareness of its product among potential customers. Advertising is crucial at this stage, so the marketing budget is often substantial. The type of advertising depends on the product. If the product is intended to reach a mass audience, than an advertising campaign built around one theme may be in order. If a product is specialized, or if a company's resources are limited, then smaller advertising campaigns can be used that target very specific audiences. As a product matures, the advertising budget associated with it will most likely shrink since audiences are already aware of the product.

Techniques used to exploit early stages make use of penetration pricing (low pricing for rapid establishment) as well as "skimming," pricing high initially and then lowering price after the "early acceptors" have been lured in.

GROWTH

The growth phase occurs when a product has survived its introduction and is beginning to be noticed in the marketplace. At this stage, a company can decide if it wants to go for increased market share or increased profitability. This is the boom time for any product. Production increases, leading to lower unit costs. Sales momentum builds as advertising campaigns target mass media audiences instead of specialized markets (if the product merits this). Competition grows as awareness of the product builds. Minor changes are made as more feedback is gathered or as new markets are targeted. The goal for any company is to stay in this phase as long as possible.

It is possible that the product will not succeed at this stage and move immediately past decline and straight to cancellation. That is a call the marketing staff has to make. It needs to evaluate just what costs the company can bear and what the product's chances for survival are. Tough choices need to be made—sticking with a losing product can be disastrous.

If the product is doing well and killing it is out of the question, then the marketing department has other responsibilities. Instead of just building awareness of the product, the goal is to build brand loyalty by adding first-time buyers and retaining repeat buyers. Sales, discounts, and advertising all play an important role in that process. For products that are well-established and further along in the growth phase, marketing options include creating variations of the initial product that appeal to additional audiences.

MATURITY

At the maturity stage, sales growth has started to slow and is approaching the point where the inevitable decline will begin. Defending market share becomes the chief concern, as marketing staffs have to spend more and more on promotion to entice customers to buy the product. Additionally, more competitors have stepped forward to challenge the product at this stage, some of which may offer a higher-quality version of the product at a lower price. This can touch off price wars, and lower prices mean lower profits, which will cause some companies to drop out of the market for that product altogether. The maturity stage is usually the longest of the four life cycle stages, and it is not uncommon for a product to be in the mature stage for several decades.

A savvy company will seek to lower unit costs as much as possible at the maturity stage so that profits can be maximized. The money earned from the mature products should then be used in research and development to come up with new product ideas to replace the maturing products. Operations should be streamlined, cost efficiencies sought, and hard decisions made.

From a marketing standpoint, experts argue that the right promotion can make more of an impact at this stage than at any other. One popular theory postulates that there are two primary marketing strategies to utilize at this stage—offensive and defensive. Defensive strategies consist of special sales, promotions, cosmetic product changes, and other means of shoring up market share. It can also mean quite literally defending the quality and integrity of your product versus your competition. Marketing offensively means looking beyond current markets and attempting to gain brand new-buyers. Relaunching the product is one option. Other offensive tactics include changing the price of a product (either higher or lower) to appeal to an entirely new audience or finding new applications for a product.

DECLINE

This occurs when the product peaks in the maturity stage and then begins a downward slide in sales. Eventually, revenues will drop to the point where it is no longer economically feasible to continue making the product. Investment is minimized. The product can simply be discontinued, or it can be sold to another company. A third option that combines those elements is also sometimes seen as viable, but comes to fruition only rarely. Under this scenario, the product is discontinued and stock is allowed to dwindle to zero, but the company sells the rights to supporting the product to another company, which then becomes responsible for servicing and maintaining the product.

PROBLEMS WITH THE PRODUCT LIFE CYCLE THEORY

While the product life cycle theory is widely accepted, it does have critics who say that the theory has so many exceptions and so few rules that it is meaningless. Among the holes in the theory that these critics highlight:

- There is no set amount of time that a product must stay in any stage; each product is different and moves through the stages at different times. Also, the four stages are not the same time period in length, which is often overlooked.

- There is no real proof that all products must die. Some products have been seen to go from maturity back to a period of rapid growth thanks to some improvement or redesign. Some argue that by saying in advance that a product must reach the end of life stage, it becomes a self-fulfilling prophecy that companies subscribe to. Critics say that some businesses interpret the first downturn in sales to mean that a product has reached decline and should be killed, thus terminating some still-viable products prematurely.

- The theory can lead to an over-emphasis on new product releases at the expense of mature products, when in fact the greater profits could possibly be derived from the mature product if a little work was done on revamping the product.

- The theory emphasizes individual products instead of taking larger brands into account.

- The theory does not adequately account for product redesign and/or reinvention.

SEE ALSO *Business Cycles; Industry Life Cycle*

BIBLIOGRAPHY

Grantham, Lisa Michelle. "The Validity of the Product Life Cycle in the High-tech Industry." *Marketing Intelligence and Planning.* June 1997.

Hedden, Carole. "From Launch to Relaunch: The Secret to Product Longevity Lies in Using the Right Strategy for Each Stage of the Life Cycle." *Marketing Tools.* September 1997.

Kumar, Sameer, and William A. Krob. *Managing Product Life Cycle In A Supply Chair.* Springer Science and Business Media, Inc., 2005.

Pavlovic, Val. "PLM Is No Passing Fad." *Manufacturers' Monthly.* 1 November 2005.

Hillstrom, Northern Lights
updated by Magee, ECDI

PRODUCT POSITIONING

"Product positioning" is a marketing technique intended to present products in the best possible light to different target audiences. The method is related to "market segmentation" in that an early step in major marketing campaigns is to discover the core market most likely to buy a product—or the bulk of the product. Once segmentation has defined this group ("active seniors," "affluent professional working women," "teens") the positioning of the product consists of creating the message likely to reach this group. Positioning involves symbol and message manipulation, including displays and packaging. Two expert definitions:

Al Ries and Jack Trout, in their book *Positioning: The Battle for Your Mind,* introduce the subject by saying: "[P]ositioning is not what you do to a product. Positioning is what you do to the mind of the prospect. That is, you position the product in the mind of the prospect. So it's incorrect to call the concept 'product positioning.' As if you were doing something to the product itself. Not that positioning doesn't involve change. It does. But changes made in the name, the price and the package are really not changes in the product at all. ... Positioning is also the first body of thought that comes to grips with the problems of getting heard in our overcommunicated society."

Louis E. Boone and David L. Kurtz, in their book *Contemporary Marketing,* put it this way: "Product positioning refers to consumers' perceptions of a product's attributes, uses, quality, and advantages and disadvantages relative to competing brands. Marketers often conduct marketing research studies to analyze consumer preferences and to construct product position maps that plot their products' positions in relation to those of competitors' offerings."

IN MASS MARKET PRACTICE

Concepts like "segmentation" and "positioning" typically arise in the "large" rather than in the "small" business context. The underlying concepts apply to both, but access to the mass market requires substantially more preparation. These methods have thus developed of necessity and in order to save money. They do not represent some kind of "high sophistication" the small business has overlooked. Small business owners practice segmentation and positioning as much as the giants and multinationals—but the small business owners think of these things differently and do not use the phrases.

The preparation of major product introductions and related packaging design, promotional and advertising campaigns, incentives for the supply channel, etc. can be very costly. Money can be wasted unless careful planning comes quite early. Market segmentation, an early step in the positioning of products, is intended both to limit the costs of sales and marketing and also to channel the money to the most cost-effective points in the communications network. Related market research, distinct from segmentation, is often used to set price points, identify competitive aspects of the product, etc.

Some product lines, of course, have obvious and built-in segmentation: the marketing of baby foods will be directed at young mothers; wheel-chairs will typically be advertised on TV channels watched by the elderly. A whole category of television drama is called the "soap opera" because these morning shows were watched by women who did the laundry. Lipsticks and cosmetics are rarely advertised on televised football games. And so on. Market segmentation is ultimately a highly developed extension of such quite common-sense linkages between social, demographic, income, and gender groups and the products these typically buy or shun. It might be argued that segmentation studies have gone too far, that the slicing and dicing of sub-sub-sub groups has reached rather silly extremes, but those who spend the money on highly elaborate market surveys and focus groups at least *believe* in the effectiveness of such techniques. And they have a certain scientific grounding.

Segmentation studies invariably attempt to capture *opinion* and then to extrapolate it using *statistical* methods. Groups are selected and interviewed based on preselected characteristics to determine their reactions to products, features, packaging concepts, price-points, appearance, symbols, and message contents. It is vital in these studies that the participants be "representative" of groups that can be measured objectively using census data, for example, urban working women between 30 and 45 with children in the home. To the extent that participants in the study meet the criteria, it is then assumed that the opinions of a small sample will be the same as the opinions of the total population in that category. Segmentation, therefore, is one category of opinion polling as a whole. Its effectiveness depends on the design of the research and is measured by results later—much as political polling is upheld or falsified by election results.

A rather vast body of knowledge, expertise, and interpretation has developed around this type of research in order properly to discern what consumers really mean, how their views and actions correspond, and so on. The amount of effort expended—and professional skills deployed—is directly related to the very large amounts of money expended on persuasion generally.

Product positioning is derived from segmentation and similar marketing studies. Research of this type will determine the different reactions of distinct and measurable groupings of consumers. Some will have a high level of enthusiasm, others will be indifferent. The largest grouping returning a favorable opinion is then selected as the target market; the marketing message is tailored to appeal most specifically to this group and will be shown most frequently in media this group routinely uses. Positioning, of course, may extend to several secondary groups as well, so that a product may be launched with somewhat different emphases and approaches in different media depending on who is watching, listening, or reading. Positioning becomes a very complex process in that attempts are made to coordinate all aspects of the symbology, to echo the very words people used in focus groups, and to select those images, packages, and life-style linkages identified earlier. Occasionally it happens, contrary to the opinion expressed by Ries and Trout, that the product itself may be significantly modified—especially if most consumer groups polled found fault with some features.

IN SMALL BUSINESS PRACTICE

Probably the biggest difference between mass marketeers and small businesses is that small operations *practice* product positioning but *without* the very costly machinery of elaborate and formal segmentation, market research, and testing paid for by the big companies. To be sure, some small businesses (those of the larger kind and able to spend such dollars) do conduct studies quite similar to the majors. But in most small businesses the positioning of products is based on the opinions of the business owner, his or her family, and selected friends and customers; *they* are the "sample." To some extent small businesses also conduct what might be called "experiential" studies once products are launched. They observe who buys most of the product, receive feedback from the market, and then later, in response, modify the ways in which they advertise, where they advertise, how they label, how they display product in the store, and even how they package. If the product is initially at least moderately successful, this type adaptation based on experience is much more effective because it reflects consumer *behavior* rather than consumer *opinion*.

BIBLIOGRAPHY

Boone, Louis E., and David L. Kurtz. *Contemporary Marketing.* Thomson South-Western, 2006.

Nunes, Paul, and Brian Johnson. *Mass Affluence: Seven New Rules of Marketing to Today's Consumer.* Accenture, 2004.

Ries, Al, and Jack Trout. *Positioning: The Battle for Your Mind, 20th Anniversary Edition.* McGraw-Hill, 2001.

Darnay, ECDI

PRODUCTIVITY

Productivity is a measure of output, and the most common use of productivity measures is in gauging economic performance at the national level. Statistics on productivity are collected routinely by the U.S. Bureau of Labor Statistics (BLS) and their publication every quarter usually brings coverage in the business press. BLS measures "labor productivity" based on dollar output per hour of labor; the agency also publishes a more complex measure known as "multifactor productivity" which takes other inputs into account. Productivity is also measured at the level of the enterprise in output of physical product by a worker. When the worker's pay is directly based on number of pieces produced, that type of work is known as "piece-work": pay is tied to the item ("collars sewn," for instance, rather than time spent).

THEORETICAL ASPECTS

In economic theory (echoed in popular opinion), labor compensation is determined by productivity. In theory a person can only earn a fixed amount by labor because the labor must be compensated by the sale of the product made, and all things being equal, competition will keep the prices competitive. This translates to an essentially stagnant economy unless, in some way, the cost of the production process can be lowered. One way to lower costs is to increase output while keeping the input the same. Thus if a worker can increase his or her production from 8 items an hour to 12 items an hour while still being paid $9 an hour, the labor costs of the items will decrease from $1.125 an item to $0.75 an item. (Economics has been called the "dreary science" because it delights in such things—but to go on...) The converse of such an improvement in productivity is that the price of the item could be held steady and the laborer could be paid *more*. In this instance the worker's pay could be increased to $13.50 an hour ($1.125 times 12, not times 8). For this reason, it is a fundamental assumption of economics that wages in a genuinely free market can only increase if *productivity increases*.

Productivity can only increase if 1) the worker's skills increase, 2) the worker's effort increases, 3) the quality of the material processed increases, 4) the worker's tooling is better, and 5) the work-process itself is improved by better arrangements of workers, work-flow, etc. Increases in skill require time and experience, increased effort requires incentives, and the remaining factors are produced by improvements in technology.

Wages, of course, can also increase as a consequence of social force. Thus workers can unionize and impose their will. Higher costs are then imposed on the public. Similarly, government can enforce a wage level with similar consequence, the minimum wage being an example. These situations, of course, no longer represent a genuine "free market"—which, to be sure, has never existed and never shall.

Throughout the period of modern industrial history, productivity has been rising steadily as a consequence of all of the factors enumerated above, namely education in general and the invention and deployment of technology which itself is based on knowledge and energy. Arguably modern civilization rests on the discovery of fossil fuels and their exploitation which have enabled humanity to have leisure to learn and power to burn.

PRODUCTIVITY MEASURES

Labor Productivity Government data on productivity are calculated by measuring and/or estimating the output of different sectors of the economy in dollars and the hours worked. The output divided by the hours produces the base of a productivity measure. But because the economy has its ups and downs as well as its seasonal swings, BLS does not publish the raw numbers but, instead, produces an index number. At present the base year of this index is 1992. This means that the values measured in that year are taken as 100. Other years are expressed as deviations from 1992. In 2000, for instance, manufacturing output per hour was 138.3, meaning that it had improved 38.3 percent over 1992. Productivity data are seasonally adjusted and adjusted dollar values are used to eliminate the influence of inflation.

The two major categories used are Manufacturing and Business as a whole. The most precise are data for manufacturing because, in that sector, the U.S. Census Bureau collects hourly compensation data separately from other employment data. In both categories, productivity is up substantially over against 1992 and in recent years as well. Manufacturing productivity (output per hour) stood at 138.3 in 2000 and at 171.2 in 2005, having increased 23.8 points since 2000. In Business as a whole, the productivity index in 2000 was 120.3; it increased to 136.7 by 2005, increasing 13.6 points.

The significantly higher growth rate in manufacturing productivity reflects the fact that tooling acts as a "multiplier" of human labor. Much more machinery is used in manufacturing than in any other sector. High output per hour is also experienced in highly automated activities like utilities and where large sums of money are transferred as in wholesale trade and in the financial sectors.

Based on data derived from the 1997 Economic Census, cited in *Social Trends & Indicators USA,* it took 4.4 people to produce $1 million in output in manufacturing, 5.7 people to produce $1 million in retail, 9 people to produce that volume in professional, scientific, and technical services, and 15.3 people to produce $1 million in health care. To produce the same dollar figure as output, the finance and insurance sector only needed 2.7 people, utilities 1.7 persons, and wholesale trade 1.4.

Multifactor Productivity (MP) Labor productivity, of course, is a very rough measure because it only incorporates sales or revenues on the one hand and hours worked on the other. It is thus used as a stand-in, a kind of abbreviation, for more complex and very difficult calculations that take other and often intangible factors into account. One attempt to do so is the effort to measure multifactor productivity.

The BLS, in its press release on this subject, provides the following comment: "Multifactor productivity is designed to measure the joint influences of economic growth on technological change, efficiency improvements, returns to scale, reallocation of resources, and other factors, allowing for the effects of capital and labor. Multifactor productivity, therefore, differs from labor productivity (output per hour worked) measures that are published quarterly by BLS since it includes information on capital services and other data that are not available on a quarterly basis."

The MP index separately measures labor and capital inputs and then combines them based on the relative importance of each in a given sector to create a "composite" input. It similarly measures outputs per hour and outputs per unit of capital employed and also combines these. The index is then computed from the two composites.

The MP index is available back to 1987, has a base year of 2000 (index at 100), and is available to 2004. The index has increased 7.7 percent between 2000 and 2004. Multifactor productivity thus produces a more sobering picture of productivity by reflecting the role of capital which, indirectly, reflects the importance and costs of technology.

The data streams required to calculate MP are difficult to get and the index therefore difficult to replicate. Cause-and-effect relationships can only be inferred indirectly. For these reasons, MP is used primarily in academic analyses.

PRODUCTIVITY, COMPENSATION, AND GLOBALIZATION

Labor productivity and compensation grow in tandem but not in precise coordination. In times of economic slow-down, inventories tend to be high but over time is cut and early layoffs take place. In times of up-turn, employers are slow to hire new labor until growth is well established. The overall growth rate of compensation lags that of productivity, in part explained by the "multifactor" influence of technology which, ultimately, accounts for productivity.

This lag has been pronounced in the early years of the 21st century. In the 1992 to 2000 period, productivity increased just 4 points more than compensation based on the indices. But in the 2000 to 2005 period, productivity increased 9.1 points over compensation. A possible explanation of this divergence may be globalization. If functions heretofore counted into hours worked are off-shored, but output continues to be counted, fewer hours will be divided into dollars. Productivity will be going up precisely because the hours are expended overseas and have become invisible.

PRODUCTIVITY AND THE SMALL BUSINESS

The small business, by its very definition ("small") will lack the scale effects often needed to justify high levels of automation. Similarly, unavoidable overhead functions will have less production to absorb their costs. Technological means of increasing productivity are, of course, also available to small business—and deployed by the alert business owner. This applies to rather esoteric areas as well as the more usual. The continued expansion in information technology (IT) and related specialties, for instance, such as computer-aided design and manufacturing (CAD/CAM), is bringing IT more and more within the "affordable range" of small business, as illustrated in several places throughout this volume. Small business, however, also has unique opportunities to achieve productivity through flexibility and creativity. It is very common in small businesses to have highly skilled and cross-trained employees who do "everything." Communications and decision-making are easier and often swifter. Small businesses tend to be innovators, not least in the novel use or invention of technology. Many of these traits are indirectly captured in multifactor productivity statistics even though they escape the simple calculation of sales divided by hours worked.

BIBLIOGRAPHY

Magee, Monique, ed. *Social Trends & Indicators USA: Work & Leisure.* Thomson Gale, 2003

Parry, Thomas, and Phil Lacy. "Promoting Productivity and Workforce Effectiveness." *Financial Executive.* November 2000.

U.S. Bureau of Labor Statistics. "Multifactor Productivity Trends, 2003 and 2004." Press Release. 23 March 2006.

U.S. Bureau of Labor Statistics. "Productivity and Costs." Press Release. 7 March 2006.

Darnay, ECDI

PROFESSIONAL CORPORATIONS

A professional corporation is a variation of the corporate form available to entrepreneurs who provide professional services—such as doctors, lawyers, accountants, consultants, and architects. "Professionals," Frederick W.

Dailey explained in his book *Tax Savvy for Small Business,* "are treated as small businesses under the tax code. Most of them operate as sole proprietorships or partnerships, and are subject to the same tax rules as other similar businesses. However, certain professionals who offer services may form and operate a special type of entity, called a professional corporation." Some states require professionals to form this type of entity if they wish to incorporate. In a professional corporation, the owners perform services for the business as employees.

The first laws that permitted the formation of professional corporations were intended to give professionals some of the tax advantages enjoyed by corporations without also giving them the benefit of limited liability. If a regular corporation—a distinct entity under the law—becomes insolvent, its creditors can only claim business assets for the repayment of debts, not the personal assets of its owners. This is in contrast to regular proprietorships and partnerships, which are not legally distinct from their owners or partners. Since personal responsibility is a key factor in being a professional, the law could not allow professionals to escape liability for their own actions by incorporating. The lines between different forms of business organization have been blurred in recent years, however, as more tax advantages have become available to sole proprietorships and partnerships, and more limited liability has been granted to professional corporations.

PERSONAL SERVICE CORPORATIONS

Most professional corporations qualify as personal service corporations (PSC) for federal tax purposes, provided that they also qualify under state law. To qualify as a PSC under Internal Revenue Service (IRS) rules, a professional corporation must be organized under state law and then pass two federal tests: the function test and the ownership test. The function test requires that substantially all (95 percent) of the business activities of the professional corporation involve services within specific occupations in the fields of health, law, engineering, accounting, actuarial science, consulting, or performing arts. The ownership test requires that substantially all the professional corporation's outstanding stock be held directly or indirectly by qualified people, either: 1) employees who are currently performing professional services for the corporation; 2) retired employees who did so prior to their retirement; 3) or their heirs or estates. If a professional corporation organized under state law does not qualify as a PSC, then it is treated as a general partnership for federal tax purposes.

PSCs are taxed like regular C corporations but with a flat corporate tax rate of 35 percent rather than a graduated rate depending on the level of income earned. The PSC files a corporate tax return and also issues Form K-1 to all shareholder/employees to show their individual shares of the corporation's profit or loss. Any income that is retained in the PSC is subject to the corporate tax rate, while any salaries paid to employees are considered tax-deductible business expenses. Like most small corporations, however, PSCs are likely to pay out all business income to shareholders in the form of salaries, bonuses, and fringe benefits, thus reducing corporate taxable income to zero. Of course, the shareholder/employees still must pay personal income taxes on the income they receive.

ADVANTAGES AND DISADVANTAGES

Organizing as a professional corporation offers many potential advantages to qualified small business owners. Some of the primary advantages involve tax breaks that are not available to unincorporated businesses. For example, professional corporations can create retirement plans and 401(k) plans for their employees that have higher contribution limits than plans available to individuals or unincorporated businesses. In addition, professional corporations can provide health and life insurance as a tax-free benefit to their employees by establishing a Voluntary Employees' Beneficiary Association (VEBA). They can also take tax deductions for disability insurance, dependent care, and other fringe benefits provided to employees. In most cases, such benefits are tax-deductible for the corporation, and also are not considered taxable income for the employees.

Another advantage available to professional corporations is perpetual existence. Unlike sole proprietorships and partnerships—which legally dissolve when an owner dies or leaves the company—professional corporations can continue operations without interruption if a shareholder/employee dies or withdraws. Another advantage is that professional corporations may enable shareholder/employees to avoid personal liability for another employee's negligence. In most cases, one owner is liable for another's actions only if he or she would have been liable as a shareholder of a regular corporation. In contrast, all members of a regular partnership are exposed to personal liability.

There are also a few potential disadvantages associated with the professional corporation form of organization. For example, passive loss limitations may apply that restrict the amount nonactive shareholders can deduct for tax purposes in the event of business losses. In the case of a partnership, all partners are able to deduct their share of business losses from their personal taxable income. Since most professional corporations have only active shareholders and do not experience losses, however, this tax liability is not usually an issue. The flat corporate tax rate that applies to professional corporations may be another source of disadvantage. Retaining earnings within the business will rarely make sense due to the higher tax bracket, and this may reduce the firm's flexibility in distributing income to shareholder/employees. In contrast, most regular corporations can "split income"—or adjust the amount paid out to shareholder/employees—so that both the company and the individual can gain the most favorable tax bracket possible.

CHOOSING AMONG THE ALTERNATIVES

Many states now provide professionals with several options about how to organize their businesses. The main alternatives to forming a professional corporation or personal service corporation include organizing as a limited liability company (LLC) or as a limited liability partnership (LLP). These options differ in the costs and tax benefits involved, as well as in the amount of liability protection afforded. For example, limited liability companies combine the liability protection afforded by professional corporations with the taxation flexibility provided by partnerships. LLCs are taxed similarly to S corporations, so the income flows through to the shareholder/employees rather than accruing to the business and then being distributed to owners and employees. Limited liability partnerships are similar to regular partnerships except that they provide additional protection for partnership assets against malpractice suits. However, the partners in an LLP are required to carry hefty insurance or guarantee deposits in exchange for this protection.

The main advantages of organizing as a professional corporation, as outlined above, include tax benefits and transferability of ownership. However, the flat corporate tax rate prevents shareholder/employees from retaining earnings in the professional corporation, which may limit opportunities for expansion and growth. In addition, professional corporation owners may face the problem of double taxation upon liquidation of the business. Income from the sale of real estate or equipment might accrue to the business, for example, where it would be taxed at the corporate rate. If this income were then distributed to shareholders as dividends (since the company was no longer in business and thus could not pay it out as salaries and benefits to employees), then it would be subject to taxation again as personal income.

BIBLIOGRAPHY

Dailey, Frederick W. *Tax Savvy for Small Business: Year-Round Tax Advice for Small Businesses.* Nolo Press, 2005.

Demkin, Joseph A. The Architect's Handbook of Professional Practice. John Wiley & Sons, Inc., 2003.

Hafter, Jacob L., and Stephen M. Greenberg. "Professional Corporations Remain the Most Popular Form of Entity for Medical Practices." *New Jersey Law Journal.* 15 December 2003.

Schneeman, Angela. The Law of Corporations, and Other Business Organizations. Thomson Learning, 2002.

Hillstrom, Northern Lights
updated by Magee, ECDI

PROFIT CENTER

A profit center is a business unit that generates revenue in excess of costs. Profit centers are expected to turn a profit by selling something. By contrast a cost center in a company provides necessary services but has no revenues. It is expected to keep costs low while providing the assigned services—within the budget. Beyond that simple definition, companies in recent years have attempted to convert service units into profit centers by two basic stratagems: charging for services rendered to internal customers (other departments) and selling a portion of cost-center outputs to outsiders in order to generate revenues. Thus "profit center" has taken on a new meaning as a search for higher profits by putting pressures on functions heretofore shielded from the "market."

All companies, of course, have both cost and profit centers—even the one-person company; in the latter case *some* things done by the entrepreneur are done to keep things going, others are directly related to revenue generation. In most companies corporate functions such as human resources, information technology (IT), purchasing, maintenance, research, and other staff-functions distant from production are cost centers—not least top management. These are service functions necessary to do other things directly related to the market. Production activities, including engineering, design, data processing tied to the factory, production itself and warehousing and testing associated with it can usually be tied to product and thus are parts of profit centers.

All companies have profit centers and cost centers, but not all companies organize their accounting practices around the "profit center concept." Where this concept has taken root, management makes attempts to view all operations under the rubric of profit and makes attempts to convert functions so that they too have bottom lines.

TRANSFORMING COST INTO A PROFIT CENTER

A cost center may actually provide services that could generate a profit if they were offered on the open market. This theoretical possibility is at the root of profit center accounting. One implementation of the concept is to require departments using a service to pay for it. This, of course, is a meaningless change in bookkeeping (and an added administrative cost) unless the purchasing departments have alternatives to buying from within. Thus implementation typically permits departments to shop around—and buy the service outside the company too. The notion is that such competition will make the "cost center" behave more responsibly in order to "keep the business." Similarly, the newly converted "cost center" is also empowered to sell its services outside. In both cases, selling in or outside, the "cost center" could mark up its costs to get a real profit margin of its own—which, of course, would increase the costs of profit centers.

All cost centers "do something" and therefore theoretically have something to sell—but the marketability of many centers is problematical or, de facto, must be relaunched as new ventures. Thus a human resources department could theoretically turn itself into a recruiting company, but to do so effectively it would have to transform itself, develop its own marketing, and lose its character as an internal service provider concentrating on achieving corporate goals first of all. The "two masters" problem arises. The accounting department's payroll function could also, similarly, head out and do battle for market share with well-entrenched independent payroll services providers.

Certain functions, like information technology, appear more suited to this concept than others because—except for the addition of a selling function—little else (except perhaps expansion) would be required. Managing external databases is functionally the same as managing those in-house. Other technically based functions would have similar advantages, e.g., product design, modeling departments, product testing, etc.

PROS AND CONS

The perceived advantages of "conversion" arise chiefly from the assumption that costs of the function would decline over time and thus make the company more profitable overall. Under competitive pressure, the former cost center would become leaner, more responsive, and more efficient. If successful externally, it would increase total revenues.

The negatives arise from the fact that corporations are "organizations" and therefore both kinds of centers, cost as well as profit, are necessary "organs" of the entity with characteristics that have evolved to make them work ideally together. (Which of our body organs do we wish to change?) The conversion of cost centers into independent functions introduces competitive forces into the organization itself. The motivations of managers running such units change; they begin to be measured by a different yardstick. At a minimum—if this policy is pursued very energetically—it will create tensions and disorders.

Primarily for these reasons, managerial initiatives to implement a profit center culture tend to translate, in practice, into greater focus on the costs and benefits of service elements, tend occasionally to lead to the exploitation of new opportunities for outside sales, but rarely result in creating a chaotic internal "auction" under which operational managers have to expend excessive time and effort to get a part, a data run, or to hire a new employee.

PROFIT CENTERING VS. OUTSOURCING

The attempt to achieve higher returns from internal service functions is conceptually and motivationally similar to moves that result in shedding entire functions—replaced by buying their services from outside vendors. This approach is administratively easier and for that reason, perhaps, growing in extent. (See *Outsourcing* in this volume.) Transforming an internal department into a service-selling entity, required to find outside customers as well, thus becomes the first stage toward the "Ah hah!" of discovery: namely that the function might not be needed at all. Some departments already buy from the outside. Why not all departments? Let's spin it off!

Companies faced with hide-bound, bureaucratic, resistant, slow-moving, and unresponsive service functions have other alternatives. The most obvious is the radical reorganization of the poorly performing function.

SEE ALSO *Outsourcing*

BIBLIOGRAPHY

Auer, Joe. "IT as Profit Center? It Can Be Done." *Computerworld.* 1 May 2000.

"Catering Grows as Profit Center." *Food Service Director.* 15 April 2006.

Deckler, Gregory J. *Achieving Process Profitability: Building the IT Profit Center."* iUniverse, 2003.

"Exclusively Online; Is Your Web Site a Profit Center?" *Advertising Age.* 3 April 2006.

Gordon, Jack. "Selling It On the Side: Maybe you could subsidize your employee training by selling courses to outsiders." *Training.* December 2005

O'Sullivan, Orla. "On-Line Markets Can Turn Web Site from Cost Center to Profit Center." *American Banker.* 4 April 2000.

Trzecesinski, Mike. "Learning to See Maintenance as a Profit Center." *Foundry Management & Technology.* February 2006.

Darnay, ECDI

PROFIT IMPACT OF MARKET STRATEGIES (PIMS)

The Profit Impact of Market Strategies (PIMS) is a comprehensive, long-term study of the performance of strategic business units (SBUs) in 3,000 companies in all major industries. The PIMS project began at General Electric in the mid-1960s. It was conducted at Harvard University between 1972 and 1974. In 1975 PIMS was taken over by a Massachusetts-based nonprofit organization, formed for that purpose, called The Strategic Planning Institute (SPI). Since then, SPI researchers and consultants have continued working on the development and application of PIMS data. The PIMS database is available to individuals for a subscription price (in 2006) of $995 for one month's use and $2,500 for three months' use. Longer periods of subscription are available from SPI by special arrangement.

According to the SPI Website, the PIMS database is "a collection of statistically documented experiences drawn from thousands of businesses, designed to help understand what kinds of strategies (e.g., quality, pricing, vertical integration, innovation, advertising) work best in what kinds of business environments. The data constitute a key resource for such critical management tasks as evaluating business performance, analyzing new business opportunities, evaluating and reality testing new strategies, and screening business portfolios."

The main function of PIMS is to highlight the relationship between a business's key strategic decisions and its results. Analyzed correctly, the data can help managers gain a better understanding of their business environment, identify critical factors in improving the position of their companies, and develop strategies that will enable them to create a sustainable advantage. PIMS principles are taught in business schools, and the data are widely used in academic research. As a result, PIMS has influenced business strategy in companies around the world.

THE PIMS DATABASE

The information comprising the PIMS database is drawn from member companies of SPI. These companies contribute profiles of their SBUs that include financial data as well as information on customers, markets, competitors, and operations. The SBUs in the database are separated into eight classifications: producers of consumer durables, consumer non-durables, capital goods, raw materials, components, or supplies; wholesale and retail distributors; and providers of services. Specific companies and industries are not identified. Each SBU profile includes financial data from the income statement and balance sheet, as well as information about quality, price, new products, market share, and competitive tactics.

The classifications are rather broad, at least from a small business perspective. The category of consumer durables, for instance, includes such diverse products as refrigerators, cell phones, air conditioners, computers, microwave ovens, lawnmowers, television sets, and much else. Thus data averaged from such a category have a rather rough granularity. The data are also drawn from large corporations and then averaged.

Judging by generic, pro-forma sample tabulations available on SPI's web site, the user comes to the database with his or her financial and other ratios as an input and can then derive comparative data from the broad categories listed above and held in the PIMS database. The outputs appear to be statistical and rely on the assumption that broad category averages can effectively guide strategy. PIMS data appear to be a good approach to benchmarking—provided that broad categories are sufficient for the PIMS data users. SPI also provides consulting services, based on PIMS, as SPI Associates, Inc.

SMALL BUSINESS RELEVANCE

Interest in PIMS as an analytical approach does not appear very high in the mid-2000s if recent coverage of the subject in the technical and business press is any indication. A search of Infotrac brings just a few references from the 1990s and 1980s. The most recent book on the subject by Paul W. Farris and Michael J. Moore is largely a look backward—an attempt to assess the contribution PIMS has made to the field of management science. Looking forward, the authors analyze how the PIMS project might be structured if it were launched in the current era. Another broad study of contemporary marketing by Louis E. Boone and David L. Kurtz mentions a comprehensive use of PIMS by the Marketing Science Institute. The MSI study came to the not-so-startling conclusion that (in Boone's and Kurtz's words) "two of the most important factors influencing profitability were product quality and market share."

PIMS was from the outset—and apparently continues as—a "big company" methodology to measure broad strategies capable of being captured by statistical measures. The reliance of this method on concepts (and measurements) like market share performance and marketing expenditures seems to make its relevance to small business marginal at best. Small companies on average find it very difficult even to guess at their own market shares and only very rarely engage in the kinds of major marketing efforts associated with the GEs, IBMs, and Coca-Colas of the world.

BIBLIOGRAPHY

Boone, Louis E., and David L. Kurtz. *Contemporary Marketing 2005.* Thomson South-Western, 2005.

Farris, Paul W., and Michael J. Moore. *The Profit Impact of Marketing Strategy Project: Retrospect and Prospects.* Cambridge University Press, 2004.

The Strategic Planning Institute. Available from http://www.pimsonline.com/. Retrieved on 5 May 2006.

Hillstrom, Northern Lights
updated by Magee, ECDI

PROFIT MARGIN

The profit margin is an accounting measure designed to gauge the financial health of a business or industry. In general, it is defined as the ratio of profits earned to total sales receipts (or costs) over some defined period. The profit margin is a measure of the amount of profit accruing to a firm from the sale of a product or service. It also provides an indication of efficiency in that it captures the amount of surplus generated per unit of the product or service sold. In order to generate a sizeable profit margin, a company must operate efficiently enough to recover not only the costs of the product or service sold, operating expenses, and the costs of debt, but also to provide compensation for its owners in exchange for their acceptance of risk.

As an example of a profit margin calculation, suppose firm A made a profit of $10 on the sale of a $100 television set. Dividing the dollar amount of earnings by the product cost, that firm's profit margin would be .10 or 10 percent, meaning that each dollar of sales generated an average of ten cents of profit. Thus, the profit margin is very important as a measure of the competitive success of a business, because it captures the firm's unit costs.

A low-cost producer in an industry would generally have a higher profit margin. Since firms tend to sell the same product at roughly the same price (adjusted for quality differences), lower costs would be reflected in a higher profit margin. Lower cost firms also have a strategic advantage in a competitive price war: they have the ability to undercut their competitors by cutting prices in order to gain market share and potentially drive higher cost firms out of business.

Firms clearly exist to expand their profits. But while increasing the absolute amount of dollar profit is desirable, it has minimal significance unless it is related to its source. This is why firms use measures such as profit margin and profit rate. Profit margin measures the flow of profits over some period compared with the costs, or sales, incurred over the same period. Thus, one could compute the profit margin on costs (profits divided by costs) or the profit margin on sales (profit margin divided by sales).

Other specific profit margin measures often calculated by businesses include: 1) gross profit margin—gross profit divided by net sales, where gross profit is the total money left over after sales and net sales is total revenues; and 2) net profit margin—net profit divided by net sales, where net profit (or net income) is profit after deducting costs such as advertising, marketing, interest payments, rental payments, and taxes. This last ratio, the most common, has hovered around 5 percent overall in all business activities.

RATE OF PROFIT

Profit margin is related to other measures such as the rate of profit (sometimes called the rate of return), which comprises various measures of the amount of profit earned relative to the total amount of capital invested (or the stock of capital) required to generate that profit. Thus, while the profit margin measures the amount of profit per unit of sales, the rate of profit on total assets indicates the efficiency of the total investment. Or, put another way, while the profit margin measures the amount of profit per unit of capital (labor, working capital, and depreciation of plant and equipment) consumed over a particular period, the profit rate measures the amount of profit per unit of capital advanced (the entire stock of capital required for the production of the good).

Using our previous example, if a $1,000 investment in plant and equipment were required to produce the $100 television set, then a profit margin of 10 percent would translate into a profit rate on total investment of only 1 percent. Thus, in this scenario, firm A's unit costs are low enough to generate a 10 percent profit margin on the capital consumed (assuming some market price) to produce the TV set; but in order to achieve that margin, a total capital expenditure of $1,000 must be made.

The difference between the profit margin measure and the profit rate concept then lies in the rate at which the capital stock depreciates, and the rate at which the production process repeats itself, or turnover time. In the first case, if the entire capital stock for a particular firm or industry is completely used up during one production cycle, then the profit margin would be exactly the same as the profit rate. In the case of turnover, if a firm succeeds in doubling the amount of times the production process repeats itself in the same period, then twice as much profit would be made on the same capital invested, even though the profit margin might not change. More formally, the rate of return = profit margin x sales / average assets, where average assets is the total capital stock divided by the number of times the production process turns over. Thus, the rate of return can be increased by increasing the profit margin or by shortening the production cycle. Of course, this will largely depend on the conditions of production in particular industries or firms.

If costs rise and sale prices do not rise to keep up, then the profit margin will fall. In times of business cycle upturns, prices tend to rise; in business cycle downturns, prices tend to fall. Of course, many factors, and not only costs, will affect the profit margin—namely, industry-specific factors that relate to investment requirements, pricing, type of market, and conditions of production (including production turnover time).

It is important for small business owners to remember that generating a profit margin does not guarantee that their business is healthy, or that they will have money in the bank. Rather, a small business must have a positive cash flow in order to pay its bills and compensate its employees. To use a profit margin figure to determine whether a start-up firm is doing well, an entrepreneur might compare it to the return that would be available from a bank or another low-risk investment opportunity.

SEE ALSO *Financial Ratios*

BIBLIOGRAPHY

Boone, Louis E., and David L. Kurtz. *Contemporary Marketing 2005.* Thomson South-Western, 2005.

Pinson, Linda. *Keeping the Books: Basic Record Keeping and Accounting for the Successful Small Business.* Dearborn Trade Publishing, 2004.

The Ultimate Small Business Guide: A Resource for Startups and Growing Businesses. Basic Books, 2004.

Hillstrom, Northern Lights
updated by Magee, ECDI

PROFIT SHARING

"Profit sharing" is a type of compensation paid to employees by companies. Payment of a profit sharing bonus to non-management employees typically takes place at the discretion of the company and does not constitute an entitlement—although if it is paid routinely and year after year, employees may come to count on it as part of their compensation. Profit sharing bonuses are treated as income for tax purposes upon receipt unless made to deferred compensation plans.

As part of its National Compensation Survey, the U.S. Bureau of Labor Statistics (BLS) collects data on cash profit sharing bonus payments to employees. Data for 2005 indicated that 5 percent of all workers had access to such bonuses. The BLS data may actually understate the prevalence of profit sharing because it also reports "end-of-year bonus" and "holiday bonus" categories, both of which are higher, 11 and 10 percent of workers receive such bonuses respectively. Many small businesses pay such bonuses at the end of the year and without labeling them as "profit sharing"—but the bonuses are only paid in good years. This interpretation of the BLS data is borne out by the fact that bonuses labeled "profit sharing" were available to 4 percent of workers employed by small firms (under 100 employees) while 6 percent of workers in larger organizations had access to such bonuses. But 13 percent of workers in small establishments had access to end-of-year and holiday bonuses (13 percent in each category) whereas only 7 percent of workers in larger organizations had access to end-of-year bonuses and 6 percent to holiday bonuses. If all three categories are combined, it would appear that small businesses used this mechanism as a form of employee recognition more than large businesses.

BLS data also indicate that profit sharing bonuses (excluding end-of year and holiday bonuses) were more likely available to blue collar workers (7 percent versus the average of 5 percent), full timers (6 percent), unionized workers (7 percent), and higher wage workers ($15 an hour and higher, 7 percent) than other categories. Eleven percent of workers in goods producing and 3 percent of workers in services producing industries had access to such bonuses.

TYPES OF PROFIT-SHARING PLANS

Companies use any number of different formulas to calculate the distribution of profits to their employees and have a variety of rules and regulations regarding eligibility. In general, however, two types of plans prevail. The first takes the form of cash bonuses under which employees receive a profit-sharing distribution at the end of the year. The main drawback to cash distribution plans is that this income is immediately subject to income tax. This also holds if the bonus is paid out in the form of company stock.

To avoid immediate taxation, companies are permitted by the Internal Revenue Service (IRS) to set up qualified deferred profit-sharing plans. Under a deferred plan, the second type of profit sharing, profit-sharing distributions are held in individual accounts for each employee. Employees are not allowed to withdraw from their profit-sharing accounts except under certain, well-defined conditions. As long as employees do not have easy access to the funds, money in the accounts is not taxed and may earn tax-deferred interest. BLS data reported on this form of profit sharing do not show extent of corporate participation or the number of employees eligible overall.

Under qualified deferred profit-sharing plans, employees may be given a range of investment choices for their accounts, including stocks or mutual funds. Such choices are common when the accounts are managed by outside investment firms. It is becoming less common for companies to manage their own profit-sharing plans due to the fiduciary duties and liabilities associated with them. A 401(k) account is a common type of deferred profit-sharing plan, with several unique features. For example, employees are allowed to voluntarily contribute a portion of their salary, before taxes, to their 401(k) account. The company may decide to match a certain percentage of such contributions. In addition, many 401(k) accounts have provisions that enable employees to borrow money under certain conditions.

OTHER ISSUES CONCERNING PROFIT-SHARING PLANS

Deferred profit-sharing plans are a type of defined contribution plan. Such employee benefit plans provide an individual account for each employee. Individual accounts grow as contributions are made to them. Funds in the accounts are invested and may earn interest or show capital appreciation. Depending on each employee's investment choices, their account balances may be subject to increases or decreases reflecting the current value of their investments.

The amount of future benefits that employees will receive from their profit-sharing accounts depends entirely on their account balance. The amount of their account balance will include the employer's contributions from profits, any interest earned, any capital gains or losses, and possibly forfeitures from other plan participants. Forfeitures result when employees leave the company before they are vested, and the funds in their accounts are distributed to the remaining plan participants.

Employees are said to be vested when they become eligible to receive the funds in their accounts. Immediate vesting means that they have the right to funds in their account as soon as their employer makes a profit-sharing distribution. Companies may establish different time requirements before employees become fully vested. Under some deferred profit-sharing plans employees may start out partially vested, perhaps being entitled to only 25 percent of their account, then gradually become fully vested over a period of years. A company's vesting policy is written into the plan document and is designed to motivate employees and reduce employee turnover.

In order for a deferred profit-sharing plan to gain qualified status from the IRS, it is important that funds in employee accounts not be readily accessible to employees. Establishing a vesting period is one way to limit access; employees have rights to the funds in their accounts only when they become partially or fully vested. Another way to limit access is to establish strict rules for making payments from employees accounts, such as upon retirement, death, permanent disability, or termination of employment. Less strict rules may allow for withdrawals under certain conditions, such as financial hardship or medical emergencies. Nevertheless, whatever rules a company may adopt for its profit-sharing plan, such rules are subject to IRS approval and must meet IRS guidelines.

The IRS also limits the amount that employers may contribute to their profit-sharing plans. The precise amount is subject to change by the IRS, but 1996 tax rules allowed companies to contribute a maximum of 15 percent of an employee's salary to his or her profit-sharing account. If a company contributed less than 15 percent in one year, it may exceed 15 percent by the difference in a subsequent year to a maximum of 25 percent of an employee's salary.

Companies may determine the amount of their profit-sharing contributions in one of two ways. One is by a set formula that is written into the plan document. Such formulas are typically based on the company's pre-tax net profits, earnings growth, or some other measure of profitability. Companies then plug the appropriate numbers into the formula and arrive at the amount of their contribution to the profit-sharing pool. Rather than using a set formula, companies may decide to contribute a discretionary amount each year. That is, the company's owners or directors—at their discretion—decide what an appropriate amount would be.

Once the amount of the company's contribution has been determined, different plans provide for different ways of allocating the funds among the company's employees. The employer's contribution may be translated into a percentage of the company's total payroll, with each employee receiving the same percentage of his or her annual pay. Other companies may use a sliding scale based on length of service or other factors. Profit-sharing plans also spell out precisely which employees are eligible to receive profit-sharing distributions. Some plans may require employees to reach a certain age or length of employment, for example, or to work a certain minimum number of hours during the year.

Although profit sharing offers some attractive benefits to small business owners, it also includes some potential pitfalls. It is important for small business owners who wish to share their success with employees to set up a formal profit sharing plan with the assistance of an accountant or financial advisor. Otherwise, both the employer and the employees may not receive the tax benefits they desire from the plan. Also, small business owners should avoid making mentions of profit sharing or stock ownership to motivate employees during the heat of battle. Such mentions could be construed as promises and lead to lawsuits if the employees do not receive the benefits they feel they deserved.

BIBLIOGRAPHY

Blencoe, Gregory J. "Utilizing Profit Sharing to Motivate Employees: The Logic Behind Sharing a Piece of the Pie." *Business Credit.* September 2000.

Dietderich, Andrew. "Survey: Pay based on performance gains ground." *Crain's Detroit Business.* 3 April 2006.

"In Depth Profit Sharing: Share Peace of Mind." *Employee Benefits.* 12 January 2006.

Jones, Dan. "How Safe is Your Retirement Plan?" *Paraplegia News.* December 2005.

"US: Chrysler to profit-share around $650 per worker." *just-auto.com.* 17 February 2006.

U.S. Department of Labor. Bureau of Labor Statistics. *National Compensation Survey: Employee Benefits in Private Industry in the United States, March 2005.* August 2005.

Hillstrom, Northern Lights
updated by Magee, ECDI

PROGRAM EVALUATION AND REVIEW TECHNIQUE (PERT)

The Program Evaluation and Review Technique (PERT) is a widely used method for planning and coordinating large-scale projects. As Harold Kerzner explained in his book *Project Management*, "PERT is basically a management planning and control tool. It can be considered as a road map for a particular program or project in which all of the major elements (events) have been completely identified, together with their corresponding interrelations.... PERT charts are often constructed from back to front because, for many projects, the end date is fixed and the contractor has front-end flexibility." A basic element of PERT-style planning is to identify critical activities on which others depend. The technique is often referred to as PERT/CPM, the CPM standing for "critical path method."

PERT was developed during the 1950s through the efforts of the U.S. Navy and some of its contractors working on the Polaris missile project. Concerned about the growing nuclear arsenal of the Soviet Union, the U.S. government wanted to complete the Polaris project as quickly as possible. The Navy used PERT to coordinate the efforts of some 3,000 contractors involved with the project. Experts credited PERT with shortening the project duration by two years. Since then, all government contractors have been required to use PERT or a similar project analysis technique for all major government contracts.

NETWORK DIAGRAMS

The chief feature of PERT analysis is a network diagram that provides a visual depiction of the major project activities and the sequence in which they must be completed. Activities are defined as distinct steps toward completion of the project that consume either time or resources. The network diagram consists of arrows and nodes and can be organized using one of two different conventions. The arrows represent activities in the activity-on-arrow convention, while the nodes represent activities in the activity-on-node convention. For each activity, managers provide an estimate of the time required to complete it.

The sequence of activities leading from the starting point of the diagram to the finishing point of the diagram is called a path. The amount of time required to complete the work involved in any path can be figured by adding up the estimated times of all activities along that path. The path with the longest total time is then called the "critical path," hence the term CPM. The critical path is the most important part of the diagram for managers: it determines the completion date of the project. Delays in completing activities along the critical path necessitate an extension of the final deadline for the project. If a manager hopes to shorten the time required to complete the project, he or she must focus on finding ways to reduce the time involved in activities along the critical path.

The time estimates managers provide for the various activities comprising a project involve different degrees of certainty. When time estimates can be made with a high degree of certainty, they are called deterministic estimates. When they are subject to variation, they are called probabilistic estimates. In using the probabilistic approach, managers provide three estimates for each activity: an optimistic or best case estimate; a pessimistic or worst case estimate; and the most likely estimate. Statistical methods can be used to describe the extent of variability in these estimates, and thus the degree of uncertainty in the time provided for each activity. Computing the standard deviation of each path provides a probabilistic estimate of the time required to complete the overall project.

PERT ANALYSIS

Managers can obtain a great deal of information by analyzing network diagrams of projects. For example, network diagrams show the sequence of activities involved in a project. From this sequence, managers can determine which activities must take place before others can begin, and which can occur independently of one another. Managers can also gain valuable insight by examining paths other than the critical path. Since these paths require less time to complete, they can often accommodate slippage without affecting the project completion time. The difference between the length of a given path and the length of the critical path is known as slack. Knowing where slack is located helps managers to allocate scarce resources and direct their efforts to control activities.

For complex problems involving hundreds of activities, computers are used to create and analyze the project networks. The project information input into the computer includes the earliest start time for each activity, earliest finish time for each activity, latest start time for each activity, and latest finish time for each activity without delaying the project completion. From these values, a computer algorithm can determine the expected project duration and the activities located on the critical path. Managers can use this information to determine where project time can be shortened by injecting additional resources, like workers or equipment. Needless to say, the solution of the algorithm is easy for the computer, but the resulting information will only be as good as the estimates originally made. Thus PERT depends on good estimates and sometimes inspired guesses.

PERT offers a number of advantages to managers. For example, it forces them to organize and quantify project information and provides them with a graphic display of the project. It also helps them to identify which activities are critical to the project completion time and should be watched closely, and which activities involve slack time and can be delayed without affecting the project completion time. The chief disadvantages of PERT lie in the nature of reality. Complex systems and plans, with many suppliers and channels of supply involved, sometimes make it difficult to predict precisely what will happen. The technique works best in well-understood engineering projects where sufficient experience exists to predict tasks accurately in advance.

BIBLIOGRAPHY

Baker, Sunny, G. Michael Campbell, and Kim Baker. *The Complete Idiot's Guide to Project Management.* Alpha Books, 2003.

Kerzner, Harold. *Project Management: A Systems Approach to Planning, Scheduling, and Controlling.* John Wiley & Sons, 2003.

Punmia, B.C. and K. Khandelwal. *Project Planning and Control P.E.R.T. and C.P.M.: For Degree Classes.* Laxmi Publications, 2006.

Hillstrom, Northern Lights
updated by Magee, ECDI

PROMISSORY NOTES

Quite simply, a promissory note is a promise to pay or IOU. It is a formal commitment (also known as a loan agreement or contract) between two parties that is usually necessary when money is borrowed and lent between them. All business loans secured from a bank or other lending institution have some sort of promissory note, but they are also recommended for loans between two individuals (even if the loan is between family members or close friends) to avoid any misunderstandings or possible legal troubles.

A promissory note should have several essential elements, including the amount of the loan, the date by which it is to be paid back, the interest rate, and a record of any collateral that is being used to secure the loan. Other interest-rate options, like discounting or compensating balance requirements, can also be included. When the promissory note is discounted, the interest is taken off the principal amount at the beginning of the loan. The borrower pays back the entire amount, even though he only received the principal minus the interest. This practice is not very common because it is a higher effective rate of interest than the stated rate for the borrower. A compensating balance is usually required for large loans or lines of credit. It requires that the borrower maintain an account with a specified minimum level account balance at the lending institution (usually a bank). This account balance earns little or no interest and also raises the effective interest rate of the loan. Default terms (what happens if a payment is missed or the loan is not paid off by its due date) should also be spelled out in the promissory note.

When signing a promissory note, both the lender and the person receiving the loan should be fully aware of the note's language. One obvious way to do this is to read the promissory note carefully and in its entirety before committing a signature to it. If there are any questions or confusion regarding the contents of the promissory note, a certified public accountant (CPA) or lawyer should be called on to make sure everything is understandable. When a casual promissory note is drawn up between two individuals, the IRS has a required interest rate. A CPA can help determine if the interest rate stated in the promissory note is too low and if it will result in penalties or automatically be raised. If the loan is interest free, the IRS may consider it a gift and require that a gift tax be paid on it.

Another point that businesses may want to consider when drafting a promissory note is what to do in case the business does not succeed. If the business is a corporation or limited liability company, it should be determined if the corporate shareholders or limited liability members will personally guarantee the loan. If this is not the case, they have no personal legal obligation to repay the loan in a worst-case scenario.

BIBLIOGRAPHY

Ashcroft, John D. *Law for Business.* Thomson South-Western, 2005.

McMillan, Dan. "Notes Causing Headaches." *Business Journal-Portland.* 28 July 2000.

Roberts, Barry S., and Richard A. Mann. *Smith and Roberson's Business Law.* Thomson West, 2006.

Hillstrom, Northern Lights
updated by Magee, ECDI

PROPRIETARY INFORMATION

Proprietary information, also known as a trade secret, is information a company wishes to keep confidential. Proprietary information can include secret formulas, processes, and methods used in production. It can also include a company's business and marketing plans, salary structure, customer lists, contracts, and details of its computer systems. In some cases, the special knowledge and skills that an employee has learned on the job are considered to be a company's proprietary information.

LEGISLATION

Federal legislation came into effect in 1996 with the enactment of The Economic Espionage Act of 1996 (EEA). The EEA was in part modeled on The Uniform Trade Secrets Act (UTSA), a model law drafted by the National Conference of Commissioners on Uniform State Laws but expands UTSA's definition. The EEA definition of trade secret follows from Section 1838, paragraph (3):

"[T]he term 'trade secret' means all forms and types of financial, business, scientific, technical, economic, or engineering information, including patterns, plans, compilations, program devices, formulas, designs, prototypes, methods, techniques, processes, procedures, programs, or codes, whether tangible or intangible, and whether or how stored, compiled, or memorialized physically, electronically, graphically, photographically, or in writing if—

"(A) the owner therefore has taken reasonable measures to keep such information secret, and

"(B) the information derives independent economic value, actual or potential, from not being generally known to, and not being readily ascertainable through proper means by, the public[.]"

With the passage of EEA, trade secrets now enjoy protection under federal law as do inventions through patents, creative works through copyright, and unique names and symbols through trademark legislation. In addition, 39 U.S. laws also define trade secrets in various ways and define the conditions under which theft has taken place. Based on such laws a significant body of case law covers proprietary information and trade secrets. This legal framework recognizes a company's right to have proprietary information and provides the company with remedies when its trade secrets have been misused or illegally appropriated.

PROTECTING TRADE SECRETS

In general, for information to be considered proprietary, companies must treat it as confidential. Courts will not treat information readily available in public sources as proprietary. In addition, proprietary information must give the firm some sort of competitive advantage and should generally be unknown outside of the firm. A company must be able to demonstrate that it has taken every reasonable step to keep the information private if it hopes to obtain court assistance in protecting its rights. "Courts require that trade secret holders take 'reasonable' steps to maintain the secrecy of their trade secrets," Randy Kay wrote in the *San Diego Business Journal*. "Courts do not require that companies take all measures conceivable to maintain the secrecy, nor do courts require absolute secrecy. Rather, the confidentiality measures must be 'reasonable under the circumstances.'"

A company has several options to keep its information proprietary. Key employees with access to such information may be required to sign restrictive covenants—also called confidentiality, nondisclosure, or noncompete agreements—that prohibit them from revealing that information to outsiders or using it to compete with their employer for a certain period of time after leaving the company. Restrictive covenants are usually enforced by the courts if they are reasonable with respect to time and place and do not unreasonably restrict the former employee's right to employment. In some cases the covenants are enforced only if the employee has gained proprietary information during the course of his or her employment.

In addition, the courts generally consider it unfair competition for one company to induce people who have acquired unique technical skills and secret knowledge at another company to terminate their employment and use their skills and knowledge for the benefit of the competing firm. In such a case the plaintiff can seek an injunction to prevent its former employees and its competitor from using the proprietary information.

Companies may also develop security systems to protect their proprietary information from being stolen by foreign or domestic competitors. Business and industrial espionage is an ongoing activity that clandestinely seeks to obtain trade secrets by illegal methods. A corporate system for protecting proprietary information would include a comprehensive plan ranging from restricting employee access, to data protection, to securing phone lines and meeting rooms. In some cases a chief information officer (CIO) would be responsible for implementing such a plan.

As Kay noted, other means of demonstrating reasonable efforts at secrecy include marking documents as "confidential," prohibiting people from making photo copies of trade secret documents or removing them from company premises, limiting the access of employees to sensitive materials, creating a written trade secret protection plan, and bringing suit for the theft of trade secrets as required.

On the other hand, small businesses are unlikely to prevail in cases involving trade secret protection if they sell a product or publish technical literature that discloses the trade secret, expose the secret to employees or colleagues who haven't signed confidentiality agreements, publish information about the secret in professional journals or on the Internet, or disclose the trade secret in public documents such as court records and government filings.

BIBLIOGRAPHY

Fitzpatrick, William M., Samual A. DiLullo, and Donald R. Burke. "Trade Secret Piracy and Protection: Corporate espionage, corporate security and the law." *Competitiveness Research*. Annual 2004.

Kay, Randy. "Guide to Trade Secret Protection—Maintaining Secrecy." *San Diego Business Journal*. 5 June 2000.

Millen, Press, and Todd Sullivan. "Commentary: The Economic Espionage Act — Is it finally catching on?" *Daily Record*. 19 March 2006.

United States Code, Title 18. "Economic Espionage Act of 1996." Available from http://www.tscm.com/USC18_90.html. Retrieved on 11 May 2006.

Hillstrom, Northern Lights
updated by Magee, ECDI

PROTOTYPE

Prototypes are working models of entrepreneurial ideas for new products. With certain types of products, prototypes are almost indispensable, and funding and building them the first test of the enterprise. On the other hand, an entrepreneur armed with a good prototype is able to show potential investors and licensees how the proposed product will work without having to rely exclusively on diagrams and his or her powers of description. Just as a picture is worth a thousand words, a prototype is worth a thousand pictures.

TYPES OF PROTOTYPES

There are basic types or stages of prototype creation, each of which can be used by the enterprising entrepreneur in securing financing and/or a licensee.

1. Breadboard—This is basically a working model of your idea, intended to serve the basic function of showing how the product will *work*—not how it will

look. Aesthetics, in other words, are secondary. The basic idea here is to show mechanical functionality. The approach is not suitable to a product that is mechanically straightforward and relies more fundamentally on such aspects as pizzazz and/or romance.

2. Presentation Prototype—This type of prototype is a representation of the product as it will be manufactured. Often used for promotional purposes, it should be able to demonstrate what the product can do, but it is not necessarily an exact copy of the final product. Presentation prototypes are, of course, hand-made. In actual practice, small changes may be introduced to fit the product for rapid and efficient manufacturing. Such prototypes are ideal in situation where a manufacturer is being sought or the product will be licensed.

3. Pre-Production Prototype—This type of prototype is for all practical purposes the final version of the product. It should be just like the finished product in every way, from how it is manufactured to its appearance, packaging, and instructions. This final-stage prototype is typically expensive to produce—and far more expensive to make than the actual unit cost once the product is in full production—but the added cost is often well worth it. It is most valuable because it enables inventors and producers to go over every aspect of the product in fine detail, which can head off potential trouble spots prior to product launch. Such prototypes, of course, also lend themselves for photographic reproduction in early promotion—or to show mockups of campaigns in order additionally to interest future participants in the venture.

THINGS TO CONSIDER IN CREATING A PROTOTYPE

Prospective entrepreneurs with a new product idea should make sure that they consider the following when putting together a prototype:

- Adequately research the requirements of the product prototype. Early planning will save a great deal of time and useless running around.

- Make sure the prototype is well-constructed and that it will stand up to rough handling if it has to be shipped to others. Be prepared to receive the prototype back broken or damaged.

- Do not shirk on presentation, even at the prototype stage.

- Recognize that complex product ideas may require outside assistance from professional prototype makers. Universities, engineering schools, local inventor organizations, and invention marketing companies are all potential sources of information on finding a good person to help you make your prototype. But before hiring a prototype maker, entrepreneurs should make certain that they can meet your expectations. To help ensure that you are satisfied, conduct research on the maker's business reputation and make certain that you adequately communicate your concept.

- Consider making multiple submissions to potential licensees. Some inventors send prototypes to several manufacturers at the same time. This harks back to planning, above, in which it is best to anticipate making five instead of one.

RAPID PROTOTYPING

A relatively recent development in the creation of prototypes is rapid prototyping (RP). Also known as desktop manufacturing, RP takes advantage of computer technology to turn designs into three-dimensional objects. Some older RP systems work by printing multiple layers of plastic ink to create a model of a computer-generated image. Some newer systems are able to freeze water into a three-dimensional ice sculpture model; the most sophisticated systems can create metal molds. RP technology saves time in the product development process. It also improves product design by allowing various people to see a model and have input without creating a full-fledged prototype. It has been used by large companies like automakers and aircraft manufacturers for several years, and it is now becoming accessible to small businesses as well.

SEE ALSO *Product Development*

BIBLIOGRAPHY

Clay, G. Thomas, and Preston G. Smith. "Rapid Prototyping Accelerates the Design Process." *Machine Design.* 9 March 2000.

Dematteis, Bob. *From Patent to Profit: Secrets and Strategies for the Successful Inventor.* Square One Publishers, 2005.

Dorf, Richard C., and Thomas H. Byers. *Technology Ventures: From Idea to Enterprise.* McGraw-Hill, 2005.

"From Concept to Crystal Clear Prototype." *Business Week.* 28 August 2000.

Gross, Neil. "Rapid Prototyping Gets Faster and Cheaper." *Business Week.* 1 December 2003.

Holay, Sanjay. "Building An Idea Store: Transforming ideas into product prototypes." *Stagnito's New Products Magazine.* June 2004.

Schrage, Michael. "How Prototypes Can Change Your Business." *Across the Board.* January 2000.

Hillstrom, Northern Lights
updated by Magee, ECDI

PROXY STATEMENTS

A proxy statement is, according to the Securities and Exchange Commission (SEC), "a document which is intended to provide security holders with the information necessary to enable them to vote in an informed manner on matters intended to be acted upon at security holders' meetings." Publicly-traded companies are required to send proxy statements to all shareholders, each of whom has a vote in the operation of the business, in advance of annual and special meetings. It includes information pertaining to issues that require a shareholder vote as well as a ballot for voting. This ballot is used for the election of the Board of Directors for the next year and may be used for other issues requiring a vote as well.

Proxy statements also provide information on all other matters which will be discussed at the annual or special meeting, such as approval of company auditors, approval of employee bonus plans, approval of changes in the company's preferred stock, etc. In addition, proxy statements contain a wealth of financial information about a company's significant shareholders, composition of the board of directors (including background and investment holdings), and compensation (salary, bonuses, stock options) paid to its top executives.

Finally, proxy statements contain SEC-mandated performance graphs detailing the company's stock performance and shareholder return when stacked up against other industry indexes, such as a national market index (like the Standard & Poor's 500), and broad industry averages. This information, if studied with a discerning eye, can help stockholders discern the fortunes and priorities of a company's top management. It serves as a financial benchmark for comparing the relationship between executive compensation and company performance. For example, proxy statements are less likely to create controversy if the company is performing well and rewarding stockholders of publicly traded companies with profits, or if the company is struggling financially and the executives are limiting their compensation accordingly. However, if key executives are pulling in enormous compensation packages while the company founders, attentive shareholders will notice. This aspect of the proxy statement cannot be hidden from public view, so experts urge leaders of growing firms to exercise appropriate judgment when establishing executive compensation packages.

Beginning in the late 1990s, analysts began to speculate that proxy statements in the future would be delivered to shareholders via the Internet. By 2006, this approach had been adopted by the SEC, as reported by Chris Kentouris in *Securities Industry News*. The SEC proposal, not yet formally required early in 2006, envisions mandatory distribution of proxy statements by the Internet, requiring investors "to opt out with a formal request for the mailing of paper documents," according to Kentouris. The securities industry was not pleased by this initiative although in agreement that it would be efficient. In the meantime, it would, according to the Securities Industry Association, "disrupt the proxy delivery system and increase the costs for issuers, and ultimately, the shareholders." In all likelihood, the proxy statement will, of course, eventually arrive by e-mail once the administrative ways of making it happen are fully ironed out by those supervising from above, the SEC, and those who have to make it happen: the issuers of stock.

BIBLIOGRAPHY

Dye, Jessica. "Secure Exchanges: The SEC's online alternative to paper proxies." *EContent.* January-February 2006.

Kentouris, Chris. "Industry Supports Efficiency But Blasts E-Proxy Proposals." *Securities Industry News.* 13 March 2006.

Partigan, John C. "Perks: What 2005 proxy statements reveal." *Financial Executive.* July-August 2005.

Roberts, Bill. "No Chads, No Rips, No Errors." *Electronic Business.* January 2001.

Sosnoff, Martin. "Forget the Annuals, Read the Proxies." *Forbes.* 4 May 1998.

Hillstrom, Northern Lights
updated by Magee, ECDI

PUBLIC RELATIONS

Public relations describes the various methods a company uses to disseminate messages about its products, services, or overall image to its customers, employees, stockholders, suppliers, or other interested members of the community. The point of public relations is to make the public think favorably about the company and its offerings. Commonly used tools of public relations include news releases, press conferences, speaking engagements, and community service programs.

Although advertising is closely related to public relations—as it too is concerned with promoting and gaining public acceptance for the company's products—the goal of advertising is generating sales, while the goal of public relations is generating good will. The effect of good public relations is to lessen the gap between how an organization sees itself and how others outside the organization perceive it.

Public relations involves two-way communication between an organization and its public. It requires listening to the constituencies on which an organization depends as well as analyzing and understanding the attitudes and behaviors of those audiences. Only then can an organization undertake an effective public relations campaign.

Many small business owners elect to handle the public relations activities for their own companies, while others choose to hire a public relations specialist. Managers of somewhat larger firms, on the other hand, frequently contract with external public relations or advertising agencies to enhance their corporate image. But whatever option is chosen, the head of a company is ultimately responsible for its public relations.

GOALS OF PUBLIC RELATIONS

Some of the main goals of public relations are to create, maintain, and protect the organization's reputation, enhance its prestige, and present a favorable image. Studies have shown that consumers often base their purchase decisions on a company's reputation, so public relations can have a definite impact on sales and revenue. Public relations can be an effective part of a company's overall marketing strategy. In the case of a for-profit company, public relations and marketing should be coordinated to be sure they are working to achieve the same objectives.

Another major public relations goal is to create good will for the organization. This involves such functions as employee relations, stockholder and investor relations, media relations, and community relations. Public relations may function to educate certain audiences about many things relevant to the organization—including the business in general, new legislation, and how to use a particular product—as well as to overcome misconceptions and prejudices. For example, a nonprofit organization may attempt to educate the public regarding a certain point of view, while trade associations may undertake educational programs regarding particular industries and their products and practices.

STEPS IN A PUBLIC RELATIONS CAMPAIGN

Effective public relations requires a knowledge, based on analysis and understanding, of all the factors that influence public attitudes toward the organization. While a specific public relations project or campaign may be undertaken proactively or reactively (to manage some sort of image crisis), the first basic step in either case involves analysis and research to identify all the relevant factors of the situation. In this first step, the organization gains an understanding of its various constituencies and the key factors that are influencing their perceptions of the organization.

In the second step, the organization establishes an overall policy with respect to the campaign. This involves defining goals and desired outcomes, as well as the constraints under which the campaign will operate. It is necessary to establish such policy guidelines in order to evaluate proposed strategies and tactics as well as the overall success of the campaign.

In step three, the organization outlines its strategies and tactics. Using its knowledge of the target audiences and its own established policies, the organization develops specific programs to achieve the desired objectives. Step four involves actual communication with the targeted public. The organization then employs specific public relations techniques, such as press conferences or special events, to reach the intended audience.

Finally, in step five the organization receives feedback from its public. How have they reacted to the public relations campaign? Are there some unexpected developments? In the final step, the organization assesses the program and makes any necessary adjustments.

AREAS OF PUBLIC RELATIONS

Public relations is a multifaceted activity involving different audiences as well as different types of organizations, all with different goals and objectives. As a result, there are several specific areas of public relations.

Product Public Relations Public relations and marketing work together closely when it comes to promoting a new or existing product or service. Public relations plays an important role in new product introductions by creating awareness, differentiating the product from other similar products, and even changing consumer behavior. Public relations can help introduce new products through staging a variety of special events and handling sensitive situations. For example, when the Prince Matchabelli division of Chesebrough-Pond's USA introduced a new men's cologne, there were twenty-one other men's fragrances being introduced that year. To differentiate its new offering, called Hero, Prince Matchabelli created a National Hero Awards Program honoring authentic male heroes and enlisted the participation of Big Brothers/Big Sisters of America to lend credibility to the program. Similarly, when Coleco introduced its Cabbage Patch Kids dolls, public relations helped increase awareness through licensed tie-in products, trade show exhibits, press parties, and even window displays in Cartier jewelry stores.

Public relations is often called on to give existing products and services a boost by creating or renewing visibility. For example, the California Raisins Advisory Board organized a national tour featuring live performances by the California Dancing Raisins to maintain interest in raisins during a summer-long advertising hiatus. The tour generated national and local publicity through media events, advance publicity, trade promotions, and media interviews with performer Ray Charles.

Other public relations programs for existing products involve stimulating secondary demand—as when Campbell Soup Co. increased overall demand for soup by publishing a recipe booklet—or identifying new uses for the product. Public relations can interest the media in familiar products and services in a number of ways, including holding seminars for journalists, staging a special media day, and supplying the media with printed materials ranging from "backgrounders" (in-depth news releases) to booklets and brochures. Changes in existing products offer additional public relations opportunities to focus consumers' attention. An effective public relations campaign can help to properly position a product and overcome negative perceptions on the part of the general public.

Employee Relations Employees are one of the more important audiences a company has, and an ongoing public relations program is necessary to maintain employee good will as well as to uphold the company's image and reputation among its employees. The essence of a good employee relations program is keeping employees informed and providing them with channels of communication to upper levels of management. Bechtel Group, a privately held complex of operating companies, published an annual report for its employees to keep them informed about the company's operations. The company used surveys to determine what information employees considered useful. A range of other communication devices were used, including a monthly tabloid and magazine, a quarterly video magazine, local newsletters, bulletin boards, a call-in telephone service, and "brown bag" lunches where live presentations were made about the company. Suggestion systems are another effective way to improve employee-management communications.

Other public relations programs focusing on employees include training them as company public relations representatives; explaining benefits programs to them; offering them educational, volunteer, and citizenship opportunities; and staging special events such as picnics or open houses for them. Other programs can improve performance and increase employee pride and motivation. Public relations can also play a role in recruiting new employees; handling reorganizations, relocations, and mergers; and resolving labor disputes.

Financial Relations Financial relations involves communicating not only with a company's stockholders, but also with the wider community of financial analysts and potential investors. An effective investor relations plan can increase the value of a company's stock and make it easier to raise additional capital. In some cases special meetings with financial analysts are necessary to overcome adverse publicity, negative perceptions about a company, or investor indifference. Such meetings may take the form of full-day briefings, formal presentations, or luncheon meetings. A tour of a company's facilities may help generate interest among the financial community. Mailings and ongoing communications can help a company achieve visibility among potential investors and financial analysts.

Annual reports and stockholder meetings are the two most important public relations tools for maintaining good investor relations. Some companies hold regional or quarterly meetings in addition to the usual annual meeting. Other companies reach more stockholders by moving the location of their annual meeting from city to city. Annual reports can be complemented by quarterly reports and dividend check inserts. Companies that wish to provide additional communications with stockholders may send them a newsletter or company magazine. Personal letters to new stockholders and a quick response to inquiries insure an additional measure of good will.

Community Relations A comprehensive, ongoing community relations program can help virtually any organization achieve visibility as a good community citizen and gain the good will of the community in which it operates. Banks, utilities, radio and television stations, and major retailers are some of the types of organizations most likely to have ongoing programs that might include supporting urban renewal, performing arts programs, social and educational programs, children's programs, community organizations, and construction projects. On a more limited scale, small businesses may achieve community visibility by sponsoring local sports teams or other events. Support may be financial or take the form of employee participation.

Organizations have the opportunity to improve good will and demonstrate a commitment to their communities when they open new offices, expand facilities, and open new factories. One company increased community awareness of its presence by converting a vacant building into a permanent meeting place. Another company built its new headquarters in an abandoned high school that it renovated. One of the more sensitive areas of community relations involves plant closings. A well-planned public relations campaign, combined with appropriate actions, can alleviate the tensions that such closings cause. Some elements of such a campaign might include offering special programs to laid-off workers, informing employees directly about proposed closings, and controlling rumors through candid and direct communications to the community and employees.

Organizations conduct a variety of special programs to improve community relations, including providing employee volunteers to work on community projects, sponsoring educational and literacy programs, staging open houses and conducting plant tours, celebrating anniversaries, and mounting special exhibits. Organizations are recognized as good community citizens when they support programs that improve the quality of life in their community, including crime prevention, employment, environmental programs, clean-up and beautification, recycling, and restoration.

Crisis Communications Public relations practitioners become heavily involved in crisis communications whenever there is a major accident or natural disaster affecting an organization and its community. Other types of crises involve bankruptcy, product failures, and management wrongdoing. In some cases, crises call for an organization to become involved in helping potential victims; in other cases, the crisis may require rebuilding an organization's image. In any case, experts recommend that business owners prepare a plan in advance to deal with potential crises in an honest and forthright manner. The main objective of such a plan is to provide accurate information quickly in order to reduce uncertainty. After the San Francisco earthquake of 1989, for example, the Bank of America utilized its public relations department to quickly establish communications with customers, the financial community, the media, and offices in 45 countries to assure them the bank was still operating.

Government and Political Relations Public relations in the political arena covers a wide range of activities, including staging debates, holding seminars for government leaders, influencing proposed legislation, and testifying before a congressional committee. Political candidates engage in public relations, as do government agencies at the federal, state, and local levels.

Trade associations and other types of organizations attempt to block unfavorable legislation and support favorable legislation in a number of ways. The liquor industry in California helped defeat a proposed tax increase by taking charge of the debate early, winning endorsements, recruiting spokespersons, and cultivating grassroots support. A speakers bureau trained some 240 industry volunteers, and key messages were communicated to the public through printed materials and radio and television commercials.

Public Relations in the Public Interest Organizations attempt to generate good will and position themselves as responsible citizens through a variety of programs conducted in the public interest. Some examples are environmental programs (including water and energy conservation) and antipollution programs. Health and medical programs are sponsored by a wide range of non-profit organizations, healthcare providers, and other businesses and industries. These range from encouraging other companies to develop AIDS-in-the-workplace policies to the American Cancer Society's Great American Smokeout. Other programs offer political education, leadership and self-improvement, recreational activities, contests, and safety instruction.

Consumer Education Organizations have undertaken a variety of programs to educate consumers, building good will and helping avoid misunderstandings in the process. Opportunities for educating consumers might include sponsoring television and radio programs, producing manuals and other printed materials, producing materials for classroom use, and releasing the results of surveys. In addition to focusing on specific issues or industries, educational programs may seek to inform consumers about economic matters and business in general.

Other Public Relations Programs Other types of programs that fall under the umbrella of public relations include corporate identity programs, ranging from name changes and new trademarks to changing a company's overall image. Special events may be held to call attention to an organization and focus the public's good will. These include anniversary celebrations, events related to trade shows, special exhibits, or fairs and festivals. Speakers bureaus and celebrity spokespersons are effective public relations tools for communicating an organization's point of view. Speakers bureaus may be organized by a trade association or an individual company. The face-to-face communication that speakers can deliver is often more effective than messages carried by printed materials, especially when the target audience is small and clearly defined.

PUBLIC RELATIONS FOR SMALL BUSINESSES

Like other types of organizations, small businesses can benefit from public relations in terms of their relationships with customers, employees, investors, suppliers, or other interested members of the community. Since small business owners are the most visible representatives of their own companies, they frequently handle many of the public relations functions in person. If the activity is principally associated with public appearances and participation in public events, the owner's natural abilities will be to the fore. But if a campaign needs to be launched, and funds are available, professional help may well be needed.

Effective PR professionals will be, above all, knowledgeable about press relations. For on-going and routine assistance, the small business is well served by engaging the services of an experienced free-lance writer with an extensive journalism background now specializing in helping companies "tell their story." Such individuals, very often one-person operations, have wide contacts and know not only how to prepare but also how to get materials placed with the right media. If a large campaign looms ahead, such consultants are also the ideal contact for selecting the right firm for a major campaign.

While communication is the essence of public relations, an effective public relations campaign is based on action as well as words. Whether it is practiced formally or informally, public relations is an essential function for the survival of any organization. Small business owners cannot afford to neglect public relations. But lavish parties and gifts are not necessary—it is possible to vastly improve a small business's image within its community while also controlling public relations expenditures. Sponsoring a local softball team, speaking at a chamber of commerce meeting, and volunteering at a neighborhood clean-up are among the wide variety of public relations activities readily available to small businesses.

SEE ALSO *Community Relations; Press Kits; Press Releases*

BIBLIOGRAPHY

Harrison, Sheena. "Spend, Target Ad Dollars Wisely." *Crain's Detroit Business.* 16 January 2006.

Newsom, Doug, and Jim Haynes. *Public Relations Writing.* Thomson Wadsworth, 2005.

Nucifora, Alf. "Small Businesses Need Positive PR." *Dallas Business Journal.* 19 May 2000.

"Opinion: Big firm versus small is not PR's most compelling battle." *PR Week.* 24 April 2006.

Treadwell, Donald, and Jill B. Treadwell. *Public Relations Writing: Principles in Practice.* Sage Publications, 2005.

Hillstrom, Northern Lights
updated by Magee, ECDI

PURCHASING

Purchasing is the act of buying the goods and services that a company needs to operate and/or manufacture products. Given that the purchasing department of an average company spends an estimated 50 to 70 percent of every revenue dollar on items ranging from raw materials to services, there has been greater focus on purchasing in recent years as firms look at ways to lower their operating costs. Purchasing is now seen as more of a strategic function that can be used to control bottom-line costs.

Companies are also seeking to improve purchasing processes as a means of improving customer satisfaction.

THE TRADITIONAL PURCHASING PROCESS

The traditional purchasing process involved several steps—requisition, soliciting bids, purchase order, shipping advice, invoice, and payment—that have come to be increasingly regarded as unacceptably slow, expensive, and labor intensive. Each transaction generated its own paper trail, and the same process had to be followed whether the item being purchased was a box of paper clips or a new bulldozer.

In this traditional model, purchasing was seen as essentially a clerical function. It was focused on getting the right quantity and quality of goods to the right place at the right time at a decent cost. The typical buyer was a shrewd negotiator whose primary responsibility was to obtain the best possible price from suppliers and ensure that minimum quality standards were met. Instead of using one supplier, the purchaser would usually take a divide-and-conquer approach to purchasing—buying small amounts from many suppliers and playing one against the other to gain price concessions. Purchasing simply was not considered to be a high-profile or career fast-track position—when surveys were taken of organizational stature, purchasing routinely rated in the lowest quartile.

That attitude has changed in recent years, in part because of highly publicized cases wherein companies have achieved stunning bottom-line gains through revamped purchasing processes. In addition, increased competition on both the domestic and global levels has led many companies to recognize that purchasing can actually have important strategic functions. As a result, new strategies are being used in purchasing departments at companies of all sizes.

Analysts observe that in this new purchasing environment, a guideline known as the total cost of ownership (TCO) has come to be a paramount concern in purchasing decisions. Instead of buying the good or service that has the lowest price, the buyer instead weighs a series of additional factors when determining what the true cost of the good or service is to his or her company. TCO calls for closer attention to *what else* should be counted in addition to price. Categories include freight, warranty requirements, financing costs, tooling requirements, storage/inventory costs, disposal costs, and the like—but netting out scrap values.

To lower TCO, companies are taking a number of steps to improve purchasing.

STRATEGIC SOURCING

Strategic sourcing is one of the key methods that purchasing departments are using to lower costs and improve

918

quality. Strategic sourcing involves analyzing what products the company buys in the highest volume, reviewing the marketplace for those products, understanding the economics and usage of the supplier of those products, developing a procurement strategy, and establishing working relationships with the suppliers that are much more integrated than such relationships were in the past. During this process, the team conducting the analysis should ask these questions:

- Why do we buy this product or service?

- What do we use it for?

- What market conditions do suppliers operate under?

- What profit margin do suppliers seek to obtain?

- What is the total price of purchasing from a particular vendor (in other words, the cost of the item plus the costs associated with quality problems)?

- Where is the good or service produced?

- What does the production process look like?

The products that are purchased in the highest volume will be the best candidates for cost reductions. That is because once those products are identified, the company can then justify the time and expense needed to closely study the industry that supplies that product. It can look at the ways key suppliers operate, study their business practices to see where the most money is added to the final cost of the product, and then work with the supplier to redesign processes and lower production costs. This maximizes the contribution that suppliers make to the process.

By knowing the market and knowing how much it costs for a supplier to do business, the purchasing department can set "target prices" on goods. If the supplier protests that the price is far too low, the purchasing company can offer to visit the supplier's site and study the matter. Such visits can occasionally spot problems in the supplier's operation that can help the vendor shave costs and thus lower price. Such "supplier alliances" can result in improved buyer/seller communication, improved planning, reductions in lead time, concurrent engineering, decreased paperwork, and better customer service.

The alliances also can sometimes register significant improvements in product quality. Buyers can build clearly-defined quality targets into their target prices. It will then work with the supplier to improve the manufacturing process until that quality target is met. Such a process can yield enormous benefits for buyers, including reduced inventory levels, faster time to market, significant cost savings, and reduced development costs.

Not all suppliers can meet the high standards demanded in this purchasing environment. Some studies indicate that companies that adapt strategic sourcing have lowered the number of suppliers they use by an average of nearly 40 percent. What characteristics make a good supplier, then? If the supplier is willing to partner, then analysts have identified several traits that good suppliers share:

- Commitment to continuous improvement

- Cost-competitive

- Cost-conscious

- Customer-oriented

- Encourages employee involvement

- Flexible

- Financially stable

- Able to provide technical assistance

Analysts indicate that suppliers receive some benefits in the emerging purchasing dynamic as well. Reduced paperwork, lower overhead, faster payment, long-term agreements that lead to more accurate business forecasts, access to new designs, and input into future materials and product needs have all been cited as gains. Other observers, meanwhile, point out that some buyer-supplier relationships have become so close that suppliers have opened offices on the site of the buyer, an arrangement that can conceivably result in even greater improvements in productivity and savings. Of course, companies are not going to form such "partnerships" with all of their suppliers. Some form of the traditional purchasing process involving bidding and standard purchase orders and invoices will continue to exist at almost every company, and especially at smaller companies that do not have the financial weight to make large demands on their suppliers.

EMPOWERING TEAMS

In addition to strategic sourcing, there are other methods companies can use to improve purchasing. One is creating cross-functional teams that involve purchasing personnel in every stage of the product design process. In the past, purchasers were not involved at all in the design process. They were simply instructed to purchase the necessary materials once a new product had been created. Now, purchasers (and suppliers) are increasingly included from the start of the new product process to ensure that the products needed to create product are readily available and are not prone to quality problems. Suppliers tend to be experts in their field, so they bring a large knowledge base to the design process that would otherwise be missing. This can help prevent poor designs or manufacturing mistakes.

These teams have broken down barriers and helped abolish the old manufacturing method that was known as the "over the wall" method of productions—each business unit would work on a project until its portion of the job was completed. It would then "throw the product over the wall" to the next functional team that was waiting to perform its part of the manufacturing process. The new cross-functional teams often include personnel from purchasing, manufacturing, engineering, and sales and marketing.

Purchasing teaches other members of the team how to deal directly with suppliers, cutting the purchasing personnel out of the loop. This is important in that it eliminates much of the time-consuming work that buyers had to deal with (soliciting bids, creating purchase orders, etc.) and frees them to concentrate on the part of their job where their expertise most pays off: finding suppliers and negotiating prices and quality standards.

JUST-IN-TIME PURCHASING

Just-in-time (JIT) manufacturing became one of the biggest trends in all facets of industry in the 1990s. JIT companies maintain only enough inventory to manufacture the products they need in the very near future. Parts are ordered on a near-continuous basis and often go directly from the loading dock to the assembly line. The benefits of this system include reduced inventory, improved quality, reduced lead time, reduced scrap and rework, and reduced equipment downtime. However, when a company shifts to JIT manufacturing, it must also shift to JIT purchasing.

JIT purchasing requires a nearly 180-degree change in purchasing philosophy. Traditional purchasing meant building a supplier list over time by constantly adding new suppliers, spreading purchases around, and maintaining higher inventory levels in case demand for a product soared or quality from a supplier dipped suddenly. JIT purchasing demands that buyers *narrow* their supplier list to a chosen few who can deliver high-quality products on-demand and in a timely fashion.

The JIT purchasers pays a fairly high cost in homework and vendor relations to achieve the "just-in-time" optimum. In addition to meeting specifications, suppliers must have the ability to make frequent, on-time deliveries and to provide very large volume commitments or single sourcing arrangements. Quality may be the toughest of these standards for suppliers to meet; the JIT purchaser should deal only with companies that utilize statistical analysis to verify the quality of their output. Failure to do so should eliminate the supplier from even being asked to submit a bid.

For frequent, on-time deliveries, it often helps if the supplier is located in the same geographic region as the buyer. That way, it is easier for the supplier to react to a sudden, unexpected demand for its product, and it costs far less to make the frequent deliveries that are needed. Those lower costs can in part be passed on to the buyer.

In single sourcing arrangements, it is not uncommon for the buyer to exert some influence over the supplier's business processes. The buyer has made such a significant commitment to the supplier, and is such a large portion of the supplier's total business, that it has the right to expect some say in the supplier's business practices. For some suppliers, this is an uncomfortable arrangement.

PURCHASING CARDS

As transaction costs soar (some companies report spending as much as $300 per transaction in clerical and other costs), companies are looking to buy smarter and cut costs any way possible. One popular method is recent years is to supply selected employees with purchasing or corporate procurement cards.

The cards are similar to credit cards; in fact the big three credit card companies—VISA, MasterCard, and American Express—are among the leaders in purchasing cards. In most cases, the cards are used to purchase small business items. A master bill is sent straight to the purchasing department. These cards are true credit cards, however. In some cases, they work only between a buyer and suppliers identified in advance, eliminating the bank that is involved with credit cards. Additionally, the cards can be coded to include a variety of important transaction information that reduces the amount of paperwork needed to track the sale, including sales tax data, customer code (such as job number or cost center), taxpayer identification number, and more. This coding allows companies to receive valuable information about each transaction and greatly streamlines the purchasing process.

The cards are beneficial to suppliers as well. The most important advantage is that the vendor receives payment much more quickly than in the past—sometimes in as short a period as two or three days. Additionally, the supplier saves money by not having to issue and mail an invoice, and the supplier knows the credit worthiness of the customer before the transaction is even processed.

BIBLIOGRAPHY

Karpak, Birsen, Rammohan R. Kasuganti, and Erdooan Kumcu. "Are You Using Costly Outmoded Techniques to Purchase Materials?" *Business Forum.* Winter 2005.

MacLean, John R. "Services Need Strategy Too." *Purchasing.* 16 February 2006.

McCrea, Bridget. "Getting Paid Faster: Government suppliers receive quicker payments with purchasing cards." *Black Enterprise.* February 2006.

Paquette, Larry. *The Sourcing Solution: A Step-By-Step Guide to Creating a Successful Purchasing Program.* AMACOM, 2004.

"Purchasing Managers Are Rethinking Supply Chain Strategies to Combat Increasing Energy Costs." *Purchasing.* 17 November 2005.

Quayle, Michael. *Purchasing And Supply Chain Management: Strategies and Realities.* Idea Group Inc., 2006.

Taylor, Nolan. "E-commerce Can Level the Playing Field." *Indianapolis Business Journal.* 27 March 2006.

Wisner, Joel D., and Keah Choon Tan. "Supply Chain Management and Its Impact on Purchasing." *Journal of Supply Chain Management.* Fall 2000.

Hillstrom, Northern Lights
updated by Magee, ECDI

Q

QUALITY CIRCLES

A quality circle is a participatory management technique that enlists the help of employees in solving problems related to their own jobs. Circles are formed of employees working together in an operation who meet at intervals to discuss problems of quality and to devise solutions for improvements. Quality circles have an autonomous character, are usually small, and are led by a supervisor or a senior worker. Employees who participate in quality circles usually receive training in formal problem-solving methods—such as brainstorming, pareto analysis, and cause-and-effect diagrams—and are then encouraged to apply these methods either to specific or general company problems. After completing an analysis, they often present their findings to management and then handle implementation of approved solutions. Pareto analysis, by the way, is named after the Italian economist, Vilfredo Pareto, who observed that 20 percent of Italians received 80 percent of the income—thus the principle that most results are determined by a few causes.

The interest of U.S. manufacturers in quality circles was sparked by dramatic improvements in the quality and economic competitiveness of Japanese goods in the post-World War II years. The emphasis of Japanese quality circles was on preventing defects from arising in the first place rather than through culling during post-production inspection. Japanese quality circles also attempted to minimize the scrap and downtime that resulted from part and product defects. In the United States, the quality circle movement evolved to encompass the broader goals of cost reduction, productivity improvement, employee involvement, and problem-solving activities.

The quality circle movement, along with total quality control, while embraced in a major way in the 1980s, has largely disappeared or undergone significant transformations for reasons discussed below.

BACKGROUND

Quality circles were originally associated with Japanese management and manufacturing techniques. The introduction of quality circles in Japan in the postwar years was inspired by the lectures of W. Edwards Deming (1900-1993), a statistician for the U.S. government. Deming based his proposals on the experience of U.S. firms operating under wartime industrial standards. Noting that American management had typically given line managers and engineers about 85 percent of the responsibility for quality control and line workers only about 15 percent, Deming argued that these shares should be reversed. He suggested redesigning production processes to account more fully for quality control, and continuously educating all employees in a firm—from the top down—in quality control techniques and statistical control technologies. Quality circles were the means by which this continuous education was to take place for production workers.

Deming predicted that if Japanese firms adopted the system of quality controls he advocated, nations around the world would be imposing import quotas on Japanese products within five years. His prediction was vindicated. Deming's ideas became very influential in Japan, and he received several prestigious awards for his contributions to the Japanese economy.

The principles of Deming's quality circles simply moved quality control to an earlier position in the production process. Rather than relying upon post-production inspections to catch errors and defects, quality circles attempted to prevent defects from occurring in the first place. As an added bonus, machine downtime and scrap materials that formerly occurred due to product defects were minimized. Deming's idea that improving quality could increase productivity led to the development in Japan of the Total Quality Control (TQC) concept, in which quality and productivity are viewed as two sides of a coin. TQC also required that a manufacturer's suppliers make use of quality circles.

Quality circles in Japan were part of a system of relatively cooperative labor-management relations, involving company unions and lifetime employment guarantees for many full-time permanent employees. Consistent with this decentralized, enterprise-oriented system, quality circles provided a means by which production workers were encouraged to participate in company matters and by which management could benefit from production workers' intimate knowledge of the production process. In 1980 alone, changes resulting from employee suggestions resulted in savings of $10 billion for Japanese firms and bonuses of $4 billion for Japanese employees.

Active American interest in Japanese quality control began in the early 1970s, when the U.S. aerospace manufacturer Lockheed organized a tour of Japanese industrial plants. This trip marked a turning point in the previously established pattern, in which Japanese managers had made educational tours of industrial plants in the United States. Thereafter quality circles spread rapidly here; by 1980, more than one-half of firms in the Fortune 500 had implemented or were planning to implement quality circles. To be sure, these were not installed uniformly everywhere but introduced for experimental purposes and later selectively expanded—and also terminated.

In the early 1990s, the U.S. National Labor Relations Board (NLRB) made several important rulings regarding the legality of certain forms of quality circles. These rulings were based on the 1935 Wagner Act, which prohibited company unions and management-dominated labor organizations. One NLRB ruling found quality programs unlawful that were established by the firm, that featured agendas dominated by the firm, and addressed the conditions of employment within the firm. Another ruling held that a company's labor-management committees were in effect labor organizations used to bypass negotiations with a labor union. As a result of these rulings, a number of employer representatives expressed their concern that quality circles, as well as other kinds of labor-management cooperation programs, would be hindered. However, the NLRB stated that these rulings were not general indictments against quality circles and labor-management cooperation programs, but were aimed specifically at the practices of the companies in question.

SILVER BULLETS AND MARKSMANSHIP

In the mid-2000s, quality circles are almost universally consigned to the dustbin of management techniques. James Zimmerman and Jamie Weiss, writing in *Quality,* summed the matter up as follows: "Quality and productivity initiatives have come and gone during the past few decades. The list of 'already rans' includes quality circles, statistical process control, total quality management, Baldrige protocol diagnostics, enterprise wide resource planning and lean manufacturing. Most have been sound in theory but inconsistent in implementation, not always delivering on their promises over the long run."

Nilewide Marketing Review said the same thing in similar words: "Management fads should be the curse of the business world—as inevitably as night follows day, the next fad follows the last. Nothing more typifies the disastrous nature of this following so-called excellence than the example of quality circles. They rose to faddish heights in the late 80s presenting the so-called secret of Japanese companies and how American companies such as Lockheed used them to their advantage. Amid all the new consultancies and management articles, everyone ignored the fact Lockheed had abandoned them in 1978 and less than 12% of the original companies still used them."

Harvey Robbins and Michael Finley, writing in their book, *Why The New Teams Don't Work,* put it most bluntly: "Now, we know what happened to quality circles nationwide—they failed, because they had no power and no one listened to them." Robbins and Finley cite the case of Honeywell which formed 625 quality circles but then, within 18 months, had abandoned all but 620 of them.

Japanese industry obviously embraced and applied quality circles (the idea of an American thinker) and QC has contributed to Japanese current dominance in many sectors, notably in automobiles. If QC became a fad in the U.S. and failed to deliver, implementation was certainly one important reason—as Zimmerman and Weiss pointed out. U.S. adapters of QC may have seen the practice as a silver bullet and did not bother shooting straight. The reason why a succession of other no doubt sensible management techniques have also, seemingly, failed to get traction may be due to a tendency by modern management to embrace mechanical recipes for success without bothering to understand and to internalize them fully and to absorb their spirit.

REQUIREMENTS FOR SUCCESS

The problems of adaptation, which have caused quality circles to be abandoned, are made plain by a look at the conditions two experts think are necessary for the success of quality circles. Ron Basu and J. Nevan Wright, in their book *Quality Beyond Six Sigma* (another quality management technique) specified seven conditions for successful implementation of quality circles. These are summarized below:

1. Quality circles must be staffed entirely by volunteers.

2. Each participant should be representative of a different functional activity.

3. The problem to be addressed by the QC should be chosen by the *circle*, not by management, and the choice honored even if it does not visibly lead to a management goal.

4. Management must be supportive of the circle and fund it appropriately even when requests are trivial and the expenditure is difficult to envision as helping toward real solutions.

5. Circle members must receive appropriate training in problem solving.

6. The circle must choose its own leader from within its own members.

7. Management should appoint a manager as the mentor of the team, charged with helping members of the circle achieve their objectives; but this person must not manage the QC.

"Quality circles have been tried in the USA and Europe, often with poor results," Basu and Wright say. "From our combined first-hand experience of quality circles in Australasia, the UK and Europe, South America, Africa, Asia and India, we believe that quality circles will work if [these] rules are applied."

Any experienced manager, contemplating the rules shown above and the typical management environments in which he or she works or has worked in the past will be able to discern quite readily why QC has not taken a firm hold in the U.S. environment. As for the small business owner, he or she may actually be in a very good position to try this approach if it feels natural. An obviously important element of success, confirmed by Basu and Wright, is that QC must be practiced in an environment of trust and empowerment.

SEE ALSO *Quality Control*

BIBLIOGRAPHY
Basu, Ron, and J. Nevan Wright. *Quality Beyond Six Sigma.* Elsevier, 2003.

Cole, Robert. *Managing Quality Fads: How America Learned to Play the Quality Game.* Oxford University Press, 1999.

"Imitate Excellence?" *Nilewide Marketing Review.* 23 October 2005.

Robbins, Harvey, and Michael Finley. *Why The New Teams Don't Work: What Goes Wrong and How to Make It Right.* Berrett-Koehler Publishers, 2000.

Zimmerman, James P., and Jamie Weiss. "Six Sigma's Seven Deadly Sins: While the seven sins can be deadly redemption is possible." *Quality.* January 2005.

Hillstrom, Northern Lights
updated by Magee, ECDI

QUALITY CONTROL

Quality control is a methodology employed in manufacturing to prevent defects in manufactured products. Abbreviated as QC, the method has been implemented in a number of ways each of which has its own name and following. Quality control is typically associated with statistical approaches. Quality management has strong philosophical aspects based on the insight that quality is as much the result of management approaches as it is of specific activities. The modern quality movement is a fusion of American know-how originally developed at Bell Laboratories and Japanese enterprise and implementation. The several waves of quality control methods that have swept U.S. manufacturing since the 1950s are almost unthinkable except against the backdrop of Japanese industry achieving a world class reputation and thus producing stimulus. The movement is very closely associated with an American mathematician and physicist, W. Edwards Deming, although Deming was one of two prominent individuals who helped the Japanese forge their approaches to manufacturing; the other was Joseph M. Juran, a Rumanian immigrant to the United States. America's embrace of QC followed its successful application in Japan. Some type of statistical quality control is practiced in connection with most demanding manufacturing processes, but the more "qualitative" (no pun intended) aspects of QC have never been wholeheartedly embraced.

ORIGINS

Modern quality control originated with Walter A. Shewhart, then working at Bell Telephone Laboratories. Shewhart devised a control chart named after him in 1923 and in 1931 published his method in *Economic Control of Quality of Manufactured Product.* Shewhart's method saw its introduction at Western Electric Company's Hawthorn plant in 1926. Joseph Juran was one of the people trained in the technique. In 1928 he wrote a pamphlet entitled *Statistical Methods Applied to Manufacturing Problems* which was later incorporated into the *AT&T Statistical Quality Control Handbook* which is still in print. In 1951 Juran published his very influential *Quality Control Handbook*.

W. Edwards Deming went to Japan to assist in the preparation of the 1951 Japanese Census. Being an expert on statistical methods, the Japanese Union of Scientists and Engineers (JUSE), having heard of Shewhart's techniques, invited Deming to lecture on statistical quality control. Deming gave a series of lectures in 1950 aimed both at describing SQC and at motivating his audience of executives. He pointed out the linkage between quality, productivity, and potential gains in market share. He found an enthusiastic audience. JUSE also invited Juran to lecture in 1954 with similar success, but by that time Deming had achieved wide prominence in Japan. With the great success enjoyed by SQC in Japan, and through his own abilities as a teacher and promoter of quality control and related management approaches, Deming became the iconic figure in the field, the "father of quality control." JUSE established the, by now, prestigious Deming Prize for quality-related achievements by individuals and organizations.

Japanese improvements in industrial performance eventually aroused interest in the United States in the early 1970s, led by Lockheed Corporation. Quality control then took on a life of its own in this country.

QUALITY CONTROL FUNDAMENTALS

Before the advent of statistical quality control, control was exercised by inspecting the output of manufacturing processes and removing defective items. The modern technique established an upstream method for detecting deviations from specified quality—early detection—used to trigger analysis of causes and then changes to manufacturing procedures.

SQC requires that the producer first identify several characteristics of a product to be measured, typically its dimensions, fit with other parts, smoothness, reflectivity, etc. Carefully conducted test runs are made first; every part is measured and its measurements are recorded. Upper and lower boundaries are set for every measurement from one or repeated test runs, with the idea that any part that falls within these boundaries conforms to the product's quality standard. The center line between the boundaries is then used as a base-line for measurement. Once this quality standard is set, production can begin.

The quality control activity during production consists of taking samples from the run continuously, taking measurements on the samples immediately, and then plotting them rapidly on a Shewhart Chart. During production, measurements typically fall close to the center line, some above it, some below it, some on the center

line. A certain amount of divergence is natural and cannot be avoided. So long as the plotted points are within the accepted boundaries, the product conforms to the quality standard. But SQC demands that if the plotted points begin to show a trend away from the center, rather than clustering randomly around it—or, worse yet, begin to fall outside the boundaries in either direction—then production must stop. The incoming raw material, the production machinery, and other inputs, such as lubricants, must next be examined to discover why results are trending in the wrong direction or fall outside the acceptable range.

SQC thus provides early warning that quality is deteriorating. When the method is applied strictly, production cannot resume until problems are detected and fixed—as shown by brief test runs. Needless to say, money is saved by preventing wasteful production of parts later, products that fail to fit, or parts that result in product failure in use. In aircraft and autos, such failures can mean injury and death and massive lawsuits. Corrective actions taken early improve the process as a whole. In due time they lead to better equipment designs.

The technique also lends itself to the gradual ratcheting up of quality. This is accomplished by setting "acceptable boundaries" more narrowly and then modifying the production process until the new quality goal is met. This, of course, may require substantial changes to the process or the raw materials used. In Deming's conceptualization of the process, quality is thus "designed in" rather than "inspected out." The concept of "continuous improvement" arose in such efforts to raise quality. Its downstream consequences are lower cost in production and in warranty service, advantages in pricing, and higher customer satisfaction leading to brand loyalty and market share.

RELATED ISSUES, PRACTICES, AND MEASURES

Statistical quality control, as described above, is the fundamental description of quality control in the modern context. It is centered on measuring deviations from a norm and then taking actions to eliminate such deviations. But quality control, almost from the outset, came to be surrounded by what might be called a "cultural" radiation—namely management approaches, philosophies, and practices aimed at creating the right environment for a quality-driven industrial process. These radiations in part came from Japanese management culture, very different from U.S. practice, the ideas of Deming—which both influenced and reflected Japanese practice—and their elaborations by others.

Deming, for instance, in his 1982 book *Out of the Crisis,* formulated "14 points for management" which generally urge greater collaboration of effort, a longer-range view, commitment to improvement, constancy of purpose, and humane treatment and involvement of people. Some of Deming's points were revolutionary (e.g., to cultivate a single supplier for a resource, to eliminate management by objectives, numerical goals, and annual reviews of employees) while others have been adopted, albeit not always in the spirit in which Deming proposed them (e.g., team approaches, continuous improvement). Deming also condemned managing for the short term, management mobility (job hopping), reliance on technology rather than real solutions, and running operations by available numbers rather than a feel for the whole.

Quality Circles Quality Circles, covered in detail elsewhere in this volume, played a role in the 1980s. These circles were envisioned as collaborative efforts by teams of workers engaged in discovering problems and the solutions to them. The cultivation of team-approaches popular in the mid-2000s for every type of activity owes much to the precedent set by quality circles.

JIT Just-in-time (JIT) procurement, which is much facilitated by the selection of a single, well-qualified supplier, arose from Japanese practice aimed at taking cost out of inventory control while maintaining very-high quality. Closely related to JIT is the practice of "supplier partnering" in which suppliers and their customers use the same quality standards.

TQM Total Quality Management (TQM), also covered elsewhere in this book, was also a method promoted by Deming. TQM is a philosophy of management in which the operational elements are continuous quality improvement, quality circles, and strong management backing.

ISO 9000 ISO 9000 is yet another result of the "quality movement." It represents a series of standards developed by the International Standards Organization which defined, for different industrial operations, managerial and operational standards that, if followed, will produce high quality. Companies can obtain ISO 9000 certification showing that they follow the standards ISO has laid out. This certification, then, can be used in advertising to inform the public that the company meets the ISO standard. The measure, of course, is somewhat indirect in that it guarantees certain practices, not necessarily what results from their use.

Lean Manufacturing Lean Manufacturing is a practice pioneered by Toyota and widely imitated. It is called "lean" because it attempts to achieve results with minimum input of labor, space, cost, and time. The method relies heavily on JIT, cross-trained and highly motivated employees, and equipment arrangements that both save space and also cluster related tooling in close proximity. Layouts and arrangements are organized so that changes between production cycles can be accomplished swiftly. Lean manufacturing thus is well-suited to predictable production orders making a single item. Quality management is intense so that one-pass production is possible.

Six Sigma Six Sigma is actually a quality goal in the achievement to which a variety of QC approaches may be applied. It was initially named by Motorola and "six sigma" was achieved there. But the concept "developed legs" when Jack Welsh, the larger-than-life CEO of General Electric adopted it at GE. So what is Six Sigma? It means production in which 1 million pieces made will have virtually no defects. "Sigma" is the Greek letter used to designate the standard deviation from a norm as measured in statistics. If every part of a 1 million production run is defective, the sigma measurement will be infinite. If 10 percent of parts are defective, sigma will be 2.8; with 1 percent defect, the sigma increases to 3.8. Thus *the higher the sigma, the greater the perfection.* A sigma of 6.0 is reached when defects are down to 3.4 items out of a million, representing 0.00034 percent—in effect about as close to perfection as one can practically get. While Six Sigma is much discussed, it is not so much a *method* as the target of a QC effort or program.

Poka-yoke The U.S. is not alone in generating ever-new buzzwords to be used in quality control. A new phrase from Japan is poka-yoke, meaning "avoid error." The coinage of a Toyota engineer, the concept refers to "designing in" methods of preventing mistakes. An example is a guard put on a drill press to stop the press before it drills too deep. The practice of poka-yoke lies in the identification of opportunities for "mistake-proofing" and then actions to make them happen. This approach is one variant for defect correction after the statistical charts show that something is amiss.

STATUS AND FUTURE

Quality control in the modern sense has come a long way since its initial formulation in the 1920s and its widespread adaptation in the 1950s, first in Japan, then across the world. It has become a routine part of many manufacturing processes, and, as signaled by Six Sigma, the goals are becoming ever-more ambitious. The more managerial and people-oriented aspects of the quality movement have a spottier history and have produced a series of initiatives that have come, have gone, and have resurfaced in various guises. Ever-new labels indicate attempts to capture something evidently difficult to hold for long: "quality circles," "teaming," the "learning organization," "knowledge management," "empowerment," and the like. The social phenomenon appears to indicate that it is ultimately easier to produce defect-free gadgets than perfect humans. The difficult we'll do immediately; the impossible will take a little time.

SEE ALSO *ISO 9000; Quality Circles; Total Quality Management (TQM)*

BIBLIOGRAPHY

Basu, Ron, and J. Nevan Wright. *Quality Beyond Six Sigma.* Elsevier, 2003.

Brownhill, Mark. "Beyond Poka-Yoke." *Fabricating & Metalworking.* February 2005.

Irwin, Stephen. "ISO 9000—A plus for airports: consultant Steve Irwin offers reasons why airports can benefit from a new standard." *Airport Business.* March 2006.

Juran, Joseph M. *Architect of Quality.* McGraw-Hill, 2004.

"The Life and Contributions of Joseph M. Juran." Carlson School of Management, University of Minnesota. Available from http://part-timemba.csom.umn.edu/Page1275.aspx. Retrieved on 12 May 2006.

Montgomery, Douglas C. *Introduction to Statistical Quality Control.* John Wiley & Sons, 2004.

"Real-World Six Sigma." *Industrial Engineer.* September 2005.

"Teachings." The W. Edwards Deming Institute. Available from http://www.deming.org/theman/teachings02.html. Retrieved on 12 May 2005.

Darnay, ECDI

R

RACIAL DISCRIMINATION

Racial discrimination is the practice of letting a person's race or skin color unfairly become a factor when deciding who receives a job, promotion, or other employment benefit. It most often affects minority individuals who feel they have been unfairly discriminated against in favor of a Caucasian (or white) individual, but there have been recent cases where whites have claimed that reverse discrimination has occurred—that is, a minority received unfairly favorable treatment at the expense of a white individual.

Court rulings handed down through the years have determined that a company's responsibility not to discriminate based on race begins even before an individual is hired. Companies can be held liable if pre-employment screening or testing is determined to be discriminatory, if applications ask unacceptable questions designed to screen for race, or if the overall selection process is deemed to be unfair. One of the main indicators that racial discrimination has occurred in the hiring process involves the qualifications of the job applicants. While a slight difference in qualifications between a minority and white candidate does not automatically indicate racial bias (if the lesser qualified white candidate is hired over the minority candidate), a substantial difference in qualifications has almost always been upheld by the courts as a sure sign of racial discrimination.

FEDERAL LAWS PROHIBIT DISCRIMINATION

Since the social unrest of the 1960s, the federal government has been actively involved in preventing racial discrimination in the workplace. The most important law covering racial discrimination on the job is the Civil Rights Act of 1964—specifically, Title VII of that act: it strictly prohibits all forms of discrimination on the basis of race, color, religion, sex, or national origin in all aspects of employment. Written during a tumultuous period in American history when many people expected the federal government to right social wrongs, the law was a monumental piece of legislation that changed the American employment landscape.

The law stated that it was unlawful for an employer to "fail or refuse to hire or to discharge any individual, or otherwise discriminate against any individual with respect to his compensation, terms, conditions, or privileges of employment, because of such individual's race, color, religion, sex, or national origin." The law covers hiring, dismissals, compensation, and all other aspects of employment, while also covering actual employment opportunities that are available. Examples of racial discrimination that would fall under the scope of the act include:

1. An employee who alleges that his or her manager only promotes nonminority employees and keeps minorities in entry-level positions.

2. An employee who alleges that a manager or other person in power tells jokes or makes statements that are demeaning, insulting, or offensive to members of a minority group.

3. A manager who makes it clear that he or she believes in racial stereotypes by admitting that he or she refuses to promote a certain minority group because "all [members of that group] are lazy."

The law covers business with 15 or more employees, and applies to all private, federal, state, and local employers. In many states, businesses with fewer than 15 employees face the same rules thanks to local or state statutes. In addition to the hiring provisions, the law dictates that employers cannot in any way limit or segregate employees based on race in any way that would adversely affect their chances at promotions. It does allow for two narrow exceptions to the law—businesses may use a "bona fide" seniority or merit system and measure performance and earnings based on a quantity or quality measuring system, and employers may use ability tests to determine the most qualified candidates for a job as long as the test does not discriminate racially in any way.

In 1991, the 1964 law was significantly amended for the first time by the passage of the Civil Rights Act of 1991. The law was passed to override several Supreme Court decisions that had made it much more difficult for employees to prove that racial discrimination had occurred. One of the many changes of the 1991 law is that it closed a loophole in the 1964 act that also involved a Civil War-era statute known as 42 U.S.C. Section 1981. The Supreme Court had held that Section 1981 applied to hiring and sometimes to promotions but did not cover racial harassment that occurred in the workplace once a person was hired. The 1991 act said that all racial discrimination was covered by U.S. law, including post-hire harassment.

The other major enhancement under the 1991 act involved monetary damages. Before the law was passed, employees who sued an employer for discrimination and won could only recover lost wages or salary, lost benefits, attorney fees, other legal costs, and the costs associated with reinstatement. The 1991 law said that employees could also recover punitive monetary damages for pain and emotional suffering, mental anguish, future lost wages and benefits, and more. Those damages could only be collected if it was proven that the discrimination was intentional and there was clearly "malice" or "reckless indifference" exhibited, but this was a radical change from the previous legislation. To protect employers from overly large court settlements, the amount of punitive damages was capped at $300,000 for certain cases of discrimination, although no caps apply in cases of ethnic or racial discrimination.

Other changes in the 1991 law involve employment practices that have a "disparate impact" on racial groups (that is, affect them more than white groups), make it easier for a plaintiff to receive damages in cases where a discriminatory practice *and* a nondiscriminatory practice both played a part in a hiring or promotion decision, and allow employees to challenge seniority systems that are put into place if the systems are later determined to be discriminatory (in the past, workers could only sue at the time the system was first put into place). Together, all of these changes made it easier for workers to prove discrimination claims, which has increased the number of lawsuits nationwide.

THE EQUAL EMPLOYMENT OPPORTUNITY COMMISSION

To oversee the federal civil rights legislation, a separate administrative body was created as part of the Civil Rights Act of 1964. The Equal Employment Opportunity Commission, or EEOC, was created to enforce laws that prevent discrimination based on race, sex, color, religion, national origin, disability, or age when hiring, firing, or promoting employees. Four categories of people—by race, color, sex, and/or creed—were given "protected status" under the law, which was to be upheld by the EEOC. The commission is an independent regulatory body that has the power to launch investigations, file lawsuits, and create programs to eliminate discrimination.

The EEOC has been a controversial organization throughout its 40-plus years of history. Liberal politicians believe that the agency was long overdue and that it is absolutely imperative that the agency be proactive in identifying and fighting discrimination in the courts, while conservatives believe that the organization is a perfect example of "big government" that intrudes far too deeply into citizens' lives. The agency's strong enforcement of affirmative action policies (which actively seek to promote minorities over equally qualified whites in order to address past discrimination) has been its most controversial action, as many Americans oppose affirmative action.

Even with political opposition, the EEOC continues to be effective in fighting racial discrimination. In FY 2005 alone, for instance, the EEOC obtained nearly $173 million in benefits for complainants through settlement and conciliation (excluding litigation awards). Litigation awards accounted for another $106 million in FY 2005.

STEPS TAKEN BY EMPLOYERS TO END DISCRIMINATION

Because racial discrimination can have adverse consequences for a company—including lower morale, a divided workplace, expensive lawsuits, and public embarrassment—some companies take highly visible steps to curtail discrimination in the workplace. These include in-house workshops and training sessions on racial sensitivity and diversity in the workplace, training on employment laws, and adopting strict new rules against discrimination.

Many other companies only become active when prodded by events and circumstances. In November of 2000, the Coca-Cola Company agreed to settle a racial discrimination suit by paying a penalty of $192.5 million. Sara Lee Corporation was forced to make a large cash settlement to a former employee who says that he was the butt of racist jokes, disparaging remarks, and was even forced to view a noose hanging in his workplace. In addition to the cash settlement, the amount of which was confidential, Sara Lee also agreed to establish training programs to raise awareness of the company's anti-discrimination policies.

To make sure that it is on the cutting edge of preventing racial discrimination, IBM has established individual employee task forces for almost every group that is employed by the huge company, including men, women, blacks, Hispanics, Asians, Native Americans, gays and lesbians, and disabled persons. The groups, which are established at many of the company's offices, meet regularly to discuss diversity and workplace concerns. This represents an extreme example of the steps companies are taking to prevent discrimination, but actions of this type are becoming more common.

AFFIRMATIVE ACTION

Affirmative action is a controversial policy intended to counteract racial discrimination. *West's Encyclopedia of American Law* defines affirmative action as referring "to both mandatory and voluntary programs intended to affirm the civil rights of designated classes of individuals by taking positive actions to protect them." In other words, affirmative action actively promotes the interest of minorities over the white majority in order to correct past discrimination. For example, in a situation where a test is required before starting a particular job or to earn a promotion, minorities may be given preference over non-minorities for that job or promotion even though they score lower on the test than the nonminority worker. While this may seem wrong to some people, those who support affirmative action argue that past acts of discrimination have been so blatant that extraordinary steps are required to overcome those acts. At the start of the twenty-first century, however, affirmative action programs are under fire across the United States, with numerous court challenges occurring across the country.

One effect of affirmative action has been an increase in "reverse discrimination" lawsuits, in which non-minority workers allege that they have been discriminated against. In situations where companies have used affirmative action to help undo decades of blatant discrimination, white workers have become upset over being passed over for jobs and promotions. They claim that, if it is unfair to not hire a qualified worker just because he

or she is a minority, then it should be equally unfair to not hire a qualified worker just because he or she is white. White employees have argued that, even though they have higher qualifications, experience, and skill, they are being passed over for jobs in favor of less-qualified candidates who are minorities.

In response to reverse discrimination lawsuits involving affirmative action programs, courts have recognized the need to overcome past racial bias, but have also sided with the white workers in many cases. For example, in an attempt to redress past problems, a public university ruled that women and minorities would no longer have to take a test to qualify for a special employment program. As a result, for nine years, every job opening in the program went to a woman or a minority, even though white males represented half of the applicant pool. When the university's program was challenged in a lawsuit brought by white males, the courts ruled that the test exemption ensured that "the sole purpose of the affirmative action plan was to circumvent a lawful ... preference program" and that the exemption violated Title VII because it caused white men to be excluded from the job in question. The school was forced to pay $113,000 to settle the case and correct the reverse discrimination.

Reverse discrimination does not always have to involve affirmative action, however. In a case decided in 2006, as reported by Shannon Duffy in *The Legal Intelligencer,* four white males prevailed in a law suit against the Philadelphia School District claiming that an African-American woman had discharged them because there were "too many white male managers in this department."

RACIAL DISCRIMINATION TRENDS

While advances have been made to improve race relations, there is statistical evidence to show that racial discrimination in the workplace is still commonplace. In 2000, the EEOC reported the results of a study of workplaces in North Carolina that showed that accusations of racial harassment on the job nearly quadrupled between 1996 and 2000, jumping from 16 reported incidents in 1996 to 62 in 2000 in just one region of the state. Mindy Weinstein, attorney at the EEOC office in Charlotte, North Carolina, was uncertain of what caused the increase, but she had some ideas. "There's a new generation of workers today who were not raised in the civil rights movement, who may not have been aware of the laws that came about because of that time," she said in the *Raleigh News & Observer.* "We think it's largely a reflection of what's going on in society as a whole."

Another potential cause of the increase is the fact that, thanks to earlier efforts to wipe out racial discrimination, there are more minorities than ever before in the workplace and also in high-level positions of power. Because minorities have been able to compete on a level playing field, they have been able to rise through the ranks more quickly, often taking jobs that were traditionally held by white workers. This can lead to resentment among the formerly dominant workers who are now lower on the employment ladder.

SEE ALSO *Affirmative Action*

BIBLIOGRAPHY

Blank, Rbecca M., Marilyn Dabady, and Constance F. Citro. *Measuring Racial Discrimination.* National Academies Press, 2004.

"The Civil Rights Act of 1964 and the Equal Opportunity Employment Commission." National Archives and Records Administration website. Available from http://www.archives.gov/education/lessons/civil-rights-act/. Retrieved on 15 May 2006.

Contini, Peter. "How to Protect Your Office from Discrimination Claims." *Real Estate Weekly.* 15 March 2006.

Duffy, Shannon P. "'Reverse Discrimination' Verdict Upheld." *The Legal Intelligencer.* 17 April 2006.

"Institutional Racism, Part II: Race, Skill, and Hiring in U.S. Cities." *Nation's Cities Weekly.* 19 June 2000.

Moss, Philip I., and Chris Tilly. *Stories Employers Tell: Race, Skill and Hiring in America (Multi-City Study of Inequality).* Russell Sage Foundation, 2001.

"Reports of Racism at Work Increasing." *Raleigh News & Observer.* 11 December 2000.

U.S. Equal Employment Opportunity Commission. "EEOC Annual Reports." Available from http://www.eeoc.gov/abouteeoc/annual_reports/index.html. Retrieved on 15 May 2006.

Hillstrom, Northern Lights
updated by Magee, ECDI

REBATES

Rebates, widely known as refunds, are a popular tool used by businesses to promote their products and services. Rebates are distinct from coupons and other forms of discounting in that they reimburse a customer for part of the purchase price following, rather than at the time of, the sale. By offering consumers cash back on the purchase price, rebates provide an incentive to buy a particular product.

A relatively new method of promotion, rebating evolved from the marketing technique of offering coupons. They were initially offered by producers of grocery-store goods and subsequently by manufacturers of nonfood items. Currently, businesses making use of rebates are diverse and include the manufacturers of health and beauty

aids, household supplies, and small and large appliances, as well as automakers, wine and liquor manufacturers, and segments of the computer industry.

The cash amounts these companies offer their customers is similarly wide-ranging; some rebates of less than a dollar are offered, while other rebates on "big ticket" items such as automobiles have reached several thousand dollars. The size of the rebate offered depends on the base retail price, the nature of the product being promoted, and the number of goods backed up in the production pipeline.

HOW REBATES WORK

A rebate is created when a manufacturer offers a rebate to all who purchase its product. Typically the offer carries an expiration date of six to eight months. The purchaser completes a form provided by the manufacturer and mails it—along with any other items the manufacturer may require, such as a cash-register receipt or the Universal Product Code (UPC) snipped from the packaging—to the address specified on the form.

Most commonly, the purchaser sends the rebate form and related "proof of purchase" items not to the manufacturer but to one of several large clearinghouses hired by the manufacturer to handle these transactions—for instance, the Young America Corporation in Minnesota or the Nielson Clearing House in Texas. The clearinghouse then processes the form and sends the purchaser a check in the manufacturer's name, usually within four to eight weeks from the time the purchaser mails in the required information.

Companies use a number of means to get their rebate forms into the hands of customers. Many companies supply a pad of tear-off rebate forms to the stores selling their products; others print the form directly on the packaging or on a tag hanging from the merchandise. To announce the rebate offer and distribute the forms, companies may also place advertisements in newspapers and magazines, utilize home mailers, and/or place ads in the myriad refunders' newsletters developed by consumers to avail themselves of these offers. In addition, companies frequently use television and radio advertisements to publicize their rebate promotions. Finally, there are several Internet sites that direct consumers to rebate offers, such as myRebates.com and CyberRebate.com.

PROS AND CONS

Rebates are highly attractive to most consumers. They provide a partial and tax-free cash reimbursement for their purchases; the Internal Revenue Service views rebates as a reduction in the price paid for a product, rather than as income. And for manufacturers, rebating provides numerous advantages: it induces prospective customers to try their products; it boosts company sales and visibility; it relieves problems of excess inventory; and it attracts interest from retailers, who often help promote the offer and expand the shelf space allotted to the manufacturer's goods accordingly. Rebate promotions can thus help a company increase its leverage with retailers and develop brand loyalty and repeat business among consumers over the long run. Indeed, a study conducted by United Marketing Services (UMS) found that rebates are an effective means of establishing product awareness with consumers. In addition, the information consumers provide on rebate forms can be used to target future promotions.

As rebates have increased in popularity, however, several common problems have emerged. For example, many companies have experienced problems honoring their rebate offers, largely due to an inability to keep up with demand. In fact, some companies offer rebates with the knowledge that only a small percentage of consumers bother to take advantage of them. Collecting on a rebate takes some trouble and concentration; consumers are forgetful, mislay the rebate coupon or the proof of purchase, and thus pay a bonus for the product. Companies relying on such probabilities sometimes fail to anticipate the level of interest the product or the rebate may generate; they plan rebate processing poorly, produce long delays, lose good will—and may even run out of money.

Due to the frequent mix-ups and delays in processing rebate submissions, some consumers now tend to view rebate offers as a sleazy marketing tactic. This means that fewer consumers will base their purchase decisions on the availability of a rebate. Experts note that consumers can increase their chances of receiving rebates due by sending all the documentation requested in the rebate offer; keeping copies of all forms and receipts; checking on the status of overdue rebates with the company; and reporting any problems to the Federal Trade Commission, the Better Business Bureaus, or the state attorneys general. Finally, experts advise consumers to never buy anything just for the rebate.

SEE ALSO *Coupons; Discount Sales*

BIBLIOGRAPHY
Davis, Douglas D., and Edward L. Millner. "Rebates, Matches, and Consumer Behavior." *Southern Economic Journal.* October 2005.

Kandra, Anne. "Rebate, Rebate, Who's Got the Rebate?" *PC World.* July 2000.

Royal, Leslie E. "Reap the Rebates." *Black Enterprise.* July 2000.

Steve, Smith. *How to Sell More Stuff: Promotional marketing that really works.* Dearborn Trade Publishing, 2005.

Hillstrom, Northern Lights
updated by Magee, ECDI

RECIPROCAL MARKETING

Reciprocal marketing describes a situation in which two businesses promote each other in order to gain a mutual benefit. Such marketing, common in the tourism industry, emerged in a new form in the 1990s and continues in the mid-2000s in electronic retail. In the online business world, reciprocal marketing is also known as reciprocal linking: the most common application involves placing links on another company's Web site. A similar concept for Internet businesses is affiliate marketing; it occurs when one of the businesses involved in a reciprocal marketing arrangement pays the other for traffic or sales generated through a link. In the brick-and-mortar business world, reciprocal marketing is more commonly known as co-op marketing, cross-promotion, or collaborative marketing.

Reciprocal marketing is equally popular among small, entrepreneurial Web sites and large, well-established ones. Writing in *Entrepreneur,* Melissa Campanelli called it "a reliable strategy employed by the most innovative dotcoms.... The tactic basically allows you to offer your paying customers discounts at your online partners' sites as well as provide discounts to your partners' customers on your site." As an example, a customer who spends $50 or more on your Web site might earn a coupon good for a discounted purchase on your partner's site. "These kinds of deals are the way the Internet will be working, going forward," Steven Bellach of the electronic florist site Proflowers told Campanelli. "The beauty of it is that no cash changes hands between merchants, and you get people when their wallets are still open."

Reciprocal marketing offers a number of potential benefits for small business owners. For example, it helps reduce the cost of attracting new customers, adds value to customers' shopping experience, and is inexpensive to implement compared with many traditional marketing schemes. As Hollis Thomases explained in an article for the *Baltimore Business Journal,* the key to successful reciprocal marketing is to find the right partners. The most suitable companies will be complementary in terms of philosophy, product line, and brand image. It may also be helpful to target Web sites that see roughly the same number of visitors as your company's, since the arrangement should be mutually beneficial rather than self-serving. But small business owners should be careful not to clutter their Web sites with dozens of links offering discounts. In addition to confusing customers, including too many links might cause traffic to leave your site before making a purchase.

Small business owners can find potential partners for reciprocal marketing arrangements through traditional forms of networking, such as attending conferences. Thomases also recommended networking online. Some possible methods include contacting the Webmasters of sites you like, e-mailing the authors of message board postings that relate to your business, and subscribing to e-mail discussion groups on subjects that relate to your business. Before approaching potential partners, it may be helpful to define the value your site has to offer. Although experts state that Internet entrepreneurs should not depend on reciprocal marketing as their only form of promotion, they do admit it is a valuable way for e-businesses to grow. "At the core of a strategic online alliance is the desire to grow your e-business," Thomases wrote. "It will allow you to extend your reach and save on marketing costs."

SEE ALSO *Banner Advertisements*

BIBLIOGRAPHY

Campanelli, Melissa. "Give and Take: Why It Pays to Partner Up on Your Marketing Efforts." *Entrepreneur.* March 2001.

"Collaborating for EDC." *R & D.* April 2002.

Fyall, Alan. *Tourism Marketing.* Channel View Marketing, 2005.

Nucifora, Alf. "Get Creative and Form That Marketing Partnership." *Orlando Business Journal.* 26 January 2001.

"OpenTV, Vizrt sign worldwide marketing agreement." *Broadcast Engineering.* 20 September 2005.

Thomases, Hollis. "Strategic Partnerships Drive Success on Internet." *Baltimore Business Journal.* 24 March 2000.

Zyman, Sergio, and Armin Brott. *The End of Advertising as We Know It.* John Wiley & Sons, 2003.

Hillstrom, Northern Lights
updated by Magee, ECDI

RECORD RETENTION

Record retention refers to the storage of records no longer active. Some records such as birth and marriage certificates, discharge papers from the armed services, naturalization papers, wills, property titles, insurance policies, and other important records are typically held for life by individuals. Businesses retain financial records for tax reasons or to maintain historical information; certain other records must be kept because required by law. Records typically fall into four categories: those securing property such as titles or shares; those that mark certain crucial events such as businesses incorporations; those used for assessing operations; and those collected or retained in compliance with government regulation.

For the small business, retention of financial records on income, expenses, and withholdings and payment of taxes are those most commonly retained. Under Internal

Revenue Service (IRS) guidelines these should be held for at least three years or until the statute of limitations on an IRS audit expires.

Records are normally retained as documents. In 1997 IRS issued new rulings related to storage of business records, essentially approving of the practice if such storage is accompanied by appropriate safeguards.

TYPES OF RECORDS

Businesses generate three main kinds of records: income, expenses, and capital expenditures. Income includes the revenue from sales of products or services, including both cash receipts and the collection of receivables. Expenses include cash disbursements and accounts payable that cover all operating expenses. These records should be maintained continuously. In the case of expenses, the records must not only prove that an expense was incurred, but also show how it was related to business. This is particularly important in the case of meals and entertainment expenses, for which the records must indicate the date, place, amount, and purpose of the expenses, as well as the type of business relationship with the person entertained.

It is also important for small business owners to keep records for major capital purchases to determine depreciation for tax purposes. These records must include the date and place of purchase, a complete description of the item, the amount paid, how it was purchased, and the date when it was put into service for the business. Keeping these basic business records enables business owners to track their progress, identify problems, and take advantage of all possible tax deductions.

Small businesses that employ people other than the owner or partners are required by the IRS to keep detailed payroll records. In fact, there are a total of 20 different types of records that must be kept for income tax withholding, FICA (Social Security) tax withholding, and FUTA (federal unemployment) taxes. These records—which include employees' names, addresses, and Social Security numbers, the amount and date of wages paid and withheld, and the amount of each type of tax paid, among other things—must be retained for at least four years from the time the relevant taxes were due or were paid, whichever was later. Experts also recommend that small businesses keep careful records regarding any automobile, life, fire, health, and other insurance coverage they hold. These records should list policy numbers and carriers, amounts of premiums and dates paid, and information on claims.

A variety of government requirements for record storage exist for specific cases. Under the Sarbanes-Oxley Act of 2001, which enacted accounting and auditing reforms for publicly traded companies, record retention requirements relating to all manner of insider dealings has imposed new costs on public companies, including stringent requirements to safeguard electronic records. Companies that work as federal contractors are bound by employment rules similar to those of the federal government itself and must retain records on hiring, firing, and other personnel actions—not least resumes received over the internet. Environmental regulations require record keeping on process effluents and hazardous waste disposal events. Recordkeeping regulations also apply under the Occupational Safety and Health Act (OSHA). Keeping up with all the rules is difficult for the small business owner unless he or she carefully reads the industry's trade publications which typically report changes in such rules. A sensible alternative is simply to retain all record related to money, people, property, safety, technology, law, and the environment.

RECORD-RETENTION POLICIES

Retaining all records or retaining some categories of records (and different categories for different periods) are part of a "record retention policy"—whether viewed as such or not. People concerned with records speak of "junk drawer" finances, indicating the worst such policy short of throwing things away: the more or less careful ferreting away of papers into a drawer on a vague hunch that they might be necessary later. More orderly arrangements, under which the company has well-developed rules on document handling, represent a genuine policy. Retention is thus part of orderly administration.

In the carefully administered business, records are typically classified into three categories and held in different places. Active records are distributed at work points in various departments, each department responsible for its own records. Such records usually cover two or three years of operations. On the same site but in remote locations will be file cabinets holding records going back two or three additional years. These records are occasionally consulted and are therefore held at the site. Transferring documents to the on-site storage may be an annual event or take place as more room is required in the active records areas—with on-site storage also divided up by departments. Finally, the company may hold a third category of archival records. These are stored either off-site in a warehouse or on site but reduced to microfilm in order to save space.

Maintaining such archives requires a fair amount of discipline. Ideally records are stored in neatly labeled file cabinets and care is exercised in removing records for reference and putting them back again. Discipline is needed because nothing seems quite so dead as the fairly deep past, and when a looking at these records most of us have trouble imagining these records ever being "needed." But occasionally tremendous anxieties can be aroused when, in the face of a threatened lawsuit, the very records proving our probity cannot be found. Record retention is akin to insurance. It's a nuisance until you need it.

The archiving of electronic records is a special category that requires attention. Most companies back up electronic records but do so on media (disks or tapes) that are periodically reused. The reuse of storage media means that the "far" past is often erased (covered over) by data from the "near" past. In the evolving record-retention climate brought about by Sarbanes-Oxley, itself the creature of corporate scandals, companies need to review their electronic data retention practices. Certain types of backups, thus, may have to be set aside as archives, the disks or tapes *not* reused. These media need to be held for archival purposes rather than to repair computer crashes.

HOW LONG TO RETAIN VARIOUS TYPES OF RECORDS

Federal income tax returns, annual financial statements, general ledgers, fixed asset records, and corporate documents (charter, bylaws, stock records, patent and trademark applications, labor contracts, pension records, etc.)—businesses typically retain such vital records for life. They tend to be looked at and in part purged only when the business changes hands. Regular business documents that support financial statements and tax payments—such as canceled checks, payroll checks, bank statements, invoices, purchase orders, and personnel records—should be retained for at least six years. These time periods allow for a margin of safety in meeting the IRS rules, which also address the means that may be used in retaining records.

Most of the IRS guidelines for record retention are included in Section 6001 of the Internal Revenue Code. The guidelines specify that the taxpayer must be able to establish on the basis of a documentary trail the amounts associated with income, costs, credits, and other relevant factors that relate to tax liability. These records can take the form of paper files or computerized data. Further IRS guidelines for record retention were issued in 1997 through Procedure 97-22. It permits taxpayers to transfer their paper files or computerized records to an adequate electronic storage medium. The storage method must be complete and reliable and be accessible for retrieval of relevant elements of information. The guidelines authorize the IRS to test the storage system periodically without actually conducting an audit, and if it does not comply with the guidelines then the taxpayer may be subject to penalties.

Record retention is part of the company's administrative work. Here an approach of routine, habitual, orderly procedure brings the best results with least costs. A good rule of record retention is: When in doubt, keep it!

SEE ALSO *Internal Revenue Service Audits; Sarbanes-Oxley*

BIBLIOGRAPHY

Baldas, Tresa. "New Federal Web Hiring Rule May Trigger More Bias Suits." *The Recorder*. 7 December 2005.

Hood, Bill. "Record Retention and E-mail." *ABA Banking Journal*. December 2005.

Occhipinti, Christina. "'Junk Drawer' Finances: Service affords individuals chance to clean up record keeping." *Westchester County Business Journal*. 23 January 2006.

Pinson, Linda. *Keeping the Books: Basic Record Keeping and Accounting for the Successful Small Business*. Dearborn Trade Publishing, 2004.

"Resource Conservation and Recovery Act (RCRA) Record Keeping." *Environs*. September 2005.

Schwartz, Ephraim. "New Regulations Loom Large in 2006—The compliance juggernaut rolls on, requiring IT to address privacy, data retention, and product lifecycle issues." *InfoWorld*. 2 January 2006.

Darnay, ECDI

RECRUITING

Recruiting in the broadest sense is the activity of acquiring new employees to fill a job "from the outside." Filling jobs internally is usually referred to as transferring, reassigning, or promoting people. Recruitment will be more intensive if the job to be filled is "permanent." Temporary hires and the act of engaging contractors to do a job tend to be less demanding because mistakes can be more easily corrected. But every serious organization looks at "new hires" as adding an important resource. The higher the responsibilities associated with the new job or the higher the skills required to do it, the more difficult the process will be. Recruiting, narrowly considered, consists of the first two steps in the total hiring process itself, which consists of 1) job definition and description, 2) sourcing of individuals by various means, 3) interviewing employees, 4) selection of individuals, 5) making the offer and negotiating the details, and 6) introducing the new employee and providing necessary initial training if that is required.

Elsewhere in this volume the hiring process is treated as a whole under the heading of *Employee Hiring*. Recruiting, the front end of the process, will be discussed more fully here: the shaping of the entire effort and then the creation and narrowing of a pool of candidates for consideration.

Job Definition Recruiting is usually triggered when an employee resigns or is released or when the workload grows and makes the need for additional help obvious. Replacing existing employees is relatively easier because the function to be fulfilled by the new hire is well-known and therefore easy to describe. Depending on the level of administrative formality practiced by the small business, a job description may already exist; if the job was created by a recruitment process a few years or months earlier, the text of the original recruitment ads may still be around. Setting about the job definition, therefore, is relatively easy. It requires review, of course, and possibly updating and revision, especially if the job "evolved" during its history and the person now being replaced carries out different tasks than those for which he or she was originally engaged.

Brand-new jobs need definition. This task is often neglected, however, because managers simply assume they know exactly what they want. If neglected, the job definition may impede recruitment. It may fail to highlight aspects of a job that will attract people and weed out others. A nursery, for instance, may need a grounds-keeper expected to wait on customers in rush periods—but this task is never mentioned. Some candidates who like to interact with people may find this feature attractive; others, of a more solitary temperament, may find this part of the job an imposition and may therefore not work out. Another example might be a computer expert who is expected to work very closely with clients to discover what they need: hence communications skills and ability to negotiate are as vital a skill as making the machine do wonders. In real life such obvious aspects may be more difficult to predict in advance—but will emerge with a little effort at visualizing the job. A good job definition, in turn, will help in the next steps.

Identifying Candidates In the vast majority of cases, canvassing for candidates takes the form of advertisements published in papers or posted on the Internet. The job definition is used as the basis for writing such texts. Beyond qualifications sought, the business usually includes additional features, in however abbreviated a form, such as something about benefits or, optionally, salary and wages, something about itself ("leading equipment seller to the elderly," "hard-charging direct sales org.") and something that might attract (or for that matter pre-select) candidates ("pleasant rural setting," "extensive travel," "significant promotional potential").

When the company is attempting to recruit high-level executives or professional skills, it may elect to use recruiting firms to do the canvassing job. In such cases also, the profile of the individual sought is almost always in written form but more extensive: the job description itself is provided to the recruiter along with information about the company, its strategies, and current needs. Similarly, the recruitment effort may take place at job fairs where the company has its own booth. In such situations one or more packets may be prepared to hand out to candidates who, after some discussion, appear to the company's representative as "possibles" or "promising."

Businesses occasionally discover that the market for people is rather competitive. In such cases, as Jennifer Wilson wrote in *Accounting Today* regarding financial experts and information technology (IT) staffs, a marketing approach must be utilized, meaning a multiple-channel advertising strategy. Bruce Markus, writing in *New Jersey Law Journal,* essentially echoed the same sentiments in the context of smaller law firms attempting to recruit lawyers.

Identifying candidates also takes places by informal word-of-mouth channels—and this at every level of skill and pay. Managers of a company may "put out the word" to friends, vendors, and customers that they are seeking someone for this or that job. The owner may "make a few calls" to potential candidates or those who might know such people. Most managers have received calls in which *they* are the target but the caller asks if they know someone with such and such qualifications.

However the job is accomplished, the objective at this stage is to build up a reasonable pool of good leads who can then be subject to—

The Screening Process No matter how much effort a business expends on writing the perfect employment ad—carefully worded, complete, informative, precise— the usual result is a flood of résumés most of which are way off the mark. A screening process thus becomes necessary. Depending on the manager's temperament, selecting good candidates may be a painful experience: it is painful (even if necessary) rapidly to put aside what may have been hours of effort by a foolishly hopeful but obviously careless person to apply for a job he or she is not qualified to fill. The most difficult cases are those where a certain doubt creeps in—and the manager sets the resume on the "reject" pile wondering if this person might be *the* candidate if a little effort is expended. Again depending on the situation, a fairly rigorous and quick decision process is needed to reduce a bagful of mail to the dozen or so survivors. In cases of genuine doubt, managers sometimes show the resumes to others and are often relieved when the consulted colleague breaks into gales of laughter.

Sometimes, alas, the résumés are less than truthful— so much so that the Small Business Administration features a Web page titled "How to Spot a Lie on a Résumé or Application." Based on SBA's advice, lies on a résumé are difficult to spot at the screening stage. But if a résumé gets past the screening, the lies can be exposed during interviews and rigorous checking of references later— beyond what we here label the front-end recruiting effort.

In the case of potential candidates presented by employment firms, the "head hunters," preliminary screening has already taken place: resumes sent by the recruiter typically represent qualifying candidates in the recruiter's opinion. Candidates sent by friends and colleagues can be checked out through these very people. And at job fairs someone in the company has usually conducted a preliminary interview.

Recruiting, narrowly considered (as in this article), usually either ends with the selection of individuals to invite for an interview or, sometimes, with a preliminary telephone call in which the manager sometimes "feels out" the candidate, asks a few clarifying questions, and, on the spot, makes a decision on whether or not the employee should be invited for an interview. Such calls can often be rather revealing and move the candidate "up" in the rankings, into the reject pile, or off the list—in cases where the promising candidate tells the manager that he or she has just taken another job. Resumes, however useful, are ultimate pieces of paper and not flesh and blood.

SEE ALSO *Employee Hiring*

BIBLIOGRAPHY

D'Amico, Gregory S. "How to Recruit and Retain the Best Employees." *Printing News.* 24 April 2006.

Davis, Martin E. "Hiring and Orienting a New Employee." *Entrepreneur.com.* Available on http://www.entrepreneur.com/article/0,4621,323632,00.html. 28 September 2005.

Ennis, Sarah J. *Manager's Pocket Guide to Interviewing and Hiring Top Performers.* Human Resource Development Press, 2002.

Marcus, Bruce W. "How to Recruit in a Competitive World." *New Jersey Law Journal.* 24 April 2006.

Wendover, Robert W. *High Performance Hiring.* Thomson Crisp Learning, 2003.

Wilson, Jennifer Lee. "Want to Attract Top Talent? Apply a marketing strategy." *Accounting Today.* 1 May 2006.

U.S. Small Business Administration. "How to Spot a Lie on a Resume or Application." Available from http://www.sba.gov/managing/growth/employeelie.html. Retrieved on 15 May 2006.

U.S. Small Business Administration. "Managing Employees." Available from http://www.sba.gov/managing/growth/employees.html. Retrieved on 15 May 2006.

Darnay, ECDI

RECYCLING

Beginning in the mid-1960s and growing alongside the environmental movement, recycling became an important aspect of municipal waste management and symbolic of personal actions to help clean up the environment. In earlier times various kinds of recycling took place; they consisted in diverting products from the waste stream before discard. Boy and Girl Scout troops collected old newspapers to raise funds—as those old enough may still remember. Beer, sodas, and milk moved in returnable glass bottles; and because most of these containers finally broke in centralized facilities like bottling plants, the residues were also collected and sold to glass companies. During World War II the government solicited metals and the public set these aside to help the war effort. Finally, automobiles that had reached their final hour were recycled, as they still are, in scrap yards—by far the most massive consumer products, alongside appliances, thus disposed.

According to the Online Etymology Dictionary, the word "environment" was first used in its current sense in 1956. It did not become a household word until the 1960s. Long before that time, however, recycling was a major *industrial* activity carried out for economic reasons but under different names: in metals it was the scrap trade, in paper the waste paper trade in two branches—newsprint gathered by volunteers and cardboard gathered from offices and warehouses; there was also a trade in broken glass ("cullet"), in rags, and in waste oil. Farmers collected restaurant wastes to feed to pigs and recycled the fertilizer value of farm animal wastes as manure. And farm and garden wastes have always been composted. None of these activities has changed and, in fact, are the recipients of wastes today extracted from the municipal waste stream. Certain forms of recycling, however, are relatively new. They include reprocessing of auto tires into rubber, synthetic fuels, or paving materials; the recovery of lead from batteries; plastics recycling; and relatively experimental methods of converting organic wastes to fuel ("bio diesel"). Then, as still today, manufacturing wastes were either immediately recycled if suitable or used for fuel to power production activities—common in wood and fiber-using operations.

MUNICIPAL SOLID WASTE RECYCLING

The movement toward municipal solid waste (MSW) recycling was probably sparked by the introduction of steel cans to package soft drinks and beer in 1953. These containers made a contrast with the returnable bottle, at that time still the dominant mode of beverage packaging; cans did not bear a deposit and were soon littering roads. Keep America Beautiful, a business-sponsored organization, began operation in 1953 as well and attempted to persuade the public not to litter. KAB's most memorable ad image was the Indian chief with the tear in his eye—sad over the despoliation of the countryside. The public noticed that packaging was proliferating and turning into a form of marketing—and solid waste tonnage was growing more rapidly than population. The "throw-away" society was born. In 1965, the first federal law on solid waste, the Solid Waste Disposal Act, passed Congress coinciding with the introduction of aluminum beverage containers that year: you could crush them in one hand! Amended versions of the act gave recycling more and more prominence until the Resource Conservation and Recovery Act of 1976 made recycling of MSW a national policy. But RCRA had no mandatory provisions. With the exception of mandatory deposit bills at the state level and local laws mandating separate collection of recyclables from waste, recycling at the national level continues still as an injunction rather than as a regulatory program.

Economics MSW recycling has always required subsidy because scrap prices do not cover the expensive separation of commingled wastes by hand or machine. At the same time, disposal of wastes, whether by the relatively expensive method of incineration or the lower-cost use of burial in landfills, is less expensive than waste separation with a portion recycled and a larger portion disposed of—even when scrap revenues were factored in. For these reasons MSW recycling has been essentially funded by the public sector and by the population's contribution of labor in separating wastes.

Even when collection, separation, and concentration costs for material components are subsidized, economic conditions cause demand for waste-derived commodities to cycle up and down. This has led to programs to increase the "recycled content" of goods produced. Companies advertise high recycled content as a way of inducing environmentally aware consumers to select their products. Where technically feasible, and the waste markets sold for a lower price than "virgin" raw materials, producers also realized a cost benefit.

Quantitative Trends Based on data from the U.S. Environmental Protection Agency (EPA), MSW generation was 236.2 million tons in 2003, of which 176.4 million tons (75 percent) was in the form of potentially recoverable materials. Of this subtotal 31.4 percent was recovered for recycling in 2003, most of it in the form of paper (72 percent). The bulk of recovered paper was in the form of old newspapers from households and corrugated cardboard from businesses. About 48 percent of all paper and board, 36 percent of metals, and 19 percent of glass is recovered; the lowest recovery rate is associated with plastics (5 percent), the highest with nonferrous metals, primarily lead batteries (67 percent). The low rate of plastics recovery is explained both by the many types of plastics on the market, the difficulties in sorting them, and the fact that some cannot be remelted.

Of the 60 million tons of organic and miscellaneous wastes not included in figures above, cities recovered about 17 million tons in 2003, 28.2 percent, the great bulk of it in the form of composted yard trimmings. For context, it is worth noting that MSW represents a mere 3 percent of total waste generation in the United States, which, based on EPA's estimates, stood at around 7.84 billion tons. The overwhelming mass of this waste, however, is the form of mine tailings. Industrial waste generation in the major categories like metals, paper, plastics, and glass is very low because production wastes are immediately recycled.

Recycling rates appear to have increased since the beginning of the recycling movement, but reliable numbers are not available. The reason for this is that waste generation by type of content is not routinely determined; in some surveys (such as the one cited above) commercial wastes are included, in some they are left out. Very substantial paperboard recoveries have always been associated with commercial sources—long before recycling took hold; and in the olden days much newsprint was diverted from MSW when demand for waste paper was high. One source, cited by EPA, *Biocycle Magazine*, showed recycling increasing from 19 percent in 1992 to 33 percent in 2000, with increases in every year in between. Such data, however, are not based on scientific or census-like measurements and, while no doubt capturing a trend, are more impressionistic.

Energy Recovery Conversion of MSW to energy, referred to as waste-to-energy, was proposed and demonstrated early in the history of waste recycling—on the model of industrial practice. Waste-to-energy conversion is tracked by the Energy Information Administration. Data provided by EIA indicate steady if somewhat cyclical growth in energy production from solid waste. Generation, expressed in equivalents of British thermal units (BTUs) was 0.354 quadrillion Btu in 1989 and had reached 0.571 quadrillion Btu by 2003. In 2003, the breakdowns of the total were 1) combustion with heat or electric power recovery at 51 percent, 2) capture of methane gases from landfills, 26 percent, and 3) heat recovery from agricultural byproducts, sludges, tires, and other biomass components of waste, 24 percent. In 2003, waste-to-energy represented 9.4 percent of all *renewable* energy consumption—more than 3 times the amount provided by solar and wind energy combined.

INDUSTRIAL RECYCLING

Commercial recycling, as distinct from industrial recycling, tends to be reported as part MSW which EPA defines as consisting of residential, commercial, and institutional sources. Commercial operations in which bulk packaging is routinely handled have always routinely collected corrugated board for sale to waste paper dealers: it is the highest grade of waste paper available and demand for it tends to be fairly steady. With the rise of environmental consciousness, offices have also participated in occasional programs of collecting waste paper used in business operations. These programs have had a mixed history—intensifying in times of high waste paper prices and slacking off in others. Unlike corrugated collection systems which are strongly institutionalized and integrated into operations, employee programs in which two separate waste cans are used, one for paper, one for all other waste, require constant management attention. Such attention is rarely sustained, with the result that programs fade away until once more reinstituted with a new initiative.

Like cardboard recovery in retail and warehousing operations, industrial recycling is strongly supported by economic motives and is hence both routine and well-managed. In industry recycling takes three basic forms: 1) reuse of production wastes in the course of normal operations, 2) use of scrap as the principal or only raw material input, and 3) the reuse of post-consumption waste products.

In the first case, reusing production wastes, the waste may be trimmings or residues from production runs which are simply collected and reintroduced at the beginning of the process. An example might be a forging operation in which defective forgings are simply remelted. Another distinct instance is an operation which uses a portion of its raw materials, namely a waste product, as a fuel. An example is a saw mill that collects wood bark in debarking operations and uses it, with other wood-wastes, as fuel to power a boiler house which runs the sawing operations.

Electric steel mills that convert scrap metal into new steel products are the best-known example of an industry which runs exclusively on scrap. Waste-oil refineries are another example: they receive spent lubricants, filter out impurities, and blend the results into various low-end products.

The steel, paper, and glass industries are examples of operations which use both "virgin" materials and waste to make new products. Certain paper mills that produce paperboard (used in folding boxes, as backings for writing pads, and in other stiffening applications—sometimes coated on one or both sides by virgin sheets) and some mills that make newsprint also rely exclusively on waste paper. Others blend in portions of waste paper with new fiber. In glass, cullet is segregated by color and if clean enough is used in clear glass; if of dark color, cullet is used in dark-colored glass.

By far the largest recycler of post-consumption scrap is the steel industry. Its products are very durable and widely used in products that are readily collected for recycling (like auto wrecks and appliances). According to the Steel Recycling Institute (SRI), the industry routinely recovers more than 70 percent of its output again as scrap; the industry reached a 75.7 percent recycling rate in 2005. Rates vary from year-to-year reflecting economic conditions. The lowest apparent recovery rates in steel coincide with the greatest dispersion of the product. Thus recycled can recovery accounted for 63 percent of steel used in cans and reinforcing bar recovery for 65 percent of re-bar production in 2005, but rates were 102 percent for autos, 96 percent for appliances, and 87.5 percent for structural beams and parts. These rates are calculated by expressing scrap collected from a category (e.g., appliances) with total steel consumed by that category; hence, in the case of autos, more steel was recovered from cars in 2005 than used in cars that year.

THE ENERGY LINK

In the energy-intensive industries—like steel, paper, aluminum, and glass—use of waste materials reduces energy costs because the wastes are already at a higher state of purity than incoming raw materials like ores, logs, and sand. To be sure, energy is required for collecting and transporting such "previously owned" raw materials back to production plants again. In many cases shredding or cutting the waste products requires additional energy. Autos are partially disassembled—seats and engine and electronics are removed. Newsprint requires deinking—another energy-consumptive activity. But energy use is almost always less than required in processing virgin raw materials. For this reason easily accessible products, especially those that are bulky and thus already "aggregated" (like junked cars), are the most easily recycled. Those that require a high degree of sorting and consume the most resources at the front end and are least reused. If energy costs rise in the future—as indeed they are very likely to do—recycling will intensify. In such an environment, human labor ("calories") will become less expensive than machine labor ("BTUs"). As we approach an era of very high energy prices, recycling may offer—as it already does—significant opportunities for small business enterprises in mining our wastes for gold.

BIBLIOGRAPHY

Davis, Mackenzie L., and Susan J. Masten. *Principles of Environmental Engineering and Sciences.* McGraw Hill, 2004

Green, Jen. *Waste and Recycling.* Chrysalis Books Group, 2004.

"Set Up an Office Recycling System." *Business Journal— Milwaukee.* 11 February 2000.

"Steel Recycling in the U.S. Continues its Record Pace in 2005." Press Release. Steel Recycling Institute. 25 April 2006.

U.S. Energy Information Administration. "Municipal Solid Waste." August 2005. Available from http://www.eia.doe.gov/cneaf/solar.renewables/page/mswaste/msw.html. Retrieved on 16 May 2006.

U.S. Environmental Protection Agency. *Municipal Solid Waste Generation, Recycling, and Disposal in the United States: Facts and Figures for 2003.* April 2005.

U.S. Environmental Protection Agency. "Recycling." Available from http://www.epa.gov/epaoswer/non-hw/muncpl/recycle.htm#Figures. Retrieved on 15 May 2006.

U.S. Environmental Protection Agency. "Summary of the EPA Municipal Solid Waste Program." Available from http://www.epa.gov/reg3wcmd/solidwastesummary.htm. Retrieved on 16 May 2006.

Darnay, ECDI

REENGINEERING

"Reengineering" as a business battle cry was first heard in the early 1990s. Most commentators cite publication of a 1993 book by consultants Michael Hammer and James Champy, entitled *Reengineering the Corporation,* as the important moment when reengineering became a movement. The book was reissued in 2003 and is cited below. "Reengineering" functionally resembles planned change and what people have traditionally called "reorganization," but, in its beginnings, it came with a definite flavor of "starting from scratch," "blank slate," and "from the ground up." Its promoters advocated radical approaches, used terms like "the big bang," and generally rendered the process of reengineering in revolutionary terminology— whereas the word itself suggested the rational approach of "engineering."

Functionally reengineering calls for rediscovering the objectives of a business, diagnosing ills and discovering new paths to the objectives, design of a process, and then its implementation. It is supposed to transform not only what is done but *how* it is done, thus to change the corporate culture. Bloated, sloppy, slow, unresponsive, expensive, unfocused organizations are supposed to become lean, quick, effective, responsive, competitive, agile, and concentrated. Since it could be applied to corporations as a whole or specific processes within the business (purchasing, marketing, production, etc.) it came to be called Business Process Reengineering and abbreviated BPR.

Reengineering came at a time when many other waves of managerial technique had already crashed on the rocky shores of corporate bureaucracy. Thus it was labeled a fad immediately by some but embraced by others. It had its predecessors and competitors in such concepts or techniques as zero-based budgeting (another from-the-ground-up approach), intrapreneuring, visioning, de-massing, de-layering, etc. Much older management approaches tied more directly to operational practices were embedded in the reengineering methodology or used in its implementation, including total quality management (TQM), continuous improvement, and the Toyota-led concept of the "lean corporation" based on just-in-time deliveries, effective operational clustering, and cross-training of employees. It is sometimes associated with Six Sigma, a Motorola-invented but GE-popularized quality control objective.

By the mid-2000s reengineering has largely lost its violent language and radical character. It has become a generic label for making change in organizations. The practice has spread beyond the business sector and is being attempted by nonprofits and governmental entities as well—usually the sign of an aging and possibly fading enthusiasm. Since reengineering—in contrast, for instance, with statistical quality control—is not based on a clearly specifiable operational methodology, it is relatively easy to label any reorganization or attempt at reform as reengineering. For this reason reengineering has also become associated with large restructurings in industry leading to mass lay-offs, off-shorings, and out-sourcings—which has tarnished its image. Based on a Louis Harris & Associates survey, cited by Balachandran Bala in his book on this subject, more than 60 percent of companies surveyed in 1996 had carried out some kind of formal reengineering program. Despite such efforts, the average profitability of companies since the 1990s has not improved by the mid-2000s—indeed, thanks to an intervening recession, profitability somewhat lags the mid-1990s level as reported by the U.S. Census Bureau.

Reengineering has a strong element of reform and, in the energetic terminology that it employed, suggested initially the reaction of a new generation of managers come of age and facing what may have looked like the decaying past. The movement roughly coincided with the maturing of the baby boom generation into managerial positions. Thus, at best, reengineering served, and still serves, some companies as an inspiration to (quoting Hammer and Champy) "achieve dramatic improvements in critical contemporary measures of performance, such as cost, quality, service, and speed." At worst reengineering was an occasional reform carried out with too much energy and therefore leaving a certain amount of ill-will behind.

THE SMALL BUSINESS PERSPECTIVE

While small business is as prone to fall into decay as large, the small business embrace of major corporate movements has always been cautious and selective—if for no other reason than the absence of the means and time to engage in too much introspection. Rodney McAdam, writing in the *International Small Business Journal,* confirmed this in a study of small and medium enterprises (SMEs). "Existing methodologies [of reengineering]," McAdam wrote, "mainly assume a large organization setting with large-scale resources dedicated to bringing about the large-scale reengineering changes. The paucity of studies in SMEs is surprising given the current and anticipated future market challenges in the SME environment that increase pressure for organizational realignment and responsiveness and market agility." After looking at the literature, McAdam concluded: "The analysis indicates that the taxonomy and nomenclature of reengineering, as defined by large organization-based studies, has not translated into SMEs, who use much more general terminology."

McAdam's conclusion, put into plain words, is that small businesses engage in similar activities but tend to use practical (what McAdam calls "phenomenological") rather than theoretical ("positivistic") approaches. As McAdam observes, the small business doesn't use reengineering phraseology but does engage in activities of occasionally radical adaptation. This, of course, is very much in line with small business practice when it comes to trendy innovations. A small business tends to pick and choose what will work in its own environment.

Reduced to the "phenomenological" level, reengineering translates into fixing things that do not seem to work. When the analysis of the problem shows that fairly drastic changes are necessary—and these changes are made effectively—results can often be dramatic and the experience occasionally wrenching. The very features of small business—its size; closer contact with employees, suppliers, and the market; and small business's more limited resources—tend to bring problems to the fore sooner. It is less likely for problems to become deeply institutionalized and to acquire large constituencies. For this reason, in usual practice, small business is also likely to take action sooner, more incrementally, and with less drama—one reason, perhaps, why McAdam encountered a "paucity of studies." Perhaps small business is, as so very often, ahead of the curve or immune to the disease.

BIBLIOGRAPHY

Bala, Balachandran. *Business Process Reengineering—Its History, Promises, and Problems.* Financial Executive Research Foundation, Inc., 1999.

Bruner, Rober F., et al. *The Portable MBA.* John Wiley & Sons, 2003.

Hammer, Michael, and James Champy. *Reengineering the Corporation.* HarperCollins, 2003.

Morgan, Jeffrey. *Creating Lean Corporations: Reengineering from the Bottom Up to Eliminate Waste.* Productivity Press, 2005.

McAdam, Rodney. "Large Scale Innovation—Reengineering methodology in SMEs: Positivistic and phenomenological approaches." *International Small Business Journal.* February 2002.

U.S. Bureau of the Census. *Quarterly Financial Report for Manufacturing, Mining, and Trade Corporations: 2005.* April 2006.

Darnay, ECDI

REFINANCING

Refinancing is the refunding or restructuring of debt with new debt, equity, or a combination of these. Businesses refinance their debts when interest rates drop. Since this tends to happen in times when money is readily available from banks or other sources of lending, the business can lower its overall costs of financing by reworking its loan portfolio. Sometimes refinancing involves the issuance of equity in order to decrease the proportion of debt in the borrower's capital structure. As a result of refinancing, the maturity of the debt may be extended or reduced, or the new debt may carry a lower interest rate, or some combination of these options.

Refinancing may be done by any issuer of debt, such as corporations and governmental bodies, as well as holders of real estate, including home owners. When a borrower retires a debt issue, the payment is made in cash and no new security takes the place of the one being paid off. The term "refunding" is used when a borrower issues new debt to refinance an existing one.

CORPORATE OR GOVERNMENT DEBT REFINANCING

The most common incentive for corporations or governmental bodies to refinance their outstanding debt is to take advantage of a decline in interest rates from the time when the original debt was issued. Another trigger for corporate debt refinancing is when the price of a company's common stock reaches a level which makes it attractive for a firm to replace its outstanding debt with equity. Aside from reducing interest costs, this latter move gives a firm additional flexibility for future financing; by retiring debt the firm will have some unused debt capacity. Regardless of the reason for the refinancing, the issuer has to deal with two decisions: 1) Is the time right to refinance, and 2) What type of security should be issued to replace the one being refinanced?

If a corporation or governmental body wishes to refinance before the maturity date of the outstanding issue, they will need to exercise the call provision of the debt. The call provision gives the borrower the right to retire outstanding bonds at a stipulated price, usually at a premium over face amount, but never less than face value. The specific price which an issuer will need to pay for a call appears in the bond's indenture. The existence of a call premium is designed to compensate the bond holder for the firm's right to pay off the debt earlier than the holder expected. Many bond issues have a deferred call, which means the firm cannot call in the bond until the expiration of the deferment period, usually between five and ten years.

The cash outlay required by exercising the call provision includes payment to the holder of the bond for any interest which has accrued to the date of the call, and the call price, including premium (if any). In addition, the firm will need to pay a variety of administrative costs, including a fee to the bond's trustee. Of course, there will also be flotation costs for any new debt or equity that is issued as part of the refinancing.

Sometimes an issuer may be prohibited from calling in the bonds (e.g., during the deferred call period). In these instances, the issuer always has the opportunity to purchase its bonds on the open market. This strategy may also be advantageous if the outstanding bond is selling in the market at a price lower than the call price. Open market purchases involve few administrative costs. The corporation will recognize a gain on the repurchase if the market value is below the amount at which the corporation is carrying the bonds on its books (face value plus or minus unamortized premium or discount), or a loss on the repurchase if the market value is above the book value.

The major difficulty with open market purchases to effect a refinancing is that typically the market for bonds is "thin." This means that a relatively small percentage of an entire issue may be available on the market over any period of time. As a result, if a firm is intent on refinancing a bond issue, it almost always needs to resort to a call. This is why virtually every new bond that is issued contains a call provision. If an outstanding issue does not permit a call, another option available to the issuer is to seek tenders (offers to sell at a predetermined price) from current bond holders.

The new debt instrument issued in refinancing can be simple or complex. A corporation could replace an existing bond with traditional bonds, serial bonds (which have various maturity dates), zero-coupon bonds (which have no periodic interest payments), or corporate shares (which have no maturity date, but which may have associated dividend payments). One factor that a firm needs to consider is that the administrative and flotation costs of issuing either common or preferred shares are higher than for new debt. Furthermore, dividend payments, if any, are not tax deductible.

The decision to refinance is a very practical matter involving time and money. Over time the opportunity to refinance varies with changing interest rates and economic conditions. When a corporation anticipates an advantageous interest rate climate, it then analyzes the cash flows associated with the refinancing. Calculating the present value of all the cash outflows and the interest savings assists in comparing refinancing alternatives that have different maturity dates and capitalization schemes.

MORTGAGE REFINANCING

Owners of residential or commercial real estate use a similar method to analyze their refinancing decisions. In residential real estate the conventional wisdom applies the "2-2-2 rule": if interest rates have fallen two points below the existing mortgage, if the owner has already paid two years of the mortgage, and if the owner plans to live in the house another two years, then refinancing is feasible. However, this approach ignores the present value of the related cash flows and the effects of the tax deductibility of interest expense and any related points.

Therefore, a better analysis of a mortgage refinancing decision should be conducted as follows: 1) Calculate the present value of the after-tax cash flows of the existing mortgage; 2) Calculate the present value of the after-tax cash flows of the proposed mortgage; 3) Compare the outcomes and select the alternative with the lower present value. The interest rate to be used in steps one and two is the after-tax interest cost of the proposed mortgage.

BIBLIOGRAPHY

"Debt Restructuring." Investopedia.com. Available from http://www.investopedia.com/terms/d/debtrestructuring.asp. Retrieved on 18 May 2006.

Fabozzi, Frank J. *Handbook of Mortgage Backed Securities.* McGraw-Hill, 2001.

Jordahl, Eric, and Kevin T. Ponton. "Synthetic Refunding: A financial tool for a low interest-rate environment." *Healthcare Financial Management.* May 2003.

Schaub, John W. *Building Wealth One House at a Time: Making it Big on Little Deals.* McGraw Hill, 2005.

Walter, Robert. *Financing Your Small Business.* Barron's Educational Series, 2004.

Hillstrom, Northern Lights
updated by Magee, ECDI

REGULATION D

Regulation D is a section of the U.S. federal securities law that provides the means for businesses to sell stock through direct public offerings (DPOs). A DPO is a financial tool that enables a company to issue stock directly to investors—without using a broker or underwriter as an intermediary—and avoid many of the costs associated with "going public" through an initial public offering (IPO). Regulation D exempts companies choosing this form of offering from many of the registration and reporting requirements of the Securities and Exchange Commission (SEC).

DPOs, private placements of stock, and other exempt offerings provide businesses with a quicker, less expensive way to raise capital than IPOs. The primary advantage of DPOs over IPOs is a dramatic reduction in cost. IPO underwriters typically charge a commission of 13 percent of the proceeds of the sale of securities, whereas the costs associated with a DPO are closer to 3 percent. DPOs also can be completed within a shorter time frame and without extensive disclosure of confidential information. Finally, since the stock sold through a DPO goes to a limited number of investors who tend to have a long-term orientation, there is often less pressure on the company's management to deliver short-term results.

DPOs and other exempt offerings also involve disadvantages, however. For example, the amount that a company can raise through a DPO within any 12-month period is limited. In addition, the stock is usually sold at a lower price than it might command through an IPO. Stock sold through exempt offerings is not usually freely traded, so no market price is established for the shares or for the overall company. This lack of a market price may make it difficult for the company to use equity as loan collateral. Finally, DPO investors are likely to demand a larger share of ownership in the company to offset the lack of liquidity in their position. Investors eventually may pressure the company to go public through an IPO so that they can realize their profits.

RULES 504, 505, AND 506

Regulation D—which was adopted in 1982 and has been revised several times since—consists of a set of rules numbered 501 through 508. Rules 504, 505, and 506 describe three different types of exempt offerings and set forth guidelines covering the amount of stock that can be sold and the number and type of investors that are allowed under each one. The most common type of DPO is the Small Corporate Offering Registration, or SCOR, which is included in Rule 504. SCOR gives an exemption to private companies that raise no more than $1 million in any 12-month period through the sale of stock. There are no restrictions on the number or types of investors, and the stock may be freely traded. The SCOR process is easy enough for a small business owner to complete with the assistance of a knowledgeable accountant and attorney. It is available in all states except Delaware, Florida, Hawaii, and Nebraska.

A related type of DPO is outlined in Rule 505. This option enables a small business to sell up to $5 million in stock during a 12-month period to an unlimited number of investors, provided that no more than 35 of them are non-accredited. To be accredited, an investor must have sufficient assets or income to make such an investment. According to the SEC rules, individual investors must have either $1 million in assets (other than their home and car) or $200,000 in net annual personal income, while institutions must hold $5 million in assets. Finally, a DPO conducted under Rule 506 allows a company to sell unlimited securities to an unlimited number of investors, provided that no more than 35 of them are non-accredited. Under Rule 506, investors must be sophisticated, or able to evaluate the merits and understand the risks of the transaction. In both of these options, the securities cannot be freely traded.

BIBLIOGRAPHY

Hicks, J. William. *Limited Offering Exemptions: Regulation D.* Thomson West, 2005.

Jennings, Marianne M. *Business: Its Legal, Ethical, and Global Environment.* Thomson West, 2006.

Roberts, Barry S., and Richard A. Mann. *Business Law and the Regulation of Business.* Thomson South-Western West, 2006.

U.S. Securities and Exchange Commission. "Regulation D." Updated 6 March 2003. Available from http://www.sec.gov/divisions/corpfin/forms/regd.htm. Retrieved on 16 May 2006.

Hillstrom, Northern Lights
updated by Magee, ECDI

REGULATORY FLEXIBILITY ACT

The Regulatory Flexibility Act (RFA) of 1980 is a law designed to make government agencies review all regulations that they impose to ensure that they do not place a disproportionate economic burden on small business owners and other small entities. The Regulatory Flexibility Act was intended to extend protection to three different types of small entities in the United States: small businesses (as defined by the Small Business Administration); small organizations (nonprofit establishments that are independently owned and operated and not dominant in their field); and small governmental jurisdictions (defined as governments of cities, counties, towns, townships, villages, school districts, and other districts with populations of less than 50,000).

In the years following the enactment of the RFA, however, many small business owners contended that agencies too often ignored the law. Periodic attempts to revise the RFA failed until March 1996, when the Small Business Regulatory Enforcement Fairness Act (SBREFA) became law. This new legislation cast the Regulatory Flexibility Act in an entirely new light, for it amended the 1980 law to allow for judicial review of government agencies' compliance with it.

Before the 1996 law was passed, small business owners had had no legal recourse when faced with regulations that they felt were unfair to smaller companies. "There was no statutory requirement that forces an agency to do an analysis," explained one spokesman for the Senate Committee on Small Business in *Nation's Restaurant News.* With the passage of the Small Business Regulatory Enforcement Fairness Act, however, "a small entity, including businesses—if an agency rule seems unfair—can challenge it in court. And if they prevail, they can modify it or strike it to reduce the impact on that entity."

LEGISLATIVE HISTORY OF THE RFA

Prior to 1980, American small businesses were forced to adhere to the same regulations as far larger companies, even though they did not have nearly the same resources to bring to bear. Entrepreneurs and directors of nonprofits repeatedly charged that when regulations put forth by the Environmental Protection Agency (EPA), the Occupational Safety and Health Administration (OSHA), and other agencies were applied evenly, without regard to the size of the enterprises affected, they sometimes did serious damage to smaller organizations. Such regulations had to do with taxes, workplace safety, and the environment, among other issues.

As the Small Business Administration noted in its *Guide to the Regulatory Flexibility Act,* "the costs of complying with a particular regulation . . . may be manageable for a business with 500 or more employees, or revenue in the millions of dollars. On the other hand, a smaller company may not have the ability to absorb the expenses as easily, to set competitive prices, to devise innovations or even to continue as a viable entity." The *Guide* added that as more businesspeople and politicians investigated the situation, "evidence indicated that uniform application of federal regulatory requirements imposed increases in the economies of scale and affected small entities' ability to compete effectively. Reports . . . cited these disproportionate economic burdens on small business as contributing to declines in productivity, competition, innovation, and the relative market shares of small business."

The passage of the RFA in 1980, then, was meant to blunt much of the burden that regulatory changes were laying on the shoulders of small businesses. According to the RFA, each agency was supposed to analyze how its regulations affected the ability of small businesses to compete. In addition, the RFA directed agencies to balance the needs of small business with the benefits of the regulation being considered. The law called for agencies to propose regulatory alternatives for smaller companies that would be unduly hurt if forced to adhere to the original regulations. The Regulatory Flexibility Act still allowed agencies to put together needed regulatory measures in such realms as workplace safety and environmental protection, but it meant to give a greater voice to small businesses by encouraging agencies to listen to small business concerns and study ways in which regulations could be adjusted for them.

During the 1980s, however, many entrepreneurs and other members of the business community came to feel that the RFA was an unacceptably weak law. The law—which actually went into effect on January 1, 1981—included no legal penalties that could be imposed on agencies that did not follow the Act's guidelines, so some agencies paid little attention to the RFA. Observers felt that some agencies were simply recalcitrant, while others, burdened by inadequate budgets, did not have the resources to satisfactorily address the issues laid out in the RFA. Most observers granted that the Regulatory Flexibility Act was valuable in certain cases, but by the early 1990s there was a growing clamor in the small business community and Congress for an amended RFA.

In September 1993 President Clinton signed Executive Order 12866, which highlighted the responsibilities of government agencies to adhere to the principles of RFA. That same year, the Clinton administration's National Performance Review task force formally recommended that agency compliance with the RFA be subject to judicial review. Less than three years later, in March 1996, a number of major amendments to the RFA—including provisions adding judicial review—became law with the passage of the Small Business Regulatory Enforcement Fairness Act.

SMALL BUSINESS REGULATORY ENFORCEMENT FAIRNESS ACT

The 1996 act included several components that drew praise from small business owners. While the addition of judicial review of agency compliance with the RFA received the bulk of attention, the amendments also gave agencies additional responsibilities in the areas of policy review and outreach, and gave non-agency entities (small businesses, Congress) more influence in the regulatory process.

Judicial Review The Small Business Regulatory Enforcement Fairness Act amended the RFA so that small

businesses finally had legal recourse when confronted with regulations that they felt did not adhere to the RFA. It created a complaint process whereby small businesses can seek review of the rule in court. Under the 1996 amendments, noted the SBA, "the court may review the final regulatory flexibility analysis, the agency's certification that the rule has no impact on small entities, and the agency's compliance with periodic reviews of current rules. Under the amendment, judicial review also applies to interpretative rulemakings promulgated by the IRS [Internal Revenue Service]." (Prior to the 1996 legislation, interpretative rulemakings of the IRS had been exempt from the RFA because of provisions of the Administrative Procedure Act.) In addition, the RFA now includes a provision that reimburses small business operators for legal fees incurred if they successfully challenge a regulation as overly harsh.

Periodic Reviews SBREFA reinforced RFA review guidelines for government agencies. Under the amended RFA, agencies are required to review all existing regulations to see if they have a significant economic impact on meaningful numbers of small entities (businesses, nonprofits, small government bodies). In situations where a "significant" impact is found, the agency in question is directed to review the regulations and determine whether they should remain in place, be revised, or be rescinded. Factors to be evaluated include: continued need for the regulation; impact of industry and economic trends on the regulation; public comments on the regulation's strengths and weaknesses; complexity of the regulation; and extent to which the regulation overlaps, duplicates, or conflicts with already existing federal, state, or local laws.

Outreach RFA now requires both OSHA and EPA to put together small business advocacy review panels every time they propose a regulation that is likely to have a big economic impact on a large number of small businesses. This information-gathering step is designed to solicit small business input on both the likely compliance costs of the regulations and possible mutually acceptable regulatory alternatives. A report reflecting the results of the review panel meetings is then prepared.

In addition, federal agencies are directed under RFA to publish a listing of all proposed or final regulations expected to be implemented during the following year. This requirement, say proponents, provides small business owners with more time to study the regulations and their likely impact on their establishments. Finally, the RFA now requires agencies to prepare easily understandable guide books to help businesses comply with regulations.

Expanded Authority for Chief Counsel for Advocacy The 1996 amendments to the RFA expanded the authority of the SBA's chief counsel for advocacy. The RFA now allows the chief counsel—who has been formally designated to monitor agency compliance with the law—to file amicus briefs in situations where regulations are being reviewed in court.

Legislative Review A provision of the 1996 legislation established a 60-day review period during which Congress will be able to reject any new regulations that are held to be unnecessary.

Despite these changes, however, some critics contend that SBREFA has not lived up to expectations in its initial years of existence. Detractors argued that Congress showed little inclination to exercise its increased powers of legislative review, and they claimed that other review panels called for in SBREFA have been slow to take shape. Others have criticized the law for giving Congress little-noticed powers to override federal regulations.

For further information on the Regulatory Enforcement Act, contact the Office of Advocacy of the Small Business Administration at 409 Third St., SW, Washington, DC 20416.

BIBLIOGRAPHY

Allen, Robin Lee. "Regulatory Bill Lets Small Operators Flex Muscles." *Nation's Restaurant News.* 22 April 1996.

Nierenberg, Danielle. "Little-Noticed Law Lurks Over Environmental Protections." *World Watch.* May 2001.

Warner, David. "Putting the Brakes on Federal Rules." *Nation's Business.* March 1995.

U.S. Small Business Administration. *Guide to the Regulatory Flexibility Act.* Available from http://www.sec.gov/divisions/corpfin/forms/regd.htm. Retrieved on 16 May 2006.

Hillstrom, Northern Lights
updated by Magee, ECDI

RELOCATION

Businesses move for the same reason that families do: they outgrow their quarters or shrink in size; they need to follow those who provide their income; they perceive new opportunities—and sometimes because they just decide to do it for altogether other reasons: a change in scene, the ocean, the mountains....

Business relocation is never simple but its expenses, complexity, the analysis and planning the move requires, and the time horizon needed to do it well will depend on the type of business it is, its size, and the distance moved. The easiest relocation will be associated with a service business which provides intellectual or information products to its clienteles from an office setting—provided it is

relatively small and moves within the same metropolitan area. But even in such a situation, moving the company's computer network will present special issues and managers will typically worry about the commuting distances imposed on some of the employees.

The most inherently difficult and potentially risky relocation is associated with a retail operation—unless the business sells a line of unusual, rare, and difficult-to-get products so that customers will find the way to the store no matter what—or unless the retail business is mostly Web-based. A well-known phrase associated with real estate applies to retail: location, location, location. For this reason, also, retail stores are often forced to move if the "location" where they find themselves suddenly or gradually loses its value, as may happen because of changes in the highway system or gradual loss of customers. Many businesses have moved from decaying urban centers to suburbs—and sometimes from decaying suburbs to areas of urban gentrification.

The move of a manufacturing operation is typically the most complex. For that reason production facilities are usually moved as part of long-range corporate modernization plans, take place in stages to minimize down-time, and extend over longer periods.

Businesses that relocate from one market to another—thus a retail store or a locally oriented consultancy, for instance, moving a significant distance, city to city—are in effect restarting their businesses and must view the relocation as a new start-up. But every relocation has some impact on customers and suppliers and will signal gains and losses in these categories.

A special category of move sometimes faced by managers is the "consolidation"—under which, for instance, a departments must absorb one or more operations located in different cities. These tend to have additional dimensions in that all the usual aspects of a move are involved along with reorganization and integration of new staff and equipment in an existing function.

THE MOTIVATION

The motivation for business relocation is *always* and unfailingly money. Businesses move because they fear that they will lose business, incur substantial new costs if they do *not* move, or because they perceive substantial new revenues resulting from the move. Even arbitrary relocations obey this rule, e.g., an owner who decides that he or she *must* live in Seattle or finally go home to Charlotte, N.C.: in such cases the move will be accomplished because the owner has the surplus funds to undergo the great adventure. Some relocations, indeed, are forms of corporate self-assertion, public ways of signaling having come of age. A new building has been erected in a fashionable business park, and the business proceeds to its new quarters with some fanfare.

THE PROCESS

Shelley Seale, writing in the *Austin Business Journal* with a focus on retail (but her words apply to all types of relocations) spoke truth when she said: "The most important aspect of relocation is allowing yourself enough time to plan for the move. Most retail stores should plan at least six months in advance—possibly as much as 12 months if your business is large or is moving a long distance. Proper planning is vital for both the logistics involved and your marketing plan. It can make the difference between your business growing and thriving or withering after a relocation." Seale expresses the process under five commands: 1) be prepared, 2) be focused, 3) be timely, 4) be realistic, and 5) be customer focused. The first command relates to planning, the second emphasizes that the relocation must be under the single command of an individual who ties the project together and delegates all other work. Timeliness refers to the scheduling and staging of the move itself. Things can go wrong, and a realistic expectation of disaster suggests that fall-back plans must be in place. Finally, no business moves effectively unless its constituencies are informed well in advance and helped to make the transition with the company.

Moves have a way of looming ahead for a long time before the first steps are actually taken—with all those directly concerned with management well aware that a move will be necessary sooner or later. The process tends to begin with looking for new quarters. By the time this begins, usually with discussions with real estate agents, the general area has already been fixed upon. Depending on the business, targeting itself may have been preceded by market analysis and visits to different areas by management. In parallel with finding the location, the business will typically begin planning on a technical level. Moves tend to be periods of renewal. Old equipment and systems are replaced; acquisition steps begin early and well before the new site is found. Difficult operations are analyzed and logistical issues examined. In many professional service businesses possibilities exist for temporarily operating from dispersed locations—and early staging of computers and people to their homes for temporary work will begin. In retail operations inventory will be sold out to reduce the amounts of goods that must be moved. In manufacturing operations production may be increased to have inventory to sell even as the factory is moved. In an operation of any scale, these many activities become complicated and need coordination. It is good practice to establish a "move committee" which regularly meets to keep the action organized.

Detailed plans for the move itself tend to be nailed down once two dates are fixed. The first is access to the new quarters and the second is the move-in date. The latter is fixed after site-improvements are completed and service installations (like telephone and computer networks and/or special power and gas facilities) have been made. Moving plans involve employees who typically assist in packing, internal and external specialists required to prepare equipment for moves, the sourcing of moving specialist, and arrangements with landlords at either end. In parallel with these activities, fall-back strategies will be tested, including communications, emergency service of selected customers, and the actual provision of services from temporary locations. A public relations campaign is always involved—even if the company is too small to call it that: customers and vendors must be notified in advance and provided with points of contact.

The move itself, for most small businesses, may be accomplished rapidly, usually over a weekend. In larger operations, of course, the move may take several weeks with different centers and departments moved in logical sequence, brought on stream and then assisting from the new location. Following the move itself, most relocations require a period of start-up at the new quarters and "mop-up" operations at the previous site. The mop-up operation can sometimes be complicated and involve the sale and movement of excess furniture or equipment. The reopening of the business at its new location is often a significant event for a retail business, long planned, and launched with appropriate hoopla. In the case of service businesses, the celebration may take the form of a formal reception to which important buyers are invited.

STRATEGY AND ADMINISTRATION

Relocations may have a predominantly strategic motivation or the strategic purpose may be minimal. Retail stores are almost always moved for strategic reasons, but office-based operations or those that deliver services to customers directly often simply move because they need more space. In either case, successful relocation is above all an exercise in well-planned, disciplined, and therefore effective administration—an art that tends to be undervalued in an era of marketing. To be sure, poor strategic choices can doom a relocation. Bad outcomes are due to neglect of necessary research of the chosen location, its demographics, and cultural traits. But the actual movement of a business from one place to another is one of the most exacting management tasks any business will undertake—requiring foresight, anticipation, and attention to the most minute details. Timing is very important, especially an ability to predict how long something will take. Unusual circumstances must be envisioned in advance and planned for, thus all manner of comfortable assumptions must be questioned. The effective manager of a relocation will *not* assume that all employees will make the move, even within the city, and have temporaries at least on call in the event this happens. Alternative systems of communications will be in place and will have been tested. Zoning ordinances and permit requirements in the new location will have been consulted. System will have been tested early enough to be reliable. The business that relocates well manages well. And nothing is as important as good plans, long to do lists, intensive attention to detail, and rigorous follow-through.

SEE ALSO *Site Selection; Zoning*

BIBLIOGRAPHY

Baltes, Sharon. "Smooth Transitions Simplifies Relocating." *Business Record*. 13 March 2006.

Lane, Marc J. *Advising Entrepreneurs: Dynamic Strategies for Financial Growth*. John Wiley & Sons, 2001.

Manzon, Gil B. Jr. "Halsey-Evans: Relocation of Operations." *Journal of Business Research*. July 2005.

Partovi, Fariborz Y. "An Analytic Model for Locating Facilities Strategically." *Omega*. January 2006.

Seale, Shelley. "Relocating Business Takes Strategic Plan." *Austin Business Journal*. 1 October 2004.

Thaler, John. *Elements of Small Business*. Silver Lake Publishing, 2005.

Darnay, ECDI

REMANUFACTURING

Remanufacturing is a process where a particular product is taken apart, cleaned, repaired, and then reassembled to be used again. Remanufacturing has long been associated with expensive technical products, but the technique is spreading. C. Franke and his coauthors, writing in *Omega* made the point as follows: "Today, the remanufacturing of expensive, long-living investment goods, e.g., machine tools, jet fans, military equipment or automobile engines, is extended to a large number of consumer goods with short life cycles and relatively low values. Reuse is an alternative to material recycling to comply with recovery rates and quantities as well as special treatment requirements" mandated by regulatory authorities. The list today includes mobile phones, tires, furniture, laser toner cartridges, computers, and electrical equipment. Essentially any product that can be manufactured can also be remanufactured. In order for a product to be considered remanufactured, most of its components must be used, although some of them can be new if the older parts are too defective to be salvaged.

Remanufacturing thus has two underpinnings. One is economic and the other is public or governmental regulatory pressure. From an environmental view point, remanufactured good are held out of the waste stream, conserve energy and thus reduce green-house gases, and protect ground-water from potentially toxic leachates—especially important in context of electronic goods. The economic motive is obvious in the case of very massive and expensive products such as machine tools and ocean-going vessels; they can also be quite real if public participation in the return of the products in part subsidizes the costs of their return to a remanufacturing facility.

While the basic concept of remanufacturing is simple, the activity is complex. It requires that a used product be completely disassembled in order to assess its actual condition. If it is determined that remanufacturing is worthwhile, various parts of the product are cleaned, restored, repaired, and replaced. Further refinements are then performed and the product is reassembled so that it once again operates in the way it was originally intended to function. The product is then ready to be used again. Each step in this process is essential to the entire concept of remanufacturing and careful precautions must be taken to ensure that each step is carried out correctly.

RELATED PROCESSES

The reuse of an object can take place after application of different kinds of processes and in various forms. The simplest form of fundamental reuse is recycling, represented by steel or aluminum beverage cans extracted from waste or separately collected which are then reintroduced into steel or aluminum furnaces scrap and may return in some other kind of form to the market.

Similar to recycling is a process of disassembly sometimes referred to as "demanufacturing"—after which the components thus obtained may be handled by recycling processes, remanufacturing methods, direct sale to end users, or by disposal. Many automobiles delivered to junk yards are demanufactured. Engines are removed and sometimes sold to remanufacturers, components pars are sold as found to individuals or repair shops, seats are removed and sold or disposed of as waste, structural components are separated and sold as scrap steel. Ship-breaking follows a similar cycle.

Certain products seen by the consumer as single entities may have the distinct roles of "container" and "content." The classical case is a returnable bottle which ends up, without its closure, at the bottling plant again to be cleaned, refilled with soda, and closed with a new cap. Toner cartridges used in laser printers are such container-content combinations, the cartridge itself designed for reuse, the toner used in printing.

In instances where the product is remanufactured, it will once again end up performing the same function it performed before after a more or less intensive remanufacturing process. To meet the "remanufactured" definition, the product must undergo some extensive process that is significantly more than "repair." A simple example of remanufacturing is the retreaded tire in which the basic inner core of the tire is retained, the remaining tread is cut off, and new rubber is applied and bonded to the core. In essence remanufactured products undergo significant processing beyond cleaning, repair, and maintenance. They are thus restored to a much higher functionality as a "used" product. Many auto parts must be remanufactured for sustained use and represent a major element of the remanufacturing industry.

INDUSTRY SIZE AND BENEFITS

The Automotive Parts Remanufacturers Association (APRA), citing research conducted by Boston University, estimated that remanufacturing had sales of $52 billion in the United States and estimated volume in excess of $100 billion worldwide. In the U.S., more than 70,000 firms are active in some kind of remanufacturing. APRA also cited data from the German Fraunhofer Institute to the effect that energy savings worldwide due to remanufacturing exceed the equivalent of 10.7 million barrels of crude oil. Substantial elimination of solid waste generation and atmospheric pollution follows.

REMANUFACTURING AND SMALL BUSINESSES

Aside from environmental benefits, there are many other reasons why remanufactured goods exist. Like many good business decisions, remanufacturing simply saves money by prolonging the economic life of a product. A small business with a tight budget can save money by using remanufactured products because they often cost less (anywhere between 40 and 60 percent less) and come with warranties and extra services that guarantee their performance.

Remanufacturing is also a business opportunity for small businesses with the appropriate technical skills and equipment deployments. For example, an auto repair business can potential branch out and begin to offer remanufactured goods as part of its services, or a small business that repairs office machines may be able to gain the necessary knowledge to remanufacture related products at the same time as it conducts its normal business activities.

If a small business decides to get into the remanufacturing industry, it must first and foremost study and understand the market. Despite the recent success of remanufacturing, there is still a negative perception among consumers regarding products that contain used parts. Many consumers feel that a remanufactured product is not durable as a brand new one and may require additional maintenance in the future. This is a serious issue that must be addressed before a small business decides whether it is worth it to pursue remanufacturing as a vocation.

Like any business venture, remanufactured products must be properly marketed in order for the company producing them to ultimately succeed. Management must target consumers who will appreciate the fact that remanufactured goods are a great financial alternative to new ones, but educate them enough so that they understand they are not sacrificing quality for price. A sound warranty plan and follow-up calls that gauge the product's performance are also suggested. Like any product or service, a remanufactured product will benefit from positive word of mouth and grow into a solid business because of it.

Inexperienced remanufacturing firms must also be careful not to compete against themselves when marketing remanufactured and new goods at the same time. In addition, management must work with their own employees so that they understand the many benefits of the remanufacturing process. Many employees may be hesitant to offer remanufactured goods to their customers for fear of a potential prejudices regarding the performance of the product.

Most importantly, a small business must have the means at its disposal to locate and recover the products and resources that will be used in the remanufacturing project and ultimately perform the task at hand. Once these products are found, they must be transported to the destination where disassembly will take place. After that, they will most likely be transported to another location that specializes in reassembly. Finally, any unusable parts and products must be collected and transported to recycling centers or other places that specialize in their disposal.

There are many legal and regulatory issues that affect the remanufacturing industry that businesses must be aware of. Intellectual property and anti-trust matters; federal, state and local recycling procedures; and government economic incentives are just a few of these issues. The Remanufacturing Institute is the watchdog organization for the entire industry and they are constantly monitoring these issues and representing the views of the businesses that are involved in remanufacturing. In addition, the federal government requires that all remanufactured goods must be labeled as such so that they cannot be passed off as new products.

SEE ALSO *Recycling*

BIBLIOGRAPHY

"APRA Urges Trade Barrier Removal." Automotive Parts Remanufacturers Association. Available from http://www.apra.org/GlobalConnection/Nov/G8_Trade_Barrier.asp. Retrieved on 17 May 2006.

Bhamra, Tracy and Bernard Hon. *Design and Manufacture for Sustainable Development 2004.* Professional Engineering Publishing Limited, 2004.

Debo, Laurens G., L. Beril Toktay, and Luk N. Van Wassenhove. "Market Segmentation and Product Technology Selection for Remanufacturable Products" *Management Science.* August 2005.

Franke, C., B. Basdere, M. Ciupek, and S. Seliger. "Remanufacturing of Mobile Phones—Capacity, Program and Facility Adaptation Planning." *Omega.* December 2006.

Hillstrom, Northern Lights
updated by Magee, ECDI

RENOVATION

Renovation describes a series of planned changes and updates made to a facility where business is conducted. Office and building renovation will take place now and again in the environment of most business, at their own or at others' initiative, in response to new needs, technological pressures, or simply the need for maintenance and renewal. Renovation, for a business, may be a response to declining sales. As an ancient Chinese saying has it: "When business slows, paint the counter red."

A well-conceived and carefully planned renovation effort can revitalize a business and provide it with much-needed room to grow. But periods of renovation also have a down-side: they can reduce productivity, create inconveniences for customers, cost money, and affect the bottom line. The inconveniences associated with office and building renovation often make it a practical impossible for businesses to maintain the exact same level of operations that they met during non-renovation periods. But owners can—whether they are building tenants or building operators—can take several steps to ensure that the negative aspects of renovation are minimized.

SMALL BUSINESS TENANTS AND RENOVATION

Many small business owners are co-tenants of a building with other businesses. These entrepreneurs may well find themselves faced with an impending renovation. This is especially true if they are operating their businesses in older buildings. Sometimes these renovations take place within the physical space of the business itself; on other occasions, the renovation may be limited to common areas—lobbies, outer building areas, stairways/elevator systems, etc.—that are shared by all the tenants. In either case, the impending arrival of a renovation crew should signal a period of preparation on the part of the small business owner. Tenants normally welcome renewal projects that make the facility more convenient and attractive, but during the period when the renovation is actually taking place, owners may find themselves feeling everything from anxiety to deep anger about the impact that it is (or seems to be) having on their company. The most effective way a small business can minimize these negatives is by establishing and maintaining good lines of communication with the building owner before and during the renovation process.

Effective building managers will typically take the initiative in talking with their business tenants so that these are more likely to feel a part of the project. But if as an owner you feel that the facility's management is doing an inadequate job of informing you of renovation issues and schedules, it is entirely within your rights to demand more information and input. Business owners should make sure that they thoroughly review their leasing contract, soliciting legal assistance if necessary, to make sure that they are being treated fairly.

Some business owners inhabiting facilities that are undergoing renovation adopt a fatalistic sort of attitude toward the process, surrendering meekly to renovation strategies without offering any workable alternatives to plans that might unnecessarily hinder their operations. Other entrepreneurs, meanwhile, err on the other end of the spectrum by making unreasonable demands that may ultimately drag out the renovation process for several extra days or weeks. Small business experts counsel owners to instead adopt a middle ground. They have to recognize that renovation efforts almost inevitably bring about some measure of inconvenience for tenants and their customers, but that they ultimately increase the value of the location for business operation. On the other hand, if a business owner spots a problem during a review of upcoming or ongoing renovation plans, he or she should bring it to the attention of building management. A renovation strategy that would render a key loading dock unavailable during a big delivery period, for example, should immediately be brought to the attention of the landlord.

Small business owners should recognize that many facility managers want to help tenants out in whatever way they reasonably can. After all, they do not want to lose tenants and go to the trouble of finding new ones. Most will bend over backwards to help the tenant get past difficulties by making accommodations.

RENOVATING PROFESSIONAL OFFICES

Office and facility renovations may also be undertaken by small business enterprises that either own or are the sole tenants of the building in which they operate. Business owners that provide professional services are especially likely to renovate to meet changing internal demands, attract new clients, and keep existing ones. Indeed, doctors, dentists, attorneys, architects, engineers, and the like recognize that the appearance of their offices can be a significant component in their overall success.

Analysts note that professional offices are more likely to renovate than relocate for two fundamental reasons: cost and client retention. Even a major renovation of an existing facility is likely to be considerably less expensive than the total costs associated with relocating to another facility. Perhaps even more importantly, existing patients and clients are accustomed to finding the office at a given location. To move may mean to lose—a following.

Renovation strategies can vary considerably, depending on the needs and concerns of the office in question. A medical practice or architectural firm may be amply equipped to integrate new technology with existing operations, only to recognize that its growth has been hampered because it is saddled with an unattractive waiting area. In this situation, the renovation may amount to little more than some new carpeting, wallpaper, and furniture. Other firms, however, may find that only a major rehabilitation effort will be sufficient to correct long-standing problems with infrastructure such as an ineffective floor plan, poor wiring to support information technology needs, or cramped office space.

Professional service firms (and many other businesses) have to meet legislated requirements as part of renovation plans. For example, businesses have to be in compliance with the Americans with Disabilities Act of 1990. Much of the renovation work that took place in the early 1990s was undertaken specifically to address this law, which called on facilities to become fully accessible by widening hallways, installing ramps, and adapting drinking fountains and bathrooms for use by people in wheelchairs. Most buildings are now in compliance with the ADA, but building owners looking to renovate need to make sure that their new plans adhere to ADA parameters. In addition, professional service firms need to factor in their attractiveness to recent graduates when weighing their renovation strategies.

Finally, before committing to a major renovation effort, professional service firms should discuss matters with appropriate experts, including architects, accountants, and lenders. Selecting a contractor should be done carefully as well; business owners are urged to check into the contractor's reputation for quality, timeliness, and financial soundness before making an agreement. Finally, firms should call in legal representation before signing a contract.

BIBLIOGRAPHY

Haughey, Jim. "Office Vacancy Rate Continues to Decline." *Building Design & Construction.* May 2006.

The Jerde Partnership. *Building Type Basics for Retail and Mixed-Use Facilities* John Wiley & Sons, 2004.

Langson, Craig. *Life-Cost Approach To Building Evaluation.* UNSW Press, 2005.

Piper, James E. *Handbook of Facility Assessment.* Fairmont Press, 2004.

Scalise, Christina. *Interior Planning and Design: Project Programs, Plans, Charettes.* Thomson Delmar Learning, 2004.

Thurm, David. "Master of the House: Why a company should take control of its building projects." *Harvard Business Review.* October 2005.

Weiss, Gail Garfinkel. "Loans, Leases, and Credentialing." *Medical Economics.* 23 April 2004.

Hillstrom, Northern Lights
updated by Magee, ECDI

REQUEST FOR PROPOSAL

A Request for Proposal (RFP) is the process by which a corporate department or government agency prepares bid documents to acquire equipment or services. RFPs are frequently published in the legal documents section of pertinent newspapers or in trade journals covering the industry in which the department operates. The RFP can also be distributed to a list of qualified potential bidders that have already been contacted and prequalified as eligible by the agency or department. "Qualified" is a key word in answering or preparing any RFP. Qualification frequently depends on follow-up investigation on the part of the hopeful bidder, and careful wording of the original RFP.

RFPs are primarily associated with government agencies, since their responsibility to get equipment and consulting talent under the most beneficial circumstances possible is closely monitored by the press and tax watchdogs. Some private companies also employ RFPs, though, usually when purchasing commodities or services that do not bear directly on the company's own products or services.

ELEMENTS OF AN ATTRACTIVE RFP

Some RFP work requests are of a scale beyond the scope of small or mid-sized companies, but others provide such businesses with valuable opportunities to expand their client base and operations. Before bidding on an RFP, however, entrepreneurs and business owners should make sure they fully understand the nature of the work request.

For instance, some RFPs are decidedly more informative than others. When scanning an RFP, vendors should make certain that it specifically describes what needs to be delivered or executed to fulfill the needs of the company or agency that posted the notice. In order to do so, it is often necessary for potential vendors to educate themselves about the nature of the agency or corporation that has issued the RFP. Vendors should also inquire whether the work request could translate into additional work on associated projects down the line. For instance, if the equipment will eventually be networked to a building that is not yet built, but is in the long range plans of the agency or company, a vendor may decide that a low price on the initial RFP is viable if it advances its prospects for a more long-term arrangement down the line.

Before making any bid, vendors should also check the RFP for other factors that might influence their response. Some possible questions follow:

- Will the asked-for equipment be subject to notable environmental conditions or regulations?

- If the equipment will be used in foreign countries, is the equipment compatible with the standards of those nations?

- Will ancillary costs associated with design, production, transportation, or some other aspect of delivery eat into the profit margin to an unacceptable extent?

- Are the RFP and the equipment or services it seeks legal under local, state, and federal laws?

- Is the RFP asking for both equipment and service? (Companies that sell equipment might not be able to adequately service it, yet that service performance may be written into the RFP in a separate section from the equipment specifications; responders must know they can fulfill the entire contract before answering it.)

- Are deadlines and performance clauses contained within the RFP reasonable?

- Will the RFP agency require the winning vendor to sign a performance bond that guarantees delivery of goods or services by a certain date?

Most companies and agencies that submit work requests provide prospective bidders with ample time to study the RFP before the deadline. Some companies give vendors as much as one month from the time the RFP is published before the bids are due. This allows bidders time to tinker with their bids, possibly allowing them to seek out new vendors of their own to help meet the needs of the RFP.

STAYING ON THE BID LIST

Companies wishing to bid on RFPs should monitor the legal notices in local newspapers and trade magazines, and contact the purchasing departments of corporations and government agencies likely to request services and equipment. They should investigate the requirements to be added to the "bid list." Finally, once the company has fulfilled all obligations necessary to be added to the list, the company's leadership needs to make certain that it stays on that list.

Government agencies and corporate departments are sometimes reluctant to delete vendors from bid lists because of fears that such cuts will elicit charges of favoritism. Nonetheless, establishments issuing RFPs do seek to keep bid lists to manageable size, since every bid requires scrutiny. One favored way to keep the bid list down is to require potential vendors to refile every few years. Another is to ask vendors to provide certain information about their companies, such as past sales and experience or number of employees available to service the account. Such requirements cull the number of bidders down, eliminating companies that are too disorganized or feeble to keep up. Conversely, a small business that meets all such requirements in a timely fashion is essentially serving notice that it has its act together.

Companies seeking RFP business should also be cognizant of the fact that winning bids are not always exclusively a matter of providing the lowest cost or the highest level of customer service. Some corporations and government agencies give special consideration on their bid lists to minority- and women-owned companies.

SEE ALSO *Competitive Bids*

BIBLIOGRAPHY

Frey, Robert S. *Successful Proposal Strategies for Small Businesses.* Artech House, 2002.

"Preparing Your Request for Proposal." *Association Management.* July 2000.

Stasiowski, Frank A. *Architect's Essentials of Winning Proposals.* John Wiley & Sons, 2003.

Thompson, Waddy. *The Complete Idiot's Guide to Grant Writing.* Alpha Books, 2003.

"Writing the Right RFP." *Health Data Management.* April 2006.

Hillstrom, Northern Lights
updated by Magee, ECDI

RESEARCH AND DEVELOPMENT

Research and development (R&D) is a process intended to create new or improved technology that can provide a competitive advantage at the business, industry, or national level. While the rewards can be very high, the process of technological innovation (of which R&D is the first phase) is complex and risky. The majority of R&D projects fail to provide the expected financial results, and the successful projects (25 to 50 percent) must also pay for the projects that are unsuccessful or terminated early by management. In addition, the originator of R&D cannot appropriate all the benefits of its innovations and must share them with customers, the public, and even competitors. For these reasons, a company's R&D efforts must be carefully organized, controlled, evaluated, and managed.

OBJECTIVES AND TYPES OF R&D

The objective of academic and institutional R&D is to obtain new knowledge, which may or may not be applied to practical uses. In contrast, the objective of industrial R&D is to obtain new knowledge, applicable to the company's business needs, that eventually will result in new or improved products, processes, systems, or services that can increase the company's sales and profits.

The National Science Foundation (NSF) defines three types of R&D: basic research, applied research, and development. Basic research has as its objectives a fuller knowledge or understanding of the subject under study, rather than a practical application thereof. As applied to the industrial sector, basic research is defined as research that advances scientific knowledge but does not have specific commercial objectives, although such investigation may be in the fields of present or potential interest to the company.

Applied research is directed towards gaining knowledge or understanding necessary for determining the means by which a recognized and specific need may be met. In industry, applied research includes investigations directed to the discovery of new knowledge having specific commercial objectives with respect to products, processes, or services. Development is the systematic utilization of the knowledge or understanding gained from research toward the production of useful materials, devices, systems, or methods, including design and development of prototypes and processes.

At this point, it is important to differentiate development from engineering. Engineering is the application of state-of-the-art knowledge to the design and production of marketable goods. Research creates knowledge, and development designs and builds prototypes and proves their feasibility. Engineering converts these prototypes into products that can be offered to the marketplace or into processes that can be used to produce commercial products and services.

R&D AND TECHNOLOGY ACQUISITION

In many cases, technology required for industrial purposes is available in the marketplace—for a price. Before embarking on the lengthy and risky process of performing its own R&D, a company can perform a "make or buy" analysis and decide whether or not the new R&D project is justified. Factors that influence the decision include the ability to protect the innovation, its timing, risk, and cost.

Proprietary Character If a technology can be safeguarded as proprietary—and protected by patents, trade secrets, nondisclosure agreements, etc.—the technology becomes exclusive property of the company and its value is much higher. In fact, a valid patent grants a company a temporary monopoly for 17 years to use the technology as it sees fit, usually to maximize sales and profits. In this case, a high-level of R&D effort is justified for a relatively long period (up to 10 years) with an acceptable risk of failure.

On the contrary, if the technology cannot be protected, as is the case with certain software programs, expensive in-house R&D is not justified since the software may be copied by a competitor or "stolen" by a disloyal employee. In this case, the secret of commercial success is staying ahead of competition by developing continuously improved software packages, supported by a strong marketing effort.

Timing If the market growth rate is slow or moderate, in-house or contracted R&D may be the best means to obtain the technology. On the other hand, if the market is growing very fast and competitors are rushing in, the "window of opportunity" may close before the technology has been developed by the new entrant. In this case, it is better to acquire the technology and related know-how, in order to enter the market before it is too late.

Risk Inherently, technology development is always riskier than technology acquisition because the technical success of R&D cannot be guaranteed. There is always the risk that the planned performance specifications will not be met, that the time to project completion will be stretched out, and that the R&D and manufacturing costs will be higher than forecasted. On the other hand, acquiring technology entails a much lower risk, since the product, process, or service, can be seen and tested before the contract is signed.

Regardless of whether the technology is acquired or developed, there is always the risk that it will soon become obsolete and be displaced by a superior technology. This risk cannot be entirely removed, but it can be considerably reduced by careful technology forecasting and planning. If market growth is slow, and no winner has emerged among the various competing technologies, it may be wiser to monitor these technologies through "technology gatekeepers" and be ready to jump in as the winner emerges.

Cost For a successful product line with relatively long life, acquisition of technology is more costly, but less risky, than technology development. Normally, royalties are paid in the form of a relatively low initial payment as "earnest money," and as periodic payments tied to sales. These payments continue throughout the period of validity of the license agreement. Since these royalties may amount to 2 to 5 percent of sales, this creates an undue burden of continuing higher cost to the licensee, everything else being equal.

On the other hand, R&D requires a high front-end investment and therefore a longer period of negative cash flow. There are also intangible costs involved in acquiring technology—the license agreements may have restrictive geographic or application clauses, and other businesses may have access to the same technology and compete with lower prices or stronger marketing. Finally, the licensee is dependent upon the licensor for technological advances, or even for keeping up to date, and this may be dangerous.

MOVING AHEAD WITH R&D

R&D can be conducted in-house, under contract, or jointly with others. In-house R&D commands a strategic advantage: the company is the sole owner of the know-how created and can protect it from unauthorized use. R&D is also basically a learning process; in-house research thus trains the company's own research people who may go on to ever better things.

External R&D is usually contracted out to specialized nonprofit research institutions or to universities. These institutions often already have experienced personnel in the disciplines to be applied and are well-equipped. The disadvantages are that the company will not benefit from the learning experience and may become overly dependent on the contractor. The trans for the technology may turn out to be difficult and leaks to competitors may develop. Using university research is sometimes slightly less expensive than engaging institutes because graduate students rather than professionals do some of the work.

Joint R&D became popular in the United States after antitrust laws were relaxed and tax incentives were offered to R&D consortia. In a consortium, several companies with congruent interests join together to perform R&D, either in a separate organization or in a university. The advantages are lower costs, since each company does not have to invest in similar equipment; a critical mass of researchers; and interchange of information among the sponsors. The disadvantages are that all the sponsors have access to the same R&D results. However, because of antitrust considerations, the R&D performed must be "precompetitive," legalese meaning that it must be basic and/or preliminary. A company must take joint research beyond the "joint" stage to make money on it; it can use this type of result as the foundation, not as the innovation itself.

R&D PROJECT SELECTION, MANAGEMENT, AND TERMINATION

Industrial R&D is generally performed according to projects (i.e., separate work activities) with specific technical and business goals, assigned personnel, and time and money budgets. These projects can either originate "top down" (for instance, from a management decision to develop a new product) or "bottom up" (from an idea originated by an individual researcher). The size of a project may vary from a part-time effort of one researcher for a few months with a budget of thousands of dollars, to major five- or ten-year projects with large, multidisciplinary teams of researchers and budgets of millions of dollars. Therefore, project selection and evaluation is one of the more critical and difficult subjects of R&D management. Of equal importance, although less emphasized in practice, is the subject of project termination, particularly in the case of unsuccessful or marginal projects.

Selection of R&D Projects Normally, a company or a laboratory will have requests for a higher number of projects than can be effectively implemented. Therefore, R&D managers are faced with the problem of allocating scarce resources of personnel, equipment, laboratory space, and funds to a broad spectrum of competing projects. Since the decision to start on an R&D project is both a technical and a business decision, R&D managers should select projects on the basis of the following objectives, in order of importance:

1. Maximize the long-term return on investment;

2. Make optimum use of the available human and physical resources;

3. Maintain a balanced R&D portfolio and control risk;

4. Foster a favorable climate for creativity and innovation.

Project selection is usually done once a year, by listing all ongoing projects and the proposals for new projects, evaluating and comparing all these projects according to quantitative and qualitative criteria, and prioritizing the projects in "totem pole" order. The funds requested by all the projects are compared with the laboratory budget for the following year and the project list is cut off at the budgeted amount. Projects above the line are funded, those below the line delayed to the following year or tabled indefinitely. Some experienced R&D managers do not allocate all the budgeted funds, but keep a small percentage on reserve to take care of new projects that may be proposed during the year, after the laboratory official budget has been approved.

Evaluation of R&D Projects Since R&D projects are subject to the risk of failure, the expected value of a project can be evaluated according to a statistical formula. The value is the payoff anticipated—but discounted by probabilities. These are the probability of technical success, the probability of commercial success, and the probability of financial success. Assuming a payoff of $100 million and a fifty-fifty rate of technical success, a commercial success rate of 90 percent, and a financial probability of 80 percent, then the expected value will be $36 million—100 discounted by 50, 90, and 80 percent respectively.

Consequently, project evaluation must be performed along two separate dimensions: technical evaluation, to establish the probability of technical success; and business evaluation, to establish the payoff and the probabilities of commercial and financial success. Once the expected value of a project has been determined it can be compared with the projected cost of the technical effort. Given a company's usual rate of return on investment, the cost may not be worth the expected value given the risks.

Needless to say, such statistical approaches to evaluation are not silver bullets but as good as the guesses that go into the formula. Businesses use such evaluations, however, when many projects compete for money and some kind of disciplined approach is needed to make choices.

Management of R&D Projects The management of R&D projects follows basically the principles and methods of project management. There is, however, one significant caveat in relation to normal engineering projects: R&D projects are risky, and it is difficult to develop an accurate budget, in terms of technical milestones, costs, and time to completion of the various tasks. Therefore, R&D budgets should be considered initially as tentative, and should be gradually refined as more information

becomes available as a result of preliminary work and the learning process. Historically, many R&D projects have exceeded, sometimes with disastrous consequences, the forecasted and budgeted times to completion and funds to be expended. In the case of R&D, measuring technical progress and completion of milestones is generally more important than measuring expenditures over time.

Termination of R&D Projects Termination of projects is a difficult subject because of the political repercussions on the laboratory. Theoretically, a project should be discontinued for one of the following three reasons:

1. There is a change in the environment—for instance, new government regulations, new competitive offerings, or price declines—that make the new product less attractive to the company;

2. Unforeseen technical obstacles are encountered and the laboratory does not have the resources to overcome them; or

3. The project falls hopelessly behind schedule and corrective actions are not forthcoming.

Due to organizational inertia, and the fear of antagonizing senior researchers or executives with pet projects, there is often the tendency to let a project continue, hoping for a miraculous breakthrough that seldom happens.

In theory, an optimal number of projects should be initiated and this number should be gradually reduced over time to make room for more deserving projects. Also, the monthly cost of a project is much lower in the early stages than in the later stages, when more personnel and equipment have been committed. Thus, from a financial risk management viewpoint, it is better to waste money on several promising young projects than on a few maturing "dogs" with low payoff and high expense. In practice, in many laboratories it is difficult to start a new project because all the resources have already been committed and just as difficult to terminate a project, for the reasons given above. Thus, an able and astute R&D manager should continuously evaluate his/her project portfolio in relation to changes in company strategy, should continuously and objectively monitor the progress of each R&D project, and should not hesitate to terminate projects that have lost their value to the company in terms of payoff and probability of success.

TAX ADVANTAGES FOR R&D

In the period 1981 through 2004, corporations had a R&D tax credit—had the ability to deduct research and development expenditures from income. The tax credit was renewed in 2004 and lasted through 2005, but the tax bill signed in May of 2006 left the provision out. This outcome no doubt pleased those who thought that government subsidies of corporate development were out of place—and energized those who saw the credit as nationally important to attempt to have the credit reinstated.

SMALL BUSINESS AND R&D

Research and development in public the public domain as well as in the media suggests big business, huge labs, vast testing fields, wind tunnels, and crash dummies flailing around as autos are crashed into walls. R&D is associated with the pharmaceutical industry, miracle cures, laser eye surgery, and super fast jet travel. To be sure, a vast amount of the money expended on formal research is expended by large corporations—often on relatively trivial improvements of products already doing quite a good job—and by government on weapons systems and space exploration. The glory and the power thus displayed before our eyes on television fail to remind us that the crucial research and development on which much else is based has been—and continues to be—the work of small entrepreneurs.

The explosive development of the oil industry was triggered by the invention of an effective kerosene lamp by Michael Dietz in 1859. Dietz ran a small lamp production business. Oil drilling began in earnest to support such lighting applications. An unwanted residue of kerosene refining was—gasoline, burned off as useless waste—until the first cars came along. The story of Thomas Edison is worth rereading occasionally to correct one's vision of modern R&D. Chester Carlson, the inventory of xerography, perfected his invention in part-time labors in a makeshift lab while working as a patent attorney. The computer revolution came about because two young men, Steve Wozniak and Steve Jobs, put together a personal computer in a garage and thus triggered the Information Age. Countless innovations large and small were made by tinkering individuals or small business people trying something new. The fact that many of these entrepreneurial, inventive, innovative, and persistent individuals are the fathers and mothers of great companies—indeed of whole industries—that now dominate formal R&D should not obscure their humble beginnings and catch-as-catch-can methods of discovering the new.

BIBLIOGRAPHY

Bock, Peter. *Getting it Right: R&D Methods for Science and Engineering.* Academic Press, 2001.

Dankbaar, Ben. *Innovation Management in the Knowledge Economy.* Imperial College Press, 2003.

Khurana, Anil. "Strategies for Global R&D: A study of 31 companies reveals different models and approaches to the conduct of low-cost R&D around the world." *Research-Technology Management.* March-April 2006.

Le Corre, Armelle, and Gerald Mischke. *Innovation Game: A New Approach to Innovation Management and R&D.* Springer, 2005.

Miller, William L. "Innovation Rules!" *Research-Technology Management.* March-April 2006.

Hillstrom, Northern Lights
updated by Magee, ECDI

RÉSUMÉS

A résumé is a document presented by a job applicant to a prospective employer outlining and summarizing that person's qualifications for employment. A résumé generally includes data on education, previous work experience, and personal information. Well-crafted résumés are concise and composed in such a way as to maximize the applicant's attractiveness as a potential employee. A résumé is generally accompanied by a cover letter which introduces the applicant and the résumé to the employer. The purpose of a résumé is to obtain an interview, not to land a job. This is an important distinction. Whether or not a person is hired is largely determined by what transpires during the job interview, not by the résumé. A résumé is extremely important, however, because it provides the employer with a first impression of the job applicant. From this first impression a decision will be made as to whether or not an interview will be granted.

RÉSUMÉ APPEARANCE AND CONTENT

Résumés are read from two perspectives: the appearance of the physical document itself and the content of the résumé. Résumé appearance concerns the presence (or absence) of typographical errors, poor grammar usage, sloppy sentence structure, garish colors, unconventional typefaces, paper stains, etc.

The content of the résumé, as indicated earlier, is the actual information included in the document. The content of most résumés falls into four broad categories: education, previous work experience, personal data, and social data. The first two are self-explanatory. Personal data includes such things as address and telephone number. Social data includes things like marital status, club memberships, military status, references, etc.

Handbooks that provide detailed advice on compiling résumés are available in most bookstores and libraries. These guides generally agree on the types of information to include on a résumé but sometimes differ on the format and hierarchical arrangement of the résumé. Some authors feel that educational information should be presented first while others feel previous work experience should be foremost. Other authors of such handbooks offer advice on tailoring a résumé to fit one's particular employment situation (looking for an entry-level position, re-entering the job market, or changing fields or vocations). Most of these handbooks, however, have one thing in common: they generally lack empirical data on what a prospective employer is looking for in a résumé. References in these handbooks to this aspect of the applicant, résumé, and employer scenario are often anecdotal.

EMPLOYERS AND RÉSUMÉS

When reading résumés, employers are usually looking for the facts. Functional résumés (résumés with no dates) are often viewed as indicators of excessive job movement or attempts to hide large gaps in one's career. Nebulous phraseology such as "exposure to" sometimes indicate a lack of depth of work experience, as does excess space devoted to education, personal, and social data. Obviously, recent college or high school graduates and other people relatively new to the work force often have little choice but to highlight such information and the discerning employer will take this factor into account.

Many small business consultants urge their clients to study résumés closely, citing the unfortunate frequency with which some applicants include outright lies. A Massachusetts-based management consultant, for instance, told *Nation's Business* writer Peter Weaver that a résumé should only be used as a starting point for launching a thorough examination of an applicant's business, professional, and interpersonal skills. "Hiring someone based on false claims in a résumé not only weakens a firm's work force but also can lead to costly legal action," said Weaver, who noted that many businesses are held legally responsible for the actions of all employees—even those who may have been placed in positions on the basis of fraudulent information.

Some employers have turned to automated résumé banks or reference checking firms to help them fill their workforce needs. Banks will, for a fee, mail out copies of résumés to prospective employers. Using technical terminology and job-related phrases a computer will match the résumés it stores in its data bank with job descriptions supplied by its clients. Résumé banks, however, are not professional recruiters; the latter are compensated for their services in terms of a percentage of a recruit's salary. Résumé banks charge a sliding fee for their services.

ELECTRONIC RÉSUMÉS

An online article posted on the Web site of a job search service, Quintessential Careers, offers the following

statistics that together highlight the reason why a print résumé, although still important, can no longer be the only résumé tool in a job-seeker's kit. "More than 80 percent of employers are now placing resumes directly into searchable databases and an equal percentage of employers prefer to receive resumes by e-mail. Eighty percent of Fortune 500 companies post jobs on their own Web sites—and expect job-seekers to respond electronically."

Some job applicants have found that the trend toward e-mailed résumés makes it more difficult for them to differentiate themselves in the eyes of prospective employers. As a result, many people have begun adding graphics and interactive elements to their electronic résumés. In fact, several Web sites exist to help users create résumés online. While including graphics and interactive elements can sometimes help applicants for some creative and technology-oriented positions, hiring executives emphasize that these features cannot make up for a lack of experience and achievements.

Job applicants who decide to create an electronic résumé and send it to potential employers via e-mail should keep a few factors in mind. First, it is generally considered bad form to use a current employer's e-mail system to send out résumés. Second, job applicants should make sure that their e-mail user name is professional and appropriate before sending out résumés. Third, applicants should consider using a standard ASCII format with a predictable layout and plain fonts, since fancy text may not be readable on some potential employers' computer systems. It may be helpful to send a test résumé to yourself and to several friends in order to check how the document appears on several systems. Fourth, experts recommend including a name, phone number, and e-mail address at the top of every page so the sender's identity will not get lost if the résumé is printed out or entered into a database. Finally, job applicants should be careful to include keywords referring to their job interests and experience in case hiring companies scan in résumés and search them to find candidates for later job openings.

POSTING A RÉSUMÉ ON AN ELECTRONIC BULLETIN BOARD

One of the reasons it is important to have an electronic résumé for job seekers in today's market is because they can be used to participate in online job bulletin boards. Some of the most popular such services are Monster.com, CareerBuilders, HotJobs.com to name the largest. Industry specific job posting services offer to assist both job seekers and employers looking for the right candidates. These electronic job posting sites are a useful tool but any job-seeker should use them as but one avenue through which to search for employment. According the CareerJournal article, "only 7 percent of 2,500 job hunters who receive outplacement counseling found new positions through the Internet, compared to 35 percent who were hired through networking."

However résumé s are used, the key to their success is their ability to communicate the most essential information about a candidate that will tweak the interest of prospective employers who have a position that will make a good fit for the job-seeker.

SEE ALSO *Employee Hiring; Recruiting*

BIBLIOGRAPHY

Hansen, Katharine. "The Top 10 Things You Need to Know about E-Resumes and Posting Your Resume Online." *Quintessential Careers.* Available from http://www.quintcareers.com/e-resumes.html. Retrieved on 18 May 2006.

Jackson, Tom. "Mastering the Electronic Job Search Monster." *CareerJouranl.com.* Available from http://www.careerjournal.com/jobhunting/strategies/20030422-jackson.html. Retrieved on 18 May 2006.

Narain, R. Kamna. "Changing Face of Résumés." *Business Journal.* 15 September 2000.

Ream, Richard. "Rules for Electronic Résumés." *Information Today.* September 2000.

U.S. Small Business Administration. Roberts, Gary, Gary Seldon, and Carlotta Roberts. *Human Resources Management.* n.d.

Weaver, Peter. "Ignoring a Résumé Can Prove Costly." *Nation's Business.* September 1997.

Hillstrom, Northern Lights
updated by Magee, ECDI

RETAIL TRADE

Retailers are business firms engaged in offering goods and services directly to consumers. In most—but not all—cases, retail outlets are primarily concerned with selling merchandise. Typically, such businesses sell individual units or small groupings of products to large numbers of customers. A minority of retailers, however, also garner income through rentals rather than outright sales of goods (as in the case of enterprises that offer furniture or gardening tools for rent) or through a combination of products and services (as in the case of a clothing store that might offer free alterations with the purchase of a suit).

The retail industry is a massive part of the overall U.S. economy. In 2005, for example, retail establishments accounted for 18 percent of all nonfarm private-sector jobs and had sales of $3.2 trillion. Moreover, many retail niches are characterized by a healthy population of

smaller enterprises; indeed, the vast majority of retail employees in the United States work at establishments with fewer than 20 employees.

Retail trade is widely known as a very competitive area of commercial endeavor, and observers note that many fledgling retail establishments do not survive for more than a few years. Indeed, competition for sales has become so great that consumers have seen a marked blurring of product lines among retailers. Increasingly, retailers have taken to stocking a much greater variety of goods than their basic industry classification would indicate (bookstores, for example, increasingly stock music products, while food, liquor, office supplies, automotive supplies, and other wares can all be found in contemporary drug stores). This development further complicates efforts to establish and maintain a healthy presence in the marketplace. But for the small business owner who launches a retail store on an adequate foundation of capital, business acumen, and attractive merchandise, involvement in the trade can be rewarding on both financial and personal fulfillment levels.

PRIMARY RETAIL TYPES

Retail enterprises can be either independently owned and operated or part of a "chain," a group of two or more stores whose activities are determined and coordinated by a single management group. Stores that are part of a chain may all be owned by a single company, but in other cases, the individual stores may be franchises that are independently owned by a small businessperson.

Many different types of retail establishments exist, and, as noted above, the overall industry has seen a significant blurring of the boundaries that had long separated the wide range of companies operating under the retail umbrella. Nonetheless, retailing establishments still generally fall into one of the following general categories:

- Specialty Stores—These establishments typically concentrate their efforts on selling a single type or very limited range of merchandise. Clothing stores, musical instrument stores, sewing shops, and party supply stores all fall within this category.

- Department Stores—These establishments are comprised of a series of departments, each of which specializes in selling a particular grouping of products. Under this compartmentalized arrangement, consumers go to one area of the store to purchase tableware and another area to acquire bedding, for example.

- Supermarkets—These retail establishments, which are primarily involved in providing food to consumers but have increasingly ventured into other product areas in recent years, account for the vast majority of total food-store sales in America.

- Discount Stores—These retail outlets offer consumers a trade-off: lower prices (typically on a broad range of products) in exchange for lower levels of service. Indeed, many discount stores operate under a basic "self-service" philosophy.

- Mail-Order Businesses and other Nonstore Retailing Establishments—Mail-order sales have become an increasingly ubiquitous part of the American retail landscape; indeed, some retail establishments subsist entirely on mail order, forsaking traditional stores entirely, while other companies maintain operations on both levels. In addition, this category includes sales made to end consumers through telemarketing, vending machines, the Internet, and other nonstore avenues.

Electronic retail has been growing at a significantly higher rate than retail trade as a whole. The subject is covered in some detail in this volume under *Dot-Coms*.

SEE ALSO *Dot-coms*

BIBLIOGRAPHY
Alexander, Tierney. *The Retail Life: A Store Manager's Companion.* iUniverse, 2002.

Barnes, Nora Ganim. "The Restructuring of the Retail Business in the US: The fall of the shopping mall." *Business Forum.* Winter 2005.

Burstiner, Irving. "How to Start and Run Your Own Retail Business." *Citadel Press.* 2001.

Heard, Geoffrey, and Gordon Woolf. *Success in Store: How to Start Or Buy a Retail Business, Enjoy Running It and Make Money.* The Worsley Press, 2003.

Koch, Lambert T. and Kati Schmengler. "Entrepreneurial Success and Low-Budget Internet Exposure: The case of online-retailing." *International Journal of Technology Management.* 13 March 2006.

U.S. Census Bureau. "Estimated Annual Retail and Food Service Sales by Kinds of Business: 1992 Through 2005." Available from http://www.census.gov/svsd/retlann/view/table2.txt. Retrieved on 16 May 2006.

Hillstrom, Northern Lights
updated by Magee, ECDI

RETIREMENT PLANNING

Retirement planning describes the financial strategies individuals employ during their working years to ensure that they will be able to meet their goals for financial security upon retirement. Making sound decisions about

retirement is particularly important for self-employed persons and small business owners. Unlike employees of some large companies, who can simply participate in the pension plans and investment programs offered by their employers, entrepreneurs must set up and administer plans for themselves and for their employees.

In recent years there has been a shift away from company-funded, defined-benefit pension plans. These plans were common within large firms during the 1950s through 1970s and into the 1980s. A defined-benefit pension plan is one in which the employer pays into and manages a plan based on calculations of how much the fund will need in order to provide an employee with a particular, **defined** post-retirement income. Such a plan guarantees all qualified employees with a predetermined retirement benefit. Many things have combined to cause a shift away from defined-benefit plans and towards defined-contribution plans. One of the more important of these, other than substantial demographic pressure that the retirement of the baby boom generation is having on all retirement issues, was the passage of an obscure provision in the Tax Revenue Act of 1978, the 401(k) provision. This provision went largely unnoticed for two years until Ted Benna, a Pennsylvania benefits consultant, devised a creative and rewarding application of the law, an application which became what is known today at the 401(k) plan.

A 401(k) plan is just one of various types of plans which fall under the umbrella of defined-contribution plans, as opposed to defined-benefit plans. A defined-contribution plan is one in which there is no guaranteed post-retirement benefit but rather a **defined** monthly or yearly contribution to a plan. How the plan's assets are invested and how much they are worth at retirement is not defined by the plans. Employees are responsible, in most cases, for investment decisions and the level of contribution made to the plan. With defined-contribution pension plans employees pay into the plan on a tax-deferred basis and in most cases, the employer agrees to a minimum contribution or agrees to match some percentage of the contribution made by the employee. Many business writers believe that this shift from defined-benefit plan to defined-contribution plan has helped to level the playing field for small businesses. Smaller companies are now able to offer the same type of retirement benefits as many larger employers.

Though establishing and funding retirement plans can be costly for small businesses, such programs also offer a number of advantages. In most cases, for example, employer contributions to retirement plans are tax-deductible expenses. In addition, offering employees a comprehensive retirement plan can help small businesses attract and retain qualified people who might otherwise seek the security of working for a larger company. The number of small firms establishing retirement plans grew during the 1990s, but small employers still lag far behind larger ones in providing this type of benefit for employees.

Retirement planning is a topic of interest to all Americans, not only to small business owners and entrepreneurs. The debate over whether Social Security will be available for the younger members of the current work force adds legitimacy to the need for early retirement planning. Longer life expectancies mean that more money must be set aside for retirement, while the uncertainty of investment returns and inflation rates makes careful planning essential. In fact, some experts recommend that individuals invest a minimum of 14 percent of their gross income from the time they enter the work force to guarantee a comfortable retirement.

Unfortunately, most of us are not doing this. In fact, most Americans approaching retirement in 2005 do not have enough to retire on according to Jack VanDerhei, Senior Research Fellow at the Employee Benefit Research Institute (EBRI). In response to an interviewer's question on the Public Broadcasting System's *Frontline* show, VanDerhei explained that most people approaching retirement now have about three times their annual salary saved for the post-retirement period. The EBRI recommends that a man have 6.3 times his annual salary available for post-retirement living and a woman 6.7 times her annual salary. (Women have a longer life expectancy than men and therefore need slightly more retirement savings.) Financial planners and insurance analysts recommend even higher retirement savings goals—10 to 15 times annual salary—as necessary for a reasonable retirement. What is clear in all studies on this subject is the fact that as Americans, we are not now saving adequately for retirement.

LAWS GOVERNING RETIREMENT PLANS

The Social Security Administration was created in the 1930s as part of President Franklin Roosevelt's New Deal. Private pension plans mushroomed shortly thereafter, offering coverage to millions of employees. In 1962 the Self-Employed Individuals Retirement Act established tax-deferred retirement plans from which account holders could withdrawals starting between the ages of 59 ½ and 70 ½. These plans—also known as Keogh plans after their originator, New York Congressman Eugene J. Keogh—were intended for the self-employed and for those who have income from self-employment on the side. Embezzlement from pension plans by trustees led to the passage of the Employee Retirement Income Security Act of 1974 (ERISA). One of the main provisions of ERISA

was to set forth vesting requirements—time periods over which employees gain full rights to the money invested by employers on their behalf. ERISA governs most large-employer-sponsored pension plans, but does not apply to those sponsored by businesses with less than 25 employees.

TYPES OF RETIREMENT PLANS

The two main categories of retirement plans are defined-contribution and defined-benefit. Perhaps the most significant difference between defined-benefit and defined-contribution plans is the voluntary nature of defined-contribution plans. Such plans are usually fully voluntary, so that hourly or salaried employees elect to have a certain percentage of money deducted—before taxes—from their paychecks. Conversely, defined-benefit plans involve automatic contributions made by the employer, with no active participation on the part of the employee.

One significant advantage of defined-contribution plans is that the amount invested by employees can be rolled over into another account with another employer. Rollover activity into similar tax-deferred plans has continued to increase as tax laws require a 20 percent withholding tax to be paid on the lump sum if it is not rolled over. Nonetheless, defined-contribution plans continued to face scrutiny by many financial advisers for two reasons: 1) the investment decisions made by the company may be too restrictive for employees to meet individual goals; and 2) many times employees are not educated about the risk and returns associated with the investment vehicles available through the company plan. Similarly, the voluntary nature of defined-contribution plans makes detractors wonder if ill-informed employees will have less money in their defined-contribution accounts at retirement than they would have had under a defined-benefit plan.

OPTIONS FOR SMALL BUSINESSES

Small business owners can set up a wide variety of retirement plans by filling out the necessary forms at any financial institution (a bank, mutual fund, insurance company, brokerage firm, etc.). The fees vary depending on the plan's complexity and the number of participants. Some employer-sponsored plans are required to file Form 5500 annually to disclose plan activities to the IRS. The preparation and filing of this complicated document can increase the administrative costs associated with a plan, as the business owner may require help from a tax advisor or plan administration professional. In addition, all the information reported on Form 5500 is open to public inspection.

The most important thing to remember is that a small business owner who wants to establish a qualified plan for him or herself must also include all other company employees who meet minimum participation standards. As an employer, the small business owner can establish retirement plans like any other business. As an employee, the small business owner can then make contributions to the plan he or she has established in order to set aside tax-deferred funds for retirement, like any other employee. The difference is that a small business owner must include all nonowner employees in any company-sponsored retirement plans and make equivalent contributions to their accounts. Unfortunately, this requirement has the effect of reducing the allowable contributions that the owner of a proprietorship or partnership can make on his or her own behalf.

For self-employed individuals, contributions to a retirement plan are based upon the net earnings of their business. The net earnings consist of the company's gross income less deductions for business expenses, salaries paid to nonowner employees, the employer's 50 percent of the Social Security tax, and—significantly—the employer's contribution to retirement plans on behalf of employees. Therefore, rather than receiving pre-tax contributions to the retirement account as a percentage of gross salary, like nonowner employees, the small business owner receives contributions as a smaller percentage of net earnings. Employing other people thus detracts from the owner's ability to build up a sizeable before-tax retirement account of his or her own. For this reason, some experts recommend that the owners of proprietorships and partnerships who sponsor plans for their employees supplement their own retirement funds through a personal after-tax savings plan.

Nevertheless, many small businesses sponsor retirement plans in order to gain tax advantages and increase the loyalty of employees. A number of different types of plans are available. The most popular plans for small businesses all fall under the category of defined-contribution plans. In nearly every case, withdrawals made before the age of 59 ½ are subject to an IRS penalty in addition to ordinary income tax. The plans differ in terms of administrative costs, eligibility requirements, employee participation, degree of discretion in making contributions, and amount of allowable contributions. Brief descriptions of some of the most common types of plans follow:

Simplified Employee Pension (SEP) Plans SEP plans are employer-funded retirement accounts that allow small businesses to direct at least 3 percent and up to 15 percent of each employee's annual salary, to a maximum of $30,000, into tax-deferred individual retirement accounts (IRAs) on a discretionary basis. SEP plans are easy to set up and inexpensive to administer, as the employer simply makes contributions to IRAs that are established by employees. The employees then take responsibility for making investment decisions regarding their own IRAs. Employers thus avoid the risk and cost involved in accounting for employee retirement funds. In addition, employers have the flexibility to make large percentage contributions during good financial years, and to reduce contributions during hard times. SEP plans are available to all types of business entities, including proprietorships, partnerships, and corporations. In general, eligibility is limited to employees 21 or older with at least three years of service to the company and a minimum level of compensation. The maximum level of compensation for SEP eligibility is $170,000.

Savings Incentive Match Plan for Employees (SIMPLE) SIMPLE plans take two forms: a SIMPLE IRA and a SIMPLE 401(k). Both plans became available in January 1997 to businesses with less than 100 employees, replacing the discontinued Salary Reduction Simplified Employee Pension (SARSEP) plans. They were intended to provide an easy, low-cost way for small businesses and their employees to contribute jointly to tax-deferred retirement accounts. An IRA or 401(k) set up as a SIMPLE account requires the employer to match up to 3 percent of an employee's annual salary, up to $6,000 per year. Employees are also allowed to contribute up to $6,000 annually to their own accounts. Companies that establish SIMPLEs are not allowed to offer any other type of retirement plan. As of early 1997, most small businesses chose the SIMPLE IRA option, as the SIMPLE 401(k) proved more expensive than a regular 401(k) due to the company matching requirements. The main problem with the plans, according to many financial planners, was that legislation is already being drafting that would make SIMPLE less simple and more expensive for the businesses that the plans were created to serve.

Profit Sharing Plans Profit sharing plans enable employers to make a discretionary, tax-deductible contribution on behalf of employees each year, based on the level of profits achieved by the business. The total annual contribution is generally allocated among employees as a percentage of their compensation. Plan costs are tax deductible for the employer, and plan earnings are tax deferred for employees. Profit sharing plans are easy to implement, offer design flexibility, and provide a wide range of investment choices. Eligibility is typically limited to employees who are at least 21 years of age and who have at least one year of service. The employer's maximum deduction is 15 percent of the total annual salaries paid to nonowner employees (adjusted to 13.04 percent for the small business owner).

A common variation is the age-based profit sharing plan, in which contributions are based on an allocation formula that factors in the age or number of years to retirement of participants. Age-based profit sharing allows employers to reward valued older employees for their length of service. Another variation is the new comparability profit sharing plan, which allows employers to define classes of employees and set up the retirement plan so that certain classes benefit the most in terms of allocation. These types of profit sharing plans are similar to defined-benefit plans, but the employer contributions are discretionary.

Money Purchase Pension Plans Money purchase pension plans are similar to regular profit sharing plans, but the employer contributions are mandatory rather than discretionary. The main advantage of money purchase plans is that they allow larger employer contributions than regular profit sharing plans. The employer determines a fixed percentage of profits that will be allocated to employee retirement accounts according to a formula. The maximum employer contribution jumps to 25 percent of payroll for nonowner employees (adjusted to 20 percent for the small business owner) or a total of $30,000 per employee. There are also combination money purchase-profit sharing plans that allow employers to select a fixed percentage for mandatory contribution and also retain the option of contributing additional funds on a discretionary basis when cash flow permits.

401(k) Profit Sharing Plans The popular 401(k) plans are profit sharing plans that include a provision for employees to defer part of their salaries for retirement. The employer can make annual profit sharing contributions on behalf of employees, the employees can contribute up to $10,000 of pre-tax income themselves, and the employer can choose to match some portion of employee contributions. 401(k) plans offer a number of advantages. First, they allow both employer and employee to make contributions and gain tax advantages. Second, they can be set up in such a way that employees can borrow money from the plan. Third, 401(k) plans enable employees to become active participants in saving and investing for their retirement, which raises the level of perceived benefits provided by the employer. The main disadvantages are relatively high set-up and administrative costs. Eligibility for 401(k) plans is typically limited to employees at least 21 years of age who have at least one year of service with the company.

Small businesses that establish 401(k)s must be careful to avoid liability for losses employees might suffer due to fluctuations in the value of plan investments.

Under ERISA, plan sponsors can avoid liability by ensuring that their 401(k) meets three criteria: offering a broad range of investment options to employees; communicating sufficient financial information to employees; and allowing employees to exercise independent control over their accounts.

Nonqualified Deferred Compensation Plans Finally, there is a type of plan often used by businesses to supplement existing qualified plans and provide an extra benefit to key personnel and highly compensated employees. In small businesses, this usually includes the owner and founder. Broadly defined, a nonqualified deferred compensation plan (NDCP) is a contractual agreement in which a participant agrees to be paid in a future year for services rendered this year.

There are two broad categories of nonqualified deferred compensation plans: elective and non-elective. In an elective NDCP an employee chooses to receive less current salary and bonus compensation than he or she would otherwise receive postponing the receipt of that compensation until a future tax year. Non-elective NDCPs are plans in which the employer funds the benefit and does not reduce current compensation in order to fund future payments. Such plans are, in essence, post-termination salary continuation plans. The argument behind such non-elective plans, funded by employers, is the retention of key employees.

One feature in particular of nonqualified deferred compensation plans that has made them a very popular tool for use by large corporations and some small businesses, is the fact that they are not limited by the same non-discrimination rules imposed on qualified plans. NDCPs may be offered to a select group of employees only, unlike qualified plans to which all employees are eligible by definition. Consequently, the cost of this benefit is lower since it accrues to fewer people. NDCPs are a type of plan that is particularly useful for small business owners in augmenting their own retirement savings plans.

WHICH PLAN TO CHOOSE

Small business owners must carefully examine their priorities when selecting a retirement plan for themselves and their employees. If the main priority is to minimize administrative costs, a SEP plan may be the best choice. If it is important to have the flexibility of discretionary contributions, a profit sharing plan might be the answer. A money purchase plan would enable a small business owner to maximize contributions, but it would require an assurance of stable income, since contributions are mandatory. If the small business counts upon key older employees, an age-based profit sharing plan or a defined-benefit plan would help reward and retain them. Conversely, an employer with a long time horizon until retirement would probably do best with a defined-contribution plan. Finally, a small business owner who wants employees to be able to fund part of their own retirement should select a SIMPLE or a 401(k) plan. There are also many possibilities for combination plans that might provide a closer fit with a small business's goals. Free information on retirement plans is available through the Department of Labor at 800-998-7542, or on the Internet at http://www.dol.gov/ebsa/savingmatters.html.

SEE ALSO *Estate Tax; 401(k) Plan; Individual Retirement Accounts; Keogh Plans; Nonqualified Deferred Compensation Plans; Pension Plans; Simplified Employee Pensions*

BIBLIOGRAPHY

"The 401(k) Paper Chase." *Business Week.* 27 March 2000.

Altieri, Mark P. "Nonqualified Deferred Compensation Plans." *The CPA Journal.* February 2005.

Clifford, Lee. "Getting Over the Hump before You're Over the Hill." *Fortune.* 14 August 2000.

Infante, Victor D. "Retirement Plan Trends." *Workforce.* November 2000.

Korn, Donald Jay. "Developing a Plan to Make Your Golden Years Brighter." *Black Enterprise.* October 2000.

Olson, John. "A Powerful Weapon in the War for Talent." *National Underwriter Life & Health-Financial Services Edition.* 23 June 2003.

Postal, Arthur D. "New Tax Bill Changes Rules on Non-qualified Deferred Comp Plans." *National Underwriter Life & Health.* 18 October 2004.

Szabo, Joan. "Pension Tension." *Entrepreneur.* November 2000.

U.S. Department of the Treasury. Internal Revenue Service. "Nonqualified Deferred Compensation Audit Techniques Guide." Available from http://www.irs.gov/businesses/corporations/article/0,,id=134878,00.html. 10 January 2005.

"What You Need To Set Aside For Retirement." Public Broadcasting Service. *Frontline* Available from http://www.pbs.org/wgbh/pages/frontline/retirement/world/need.html. Retrieved on 30 May 2006.

Wyss, David. "The Gathering Pensions Storm: Boomers will soon find their retirement kitty has been underfunded. Making up the shortfall will buffet corporations—and the economy" *Business Week Online.* 5 June 2006.

Hillstrom, Northern Lights
updated by Magee, ECDI

RETURN ON ASSETS (ROA)

Return on assets (ROA) is a financial ratio that shows the percentage of profit a company earns in relation to its overall resources. It is commonly defined as net income divided by total assets. Net income is derived from the income statement of the company and is the profit after taxes. The assets are read from the balance sheet and include cash and cash-equivalent items such as receivables, inventories, land, capital equipment as depreciated, and the value of intellectual property such as patents. Companies that have been acquired may also have a category called "good will" representing the extra money paid for the company over and above its actual book value at the time of acquisition. Because assets will tend to have swings over time, an average of assets over the period to be measured should be used. Thus the ROA for a quarter should be based on net income for the quarter divided by average assets in that quarter. ROA is a ratio but usually presented as a percentage.

ROA answers the question: "What can you do with the assets that you have available?" The higher the ROA, the better the management. But this measure is best applied in comparing companies with the same level of capitalization. The more capital-intensive a business is, the more difficult it will be to achieve a high ROA. A major equipment manufacturer, for instance, will require very substantial assets simply to do what it does; the same will be true for a power plant or a pipeline. A fashion designer, an ad agency, a software firm, or a publisher may require only minimal capital equipment and will thus produce a high ROA. To compare Microsoft with General Motors on the basis of ROA is to compare apples to oranges. The industry average ROA for software companies in mid-2006 was 13.1 and Microsoft's own stood at 20.1. The industry ROA for autos was 1.1 and GM's was a negative 1.8.

The difference between a highly capitalized business and one running largely on intellectual property or creative assets is that, in the case of failure, the capital-intensive company will still have major assets that can be turned into real money whereas a concept-based enterprise will fail when its art is no longer favored; it will leave a few computers and furniture behind. Therefore ROA is used by investors as one of several ways of measuring a company *within* an industry, comparing it with others playing by the same rules.

USES FOR ROA

Unlike other profitability ratios, such as return on equity (ROE), ROA measurements include all of a business's assets—those which arise out of liabilities to creditors as well capital paid in by investors. Total assets are used rather than net assets. Thus, for instance, the cash holdings of a company have been borrowed and are thus balanced by a liability. Similarly, the company's receivables are definitely an asset but are balanced by its payables, a liability. For this reason, ROA is usually of less interest to shareholders than some other financial ratios; stockholders are more interested in return on *their* input. But the inclusion of all assets, whether derived from debt or equity, is of more interest to management which wants to assess the use of all money put to work.

ROA is used internally by companies to track asset-use over time, to monitor the company's performance in light of industry performance, and to look at different operations or divisions by comparing them one to the other. For this to be accomplished effectively, however, accounting systems must be in place to allocate assets accurately to different operations. ROA can signal both effective use of assets as well as under-capitalization. If the ROA begins to grow in relation to the industry's as a whole, and management cannot pinpoint the unique efficiencies that produce the profitability, the favorable signal may be negative: investment in new equipment may be overdue.

Another common internal use for ROA involves evaluating the benefits of investing in a new system versus expanding a current operation. The best choice will ideally increase productivity and income as well as reduce asset costs, resulting in an improved ROA ratio. For example, say that a small manufacturing company with a current sales volume of $50,000, average assets of $30,000, and a net profit of $6,000 (giving it an ROA of $6,000 / $30,000 or 20 percent) must decide whether to improve its current inventory management system or install a new one. Expanding the current system would allow an increase in sales volume to $65,000 and in net profit to $7,800, but would also increase average assets to $39,000. Although sales would increase, the ROA of this option would be the same—20 percent. On the other hand, installing a new system would increase sales to $70,000 and net profit to $12,250. Because the new system would allow the company to manage its inventory more efficiently, the average assets would increase only to $35,000. As a result, the ROA for this option would increase to 35 percent, meaning that the company should choose to install the new system.

BIBLIOGRAPHY

Albrecht, W. Steve, James D. Stice, Earl Kay Stice, and Monte Swain. *Financial Accounting.* Thomson South-Western, 2005.

Baker, H. Kent, Erik Benrud, and Gary N. Powell. *Understanding Financial Management.* Blackwell Publishing, 2005.

Bernstein, Leopold A., and John J. Wild. *Analysis of Financial Statements.* New York: McGraw-Hill, 2000.

MSN Money. Available from http://moneycentral.msn.com/home.asp. Retrieved on 21 May 2006.

Hillstrom, Northern Lights
updated by Magee, ECDI

RETURN ON INVESTMENT (ROI)

Return on investment (ROI) is a financial ratio intended to measure the benefit obtained from an investment. Time is usually of the essence in this measurement because it takes time for an investment to realize a benefit. An ROI calculation can be illustrated by the purchase and subsequent sale of a house. Let us assume a cash purchase of a residence for $100,000. The house is held for 10 years and is then sold for $150,000; during its 10 years of ownership, maintenance costs have been $1,000 per year, so that the net sales value is $140,000. This sum, less the purchase price, nets out to $40,000. That $40,000 divided by the purchase price produces 0.4 or 40 percent. The ROI of this transaction has therefore been 40 percent. This elaborate example is presented with a purpose. ROIs are typically calculated in different ways. In this example, for instance, the owner may have rented the house for $200 per month and realized a 10-year income stream of $24,000 as well. If that income is factored in, the net benefit will be $64,000 rather than $40,000, and the ROI will be 64 percent.

The general rule to keep in mind is that ROI is the ratio produced when all gains from a transaction, less the costs associated with that transaction, are divided by the initial investment. The most common use of ROI is to assess the profitability of a company (or an operation within a company) based on investment. There are other measures of profitability—as a percent of *sales*, for instance, or as a percent of total *assets* used. ROI is of special interest to those who put their money into stocks or invest their savings into their own business: they have different choices available, and ROI can help to guide them to where to put their money.

ALTERNATIVE WAYS OF CALCULATING ROI

The general formula for computing the ROI of a business is to divide the company's net income for a period by its invested capital. But the term "invested capital" does not have a universally or uniformly accepted definition. It is sometimes defined as net work or owners' equity. Other definitions include the company's long-term debt on the principle that, for operational purposes, money derived from debt is equivalent to paid-in capital. Barron's *Dictionary of Finance and Investment Terms* (1985), for instance, includes long-term debt in its definition of "return on invested capital," which it uses synonymously with ROI. When the company has no long-term debt, the measure becomes Return on Equity. *MSN Money* uses the same definition as Barron's and showed, in mid-2006, that the average return on capital (ROI including long-term debt) of the S&P 500 companies was 7.9 percent. Return on equity was 12.4 percent.

The small business can, thus, calculate its ROI simply by dividing its after-tax income by its net worth (the residue after total liabilities are deducted from total assets on the balance sheet) or can use net worth *plus* long-term debt. Consistency in the use of the formula is, of course, advisable. When asked by a lender or investor for the company's ROI, the owner might be well advised to find out the party's own definition. ROI will be lower if long-term debt is present.

ROI calculations are also typically employed to monitor the performance of divisions or of product lines within a company. The approaches used tend to be varied, but a common form of measurement is to use operating income for the division (income before taxes) as the "gain" and a composite measure to represent investment—funds expended on behalf of the division's operations including the depreciated value of capital equipment, the value of inventories carried, and the net value of receivables less payables. When all divisions are measured the same way, comparisons are possible across the board.

ROI can also be used to evaluate a proposed investment in new equipment by dividing the increase in profit attributable to the new equipment by the increase in invested capital needed to acquire it. For example, a small business may be able to save $5,000 in operating expenses (and thus raise profit by the same amount) by spending $25,000 on a piece of new equipment. This yields an ROI of $5,000 divided by $25,000 or 20 percent. If this figure is higher than the company's cost of capital (the interest paid on debt and the dividends paid to investors) prior to the investment, and no better investment opportunities exist for those funds, it may make sense to purchase the equipment.

In addition to the various uses ROI holds for small business managers, it is routinely used by investors in the stock market to compare the performance of different companies and by people buying and selling companies in merger and acquisition activity.

SEE ALSO *Financial Ratios*

BIBLIOGRAPHY
Albrecht, W. Steve, James D. Stice, Earl Kay Stice, and Monte Swain. *Financial Accounting.* Thomson South-Western, 2005.

Baker, H. Kent, Erik Benrud, and Gary N. Powell. *Understanding Financial Management.* Blackwell Publishing, 2005.

Bernstein, Leopold A., and John J. Wild. *Analysis of Financial Statements.* New York: McGraw-Hill, 2000.

MSN Money. Available from http://moneycentral.msn.com/ home.asp. Retrieved on 21 May 2006.

"Return on Investment – ROI." *Investopedia.com.* Available from http://www.investopedia.com/terms/r/ returnoninvestment.asp. Retrieved on 21 May 2006.

Hillstrom, Northern Lights
updated by Magee, ECDI

RETURN POLICIES

Return policies are the rules retail merchants establish to manage the process by which customers return or exchange unwanted or defective merchandise that they have purchased previously. Return policies are an extension of the customer service retailers provide; they tend to be fairly liberal as a consequence. For this reason many consumers hold the mistaken belief that they can always return merchandise for a full refund regardless of the circumstances. In reality, both regular and online merchants enjoy great leeway in establishing individual policies. As returns have become more prevalent and more costly, some merchants have imposed tighter restrictions on merchandise returns.

The most generous return policies—which are usually found at large, upscale retailers—permit customers to return any merchandise at any time for a full refund, with or without a receipt. But most retailers place restrictions on one or more aspects of this process. For example, many merchants will not accept merchandise for return unless the customer can produce a dated receipt proving that he or she actually purchased the item at that store within a reasonable amount of time. Other merchants have slightly more liberal return policies and will accept items without a receipt as long as the sale tag is still attached. Still others will provide a store credit rather than a cash refund when no receipt is forthcoming. Some retailers have even tighter return policies and prohibit returns on sale merchandise or on certain types of items, like bathing suits, or impose a limited window of time when returns are accepted.

The goal for retailers is to balance the need to satisfy customers against the cost and hassle associated with merchandise returns. Setting too liberal policies may encourage customers to abuse the system. For example, a customer might purchase a dress for a formal occasion, wear it once, and then return it. Similarly, a consumer might purchase a top-of-the line computer, use it for several months until an even faster model becomes available, and then return it. Finding the right balance between self-protection and customer service can be a particularly important issue for small business owners. Much more than big retailers, they depend on superior customer service to keep people coming back to their shops and Web sites. Larger merchants can generally afford to be more liberal in allowing returns; smaller outfits may need to raise prices in order to compensate for the added expense. After all, returned items that cannot be resold must either be returned to the manufacturer or sold to a jobber, which costs the retailer extra in transaction and transportation fees.

There are several steps brick-and-mortar retailers can take to discourage abuse of their return policies. For example, they can attempt to reduce the volume of sales returns by posting their policy for customers to see. Although some types of products are easier to resell after being returned, it is advisable to have a single policy and to adhere to it rather than attempt to attach different rules to different types of items sold in a store.

RETURNS IN E-COMMERCE

Establishing fair return policies while limiting the cost of returns is of particular importance to online retailers. After all, returns are a fact of life in electronic commerce. "How well you handle online returns will likely determine your future success—or failure—in the dotcom world," Melissa Campanelli wrote in *Entrepreneur*. "Unfortunately, returned merchandise is a major byproduct of increased Internet growth, especially as consumers become much more comfortable purchasing items over the Net." Some experts claim that the nature of electronic commerce invites large numbers of merchandise returns because consumers are not able to see and touch the items they purchase online. Recent technological developments promise to address this problem, however, and enhance the online shopping experience. "There's incredible technology at work in making touch, feel, color, look, size, and fit issues more user-friendly," Irwin Barkan of the data services organization e-BuyersGuide.com told Campanelli.

A survey by e-BuyersGuide.com found that 86 percent of online shoppers rated return policies of significant importance in choosing an online merchant. Consumers were especially concerned about whether the policies permitted them to receive a refund immediately after items were returned, return online purchases to a brick-and-mortar store, exchange items as needed, and have the convenience of postal pickup at their homes. But the number-one priority of online shoppers was not having to pay return postage for items they ship back to e-tailers. In a survey of the top 50 online merchants, however, 85 percent said that they required customers to pay return postage. Requiring customers to pay for shipping tends to discourage frivolous returns, according to some online retailers.

According to the e-BuyersGuide.com survey reported in *Entrepreneur,* the main reasons online shoppers returned their purchases included: that the product was not what they expected (25 percent); that the product did not fit properly (17 percent); that the merchandise was damaged (17 percent); that the wrong items were delivered (16 percent); that the products were of poor quality (10 percent); and that they simply changed their minds and did not want the product (15 percent). Of the consumers who returned items purchased online, 78 percent said they were satisfied with the experience, while only 6 percent described it as unsatisfactory. Of those who had a bad experience returning merchandise, however, 62 percent said they would not return to the offending Web site afterward.

The most popular way to handle online returns is to provide postage-paid return labels. Both the U.S. Postal Service and United Parcel Service (UPS) provide merchants with a service where customers can generate labels online and print them on their home computers. Retailers can open an account at a local post office to use the U.S. Postal Service's easy return system. There is a minimum charge of 30 cents per return for the merchant. The UPS system is similar but also separates merchandise that is returned because it is faulty or damaged from that returned because the customer changed his/her mind. Both systems allow retailers to track packages online.

Another option for electronic retailers is outsourcing returns to a return management solution (RMS) company, like Return.com. These firms handle all aspects of merchandise returns, from generating labels and return authorizations to the physical handling and processing of merchandise. Some RMS companies integrate their computer systems with retailers' in order to facilitate tracking and routing of packages. According to Campanelli, using an RMS firm generally involves an installation fee of around $10,000 plus a transaction fee for each package handled.

BIBLIOGRAPHY

Arya, Anil and Brian Mittendorf. "Using Return Policies to Elicit Retail Information." *RAND Journal of Economics.* Autumn 2004.

Biederman, David. "Many Happy Returns: Companies wrestle with post-holiday merchandise returns." *Journal of Commerce.* 5 December 2005.

Campanelli, Melissa. "Many Happy Returns." *Entrepreneur.* January 2001.

Haeberle, Matthew. "Return to Sender: Best Buy streamlines its merchandise returns through a third party." *Chain Store Age.* September 2004.

Plunkett, Jack W. *Plunkett's Retail Industry Almanac 2006: The Only Complete Reference To The Retail Industry.* Plunkett Research, Ltd., 2005.

Hillstrom, Northern Lights
updated by Magee, ECDI

REVENUE STREAMS

A "revenue stream" is simply another name for income, but possibly because it sounds more sophisticated than the word "sales" or "salary," was borrowed from investment talk where assets are said to have a "future revenue stream" or from government where it is less crass-sounding than "taxes"—the phrase has come into current use in business to mean sales. More specifically, the phrase is often qualified by modifiers such as "new" or "additional"; it has thus gradually taken on a distinct and specialized meaning in certain contexts to mean a new, novel, undiscovered, potentially lucrative, innovative, and creative means of generating income or exploiting a potential. The phrase also comes in handy in the new Internet age where revenues are sometimes generated in novel ways that do not resemble the old-fashioned sale across a counter. Some headlines picked at random, for instance, proclaim: "Keyhole: Another Google Revenue Stream," "Same Day Payments: A New Revenue Stream from the Online Channel," "On demand games offer new revenue stream," and "Radio Wades into Podcast Revenue Stream."

In the following discussion this narrower context of "revenue stream," as an opportunity for additional income, will be further explored as an business activity. Measuring and reporting revenues is the job of accounting departments, but generation of revenues is a top management job. It is by nature an entrepreneurial activity with just a touch of the magical implied—as a phrase common in law practices reveals: the principal in a law firm is often referred to as the "rain maker." Making it rain when drought parches the land takes a bit of luck, pluck, or both.

THE STIMULUS OF CHANGE

The quest for new streams of revenue is stimulated by change. The change can be negative or positive. The discovery of vast prairies was eventually exploited by the formation of many great cattle ranches. But when in time ranching declined, some innovator coped with the problem by creating the first dude ranch. U.S. business history is rife with the discovery of endlessly new revenue streams in response to technological development, and the buzz about new revenue streams surrounding the Internet is just the most recent example. Change creates opportunities, the ability to see a potential and then to exploit it—that's what creates new revenue streams. The change may hurt or may entice. Either way, effective innovation makes use of the stimulus.

Classical examples of positive stimulus provided by the appearance of home computers are the invention of joy-sticks to enable kids and adults to play games on the computer, the invention of a visual interface first introduced on the Apple Macintosh (although invented by Xerox, along with the mouse, which is required for it). Games, joy-sticks, and visual interfaces and pointer devices all produced massive, global revenue streams—and stimulated others.

Interesting innovations by institutions plagued by income problems show how these institutions are coping with negative change. Public Television, for example, once wholly funded by government, was forced eventually to develop skills in on-air fundraising. This new stream of revenue suggested yet another approach—so that most public television stations nowadays also hold annual auctions. And these auctions are, in turn, making more and more use of the Internet. Museums, seeking additional funding, have developed lucrative new revenue streams by developing memberships and establishing very attractive specialized retail activities selling art objects, souvenirs, books, music, toys, and much more. Some museums have then ventured beyond the museum's walls and have established retail outlets in malls. Theatrical companies are moving in this direction as well.

NODES OF INNOVATION

Certain features of the market act as nodes around which new revenue streams tend to be established in response to positive or negative stimulus. Among these are 1) location, 2) existing traffic, 3) a purchasing context, 4) an expandable cluster of skills, and, of course, 5) a technology.

Location In the past several decades, companies have more and more exploited convenient locations to add new product categories to once sharply differentiated specializations. The best example of this has been the addition of limited but basic grocery lines to the offerings of drug stores so that consumers can pick up such staples as milk, ice cream, cereals, and toilet paper nearer to home—thus transforming themselves into convenience stores. In the early days of video rental, small grocers and drug stores also, for a while, turned this new product category into income streams for themselves until the market changed.

Traffic Drug stores, of course, also benefit from established traffic. Another traffic-based example is the transformation that took place in gasoline stations. Beginning in the 1960s, many of these operations, once strictly confined to selling gas, changing oil, and occasionally fixing and selling tires have become drug/grocery/convenience outlets to take advantage of the visits consumers were forced to make to fill the tank. Gas stations also sometimes benefited by being closer than larger stores. The sheer command over traffic has acted, in effect, to turn many large retail operations into all-purpose bazaars in which consumers have access to products across a wide range, restaurants, banks, means of communication, even entertainment. Quite small shops by coincidence located at the entrance to malls occasionally exploit the traffic passing by them by selling specialty items not even vaguely related to their main business.

Purchasing Context People going to the dentist have learned to expect to see displays discreetly offering the electric tooth-cleaning systems the dentist recommends. People buying shoes can expect also to purchase on-site all manner of goods associated with foot-gear, including sometimes inner soles and other more medically related goods. Well-organized computer service firms have learned that they can use the service context of their specialization to sell software services, Web-page design, computers and peripherals, and training. Sometimes the entrepreneurial energy is very high indeed—so that Martha Stewart exploited her skills in catering into a publishing, television, product promotion, and endorsement empire all based on the rather extensive purchasing context of the homemaker.

Cluster of Skills Virtually any well-developed professional or managerial skills offer opportunities to discover and tap into new streams of revenue—even those rarely imagined to have such leverage. But Richard Muhlback and David Buntin, writing for *Journal of Property Management* took on the seemingly mundane function of property management and showed the opportunities for consulting, legal support, public lecturing, and writing available for the creative property manager. But in the exploitation of personal skills, the most important innovation, as Anita Campbell pointed out, writing in *Small Business Trends* is to discover a way of selling one's *work* rather than one's *time*. Personal time is very limited and one's expertise must be multiplied in some way and sold over and over again. Publications multiply a message; and organizations can do the job too by means of training others to deliver a unique service. It is for this reason that new revenue streams require entrepreneurial "packaging" of skills in saleable quantities.

Technology Technology is itself a powerful multiplier of personal skill—in its exploitation alone, much less in its modification and improvement. The sculptor who exploits chain saws rapidly to create ice sculptures for weddings is doing something very similar to the skilled writer who exploits the Internet, analytical skills, and statistical data to create books that reveal modern trends of interest either to specialist audiences or the public. One of the reasons why "new revenue stream" is such a common phrase in the mid-2000s is that computer technology and the communications systems that have proliferated like a primordial jungle all around it offer an enormous variety of opportunities for exploitation, both in technological extensions and in the use of it.

THE VITAL INGREDIENT

When, however, all is said and done, the vital ingredient in the creation of new revenue streams remains something perennial and ancient. It is individual creativeness coupled with enterprise. Revenue streams are created by people who are more than simply threatened by change or fascinated by the new. They must have their eyes open to see the opportunities and the discipline and skill to turn ideas and notions into actually saleable products or services. Not surprisingly, small business has been particularly active in the creation of the digital age. Virtually every big-name corporation in the field began as one or a pair of creative people. They saw, they acted, and they have in consequence created what amounts to much more than a stream. Call it a Mississippi, a Niagara Falls of revenue.

BIBLIOGRAPHY

Berkowitz, Hank. "CPAs Building Financial Services Practices: Firms of all sizes are successfully balancing client interests and pressures for new revenue." *Journal of Accountancy.* July 2005.

"Building Joint Ventures that Work." *Healthcare Financial Management.* January 2006.

Cameron, Ben. "The Entrepreneur's Lament." *American Theatre.* November 2004.

Campbell, Anita. "Recurring Revenue Streams – How to Create Them." *Small Business Trends.* 8 November 2005.

Muhlback, Richard F., and David Buntin. "Tap Into Paired Profits: Convert your expertise to income by consulting for owners or attorneys, lecturing or writing." *Journal of Property Management.* September-October 2004.

Darnay, ECDI

RIGHT-TO-KNOW (RTK) LAWS

Right-to-know laws are a group of rules and regulations at the state and national levels that mandate that employers share scientific information with workers and local communities about the toxicity and other characteristics of chemicals and materials used in business processes. This information encompasses all substances to which workers might be exposed in the workplace, including materials and chemicals utilized in producing goods or providing services, chemical releases into the environment, waste management, and long-term exposure to substances. Right-to-know laws place special emphasis on maintaining and disseminating information on the potential long-term health effects (cancer, infertility, etc.) sometimes associated with longtime work exposure to high concentrations of industrial materials.

Experts in the fields of risk management and hazardous materials management generally separate employer obligations under "right-to-know" (RTK) into four broad categories: obligation to compile and retain relevant records; obligation to disclose any available information to workers, community members, or organizations on any potentially hazardous materials and processes used; obligation to provide adequate training to employees working with potentially dangerous materials; and obligation to disclose information on sudden health risks. This information, which must be presented even if it is not formally requested, should cover the potential risks of sudden and accidental chemical releases, explain the scope of the company's technological and human resources to effectively address such events; and identify other options that could also be considered.

THE MOVEMENT TOWARD RIGHT-TO-KNOW

The first U.S. efforts to inform workers and communities about hazardous substances used in the workplace were voluntary industry labeling practices. These labeling practices—now incorporated into the Federal Hazardous Substances Labeling Act—provided workers with basic information on hazardous materials, including descriptions of the nature of the hazard and instructions for safe handling (and medical treatment in case of exposure to the chemical in question). But as recognition increased of the potential long-term health effects of prolonged exposure to certain chemicals and materials, employee groups, companies, and government agencies all recognized that these safety measures needed to be bolstered.

In 1970 the federal Occupational Safety and Health Administration (OSHA) was formed to help assure that American workers enjoyed safe and healthy working environments. In subsequent years, the agency established a body of regulations designed to ensure that workers were adequately informed about workplace risks (both short- and long-term) through training programs, labeling, and material safety data sheets (MSDS), in which original manufacturers provide complete information on all hazardous substances shipped to customers (downstream users are also required to supply end-users with MSDSs.) Contents of material safety data sheets must include the following for each chemical: identity, physical and chemical characteristics; primary routes of entry; health hazards; permissible exposure limits and control measures for reducing exposure; instructions for safe use, handling, and storage; emergency and first aid steps; name and address of manufacturer; date of production; and date at which the information contained in the MSDS was last changed. This bounty of centralized information makes the MSDS a cornerstone of all right-to-know programs. Moreover, during the 1990s some states initiated efforts to make these information-crammed forms more concise and understandable to lay readers, making them even more valuable.

OSHA's mandate remains in place in the mid-2000s. It requires employers to maintain safe workplaces and jobs for their workers and maintains exposure standards for a wide variety of substances that are used in all industry sectors. In addition, many states have also developed their own right-to-know programs. These programs, if certified by the OSHA, allow individual states to assume responsibility for administration and enforcement.

COMPLIANCE WITH RTK PROGRAMS

Many employers erroneously believe that the nature of their business operation renders them immune to right-to-know regulations. Typical misconceptions include the belief that the workplace does not have any hazardous chemicals or that the quantities used in the workplace are so small that RTK rules do not apply. In reality, however, these regulations do not distinguish between quantity or size, and nearly every place of employment in the United States contains some substance that meets the definition of a hazardous chemical. For example, many paints, cleaning solutions, solvents, corrosives, compressed gases, glues, and other common substances fall under RTK regulations.

Business owners, though, can take a number of steps to ensure that they are in compliance with right-to-know rules and are promoting safety and healthy working conditions for all of their employees. Many of these steps can be undertaken quickly, and none requires the knowledge or skills of a chemist or materials expert.

Inventory Employers are encouraged to complete a comprehensive written inventory of all materials in the workplace that may be hazardous, irrespective of the quantity or size of the materials on hand. The written inventory should include chemicals used and/or stored in work areas outside the building proper. This inventory should also include by-products and intermediate products resulting from workplace processes. These materials inventories should include the name of the product, contact information for the manufacturer and distributor, and general work area in which the material is used and/or stored (chemicals used throughout the facility can be so designated).

Material Safety Data Sheets Each substance noted as a result of the materials inventory should have a corresponding material safety data sheet, for manufacturers must provide MSDSs to each purchaser of a hazardous chemical when making the initial shipment (recipients of these information sheets, whether distributors or purchasers, must provide updated information with the first shipment after each update). If you do not have an MSDS for a chemical, immediately request a replacement data sheet from the manufacturer or distributor. Some businesses even stipulate delivery of an MSDS as a condition of purchase when ordering hazardous chemicals.

Chemical Information List Once all material safety data sheets have been gathered, they should be reviewed to identify the substance and understand specific hazards associated with the material. The MSDS can also be used to prepare a chemical information list for the workplace. This list, required by law, must be 1) arranged in alphabetical order according to common name; 2) contain the chemical name; and 3) identify the area of the workplace in which it can be found. According to right-to-know regulations, employers must provide access to and copies of the chemical information list to employees and their representatives, OSHA inspectors, and other employers sharing the same workplace.

Not all chemicals used in the workplace are required on these information lists. For example, a chemical list is not required in situations where employees handle chemicals only in sealed, unopened containers under normal working conditions, such as in warehousing or retail sales.

Clear Labeling Businesses should make certain that all containers used to hold hazardous materials, whether on the factory floor or in the office, are labeled, tagged, or otherwise identified. This includes temporary portable containers if the container is going to be used by more than one person, utilized for an extended period of time (for example, more than one shift), or left unattended for any period of time. All hazardous substance container labels should clearly identify the material and detail potential hazards. Employers who receive unlabeled containers should either obtain an accurate label from the manufacturer or gather pertinent information from the manufacturer so that they can ready their own label.

Some businesses utilize commercially available labeling systems that use non-text methods to convey hazard warnings. These alternative systems may use icons, color coded numbers, or pictographs to describe levels of hazard and required personal protection equipment.

Institute Updating System Employers should develop a system that allows them to efficiently update their chemical information list and MSDS holdings as each new substance arrives in their workplace. Updates should take place within 30 days of receiving the materials in question, as state and federal right-to-know programs require chemical lists to be updated regularly.

Hazard Assessment Many employers use the hazard information contained in each MSDS to carefully review all processes in which the material is used. At this time, business owners can decide whether current workplace practices are adequate to ensure the safety and health of employees. Specific elements to review include level of engineering controls, adequacy of personal protective equipment, emergency procedures, and work practices.

Hazard Communication Program Employers should put together a written hazard communication program for their employees. This program should explain how the company is meeting state/federal right-to-know requirements. Effective hazard communication programs will also include detailed explanations of the company's system of identifying and labeling hazardous substances; information about the company's material safety data sheets and chemical information lists, including how they are maintained and how they can be accessed by workers; and details on policies and procedures that employees should follow when engaged in non-routine tasks that require usage of hazardous chemicals and other potentially dangerous materials.

Training Effective training programs must be implemented in conjunction with RTK laws. Right-to-know training programs should provide guidance and information in several key areas, including the purpose and content of the law; the nature of the hazardous substances in the workplace; protection from hazards; location and usage of information on these workplace materials, including material safety data sheets, labels, and chemical information lists; and overall employee rights. In essence, all right-to-know training programs should be based on the knowledge that information that is not understood by workers will be of little utility to them in preventing or limiting their exposure to hazardous chemicals in the workplace.

Business experts and state and federal administrators cite several keys to shaping and implementing an effective training program for your workforce:

- Identify who needs training. Employers should utilize organizational charts and personnel records to identify the training needs of various staff. Assess each employee's actual and potential exposure to hazardous chemicals during normal working situations and in potential emergencies (for example, production and custodial workers are likely to have a higher level of training than salespeople and secretaries).

- Determine which chemicals your employees may be exposed to, either under normal working conditions or emergency situations.

- Ensure that employees are aware of the location of chemical information lists and material safety data sheets.

- Make sure that employees know how to use labels, MSDSs, and chemical information lists to obtain information on hazardous materials.

- Make sure that employees understand control programs and personal protective equipment.

- Institute measures to ensure that new and transferred workers receive training. Many businesses integrate Right-to-Know training into general orientation programs or existing departmental safety programs.

- Make contingency plans to provide additional training if new hazards are introduced into the workplace.

- Evaluate effectiveness of training programs after workers have completed them. This can be done through written tests, one-on-one meetings with employees who completed the program, or employee demonstrations of acquired skills and knowledge. Employee feedback on the training program should also be encouraged. Business owners and managers should ask workers which aspects of the program were most valuable and informative, and which aspects were least useful. In some cases, this feedback phase may reveal that the training program did not provide staff with the necessary level of knowledge to safely and effectively deal with hazardous materials they encounter in the workplace. In those cases, programs should be revised until they meet expectations.

Experts note that many facilities utilize literally thousands of chemicals in their operations. Training all employees about the characteristics of each one is an unrealistic burden for any employer. Over the years, OSHA policies have shown a general recognition of this reality. According to OSHA, "information and training may be designed to cover categories of hazards (e.g., flammability, carcinogenicity) or specific chemicals. Chemical-specific information must always be available through labels and material safety data sheets .... If there are only a few chemicals in the workplace, then you may

want to discuss each one individually. Where there are large numbers of chemicals, or the chemicals change frequently, you will probably want to train generally based on the hazard categories (e.g., flammable liquids, corrosive materials, carcinogens)." The market has also responded with helpful products. Thus Del Williams reported, in *Medical Laboratory Observer,* on Windows-based right-to-know labeling software which enables OSHA compliance officers to prepare labels on ordinary printers—having done so by hand before. Williams' report was based on an interview with a supplier servicing 200 hospitals—indicating the often massive size of the compliance task. Suzanne Shelley, reporting on the same product (called RTKV2 HazCom) in *Chemical Engineering* made the point that the product comes with online access to a database of 160,000 MSDS records—thus making the job significantly easier.

BIBLIOGRAPHY

Shelley, Suzanne. "Save Time and Money with This Chemical-Labeling System." *Chemical Engineering.* November 2004.

U.S. Department of Labor. *Hazard Communication in the 21st Century Workplace.* March 2004.

U.S. Department of Labor. Occupational Safety & Health Administration. "Hazard Communication: Foundation of Workplace Chemical Safety Programs." Available from http://www.osha.gov/SLTC/hazardcommunications/index.html. Retrieved on 25 May 2006.

Williams, Del. "OSHA HazCom Compliance on Your Terms." *Medical Laboratory Observer.* March 2006.

Hillstrom, Northern Lights
updated by Magee, ECDI

RISK MANAGEMENT

Risk management involves identifying, analyzing, and taking steps to reduce or eliminate the exposures to loss faced by an organization or individual. The practice utilizes many tools and techniques, including insurance, to manage a wide variety of risks. Every business encounters risks, some of which are predictable and under management's control; others are unpredictable and uncontrollable. Risk management is particularly vital for small businesses, since some common types of losses—such as theft, fire, flood, legal liability, injury, or disability—can destroy in a few minutes what may have taken an entrepreneur years to build. Such losses and liabilities can affect day-to-day operations, reduce profits, and cause financial hardship severe enough to cripple or bankrupt a small business. But while many large companies employ a full-time risk manager to identify risks and take the necessary steps to protect the firm against them, small companies rarely have that luxury. Instead, the responsibility for risk management is likely to fall on the small business owner.

The term is a relatively recent evolution of the term "insurance management." The concept of risk management encompasses a much broader scope of activities and responsibilities than does insurance management. Risk management is now a widely accepted description of a discipline within most large organizations. Basic risks such as fire, windstorm, employee injuries, and automobile accidents, as well as more sophisticated exposures such as product liability, environmental impairment, and employment practices, are the province of the risk management department in a typical corporation. Although risk management has usually pertained to property and casualty exposures to loss, it has recently been expanded to include financial risk management—such as interest rates, foreign exchange rates, and derivatives—as well as the unique threats to businesses engaged in E-commerce. As the role of risk management has increased, some large companies have begun implementing large-scale, organization-wide programs known as enterprise risk management.

THE PROCESS

Businesses have several alternatives for the management of risk, including avoiding, assuming, reducing, or transferring the risks. Avoiding risks, or loss prevention, involves taking steps to prevent a loss from occurring by such methods as employee safety training. As another example, a pharmaceutical company may decide not to market a drug because of the potential liability. Assuming risks simply means accepting the possibility that a loss may occur and being prepared to pay the consequences. Reducing risks, or loss reduction, involves taking steps to reduce the probability or the severity of a loss, for example by installing fire sprinklers.

Transferring risk refers to the practice of placing responsibility for a loss on another party by contract. The most common example of risk transference is insurance; it allows a company to pay a small monthly premium in exchange for protection against automobile accidents, theft or destruction of property, employee disability, or a variety of other risks. Because of its costs, the insurance option is usually chosen when the other options don't provide sufficient protection. Awareness of, and familiarity with, various types of insurance policies is a necessary part of the risk management process. A final risk management tool is self-retention of risks—sometimes referred to as "self-insurance." Companies that choose this option set up a special account or fund to be used in the event of a loss.

Any combination of these risk management tools may be applied in the last step of the process, implementation. This step, monitoring, involves a regular review of the company's risk management tools to determine if they have obtained the desired result or if they require modification. Tools in that process include maintaining a high quality of work; training employees well and maintaining equipment properly; installing strong locks, smoke detectors, and fire extinguishers; keeping the office clean and free of hazards; backing up computer data often; and storing records securely off-site.

RISK MANAGEMENT IN THE INTERNET AGE

Small businesses encounter a number of risks when they use the Internet. Increased reliance on Web-based operations demands that small business owners decide how much risk to accept and implement security systems to manage the risk associated with online business activities. Conducting business online exposes a company to liability due to infringement on copyrights, patents, or trademarks; charges of defamation due to statements made on a Web site or by e-mail; charges of invasion of privacy due to unauthorized use of personal information or excessive monitoring of employee communications; liability for harassment due to employee behavior online; and legal issues due to accidental noncompliance with foreign laws. In addition, businesses connected to the Internet also face a number of potential threats from computer hackers and viruses, including a loss of business and productivity due to computer system damage, and the theft of customer information or intellectual property. If the small business is publicly traded, the requirements of the Sarbanes-Oxley Act, specifically record retention, including the archiving of computer-based records, apply as well.

In the early 2000s new forms of insurance coverage emerged to cover risks businesses run in cyberspace, and this branch of protection is expected to develop along with new risks as they emerge. In the meanwhile attentive care to e-commerce implementation, the installation of firewalls, and effective disciplines inside the business can largely prevent serious problems. As pointed out elsewhere in this volume (see *Computer Crimes*) the largest risks most business run these days are from actions of employees inside the company.

ENTERPRISE RISK MANAGEMENT

In the 1990s, the field of risk management expanded to include managing financial risks as well as those associated with changing technology and Internet commerce. In the early 2000s, the role of risk management began to expand even further to protect entire companies during periods of change and growth. As businesses grow, they experience rapid changes in nearly every aspect of their operations, including production, marketing, distribution, and human resources. Such rapid change also exposes the business to increased risk. In response, risk management professionals created the concept of enterprise risk management, which was intended to implement risk awareness and prevention programs on a company-wide basis.

The main focus of enterprise risk management is to establish a culture of risk management throughout a company to handle the risks associated with growth and a rapidly changing business environment. Writing in *Best's Review*, Tim Tongson recommended that business owners take the following steps in implementing an enterprise-wide risk management program: 1) incorporate risk management into the core values of the company; 2) support those values with actions; 3) conduct a risk analysis; 4) implement specific strategies to reduce risk; 5) develop monitoring systems to provide early warnings about potential risks; and 6) perform periodic reviews of the program.

Finally, it is important that the small business owner and top managers show their support for employee efforts at managing risk. "To bring together the various disciplines and implement integrated risk management, ensuring the buy-in of top-level executives is vital," Luis Ramiro Hernandez wrote in *Risk Management*. "These executives can institute the processes that enable people and resources across the company to participate in identifying and assessing risks, and tracking the actions taken to mitigate or eliminate those risks."

SEE ALSO *Business Insurance; Computer Crimes*

BIBLIOGRAPHY
Anastasio, Susan. *Small Business Insurance and Risk Management Guide.* U.S. Small Business Administration. Available from http://www.sba.gov/library/pubs/mp-28.txt. Retrieved on 22 May 2006.

Hernandez, Luis Ramiro. "Integrated Risk Management in the Internet Age." *Risk Management.* June 2000.

Hommel, Ulrich, Michael Frenkel, and Markus Rudolf. *Risk Management: Challenge and Opportunity.* Springer, 2005.

Lam, James. *Enterprise Risk Management: From Incentives to Controls."* John Wiley & Sons, 2003.

O'Neill, David T. "Guard Against Cyber Exposures: New e-commerce risk insurance offers coverages beyond your standard policies." *Risk Management.* April 2003.

Sandgrove, Kit. *The Complete Guide to Business Risk Management.* Grower Publishing, 2005.

Tongson, Tim. "Turning Risk into Reward." *Best's Review.* December 2000.

Williams, Kathy. "How is Your Company Managing Risk?" *Strategic Finance.* September 2005.

Hillstrom, Northern Lights
updated by Magee, ECDI

RISK AND RETURN

It is an axiom of financial transactions that the highest returns go with the highest risks and, conversely, the safest investments have the lowest returns. The only real difference between buying something and investing in something is the level of uncertainty involved. When the certainty of reward is virtually assured, we call it purchasing; when there is risk but it is low, we speak of lending; when risks are higher, we call it investing; when even higher we call it speculation; and the most extreme form of this activity is gambling. Moving up this chain both the returns and the risks increase—moving down the reverse is true. Even a person buying a car can sometimes end up with a lemon—but he or she has warranty claims to exercise. But the person putting a large sum on red or black on the roulette table has a 50-50 chance of losing it all.

The investment world has developed a rich array of instruments to enable those who lack money but have ideas for creating new wealth to obtain money from those who have the funds but either lack the time, skill, or enterprise to go venturing themselves. The fundamental divisions are described by the common phrase of "stocks and bonds." In a very general sense stocks are risky and have high yield and bonds are safe but produce low returns. But this formulation is far too broad for general use. Sorting out the nuances of risk and return requires a closer look. Financial markets are both innovative and competitive. For this reason virtually every conceivable niche available has been populated by financial instruments that attempt to minimize the negatives involved and to hedge the risks—not least hedge funds.

BASIC DIVISIONS

In the first quarter of 2006, more than two-thirds of roughly $38 trillion in investment funds (68.7 percent) were allocated to debt instruments of one sort or another and somewhat under a third (31.3 percent) were held in the form of stock. These were domestic figures for bond debt (of $25.86 trillion in the first quarter of 2006) as reported by the Bond Market Association and figures for the market capitalization of U.S. stocks (at $11.8 trillion) as reported by Charles Schwab, citing Morgan Stanley Capital International. These ratios change over time, of course. In 2000 investment funds were divided almost equally between bond debt and market capitalization, 2000 having experienced a peak of stock capitalization of $17 trillion. The allocation of money between these two major categories is itself a reflection of risk: in periods of expansion (one of which peaked in 2000) money is drawn to stocks; in times of decline, money is invested in bonds. Both bonds and stocks are discussed in more detail elsewhere in this volume.

Stocks Stocks are typically classified by market capitalization and divided into Large, Medium or Mid, and Small capitalizations ("large-caps," "mid-caps," etc.). Large-caps have $10 to $200 billion in capitalization, mid-caps $2 to $10 billion, small-caps $300 million to $2 billion. The market capitalization is the value per share multiplied by the shares outstanding. Risks are greatest with small-caps but upward potential is greatest as well—so that financial journals routinely report on the exciting promise of small-caps. The great and massive large-caps, however, are unlikely to surprise anyone—except perhaps by spectacular and sudden failure, like Enron Corporation.

Most ordinary people participate in the stock market by buying mutual funds offered by fund managers. Funds come in a great many varieties but have the common feature of combining different kinds of stocks to maximize returns, stock appreciation, safety, and even stockholder aspirations. Some funds favor "green" companies, others avoid tobacco or alcohol or favor companies owned or controlled by religious affiliations. In that they combine many companies into a single instrument, a mutual fund is often less risky than the stock of a single company. Fund managers are rewarded for closely tracking trends in the market and making swift changes to maintain the fund's value.

A particularly interesting and complex type of fund is the hedge fund. Hedge funds are not regulated on the assumption that only highly sophisticated investors will participate in them. Some restrictions apply, including the number of investors and minimum assets that investors must have to participate. Being otherwise unregulated, they are opaque to view and thus on the face of it highly risky—although their intention is to "hedge" against the risk of the stock market. Hedging is to balance one risk by another—thus to invest in oil but to balance it by investing in windmills as well. In actual practice, hedge funds combine many different techniques, including selling stocks short, buying on one market and selling on another in order to realize a temporary differential in prices between the two, buying futures, and leveraging investor funds by borrowing. Sophisticated market knowledge and rapid execution are hall marks of hedge funds. But pure leverage would rarely make money. For this reason hedge funds are somewhat misnamed.

BONDS

It is useful to remember that "bonds"—whatever name they might actually bear—are ultimately loans. Thus in a sense all loans are bonds and all bonds are loans. A certificate of deposit (CD), a private placement, a savings account, a corporate bond, a treasury bill, a bank loan—all can be clustered under the generic "bond" designation because all types of loan instruments are ultimately bought, sold, and traded.

Bond debt is reported under seven major categories by the Bond Market Association. In order of magnitude the categories are mortgage-backed securities (23.6 percent), corporate bonds (19.7), Treasury notes (16.7), money market funds (13.5), federal agency bonds (10.2), municipal bonds (8.6), and asset-backed instruments (public and private placements—7.6 percent of total). Money market funds are commercial loans, bankers' acceptances, and large time deposits. These instruments represent different mixtures of security, time commitment, and return. Mortgage-backed securities are long-term debt on homes and other real estate and thus well-secured. Corporate bonds depend on the bond rating and may be quite secure or risky ("junk bonds"). Treasury notes are considered the most secure debt instruments of all; they are short-term instruments. Municipal bond yields are tax-free and hence desirable for that reason.

Bonds carry a rating set by rating agencies such as Moody's Investor Service, Standard & Poors, Fitch Bond Rating Agency, and others. Using Moody's ratings, a bond rated Aaa has the highest quality; Aa is high quality, A is strong, and Baa is medium grade; all of the above are "investment grade." Bonds rated Ba, or B are speculative "junk grade" bonds, those classified as Caa/Ca/C are highly speculative junk bonds, and a rating of C means that a junk bond is in default. S&P and Fitch use D to indicate a bond in default. The label "junk" in all cases indicates that the bond holder is in some kind of financial difficulty. The investor, therefore, is not left to fend for him- or herself. Those who trade in junk bonds typically know (or think they know) what they are doing.

LONGER-TERM TRACKING

Viewed over a number of decades, the literature on investment displays a see-saw of opinion in which optimistic and realistic views are applauded all depending on the volatile moods of the market. Thus in the high-flying 1990s, James Glassman and Kevin Hasset, in a 2000 book titled *Dow 36,000* promoted what Harvard Professor John Campbell calls the "revisionist" view. "In recent years," Campbell wrote in a paper cited below, "it has become commonplace to argue that equities are actually relatively safe assets for investors who are able to hold for the long term." Campbell himself does not subscribe to this view but sides with the realists who hold that the high returns of stocks *compensate* investors for the high risks.

Data published in the *Statistical Abstract of the United States,*, based on research conducted by Global

Financial Data (GFD), clearly show the longer-range differences between stocks and bonds—and between Treasury notes and other bonds. In the 1970 through 2004 time frame, GFD calculated total return on stocks and bonds by periods, expressed as percentages based on real (inflation-adjusted) dollars. In the period 1970-1979 and 2000-2004, returns on stocks were negative—producing a percentage loss of 1.38 in the first and 4.67 in the second decade shown. In the 1980-1989 and 1990-1999 periods, however, stocks had very nice returns of 11.85 and 14.85 percent respectively. During these same decades, Treasuries and bonds invariably provided positive returns. Both Treasuries and bonds had their highest performance in the 1980-1989 period, returning 9.13 and 13.01 percent to investors. During that period, money was moving into the stock market and borrowers, consequently, had to lift returns to attract money.

Investors, of course, have the option to put their money where they expect the best return. Therefore money tends to move between investment vehicles depending on the economic weather. In the world of "risk and return"—as in so many other areas—change is a constant, alertness is rewarded, no system of gambling ever works, and there are no silver bullets.

SEE ALSO *Bonds; Stocks*

BIBLIOGRAPHY

Brennan, Jack. Straight Talk on Investing: What You Need to Know. John Wiley & Sons, 2002.

Campbell, John Y. "Is the Stock Market Safer for Long-Term Investors?" Harvard University. Available from http://kuznets.fas.harvard.edu/~campbell/papers/stockrisk.pdf. Retrieved on 22 May 2006.

Cooper, James C. "The Bond Market: Don't Watch This Curve Too Closely." *Business Week*. 9 January 2006.

Estrada, Javier. *Finance in a Nutshell: A no-nonsense companion to the tools and techniques of finance.* Financial Times Prentice Hall, 2005.

Glassman, James, and Kevin A. Hasset. *Dow 36,000: The New Strategy for Profiting From the Coming Rise in the Stock Market.* Three Rivers Press, November 2000.

"Outstanding Level of Public & Private Bond Market Debt." The Bond Market Association Available from http://www.bondmarkets.com/story.asp?id=323. Retrieved on 7 January 2006

Picerno, James. "Rising Inflation? Protect Your Investments!" *The Scientist*. January 2006.

Mun, Jonathan. *Applied Risk Analysis: Moving Beyond Uncertainty in Business.* John Wiley & Sons, 2004.

"Schwab Report." Charles Schwab. 3 May 2006.

U.S. Census Bureau. *Statistical Abstract of the United States: 2006.* 2006.

Darnay, ECDI

ROBOTICS

The Robotic Industries Association (RIA) defines *robot* as follows: "A robot is a reprogrammable, multifunctional manipulator designed to move material, parts, tools or specialized devices through variable programmed motions for the performance of a variety of tasks." Recently, however, the industry's current working definition of a robot has come to be understood as any piece of equipment that has three or more degrees of movement or freedom.

Robotics is an increasingly visible and important component of modern business, especially in certain industries. Robotics-oriented production processes are most obvious in factories and manufacturing facilities; in fact, approximately 90 percent of all robots in operation today can be found in such facilities. These robots, termed "industrial robots," were found almost exclusively in automobile manufacturing plants 20 years ago. But industrial robots are now being used in laboratories, research and development facilities, warehouses, hospitals, energy-oriented industries (petroleum, nuclear power, etc.), and, above all, in research.

According to RIA, some 160,000 robots were installed and operating in the U.S. in 2006. In 2005, 19,594 robots valued at $1.18 billion were shipped to North American companies. In the first quarter of 2006, orders by RIA members (about 90 percent of the industry) were valued at $272 million and represented 3,722 such machines. Robotics thus is already a well-established and one might say mature industry—and yet its future is unimaginably large and diverse.

TECHNOLOGY

Today's robotics systems operate like most machines by way of hydraulic, pneumatic, and electrical power. Electric motors have become progressively smaller, with high power-to-weight ratios, enabling them to become the dominant means by which robots are powered. The crucial element in robotics is the artificial intelligence carried in the programmable circuitry of the machines.

Robots are comprised of elements that differ depending on end use. The hand of a robot, for instance, is referred to in the industry as an "end effector." End effectors may be specialized tools, such as spot welders or spray guns, or more general-purpose grippers. Common grippers include fingered and vacuum types. Another central element of robotics control technology is the sensor. It is through sensors that a robotic system receives knowledge of its environment, to which subsequent actions of the robot can be adjusted. Sensors are used to enable a robot to adjust to variations in the position of objects to be picked up, to inspect objects, and to monitor proper operation (although some robots are able to adjust to variations in object placement without the use of sensors, provided they have sufficient end effector flexibility). Important sensor types include visual, force and torque, speed and acceleration, tactile, and distance sensors. The majority of industrial robots use simple binary sensing, analogous to an on/off switch. This does not permit sophisticated feedback to the robot as to how successfully an operation was performed. Lack of adequate feedback also often requires the use of guides and fixtures to constrain the motions of a robot through an operation, which implies substantial inflexibility in changing operations.

Robots are programmed either by guiding or by off-line programming. Most industrial robots are programmed by the former method. This involves manually guiding a robot from point to point through the phases of an operation, with each point stored in the robotic control system. With off-line programming, the points of an operation are defined through computer commands. This is referred to as manipulator level off-line programming. An important area of research is the development of off-line programming that makes use of higher-level languages, in which robotic actions are defined by tasks or objectives.

Robots may be programmed to move through a specified continuous path instead of from point to point. Continuous path control is necessary for operations such as spray painting or arc welding a curved joint. Programming also requires that a robot be synchronized with the automated machine tools or other robots with which it is working. Thus robot control systems are generally interfaced with a more centralized control system.

COMMON USES OF ROBOTICS

Industrial robotics has emerged as a popular manufacturing methodology in several areas in recent years, including welding, materials transport, assembly, and spray finishing operations.

Spot and Electric Arc Welding Welding guns are heavy and the speed of assembly lines requires precise movement, thus creating an ideal niche for robotics. Parts can be welded either through the movement of the robot or by keeping the robot relatively stationary and moving the part past the robot. The latter method has come into widespread use since it generally requires less expensive conveyor systems. The control system of the robot must synchronize the robot with the speed of the assembly line and with other robots working on the line. Control systems may also count the number of welds completed and derive productivity data.

Pick-and-Place Operations Industrial robots also perform what are referred to as pick-and-place operations. Among the most common of these operations is loading and unloading pallets, used across a broad range of industries. This requires relatively complex programming, as the robot must sense how full a pallet is and adjust its placements or removals accordingly. Robots have been vital in pick-and-place operations in the casting of metals and plastics. In the die casting of metals, for instance, productivity using the same die-casting machinery has increased up to three times, the result of robots' greater speed, strength, and ability to withstand heat in parts removal operations.

Assembly Assembly is one of the most demanding operations for industrial robots. A number of conditions must be met for robotic assembly to be viable, among them that the overall production system be highly coordinated and that the product be designed with robotic assembly in mind. The sophistication of the control system required implies a large initial capital outlay, which generally requires production of 100,000 to one million units per year in order to be profitable. Robotic assembly has come to be used in the production of a wide range of goods, including circuit boards, electronic components and equipment, household appliances, and automotive subassemblies.

Spray Finishing Operations Industrial robots are widely used in spray finishing operations, particularly in the automobile industry. One of the reasons these operations are cost-effective is that they minimize the need for environmental control to protect workers from fumes.

Robots are also used for quality control inspections, since they can be programmed to quantitatively measure various aspects of a product's creation. In addition, the use of robots in environmental applications, such as the cleaning of contaminated sites and the handling and analysis of hazardous materials, represents an important growth market for robotics producers. Non-industrial applications for robots in security, commercial cleaning, food service, and health care are also on the rise.

FUTURE OF ROBOTICS

Recent research and development has addressed a number of aspects of robotics. Robotic hands have been developed which offer greater dexterity and flexibility, and improvements have been made in visual sensors as well (earlier generations of visual sensors were designed for use with television and home video, and did not process information quickly for optimal performance in many robotics applications; as a consequence, solid-state vision sensors came into increased use, and developments were also made with fiber optics). The use of superconducting materials, meanwhile, offers the possibility of substantial improvements in the electric motors that drive robotic arms. Attempts have also been made to develop lighter robotic arms and increase their rigidity. Standardization of software and hardware to facilitate the centralization of control systems has also been an important area of development in recent years.

Research in robotics is a large and thriving enterprise ranging at one end from artificial intelligence studies attempting to decompose the processes of human thought—so that these can be mechanized and put into robots—to complex and independent movement needed to turn industrial robots into walking, talking, and manipulating human look-alikes—the way ordinary people picture robots. Communication between people and robots—and robot-to-robot dialogue—fit into this spectrum somewhere. Motivations for creating robots arise from the field of medicine where robots are being developed to act as nursing aides on the one hand and as intelligent miniaturized agents on the other. Environmental issues have engaged robotics designers, e.g., the demanufacturing of electronic equipment which is a form of toxic waste and the handling of nuclear wastes. Robot miners may someday replace humans in dangerous environments. And, of course, robotics is a major area of research in defense applications.

Participation in this business by small business has centered around research and development—either directly in developing applications or in providing support services. High levels of engineering, electronics, and computer science skills are the keys of entry—and not least an interest in what is a genuinely fascinating subject.

SEE ALSO *Automation*

BIBLIOGRAPHY

"Age of Robotic Care for the Elderly?" *Healthcare Financial Management.* May 2006.

"Almost Human: They walk, talk and handle objects like we do. Get ready for a new era in robotics." *New Scientist.* 4 February 2006.

"Deployment of Robotics for Demanufacturing of Electronic Products." *Advanced Manufacturing Technology.* 15 April 2006.

Dubey, Venketesh N., and Jian S. Dai. "A Packaging Robot for Complex Cartons." *Industrial Robot.* March-April 2006.

"First Quarter 2006 Robot Sales Impacted by Downturn in Automotive Market." *Robotics Online.* 3 May 2006.

Nowak, Rachel. "And they call it robot love." *New Scientist.* 14 January 2006.

"Robotic Sensing for the Mining Industry." *Advanced Manufacturing Technology.* 15 March 2006.

"Robotic Surgery: Medic-aid." *The Engineer.* 3 October 2005.

Sands, David. "Cost Effective Robotics in the Nuclear Industry." *Industrial Robot.* May-June 2006.

Thilmany, Jean. "Space Robots Like Us." *Mechanical Engineering-CIME.* April 2006.

Hillstrom, Northern Lights
updated by Magee, ECDI

ROYALTIES

Royalties are payments made by one company (the licensee) to another company (the licensor) in exchange for the right to use intellectual property or physical assets owned by the licensor. For example, software giant Microsoft invented the Windows operating system for personal computers as a means of managing files and performing operations. Computer manufacturers such as IBM and Compaq pay a royalty to Microsoft in exchange for being allowed to use the Windows operating system in their computers. Other common situations in which royalties are paid include the following:

1. In the fashion industry, designers such as Ralph Lauren and Calvin Klein license the right to use their names on items of clothing in exchange for royalties. For example, they may sign a contract with a company that makes jeans that allows the company to place the designer's name on the jeans.

2. In book publishing, authors are commonly paid an advance on future royalties based on percentage of sales price; after sufficient sales have been made to "pay back" the advance, the authors received additional royalties paid periodically.

3. In the music industry, royalties are paid to music copyright holders and to songwriters by radio stations and anyone else who derives a commercial benefit from the copyrighted material.

4. In the television industry, popular satellite TV services such as Direct TV and cable television services pay network stations and superstations a royalty rate so that they can broadcast those channels over their systems.

5. In the oil and gas industry, companies pay landowners a royalty rate for the right to extract natural resources, such as petroleum and natural gas, from the landowner's property. Similar agreements exist in the mining industry for minerals such as copper and silver.

HOW RATES ARE ESTABLISHED

Royalty agreements are intended to benefit both the licensor (the person receiving the royalty) and the licensee (the person paying the royalty). For the licensor, signing a royalty agreement to allow another company to use its product or intellectual property can mean expanding into a new market, or increasing market share in an existing market. For the licensee, the agreement can mean gaining access to products that may have been too expensive or too difficult to produce on its own, or that were protected by patents it did not own. If done right, the royalty arrangement is a win-win situation.

Royalty agreements generally are one of two types. The fixed price-per-unit agreement pays the licensor a set price for every one of its products sold by the licensee. Often, this type of agreement is used when the licensor's product is one that will be a small part of a larger product produced by the licensee. An example of this might be a new type of windshield wiper motor developed by Company A. The motor drastically changes the way windshield wipers work and is granted a patent by the U.S. Patent Office. Company A approaches BBB Autos and offers to license the motor to the automaker so that it can be included in all BBB cars and trucks. In return, BBB agrees to pay Company A $10 per unit for every motor it purchases. This price would cover the materials and labor needed to produce the motor, as well as include an extra sum to cover Company's A investment in developing the motor. In fixed price arrangements, the amount per unit can be adjusted for inflation, or a minimum royalty amount can be specified.

The second type of agreement is a royalty that pays a percentage of revenues or operating profit that results from the sale of the licensed product. This is more likely to be used when the item covered by the royalty agreement stands alone or when the cost of using the item can be clearly itemized. Percentage agreements are generally more intricate than fixed price agreements because more terms must be defined—what rate will be paid for discounted items, what happens to items that are returned, whether sales commissions affect the percentage paid, whether updated versions of the item are covered by the agreement, and more. Agreements based on a percentage of the operating profit generally result in a more equitable settlement for both parties, but those agreements are also more complicated. As a result, it is more common for companies to agree on a percentage of revenues.

In percentage agreements, it is essential that the percentage chosen be fair to both sides. There are three areas to consider when determining a rate: 1) the specifications of the actual product or intellectual property being licensed; 2) the length and the geographic scope of the agreement; and 3) the capabilities of the licensor and licensee to live up to the agreement.

Factors related to the product that can affect the agreement include the uniqueness of the product, includ-ing any patents that may be included as well as any new versions of the product that may or may not be included in the agreement; the markets in which the product will be sold; and whether or not the product needs to be customized to meet the needs of the licensee. If customization is required, then the licensee should pay the licensor a higher percentage to cover additional manufacturing costs.

As for the agreement itself, it should clearly state the duration and should include the terms under which termination will occur. Whether or not the agreement can be renewed if certain goals are met should also be clearly spelled out. If a contract is too restrictive, the licensor may find at the end of the contract that it has limited itself in such a way that it can only renew the agreement with the current licensee, at less desirable financial terms. To try to find a new partner would be too cost intensive, so the licensor must renew with the original licensee. In addition to duration, the agreement should spell out the geographic rights granted to the licensee—does the agreement cover U.S. sales only, or are international rights included? Finally, the agreement should have a provision to handle "third party assignment." That is, what happens if the licensee assigns the rights to the product to a third party, possibly as a means to lower production costs? In some cases, the contract is invalidated if a third party assignment occurs, so it is an important area to cover.

When approaching a licensor, a licensee should examine the company's business practices before signing an agreement. Things to watch for include the licensor's ability to keep up with technological advances and its financial stability. If the licensee feels there is a chance the licensor may not be able to keep up with industry shifts and may even go out of business during the life of the agreement, than the licensee should seek to negotiate more favorable royalty terms. The licensee should also expect the licensor to have a clear plan outlining research and development plans, goals for the product, and plans to develop new or related products that could possibly expand the agreement. Evidence of planning and clear goals for the future by the licensor should instill confidence in the licensee. Finally, does the licensor have the ability to provide the licensee (and consumers) with needed levels of customer service and support? This is especially important for high-tech products or for complex products. The better the support that is in place, the better the terms the licensor can expect to receive.

Conversely, the licensor should expect certain things from the licensee. Can the licensee live up to its promises as far as units sold and territory covered? Has the licensee sold products of this nature before, and does it have a strong history? Is the company financially viable, and does it show clear plans for future growth? Can the licensee offer something other than cash as part of the agreement—for example, does the licensee have the ability to enhance the original product with its own products, or does it offer the licensor a market credibility that was previously lacking? All of these situations can affect how much money the licensor expects in the royalty contract.

LICENSING INTELLECTUAL PROPERTY

Intellectual property owned by one company is considered to be an intangible asset of that company. An intangible asset is something abstract, such as a patent or copyright, as opposed to a tangible asset, such as a factory or manufacturing equipment, or even cash. Intellectual property will, of course, have a physical form. It is structured information which can be and is recorded. Xerography or the chemical content of an important drug are examples. They reflect real wealth.

Not all intangible assets are intellectual property, however. For example, a company's workforce has skills that make it an intangible asset, but it is not intellectual property. Intellectual property is protected by law and may be sold, licensed, or transferred. Patents are perhaps the most common form of intellectual property. A patent is essentially a license granted by the U.S. Patent Office that gives one company the exclusive right to make and sell a patented invention for a period of 17 years. Any other company that desires to use that invention must negotiate terms of use with the company that receives the patent. Most often, those terms of use will involve a royalty agreement.

The Internal Revenue Service of the United States has developed definitions of what qualifies as intellectual property and oversees the regulation of royalty payments involving intellectual property. Among the intangible assets that are considered to be intellectual property are:

- Patents, inventions, formulas, processes, or designs;

- Copyrights and artistic compositions, including books and music;

- Trademarks, trade names, or brand names;

- Franchises, licenses, or contracts;

- Items specifically compiled or created by a company, such as methods, programs, systems, procedures, campaigns, surveys, studies, forecasts, estimates, customer lists, or technical data; and

- Any other items that are not physical in nature, but rather intellectual.

Whenever any intangible assets that fit these criteria are sold or licensed from one company to another, a royalty must be paid. There are two types of transactions that may occur. The first involves the sale or license from one company to another, which is called a third-party transaction. In this type of transaction, Company A licenses the rights to its product or process to Company B, which pays a royalty rate for the right to use the product or process. This is the type of transaction that is most commonly thought of when royalties are considered. However, the second type of transaction, the intercompany transfer, is actually more common. The law in the U.S. makes it illegal for an American firm to transfer intellectual property rights to a foreign subsidiary unless royalties are paid. The IRS has very strict rules that it applies to all intercompany situations and has come up with a number of formulas that it uses to determine if a fair royalty rate is being paid.

The simplest formula used by the IRS is called the cost-based method. Using the cost-based method, a company can establish a royalty rate that recaptures the costs of developing the item that is being licensed while also providing a fair rate of return on the item. To use the cost-based method, a company must determine what it cost to develop the intellectual property, the life expectancy of the property, the total revenue generated by products that use the property, and a fair rate of return that will cover the risks the company took in developing the property.

The cost-based method is the most straightforward, but it has flaws that limit its effectiveness. In most cases, the costs of developing the intellectual property do not have a direct correlation to the actual value of the property, so the method will not produce accurate results. As a result, the most commonly used formula for determining a royalty rate is the "comparable uncontrolled transaction (CUT)" method. This method relies on historical data and the performance results for products or processes that are similar to the intellectual property that is being licensed. For example, a book publisher lining up an author to write a book may look at the rates that were paid to other authors to write similar books when they determine how much to pay an author for the new project. Similarly, a clothing designer may look at other licensing deals in the industry when it comes time to license his name for use on a line of handbags or accessories.

When applying the CUT method, the intellectual property in question can only be measured against other intellectual property that was used in similar products within the same basic industry or market, and that has similar profit potential. Additional factors, such as the length of the agreement, geographic restrictions, and the right to receive updates, also factor into determining if the CUT method can be utilized. The CUT method is preferred by the IRS and is used in most third-party licensing agreements.

Beyond the two most common methods of evaluating royalty rates, the IRS uses four other formulas that are less common. These include the comparable profits method (CPM), which compares the profits of companies that use the intellectual property in question to the profits of similar companies that do not use the intellectual property; the hybrid CPM, which uses a combination of the CUT method and the CPM method in order to take the profit-making potential of the intellectual property into account; the profit split method (PSM), which accounts for situations where the licensor takes the intellectual property and adds value to it through its own processes, thereby enhancing the profitability of the property at its own expense; and the residual market value (RMV) method, which recognizes that a company's financial performance can affect the value of intellectual property and thus uses stock market data to determine the estimated value of the intellectual property that is being licensed.

COPYRIGHTS, PATENTS, AND ROYALTIES

Perhaps the most common day-to-day application of royalties that most consumers can relate to involves those paid for the use of copyrighted material. Every time a song is played on the radio, a royalty fee is paid by the station for playing that song. Every time a cable television provider transmits the signal of a broadcast television channel, such as superstation WTBS out of Atlanta, it pays that station a royalty for the right to show it. Every book, magazine, and newspaper published in the United States is protected by a copyright, and royalties must be paid any time a portion of a print product is reproduced by anyone other than the publisher.

In the United States, several organizations are involved in the oversight and management of royalty agreements involving copyrighted material. These primarily consist of government agencies and nonprofit associations that monitor intellectual property rights and, in some cases, actually collect royalties due to member companies.

The primary government agencies that are involved in royalty situations are the U.S. Copyright Office and the U.S. Patent and Trademark Office. Neither agency is directly involved in royalty payments, but both play an important role in the process. The Copyright Office provides all original authored works (including literary, dramatic, musical, and artistic works) with full protection under the law. When an author, artist, or publisher applies for a copyright, he or she receives the right to reproduce the work, to prepare derivative works based upon the work, to distribute copies of the work, to perform the work publicly, to display the work publicly, and, in the case of records, to perform the works by way of digital audio transmission. The length of time that a copyright lasts varies depending on the work and when it was published, but it is a minimum of several decades in every case. This means that only the person or company that holds the copyright for a work can license that work and receive royalties for it.

The Copyright Office determines when royalties are required, and its latest target is the Internet. Just as it requires cable and satellite television systems to pay licensing fees for content, the office is close to requiring Internet "Webcasters" to pay royalties as well for broadcasting the copyrighted work of artists. Webcasters include online services that broadcast radio and television programming and movies over the World Wide Web.

Similarly, the Patent Office protects inventors and their inventions. Whenever a person or company invents a new product or process, he or she can apply for a patent to indicate that he or she did invent that product or process, which grants him or her full protection under the law. If the work submitted is found to already exist or to be too derivative of an existing patent, then the new patent is not granted. Like a copyright, a patent gives the holder of that patent the right to license the product or service under royalty agreements, in this case for 17 years.

In the private sector, one of the major royalty organizations is the American Society of Composers, Authors, and Publishers (ASCAP), an association that protects the rights of its members working in the music industry (primarily composers, songwriters, lyricists, and music publishers). ASCAP monitors all public venues where music is played and collects royalties for its members by negotiating licensing agreements and fees with those venues, mainly radio stations. In addition to radio, however, ASCAP also closely monitors network, local, and cable television; live concert venues; college radio stations; bars, clubs, and restaurants; and background music services such as MUZAK. Every single time a songwriter's song is played, ASCAP collects money for the songwriter. This greatly simplifies the process of collecting royalties for creative works, and other similar organizations exist for writers and other creative professionals.

Another example of an umbrella organization that gathers royalty payments for a large number of clients is the Copyright Clearance Center, Inc. (CCC). Created at the suggestion of Congress in 1978, the CCC is a central body for licensing, recording, and collecting royalty fees.

CCC describes its own scope on its Web site as follows: "Copyright Clearance Center manages the rights to over 1.75 million works and represents more than 9,600 publishers and hundreds of thousands of authors and other creators. The company's streamlined, convenient compliance solutions enable more than 10,000 corporations and subsidiaries, including most of the *Fortune 100,* and thousands of government agencies, law firms, document suppliers, libraries, academic institutions, copy shops and bookstores to respect the rights of copyright holders and lawfully reuse the copyright-protected information they need to drive their business." This service is not necessarily intended to capture royalties from the average person when they make a copy of an article at their local library; instead, the CCC is intended to ensure that large-scale copying is monitored so that publishers can be fairly compensated for their work.

More than 3,500 high-volume users are registered with the CCC as part of its Transactional Reporting Service so that their payments for copying materials can be easily processed (the alternative would be to contact each publisher individually and negotiate separate royalty agreements with each).

A CHANGING ENVIRONMENT

Royalties have long compensated authors, artists, composers, and other creative producers as copyrights have protected their creations from piracy. The Internet has introduced a formidable new factor into the old equation both by making the electronic duplication of works easy and rendering such works readily searchable using programmatic means. As reported by Kevin Kelly in *The New York Times Magazine,* massive ventures are underway to digitize the world's books in efforts led by Google but also carried out by Amazon.com, by Superstar (in China, on Chinese books), and others. Major libraries, e.g., the New York Public Library, and universities are participating. Kelly, peering into the future, foresees a weakening of the old model based on copyright and royalties as the Internet appears irresistibly to swallow all information. Depending on how copyright issues are eventually resolved, royalties, at least in relation to intangible products of the human mind, may give place to other forms of compensation. Ad revenues, anyone?

SEE ALSO *Licensing; Royalty Financing*

BIBLIOGRAPHY

"Creating Copyright Solutions." Copyright.com. Available from http://www.copyright.com/ccc/do/viewPage?pageCode=au1. Retrieved on 25 May 2006.

Harrower, Andy. "Copyright Issues in Internet Music." *Contemporary Music Review.* December 2005.

Kelly, Kevin. "Scan This Book!" *The New York Times Magazine.* 14 May 2006.

Stoddard, Steven A. "Maximizing Federal Natural Gas Royalties." *Interfaces.* September-October 2005.

U.S. Copyright Office. "Notice of Inquiry Concerning Orphan Works." 26 January 2005.

Hillstrom, Northern Lights
updated by Magee, ECDI

ROYALTY FINANCING

Royalty financing is a relatively new concept that offers an alternative to regular debt financing (loans and trade credit) and equity financing (venture capital and stock sales). In a royalty financing arrangement, a business receives a specific amount of money from an investor or group of investors. The money might be put toward launching a new product or expanding the company's marketing efforts. In exchange, the investor receives a percentage of the company's future revenues over a certain period of time, up to a specific amount. The investment can be considered an "advance" to the company, and the periodic percentage payments can be considered "royalties" to the investors.

Royalty financing arrangements offer a number of advantages to small businesses. Compared to equity financing, royalty financing enables entrepreneurs to obtain capital without giving up a significant ownership position in the company to outside investors. The founders of the company are thus able to preserve their equity position, which may help motivate them toward continued success. In addition, royalty financing arrangements—since they most resemble loans—are not subject to state and federal securities laws as some equity financing deals are. Thus the company is able to save the time and money it might otherwise devote to complex filings and legal fees. Royalty financing also increases a company's ability to structure deals with individual investors, who might be attracted to the idea of receiving a monthly or quarterly yield over the life of their investment. In contrast, equity financing arrangements often show no yield until the stock is sold.

Compared to debt financing, royalty financing provides more convenient payback terms and less severe penalties for default. In addition, the infusion of cash may help the company increase sales, which may make it a better candidate to obtain more financing later. Finally, royalty financing enables a small business to keep its options open for later financing rounds. In contrast, a company that incurs significant debt or sells a great deal of equity in its early stages may find it difficult to attract investment later.

DETAILS OF ROYALTY FINANCING

As an example, suppose that a small business obtains an "advance" of $100,000 against future sales from individual investors or an economic development organization. In exchange, the investors would receive 3 percent of the company's total sales for a 10-year period, to a maximum of $300,000. If the company repaid the investment over 10 years, then the investors would earn a compound annual return of 11.6 percent. However, if the investors reached their maximum royalties of $300,000 in half that time, the initial investment would yield an annual return of 24.5 percent.

A small business interested in royalty financing may be able to negotiate a grace period so that royalties will not begin to accrue for a quarter or more following the close of the deal. It may also be possible to establish a lag between the time revenues are realized by the company and the time royalties are paid to investors. This sort of arrangement can give the small business time to put the capital to work and increase sales before paying a percentage of sales as royalties. In most cases, these arrangements are acceptable to investors since they still offer a better deal than most equity financing arrangements, which only pay when the stock is sold.

Royalty financing may tend to work best for small businesses that have some elasticity in pricing, so that they can raise prices to cover the percentage of royalties without losing customers. Royalty financing is also suitable for companies for which increased marketing efforts have an immediate impact on sales. However, royalty financing may not be a good option for companies with very tight profit margins. In summary, the capital gained through royalty financing can enable a fledgling business to launch a new product or expand its marketing efforts without having to give up too much equity in the early stages. In royalty financing, investors own a piece of the company's revenue stream rather than a piece of the company itself.

BIBLIOGRAPHY

Evanson, David R. "Royalty Treatment – using royalties as a form of business financing." *Entrepreneur.* September 2001.

Marks, Kenneth, Larry E. Robbins, Gonzalo Fernandez, John P. Funkhouser. *The Handbook of Financing Growth: Strategies and Capital Structure.* John Wiley & Sons, 2005.

"Royalty Financing." *Entrepreneur.* 1 December 2005.

Hillstrom, Northern Lights
updated by Magee, ECDI

RURAL BUSINESSES

Data from the last population census, held in 2000, showed that just under a fifth of the people in the U.S. (slightly over 55 million people) lived in rural areas defined as areas outside urbanized places—counties with a population of 50,000 or fewer—and the suburbs, if any, that surround them. Thus "rural," in the official definition, which is set by the U.S. Office of Management and Budget, means small towns and the countryside beyond these. Consequently, rural businesses are all those located in small towns and along the highways of the country well outside the metro centers.

Until 1920, a cross-over year, more people lived in rural areas than in cities. For city dwellers fighting commutes, bureaucracy, crowding, decay and bigness, life out on the farm or in small towns carries an aura of romance and of nostalgia. Traditional American value systems were shaped by our rural past and are in the process of transformation. In reflection of public sentiment, substantial efforts continue to be made by the federal and state governments to preserve the family farm and to foster life in rural areas by various support programs. For these reasons, perhaps, a certain sentimental flavor attaches to rural business activity—which happens not to be shared by the people actually engaged in such activities. For them the old adage still applies: business is business.

Rural business, in other words, encompasses exactly the same types of activities as business in general, although there are some important differences. Rural areas are the location of agricultural and mining activities—despite the very rare oil well still pumping in a big city here and there and the occasional suburban orchards. These two activities in 2005, measured by value added, represented 3 percent of Gross Domestic Product and 2 percent of total full-time employment. Agriculture, in this context, includes forestry, animal husbandry, and fishing—and, in addition to the output and employment already mentioned often also employ additional people in first-stage processing in rural settings. Mining includes, along with metals and minerals, oil and gas extraction, including some refining and certain transportation services located in rural areas such as pipeline compressor and pumping stations.

The distribution of farming products has also produced a unique form of institution, the farmers' cooperative. The most recent data on this institutional form, from the U.S. Department of Agriculture (USDA), indicates that 3,086 cooperatives were in operation in 2003, made up of 2.8 million members (a number greater than farms in operation), employing 165,000 full time and 62,000 part time workers.

In addition to the important sectors of agriculture and mining—which are more or less monopolized by rural areas, employ a lot of people, and together represent a large number of small businesses—rural areas also have a high share of tourism. Rural areas house travel service businesses in large number. Found in rural areas are most ski resorts, all dude ranches. Rural hospitality businesses attract hunting and fishing enthusiasts, hold snowmobile, bicycle, and other races, and operate many small hotels, restaurants, and bars.

Finally, rural areas also have every other type of activity present in major cities except those most specialized (like stock exchanges, research hospitals, etc.), including manufacturing operations of the most sophisticated character.

SMALL BUSINESS

In the U.S. as a whole, total company counts indicate that roughly 98 percent of 5.8 million companies, *not* counting farms, were small business. The same proportion must hold for rural businesses as well. No data breaking down businesses by rural or urban locations are available, but assuming that small businesses are distributed based on population, about 1.1 million small businesses operate in rural areas, including small towns. In 2004, using data from USDA, published in the *Statistical Abstract of the United States,* some 2.1 million farms were also operating in the United States. Of these, 84 percent were farms under 500 acres—thus, in terms of business size, they were small farms. Given these estimates, small commercial operations appear to be more numerous in rural areas than in urban areas.

Small Business Influx Demographic trends show that population growth has been highest in suburban areas (1.57 percent a year, 1970 to 2000) and lowest in central cities (0.57 percent), rural areas (with a growth of 0.83 percent a year) lag metro areas as a whole (1.16 percent). There is, however, a contrarian flow of small business enterprise out of cities and suburbs to rural places as individuals fed up with corporate life migrate out of congestion into the countryside. The evidence for this is anecdotal but apparently real. This shift is driven, in part, by corporate downsizing that provides an impulse to many to establish their own businesses. The Internet is another contributing factor because it enables people to set up many of those new businesses wherever they'd like. For a service business that uses the Internet to communicate and coordinate with suppliers and customers, location of its physical premises is a matter of less concern than for a goods producing business. Many small businesses that exit the urban arena physically still service clients in the cities. Also influential in this shift towards rural areas has been the plethora of government programs that offer financial support to those willing to set up businesses in rural areas. These programs are part of efforts to foster rural development.

Government Subsidies In Fiscal Year 2005, for instance, the USDA oversaw the distribution of $821 million in support of 12,000 businesses. These funds either created or saved nearly 74,000 jobs. Eight major programs were supported and of these the one that impacted the greatest number of companies, nearly 11,000, was one offering rural business enterprise grants intended to start things up. Other categories were loan guarantees, opportunity grants, relending programs, development loans, development grants, renewal energy loans, and renewal energy grants.

LOOKING AHEAD

Trends emerging in the mid-2000s suggest that the environment for business in rural areas will at least continue to be favorable and likely improve for four reasons: 1) rising energy costs will increase renewable energy initiatives; 2) Internet-based communications are making working from remote locations ever easier; 3) continued outsourcing activities will favor dispersal of professional work from dense urban centers; and 4) security issues may result in relocation of activities to rural areas where they will require new services. The individual or couple pondering a future in the country—or a small business thinking of relocation to or expanding in rural areas—will thus have opportunities to ponder. And the means may be there, using government help, to get start-up capital as well.

SEE ALSO *Small Business*

BIBLIOGRAPHY

Garrod, Brian, Roz Wornell, and Ray Youell. "Re-Conceptualising Rural Resources as Countryside Capital: The case of rural tourism." *Journal of Rural Studies.* January 2006.

Kraenzle, Charles A. "Statistics Show Cooperative Status, Progress and Trends." *Rural Cooperatives.* July 2001.

U.S. Census Bureau. *Statistical Abstract of the United States: 2006.* 2006.

U.S. Department of Agriculture. *Business Programs Activity Report: Fiscal Year 2005.* Available fromhttp://www.rurdev.usda.gov/rbs/pub/BPAReport05.pdf. Retrieved on 23 May 2006.

U.S. Department of Agriculture. *Farmer Cooperative Statistics, 2003.* Available from http://www.rurdev.usda.gov/rbs/pub/sr64.pdf. Retrieved on 23 May 2006.

"Wireless Internet for Rural Areas." *Science Activities.* Winter 2006.

Darnay, ECDI

S

S CORPORATIONS

A small business may operate under various legal forms. The most common of these, particularly for new start-ups, is the sole proprietorship. The individual who owns the business receives all of its income and is responsible for all of the business's debts—including other liabilities to which the business may be subject (e.g. a customer slipping on that banana peel in the store). Under a sole proprietorship, the individual and the business are the same thing. If the business fails, the owner may have to sell his or her house and other goods to satisfy its debts. The principal advantage of incorporation is that the owner as a person is separated from the corporation, the latter viewed as an artificial "person." They are now two, not one. The corporation carries its own liabilities. When the corporation fails, the liability of its owners is limited to whatever they have invested—and no more. The business owner who started a business with $10,000 may lose the $10,000—but not the $300,000 he or she owns in other assets. The downside of incorporation is that the income of the corporation is taxed separately—and the owner gets his or her share only *after* the corporate tax has been deducted. The owner also then owes *additional* taxes on his or her earnings. Thus double taxation is involved. As a sole proprietor, the owner is taxed once but is personally exposed to all of the liabilities of the business. As a corporate entity, the owner is shielded from liabilities but is taxed twice. Is there a way to have the best of both worlds? Yes, there is. It is called the S Corporation.

The S corporation derives its name from Subchapter S of the Internal Revenue Code which provides corporations a "tax election" option—a choice on how they want to be taxed. Under Subchapter S, a company may elect to pass all of its profits to its shareholders directly. The shareholders are then responsible for paying taxes on this income stream. The corporation itself is not taxed. Meanwhile the limited liability benefits of the regular corporate form continue. Not all corporations, however, qualify for the Subchapter S tax election. The company may only have a maximum of 75 investors. They must all agree to this choice. All must be residents in the U.S. or U.S. citizens. The IRS also excludes certain types of companies described below. A regular corporation, called a C corporation, can convert itself to S status—and thus have it both ways.

BECOMING AN S CORPORATION

Filing with the Internal Revenue Service Once a business has incorporated in the usual way and has filed its articles of incorporation, it can elect S corporation status by filing Form 2553 with the IRS. All of the corporation's shareholders must sign this form or file special shareholder consent forms. The rules apply to anyone who has held stock in the company during the current tax year. To be eligible for S corporation status for the current tax year, a corporation must file the form by the fifteenth day of the third month of the corporation's tax year. Once the form has been filed, it is not necessary to file every year.

Eligibility For a corporation to be eligible for S corporation status, the following conditions must be met and maintained:

- The business must have become a corporation prior to filing for S corporation status. See the entry *Incorporation* for more information on this process.

- The business must also have no more than 75 stockholders. Until the Small Business Job Protection Act of 1996 was passed, corporations with more than 35 shareholders were disqualified.

- All of the business's stock must be owned by individuals who reside in or are citizens of the United States. Estates or trusts may be allowed as stockholders, but corporate or foreign investors are not allowed. This includes other businesses that are not corporations, such as partnerships or sole proprietorships. This provision, therefore, excludes corporate subsidiaries from claiming S corporation status.

- The business must issue only one class of stock. This means that with the purchase of stock must come the same economic rights, such as receiving dividends or compensation in the event of liquidation at the same time and in the same amount per share as all other shareholders. Voting rights may differ amongst the shareholders without being considered a sign of the possession of different classes of stock.

Ineligible Businesses Those businesses that are ineligible for S corporation status include:

- All financial institutions, such as banks and savings and loans.

- Insurance companies.

- Businesses that receive 95 percent or more of their gross income from exports (also known as DISCs, Domestic International Sales Corporations).

- Corporations that use the possessions tax credit (a type of foreign tax credit).

- C Corporations that have been S corporations within the last five years.

ADVANTAGES

The chief advantage of the S corporation is its treatment under the tax law, particularly if the company routinely pays high dividends. Under the C form, stockholders actually "feel" the double taxation of corporate profits only when they get dividends: under an S form, they would get more money. S corporation stockholders also get assigned losses if the company sustains them. These losses do not require stockholders to pay any money to the company but allow them to factor the reported losses into their own income taxes and thus reduce their taxes on other income.

DISADVANTAGES

Paying Taxes on "Absent" Income Most healthy corporations reinvest all or substantial portions of their profits into operations to fund growth. Dividends paid are therefore just a portion of all profits. In C corporations, stockholders only pay taxes on dividends, year to year, and are not liable for taxes on the total profit made. But when the S corporation retains its profits for growth, stockholders must pay taxes on that profit even though they do not get a check in the mail—and the higher the profits, the more rapid the growth, the higher the taxes. This structural arrangement can thus produce tensions between stockholder and the corporation—stockholders either required to keep "investing" in a going concern indirectly by paying its taxes or, conversely, pressuring the corporation to distribute more of its profits and thus potentially slowing the company's growth.

Taxed Fringe Benefits Unlike C corporations—but like partnerships—S corporations may not deduct fringe benefits, given to shareholders who are also employees, as a business expense. As a result, shareholder-employees must pay taxes on those benefits. These rules apply to all shareholders who own more than two percent of the corporation's stock and are employees of the corporation. But all employees who are not stockholders may receive benefits without paying taxes.

Pay Vs. Profit Sharing S corporations must be careful to pay stockholders who work for the corporation salaries "deemed reasonable" by industry standards. The temptation exists to pay stockholders low salaries and to compensate them, instead, from profits—thus avoiding payroll taxes. But if the stockholder-employee is not paid at a reasonable rate, the IRS may require the stockholder to pay payroll taxes on the totality of the income received from the S corporation—which may be substantial.

State and Local Taxes S corporations are sanctioned under federal tax laws which may not be matched by local and state governments. Thus S corporations may still have to pay taxes as corporations to states and localities.

Record Keeping S corporations must act like S corporations and maintain careful records. This is not, per se, a disadvantage of the form: after all, *all* businesses should keep good records. But some business owners see the S corporation as merely one way to escape liabilities by gaining the benefits of limited liability while continuing to operate as sole proprietorships. Under prevailing law, a corporation (S or C) must adhere to regular forms: it must separate personal from corporate accounts, hold regular directors' and shareholders' meetings, take minutes, and also use the appropriate corporate designation on its documents and stationary. Failing to adhere to these requirements, the S corporation may not prevail in court in the case of a liability action, with the result that the stockholders are severally and individually held to be liable.

TERMINATING S CORPORATION STATUS

An S corporation may voluntarily revoke its status if it finds that S status is no longer beneficial; it may also lose the status involuntarily. In the first case, a majority of the stockholders is required to make the decision, and a simple notice to the IRS is all that is required. In the second case, any act which disqualifies the corporation's eligibility for S status will result in the termination of that status effective on the date that the infraction occurs. An example of such a disqualification would be acquiring a single foreign stockholder living abroad. In either case, the corporation becomes a C corporation in the absence of S corporation status.

SEE ALSO *C Corporation; Incorporation; Professional Corporation*

BIBLIOGRAPHY

Adkisson, Jay, and Chris Riser. *Asset Protection.* McGraw-Hill, 2004.

Fishman, Stephen. *Working for Yourself: Law and Taxes for Independent Contractors, Freelancers and Consultants.* Nolo, 2004.

Mancuso, Anthony. *LLC Or Corporation?* Nolo, 2005.

Nathan, Karen, and Alice Magos. *Incorporate!* McGraw-Hill, 2003.

U.S. Small Business Administration. "Forms of Business Ownership." Available from http://www.sba.gov/starting_business/legal/forms.html. Retrieved on 5 June 2006.

Hillstrom, Northern Lights
updated by Magee, ECDI

SALES COMMISSIONS

Paying a sales commission is a way of compensating salespeople. Under so-called "straight" commission arrangements, the salesperson receives an agreed-upon percentage of the revenue brought in by a sale that he or she makes. Companies use commission arrangements to sell products as well as services. But some employers choose to pay salespeople a straight salary instead. The most common form of sales compensation—other than in retail sales—is to combine a salary with commissions.

The chief advantage cited for straight commission is that commissions cause salespeople to work harder. Detractors contend that uncertainties surrounding such a form of compensation may drive off good salespeople. Furthermore, their complete dependence on commissions may lead them to develop bad business habits. But even detractors admit that pure commissions incentivize and move people to try harder. As a consequence the majority of businesses that employ a sales force use some combination of base pay and commission—also known as incentive pay—to compensate their salespeople. Sales clerks, however, tend to be paid salaries or wages.

BASIC COMPENSATION PLANS

Straight Commission Under straight commission arrangements, the seller gets a percentage of the sales price. The percentage may vary from product to product. Observers of the sales function estimate or guess that fewer than 15 percent of American firms pay their salespeople a straight commission—but those that do are satisfied with it: it motivates people to work hard enough to get the sales such companies need. Salespeople prosper in good times but are not a cost in during a downturn.

The straight salary route has its disadvantages as well. Some very able salespeople may also be lazy: they may work hard until they have what they need and then tend to sit back. They cherry-pick what they sell, moving high-commission product at the neglect of other lines. They by-pass difficult-to-reach customers when traveling or favor large buyers over small. Other, highly motivated salespeople view straight-commission selling as demeaning and cannot be attracted. Others view themselves as independents and move at frequent intervals, able to secure new jobs relatively easily. Pure commission salespeople tend not to develop high loyalties to the company that employs them: the company, after all, is not sharing the risk of the downside with them. Thus many also resist doing necessary work that is in the non-selling category, such as, for instance, attendance at trade fairs, participation in promotional visits, and providing follow-up work or technical assistance. A good deal of the sales management effort in companies that use straight-commission forces is devoted to get around problems of this type by a succession of tinkerings with incentives, supervision, and attempts at motivation. In such organizations the sales function is also often in a permanent recruiting mode.

Straight Salary The most frequent criticism of compensation plans that pay sales representatives a straight salary is that they eliminate the employees' incentive to perform. But such criticism is rarely heard in situations where, for instance, the sales function in performed by

987

principals or executives—common in consulting, engineering, and service operations—or in organizations where professional level individuals are engaged in selling, the sales activity itself has significant technical complexity, and the sales function is valued and well compensated.

Salary Plus Commission or Other Incentives This arrangement is by far the most common employed by organizations that use salespeople. Proponents tout several meaningful advantages associated with compensation plans that combine base salaries with commissions:

- Motivates sales force to expend greater effort.

- Provides company with a way to extend additional rewards to its best sales performers.

- Closely ties compensation to performance (though not to the same degree as straight commission arrangements).

- Generally easy to administer.

- Depending on the arrangement, the bestowal of increased security to employees may allow the company to take a greater percentage of sales profits.

Criticisms of compensation plans that combine salary with commissions or other incentives are usually framed not as rebukes of its philosophical underpinnings but as laments concerning its execution. For example, some companies may offer only token commissions, which do little to foster aggressive salesmanship.

In addition to commissions, some companies choose to provide non-salary compensation to their sales force through expense accounts, automobile leasing, advances against future earnings (usually commission), or sales contests.

Expense accounts are common features in many industries. Indeed, salespeople in a wide range of industry sectors depend a great deal on business lunches, etc. to close deals. Moreover, salespeople are often responsible for large territories, which makes long hours of travel a fundamental element of their job description. Organizations that do not compensate such individuals with expense accounts—or free use of leased automobiles—are likely to have considerable difficulty finding and retaining gifted salespeople. Indeed, most prospective hires will view refusal to take care of expenses as a sure sign of company stinginess and an indication that the company's ownership may not be cognizant of basic business realities.

Sales contests are another popular tool used by business owners to encourage sales activities. Under these programs, sales personnel who meet certain sales goals are rewarded with cash bonuses, paid vacations, etc. But business experts contend that sales contests can have unintended consequences for organizations if they are poorly defined or structured so that only a small segment of the sales force is rewarded. Indeed, some organizations provide incentives only to a certain percentage of top-level performers. Such programs—whether commissions or sales contests—are usually implemented in hopes of creating a competitive environment, but all too often they have the opposite effect. After all, if 25 people participate in a contest that only one person can win, 24 must also lose. In order to counteract the negative characteristics associated with traditional sales contests, sales consultants recommend that businesses instead institute so-called "open-ended" incentive programs. Such programs are designed so that participants compete against their own past performances rather than their fellow salespeople.

Open-ended programs can be shaped in two-tiered fashion so that a business's very best sales performers receive some extra recognition. For example, salespeople who increase their sales by 10 percent might receive a nice prize, while those that increase their sales by 20 percent would receive an even better one. Two objections are commonly raised to open-ended sales incentives. The first is that such initiatives cast greater uncertainty on sales budgeting efforts. After all, companies that offer an open program cannot know how many prizes to budget for. In addition, some observers contend that open programs can actually detract from the performance of a business's top salespeople—who might reach a goal too early and therefore slack off. But the impact of both of these negative attributes can be neutralized by careful planning (such as studying multi-tiered programs) and continuous monitoring.

THE FUTURE IS THE PAST

The sales function in any organization is a perpetual focus of concern. Sales are rarely overwhelming—and when they are they become a major problem of production, fulfillment, service, and the potential of losing the customer's good will. Selling is almost invariable beset by uncertainties, stresses, and the occasional (short-lived) triumph: every success is followed, not too soon after, by the question that haunts all those engaged in making or managing sales: "What have you done for me *lately?*" Not surprisingly, continuous examination of the sales function is a perennial preoccupation of business, has been so in the past, and is likely to be there in the future as well. In the future mix, whether the sales are predominantly direct, business-to-business, business-to-consumer, by electronic means, face to face, or take place in some other manner, finding the right mix of compensating salespeople will be a business concern, be that operation big or small. Commission sales will no doubt be one of the tools the small business owner will be using in certain circumstances.

SEE ALSO *Multilevel Marketing; Personal Selling*

BIBLIOGRAPHY
Calvin, Robert J. *Sales Management.* McGraw-Hill, 2004.

Cichelli, David J. *Compensating the Sales Force: A Practical Guide to Designing Winning Sales Compensation Plans."* McGraw-Hill, 2004.

Ingram, Thomas N. et al. *Sales Management: Analysis and decision making.* South-Western College Publishing, 2006.

"Job Performance—Productivity—Effectives—Effort—Failure." *Journal of Personal Selling and Sales Management.* Winter 2005.

"Sales Compensation Plans That Work for Entrepreneurial Companies Featured on Kauffman eVenturing." *Business Wire.* 3 April 2006.

Simpkins, Robert A. *The Secrets of Great Sales Management: Advanced Strategies for Maximizing Performance.* AMACOM, 2004.

Hillstrom, Northern Lights
updated by Magee, ECDI

SALES CONTRACTS

A sales contract is an agreement between a buyer and seller covering the sale and delivery of goods, securities, and other personal property. In the United States, domestic sales contracts are governed by the Uniform Commercial Code. International sales contracts fall under the United Nations Convention on Contracts for the International Sale of Goods (CISG), also known as the Vienna Sale Convention.

Under Article 2 of the UCC, a contract for the sale of goods for more than $500 must be in writing in order to be enforceable (UCC 2-201). The sale of securities is a special case covered in Article 8 (UCC 8-319); to be enforceable a contract for the sale of securities must be in writing regardless of the amount involved. For the sale of other kinds of personal property, a minimum of $5,000 must be involved before an enforceable contract must be in writing. Otherwise, an oral agreement is enforceable as a binding contract.

Contracts that must be in writing to be enforceable are said to be within the Statute of Frauds. The Statute of Frauds dates back to 1677, when the English Parliament decreed that certain types of contracts must be in writing. The applicable parts of the UCC effectively define the types of sales contracts that must be in writing. In addition, every state has its own version of the Statute of Frauds.

Under the UCC a written sales contract should specify the parties involved, the subject matter to be sold, and any material or special terms or conditions. Some states also require that the consideration—the amount and type of payment—be specified. But the UCC does not require a formal sales contract. In many cases a memorandum or collection of papers is sufficient compliance. The courts have held that a written check can be considered a written memorandum of a sales agreement. The UCC allows a written sales contract to be enforced even if it leaves out material terms and is not signed by both parties. However, one party may not create a sales contract on its own that is binding against another party, and an enforceable contract must be signed by the defendant or the one against whom the contract is sought to be enforced.

In many cases a purchase order, pro forma invoice, or order acknowledgment may serve in place of a formal sales contract. A purchase order is issued by the buyer and sent to the seller, stating the type and amount of goods to be purchased, the price, and any other material terms such as a time limit on filling the order. A pro forma invoice is issued by the seller and sent to the buyer, often in response to a purchase order or oral agreement. In international transactions, the pro forma invoice may enable the buyer to open a line of credit with which to pay for the goods ordered. The pro forma invoice typically includes relevant terms and conditions that apply to the sale.

A formal order acknowledgment is useful for establishing the seller's position in case a dispute should arise. The order acknowledgment is drawn up by the seller in response to a received purchase order. It does not necessarily repeat the details of the purchase order, but it may clarify details such as delivery schedules. When a formal order acknowledgment is countersigned by the buyer, it becomes a type of sales contract.

For international transactions, the Vienna Sale Convention is binding on signatory countries, of which the United States is one. Each of the nations that has signed the convention may state up to five reservations. For example, the United States has stipulated that it shall apply to U.S. companies only when the transaction involves another signatory country. Much of the convention parallels the UCC, with these notable exceptions:

- Acceptance of an offer that includes a request for additions or modifications constitutes a counteroffer.

- There is no provision requiring a contract be written in order to be enforceable.

- The period for discovering defective merchandise may be as long as two years.

Sales contracts are useful in providing for a common understanding between buyer and seller, thus minimizing disputes. When a dispute does occur, the sales contract can help provide for a fair settlement.

BIBLIOGRAPHY

Ashcroft, John D. *Law For Business.* Thomson South-Western, 2005.

Miller, Roger LeRoy, and Gaylord A. Jentz. *Fundamentals of Business Law.* Thomson South-Western, 2005.

Roberts, Barry S., and Richard A Mann. *Smith and Roberson's Business Law.* Thomson West, 2006.

Wayne, Jonathan, and Karla C. Shippey. *A Short Course in International Contracts.* World Trade Press, 2003.

Hillstrom, Northern Lights
updated by Magee, ECDI

SALES FORCE

A company's sales force consists of its staff of salespeople. The role of the sales force depends to a large extent on whether a company is selling directly to consumers or to other businesses. In consumer sales, the sales force is typically concerned simply with taking and closing orders. These salespeople are not responsible for creating demand for the product, since, theoretically, demand for the product has already been created by marketing efforts such as advertising campaigns and promotional activities. Salespeople may provide the consumer with some product information, but individuals involved in consumer sales are often not concerned with maintaining long-term customer relationships. Examples of consumer sales forces include automobile salespersons and the sales staffs found in a variety of retail stores.

The sales force takes on a completely different role in business-to-business sales. Industrial sales forces, for example, may be required to perform a variety of functions. These include prospecting for new customers and qualifying leads, explaining who the company is and what its products can do, closing orders, negotiating prices, servicing accounts, gathering competitive and market information, and allocating products during times of shortages.

Within the business-to-business market, a distinction can be made between selling to retailers, industrial sales, and other types of business-to-business sales and marketing. The concerns and activities of the sales force tend to vary in each type of business market. What they have in common, however, is the desire of the sales force to establish a long-term relationship with each of its customers and to provide service in a variety of ways.

In selling to retailers, for example, the sales force is not concerned with creating demand. Since consumer demand is more a function of advertising and promotion, the sales force is more concerned with obtaining shelf space in the retailer's store. The sales force may also attempt to obtain more promotion support from the retailer. The sales force relies on sophisticated marketing data to make a convincing presentation to the retailer in order to achieve its sales and marketing objectives.

The largest sales forces are involved in industrial selling. An average industrial field sales force ranges in size from 20 to 60 people and is responsible for selling throughout the United States. The sales force may be organized around traditional geographic territories or around specific customers, markets, and products. An effective sales force consists of individuals who can relate well to decision makers and help them solve their problems. A sales manager or supervisor typically provides the sales force with guidance and discipline. Within the company the sales force may receive support in the form of specialized training, technical backup, inside sales staff, and product literature. Direct mail and other types of marketing efforts can be employed to provide the sales force with qualified leads.

In recent years, costs associated with making single business-to-business industrial sales calls have risen dramatically. As a consequence, many businesses have redoubled their efforts to make sure that they get the most possible efficiency out of their sales force (by expanding their territories, increasing their duties, etc.).

Sales managers and supervisors can measure the efficiency of their sales force using several criteria. These include the average number of sales calls per salesperson per day, the average sales-call time per contact, the average revenue and cost per sales call, the entertainment cost per sales call, and the percentage of orders per 100 sales calls. The sales force can also be evaluated in terms of how many new customers were acquired and how many customers were lost during a specific period. The expense of a sales-force can be measured by monitoring the sales-force-to-sales ratio, or sales force cost as a percentage of total sales.

Using such criteria to evaluate the effectiveness of the sales force allows companies to make adjustments to improve its efficiency. If the sales force is calling on customers too often, for example, it may be possible to reduce the size of the sales force. If the sales force is servicing customers as well as selling to them, it may be possible to shift the service function to lower-paid personnel.

In industrial and other business-to-business sales, the sales force represents a key link between the manufacturer and the buyer. The sales force is often involved in selling

990

technical applications and must work with several different contacts within a customer's organization. Industrial salespeople tend, on average, to be better educated than their consumer counterparts, and to be better paid. However, their cost as a percentage of sales is lower than in consumer sales, because industrial and business-to-business sales generally involve higher-ticket items or a larger volume of goods and services.

The sales force may be compensated in one of three ways: straight salary, straight commission, or a combination of salary plus commission. The majority of today's businesses utilize a combination of salary plus commission to compensate their sales forces, and fewer companies based their sales force compensation on straight commission. It appears that, as a percentage of all sales forces, the use of straight salaries remains constant. Whatever type of compensation system is used for the sales force, the important consideration is that the compensation adequately motivates the sales force to perform its best.

SEE ALSO *Business-to-Consumer; Business-to-Business; Manufacturers' Agents; Personal Selling; Sales Commissions*

BIBLIOGRAPHY

Boone, Louis E., and David L. Kurtz. *Contemporary Marketing 2005.* Thomson South-Western, 2005.

Calvin, Robert J. *Sales Management.* McGraw-Hill, 2004.

Cichelli, David J. *Compensating the Sales Force: A Practical Guide to Designing Winning Sales Compensation Plans."* McGraw-Hill, 2004.

Cohon, Charles M. *The Sales Force.* Manufacturers and Agents National Education Foundation, 2004.

Gitomer, Jeffrey. *The Sales Bible: The Ultimate Sales Resource.* John Wiley & Sons, 2003.

Hillstrom, Northern Lights
updated by Magee, ECDI

SALES FORECASTS

Companies large and small engage in forecasting their sales in order to decide with the greatest accuracy possible what and how much to build or what and how much to buy. Sales forecasts support operational planning and supply chain management—not marketing or sales efforts. To be sure, sometimes accurate sales forecasts can also lead to intensified selling or its reverse: sales forces fanning out to dampen buyer enthusiasm because the company cannot actually supply the demand foreseen. But such efforts are not central to forecasting. Forecasts are made to project the business into the future accurately in order to avoid costly mistakes.

A classical example of sales forecasting is the determination of "the build." This phrase is used in industries where production falls into one season and sales into another. Thus snowmobiles are manufactured in the summer and sold in late fall and winter. How many sleds to build, how many of the low end and how many of the expensive models—"the build," in other words—must be decided long before the winter season actually arrives, before likely snowfall is predictable, before economic conditions influencing sales *then* can be known with certainty *now*. In "bad snow years" demand tends to drop, in "good snow years" it spikes. Snowmobiles are big-ticket items. Overbuilding can hurt the company and its dealer structure for longer than one season; underbuilding leaves substantial money on the table and may lead to a loss of market share if the competitor made a better forecast. Builders of boats and similar "water toys" have the reverse problem: they build in the winter for spring and summer sales. Boat builders, like snowmobile manufacturers, require positive economic times in that they sell high-end recreational products users can do without. Both are influenced by weather. Boat sellers can also be hurt by high prices for fuels.

"The build" serves as an easy illustration of the need for good sales forecasts, but every producer and every merchant faces exactly the same problem in looking ahead. In every case more or less irreversible actions must be taken in advance of actual sales; in every case multiple factors influence future demand which may change in response to yet other factors; in every case bad forecasts may mean being saddled by large inventories or having to turn customers away. Not surprisingly, every business, even the smallest, engages in some kind of sales forecasting. It may be quite instinctive and informal—a gut feel by the owner that more or less should be purchased or made, based simply on experience leading up to the purchasing decision. Sales forecasting is often a process involving contact with the sales channel. In many large companies producing for mass markets, sales forecasting is a very complex, formal, and highly structured activity involving expensive surveys, computer modeling, and statistical analyses.

BASIC TECHNIQUES

Fundamental approaches to forecasting sales rely on 1) looking at the company's own history (internal numbers), on 2) looking at the product's or category's market history (external numbers), 3) soliciting external opinion (channel surveys), and 4) examining other sources of information which indirectly influence the future.

In the first case the company will look at its own past sales and determine a trend, ideally based on units rather than on dollars to eliminate the effect of price changes. If the item is growing at 2 percent a year, the company may feel safe in increasing its production/purchasing by 2 percent for the next period. Such a forecast is typically just the start of a process of review. The company may wish to eliminate the product because its margin is low and decreasing, its warranty service requirements are too great, etc. Alternatively, the company may wish to increase its growth in the category by additional promotional, discount, and sales efforts—and, betting on success, may order above its historical trend projection. Quite complicated formulas are sometimes applied. An example is production of replacement parts for outdated models of a product—in which the forecast is dated on an estimate of the models still remaining "out there" in active use—with the production reduced each year.

The second case, looking at the total market for the item, requires access to data on such sales. If these are available, the company can compare its own performance against the product's growth/decline as a whole and make adjustments accordingly. Suppose the category, e.g., a certain type of garden tool, has been declining as a whole in the gardening field while the company's own sales of that product have been increasing at 5 percent a year. This may mean that the company may have become the last active supplier of a product in its locality thus drawing a segment of the public that still wants the product. Such a finding may lead to energetic stocking *up*. Conversely, if the company's sales are poor but the product as a whole is making waves, adjustments in price, promotion, display, and the like may justify much more ambitious stocking. In practice it is often very difficult to get objective data on the performance of a specific item for comparison. Similarly, even if overall sales data can be found, it may be very difficult for a merchant to discover why he or she is selling more or less of an item. The merchant's location, clientele, region of operation, and many other factors may influence the result. The small business typically lacks the time and money to go deeply into such a subject unless the product is rather expensive and central, e.g., the business sells farm equipment.

Many small manufacturers make heavy use of the third basic technique (along with the others): asking the channel what it expects to purchase in the coming planning period (quarter, year). Companies typically survey their distributors, dealers, or major customers at regular intervals to get a feel for what they plan on buying. In many fields such surveys are routine—the buyers as anxious as the sellers in getting the production numbers right so that, in the future, shortages on the one hand and pressure to buy on the other can be avoided. These types of surveys are usually conducted outside the usual "selling" context—the channel made to understand that these estimates are intended for planning production. To be sure, the channel will nevertheless feel a certain pressure.

Unless there is a known shortage in a field, buyers will thus typically somewhat understate their buying intentions; they don't want to have the numbers misunderstood as commitments to buy; they hedge in the lower direction; producers in turn typically plan on slightly higher production rates, all else being equal.

The fourth technique of developing forecasts—eyeballing indirect forces—is often the most tricky and occasionally the most important. This, in the snowmobile business, for instance, is guessing at the weather, but it takes innumerable other forms. Indicators of the economy are the most closely watched: almost all businesses are affected by rising or declining economies. Hot economies lift costs of supplies and of labor—and also lift sales. Consumer durables turn sluggish in times of decline—as do capital goods bought by industry. Interest rates powerfully influence new home construction—as does the demographic phenomenon of new family formation—which, in turn, depends on the age structure of the population and the average age of marriage, etc. Energy and fuel prices influence virtually every sector— and these, in turn, are influenced by international events. Sociological trends are more subtle and difficult to exploit effectively. In the mid-2000s a certain and very important trend is the aging of the baby boom generation, for example, but this generation is very large and pin-pointing its immediate influence on a small business during a brief period, like the next fiscal year, is not exactly simple. The small business that at least attempts consciously to look for and to analyze such trends—using the broadly available statistical sources as well as its own experience with the public—will outperform a company that simply looks at past sales and uses these to predict future sales.

FORECASTS, OUTCOMES, AND LIMITATIONS

Well-conducted sales forecasting programs have an impact on every aspect of the business—on financial performance first of all, of course, but also on market share, channel relations, and consumer satisfaction. An accurate forecast buys the company time—and time is money. If the market is projected to experience a sharp decline and the forecast is correct, the company can scale back its production and purchases early, will have more time to adjust to these changes—and will be able to retain its place in the market with a properly priced product. The downward adjustment will be no less painful when taken early rather than later—but if taken later, it will be more costly: the company will be sitting on and required to finance a large inventory; it will have to move goods at large discounts, eroding its margins; at the same time it will bear high costs of severance from layoffs.

Companies, however, are rarely able to get themselves to shrink deliberately in advance of facts clear and evident on the ground. For this reason, even very effective managements will compromise and simply scale back a little. But even that will be more adaptive than projecting lasts year's sales with a small increase.

Companies, similarly, are rarely able to believe a forecast that predicts a sudden surge in sales. Such things are rare and therefore too good to be true. But the company that has a decent sales forecasting program and dares to act on it, at least up to a point, will find itself with product in the channel when everyone else is out. It will thus garner new buyers and, if the new customers are pleased, it will gain market share as well as channel loyalties.

These two cases illustrate the benefits as well as limitations of sales forecasting. The technique works best when projected changes are relatively small. Both sharp down and up adjustments from a company's or a market's history will tend to be resisted. But those with the best techniques, combining every major approach, are likely to go farthest in the right direction and will ultimately emerge as the winners.

BIBLIOGRAPHY

Burton, James E., and Steven M. Bragg. Sales and Operations for Your Small Business. John Wiley & Sons, 2001.

Crosby, John V. *Cycles, Trends, and Turning Points: Practical Marketing and Sales Forecasting Techniques.* NTC Publishing, 2000.

Evans, Michael. *Practical Business Forecasting.* Blackwell, 2003.

Forgang, William G. *Strategy-Specific Decision Making.* M.E. Sharpe, 2004.

Mentzer, John T., and Mark A. Moon. *Sales Forecasting Management: A Demand Management Approach.* Sage Publications, 2005.

Wallace, Thomas F., and Robert A. Stahl. *Master Scheduling in the 21st Century.* T.F. Wallace, 2003.

Darnay, ECDI

SALES MANAGEMENT

Sales management refers to the administration of the personal selling a company's product line(s). It includes the planning, implementation, and control of sales programs, as well as recruiting, training, motivating, and evaluating members of the sales force. In a small business, these various functions may be performed by the owner or by the sales manager. The fundamental role of the sales manager is to develop and administer a selling program that effectively contributes to the organization's goals. The sales manager for a small business would likely decide how many salespeople to employ, how best to select and train them, what sort of compensation and incentives to use to motivate them, what type of presentation they should make, and how the sales function should be structured for maximum contact with customers.

Sales management is just one facet of a company's overall marketing mix, which encompasses strategies related to the "four Ps": products, pricing, promotion, and place (distribution). Objectives related to promotion are achieved through three supporting functions: 1) advertising, which includes direct mail, radio, television, and print advertisements, among other media; 2) sales promotion, which includes tools such as coupons, rebates, contests, and samples; and (3) personal selling, which is the domain of the sales manager.

Although the role of sales managers is multidisciplinary in scope, their primary responsibilities are: 1) setting goals for a sales force; 2) planning, budgeting, and organizing a program to achieve those goals; 3) implementing the program; and 4) controlling and evaluating the results. Even when a sales force is already in place, the sales manager will likely view these responsibilities as an ongoing process necessary to adapt to both internal and external changes.

GOAL SETTING

Goal setting is usually based on a company's overall sales goals, modified by the mix of products to be moved. Overall sales goals must be met, of course, but balance must also be maintained. A company that makes three different types of boats, for instance, of which the highest-priced model has the highest profit margins but the lowest-priced boat is easiest to sell, the goal will be structured to move as many of the highest-priced models as possible. Balance between regions also enters the goal-setting process. Sales to some regions may be more difficult (far fewer lakes) but necessary to maintain the company's total volume. If multiple lines are sold (tenting and trailers, for instance), different goals will apply to each category. Goal setting will depend on product mix. In the usual case, past history will be a guide and goals will be set in light of the history—and desires to change past performance—by lifting all sales, high-margin sales, creating sales for new products, etc.

PLANNING, BUDGETING, AND ORGANIZING

After goals are set, the sales manager may accept, or be required to modify, the general approach to sales in the current year. Both ongoing patterns and new ones require budgeting and, occasionally, changes to the organization.

Fundamental structural issues are involved such as the distribution channel, the forces to be deployed, and the sales program (incentives, pricing schedules, cooperative advertising programs, etc.) that will be used. A company, for instance, may be engaged in making a transition from direct sales using its own sales branches as distributors to using independent distributors. The planning process in the first year may involve finding and starting three new distributors and closing two company branches and relocating its best sales people. In another operation, the goal may simply require adding four new sales people and training them. In yet another case, the company may have decided to distribute some of its production through a "Big Box," thus creating ill-will among its servicing retailers—and in consequence has decided to offer the retailers a more attractive sales program, higher co-op advertising participation, and high discounts on four occasions if they hold seasonal sales. Finally, in yet another case, no big changes are in the offing, but budgets must be formulated anyway, retiring salespeople replaced, and programs launched in the past continued.

For start-ups, of course, the sales organization must be built from scratch after its general structure has been determined. In such situations planning, budgeting, and organizing take on rather formidable dimensions. The ideal approach is to concentrate on hiring the best possible sales people, to bring them on board as rapidly as possible, and then using them to help with the process.

IMPLEMENTATION

Implementation of the plan will have different emphases depending on whether the operation is up and running or required to be built or rebuilt. Recruiting, training, and setting compensation are primary implementation activities of start-ups or expansions. So are designing sales territories and assigning sales goals to each.

Recruiting Recruiting salespeople ideally requires understanding of the customers and the market, not least its physical aspects, travel time needed to reach targeted points, and the type of selling involved. Experienced sales managers typically bring such skills to the job or, if brought in from a different field, will make some preliminary field trips to get a feel.

The manager may seek candidates through advertising, college recruiting, company sources, and employment agencies. Another excellent source of salespeople is—other salespeople. In this field, to be one is to know one. Sales recruiting has special characteristics difficult to describe in analytical terms—especially in the small business environment where relationships tend to be closer. But, indeed, in all areas of sales, managers rely a great deal on their experience of sales to find people

who have the special knack. Generalizations are dangerous, but good sales people have good communications skills, enjoy human contact, are disciplined, can tolerate rejection with good humor, respond to rewards, and have a high level of energy—often needed because sales may be tiring, may require many hours of standing, and occasionally physical effort in demonstrating products. In technical sales, an engineering background is often required in addition to favorable personality traits. Generalizations are dangerous because experienced people in this business know that often the outwardly least likely people turn out to be great producers whereas those who seem ideal miserably fail. Not everything can be determined by administering personality tests. Good sales people have something in common with entrepreneurs; both categories are notoriously diverse.

Training After recruiting a suitable sales force, the manager must determine how much and what type of training to provide. Most sales training emphasizes product, company, and industry knowledge. Only about 25 percent of the average company training program, in fact, addresses selling techniques. Because of the high cost, many small businesses try to limit the amount of training they provide. The average cost of training a person to sell industrial products, for example, commonly exceeds $30,000. Sales managers can achieve many benefits with competent training programs, however. For instance, research indicates that training reduces employee turnover, thereby lowering the effective cost of hiring new workers. Good training can also improve customer relations, increase employee morale, and boost sales. Common training methods include lectures, cases studies, role playing, demonstrations, on-the-job training, and self-study courses. Ideally, training should be an ongoing process that continually reinforces the company's goals.

Compensation After the sales force is in place, the manager must devise a means of compensating individuals. The ideal system of compensation reaches a balance between the needs of the person (income, recognition, prestige, etc.) and the goals of the company (controlling costs, boosting market share, increasing cash flow, etc.), so that a salesperson may achieve both through the same means. Most approaches to sales force compensation utilize a combination of salary and commission or salary and bonus. Salary gives a sales manager added control over the salesperson's activities, while commission provides the salesperson with greater motivation to sell.

Although financial rewards are the primary means of motivating workers, most sales organizations also employ other motivational techniques. Good sales managers recognize that salespeople have needs other than the basic ones satisfied by money. For example, they want to feel they are part of a winning team, that their jobs are secure, and that their efforts and contributions to the organization are recognized. Methods of meeting those needs include contests, vacations, and other performance-based prizes, in addition to self-improvement benefits such as tuition for graduate school. Another tool managers commonly use to stimulate their salespeople is quotas. Quotas, which can be set for factors such as the number of calls made per day, expenses consumed per month, or the number of new customers added annually, give salespeople a standard against which they can measure success.

Designing Territories and Allocating Sales Efforts In addition to recruiting, training, and motivating a sales force to achieve the company's goals, sales managers at most small businesses must decide how to designate sales territories and allocate the efforts of the sales team. Territories are geographic areas assigned to individual salespeople. The advantages of establishing territories are that they improve coverage of the market, reduce wasteful overlap of sales efforts, and allow each salesperson to define personal responsibility and judge individual success. However, many types of businesses, such as real estate and insurance companies, do not use territories.

Allocating people to different territories is an important sales management task. Typically, the top few territories produce a disproportionately high sales volume. This occurs because managers usually create smaller areas for trainees, medium-sized territories for more experienced team members, and larger areas for senior sellers. A drawback of that strategy, however, is that it becomes difficult to compare performance across territories. An alternate approach is to divide regions by existing and potential customer base. A number of computer programs exist to help sales managers effectively create territories according to their goals. Good scheduling and routing of sales calls can reduce waiting and travel time. Other common methods of reducing the costs associated with sales calls include contacting numerous customers at once during trade shows, and using telemarketing to qualify prospects before sending a salesperson to make a personal call.

CONTROLLING AND EVALUATING

After the sales plan has been implemented, the sales manager's responsibility becomes controlling and evaluating the program. During this stage, the sales manager compares the original goals and objectives with the actual accomplishments of the sales force. The performance of each individual is compared with goals or quotas, looking at elements such as expenses, sales volume, customer satisfaction, and cash flow.

An important consideration for the sales manager is profitability. Indeed, simple sales figures may not reflect an accurate image of the performance of the sales force. The manager must dig deeper by analyzing expenses, price-cutting initiatives, and long-term contracts with customers that will impact future income. An in-depth analysis of these and related influences will help the manager to determine true performance based on profits. For use in future goal-setting and planning efforts, the manager may also evaluate sales trends by different factors, such as product line, volume, territory, and market. After the manager analyzes and evaluates the achievements of the sales force, that information is used to make corrections to the current strategy and sales program. In other words, the sales manager returns to the initial goal-setting stage.

ENVIRONMENTS AND STRATEGIES

The goals and plans adopted by the sales manager will be greatly influenced by the company's industry orientation, competitive position, and market strategy. The basic industry orientations available to a firm include industrial goods, consumer durables, consumer nondurables, and services. Companies that manufacture industrial goods or sell highly technical services tend to be heavily dependent on personal selling as a marketing tool. Sales managers in those organizations characteristically focus on customer service and education and employ and train a relatively high-level sales force. In contrast, sales managers that sell consumer durables will likely integrate the efforts of their sales force into related advertising and promotional initiatives. Sales management efforts related to consumer nondurables and consumer services will generally emphasize volume sales, a comparatively low-caliber sales force, and an emphasis on high-volume customers. In certain types of service activities, e.g., consulting, market research, and advertising, sales are very often conducted by high-level executives or the principals who actually supervise the work to be performed—for example senior researchers or account executives.

REGULATION

Besides markets and industries, another chief environmental influence on the sales management process is government regulation. Indeed, selling activities at companies are regulated by a multitude of state and federal laws designed to protect consumers, foster competitive markets, and discourage unfair business practices.

Chief among anti-trust provisions affecting sales managers is the Robinson-Patman Act, which prohibits companies from engaging in price or service discrimination. In other words, a firm cannot offer special incentives to large customers based solely on volume, because such practices tend to hurt smaller customers. Companies can give discounts to buyers, but only if those incentives are based on real savings gleaned from manufacturing and distribution processes.

Similarly, the Sherman Act makes it illegal for a seller to force a buyer to purchase one product (or service) in order to get the opportunity to purchase another product—a practice referred to as a "tying agreement." A long-distance telephone company, for instance, cannot require its customers to purchase its telephone equipment as a prerequisite to buying its long-distance service. The Sherman Act also regulates reciprocal dealing arrangements, whereby companies agree to buy products from each other. Reciprocal dealing is considered anticompetitive because large buyers and sellers tend to have an unfair advantage over their smaller competitors.

Several consumer protection regulations also impact sales managers. The Fair Packaging and Labeling Act of 1966, for example, restricts deceptive labeling, and the Truth in Lending Act requires sellers to fully disclose all finance charges incorporated into consumer credit agreements. Cooling-off laws, which commonly exist at the state level, allow buyers to cancel contracts made with door-to-door sellers within a certain time frame. Additionally, the Federal Trade Commission (FTC) requires door-to-door sellers who work for companies engaged in interstate trade to clearly announce their purpose when calling on prospects.

BIBLIOGRAPHY

Calvin, Robert J. *Sales Management.* McGraw-Hill, 2001.

Cichelli, David J. *Compensating the Sales Force: A Practical Guide to Designing Winning Sales Compensation Plans.* McGraw-Hill, 2004.

"Sales Force Control." *Journal of Personal Selling & Sales Management.* Winter 2005.

"Sales Management Functions—analysis—planning—strategy—implementation—decision making—quotas." *Journal of Personal Selling & Sales Management.* Winter 2005.

Simpkins, Robert A. *The Secrets of Great Sales Management.* AMACOM, 2004.

Hillstrom, Northern Lights
updated by Magee, ECDI

SALES PROMOTION

Sales promotion is one level or type of marketing aimed either at the consumer or at the distribution channel (in the form of sales-incentives). It is used to introduce new product, clear out inventories, attract traffic, and to lift sales temporarily. It is more closely associated with the marketing of products than of services. The American Marketing Association (AMA), in its Web-based "Dictionary of Marketing Terms," defines sales promotion as "media and nonmedia marketing pressure applied for a predetermined, limited period of time in order to stimulate trial, increase consumer demand, or improve product availability." Business pundits and academic students of business have developed almost fancifully sophisticated views of sales promotion. In down-to-earth terms it is a way of lifting sales temporarily by appealing to economic motives and impulse-buying behavior. The chief tools of sales promotion are discounts ("sales"), distribution of samples and coupons, the holding of sweepstakes and contests, special store displays, and offering premiums and rebates. All of these techniques require some kind of communication. Thus sales promotion and advertising are difficult to distinguish.

The need for promotion arises from the intensity of competition. Sellers must somehow attract customers' attention. In the open markets of old (and farmers markets of today), sellers did and do this by shouting, joking with customers, and sometimes by holding up a squealing piglet for everyone to see. Priya Raghubir and his coauthors, writing in *California Management Review,* identify "three faces" of consumer promotions: these are information, economic incentive, and emotional appeal. Information may take the form of advertising the availability of something, incentives are offered in the form of discounts, and emotional appeals are made by displays and, of course, by the low price itself.

Precisely because sales promotions must provide *incentives*—whether to the distribution channel, the company's own sales people, or to the consumer—they cost money by definition and must produce additional volume to pay for the expenditures. A grand sale that clears out the inventory but, with added advertising costs factored in, reduces margin too is—a failure. Sales promotions therefore must be carefully calibrated to achieve the purpose. Holding promotions too frequently will habituate customers to buy only when promotions are in effect. Avoiding promotions altogether will let competitors draw customers away. Alas, business never fails but to challenge the participant....

GROWTH OF SALES PROMOTION

Craig Endicott and Kenneth Wylie, writing for *Advertising Age* in the magazine's 62nd annual Agency Report, indicate a continued shift of revenues in advertising from traditional to new forms of media. They label the new forms as "marketing services" and comment as follows: "Marketing services—identified as all forms of interactive, sales promotion and direct marketing in this report—grew 11.3% to $7.66 billion in revenue in the U.S. [in 2005]; traditional advertising and its media component advanced to $12.02 billion, a 5.1% advance that was slightly stronger than last year." The growth of sales promotion, a significant portion of total marketing services expenditures, is no doubt in part due to the proliferation of media channels by cable, the availability of the Internet to channel direct marketing messages, and simply the fact that advertising has become so ubiquitous it has become less effective: people tune (or mute) it out.

CONSUMER PROMOTIONS

Consumer sales promotions are steered toward the ultimate product users—typically individual shoppers in the local market—but the same techniques can be used to promote products sold by one business to another, such as computer systems, cleaning supplies, and machinery. In contrast, trade sales promotions target resellers—wholesalers and retailers—who carry the marketer's product. Following are some of the key techniques used in consumer-oriented sales promotions.

Price Deals A consumer price deal saves the buyer money when a product is purchased. The main types of price deals include discounts, bonus pack deals, refunds or rebates, and coupons. Price deals are usually intended to encourage trial use of a new product or line extension, to recruit new buyers for a mature product, or to convince existing customers to increase their purchases, accelerate their use, or purchase multiple units. Price deals work most effectively when price is the consumer's foremost criterion or when brand loyalty is low.

Buyers may learn about price discounts either at the point of sale or through advertising. At the point of sale, price reductions may be posted on the package, on signs near the product, or in storefront windows. Many types of advertisements can be used to notify consumers of upcoming discounts, including fliers and newspaper and television ads. Price discounts are especially common in the food industry, where local supermarkets run weekly specials. Price discounts may be initiated by the manufacturer, the retailer, or the distributor. For instance, a manufacturer may "pre-price" a product and then convince the retailer to participate in this short-term discount through extra incentives. For price reduction strategies to be effective, they must have the support of all distributors in the channel. Existing customers perceive discounts as rewards and often respond by buying in larger quantities. Price discounts alone, however, usually do not induce first-time buyers.

Another type of price deal is the bonus pack or banded pack. When a bonus pack is offered, an extra amount of the product is free when a standard size of the product is bought at the regular price. This technique is routinely used in the marketing of cleaning products, food, and health and beauty aids to introduce a new or larger size. A bonus pack rewards present users but may have little appeal to users of competitive brands. A banded pack offer is when two or more units of a product are sold at a reduction of the regular single-unit price. Sometimes the products are physically banded together, such as in toothbrush and toothpaste offers.

A refund or rebate promotion is an offer by a marketer to return a certain amount of money when the product is purchased alone or in combination with other products. Refunds aim to increase the quantity or frequency of purchase, to encourage customers to "load up" on the product. This strategy dampens competition by temporarily taking consumers out of the market, stimulates the purchase of postponable goods such as major appliances, and creates on-shelf excitement by encouraging special displays. Refunds and rebates are generally viewed as a reward for purchase, and they appear to build brand loyalty rather than diminish it.

Coupons are legal certificates offered by manufacturers and retailers. They grant specified savings on selected products when presented for redemption at the point of purchase. Manufacturers sustain the cost of advertising and distributing their coupons, redeeming their face values, and paying retailers a handling fee. Retailers who offer double or triple the amount of the coupon shoulder the extra cost. Retailers who offer their own coupons incur the total cost, including paying the face value. In this way, retail coupons are equivalent to a cents-off deal.

Manufacturers disseminate coupons in many ways. They may be delivered directly by mail, dropped door to door, or distributed through a central location such as a shopping mall. Coupons may also be distributed through the media—magazines, newspapers, Sunday supplements, or free-standing inserts (FSI) in newspapers. Coupons can be inserted into, attached to, or printed on a package, or they may be distributed by a retailer who uses them to generate store traffic or to tie in with a manufacturer's promotional tactic. Retailer-sponsored coupons are typically distributed through print advertising or at the point of sale. Sometimes, though, specialty retailers or newly opened retailers will distribute coupons door to door or through direct mail.

Contests/Sweepstakes The main difference between contests and sweepstakes is that contests require entrants to perform a task or demonstrate a skill that is judged in order to be deemed a winner, while sweepstakes involve a random drawing or chance contest that may or may not have an entry requirement. At one time, contests were more commonly used as sales promotions, mostly due to legal restrictions on gambling that many marketers feared might apply to sweepstakes. But the use of sweepstakes as a promotional tactic has grown dramatically in recent decades, partly because of legal changes and partly because of their lower cost. Administering a contest once cost about $350 per thousand entries, compared to just $2.75 to $3.75 per thousand entries in a sweepstakes. Furthermore, participation in contests is very low compared to sweepstakes, since they require some sort of skill or ability.

Special Events According to the consulting firm International Events Group (IEG), businesses spend over $2 billion annually to link their products with everything from jazz festivals to golf tournaments to stock car races. In fact, large companies like RJR Nabisco and Anheuser-Busch have special divisions that handle only special events. Special events marketing offers a number of advantages. First, events tend to attract a homogeneous audience that is very appreciative of the sponsors. Therefore, if a product fits well with the event and its audience, the impact of the sales promotion will be high. Second, event sponsorship often builds support among employees—who may receive acknowledgment for their participation—and within the trade. Finally, compared to producing a series of ads, event management is relatively simple. Many elements of event sponsorship are prepackaged and reusable, such as booths, displays, and ads. Special events marketing is available to small businesses, as well, through sponsorship of events on the community level.

Premiums A premium is tangible compensation that is given as an incentive for performing a particular act—usually buying a product. The premium may be given for free, or may be offered to consumers for a significantly reduced price. Some examples of premiums include receiving a prize in a cereal box or a free garden tool for visiting the grand opening of a hardware store. Incentives that are given for free at the time of purchase are called direct premiums. These offers provide instant gratification, plus there is no confusion about returning coupons or box tops, or saving bar codes or proofs of purchase.

Other types of direct premiums include traffic builders, door openers, and referral premiums. The garden tool is an example of a traffic-builder premium—an incentive to lure a prospective buyer to a store. A door-opener premium is directed to customers at home or to business people in their offices. For example, a homeowner may receive a free clock radio for allowing an insurance

agent to enter their home and listening to his sales pitch. Similarly, an electronics manufacturer might offer free software to an office manager who agrees to an on-site demonstration. The final category of direct premiums, referral premiums, reward the purchaser for referring the seller to other possible customers.

Mail premiums, unlike direct premiums, require the customer to perform some act in order to obtain a premium through return mail. An example might be a limited edition toy car offered by a marketer in exchange for one or more proofs-of-purchase and a payment covering the cost of the item plus handling. The premium is still valuable to the consumer because he or she cannot readily buy the item for the same amount.

Continuity Programs Continuity programs retain brand users over a long time period by offering ongoing motivation or incentives. Continuity programs demand that consumers keep buying the product in order to get the premium in the future. Trading stamps, popularized in the 1950s and 1960s, are prime examples. Consumers usually received one stamp for every dime spent at a participating store. The stamp company provided redemption centers where the stamps were traded for merchandise. A catalog listing the quantity of stamps required for each item was available at the participating stores. Today, airlines' frequent-flyer clubs, hotels' frequent-traveler plans, retailers' frequent-shopper programs, and bonus-paying credit cards are common continuity programs. When competing brands have reached parity in terms of price and service, continuity programs sometimes prove a deciding factor among those competitors. By rewarding long-standing customers for their loyalty, continuity programs also reduce the threat of new competitors entering a market.

Sampling A sign of a successful marketer is getting the product into the hands of the consumer. Sometimes, particularly when a product is new or is not a market leader, an effective strategy is giving a sample product to the consumer, either free or for a small fee. But in order for sampling to change people's future purchase decisions, the product must have benefits or features that will be obvious during the trial.

There are several means of disseminating samples to consumers. The most popular has been through the mail, but increases in postage costs and packaging requirements have made this method less attractive. An alternative is door-to-door distribution, particularly when the items are bulky and when reputable distribution organizations exist. This method permits selective sampling of neighborhoods, dwellings, or even people. Another method is distributing samples in conjunction with advertising. An ad may include a coupon that the consumer can mail in for the product, or it may include an address or phone number for ordering. Direct sampling can be achieved through prime media using scratch-and-sniff cards and slim foil pouches, or through retailers using special displays or a person hired to hand out samples to passing customers. Though this last technique may build goodwill for the retailer, some retailers resent the inconvenience and require high payments for their cooperation.

A final form of sample distribution deals with specialty types of sampling. For instance, some companies specialize in packing samples together for delivery to homogeneous consumer groups, such as newlyweds, new parents, students, or tourists. Such packages may be delivered at hospitals, hotels, or dormitories and include a number of different types of products.

TRADE PROMOTIONS

A trade sales promotion is targeted at resellers—wholesalers and retailers—who distribute manufacturers' products to the ultimate consumers. The objectives of sales promotions aimed at the trade are different from those directed at consumers. In general, trade sales promotions hope to accomplish four goals: 1) Develop in-store merchandising support, as strong support at the retail store level is the key to closing the loop between the customer and the sale. 2) Control inventory by increasing or depleting inventory levels, thus helping to eliminate seasonal peaks and valleys. 3) Expand or improve distribution by opening up new sales areas (trade promotions are also sometimes used to distribute a new size of the product). 4) Generate excitement about the product among those responsible for selling it. Some of the more common forms of trade promotions—profiled below—include point-of-purchase displays, trade shows, sales meetings, sales contests, push money, deal loaders, and promotional allowances.

Point-of-Purchase (POP) Displays Manufacturers provide point-of-purchase (POP) display units free to retailers in order to promote a particular brand or group of products. The forms of POP displays include special racks, display cartons, banners, signs, price cards, and mechanical product dispensers. Probably the most effective way to ensure that a reseller will use a POP display is to design it so that it will generate sales for the retailer. High product visibility is the basic goal of POP displays. In industries such as the grocery field where a shopper spends about three-tenths of a second viewing a product, anything increasing product visibility is valuable. POP displays also provide or remind consumers about important decision information, such as the product's name,

appearance, and sizes. The theme of the POP display should coordinate with the theme used in ads and by salespeople.

Trade Shows Thousands of manufacturers display their wares and take orders at trade shows. In fact, companies spend over $9 billion yearly on these shows. Trade shows provide a major opportunity to write orders for products. They also provide a chance to demonstrate products, disseminate information, answer questions, and be compared directly to competitors. Related to trade shows, but on a smaller scale, are sales meetings sponsored by manufacturers or wholesalers. Whereas trade shows are open to all potential customers, sales meetings are targeted toward the company's sales force and/or independent sales agents. These meetings are usually conducted regionally and directed by sales managers. The meetings may be used to motivate sales agents, to explain the product or the promotional campaign, or simply to answer questions. For resellers and salespeople, sales contests can also be an effective motivation. Typically, a prize is awarded to the organization or person who exceeds a quota by the largest percentage.

Push Money Similarly, push money (PM)—also known as spiffs—is an extra payment given to salespeople for meeting a specified sales goal. For example, a manufacturer of refrigerators might pay a $30 bonus for each unit of model A, and a $20 bonus for each unit of model B, sold between March 1 and September 1. At the end of that period, the salesperson would send evidence of these sales to the manufacturer and receive a check in return. Although some people see push money as akin to bribery, many manufacturers offer it.

Deal Loaders A deal loader is a premium given by a manufacturer to a retailer for ordering a certain quantity of product. Two types of deal loaders are most typical. The first is a buying loader, which is a gift given for making a specified order size. The second is a display loader, which means the display is given to the retailer after the campaign. For instance, General Electric may have a display containing appliances as part of a special program. When the program is over, the retailer receives all the appliances on the display if a specified order size was achieved.

Trade Deals Trade deals are special price concessions superseding, for a limited time, the normal purchasing discounts given to the trade. Trade deals include a group of tactics having a common theme—to encourage sellers to specially promote a product. The marketer might receive special displays, larger-than-usual orders, superior in-store locations, or greater advertising effort. In exchange, the retailer might receive special allowances, discounts, goods, or money. In many industries, trade deals are the primary expectation for retail support, and the marketing funds spent in this area are considerable. There are two main types of trade deals: buying allowances and advertising/display allowances.

Buying Allowances A buying allowance is a bonus paid by a manufacturer to a reseller when a certain amount of product is purchased during a specific time period. For example, a reseller who purchases at least 15 cases of product might receive a buying allowance of $6.00 off per case, while a purchase of at least 20 cases would result in $7.00 off per case, and so forth. The payment may take the form of a check or a reduction in the face value of an invoice. In order to take advantage of a buying allowance, some retailers engage in "forward buying." In essence, they order more merchandise than is needed during the deal period, then store the extra merchandise to sell later at regular prices. This assumes that the savings gained through the buying allowance is greater than the cost of warehousing and transporting the extra merchandise. Some marketers try to discourage forward buying, since it reduces profit margins and tends to create cyclical peaks and troughs in demand for the product.

The slotting allowance is a controversial form of buying allowance. Slotting allowances are fees retailers charge manufacturers for each space or slot on the shelf or in the warehouse that new products will occupy. The controversy stems from the fact that in many instances this allowance amounts to little more than paying a bribe to the retailer to convince him or her to carry your company's products. But many marketers are willing to pay extra to bring their products to the attention of consumers who are pressed for time in the store. Slotting allowances sometimes buy marketers prime spaces on retail shelves, at eye level or near the end of aisles.

The final type of buying allowance is a free goods allowance. In this case, the manufacturer offers a certain amount of product to wholesalers or retailers at no cost if they purchase a stated amount of the same or a different product. The allowance takes the form of free merchandise rather than money.

Advertising Allowances An advertising allowance is a dividend paid by a marketer to a reseller for advertising its product. The money can only be used to purchase advertising—for example, to print flyers or run ads in a local newspaper. But some resellers take advantage of the system, so many manufacturers require verification. A display allowance is the final form of trade promotional allowance. Some manufacturers pay retailers extra to highlight their display from the many available every week. The payment can take the form of cash or goods. Retailers must furnish written certification of compliance with the terms of the contract before they are paid. Retailers are most likely to select displays that yield high volume and are easy to assemble.

BIBLIOGRAPHY

Boone, Louis E. *Contemporary Marketing 2006.* Thomson South-Western, 2006.

Cummins, Julian, and Roddy Mullin. *Sales Promotion: How to Create, Implement and Integrate Campaigns That Really Work.* Kogan Page, 2002.

Endicott, Craig R., and Kenneth Wylie. Agency Report. *Advertising Age.* 1 May 2006.

Raghubir, Priya, J. Jeffrey Inman, and Hans Grande. "The Three Faces of Consumer Promotions." *California Management Review.* Summer 2004.

Taylor, Derek. *Hospitality Sales and Promotion.* Butterworth-Heinemann, 2001.

van Heerde, Harold J., Peter S.H. Leeflang, and Dick R. Wittink. "Decomposing the Sales Promotion Bump with Store Data." Marketing Science. *Summer 2004.*

Hillstrom, Northern Lights
updated by Magee, ECDI

SARBANES-OXLEY

On December 2, 2001, the Enron Corporation, a highly-respected and rapidly growing energy-trading company filed for bankruptcy. It had inflated its earnings by nearly $600 million in the 1994-2001 period. This had become known less than a month before. Enron, with assets of $62.8 billion, became the largest bankruptcy in U.S. history. Its stock closed at 72 cents on December 2. It had been over $75 a share one year earlier. Investors lost billions and employees lost their life savings. Exactly 241 days later, on July 30, 2002, the President signed into law the Public Company Accounting Reform and Investor Protection Act of 2002. The act's two chief sponsors were Senator Paul Sarbanes (D-MD) and Representative Michael G. Oxley (R-OH). The legislation thus carried the short title of Sarbanes-Oxley Act of 2002, subsequently abbreviated as SOX or SarbOx. In the opinion of most observers of securities legislation, SOX is viewed as the most important new law enacted since the passage of the Securities and Exchange Act of 1934.

The Enron debacle would have been prevented if audits of the company had detected accounting irregularities or if the company would have been required to disclose transactions not directly reflected on its balance sheet. Incentives and rewards used within the company and dealings with entities imprecisely associated with Enron contributed to the massive failure. Furthermore, insider trading took place toward the end while employees holding company stock as part of their pensions were prevented from trading them during a so-called "blackout" period.

Sarbanes-Oxley was principally a reaction to this failure. However, during this same period, the equally dramatic actual or pending bankruptcies of WorldCom, a long-distance telecommunications company, and Tyco, a diversified equipment manufacturer, influenced the content of the legislation. SOX thus deals with 1) reform of auditing and accounting procedures, including internal controls, 2) the oversight responsibilities of corporate directors and officers and regulation of conflicts of interest, insider dealings, and the disclosure of special compensation and bonuses, 3) conflicts of interest by stock analysts, 4) earlier and more complete disclosure of information on anything that directly and indirectly influences or might influence financial results, 5) criminalization of fraudulent handling of documents, interference with investigations, and violation of disclosure rules, and 6) requiring chief executives to certify financial results personally and to sign federal income tax documents.

SUMMARY OF PROVISIONS

Sarbanes-Oxley governs the activities of *publicly traded* companies. It aims at protecting investors who, unlike investors in privately held corporations, are presumed to be at a greater distance from management and therefore more vulnerable. Any and all companies, of any size, the stock of which is publicly traded (whether on a stock exchange or over the counter) are subject to SOX; thus it touches a certain range of small business as well.

The act has 11 titles, i.e., major subdivisions. These in turn are divided into sections. The sections of Title IV, for instance, begin with Section 401 and end with Section 409. It is common practice in referencing pieces of legislation to refer to section numbers. Some sections are more controversial or difficult than others and will be more frequently mentioned in articles. An example is Section 404 in SOX which deals with internal accounting controls—which has imposed significant data processing costs. In the following explanations sectional references are omitted. A title-by-title summary follows.

Title I – Public Accounting Oversight Board Title I creates an independent Public Accounting Oversight Board under the general oversight of the Securities and Exchange Commission. PAOB is charged with newly registering, regulating, inspecting, and generally overseeing companies that audit publicly traded companies. PAOB owes its origin to auditing failures that surfaced during the Enron bankruptcy. The Board is self-funded by the fees that it is authorized to charge.

Title II – Auditor Independence Next is Title II which legislates the behavior of auditing firms in particular. Its most important provisions severely restrict auditing firms from carrying out compensated activities for their auditing clients that fall outside the boundaries of auditing narrowly viewed. Such "outside" activities include the provision of services like bookkeeping, accounting, financial information systems design, appraisals, and many other jobs. This prohibition is based on the notion that audit firms may be influenced in their *audit* practices *in favor* of a client from whom they are getting other profitable business. Other provisions of Title II require that audit partners are rotated after five years of service auditing a client (lest relations become too cozy) and also prohibit financial officers of the audited firm from having been employed by the audit company.

Title III – Corporate Responsibility Title III specifies the responsibilities of public companies in relation to financial and accounting behavior. It requires that companies establish audit committees made up of independent board members who have no financial ties to the company; they may, of course, be paid for their board duties. The chief executive and the chief financial officer both must certify the material correctness of financial statements underlying audit reports. It forbids officers and board members from attempt improperly to influence audits. If financial statements must be revised because of misconduct, the CEO and CFO forfeit bonuses or incentives or profits from securities sales. Directors and officers may be barred from service for violating certain SEC requirements. While the trading of a pension fund is suspended (a "blackout" period), insider trading is prohibited as well—a provision that also harks back to Enron where insiders traded while pension funds were frozen.

Title IV – Enhanced Financial Disclosures The intention of Title IV is to cause corporations to make public transactions not heretofore normally required to be discussed, such as off-balance sheet transactions (of the sort that, in part, caused Enron's failure) and relationships with "unconsolidated entities" that could influence the company's finances. The SEC is charged with studying the matter in greater detail as well. Directors, officers, and stockholders with 10 percent or more holdings are required to make certain transactions public—such as special bonuses and stock grants or large dispositions of stock. Companies are prohibited from making loans to any director or executive (echoing a problem discovered at WorldCom). The Title also mandates that companies with codes of ethics make these codes public. Changes in financial conditions must be disclosed in real time. Another important requirement of the Title is that every annual report must contain a special report on internal controls. Such controls must be established and maintained and then assessed every year. (This is the "costly" Section 404.) Such controls consist of special methods of testing financial reports and data to determine their truth and coherence.

Title V – Analyst Conflicts of Interest Securities analysts who recommend the purchase of securities to the public are addressed by Title V. It requires that National Securities Exchanges and associations of registered securities formulate and adopt rules governing conflicts of interest for analysts. The aim of the Title is to prevent situations in which favorable recommendations are in effect "bought" by indirect favors of one sort or another.

Titles VI and VII – SEC Role and Studies These titles address the SEC's role and specify studies to be undertaken.

Title VIII - Corporate and Criminal Fraud Accountability Title VIII makes it a felony to destroy documents and to create fraudulent documents in order to thwart federal investigations. It mandates auditors to keep all paper work related to an audit for five years. It changes the statute of limitations on securities fraud claims and extends whistleblower protections to those who disclose closely held company information to parties in a lawsuit. Title VIII also establishes a new crime for securities frauds punishable by up to10 years in prison and fines.

Title IX - White Collar Crime Penalty Enhancements The best-known provision of Title IX is that financial reports made to the SEC must be certified by the CEO and CFO who must state that such reports are in compliance with the securities act and include all material aspects of the company's finances. Violations of this provision carry a fine of $500,000 and up to five years in prison. Other provisions in this Title address mail and wire fraud, making it a crime to interfere with official proceedings and tampering with records; give the SEC the right to seek a court-ordered freeze of payments to company directors, agents, and employees; and enable the SEC to prevent any person convicted of securities fraud from holding office as a director or officer of a publicly traded company.

Title X – Corporate Tax Returns This Title requires that the CEO sign corporate income tax returns.

Title XI – Corporate Fraud and Accountability This Title, which Congress entitles as the "Corporate Fraud Accountability Act of 2002," specifically amends the U.S. Code to make tampering with records and interfering with official proceedings a crime and sets the penalty for this crime (a fine or imprisonment for no more than 20 years). It gives the SEC authority to temporarily freeze extraordinary payments to directors, officers, agents and employees of a company during investigations of security law violations, and codifies the SEC's right to prohibit persons convicted of securities fraud from serving as a director or officer of a public company.

MAJOR DOS AND DON'TS

Sarbanes-Oxley can also be reduced to 13 dos and don'ts—provided here strictly for reference and as reminders. The publicly traded company, needless to say, is well advised to implement SOX requirement only after close study of the law itself with the help of experts. The list follows:

1. Audit firms shall be registered. They must do audits only. If they do other work for a company, they must *not* do audits for that company.

2. The company's audit committee members shall be independent board members.

3. Stock analysts shall be subject to conflict of interest rules.

4. Companies must disclose *all* pertinent information that may in any way affect company finances, whether on or off the balance sheet.

5. Companies shall not lend money to executive officers or directors.

6. CEO and CFO compensation, bonuses, and profit sharing shall be reported to the public.

7. Insider trades must be made public immediately.

8. Insiders shall not trade company stock during periods of pension fund blackouts.

9. Financial reports must be certified by the CEO and CFO.

10. Financial reports must be accompanied by a special report on internal controls and an assessment on how well they work.

11. Federal income tax filings must be signed by the CEO.

12. Whistleblowers shall be protected.

13. Violators shall pay higher fines and spend longer times in prison than heretofore.

EVOLUTION AND COST

In early 2006, implementation of Sarbanes-Oxley was well underway. The Public Company Accounting Oversight Board was in operation and had issued interim standards as of April 16, 2003. Costs of implementation have shown up most dramatically as information technology expenditures in support of Section 404 compliance (accounting controls). Wikipedia, in its article on SOX, citing Financial Executives International (FEI) data, based on 217 companies with revenues over $5 billion, indicated average compliance to have been $4.36 million per company. Compliance costs for companies with lower revenues have averaged $1.9 million. Opinion on the overall benefits of Sarbanes-Oxley is divided. Some claim that the financial activities of publicly traded companies are still severely under-regulated while others hold that SOX was necessary but that some of its requirements are not cost-effective.

BIBLIOGRAPHY

"A Bird's Eye View of the Enron Debacle." American Institute of Certified Public Accountants (AICPA). Available from http://www.aicpa.org/info/birdseye02.htm. Retrieved on 20 April 2006.

Public Company Accounting Oversight Board (PCAOB). PCAOB Web Page. Available from http://www.pcaobus.org/index.aspx. Retrieved on 20 April 2006.

"Sarbanes-Oxley Act." Wikipedia. Available from http://en.wikipedia.org/wiki/Sarbanes-Oxley_Act. Retrieved on 21 April 2006.

"Summary of Sarbanes-Oxley Act of 2002." American Institute of Certified Public Accountants (AICPA). Available from http://www.aicpa.org/info/sarbanes_oxley_summary.htm. Retrieved on 20 April 2006.

U.S. Congress. *Sarbanes-Oxley Act of 2002.* Available from http://www.law.uc.edu/CCL/SOact/soact.pdf. Retrieved on 20 April 2006.

Darnay, ECDI

SCALABILITY

While the word "scalability" refers generally to the ability to increase the size of any system in a linear manner without changing its fundamental properties, in the Internet environment and, more broadly in the world of networked computers, the word has come to refer to the ability to grow a network or Web site at the same rate at which use of the system is growing. Peter Loshin and his co-authors, writing in their book, *Electronic Commerce*, define scalability as follow: "The ability of a system with multiple available processors to call as many of those processors into service as necessary when system load increases, as well as the ability of that system to be expanded." Since all of the work on a Web site must be performed by central processing units (CPUs), the number of those processors and the manner in which they are linked is central to the concept. Loshin et al. link the concept to "performance," which they define, citing others, as "the ability to effectively increase throughput as needed on a single CPU in response to increased systems load." Performance is often an important aspect of adding users to a network.

Scalability became a central concern in the dot-com industry because popular Web sites can exhibit explosive growth. If they are poorly designed or difficult to scale up (because they slow down substantially as more nodes are added) demand is difficult to satisfy and traffic will decline.

While specialized software exists for those who want to attempt scalability projects on their own, many firms offer this service and help businesses design their sites to become efficient models of scalability. These firms are experts in the latest technological innovations and specialize in tiered Internet architecture that allows the site to grow without having to rewrite mainframe systems, while at the same time making better use of existing servers. They also help larger sites set up subdirectories within the domain directory to help serve a large number of accounts simultaneously. By performing these functions, scalability experts can help prevent Web site crashes and save the company lost revenue and damaged reputations.

The inability for an e-commerce site to scale properly could cripple their business. As Nicholas G. Carr stated in an article that appeared in *The Standard:* "On the Internet, if you can't scale—if you can't get really big really fast—you're nowhere. And it's not enough for just your technology to be scalable. Your entire business model has to have scalability, as well; you need to be able to quickly extend your business into new markets, either horizontally or vertically. 'Will it scale?' is one of the first questions venture capitalists ask."

While scalability is a critical issue for dot-coms, the actual advantage that comes with growing up to become a large Web site can still be debated. A larger site can appear to be more of a threat to a possible competitor that is thinking about entering the market, so much so that small sites are being bought up by larger sites in an effort cut down on the competition. This sort of consolidation can get pretty expensive, and presents a whole new set of scalability issues for the company that is doing the consolidating. Many dot-coms have learned the hard way about the problems that come with rapid and immense growth. A lot of the time, it is the consumer that gets hurt the most.

Carr sums it up by stating: "While scalability will continue to be critical for e-businesses, I doubt scale itself will provide much of an advantage. Companies will need to be able to expand their businesses fast, but their bigness won't ensure lasting success. Rather, once they've scaled up in one market, they'll need to immediately look for new markets in which to replicate their growth. Defense was the name of the game in the old economy. In the new one, offense is everything."

SEE ALSO *Web Site Design*

BIBLIOGRAPHY

Carr, Nicholas G. "The Myth of Scalability." *The Standard.* 10 January 2000.

Killelea, Patrick. *Web Performance Tuning.* O'Reilly, 2002.

Loshin, Peter, John Vacca, and Paul Murphy. *Electronic Commerce.* Charles River Media, 2004.

Hillstrom, Northern Lights
updated by Magee, ECDI

SEARCH ENGINES

What is almost certain is that this entry on search engines will soon be obsolete—so rapid and dynamic are the changes that affect this central technology and service on the Internet. Thus in the entry published in the last edition of this volume the name Google did not even appear, but just a few years later Google has become the leading search engine provider the world over. So what *is* a search engine?

GENERAL ASPECTS

Search engines are software systems that associate search words entered by a user, looking for information, with websites on the World Wide Web that contain the words of the query. To accomplish this linking, search engines must be backed by databases that hold words that Web sites use as linked lists. Search words may produce just a handful or a very large number of Web sites. The search word "supercalifragilisticexpialidocious" produced around 294,000 hits in 2006 on Google; the somewhat obscure and specialized word "nunciature" (the office or period of office of a nuncio) produced 82,400 hits; the word "nuncio" itself (an ambassador for the papacy) yielded 1,050,000 hits. The name Chu Yuan-chang, the 14th century founder of the Ming Dynasty in China, produced 725 hits. It is difficult to find stand-alone search words with a low number of hits; even misspellings bring rich results—because words are often misspelled on Web pages too and dutifully indexed by the search engines. This very wealth of hits makes it necessary for search engines to store additional information about every Web site in order to enable the engine somehow to present results in some kind of rationally ranked order. Complex algorithms are used to rank hits. The principal method is to present those sites first which have been clicked on most frequently in the past; and sites with more links to other sites get preference, all things equal.

A search engine, thus, requires its own internal logic and functionality, the software, and a database. But this database must first be built, maintained, updated, and grown as new sites are added to the Internet. Search engines, therefore, have a massive data acquisition function. In the early days the databases were built by people who scanned the web, followed links on Web sites, and indexed new pages they found. This technique is still in use with specialized Web sites and, until October 2002, was used by the world's second-ranking search engine, Yahoo. In the mid-2000s the databases of almost all search engines are built and maintained by search robots that seek out sites and capture their contents for indexing—unless the site itself prohibits this activity. The robots are themselves software programs. They are known as "crawlers" because they "crawl the Web" acquiring information. Alternatively, Web site owners can also register their sites with search engines—a technique used by commercial sites eager to be found.

Search engines are 1) technologies of searching, 2) databases in support of searching, and 3) services provided to users. Search engine owners can cover their costs by all three means. The technology they own can be licensed or deployed for others at a fee; the databases can be made available for money; and the services provided can be paid for using advertising. The most effective linking of the search function itself with advertising was pioneered by Google under the name "Adwords." Specific words are sold to advertisers. When searches using the words appear, the advertisers' small ads are displayed with search results. Advertisers pay a fee when the engine users "click through" to the advertiser's own site. Other techniques make use of search words or phrases and display closely matching spot ads on the Web page.

ENGINES AND THE INTERNET

The Internet owes its dramatic growth to the development of search engines. The first such engine was Lycos, launched in mid-1994 with 54,000 documents. Using its crawler technology, it had expanded its database to 1.5 million documents by early 1995 and had 60 million by the end of 1996. Another claimant to the founding role was AltaVista, introduced in 1995 and still active on the Web. Until Lycos and AltaVista appeared, access to the Internet required advanced knowledge of Web addresses, and roaming the Internet involved following links from site to site as these referred to each other.

The services provided by search engines become obvious with a few statistics. According to the Internet Systems Consortium (ISC), which conducts four surveys every year, in January 2006 around 395 million Internet hosts were in operation, each one hosting multiple sites, each site consisting of several Web pages on average. Extremely simple searches on leading engines provided up to 17 billion hits on Google in 2006 (for the word "the," for instance); AltaVista produced 7.4 billion, Ask.com 2.1 billion, and MSN 2.4 billion hits on the word. AltaVista uses Yahoo technology; Yahoo itself, asked to search for "the," simply shrugged off the labor and provided a single hit on a corporation with the THE acronym. Some estimates put the number of pages on the Internet at hundreds of billions, but as the ISC points out from a depth of survey experience, it is not possible to determine the actual size of the Internet. In any case, several million hosts, never mind 17 billion pages, are already astronomically big numbers. The ability of search engines to provide access to such magnitudes in matters of a second or so makes the Internet the useful phenomenon that it is. The rankings of hits, which actually reflect frequency of use by others, makes using very massive search results practical. Who, after all, can afford to review 60,000 hits—or even 700.

STRUCTURE OF THE INDUSTRY

Search Engine Watch, a Web journal concentrating on search engines and related matters, began operations in 1997, thus three years after the first search engine appeared. The company offers prizes, has public information as well as a membership service, and is an excellent source of developments in this field. Search Engine Watch (hereafter referred to as SEW) produces rankings and technical information about this industry. What follows has been gleaned largely from searchenginewatch.com.

Search Engines SEW identifies Google, Yahoo, and Ask.com as the top search engines on the Internet. Ask.com may be more familiar to users as AskJeeves.com; the company simplified its name in 2006. All three of these leaders began with proprietary methods and technologies. Google's search engine is the most widely used by others under license. Yahoo, which began by using human indexers, began to shift its data acquisition processes to crawlers in October 2002 after a period of using Google technology. Ask.com's basic search engine was developed by Teoma, a company that it owns, but Ask also developed an expert-based indexing technique that, in the past, enabled it to serve more "human language" queries.

In a second tier SEW lists AllTheWeb.com (powered by Yahoo), AOL Search (powered by Google), and HotBot (using Google, Yahoo, and Teoma—currently merged with Ask).

Under a category SEW calls "Other Choices," it lists AltaVista (using Yahoo), Gigablast (a tiny engine with propriety technology), LookSmart (compiled by people), Lycos (using HotBot and others), MSN (Microsoft's search engine, developing proprietary methods), Netscape (using Google), and Open Directory (using Google).

As is evident from this listing, the number of proprietary technologies widely used is much smaller than the search engines on offer—many of them on the Web using Google and Yahoo. But each of the search engines has its special features and add-ons.

Metacrawlers Chris Sherman, writing for Search Engine Watch, defined this category as follows: "Unlike search engines, metacrawlers don't crawl the Web themselves to build listings. Instead, they allow searches to be sent to several search engines all at once. The results are then blended together onto one page." Thus metalcrawlers, also called metasearch engines, have carried the basic strategies of search engine companies a step further: they simply *use* search engines, being an intermediate between others. Sherman listed 21 such metacrawlers operating in 2005. Those that had won SEW awards included Dogpile, Vivisimo, Kartoo, Mamma, and Surfwax.

GETTING VISIBILITY

From the viewpoint of the small business hoping that its Web site is found as often as possible by searchers on the Web (traffic equals sales, after all), the chief issue regarding search engines is how to be found by them and—more importantly—how to be ranked high enough actually to be seen at all. Being 82nd in a list of 200 hits is almost equivalent to invisibility. On a typical Google search result, the entry will be on the 9th page—and rare the user who will examine nine pages of a search.

Creating, promoting, and structuring a company's site for maximum visibility is a very complex subject and will require substantial homework or expert advice. A good beginning point is SEW's Web page entitled "Search Engine Submission Tips." It provides a systematic tutorial on the major aspects, including registering the site with search engines, which may be free or may have to be paid for, using advertising services such as Google's Adwords program, and internally structuring the Web site to present the most favorable features to Web crawlers. Rankings go up when a site offers multiple links to other sites—and also when many other sites point to one's own. Self-contained sites (one might say solitary or self-centered sites) tend to be ranked low. Search engines inherently favoring a communal spirit of interconnectedness—the very essence of the Internet. The small business intent on maximizing its exposure should engage an experienced Web page design firm. Such organizations typically have the know-how to structure the Web page appropriately and also to guide the owner on additional steps to take.

FRUSTRATIONS AND PLEASURES

A discussion of search engines would be incomplete without pointing to the frustrations and pleasures of using such services. Thus, for instance, it may be possible to find 700-some-odd pages on an ancient Chinese emperor—but frustrating sometimes when a specific phrase is sought, usually entered into the search engine between quotes, and getting the standard "Your search – 'X' – did not match any documents." At the same time, it is often quite easy, remembering just a little snatch of a song's lyrics, to enter that truncated phrase and to get pages and pages of hits with the lyrics—and more: the music itself, played on the sound system to bring back the tune. This experience—whether in a serious business context or just for fun—is exhilarating. And things are moving so rapidly that by the time this text is out in print or visible on the Internet it may well be possible that search engines will provide genuinely helpful suggestions when the "did not match" message appears. Currently the advice is next to useless. But just wait a while.

SEE ALSO *Internet Domain Name; Web Site Design*

BIBLIOGRAPHY

"ISC Internet Domain Survey." Internet Systems Consortium. Available from http://www.isc.org/index.pl?/ops/ds/. Retrieved on 27 May 2006.

"Lycos: A brief history of the Lycos search engine." The Web Marketing Workshop. Available from http://www.websearch workshop.co.uk/lycos_history.php. Retrieved on 27 May 2006.

"Search Engine Submission Tips." Search Engine Watch. Available from http://searchenginewatch.com/webmasters/. Retrieved on 25 May 2006.

SearchEngineWatch. Web Site. Available from http:// searchenginewatch.com/. Retrieved on 26 May 2006.

Sherman, Chris. "Metacrawlers and Metasearch Engines." SearchEngineWatch. 23 March 2005. Available from http:// searchenginewatch.com/links/article.php/2156241. Retrieved on 27 May 2006.

Sullivan, Danny. "Major Search Engines and Directories." SearchEngineWatch. 28 April 2004. Available from http:// searchenginewatch.com/links/article.php/2156221. Retrieved on 26 May 2006.

Darnay, ECDI

SEASONAL BUSINESSES

Most businesses experience some ebb and flow in business and in many cases these fluctuations correspond with the seasons. Seasonal business is a term that refers to the fluctuations in business that correspond to changes in season. Season can be understood in this context to include a) seasons of the year and their weather-related changes, b) holidays, and c) events like the summer school holiday, the fall return to school, or the Super Bowl. Although most businesses experience some seasonal business fluctuations, others experience severe seasonal fluctuations and may even limit their operations to particular seasons. Examples of such businesses include operators of vacation cottages, lawn care service businesses, and businesses that contract to do snow removal. Extremely seasonal businesses may close down completely for part of the year or drastically scale back operations during their off-season, managing only basic services such as accounts payable and/or maintenance work. Many retail businesses have a strong seasonal component and see the majority of their profits generated in one or two seasons of the year, the year-end or Christmas season being a typically busy period.

There are predictable events that can influence sales in every month of the year. These seasonal events affect different industries and businesses differently. For example, January is a good month for health club memberships as well as self-help books and programs. February is generally the slowest month of the year, but it does feature Valentine's Day, which triggers a great deal of seasonal business. In March, attendance at church and other religious activities jumps 60 percent. April is the month to market household cleaners and other spring cleaning products, while May features the cash cow that is Mother's Day. June features a lot of family activities, such as weddings, graduations, and vacations. July is the best month for all summer products. August is the busiest travel month of the year. September features back-to-school sales, while October is a marketing bonanza thanks to Halloween and the World Series. Finally, November and December are the biggest months of the year for almost every retailer because of the holidays—Thanksgiving, Hanukkah, Kwanza, Christmas, and New Year's.

BUSINESSES BASED ON THE ACTUAL SEASONS

Throughout the business world, there are numerous types of businesses that operate on a strictly seasonal basis, while many others stay open year-round but make a significant portion of their annual profits in one, or possibly two, seasons. Examples include vacation resorts, which in some regions of the United States are only open for part of the year (spring and summer in the northern

U.S., fall and winter in the southern half of the country); cross-country and downhill skiing facilities; youth summer camps; lawn care and landscaping firms; golf courses; and sports leagues, from amateur all the way to the top professional leagues. Smaller-scale examples include snow removal services, pool cleaning services (in the northern U.S.), ice cream stands, golf driving ranges, and drive-in movie theaters, just to name a few.

If it is feasible, a business that relies heavily on one season tries to at least make some money during the remaining months of the year. If it absolutely cannot turn a profit, then the business often closes during its off-season to avoid paying employees and to reduce the cost of supplies and overhead. For example, in the northern United States, ice cream shops other than those located inside shopping malls simply close for the winter once the temperature dips down to the freezing level. On the other hand, some lawn care businesses in the northern United States may attempt to put their equipment and machinery to use during their off-season by cultivating a snow removal service in the winter months.

The movie industry remains one of the largest industries in the world driven by seasonal buying habits. The two biggest seasons of the year for the movie industry are summer and winter. Movie theaters do not shut down like some other seasonal businesses, but they hire extra employees for those two seasons and create budgets that reflect the dominance of those two seasons. Each year, the movie studios' most important releases are planned for those two times of year. High-budget, wide-appeal movies that have blockbuster potential are usually released in the summer, often at either the Memorial Day or Fourth of July holiday weekend. Around Christmas, the studios release serious pictures expected to gain Academy Award attention together with big-budget films that are aimed at the entire family.

EVEN DURING BUSY SEASONS, THINGS CAN FLUCTUATE

For truly seasonal businesses, there are often situations beyond the business's control that cause sales to fluctuate wildly each year, with almost no way to predict what will happen in any given year. Perhaps the best example of this, in cold climates, is the amount of snow that falls. Snowfall levels can affect any number of businesses, from ski resorts to hardware stores that sell snowblowers, salt, and chemical de-icers. (The reverse of this situation for summer resorts is a summer that is colder and rainier than usual.) One winter can be extremely snowy, while the next can see almost no snowfall, with very little chance of consistently predicting which way a winter will turn out in advance.

Some businesses use this uncertainty to their advantage, offering unique sales pitches revolving around the snow, or lack of it. For example, it is not unusual for a creative hardware store to run a special on snowblowers late in the fall. As a gimmick to lure buyers, the store offers to refund the entire purchase price of a new snowblowers if a certain amount of snow does not fall that winter. If the snow does fall, then all sales are final, and the merchant was able to sell all his snowblowers at full price.

If the snow does not fall, then the merchant normally has taken out a special insurance policy that will cover most of his or her losses from the special sale, which has now turned out to be a worst-case scenario. Businesses that offer this kind of seasonal gimmick usually do their homework before they make what seems to be an outlandish offer. For example, the hardware store owner might know from studying statistical data that only twice in the last 100 years has the designated amount of snow not fallen, and therefore his odds of having to pay for the customers' snowblowers are extremely slim.

SUCCEEDING AT A TRULY SEASONAL BUSINESSES

In a business that is truly driven by the seasons, there are steps that can be taken to ensure greater success. The two most important factors are managing cash flow and hiring the right employees. Cash flow management is important to any business but for companies whose cash flow fluctuates dramatically from one period to the next this task is especially critical. Cash flow management does not need to be mysterious or complex. Cash flow management is, quite simply, all about timing cash inflows and outflows. Since a seasonal business can anticipate the inflows being heavier during one period than in others the key is to match the outflows to the same period as much as possible and create reserves to use during the off-season.

Finding and keeping good employees is another key to succeeding in a seasonal business. Paying well and creating a positive work environment are obvious ways to gain good employees, but there are other tactics a small business owner can use. Keeping employees informed of how the seasonal shift affects the company is a good idea, as the employees feel as if they matter more and are an important part of the business. It also helps employees identify the best time to take a vacation. When hiring new employees, two sources of good seasonal employees should be kept foremost in mind—students and retirees. Students are perfect for summer jobs because their time off from school matches the business's busy season perfectly, and most students need to earn money in the summer to pay for school in the fall. Retirees tend to make good employees because they may have years of experience in their field, but they no longer desire to work full time. Therefore, a job that lasts a few months each year is perfect.

One other tactic that seasonal business owners can use to succeed is to expand their business to include a new product line that is seasonal in the opposite way as their original line. For example, a lawn and garden company that sells lawn mowers and offers mowing and landscaping services can add snowblowers to their product mix and offer snow removal services to complement their landscaping services. The new product should be similar to the existing product so that an owner does not have to learn a brand new business or invest a great deal of money.

EVENT- OR HOLIDAY-BASED SEASONAL BUSINESS

The retail sector is one that tends to be very sensitive to seasonal fluctuations. This type of seasonal business is driven by holidays or events that greatly influence consumer spending. Christmas is by far the largest holiday that creates seasonal shopping. In fact, it is not unusual for many retail businesses to see sales rise by 15 percent above normal monthly sales in December and then drop 30 percent below normal monthly sales in January each year. Other examples of event- or holiday-based seasonal periods include Halloween, Mother's Day, graduation, and back-to-school. These events are held at the same time each year, which makes it easy for a businessperson to establish an annual schedule.

SEE ALSO *Business Cycles; Fiscal Year*

BIBLIOGRAPHY
"Broad Mix Meets Variety of Needs." *Chain Drug Review.* 2 May 2005.

Ellis, Suzanne M. "Sledders an Inspiration: Fulton Drive-In Restaurant Opening for Snowmobilers." *The Post-Standard (Syracuse, NY).* 30 December 2004.

Erickson, Tim. "The Off-Season? One of the most frequent questions I am asked is 'What do you do all summer?'" *Snow Goer.* August 2005.

Getz, Donald, J. Carlsen, and A. Morrison. *The Family Business in Tourism and Hospitality.* CABI Publishing, 2004.

Gogoi, Pallavi. "Goodbye, Dracula. Hello, Hollywood: As retailers jockey for seasonal sales, the most popular costumes come from movies and TV." *Business Week Online.* 26 October 2005.

Heath, Erica. "Season-Related Excuses Always are in Season." *Rocky Mountain News.* 6 August 2005.

Kim, Ryan. "Seasonal Businesses Get Ready to Twinkle: It's a tough living, but they love it." *San Francisco Chronicle.* 26 November 2005.

Partyka, Paul M. "At Your Service: Car washing is more than a seasonal business." *American Coin-Op.* October 2004.

"There's a Gift for Simply Every Celebration: After the Christmas glut, the gifting engine shows no signs of dieting." *Grocer.* 14 January 2006.

Torres, Nichole L. "A Festive Focus: Turn your passion for a specific holiday into a thriving business by getting your timing right." *Entrepreneur.* April 2006.

Waldrop, Judith. "The Seasons of Business." *American Demographics.* May 1992.

Hillstrom, Northern Lights
updated by Magee, ECDI

SEC DISCLOSURE LAWS AND REGULATIONS

Companies that are privately owned are not required by law to disclose detailed financial and operating information in most instances. They enjoy wide latitude in deciding what types of information to make available to the public. Small businesses and other enterprises that are privately owned may shield information from public knowledge and determine for themselves who needs to know specific types of information. Companies that are publicly owned, on the other hand, are subject to detailed disclosure laws about their financial condition, operating results, management compensation, and other areas of their business. While these disclosure obligations are primarily linked with large publicly traded companies, many smaller companies choose to raise capital by making shares in the company available to investors. In such instances, the small business is subject to many of the same disclosure laws that apply to large corporations. Disclosure laws and regulations are monitored and enforced by the U.S. Securities and Exchange Commission (SEC).

All of the SEC's disclosure requirements have statutory authority, and these rules and regulations are subject to changes and amendments over time. Some changes are made as the result of new accounting rules adopted by the principal rule-making bodies of the accounting profession. In other cases, changes in accounting rules follow changes in SEC guidelines. For example, in 2000 the SEC imposed new regulations to eliminate the practice of "selective disclosure," in which business leaders provided earnings estimates and other vital information to analysts and large institutional shareholders before informing smaller investors and the rest of the general public. The regulation forces companies to make market-sensitive information available to all parties at the same time. Dramatic and sweeping amendments were made to the SEC's disclosure rules in the summer of 2002 with the passage of the Sarbanes-Oxley Act, often referred to simply as Sarbanes-Oxley, Sarbanes, or SOX.

The Sarbanes-Oxley Act came about because of the stunning and unexpected bankruptcy filed by Enron, an enormous energy-trading company in late 2001. This bankruptcy filing was the largest to date in 2001, it cost investors billions and employees lost far more than their jobs, many lost their life savings. The Enron debacle would have been prevented if audits of the company had detected accounting irregularities or if the company would have been required to disclose transactions not directly reflected on its balance sheet. To a large extent, Enron's failure was the result of corrupt practices. Concern quickly grew about how easily these practices had been carried out and hidden from investors and employees alike.

Sarbanes-Oxley was principally a reaction to this failure. However, during this same period, the equally dramatic actual or pending bankruptcies of WorldCom, a long-distance telecommunications company, and Tyco, a diversified equipment manufacturer, influenced the content of the legislation. SOX thus deals with 1) reform of auditing and accounting procedures, including internal controls, 2) the oversight responsibilities of corporate directors and officers and regulation of conflicts of interest, insider dealings, and the disclosure of special compensation and bonuses, 3) conflicts of interest by stock analysts, 4) earlier and more complete disclosure of information on anything that directly and indirectly influences or might influence financial results, 5) criminalization of fraudulent handling of documents, interference with investigations, and violation of disclosure rules, and 6) requiring chief executives to certify financial results personally and to sign federal income tax documents. The provisions of SOX have significantly changed SEC disclosure requirements.

In a very real sense, SOX has changed the very regulatory authority upon which the SEC operates. For a detailed discussion of the provisions of Sarbanes-Oxley, refer to the essay by the same name in this volume.

SEC DISCLOSURE OBLIGATIONS

SEC regulations require publicly owned companies to disclose certain types of business and financial data on a regular basis to the SEC and to the company's stockholders. The SEC also requires disclosure of relevant business and financial information to potential investors when new securities, such as stocks and bonds, are issued to the public, although exceptions are made for small issues and private placements. The current system of mandatory corporate disclosure is known as the integrated disclosure system. By amending some of its regulations, the SEC has attempted to make this system less burdensome on corporations by standardizing various forms and eliminating some differences in reporting requirements to the SEC and to shareholders.

Publicly owned companies prepare two annual reports, one for the SEC and one for their shareholders. Form 10-K is the annual report made to the SEC, and its content and form are strictly governed by federal statutes. It contains detailed financial and operating information, as well as a management response to specific questions about the company's operations.

Historically, companies have had more leeway in what they include in their annual reports to stockholders. Over the years, however, the SEC has gained more influence over the content of such annual reports, primarily through amending its rules on proxy statements. Since most companies mail annual reports along with their proxy statements, they must make their annual stockholder reports comply with SEC requirements.

SEC regulations require that annual reports to stockholders contain certified financial statements and other specific items. The certified financial statement must include a two-year audited balance sheet and a three-year audited statement of income and cash flows. In addition, annual reports must contain five years of selected financial data, including net sales or operating revenues, income or loss from continuing operations, total assets, long-term obligations and redeemable preferred stock, and cash dividends declared per common share.

Annual reports to stockholders must also contain management's discussion and analysis of the firm's financial condition and results of operations. Information contained therein includes discussions of the firm's liquidity, capital resources, results of operations, any favorable or unfavorable trends in the industry, and any significant events or uncertainties. Other information to be included in annual reports to stockholders includes a brief description of the business covering such matters as main products and services, sources of materials, and status of new products. Directors and officers of the corporation must be identified. Specific market data on common stock must also be supplied.

Registration of New Securities Private companies that wish to become publicly owned must comply with the registration requirements of the SEC. In addition, companies floating new securities must follow similar disclosure requirements. The required disclosures are made in a two-part registration statement that consists of a prospectus as one part and a second section containing additional information. The prospectus contains all of the information that is to be presented to potential investors. It should be noted that SEC rules and regulations governing registration statements are subject to change.

In order to meet the disclosure requirements of new issue registration, companies prepare a basic information package similar to that used by publicly owned companies for their annual reporting. The prospectus, which contains all information to be presented to potential investors, must include such items as audited financial statements, a summary of selected financial data, and management's description of the company's business and financial condition. The statement should also include a summary of the company's material business contracts and list all forms of cash and noncash compensation given to the chief executive officer (CEO) and the top five officers. Compensation paid to all officers and directors as a group must also be disclosed. In essence, a company seeking to go public must disclose its entire business plan.

Securities Industry Regulations Additional disclosure laws apply to the securities industry and to the ownership of securities. Officers, directors, and principal stockholders (defined as holding 10 percent or more of the company's stock) of publicly owned companies must submit two reports to the SEC. These are Form 3 and Form 4. Form 3 is a personal statement of beneficial ownership of securities of their company. Form 4 records changes in such ownership. These reporting requirements also apply to the immediate families of the company's officers, directors, and principal stockholders. Individuals who acquire 5 percent or more of the voting stock of a SEC-registered company, meanwhile, must also submit notification of that fact to the SEC.

Securities broker-dealers must provide their customers with a confirmation form as soon as possible after the execution of an order. These forms provide customers with minimum basic information required for every trade. Broker-dealers are also responsible for presenting the prospectus to each customer for new securities issues. Finally, members of the securities industry are subject to reporting requirements of their own self-regulating organizations. These organizations include the New York Stock Exchange (for listed securities transactions) and the National Association of Securities Dealers (for over-the-counter traded securities).

DISCLOSURE RULES OF THE ACCOUNTING PROFESSION

Generally accepted accounting principles (GAAP) and specific rules of the accounting profession require that certain types of information be disclosed in a business's audited financial statements. As noted above, these rules and principles do not have the same force of law as SEC rules and regulations. Once adopted, however, they are widely accepted and followed by the accounting profes-

sion. Indeed, in some instances, disclosures required by the rules and regulations of the accounting profession may exceed those required by the SEC.

It is a generally accepted accounting principle that financial statements must disclose all significant information that would be of interest to a concerned investor, creditor, or buyer. Among the types of information that must be disclosed are financial records, accounting policies employed, litigation in progress, lease information, and details of pension plan funding. Generally, full disclosure is required when alternative accounting policies are available, as with inventory valuation, depreciation, and long-term contract accounting. In addition, accounting practices applicable to a particular industry and other unusual applications of accounting principles are usually disclosed.

Certified financial statements contain a statement of opinion from an auditor, in which the auditor states that it is his or her opinion that the financial statements were prepared in accordance with GAAP and that no material information was left undisclosed. If the auditor has any doubts, then a qualified or adverse opinion statement is written.

SEE ALSO *Sarbanes-Oxley*

BIBLIOGRAPHY

"A Bird's Eye View of the Enron Debacle." American Institute of Certified Public Accountants (AICPA). Available from http://www.aicpa.org/info/birdseye02.htm. Retrieved on 20 April 2006.

Culp, Christopher L, and William A. Naskanen. *Corporate Aftershock: The Public Policy Lessons from the Collapse of Enron and Other Major Corporations.* John Wiley & Sons, June 2003.

Nocera, Joseph. "No Whispering Allowed: Why the SEC's Crackdown on Selective Disclosure is Good News." *Money.* 1 December 2000.

"Proposed Changes to Disclosures." *California CPA.* March-April 2006.

Public Company Accounting Oversight Board (PCAOB). PCAOB Web Page. Available from http://www.pcaobus.org/index.aspx. Retrieved on 20 April 2006.

"Sarbanes-Oxley Act." Wikipedia. Available from http://en.wikipedia.org/wiki/Sarbanes-Oxley_Act. Retrieved on 21 April 2006.

"Summary of Sarbanes-Oxley Act of 2002." American Institute of Certified Public Accountants (AICPA). Available from http://www.aicpa.org/info/sarbanes_oxley_summary.htm. Retrieved on 20 April 2006.

U.S. Congress. *Sarbanes-Oxley Act of 2002.* Available from http://www.law.uc.edu/CCL/SOact/soact.pdf. Retrieved on 20 April 2006.

Hillstrom, Northern Lights
updated by Magee, ECDI

SECURITIES AND EXCHANGE COMMISSION (SEC)

The U.S. Securities and Exchange Commission (SEC) is a federal agency responsible for administering federal securities laws that protect investors. The SEC also ensures that securities markets are fair and honest and, if necessary, enforces securities laws through the appropriate sanctions. Basically, the SEC oversees the activities of all participants in the securities markets—including publicly held corporations, public utilities, investment companies and advisers, and securities brokers and dealers—to ensure that investors are adequately informed and their interests are protected. Small businesses are most likely to come into contact with the SEC when they decide to make a public offering of debt or securities. Any business wishing to issue stock must first file a registration statement with the SEC. Another role of the SEC is to serve as adviser to the federal courts in Chapter 11 cases (corporate reorganization proceedings under Chapter 11 of the Bankruptcy Reform Act of 1978).

ORGANIZATION AND RESPONSIBILITIES OF THE SEC

The SEC was created by Congress in 1934 under the Securities Exchange Act as an independent, nonpartisan, quasi-judicial regulatory agency. The commission is made up of five members: one chairman and four commissioners. Each member is appointed by the president to a five-year term, with the terms staggered. The commission's staff is made up of lawyers, accountants, financial analysts, engineers, investigators, economists, and other professionals. The SEC staff is divided into divisions and offices, which includes 12 regional and branch offices, each directed by officials appointed by the SEC chairman.

The chairman and commissioners of the SEC are responsible for ensuring that publicly held corporations, brokers or dealers in securities, investment companies and advisers, and other participants in the securities markets comply with federal securities law. These laws were designed to help public investors make informed investment analysis and decisions—principally by ensuring adequate disclosure of material information. The SEC does not, however, make any evaluations of the quality of the company making the IPO; it is concerned only with assuring that the registration statement and prospectus documents contain the information necessary for potential investors to make informed decisions. The SEC also has the authority to initiate legal penalties—both civil and criminal—against companies if the agency determines that the IPO materials contain serious omissions, misleading information, or outright falsehoods. "If

the SEC finds mistakes during the registration process, it can delay your IPO," said Chuck Berg in *Cincinnati Business Courier*. "If it finds mistakes or omissions after your company goes public, your company may soon have a thorough—and unpleasant—understanding of legal liability."

There are seven major laws that the SEC is responsible for administering:

- Securities Act of 1933
- Securities Exchange Act of 1934
- Public Utility Holding Company Act of 1935
- Trust Indenture Act of 1939
- Investment Company Act of 1940
- Investment Advisers Act of 1940
- Sarbanes-Oxley Act of 2002

The Securities Act of 1933, also known as the "truth in securities" law has two primary objectives: 1) to require that investors be provided with material information concerning securities offered for public sale; and 2) to prevent misrepresentation, deceit, and other fraud in the sale of securities. The SEC ensures that both of these objectives are met.

The Securities Exchange Act of 1934 extended the "disclosure" doctrine (from the Securities Act of 1933) to securities listed and registered for public trading on the U.S. securities exchanges. In 1964, the Securities Act Amendments extended disclosure and reporting provisions to equity securities in the over-the-counter market. The act seeks to ensure (through the SEC) fair and orderly securities markets by prohibiting certain types of activities and by setting forth rules regarding the operation of the markets and participants.

The SEC also administers the Public Utility Holding Company Act of 1935. Subject to regulation under this act are interstate holding companies engaged in the electric utility business or in the retail distribution of natural or manufactured gas. Reports to be filed with the SEC by these holding companies include detailed information concerning the organization, financial structure, and operations of the holding company and its subsidiaries. Holding companies are subject to SEC regulation in areas such as corporate structure, acquisitions, and issue and sales of securities.

The Trust Indenture Act of 1939 applies to bonds, debentures, notes, and similar debt securities offered for public sale and issued under trust indentures with more than $7.5 million of securities outstanding at any one time. Other provisions of the act prohibit the indenture trustee from having conflicts of interest; require the trustee to be a corporation with minimal combined capital and surplus; and impose high standards of conduct and responsibility on the trustee.

The SEC also ensures compliance with the Investment Company Act of 1940. This act seeks to regulate the activities of companies engaged primarily in investing, reinvesting, and trading in securities, and whose own securities are publicly offered. It is important for potential investors to understand that although the SEC serves as a regulatory agency in these cases, the SEC does not supervise a company's investment activities, and the mere presence of the SEC as a regulatory agency does not guarantee a safe investment.

The Investment Advisers Act of 1940—also overseen by the SEC—establishes a style, or a system, of regulating investment advisers. The main thrust of this act requires all persons, or firms, that are compensated for advising anyone about securities investment opportunities to be registered with the SEC and conform to the established standards of investor protection. The SEC has the power and ability to strip an investment adviser of his or her registration if a statutory violation has occurred.

In 2002 Congress passed the Sarbanes-Oxley Act and it was signed into law. Parts of this sweeping legislation are the responsibility of the SEC to administer. The act came about in the wake of serious allegations of accounting fraud and a string of bankruptcies of very high-profile, publicly traded companies. The act established stricter reporting requirements and increased the personal responsibility that both CEOs and CFOs must take on when signing corporate reports. Meeting the requirements of this law has increased the workload for publicly traded firms and the firms that do their auditing work. In particular, Section 404 of the Sarbanes-Oxley Act requires that a company's annual report include an official write-up by management about the effectiveness of the company's internal controls. The section also requires that outside auditors attest to management's report on internal controls. An external audit is required in order to attest to the management report.

Finally, the SEC is given some responsibility connected with corporate bankruptcy reorganizations, commonly referred to as Chapter 11 proceedings. Chapter 11 of the Bankruptcy Code grants the SEC permission to become involved in any proceedings, but the SEC is primarily concerned with proceedings directly involving significant public investor interest.

BIBLIOGRAPHY

"Fresh Strategies are Needed for the New SEC Reporting Requirements." *Corporate Board.* March-April 2003.

MacAdam, Donald H. *Startup to IPO.* Xlibris Corporation, 2004.

Mirza, Patrick. "Some Companies Struggle to Meet SEC Reporting Requirements." *HRMagazine.* May 2004.

Skousen, K. Fred. *An Introduction to the SEC.* South-Western College Publishing, 1991.

U.S. Securities and Exchange Commission. "Summary of SEC Actions and SEC Related Provisions Pursuant to the Sarbanes-Oxley Act of 2002." Available from http://www.sec.gov/news/press/2003-89a.htm. 30 July 2003.

Hillstrom, Northern Lights
updated by Magee, ECDI

SEED MONEY

Seed money, or seed capital, is the first round of capital for a start-up business. It gets its name from the idea that early stage financing plants the seed that enables a small business to grow. Obtaining funding is one of the most critical aspects of starting a small business. In fact, many businesses fail or are prevented from even starting due to a lack of capital. Although obtaining financing can be difficult for any small business, it is particularly hard for new ventures. Since new ventures lack a track record, potential lenders and investors are often skeptical about their prospects for success. Nonetheless, the persistent would-be entrepreneur, if armed with a sound business plan and the necessary skills, can usually obtain funding for his/her dream eventually.

Many entrepreneurs approach their family, friends, and colleagues for seed money after exhausting their own finances. Since these investors know the entrepreneur, they are more likely to take a risk on funding a new venture than are traditional financing sources, such as banks or venture capital firms. An entrepreneur must be committed and enthusiastic in pursuing seed money since he or she has little else with which to entice investors. Because it is almost impossible to predict how successful the project may eventually be, the only outsiders likely to invest in the venture are those who respect the entrepreneur's judgment and abilities. Those people are the ones who know the entrepreneur best. By getting in on the ground floor, the providers of seed money hope to participate in the entrepreneur's success and realize a healthy return as their investment appreciates over time. Nonetheless, seed money is a risky investment and most investors know this, or should. Investing seed money is, in many instances, more like buying a lottery ticket than making an investment.

Seed money usually takes the form of equity financing, so investors receive partial ownership of the fledgling company in exchange for their funds. As a result, it is important for the entrepreneur to take potential investors' personalities and business reputations into consideration when seeking seed money. Since these people will be part owners of the company—and may insist upon having some control over decision making—it is vital to ascertain whether their interests and personalities are compatible with those of the entrepreneur. Once suitable investors have been located, the entrepreneur must convince them that the new business venture has a good chance of success. The first step in this process is creating a formal, written business plan, including plausible projections of income and expenses.

Having a clearly defined purpose for seed money can be an important factor in securing these funds. The purpose of seed capital usually involves moving the business out of the idea stage—by building a prototype product or conducting market research, for example—and gathering concrete evidence that it can succeed. In this way, seed money helps the entrepreneur to prove the merit of his or her idea in order to attract the interest of formal investment sources.

As far as the amount of seed money the entrepreneur should try to obtain, experts recommend targeting only what is needed to accomplish the business's initial objectives. Given its risk, seed capital is usually more expensive for the firm than later stage financing. Thus, raising a small amount at a time helps the entrepreneur to preserve equity for later financing rounds. Ideally, an arrangement can be made that links seed money to launch financing, so the entrepreneur can go back to the same investors for future funding needs. For example, the entrepreneur might set goals for a successful market test of a new product. If the goals are met, then the original investors agree to provide additional funds for a product launch. This approach protects the entrepreneur against the possibility of having a successful test and then running out of money before being able to launch the product. Even if the original investors cannot provide additional funds directly, their vested interest may encourage them to help the venture succeed in other ways.

There are other sources of seed money available to entrepreneurs besides friends and family members. For example, some venture capital firms reserve a limited amount of capital for financing new ventures or business ideas. Since start-ups involve greater risks than established businesses, however, the venture capital investors generally require a larger equity position in exchange. On average, venture capitalists providing seed money will expect a 50 to 100 percent higher return on investment than in a standard venture capital arrangement. There are also nonprofit organizations dedicated to providing seed capital for new businesses. In many cases, these organizations will also assist the entrepreneur in creating a business plan or marketing materials, and establishing cash flow controls or other systems.

Angel Investors Successful business owners looking to invest in new enterprises are a good potential source of start up capital or seed money. These people are often referred to as angel investors. They are known as "angels" because they often invest in risky, unproven business ventures for which other sources of funds—such as bank loans and formal venture capital—are not available. New startup companies often turn to the private equity market for seed money because the formal equity market is reluctant to fund risky undertakings. In addition to their willingness to invest in a startup, angel investors may bring other assets to the partnership. They are often a source of encouragement, they may be mentors in how best to guide a new business through the startup phase and they are often willing to do this while staying out of the day-to-day management of the business.

Although angel investors usually work on an individual basis there has been a trend towards the formation of angel investor groups within the last decade. An article in *Fortune Small Business (FSB)* discusses the trend towards angle investment groups. According to the author, Jennie Lee, "Last year [2005] some 227,000 angles in the U.S. pumped $23 billion into startups, up about 3 percent from 2004.... One reason for the growth: the void left by venture capitalist, who have started to favor larger, later-stage investments."

These angel investment groups usually meet on a regular basis and invite prospective entrepreneurs to present their business ideas for consideration. David Worrell discusses what such a presentation may involve in his article entitled "Taking Flight: Angel Investors are Flocking Together to Your Advantage." If invited to present ideas before an angel investor group, "expect to be one of two or three presenters, each given 10 to 30 minutes to showcase an investment opportunity. Speak loudly, as most groups mix presentations with a meal."

Despite the potential for funding through an angel investor group, according to Worrell, individual angels are still likely to be the best source of seed and early stage money for a small business or startup. "Angel groups can bring more money and other resources, which makes them more effective at later stages."

SEE ALSO *Angel Investors; Financial Planning; Venture Capital*

BIBLIOGRAPHY
"About ACA." Angel Capital Association, Available from http://www.angelcapitalassociation.org/. January 2006,

Benjamin, Gerald A., and Joel Margulis. *The Angel Investor's Handbook.* Bloomberg Press, January 2001.

Chung, Joe. "Panning Out." *Technology Review.* October 2004.

Lee, Jeannie. "How to Fund Other Startups and Get Rich." *FSB.* June 2006.

National Venture Capital Association. "The Venture Capital Industry—An Overview." Available from http://www.nvca.org/def.html. Retrieved on 3 May 2006.

Phalon, Richard. *Forbes Greatest Investing Stories.* John Wiley & Sons, April 2004.

"Where the Seed Money Is." *Industry Standard.* 26 February 2001.

Worrell, David. "Taking Flight: Angel Investors are Flocking Together to Your Advantage." *Entrepreneur.* October 2004.

Hillstrom, Northern Lights
updated by Magee, ECDI

SELF-ASSESSMENT

Self-assessment has been around since the most ancient times in the form of the admonition: Know Thyself. It emerged roughly four decades ago from work in psychology; it has been applied in that field, in medicine, and increasingly also in business. In business or professional activity, it is a tool that involves performing a critical analysis of one's own goals, interests, skills, and experience. It is also used by organizations as a self-evaluation tool. Among its many applications in the business world are employee development, team performance, and organizational change efforts. But self-assessment is perhaps most valuable for would-be entrepreneurs considering starting a new business. Are you really ready to make it on your own? Conduct a self-assessment. Future entrepreneurs, in others words, may be able to improve their chances of success in business by undertaking an honest and detailed self-assessment. By evaluating such personal traits as business skills, experience, and knowledge, financial goals, likes and dislikes, willingness to expend effort, and ability to meet challenges, entrepreneurs may be able to identify the business opportunities for which they are best suited. In some cases, self-assessment may even lead to innovative new business ideas. In addition, completing a self-assessment can help entrepreneurs recognize areas where they will need assistance or training. Increasing self-knowledge may also help entrepreneurs to attract investors and impress lenders.

A good way to start in performing a self-assessment is to prepare a detailed resume. This document should list the entrepreneur's educational background and professional experience—describing the requirements and responsibilities of each job in detail—along with hobbies and outside interests. Using the resume as a guide, it may then be helpful for the entrepreneur to separate his or her professional attributes by functional area—such as marketing, accounting, or human resource management—and assign a competency level to each one. Finally, the entrepreneur may wish to create a list of personal attributes—such as ability with numbers, common sense, communication skills, organization skills, people skills, etc.—that may be useful in starting and running a small business. The mere process of thinking about and categorizing one's skills and experience can be informative.

Not surprisingly, the tool of self-assessment can be applied to a wide variety of other business situations as well. For example, it can be used as an aid in employee development as part of a company's performance evaluation and training efforts. A common application is "360-degree feedback" systems—in addition to being evaluated by supervisors, peers, and subordinates, employees evaluate their own performance and participate in setting goals. Self-assessment can also be applied to teams of workers or even overall organizations to help identify strengths and weaknesses and improve performance. Teams might evaluate such elements of team performance as goal setting, communication, decision making, problem solving, and conflict management. At the organizational level, self-assessment performed with the participation of employees can help clarify a company's mission and goals, identify shortcomings, and generate ideas to increase competitiveness.

Self-assessment, of course, especially in discovering one's personal goals, tends to depend rather highly on the person's thoroughness, honesty, and objectivity. People tend to overlook their own shortcomings—and there is the old proverb which says: "He who is his own lawyer has a fool for a client." Edward Inderrieden and his co-authors, writing in *Journal of Managerial Issues* on the subject of self-appraisals refer to what they call the "leniency effect," a phrase dating to studies of self-assessment and coined in the 1980s: people "cut themselves a lot of slack." Perhaps for this reason, self-assessment is often accompanied by interaction with at least one other person who can apply some critique to the perhaps too lenient views of the assessor. In the case of the entrepreneur, a trusted but senior mentor would seem best suited for this role.

BIBLIOGRAPHY

Branham, Leigh. *The 7 Hidden Reasons Employees Leave: How to Recognize the Subtle Signs and Act Before It's Too Late.* AMACOM, 2005.

Caffyn, Sarah. "Development of a Continuous Improvement Self-Assessment Tool." *International Journal of Operations and Production Management.* November 2000.

Hoag, Kevin L. *Skill Development for Engineers: An Innovative Model for Advanced Learning in the Workplace.* The Institution of Electrical Engineers, 2001.

Inderrieden, Edward J., Robert E. Allen, and Timothy Keaveny. "Managerial Discretion in the Use of self-Ratings in an Appraisal System: The antecedents and consequences." *Journal of Managerial Issues.* Winter 2004.

Muchinsky, Paul M. *Psychology Applied to Work.* Thomson Wadsworth, 2006.

Hillstrom, Northern Lights
updated by Magee, ECDI

SELF-EMPLOYMENT

Self-employment has always been a fundamental feature of American life, not just in colonial times and during early U.S. history—during which, of course, the predominant form of work was agriculture—but also in the most recent period of modern times since World War II. Data on self-employment are collected by the U.S. Bureau of Labor Statistics (BLS) as part of the Current Population Survey. The most recent such data are for the year 2003. In the period 1948 through 2003, those self-employed in non-agricultural industries have represented around 7 percent of total employment. The highest levels came in the early decades of this period, with 1948 being the highest year: 12 percent of all those working outside agriculture were working for themselves. The lowest level was reached in 2002 (6.7 percent), and, generally the trend has been downward. In 2003, 9.3 million individuals were self-employed and represented 6.9 percent of non-agricultural employment. Self-employment rates fluctuate up and down. They tend to rise during recessions—but sometimes also rise with the rising economy. Self-employment is highest in the agricultural sector where, in 1948, 61.1 percent of all workers were self-employed. In 2003, 951,000 agricultural workers, 41.8 percent of all those engaged in agriculture, worked for themselves.

LEGAL DEFINITIONS

Individuals who choose self-employment must be aware of the rules governing the treatment of free-lance employees (also known as independent contractors). Classification of someone as an employee or a self-employee is somewhat ambiguous and depends on several factors, including the degree of independence, the freedom to hire others to do the work taken on, the freedom to work for others, and the assumption of risks. Independent contractors typically accept no fringe benefits and pay Social Security, Medicare, and income tax installments directly. Employees have more statutory rights, benefits, and protections than subcontractors, who must generally provide these for themselves. But independent contractors have advantages in terms of freedom, flexibility, and tax deductions.

The IRS applies a 20-part test in order to determine whether a certain worker should be classified as an employee or an independent contractor. The main issue underpinning the test is who sets the work rules: employees must follow rules set by their bosses, while independent contractors set their own rules. For example, an individual who sets his own hours, receives payment by the job, and divides his time between work for several different employers would probably be classified as an independent contractor. Other criteria involve who provides the tools and materials needed to complete the work. For example, an individual who works at an employer's facility and uses the employer's equipment would be considered an employee, while one who works at a separate location and provides her own equipment would be classified as an independent contractor. Finally, an independent contractor usually pays his own expenses of doing business and takes the risk of not receiving payment when work is not completed in accordance with a contract, while an employee is usually reimbursed for business-related expenses by the employer and receives a paycheck whether his work is completed or not.

An individual's status as a self-employed, independent contractor can be reinforced by having multiple clients, being paid by the amount of work done rather than by the hour, or obtaining an employer identification number from the IRS. Working under a business name also helps reinforce this status. Printing invoices, business cards, and stationery can also help identify someone as a self-employed person. In general, the person must demonstrate that he or she is in business for the purpose of making a profit.

CHARACTERISTICS

Of those self-employed in industry (versus agriculture), slightly over half (51.5 percent) were working as incorporated entities. The self-employed are predominantly older. Among those unincorporated, those aged 24-44 represented 42 percent and those aged 44 and older 54.5 percent of this segment of the self-employed. Among those incorporated, the older were even more numerous, representing 58.5 percent of those over 44 and 42 percent of those in the 24-44 bracket. In the wages and salary-earning population as a whole the 24-44 group was 48.1 percent and those over 44 were 36.5 percent. The self-employed are overwhelmingly white (88.2 percent of unincorporated, 90.1 percent of those incorporated) and U.S. born (87 percent in both categories). The educational attainment of the incorporated self-employed was high in 2003. Of these individuals, on average, 72 percent had some college on up to advanced degrees; among the unincorporated 58 percent had such attainment, slightly below the wages and salary-earning population, of which 60 percent had some college or higher attainment. Males are more present in both categories, representing 62 percent of the unincorporated and 73 percent of the incorporated self-employed.

Beyond such demographic measurements, the motivation for self-employment is more difficult to determine. Motivations routinely mentioned by commentators no doubt rest on experience and observation—namely that some women choose self-employment to be more available to care for a member of the household. Some of the elderly continue working on their own as they reach retirement age—and beyond. A certain segment of the self-employed population is motivated by enterprise. Many, however, do not choose this type of work but do it as a way of coping with inability to find good jobs, especially in middle age. And of these some succeed well enough to found organizations and thus, after a period, migrate back into employment—but in companies that they now own. Fluctuations in self-employment data may in part be explained as an indirect effect of new business formation: these begin as single-person businesses but then become providers of wages and salaries—for the owners as for others.

SELF-EMPLOYMENT AND THE VERY SMALL BUSINESS

Elsewhere in this volume (see *Small Business*) are presented data on the so-called nonemployer businesses, labeled "the micros." In 2003, there were some 18.6 million such businesses grossing $830 billion in revenues, equivalent to $44,623 per entity. This number was twice as high as the 9.3 million self-employed persons in 2003—but also includes them. The self-employed, thus, are roughly half of the population of "micro" of business, the seedlings from which larger entities often emerge. But obviously many nonemployer businesses are also operated "on the side" by people employed in ordinary jobs but doing some trading, producing, and service providing in their spare time: moonlighting, in other words. In 2001, 7.8 million people reported working at multiple jobs. Of these, 4.6 percent (359,000) told the BLS that they were doing this in order to build a business or to get experience—preparing, perhaps, to launch their own operations. Nonemployer businesses grew by 20.8 percent between 1997 and 2003; during the same period, total employment increased 7.3 percent and self-employment by 3.1 percent, losing share, in other words. Thus it is plain that the growth of seedling businesses is far less attributable to self-employment than to entrepreneurial activity.

CONSIDERATIONS IN SELF-EMPLOYMENT

Self-employed individuals as a whole tend to work longer (an additional 17.5 hours per week, according to one study) and harder than their colleagues who are organizationally employed. Moreover, self-employed people often operate under uncertain payment schedules and must make outlays from personal earnings for insurance and retirement. In addition, their salaries and assets are dependent on their work contributions in a more intimate way than are those of their colleagues. The entrepreneurial role is also often more physically and psychologically stressful due to the investments in energy the jobs demand.

Isolation and Networking Isolation often proves to be an important source of psychological strain for self-employed individuals. The environment of the typical self-employed individual is quite different from the corporate environment where many professionals gain their experience. This is one reason contact with supportive colleagues becomes crucial. Mentors can provide advice regarding business aspects of a new business owner's operation. Trade and professional organizations can be an excellent way to establish contacts with peers. Tenacity in networking has been cited as a key to survival for business owners, some of whom maintain databases of thousands of contacts. These contacts are also vital in referring clients and providing market information. The role of the contact is made more important as the self-employed individual typically has no staff for marketing support.

It is difficult to exaggerate the importance of referrals to the typical independent professional. Since relationships are so vital, one must exercise the utmost delicacy in terminating employment with one's former employer or turning down a job. One's former employer can even become a good client, besides providing valuable referrals. When turning down clients, the self-employed person can protect those relationships by making referrals or even subcontracting to other colleagues in their network. Provided the work done is of quality, this can strengthen one's reputation as a purveyor of talent—whether one's own or an associate's. When the client calls back with a more appropriate assignment, the contractor has the choice of the business.

As they begin their enterprises, many self-employed individuals feel compelled to accept a variety of assignments due to sheer scarcity of work. However, specialization can help ensure their long-term survival. For one thing, corporate clients can often find a generalist's abilities in-house. Also, specialization may allow professionals to broaden their client base geographically, thus freeing their fortunes from fluctuations in the local economy. These factors can enable the specialist to earn higher fees and work more consistently. Paradoxically, one's work as a specialist can garner referrals outside one's specialty, so specialization might not be as limiting as a strict definition would imply. The self-employed should be cautioned against changing their specialties too often, as this can confuse clients and make their own operations inefficient.

Tax Implications Self-employment entails both tax advantages and disadvantages. In terms of advantages, individuals who are classified as independent contractors can deduct work-related expenses for tax purposes. In addition, independent contractors often qualify for tax deductions for using part of their home as an office and for salaries paid to other people, while employees usually do not. Independent contractors also can claim significant deductions for medical insurance, transportation, office supplies, and a host of other operating costs.

The main tax disadvantage for self-employed persons is that they must pay the full amount of Social Security and Medicare taxes themselves and make quarterly estimated tax payments to the federal government. For those who are organizationally employed, the employer withholds income taxes and pays half of their Social Security and Medicare taxes. Although the payment of Social Security and Medicare increases the tax burden of self-employed individuals, these amounts are based on net, rather than gross, earnings. For this reason, it is essential for small business owners to keep an accurate record of expenses. Self-employed individuals also file quarterly taxes.

INCREASING THE CHANCE OF SUCCESS IN SELF-EMPLOYMENT

Self-employment, whether by choice or necessity, does not guarantee success. In fact, nearly two out of every three new businesses fail within five years. But the chances of success can be improved with careful planning, prior savings, and a sound marketing strategy. It may also be helpful to make the transition to full-time self-employment gradually. As already mentioned, one option is to "moonlight" on the new job first. Those planning home-based businesses should also take time to prepare family members for the changes that will take place.

Some prospective new business owners also try to establish one stable client relationship that will provide steady income during the search for additional clients. A particularly attractive option may be an individual's former employer, who will already be familiar with the would-be entrepreneur's reputation and abilities. For this relationship to succeed, however, it is important that the individual use an honest and professional approach when severing ties with their employer. Of course, your employer may not react warmly to such an arrangement if your new business is a potential threat to its own financial fortunes.

Although one stable client relationship can help establish a new business, it is also important that the self-employed person develop a marketing strategy to find new clients and grow. Many new business owners become so busy serving their existing clients that they do not devote sufficient time to marketing. Sending out brochures, networking, and joining professional organizations are a few possible marketing strategies.

Finally, self-employed individuals should take an organized approach to all business activities in order to increase their chances of success. A business plan, however rudimentary, is often helpful to set the path ahead with some consciousness and formality. A plan can help a self-employed person evaluate strategies, plan expenditures, and motivate him or herself. It is also important to keep careful records of income and expenses, set aside money for taxes, and insist upon contracts for all work performed.

SEE ALSO *Self-Employment Contributions Act (SECA); Small Business*

BIBLIOGRAPHY
Hipple, Steve. "Self-Employment in the United States: An update." *Monthly Labor Review.* U.S. Department of Labor. 23 July 2004.

Karoly, Lynn A., and Julie Zissimompoulos. "Self-Employment Among Older U.S. Workers." *Monthly Labor Review Online.* U.S. Department of Labor. Available from http://www.bls.gov/opub/mlr/2004/07/art3exc.htm. July 2004.

"Moonlighting in 2001." *Monthly Labor Review.* U.S. Department of Labor. 16 October 2002.

U.S. Bureau of Labor Statistics. "Work at Home in 2004." Press Release. 22 September 2005.

U.S. Census Bureau News. "Small Business Week 2006." Press Release. 27 March 2006.

Hillstrom, Northern Lights
updated by Magee, ECDI

SELF-EMPLOYMENT CONTRIBUTIONS ACT (SECA)

The Self-Employment Contributions Act (SECA) of 1954 is a tax law that requires the owners of small businesses—such as S corporations, partnerships, and sole proprietorships—to pay a tax of 15.3 percent of their net income from self-employment to cover their own Social Security, Medicare, and Old Age Survivors and Disability Insurance (OASDI) costs. Workers who are employed by a company or another person (rather than being self-employed) only have to pay half of this amount, which is withheld from their paychecks. Their employer pays the other half. In effect, SECA requires self-employed persons to pay both the employer and employee portions of the Federal Insurance Contributions Act (FICA) tax (a combination of Social Security and Medicare). To make this situation more equitable, small business owners subject to SECA are allowed to deduct half of their SECA tax amount on their personal federal tax returns.

SECA taxes are paid on self-employment income after costs associated with the activity have been deducted. The Internal Revenue Service refers to this as net profit (or loss), usually reported on Schedule C of Form 1040. Thus the base amount used for SECA calculation is profit before taxes. The first step in calculating the SECA is to multiply this value by .92235 (taking 92.35 percent of it). IRS calls the result "net earnings from self-employment." If this amount is under $400, no tax is owed at all. If the amount is $94,200 or less (in 2006), the self employment tax is 15.3 percent of these "net earnings." If the net earnings exceed $94,200, the first $94,200 are taxed at 15.3 percent, the amount above this sum at 2.9 percent. For example, suppose a person had net earnings of exactly $100,000. The tax would be $14,413 on the first $94,2000 (15.3 percent) and $168 on the $5,800 (2.9 percent) exceeding the base value, for a total tax of $14,581.

Why this curious two-tiered calculation? The base rate of 15.3 percent is made up of two contributions. The first is the Social Security tax, 12.4 percent of income, but ordinarily paid at the rate of 6.2 percent by the employee, an amount matched by the employer. This 12.4 percent tax applies only to a base income, in 2006 to income up to a maximum of $94,200 (the "contribution base."). The balance of the FICA contribution, 2.9 percent, is for Medicare, again paid at the rate of 1.45 percent by the employee and matched by the employer, but this rate is applied to *all* net earnings. The self-employed individual is *both* an employee and an employer rolled into one and thus is taxed at 12.4 percent for Social Security (up to the maximum level) and 2.9 percent for Medicare on all income.

The base income to which SECA tax applies has gradually increased over time. Thus in 1986 the maximum taxable income for Social Security purposes was $42,000, in 1996 $62,700, and in 2006 $94,200. Since 1982 the rate is set by the Social Security Administration under the automatic adjustment provisions of the Social Security Act; thus new base income figures are announced late each year for the following year. In the periods 1937-1974 and 1979-1981 these levels were set by statute. As this entry was being prepared, the contribution base for the years 2007 and beyond had not yet been published. The Social Security contribution rate (6.2 percent or, doubled, 12.4 percent) was last increased in 1990; the Medicare contribution (1.45 percent, 2.9 percent doubled) was last increased in 1986.

Each individual must calculate his or her self-employment tax separately—even when filing a joint return with another self-employed person. For example, a wife and a husband may both operate sole proprietorships, the wife having earnings ("net earnings" in the IRA sense) of $80,000 and the husband $45,000. The total tax to be paid by the couple in 2006 would be $12,240 for the wife and $6,885 for the husband (each income times .153). The total tax would thus be $19,125. If the law permitted these two incomes to be merged and treated as one—which it does *not*—the SECA tax would be lower. Of the combined earnings of $125,000, only $94,200 would be taxed at 15.3 percent and the remainder of $30,800 at 2.9 percent, for a total tax of $15,306. Joint filing in this case still produces benefits, but not benefits derivable from the rules that govern SECA.

When a person has income from an employer as well as from self-employment, however, the person may combine the two incomes for purposes of calculating SECA. An example is provided by Diane Weber writing for *Medical Economics* concerning a person who earned a salary of $80,000 and self-employment income of $30,000 in 2006, with a "contribution base," that year of $94,200. The total income thus was $110,000. In addition to deductions already made by the employer on the $80,000 in salary, the person would be required to pay in addition 15.3 percent on $14,200 of the $30,000 (calculated by taking $80,000 from $94,200) and 2.9 percent on $15,800 (calculated by deducting $94,200 from total income of $110,000).

The person who first sets off on his or her own usually experiences the self-employment tax as something of a shock. The political and business hype seem to promote the values and virtues of small business—but the first experience of being self-employed is paying *higher* tributes to the government than heretofore, almost as if government policy were designed to discourage enterprise. Legislators are, of course, both aware of this reaction and inclined to be helpful, but many other issues enter into the broader policy. Growing pressures on the Social Security system, and even greater pressures on the Medicare system, indicate that cuts for the self-employed are unlikely to pass soon. The self-employed person is thus likely to continue to have to pay the costs of independent operation—whether as an individual or as a sole proprietor. Once a business is incorporated, the self-employed person can become an employee of his or her company, and revert to paying half the FICA total. To be sure, the *company* now has to pay the matching amounts, but the matching amount, in any case, can be deducted from income. Meanwhile the two identities, employer and employee, are once more separated.

BIBLIOGRAPHY

Weber, Diane. "Employment Taxes on Mixed Earnings." *Medical Economics.* 17 February 2006.

U.S. Internal Revenue Service. "Self-employment Tax." Available from http://www.irs.gov/faqs/faq-kw167.html. Retrieved on 29 May 2006.

U.S. Internal Revenue Service. Schedule SE (Form 1040). 2005.

U.S. Social Security Administration. "Contribution and Benefit Base." 14 October 2005. Available from http://www.socialsecurity.gov/OACT/COLA/cbb.html#Series. Retrieved on 29 May 2006.

Hillstrom, Northern Lights
updated by Magee, ECDI

SELLING A BUSINESS

Many small business owners eventually decide to sell their companies. Some wish to retire, while others are impatient to investigate new challenges—whether in business or in some other sector—or they have grown weary of the frustrations that come with business. Others decide to sell for reasons more closely associated with the health of the business itself. Disputes with partners, incapacitation or death of principals, or downturns in the company's financial performance can all spur business owners to ponder putting the business on the block. Whatever their ultimate reason, business owners can get the most out of selling their company by carefully considering a number of factors.

TIMING THE SALE

The financial performance and history of the company in question are often the most important factors in determining price at the time of sale. A business owner who chooses to sell after posting several years of steady growth will naturally command a higher price than will the business owner who decides to sell only a year or two into that growth trend, even if the environment continues to appear friendly to the business for the foreseeable future.

The business environment in which the company operates is also an important factor in determining the asking price that the market will bear. If the company in question operates in an industry struggling through a downturn, the owner should wait for better times if possible. Few companies are able to buck the tide when the industry in which they operate is stuck in a sluggish cycle, and even attractive businesses will lose their luster in such times. Of course, some industries never post a recovery; business owners engaged in underperforming industries need to determine whether the downturns they experience are simply an inevitable part of the business cycle within a basically healthy industry or whether times are leaving an industry behind. There was a time once to hurry to establish a miniature golf course or to expand that business in men's hats. There are times when it's best to make a graceful exit.

The stock market is a third factor that can signal good and bad times to sell. A surging market tends to produce energetic buying activity because others are ambitious to expand. A slumping market is a good time to hunker down.

STOCK SALES AND ASSET SALES

Business owners need to decide early whether to sell stock or assets—a choice available if the company is incorporated. Sole proprietorships and partnerships undergo asset sales. Under the terms of a stock sale, the seller receives an agreed-upon price for his or her shares in the company. After ownership of the stock changes hands, the buyer steps in and operates the still-running business. Typically, such a purchase means that the buyer receives not only all company assets, but all company liabilities as well. This arrangement is often appealing to the seller because of its tax advantages. The sale of stock qualifies as a capital gain, and it enables the seller to avoid double taxation, since sale proceeds flow directly to the seller without passing through the corporation. In addition, a stock sale frees the seller from any future legal action that might be leveled against the company. Lawsuits and claims against the company become the sole responsibility of the new stock owner(s).

Partnerships and sole proprietorships must change hands by means of asset sale arrangements; stock is not a part of the picture. Under asset sale agreements, the seller hands over business equipment, inventory, trademarks and patents, trade names, "goodwill," and other assets for an agreed-upon price. The seller then uses the money to pay off any debts; the remainder is his or her profit. Changes in ownership accomplished through asset transactions are generally favored by buyers. First, the transaction sometimes allows the buyer to claim larger depreciation deductions on his or her taxes. Second, an asset sale provides the buyer with greater protection from unknown or undisclosed liabilities—such as lawsuits or problems with income taxes or payroll withholding taxes—incurred by the previous owner.

PREPARING TO SELL

When preparing to sell a business, owners need to gather a wide variety of information for potential buyers to review. Financial, legal, marketing, and operations information all need to be prepared for examination.

Financial Information Most privately held businesses are operated in ways that serve to minimize the seller's tax liability. As John A. Johansen observed in the SBA brochure *How to Buy or Sell a Business,* however, "the same operating techniques and accounting practices that minimize tax liability also minimize the value of a business.... It is possible to reconstruct financial statements to reflect the actual operating performance of the business, [but] this process may also put the owner in a position of having to pay back income taxes and penalties. Therefore, plans to sell a business should be made years in advance of the actual sale." Such a period of time allows the owner to make the accounting changes that will put his or her business in the best financial light. Certainly, a business venture that can point to several years of optimum fiscal success is apt to receive more inquiries than a business whose accounting practices—while quite sensible in terms of creating a favorable tax environment for the owner—blunt those bottom line financial numbers.

Would-be business sellers also need to prepare financial statements and other documents for potential buyers to review. These include a complete balance sheet (with detailed information on accounts receivable and payable, inventory, real estate, machinery and other equipment, liabilities, marketable securities, and schedules of notes payable and mortgages payable), an income statement, and a valuation report. The latter is an appraisal of the business's market value.

Legal Information The seller should also prepare the necessary information on legal issues pertaining to the company. These range from such basic operating documents as articles of incorporation, bylaws, partnership agreements, supplier agreements, and franchise agreements to data on regulatory requirements (and whether they are being adhered to), current or pending legal actions against the company, zoning requirements, lease terms, and stock status.

Marketing Information Intelligent buyers will want detailed marketing information on the company as well, including data on the business's chief market area, its market share, and marketing expenditures (on advertising, consultants, etc.). In addition, product line information will also be expected. Buyers, for instance, will want to know whether any of the company's products are proprietary, or whether there are potentially valuable new goods in the production pipeline. Descriptions of pricing strategies, customer demographics, and competition should also be available for potential buyers to review.

Operations Information Finally, business owners looking to sell their companies should be prepared to provide detailed information on various aspects of the business's day-to-day operations. The "operations" umbrella encompasses everything from company policies to historical hours of operation to personnel listings, including organizational chart (if applicable), job descriptions, rates of pay, and benefits. Other factors that can potentially impact one or more aspects of the company's operations, such as the presence or absence of an employee union, will also have to be detailed.

Once information on all facets of the business has been gathered, it should be organized into a comprehensive business presentation package. A complete business presentation package, remarked Johansen, should include the following:

- History of the business
- Description of business operations
- Description of physical facilities
- Discussion of suppliers (if any) and agreements with those suppliers
- Review of current and historical marketing practices
- Description of competition
- Coverage of personnel and employee issues
- Identification of owners
- Description of insurance coverage for business
- Discussion of pending legal issues or contingent liabilities
- Financial statements for the past three to five years

LOCATING PROSPECTIVE BUYERS

Most business owners sell their companies to external buyers—buyers other than current partners or employees in the organization. The seller can advertise the business, use his or her industry contacts to the get the word out, or engage intermediaries. Increasingly, online services with many options are available for advertising the business. Examples of sites, one on which a business can be advertised for sale directly (cityfeetBiz) and of one of brokers (United Business Brokers, serving cities in Utah, Nevada, California, and Idaho) able to act as intermediaries, are provided in the references; there are many more.

Many people hoping to sell their businesses make arrangements for advertisements in the Thursday edition of the *Wall Street Journal,* which produces several regional versions of its paper around the country. The *Journal* is a particularly popular option for owners of large, privately held businesses. Owners of smaller businesses, meanwhile, often turn to the classified sections of their own local newspapers to advertise the availability of their company for acquisition. When submitting a "business opportunity" advertisement for publication in the newspaper, however, sellers need to take a sensible approach. Ads must be framed to convey essential information without details that let others (including competitors) guess who the seller actually is. Advertisements should provide a brief description of the type of business for sale, its primary assets (location, popularity, profitability, etc.), and a way interested buyers can make contact. Sellers who wish to maintain some degree of anonymity while looking for a buyer may wish to arrange for a post office box rather than include their telephone number.

Industry sources also can be valuable when a business owner decides to sell his or her business. Suppliers may know of potential buyers elsewhere in the industry or the community. In addition, trade associations and trade journals can be used to get the word out about a company's availability.

A third option is to secure the services of a business broker or merger and acquisition consultant. Business brokers, who generally handle the sale of smaller companies (though this is by no means an absolute rule), typically charge the seller a fee of about 10% of the final purchase price. Merger and acquisition consultants typically specialize in handling larger middle-market companies. Payments to "M&A" consultants are usually less than 10%, but this is in part because of the larger scale of the deals in which they are typically involved. In addition, many consultants ask for a monthly retainer fee. One of the benefits of securing the services of a merger and acquisition consultant is that he or she will typically provide help in preparing presentation packages, valuing businesses, and negotiating with prospective buyers.

A well-chosen business broker or merger and acquisition consultant can save the seller of a business a considerable amount of time and effort. However, both groups include hucksters who prey on unwary business owners, so it is important for sellers to conduct the appropriate background research before soliciting services in these areas.

Another option sometimes available to business owners is to sell the company to "internal" buyers—employees, business partners, or family members. Selling to employees through employee stock ownership plans (ESOPs) or other arrangements are particularly attractive because they accrue significant tax advantages for owners through such sales. Employees interested in assuming ownership of the company by a management buyout (MBO) could range from a single key employee, such as a general manager who already has a good grasp on many aspects of the enterprise, to a group of employees (or even all of the company's employees). MBOs that rely on external financing typically require that one or more members of the purchasing group have management training in all aspects of the business; if such expertise is lacking, the seller will need to implement a training schedule for one or more employees to fulfill this requirement.

Business partners, meanwhile, are often ideal business buyers when an owner is ready to get out. Indeed, many business owners—especially in professional practices—bring in partners for this express purpose. The advantages of selling to a partner are numerous: the need to search for a buyer—or to use an intermediary—is obviated; terms of payment are often easier to arrange; and the business transition is eased because of the familiarity that already exists between the partner and the enterprise's suppliers, clients, and customers. Small business owners looking to hand over the reins of a company to a partner, however, need to adequately prepare for such a step. Locating a suitable partner, structuring a partnership buyout, and financing a partnership buyout are all important and complex issues that require care and attention.

Finally, business owners also groom people within their organization to take over the business upon their retirement (or death or disability). Family-owned businesses often hand over the reins from generation to generation in this fashion. In many cases this transfer of ownership is made as a gift or included as part of the owner's estate.

MAKING THE SALE

Once the seller has found a buyer for his or her company, the next step is to arrange the structure of the transaction. In addition to determining whether to make a stock or asset sale (in the case of corporations), the seller and the buyer need to reach agreement on other terms of the sale as well.

Earn-Outs An earn out is an agreement wherein the seller takes a portion of the selling price each year for a fixed period of time out of the earnings of the company under its new ownership. These agreements are sometimes employed when a seller cannot get his or her full asking price because of buyer concerns about some aspect of the business. As a result, some sellers insist on minimum payment amounts. In addition, since the seller's total compensation under this arrangement depends on the company's performance during the specified earn-out period, sellers often require that they be involved in management decisions during this period. Earn-outs can be calculated as a percentage of gross profit, net profit, sales, or some other mutually agreed-upon figure. Sellers, however, need to make sure that the measurement used is fair and easily verifiable.

Installment Sales Under this common arrangement, the seller of the business receives some cash, but the majority of the purchase price is received over a period of years. The down payment for small businesses may range from as little as 10 to as much as 40 percent or more, with the rest paid out—with interest—over a period of 3-15 years.

Leveraged Buyout A leveraged buyout or LBO is the purchase of a company through a loan secured by using the assets of the business as collateral. This option, however, places a greater debt burden on the company than do other types of financing.

Stock Exchanges In instances where a large, publicly held company is the purchaser, business owners sometimes ask to be compensated with stock in the purchasing corporation. In such cases, the seller is usually required to hold on to the stock for a certain period of time—usually two years—before he or she has the option to resell it.

Buyers sometimes insist on a noncompetition clause as well. Such a covenant, which can be incorporated into the purchase and sale agreement or created as a separate document, usually stipulates a market area and/or a period of time (three to five years is common) in which the seller may not open a business that would compete with the enterprise that he or she previously sold.

CLOSING THE DEAL

Once a deal has been struck between the seller and the buyer of the business, various conditions of sale often have to be addressed before the deal is closed. These include verification of financial statements, transfer of licenses, obtaining financing, and other conditions. Most contracts call for these conditions of sale to be addressed by a specified date; if one or more of these conditions is not taken care of by that time, the agreement is no longer valid.

Provided that these conditions have been attended to, however, the parties can move on to the closing. Closings are generally done either via an escrow settlement or via an attorney who performs settlement. In an escrow settlement, the money to be deposited, the bill of sale, and other relevant documents are placed with a neutral third party known as an escrow agent until all conditions of sale have been met. The escrow agent then distributes the held documents and funds in accordance with the terms of the contract.

If an attorney performs settlement, meanwhile, he or she—acting on behalf of both buyer or seller, or for the buyer—draws up a contract and acts as an escrow agent until all stipulated conditions of sale have been met. Whereas escrow settlements do not require the buyer and the seller to get together to sign the final documents, an attorney who performs settlements does include this step.

Several documents are required to complete the transaction between business seller and business buyer. The purchase and sale agreement is the most important of these, but other documents often used in closings include the escrow agreement; bill of sale; promissory note; security agreement; settlement sheet; financing statement; and employment agreement.

SEE ALSO *Business Appraisers; Valuation*

BIBLIOGRAPHY
cityfeetBiz. Web Site. Available from http://www.cityfeet businessesforsale.com/. Retrieved on 26 May 2006.

Klueger, Robert F. *Buying and Selling a Business: A Step-by-Step Guide.* John Wiley & Sons, 2004.

Steingold, Fred. *The Complete Guide to Selling a Business: The Step by Step Legal Guide.* Nolo, 2005.

Tuttle, Samuel S. *Small Business Primer: How To Buy, Sell, and Evaluate a Business.* streetsmartbooks, 2002.

United Business Brokers. Web Site. Available from http://unitedbusinessbrokers.com/. Retrieved on 26 May 2006.

U.S. Small Business Administration. Johansen, John A. *How to Buy or Sell a Business.* n.a.

Hillstrom, Northern Lights
updated by Magee, ECDI

SENIORITY

Seniority, defined broadly, means the length of service with an employer. Historically, those who had more experience with a task or in a job position managed those with less experience. Formal seniority policies grew out of this natural state of affairs. Based on an employee's seniority, preference can be accorded him or her in such areas as promotion, transfer, shift assignment, scheduling, vacation accrual, layoff, and recall after temporary layoff. Seniority is used as a means of gauging the relative status of one employee with respect to another based on length of service. As an employee's seniority grows, he or she accrues certain rights and privileges.

How exactly seniority is defined will differ from company to company. Some will track longevity without concern for the position worked while others will restart the clock every time an employee changes positions within the company. For some companies, seniority measurement is indifferent to whether an employee holds a part-time position or a full-time job. Other companies only measure seniority based on time worked in a full-time position. What all seniority calculations have in common is that they measure, in some fashion, an employee's longevity with a company. Collective bargaining agreements usually calculate seniority by total length of service, sometimes with consideration for length of service within a particular craft or department.

The rights that accrue to senior employees also differ from company to company. Seniority may be used in making determinations about the order in which to hire back from a layoff list. It is often used to allocate vacation time providing those with more seniority a greater number of vacation days. It may also be used to determine pay in organizations instead of or in addition to a merit-based pay system. If organizations do not pay employees on the basis of doing the same work and holding the same level or rank in the organization, they must determine a basis to make a pay distinction or differentiation. In a large organization, compensation specialists within the human resources area may make these determinations and may consider an employee's seniority in the pay decision.

SENIORITY'S DECLINING ROLE

As the economy has changed over the past 40 to 60 years—shifting from a manufacturing economy to an economy based on services, absorbing large numbers of women into the workforce, and becoming more globally interdependent—expectations of work have changed. In the past it was far more likely that a person would work much, if not all, of his or her career with a single employer. This in no longer the case. As mobility has increased in the workforce, the role of seniority has diminished. Declining union membership as a percentage of the workforce has also contributed to the reduced role of seniority as an important factor in employment decisions.

While seniority was valued in the past, for many people today, the longer you have been with a company, the more your job may be in jeopardy. Technology is cited as a primary reason for this change. Younger workers are perceived as more creative and innovative and may have more relevant educational experiences and training. Just as the product life cycle has shortened, so too has the career cycle of employees. Today job change and diversity of experiences is valued more than seniority.

Companies are under great competitive pressure and have less tolerance for employees who are earning in excess of their output, a situation more common among the most senior members of an organization. Today an older employee can be replaced by someone younger earning less than half as much salary.

But will that always be the case? As the influential baby boom generation begins to depart the workforce, most observers see a shortage of skills and a potentially serious shortfall in the supply of labor looming in the very near future. The conclusion of a report on a human resource director's survey, conducted by IBM and reported on in the *Economist,* states the situation this way: "When the baby-boom generation retires, many companies will find out too late that a career's worth of experience has walked out the door, leaving insufficient talent to fill the void."

In anticipation of this demographic shift, efforts are being made by some foresighted firms to maintain those with seniority and experience. Employees who are reaching retirement age are being encouraged to consider a phased withdrawal from the labor force. The use of job-sharing arrangements and part-time work schedules are two ways that are becoming more common for senior personnel in the stage a phased retirement. These flexible work arrangements allow an employee to ease out of the work habit while providing the company with an opportunity to use the senior employee's skills to train newer employees before the departure of senior employees.

SENIORITY IN JAPAN

Japan has long been known for its cradle-to-grave employment relationship. But, even in Japan things are changing. In the past, the seniority system in organizations was a measure of job security in the employment relationship. Many companies are abandoning traditional employment relationships and no longer offering lifetime employment.

Employment practices in Japan—which were once characterized by seniority, company unions, and lifetime employment—have been undergoing a structural transformation as the nation struggles to cope with an ever more competitive economy. Since the collapse of the Japanese bubble economy early in the 1990s, Japanese companies, like their American counterparts, have been forced to restructure and have adopted a system of determining promotions and salaries based not on seniority but on merit. This has dramatically changed their once-treasured code of seniority, according to *Focus Japan.*

In addition, just as this happened in the United States, the percentage of workers belonging to labor unions has steadily dropped, eroding the influence of the once-powerful Japanese company unions. Today's younger workers and new entrants to the job market are becoming less interested in the prospect of lifetime employment. As a result, many are considering entrepreneurship and self-employment as a more viable career choice.

SEE ALSO *Age Discrimination; Flexible Work Arrangements; Retirement Planning*

BIBLIOGRAPHY

"The Growing Mobility of Labor." *Focus Japan* October 2000.

Munk, Nina. "Finished at Forty." *Fortune.* 1 February 1999.

"Turning Boomers into Boomerangs – The Ageing Workforce." *The Economist.* 18 February 2006.

Wyss, David. "The Gathering Pension Storm: Boomers Will Soon Find Their Retirement Kitty Has Been Underfunded. Making up the shortfall with buffet corporations – and the economy." *The Economist.* 18 February 2006.

Hillstrom, Northern Lights
updated by Magee, ECDI

SERVICE BUSINESSES

INDUSTRIAL CLASSIFICATION

Industries are broadly classified as goods-producing and services-producing, but in the gradual evolution of industrial classification, ever new definitions of the services-producing sectors have emerged, indeed continue to emerge. Thus, for example, until 1997 U.S. industry was classified using the Standard Industrial Classification (SIC) system. It broke down industrial activity into nine major divisions: Agriculture, Mining, Construction, Manufacturing, Transportation and Utilities, Wholesale Trade, Retail Trade; Finance, Insurance, and Real Estate (FIRE); and, finally, Services. At that point the "services" component at least had a division of its own—although, in common parlance, people tended to include the Retail and the FIRE categories as part of the services sector.

Then came the North American Industrial Classification System (NAICS). It greatly expanded the divisional breakdown of industry, creating some 19 sectors. For example, Utilities were separated from Transportation; an Information sector was cut out of Manufacturing. FIRE lost Real Estate, which came to stand alone. And Retail lost Food Services. Most importantly, the Services Sector, which had become very important over the decades, was split apart into eight separate categories: Professional and Technical Services (which include law and engineering, for instance), Management Services (including holding companies), Administrative Support and Waste and Remediation Services, Educational Services, Health Services, Arts and Entertainment, Accommodations and Food Services, and Other Services (including household services, for instance).

The transition from SIC to NAICS, which had been a difficult path for industrial analysts in any case, was still not entirely traveled in the mid-2000s. During this period, the Census Bureau, working with Canada and Mexico (co-authors of NAICS), are working on NAPCS (for North American Product Classification System). NAPCS is causing the Census Bureau to revisit the services classifications. As a consequence of this new initiative, certain elements of other industries are now coming to be classified as "services," as indicated by the Census Bureau's *Services Annual Survey: 2004,* issued in April 2006. Important additions to the list include Truck Transportation, Couriers and Messengers, Warehousing and Storage, all of Information (which includes communications and publishing among others), Securities Brokerage (taken from Finance and Insurance), and Rental and Leasing (taken from Real Estate).

DEFINITION, CHARACTERISTICS, AND EXTENT

Given this still dynamically changing structure of classification, defining with any precision just exactly what a "service business" is presents some challenges. Service businesses are major movie studios, gigantic telecommunications firms, major publishers, enormous engineering concerns, the shoe repair shop down the street, the law firm, the payroll service, the auto rental organization, the apartment house, the fast food chain, the dental clinic, and so on and on.

Given the very great diversity that the term "service business" encompasses, its characteristics must, by definition, be rather broad. A service business is not primarily engaged in extractive, harvesting, and goods producing activities but in delivering results, often based on symbolical processes or the rearrangement of physical environments (landscaping, redecorating, waste handling, repairing), on personal services (healing, counseling, litigating, advising, persuading, amusing, caring for, teaching, etc.), on transporting goods and messages, and in structuring and managing ongoing or future activities by others (planning, engineering, management).

A service business, however, may also, if only incidentally, sell and deliver goods: people in the entertainment business sell CDs—although it is the *films* and the *music* that people are buying; in the information sector businesses sell newspapers and books—although it is the *content* of these media consumers are paying for; in the landscaping trade the businesses sell shrubs, plants, and decorative rock—but the buyer hires a landscape architect for the *design*; and in waste management, companies physically remove the waste—although the consumer is buying *the absence* of trash.

According to the Bureau of Economic Analysis (BEA), which produces the Gross Domestic Product estimates, the goods-producing sectors represented 21.3 percent, the service-producing sectors 74.5 percent, and the information, communications, and technology producing sectors 4.2 percent of GDP in 2004. BEA uses the "value added" measure, meaning the difference between a sector's outlays for input and receipts for sales. The Census Bureau, also using the 2004 base year, estimates that non-goods producing sectors accounted for 70 percent of business activity (using revenues, this time); services, more narrowly viewed, i.e., based on the categories presented above, accounted for 55 percent of the economy. Thus by any measure, a company in the "service business" could count itself as a member of the majority.

MASSIVE AND GROWING

The services sectors—however defined, whatever industries happen to be parts of it today—are the consequence of a mature and wealthy economy—as illustrated by historical statistics provided by the Census Bureau. In 1900 services represented 25.4 percent of all employment (business and other but excluding government); this percentage had changed to 50.6 percent by 1980, 57.7 percent by 1990, and stood at 62.5 percent in the census year of 2000. With productivity in the goods-producing industries increasing (fewer people needed to produce the same dollar output) but much more sluggish in growth in the services sectors, employment in the mid-2000s stands even higher.

SMALL BUSINESS IN THE SERVICES SECTORS

In terms of sheer numbers, small business has always dominated the corporate population, with well over 90 percent of all business firms being small, even when excluding the tiny operations that do not employ people, the owner alone participating. The usual—but not the formal—definition of a small business is one with fewer than 100 employees. (For a more detailed discussion, see the entry *Small Business.*) A look at small business in the services sectors shows that these not only dominate services but very small companies, those with fewer than 20 employees, are the overwhelming majority.

These data, for the year 2003 and provided by the Census Bureau, include only the traditional services sectors, thus Professional and Technical, Management, Administrative and Waste Handling, Educational, and Health Services. Also included are Arts and Entertainment, Accommodations and Food Service, and the "Other" category. In the aggregate 88 percent of all firms participating in these industries had fewer than 20-employees—but those counted all had some paid employees. The two sectors with the most "under-20 employee" firms were Professional and Technical Services and Other Services; in both, very small firms were 93 percent of all companies. Management firms (which include holding companies) had the fewest—only 24 percent were companies with under-20 employees. Educational service companies were next to the lowest—but among these the small companies already represented 75.7 percent of the participants.

In terms of employment, the largest of these sectors was Health Care and Social Assistance, with 15.4 million employees, followed by Accommodation and Food Services, with some 10.4 million employees in the aggregate; the smallest sector was Arts, Entertainment, and Recreation, with 1.8 million workers and Educational Services with 2.8 million employees.

TRENDS LIKELY TO CONTINUE

With services a dominant expression of the U.S. economy, with manufacturing productivity still growing, and outsourcing of function a favorite activity of very large organizations—almost always outsourcing service functions—the service sectors are likely to continue growing. With the majority of people employed in services industries, moreover, those thinking of striking out on their own will also, on average, be experienced in services activities—and start up service businesses themselves. Entry into the services sector requires more education and know-how than capital resources, which favors the entrepreneur with limited means. He or she, looking "to be of service" to society, will find a rather favorable environment for venturing out.

BIBLIOGRAPHY

Alexander, James A. *S-Business: Reinventing the Services Organization.* Select Books, 2003.

Baskin, Elizabeth Cogswell. *How to Run Your Business Like A Girl.* Adams Media, 2005.

Blumberg, Donald. *Managing High-Tech Services Using a CRM (Customer Relations Management) Strategy.* CRC Press, 2003.

Lake, Neville, and Cristin Hickey. *The Customer Service Workbook.* Kogan Page, 2002.

"Software Helps Manage Small Service Businesses." *Product News Network.* 11 May 2006.

U.S. Census Bureau. "Statistics of U.S. Businesses: 2003." Available from http://www.census.gov/epcd/susb/2003/us/US--.HTM. Retrieved on 7 June 2006.

U.S. Bureau of the Census. *Service Annual Survey: 2004.* April 2006.

Darnay, ECDI

SERVICE CORPS OF RETIRED EXECUTIVES (SCORE)

The Service Corps of Retired Executives (SCORE) is a national non-profit organization that counsels business owners and aspiring entrepreneurs. There are 389 SCORE chapters throughout the United States offering counseling services to small businesses in all areas at no charge to the client. There is no membership requirement to receive SCORE counseling—a phone call to make an appointment with a local SCORE chapter is sufficient to put the small business owner in touch with this valuable organization.

History SCORE was founded in 1964 specifically to provide business counseling to entrepreneurs. A national non-profit organization, SCORE is funded primarily by the U.S. Small Business Administration (founded in 1953). The group is made up of more than 10,000 active and retired business executives familiar with all areas of business management. This group donates its services, conducting one-to-one counseling as well as team counseling and training sessions. SCORE provides assistance to an estimated 300,000 plus would-be entrepreneurs and business owners annually. According to the SCORE Web site, the organization has helped 7.2 million small businesses since its founding.

Mission and Programs According to SCORE, volunteers "serve as 'Counselors to America's Small Business.'" The volunteer members of the organization are "dedicated to entrepreneur education and the formation, growth and success of small business nationwide."

SCORE counselors provide general business advice on all aspects of business formation and management. This service is provided free of charge and in confidential fashion. Counselors may assist in anything from investigating market potential for a product or service to providing guidance on cash flow management. They may provide insight into how to start or operate a business, how to buy a business or franchise, or how to sell a business. Volunteers also review business plans, often offering suggestions before the plans are submitted to a bank for financing consideration (in one survey of SCORE offices in 14 states, 27 percent of respondents indicated they delayed or canceled plans to start their own business after talking with a SCORE counselor, usually because the meetings illuminated shortcomings in training or strategy). Finally, individual SCORE offices offer free and confidential counseling and business advice via electronic mail on the Internet. According to the organization, these e-mail counseling sessions are

its fastest growing service (SCORE offices conducted 75,000 such sessions in 2000).

SCORE also holds workshops throughout the country. Workshops and seminars on specialized areas of business training such as writing business plans, inventory control, advertising, financing and international trade are available at reduced cost (usually a nominal fee of $100 or so, to cover cost of facilities and materials). For more information on this and other SCORE services, the organization maintains a Web site (www.score.org) detailing its offerings.

SCORE Volunteers SCORE volunteers are usually between the ages of 60 and 70, but there is no age limit for a volunteer. Retired executives interested in joining SCORE fill out a formal application and usually supply a resume for consideration by their local chapter. There is a 90 day probation period during which performance is monitored. To insure quality, SCORE counselors are matched to cases according to the type of business or client seeking advice and the counselor's area of specialty. SCORE is not an employment service, however. Members may give advice, but may not accept positions with client companies, nor may they direct a business owner to individuals or firms which may provide employees. SCORE's main function is to provide free advice to small businesses.

BIBLIOGRAPHY

Aglar, Robert. "SCORE: America's Small Business Counselors Score with Professional, Confidential, No-Cost Counseling." *Denver Business Journal.* 26 May 2000.

Broome, Jr., J. "SCORE's Impact on Small Firms." *Nation's Business.* January 1999.

Campanelli, Melissa. "Getting Good Advice." *Sales and Marketing Management.* March 1995.

Dawkins, Pam. "SCORE Pays Big Dividends." *Connecticut Post.* 3 May 2005.

"Explore SCORE." *SCORE Counselors to America's Small Business.* Available from http://www.score.org/explore_score.html. Retrieved on 6 June 2006.

"SCORE Volunteers Score Kudos from Businesses." *The Bellingham Herald.* 15 October 2005.

Hillstrom, Northern Lights
updated by Magee, ECDI

SEXUAL HARASSMENT

Sexual harassment is a term used to describe actions that make use of sexual comments or acts in order to intimidate those with whom one works. Sexual harassment is illegal. Sexual harassment is a form of sex discrimination, it is a violation of Title VII of the Civil Rights Act of 1964. Title VII applies to all employers with 15 or more employees.

Many actions can be legally shown to be either sexual harassment or to contribute to a hostile or offensive work environment. The Equal Employment Opportunity Commission (EEOC) defines sexual harassment as follows: "Unwelcome sexual advances, requests for sexual favors, and other verbal or physical contact of a sexual nature constitute sexual harassment when: 1) Submission to such conduct is made either explicitly or implicitly a term or condition of an individual's employment. 2) Submission to or rejection of such conduct by an individual is used as the basis for employment decisions affecting such individuals. 3) Such conduct has the purpose or effect of unreasonably interfering with an individual's work performance or creating an intimidating, hostile, or offensive working environment." But legal experts warn managers and business owners that definitions of sexual harassment extend beyond these boundaries. Although most people think that sexual harassment involves **conduct** of a sexual nature, based on a study of case law, this is not true. Sexual harassment includes acts that are not overtly sexual but rather are directed at individuals based on their gender. Therefore, profanity or rude behavior that is gender-specific may create a work environment that legally supports claims of sexual harassment.

Some observers believe that small businesses are particularly susceptible to sexual harassment problems. This is because small businesses often have an informal office atmosphere that may seem to allow sexual banter and innuendo. Small businesses are also less likely to have an official sexual harassment policy and training program than are larger firms. Savvy small business owners adopt proactive stances to make certain that their employees know that inappropriate behavior—whether it takes the form of displaying sexually explicit photographs, using offensive language, making suggestive or otherwise inappropriate comments, badgering an employee for dates or other interactions outside the workplace, or suggesting that one gender is inferior to another—will not be tolerated in their company. Indeed, firms that do not do so leave themselves open to financial loss via lawsuits as well as other problems like low morale, employee turnover, and absenteeism. These negative side effects can ultimately impact on financial performance. As EEOC guidelines state, "with respect to conduct between fellow employees, an employer is responsible for acts of sexual harassment in the workplace where the employer (or its agents or supervisory employees) knows or should have known of the conduct, unless it can show that it took immediate and appropriate corrective action."

HARASSMENT AND EMPLOYEE RIGHTS

Over the past several years, sexual harassment has become a subject of considerable discussion. Previous generations

of business owners and managers rarely had to address the issue. Business historians and social observers point to several possible factors for this. Some note that women used to comprise a much smaller component of the workforce, and that various societal pressures may have made them less likely to come forward with complaints. Others point out that many of the legal protections that are now in place against harassment have only developed over the last 25 to 35 years. Still other observers contend that the rise in sexual harassment claims simply reflects a general decline in civility in American society. Whatever the reasons, sexual harassment complaints have risen throughout the 1990s and remained fairly steady throughout the first five years of the 2000s. The Equal Employment Opportunity Commission is the governing body that is authorized to administer laws prohibiting sexual harassment. Charges of harassment are filed with the EEOC. The EEOC reported that it received 12,679 charges of sexual harassment in fiscal year 2005, of which 14.3 percent were filed by men. The EEOC resolved 12,859 sexual harassment charges in FY 2005 (some charges take longer than a year to resolve and thus the number of charges filed in a single year may be lower than the number of resolutions) and recovered $47.9 million in monetary benefits for charging parties and other aggrieved individuals. This figures does not including monetary benefits obtained through litigation. To these totals, it should be understood that many charges of sexual harassment are resolved quietly, some at substantial cost, before they ever reach the point at which the charge is officially made with the EEOC. Clearly, the potential for losses, both financial and in terms of reputation, as a result of sexual harassment are great and it is a subject that should be dealt with in a very visible and up-front manner within companies of all sizes.

But small business owners and corporate executives alike need to make sure that in their zeal to protect the legitimate rights of employees not to be harassed in the workplace, they do not trample on the rights of those accused of misbehavior. Just because sexual harassment is a significant social and business problem does not mean it has in fact occurred in a particular instance. Indeed, an employee who is punished or dismissed on the basis of a frivolous sexual harassment claim has the same recourse to the law as the victim of sexual harassment who is left unprotected by indifferent managers/owners. Business owners and managers thus need to consider the rights of all parties involved when investigating sexual harassment complaints.

DEVELOPING AND MAINTAINING SEXUAL HARASSMENT POLICIES

A well-drafted, carefully thought-out policy statement on sexual harassment is an important human resource policy for all companies. It's valuable in at least three major ways:

1. As an employee relations tool

2. As basic education for both managers and employees on the subject of sexual harassment

3. As a way of minimizing legal liability to the organization in hostile-environment sexual harassment cases.

Such a policy statement is evidence of a company's good-faith effort to provide a work environment that is free of harassment. When coupled with a proper investigation that successfully ends illegal or inappropriate conduct, it can also provide a major offensive weapon in employer efforts to demonstrate that all reasonable steps were taken and that they were effective in the case of a sexual harassment charge.

Indeed, business consultants universally counsel both small businesses and multinational corporations to establish formal written policies that make it explicitly clear that no forms of sexual harassment will be tolerated. Some companies prefer to disseminate this information as part of their larger general policy statements because of their sensitivity to giving extra attention to a sometimes awkward subject. But others believe that doing so can have the effect of burying the company's sexual harassment policies under the weight of all its other statements. These observers claim that dissemination of a separate policy statement not only better informs employees of the policy itself, but also underlines the company's serious approach to the subject.

Whether a business chooses to distribute its policies on sexual harassment via general information sources (employee handbook) or separate statements, its policies should list all the various forms that sexual harassment can take (sexually loaded "compliments," sexual advances, denigration of a person's gender, etc.) and explain how the company proceeds when confronted with a sexual harassment complaint. The policy statement should also discuss possible disciplinary consequences for workers who are found guilty of engaging in harassment.

Other steps that businesses can take to establish an harassment-free workplace include: establishing internal procedures that address complaints promptly and thoroughly; establishing training programs that educate workers—and especially managers, supervisors, and other people wielding power—about components of sexual harassment and their responsibilities when exposed to such behavior; establishing alternative routes for workers to lodge complaints (in instances where his or her supervisor is the alleged harasser, for instance).

BUILDING A COMPREHENSIVE POLICY

Legal experts warn businesses that they need to make certain that their policies reflect a true understanding of the legal responsibilities of the employer, and a full recognition of the multitude of forms that sexual harassment can take. They point out that some companies have put together policies that, while sensible and effective in some or even most areas, are flawed in other areas, either because their policies did not adequately cover all the ways in which sexual harassment can occur, or because their understanding of sexual harassment was incomplete from the outset. For example, many people have long operated under the misconception that for sexual harassment to occur, the harasser must have a bad intent. The reality, however, is that what may be viewed as perfectly harmless by some people, may be viewed as offensive by others. Courts have dealt with this difference by developing a new standard for analyzing claims of sexual harassment. The old standard was the traditional gender-neutral reasonable person standard, which is thought to be biased toward the male viewpoint. Sexual harassment claims are now analyzed in many jurisdictions from the perspective of a reasonable person of the same sex so as to eliminate the potential for differences in perspective that are based on gender.

Another important factor that is not always sufficiently appreciated by employers is that they can be held liable for harassing conduct by a third party such as a customer or vendor. Cases of this type are rare. Nonetheless, business owners should be aware of their responsibility to address complaints of this type. Just as an employer is responsible to provide employees with a safe work environment, it is responsible to confront customers, clients or other third parties if they harass employees in any way.

Sexual harassment complaints often arise after the failure of a romantic liaison between employees. As a result, many companies attempt to limit such romantic involvement between employees by establishing anti-nepotism and anti-dating policies. Assessments of the dangers of office romance vary dramatically. Some observers view it as a wholly undesirable condition that should be avoided by business owners and managers if at all possible, while others view it as a potential positive development, provided that the relationship lies within certain parameters. But what happens when a philanderer dates and discards casually within a company, leaving angry, litigation-prone employees in his/her wake? Reasons for dating policies to address supervisors, subordinates, and clients, not to mention patients and vendors, are understandable.

The risks that a deteriorating romance poses for a company that employs both parties are undeniable. Perhaps, however, the benefits of happily partnered employees is another possible outcome to an office romance. Famous cases abound: Microsoft's founder Bill Gates and opera impresario Luciano Pavarotti both married employees of their organizations. Obviously, businesses create dating policies to try and manage the negative aspects of office romances, and those that crash and burn. But, since perfectly happy relationships may result from office romances, policies that are clear and specific about exactly what they prohibit are best. The subject is complex, the potential threats serious, and the need for clarity is essential.

INVESTIGATING SEXUAL HARASSMENT COMPLAINTS

Companies must investigate every sexual harassment complaint seriously and thoroughly, and take action accordingly. A key foundation of this process is to make certain that the person who will investigate the complaint has credibility with the workforce. Ideally, the individual will be knowledgeable about the legal dimensions of sexual harassment, experienced in handling employee issues, familiar with the organization's policies, and socially and organizationally distant from both the alleged victim and the alleged harasser (the investigator should not be friends with the alleged victim, nor directly report to the alleged harasser, or vice versa). With smaller companies, however, it can be more difficult to adhere to such guidelines. If a small business owner has only four employees, and two of them become embroiled in a harassment case, finding an investigator with the above qualities is next to impossible. The owner may be tempted to look into the complaint him or herself in such instances, but business advisors often counsel against this. Instead, they recommend that the owner turn to an outside counsel or external consultant to pursue the complaint.

Whether the person doing the investigating is a third party, an employee, or the owner of the business, he or she should have a focused, carefully thought-out investigation plan designed to settle the issue in as timely a fashion as possible. This typically includes a review of relevant organizational records, including complainant's personnel file, alleged harasser's personnel file, performance reviews, and promotional and salary records. Such reviews can turn up everything from prior disciplinary warnings aimed at the accused to possibly relevant indications that the involved parties had previously competed against one another for promotions or other job opportunities. Such data may well be completely irrelevant to the legitimacy of the complaint, but it is the investigator's duty to check into all possible aspects of the complaint.

Every claim should be treated seriously, no matter how unusual or seemingly frivolous it might first appear, until an informed decision can be made. Conversely, an investigator should also suspend judgment on complaints that seem obviously legitimate until a thorough investigation has been completed. This may seem obvious advice but it is as difficult to adhere to as it is obvious.

The first step in an investigation usually involves an in-depth interview of the complainant. Areas that should be pursued during this interview include the cultural background of the complainant (if dramatically different from that of the accused), a detailed reconstruction of the incident(s) that prompted the complaint, the context and circumstances in which it occurred, the involved parties' prior relationship (if any), the nature of the allegations against each individual in instances where incidents involved the participation of more than one person (common in hostile workplace complaints), and the complainant's expectations regarding how the alleged offender should be disciplined.

The investigation then turns to getting the accused's account of events. This step has different nuances, depending on whether the alleged harasser is a supervisor, a coworker, or a third party such as a customer, but basically this part of the investigation aims to secure the accused's perspective. In some instances, the accused may appear angry or shocked when confronted with a sexual harassment charge, so the investigator needs to allow time for the return of some measure of emotional equilibrium. When the initial reaction has subsided the investigator should ask the worker to relate what he or she believed happened during the incidents cited. Allow the accused to relate his or her understanding of the situation completely once, then return to it for specific, step-by-step review. As with the complainant, make sure the discussion is specific and detailed enough to provide the necessary information for later decision making. Note dates, times, places, circumstances, dress, words exchanged, as well as the specifics of the alleged acts. Again, issues such as prevailing work environment, prior relationships, etc. should be discussed.

Once the investigator has finished gathering information from the principal parties, he or she should then turn to possible witnesses. These could range from coworkers who were present when the alleged incident took place to those who have relevant information on either or both of the parties involved. The investigator should not be concerned with unsubstantiated rumors at this juncture; rather, he or she should concentrate on gathering factual data. This can be a very important part of the investigation, for accusations that turn into basic "he said, she said" disputes can be profoundly difficult for employers to resolve. Immediate action may be almost impossible when an employer is faced with unsub-stantiated accusation on one side and a categorical denial on the other. But experts point out that workplace behavior often can be corroborated by other staffers. Employers need to interview these witnesses carefully, being careful not to fuel rumors, and/or be seen to have taken sides. The objective of these interviews is to gather factual data, nothing more. It does offer the opportunity, however, to show that the company is handling the investigation seriously, professionally, and carefully. Securing written statements is helpful.

Once the investigation into the sexual harassment complaint has been completed, corrective action (if any) needs to be implemented. When corrective action is warranted, it can range from counseling to transfer to dismissal. The key factors that usually determine the severity of the corrective action are: 1) the nature of the offense, 2) the desires of the complainant, and 3) the impact that the incident had on the workplace as a whole.

HARASSMENT OF THE SELF-EMPLOYED

Self-employed individuals who work as independent con-tractors enjoy fewer legal protections from sexual harass-ment at the hands of clients. Experts recommend that self-employed people confronted with such unpleasant-ness react strongly and decisively. They should make it immediately clear that the harassment (which in these situations typically takes the form of unwanted sexual advances) is unwelcome, and that they would prefer to keep their association with their client a professional one. If this line of defense does not work, the self-employed worker may wish to consult an attorney about his or her state's tort law, which regulates conduct between people and provides monetary damages. In addition, national women's organizations can often provide guidance and legal assistance in these matters.

SEE ALSO *Gender Discrimination; Office Romance; Nepotism*

BIBLIOGRAPHY
Buhler, Patricia M. "The Manager's Role in Preventing Sexual Harassment." *Supervision*. April 1999.

"The Downside of Office Romance." *OfficeSolutions*. March-April 2006.

Lynn, Jacquelyn. "Lawfully Wedded Employees." *Entrepreneur*. April 2000.

Moses, Jeffrey. "Office Romance in the New Millennium." National Federation of Independent Business. Available from http://www.nfib.com/object/IO_22940.html. 21 June 2005.

Penttila, Chris. "In the Hot Seat: One person's promotion is another's harassment claim." *Entrepreneur*. January 2006.

Pfeiffer, Sacha. "Grey Areas Complicate Sexual Harassment Cases." *Boston Globe*. 25 May 2006.

Petrocelli, William, and Barbara Kate Repa. *Sexual Harassment on the Job: What It Is and How to Stop It*. Fourth Edition. Nolo Press, 1998.

Risser, Rita. "Sexual Harassment Training: Truth and Consequences." *Training and Development*. August 1999.

U.S. Equal Employment Opportunity Commission. "Sexual Harassment." Available from http://www.eeoc.gov/types/sexual_harassment.html. Retrieved on 7 June 2006.

Weiss, Donald H. *Fair, Square, and Legal*. AMACOM, 1 April 2004.

Hillstrom, Northern Lights
updated by Magee, ECDI

SHARED SERVICES

"Shared services" is a term defining an operational phil-osophy that involves centralizing those administrative functions of a company that were once performed in separate divisions or locations. Services that can be shared among the various business units of a company include finance, purchasing, inventory, payroll, hiring, and infor-mation technology. For example, a central headquarters might control all the hiring for an entire chain of retail stores. The term "shared services" can also apply to part-nerships formed between separate businesses. In this case, the tenants of an office building might share telecommu-nications or maintenance service. Shared services are also available on the Internet. An example of this form of shared services is Application Service Providers (ASPs) who offer numerous business clients access to online appli-cations so they can avoid purchasing special systems and software.

Ideally, companies that implement shared services enjoy significant cost savings by standardizing practices and procedures and by creating economies of scale. Proponents argue that performing a function in one location usually requires less investment in technology and office space, as well as up to 30 percent fewer employees, than performing the function in multiple locations. "Under shared services, a company centralizes back-office functions, such as accounting, warehousing, and even information technology, and treats them as internal vendors," Erik Sherman explained in *Computerworld*. "The rest of the company can use out-side service providers instead, so competitive pressures promote responsive service, and reduced staffing saves money." In some cases, the centralized functions—or shared services organizations—charge the different divi-sions for the use of their services. Other shared services organizations even offer their services to outside firms on the open market.

The application of shared services is a popular business strategy. In fact, Elizabeth Ferrarini noted in *Computerworld* that it has been adopted by half of all Fortune 500 companies. "Centralizing company functions—in a manner now known as the 'shared services' model—is one of the hottest trends in business today," Mark Henricks wrote in *Entrepreneur*. "Those who practice it say they can cut costs while improving the quality of the services shared." The concept of shared services was introduced in the 1980s, when a number of large companies with multiple business units began looking for ways to reduce their administrative costs. Since then, Henricks noted, "shared services has evolved into a more comprehensive and flexible tool for improving processes, enabling technology investment, generating profits, and reducing costs."

There are a number of potential drawbacks associated with shared services, however. For example, companies switching to a shared services model often incur the cost of hiring new people and installing new technology. In addition, implementing shared services takes time—often more than one year. Furthermore, as Henricks warned, centralization is not appropriate for every function. Companies should not centralize their core competencies or functions that involve direct customer contact, particularly if outside firms also use the shared services.

The implementation of shared services can also create problems within a company. For example, the employees who used to provide the services in various business units might be upset with the loss of control they experience under the new arrangement. In addition, the headquarters employees who provide shared services from a central location might be uncomfortable treating business units as customers. In fact, switching to a shared services environment requires employees to develop new skills, with an increased emphasis on flexibility and customer service. "To be the preferred supplier—and even to have a secure corporate existence—the shared service has to cost-effectively deliver superior results," Sherman stated. As a result, a shared services system is not appropriate for every business. "For many companies, shared services will remain an intriguing concept that just doesn't fit their needs," Henricks noted. "For others, it will represent exactly the right model to take advantage of a promising opportunity to make the most of home-office skills that other divisions, locations, and even other companies can also use."

SEE ALSO *Cost Sharing*

BIBLIOGRAPHY
Bangemann, Tom. *Shared Services In Finance And Accounting.* Gower Publishing Ltd., December 2005.

Ferrarini, Elizabeth. "Shared Services." *Computerworld.* 27 November 2000.

Henricks, Mark. "Learn to Share." *Entrepreneur.* March 2001.

Herman, Jim. "Shared Business Services on the Net." *Business Communications Review.* June 2000.

Reilly, Peter A. *How to Get Best Value from HR: The Shared Services Option.* Gower Publishing Ltd., January 2003.

Quinn, Barbara. *Shared Services: Mining for Corporate Gold.* Prentice-Hall, 2000.

Schwartz, Ephraim. "HP Set to Unveil IT Shared Services Offering: IT as internal service provider promises greater flexibility." *InfoWorld.* 23 May 2006.

Sherman, Erik. "The Shared Services Challenge: Retooling IT as an Internal Vendor to Deliver Better Service Works for Many, but It's Easy to Hit Snafus along the Way." *Computerworld.* 2 August 1999.

Whitehead, William T. "Shared Services: A Business Strategy for Increasing Shareholder Value." *Site Selection.* July 2000.

Hillstrom, Northern Lights
updated by Magee, ECDI

SHOPLIFTING

Shoplifting is the practice of stealing merchandise from retail establishments. Unfortunately, shoplifting is a serious and persistent problem for most retailers. The results of an annual National Retail Security Survey were reported in the *St. Louis Post-Dispatch.* They found that shoplifting cost retailers an estimated $10 billion annually and that 30 percent of these losses are the result of organized retail crime. These professional shoplifters are of concern to retailers because they tend to steal higher priced items or work from the inside, through employees. Nonetheless, the fact that 70 percent of shoplifting losses result from unorganized stealing means that attempts to stop these losses must focus on both professional as well as casual shoplifters. Among the most commonly stolen items are tobacco products, athletic shoes, brand-name clothing, small appliances, jewelry, leather goods, and food items.

The costs of shoplifting are many. Most obvious of these costs are the losses suffered by retailers. The inventory lost to shoplifters is only part of the retailer's costs. They also absorb the costs of increased security measures and higher legal expenses associated with prosecuting the thieves. But shoplifting also costs the community in which it takes place by affecting store location decision. Stores in high-theft areas will often relocate and in so doing they end up contributing to the deterioration of these troubled areas. Finally, shoplifting costs consumers in terms of higher priced goods. "The cost [of shoplifting] is very high," said business professor Ed Mazze in *Providence Business News*. "It cuts into the profit margin of the retailer and is paid for by the consumer. It requires stores to invest in more complex security devices."

PREVENTING THEFT

The first step for retailers hoping to reduce their losses to shoplifting is to create a strong antitheft policy and publicize it among customers and employees alike. In preparing a policy, it is important to note that deterring theft is usually less expensive than apprehending and prosecuting thieves. In addition, retailers must be familiar with the shoplifting laws in their states, particularly in light of recent incidents involving the assault of alleged shoplifters by store security guards. Some states require individuals to exit a store before they can be accused of shoplifting, for example. Experts suggest that small business owners consult with local police or their insurance company to obtain assistance in setting up an antitheft program.

In order to address the problem of employee theft, retailers can use integrity questionnaires and conduct reference checks when hiring new employees. In addition, software solutions exist to help retailers detect point-of-sale errors and fraud. Another way that small retailers can help prevent shoplifting is to buy merchandise from established sources. In many cases, professional shoplifters steal from major retail chains and then resell the merchandise to small, local stores. A good rule of thumb is that if you are able to buy merchandise less expensively than a big chain, then it is probably stolen merchandise.

SECURITY MEASURES

Retailers have a number of security measures available to them to help deter potential shoplifters. A good place to start is by training employees to recognize and report suspicious behavior. Visible security measures are another valuable way to deter shoplifters. Security gates in doorways, security cameras in obvious locations, and uniformed security guards patrolling the store are all strong deterrents. Many retailers choose to reduce the temptation to steal by putting items that have high theft rates behind counters or giving them electronic article surveillance (EAS) tags. These methods have drawbacks, however, because limiting customer access to items reduces sales, while applying antitheft tags to items is labor intensive.

A relatively new weapon in the fight against shoplifting is the use of source tags. A source tag is a type of EAS tag that is applied by the manufacturer—usually inside the container or packaging—rather than by the retailer. The usage of source tags is growing, particularly in the areas of health and beauty aids and over-the-counter drugs. Some source tags can be used for both

security and inventory control. In the future, the technology might even be used for tracing stolen merchandise that is resold to other stores. "Source tagging helps us provide our valued customers with low-cost products and the perpetual inventory they are looking for," Tom Coughlin, CEO of Wal-Mart USA, told Hallie Forcinio in *Pharmaceutical Technology*. "It allows us to enhance sales and focus our resources on how we can better serve our customers."

BIBLIOGRAPHY

Feldstein, Mary Jo. "Retailers Turn to Technology to Thwart Bogus Returns." *St. Louis Post-Dispatch.* 14 December 2005.

Forcinio, Hallie. "Electronic Article Surveillance—Source Tag to Smart Tag." *Pharmaceutical Technology.* October 2000.

Mavromatis, K. Alexa. "'Tis the Season—to Shoplift." *Providence Business News.* 27 November 2000.

"Protect High-Risk Items from Shoplifters." *Chain Store Age Executive with Shopping Center Age.* June 1998.

Seigel, Larry J. *Criminology With Infotrac.* Thomson Wadsworth, 2005.

Wilson, William. "Being Prepared Is the Best Strategy Against Shoplifters and Robbers." *Discount Store News.* 3 April 2000.

Hillstrom, Northern Lights
updated by Magee, ECDI

SICK LEAVE AND PERSONAL DAYS

Sick leave and personal days are a form of employment benefit in the form of paid time off for illness or to deal with a personal/private matter. Since nearly everyone occasionally needs such time off, all businesses should have a clear policy established regarding sick leave and personal days. A sick day is fairly self-explanatory and can be used for everything from a common cold to a more serious illness that could require hospitalization or even surgery. Personal days can cover things like the illness of a child, a death in the family, jury duty, military obligations, or religious holidays. Most companies also allow vacation time for employees in addition to their set amount of sick leave and personal days.

Most companies allocate only a certain number of days for sick leave and personal time. For example, in a calendar year an employee could have five sick days and three personal days. If the employee fails to use them all in the given amount of time, the company must decide whether to allow employees to roll them over (that is, add or bank them to the number of sick days for the following year). The company could also reward the employee for not taking all available sick and personal days by offering cash bonuses, perks, or additional vacation days.

In an article for *Business First,* Dr. James D. Levy discussed employee attendance issues and described the three employee types that most businesses have to contend with. "On average, a small portion of employees will rarely, if ever, be absent because of illness. They pride themselves on being the iron man or iron woman and prove that people can, and do fulfill their responsibilities even when they don't feel well," he explained. "A second group, the great majority, will use a few sick days a year, well within most organizations' guidelines. The third group, usually only 5 percent or so, use their sick days plus most or all of their vacation time and additional lost time because of illness. It's this group that blurs the line between actual illness and the kind of 'not feeling well' that can be an excuse for poor performance or absences. Improvement in the attendance and performance of that small group would pay big dividends to organizations."

PROBLEMS WITH SICK LEAVE AND PERSONAL DAYS

From a business standpoint, the main problem that companies face when an employee takes time off because of an illness or personal matter is the loss of production. This in turn leads to a loss of money (in most instances, an employee is paid when they take a sick or personal day). The loss of productivity occurs simply because the work that the employee was supposed to do that particular day has to be done by one or more other employees or by a temporary employee. There is also the chance that the work could not get done at all.

The existence of sick and personal days also leaves the door wide open for them to be abused by employees who are less than honest about their health or personal lives. Most everyone has played hooky by calling in sick to work at one time or another, but those who make a habit of it are costing their employers a lot of money over the long run. In addition, the other employees who have to cover for them while they are taking time off may start to build up resentment if this situation occurs over and over again with the same individuals. This dip in morale can also hurt the company over a long period of time.

WAYS TO COMBAT ABUSE OF SICK LEAVE AND PERSONAL DAYS

There are many ways employers can fight back and make sure that their employees are not abusing the sick and personal days that they have been allotted. The first step would be to examine the existing policy and determine if it encourages unscheduled absenteeism. Management and supervisors can also force themselves to become more aware of their employees' habits and be on the lookout

for things like stress or specific types of lifestyles that may force an employee to take more time off. Single parents or recent divorcees would fall into this category.

In some instances, the company could consider providing counseling or other assistance to employees who suffer from problems that cause them to miss work (including alcoholism, drug abuse, and psychological problems). In addition, many employers can combat an attendance problem before it gets out of hand simply by confronting the employee and discussing the reasons why he or she has missed so much work. An official attendance record could be kept just in case the employee disputes the employer's claims. Policies requiring an employee to file a report stating why they missed work can also be helpful in these types of situations. Also, since many employees spend a lot of time in the workplace, an employer can also reduce the chances of them getting sick in the first place by promoting a clean, safe, and healthy office environment.

Another concept that many employers have found useful in cutting down on unscheduled absences is known either as a paid leave bank (PLB) or a paid time off program (PTO). This program requires employees to consider all of their vacation, sick, and personal days as one unit to be used either for PTO or serious catastrophic situations. This system forces an employee who is abusing his or her sick day privileges to subtract them from vacation time or personal days if he or she continues to do so. Since the time that falls under the PTO plan is essentially the employee's time, they would be less likely to abuse it. This plan also helps to cut down on unscheduled absences that disrupt the workplace. On the positive side, a company is better able to control costs under this system while still allowing an employee to take additional time if something catastrophic happens. A reward system can also be built into this plan to encourage employees from taking unscheduled absences off.

If a company offers employment options like flextime or the opportunity to work from home, they also stand the chance of cutting back on unscheduled absences. With a flexible schedule, employees can rearrange their work times to attend to a personal situation like taking their child to the doctor in the morning. After their personal business is taken care of, they can still come in and put in a full day at the office and not have to use a personal day. The option to work at home can also cut down on an unscheduled absence if employees are too sick to report to work but healthy enough to perform their duties. Many such duties can be done at home with the help of a laptop or other device that is useful in telecommuting. Another benefit to this option is that other employees will stand less of a chance of coming down with an illness if the employee who is already sick just works from home.

If constant abuse of sick and personal days continue to be a problem between a company and a particular employee, more drastic measures can be taken. One tried and true method requires that the employer insist on a note from a doctor before allowing an employee who has been out for more than several days to return to work. Policies regarding raises or other rewards can also be tied directly to employees' attendance records, therefore encouraging them not to take an unscheduled absence.

In serious circumstances, an employee can be fired for taking too many days off. The employer should make sure that they have a legitimate case against the employee in this instance because many situations are covered by the Family and Medical Leave Act (FMLA) and other laws that protect employees. If an employer is found to have wrongfully terminated an employee under one of these laws, it could stand to lose a considerable amount of money in a settlement.

But the best policies for reducing employee absenteeism have to do with creating a health workplace. Stephen Moir put it this way in an article on the subject that appeared in *Personnel Today*. "Staff wellbeing is about providing an environment that is conducive to people wanting to come to work and doing a good job. It is about having managers who manage well, and an organizational culture that is mature enough to recognize that a degree of absence is a natural side effect of employing real people. It is also about creating greater access to flexible working, and a broad range of benefits that motivate and encourage individuals. A truly successful approach to absence management is a holistic one that doesn't just do the hard stuff, but also thinks about the total package that you offer as an employer—friendly colleagues, access to learning opportunities, work-life balance, fair pay and rewards and so on."

SICK LEAVE AND PERSONAL DAY POLICIES FOR SMALL BUSINESSES

Small businesses that pay their employees by the hour often have no sick leave and personal day policies. In most cases, companies in this situation experience fewer cases of abuse of sick days off because when employees do not show up for work, then they do not get paid. Time clocks or official attendance ledgers are also used to let employers know exactly how many hours a particular employee works per day so that they can be paid accordingly. Of course, things like extended illnesses, a death in the family, or religious holidays can always force an employee to miss work.

For companies that employ salaried staff, a clear and defined policy for handling necessary sick days and per-

sonal days should be in place and followed carefully. In the case of an abuse of the system serious enough to motivate a termination, care must be taken. As Phillip M. Perry stated in *Industrial Distribution*: "If your business is small enough that you operate as the sole supervisor, you are still open to legal problems if you don't have a written policy followed to the letter. Employees who are terminated for excessive absenteeism will sue, claiming discrimination over those employees—possibly the ones who are more vital to your business success—who are absent just as often."

SEE ALSO *Absenteeism; Employee Benefits*

BIBLIOGRAPHY
Collis, Leighton. "The Hidden Costs of Sniffles and Sneezes." *HR Magazine*. July 1997.

Kaiser, Carl P. "What Do We Know About Employee Absence Behavior? An Interdisciplinary Interpretation." *The Journal of Socio-Economics*. January-February 1998.

Levy, Dr. James D. "Employers Can Make Sick Leave Less Debilitating." *Business First-Columbus*. 8 December 2000.

Moir, Stephen. "Tightening Sickness Absence Policies Is Not Necessarily the Answer." *Personnel Today*. 4 April 2006.

Perry, Phillip M. "Where's Jones? It's 9 A.M., Do You Know Where Your Employees Are?" *Industrial Distribution*. June 1996.

Hillstrom, Northern Lights
updated by Magee, ECDI

SIMPLIFIED EMPLOYEE PENSION (SEP) PLANS

Simplified employee pension (SEP) plans—also known as SEP/IRAs since they make use of individual retirement accounts—are pension plans intended specifically for self-employed persons and small businesses. Created by Congress and monitored by the Internal Revenue Service, SEPs are designed to give small business owners and employees the same ability to set aside money for retirement as traditional large corporate pension funds. SEP plans are available to all types of business entities, including proprietorships, partnerships, and corporations.

As employer-funded retirement plans, SEPs allow small businesses to direct at least 3 percent and up to 15 percent of each employee's annual salary into tax-deferred IRAs on a discretionary basis. SEP plans are easy to set up and inexpensive to administer, as the employer simply makes contributions to IRAs that are established by employees. The employees then take responsibility for making investment decisions regarding their own SEP accounts. Employers thus avoid the risk and cost involved in accounting for employee retirement funds. In addition, employers have the flexibility to make large percentage contributions during good financial years, and to reduce contributions during hard times. Like other tax-deferred retirement plans, SEPs provide a tax break for employers and a valuable benefit for employees.

In many ways, SEPs can be more flexible and attractive than corporate pensions. They can even be used to supplement corporate pensions and 401(k) plans. Many people who are employed full-time use SEPs as a way to save and invest more money for retirement than they might normally be able to put away under IRS rules. In fact, an article in *Forbes* magazine called SEPs a "moonlighter's delight," in that they enable full-time employees to contribute a portion of their self-employment income from consulting or free-lancing outside of their regular jobs.

RULES GOVERNING SEPs

The rules governing SEPs are fairly simple but are subject to frequent changes, so annual reviews of IRS publications 560 (retirement plans for the self-employed) and 590 (IRAs) are recommended. As of 2000, SEPs could be set up using a simple form (IRS Form 5305-SEP) and—unlike larger, more complicated pension plans—did not require a separate trustee. As of 2006 the maximum allowable contribution per employee was 25 percent of the first $220,000 of an employee's eligible compensation, or $44,000, whichever is less. In general, eligibility is limited to employees 21 or older with at least one year of service to the company and a minimum level of compensation. The maximum level of compensation for SEP eligibility is $170,000.

SIMPLE IRAs A similar program to the SEP program is the Savings Incentive Match Plan for Employees (SIMPLE) IRA. SIMPLE plans became available in January 1997 to businesses with fewer than 100 employees, replacing the discontinued Salary Reduction Simplified Employee Pension (SARSEP) plans. They are intended to provide an easy, low-cost way for small businesses and their employees to contribute jointly to tax-deferred retirement accounts. An IRA set up as a SIMPLE account requires the employer to match up to 3 percent of an employee's annual salary, up to $10,000 per year (as of 2006). Employees are also allowed to contribute up to $10,000 annually to their own accounts. In this way, a SIMPLE IRA is similar to a 401(k), but it is generally less complex and has fewer administrative requirements.

Companies that establish SIMPLEs are not allowed to offer any other type of retirement plan. The main problem with the plans, according to Stephen Blakely in *Nation's Business*, was that "Congress is already drafting legislation that would make SIMPLE less simple and

more costly for the very businesses the plans were created to serve."

OWNERS BENEFIT LESS THAN NONOWNER EMPLOYEES

A note of caution is in order. A small business owner who wants to establish a SEP—or any other qualified retirement plan—for him or herself must also include all other company employees who meet minimum participation standards. As an employer, the small business owner can establish retirement plans like any other business. As an employee, the small business owner can then make contributions to the plan he or she has established in order to set aside tax-deferred funds for retirement, like any other employee. The difference is that a small business owner must include all nonowner employees in any company-sponsored retirement plans and make equivalent contributions to their accounts. Unfortunately, this requirement has the effect of reducing the allowable contributions that the owner of a proprietorship or partnership can make on his or her own behalf.

For self-employed individuals, contributions to a retirement plan are based upon the net earnings of their business. The net earnings consist of the company's gross income less deductions for business expenses, salaries paid to nonowner employees, the employer's 50 percent of the Social Security tax, and—significantly—the employer's contribution to retirement plans on behalf of employees. Therefore, rather than receiving pre-tax contributions to the retirement account as a percentage of gross salary, like nonowner employees, the small business owner receives contributions as a smaller percentage of net earnings. Employing other people thus detracts from the owner's ability to build up a sizeable before-tax retirement account of his or her own.

Still, a SEP plan offers significant advantages for self-employed persons and small business owners. It allows a much greater annual pre-tax contribution than a standard IRA (at $4,500 or less, depending on the individual's financial status and participation in other retirement plans). In addition, individuals can contribute to their existing IRAs and 401(k)s, and still participate in a SEP plan.

SEE ALSO *Individual Retirement Accounts; Pension Plans; Retirement Planning*

BIBLIOGRAPHY
Basi, Bart A. "Look at SEP for Retirement Plan." *Supply House Times.* May 2000.

Blakely, Stephen. "Pension Power." *Nation's Business.* July 1997.

Crouch, Holmes F. *Decisions When Retiring.* Allyear Tax Guides, 1995.

Internal Revenue Service. *Form 5305-SEP.* "Simplified Employee Pension Individual Retirement Accounts Contribution Agreement." December 2005.

Lee, Mie-Yun. "Retirement Plans Don't Have to Be Expensive." *Philadelphia Business Journal.* 22 October 1999.

Olson, John. "A Powerful Weapon in the War for Talent." *National Underwriter Life & Health-Financial Services Edition.* 23 June 2003.

"What You Need To Set Aside For Retirement." Public Broadcasting Service. *Frontline* Available from http://www.pbs.org/wgbh/pages/frontline/retirement/world/need.html. Retrieved on 30 May 2006.

Hillstrom, Northern Lights
updated by Magee, ECDI

SITE SELECTION

For many small businesses, business location is an essential component in its eventual success or failure. Site selection can be pivotal in all sorts of businesses, including retail, service, wholesale, and manufacturing efforts. In fact, studies conducted by the Small Business Administration (SBA) and other organizations indicate that poor location is one of the primary causes of business failure in America. Conversely, a good business location can be enormously beneficial to a small firm. In the retail business especially, the adage from real estate applies: Location, location, location.

LOCATION NEEDS OF VARIOUS BUSINESS TYPES

Each of the above-mentioned business types—retail, service, wholesale, and manufacturing—have different site needs that need to be considered when settling upon a location for starting or relocating a business.

Retail Businesses The success of retail establishments is often predicated to a large degree on their location.

Since location is so important, small business retailers often have to make significant expenditures to secure a good site on which to operate. Property owners that offer land or buildings or office space for lease or sale in already-thriving retail areas know that they can command a higher price because of the volume and quality of business that the location will bring to the company.

Service Businesses Many service-oriented businesses also need to operate in "high traffic" regions, but there are exceptions to this. Most home-based business owners, for example, package their talents in service-oriented businesses (software development, freelance writing, home improvement, etc.). Others, such as pest control services or landscaping services, secure the majority of their customers through the Yellow Pages, etc., and thus do not need to worry as much about their location (although location can become a problem because of other factors; for example, a service business that has to travel great distances to take care of the majority of its customers might consider relocating closer to its primary customer base). Still other service-oriented businesses, of course, rely to a great degree on their location. Dry cleaners, hair salons, and other businesses can not afford to locate themselves on the outskirts of a business district. Many of their customers frequent their business precisely because of the convenience of their location; if that benefit dries up, so too do the customers.

Wholesale Businesses Whereas the primary consideration for retailers and some service businesses is to locate themselves in high traffic areas—hence the ubiquity of such businesses in shopping centers and malls—the major location concern of wholesalers is to find a site that has good shipping and receiving facilities and close proximity to transportation routes. Zoning laws are also a consideration. Most communities maintain zoning laws that restrict where wholesalers can set up their businesses.

Manufacturing Businesses As with wholesalers, businesses engaged in manufacturing usually have limited site location options because of local zoning laws. But manufacturers generally do not lack for options when the time comes to build or relocate a facility. Most communities have any number of sites to choose from. The key is to select the land or building that will be most beneficial to the company in the long run, taking into consideration the company's primary market, the available labor force, transportation factors, availability of raw materials, available buildings or building sites, community attitudes toward the industry, expense, and convenience of access for customers.

LOCATION OPTIONS

Small business have a number of different choices in the realm of site selection. The type of facility most often embraced by retail and many service establishments is the shopping center. The shopping center, which houses a variety of different stores (often including well-known chain stores), can take several different forms, but the best known of these is the mall. These establishments provide their tenants with large numbers of potential customers and professional marketing and maintenance services, but in return, tenants often pay high rent and additional fees (to cover maintenance costs, etc.) Many other small businesses, meanwhile, are located in smaller shopping centers that are sometimes known as strip malls or neighborhood shopping centers. These centers, which rely on a smaller customer base than their mega-mall cousins, are typically anchored by one or two super-markets or discount stores. The rest of the stores are usually small retail or service establishments of one type or another. The rent at strip malls is generally much less than it is at major malls, but of course, the level of traffic is generally not as high either. The small business owner who wishes to establish his or her store in a shopping center must carefully weigh the financial advantages and pitfalls of each of these options before moving forward. Other retailers or service businesses prefer to set up their businesses in freestanding locations. Restaurants, for instance, often choose to set up their business in a lone building, attracted by the lower fixed rent that often accompany such arrangements.

Another facility option for the small business is the business park or office building. Indeed, many professionals (doctors, architects, attorneys) choose this option, attracted by the professional image that such trappings convey and the ability to share maintenance costs with other tenants. Some service businesses also operate from these facilities, especially if their primary clientele are other businesses.

OTHER FACTORS IN BUSINESS SITE SELECTION

There are myriad factors that need to be evaluated when deciding where to locate a business. Settling on a site that is both convenient and comfortable for the company's primary customers is, of course, vital, but that is only one piece of the site selection puzzle. These considerations include:

- Will projected revenues cover the total costs of leasing or purchasing the site?

- Will ancillary costs associated with business establishment or relocation (purchase and/or transportation of equipment, computer wiring requirements, etc.) be prohibitive?

- Will it be possible to secure lenders to help cover costs associated with moving into the new business site?

- Are there restrictive ordinances that will unduly interfere with business operations?

- Is the facility itself in good condition (including both exterior and interior), and does it meet layout requirements? If not, how expensive will refurbishment be?

- Are the grounds (landscaping, light fixtures, drainage, storage facilities) in good condition?

- If sharing costs of maintenance/housekeeping services, do other tenants view services favorably?

- How secure is the facility?

- Is the site large enough for your business?

- Can the site accommodate future growth?

- Are nearby business establishments successful, and are they likely to attract customers to your business?

- Are regional competitors successful?

- Does the site provide for adequate parking and access for customers?

- Might the area surrounding the facility (neighboring lots, parking facilities, buildings) undergo a dramatic change because of sale and/or construction?

- What sort of advertising expenditures (if any, in the case of malls, etc.) will be necessary?

- What sort of leasehold improvements (if any) will be necessary?

- Will customer service be interrupted by a relocation? If so, for how long?

- Will major system changes (addition or subtraction of equipment or processes) be necessary?

- What impact will the business site have on workforce needs?

- Should the choice of facility reflect changes in the industry or market in which you are operating?

- Are there any existing or proposed government regulations that could change the value of the facility?

- What is the climate as far as business taxation is concerned?

- Are important suppliers located nearby?

OWNERSHIP VS. LEASING

Whether starting up a new business or moving an already established one, small business owners are faced with the question of whether to lease or purchase the land and/or facility that they choose as the site for their company. Most small businesses operate under lease arrangements—indeed, many small business owners do not have the necessary capital to buy the facility where they will operate—but some do choose to go the purchase route, swayed by the following advantages:

- Increased sense of permanence and credibility in the marketplace

- Property taxes and interest payments are tax-deductible

- Facility improvements increase the value of the business's property rather than the landlord's property

- Increased net worth through appreciation of both the business and the facility (including land and buildings)

- No forfeiture of asset at the end of term

- Ability to liquidate (lessors often have far less freedom in this area)

Of course, there are also factors associated with ownership that either convince small business owners to stick with lease agreements or preclude ownership as a viable option.

- Risk that value of the land and/or facilities will actually go down over time because of business trends (a neighboring anchor store goes bankrupt) or regional events (a flood, massive layoffs)

- Financial risks associated with purchasing are greater, and put a greater financial drain on small establishments that often have other needs (purchasing typically requires greater initial capital investment and entails higher monthly costs)

- Property can be claimed by creditors as an asset if the business goes bankrupt

PLANNING FOR THE FUTURE

An important factor that small business owners need to consider when weighing various business location alternatives is the site's ability to address the company's future needs. It is usually easier to shrink than to expand space in the same location. Thus the growing company is wise to locate in a building or a shopping center where there is room to expand without undertaking the costs of a big move. Sometimes technological considerations enter into planning. The higher lease costs of a building located on a railroad siding may be a worthwhile anticipation of volume climbing to levels where rail service will be needed either to supply or to distribute the businesses volume—or both. If relocation becomes unavoidable, it can sometimes be done in stages—moving operations to new locations one at a time.

SOURCES TO CONSULT WHEN SELECTING A BUSINESS SITE

Local assistance in selecting a site for a new business can usually be found from a number of sources. These include local utilities, some of which have departments designed to provide help in this area; local Chambers of Commerce; banks and insurance agencies; real estate agents who specialize in commercial and industrial property; and state agencies. More informal networking with members of the local business community can also provide both leads and warnings about various regional properties.

SEE ALSO *Relocation*

BIBLIOGRAPHY

Cannon, Howard. *The Complete Idiot's Guide to Starting Your Own Restaurant.* Alpha Books, 2002.

Hamacher, Horst W., and Zvi Drezner. *Facility Location: Theory and Applications.* Springer, 2002.

Manzon, Gil B. Jr. "Halsey-Evans: Relocation of Operations." *Journal of Business Research.* July 2005.

Partovi, Fariborz Y. "An Analytic Model for Locating Facilities Strategically." *Omega.* January 2006.

Thaler, John. *Elements of Small Business.* Silver Lake Publishing, 2005.

Wheaton, William C., and Gleb Nechayev. "Does Location Matter? Do property fundamentals vary within markets, and is this reflected in pricing?" *Journal of Portfolio Management.* Fall 2005.

Hillstrom, Northern Lights
updated by Magee, ECDI

SMALL BUSINESS

Most people get their definition of "small business" from personal experience in dealing with small retail stores and service organizations. Most people also have a minimum size in mind and overlook a whole category of small business, the very small operations Europeans call "micros"; furthermore, most people do not realize that quite sizeable businesses are considered "small" under U.S. law. Definitions are typically based on the number of people employed or on sales volume, but in defining small business, there is no "one-size fits all." More true is the expression: "Different strokes for different folks," meaning that definitions are based on the economic sector in which a business operates. Small business may also be defined by a way of looking at the world; it has a cultural meaning; it is a way of life. Thus the definition has qualitative aspects the law doesn't care about. A quite small business may behave like a very large one because its owners have a certain view; conversely quite large corporations are sometimes still run like small businesses and exemplify the values of small business.

OFFICIAL SIZE DEFINITIONS

In most industrialized countries small businesses are treated in special ways. They are eligible for financial programs or get favored treatment under the tax laws. For this purpose governments publish official size standards. In the U.S. such definitions are issued by the U.S. Small Business Administration's Office of Size Standards. SBA's basic definition begins with a listing of common features. A small business must be 1) organized for profit; 2) have a place of business in the United States; 3) make a significant contribution to the U.S. economy by paying taxes or using American products, materials, or labor; and 4) be at or below the numerical size standard for its industry. So what is this size standard?

U.S. Size by NAICS SBA determines size for businesses in Manufacturing, Wholesale Trade, Mining, and certain other specific industries by employment size. For others it uses revenue size except in Banking, where asset size rules. Manufacturing enterprises with 500 and fewer employees are small businesses, although there are some industries within that sector with higher tilt-points, as discussed below; in the Wholesale Trade sector, the upper limit is 100 employees. This number is widely used as *the* definition of smallness in ordinary assessments and in eyeballing small business generally. The number is easy to remember; it is easier to get a headcount than revenue data; and Census data on employment by firm are readily available. But the "100-and-under" definition is official only for businesses in the wholesale trades.

For businesses in all other fields the definitions are based on revenue; this makes it easy for the small business to establish its own eligibility but much more difficult for analysts of small business to classify a population of companies as "small" or "large." In descending order of revenues, the major sectors (as summarized by SBA) are:

- General and Heavy Construction, $31 million
- Dredging (technically part of construction but singled out here), $18.5 million
- Special Trade Contractors, $13 million
- Retail Trade and Business and Personal Services, $6.5 million
- Architectural, Engineering, Mapping Services, Dry Cleaning and Carpet Cleaning Services, $4.5 million
- Travel Agencies, $3.5 million
- Agriculture, $750,000.

Businesses in these categories may *maximally* have the revenues shown and still be considered small businesses. The values thus represent upper limits.

These summaries, however, are not the detailed definitions. Those are published by the SBA in a special Table organized by North American Industrial Classification System (NAICS) codes (see references). The Table lists exceptions, typically showing *larger* sizes for certain NAICS industries. To illustrate, within the Agriculture Sector, where the top is generally defined as $750,000 in revenues, Feedlots may have revenues up to $2 million, Chicken Egg Production up to $11.5 million, Forestry operations up to $6.5 million, and Logging may have 500 employees. Fishing operations top out at $4 million, and Agricultural and Forestry Support activities are $6.5 million except Forest Fire Suppression and Fuel Management Services where the top size is $16.5 million. The example illustrates that summary data are very general. The business owner needs to obtain his or her NAICS code and then look at the Table for the precise definition for his or her operation.

The Table also includes whole sectors left out of the summary such as Mining (generally 500 employees); Utilities (4 million megawatt hours a year or less); Transportation (1,500 employees for airlines, long haul rail, and pipelines; 500 for water transport; $23.5 million in revenues for Trucking; $6.5 million for others); Information (500 employees for Publishing, 1,500 for Telecommunications); Real Estate and Rental ($2 million is the smallest revenue category for Real Estate Offices, $23.5 the largest for Vehicle and Truck Leasing); Finance and Insurance ($165 million in assets for Banks; $6.5 million in revenues for an insurance brokerage); and there are others.

IN CANADA AND EUROPE

As reported by GDSourcing, a company that retails Canadian federal statistics, Canada divides its small business into two categories, "small" and "medium." The small business is defined as one with revenues between $30,000 and $5 million whereas a medium-sized business has revenues between $5 million and $25 million. The dollars are Canadian. Generally, in Canada, the United Kingdom, and other former British Commonwealth countries the small business sector is referred to as the SMEs, which includes both categories: small and medium enterprises.

Based on data from the University of Strathclyed in the UK, the British definition of "small" is sales ("turnover") of not more than £5.6 million, assets of not more than £2.8 million, and not more than 50 employees. A medium-sized company has sales of £22.8 million, assets of £11.4 million and not more than 250 employees. The definitions were set by the UK's Companies Act of 1985, as amended in 2004, for tax purposes. The British Bankers Association defines small business customers as proprietorships, partnerships, and companies with annual sales under £1 million.

The European Commission, in its Recommendation 2003/361/EC (May 6, 2003, effective January 1, 2005) has three categories for small business: micro enterprises have fewer than 10 employees and sales and assets both less than €2 million each. Small enterprises are defined as having fewer than 50 employees and sales and assets of €10 million each or less. A medium-sized enterprise has fewer than 250 employees, sales of not more than €50 million, and assets of not more than €43 million.

COMPANY DISTRIBUTION BY EMPLOYMENT

Just how big a role does small business play in American commerce? Data for 2003 available from the U.S. Census Bureau enable us to get a general feel. In that year the U.S. economy had 5.8 million companies employing 113.4 million people. The census provides breakdowns by employment range such as 1-4, 5-9, 10-19, 20-99, and 100-499 employees. Using all employment brackets up to the 20-99 category, the closest approximation to the "100-and-under" category generally used for defining a small business, data for 2003 showed that 98.2 percent of all firms could be classified as small. These companies employed 36.2 percent of all people working for the profit-making private sector. This means that the overwhelming majority of all companies are small and employ well over a third of private-sector workers. Big business, with just 1.8 percent of companies, however, employs the majority of people, 63.8 percent. This rough approximation, of course, *understates* the total for small businesses because in major industries a much higher employment cut-off is used (e.g. 500 employees). But we can test this number by looking at three major industries for which the SBA specifically identifies employment size as the cut-off: Manufacturing and Mining (500 in each case) and Wholesale Trade (100 employees).

In Manufacturing, 295,596 companies were active in 2003. Of these 291,494 had 499 or fewer employees. Thus 98.6 percent of Manufacturing firms were classified as small business. They employed 43.2 percent of the manufacturing workforce. In Mining 98.3 percent of companies were small (17,896 of 18,210) and employed 44.2 percent of the workforce in the industry. Finally, in Wholesale Trade, 331,633 of 342,450 firms fell into the 99 or fewer employee category—96.8 percent of companies. They employed 45.3 percent of those engaged in wholesale trade.

These three sectors in aggregate represented 11.4 percent of all firms and 18 percent of total employment. Small businesses within them were 11.3 percent of all small businesses and represented 21.8 percent of small business employment.

AMERICA'S "MICROS"

The data cited above *exclude* a very large category of tiny businesses—those that do not have employees at all. Their owners earn business income and are not paid a salary. The Census Bureau classifies these entities as "nonemployer businesses." They are America's own "micro" enterprises—the seeds from which small businesses with employees develop. Data released by the Bureau in connection with Small Business Week in 2006 indicate (again for the year 2003) that 18.6 million

such businesses existed. They had revenues of $830 billion, equivalent to $44,623 per entity.

Who are these people? They are engaged across the board in every industrial sector, albeit, obviously, at a very small scale. An indication is provided by categories that had particularly strong growth between 2002 and 2003. They were real estate appraisers growing by 19.1 percent, nail salons (15.9 percent), landscape architectural services (14.6 percent), software publishers (14.4 percent), clothing accessories stores (12.9 percent), bed and breakfast inns (8.5 percent), carpet and upholstery cleaning services (7.5 percent), and confectionery and nut stores, growing 6.5 percent between 2002 and 2003.

The Census Bureau's press release also identified the biggest sectors as follows: "Four economic sectors accounted for almost 60 percent of nonemployer receipts in 2003—real estate and rental and leasing ($176.0 billion, or 21.2 percent); construction ($126.4 billion, or 15.2 percent); professional, scientific and technical services ($102.9 billion, or 12.4 percent) and retail trade ($80.5 billion, or 9.7 percent)."

The growth rate of nonemployer revenues was 5.7 percent between 2002 and 2003, the largest annual increase since the Bureau began collecting such statistics in 1997. The growth rate, of course, may in part be a reflection of bad news: individuals affected by slow recovery, outsourcings, and layoffs may have been, as it were, "fighting back" by creating a modest income for themselves by enterprise.

A DIFFERENT CULTURE

Anybody who has ever worked in or run a small business will be aware of a difference in culture between "small" and "big" business. The difference arises from structural factors, of course, but equally from different values. To be sure, in specific cases a small business may have "big business" values and attitudes arising from the experience and intentions of the owners. On the whole, however, the small business culture is marked by close and familiar contact between owners and employees; and the business as a whole is close to the outside world—customers, neighbors, and suppliers. Structural factors arise because communications in a small business are easy and informal; there is much less layering; contact with the world is immediate and does not require expensive market surveys. The owners very often work within the business and are not the abstract and distant symbol of a faceless stockholder somewhere out there. Much more so in small businesses than in large, the enterprise has a "family" or "tribal" atmosphere and the predominant value is continuity and survival rather than abstract concepts like profit, return, and asset appreciation. Being in close and direct contact with the environment ("belly-to-belly" as

Japanese business people say), with information flow rapid and decisions easier to make and to implement, small businesses tend on the whole to be capable of rapid reaction—but are also limited by limited means.

The small business environment is both more open, free, quick, and "organic" than large structures where size alone imposes bureaucratic methods of control and slow communications through many layers of decision-makers. For this reason a highly disproportionate number of innovations arise first in small businesses. And, as the SBA points out, small business is also the source of most new jobs: 75 percent of net new jobs added to the economy come from small business. When it comes to the future, one can confidently say: "Small is beautiful."

BIBLIOGRAPHY

"Canada's Small Business Data Centre." GDSourcing. Available from http://www.gdsourcing.ca/SBDC.htm. Retrieved on 18 April 2006.

"Small and Medium Sized Enterprises: Definitions." University of Strathclyed. Available from http://www.lib.strath.ac.uk/busweb/guides/smedefine.htm. Retrieved on 18 April 2006.

U.S. Census Bureau. "Statistics of U.S. Businesses: 2003." Available from http://www.census.gov/epcd/susb/2003/us/US-.HTM. Retrieved on 18 April 2006.

U.S. Census Bureau News. "Small Business Week 2006." Press Release. 27 March 2006.

U.S. Small Business Administration. "Small Business Statistics." Available from http://www.sba.gov/aboutsba/sbastats.html. Retrieved on 18 April 2006.

U.S. Small Business Administration. "Summary of Small Business Size Standards." Available from http://www.sba.gov/size/summary-whatis.html. Retrieved on 18 April 2006.

U.S. Small Business Administration. "Table of Small Business Size Standards Matched to North American Industry Classification System Codes." 5 January 2006. Available from http://www.sba.gov/size/sizetable2002.pdf. Retrieved on 18 April 2006.

Darnay, ECDI

SMALL BUSINESS ADMINISTRATION

The Small Business Administration (SBA), which was created in 1953, is an independent federal agency charged with aiding, counseling, and protecting the interests of American small businesses. The agency maintains a wide range of programs designed to address various aspects of this mandate. These programs, each of which seeks to assist small business owners in one or more areas of their enterprise, are maintained in the following areas: lending and investment; surety bonds; international

expansion and development; disaster assistance; federal procurement contracts; minority small business assistance; veterans' assistance; research and development; business and training; and business information and counseling. The SBA also serves as an advocate for American small businesses in government.

STRUCTURE OF THE SBA

Most SBA programs and services are implemented through Small Business Administration district offices. District offices are maintained in all 50 states, as well as Washington, D.C., and Puerto Rico (some larger states, such as California, New York, and Texas, have as many as half a dozen offices). Personnel in these offices work directly with small business owners and various cooperating institutions to implement SBA programs.

These field offices report to regional offices of the SBA. In addition to their supervisory responsibilities, the regional headquarters are charged with educating small business owners, lending institutions, and others on issues that affect them; fostering regional economic development; and providing the Office of Field Operations (OFO) with information on SBA programs and small business developments at the district level. OFO is responsible for all aspects of the SBA's field operations, including communications, policy formation, and general performance. It reports directly to the SBA's chief administrator.

Collateral offices maintained by the Small Business Administration include administration; comptroller; personnel; external affairs; marketing and customer service; public communications, congressional and legislative affairs; Hearings and Appeals; Inspector General; Office of Information Resources Management (OIRM); Equal Employment Opportunity and Civil Rights Compliance; and Office of General Counsel.

Finally, the SBA maintains several departments devoted to providing advocacy services on behalf of American small business owners. The Office of Interagency Affairs oversees enforcement of the Regulatory Flexibility Act, analyzes small business issues, develops governmental policy options, and prepares testimony for use before various legislative and regulatory bodies. The Office of Economic Research oversees the SBA's research contracting program, and compiles and interprets various economic data on small businesses. The Office of Information publishes books and economic reports on small business issues, and serves as a distributor of advocacy publications and other materials. Finally, the Office of Advocacy attempts to evaluate the effect of proposed legislation and other policy issues on small businesses. The chief counsel for advocacy acts as the primary spokesperson for America's small business community and represents its views before Congress, local governments, and other agencies. The Office of Advocacy also utilizes regional advocates who work directly with local communities and small businesses, gathering information on policies and regulations that are helping and hurting small businesses and the communities in which they operate.

SMALL BUSINESS ADMINISTRATION PROGRAMS

Lending Programs The SBA provides a number of lending options to small business owners. The best known of these is the 7(a) Loan Guaranty, but there are many others that are widely used as well. In all of these cases, the loan is actually delivered through commercial lending institutions and other intermediaries. The SBA helps secure the loans, though, by consenting to cover the cost of the loan should the borrower be unable to pay. Lending institutions value this added protection very highly.

The 7(a) Loan Guaranty Program, which was authorized by the passage of the Small Business Act, is primarily designed to address the long-term funding needs of small businesses by guaranteeing loans to qualified enterprises. These loans can be used for all sorts of purposes, including inventory, working capital, equipment, and real estate. Maturities are up to 10 years for working capital and up to 25 years for fixed assets. The SBA can guarantee 80 percent of loans of $100,000 or less, and 75 percent of loans between $100,000 and $750,000. There are several other loan programs available through the 7(a) Loan Guaranty plan as well.

The Low Documentation Loan (LowDoc) program is a streamlined version of the 7(a) loan for businesses seeking less than $150,000. Limited to applicants with a strong credit history, LowDoc loans can be secured with a one-page application (in cases where the loan request is for $50,000 or less). The SBA has made a strong effort to improve response time under this plan, in large measure because it had long been criticized for the bureaucratic red tape associated with even the smallest of its loan programs.

The CAPLines program is an option designed to meet the short-term and cyclical working capital needs of small businesses. There are several different loan options available under this program, which replaced the SBA's earlier GreenLine program. Loans under CAPLines are generally limited to $750,000.

The SBAExpress program is shaped to increase the capital available to small businesses seeking loans up to $150,000; it is currently offered as a pilot program, with a limited number of participating lenders.

SBA MicroLoans, meanwhile, are short-term loans of up to $25,000. Disseminated through non-profit groups, MicroLoans are intended for the purchase of machinery and other equipment, office furniture, inventory, supplies, and working capital.

The SBA also offers several targeted lending programs for small businesses. These include the Defense Loan and Technical Assistance (DELTA) program, which provides financial assistance to defense-dependent small businesses impacted by defense cuts (maximum loan amounts under the DELTA plan through the 7(a) Program is $1.25 million, usable for working capital, acquisition of assets, raw materials or inventory, capital improvements, or refinancing of current debt); prequalification pilot loan programs for women and minorities; the Export Working Capital Program (EWCP), which guarantees loans for qualified small businesses engaged in export transactions; the International Trade Loan (ITL), which provides long-term financing assistance to small businesses engaged in international trade and/ or hurt by imports; and the Pollution Control Program, which gives loan guarantees to eligible small businesses proposing to design and install pollution control facilities.

The SBA also maintains a loan program known as the 504 CDC (Certified Development Companies), which makes available up to $1 million to qualified applicants. Under this system, long-term, fixed-rate financing is made available to small businesses interested in expanding or modernizing their operations through the purchase of new machinery, equipment, and/ or real estate. DELTA loans are available through this program as well.

Another SBA loan program is the U.S. Community Adjustment and Investment Program (CAIP), created to help communities that suffered economic and workforce losses due to changing trade patterns following implementation of the North American Free Trade Agreement (NAFTA). According to the SBA, this program utilizes both the SBA 7(a) Program and the SBA 504 Program to "promote economic implementation of the adjustment [to NAFTA] by increasing the availability and flow of credit and [encourage] business development and expansion in impacted areas. Through the CAIP, credit is available to businesses in eligible communities to create new, sustainable jobs or to preserve existing jobs." Small companies interested in pursuing CAIP assistance should contact their local CDC for more information.

The Small Business Administration relies on lending institutions and other intermediaries (such as non-profit organizations, in the case of MicroLoans). But the SBA is careful about the banks and savings and loans companies with which it does business. The most reliable of these lending institutions are eventually designated as "preferred lenders." This status gives them increased powers of loan approval and processing (although the SBA still conducts a final review of loan applications). To become a preferred lender, an institution needs to have established a reputation for solid community lending (to small businesses and minority- and women-owned firms) and a strong history of being repaid by loan applicants.

Investment The SBA also maintains investment programs for small businesses. The Main Street Investment Program, for example, is described by the SBA as "a public/private partnership between the SBA and state governments to make capital more available to lenders who, in turn, make loans to small businesses. Participating states invest tax revenues in community banks that agree to make LowDoc loans." Small Business Investment Companies (SBICs), meanwhile, are SBA-licensed investment firms who—armed with U.S. government-guaranteed debentures or participating securities—make investments and loans to small businesses. Indeed, SBICs exist for the express purpose of funding start-up companies. They operate under extremely stringent guidelines, however, and turn down many applicants. Similar to SBICs are Minority Enterprise Small Business Investment Companies (MESBICs), which provide funding to businesses owned or operated by minorities.

Surety Bonds In recognition of the fact that contractors to construction projects must post surety bonds on federal construction projects valued at $25,000 or more, the SBA established a program wherein they guarantee bid, performance, and payment bonds for contracts up to $1.25 million for eligible small firms unable to secure surety bonds through commercial lenders. Under this program, bonds may be obtained either via prior approval, in which contractors apply through a surety bonding agent; or preferred sureties, authorized by the SBA to issue, monitor, and service bonds without prior SBA approval.

International Trade The SBA's International Trade Loan Program is designed for small companies engaged or preparing to engage in international commerce. Under this program, the SBA guarantees up to $1.25 million for a combination of fixed asset financing and Export Working Capital Program (EWCP) assistance. The fixed-asset portion of the loan may not exceed $1 million, while the EWCP segment may not exceed $750,000. According to the SBA, the small business applicant must do the following in order to qualify: "establish that the loan will significantly expand or develop an export market, is currently adversely affected by import competition, will upgrade equipment or facilities to improve competitive position, or must be able to provide a business plan that reasonably projects export sales sufficient to cover the loan."

In addition to maintaining loan programs for small businesses engaged in international commerce, the Small Business Administration provides a number of other services to these enterprises. The Export Legal Assistance Network (ELAN), for instance, is the product of an agreement between the SBA, the Federal Bar Association, and the U.S. Department of Commerce. Under this program, trade attorneys provide free legal consultations to small business exporters.

The SBA also operates information centers called U.S. Export Assistance Centers (USEACs). As with ELAN, the USEACs are the product of an alliance between the SBA and other organizations (in USEACs' case, the Department of Commerce and the Export-Import Bank). These centers are designed to disseminate trade promotion and export financing information to small businesses engaged in international trade. In addition, the SBA maintains a computer database known as the Small Business Automated Trade Locator Assistance System (SBAtlas), which includes market data of interest to exporters.

Assistance Programs The SBA makes available Physical Disaster Business Loans to businesses of any size that need to repair or replace business property to "pre-disaster" conditions. These loans, which can be used for equipment, fixtures, and inventory, are limited to $1.5 million and are not available to businesses who were insured for their losses. Economic Injury Disaster Loans (EIDLs), meanwhile, are targeted at businesses that have "sustained economic injury as a direct result of a disaster," said the SBA. "These working capital loans are made to help businesses pay ordinary and necessary operating expenses which would have been payable barring disaster." The maximum amount of an EIDL loan is $1.5 million, but small business experts note that businesses can receive no more than $1.5 million in combined EIDL and physical disaster business loans. An exception to this stipulation is made, however, for those places of business that qualify as major sources of employment. Under the SBA's Major Source of Employment (MSE) program, the $1.5 million loan limit is waived for those businesses that employ 250 or more people in an affected area.

Federal Procurement The Small Business Administration maintains several programs designed to help small businesses secure government contracts. These include:

- Breakout Procurement Program—promotes the breakout of historically sole-source contracts for open competition with the aim of aiding small businesses and effecting government savings.

- Prime Contracting Program—designed to help small businesses interested in securing federal contracts;

services include support for small business set-asides, counseling, identification of new small business sources, and "assessment of compliance with the Small Business Act through surveillance reviews."

- Subcontracting Program—designed to aid small businesses in their efforts to secure federal contracts as suppliers and subcontractors.

- Certificates of Competency—appeal process that can be used by small businesses that have been denied government contracts because of alleged lack of ability to fulfill job requirements.

The most recent program in this area introduced by the SBA is the HUBzone Empowerment Contracting Program. This initiative, unveiled in 1997, provides federal contracting opportunities for qualified small businesses located in economically distressed areas.

Minority Assistance The SBA has several programs intended to provide support to small businesses owned and operated by minorities. Programs maintained by the SBA's Minority Enterprise Development office include 8(a) Small Disadvantaged Business Development, which arranges federal procurement opportunities for minority- and disadvantaged-owned firms, and initiatives which provide management and technical assistance to those firms. The SBA also operates an Office of Native American Affairs (ONAA), which works to provide Native American communities with business development and job creation opportunities.

Business Training and Counseling SBA-sponsored training and counseling services are available through the following programs:

- Small Business Development Centers—provides management and technical assistance to both current and prospective small business owners through an alliance of educators, the private sector, and federal, state, and local governments. All areas of business are covered, from market research and accounting systems to inventory control and cost-benefit analysis.

- Business Information Centers (BICs)—specializes in providing technology information to small businesses. Subjects covered include advances in telecommunications, software, and computers.

- Service Corps of Retired Executives (SCORE)—matches retired business executives with small businesses seeking advice on business issues. SCORE includes more than 12,300 members in hundreds of chapters around the country.

Women's Business Ownership SBA programs specifically directed at women small business owners include the Women's Demonstration Program, which provides women with training and advice on all aspects of business ownership and management, and the Women's Network for Entrepreneurial Training (WNET), wherein established women business owners serve as mentors to other women entrepreneurs.

Veterans' Affairs The SBA maintains several programs intended to provide information and training to veterans. These include the VET (Veterans' Entrepreneurial Training) Program, the Transition Assistance Program (TAP), and "business opportunity conferences," which helps veteran-owned companies previously reliant on the defense industry to secure other clients.

Research and Development The two principal programs administered by the SBA in this area are the Small Business Innovation Research (SBIR) Program and the Small Business Technology Transfer (STTR) Program. STTR is a program that seeks to form research and development partnerships between small firms and non-profit research institutions. It provides up to $100,000 to companies for the first phase of research, though there are stipulations attached to that figure. SBIR, meanwhile, provides financial rewards to small businesses who propose innovative ideas to problems faced by participating federal agencies. Initially established in the early 1980s, as a result of the 1982 Small Business Innovation Development Act, SBIR has been warmly received by many small companies with expertise in science and high-technology areas.

One-Stop Capital Shop (OSCS) The SBA expects to contribute to the Empowerment Zone/Enterprise Communities Program initiative headed by the Department of Housing and Urban Development and the Department of Agriculture through its "One-Stop Capital Shops." These centers, located in federally designated empowerment zones and enterprise communities, are expected to be headed up by local nonprofit organizations, but they are intended to include access to complete information on various SBA programs and offerings. "A One Stop Capital Shop is a partnership between SBA and a local community designed to offer small business assistance from an easy to access, retail location, all under one roof," explained the SBA. "Small business clients require a wide range of assistance, from the simple: accessing the Internet or gathering basic information on writing a business plan, to the complex: learning how to compete for a federal contract or applying for a city permit. Whether a small business needs information or has to complete a transaction, requires training or counseling, is applying for a loan or seeking a government contract, a One Stop Capital Shop is designed to make all those services available in one location.... No other SBA program or federal agency plays a more prominent role in generating economic revitalization in distressed communities than the One Stop Capital Shop Initiative."

Business Information Services A comprehensive range of business development booklets is published by and made available from the SBA. A diverse range of topics are covered in these brochures; sample titles include *Strategic Planning for Growing Businesses, Budgeting in a Small Service Firm, Inventory Management,* and *Evaluating Franchise Opportunities.* SBA also maintains SBA Online, a computer-based electronic bulletin board of small business information, and a toll-free answer desk for small business owners with questions about aspects of their operation. The answer desk is open 24 hours a day, seven days a week, but counselors are only available Monday through Friday, 9 a.m. to 5 p.m. Eastern Time. The toll-free number is (800) 8-ASK-SBA. Finally, the Small Business Administration maintains a page on the World Wide Web at http://www.sba.gov.

SEE ALSO *8(a) Program; Service Corp of Retired Executives (SCORE); Small Business Development Centers (SBDC); Small Business Innovation Research (SBIR); Small Business Technology Transfer (STTR)*

BIBLIOGRAPHY

Barlas, Stephen. "Looking Ahead: Three SBA Programs Face Closer Scrutiny." *Entrepreneur.* January 1997.

Emerich, Amy., ed. *Small Business Sourcebook.* Gale Group, 1996.

Murphy, Richard McGill. "Now is the Time to Tear Down the SBA." *FSB.* June 2006.

U.S. Small Business Administration. *SBA Profile: Who We Are and What We Do.* 2000.

Hillstrom, Northern Lights
updated by Magee, ECDI

SMALL BUSINESS CONSORTIA

Business consortia are alliances of individual business enterprises. Businesses involved in these sorts of consortia are often in the same broad field or industry, though they are rarely in direct competition with one another. Instead, members usually offer products or services that are complementary to those available through other consortium members. Unlike associations and other similar organizations, which engage in efforts to shape legislation and present a unified industry front, business consortia ally themselves for basic business functions, such as marketing. These alliances are not commonplace, but some analysts indicate that in the future, increasing numbers of small business owners may investigate consortiums as a way of sharing common costs, increasing purchasing power, and competing with larger companies.

Business consortia that do form usually come into being for specific reasons, such as competitive threats from a common enemy (whether another business or an unwelcome economic trend), changes in competitive structures, or deregulation. By forming a consortium, the member companies that are involved are usually admitting that for the tie being competitive pressures are so great that the member businesses' ability to survive as completely independent entities is in question.

Participants in business consortia admit that striking such alliances can sometimes curb a firm's ability to act independently, since it's words and actions will reflect on other consortia members. This can be difficult for some entrepreneurs to handle. Moreover, consortia can become crippled if their membership grows too large and unwieldy to make quick decisions, or if individual members fall victim to squabbling or worse as a result of personality conflicts, similar customer bases, or other business disputes. But proponents point out that a business consortium can provide several meaningful advantages to members as well. These include:

Increased clout. Whereas individual small businesses sometimes do not enjoy the same name recognition or respect as do larger companies, the collective bargaining and purchasing power of a consortium as well as the individual marketing efforts of members can provide individual businesses with increased recognition and stature in the community.

Savings of time and money. Joint marketing and advertising efforts save members money because they can pool their resources for better rates; they also save member businesses time because they do not have to undertake as much work themselves.

Expanded customer base. Membership in business consortia can provide participating businesses with increased exposure to new revenue streams.

SEE ALSO *Cooperatives*

BIBLIOGRAPHY

Bigbie, John Eric. "Consortia Back in Business." *Acquisitions Monthly.* April 1994.

Doz, Yves L., and Gary Hamel. *Alliance Advantage: The Art of Creating Value Through Partnerships.* Harvard Business School Press, 1998.

Smith, Jerd. "Strength in Their Number." *Denver Business Journal.* 3 March 1995.

U.S. General Accounting Office. *Small Business: Workforce Development Consortia Provide Needed Services.* Available from www.gao.gov/new.items/d0280.pdf. Retrieved on 13 June 2006.

Vaanderdorpe, Laura. "Capitalizing on Consortia: Cooperation Bolsters Research." *R & D.* October 1997.

Hillstrom, Northern Lights
updated by Magee, ECDI

SMALL BUSINESS DEVELOPMENT CENTERS (SBDC)

One of many programs administered by the Small Business Administration (SBA), the Small Business Development Center (SBDC) program is intended to provide management assistance to both established and prospective small business owners. The SBA characterizes the program, which was established in 1976, as a "cooperative effort of the private sector, the educational community, and federal, state, and local governments. It enhances economic development by providing small businesses with management and technical assistance."

The SBA maintains small business development centers in all 50 states, as well as Puerto Rico, Guam, the U.S. Virgin Islands, and the District of Columbia. Many of these centers have satellite service locations as well. These satellite locations are housed primarily at colleges, universities, and community colleges, but they may also be found at vocational schools, chambers of commerce, and economic development corporations.

SBDCs are typically headed up by a director and include paid staff members, but the services of volunteers—qualified individuals from professional and trade associations, members of the legal, banking, and academic community, chambers of commerce representatives, and members of the Service Corps of Retired Executives—are integral to most SBDCs. In addition, SBDCs commonly compensate consultants, consulting engineers, and testing laboratories for services rendered on behalf of SBDC clients.

While Small Business Development Centers are administered by the SBA, that organization is prevented by law from providing more than 50 percent of the operating funds for each state SBDC. The centers turn to state legislatures, private sector foundations and grants, state and local chambers of commerce, economic development corporations, public and private universities, vocational and technical schools, and community colleges for the remainder of their operating funds. In recent years, non-SBA sponsors have accounted for more than 50 percent of their required matching share at a number of centers.

THE SBDC PROGRAM

According to the SBA, Small Business Development Centers are designed to deliver timely and accurate counseling, training, and technical assistance in all aspects of small business management, including financial management, marketing, production and operations, organization, engineering and technical issues, personnel management, and feasibility studies. Some centers also offer assistance in such areas as venture capital formation, rural development, exporting and importing, and procurement of funding (including Small Business Innovation and Research grants), depending on the needs of their business clients and the communities in which the centers operate.

SBDC assistance to small business owners takes many forms, from counseling on legal issues to seminars on business finance to aid in putting together a business plan. Many centers also maintain extensive business libraries that contain a great deal of information of value to entrepreneurs and small business owners.

Anyone interested in starting a small business or making improvements to an existing small business is free to make use of the SBDC program, provided that they do not have the financial resources to secure the services of a private consultant. Indeed, the SBDC centers regard their primary clientele to be businesspeople from disadvantaged socioeconomic backgrounds. The SBDC program also makes special efforts to provide assistance to women, the disabled, and military veterans. To locate the SBDC nearest you, call (800) 8-ASK-SBA or see the Small Business Administration Web site at www.sba.gov/sbdc/.

BIBLIOGRAPHY

Lesonsky, Rieva. "The Long Road: Enlightening travels find SBDC funding reaching new lows, generous big guys and inspiring entrepreneurs." *Entrepreneur.* November 2005.

Tiffany, Laura. "Show Me the Way: SBDCs Put You on the Road to Success." *Entrepreneur.* July 1998.

U.S. Small Business Administration. *SBA Profile: Who We Are and What We Do.* 1996.

Hillstrom, Northern Lights
updated by Magee, ECDI

SMALL BUSINESS INNOVATION RESEARCH (SBIR) PROGRAM

The Small Business Innovation Research Program (SBIR) is the federal government's most important research and development funding program for small businesses. It was established by the passage of the Small Business

Innovation Development Act of 1982. SBIR, at the time of its passage, required by law that any federal government agency with an extramural research and development budget of more than $100 million set aside 1.25 percent of those funds for the development of high tech small businesses. When the original law expired after ten years, Congress reauthorized SBIR and increased the agencies' contributions to 2.5 percent in 1992. By the latter part of the 1990s, total SBIR funding had reached some $1.2 billion. In December 2000 the program was reauthorized—with $1.5 billion in annual funding—for another seven years.

The Small Business Administration (SBA) serves as the coordinating agency for the SBIR program. It directs implementation of the program among participating agencies, reviews their progress, and reports annually to Congress on the status of the program. The SBA is also the information link to the program, collecting solicitation information from participating agencies and publishing it in quarterly Pre-Solicitation Announcements (PSA). These announcements are the single source for the topics and anticipated release and closing dates for each federal agency's solicitations.

By 2006, 11 federal agencies were participating in SBIR, bestowing research and development funds to small businesses in an array of industries. Participating agencies include the Departments of Agriculture, Commerce, Defense, Education, Energy, Health and Human Services, Homeland Security, and Transportation, as well as the Environmental Protection Agency, the National Aeronautics and Space Administration and the National Science Foundation. According to *Science* magazine, 96 percent of the total SBIR budget from all agencies comes from the Departments of Defense and Energy, the National Institutes of Health, National Aeronautics and Space Administration, and the National Science Foundation.

These agencies set aside seed funds to help small businesses develop innovative high-tech ideas whose commercial appeal may by some time in coming. Each year the agencies release for consideration more than 3,000 technology topics under which businesses may apply. The topics speak to specific program problems or needs and may be found in the quarterly *Pre-Solicitation Announcement (PSA),* which is only provided online.

SBIR ELIGIBILITY AND FRAMEWORK

To be eligible for SBIR funding, a small business concern must be American-owned, independently operated, for-profit, and employ fewer than 500 people. Nonprofit organizations are not eligible for SBIR awards.

The SBIR program comprises three phases. This approach allows the government agency to invest a small amount in the beginning and then increase their financial support later should the idea show promise. Once the project nears completion, funding drops off and the business must solicit capital from other sources.

Phase One - The Concept Stage. In this stage, individual awards of up to $100,000 are distributed to enable businesses to conduct approximately 6 months of preliminary investigations into the feasibility of their proposed project. At this point, business owners must have a well-formed idea for an innovative product and a specific plan for how to transform it into a commercially viable form.

Phase Two - The Prototype Development Phase. This phase, for which only Phase One entrepreneurs are eligible, provides additional monies (up to $750,000 over 24 months) to be used toward developing a prototype. From here, determinations are made about whether the product is a success or a failure and whether or not it is commercially viable. About 40 percent of Phase One ideas reach this second stage.

Phase Three - The Commercialization Stage. In this stage, states the SBA, "Phase Two innovation moves from the laboratory into the marketplace." No SBIR funds are used in this stage. Instead, funding must be secured from the private sector or other non-SBIR federal agency funding.

For more information on the SBIR program, contact the Small Business Administration's Office of Technology at 409 Third Street SW, Washington, DC 20416, (202) 205-6450. The SBA's Web site with information about the SBIR program is http://www.sba.gov/sbir/indexsbir-sttr.html.

BIBLIOGRAPHY

Barlas, Stephen. "Teaming Up: Universities and Businesses Come Together in a Pilot Program to Fund Innovation." *Entrepreneur.* August 1996.

Giannone, Michael A. "A Wealth of New Ideas." *Environmental Technology.* November-December 1999.

Gillis, Tom S. *Guts & Borrowed Money: Straight Talk for Starting & Growing Your Small Business.* Bard Press, 1997.

"SBIR project to develop novel electrode fabrication methods for thermal batteries." *Advanced Manufacturing Technology.* 15 January 2006.

U.S. Small Business Administration. "Technology SBRI/STTR." Available from http://www.sba.gov/sbir/indexsbir-sttr.html. Retrieved on 5 June 2006.

Wallsten, Scott J. "The Effects of Government-Industry R&D Programs on Private R&D: The Case of the Small Business Innovation Research Program." *RAND Journal of Economics.* Spring 2000.

Hillstrom, Northern Lights
updated by Magee, ECDI

SMALL BUSINESS INVESTMENT COMPANIES (SBIC)

The Small Business Investment Company (SBIC) program was created in 1958 with the passage of the Small Business Investment Act of 1958. Licensed by the Small Business Administration (SBA), SBICs are privately organized and privately managed investment firms that provide venture capital to small independent businesses. These loans, which are available both to new and established businesses, consist of funds borrowed (at favorable rates) from the U.S. government or from the lending institutions' own capital stock. In essence, an SBIC uses its own capital, combined with funds borrowed from investors and supported by an SBA guarantee, to make investments in qualifying small businesses. The SBIC program is designed to assure that there are institutions within the marketplace able and willing to facilitate the capital needs of a vibrant small business community.

Two different kinds of Small Business Investment Companies operate in the United States. In addition to regular SBICs, investment firms known as Specialized Small Business Investment Companies (SSBICs) also exist; this latter type of firm emphasizes service to entrepreneurs who "have been denied the opportunity to own and operate a business because of social or economic disadvantage," according to the SBA. Formerly known as Minority Enterprise Small Business Investment Companies (MESBICs), SSBICs are now officially called Section 301(d) SBICs. However, since the differences between SSBICs and regular SBICs are minor they are generally lumped together under the SBIC heading.

THE SBIC ORGANIZATION

Ownership of SBICs generally takes two different forms. The majority of SBICs are relatively small, privately owned and operated firms, but many others are firms owned by commercial banks or insurance companies. For banks, establishment of an SBIC subsidiary is often an attractive proposition, because it enables them to make small business investments that would otherwise be closed to them because of U.S. banking laws and requirements. United States law places few restrictions on SBIC ownership. As the SBA itself said, "almost any person or organization with a minimum initial private capitalization of $5 million and an SBA-approved full time manager who will be in charge of the licensee's operations and who is able to serve the licensee's small business concerns, may be approved for ownership." Indeed, the SBA's interest in encouraging SBICs is evident in the relatively hands-off regulatory environment that they have established for such enterprises. Those regulations that the SBA does enforce are concerned with ensuring the continued financial and ethical health of the SBIC program.

SBICs, then, range from limited partnerships to subsidiaries of multinational corporations. Whatever their ownership situation, however, their ultimate goal is to realize a profit from their various business transactions. Some SBICs make most of their revenue from straight debt financing, with their profit coming from the differential between the cost of borrowing from the SBA and the interest rate they charge the small business borrower. Other SBICs take a more aggressive tack in seeking profits by making equity-participation loans.

According to the SBA, prospective SBICs (and SSBICs) must have a minimum private capital investment of $5 million to form (the minimum requirement for those firms wishing to utilize participating securities is $10 million). The amount of private capital that an SBIC has at its disposal is important, for the SBA limits its loan guarantees to SBICs to 300 percent of its private capital. The SBA notes, however, that an SBIC "with at least 50 percent of its 'total funds available for investment' invested or committed in 'venture capital' may receive an additional tier of leverage per dollar of private capital for total leverage of 400 percent of private capital. However, in no event may any SBIC or SSBIC draw down leverage in excess of $90 million." An SBIC that engages in leveraging is in essence borrowing additional investment funds from the U.S. Treasury. Only those SBICs that have invested the bulk of its initial private capital and are in full compliance with state and federal regulations are eligible to do this.

Small Business Investment Companies have several different options to choose from in providing financing to small businesses. Most SBICs provide long-term loans to qualified small businesses that need funding for needs that range from expansion of existing facilities to modernization of operations. Sometimes this loan will take the form of equity or debt securities.

OPERATING RESTRICTIONS FOR SBICS

While the SBA provides SBICs with considerable freedom to operate, they do require that these organizations adhere to certain rules. For example, SBICs are not permitted to invest in the following entities: companies with less than one-half of their assets and operations in the United States; unimproved real estate; finance and investment companies; or companies seeking to purchase or improve farmland, cemeteries, or certain other stipulated types of real estate (exceptions are made for subdividers and developers, title abstract companies, and real estate agents and brokers. Small Business Investment Companies also are forbidden from investing in other

SBICs, or in business enterprises that do not fit federal definitions of a "small business."

The SBA also has established regulations in the following areas:

- Conflict of Interest—SBICs are not allowed to make business transactions with any of its associates, which are defined as officers, directors, employees, key "control persons," and certain shareholders.

- Control—the SBA has stipulated that no SBIC may exercise either direct or indirect control over the operations of any small business on a permanent basis. The SBA has, under some circumstances, permitted SBICs to assume temporary control of a business enterprise in order to protect its investment. Before doing so, however, the SBIC and the small business must submit a plan of divestiture for SBA approval.

- Overline Limitations—The SBA has established investment ceilings for both SBICs and SSBICs in their dealings with individual small businesses. SBICs are not allowed to invest more than 20 percent of its private capital with any one small business, while the limit for SSBICs is 30 percent. The SBA does, however, occasionally grant waivers to this rule.

- Cost of Money—The SBA regulates the cost of money on SBIC loans and debt securities issued by SBIC clients.

- Financing Proceeds—The SBA has established regulations designed to ensure that investment funds that are used to purchase securities go directly to the small business that has offered those securities.

- Length of Financing Agreements—SBA rules stipulate (in most cases) that SBIC loan agreements with small business enterprises be made for at least five years, and that the small business taking the loan be given adequate opportunity to fulfill its obligations ahead of schedule if it is able to do so. According to the SBA, loan and debt securities of less than five years' duration are permissible only on those occasions when they are necessary to protect existing financing agreements, are made in contemplation of long-term financing, or are made to finance a change in ownership.

BORROWING FROM AN SBIC

"As is true with venture capitalists in general, SBICs have divergent philosophies and operating policies," wrote Art DeThomas in *Financing Your Small Business*. "Some specialize in equity financing while others provide debt financing in several different forms.

This latter group of SBICs is the richest source of debt financing for small businesses outside commercial banks." Small business owners, however, need to weigh several factors before making a loan arrangement with an SBIC.

Entrepreneurs and small business owners seeking financing from SBICs first need to determine how many options they have. Regional SBA offices maintain information on SBICs that operate in their areas, and while they do not provide guidance in directing businesses to particular SBICs, they can give information on the industries and types of investments in which area SBICs have historically shown interest. In addition, a free directory of SBICs is available through the National Association of SBICs.

As many experts note, small businesses should narrow their search for a suitable SBIC by eliminating those that do not provide the business's desired financing route or display adequate management experience in the industry in which the business is involved. Analysts also caution small business owners not to rush through the decision making process. Given the latitude that SBICs have in shaping their loan policies, individual SBICs often maintain dramatically varied lending policies. Entrepreneurs and small business owners should take the time to find the program that best meets their needs.

Business consultants also encourage prospective borrowers to negotiate the best possible loan agreement for themselves when talking with SBICs. "Aside from the specifics of SBIC lending that are mandated by existing law or regulation," noted DeThomas, "particulars such as interest rate, maturity, equity participation, and collateral requirements can be negotiated. In general, the more attractive your firm as a financing opportunity—that is, the stronger the business plan—the more negotiating leverage you possess."

BIBLIOGRAPHY

DeThomas, Art. *Financing Your Small Business: Techniques for Planning, Acquiring & Managing Debt*. Oasis Press, 1992.

"Senators Propose New SBA Program: Under the bill, the SBA would get a bigger chunk of an SBIC's profits. *Private Equity Week*. 7 November 2005.

U.S. Small Business Administration. *SBA Profile: Who We Are and What We Do*. 1996.

U.S. Small Business Administration. Small Business Innovation Companies Program. Available from http://www.sba.gov/INV/forentre.html. Retrieved on 5 June 2006.

Hillstrom, Northern Lights
updated by Magee, ECDI

SMALL BUSINESS JOB PROTECTION ACT

The Small Business Job Protection Act (SBJPA), signed into law in 1996, contains a number of provisions that impact various aspects of small business operations, from retirement plans to changes in S Corporation structures. The small business community greeted many of the changes contained in SBJPA with considerable enthusiasm, since it was widely interpreted as an act that eliminated a number of unnecessarily burdensome provisions. The act touched on a wide variety of areas relevant to small businesses, especially in the area of pensions. Changes made by the law can be found in such areas as the definition of highly compensated employees, deferred compensation arrangements, family aggregation rules, minimum pension participation rules, "safe harbor" rules for qualified cash or deferred arrangements (CODAs), notice requirements, limits on matching contributions, distributions of excess contributions, elective deferrals that may be included as compensation, early participation nondiscrimination rules, plan distributions and QJSA waivers, employee leasing provisions, and modification of GATT interest and mortality rate rules. Small business consultants strongly advise business owners who wish to take full advantage of the myriad changes included within SBJPA to consult with a tax advisor or other accounting professional.

IMPACT ON SUBCHAPTER S CORPORATIONS

Some observers estimate that the Small Business Job Protection Act has directly impacted as many as two million small businesses currently structured as Subchapter S Corporations. For instance, the law allows S Corporations to increase its shareholders from 35 to 75, giving businesses heightened capacity to attract additional investors and capital. Another change that benefited small business owners concerned an expansion in the kinds of organizations that can be shareholders. Under the SBJPA, qualified pension plans became eligible to be shareholders in S Corporations after January 1998. Since many pension plans are willing to invest in promising young businesses, S Corporation owners have been able to turn to these entities as a source of significant capital.

The Small Business Job Protection Act also provided S Corporation owners with greater flexibility in structuring their businesses. Prior to the passage of the SBJPA, S corporations could not own more than 79 percent of another company, but with the new law, they may now own 100 percent of affiliated companies. Finally, business experts note that the SBJPA expands the number of allowable beneficiaries when an S Corporation puts together a small business trust.

CHANGES TO RETIREMENT PLANS

The SBJPA established a simplified retirement plan for small businesses that is known as the A SIMPLE retirement plan. Under these plans, which are designed for employers with 100 or fewer employees who do not maintain another employer-sponsored plan, employers and employees work together to help ensure that workers have adequate financial security when they reach retirement age. Under the law, employees may make elective pre-tax contributions of up to $6,000 annually, a total that has moved up at regular intervals to adjust for cost of living increases and in 2005 was set by the Internal Revenue Service (IRS) at $10,000. The employer is required to make matching contributions and do so every year. The SBJPA also requires that businesses contribute at least 1 percent of all employees' compensation or be subject to significant penalties.

The law also impacts other elements of pension plans. For example, for the years 1997, 1998, and 1999, the 15 percent excise tax on excess distributions from pension plans was suspended. Moreover, the act introduced safe-harbor formulas for 401(k) salary deferral and matching contributions that eliminated requirements that employers conduct annual nondiscrimination testing. "Under the 1996 act, small employers can adopt matching 401(k) plans without concern about whether non-HCEs [highly compensated employees] elect to participate," wrote Michael Collins and Charles Sherman Jr. in *Journal of Accountancy.* "Depending on how attractive non-HCEs find the safe-harbor matching formula, the use of the safe harbors may reduce substantially the employer contributions businesses must make on behalf of these employees.... The safe-harbor formulas provide a way for employers to avoid nondiscrimination testing by adopting a plan with a relatively generous employer match—one that includes a contribution of at least 4 percent of pay on behalf of all eligible employees (depending on employee contributions). Safe-harbor matching contributions must be 100 percent vested at all times. Such contributions generally may not be distributed to employees until the earlier of when they terminate employment or reach age 59 ½." In addition, under the SBJPA, distributions from a qualified plan must begin by April of the calendar year following the later of: 1) the calendar year in which the employee reaches 70 ½ years of age, or 2) the calendar year in which the worker retires.

BIBLIOGRAPHY

Day, Sally E. "ESBTs [electing small business trusts]: Perhaps More Advantages than Disadvantages." *The Tax Adviser.* September 2005.

Mulleneaux, Natasha M. "Retirement Plan Reform: The Aftermath of the Small Business Job Protection Act of 1996." *Taxes: The Tax Magazine.* August 1997.

Schneider, Mark N., and Marilyn C. Doolittle. "Small Business Job Protection Act Adds Simplicity (and Complexity)." *The Tax Advisor.* June 1997.

Sharp, Joel, Jr., and Hewitt D. Shaw Jr. "Subchapter S Reform: The Small Business Job Protection Act of 1996." *Journal of Corporate Taxation.* Spring 1997.

Sherman, Jr., Charles W., and Michael J. Collins. "The Safe-Harbor Solution." *Journal of Accountancy.* July 1999.

U.S. Department of Labor. Employment and Training Administration. Wyrsch, Mary Anne. "The Small Business Job Protection Act of 1996 and the Health Coverage Availability and Affordability Act of 1996." Available from http://workforcesecurity.doleta.gov/dmstree/uipl/uipl96/uipl_3696.htm. Retrieved on 5 June 2006.

Hillstrom, Northern Lights
updated by Magee, ECDI

SMALL BUSINESS/LARGE BUSINESS RELATIONSHIPS

Many small business owners see large businesses exclusively in competitive terms. For small enterprises that compete directly with larger companies, this characterization is an accurate one. An independent record store owner, for example, will undoubtedly—and legitimately—regard the arrival of a new record store operating under the banner of a national chain as a threat. Similarly, a small plastics manufacturer will view larger firms engaged in the same industry sector as competition. But small businesses should recognize that large regional, national, or even international companies can take on other, decidedly more attractive, identities as well. Larger companies may assume roles as business partners, product distributors, or customers. Indeed, large enterprises wear different hats to different observers. One small business's aggressive competitor may be another small firm's business ally, distributor, or client.

LARGE BUSINESSES AS PARTNERS

The 1990s saw a general increase in business partnerships between small and large companies. Alliances between large companies are still more prevalent, and many large firms continue to prefer to simply swallow up smaller enterprises via acquisition, but analysts and consultants alike contend that growing numbers of large companies are recognizing the benefits that can accrue from establishing partnerships with nimble, entrepreneurial firms. Small but growing companies can offer mature partners access to new customers, innovative products and management practices, and opportunities to bask in the glow of the small business's innovative, contemporary image. This is especially true in the biotechnology sector and in other industrial sectors characterized by rapid change and innovation. Partnerships of this sort often cross industry boundaries as Myron Gould explained in *Direct Marketing,* "Partnerships can be formed in the profit and nonprofit sectors, in the same or different industries, within different divisions of the same company, and in similar market segments/demographics in non-competitive industries."

Indeed, many observers believe that in recent years, festering suspicions and stereotypes in both the large- and small-business camps about the motivations and abilities of the other have begun to give way to an increasing recognition of the positives that can be gained by working cooperatively. James W. Botkin and Jana B. Matthews, authors of *Winning Combinations: The Coming Wave of Entrepreneurial Partnerships Between Large and Small Companies,* stated that "entrepreneurs and corporate executives now need each other more than ever. Their needs and their strengths are often opposite and complementary. Both large corporations and small companies can brighten their global prospects by forming collaborative partnerships that capitalize on their complementary strengths while respecting the independence of each party."

Well-managed smaller companies have long proven themselves to be very adept at anticipating market trends, capitalizing on new technologies, and using their lean structures to outpace larger companies. But while their small size enables them to evade the lumbering bureaucracies that hamper the actions of all but the most progressive larger companies, small companies are also limited by certain realities that can be easily addressed by big firms, and these impediments are often emphasized if the small firm hopes to establish a presence beyond its domestic borders. "Increasing globalization ... makes it difficult for small entrepreneurial companies to act alone effectively," wrote Botkin and Matthews. "Their marketing and distribution channels are frequently inadequate for getting their innovative products and services to an international marketplace. The continual need of small companies for capital also limits their maneuverability. The time and attention of their entrepreneurial management is often diverted to finding and negotiating financing instead of developing markets and distribution systems.... Though their innovations may be exactly what the marketplace needs and wants, they are likely to be handicapped in reaching it."

Large firms are an obvious source of assistance in many of the above areas—distribution, financing, marketing, etc.—but small businesspeople have a tendency to regard large corporations with suspicion. After all, many entrepreneurs come from corporate environments that were not necessarily characterized by adherence to any code of business ethics, and American corporations have not always shown respect for small business autonomy. "Given the 'big fish eats little fish' history of large-to-small encounters, founders of small companies may understandably be leery of forming partnerships that they fear will destroy their company's autonomy and identity," admitted Botkin and Matthews. "But this need not be the case. We suggest that any partnership offer be examined critically and carefully. Entrepreneurs must learn to discriminate between corporate sharks with a bite and swallow mentality and those suitors who have a mutually beneficial arrangement in mind. It's natural to be suspicious. However, many founders of small businesses write off strategic alliances altogether, closing off what might be an increasingly important avenue of rapid growth."

Keys to Successful Partnerships with Larger Companies

Following are several tips that entrepreneurs should consider when negotiating and maintaining a partnership with a larger company:

Research. Some partnership offers sound great on the surface, but are fraught with unpleasantness under the surface. Entrepreneurs should make sure that they undertake diligent research so that they can best assure themselves of finding the right partner, for as Botkin and Matthews admitted, "not every partnership yields happy results; ill-conceived partnerships can leave your company in worse shape than before. Bad partnerships, like bad marriages, can drain resources, end up in costly litigation, and sour both partners on future relationships." Typically, however, warning signs will be there for the small business owner who takes the time to look.

Fundamentally sound business practices. Entrepreneurs hoping to secure a partner to bankroll their R&D efforts or market their products are wasting their time if they do not have a viable business already in place. If the small company's business practices are shoddy, disorganized, or incomplete, large companies will be sure to notice.

Recognition of own responsibilities. Entrepreneurial companies can reap many benefits from partnering with large firms, but they need to recognize that those big companies are for-profit enterprises; they expect something in return for their financial, marketing, and/or management help.

Monitor requirements of successful partnership. Many partnerships with larger companies require entrepreneurs to make a greater commitment to their business in order to meet the obligations and conditions explicated in the partnership agreement. If the entrepreneur in question

launched his or her business for the express purpose of realizing greater personal wealth or establishing a significant presence in a given industry, finding the desire to meet those partnership obligations should not be a problem. If, however, the entrepreneur launched his or her venture in order to stake out a lifestyle of independence and travel, that person may want to weigh the sort of impact that the partnership could have on those aspects of his or her life.

Do not be intimidated. The trappings of the corporate world (high-rise buildings, cavernous conference rooms, legions of blue suits, etc.) can be intimidating, but small business owners have to remember that they run viable businesses of value themselves, and they should negotiate accordingly.

Maintain independence. Autonomy is assured if you maintain ownership, so be leery of turning over too much equity in the business in exchange for financial help.

Establish clear and open lines of communication. Good communication practices are essential to all business relationships, both internal and external, and alliances with large companies are no exception.

LARGE BUSINESSES AS PRODUCT DISTRIBUTORS

Myriad small manufacturers rely on major mass merchandisers (regional, national, or international) to sell their goods. Indeed, these distributors can dramatically heighten a small business's fortunes in a matter of weeks or months. But entrepreneurs seeking to establish such relationships will find that 1) competition to secure a place on the shelves of major retail outlets is fierce, and 2) some mass merchandisers will be better suited for the small business's product than others.

Competition The single most important factor in securing a distribution agreement with a major retailer is, of course, having a quality product that will sell. But small business owners seeking to establish themselves with a major mass merchandiser also need to make sure that they attend to myriad other business matters every step of the way. After all, the mass merchandiser in question has plenty of product options from which to choose; if your company stumbles at any point, there are plenty of other competitors waiting to take your place on the merchandiser's shelf. Given that reality, entrepreneurs have to make sure that they have a dependable production/delivery operation in place. In addition, small business owners should be prepared to provide prospective distributors with information on the firm's management and financial situation.

Compatibility Moreover, entrepreneurs need to make sure that they concentrate their efforts on finding mass merchandisers that already sell products to the new product's probable demographic audience. For example, an expensive, "high-end" home furnishing product is more likely to be compatible with the existing product lines of an upscale retailer than one of the major discount retailers (Kmart, Wal-Mart, etc.). Conversely, an inexpensive but functional item that would be commonly used might be better suited to discount outlets rather than Nordstrom's or some other high-end retailer.

LARGE BUSINESSES AS CUSTOMERS

Many small businesses, whether involved in retail, wholesale, manufacturing, or services, count fellow businesses as significant or primary customers. Pleasing corporate clients is in many fundamental respects no different than pleasing individual customers. As Richard Gerson observed in *Great Customer Service for Your Small Business,* "much of customer service comes down to plain old common sense. Simply put, customer service involves everything you and your employees do to satisfy customers. That means you give them what they want and make sure they are happy when they leave. If you just manage complaints, offer refunds or exchanges on returns, and smile at customers, you only provide a small part of excellent customer service. Customer service also means going out of your way for the customer, doing everything possible to satisfy the customer, and making decisions that benefit the customer—sometimes even at the expense of the business [depending on the customer's future potential]."

However, corporate customers sometimes have different needs and priorities than do private individuals, and small businesses that do not recognize these differences are unlikely to provide service that will be acceptable in the long term. For example, delivery deadlines are often far more important for businesses than they are for regular customers. Late delivery of a service or product may constitute no more than a minor convenience to a private-sector customer, but it might mean significant monetary loss for a corporate customer that was depending on that delivery to meet deadlines imposed by its own customers.

Small business owners are painfully aware of the fact that the loss of a single corporate customer often constitutes a much more severe blow to a business's health than does the loss of a single retail consumer. Whereas businesses that provide goods or services to the general public will have many customers, establishments that provide their goods or services to corporate clients will in all likelihood have far fewer customers. The loss of even one such client, then, can have a significant impact because of the percentage of total business that the customer represents. Finally, businesses that rely on corporate clients are more likely to encounter higher levels of paperwork and bureaucracy to satisfy the recordkeeping apparatus of their clients.

BIBLIOGRAPHY

Ansary, Mir Tamim, and John De La Mothe. *Networks, Alliances and Partnerships in the Innovation Process.* Springer, 2002.

Botkin, James W., and Jana B. Matthews. *Winning Combinations: The Coming Wave of Entrepreneurial Partnerships Between Large and Small Companies.* John Wiley & Sons, 1992.

Buvik, Arnt, and Kjell Gronhaug. "Inter-firm Dependence, Environmental Uncertainty, and Vertical Coordination in Industrial Buyer-Seller Relationships. *Omega.* August 2000.

Doz, Yvez L., and Gary Hamel. *Alliance Advantage: The Art of Creating Value through Partnerships.* Harvard Business School Press, 1998.

Gerson, Richard F. *Great Customer Service for Your Small Business.* Crisp Publications, 1996.

Gould, Myron. "Partnering for Profit—How to Achieve Impressive Cost-Benefit Results." *Direct Marketing.* February 1997.

Neuborne, Ellen. "Small Business, Big Client: Leveraging your size to snag a mammoth customer." *Sales & Marketing Management.* October 2003.

"Small Firms Have Big Advantages." *Mortgage Strategy.* 30 May 2005.

Wilhelm, Wayne, and Bill Rossello. "The Care and Feeding of Customers." *Management Review.* March 1997.

Hillstrom, Northern Lights
updated by Magee, ECDI

SMALL BUSINESS TECHNOLOGY TRANSFER (STTR) PROGRAM

The Small Business Technology Transfer (STTR) Program is an initiative, coordinated and overseen by the Small Business Administration (SBA), to provide small businesses with greater access to funding in the federal innovation research and development arena. "Central to the program," notes the SBA, "is expansion of the public-private sector partnership to include the joint venture opportunities for small business and the nation's premier nonprofit research institutions. STTR's most important role is to foster the innovation necessary to meet the nation's scientific and technological challenges in the 21st century."

STTR is a parallel program to the Small Business Innovation Research (SBIR) Program, and was created by

Congress when it reauthorized SBIR in 1992. The STTR program is a cooperative research partnership between small business concerns and research institutions. It differs from SBIR in two ways. First, it places a greater emphasis on the potential for commercial success. This has spurred participating agencies to be more stringent in their evaluations of applicants. Secondly, it requires that universities, federal laboratories, or nonprofit research centers team with businesses to get product into the marketplace. These research partnerships between small businesses and nonprofit institutions enable participants to combine entrepreneurial initiative and creativity with the expertise, equipment, and other assets of nonprofit research laboratories.

The SBA summarizes the program's development and rapid growth this way. "The STTR Pilot program began making awards in FY 1994. In that year, 198 awards were issued for approximately $19 million to small high technology businesses that collaborated with nonprofit research institutions to undertake R & D projects. In FY 2004, Federal participating agencies awarded 614 Phase I awards and 195 Phase II awards totaling just over $198 million dollars."

STTR QUALIFICATIONS

In order to be considered for the STTR program, interested small businesses must meet several criteria. For instance, they must be American-owned and independently operated for-profit enterprises. In addition, the size of the company may not exceed 500 employees. There is no workforce size limit for participating nonprofit research institutions, but they must also meet certain parameters of the program. They must be principally located in the United States, and they must meet one of the following three definitions: nonprofit college or university, domestic nonprofit research organization, or federally funded research and development center.

Five federal departments and agencies—the departments of Defense, Energy, and Health and Human Services, along with the National Science Foundation and the National Aeronautics and Space Administration—are required by STTR rules to reserve a portion of their research and development funds for the program. As the distributors of STTR funding, they also designate those subjects suitable for additional R&D and determine whether to accept or reject STTR proposals.

These agencies make STTR awards based on the following factors: qualifications of the nonprofit research institution and its small business partner; degree of innovation; and future market potential. Small businesses that secure STTR funding are then routed through a three-phase program.

Phase One: Startup. In this initial stage, awards of up to $100,000 are given to pay for approximately one year's worth of study and research into the scientific, technical, and commercial feasibility of an idea or technology.

Phase Two: Development. These awards, available to Phase One participants, reach up to $500,000 for two years. During this period, business/research partnerships engage in research and development work with an eye toward commercial potential.

Phase Three: Introduction to Market. During this phase, the completed project is introduced into the commercial marketplace to succeed or fail. No STTR funds support this phase. Instead, participants must secure funding from private parties or other federal agencies that do not allocate STTR monies.

For more information on the STTR program, contact the Small Business Administration's Office of Technology in Washington, DC, or visit the SBA's Web site at www.sba.gov.

SEE ALSO *Innovation; Research and Development; Small Business Administration*

BIBLIOGRAPHY
U.S. Small Business Administration. Office of Technology. "What We Do." Available from http://www.sba.gov/sbir/indexwhatwedo.html. Retrieved on 2 June 2006.

Hillstrom, Northern Lights
updated by Magee, ECDI

SMALL BUSINESS-DOMINATED INDUSTRIES

The United States supports many industries that are dominated by or heavily populated with small firms. The majority of these are in the services sector, a fact that reflects the growing dominance of this sector in the overall American economy. Industries that tend to be more easily entered tend to be favorable for small businesses. A need within some industries for heavy investment early on, as would be the case for somebody wishing to enter the cement manufacturing business, makes these industries less hospitable to the small business. It is not surprising, therefore to see the list of industries that the U.S. Census Bureau reports as having the fewest small businesses involved. They are: Accommodation and Food Service; Educational Services; Manufacturing; Mining, and Utilities. When it comes to industries in which the small business plays a dominant role, the U.S. Small Business Administration reported that the fastest-growing such industries in the country were as follows:

1. Employment Agencies
2. Real Estate
3. Automotive Dealers and Service Stations
4. Building Materials and Garden Supplies
5. Automotive Services, Except Repair
6. Millwork, Veneer, and Plywood Manufacturing
7. Paint, Paper Hanging, and Decorating
8. Meat Markets and Freezer Provisioners
9. Retail Stores
10. Agricultural Services

These industries are expected to see continued growth over the coming years, as increasing numbers of small businesses enter the marketplace. But many analysts, citing studies conducted by the SBA's Small Business Advocate office, believe that some other industries friendly to small business are poised for even greater growth. Indeed, statistics compiled by the SBA, the Department of Labor, the Bureau of Labor Statistics, and *Monthly Labor Review* indicated that high rates of growth can also be expected in such business areas as residential care, collection agencies, child day care services, travel arrangement services, equipment rental companies, accounting and bookkeeping services, public relations, and family services.

Residential Care Residential care encompasses a variety of facilities, including those devoted to caring for emotionally disturbed adolescents and mentally retarded individuals, but government data indicates that the area in which residential care will see its greatest growth is in the realm of elder care. Analysts expect growth in assisted-living facilities—which range from domiciliary care homes and personal care homes to adult congregate living facilities—to serve as the engine that drives this industry forward over the next few years, as the American population ages and workers explore various elder care options. "These facilities," wrote Jenny McCune in *Journal of Business Strategy,* "are a bridge between traditional nursing homes, which offer round-the-clock, skilled medical care in an institutional setting, and independent retirement housing, in which residents receive no outside help. In assisted living, the elderly live as independently as possible—usually in suites or cottages—but also have access to meal and laundry facilities and get assistance with daily chores such as bathing and dressing." Business consultants and current participants in the industry warn, however, that while demand for

these services will continue to grow in the coming years, entrance into this business area is costly.

SELECTED HIGH-GROWTH INDUSTRIES FOR SMALL BUSINESS

Child-Care The child-care services industry has enjoyed steady growth for a number of years, due to population increases and the growing presence of women in the business world. And as McCune noted, the popularity of child-care facilities in recent years has also been driven by the increased professionalism of the industry, as evidenced by the development of accreditation standards. The sheer demand for child-care services is expected to insure the continued health of many businesses engaged in this area for years to come, but entrepreneurs should be aware of the hazards that lurk here as well. Business experts note that concerns about child welfare have sparked increased calls for regulation of the industry by OSHA and other government agencies, and that participants face a host of competitors. "A for-profit center may be competing with non-profit centers sponsored by religious organizations, the local Head Start program, family members who baby-sit for little or no cost, caregivers who work in the home, and even after-hours programs run by local elementary schools." Finally, professional day care centers have to grapple with liability issues, encroaching involvement of larger firms, and historically high levels of turnover both among clients and employees.

Collection Agencies The surge in credit availability in American households has sparked a corresponding increase in demand for businesses willing to pursue collections for clients. As one industry participant told *Journal of Business Strategy,* establishing a business in this area is attractive to some entrepreneurs "because the cost of entry is low—someone can start out with a phone and a personal computer in a spare bedroom—and clients generally accept smaller vendors." Another business owner in the industry observed that effective collection agencies will particularly benefit from increasing demands from clients such as credit card companies; doctors, lawyers, and other professionals; and health care firms. Moreover, many observers believe that privatization initiatives by local, state, and federal government agencies will provide collection agencies with additional business.

Travel Agencies Travel and tourism is a huge business area both in the United States and around the world, and independent travel agencies have benefited accordingly. Both business and recreational travel continue to rise in all geographic regions of America, but the hectic pace of modern life has made many of these travelers look to agencies to take care of the specifics of their journeys, from itinerary planning to plane reservations. McCune noted that travel agents do face some challenges today, including slimmer profit margins (because of competitive fares, etc.) and what amounts to a mandate to provide top-level service (since travelers can either go to competitors or make travel arrangements themselves). But she added that travel agencies that are able to improve productivity through available technology can dramatically increase their prospects for success, and noted that "becoming a specialist in a particular type of travel also gives agencies an edge. [In the mid-1990s], cruises, adventure travel, and eco-tours are what's hot. In addition to being in demand by consumers, such packaged tours also offer better margins. Of course, the key to succeeding in the long run is an ability to uncover the next trendy market in travel. That requires a study of demographics—like the aging of the population and the rise of dual-income families—to identify up-and-coming niches."

SEE ALSO *Clusters; Economies of Scale*

BIBLIOGRAPHY

McCune, Jenny. "The Face of Tomorrow." *Journal of Business Strategy.* May-June 1995.

Porter, Michael E. *Competitive Strategy: Techniques for Analyzing Industries and Competitors.* Free Press, 1998.

Schiffer, Mirjam. *Firm Size and the Business Environment: Worldwide Survey Results.* World Bank Publications, 2001.

"Top 10 Small-Business-Dominated Industries." *Journal of Accountancy.* January 1995.

U.S. Census Bureau. "U.S. - All industries - by Employment Size of Enterprise." Available from http://www.census.gov/epcd/susb/2003/us/US--.HTM. Retrieved on 2 June 2006.

Hillstrom, Northern Lights
updated by Magee, ECDI

SMALL CLAIMS COURT

Small claims court is a legal court of law designed to resolve disputes involving relatively small amounts of money in an expeditious manner. Unlike other legal courts, small claims court does not operate by formal rules of evidence, and attorneys are not usually employed to plead such cases. Instead, plaintiffs and defendants appear before the court and present what evidence they have and their perspectives on the dispute. The court makes a judgment based on the evidence presented. Claims made in small claims court typically involve consumer purchases, landlord tenant relations, unpaid

obligations and bills, and other types of property disputes. Small businesses occasionally go before small claims courts when the magnitude of the claim that they pursue fits the court's parameters. This form of litigation has the lowest costs. Unfortunately it is occasionally difficult also to enforce the court's rulings.

CHARACTERISTICS

All 50 states and the District of Columbia have small claims courts or equivalents. In Delaware the function is performed by the Justice of The Peace, in Georgia by the Magistrate Court, and in Mississippi by the Justice Court. In all other jurisdictions a small claims court structure exists. As the name of this institution suggests, such courts limit the size of the claims that they will adjudicate. In 19 states, the maximum claim permitted to be brought is under $5,000; the highest is in New Jersey ($4,500) and the lowest in Kentucky and Tennessee ($1,500). In 17 states the claim is fixed at no more than $5,000. In 15 states the claim may be higher, averaging $8,500 in these states, the lowest being in Indiana and Oklahoma ($6,000) and the highest in Delaware and in Georgia ($15,000).

Halt, which describes itself as "an organization of Americans for legal reform," provides on its Web site small capsules on the characteristics of small claims courts in every state. Their descriptions are offered under a nine-rubric structure. The nine rubrics are: 1) the applicable statutes, 2) the dollar limits, 3) where to sue, 4) service (how notice of a proceeding is brought), 5) hearing date from time of filing, 6) attorneys (permitted to participate or not), 7) transfer (of the case to another court), 8) appeals available, and 9) special provisions—most importantly whether or not the court will assist the successful claimant in collected his or her judgment. The web site is identified in the references below.

Halt advocates reforms in small claims court operations across the board, aiming to raise the maximum level of claims that may be presented, improving access and user-friendliness, and ensuring that claimants are able actually to collect moneys owed to them after a favorable judgment with help from the court. In this effort Halt issues a report card to states. In its most recent report card, Halt gave no As, gave a B to California, Colorado, Georgia, New Mexico, and Utah—singling out Georgia as the best. Halt also gave failing grades to Delaware, Kentucky, Mississippi, and Missouri. The rest got Cs and Ds.

Appearing as a Plaintiff Most small business owners who appear in small claims court as plaintiffs do so because they are having difficulty securing payment for some product or service that they have provided to the defendant. To file a small claims action, the owner needs to first find out if he or she has a case that can even be heard in the state's court. If the size of the claim fits, the owner can check with the local county clerk's office for information on procedures for bringing suit. Again, guidelines vary from state to state, although the basic set-up is consistent. The plaintiff also needs to file the claim in the jurisdiction where the defendant resides.

Once the business owner has familiarized him or herself with the basic procedures, he/she should proceed with the filing. This is a fairly basic document, usually only one page in length. The document briefly delineates the reasons for the suit. Also known as a summons or complaint, the document should describe the dispute; the time, date, and location that it took place; names of witnesses (if any); and desired compensation. The plaintiff should also try to name the defendant as accurately as possible when filing. The filing should name the actual corporate entity rather than, for instance, some brand name or "doing business as" designation under which the defendant operates. When the complaint has been filed, the court clerk will inform the plaintiff when the case will be tried. A filing charge will typically have to be paid.

In the weeks leading up to the court date, the plaintiff needs to gather whatever evidence is available to bolster his or her claim, including photographs, written agreements, itemized bills and invoices, written cost estimates for service or repairs, receipts, canceled checks, and other correspondence.

Appearing as a Defendant When a small business owner receives notice of claim (this is usually sent by both certified and first-class mail), he or she should study the summary of the plaintiff's claims, the amount being sought, and begin preparing for the trial date (which is also included in the notification). If the copy of the claim sent by regular mail is not returned to the court as undeliverable within 21 days, it is assumed that the defendant has received the notice.

Once notified, the defendant can either settle the matter before the trial date or begin preparing for the case by gathering all favorable evidence available (itemized bills or invoices, written agreements, etc.). Untrue claims must be denied unequivocally. If the facts are true, the reasons for failing to pay must be argued with appropriate factual backing. The defendant may also make counter charges and files these in the process of answering the claim. The time frame for accomplishing all this is set by state law and will not be uniform across the nation.

RESOLVING CASES

Small claims court cases are resolved by trial, arbitration, settlement, or default judgment.

Trial. This is the method that is most familiar to most Americans. Under this arrangement, the plaintiff makes his case, the defendant offers a rebuttal, and the presiding judge makes a judgment based on the evidence presented by both sides. If either the plaintiff or the defendant is unhappy with the judge's verdict, he or she can file an appeal. This step is rarely taken, however, because of the added expense involved (filing an appeal is more expensive than filing an initial claim, and it sometimes requires soliciting the services of an attorney).

Arbitration. If both sides agree, the dispute can be resolved by way of arbitration. Arbitration is typically conducted immediately and is less formal than a trial, but no appeal from an arbitrated decision is available to either party.

Settlement. Plaintiffs and defendants also have the option of settling the case out of court prior to the trial. Out of court settlements, of course, are simply yet another commercial agreement, and if not formulated in a properly binding manner, enforceable in the courts, the settlement will be meaningless—unless, of course, it takes the form of a cash payment on the spot.

Default Judgment. A default judgment—also sometimes referred to as a liquidated complaint—can be handed down in the event that one of the sides involved in the dispute does not appear at the scheduled trial time. In such instances, the judge is presented with the evidence provided by whichever side is present. If the person adequately proves his or her case, a default judgment for the amount claimed is entered, or (in instances wherein the plaintiff does not show up) the case may be dismissed.

COLLECTING MONEY THAT IS OWED

Winning a case in small claims court does not necessarily mean that the dispute has been wholly settled. Certainly, if the small business owner mounts a successful defense of a claim, then he or she can return to his business secure in the knowledge that the affair is over. But if the small business owner was a successful plaintiff, he or she still needs to make sure that the amount owed is turned over. The problem of collections, as Halt points out, is that "In most states, small claims courts can only award money damages. Small claims courts cannot issue court orders that require someone to 'cease and desist' from actions that harm others. This limitation means that many small disputes between neighbors or over contract rights, cannot be dealt with in small claims court. The lack of the ability to issue court orders also means that small claims judges often cannot help people collect a judgment they have won. Fully empowering small claims judges to handle cases and problems that require a court order is the second major reform that would improve consumer service by the small claims system." Thus where money is at issue, the small business person should first carefully study the applicable state law and, if it is unfavorable to collections, pursue his or her claim in regular court.

BIBLIOGRAPHY

Randolph, Mary. *Every Dog's Legal Guide: A Must-Have Book for your Owner.* Nolo, 2005.

"Small Claims." Halt. Available from http://www.halt.org/reform_projects/small_claims/. Retrieved on 31 May 2006.

Stewart, Marcia, Janet Portman, and Ralph E. Warner. *Every Landlord's Legal Guide.* Nolo, 2004.

Warner, Ralph E. *Everybody's Guide to Small Claims Court.* Nolo, 2004.

Hillstrom, Northern Lights
updated by Magee, ECDI

SMOKE FREE ENVIRONMENT

The term smoke free environment is sometimes used indiscriminately to discuss both 100 percent smoke free areas as well as segregated and ventilated areas. A truly smoke free environment in a business is one in which no smoking is allowed within any company building or vehicle. Depending on the company, smoking may be permitted in certain outdoor areas designated for that purpose. In other companies, the smoke free policy prohibits smoking on *any* company property. Employees who smoke must abstain from smoking while at work or must leave company grounds to smoke. Other companies allow smoking in special rooms or areas dedicated to that purpose. For smoking areas within the building, a special and separate ventilation system must be installed in order to prevent smoke from leaking into other areas of the structure.

The concept of creating a smoke free workplace has gained many supporters over the last decades. As reported by the American Lung Association, a recent Gallup poll showed that 95 percent of Americans, smokers and non-smokers, believe companies should either ban smoking totally in the workplace or restrict it to separately ventilated areas. In a Centers for Disease Control (CDC) study published in *JAMA*, the number of respondents reporting that smoking was not allowed in public or work areas at their companies increased from 46.5 percent in 1992-93 to 63.7 percent in 1995-96. The CDC

also noted that in 1999, 43 states and the District of Columbia had laws restricting smoking in governmental work areas. Eleven of these states completely prohibited smoking in these areas. Yet the CDC also noted that only one state (Utah) had achieved a CDC national health objective (under the Healthy People 2000 program) of reducing the prevalence of adult cigarette smoking to 15 percent or less. A more recent CDC study reported on in the *American News Wire* underscored the strong momentum across the country to pass comprehensive smoke-free workplace laws to protect everyone from secondhand smoke. But the study also shows that there is much further to go. At the end of 2004, 16 states still had no laws restricting workplace smoking, and many other states did not have comprehensive laws that cover all indoor workplaces, including restaurants and bars.

The CDC has established a series of national public health goals that it works to see met by the year 2010. With regard to smoking issues they are focused extensively on reducing the number of nonsmokers exposed to environmental smoke. There are specific objectives to increase the number of work sites that have smoking restrictions, and to address ETS in more restrictive clean indoor air laws. According to the CDC, the existence of smoke free work environments will increase the likelihood that affected employees will either reduce or eliminate cigarette use.

DEVELOPING AND IMPLEMENTING A SMOKE FREE WORK ENVIRONMENT

In addition to its impact on employee health and welfare, there are a number of costs associated with smoking. According to Lin Grensing-Pophal in *HR Magazine,* expenditures in the United States related to smoking equal roughly $72 billion every year. These include property loss from fires started by smoking products (over $500 million), work productivity loss ($40 billion), and the costs of additional tobacco-related cleaning and maintenance ($4 billion).

Despite the many reasons to help reduce the incidence of employee smoking, the implementation of a smoke free workplace policy needs to be considered carefully. Between the 1960s and the 1990s, the number of smokers in the U.S. dropped steadily. However, the number leveled off during the 1990s, despite increased numbers of smoke free work sites. Smokers have rights too, as has been proven by litigation attempts. Human resources director Arthur Friedson, quoted in *HR Magazine,* stated that developing a smoke free policy rooted in "the basic respect of one co-worker to another" can be most successful, from both an ethical and a legal standpoint.

Prior to establishing a smoke free policy, a company should investigate any existing local and state laws on smoking. Despite highly publicized trials and settlements between the federal government and tobacco companies, there is no federal oversight with respect to the institution of a smoke free environment. *HR Magazine* quotes a figure of over 560 local governments which have enacted ordinances dealing with the rights of nonsmokers. These tend to be stricter than state laws and generally address smoking in public areas such as restaurants, grocery stores, and malls.

On the other side, a careful review of Occupational Safety and Health Administration (OSHA) regulations, protections under the Americans with Disabilities Act (ADA), and state and local law with regards to the rights of smokers and nonsmokers is also warranted. Litigation in which a smoker claims that his or her addiction to tobacco is a disability covered by state and federal laws has occurred with more frequency, although not usually successfully. However, given that any litigation, successful or not, is an enormous burden both financially and emotionally for a small business, it is important to proceed carefully. Work closely with your lawyer to determine applicable laws and regulations.

It may also be helpful to determine how many other businesses in your area are addressing the issue of smoking in the workplace. This can serve as support for your own policies in the case of litigation. You can also get a good idea of what has been successful in other organizations in order to establish a smoke free environment of your own. Other sources for ideas on how to develop or update a nonsmoking policy include a report published by the CDC, *Best Practices for Comprehensive Tobacco Control Programs,* as well as organizations such as the American Cancer Society.

The most important factor in creating a smoke free business environment is having a solid understanding of the workforce. By factoring in the needs of each employee segment, smokers and nonsmokers, and achieving some "buy-in," a small business can reduce or avoid problems down the road. From the very beginning, the involvement of individual employees (again, smokers and nonsmokers alike) in the development of a nonsmoking policy is crucial. Be supportive of employee efforts to stop smoking as well. Many businesses have found the investment in or reimbursement for smoking cessation programs and tools to be money well spent. Some companies even provide a monetary award to successful quitters.

Depending on the elements of your policy, you may need to establish a designated area for smoking. Placing the area outdoors eliminates the expense of a separate ventilation system but may have undesired consequences

such as longer break times, and possibly the additional expense of building a shelter, if this is needed.

Be sure to focus efforts on how employee habits, such as frequent breaks, impact an employee's job. In other words, keep policy and discussions steered toward job performance, rather than the issue of smoking. It is important to establish guidelines that impact all employees such as those regarding breaks and then enforce them on a consistent basis for the entire staff. Any discussions of violations to these guidelines should address the impact of employee actions on performance. Leave smoking out of the discussion entirely.

Once a small business has developed its nonsmoking policy, it should provide early notice of the policy, prior to implementation. This allows employees to consider the consequences of behavior and, if need be, to make efforts to quit smoking. At this time, the company should also publicize any assistance in quitting smoking, such as a cessation program or monetary rewards. It may be more successful to implement a smoke free policy in stages. For example, smoking might first be restricted to a designated area, then eliminated from company property entirely. However, the success of gradual implementation can vary from workplace to workplace.

Once established, a small business's smoke free environment should also take into account new employees. While there are no laws prohibiting discrimination against smokers, questioning prospective staff as to their smoking habits is ill advised. Not hiring smokers may be defensible for an organization such as the American Cancer Society, but not for most small employers. A more acceptable position is to alert candidates at the time of the interview to the small business's nonsmoking policy and its associated standards of acceptable behavior.

Finally, it is especially important for a small business to regularly revisit its smoking policy, along with other human resources policies. Local, state, and federal laws and regulations are in a constant state of flux over this issue. It pays to review these laws regularly and in conjunction with a legal advisor. The burden of litigation over such issues is a heavy one for a small business to bear. In addition, a shifting employee population may make some changes necessary. Seeking input from employees helps to both promote and refine the policy.

EFFECTS OF A SMOKE FREE ENVIRONMENT ON CUSTOMERS

The implications of a smoke free environment in small businesses such as restaurants, bars, and shops also extend to customers. For these types of businesses, local and state laws and regulations may also be more straightforward. Many states and municipalities already limit or eliminate smoking in the public areas of these businesses. In the state of California, for example, no smoking is permitted in any public establishment. California lawmakers alerted the public of the change six months prior to implementing this legislation to allow businesses time to address the issue in their workplace policies and to provide consumers with time to get used to the idea. There also may be legal issues to consider. According to an article in *Business-First Columbus*, the National Restaurant Association states that employers can be held liable if staff members become ill from second-hand smoke.

Other states require a public establishment to have both smoking and nonsmoking areas within a restaurant, with space and sometimes ventilation requirements for each. As noted with work environments, a separate ventilation system may be used to divert smoky air. Working with local authorities as well as reviewing policies from similar businesses in the area can help a small business to determine its needs.

If the institution of a smoke free environment at a small business is not tied to any governmental regulations or requirements that are already known by the general public, a small business should consider giving advance notice of the new policy to their customers. A simple posting at the door as well as personal verbal or written notice to regular clients can go a long way to ensure customers' responsiveness and compliance. Finally, in cases where customers ignore the policy, it is important to courteously but consistently administer it, even at the risk of losing those customers.

The implementation of a smoke free environment is a complex process for any small business. By using legal counsel to wade through the maze of pertinent laws and regulations, working with employees to develop a policy, and communicating the policy regularly to both employees and customers, a small business can ensure its efforts are successful.

BIBLIOGRAPHY

Bellotti, Mary. "Who's Taking the Hit?" *Business Journal-Portland*. 22 September 2000.

Cronan, Carl. "Cancer Society Offers 'How-To' Help On Smoking Policies." *Tampa Bay Business Journal*. 26 January 2001.

"DOD to Phase Out Smoking at Recreation Facilities." *All Hands*. August 2000.

Downey Grimsley, Kirstin. "Dumped, Stiffed and Delinquent." *Washington Post*. 31 May 2000.

Linn, Diane. "Ordinance 937: A Business-Friendly Smoking Ban." *Business Journal-Portland*. 22 September 2000.

Millar, Michael. "Health Benefits Justify Smoking Ban Job Losses." *Personnel Today*. 18 January 2005.

Pavilkey, Susan. "Clearing the Air." *Business First-Columbus*. 2 February 2001.

"Smoking Policies in the Workplace Fact Sheet." American Lung Association. Available from http://www.lungusa.org/site/pp.asp?c=dvLUK9O0E&b=36000. Retrieved on 31 May 2006.

"State-Specific Prevalence of Current Cigarette Smoking Among Adults and the Proportion of Adults Who Work in a Smoke Free Environment—United States, 1999." *JAMA, The Journal of the American Medical Association*. 13 December 2000.

Hillstrom, Northern Lights
updated by Magee, ECDI

SOLE PROPRIETORSHIP

The sole proprietorship is both the simplest and most common type of business operating in the United States today. Most businesses that are owned and operated by one person take this form; in fact, small business owners who have sole ownership of their enterprises are automatically categorized under this business type if they do not take steps to legally establish themselves as another type of business. The essential feature of a sole proprietorship is that the law makes no distinction between the person, the sole proprietor, and the business. Virtually all of the legal and tax consequences associated with sole proprietorships flow from this basic fact.

ADVANTAGES OF SOLE PROPRIETORSHIP

Many aspects of sole proprietorship are attractive to entrepreneurs. Primary reasons why small business owners choose to operate in this fashion include:

- Sole proprietors enjoy a great deal of independence and autonomy. The sole proprietor makes all the decisions. As a sole proprietor, you alone can decide what to sell and how to sell it, when to expand and when to pull back, when to look for financing, when to buy new equipment, when and how long to work, and when to take the day off. In some instances, sole proprietorships can benefit enormously as a result of this streamlined management structure. An entrepreneur who keeps abreast of business trends, community events, and other factors that can impact on a company's fortunes may, in some cases, be able to adjust to changing business realities far more quickly than a partnership or corporation, where multiple owners and/or managers need to reach agreement on appropriate responses to changes in their business environment.

ENCYCLOPEDIA OF SMALL BUSINESS

- Figuring taxes is fairly straightforward. Unlike other business types, sole proprietorships do not have to file separate income tax returns. In addition, FICA (Federal Insurance Contributions Act) taxes for such businesses are less than they are for partnerships or other legal operating forms.

- Accounting is a relatively simple affair, although small business experts encourage the owners of even the most modest business ventures to establish separate bank accounts and record keeping practices for their enterprise.

- Business operations, too, are generally simpler in a sole proprietorship. Other forms of business often have to contend with more cumbersome or time-consuming regulatory requirements in conducting or reporting on their operations.

- Start-up costs are often modest. This is due in part to the fact that entrepreneurs who intend to establish sole proprietorships do not need to secure the services of an attorney to prepare documents required by state or federal agencies, since none are needed.

- Business losses can be used to offset other income on personal tax returns. Conversely, business profits do not have to be shared with any other owners.

- Sole proprietors are not forbidden from securing and building a work force. Indeed, many businesses that qualify as sole proprietorships (delicatessens, landscaping firms, canoe liveries, flower shops, etc.) have employees.

DISADVANTAGES OF SOLE PROPRIETORSHIP

While business owners who choose sole proprietorship understandably enjoy their autonomy and their freedom from the paperwork that can be considerable in other, more complicated, business types, they still need to consider the following drawbacks in the areas of liability and business financing.

"In a sole proprietorship," warned Jocelyn West Brittin in *Selecting the Legal Structure for Your Business,* "the business and the owner are one and the same. There is no separate legal entity and thus no separate legal 'person.' This means that as a sole proprietor you will have unlimited personal responsibility for your business's liabilities. For example, if your business cannot pay for its supplies, the suppliers can sue you individually. The business creditors can go against both the business's assets, including your bank account, car or house.... The reverse is also true; i.e., your personal creditors can make claims against your business's assets." She does note that some states offer sole proprietors protection of their personal assets from business risks through legal designations that involve the owner's spouse and/or children, but such arrangements are complex, and should not be entered into without first consulting with an attorney. Business owners can also elect to purchase liability insurance for protection from lawsuits and other threats. In addition to general liability insurance, producers or sellers of goods may also want to consider securing product liability insurance. The cost of such insurance varies considerably depending on the type of business under consideration.

Raising capital for a sole proprietorship can be quite difficult as well (though many businesses that operate as sole proprietorships are of modest size and thus are not impacted by this reality). Many lenders are reluctant to provide financing to owners of sole proprietorships—in large part because of fears about their ability to recover the funds should the owner die or become disabled—and even those who make such loans require borrowers to provide personal guaranties on the loan. Sole proprietors who consent to such arrangements are in effect pledging their personal assets as collateral on the loan. Small business advisors counsel clients who are considering these stipulations to proceed cautiously. If a potential lender is taking extra measures to protect itself from default, it may be an indication that the prospective borrower's business plan is viewed—legitimately, perhaps—as flawed or risky. In addition, even well-conceived businesses sometimes fail as a result of circumstances beyond the owner's control. An entrepreneur might, for example, establish a store that is enormously successful for its first few years of operation, only to see it suffer a dramatic downturn in performance with the arrival in town of a much larger competitor that provides its customers with a wider variety of services and goods. Banks and other lending institutions are aware that such scenarios occur, and they plan accordingly.

Continuity and Transferability Unlike other businesses that can be passed down from generation to generation or continue to exist long after the passage of its original board of directors, sole proprietorships have a limited life. As Brittin wrote, "a sole proprietorship can exist as long as its owner is alive and desires to continue the business. When the owner dies, the sole proprietorship no longer exists. The assets and liabilities of the business become part of the owner's estate."

A sole proprietor is free to sell all or a portion of his or her business to a buyer, but any transaction that transfers ownership or turns the business into one with two or more owners puts an end to the sole proprietorship that had been in existence.

STARTING A SOLE PROPRIETORSHIP

Sole proprietorships often operate under the name of the owner of the business, but this is not a requirement. If the owner decides to select a fictitious name, however, he or she may be required to file a certificate explaining the arrangement in the region in which he or she is operating the business in question (this requirement also gives the sole proprietor legal protection, for it serves to protect them from other persons who might otherwise use the name for their own business enterprises). In addition, many states forbid business establishments from using words like "incorporated," "Co.," or "Inc." unless they actually qualify as corporations. Some cities and counties also require sole proprietorships to secure a business license before launching their business. Owners who subsequently change their business location or add new locations to their operation are often required to obtain new business licenses for those sites as well.

Many sole proprietorships also will need to obtain federal and state payroll ID numbers. These numbers are required for any businesses that will have employees or will do business with establishments that have employees. Finally, owners of sole proprietorships will, like all other business owners, have to obtain the appropriate operating licenses and certificates, if any, for the area in which they will be conducting business. Business licenses and zoning permits are among the types of licenses that are sometimes required. Once these few minor licensing issues have been addressed, the sole proprietor is free to conduct business.

Once a sole proprietorship has been established and proven viable, many business owners eventually choose to incorporate. Incorporation is both more expensive and more time-consuming than sole proprietorship, but it also affords the business owner considerably more legal protection from lawsuits and other liabilities than does sole proprietorship, and it also makes it easier to secure financing for business expansion.

SEE ALSO *Partnership; Incorporation; Organizational Structure*

BIBLIOGRAPHY

Anderson, Brian L. "Benefit Issues Regarding Partnerships, S Corporations, and Sole Proprietorships." *Jouranl of Pension Benefits.* Spring 2004.

Fraser, Jill Andresky. "Perfect Form." *Inc.* December 1997.

Hawkins, Carole. "Beyond the Sole Proprietorship." *Home Office Computing.* March 2001.

How to Set Up Your Own Small Business. American Institute of Small Business, 1990.

Schneeman, Angela. *The Law of Corporations, and Other Business Organizations.* Thomson Delmar Learning, 2002.

Sitarz, Daniel. *Sole Proprietorship: Small Business Start-Up Kit.* Nova, 2000.

U.S. Small Business Administration. Brittin, Jocelyn West. *Selecting the Legal Structure for Your Business.* n.d.

Hillstrom, Northern Lights
updated by Magee, ECDI

SPAM

Spam is a slang term that describes unsolicited commercial advertisements sent by e-mail over the Internet. Spam, which can be used as a noun or as a verb, is also known as junk e-mail or unsolicited bulk e-mail. According to Heather Newman in the *Detroit Free Press,* the term comes from a skit by the Monty Python comedy troupe, in which a group of Vikings chants "spam, spam, spam, spam," to drown out all other conversation. It was adopted by early Internet users to describe annoying, unsolicited e-mail advertisements that crowd out legitimate communication. "Spam is an overwhelming fact of life for nearly every e-mail user," Newman wrote. "Some Internet webmasters say that more than half the traffic their computers handle is spam."

THE COSTS OF SPAM

"The financial and psychological costs of spam are eroding the Internet's goodwill," Karen Rodriguez wrote in the *Phoenix Business Journal.* Spam causes problems for both e-mail users and the Internet Service Providers (ISPs) that offer access to the Internet to customers for a fee. Most e-mail users resent receiving spam messages because they fill up electronic mailboxes and are time-consuming to sort through. In addition, a large proportion of spam messages contain material that could be considered offensive or fraudulent. A survey of spam content conducted on behalf of Representative Gary Miller of California, co-sponsor of proposed legislation to ban spam, found that 30 percent consisted of pornographic materials, another 30 percent consisted of get-rich-quick schemes, and the remainder included a variety of questionable business proposals and gambling opportunities.

According to Ryan P. Wallace, Adam M. Lusthaus, and Jong Hwan Kim in their book *Computer Crimes,* "Estimates put the total cost of spam to American businesses in 2003 at more than $10 million in lost productivity and anti-spam measures."

Companies that send out bulk e-mail defend the practice on several grounds. For example, they say that some small businesses cannot afford other forms of marketing. Sending bulk e-mail helps these businesses reach potential customers and compete with larger firms. Proponents of e-mail marketing also claim that their advertisements are a constitutionally protected form of free speech. Spammers try to justify their actions by claiming that companies should be allowed to take advantage of the online market and that people have no right to filter their mail.

But opponents of spam argue that Internet users end up paying to receive unwanted advertisements. By sending bulk e-mail to thousands of recipients, spammers create an increase in the load placed on ISP mail servers. ISPs must purchase bandwidth in order to connect their servers to the Internet. They buy bandwidth based on expected usage by their paying customers, and the cost accounts for a large percentage of their operating budgets. Spam ties up bandwidth and reduces processing speed, which causes an increase in costs for ISPs and a decrease in performance for their customers. So while it may cost a spammer only a few dollars to create and send an advertisement via e-mail, it may cost an ISP thousands of dollars to accommodate the spam. These costs are usually passed on to the ISP's customers, most of whom did not want to receive the spam in the first place.

LEGISLATION TO CURB SPAM

Complaints from ISPs and Internet users have prompted several states to pass laws regulating spam. In 2003 the federal government also took action. Spam came under relatively mild regulation with the passage of the Controlling the Assault of Non-Solicited Pornography and Marketing Act, also officially called the CAN-SPAM Act of 2003 (Public Law 108-197). It became effective in December of 2003 and took effect on January 1, 2004. The Act requires that senders of unsolicited commercial e-mail label their messages, but Congress did not require a standard labeling language. Such messages are required to carry instructions on how to opt-out of receiving such mail; the sender must also provide its actual physical address. Misleading headers and titles are prohibited. Congress authorized the Federal Trade Commission to establish a "do-not-mail" registry but did not require that the FTC do so. As of 2006 the FTC has not taken action to create a do-not-mail registry. CAN-SPAM also prevents states from outlawing commercial e-mail or to require their own labeling. Since 2003 other bills have been proposed but have not been enacted.

In effect, based on the provisions of CAN-SPAM, spam is not a computer crime unless, according to U.S. Code, Title 18, No. 1037, violation is committed "in furtherance of any felony under the laws of the United States or of any State." Despite its legal status, spam is both a major annoyance and extracts a cost.

After two plus years in force, the CAN-SPAM law appears to have done little to reduce the volume of spam that clutters cyberspace. As Roger A. Grimes reports in *InfoWorld,* much of the problem with the law is the fact that it requires e-mail recipients to opt-out of receiving mail by replying to a spam note and asking to be removed from the mailing list. Grimes provides in his article a rather stark assessment of the CAN-SPAM law and its likelihood to ever curb spam. "If you don't have time to read the FTC's report [on the first two year's impact of CAN-SPAM], let me give you my Executive Summary of whether CAN-SPAM has led to a decrease in spam: No! . . . The real question is whether or not the percentage of spam as compared with total e-mail sent is decreasing. Although several entities report drops in the amount of spam reaching end-users because of improved filtering capabilities, the real rate of spam is leveling off at between 50 percent and 70 percent of e-mail traffic, depending on which statistics you read. And if spam reaching the end-user has decreased because of better filtering devices, then the CAN-SPAM Act has had no part in any so-called success." Grimes concludes with the suggestion that the law be abolished and a new one written which would criminalize the practice and add teeth to the legislation.

WAYS TO REDUCE SPAM

As Grimes' assessment of the CAN-SPAM Act suggests, strides have been made to curtail the number of spam messages that reach their intended audience. These strides appear to be the result, however, of companies spending time and money on spam filtering systems. The market for spam filtering and blocking services and software has grown rapidly in the last 5 years and is likely to continue growing. And while choice is good, the plethora of anti-spam options can be confusing.

"Before attempting to sift through the various anti-spam approaches, companies should make a few key decisions to help guide their search. Are you comfortable outsourcing your spam headache to a service provider, which means letting your e-mail traffic flow through their data centers before hitting your corporate network? If you prefer an in-house solution, should it sit at your mail gateway to ward off spam before it enters your network, saving valuable resources, or at the mail server where it can perform additional tasks as well? Or does a dedicated appliance that can't be tampered with sound more secure? And what about offerings from established messaging security vendors?" This is how the authors, Cara Garretson and Ellen Messmer, of an article in *Network World* begin a lengthy review of anti-spam products. Three options exist for implementing an anti-spamming program: anti-spam services provided by a third party; server software that can be loaded onto the company server, and a dedicated server used for this purpose only called a gateway appliance. For most small companies, one of the first two options is probably the most cost effective, the third being costly for smaller installations.

Anti-spam services are a good choice for companies that wish to dedicate minimal information technology resources to handling spam. Providers of this service divert a company's incoming mail to their own data centers, where a number of techniques are used to quarantine unwanted e-mail messages, and the remainder of the traffic is passed on to the customer. The benefits of anti-spam services can be put in place very quickly but over time they may prove to be more costly than a software option. Contracts with service providers usually cost between $1.50 and $4.00 per e-mail account per month after the minimum monthly charge.

Spam filtering software packages vary and provide a differing level of functionality and customization options. Anti-spam software packages usually sit at a company's mail gateway to filter spam out of the incoming messages. These products give companies many options for handling spam once it's caught, options like quarantine areas managed by end users where spam messages are held. Many products also offer lists, which dictate e-mail senders that should always be blocked and those who should never be blocked, respectively.

Other actions which can be taken to reduce the volume of incoming spam messages all have to do with limiting the ways in which your e-mail address is exposed to the public. Spammers obtain e-mail addresses from a wide range of legal sources, including business cards, newspaper articles, Web pages, member lists, customer lists, and message postings. They even collect jokes, chain letters, and other frequently forwarded e-mail messages that have hundreds of addresses on the top. Prudent rules to follow to minimize e-mail address exposure include: never replying to an e-mail message from spammers, even in order to use their "opt-out" buttons; hiding the addresses of recipients if you forward e-mail messages to large groups of people, and not including linked e-mail addresses in the company Web site.

Finally, it may be helpful to inform your own ISP when you receive spam, so that the system administrator can filter out future messages from that address. Many e-mail programs also feature filtering capabilities. Finally, if you are bombarded with e-mail from a company with which you have done business, or you find out that such a company has sold your e-mail address to a spammer, you can boycott the company's products or send an e-mail of protest to the company president.

SEE ALSO *Computer Crime; Electronic Mail*

BIBLIOGRAPHY

Garretson, Cara, and Ellen Messmer. "How To: Fighting Spam." *Network World.* 1 December 2003.

Gordon, Lawrence A., Martin P. Loeb, William Lucyshyn, and Robert Richardson. *2005 CSI/FBI Computer Crime and Security Survey.* Computer Security Institute. Available from www.gocsi.com. Retrieved on 29 January 2006.

Grimes, Roger A. "SECURITY ADVISER: Time to Can the CAN-SPAM Act - Despite the FTC's Declaration of Success, Spam Isn't Getting Better, and It's Partly the CAN-SPAM Act's Fault." *InfoWorld.* 23 January 2006.

Hinde, Stephen. "Smurfing, Swamping, Spamming, Spoofing, Squatting, Slandering, Surfing, Scamming, and Other Mischiefs of the World Wide Web." *Computers and Security.* May 2000.

Newman, Heather. "Do a Little Work to Give Spammer Unhappy Returns." *Detroit Free Press.* 28 February 2001.

Rodriguez, Karen. "Federal Lawmakers Propose Bill to End Spamming." *Phoenix Business Journal.* 12 May 2000.

Wallace, Ryan P., Adam M. Lusthaus, and Jong Hwan Kim. "Computer Crimes." *American Criminal Law Review.* Spring 2005.

Hillstrom, Northern Lights
updated by Magee, ECDI

SPAN OF CONTROL

The concept of "span of control," also known as management ratio, refers to the number of subordinates controlled directly by a superior. It is a particularly important concept for small business owners to understand because small businesses often get into trouble when the founder ends up with too wide a span of control. Span of control is a topic taught in management schools and widely employed in large organizations like the military, government agencies, and educational institutions. "Yet few entrepreneurs know the term or are willing to admit any limit to the number of people they directly oversee," explained Mark Hendricks in an article for *Entrepreneur* magazine. When a small business owner's span of control becomes too large, it can limit the growth of his or her company. Even the best managers tend to lose their effectiveness when they spend all their time managing people and their issues and are unable to focus on long-term plans and competitive positioning for the business as a whole.

The concept of span of control was developed in the United Kingdom in 1922 by Sir Ian Hamilton. It arose from the assumption that managers have finite amounts of time, energy, and attention to devote to their jobs. In studies of British military leaders, Hamilton found that they could not effectively control more than three to six people directly. These figures have been generally accepted as the "rule of thumb" for span of control ever since. More than a decade later, A.V. Graicumas illustrated the concept of span of control mathematically. His research showed that the number of interactions between managers and their subordinates—and thus the amount of time managers spent on supervision—increased geometrically as the managers' span of control became larger.

It is important to note that all managers experience a decrease in effectiveness as their span of control exceeds the optimal level. In other words, the limitations implied by span of control are not shortcomings of certain individual managers but rather of managers in general. In addition, it is important to understand that span of control refers only to direct reports, rather than to an entire corporate hierarchy. Even though a CEO may technically control hundreds of employees, his or her span of control would only include the department heads or functional managers who reported to the CEO directly. "When given enough levels of hierarchy, any manager can control any number of people—albeit indirectly," Hendricks noted. "But when it comes to direct reports, the theory [of span of control] suggests entrepreneurs must respect managers' inborn limits."

Entrepreneurs and small business owners are particularly susceptible to overextending their span of control. After all, many of these people have started a business from the ground up and are wary of losing control over its operations. They thus choose to manage lots of people directly, rather than delegating tasks to middle managers, in an effort to continue being involved in key decisions as the business grows. But this strategy can backfire, as Hendricks explained: "Extending span of control beyond the recommended limits engenders poor morale, hinders effective decision making, and may cause loss of the agility and flexibility that give many entrepreneurial firms their edge."

ORGANIZING TO OPTIMIZE MANAGERS' SPAN OF CONTROL

Establishing the optimal span of control for managers is one of the most important tasks in structuring organizations. Finding the optimal span involves balancing the relative advantages and disadvantages of retaining responsibility for decisions and delegating those decisions. In general, studies have shown that the larger the organization, the fewer people should report to the top person. Managers should also have fewer direct reports if those subordinates interact with each other frequently. In this situation, the supervisor ends up managing both his or her relationship with the subordinates and the subordinates' relationships with one another.

Some other factors affecting the optimal span of control include whether workers perform tasks of a routine nature (which might permit a broader span of control) or of great variety and complexity (which might require a narrower span of control), and whether the overall business situation is stable (which would indicate a broader span) or dynamic (which would require a narrower span). Other situations in which a broader span of control might be possible include when the manager delegates effectively; when there are staff assistants to screen interactions between the manager and subordinates; when subordinates are competent, well-trained, and able to work independently; and when subordinates' goals are well-aligned with those of other workers and the organization.

There are advantages and disadvantages to different spans of control. A narrow span of control tends to give managers close control over operations and to facilitate fast communication between managers and employees. On the other hand, a narrow span of control can also create a situation where managers are too involved in their subordinates' work, which can reduce innovation and morale among employees. A wide span of control forces managers to develop clear goals and policies, delegate tasks effectively, and select and train employees carefully. Since employees get less supervision, they tend to take on more responsibility and have higher morale with a wide span of control. On the other hand, managers with a wide span of control might become overloaded with work, have trouble making decisions, and lose control over their subordinates.

With all of these factors to consider, small business owners might become overwhelmed with the task of finding the optimal span of control. But Hendricks claimed that evaluating the situation and making a decision should not be too difficult. "The rule of thumb that an executive should supervise three to six people directly held up fairly well against challenges from efficiency experts, team-building zealots, technology buffs, empowerment boosters, megalomaniacs, and others determined to increase the accepted span of control," Hendricks wrote. "If the calculations are too much for you, just take a look at the amount of hours you're working. When workdays for the people at the top are twice what they are for others, span of control is out of whack."

For small business owners who feel that they have too many direct reports and need to reduce their span of control, the solution may involve either hiring middle managers to take on a portion of the owner's responsibilities, or reorganizing the reporting structure of the company. In either case, small business owners must balance their own capabilities and workload against the need to control costs. After all, reducing the entrepreneur's span of control may involve the costs of paying additional salaries for new hires or training existing employees to take on supervisory responsibilities. Despite the potential costs involved, Hendricks argued that adjusting span of control toward the optimal level can lead to vast improvements for small businesses. "There's the real possibility that paying attention to span of control could usher your business into a new era of rapid, sustained, profitable growth," he told entrepreneurs. "You could even find running your business easier and more fun."

SEE ALSO *Delegation; Manager Recruitment; Organizational Structure*

BIBLIOGRAPHY

Harrison, Simon. "Is There a Right Span of Control?" *Business Review.* February 2004.

Hendricks, Mark. "Span Control." *Entrepreneur.* January 2001.

Visser, Bauke. "Organizational Communication Structure and Performance." *Journal of Economic Behavior and Organization.* June 2000.

Hillstrom, Northern Lights
updated by Magee, ECDI

STANDARD MILEAGE RATE

The standard mileage rate (SMR), also known as mileage per diem, is the amount per mile that the Internal Revenue Service (IRS) allows small businesses and self-employed persons to use to calculate their vehicle expenses for tax deduction purposes. Businesses that choose to use the standard mileage rate do so because it is easier to use than the actual costs method, which requires keeping complete records of expenses like gasoline, maintenance, tires, insurance, and license and registration fees. The standard mileage rate for business can be used for all mileage accumulated for work-related trips. Normal commuting between home and work does not qualify for this type of deduction.

The standard mileage rate is determined by the IRS and is routinely adjusted, but not more often than once a year. As of January 1, 2006 the standard mileage rate was set to 44.5 cents per mile for the year. In the late summer of 2005 the IRS did make a rare midyear adjustment to the standard mileage rate in an attempt to deal with the unusual circumstances resulting from a summer of devastating hurricanes and the loss of oil refining capacity in the Gulf of Mexico. The IRS explained the one time adjustment this way: "In September, the IRS made a special one-time adjustment for the last four months of 2005, raising the rate for business miles to 48.5 cents per mile in response to a sharp increase in gas prices, which topped $3 a gallon." The 2006 rate was lowered

following stabilization in gas prices but still represents the highest annual rate ever set by the IRS.

A different rate is set by the service for miles driven "for medical or moving purposes" and those driven "in service of charitable organizations." The 2006 standard mileage rates per mile driven for these two categories were 18 cents and 14 cents respectively.

The standard mileage rate can be used for vehicles that a business owns. In addition, the IRS decided in 1998 that the SMR can also be used for leased vehicles, provided that one uses the standard mileage rate for the duration of the lease (or the balance of the lease if it began before 1998).

RESTRICTIONS ASSOCIATED WITH THE STANDARD MILEAGE RATE

While the standard mileage rate is quite practical, it may not be used in several situations. One instance would include taxis and other vehicles for hire that charge for mileage in the first place. Also, if a fleet-type business is using more than one vehicle at the same time, they cannot use the standard mileage rate, although they can use it if they own two or more vehicles that aren't being used concurrently. Rural mail carriers that already receive a qualified reimbursement are also not eligible for the standard mileage rate.

In addition, small businesses that decide to use the standard mileage rate for a vehicle must do so in the first year that the vehicle is placed into service. In later years, a business can switch to the actual cost method if they so desire. However, a straight-line method of depreciation, which yields a smaller deduction, must be used in all subsequent years for vehicles that initially used the standard mileage rate.

The standard mileage rate already has vehicle depreciation built into it, meaning that one cannot claim additional depreciation when using this form of deduction. Also, businesses that sell a car that has used the standard mileage rate will have to figure out whether any taxable gains were made on the sale and adjust the tax basis of the vehicle for each year the SMR was applied. Finally, the standard mileage rate and the 'actual costs' method cannot be used at the same time.

SEE ALSO *Business Travel*

BIBLIOGRAPHY

Internatl Revenue Service "IRS Announced Standard Mileage Rates for 2006." Available from http://www.irs.gov/newsroom/article/0,,id=151226,00.html. Retrieved on 31 May 2006.

Hillstrom, Northern Lights
updated by Magee, ECDI

STOCKS

Securities issued by a corporation are classified as debt, equity, or some hybrid of these two forms. Debt usually takes the form of a loan and must be repaid; equity usually takes the form of an ownership claim upon the corporation. The two main types of equity claims are common stock and preferred stock, although there are also related claims, such as rights, warrants, and convertible securities. Growing companies, which tend to lack the assets necessary to secure debt, often decide to issue equity securities. Although issuing common stock can be traumatic for a small business—because it can be costly, and because it causes a dramatic redistribution of ownership and control—it can also provide a solid foundation upon which to build a company. Preferred stock offers holders priority in receiving dividends and in claiming assets in the event of business liquidation, but it also lacks the voting rights afforded to common stockholders. Many venture capitalists require convertible preferred stock—which can be converted to common stock at some time in the future at a favorable price—as incentive to invest in start-up ventures.

COMMON STOCK

A share of common stock is quite literally a share in the business, a partial claim to ownership of the firm. Owning a share of common stock provides a number of rights and privileges. These include sharing in the income of the firm, exercising a voice in the management of the firm, and holding a claim on the assets of the firm.

Dividends Sharing in the income of the firm is generally in the form of a cash dividend. The firm is not obligated to pay dividends, which must be declared by the board of directors. The size and timing of the dividends is uncertain. In a strictly rational economic environment, dividends would be considered as a "residual." In this view, the firm would weigh payment of dividends against other uses for the funds. Dividends would be paid only if the firm had no better use for the funds. In this case, declaring or increasing dividends would be a negative signal, since the firm would be admitting that it lacked possibilities for growth.

For widely held, publicly traded firms there are a number of indications that this is not the case, and that shareholders and investors like dividends and dividend increases. In these contexts, dividends are taken as a signal that the firm is financially healthy. A decrease in dividends would indicate inability to maintain the level of dividends, signaling a decline in prospects. An increase would signal an improvement in prospects. The signal from a dividend decrease is strong because management will wish to give only positive signals by at least maintaining the dividend, making cuts only when absolutely necessary. The signal from a dividend increase is also strong because management would be hesitant to increase dividends unless they could be maintained. The signaling nature of dividends is supported by cases in which the dividend is maintained in the face of declining earnings, sometimes even using borrowed funds. It is also supported by the occurrence of "extraordinary" or one-time-only dividends, a label by which management attempts to avoid increasing expectations.

This signaling approach is not applicable to closely held firms. In this situation, communication between management and shareholders is more direct and signals are not required. When owners are also the managers, sharing in earnings may take the indirect form of salaries and fringe benefits. In fact, shareholders in closely held firms may prefer that dividends be reinvested, even in relatively low return projects, as a form of tax protection. The investment is on a pretax (before personal tax) basis for the investor, avoiding immediate double taxation and converting the income to capital gains that will be paid at a later date.

Dividends are declared for stockholders at a particular date, called the date of record. Since stock transactions ordinarily take five business days for completion, the stock goes "ex-dividend" four days before the date of record, unless special arrangement is made for immediate delivery. Since the dividend removes funds from the firm, it can be expected that the per share price will decrease by the amount of the dividend on the ex-dividend date.

Stock dividends are quite different in form and nature from cash dividends. In a stock dividend, the investor is given more shares in proportion to the number already held. A stock split is similar, with a difference in accounting treatment and a greater increase in the number of shares. The use of the word "dividends" in stock dividends is actually a misuse of the word, since there is no flow of cash, and the proportional and absolute ownership of the investor is unchanged. The stockholder receives nothing more than a repackaging of ownership: the number of shares increases, but the price per share will drop. There are, however, some arguments in favor of stock dividends. One of these is the argument that investors will avoid stocks of unusually high price, possibly due to required size of investment and round lot (100 share) trading. On the other hand, stocks with unusually low price are also avoided, perhaps perceived as "cheap." The price drop accompanying stock dividends can be used to adjust price. Stock dividends have also been suggested as a way to make cash dividends elective while also providing tax-advantaged reinvestment.

With a cash dividend, an investor who wishes to reinvest must pay taxes and then reinvest the reduced amount. With a stock dividend, the entire amount is reinvested. Although taxes will ultimately be paid, in the interim a return is earned on the entire pretax amount. This is the same argument as that for low dividends in a closely held firm. Investors who wish cash dividends can simply sell the stock. Using stock dividends in this way faces restrictions from the Internal Revenue Service.

Control The corporate form allows the separation of management and ownership, with the manager serving as the agent of the owner. Separation raises the problem of control, or what is termed the agency problem. Stockholders have only indirect control by voting for the directors. The directors in turn choose management and are responsible for monitoring and controlling management's conduct. In fact, the stockholders' ability to influence the conduct of the firm may be quite small, and management may have virtually total control within very broad limits.

Voting for the directors takes either of two forms. The first form is majority voting. In this form, each stockholder receives votes for each open position according to the number of shares held, and may cast those votes only for candidates for that position. The winning candidate is the candidate winning a majority of the votes cast. The second form is called cumulative voting. In this form, stockholders again receive votes for each open position according to the number of shares held, but may apportion the votes among the positions and candidates as desired. The candidates receiving the most votes are elected.

Excluding minority stockholders from representation on the board is more difficult under cumulative voting. For example, if there are four directors to be elected and one million shares eligible to vote at one vote per share, a stockholder with 500,001 shares would control the election. Under majority voting a dissident stockholder with 200,001 shares could cast only 200,001 votes apiece for candidates for each of the four positions, which would not be sufficient to ensure representation on the board. Under cumulative voting, a dissident stockholder with a minimum of 200,001 shares could be sure of representation by electing one candidate of choice, casting a cumulative 800,004 votes for that candidate. The remaining 799,999 shares could be sure of electing three chosen candidates, but could not command sufficient votes to exceed the cumulative dissident vote four times.

Although the board of directors is supposedly independent of management, the degree of independence is sometimes small. Typically, some members of the board are "insiders" drawn from management, while others are "outside" directors. Even the outside directors may not be completely independent of management for several reasons. One reason is that few shareholders can afford the time and expense to attend the annual meetings, so that voting is done through the mail. This usually takes the form of a "proxy" giving management the power to vote for the shareholder, as instructed. While the shareholder may instruct management on how to vote, the choices may be few and are controlled by management. Management will tend to nominate safe candidates for directorship, who will not be likely to challenge the status quo. As a result, directorship is at times an honor or sinecure, treated as having few real obligations.

Dissidents may mount opposition and seek the proxy votes, but such opposition is liable to face legal challenges and must overcome both psychological barriers and shareholder apathy. Many shareholders either do not vote or routinely vote for existing management. Further, dissidents must spend their own money, while management has the resources of the firm at its disposal.

In addition to controlling the proxy system, managements have instituted a number of other defensive mechanisms in the face of takeover threats. It is not unusual to find several "classes" of stock with different voting power, with some classes having no voting power at all. A number of firms have changed from cumulative to majority voting. Staggered boards, in which only a portion of the board terms expire in a given year, and supermajority voting policies have also been used. Takeover defenses include the golden parachute, or extremely generous severance compensation in the face of a takeover, and the poison pill, an action that is triggered by a takeover and has the effect of reducing the value of the firm. All of these measures act to make stockholder power appear more tenuous.

There has been some recent movement towards greater stockholder power. One factor in this movement is the increasing size of institutional investors such as pensions and mutual funds. This has led to a more activist stance, and a willingness to use the power of large stock positions to influence management. Another factor is a renewed emphasis on the duties of the directors, who may be personally liable for management's misconduct.

Residual Ownership The common stockholder has a claim on the assets of the firm. This is an undifferentiated or general claim which does not apply to any specific asset. The claim cannot be exercised except at the breakup of the firm. The firm may be dissolved by a vote of the stockholders, or by bankruptcy. In either case, there is a well-defined priority in which the liabilities of the firm will be met. The common stockholders have the lowest priority, and receive a distribution only if prior claims are paid in full. For this reason the common stockholder is referred to as the residual owner of the firm.

Preemptive Right The corporate charter will often provide common stockholders with the right to maintain their proportional ownership in the firm, called the preemptive right. For example, if a stockholder owns 10 percent of the stock outstanding and 100,000 new shares are to be issued, the stockholder has the right to purchase 10,000 shares (10 percent) of the new issue. This preemptive right can be honored in a rights offering. In a rights offering, each stockholder receives one right for each share held. Buying shares or subscribing to the issue then requires the surrender of a set number of rights, as well as payment of the offering price. The offering is often underpriced in order to assure its success. The rights are then valuable because possession of the rights allows subscription to the underpriced issue. The rights can be transferred, and are often traded.

A rights offering may be attractive to management because the stockholders, who thought enough of the firm to buy its stock, are a pre-sold group. The value of the preemptive right to the common stockholders, however, is questionable. The preemptive right of proportional ownership is important only if proportional control is important to the stockholder. The stockholder may be quite willing to waive the preemptive right. If the funds are used properly, the price of the stock will increase, and all stockholders will benefit. Without buying part of the new issue, the stockholder may have a smaller proportional share, but the share will be worth more. While rights are usually valuable, this value arises from under-pricing of the issue rather than from an inherent value of rights. The value of the rights ultimately depends on the use of the funds and whether or not the market views that use as valuable.

Valuation In investment practice, decisions are more often expressed and made in terms of the comparative expected rates of return, rather than on price. A number of models and techniques are used for valuation. A common approach to valuation of common stock is present value. This approach is based on an estimate of the future cash dividends. The present value is then the amount which, if invested at the required rate of return on the stock, could exactly recreate the estimated dividends. This required rate of return can be estimated from models such as the capital asset pricing model (CAPM), using the systematic risk of the stock, or from the estimated rate of return on stocks of similar risk. Another common approach is based on the price-earnings ratios, or P/E. In this approach, the estimated earnings of the firm are multiplied by the appropriate P/E to obtain the estimated price. This approach can be shown to be a special case of present value analysis, with restrictive assumptions. Since various models and minor differences in assumptions can produce widely different results, valuation is best applied as a comparative analysis.

In some cases, such as estate valuation, the dollar value of the stock must be estimated for legal purposes. For assets that are widely publicly traded, the market price is generally taken as an objective estimate of asset value for legal purposes, since this is sale value of the stock. For stock that is not widely traded, valuation is based on models such as present value, combined with a comparison with similar publicly traded stock. Often, however, a number of discounts are applied for various reasons. It is widely accepted that, compared to publicly traded stock, stock that is not publicly traded should be valued at a discount because of a lack of liquidity. This discount may be 60 percent or more. Another discount is applied for a minority position in a closely held stock or a family firm, since the minority position would have no control This discount does not apply if the value is estimated from the value of publicly traded stock, because the market price of a stock is traded already the price of a minority position. There is an inverse effect for publicly traded stock in the form of a control premium. A large block of stock which would give control of the firm might be priced above market.

Finally, it should be noted that the accounting book value is only rarely more than tangentially relevant to market value. This is due to the use of accounting assumptions such as historic cost. While accounting information may be useful in a careful valuation study, accounting definitions of value differ sharply from economic value.

PREFERRED STOCK

Preferred stock is sometimes called a hybrid, since it has some of the properties of equity and some of the properties of debt. Like debt, the cash flows to be received are specified in advance. Unlike debt, these specified flows are in the form of promises rather than of legal obligations. It is not unusual for firms to have several issues of preferred stock outstanding, with differing characteristics. Other differences arise in the areas of control and claims on assets.

Dividends Because the specified payments on preferred stock are not obligations, they are referred to as dividends. Preferred dividends are not tax-deductible expenses for the firm, and consequently the cost to the firm of raising capital from this source is higher than for debt. The firm is unlikely to skip or fail to declare the dividend, however, for several reasons. One of the reasons is that the dividends are typically (but not always) cumulative. Any skipped dividend remains due and payable by the firm, although no interest is due. One source of the preferred designation is that all preferred dividends in arrears must be paid before any dividend can be paid to common stockholders (although bond payments have priority over all dividends). Failure to declare preferred dividends may also trigger restrictive conditions of the issue. A very important consideration is that, just as for common dividends, preferred dividends are a signal to stockholders, both actual and potential. A skipped preferred dividend would indicate that common dividends will also be skipped, and would be a very negative signal that the firm was encountering problems. This would also close off access to most lenders.

There is also a form of preferred stock, called participating preferred stock, in which there may be a share in earnings above the specified dividends. Such participation would typically only occur if earnings or common dividends rose over some threshold, and might be limited in other ways. A more recent innovation is adjustable-rate preferred stock, with a variable dividend based on prevailing interest rates.

Control Under normal circumstances, preferred stockholders do not have any voting power. As a result, they have little control over or direct influence on the conduct of the firm. Some minimal control would be provided by the indenture under which the stock was issued, and would be exercised passively—i.e., the trustees for the issue would be responsible for assuring that all conditions were observed. In some circumstances, the conditions of the issue could result in increased control on the part of the preferred stockholders. For instance, it is not unusual for the preferred stockholders to be given voting rights if more than a specified number of preferred dividends are skipped. Other provisions may restrict the payment of common dividends if certain conditions are not met. Preferred stockholders also may have a preemptive right.

Claim on Assets and Other Features Another source of the preferred designation is that preferred stock has a prior claim on assets over that of common stock. The claim of bondholders is prior to that of the preferred stockholders. Although preferred stock typically has no maturity date, there is often some provision for retirement. One such provision is the call provision, under which the firm may buy back or recall the stock at a stated price. This price may vary over time, normally dropping as time passes. Another provision is the sinking fund, under which the firm will recall and retire a set

number of shares each year. Alternately, the firm may repurchase the shares for retirement on the open market, and would prefer to do so if the market price of the preferred is below the call price. Preferred stock is sometimes convertible, i.e., it can be exchanged for common stock at the discretion of the holder. The conversion takes place at a set rate, but this rate may vary over time.

Valuation The par value of a preferred stock is not related to market value, except that it is often used to define the dividend. Since the cash flow of dividends to preferred stockholders is specified, valuation of preferred stock is much simpler than for common stock. The valuation techniques are actually similar to those used for bonds, drawing heavily on the present value concept. The required rate of return on preferred stock is closely correlated with interest rates, but is above that of bonds because the bond payments are contractual obligations. As a result, preferred stock prices fluctuate with interest rates. The introduction of adjustable-rate preferred stock is an attempt to reduce this price sensitivity to interest rates.

FOREIGN STOCK

Purchases of foreign stock have greatly increased in recent years. One motivation behind this increase is that national economies are not perfectly correlated, so that greater diversification is possible than with a purely domestic portfolio. Another reason is that a number of foreign economies are growing, or are expected to grow, rapidly. Additionally, a number of developing countries have consciously promoted the development of secondary markets as an aid to economic development. Finally, developments in communications and an increasing familiarity with international affairs and opportunities has reduced the hesitance of investors to venture into what once was unfamiliar territory.

Foreign investment is not without problems. International communication is still more expensive and sometimes slower than domestic communication. Social and business customs often vary greatly between countries. Trading practices on some foreign exchanges are different than in the United States. Accounting differs not only in procedures, but often in degree of information disclosed. Although double taxation is generally avoided by international treaties, procedures are cumbersome. Political instability can be a consideration, particularly in developing countries. Finally, the investor faces exchange rate risk. A handsome gain in a foreign currency can be diminished, or even turned into a loss, by shifting exchange rates. These difficulties are felt less by professional managers of large institutions, and much of the foreign investment is through this channel.

An alternative vehicle for foreign investing is the American Depositary Receipt (ADR). This is simply a certificate of ownership of foreign stock that is deposited with a U.S. trustee. The depository institution also exchanges and distributes any dividends, and provides other administrative chores. ADRs are appealing to individual investors. It has also been suggested that the benefits of international investing can be obtained by investing in international firms.

INVESTMENT CHARACTERISTICS

Stocks are diverse in nature and can be classified many ways for investment purposes. For example, stocks can be classified according to the level of risk. Risky stocks are sometimes referred to as aggressive or speculative. They may also be growth stocks, which are expected to experience high rates of growth in size and earnings. If risk is measured by the beta (systematic or nondiversifiable risk), then the term applies to a stock with a beta greater than one. These stocks are quite sensitive to economic cycles, and are also called cyclical. Contrasted are the blue-chip stocks—high-quality stocks of major firms that have long and stable records of earnings and dividends. Stocks with low risk, or a beta of less than one, are referred to as defensive. One form of investment strategy, called timing, is to switch among cyclical and defensive stocks according to expected evolution of the economic cycle. This strategy is sometimes refined to movement among various types of stock or sectors of the economy. Another stock category is income stocks—stocks that have a long and stable record of comparatively high dividends.

Common stock has been suggested as a hedge against inflation. This suggestion arises from two lines of thought. The first is that stocks ultimately are claims to real assets and productivity, and the prices of such claims should rise with inflation. The second line of thought is that the total returns to common stock are high enough to overcome inflation. While this is apparently true over longer periods, it has not held true over shorter periods.

Preferred stock is generally not considered a desirable investment for individuals. While the junior position of preferred stockholders as compared to bondholders indicates that the required rate of return on preferred will be above that of bonds, observation indicates that the yield on bonds has generally been above that of preferred stock of similar quality. The reason for this is a provision of the tax codes that 70 percent of the preferred dividends received by a corporation are tax exempt. This provision is intended to avoid double taxation. Because of the tax exemption, the effective after-tax yield on preferred stock is higher for corporations, and buying of preferred stock by corporations drives the yields down. The resulting realized return for individuals, who cannot take advantage of this tax treatment, would generally be below acceptable levels.

BIBLIOGRAPHY

Geddes, Ross. *IPOs and Equity Offerings.* Elsevier, 2003.

Goodman, Jordan Elliott. *Everyone's Money Book on Stocks, Bonds, and Mutual Funds.* Dearborn, 2002.

Madular, Jeff. *Financial Markets and Institutions.* Thomson South-Western, 2006.

Scott, David Logan. *David Scott's Guide to Investing in Common Stocks.* Houghton-Mifflin, 2005.

Sincere, Michael. *Understanding Stocks.* McGraw-Hill, 2004.

Williams, Ellie. *The McGraw-Hill Investor's Desk Reference.* McGraw-Hill, 2001.

Hillstrom, Northern Lights
updated by Magee, ECDI

STRATEGY

"Strategy" is a somewhat over-used word to indicate a general plan or an approach to doing just about anything—so that one reads about strategies for winning in poker, finding the right woman or man, shaping a business, or preparing prize animals for an exhibition. The word came to be adopted from military usage after World War II. Etymologically the word comes from the Greek *stratos,* meaning army, and more narrowly from *strategos,* meaning a general. Thus it derives from "generalship" or, more precisely, a general's battle plan. It is normally coupled with the word "tactics," which comes from the Greek for "arranging things." The general formulated his plan and lesser officers then "arranged things" so that the plan would work out in detail. "Strategy" thus sounds both more martial and exalted than the ho-hum word "planning"—which, in addition, carries a faint reminder of socialist economics. Strategy has therefore, as it were, invaded business discourse and spread from broad concepts of corporate planning to such matters as marketing, advertising, human resources, accounts receivable collections and on to every specialty of business, suggesting that everyone is now a strategic thinker, not just the person at the top.

DEFINITIONS AND EXAMPLES

When the word is appropriately used, a strategy is a broad and general approach to an enterprise in which certain *structural elements* are determined in advance and *courses of action* have been selected from among others by preference in order to *differentiate* this enterprise from

1071

others in light of the *environment* as it is perceived to be and the anticipated action of *opponents* in particular.

A strategy is thus characterized by choices and decisions concerning future action at a level of generality which permits flexible implementation within the broad outline that the strategy presents. A strategy is more specific than a policy but more general than a plan yet has aspects of both.

A classical example of corporate strategy was that developed by Alfred P. Sloan for General Motors after he became its president in 1923. Sloan introduced annual styling changes, thus launching planned obsolescence as a motivator for replacing the car, and organized the different car lines based on pricing, with Chevrolet, Pontiac, Oldsmobile, Buick, and Cadillac each positioned in a unique price range and not competing with each other. The strategy worked very well for its time and consequently has led to widespread imitation. But it was a high-cost strategy in that it imposed significant, expensive redesign and reengineering annually—and is now followed only with token symbolic gestures. Another strategy, the basic platform on which multiple models can be built, has gradually taken over—and the competition now is between categories: sedans, SUVs, and pickups.

It is worth noting that strategies in business (as also in war) frequently *evolve* from circumstances; the significance of the circumstances is then consciously noted and formalized. Thus, for instance, 7-Eleven, credited with pioneering the convenience store, began in 1927 as an ice cream company that started selling bread, milk, and eggs at its ice docks to customers. It was called The Southland Corporation then and did not adopt its current name until 1946, choosing the name then because its stores were open from 7 a.m. to 11 p.m. These days, of course, 7-Eleven is open 24 hours a day and seven days a week—but has not chosen to rename itself to fits its new strategy of delivering convenience 24-Seven.

It is conventional management wisdom to say that businesses must have a strategy in order to succeed. It is closer to the truth to say that all businesses by definition *have* a strategy; it may be consciously realized or not, formally rendered or not. The manner in which a company is organized and run is the expression of its strategy. The difference between two companies is that in one the strategy may be well known by all and operating as a set of conscious guiding principles; in the other it may be unconscious or simply perceived as "the way we do things around here." Consciously formulated strategies are superior to "traditional" approaches only if the planning is insightful, well done, and adapted to the circumstances. The business owner with a good smell for the market, a good sense of his or her customers, and a

history of good "seat of the pants" judgment will outperform another business no matter how formal the strategizing of its owners—if they do not have the touch. For these reasons "strategy" is not a cure-all for a business in trouble, large or small, but a technique of discovering solutions and setting a course.

STRATEGIZING: BIG AND SMALL

Strategy formulation as a discipline—meaning as a special kind of business activity—is much more common in large corporations than in small business. In small business the same activity takes place but tends to be less formal, more adaptive, and more the product of one or two individuals in the company's leadership. In the big corporations strategy development flows in two directions. From the top will come a general sense of direction and emphasis: "We are a marketing company." "We are a technology company." "We are bottom-line oriented." Operating elements within the company then respond to this general message in annual plans in which each division or element responds with a plan of which the top few paragraphs are a strategic statement further elaborated into specific action initiatives in the body. This general approach arises from the very complexity of large organizations serving many diverse markets with dozens or hundreds of products or services—each of which requires different adaptations. In a company principally interested in short-term returns, for instance, individual strategies reliant on capital investments over longer periods will fare more poorly than highly leveraged approaches. In a technology company dominated by an engineering mindset, very exciting ("sexy") marketing concepts may be sidelined because they lack technical sophistication. In well-run large corporations, top management will make the effort to formulate different broad strategies for lower elements based on realities in the market and not permit vague, broad, but restrictive concepts to preempt appropriate responses. Such a stance, of course, requires high-level executives who actually understand a business rather than shining in some specialty like finance or marketing.

In a small business the formulation of strategy is typically closer to the market simply because the principals are engaged in the business itself at the point where, proverbially put, the rubber meets the road: where the business interfaces with the customer. Most small businesses owe their origin to the perception of what is, in actually, a strategic opportunity. The very idea of the business expresses the strategy: "I swear I've driven fifty miles this afternoon and I still can't find a decent art supply store anywhere." "What this town needs is a [fill in the blank]" has launched many a business. So have two unrelated objects that, for a brilliant moment, combine in the mind of an entrepreneur—and a new product is born.

In his book, *My Years at General Motors,* Sloan spoke about "the concept of the organization." Behind every small business there is a concept of the organization—a complex perception of needs and of responses to that need. That concept, in effect, is the strategy of the business. It is equivalent to the theme of a novel or of a nonfiction work: it is the organizing idea behind it which often escapes analysis—the entrepreneurial insight. It might be argued that, in its absence, strategies will tend to be pretty much the same and quite conventional. Robert Kennedy, writing in the *Journal of Industrial Economics* on "strategy fads" made this point by analyzing prime-time television programs—showing that, despite a great deal of strategizing, networks produce lackluster imitations. These findings are echoed in a broader context by Cass Sunstein of the University of Chicago in a paper titled *Conformity and Dissent.*

Analysis applied to strategy decomposes the concept into its visible inputs. These are the needs of the market, products that can meet the need, their differentiation from competing products, alternative means of production and of reaching the market, different messages to reach the consumer, the positioning of products to reach the best segments, pricing and incentives, and much more. There is little doubt that intense examination of the market is desirable—as is the consideration of alternative approaches. But what makes a winning strategy is that secret ingredient the entrepreneurial mind adds after everyone has left for home.

SEE ALSO *Business Planning*

BIBLIOGRAPHY

Colley, John L, Jacqueline L. Doyle, and Robert D. Hardie. *Corporate Strategy.* McGraw-Hill, 2002.

Grant, Robert M. *Contemporary Strategy Analysis.* Blackwell Publishing, 2002.

Kennedy, Robert E. "Strategy Fads and Competitive Convergence: An Empirical Test for Herd Behavior in Prime-Time Television Programming." *Journal of Industrial Economics.* March 2002.

Lake, Neville. *The Strategic Planning Workbook.* Second Edition. Kogan Page, 2006.

Mourdoukoutas, Panos. *Business Strategy in a Semiglobal Economy.* M.E. Sharpe, 2006.

Navarro, Peter. "Sustainable Strategies for a World of Economic Shocks." *Financial Executive.* April 2006.

Pettigrew Andrew M., Howard Thomas, and Richard Whittington eds. *Handbook of Strategy and Management.* Sage, 2002.

Schmetterer, Bob. *Leap: A Revolution in Creative Business Strategy.* John Wiley & Sons, 2003.

Sloan, Alfred P. *My Years with General Motors.* Currency, 1990.

Sunstein, Cass R. *Conformity and Dissent.* University of Chicago. 30 October 2002. Available from http://www.law.uchicago.edu/academics/publiclaw/resources/34.crs.conformity.pdf. Retrieved on 31 May 2006.

Darnay, ECDI

SUBCONTRACTING

Strictly speaking, "subcontracting" is practiced only by a contractor, namely an individual or a company working for another entity under a contractual agreement. If the contractor then hires out some of the work to yet another organization, it is said to have subcontracted the work out. Subcontracting is most common in the construction industry: builders often subcontract plumbing, electrical work, drywalling, painting, and other tasks. But many other sectors engage in contract work as well, most notably government contractors of all kinds. The whole industry that supplies the U.S. Department of Defense typically operates under contract and uses many subcontractors in turn.

In recent times the term has come to be used in a more general sense to refer to any kind of work contracted or "farmed" out. Outsourcing tasks and functions has become a common tactic used to lower costs. Companies that operate on their own behalf selling goods and services to the public may also engage in contracting or "subbing" some of the work. In such cases no contract is in existence, hence the prefix "sub" is unnecessary; it is often used anyway and thus the commonly used abbreviation, "subbing." In the discussion that follows both kinds of contract relationship will be included, thus also the use of so-called independent contractors and hiring free-lancers.

WHY CONTRACTORS ARE USED

Contracting and subcontracting are institutional expressions of the division of labor or of specialization. Such forms are used for the simple reason that they cost less than providing the service in-house. Certain types of work require specialized and often expensive tooling and skills not required in a company on a daily basis; to provide such services in-house would not be cost-effective. By specializing in a particular function, equipping it and staffing it to serve a large clientele, service organizations can achieve scale effects simply not available to the ordinary business. An example of this is payroll services under which a small firm can contract out its payroll administration to a company for a small fee; the company gets excellent service, guaranteed conformity to tax law, and saves money. Saving money is also at the root of the more questionable practice of laying off people and then hiring them back as "independent contractors" at fees that cost less than their previous salaries, payroll tax, plus fringes. Such forms are frowned upon by government and are sustained only so long as the supply of such labor exceeds the demand. The chief disadvantages of using contractors are diminished control over the function and less ability to predict its future costs.

CONTRACTORS VS. EMPLOYEES

A contractor who behaves and is treated like an employee *is* an employee from the viewpoint of the U.S. Internal Revenue Service (IRS). The IRS applies a 20-part test in order to determine whether a certain worker should be classified as an employee or an independent contractor. The main issue underpinning the test is who sets the work rules: employees must follow rules set by their bosses; independent contractors set their own rules. An individual who sets his or her own hours, receives payment by the job, and divides his or her time between work for several different employers would typically be classified as an independent contractor. Other criteria involve who provides the tools and materials needed to complete the work. An individual who works at an employer's facility and uses the employer's equipment may be considered an employee—unless the individual is providing software consulting, for instance; one who works at a separate location and provides his or her own equipment would be classified as an independent contractor. Finally, an independent contractor usually pays his or her own business expenses and takes the risk of not receiving payment when work is not completed in accordance with a contract; an employee is usually reimbursed for business-related expenses by the employer and receives a paycheck whether his or her work is completed or not.

A small business may be on either side of this equation: providing contractual services or purchasing such services. As a seller, the business must retain its independence; as a buyer, the business must avoid directing the contractor in such detail as to qualify him or her as an employee. Problems often arise when the seller *wishes* to be a contractor, has chosen that path willingly, but is using the buyer as his or her first customer, having worked there many years. In such cases the old relationship may be habitual.

WORKING WITH SUBS AND CONTRACTORS

Small business owners may be highly experienced in using subcontractors because subs are a natural part of their industry—as in construction. In cases where a large company provides a service, such as a payroll firm, the relationship is again clear and unambiguous—as is, for instance, working with an outside accountant in business for him or herself. Nor are problems likely to arise when surges in business must be accommodated by hiring temporary workers from a temp firm. In yet other cases, such as buying advertising services, the relationship is traditional and not viewed as contracting out a service—even when the relationship is on-going rather than singular. Most companies working with ad agencies also have an internal advertising manager. Problems for the small business arise when it works with independent contractors, usually individuals, who carry out tasks that either have been or could be done in-house. Problems also arise when the business works in such close partnership with a contractor that interactions between the contractor's employees (and executives) and the company's own staff arise.

The skilled small business owner will, of course, avoid any contracting arrangements that may be seen by his or her own people as exploitive. The owner who makes use of people down on their luck in order to avoid having to pay their payroll taxes, for example, will likely pay a high price for this in another the form: eroding morale and key people quitting to seek their fortunes elsewhere. But it is sometimes difficult to hire talented individuals because they do not wish to work for the company as employees. If that is the case, the company's own employees should be informed of the fact.

More difficult are situations where a very useful contractor becomes a problem. An example might be a sales organization working closely with a small manufacturer—effectively lifting the manufacturer's sales. Close contact between the contractor and elements of the company may lead to situations where employees start to wonder "who's in charge around here?" In this case the sales contractor, well-meaning in every way, may become too assertive in asking for changes in product or in packaging. Such situations can be avoided by setting clear rules early, monitoring interactions, and maintaining open communications at all times. Situations of this sort also arise in companies where two different internal functions develop conflicts—engineering versus market, marketing versus accounting, etc. The same solutions apply whether the function is contracted or internal—but an external provider of a service will invariably appear as more threatening or annoying to the company's own people.

Apart from these issues, working with contractors has exactly the same requirements as working with any vendor. Aims must be clear, specifications well-developed, sourcing should be as competitive as possible, and the purchasing decision must be a careful blend of price and quality.

BIBLIOGRAPHY

Hartman, Francis T. *Ten Commandments of Better Contracting.* ASCE Publications, 2003.

Moskin, Morton. Commercial Contracts: Strategies for Drafting and Negotiating. Aspen, 2005.

Stanberry, Scott A. *Federal Contracting Made Easy.* Management Concepts, 2004.

Walker, Anthony. *Project Management in Construction.* Blackwell, 2002.

Waxman, Shelly. *All Anybody Needs to Know About Independent Contracting.* iUniverse, 2003.

Darnay, ECDI

SUBSTANCE ABUSE

Substance abuse in the workplace is a subject of concern to many small business owners, to one degree or another. Oftentimes the issue is a sensitive one to confront, but business owners and researchers alike agree that if left unchecked, substance abuse has the capacity to cripple or destroy a company.

IMPACT IN THE WORKPLACE

Substance abuse is a hard problem to eradicate in any business setting, but it can be particularly difficult to address in small business settings. After all, many small business owners develop close—or at least friendly—relationships with their employees because they often work together on projects and share smaller work areas. "Because many small business owners have one-on-one relationships with each employee, dealing with an employee who is addicted to alcohol or drugs is a personal as well as a personnel problem," wrote Barbara Mooney in *Crain's Cleveland Business.*

But substance abuse experts and business researchers alike warn that substance abuse problems are not the sort of problems that tend to go away by themselves. Rather, they often continue to grow and fester, further strangulating the business's productivity and profitability. Indeed, substance abuse often ends up being a tremendous drain on a company's fiscal well-being. This drain takes many forms, including decreased productivity, increased absences, rising numbers of accidents, use of sick leave, and jumps in workers' compensation claims. Indeed, *HR Focus* reported in 1997 that "alcohol and drug abusers are absent from work two-and-a-half times more frequently than nonusers; they use three times the amount of sick leave as nonusers; their worker's compensation claims are five times higher; and they are generally less productive." This latter factor—what *HR Focus* termed "the less dramatic, day-to-day financial losses that accrue in a company when its workers are impaired and performing below potential"—can be particularly deadly to a business precisely because its impact is so hard to detect and quantify. Finally, substance abusers often compromise the efficiency of other workers within the business. Co-workers are often hampered by the substandard work of the abuser, and in many cases their effectiveness may be further curtailed by a sense of obligation to cover for their co-workers—who, after all, are often their friends as well.

Substance abuse problems also open companies up to greater legal liability. According to *Occupational Medicine,* Studies indicate that 1) alcohol and drug abusers are two to four times as likely to have an accident as people who do not use drugs and alcohol, and 2) substance abusers can be linked to approximately 40 percent of American industrial fatalities. Moreover, business consultant Tim Plant indicated to *HR Focus* that drug- or alcohol-addled employees can also wreak harm on people and places outside the company: "When drivers come to work under the influence of drugs or alcohol," he said, "accidents could happen, causing the disruption of deliveries or other activities. Vehicles could be damaged; people could be hurt or killed. These have an immediate impact on the bottom line for a small- or medium-sized company."

Finally, in situations where a partner or owner of the business is the one with the substance abuse problem, the very life of the company is often jeopardized. Such people obviously wield a tremendous amount of influence over a company, and if their ability to make reasonable, intelligent decisions in a timely manner is compromised, the financial health of the company will likely deteriorate as well.

CHARACTERISTICS OF SUBSTANCE ABUSERS

Substance abuse experts and business owners who have been forced to deal with drug and/or alcohol abusers in their workplace cited a variety of warning signs that owners and managers should look for if they suspect a problem:

- Increased absenteeism and tardiness, especially immediately before and after weekends and holidays

- Deteriorating work performance, as manifested in big changes in work quality and/or productivity

- Frequent colds, flus, headaches, and other ailments

- High rates of mishaps, both on and off the job

- Unusually high medical claims

- Excessive mood swings, which may manifest themselves in immoderate levels of talking, anxiety, or moodiness

- Overreactions to criticism, both real or imagined

- Avoidance of supervisors

- Deterioration in physical appearance or grooming

- Financial problems

Researchers also note that certain industries and business dynamics seem especially prone to substance abuse problems. One substance abuse counselor flatly told Barbara Mooney of *Crain's Cleveland Business* that the extent of substance abuse problems in small businesses often depends on the makeup of its work force: "It's a problem prevalent among employers who hire a lot of entry-level people in industries with high turnover rates and high stress levels." Such conditions can be found in some retail establishments and especially in the restaurant industry, where late working hours, proximity to liquor, and demographic characteristics (prevalently young and single) provide a fertile atmosphere for substance abuse. Family-owned businesses are also cited as being particularly vulnerable to substance abuse problems, in part because family members may have a more difficult time being objective about a relative's work performance.

POLICIES AND STRATEGIES TO CURB SUBSTANCE ABUSE

Although tackling the problem of substance abuse can be a daunting one for small business enterprises, substance abuse experts and business researchers note that affected businesses can utilize a variety of steps that have a track record of effectiveness in curbing workplace drug and alcohol abuse.

One of the most commonly practiced policies employed by businesses of all sizes is random drug testing, wherein employees (and prospective employees) are required to submit to scientific tests to determine whether they have been using illegal drugs. Many experts cite the growing popularity of such policies for the apparent downturn in workplace substance abuse incidents in recent years. Drug testing remains controversial, however, as opponents argue that it violates individual privacy rights and sometimes hurts employee morale.

Another option for small business owners is to actively utilize the hiring/interviewing process to screen for substance abusers. "You get what you ask for," contended Gregory Lousig-Nont and Paul Leckinger in *Security Management.* "If you want people who are free from substance abuse problems—just ask for them in your ad." They point out that studies and anecdotal

evidence suggests that want ads that include phrases like "Applicant must have a clean drug history" effectively dissuade many applicants with substance abuse problems from submitting an application. "Another commonsense approach to screening applicants," say Lousig-Nont and Leckinger, "is to broach the subject on the application form" by bluntly inquiring whether the applicant has used illicit drugs in the past. "Surprisingly, many people will actually list the drugs they have used. People who use drugs but do not want to tell you about it will leave the answer blank or put a dash on the answer line. People who have not used drugs will usually write a bold 'NONE' in the space provided." They note, however, that even though federal laws do not restrict asking questions about drug abuse, companies should check with their state employment commission to see if any state laws might apply in this area.

With current employees, business owners are encouraged to establish clear, written guidelines that explicitly detail the company's stance on substance abuse. "The policy should take a clear stand against the use, possession, sale or distribution (particularly on company time) of any mood altering substances," stated *HR Focus.* "It should also outline a very clear sequence of events that will ensue if the rules are broken." Small business owners need to make sure that their substance abuse policies abide by various state and federal laws.

Small business owners should also make an effort to enlist the support of employees in establishing a drug-free workplace. "Everyone ... has an interest in securing a safe workplace and making sure that colleagues pull their loads," commented *HR Focus.* "One of the most effective ways to fight substance abuse is for employees to unite against it," concurred W.H. Weiss in *Supervisor's Standard Reference Handbook.* "Supervisors can spur such a move by making it clear to their people that alcohol or drug use on the job is absolutely unacceptable."

Business owners should also consider providing an employee assistance program (EAP) for its workers. "Adopting an employee assistance program is viewed favorably by both management and employees," wrote Lousig-Nont and Leckinger. "Under such a policy, the company agrees to assist employees who have a substance abuse problem. Assistance generally comes in the form of granting the employee sick leave and paying for a rehabilitation program, and a promise by the company that there will be no retribution against the employee." The responsibility for initiating enrollment in such programs, however, rests with the employee. If management discovers that a worker who has not pursued help through an EAP has a substance abuse problem, he or she may face termination. Employee assistance programs have been hailed by substance abuse experts and businesspeople alike as an effective tool in curbing workplace drug and alcohol abuse, and proponents point out that the cost of such programs is usually far less than the costs that often accrue when a substance-abusing employee is not dealt with.

Finally, when confronted with evidence of workplace substance abuse, managers and owners of small companies are urged to intervene immediately and determine whether a problem exists. If a problem is found, then the business needs to document the performance of the employee. This will offer the company a greater measure of legal protection in case they need to fire the employee or the employee's performance spurs legal claims from outside parties.

BIBLIOGRAPHY

Carr, Elena. "Re-Energizing the Roots of Employee Assistance: Tapping federal workplace substance abuse efforts." *The Journal of Employee Assistance.* January-March 2006.

"Drug Trends: A Shot in the Arm?" *Security Management.* August 1996.

Gray, George R., and Darrel R. Brown. "Issues in Drug Testing for the Private Sector." *HR Focus.* November 1992.

Humphreys, Richard M. "Substance Abuse: The Employer's Perspective." *Employment Relations Today.* Spring 1990.

Lousig-Nont, Gregory M., and Paul M. Leckinger. "Alternatives to Drug Testing." *Security Management.* May 1990.

Martin, Lynn. "Drug Free Policy: Key to Success for Small Businesses." *HR Focus.* September 1992.

Mooney, Barbara. "Addiction: A Downer for All; Substance Abuse can be an Owner's Toughest Problem." *Crain's Cleveland Business.* August 8, 1994.

"Substance Abuse in the Workplace." *HR Focus.* February 1997.

Hillstrom, Northern Lights
updated by Magee, ECDI

SUCCESSION PLANS

A succession plan is a written document that provides for the continued operation of a business in the event that the owner—or a key member of the management team—leaves the company, is terminated, becomes incapacitated, retires, or dies. It details the changes that will take place as leadership is transferred from one generation to the next. In the case of small businesses, succession plans are often known as continuity plans, since without them the businesses may cease to exist. Succession plans can provide a number of important benefits for companies that develop them. For example, a succession plan may help a business retain key employees, reduce its tax burden, and maintain the value of its stock and assets during a management or ownership transition. Succession plans may also prove valuable in allowing a business owner to retire in comfort and continue to provide for family members who may be involved with the company.

Despite the many benefits of having a succession plan in place, many companies neglect to develop one. This oversight may occur because the business owner does not want to confront his or her own mortality, is reluctant to choose a successor, or does not have many interests beyond the business. Although less than one-third of family businesses survive the transition from the first generation to the second—and only 13 percent remain in the family for more than 60 years—fewer than half of business owners establish a formal succession plan. Succession and the planning it entails can be much like planning one's own funeral. Perhaps in part because of this discomfort of the process, the transfer of power from the first to the second generation seldom happens while the founder is alive and active in the business. Yet it is one that must be prepared for, if the business owner hopes to avoid having hard-earned assets go to unwanted individuals and institutions. "The economic costs are significant," stated James Bieneman in *Business First-Columbus.* "[But] the human costs are even greater in terms of spoiled family relationships, missed career opportunities, and the discomfort of living in a state of misalignment."

PREPARING FOR SUCCESSION

Experts claim that the succession planning process should ideally begin when the business owner is between the ages of 45 and 50 if he or she plans to retire at 65. Since succession can be an emotionally charged issue, sometimes the assistance of outside advisors and mediators is required. Developing a succession plan can take more than two years, and implementing it can take up to ten years. The plan must be carefully structured to fit the company's specific situation and goals. When completed, the plan should be reviewed by the company's lawyer, accountant, and bank.

One of the main reasons business owners should take the time to create a successful continuity plan is that it is one of the few ways for most to assure themselves a way out of the business with assets enough for retirement. To do this, the business owner has a few basic options: sell the company to employees, family members, or an outsider; retain ownership of the company but hire new management; or liquidate the business. An Employee Stock Ownership Plan, or ESOP, can be a useful tool for the owner of a corporation who is nearing retirement age. The owner can sell his or her stake in the company to the ESOP in order to gain tax advantages and provide for the continuation of the business. If, after the stock purchase, the ESOP holds over 30 percent of the company's shares, then the owner can defer capital-gains taxes by investing the proceeds in a Qualified Replacement Property (QRP). QRPs can include stocks, bonds, and certain retirement accounts. The income stream generated by the QRP can help provide the business owner with income during retirement.

In *Family Business Succession: The Final Test of Greatness,* Craig E. Aronoff, Stephen L. McClure, and John L. Ward outline a number of steps companies should follow in preparing for succession. These steps include:

1. Establishing a formal policy regarding family participation in the business

2. Providing solid work experience for all employees, to ensure that succession is based on performance rather than heredity

3. Creating a family mission statement based on the members' beliefs and goals for the business

4. Designing a leadership development plan with specific job requirements for the successor

5. Developing a strategic plan for the business

6. Making plans for the preceding generation's financial security

7. Identifying a successor or determining the selection process

8. Setting up a succession transition team to keep decision-makers informed about their role in the changes

9. Completing the transfer of ownership and control.

Succession should be viewed as a process rather than as an event. There are four main stages in the succession process: initiation, selection, education, and transition. In the initiation phase, possible successors learn about the family business. It is important for the business owners to speak openly about the business, in a positive but realistic manner, in order to transmit information about the company's values, culture, and future direction to the next generation.

The selection phase involves actually designating a successor among the candidates for the job. Because rivalry often develops between possible successors—who, in the case of a family business, are likely to be siblings—this can be the most difficult stage of the process. For this reason, many business owners either avoid the issue outright—or indirectly through the naming of multiple successors—or make the selection on the basis of age, gender, or other factors other than merit. A wiser course would be to develop specific objectives and goals for the next generation of management, including a detailed job description for the successor. Then a

candidate can be chosen who best meets the qualifications. This strategy helps reduce the emotional aspect from the selection process and also may help the business owners feel more comfortable with their selection. The decision about when to announce the successor and the schedule for succession depend upon the business, but an early announcement can help reassure employees and customers and enable other key employees to make alternative career plans as needed.

Once a potential successor has been selected, the company then enters the training phase. Ideally, a program is developed through which the successor can meet goals and gradually increase his or her level of responsibility. The owner may want to take a number of planned absences so that the successor has a chance to actually run the business for limited periods of time. The training phase also provides the business owner with an opportunity to evaluate the successor's decision-making processes, leadership abilities, interpersonal skills, and performance under pressure. It is also important for the successor to be introduced to the business owner's outside network during this time, including customers, bankers, and business associates.

The final stage in the process occurs when the business owner retires and the successor formally makes the transition to his or her new leadership role. This transition can be made as smooth as possible for the company by publicly committing to the succession plan, having the departing executive leave in a timely manner, and eliminating his or her involvement in the company's daily activities completely. In order to make the transition as painless as possible for himself or herself, the business owner should also be sure to have a sound financial plan for retirement and to engage in relationships and activities outside of the business.

Business owners who fail to adhere to the above steps may end up cobbling together succession plans that do not reflect the best interests of the company or of its stakeholders (valued staffers, family members, partners, etc.). "Why and how often do succession plans fail?" wrote Bieneman. "Succession plans fail when serious conflict (some call it dysfunctional behavior) cannot be overcome, when family members have and cannot abandon unrealistic expectations, or when the family business has run its course and should be sold but isn't. Succession plans are an exercise in compromise, tough love, forthrightness, and making difficult but necessary decisions."

SEE ALSO *Estate Tax; Family-Owned Business*

BIBLIOGRAPHY
Aronoff, Craig E., Stephen L. McClure, and John L. Ward. *Family Business Succession: The Final Test of Greatness.* Second Edition. Business Owner Resources, 2003.

Bialyj, Mike. "Will Your Business Survive After Your Retirement?" *Contract Flooring Journal.* May 2006.

Bieneman, James N. "Succession Plans Provide Blueprint for Peace of Mind." *Business First-Columbus.* 6 October 2000.

Dammon Loyalka, Michelle. "Family-Biz Circle: The Boomer Handoff." *Business Week.* 14 February 2006.

Gangemi, Jeff, and Francesca Di Meglio. "Making an Educated Decision." *Business Week Online.* 15 February 2006.

Karofsky, Paul. "Can Business Bring a Family Together?" *Business Week.* 22 February 2006.

Powell, Larry, and John Venturella. "Succession Planning Two Ways: Business Items and Emotional Items." *Production Machining.* May 2006.

Hillstrom, Northern Lights
updated by Magee, ECDI

SUPPLIER RELATIONS

Good purchasing practices are an integral part of small business success, and few factors are as vital in ensuring sound purchasing methodologies as the selection of quality suppliers. Indeed, finding good suppliers and maintaining solid relations with them can be an invaluable tool in the quest for business success and expansion. In fact, a business can only be as good as are the suppliers with whom it works. Suppliers provide the materials a company uses to produce its own goods and/or services. Suppliers provide the transportation of those materials. Suppliers provide a company with the services it uses in providing goods and service to its customer. Without a solid relationship with its suppliers, a company can not offer its own customers a consistently high quality product or service.

For many procurement organizations, suppliers have become an important factor in their planning. Suppliers are often a procurement organization's secret competitive weapon, their hidden resource, their competitive edge. These competitive gains can manifest themselves in a wide range of areas, from better prices and delivery times to increased opportunities to consider and implement innovative practices. Such improvements will not be realized without meaningful leadership from business owners and executives. Leading companies develop tailored supply strategies that are directly linked to their corporate strategies. These leaders emphasize shareholder-value creation, revenue growth, and cost competitiveness, and establish specific programs with their key suppliers in order to ensure that these priorities are addressed. Whenever possible, business leaders use suppliers to maximize their own product competitiveness, going beyond the narrow focus of cost reduction.

SUPPLY CHAINS AND PARTNERSHIPS

In recent years, countless management experts and analysts have touted the benefits that businesses of all sizes can realize by establishing "partnerships" with their suppliers. Under such a plan, which is also sometimes referred to as "supply chain management," distribution channels are set up across organizations so that all the members of the channel, from suppliers to end users, coordinate their business activities and processes to minimize their total costs and maximize their effectiveness in the marketplace. But while this trend has become more prevalent in today's business environment, it is still practiced in only spotty fashion in many industries. Common impediments to establishing true business partnerships with suppliers include: attachment of greater importance to other initiatives; comfortable relationships with existing suppliers; dearth of cross-business unit cooperation; doubts about the benefits of instituting such practices; lack of cross-functional cooperation; poor monitoring and control systems; inexperience at managing improvement programs; and distrust of suppliers. Companies that feature many of these characteristics typically cling to old competitive bidding practices that center on perfectly legitimate concerns about price, but at the exclusion of all else.

As a result, these businesses miss out on the many benefits that can accrue when effective partnering initiatives are established with suppliers. Suppliers can be an important source of information on ways in which both small and large businesses can improve performance and productivity. Five general categories exist in which supplier involvement can help buyers compete in the marketplace:

1. Improvement of products through contributions to product design, technology, or ideas for producing new products. In most such instances, suppliers help buyers by pointing out ways in which designs can be improved or more desirable materials can be used.

2. Improvements in product quality. In addition to providing design recommendations that result in improved products, suppliers are often sources of suggestions that allow buyers to hold consistent tolerances in production.

3. Improvements in "speed to market." Some of the most significant contributions in this area came from suppliers to original equipment manufacturers.

4. Reductions in total product cost, either through streamlining of work processes (inventory management, new product design, scheduling, etc.) or replacement of costly components with less expensive—but still effective—ones.

5. Improvements in customer satisfaction.

Analysts indicate that suppliers receive some benefits in the emerging purchasing dynamic as well. Reduced paperwork, lower overhead, faster payment, long-term agreements that lead to more accurate business forecasts, access to new designs, and input into future materials and product needs have all been cited as gains. Other observers, meanwhile, point out that some buyer-supplier relationships have become so close that suppliers have opened offices on the site of the buyer, an arrangement that can conceivably result in even greater improvements in productivity and savings. Of course, companies are not going to form such "partnerships" with all of their suppliers. Some form of the traditional purchasing process involving bidding and standard purchase orders and invoices will continue to exist at almost every company, and especially at smaller companies that do not have the financial clout to pressure suppliers for price or delivery concessions.

But many management consultants and business experts contend that even those businesses that are not ideally positioned to create partnerships with suppliers can benefit from the establishment of effective supply chain management practices. Buyer-seller alliances unleash a capacity for innovation that far outweighs the short-term cost savings offered by arm's-length competitive bidding. Businesses should explain their overarching needs to several dedicated suppliers and open lines of communication with them rather than simply defining their requirements and waiting for a flurry of bids that are primarily—or exclusively—concerned with submitting the lowest bid.

Potential Drawbacks of Supplier Partnerships
Establishing close relationships with suppliers, though, means that buyers have to conduct the necessary research to make sure that they select the right companies. Purchasers need to know a great deal more about suppliers' capabilities than they did when everything depended on a bid/buy relationship. Today's emphasis on partnerships is contingent on suppliers who can become part of a whole supply system. In fact, major suppliers need to be critically screened and evaluated before they are brought into any supply chain system. Thriving small- and mid-sized businesses that are already well-established will be better able to take on such tasks than will fledgling businesses, but even start-ups should take the time to learn more about their suppliers than their prices.

Of course, desired supplier traits vary somewhat depending on who is being surveyed. For example, design engineers tend to place the most weight on product quality when analyzing suppliers, while purchasing professionals place greater importance on cost considerations in conjunction with product quality. Criteria to be evaluated will also vary depending on product category. The objective of all evaluations is the same: To compare all potential suppliers in a market segment to determine the one best qualified partner with whom to work. The evaluation of potential suppliers should include an assessment about whether the supplier is suited to assist the purchaser to meet its prime business objectives. Typical the objectives to which the supplier should provide assistance include inventory reduction, quality improvement, elimination of paperwork, and improved handling of incoming goods.

Companies that do not do the necessary legwork, on the other hand, may find themselves linked to a poor or untrustworthy supplier that can erode a business's financial fortunes and industry/community reputation in a remarkably short span of time. Poor supplier performance is not the only risk a purchaser faces in situations where it has linked with a bad supplier. Another potential threat that arises when partnering with suppliers is the loss of trade secrets to competitors. Additionally, a supplier may venture out on its own once it has acquired new abilities and may in fact become a competitor. A company that abdicates too much to its suppliers may weaken itself. All of these risks are especially great in fast-moving, knowledge-intensive industries, which are precisely those for which integrated supply chains may be of particular usefulness. Given these potential pitfalls, businesses seeking to establish partnerships with suppliers are urged to proceed with caution.

EVALUATING SUPPLIERS
Whether searching out new suppliers or benchmarking the performance of current suppliers, businesses are urged to consider the following when evaluating their options:

- Commitment to quality—Not surprisingly, product quality is regarded as an essential factor in selecting a supplier. Specifics in this realm include the suppliers' statistical process control methods, its QS-9000 registration, its approaches to problem solving and preventive maintenance, and its methods of equipment calibration.

- Cost-competitive—Competitive pricing is another huge factor, especially for businesses that are smaller or experiencing financial difficulties.

- Communication—Suppliers that do not maintain a policy of open communication—or even worse, actively practice deception—should be avoided at all costs. The frustrations of dealing with such companies can sometimes assume debilitating dimensions. Moreover, constant exposure to such tactics can have a corrosive effect on internal staff.

- Timely Service—Businesses' strategies are predicated on schedules, which in turn are based on receiving shipments at agreed-upon times. When those shipments slip, business strategies suffer. The blow can be particularly severe if the supplier is negligent or late in reporting the problem.

- Flexibility and Special Services—Many purchasers express appreciation for suppliers that take extra measures to satisfy their customers. These "perks" can range from after-hours accessibility to training or inventory support.

- Market Knowledge—Suppliers with extensive knowledge of market conditions and mastery of contemporary issues impacting your business can be immensely valuable in helping small companies chart a course to sustained financial success.

- Production Capabilities—the supplier's capacity for program management and production should be considered, including its ability to integrate design and manufacturing functions, its approach to design changes, and its program measurement features.

- Financial Stability—Businesses that allocate large sums for purchasing materials often prefer to make long-term deals with suppliers that are financially stable. Such arrangements not only convey security, but they allow companies to learn about one another and gain a fuller understanding of each business's needs, desires, operating practices, and future objectives.

- Logistics/Location—Supplier capabilities in this area include transportation capacity, sourcing capabilities, and 'just-in-time' performance.

- Inventory—Evaluation of this consideration is dependent somewhat on the supplier's business. If the supplier is a distributor, the emphasis will be on how well his inventory is set up to avoid stockouts. With a manufacturer, emphasis has to be on inventory accessibility. If the supplier has a just-in-time program with 24-hour assured delivery, it's in better condition than the manufacturer with a lot of raw material inventory and an eight-week lead-time for raw material.

- Ability to Provide Technical Assistance—Suppliers with top research and development capacities can be quite valuable to buyers, providing them with significant savings in both price and quality.

OTHER KEYS TO SUCCESSFUL SUPPLIER RELATIONSHIPS

A common lament of suppliers is that buyer organizations all too often have unrealistic expectations about the supplier's ability to anticipate buyer needs. As one purchasing executive admitted to *Purchasing*, "In new technology areas we have great difficulty getting the users in our own company to define what they want. Most have an attitude of 'I'll know it when I see it.' And many of these users keep changing their minds."

Honesty on both sides is another important quality in effective buyer-supplier relations. Small business owners hate being misled by their suppliers, yet they are often less than above-board in their own communications with suppliers. This is most common when the business is grappling with past-due payments, but entrepreneurs should avoid subterfuge and be upfront with suppliers about their situations. "Instead of lying and saying the check's in the mail, tell suppliers what's happening and what you propose to do about it," one small business owner told *Nation's Business*. "If you have a note that's due, you call them, instead of waiting for them to call you. They appreciate that. Business people are afraid to make that phone call; they want to make it all sound rosy. But ... if you owe them, suppliers are eager to find a way to work with you."

SEE ALSO *Competitive Bids; Cooperatives; Inventory Control Systems; Supply Chain*

BIBLIOGRAPHY

Fitzgerald, Kevin R. "What OEM Engineers Want from Suppliers." *Purchasing*. 14 August 1997.

Harrington, Lisa H. "Buying Better: Strategic Sourcing Can Improve Suppliers' Productivity, Component and Product Quality—and Improve the Bottom Line." *Industry Week*. 21 July 1997.

Harrison, Terry P., Hau L Lee, and John J. Neale *The Practice of Supply Chain Management*. Springer, 2003.

McIvor, Ronan, Paul Humphreys, and Eddie McAleer. "Implications of Partnership Sourcing on Buyer-Supplier Relations." *Journal of General Management*. Autumn 1997.

Munson, Charles L., Meir J. Rosenblatt, and Zehava Rosenblatt. "The Use and Abuse of Power in Supply Chains." *Business Horizons*. January-February 1999.

"The Nuts and Bolts of Supplier Relations." *Nation's Business*. August 1997.

Porter, Anne Millen. "Purchasing Pros Insist They Buy On Far More than Price." *Purchasing*. 1 May 1997.

"Strong Supply Relationships Reduce Cost, Spark Innovation." *Purchasing*. 15 January 1998.

Teague, Paul E. "Ultra Tells Suppliers Quality is Critical." *Purchasing*. 18 May 2006.

Wilson, Amy. "A New Way to Pay Purchasing Execs: Ford buyers will be rewarded for improving supplier relations." *Automotive News*. 5 December 2005.

Hillstrom, Northern Lights
updated by Magee, ECDI

SUPPLY AND DEMAND

Supply and demand is a fundamental factor in shaping the character of the marketplace, for it is understood as the principal determinant in establishing the cost of goods and services. The availability, or "supply," of goods or services is a key consideration in determining the price at which those goods or services can be obtained. For example, a landscaping company with little competition that operates in an area of high demand for such services will in all likelihood be able to command a higher price than will a business operating in a highly competitive environment. But availability is only one-half of the equation that determines pricing structures in the marketplace. The other half is "demand." A company may be able to produce huge quantities of a product at low cost, but if there is little or no demand for that product in the marketplace, the company will be forced to sell units at a very low price. Conversely, if the marketplace proves receptive to the product that is being sold, the company can establish a higher unit price. "Supply" and "demand," then, are closely intertwined economic concepts; indeed, the law of supply and demand is often cited as among the most fundamental in all of economics.

FACTORS IMPACTING SUPPLY AND DEMAND

When using the term "demand" most people think the word means a certain volume of spending, as when we say that the demand for cars has fallen off or the demand for paper is high. But that is not what economists mean when using the term. For economists, demand means not just how much we are spending for a given item, but how much we are spending for that item *at its price,* and how much we would spend *if its price changed.*

The demand for products and services is predicated on a number of factors. The most important of these are the tastes, customs, and preferences of the target market, the consumer's income level, the quality of the goods or services being offered, and the availability of competitors' goods or services. All of the above elements are vital in determining the price that a business can command for its products or services, whether the business in question is a hair salon, a graphic arts firm, or a cabinet manufacturer.

The supply of goods and services in the marketplace is predicated on several factors as well, including production capacity, production costs (including wages, interest charges, and raw materials costs), and the number of other businesses engaged in providing the goods or services in question. Of course, some factors that are integral in determining supply in one area may be inconsequential in another. Weather, for example, is an important factor in determining the supplies of wheat, oranges, cherries, and myriad other agricultural products. But weather rarely impacts on the operations of businesses such as bookstores or auto supply stores except under the most exceptional of circumstances.

"When we are willing and able to buy more, we say that demand rises, and everyone knows that the effect of rising demand is to lift prices," summarized Robert Heilbroner and Lester Thurow in their book *Economics Explained: Everything You Need to Know About How the Economy Works and Where It's Going.* "Of course the mechanism works in reverse. If incomes fall, so does demand, and so does price." They point out that supply can also dwindle as a result of other business conditions, such as a rise in production costs for the producer or changes in regulatory or tax policies. "And of course both supply and demand can change at the same time, and often do," added Heilbroner and Thurow. "The outcome can be higher or lower prices, or even unchanged prices, depending on how the new balance of market forces works out."

SUPPLY AND DEMAND ELASTICITY

The demand for goods depends on the price for those goods, as well as on consumer income and on the prices of other goods. Similarly, supply depends on price, as well as on variables that affect production cost. How much the supply and demand will rise or fall is often difficult to predict. This measurement of a product or service's responsiveness to market changes is known as elasticity. Elasticity is a measure of the responsiveness of one economic variable to another. For example, price elasticity is the relationship between a change in the supply of a good and the demand for that good. Economists are often interested in the price elasticity of demand, which measures the response of the quantity of an item purchased to a change in the item's price. A good or service is considered to be highly elastic if a slight change in price leads to a sharp change in demand for the product or service. Products and services that are highly elastic are usually more discretionary in nature—readily available in the market and something that a consumer may not necessarily need in his or her daily life. On the other hand, an inelastic good or service is one for which changes in price result in only modest changes in demand. These goods and services tend to be necessities.

The quality and degree of marketplace reaction to price changes depend on several factors. These include: 1) the presence or absence of alternative sources for the product or service in question; 2) the time available to customers to investigate alternatives; 3) the size of the investment made by the purchaser. Elasticity, then, is an important factor for small business owners to consider when entertaining thoughts about changing the prices of the goods or services that they offer.

SEE ALSO *Elasticity; Product Costs*

BIBLIOGRAPHY

Hall, Robert Ernest. *Microeconomics: Principles and Applications.* Thomson South-Western, January 2004.

Heilbroner, Robert, and Lester Thurow. *Economics Explained: Everything You Need to Know About How the Economy Works and Where It's Going.* Revised Edition. Touchstone, 1998.

Langabeer II, Jim R. "Aligning Demand Management with Business Strategy." *Supply Chain Management Review.* May 2000.

"No Conspiracy: Law of Supply and Demand At Work." *Paducah Sun.* 5 May 2006.

Hillstrom, Northern Lights
updated by Magee, ECDI

SUSTAINABLE GROWTH

In simple terms and with reference to a business, sustainable growth is the realistically attainable growth that a company could maintain without running into problems. A business that grows too quickly may find it difficult to fund the growth. A business that grows too slowly or not at all may stagnate. Finding the optimum growth rate is the goal. A sustainable growth rate (SGR) is the maximum growth rate that a company can sustain without having to increase financial leverage. In essence, finding a company's sustainable growth rate answers the question: how much can this company grow before it must borrow money?

The models used to calculate sustainable growth assume that the business wants to: 1) maintain a target capital structure without issuing new equity; 2) maintain a target dividend payment ratio; and 3) increase sales as rapidly as market conditions allow. Since the asset to beginning of period equity ratio is constant and the firm's only source of new equity is retained earnings, sales and assets cannot grow any faster than the retained earnings plus the additional debt that the retained earnings can support. The sustainable growth rate is consistent with the observed evidence that most corporations are reluctant to issue new equity. If, however, the firm is willing to issue additional equity, there is in principle no financial constraint on its growth rate. Indeed, the sustainable growth rate formula is directly predicated on return on equity.

To calculate the sustainable growth rate for a company, one must know how profitable the company is based on a measure of its return on equity (ROE). One must also know what percentage of a company's earnings per share it pays out in dividends, which is called the dividend-payout ratio. With these figures one can multiply the company's ROE by its plowback ratio, which is equal to 1 minus the dividend-payout ratio. [Sustainable growth rate = ROE x (1 - dividend-payout ratio). Just as the break-even point for a business is the 'floor' for minimum sales required to cover operating expenses, the SGR is an estimate of the 'ceiling' for maximum sales growth that can be achieved without exhausting operating cash flows. The SGR can be thought of as a growth break-even point.

THE CHALLENGE OF ATTAINING SUSTAINABLE GROWTH

Creation of sustainable growth is a prime concern of small business owners and big corporate executives alike. Obviously, however, achieving this goal is no easy task, given rapidly changing political, economic, competitive, and consumer trends. Each of these trends presents unique challenges to business leaders searching for the elusive grail of sustainable growth. Customer expectations, for example, have changed considerably over the last few generations. Modern consumers have less disposable wealth than their parents, which makes them more discriminating buyers. This fact, coupled with the legacy of a decade of quality and cost reduction programs, means that companies must try to attract customers by redefining value and keep those customers by beating their competitors in enhancing value. Similarly, competition is keen in nearly all industries, which have seen unprecedented breakdowns in the barriers that formerly separated them.

The growth challenge is articulated differently by different companies and within different industries. For some, developing and launching new products and services to meet the evolving needs of their customers is the issue. For others, capitalizing on global opportunities is key. Some companies look to new business areas that will represent the next major thrust for their business. And for a few companies, all of these strategic efforts are simultaneously used, along with ongoing efforts to rebuild organizational capabilities.

Economists and business researchers contend that achieving sustainable growth is not possible without paying heed to twin cornerstones: growth strategy and growth capability. Companies that pay inadequate attention to one aspect or the other are doomed to failure in their efforts to establish practices of *sustainable* growth (though short-term gains may be realized). After all, if a company has an excellent growth strategy in place, but has not put the necessary infrastructure in place to execute that strategy, long-term growth is impossible. The reverse is true as well.

USING THE SUSTAINABLE GROWTH RATE

The concept of sustainable growth can be helpful for planning healthy corporate growth. This concept forces managers to consider the financial consequences of sales increases and to set sales growth goals that are consistent with the operating and financial policies of the firm. Often, a conflict can arise if growth objectives are not consistent with the value of the organization's sustainable growth.

According to economists, if a company's sales expand at any rate other than the sustainable rate, one or more of the basic business ratios must change. If a company's actual growth rate temporarily exceeds its sustainable rate, the required cash can likely be borrowed. When actual growth exceeds sustainable growth for longer periods, management must formulate a financial strategy from among the following options: 1) sell new equity; 2) permanently increase financial leverage (i.e, take on more debt); 3) reduce dividends; 4) increase the profit margin; or 5) decrease the percentage of total assets to sales.

In practice, companies are often reluctant to undertake these measures. Firms dislike issuing equity because of high issue costs, possible dilution of earnings per share, and the unreliable nature of equity funding on terms favorable to the issuer. A firm can only increase financial leverage if there are assets that can be pledged and if its debt-to-equity ratio is reasonable in relation to its industry. The reduction of dividends typically has a negative impact on the company's stock price. Companies can attempt to liquidate marginal operations, increase prices, or enhance manufacturing and distribution efficiencies to improve the profit margin. In addition, firms can source more activities from outside vendors or rent production facilities and equipment, which has the effect of improving the asset turnover ratio. Increasing the profit margin is difficult, however, and large sustainable increases may not be possible. Therefore, it is possible for a firm to grow too rapidly, which in turn can result in reduced liquidity and the unwanted depletion of financial resources.

The sustainable growth model is particularly helpful in situations in which a borrower requests additional financing. The need for additional loans creates a potentially risky situation of too much debt and too little equity. Either additional equity must be raised or the borrower will have to reduce the rate of expansion to a level that can be sustained without an increase in financial leverage.

Mature firms often have actual growth rates that are less than the sustainable growth rate. In these cases, management's principal objective is finding productive uses for the cash flows that exist in excess of their needs. Options available to business owners and executives in such cases include returning the money to shareholders through increased dividends or common stock repurchases, reducing the firm's debt load, or increasing possession of lower earning liquid assets. Note that these actions serve to decrease the sustainable growth rate. Alternatively, these firms can attempt to enhance their actual growth rates through the acquisition of rapidly growing companies.

Growth can come from two sources: increased volume and inflation. The inflationary increase in assets must be financed as though it were real growth. Inflation increases the amount of external financing required and increases the debt-to-equity ratio when this ratio is measured on a historical cost basis. Thus, if creditors require that a firm's historical debt-to-equity ratio stay constant, inflation lowers the firm's sustainable growth rate.

SEE ALSO *Financial Ratios*

BIBLIOGRAPHY

Gallinger, George W. "Tax Effects on Profitability and Sustainable Growth." *Business Credit*. April 2000.

Galpin, Timothy. *Making Strategy Work: Building Sustainable Growth Capability*. John Wiley & Sons, 1997.

Sowinski, Lara L. "The Trucking Industry's On a Roll--Or Is It? While demand in the sector remains strong, the state of the nation's infrastructure is threatening to put the brakes on sustainable growth." *World Trade*. March 2006.

"Sustainable Growth: Is There Room to Grow?" A Deloitte Research Viewpoint. Available from http://www.deloitte.com/dtt/research/0,1015,sid%253D15582%2526cid%253D100764,00.html. 2005.

Hillstrom, Northern Lights
updated by Magee, ECDI

SYNDICATED LOANS

Syndicated loans are large loans made by two or more lenders and administered by a common agent using similar terms and conditions and common documentation. Most loan syndications take the form of a direct-lender relationship, in which the lead lender is the agent for the other lenders in the origination and administration of the loan, and the other lending banks are signatories to the loan agreement. In the last several years the popularity of this type of loan has exploded. According to an article in *Bank Loan Report*, by 2004, the total annual volume of syndicated loan issuance had risen to $1.35 trillion. "Total US syndicated loans were up by nearly $364 billion, or 37%, over 2003 levels and 9% over

2000 levels.... Even so, although the numbers seemed to paint a picture of prolific loan supply in 2004, issuance still could not keep up with demand last year, as an increased amount of entrants on the lending side caused paper to remain scarce." The businesses that are choosing this option to finance their growth have expanded beyond the Fortune 500 companies that were its first users. Initially developed to address the needs of huge, acquisition-hungry companies, they have now become a flexible funding source for both mid-sized companies and smaller companies that are on the cusp of moving into mid-sized status. In fact, although syndicated loans are by nature very large loans—measured in the $100s of millions—it has become somewhat more common to see smaller syndicated loans in the mid 2000s—loans in the range of $10 million.

Most successful small companies that have evolved to the point where they are straining at the boundaries of that "small" designation have always dealt with one or a few individual banks, negotiating individual loans and lines of credit separately with each institution. The next financing step, however, may be to consolidate banking activity through one syndicated facility. While business owners and executives are sometimes loath to run the risk of alienating banks with which they have long done business, the simple reality is that companies can outgrow their traditional banks. As they grow, such companies may need access to more capital than can be handled comfortably by a single bank. An expanded bank group may be needed to fund their continued growth.

Of course, businesses can always choose to simply increase their stable of lending institutions, but this has several drawbacks. Managing multiple bank relationships is a time-consuming job. Each bank must be provided a lot of information about a potential borrower and how its financial activities are conducted. A comfort level must be established on both sides of the transaction, which requires time and effort.... Negotiating a document with a single bank can take days. To negotiate documents with four to five banks separately is a much bigger job. Staggered maturities must be monitored and orchestrated. Multiple lines of credit require an inter-creditor agreement among the banks, which takes additional time to negotiate.

Given these obstacles, business owners and executives often express interest in syndicated loans, which offer consolidation of effort and the possibility of making new banking contacts. Lenders support their use as well. Lenders tend to favor syndications because these arrangements permit then to make more loans, while limiting individual exposures and spreading the lenders' risk within portfolios more widely. In addition, lenders like the fact that administration of syndicated loans is extremely efficient, with the agent managing much of the process on behalf of the participants.

Syndicated loans hinge on the creation of an alliance of smaller banking institutions that, by joining forces, are able to meet the credit needs of the borrower. This creation is spurred by selection of an agent or arranger who manages the account. In consultation with the borrower, the agent will assemble a group of banks to form a syndicate. Each member of the syndicate then lends a portion of the total loan amount. Such a syndicated loan is normally signed six to eight weeks after the mandate has been awarded, and after signing, the borrower can begin to draw down funds.

Borrowers taking out syndicated loans pay up-front fees and annual charges to the participating banks, with interest accruing (on a quarterly, monthly, or semiannual basis) from the initial draw-down date. Nonetheless, on large loans that would otherwise be handled by several different lending institutions under separate loan agreements, syndicated loans can still be more cost-effective. This cost saving increases as the amount required rises.

OTHER ADVANTAGES OF SYNDICATED LOANS

Economists and syndicate executives contend that there are other, less obvious advantages to going with a syndicated loan. These benefits include:

- Syndicated loan facilities can increase competition for your business, prompting other banks to increase their efforts to put market information in front of you in hopes of being recognized.

- Flexibility in structure and pricing. Borrowers have a variety of options in shaping their syndicated loan, including multi-currency options, risk management techniques, and prepayment rights without penalty.

- Syndicated facilities bring businesses the best prices in aggregate and spare companies the time and effort of negotiating individually with each bank.

- Loan terms can be abbreviated.

- Increased feedback. Syndicate banks sometimes are willing to share perspectives on business issues with the agent that they would be reluctant to share with the borrowing business.

- Syndicated loans bring the borrower greater visibility in the open market.

SYNDICATE FORMATION

A borrower's ability to secure a syndicated loan, though, is predicated on its ability to spur the creation of a syndicate in the first place. No two syndications are identical. The lending environment changes every day. Many intangibles influence the structure and pricing of credit. These include the experience and depth of a borrowing company's management team; trends in the industry and market in which the borrower is active; and financial trends within a company.

The first thing the company has to do is select an agent to facilitate communications and transactions between the borrower and the banking institutions that will form the syndicate. The first place to look for an agent is among existing contacts. The agent is often, though need not be, the largest participant in the syndication. The agent must, however, have sufficient capital strength to be the anchor of the credit. Because it is important for a borrower to feel comfortable with the agent, and vice-a-versa, working with an institution with whom one has a solid history often works best.

Once an agent has been selected, the process of finding willing banks is undertaken. This phase of the process can vary considerably in terms of complexity. Some agents gauge the interest level of other lenders by simply sending them necessary financial information on the borrower and the intended shape and size of the syndicate group, as well as data on borrower operations, background, management, and marketing. In other cases, however, this process can be more complex, involving extensive due diligence, the preparation of a complete syndication offering memorandum (including financial projections), and a formal bank presentation.

By and large, the length of time necessary to form a bank group is roughly equivalent to the complexity of the proposed deal. Creation of a syndicate can take place over the course of a few weeks or a few months. Analysts note, however, that the length of time necessary to conclude the deal is usually less if the banks are already familiar with the borrower's operations. Once the membership of the group has been determined, the relationship quickly assumes the character that the borrowing business would expect when dealing with a single lending institution. Participating banks will still call on the borrower if need be but these interactions will be infrequent. The agent or arranger will be the primary contact for the borrower.

Indeed, the agent's responsibilities are many and varied. The agent is charged with administering the syndicated facility itself, as well as all borrowings, repayments, interest settlements, and fee payments. A chief component of the administration function is to make sure that communications between the lending institutions and the borrower remain open so that both sides remain informed about changing business and market realities. In return for providing these services, the agent is compensated with an annual fee.

SEE ALSO *Finance and Financial Management; Loans*

BIBLIOGRAPHY

Kantin, Kerry. "Record Volume For US Syn Loan Mart In 04." *Bank Loan Report.* 10 January 2005.

Madura, Jeff. *Financial Markets and Institutions.* Thomson South-Western, January 2005.

"Syndicated Loans." *Wall Street Journal.* 22 November 2000.

Hillstrom, Northern Lights
updated by Magee, ECDI

T

TARGET MARKETS

A target market is a group of customers with similar needs that forms the focus of a company's marketing efforts. Similarly, target marketing involves tailoring the company's marketing efforts to appeal to a specific group of customers. Selecting target markets is part of the process of market segmentation—dividing an overall market into key customer subsets or segments, whose members share similar demographic characteristics and needs. Demographic characteristics that are analyzed for target marketing purposes include age, income, geographic origins and current location, ethnicity, marital status, education, interests, level of discretionary income, net worth, home ownership, and a host of other factors. A company wishing to focus its efforts on a well-defined market segment can select from among these characteristics the particular segments it wishes to target. For a small company, the act of identifying a target market and then working to satisfy the needs of that market is a sound basis upon which to build the business. For any company, making the most of marketing expenditures means getting the message to the intended audience—focusing the marketing effort in such a way that it reaches and appeals precisely to the audience being targeted.

Target marketing can be a particularly valuable tool for small businesses, which often lack the resources to appeal to large aggregate markets or to maintain a wide range of differentiated products for varied markets. Target marketing allows a small business to develop a product and a marketing mix that fit a relatively homogenous part of the total market. By focusing its resources on a specific customer base in this way, a small business may be able to carve out a market niche that it can serve better than its larger competitors.

Identifying specific target markets—and then delivering products and promotions that ultimately maximize the profit potential of those targeted markets—is the primary function of marketing management for many smaller companies. For instance, a manufacturer of fishing equipment would not randomly market its product to the entire U.S. population. Instead, it would conduct market research, using such tools as demographic reports, market surveys, and trade shows, to determine which customers would be most likely to purchase what it offers. It could then spend its limited resources in an effort to persuade members of its target group(s) to buy. Advertisements and promotions could be tailored for each segment of the target market.

There are infinite ways to address the wants and needs of a target market. For example, product packaging can be designed in different sizes and colors, or the product itself can be altered to appeal to different personality types or age groups. Producers can also change the warranty or durability of the good or provide different levels of follow-up service. Other influences, such as distribution and sales methods, licensing strategies, and advertising media, also play an important role. It is the responsibility of the marketing manager to take all of these factors into account and to devise a cohesive marketing program that will appeal to the target customer.

Small business enterprises are also encouraged to continually examine their marketing efforts to make sure that they keep pace with changing business realities. For example, business start-ups typically accept any kind of legitimate business in order to pay the bills and establish themselves as a viable entity. But long after the start-up has blossomed into a solid member of the local business community, it may continue to rely on these early accounts rather than casting its net for more promising clients. "Are you happy with the makeup of your customer base and the nature of the work you do now?," asked Kim Gordon in *Entrepreneur*. "Altering the types of accounts you serve, their size, location or other criteria can have a big impact on your bottom line.... Instead of letting your current customer base define you, use target marketing to determine who your next customers or clients should be." The process of redefining ideal clients and customers can be painstaking and time-consuming, for creating profiles of your new target audience necessitates extensive research into ideal prospects and the marketing measures that will be most effective in reaching them, as well as your own desires for your company's future direction. But for many small business owners, the effort is worthwhile. "By targeting your ideal prospects, you'll avoid detours and grow your business in all the right directions," wrote Gordon. "Soon you'll have the kind of company that matches your vision and grows increasingly profitable over time."

SEE ALSO *Advertising Strategy; Market Research; Market Segmentation*

BIBLIOGRAPHY

Burke, Colette. "Promotion: Identify Your Target Market." *Farmers Guardian.* 16 May 2006.

Gordon, Kim T. "Selecting the Best Media for Your Ad." *Entrepreneur.* September 2003.

"Insight — Women: Tying Down Inconstant Women." *Marketing Week.* 27 April 2006.

Madler, Mark R. "Firms Find Different Way of Targeting Latino Market." *San Fernando Valley Business Journal.* 24 April 2006.

Ries, Al, and Laura Ries. *The Fall of Advertising and the Rise of PR.* HarperCollins, May 2004.

Stafford, Marla R., and Ronald J. Faber. *Advertising, Promotion, and New Media.* M.E. Sharpe, October 2004.

Hillstrom, Northern Lights
updated by Magee, ECDI

TARIFFS

A tariff is a tax or duty imposed by one nation on the imported goods or services of another nation. Tariffs are a political tool that have been used throughout history to control the amount of imports that flow into a country and to determine which nations will be granted the most favorable trading conditions. High tariffs create protectionism, shielding a domestic industry's products against foreign competition. High tariffs usually reduce the importation of a given product because the high tariff leads to a high price for the customers of that product.

There are two basic types of tariffs imposed by governments on imported goods. First is the *ad valorem* tax which is a percentage of the value of the item. The second is a *specific tariff* which is a tax levied based on a set fee per number of items or by weight.

Tariffs are generally imposed for one of four reasons:

- To protect newly established domestic industries from foreign competition.

- To protect aging and inefficient domestic industries from foreign competition.

- To protect domestic producers from "dumping" by foreign companies or governments. Dumping occurs when a foreign company charges a price in the domestic market which is below its own cost or under the cost for which it sells the item in its own domestic market.

- To raise revenue. Many developing nations use tariffs as a way of raising revenue. For example, a tariff on oil imposed by the government of a company that has no domestic oil reserves may be a way to raise a steady flow of revenue.

Since the early 1990s, the trend has been decreased tariffs on a global scale, as evidenced by the passage of well-known treaties such as the General Agreement on Tariffs and Trade (GATT) and the North American Free Trade Agreement (NAFTA), as well as the lowering of trade barriers in the European Economic Community, reducing or even abolishing tariffs. These changes reflect the conviction among some politicians and economists that lower tariffs spur growth and reduce prices generally.

Opponents of tariffs argue that tariffs hurt both (or all) countries involved, those that impose the tariff and those whose products are the target of the tariffs. For the country whose products are the target of tariffs, costs of production and sale prices rise and for most this leads to fewer exports and fewer sales. A decline in business leads to fewer jobs and spreads the slowdown in economic activity.

The argument that tariffs actually harm the country that imposes them is somewhat more complex. Although tariffs may initially be a boon to domestic producers who are faced with reduced competition as a result of the tariffs, the reduced competition then allows prices to rise. The sales of domestic producers should rise, all else being equal. The increased production and higher price lead to domestic increases in employment and consumer spending. The tariffs also increase government revenues that can be used to the benefit of the economy. All of this sounds positive. However, tariff opponents argue that the costs of tariffs can not be ignored. These costs come when the price of the goods on which the tariffs were imposed has increased, the consumer is forced to either buy less of these goods or less/fewer of some other goods. The price increase can be thought of as a reduction in consumer income. Since consumers are purchasing less, domestic producers in other industries are selling less, causing a decline in the economy.

Despite these arguments that tariffs are eventually harmful to all parties in a trade relationship, they have been used by all nations from time to time. Most developing countries use tariff to try and protect their fledgling industries or industries they feel the nation needs domestically in order to remain independent. The United States used tariffs extensively throughout its early years as a nation, and continues to do so today when the political will exists. Even proponent of free trade sometimes determine that tariffs may serve a useful purpose. In 2002, for example, President George W. Bush announced the imposition of steel tariffs for a three year period on imports from the European Union, Japan, China, South Korea and Taiwan. The reaction to these tariffs was swift and threatening. The U.S. ended up withdrawing the tariff in December of 2003 in order to avert the trade war that was brewing in reaction to the steel tariff.

How companies are impacted by tariffs differs from company to company based on a number of factors—proximity of industry sector to the tariff imposed, how directly the company's inputs and outputs are touched by the tariff, whether or not the company is involved in exporting or importing, etc. Businesses that do most of their business within a domestic market may benefit from the imposition of tariffs on competitive products. If, however, the material inputs to the products of a business are the targets of tariffs, then the business may well be harmed by rising prices on its material inputs. In another possible scenario, a business that is involved with exporting may be harmed if it sees the imposition of a tariff on products similar to those it exports, and retaliatory tariffs are imposed by other nations on the products it exports. As these examples show, the impact of tariffs on one business may be very different than those experienced by another business and the impacts differ based on characteristic other than the size of the businesses.

Exporters are usually well aware of the potential harm that may befall them if tariffs are unexpectedly imposed on their products and for that reason they usual include a disclaimer of responsibility for such tariffs that are imposed after a purchase agreement is signed. Such clauses to a purchase agreement usually state something like:

"Prices quoted do not include (and Customer agrees to pay) taxes, tariffs, duties, or fees of any kind which may be levied or imposed on either party by federal, state, municipal, or other governmental authorities in connection with the sale or delivery of the product." The key is to protect the business from liability for potential unpredictable and potentially arbitrary government actions.

NON-TARIFF BARRIERS
Worth noting is the fact that non-tariff barriers are also used quite frequently by nations of all sizes in their attempt to bolster their own economies and protect domestic interests. The Small Business Administration defines non-tariff barriers as "laws or regulations that a country enacts to protect domestic industries against foreign competition. Such non-tariff barriers may include subsidies for domestic goods, import quotas or regulations on import quality."

SEE ALSO *Exporting; Globalization*

BIBLIOGRAPHY
Allen, Mike. "President To Drop Tariffs On Steel. Bush Seeks to Avoid a Trade War and Its Political Fallout." *Washington Post.* 1 December 2003.

Ethier, Wilfred J. "The Theory of Trade Policy and Trade Agreements: A Critique." University of Pennsylvania. Department of Economics. Second Edition. 23 March 2005.

Rushford, Greg. "Quit Hiding Behind Tariffs and Embrace Globalization." *Seafood Business.* August 2005.

Tirschwell, Peter. "An Emerging Trade Barrier." *The Journal of Commerce.* 15 December 2003.

U.S. Small Business Administration. "Breaking Into the Trade Game: A Small Business Guide." Available from http://www.sba.gov/oit/txt/info/Guide-To-Exporting/trad7.html. Retrieved on 20 May 2006.

Magee, ECDI

TAX DEDUCTIBLE BUSINESS EXPENSES

Tax deductible expenses are almost any "ordinary, necessary, and reasonable" expenses that help to earn business income. Deductible expenses are those that can be subtracted from a company's income before it is subject to taxation. When it comes to what exactly is meant by ordinary, necessary, and reasonable expenses, the Internal Revenue Service (IRS) has defined these as any expenses that are "helpful and appropriate" for a business. The standard business deductions—which include general and administrative expenses, business-related travel and entertainment, automobile expenses, and employee benefits—are outlined in Section 162 of the Internal Revenue Code. Some expenses are considered "current" and are deducted in the year that they are paid, while others are considered "capitalized" and must be spread out or depreciated over time. There are a few business expenses that are specifically prohibited by law from being deductible, even though they may be used by the business to earn income. These include such things as a bribe paid to a public official, traffic tickets, the clothing one wears for work unless they are a required uniform, and expenditures deemed to be unreasonably large (like a corporate jet for a small retail business to use in visiting a few suppliers).

Good management of a business must include efficient management of the company's tax liabilities, maximizing the deductions and minimizing the obligations within the boundaries of the law. Taking advantage of allowable tax deductions can benefit to small business owners in many ways. "Knowing how to maximize your deductible business expenses lowers your taxable profit," noted Frederick W. Dailey in his book, *Tax Savvy for Small Business*. "To boot, you may enjoy a personal benefit from a business expenditure—a nice car to drive, a combination business trip/vacation and a retirement savings plan—if you follow the myriad of tax rules." Solid record-keeping is vital for small businesses that hope to claim their allowable tax credits and deductions. After all, deductions can be disallowed for even legitimate business expenditures if those expenditures are not adequately supported by business records. Some of the major categories of tax deductible business expenses are described below:

GENERAL AND ADMINISTRATIVE EXPENSES

All of the basic expenses necessary to run a business are generally tax-deductible, including office rent, salaries, equipment and supplies, telephone and utility costs, legal and accounting services, professional dues, and subscriptions to business publications. Education expenses are deductible if they are necessary to improve or maintain the skills involved in one's present employment or are required by an employer. However, education costs cannot be deducted when they are incurred in order to qualify for a different job. Some other miscellaneous expenses that may be deductible in this category include computer software, charitable contributions, repairs and improvements to business property, bank service charges, consultant fees, postage, and online services.

In most cases, general and administrative business expenses are deductible in the year in which they are incurred. An exception applies to the costs of starting a business, costs that may be incurred prior to beginning operations. These expenses must be capitalized over five years, which may seem strange since they are deductible immediately once the business is open. Depreciating the costs of starting a business might be preferable if the business is expected to show a loss for the first year or two. Otherwise, it may be possible to avoid the need to capitalize these expenses by delaying payment on invoices until the business opens or by doing a trivial amount of business during the startup period.

Home Office Deduction The use of part of a home as a business office may enable an individual to qualify for significant tax deductions. The "home office deduction" allows individuals who meet certain criteria to deduct a portion of mortgage interest or rent, depreciation of the space used as an office, utility bills, home insurance costs, and cleaning, repairs, and security costs from their federal income taxes. Although IRS has established strict regulations about who qualifies for the deduction, about 1.6 million people claim the deduction each year. The savings that this deduction enables can be considerable, as much as $3,000 annually for a sole proprietor living in a home valued at $150,000.

Home office operators may claim a deduction for those offices on IRS Form 8829 (Expenses for Business Use of Your Home), which is filed along with Schedule C (Profit or Loss From Your Business). There are restrictions, however, which are covered in IRS Publication 587 (*Business Use of Your Home*). The restrictions were eased somewhat with the passage of the Taxpayer Relief Act of 1997, which will take effect beginning with returns filed in 2000.

In general, a home office deduction is allowed if the home office meets at least one of three criteria: 1) the home office is the principal place of business; 2) the home office is the place where the business owner meets with clients and customers as part of the normal business day; or 3) the place of business is a separate structure on the property, but is not attached to the house or residence. The 1997 changes expanded the definition of "principal place of business" to include a place that is used by the taxpayer for administrative or management activities of the business, provided there is no other fixed location where these activities take place.

The deduction is figured on the size of the home office as a percentage of the total house or residence. For example, if the total house size is 2,400 square feet and the home office is 240 square feet, 10 percent of the total house is considered used for business. That would allow the business owner to deduct 10 percent of the household's costs for electricity, real estate taxes, mortgage interest, insurance, repairs, etc. as business expenses.

The total amount of the deduction is limited to the gross income derived from the business activity, less other business expenses. In other words, the home office deduction cannot be used to make an otherwise profitable business show a loss.

AUTOMOBILE EXPENSES

Most people have occasion to drive a car while conducting business. Business-related automobile mileage is tax deductible, with the exception of commuting to and from work. Any other mileage from the place of business to another location can be considered a business expense as long as the travel was made for business purposes. The IRS allows the mileage deduction to be calculated using two different approaches. The straight-mileage approach multiplies the cents-per-mile allowed by the IRS (40.5 cents in 2006) by the number of miles attributable to business use of the automobile. For example, a small business owner who drove 1,000 miles at .405 per mile would gain a deduction of $405.

In contrast, the actual-expense approach adds up all the costs of operating the car for a year—such as gasoline, insurance, maintenance, and depreciation—and multiplies that total by the percentage of the annual mileage that was attributable to business purposes. For example, a small business owner who paid a total of $3,000 in operating costs and drove a total of 15,000 miles, only 1,500 of which were business-related, would gain a deduction of $3,000 x .10 or $300. Businesses are required to use the actual-expense approach under certain circumstances—if the vehicle is leased, if more than one vehicle is used for the business, or if the approach was used for that vehicle during its first year of service—but otherwise can choose the approach that yields the larger deduction. In either case, it is necessary to maintain an accurate log of business mileage and associated automobile expenses.

ENTERTAINMENT AND TRAVEL

Reasonable travel and entertainment costs are tax deductible if they are: 1) directly related to business, meaning that business took place or was discussed during the entertainment; or 2) associated with business, meaning that business took place or was discussed immediately before or after the entertainment (i.e., a small business owner took a client out to dinner or to a sporting event following a meeting). Because they include a personal element, only 50 percent of meals and entertainment expenses are deductible as business expenses. Business-related travel, however, is fully deductible.

Careful records are necessary to substantiate the deductions. For business-related meals and entertainment, these records should include the amount, place, date, reason for entertainment, nature of business discussion, and name and occupation of the person being entertained. It is not necessary to retain receipts for expenditures less than $75. Entertainment that is done within the home is also deductible in some cases. Company parties that involve all employees are 100 percent deductible, although they must be infrequent and not overly extravagant. In addition, gifts to clients and customers are deductible to a maximum of $25 per year, or $400 if the business name is imprinted on them.

The costs of reasonable and necessary business travel—including meetings with clients and suppliers as well as conferences and seminars intended to expand a business person's expertise—are fully deductible as business expenses. The costs that can be deducted include airfare, bus or train fare, car rental, and taxi fare, hotels and meals, and incidentals such as tips and dry cleaning expenses. Restrictions apply to travel in foreign countries or on cruise ships. In addition, travel to investment-related seminars are not deductible, though the cost of the seminars may be. A variety of rules apply to deducting business travel expenses, so it is necessary to review them in detail or enlist the help of a tax professional.

DEPRECIATION

According to Section 179 of the Internal Revenue Code, small business owners can write off the first $18,000 of equipment purchased for business use each year during the year in which it was purchased. In many cases, it makes sense to take advantage of this tax break immediately, particularly if purchases will be fairly regular from year to year. If the item is a one-time purchase or if the total amount spent is greater than the limit, however, the business owner may wish to depreciate the cost over future time periods. Depreciation is a tax-deductible business expense.

Depreciation for tax purposes is determined by an IRS formula and has nothing to do with the actual value of equipment at year end. Instead, the amount claimed as depreciation is designed to spread the cost of the equipment over time and maximize the annual tax deductions associated with it. Most companies use a straight-line depreciation method for their financial statements, because the even amounts approximate the rate at which the equipment is used up and will need to be replaced. However, they tend to use accelerated depreciation methods for tax purposes in order to deduct a larger portion of the equipment's cost sooner. The IRS applies different "life spans" to different types of equipment for the purposes of depreciation. For example, it applies a five-year life to telecommunications equipment and automobiles, and a seven-year life to computers and office equipment like desks, chairs, and fixtures.

EMPLOYEE BENEFITS

The cost of providing employees with a wide variety of fringe benefits is considered a tax deductible business expense for employers. Most of these benefits are not considered income for employees, so they receive a tax break as well. Certain types of benefits—particularly retirement and pension plans—are also deductible for self-employed persons and small business owners. However, it is important to keep up with the rapidly changing tax laws regarding these matters. Some of the types of employee benefits that may be considered tax deductible business expenses include: retirement plans, health insurance, disability and life insurance, company cars, membership in clubs and athletic facilities, dependent care assistance, education assistance, employee discounts, and business meals, travel, and lodging.

Retirement and Pension Plans Small business owners have a wide variety of retirement plans from which to choose in order to gain tax advantages. In most cases, employer contributions are tax-deductible business expenses, and the money is allowed to grow tax-deferred until employees reach retirement age, at which point, it is assumed, they will be in a lower tax bracket than during their working years. The most important thing to remember is that a small business owner who wants to establish a qualified plan for him or herself must also include all other company employees who meet minimum participation standards. As an employer, the small business owner can establish retirement plans like any other business. As an employee, the small business owner can then make contributions to the plan he or she has established in order to set aside tax-deferred funds for retirement, like any other employee. The difference is that a small business owner must include all nonowner employees in any company-sponsored qualified retirement plans and make equivalent contributions to their accounts.

For self-employed individuals, contributions to a retirement plan are based upon the net earnings of their business. The net earnings consist of the company's gross income less deductions for business expenses, salaries paid to nonowner employees, the employer's 50 percent of the Social Security tax, and—significantly—the employer's contribution to retirement plans on behalf of employees. Therefore, rather than receiving pre-tax contributions to the retirement account as a percentage of gross salary, like nonowner employees, the small business owner receives contributions as a smaller percentage of net earnings. Employing other people thus detracts from the owner's ability to build up a sizeable before-tax retirement account of his or her own. For this reason, some experts recommend that the owners of proprietorships and partnerships who sponsor plans for their employees supplement their own retirement funds through a personal after-tax savings plan.

Nevertheless, many small businesses sponsor retirement plans in order to gain tax advantages and increase the loyalty of employees. A number of different types of plans are available. In nearly every case, withdrawals made before the age of 59 ½ are subject to an IRS penalty in addition to ordinary income tax. The plans differ in terms of administrative costs, eligibility requirements, employee participation, degree of discretion in making contributions, and amount of allowable contributions.

Health Insurance Health insurance benefits provided to employees are also tax deductible. However, self-employed persons are only able to deduct a portion of their own payments for health insurance (40 percent in 1997, gradually increasing to 80 percent in 2006). An exception to this rule is included under Section 105 of the Internal Revenue Code. This loophole allows a small business owner whose spouse works in the business to fully deduct his or her health insurance and unreimbursed medical expenses by creating a medical reimbursement plan for employees. The spouse is then covered under the plan, the small business owner is covered under his or her spouse's insurance, and the entire bill is a tax-deductible business expense. Many tax professionals and insurance providers offer this sort of plan to their clients. It is important to note, however, that the same plan must be available to all of the business's employees.

BIBLIOGRAPHY

Carter, Gary W. *Small Business Tax Secrets: Ultimate Tax Savings for the Self-Employed!*. John Wiley & Sons, March 2003.

Cash, L. Stephen, and Thomas L. Dickens. "New Home Office Rule Applies for 2000 Filing Season." *Strategic Finance.* February 2000.

Dailey, Frederick W. *Tax Savvy for Small Business.* Ninth Edition. Nolo Press, 2005.

Ennico, Cliff. "Preparing Your IRS Forms 1099 and W-2." *Entrepreneur.com.* 27 January 2003.

Fink, Philip R. "Individuals and Small Business Tax Planning Guide." *The Tax Adviser.* September 2005.

U.S. Department of Treasury. Internal Revenue Service. "Business Expenses." Publication 535. 2005.

U.S. Department of Treasury. Internal Revenue Service. "Forms and Instruction." Available from http://www.irs.gov/formspubs/lists/0,id=97817,00.html. Retrieved on 17 May 2006.

Hillstrom, Northern Lights
updated by Magee, ECDI

TAX PLANNING

Tax planning involves conceiving of and implementing various strategies in order to minimize the amount of taxes paid for a given period. For a small business, minimizing the tax liability can provide more money for expenses, investment, or growth. In this way, tax planning can be a source of working capital. Two basic rules apply to tax planning. First, a small business should never incur additional expenses only to gain a tax deduction. While purchasing necessary equipment prior to the end of the tax year can be a valuable tax planning strategy, making unnecessary purchases is not recommended. Second, a small business should always attempt to defer taxes when possible. Deferring taxes enables the business to use that money interest-free, and sometimes even earn interest on it, until the next time taxes are due.

Experts recommend that entrepreneurs and small business owners conduct formal tax planning sessions in the middle of each tax year. This approach will give them time to apply their strategies to the current year as well as allow them to get a jump on the following year. It is important for small business owners to maintain a personal awareness of tax planning issues in order to save money. Even if they employ a professional bookkeeper or accountant, small business owners should keep careful tabs on their own tax preparation in order to take advantage of all possible opportunities for deductions and tax savings. Whether or not an entrepreneur enlists the aid of an outside expert, he or she should understand the basic provisions of the tax code.

GENERAL AREAS OF TAX PLANNING

There are several general areas of tax planning that apply to all sorts of small businesses. These areas include the choice of accounting and inventory-valuation methods, the timing of equipment purchases, the spreading of business income among family members, and the selection of tax-favored benefit plans and investments. There are also some areas of tax planning that are specific to certain business forms—i.e., sole proprietorships, partnerships, C corporations, and S corporations. Some of the general tax planning strategies are described below:

Accounting Methods Accounting methods refer to the basic rules and guidelines under which businesses keep their financial records and prepare their financial reports. There are two main accounting methods used for recordkeeping: the cash basis and the accrual basis. Small business owners must decide which method to use depending on the legal form of the business, its sales volume, whether it extends credit to customers, and the tax requirements set forth by the Internal Revenue Service (IRS). The choice of accounting method is an issue in tax planning, as it can affect the amount of taxes owed by a small business in a given year.

Accounting records prepared using the cash basis recognize income and expenses according to real-time cash flow. Income is recorded upon receipt of funds, rather than based upon when it is actually earned, and expenses are recorded as they are paid, rather than as they are actually incurred. Under this accounting method, therefore, it is possible to defer taxable income by delaying billing so that payment is not received in the current year. Likewise, it is possible to accelerate expenses by paying them as soon as the bills are received, in advance of the due date. The cash method is simpler than the accrual method, it provides a more accurate picture of cash flow, and income is not subject to taxation until the money is actually received.

In contrast, the accrual basis makes a greater effort to recognize income and expenses in the period to which they apply, regardless of whether or not money has changed hands. Under this system, revenue is recorded when it is earned, rather than when payment is received, and expenses recorded when they are incurred, rather than when payment is made. The main advantage of the accrual method is that it provides a more accurate picture of how a business is performing over the long-term than the cash method. The main disadvantages are that it is more complex than the cash basis, and that income taxes may be owed on revenue before payment is actually received. However, the accrual basis may yield favorable tax results for companies that have few receivables and large current liabilities.

Under generally accepted accounting principles (GAAP), the accrual basis of accounting is required for all businesses that handle inventory, from small retailers to large manufacturers. It is also required for corporations and partnerships that have gross sales over $5 million per year, though there are exceptions for farming businesses and qualified personal service corporations—such as doctors, lawyers, accountants, and consultants. Other businesses generally can decide which accounting method to use based on the relative tax savings it provides.

Inventory Valuation Methods The method a small business chooses for inventory valuation can also lead to substantial tax savings. Inventory valuation is important because businesses are required to reduce the amount they deduct for inventory purchases over the course of a year by the amount remaining in inventory at the end of the year. For example, a business that purchased $10,000 in inventory during the year but had $6,000 remaining in inventory at the end of the year could only count $4,000 as an expense for inventory purchases, even though the actual cash outlay was much larger. Valuing the remaining inventory differently could increase the amount deducted from income and thus reduce the amount of tax owed by the business.

The tax law provides two possible methods for inventory valuation: the first-in, first-out method (FIFO); and the last-in, first-out method (LIFO). As the names suggest, these inventory methods differ in the assumption they make about the way items are sold from inventory. FIFO assumes that the items purchased the earliest are the first to be removed from inventory, while LIFO assumes that the items purchased most recently are the first to be removed from inventory. In this way, FIFO values the remaining inventory at the most current cost, while LIFO values the remaining inventory at the earliest cost paid that year.

LIFO is generally the preferred inventory valuation method during times of rising costs. It places a lower value on the remaining inventory and a higher value on the cost of goods sold, thus reducing income and taxes. On the other hand, FIFO is generally preferred during periods of deflation or in industries where inventory can tend to lose its value rapidly, such as high technology. Companies are allowed to file IRS Form 970 and switch from FIFO to LIFO at any time to take advantage of tax savings. However, they must then either wait ten years or get permission from the IRS to switch back to FIFO.

Equipment Purchases Under Section 179 of the Internal Revenue Code, businesses are allowed to deduct a total of $18,000 in equipment purchases during the year in which the purchases are made. Any purchases above this amount must be depreciated over several future tax periods. It is often advantageous for small businesses to use this tax incentive to increase their deductions for business expenses, thus reducing their taxable income and their tax liability. Necessary equipment purchases up to the limit can be timed at year end and still be fully deductible for the year. This tax incentive also applies to personal property put into service for business use, with the exception of automobiles and real estate.

Wages Paid to Family Members Self-employed persons can also reduce their tax burden by paying wages to a spouse or to dependent children. Wages paid to children under the age of 18 are not subject to FICA (Social Security and Medicare) taxes. Under normal circumstances, employers are required to withhold 7.65 percent of the first $94,200 of an employee's income for FICA taxes. Employers are also required to match the 7.65 percent contributed by every employee, so that the total FICA contribution is 15.3 percent. Self-employed persons are required to pay both the employer and employee portions of the FICA tax.

But the FICA taxes are waived when the employee is a dependent child of the small business owner, saving the child and the parent 7.65 percent each. In addition, the child's wages are still considered a tax deductible business expense for the parent—thus reducing the parent's taxable income. Although the child must pay normal income taxes on the wages he or she receives, it is likely to be at a lower tax rate than the parent pays. Some business owners are able to further reduce their tax burden by paying wages to their spouse. If these wages bring the business owner's net income below $94,200—the threshold for FICA taxes—then they may reduce the self-employment tax owed by business owner. It is important to note, however, that the child or spouse must actually work for the business and that the wages must be reasonable for the work performed.

Benefits Plans and Investments Tax planning also applies to various types of employee benefits that can provide a business with tax deductions, such as contributions to life insurance, health insurance, or retirement plans. As an added bonus, many such benefit programs are not considered taxable income for employees. Finally, tax planning applies to various types of investments that can shift tax liability to future periods, such as treasury bills, bank certificates, savings bonds, and deferred annuities. Companies can avoid paying taxes during the current period for income that is reinvested in such tax-deferred instruments.

TAX PLANNING FOR DIFFERENT BUSINESS FORMS

Selection of the form of organization that one uses for a company has a considerable impact on the rate at which tax liabilities accrue. Many aspects of tax planning are specific to certain business forms; some of these are discussed below:

Sole Proprietorships and Partnerships Tax planning for sole proprietorships and partnerships is in many ways similar to tax planning for individuals. This is because the owners of businesses organized as sole proprietors and partnerships pay personal income tax rather than business income tax. These small business owners file an informational return for their business with the IRS, and then report any income taken from the business for personal use on their own personal tax return. No special taxes are imposed except for the self-employment tax, which requires all self-employed persons to pay both the employer and employee portions of the FICA tax, for a total of 15.3 percent.

Since they do not receive an ordinary salary, the owners of sole proprietorships and partnerships are not required to withhold income taxes for themselves. Instead, they are required to estimate their total tax liability and remit it to the IRS in quarterly installments, using Form 1040 ES. It is important that the amount of tax paid in quarterly installments equal either the total amount owed during the previous year or 90 percent of their total current tax liability. Otherwise, the IRS may charge interest and impose a stiff penalty for underpayment of estimated taxes.

Since the IRS calculates the amount owed quarterly, a large lump-sum payment in the fourth quarter will not enable a taxpayer to escape penalties. On the other hand, a significant increase in withholding in the fourth quarter may help, because tax that is withheld by an employer is considered to be paid evenly throughout the year no matter when it was withheld. This leads to a possible tax planning strategy for a self-employed person who falls behind in his or her estimated tax payments. By having an employed spouse increase his or her withholding, the self-employed person can make up for the deficiency and avoid a penalty. The IRS has also been known to waive underpayment penalties for people in special circumstances. For example, they might waive the penalty for newly self-employed taxpayers who underpay their income taxes because they are making estimated tax payments for the first time.

Another possible tax planning strategy applies to partnerships that anticipate a loss. At the end of each tax year, partnerships file the informational Form 1065 (Partnership Statement of Income) with the IRS, and then report the amount of income that accrued to each partner on Schedule K1. This income can be divided in any number of ways, depending on the nature of the partnership agreement. In this way, it is possible to pass all of a partnership's early losses to one partner in order to maximize his or her tax advantages.

C Corporations Tax planning strategies for C corporations are different from those used for sole proprietorships and partnerships. This is because profits earned by C corporations accrue to the corporation rather than to the individual owners, or shareholders. A corporation is a separate, taxable entity under the law, and different corporate tax rates apply based on the amount of net income received. As of 2005, the corporate tax rates were 15 percent on income up to $50,000, 25 percent on income between $50,001 and $75,000, 34 percent on income between $75,001 and $100,000, 39 percent on income between $100,001 and $335,000, 34 percent on income between $335,001 and $10 million, 35 percent on income between $10 million and $15 million, 38 percent on income between $15 million and $18,333,333, and 35 percent on all income over $18,333,334. Businesses involved in manufacturing are charged a top tax rate of 32 percent. Personal service corporations, like medical and law practices, pay a flat rate of 35 percent. In addition to the basic corporate tax, corporations may be subject to several special taxes.

Corporations must prepare an annual corporate tax return on either a calendar-year basis (the tax year ends December 31, and taxes must be filed by March 15) or a fiscal-year basis (the tax year ends whenever the officers determine). Most Subchapter S corporations, as well as C corporations that derive most of their income from the personal services of shareholders, are required to use the calendar-year basis for tax purposes. Most other corporations can choose whichever basis provides them with the most tax benefits. Using a fiscal-year basis to stagger the corporate tax year and the personal one can provide several advantages. For example, many corporations choose to end their fiscal year on January 31 and give their shareholder/employees bonuses at that time. The bonuses are still tax deductible for the corporation, while the individual shareholders enjoy use of that money without owing taxes on it until April 15 of the following year.

Both the owners and employees of C corporations receive salaries for their work, and the corporation must withhold taxes on the wages paid. All such salaries are tax deductible for the corporations, as are fringe benefits supplied to employees. Many smaller corporations can arrange to pay out all corporate income in salaries and benefits, leaving no income subject to the corporate income tax. Of course, the individual shareholder/employees are required to pay personal income taxes. Still, corporations can use tax planning strategies to defer or accrue income between the corporation and individuals in order to pay taxes in the lowest possible tax bracket. The one major disadvantage to corporate taxation is that corporate income is subject to corporate taxes, and then income distributions to shareholders in the form of dividends are also taxable for the shareholders. This situation is known as "double taxation."

S Corporations Subchapter S corporations avoid the problem of double taxation by passing their earnings (or losses) through directly to shareholders, without having to pay dividends. Experts note that it is often preferable for tax planning purposes to begin a new business as an S corporation rather than a C corporation. Many businesses show a loss for a year or more when they first begin operations. At the same time, individual owners often cash out investments and sell assets in order to accumulate the funds needed to start the business. The owners would have to pay tax on this income unless the corporate losses were passed through to offset it.

Another tax planning strategy available to shareholder/employees of S corporations involves keeping FICA taxes low by setting modest salaries for themselves, below the Social Security base. S corporation shareholder/employees are only required to pay FICA taxes on the income that they receive as salaries, not on income that they receive as dividends or on earnings that are retained in the corporation. It is important to note, however, that unreasonably low salaries may be challenged by the IRS.

SEE ALSO *Accounting Methods; Capital Structure; Financial Planning; Organizational Structure*

BIBLIOGRAPHY

Carter, Gary W. *Small Business Tax Secrets.* John Wiley & Sons, 2003.

Dailey, Frederick W. *Tax Savvy for Small Business.* Ninth Edition. Nolo Press, 2005.

Fink, Philip R. "Individual and Small Business Tax Planning Guide." *The Tax Adviser.* September 2005.

Fink, Philip R. "Strategic Corporate Tax Planning." *The Tax Adviser.* December 2004.

Hoover, Kent. "Critics Blast IRS Rule Change." *Triangle Business Journal.* 21 April 2000.

Karayan, John E., Charles W. Swenson, and Joseph W. Neff, *Strategic Corporate Tax Planning.* Wiley, 2004.

Hillstrom, Northern Lights
updated by Magee, ECDI

TAX PREPARATION SOFTWARE

Faced with a tax code which inevitably changes from year to year, many small business owners choose to use one of the many tax preparation software packages which are now widely available. These packages are available for computers running any of the more popular operating systems—Apple OS, Unix, or Windows—and most use a spreadsheet format.

The advantages to using tax preparation software are many. First, they result in more complete and accurate returns. The typical paper tax return has an error rate of 20 percent. Because of built-in math calculators and other automatic checks, electronic tax preparation reduces this error rate to less than 1 percent. Tax preparation software packages may also steer the taxpayer toward greater savings or little-known deductions, paying for themselves with the returns they yield. But even if no direct tax savings are realized, many analysts believe that use of the software saves many business owners a considerable amount of time, thus freeing them to use their talents in other business areas.

Purchasing the software to prepare tax returns, no matter which package is purchased, will undoubtedly be less expensive than hiring an accountant. Of course, a CPA can be creative and intuitive about individual circumstances in a way that a computer program can not. But unless the finances for the year are extremely complicated, the best of these software programs should be sufficient to meet the requirements of most small enterprises. Of course, the old adage "garbage in, garbage out" applies here. A small business owner that is not comfortable with accounting and finance may choose to enlist the aid of an accountant even if the software option seems alluring. Some entrepreneurs prepare the taxes themselves and then have an accountant review and sign off on the results. Using an accountant may also be comforting for some because in the event of an audit, the small business owner will not have to face the IRS without the expert knowledge of the CPA that originally prepared the tax return.

COMPONENTS OF THE PACKAGES

Data Entry All of the software packages have more than one option for entering data into the IRS-accepted forms. The user can always opt for the simple method of entering figures into the forms without assistance from the program, using the software mainly to double-check figures and calculate final amounts. All of the software packages also have an interview function, which asks easily understandable questions to which the user responds by clicking yes or no boxes. This function specifies which schedules are required by the IRS, and which sections of the basic 1040 and schedules can be bypassed. Depending on the program, there may be a third route—a "fast track" interview, through which the user can select specific parts of the interview to fill out, speeding up the process and avoiding the sections which are not pertinent to the case at hand.

Many of the programs also have importing features, which allow the user to pull data from other programs directly into the tax preparation. Generally, these work primarily with Quicken and QuickBooks. If the small business owner already uses one of these applications to calculate tax-related expenses, it is relatively quick and easy to transfer information, cutting down on duplicated work. Almost all of the packages also allow the user to import last year's tax information, provided it was prepared with the same package.

Filing When it comes to methods of filing, most of the packages provide several options for the user to choose between. The forms can be filled out electronically and then printed and mailed to the IRS to be processed in a paper version. Some of the packages offer the abbreviated

Form 1040PC, which is also submitted as a hard copy. And some of the packages allow the user to file electronically, although most charge an additional fee for this option (around $10).

Features and Help All of the software packages automatically check for mathematical mistakes and warn of possible errors when questionable data is entered into a field. Most of the programs can offer advice—some from specific tax experts—about how to maximize the return and minimize taxes paid. Some of the programs offer complete IRS tax guides which can be directly accessed, and some offer only abbreviated versions of this information. Another feature often offered in these tax preparation software packages is one that can alert the user to potential audit flags resulting from data entered. Several packages offer a review option after the forms are completed; this option can provide advice on what to do differently to pay fewer taxes the next time around.

Most software packages include the option to do state tax preparation in addition to the federal forms. Since some packages do not cover all 50 states, it is important when buying the software to be sure that it includes the forms necessary for the state in which one is operating. The state return supplement may be included in the original price or may be priced separately. Prices for the packages range from around $20 to more than $75, plus state supplements and filing fees.

DECIDING WHICH PACKAGE TO USE

Choosing a package will depend on how complicated the company's tax return is likely to be. A few of the products can manage even very complicated scenarios, while the few at the bottom of the price range tend to be better for simple personal tax returns. For the small business owner, who may be dealing with self-employment taxes, home-work environments, and partnerships, it is probably worthwhile to purchase one of the more detailed programs. As of 2005, the two most popular tax software packages were Turbo Tax by Intuit, and Tax Cut by H&R Block.

With the advent of high-speed Internet connections and improved Internet security, more and more tax preparation is taking place online. Growing numbers of small businesses are contracting with application service providers (ASPs) that specialize in tax preparation. ASPs provide tax preparation applications on their Web sites and also maintain huge databases to store clients' data. Users connect to the ASP's remote computer over the Internet, access their files with a password, and use the software provided to prepare their taxes online.

SEE ALSO *Electronic Tax Filing*

BIBLIOGRAPHY

Dailey, Frederick W. *Tax Savvy for Small Business.* Ninth Edition. Nolo Press, 2005.

Higginbotham, Keith. "IRS Expands Electronic Tax Filing." *Knight-Ridder/Tribune Business News.* 5 January 2001.

"A Necessary Strategic Partner." *Accounting Technology.* May 2006.

Whittenburg, Gerald E., and Martha Altus-Buller. *Income Tax Foundations 2005.* Thomson West, December 2004.

Zarowin, Stanley. "Expanding into Cyberspace." *Journal of Accountancy.* September 2000.

Hillstrom, Northern Lights
updated by Magee, ECDI

TAX RETURNS

Tax returns include all the required paperwork that accompanies the remittance of taxes to the appropriate government agencies, the largest of these being the Internal Revenue Service (IRS). The IRS issues more than 650 different forms for taxpayers to use in calculating and paying their taxes (the complete list is available through IRS publication 676, *Catalog of Federal Tax Forms*). Each form applies to a different situation or purpose. For example, Form 1065 details the income received by a business operating as a partnership, and Form 8826 relates to expenses claimed for business use of a home. Perhaps the most familiar type of tax form is the annual personal tax return, Form 1040, that must be completed by millions of taxpayers each year.

Considering that the laws have undergone no fewer than eight major revisions in the past two decades, as well as numerous minor changes, it is no wonder that tax return preparation can be exceedingly difficult and time consuming for small business owners. Since the average small business person can ill afford to call a tax pro with every question, time will be necessary to make one's way through the maze of tax forms and instructions. Fortunately, a great deal of information is available to help in this task. Sources include IRS publications and help lines, self-help tax preparation guides and software, trade associations, periodicals, and online services.

It is important for small business owners to maintain a personal awareness of tax-related issues in order to save money. Even if they employ a professional bookkeeper or accountant, small business owners should keep careful tabs on their own tax preparation in order to take advantage of all possible opportunities for deductions and tax savings. Whether or not a small business owner enlists the aid of an outside accountant, she should understand the basic provisions of the tax code. Just as one would not turn over the management of his money to another person, he should not blindly allow someone else to take complete charge of his taxpaying responsibilities. Knowledge of tax structures and provisions can have a powerful impact on the potential for maximizing profits. Knowing what the tax law has to offer can provide a company with an advantage over competitors who don't use tax planning efficiently.

COMMON BUSINESS TAX FORMS AND FILING DEADLINES

Small businesses that employ persons other than the owner or partners are required to withhold payroll taxes from the wages paid to employees, remit these taxes to the Internal Revenue Service (IRS), and make regularly scheduled reports to the IRS about the amount of payroll taxes owed and paid. Payroll taxes include regular income taxes, FICA (Social Security and Medicare) taxes, and FUTA (federal unemployment) taxes. In addition to withholding payroll taxes for employees, employers must remit these taxes to the IRS in a timely manner. The regular income taxes and the portion of the FICA taxes that are withheld from employees' wages each pay period must be remitted to the IRS monthly, along with a Federal Tax Deposit Coupon (Form 8109-B). If the total withheld is less than $500, however, the business is allowed to make the payments quarterly.

Employers must also file four different reports regarding payroll taxes. The first report, Form 941, is the Employer's Quarterly Federal Tax Return. This report details the number of employees the business had, the amount of wages they were paid, and the amount of taxes that were withheld for the quarter. The other three reports are filed annually. Form W-2—the Annual Statement of Taxes Withheld—must be sent to each employee before January 31 of the following year. It details how much each employee received in wages and how much was withheld for taxes over the course of the year. Copies of the W-2 forms for all employees also must be sent to the Social Security Administration. The third payroll tax report, Form W-3, must be sent to the IRS by February 28 of the following year. It provides a formal reconciliation of the quarterly tax payments made on Form 941 and the annual totals reported on Form W-2 for all employees. The final report is the Federal Unemployment Tax Return, Form 940, which outlines the total FUTA taxes owed and paid for the year.

Independent contractors to whom a business pays more than $600 during the tax year must be sent a Form 1099 by the business no later than January 31 of the following year. This form is like a W-2 form for non-employees. And like the W-2 form, it has a related summary form that must be sent to the IRS—along with copies of all 1099 forms—no later than February 28. This summary report is IRS Form 1096.

Since they do not receive an ordinary salary, the owners of sole proprietorships and partnerships are not required to withhold income taxes for themselves. Instead, they are required to estimate their total tax liability and remit it to the IRS in quarterly installments, using Form 1040 ES. It is important that the amount of tax paid in quarterly installments equal either the total amount owed during the previous year or 90 percent of their total current tax liability. Otherwise, the IRS may charge interest and impose a stiff penalty for underpayment of estimated taxes. At the end of the tax year, the income for sole proprietorships is simply reported on the personal tax return of the business owner. Partnerships must file the informational Form 1065 (Partnership Statement of Income) with the IRS, and then report the amount of income that accrued to each partner on Schedule K1.

Corporations must prepare an annual corporate tax return on either a calendar-year basis (the tax year ends December 31, and taxes must be filed by March 15) or a fiscal-year basis (the tax year ends whenever the officers determine). Most Subchapter S corporations, as well as C corporations that derive most of their income from the personal services of shareholders, are required to use the calendar-year basis for tax purposes. Most other corporations can choose whichever basis provides them with the most tax benefits. At the end of their tax year, corporations file either Form 1120, the U.S. Corporate Income Tax Return, or the shorter Form 1120A. If they expect to owe taxes, corporations are required to make quarterly estimated payments, like other businesses.

BIBLIOGRAPHY

Carter, Gary W. *Small Business Tax Secrets: Ultimate Tax Savings for the Self-Employed!*. John Wiley & Sons, March 2003.

Dailey, Frederick W. *Tax Savvy for Small Business.* Ninth Edition. Nolo Press, 2005.

Ennico, Cliff. "Preparing Your IRS Forms 1099 and W-2." *Entrepreneur.com.* 27 January 2003.

Fink, Philip R. "Individuals and Small Business Tax Planning Guide." *The Tax Adviser.* September 2005.

"Top Errors Preparers Make." *Journal of Accountancy.* June 2000.

U.S. Department of Treasury. Internal Revenue Service. "Forms and Instruction." Available from http://www.irs.gov/formspubs/lists/0,id=97817,00.html. Retrieved on 17 May 2006.

Hillstrom, Northern Lights
updated by Magee, ECDI

TAX WITHHOLDING

Tax withholding refers to the portion of an employee's gross wages that is retained by an employer for remittance to the Internal Revenue Service (IRS). Two main types of taxes are typically withheld—regular income taxes and Federal Insurance Contribution Act (FICA) taxes, which include contributions to the federal Social Security and Medicare programs. Many states and some cities and municipalities also apply taxes and in some cases these taxes too must be withheld by employers.

At the federal tax level, the two types of taxes that employers are required to withhold are amounts for regular income taxes and a set percentage of gross pay for FICA taxes.

Income Tax Withholding The amount that is withheld from an employee's paycheck in order to pay income taxes is determined based on the person's income level and the number of exemptions that the person claims. Withholding is usually done in standard amounts based on formulas provided by the IRS. Employees can adjust their income tax withholding by filing Form W-4 with their employer and designating the number of withholding allowances they wish to claim. Employees decide upon the number of withholding allowances they wish to claim based on their expected tax liability, which depends on their filing status, family circumstances, other sources of income, and available deductions or tax credits. It is not advisable to overpay taxes—even though the extra amount is eventually refunded to the taxpayer—because it is like giving the government an interest-free loan. At the same time, it is not advisable to underpay taxes because it may be difficult to come up with a lump-sum payment when it is due on April 15. In addition, a taxpayer who underpays his or her income taxes by more than 10 percent may face a penalty and have to pay the government interest on the funds owed.

Unfortunately, the IRS guidelines for withholding can cause problems with overpayment or underpayment of taxes even in simple cases. For example, a single taxpayer with no dependents and only one source of income would be instructed to claim two withholding allowances to best approximate the total tax owed. But this strategy may cause the taxpayer in question to owe around $200 on April 15. Similarly, a married couple with one income would be instructed to claim three withholding allowances, but this would cause a balance due for the year of nearly $400. Because the IRS guidelines are general, some small underpayment or overpayment is likely even if the number of withholding allowances or exemptions is chosen with care.

There is another factor that needs to be considered when an employee decides about the number of exemptions to choose, and thus a tax withholding level. Many people supplement their regular employment income with interest, dividends, capital gains, rental property, or self-employment income. In many cases, this means that regular withholding from employment income—based on the IRS formulas—is not enough to cover the taxes owed. In a situation in which an employee anticipates income from other sources, he or she may choose to maximize the amount withheld by the employer so that the taxes withheld will help to pay for tax obligations arising from another source of income.

Taxpayers are required to pay at least 90 percent of their total tax liability in installments prior to April 15. If they do not, they may be subject to a penalty. However, the penalty is waived for taxpayers who pay at least as much in total taxes as they had owed the previous year, or for whom the amount underpaid is less than $500. Since the IRS calculates the amount owed quarterly, a large lump-sum payment in the fourth quarter will not enable a taxpayer to escape penalties. On the other hand, a significant increase in withholding in the fourth quarter may help, because tax that is withheld by an employer is considered to be paid evenly throughout the year no matter when it was withheld. For this reason, taxpayers who see a significant underpayment problem looming should have additional taxes withheld by their employers. An employee may request that his or her employer withhold and send to the IRS as large a percentage of his or her gross income as desired. So, for example, if a person who does Web site design work as a supplement to her regular job receives a large Web design project late in the tax year, she may ask her employer to increase her income tax withholding to 50 percent for the remainder of the year in order to try and make up for the unexpected rise in income tax liability for that year. To avoid a penalty, the total tax withheld must reach 90 percent of what will be owed in the current year or 100 percent of what was owed in the previous year.

This strategy can also work for a self-employed person who falls behind in his or her estimated tax payments. By having an employed spouse increase his or her withholding, the self-employed person can make up for the deficiency and avoid a penalty. The IRS has also been known to waive underpayment penalties for people in special circumstances. For example, they might waive the penalty for newly self-employed taxpayers who underpay their income taxes because they are making estimated tax payments for the first time.

FICA Tax Withholding The second type of federal tax which employers are required to withhold from their employees' payroll checks is the Federal Insurance Contribution Act (FICA) tax. The FICA tax includes contributions to two federal programs, Social Security and Medicare. The tax rate for FICA taxes does not often change but the earnings on which those taxes are applied changes from year to year. In 2006, full FICA taxes of 7.65 percent were due on the first $94,200 earned. Only the Medicare portion of the FICA tax, 1.45 percent, was due on earnings over $94,200. Employers are required to match the FICA amount withheld for every employee, so that the total FICA contribution is 15.3 percent on the first $94,200 earned. Self-employed persons are required to pay both the employer and employee portions of the FICA tax.

Employers are required to withhold 7.65 percent of the first $94,200 of an employee's income for FICA taxes. Employers are also required to match that amount for every employee, so that the total FICA contribution is 15.3 percent. Self-employed persons are required to pay both the employer and employee portions of the FICA tax. The amount of regular income tax that must be withheld from an employee's paycheck depends on the individual's tax status. Ideally, the total income tax withheld should come close to equaling the employee's overall tax liability at the end of the year. Employees can adjust their income tax withholding by filing Form W-4 with their employer and designating the number of withholding allowances they wish to claim.

SEE ALSO *Electronic Tax Filing; FICA Taxes; Payroll Taxes*

BIBLIOGRAPHY

Aaron, Henry J., and Joel Slemrod. *Crisis in Tax Administration.* Brookings Institute Press, December 2003.

"Bad Health Will Not Excuse Penalty for Unpaid Payroll Tax." *The Kiplinger Tax Letter.* 10 March 2006.

Bieg, Bernard J. *Payroll Accounting 2005.* Thomson South-Western, November 2004.

Daily, Frederick W. *Tax Savvy for Small Business.* Nolo, November 2004.

Fishman, Stephen. *Deduct It!: Lower Your Small Business Taxes.* Nolo, September 2005.

Grassi, Carl. "Federal Withholding Rules Enforced with an Iron Fist." *Crain's Cleveland Business.* 12 June 2000.

Longenecker, Justin G., Carlos W. Moore, J. William Petty, and Leslie E. Palich. *Small Business Management with Infotrac: An Entrepreneurial Emphasis.* Thomson South-Western, 2005.

U.S. Department of the Treasury. Internal Revenue Service. "What is the difference between a Form W-2 and a Form 1099-MISC?" Available from http://www.irs.gov/faqs/faq12-2.html. Retrieved on 1 May 2006.

Hillstrom, Northern Lights
updated by Magee, ECDI

TELECOMMUTING

Telecommuting is a practice in which an employee works at a location—often his or her home—that is remote from the actual business facility at which he/she is employed. Under this arrangement, the employee maintains close contact with coworkers and supervisors via various forms of computer, Internet, and communication technology (i.e, electronic mail, telephone, computer networks, etc.)

Advances with communications devices and computer networking systems have made it possible for more people to work from remote locations and for telecommuting to become an ever-more feasible option for many companies. During the 1990s the number of companies offering employees the opportunity to telecommute—if not full-time, on a part-time basis—increased rapidly and became very popular within some industries. According to the Bureau of Labor Statistics, in a report entitled simply *Telecommuting*, data they collect in the Current Population Survey do not identify telecommuters as such. This makes getting clear statistics about the size of the telecommuting workforce very difficult. Further complicating the task of counting telecommuters is the fact that many telecommuting arrangements are informal as opposed to formal telecommuting agreements. Informal telecommuting involves the periodic working from home as projects or family needs dictate. Formal telecommuting arrangements are those in which an employee regularly works from an off-site location.

According to the Bureau of Labor Statistics report, most telecommuters belong to one of four major occupational groups. These broad occupational categories include professional specialists, executives, administrative staffers, and managers. From an industrial standpoint, the service industry stands above all others in terms of the number of telecommuters it employs. The spread of telecommuting was so popular in the 1990s that many predicted that its numbers would continue to grow rapidly. But, the recession of 2001 slowed growth. And, as *The Kiplinger Letter* explains, "telecommuting is losing some appeal, putting the lie to forecasts that by 2006 some 70 million U.S. workers would quit heading to offices. One reason: Telecommuting is maxing out at industries most open to it, publishing, telecom, finance, where nearly everyone who can already does.... The tough economic climate is dampening employee ardor, too, Workers fear that being out of sight makes them more vulnerable to layoffs. Employers trimming office and relocation costs are still enticed, though."

ADVANTAGES OF TELECOMMUTING

Both employers and employees have found telecommuting to be a mutually beneficial arrangement in many instances. Proponents cite several positive factors in particular:

Happier employees. Telecommuting arrangements can help workers realize a general improvement in their personal "quality of life." They avoid long, stressful commutes, thus gaining more time for pleasurable activities and more flexibility for changeable tasks like child and elder care.

Increased retention of valued employees. Many businesses lose workers when those employees undergo significant life changes, such as starting a family or relocating to another region or state because of a spouse's career. Telecommuting is one way in which a business may be able to continue to utilize the services of an otherwise unavailable worker. It is also touted as a tool that permits workers to minimize use of "personal days" in instances where they have to stay home and care for a sick child, etc.

Increased productivity. Business studies and anecdotal evidence both suggest that employees are often much more productive at home, where "drop-in" interruptions and meetings are not distractions. Instead, the teleworker can focus on the job at hand. Of course, productivity at home is directly related to the employee's level of self-discipline and abilities.

Cost savings. Businesses can often gain significant savings in facilities costs like office space and parking space requirements when staff members telecommute.

DISADVANTAGES OF TELECOMMUTING

But while telecommuting programs have been highly successful for many businesses of all shapes, sizes, and industry orientations, there are potential pitfalls associated with them. Commonly cited drawbacks include the following:

Lack of oversight. Direct supervision of teleworkers is not possible.

Diminished productivity. Some people are unable to be productive in at-home work settings, either because of family distractions or their own limited capacity to focus on tasks when more pleasurable activities (bicycling, gardening, watching television, etc.) beckon.

Cost of added security requriements. Telecommuting arrangements usually require some form of added openness in a company's computer networks. Consequently, additional steps must be taken to secure networks in ways that allow remote access by some while protecting against unwanted intruders. These measures necessitate a cost that may not be required if employees did not work remotely.

Isolation. The freedom of working alone comes with a price, namely the burden of isolation. Some people deal with this trade-off more easily than others. Partial teleworking arrangements, in which the employee spends a portion of each week (1-3 days) in the office and the remainder working from home, can sometimes be an effective means of addressing this problem.

Erosion of company culture and/or departmental morale. Many businesses include certain employees who have a major positive impact on the prevailing office environment. When these employees enter into telecommuting programs, their absence is often deeply felt by the staff members left behind. In some cases, this departure from the company's everyday operations can even have a deleterious effect on the operation's overall culture.

Loss of "brainstorming" ability. In the information age, much of the value added to the production process is in the form of 'knowledge' and the dispersal of key employees may make it less likey that these knowledgeable workers will interact vigorously as a part of the normal daily exchange in a workplace. The informal bouncing around of ideas is difficult, or even impossible, without the face-to-face contact of a common workplace.

Perceived damage to career. A common perception among employees of businesses that embrace teleworking options is that telecommuters are placed at a disadvantage in terms of career advancement and opportunity. Certainly, some professional avenues—such as supervisor positions—may be shut off to workers who want to continue telecommuting, but employers should make every effort to avoid an "out of sight, out of mind" perspective from taking shape.

Legal vulnerability. Some analysts have expressed concern that some employer liability issues regarding telecommuting practices have yet to be completely settled. They cite issues such as employer liability for home-office accidents under common law; applicability of the employer's insurance coverage when they work at home; and responsibility for equipment located in the home as particular concerns.

INSTITUTING A TELECOMMUTING PROGRAM

Experts cite several key elements in creating and maintaining a successful telecommuting policy in your business. First, business owners and/or managers should make sure that such a program will actually benefit their company's ability to efficiently address its various operational needs. For example, some positions require an extensive on-site presence. These range from management positions to those in which face-to-face communication with clients or other members of the workforce is imperative. Consultants urge employers to consider telecommuting proposals on a position-by-position basis, rather than adopting "one size fits all" parameters.

Companies should also conduct extensive research before buying and implementing new technologies necessary to institute a telecommuting program. Information technology (IT) personnel can be particularly useful in shaping program policies and anticipating remote workplace needs of teleworkers. In addition, you should consider the impact of telecommuting on other departments, both in terms of operational efficiency and morale.

Business owners should draft specific guidelines and policies for any telecommuting program. These policies may delineate reporting guidelines, delivery schedules for completing and submitting work, selected hours during which employee guarantees his or her availability, employee performance evaluation criteria, and telecommuting work option evaluation criteria. Once such a program has been put in place, it is essential that it be actively monitored. Analysts urge business owners and managers to maintain open lines of communication with teleworkers, so that problems can be addressed in a timely manner.

Finally, business owners and managers need to recognize that some employees are better suited than others to thrive in a telecommuting program. Prospective workers should be self-motivated; self-disciplined; and possessed of good problem-solving skills and communication skills (both written and verbal). They should also have a home environment which will enable them to maintain or exceed the levels of productivity they attain in an office setting.

SEE ALSO *Flexible Work Arrangements; Home-Based Business; Hoteling; Mobile Office*

BIBLIOGRAPHY
Bray, Laura. "Consider the Alternatives." *Association Management.* November 1999.

Dunham, Kemba J. "Telecommuters' Lament: Once Touted as the Future, Work-at-Home Situations Lose Favor with Employers." *Wall Street Journal.* 31 October 2000.

"Flexible Working Practices Boost Business Success." *Leadership and Organization Development Journal.* February-March 1997.

Gillentine, Amy. "Telecommuting is Still Far from the Mainstream." *St. Charles County Business Record.* 6 May 2006.

McNeely, Kevin. "Pitfalls of an Electronic Workplace." *Providence Business Journal.* 27 March 2000.

Naylor, Mary A. "There's No Workforce Like Home: Want to help keep jobs in this country, serve customers better, and lower your costs? Telework lets companies tap an accomplished but underutilized talent pool." *Business Week Online.* 2 May 2006.

"Telecommuting Trends." *The Kiplinger Letter.* 6 December 2002.

U.S. Department of Labor. Bureau of Labor Statistics. Mariani, Mattthew. "Telecommuting." *Occupational Outlook Quarterly.* Fall 2000.

Hillstrom, Northern Lights
updated by Magee, ECDI

TELEMARKETING

Telemarketing is the process of using the telephone to generate leads, make sales, or gather marketing information. Telemarketing can be a particularly valuable tool for small businesses, in that it saves time and money as compared to personal selling, but offers many of the same benefits in terms of direct contact with customers. In fact, experts have estimated that closing a sale through telemarketing usually costs less than one-fifth of what it would cost to send a salesperson to make a sale in person. Though telemarketing is more expensive than direct mail, it tends to be more efficient in closing sales and thus provides a greater yield on the marketing dollar.

Telemarketing is especially useful when the customers for a small business's products or services are located in hard-to-reach places, or when many prospects must be contacted in order to find one interested in making a purchase. Although some small businesses operate exclusively by telephone, telemarketing is most often used as part of an overall marketing program to tie together advertising and personal selling efforts. For example, a company might send introductory information through the mail, then follow-up with a telemarketing call to assess the prospect's interest, and finally send a salesperson to visit.

Telemarketing can be either inbound or outbound in scope. Inbound telemarketing consists of handling incoming telephone calls—often generated by broadcast advertising, direct mail, or catalogs—and taking orders for a wide range of products. Representatives working in this type of telemarketing program normally do not need as much training as outbound reps because the customer already has shown an interest by calling in.

Outbound telemarketing can be aimed directly at the end consumer—for example, a home repair business may call people in its community to search for prospects—or can be part of a business-to-business marketing program. Representatives working on this side of the industry generally require more training and product knowledge, as more actual selling is involved than with inbound operations.

Major applications of business-to-business telemarketing include selling to existing accounts, outbound new account development, inbound order processing and inquiry handling, customer service, and supporting the existing field sales force. As the costs of field sales continue to escalate, businesses are using telemarketing as a way to reduce the cost of selling and give more attention to marginal accounts. Telemarketing programs can be either handled in-house by a company or farmed out to service bureaus. Operations range in size from a one-person in-house staff member at a small business to a major corporation or service center that may have as many as 1,000 telephone stations.

One of the advantages telemarketing has over other direct marketing methods is that it involves human interaction. Used correctly and by professionals, the telephone is a very cost-efficient, flexible and statistically accountable medium. At the same time, the telephone is still very intimate and personal, one person speaking with another.

Although telemarketing has been the center of some controversies—ranging from scams run over the phone to a number of legal issues that have been the center of debate at both the state and national levels—the industry continues to grow. In fact, the American Telemarketing Association found that spending on telemarketing activities increased from $1 billion to $60 billion between 1981 and 1991. By the mid-1990s, telemarketing accounted for more than $450 billion in annual sales. This increased use of telemarketing resulted in an unexpectedly strong backlash and for telemarketing firms the landscape in the early 21st century has changed dramatically.

FEDERAL DO-NOT-CALL LIST

In 2003, the popular uproar against telemarketing calls grew so loud that legislators in Washington took notice and took action. Following the lead of several states, federal legislators passed a law in 2003 that made it possible for people to register to have their home phones included on a do-not-call list and by so doing "opt-out of telemarketing." The law is the Do-Not-Call Registry Act of 2003. This act authorized the Federal Trade Commission (FTC), under sections of the Telemarketing and Consumer Fraud and Abuse Prevention Act, to implement and enforce a do-not-call registry to be established and run by the commission. The registry is nationwide in scope, applies to all telemarketers (with the exception of certain non-profit organizations), and covers both interstate and intrastate telemarketing calls. Commercial telemarketers are not allowed to call a number that is on the registry, subject to certain exceptions.

Organizations not covered by the law include non-profit organizations, political campaigns and companies that have an existing business relationship with a call recipient. The goal is to eliminate cold calls for all

those who chose to "opt-out" of telemarketing, it is not designed to keep companies from calling their customers for repeat sales. As of early 2005, the FTC reported having close to 65 million numbers in the do-not-call registry with an additional 150,000 added monthly. Under the law, telemarketers are required to purchase a copy of the list for the area codes they wish to call and then remove from their call lists all numbers that appear on the FTC list. Those companies that fail to comply with this law face the imposition of heavy fines. In late 2005, the largest fine to-date was imposed on the satellite television company, DirectTV. The fine charged DirectTV was $5.3 million. The underlying complaint named as defendants DirectTV, five firms that telemarketed on its behalf and six principals of those telemarketing firms. "This multimillion-dollar penalty drives home a simple point: Sellers are on the hook for calls placed on their behalf," said FTC chairman Deborah Platt Majoras in an article in the magazine *Brandweek.*

Although solid numbers are hard to find, one commonly accepted estimate is that the do-not-call regulation had cut the number of telemarketing calls by half during the first two years in effect. Telemarketing firms report seeing their lists cut from 35 to 55 percent.

The industry is still adjusting to the new reality that has been created by the do-not-call registry. They will continue to search for ways in which to generate new telephone lists that include potential clients that are not on the do-not-call list or clients who by virtue of signing up for a sweepstakes event have created for themselves a "relationship" with the seller. Companies with whom a person has done business or with whom a person has signed up for a drawing are allowed to call that individual whether or not his or her phone number is on the do-not-call list. Consequently, companies that use telemarketing are researching ways to go about rebuilding their calling lists.

Although much reduced during the first years of the 21st Century, telemarketing is still an option for some types of businesses. In particular, business-to-business telemarketing is still a useful tool within a larger marketing strategy for companies that sell to other companies.

Selling Telemarketing can either supplement or replace face-to-face selling to existing accounts. It can complement the field sales effort by reaching new customer bases or geographic markets at relatively low cost. It can also be used to sell goods and services independently, with no field sales force in place. This method often is used for repetitive supply purchases or readily identifiable products, though it can be effectively applied to other products as well.

The inside sales force can be used to replace direct contact for marginally profitable customers. A general rule of thumb in business says that 20 percent of customers account for 80 percent of sales, so conversely the remaining 80 percent of customers generate just 20 percent of sales. But businesses must keep in mind that marginal does not necessarily mean unprofitable. And the existing customer base is perhaps the most important asset in any business; increases in sales most often come from current accounts, and it generally is less costly to maintain current customers than to search out new business, particularly with the reduction of access resulting from the FTC do-not-call list. Telemarketers can give these reliable customers the attention they deserve. The reps can phone as often as needed, determine the customers' purchasing cycles, and contact them at appropriate reorder times.

In making such a consolidation between a direct and inside sales force, the company must be careful in determining which accounts should stay with field sales and which should be handled by telemarketing. Some businesses start their telemarketing operations with just small or inactive accounts, gradually increasing the size of accounts handled.

Lead Generation Through telemarketing, a company can compile and update lists of customer prospect leads and then go through these lists searching for sales leads. Telemarketing can screen the leads and qualify them according to priority, passing the best leads to the field sales force for immediate action. The inside sales force also can identify the decision maker with the buying power and set up appointments for the outside sales force.

Gathering Information Telemarketing can provide accurate information on advertising effectiveness, what customers are buying, from whom they're buying, and when they will buy again. It is also commonly used in conducting surveys.

Improving Customer Service Studies show it costs five times more to win over a new customer than to keep an existing one. By using telemarketing as a main facet of customer service, companies can go a long way toward keeping customers happy.

In addition, when used in conjunction with current computer technology, a telemarketing program can be analyzed in terms of costs and benefits, using quantitative data on the number of contacts, number of presentations, total sales, cost per sale, and income per sale.

ESTABLISHING A SUCCESSFUL PROGRAM

Not all telemarketing programs are successful. Improper execution, unrealistic goals over a short time period,

oversimplification, and lack of top management support have caused the ultimate failure of more telephone sales programs than can be imagined. Like any marketing strategy, telemarketing takes time to plan and develop. It takes time to gain confidence in the message, to identify weak areas, and to predict bottom-line results. Some of the most common telemarketing mistakes include: not giving it a total commitment; not utilizing the proper expertise; failing to develop a proper database; improper human resource planning; lack of proper scripts and call guides; lack of quality control, and failing to understand the synergy with other direct marketing disciplines. To create a successful telemarketing program, management must understand and agree to the necessary personnel and financial resources, as well as devoting adequate time for program development and testing. Telemarketing and related direct marketing techniques can produce solid sales. But they need a chance to develop and demonstrate that success. Very simply, it takes time.

Experts agree that companies must be careful in forming telemarketing goals and objectives. Some of the most important factors for success include: developing a complete marketing plan with built-in criteria for accounting and analysis; writing scripts, sales outlines, and presentations to be performed; establishing training and hiring procedures for both supervisors and sales personnel; analyzing and evaluating campaigns, personnel, and cost effectiveness; having support and commitment from management for the telemarketing's role in the overall marketing effort; establishing reachable goals; and placing a continuous emphasis on follow-up.

IN-HOUSE VS. OUTSIDE SERVICE BUREAUS

When establishing a telemarketing program, a company has the option of setting up the operation in-house, or subcontracting it to an outside service bureau. Both have advantages and disadvantages. In-house programs usually are better if products and/or services require extensive technical expertise to explain. They also can be better for firms making a long-term commitment to telemarketing. Service bureaus, on the other hand, can help firms that need around-the-clock coverage for inbound programs, are supporting television ad campaigns, or are running a seasonal marketing program.

Service Bureaus One of the main advantages of service bureaus is that they likely can offer lower costs. By grouping programs from several different companies, service bureaus can generate sufficient volume to reduce labor and telephone costs, which make up a majority of total costs. They can also get a program started more quickly because they have experienced telephone reps on staff, along with necessary equipment.

When 24-hour coverage is needed on an inbound telemarketing program, it probably is more cost-effective to go with a bureau. When setting up an outbound program, the experienced managers at a bureau can help a company avoid making mistakes and often can accurately project call volumes and sales per hour. Service bureaus also can help with testing new programs and have a greater ability to handle demand peaks.

On the downside, several client companies often must compete for a service bureau's attention, and for firms that share service with a broadcast advertiser whose response rates are underestimated, that can be a decided drawback. Stability of service bureaus has also been a problem at times.

In-house Operations The main reason companies decide to run their own telemarketing campaign is that they can maintain total control over all facets, including hiring and firing, scripts and presentations, budgets, advertising, and compensation and incentive policies. When telemarketing programs are kept in-house, phone reps have ready access to company information, so they can confirm delivery, authorize credit, and suggest alternatives to out-of-stock items.

Since in-house reps are trained on individual product lines, they can handle highly technical calls no service bureau likely would attempt. Such technical expertise also helps companies maintain effective customer service programs through observation (such as via call monitoring). In addition, it is easier to gain company loyalty from actual employees than from people employed by an outside bureau. The biggest drawback to taking a program in-house is the large capital investment needed to get a telemarketing program started. It involves hiring and training new personnel, purchasing new communications equipment, and dealing with a process that is unfamiliar to many in business.

TECHNOLOGICAL AND HUMAN ELEMENTS

Computers have played an important role in the growth of telemarketing. Access to databases provides phone reps with account histories, stock status, order-taking formats, and other vital information. Besides analyzing data, computers are used for scheduling, scripting, and follow-ups. Computers also can be programmed to automatically dial phone numbers and connect the calls to telemarketers only if they are answered, screen out answering machines, and guide the phone rep through the telemarketing presentation.

While technology plays a vital role in keeping telemarketing cost-effective, the human element is critical in making the effort successful. Unfortunately, many firms still view telemarketing positions as clerical-level jobs staffed by people with few skills, no training, and little understanding of the product or service being sold. Often, the manager of a telemarketing operation is the only person in an organization familiar with the discipline. Some firms, though, have come to realize the importance of the telemarketers, as the firm's image is on the line with every call. They realize the position needs skilled, trained professionals who must be adequately compensated.

For compensation, most companies use a combination of salary, commission, and/or bonuses. Studies indicate that incentives generally aid in sales success, but it is important to link the inducements to the performance desired, be it total sales, calls completed, or presentations given. Some form of quotas are also commonly used so that sales reps know what is expected of them. Firms should be reasonable in setting quotas. If the goals are too high, the reps will become frustrated, leading to morale and worker retention problems. Conversely, low quotas can create an environment in which effort is lacking, especially if the compensation package in place is heavily weighted toward base salary.

Telemarketing positions typically show high levels of turnover, in large measure because the majority of interactions with potential customers end in rejection. Working shorter shifts or using computers to prescreen customers can help reduce the amount of rejection telemarketers experience. Training is another important factor. If the individuals that comprise your telemarketing staff are trained to be specific, control the time and pace of conversation, ask questions and listen without interrupting or rushing the customer's response, and respond to objections or concerns in a positive manner, they will experience greater levels of success—and hence, a more positive outlook on their duties.

SEE ALSO *Advertising Strategy; Marketing*

BIBLIOGRAPHY

Cleveland, Brad. "What You Need to Understand About Abandoned Calls—How to lower your call center's abandonment rates." *Call Center.* 1 April 2006.

"DirectTV to Pay Record Fine for Do Not Call Violations." *The Computer & Internet Lawyer.* February 2006.

McCullagh, DeClan. "Hanging Up on Telemarketers." *CNET news.com.* 1 October 2004.

McLuhan, Robert. "Warm Calling Builds Results." *Marketing.* 5 August 1999.

Rosen, Judith. "Telemarketing: Pros and Cons." *Publishers Weekly.* 11 January 1999.

U. S. Federal Trade Commission. *National Do Not Call Registry.* Available from http://www.ftc.gov/donotcall/. Retrieved on 23 February 2006.

"Where Marketers Can Obtain State Do-Not-Call Lists." Direct Marketing Association. Available from http://www.the-dma.org/government/donotcalllists.shtml. Retrieved on 10 May 2006.

Wilkins, Tony. *The Telemarketing Success for The Small to Mid Size Firm.* Xlibris Corporation, 2004.

Hillstrom, Northern Lights
updated by Magee, ECDI

TEMPORARY EMPLOYMENT SERVICES

Temporary employment services (often referred to as temporary employment agencies or firms) offer client companies the services of temporary employees who possess specific skills. This arrangement can provide a client company with needed help during peak demand periods, staffing shortages, or the vacations of regular employees, without requiring the time, expense, and long-term commitment of hiring a new employee. Temporary employment firms typically undertake hiring and firing decisions, issue paychecks, withhold payroll taxes, and make contributions for unemployment insurance, workers' compensation, and Social Security for the employees serving in their client's places of business. Client companies simply describe their staffing needs and time frame, then pay a set hourly rate to the temporary employment agency for the services of a "temp." The business scenarios in which temporary staff can be useful are virtually endless, noted *Arkansas Business.* "A large staffing service can bring in any number of temporaries to work days, nights, weekends, or holidays—and not just to perform low-skill tasks. Specialized temporary services can routinely handle specific, time-sensitive and highly skilled projects. In fact, very often temporary workers are so qualified, employers end up adding them to the full-time staff, saving the high cost of hiring and training. Additionally, a temporary employee allows you to judge whether you need a full-time person for a particular job or if ongoing temporaries can complete the tasks."

The use of temporary employment grew rapidly in the 1980s and early 1990s during the trend toward business downsizing and restructuring, in which many companies reduced the size of their core work forces. Companies began to substitute temporary for permanent employees for cost savings in payroll administration and fringe benefits, and to gain greater flexibility in the face of changing business conditions. After a slowdown in 2000 because of the tech bubble and in 2001 because of the recession, "the temp industry is thriving again, placing day laborers, secretaries, accountants and engineers in projects that last from a few days to six months or more," according to H. Lee Murphy writing in *Crain's Chicago Business.* And, although in the past, most temporary employment services specialized in providing general secretarial and clerical help to client companies, this is changing. Use of temporary workers has expanded in the manufacturing sector—coinciding with the advent of "just-in-time" production systems—and in professional occupations, such as accountants, lawyers, and engineers. Growth in these areas enabled the temporary staffing industry to register annual double-digit gains in revenue throughout the 1990s and again after the 2001 recession. According to an estimate by the American Staffing Association, reported on in a *Fairfield County Business Journal* article in early 2006, there are an estimated 2.5 million people per day employed by staffing companies. This figure represents nearly 2 percent of the entire U.S. workforce.

Changes in the nature of the work force—such as an increase in the number of working mothers—have contributed to the popularity of temporary employment arrangements. Part-time workers who are employed as "temps" enjoy a great deal of flexibility in setting schedules and choosing assignments. For example, a mother with young children in school might opt to work fairly consistently during the school year, but not at all during the summer months. Some professional workers use temporary assignments as a way to add variety to their jobs, while recent college graduates might view temp work as a stepping stone to permanent employment. But even though temporary employment offers advantages for some workers, many others—who have been laid off or are unable to find permanent positions—work as temps out of necessity rather than preference.

The economic and demographic forces that have stimulated growth in the temporary staffing industry as an alternative to hiring permanent employees are not likely to change in the near future. These forces include the shift from production of goods to processing of information; employer reluctance to add permanent staff in the face of economic uncertainly and volatility; technological changes that require special expertise to deploy and operate; a desire to avoid seemingly ever more expensive benefit packages, and the availability of capable individuals who either must, or prefer to enter the temporary labor market.

Nonetheless, there are potential drawbacks associated with going the "temp service" route that must be weighed. One factor commonly cited is the greater

1106

allocation of time and resources to training that may be necessary if a company receives several different temp workers in succession for one job. Another criticism that is sometimes raised in conjunction with reliance on temp services is that some temporary staffers do not feel a connection to the company for which they are working, which can have a deleterious impact on effort and effectiveness. Companies can do much to address these potential problem areas, however, by establishing and maintaining a program that continually monitors and reviews the contributions of temp workers.

CHOOSING A TEMPORARY SERVICE

Temporary employment services are a particularly attractive option for small businesses, which often need help on a limited basis but lack the resources to recruit, screen, and pay new, full-time employees. A small business considering the services of a temporary employment agency should first consider several factors:

Gauge need. Business owners should examine production schedules, composition of employee benefits (number of sick days and vacation days, etc.), and seasonal workloads when weighing whether to pursue temporary staff. Shortcomings in specific areas of business knowledge should be factored in as well. Another key factor that should be weighed is less quantifiable but even more important: quality of customer service. "Check the quality of the work not just during the times when employees are covering for another worker, but on a regular basis," said Don Owens in *Sacramento Business Journal.* "Judge the way employees react when asked to do more from each other and from managers. Most importantly, look at how employees treat people outside the company—from the vendors and suppliers to the customers themselves. Are they harried, short and tense?" If so, temporary additions to the workforce may be in order.

Put an effective screening process in place. It is important to understand the temporary services firm's screening process for temporary employees. Though minimal screening is acceptable for low-level jobs, the process should include more sophisticated screening methods—such as personal interviews, computer testing, or psychological evaluations—for positions requiring specialized skills. Existing employee job descriptions can be used to determine temp staffers' suitability for jobs and to measure their performance once they have begun work.

Evaluate potential temporary staffing services. Experts urge business owners to seek out recommendations for temp services from other members of the business community. Once you have targeted specific services for consideration, conduct extensive interviews with management to explain your company's needs and determine their ability to meet those needs. "The natural inclination is to look for the lowest rate," observed *Arkansas Business.* "Yet quality of service is just as important.... A firm that carefully screens and evaluates the skills of all its temporaries will provide you with workers who do the job right the first time."

Establish partnership with the temp service. The temporary services firm your company selects should be able to evaluate the client company's project requirements, time frame, budget, and working environment, and provide temporary employee who have the appropriate skills, availability, and personality to meet its client's needs. Ideally, the temp services firm should be flexible in accepting last-minute requests for temps or in changing temps in the middle of a project if the first one does not work out. Payment rates should be negotiable, based on the skill level required and the quantity of work.

Make you workplace one in which temporary workers can succeed. Companies should make sure that temporary workers are made to feel welcome upon arrival, and that they receive solid training. Do not abandon temporary workers to "sink or swim" on their own.

Monitor temporary staffing initiatives. Put programs in place to monitor and review temp staff performance and determine the impact of the temp service on bottom-line financial performance and customer service.

SEE ALSO *Employee Leasing Programs*

BIBLIOGRAPHY

Butterfield, L.J. "Temp Workers Fill Labor Pool." *Fairfield County Business Journal.* 23 January 2003.

Lee, Mie-Yun. "Temp Choices Put Longtime Mark on Firms." *Crain's Cleveland Business.* 9 September 1996.

Murphy, A. Lee. "Temps Are Back, and Cheaper: Using an agency also can be a time-saver." *Crain's Chicago Business.* 14 February 2005.

Owens, Don L. "Employees Know if You Need Temporary Staffing." *Sacramento Business Journal.* 11 February 2000.

"Staffing Industry Economic Analysis." American Staffing Association. Available from http://www.americanstaffing.net/statistics/economic.cfm. Retrieved on 15 May 2006.

"Temporary Employees Take Up Slack, Save the Day with a Variety of Skills." *Arkansas Business.* 27 December 1999.

Hillstrom, Northern Lights
updated by Magee, ECDI

TESTING LABORATORIES

Testing laboratories are utilized by all manner of businesses to provide objective analytical data on the quality of a product or a process. Some companies look to testing labs for product certification, which can be a significant marketing tool, while others use testing labs to analyze the results of employee drug tests. Still other companies secure the services of environmental testing laboratories to check on water and soil quality before making a major land and/or facility purchase. Whatever the reason, the services offered by testing laboratories are often of great usefulness to businesses in a wide range of industry sectors.

The number and size of testing laboratories operating in the United States and many other industrialized nations has increased significantly over the last few decades. There are myriad reasons for this growth, but observers generally point to the rise in product testing for the bulk of the increase. "It's the significant diversity in products, growth in consumer demand, and the globalization of sourcing that are providing the major thrust behind testing and certification," claimed a testing industry executive in *Appliance Manufacturer.* Experts agree that these product analysis factors have had a significant impact, but several other trends have also been cited as key to the increased reliance on external testing labs. The rising expense of product liability insurance, for instance, has led many companies to utilize testing labs to check out new or "improved" products prior to general release. Small- to mid-sized companies often look to independent labs to serve as their quality control department. Testing laboratories have assumed this role with smaller companies in large measure because of the expense of maintaining comparable facilities in-house. Still, many big firms use them as well in order to secure independent results in areas of quality control and failure analysis.

It should be noted, however, that testing laboratories generally limit themselves to one specific testing area. For example, a company that conducts analysis of employee drug tests will rarely offer services in the realm of environmental analysis; similarly, a company that conducts tests on soil or water will not be of use to a small business owner who is seeking product quality testing services.

ADVANTAGES OF USING A TESTING LABORATORY

Business analysts, laboratory managers, and business owners—for both large and small organizations—agree that there are several significant advantages associated with utilizing the services of an independent testing lab. Three primary reasons that businesses choose off-site independent laboratories are: objectivity, economic considerations, and safety.

Objectivity The independent, off-site testing laboratory focuses on its testing procedures to ensure accurate results. Companies often use the terms "third-party testing" or "tested by an independent laboratory" in advertising claims that guarantee that their test results are objective and free from the influence, guidance or control of interested parties. The independent laboratory exists for only one purpose: to provide objective, analytical data on the quality of a product or process. Testing laboratories invests considerable time, money and effort to ensure this objectivity. In keeping with this agenda, testing labs usually keep copious documentation on the internal processes that they follow to ensure objectivity and accuracy. Such information usually includes requirements for: training of personnel, especially analysts; maintenance and calibration of equipment; standardization and adoption of analytical methods; verification of results; sample recovery and handling procedures; quality control measurement procedures; internal and external proficiency programs and certifications; and accreditations.

Economic Considerations Economics play a central role in the decision to utilize an outside testing laboratory to conduct quality and safety tests. This is especially true for small firms. Indeed, small business owners engaged in establishing or fortifying their enterprises will likely have a host of things on which they will want to spend their money, from new equipment to new advertising campaigns to work force or facility expansion. These businesses may well be better off financially by securing the services of an outside entity, despite the expense involved there, rather than setting up internal testing facilities. Moreover, many businesses that decide to establish internal testing facilities do so without fully factoring in the ancillary costs associated with such activity. Running a testing laboratory includes many costs that may be overlooked in an initial analysis of the undertaking. These include corporate or upper management salaries and benefits; liability insurance; additional professional services (legal or accounting); and finally the opportunity cost associated with investing the funds necessary for such an undertaking in a more profit-making activities.

Safety Many companies engaged in producing potentially hazardous materials prefer to utilize an outside testing firm to minimize the danger of in-house exposure to hazardous agents.

CHOOSING A TESTING LABORATORY

There are many criteria to consider when selecting a testing laboratory. These criteria will be shaped to some degree by the situation of the company making the selection; for example, a smaller company that needs only limited testing done may well make its selection exclusively on the basis of price and quality. But for many companies of varying sizes, several other factors are usually considered as well. It's important to take as much care in selecting a laboratory as one might in selecting a financial advisor—the accuracy of the results may affect decisions worth thousands or even millions of dollars.

There are several basic criteria upon which testing laboratories should be selected:

- Quality and accuracy of testing
- Turnaround time
- Nature of analysis services provided
- Additional services
- Cost
- Certification/accreditation

Quality This is the most vital consideration in judging any testing lab. Small business owners should look for labs that maintain and adhere to documented quality control programs. A good laboratory should be eager to discuss its quality control program with potential clients. It should have a quality assurance manager whose sole responsibility is the implementation of quality control programs and the monitoring of the same. Those quality control programs should also: perform multi-point calibrations; analyze control standards; use analytical methods in testing; test for inadvertent skewing of results; and test for reproducible results.

Turnaround The amount of time necessary to get results on tests from independent labs depends to a large extent on the area in which the labs are involved. Product testing labs, for example, typically take months to complete their tests, and environmental analyses take longer than do medical or clinical tests. Still, most environmental tests can be completed in a week or two, and some environmental, clinical, or medical labs are able to speed up analyses in exchange for additional compensation.

Nature of Services Businesses requiring environmental, clinical, or medical tests should find out about the following before committing to a testing laboratory:

- Can the laboratory supply the necessary sample collection equipment and/or guidance?
- Can the laboratory take the sample itself?
- Do the samples have to be delivered or will the lab pick them up?
- Are you given the opportunity to communicate with personnel directly involved in the testing process?

- If the laboratory can not offer a certain kind of test, will it provide good referrals to other facilities that can do so?

Expense Cost is always a concern, especially for smaller businesses with more modest financial resources. But small business owners should make sure that they fully understand the extent of the testing and other services that they are receiving before signing an agreement.

Certification All testing laboratory candidates should be asked to provide prospective clients with documentation as to the certifications and/or accreditations the lab carries. Certification requirements differs from state to state and from application to application. This is one reason why testing labs often specialize in one or two areas of expertise. For the client, the consequences of a poorly produced testing result may range from worthless data to the potentially staggering costs associated with correcting for actions taken based on incorrect data.

Companies preparing a product for testing and certification should make arrangements with a reliable testing laboratory early in the process, so that all procedural issues can be addressed in advance and so both sides are on the same page regarding such issues as timeline and necessary information exchange. "Communication is probably the most important aspect of dealing with an outside certification agency," stated one executive in *Appliance Manufacturer.*

Future Challenges Several challenges loom for both the testing industry and those companies that utilize its services in the next few years. For example, the rapid expansion of the global marketplace has brought with it a corresponding expansion in the testing and certification offerings of laboratories. Most observers believe that American firms' ability to make inroads into international markets will partially depend on the pace at which the international business community is able to settle on common testing and certification standards. Observers point to the European Community's CE Mark as a key component of any harmonization. (The CE Mark is a visible declaration by the manufacturer that the equipment which is marked complies with all the requirements of all the applicable European Union (EU) directives.) "[Harmonization is] becoming a major thrust mainly because testing and certification are built into the CE-Marking approach created by the Europeans," one American executive told *Appliance Manufacturer.* "The CE Mark is the EU-required safety mark that must be affixed in order for products to travel freely throughout the EU." Most experts agree that the development of one globally accepted mark of certification lies some time off because of the lack of a single international legal system that can ensure compliance.

Another factor that is expected to have a significant impact on independent laboratory practices is the Internet. "The laboratory-services industry is eyeing the Internet as a potential tool for expansion," said Sue Robinson in *Seafood Business*. She noted that many analysts believe that testing companies will become even more vital as products are sold online because such sight-unseen transactions will place an even greater premium on third-party assurances of quality.

BIBLIOGRAPHY

"Circling the Globe." *Appliance Manufacturer*. August 1997.

Cook, Robert C. "A Tale of UL Testing." *Security Management*. July 1995.

Crowe, Michelle. "Testing Lab Provides Other Firms with a Competitive Edge." *The Business Journal*. 9 February 1998.

Feldman, Jonathan. "Justify My Lab — Testing Labs Have Real Costs and Benefits: They're just difficult to quantify. Be prepared to make your pitch in terms that management can understand." *Network Computing*. 25 September 2003.

Litsikas, Mary. "Put Products Through Their Environmental Paces." *Quality*. February 1997.

Morgan, Robert. "Off-Site Labs Right on Target: An Independent Lab May Be Better than Doing Your Own Testing." *Food Processing*. August 1995.

Munzer, Michael. "Research: Outsourcing of R&D, Testing Seen Increasing in Popularity." *American Metal Market*. 14 May 1996.

Robinson, Sue. "Lab Services." *Seafood Business*. December 2000.

Zuckerman, Amy. "Sorting Out the Seals of Approval." *New York Times*. 16 July 2000.

Hillstrom, Northern Lights
updated by Magee, ECDI

TOLL-FREE TELEPHONE NUMBERS

Toll-free telephone numbers are a staple of business efforts to garner new customers and retain existing ones. By utilizing toll-free phone numbers, businesses provide clients and others with a means of communicating with them at no charge; instead, the business that maintains the toll-free line pays all costs associated with the line including incoming calls.

At one time, toll-free telephone numbers were a novelty. Since their inception in 1967, however, the U.S. economy has become increasingly service-based and competitive, creating an environment in which toll-free numbers have come to be expected by customers seeking to make purchases of all kinds of goods and

services. But the popularity of toll-free numbers has created a growing shortage of the numbers in recent years. Indeed, reports indicate that the mid-1990s saw the same number of new toll-free numbers introduced as were assigned during the first two and a half decades of toll-free usage. This increase can be attributed both to improved technologies, which gave rise to the usage of pagers, modems, and cellular phones (many of which have 800 numbers); the ease in obtaining toll-free telephone numbers through promotional packages; 800 number portability from carrier to carrier; and the growth in use of "vanity" numbers (i.e., 800-FLOWERS, 800-HOLIDAY). Another key factor in the explosion of toll-free numbers was an FCC ruling that took effect in 1993, granting companies ownership of their toll-free numbers. "Before that time, a company with an 800 number that wanted to change from AT&T to Spring for long-distance had to have its number deleted from the AT&T database, then see if Sprint had the same toll-free number available, which was unlikely," wrote *Telephony*'s Phil Britt. "So rather than change toll-free numbers, the company would stay with its original long-distance carrier. After the ruling took effect, the toll-free numbers were maintained ... on a centralized database rather than on separate databases by each of the long-distance companies.... That meant lower cost and keener competition."

The popularity and demand for toll-free numbers resulted in the 800 prefix running out. New toll-free telephone numbers were assigned by the Federal Communications Commission (FCC) and now include the original 800 prefix, as well as 888 and 887 (since 1995), 866 (since 1997), 855 (since 2000). For future use are 844, 833, and 822 which have all been reserved but have yet to be activated as of early 2006.

ADVANTAGES OF TOLL-FREE NUMBERS

Toll-free service offers several advantages to small business owners that traditional toll phone service cannot provide. First and foremost, a toll-free telephone number makes your company more accessible to clients, customers, employees, and business associates. It enhances a business's image as a successful, professional company, and many experts contend that it shows clients that customer service is an important component of the business's operating philosophy. Additionally, toll-free service can help lower business costs if you are currently accepting collect calls or are finding it expensive to keep in touch with the home office while on the road. Lastly, toll-free service usually details incoming calls on your statement, with names and numbers allowing easier customer tracking.

Obtaining a toll-free number is a relatively simple process. Consumers can simply request one from their local or long-distance phone company. The cost of securing and maintaining a toll-free line will vary depending on geographic region and the amount of calls that are transmitted through the line. Some small business owners who request vanity toll-free numbers have reported tremendous success with them, but other experts counsel small business owners to avoid vanity numbers altogether, saying that customers may become frustrated by being forced to hunt and peck their way through an alphabetic toll-free number. Firms that do choose to secure a vanity number can eliminate much of this frustration by advertising both the spelled-out and numeric versions of the number.

BIBLIOGRAPHY
Britt, Phil. "Toll-Free Help Is On the Way: But 888 Numbers Must Last a Little Longer." *Telephony.* 17 November 1997.

Delor, Tom. "Vanity Toll-Free Numbers Improve the Effectiveness of Advertising." *Response.* May 2003.

De Marco, Donna. "Residences Can Now Get Toll-Free 1-800 Numbers." *Knight-Ridder/Tribune Business News.* 21 April 1999.

Federal Communications Commission. "What is a Toll-Free Number and How Does it Work?" Available from http://www.fcc.gov/cgb/consumerfacts/tollfree.html. 28 October 2005.

Gable, Robert A. "Establishing a Corporate Toll-Free Strategy." *Telecommunications.* October 1996.

Luove, Seth "Numbers Game." *Forbes.* 25 July 2005.

Hillstrom, Northern Lights
updated by Magee, ECDI

TOTAL PREVENTIVE MAINTENANCE

Total Preventive Maintenance (TPM) is the application of preventive maintenance strategies in an organized and standardized method. Total preventive maintenance is an approach that places the responsibility for routine maintenance on the workers who operate the machinery, rather then employing separate maintenance personnel for that function. Used in many Japanese companies, TPM gives employees a sense of responsibility and awareness of the equipment they use. It has the side benefit of reducing the abuse and misuse of the equipment as operators who are also in charge of the maintenance of equipment are more careful about using it. TPM is increasingly being used in manufacturing environments in the United States. It holds particular appeal for small manufacturers.

The term *maintenance* is used to describe the various efforts businesses make toward keeping their facilities and equipment in good working order. It encompasses both breakdown maintenance—a policy that involves dealing with problems as they occur and attempting to reduce their impact on operations—and preventive maintenance—a policy that involves using such measures as inspecting, cleaning, adjusting, and replacing worn parts to prevent breakdowns from occurring in the first place.

Making the most of maintenance dollars means intelligent planning and good implementation. Preventive maintenance is performed periodically in order to reduce the incidence of equipment failure and the costs associated with it. These costs include disrupted production schedules, idled workers, loss of output, and damage to products or other equipment. Preventive maintenance can be scheduled to avoid interfering with production. Common methods of planning preventive maintenance are based on the passage of time, on the amount of usage the equipment receives, and on an as-needed basis when problems are uncovered through inspections. Ideally, preventive maintenance will take place just before failure occurs in order to maximize the time that equipment is in use between scheduled maintenance activities.

The goal for production managers is to find a balance between preventive maintenance and breakdown maintenance that will minimize the company's overall maintenance costs. Those in charge of the TPM must balance these two factors in order to minimize their combined cost. If maintenance work is done only in a reactive manner, after breakdown occurs, repair costs are very high. Furthermore, hidden costs, such as lost production and the cost of wages while equipment is not in service, must be factored in. So must the cost of injuries or damage to other equipment and facilities or to other units in production. All of the costs associated with these side effects can by minimized by TPM. There is, however, a point at which the cost of preventive maintenance exceeds the benefit.

The decision of how much maintenance to perform involves the age and condition of the equipment, the complexity of technology used, the type of production process, and other factors. For example, managers would tend to perform more preventive maintenance on older machines because new ones have only a slight risk of breakdown and need less work to stay in good condition. It is also important to perform routine maintenance prior to beginning a particularly large or important production run.

In TPM, production employees are trained in both operating procedures and routine maintenance of equipment. They perform regular inspections of the machinery they operate and replace parts that have become worn through use before they fail. Since the production employees spend so much time working with the equipment, they are likely to pick up small signals that a machine is in need of maintenance. Among the main benefits of TPM is that employees gain a more complete understanding of the functioning of the system. TPM also gives them increased input into their own productivity and the quality of their work.

BIBLIOGRAPHY

Brikland, Carol. "PM Optimization: Fleet equipment managers talk about the ways they have successfully managed preventive maintenance." *Fleet Equipment.* March 2006.

Levitt, Joel. *Complete Guide to Preventive and Predictive Maintenance.* Industrial Press, 2002.

Minty, Gordon. *Production Planning and Controlling.* Goodheart-Willcox, 1998.

Smith, Marc, and Glenn Hinchcliff. "Four Task Categories to Understand in Undertaking Preventive Maintenance." *Plant Engineering.* December 2005.

Stevenson, William J. *Production/Operations Management.* Fifth Edition. McGraw-Hill, 1996.

Wireman, Terry. *Preventive Maintenance.* Reston Publishing, 1984.

Hillstrom, Northern Lights
updated by Magee, ECDI

TOTAL QUALITY MANAGEMENT (TQM)

Total Quality Management (TQM) refers to management methods used to enhance quality and productivity in business organizations. TQM is a comprehensive management approach that works horizontally across an organization, involving all departments and employees and extending backward and forward to include both suppliers and clients/customers.

TQM is only one of many acronyms used to label management systems that focus on quality. Other acronyms include CQI (continuous quality improvement), SQC (statistical quality control), QFD (quality function deployment), QIDW (quality in daily work), TQC (total quality control), etc. Like many of these other systems, TQM provides a framework for implementing effective quality and productivity initiatives that can increase the profitability and competitiveness of organizations.

ORIGINS

TQM, in the form of statistical quality control, was invented by Walter A. Shewhart. It was initially implemented at

Western Electric Company, in the form developed by Joseph Juran who had worked there with the method. TQM was demonstrated on a grand scale by Japanese industry through the intervention of W. Edwards Deming—who, in consequence, and thanks to his missionary labors in the U.S. and across the world, has come to be viewed as the "father" of quality control, quality circles, and the quality movement generally.

Walter Shewhart, then working at Bell Telephone Laboratories first devised a statistical control chart in 1923; it is still named after him. He published his method in 1931 as *Economic Control of Quality of Manufactured Product.* The method was first introduced at Western Electric Company's Hawthorn plant in 1926. Joseph Juran was one of the people trained in the technique. In 1928 he wrote a pamphlet entitled *Statistical Methods Applied to Manufacturing Problems.* This pamphlet was later incorporated into the *AT&T Statistical Quality Control Handbook,* still in print. In 1951 Juran published his very influential *Quality Control Handbook.*

W. Edwards Deming, trained as a mathematician and statistician, went to Japan at the behest of the U.S. State Department to help Japan in the preparation of the 1951 Japanese Census. The Japanese were already aware of Shewhart's methods of statistical quality control. They invited Deming to lecture on the subject. A series of lectures took place in 1950 under the auspices of the Japanese Union of Scientists and Engineers (JUSE). Deming had developed a critical view of production methods in the U.S. during the war, particularly methods of quality control. Management and engineers controlled the process; line workers played a small role. In his lectures on SQC Deming promoted his own ideas along with the technique, namely a much greater involvement of the ordinary worker in the quality process and the application of the new statistical tools. He found Japanese executive receptive to his ideas. Japan began a process of implementing what came to be known as TQM. They also invited Joseph Juran to lecture in 1954; Juran was also enthusiastically received.

Japanese application of the method had significant and undeniable results manifesting as dramatic increases in Japanese product quality—and Japanese success in exports. This led to the spread of the quality movement across the world. In the late 1970s and 1980s, U.S. producers scrambled to adopt quality and productivity techniques that might restore their competitiveness. Deming's approach to quality control came to be recognized in the United States, and Deming himself became a sought-after lecturer and author. Total Quality Management, the phrase applied to quality initiatives proffered by Deming and other management gurus, became a staple of American enterprise by the late

1980s. But while the quality movement has continued to evolve beyond its beginnings, many of Deming's particular emphases, particularly those associated with management principles and employee relations, were not adopted in Deming's sense but continued as changing fads, including, for example, the movement to "empower" employees and to make "teams" central to all activities.

TQM PRINCIPLES

Different consultants and schools of thought emphasize different aspects of TQM as it has developed over time. These aspects may be technical, operational, or social/managerial.

The basic elements of TQM, as expounded by the American Society for Quality Control, are 1) policy, planning, and administration; 2) product design and design change control; 3) control of purchased material; 4) production quality control; 5) user contact and field performance; 6) corrective action; and 7) employee selection, training, and motivation.

The real root of the quality movement, the "invention" on which it really rests, is statistical quality control. SQC is retained in TQM in the fourth element, above, "production quality control." It may also be reflected in the third element, "control of purchased material," because SQC may be imposed on vendors by contract.

In a nutshell, this core method requires that quality standards are first set by establishing measurements for a particular item and thus defining what constitutes quality. The measurements may be dimensions, chemical composition, reflectivity, etc.—in effect any measurable feature of the object. Test runs are made to establish divergences from a base measurement (up or down) which are still acceptable. This "band" of acceptable outcomes is then recorded on one or several Shewhart charts. Quality control then begins during the production process itself. Samples are continuously taken and immediately measured, the measurements recorded on the chart(s). If measurements begin to fall outside the band or show an undesirable trend (up or down), the process is stopped and production discontinued until the causes of divergence are found and corrected. Thus SQC, as distinct from TQM, is based on continuous sampling and measurement against a standard and immediate corrective action if measurements deviate from an acceptable range.

TQM is SQC—plus all the other elements. Deming saw all of the elements as vital in achieving TQM. In his 1982 book, *Out of the Crisis,* he contended that companies needed to create an overarching business environment that emphasized improvement of products and services over short-term financial goals—a common

strategy of Japanese business. He argued that if management adhered to such a philosophy, various aspects of business—ranging from training to system improvement to manager-worker relationships—would become far healthier and, ultimately, more profitable. But while Deming was contemptuous of companies that based their business decisions on numbers that emphasized quantity over quality, he firmly believed that a well-conceived system of statistical process control could be an invaluable TQM tool. Only through the use of statistics, Deming argued, can managers know exactly what their problems are, learn how to fix them, and gauge the company's progress in achieving quality and other organizational objectives.

MAKING TQM WORK

In the modern context TQM is thought to require participative management; continuous process improvement; and the utilization of teams. Participative management refers to the intimate involvement of all members of a company in the management process, thus de-emphasizing traditional top-down management methods. In other words, managers set policies and make key decisions only with the input and guidance of the subordinates who will have to implement and adhere to the directives. This technique improves upper management's grasp of operations and, more importantly, is an important motivator for workers who begin to feel like they have control and ownership of the process in which they participate.

Continuous process improvement, the second characteristic, entails the recognition of small, incremental gains toward the goal of total quality. Large gains are accomplished by small, sustainable improvements over a long term. This concept necessitates a long-term approach by managers and the willingness to invest in the present for benefits that manifest themselves in the future. A corollary of continuous improvement is that workers and managers develop an appreciation for, and confidence in, TQM over a period of time.

Teamwork, the third necessary ingredient for TQM, involves the organization of cross-functional teams within the company. This multidisciplinary team approach helps workers to share knowledge, identify problems and opportunities, derive a comprehensive understanding of their role in the overall process, and align their work goals with those of the organization. The modern "team" was once the "quality circle," a type of unit promoted by Deming. Quality circles are discussed elsewhere in this volume.

For best results TQM requires a long-term, co-operative, planned, holistic approach to business, what some have dubbed a "market share" rather than a "profitability" approach. Thus a company strives to control its market by gaining and holding market share through continuous cost and quality improvements—and will shave profits to achieve control. The profitability approach, on the other hand, emphasizes short-term stockholder returns—and the higher the better. TQM thus suits Japanese corporate culture better than American corporate culture. In the corporate environment of the U.S., the short-term is very important; quarterly results are closely watched and impact the value of stocks; for this reason financial incentives are used to achieve short term results and to reward managers at all levels. Managers are therefore much more empowered than employees—despite attempts to change the corporate culture. For these reasons, possibly, TQM has undergone various changes in emphasis so that different implementations of it are sometimes unrecognizable as the same thing. In fact, the quality movement in the U.S. has moved on to other things: the lean corporation (based on just-in-time sourcing), Six Sigma (a quality measure and related programs of achieving it), and other techniques.

PRACTICING TQM

As evident from all of the foregoing, TQM, while emphasizing "quality" in its name, is really a philosophy of management. Quality and price are central in this philosophy because they are seen as effective methods of gaining the customer's attention and holding consumer loyalty. A somewhat discriminating public is thus part of the equation. In an environment where only price matters and consumers meekly put up with the successive removal of services or features in order to get products as cheaply as possible, the strategy will be less successful. Not surprisingly, in the auto sector, where the investment is large and failure can be very costly, the Japanese have made great gains in market share; but trends in other sectors—in retailing, for instance, where labor is imposed on customers through self-service stratagems—a quality orientation seems less obviously rewarding.

For these reasons, the small business looking at an approach to business ideal for its own environment may well adapt TQM if it can see that its clientele will reward this approach. The technique can be applied in service and retail settings as readily as in manufacturing, although measurement of quality will be achieved differently. TQM may, indeed, be a good way for a small business, surrounded by "Big Box" outlets, to reach precisely that small segment of the consuming public that, like the business itself, appreciates a high level of service and high quality products delivered at the most reasonable prices possible.

SEE ALSO *ISO 9000; Quality Circles; Quality Control*

BIBLIOGRAPHY

Basu, Ron, and J. Nevan Wright. *Quality Beyond Six Sigma.* Elsevier, 2003.

Deming, W. Edwards. *Out of the Crisis.* MIT Center for Advanced Engineering Study, 1982.

Juran, Joseph M. *Architect of Quality.* McGraw-Hill, 2004.

"The Life and Contributions of Joseph M. Juran." Carlson School of Management, University of Minnesota. Available from http://part-timemba.csom.umn.edu/Page1275.aspx. Retrieved on 12 May 2006.

Montgomery, Douglas C. *Introduction to Statistical Quality Control.* John Wiley & Sons, 2004.

"Teachings." The W. Edwards Deming Institute. Available from http://www.deming.org/theman/teachings02.html. Retrieved on 12 May 2005.

Youngless, Jay. "Total Quality Misconception." *Quality in Manufacturing.* January 2000.

Hillstrom, Northern Lights
updated by Magee, ECDI

TRADE SHOWS

A trade show is an event where companies that are involved in a certain industry gather to exhibit their products, learn about current trends in their industry, and gain knowledge about their competitors. Trade shows provide opportunities for selling, reinforcing existing business relationships, and launching new products. These events can range in size from small regional shows featuring fewer than two dozen participants to massive national shows, which may draw hundreds of exhibitors and tens of thousands of visitors over a period of several days to a week.

During the 1990s, business analysts, consultants, and participants alike debated whether the surge in electronic commerce and Internet purchasing options might soon render the trade show an irrelevant relic of a bygone business era. But, after a slow down in growth in the first three years of the 21st century—due to post 9/11 decline in travel and a general economic slowdown—the trade show industry has grown steadily. These trade shows accounted for more than $100 billion in annual direct spending and attracted nearly 125 million individuals in 2004. "In many industries, the trade show has become a must-seize marketing opportunity," stated *Business Week*. "It's a time to meet prospective customers, get valuable feedback on your product or service, and close sales."

The continued vitality of trade show exhibitions provide small businesses with excellent opportunities to stand on equal footing with far larger competitors. For small companies with limited marketing budgets, trade shows can serve as an economical and effective pathway to new clients and increased industry visibility. Moreover, trade shows provide entrepreneurs and their small business managers with priceless opportunities to gather information about new industry innovations and competitor products and/or services.

SELECTING THE APPROPRIATE TRADE SHOW

The first step in establishing a presence at a trade show is choosing the right show. Finding the show that best meets your company's needs is crucial, since exhibiting is a costly proposition. Attending the wrong show is a frustrating waste of time and money. In order to avoid committing to a trade show that provides little in the way of new business or contacts, companies can take several precautions:

Crunch the Numbers. Businesses should request detailed statistical and other information on past trade shows from the organizers.

- What was last year's attendance? Was the show visited most by serious buyers or by browsers? Savvy small business owners are aware that some trade shows pad their attendance numbers by counting every person who walks through the doors, including exhibitors and repeat visitors.

- Is there demographic data available on attendees? For example, how old is the average attendee? Male or female? What is his or her income?

- Who else will be exhibiting? Will your competitors be there?

- How stable and successful is the show promoter? Are they experienced in managing a show and delivering an audience, or is this a new, untested exhibition?

- What will the cost be? Expenses include booth space (typically about 25 percent of your expenses); furnishings, equipment, and other exhibit expenses (30 percent); utilities (20 percent); transportation of staff and materials to and from the trade show (15 percent); and pre-show promotions (10 percent). Booths that incorporate new electronic technologies (Webcasts, videoconferencing, etc.) will add to the expense as well. Some companies that exhibit infrequently rent displays—typically portable booths that come in easy-to-assemble kits—rather than invest in booths.

Identify target audience. If you are a small vendor with a new and exciting product seeking national distributors, then the goal would be to attend a national show with high visibility and attendance by all key players. If, on the other hand, you have an existing product that you want to expose to new markets, you would target

potential buyers. For example, if a company decides that one of its software packages—originally designed for and used by the publishing industry—also would be useful to teachers and educators, the sensible strategy would be to attend trade shows aimed at teachers instead of computer software industry shows.

Scout potential shows. Experts counsel entrepreneurs to scout potential trade shows before committing resources to a booth. Business owners can often get an accurate sense of a trade show's value simply by visiting a show, sponsoring a show-related event, or participating in a show-related seminar or conference. All of these avenues can be excellent ways of gauging the quality of the attendees.

Weigh value of exhibiting. Business owners are also urged to consider whether or not he/she should even be exhibiting at trade shows. A very small business with limited funds and a clear business model might decide that the best route to go is direct mail and promotions to a well-defined target audience. On the other hand, a business that is attempting to publicize an established product with low profit margins might well decide that attendance at large national and regional shows with heavy traffic is a good strategic move. And some industry sectors—such as high tech, transportation, communications, and manufacturing—place a heavy emphasis on trade shows.

PREPARING FOR A SUCCESSFUL TRADE SHOW EXHIBIT

Once a small business owner has decided to attend a specific trade show, there are steps that he or she can take to ensure that it is a successful and profitable endeavor. Of course, shows will vary in content, character, and tone from industry to industry, but for the most part, these guidelines can be followed no matter what field your small business is in.

Set specific and measurable goals. Perhaps the most important first step to take is to approach the show with enthusiasm and treat it as a sales opportunity and not a money drain. To take advantage of the opportunity, set specific goals. If the purpose of the show is to gather leads, then set a number in advance that would make the show, in your mind, a success. Compare actual leads gathered to that target number to gauge whether or not the show was worthwhile.

Publicize your involvement. According to the Trade Show Bureau, 45 percent of trade show attendees are drawn to a company's exhibit as the direct result of a personal invitation (via direct mail, e-mail, or telephone), trade journal publicity, or pre-show advertising. A trade show is worthless unless prospective customers visit the booth, and the best way to ensure that those visits occur is to make them aware of your location on the floor. Indeed, industry surveys indicate that about 75 percent of all trade show attendees make out their schedules in advance of arrival. This is an important step, then, so companies should make sure that they allocate sufficient funds for marketing needs.

Prepare personnel. Staffers manning trade show booths should be personable, well-informed, and well-trained to demonstrate and sell your product and/or service. Conduct a pre-show meeting with all key personnel who will be a part of the show, from employees who will spend their time at the booth to the shipper who will send your products to the show and be responsible for set-up. Let each person know what is expected of him or her at the show, and make sure that they know about all pertinent facets of the effort, from the location of promotional brochures to products that should be highlighted. Other assignments, like observation of competitor's booths and materials or breaking down the booth at the end of the show, may be assigned to specific people.

SUCCESSFUL EXHIBITING

"Getting attention on a crowded show floor isn't easy for a newcomer," admitted *Business Week*. "However, you can create a respectable-looking booth inexpensively without being tacky: Buy good quality, three-sided skirts for your tables and portable banner stands for signage, and make flyers on your computer to set on plastic literature racks. Don't clutter the space with lots of give-aways, but do hand out your business card and a small gift with your logo and phone number on it to qualified leads."

There are two types of booths you can set up at a show, with different sales techniques needed for each. One is designed to make sales at the show, so salespeople should be trained in "one interview selling"—quickly identifying a customer's needs and selling him or her your product to meet that need. At such a booth, it is common to have smaller and less expensive items on display and for sale at the show. Larger and more expensive items can be sold at the show and delivered later. All sales at the show should be at a discount over the regular list price, at least 20 percent. If sales are your goal, be prepared to deal with cash, credit cards, and checks.

The other kind of booth is more informational and less sales-oriented. It is primarily designed to meet people, to demonstrate a presence in the industry, to promote customer relations, or to generate new business leads. It can also serve as an excellent meeting point for people you are hoping will invest in your company or join you in a partnership. Since the focus of this type of booth is not sales, the booth personnel should approach

their role differently than that of pure salesperson. Interaction produced valuable feedback. "Unlike the social vacuum of the Web, you can see immediately what customers think of your product," observed *Business Week*.

In the booth itself, try to have at least two people on duty at all times so that visitors receive a healthy measure of personal attention. Arrange the booth to maximize flow of traffic, for overcrowded booths will lead many potential visitors to pass on by. Booth staff should not hover over visitors. Instead, they should encourage browsing and be attentive to signals of interest in products/services from visitors. Make sure everyone who will be manning the booth understands the rules of etiquette at trade shows. There should be no eating or drinking in the booth, and no smoking. Do not spend time talking to the other salespeople in the booth. Assume friendly body posture and look receptive to questions. Perhaps most importantly, do not be in a hurry to get out of the show, since many people wait until the end of the show to make their purchases.

POST-EXHIBITION FOLLOW UP

Small businesses that maintain a quality presence at a trade show are likely to obtain a number of business leads during the show's duration. Yet many companies never follow up on these leads. According to the Trade Show Bureau, as many as 83 percent of exhibitors do not engage in any sort of organized post-exhibition marketing to trade show visitors. This is a terrible oversight that blunts much of the business potential of trade shows. With this in mind, trade show experts offer a variety of tips to make sure that small business owners make the most of their trade show experiences:

- Allocate money wisely. Many analysts believe that businesses should devote at least one third of their total trade show budgets to post-exhibition follow-up.

- Separate hot leads from those that seemed lukewarm or ambivalent and concentrate on those.

- Use a lead sheet to collect information on prospective customers who visit the booth.

- If applicable, send new leads back to the home office every night.

- Make sure that salespeople follow up on a lead within one or two weeks after the show; time is often of the essence in these cases.

- Do not gather more leads than you can follow up on. Analysts contend that many businesses owners or representatives that gather a surplus of leads at trade shows are likely to break promises made (sending literature, following up with an answer to a question, etc.) at the show, which will reflect badly on the company.

- Do not let new leads keep you from servicing existing customers. If you cannot handle new leads without neglecting the existing customer base, then maybe you should not be at the trade show.

ATTENDING A SHOW

Even if a small business owner considers trade shows to be an important part of his or her marketing strategy, there will be some trade shows that are not worth exhibiting at but that would still be useful to attend. For those shows, there are tips to follow to make the most out of the show.

The most important step is to find a good show that is worth the time and trouble it takes to attend. Watch the local papers or industry journals for leads. The biggest shows are typically held in major metropolitan areas, so concentrate on the largest cities in your region. Once you have identified a list of potential shows, contact each and ask for information.

Once you have identified a show to attend, good planning is the key to a successful trip. Make your travel arrangements and submit the show registration far in advance. Allow at least 90 days to avoid snags and delays. Decide in advance what you are hoping to get out of the show—if it is a buying trip, know in advance what you hope to purchase.

Once you arrive at the show, review the list of exhibitors to see which companies interest you the most. Highlight those companies and check them off as you visit each one. Some people like to make one general trip around the entire exhibit floor, highlighting interesting exhibits as they go and making a second, more serious trip to those booths. Be warned that this approach may not be practical for the largest national trade shows, which are often spread over several floors of a huge convention center. Also, do not ignore the seminars that are offered as part of most trade shows. These may be just as useful as the booths in the exhibit hall. The seminars are educational and are also a great way to meet people.

Prepare to spend the entire day at the show. It is often helpful to take a tote bag along with supplies you might need—a notepad and pens, a personal tape recorder to record notes along the way, traveler's checks and credit cards, business credentials (a list of creditors, for example, if this is a buying trip), business cards, and personal identification. The tote bag will also hold all the product literature you gather at the show. Finally, trade show visitors should make certain that they pack comfortable walking shoes. This may sound like a minor

issue, but after eight hours on your feet walking the floor, it will seem like a very important item to remember.

BIBLIOGRAPHY

Cohen, Stephanie. "The Abracadabras of Trade Shows." *The Columbia News Service.* Available from http://jscms.jrn.columbia.edu/cns/2005-04-19/cohen-trademagic. 19 April 2005.

Hart, Michael. "What's first? The Tradeshow or Industry?" *Tradeshow Week.* 6 February 2006.

Lynch, Brenda M., "Showdown: The Rise and Fall of the Tech Show Market: Why Some Survived and Others Short-Circuited." *Meetings & Conventions.* November 2004.

Miller, Steve. *How to Get the Most Out of Trade Shows.* NTC Publishing, 2000.

"Trade Secrets." *Business Week.* 16 August 1999.

U.S. Small Business Administration. Trade Show Bureau. "Trade Shows." Available from http://www.sba.gov/starting_business/marketing/tradeshows.html. Retrieved on 15 May 2006.

Hillstrom, Northern Lights
updated by Magee, ECDI

TRADEMARKS

A trademark is a word, phrase, symbol or design—or a combination of these—adopted and used by a manufacturer or merchant to identify its goods and distinguish them from those manufactured or sold by its competitors. The symbol used to identify a trademarked product are the letters TM presented in upper case, superscript—^{TM}. In recent years, colors (such as John Deere green), sounds (such as the National Broadcasting Company's use of distinctive chimes), and scents have also been registered as trademarks. Service marks, meanwhile, are identical to trademarks except that they identify and distinguish the source of a *service* rather than a product. The term "trademark," however, is commonly utilized to refer to both trademarks and service marks.

Whereas exclusive rights to other items of intellectual property such as copyrights and patents eventually expire, trademark rights can last indefinitely, provided the owner of the mark continues to use it to identify its goods or services. The initial term for a federal trademark registration is ten years, but the owner has the option to renew for additional ten-year terms. The Patent and Trademark Office (PTO), however, has stipulated that between the fifth and sixth years of the initial registration term, the registrant must file an affidavit confirming the need to keep the registration alive. If no affidavit is filed, the registration is canceled, and other companies can pursue the mark for their own use if they so desire.

OTHER TYPES OF TRADEMARKS

In addition to trademarks and service marks, there are two other kinds of marks that generally fit under the generic "trademark" umbrella: certification marks and collective marks.

Certification Mark A certification mark is a mark used in connection with products or services in order to certify the region of origin of those products and services, or to certify some other characteristic of those products and services. Other characteristics may be 1) the origin of the materials used to make a product; 2) the procedures used to assure the quality of the product or service, or 3) the union membership of those involved in the manufacture of a product or service. Examples of certification marks include the UL symbol of Underwriters Laboratories (for quality), "Made in the U.S.A." designations (for place of origin), and the Motion Picture Association of America's movie ratings (for service).

Collective Mark Collective marks are trademarks or service marks used by members of an association, cooperative, or other group. Organizations as diverse as the National Rifle Association, the Big Ten Athletic Conference, and the Sierra Club all utilize collective marks.

TRADEMARK RIGHTS

Trademark rights to an identifying word, phrase, symbol, design, sound, or color can be secured either by actually using the mark in commerce or by registering the mark with the Trademark Office, a division of the Patent and Trademark Office (PTO). "Federal registration [with the PTO] is not required to establish rights in a mark, nor is it required to begin use of a mark," noted the PTO in its booklet, *Basic Facts About Registering a Trademark.* "However, federal registration can secure benefits beyond the rights acquired by merely using a mark. For example, the owner of a federal registration is presumed to be the owner of the mark for the goods and services specified in the registration, and to be entitled to use the mark nationwide." In addition, owners of federal registration for a trademark often enjoy an advantage if legal disputes over use of a trademark arise.

The "Right to Register" According to the Patent and Trademark Office, the ultimate right to register a trademark generally belongs to the first party—whether it is a small business or a large corporation—to use a trademark "in commerce" or file a trademark application with the PTO. ("Commerce" in this situation means commerce regulated by the U.S. Congress, i.e., interstate commerce or commerce between America and another nation; use of a trademark in purely local commerce within a state does not qualify as "use in commerce.")

The "Right to Use" As the PTO itself admitted in its *Basic Facts About Registering a Trademark,* "the right to use a mark can be more complicated to determine. This is particularly true when two parties have begun use of the same or similar marks without knowledge of one another and neither has a federal registration. Only a court can render a decision about the right to use, such as issuing an injunction or awarding damages for infringement." As indicated above, possession of federal registration can be a valuable weapon if a court fight erupts over use of a disputed trademark.

TRADEMARK SEARCHES

A small business owner who has come up with a trademark that he or she wishes to use may want to conduct a trademark search before going to the trouble and expense of sending an application to the PTO. Infringing on another's marks can often happen unintentionally, without copying the marks outright or even being in direct competition with their owner. All that is necessary is to use the same mark or a similar mark in a way that may cause consumers some confusion as to the source or sponsorship of the goods or services. A trademark search can uncover whether the mark (or a similar one) has already been registered with the PTO.

APPLICATIONS FOR FEDERAL REGISTRATION

There are two primary ways in which a U.S. applicant can apply to register his or her trademark with the PTO, depending on whether or not the mark has already been used in commerce. An applicant who has already begun using the trademark in commerce may file with the PTO based on that use. This is commonly known as a "Use" application. If an applicant has not yet used the trademark in question in commerce, but has an honest intention to do so, he or she may file an "Intent-to-Use" application with the PTO. A third option, which can only be used by applicants from outside the United States, allows the applicant to file in the United States based on an application or registration made in another country.

Applications for federal registration should include the following:

- PTO Form 1478—this application, also known as "Trademark/Service Mark Application, Principal Register, with Declaration," should be carefully completed and fully signed.

- Drawing of the mark—this drawing must be included on a separate piece of paper; the specifications for the drawing—and the paper itself—are quite extensive, so make sure that the drawing adheres to all guidelines. If a separate drawing page is not included, then the application will be returned to the applicant without a filing date.

- Filing fee—For current information on the application filing fee for trademarks, call the Patent and Trademark Office or consult its Web site ("Intent-to-Use" applications are more expensive). If the full amount of the fee is not included in the application, then the application will not be considered. Fees are not refundable, even in instances where trademark ownership applications are turned down.

- Specimens—These are actual samples of how the mark is actually used—or will be used—in commerce. For products, examples of acceptable specimens are tags or labels attached to the goods, to the containers in which those goods are packaged, to displays associated with the goods, or to photographs of the goods showing use of the mark on the goods themselves. For services, examples of acceptable specimens include signs, brochures about the services, advertisements for the services, business cards or stationery showing the mark in connection with the services, or photographs which show the mark as it is used either in the rendering or advertising of the services. Each application must include three specimens, but they do not necessarily have to be of three different uses.

PTO Acceptance and Rejection The federal registration of trademarks is governed by the Trademark Act of 1946 (and amendments thereof), the Trademark Rules, 37 C.F.R. Part 2, and the Trademark Manual of Examining Procedure. When the PTO receives an application for trademark registration, it checks the application in accordance with the above-mentioned guidelines. First, the Office reviews it to see if it meets the minimum requirements for receiving a filing date. If it meets those requirements, the PTO assigns it a serial number and sends the applicant a notification of receipt. If the minimum requirements are not met, the entire thing (including the filing fee) is returned to the applicant.

Applications that pass this first stage are then reviewed by an examining attorney at the PTO, who determines if there are any reasons why the mark cannot be registered. A mark may be turned down for any of the following reasons:

- The mark too closely resembles a mark already registered in the PTO.

- The mark's capacity for causing confusion among relevant consumers with goods or services associated with other parties.

- The mark includes a name, portrait, or signature identifying a particular living individual except by his written consent, or the name, signature, or portrait of a deceased president of the United States during the life of his wife, except in instances where the widow has given her written consent to such use.

- The mark includes the flag or coat of arms or other insignia of the United States or any of its states or municipalities, or of any foreign nation, or any simulation thereof.

- The mark has immoral, deceptive, or scandalous connotations.

- The mark disparages or falsely suggests a connection with persons (living or dead), institutions, beliefs, or national symbols.

- The mark brings such persons, institutions, beliefs, or national symbols into contempt or disrepute.

Objections raised during this stage of the review are sent along to the applicant. Remedies that might make the mark acceptable are sometimes suggested in these letters as well. The application will be deemed abandoned if the applicant does not respond within six months of the mailing date of that letter. In cases in which the applicant's response does not sway the PTO examiner to give approval for the mark, the applicant can turn to the PTO's Trademark Trial and Appeal Board.

If there are no objections, or if the applicant overcomes all objections, the examining attorney will approve the mark for publication in the *Official Gazette,* a weekly publication of the PTO. At this point, anyone who believes he or she may be damaged by the registration of the mark has 30 days from the date of publication to file an opposition to registration. An opposition is similar to a formal proceeding in the federal courts, but it is held before the Trademark Trial and Appeal Board. If no opposition is filed, the application enters the next stage of the registration process.

If the application is approved and no opposition is filed, applicants may have a little or a lot to do, depending on their situation. For applicants who filed "Use" applications, most of the work is over. The PTO will register the trademark and issue a registration certificate a few months after the date the mark was published in the *Gazette.* Applicants who filed based on their intent to use the trademark down the line, though, need to attend to several matters to make sure that their rights do not slip away. In situations where it has approved an "Intent-to-Use" application, the PTO issues a Notice of Allowance approximately 12 weeks after the mark was published. After receiving the Notice, the applicant has six months in which to either use the trademark in commerce and submit documentation of that use or request a six-month extension. If the documentation of use—called the Statement of Use—is filed and approved, then the PTO will issue the registration certificate for the trademark.

Even if the PTO grants an applicant a trademark registration, business experts warn that such registration only provides protection to the owner in the United States and its territories. "If the owner of a mark wishes to protect a mark in other countries, the owner must seek protection in each country separately under the relevant laws," warned the PTO in its *Basic Facts About Registering a Trademark*. "The PTO cannot provide information or advice concerning protection in other countries."

SEE ALSO *Brands and Brand Names; Copyrights; Corporate Logos*

BIBLIOGRAPHY

"First Circuit Decision Reminds Trademark Owners of the Importance of Claiming Incontestability for Registered Trademarks." *Mondaq Business Briefing.* 3 May 2006.

Miller, Arthur R., and Michael H. Davis. *Intellectual Property: Patents, Trademarks and Copyright.* West/Wadsworth, 2000.

U.S. Patent and Trademark Office. *Basic Facts About Registering a Trademark.* 1995.

U.S. Small Business Administration. Field, Thomas. *Avoiding Patent, Trademark and Copyright Problems.* 1992.

The Value of Good Idea: Copyright, Trademarks and Intellectual Property in an Information Economy. Silver Lake Publishing, 2002.

Hillstrom, Northern Lights
updated by Magee, ECDI

TRAINING AND DEVELOPMENT

Training and development describes the formal, ongoing efforts that are made within organizations to improve the performance and self-fulfillment of their employees through a variety of educational methods and programs. In the modern workplace, these efforts have taken on a broad range of applications—from instruction in highly specific job skills to long-term professional development. In recent years, training and development has emerged as a formal business function, an integral element of strategy, and a recognized profession with distinct theories and methodologies. More and more companies of all sizes have embraced "continual learning" and other

aspects of training and development as a means of promoting employee growth and acquiring a highly skilled work force. In fact, the quality of employees and the continual improvement of their skills and productivity through training, are now widely recognized as vital factors in ensuring the long-term success and profitability of small businesses. "Create a corporate culture that supports continual learning," counseled Charlene Marmer Solomon in *Workforce*. "Employees today must have access to continual training of all types just to keep up.... If you don't actively stride against the momentum of skills deficiency, you lose ground. If your workers stand still, your firm will lose the competency race."

For the most part, the terms "training" and "development" are used together to describe the overall improvement and education of an organization's employees. However, while closely related, there are important differences between the terms that center around the scope of the application. In general, training programs have very specific and quantifiable goals, like operating a particular piece of machinery, understanding a specific process, or performing certain procedures with great precision. Developmental programs, on the other hand, concentrate on broader skills that are applicable to a wider variety of situations, such as decision making, leadership skills, and goal setting.

TRAINING IN SMALL BUSINESSES

Implementation of formal training and development programs offers several potential advantages to small businesses. For example, training helps companies create pools of qualified replacements for employees who may leave or be promoted to positions of greater responsibility. It also helps ensure that companies will have the human resources needed to support business growth and expansion. Furthermore, training can enable a small business to make use of advanced technology and to adapt to a rapidly changing competitive environment. Finally, training can improve employees' efficiency and motivation, leading to gains in both productivity and job satisfaction. According to the U.S. Small Business Administration (SBA), small businesses stand to receive a variety of benefits from effective training and development of employees, including reduced turnover, a decreased need for supervision, increased efficiency, and improved employee morale. All of these benefits are likely to contribute directly to a small business's fundamental financial health and vitality

Effective training and development begins with the overall strategy and objectives of the small business. The entire training process should be planned in advance with specific company goals in mind. In developing a training strategy, it may be helpful to assess the company's customers and competitors, strengths and weaknesses, and any relevant industry or societal trends. The next step is to use this information to identify where training is needed by the organization as a whole or by individual employees. It may also be helpful to conduct an internal audit to find general areas that might benefit from training, or to complete a skills inventory to determine the types of skills employees possess and the types they may need in the future. Each different job within the company should be broken down on a task-by-task basis in order to help determine the content of the training program.

The training program should relate not only to the specific needs identified through the company and individual assessments, but also to the overall goals of the company. The objectives of the training should be clearly outlined, specifying what behaviors or skills will be affected and how they relate to the strategic mission of the company. In addition, the objectives should include several intermediate steps or milestones in order to motivate the trainees and allow the company to evaluate their progress. Since training employees is expensive, a small business needs to give careful consideration to the question of which employees to train. This decision should be based on the ability of the employee to learn the material and the likelihood that they will be motivated by the training experience. If the chosen employees fail to benefit from the training program or leave the company soon after receiving training, the small business has wasted its limited training funds.

The design of training programs is the core activity of the training and development function. In recent years, the development of training programs has evolved into a profession that utilizes systematic models, methods, and processes of instructional systems design (ISD). ISD describes the systematic design and development of instructional methods and materials to facilitate the process of training and development and ensure that training programs are necessary, valid, and effective. The instructional design process includes the collection of data on the tasks or skills to be learned or improved, the analysis of these skills and tasks, the development of methods and materials, delivery of the program, and finally the evaluation of the training's effectiveness.

Small businesses tend to use two general types of training methods, on-the-job techniques and off-the-job techniques. On-the-job training describes a variety of methods that are applied while employees are actually performing their jobs. These methods might include orientations, coaching, apprenticeships, internships, job instruction training, and job rotation. The main advantages of on-the-job techniques is that they are highly practical, and employees do not lose working time while they are learning. Off-the-job training, on the other hand, describes a number of training methods that are delivered to employees outside of the regular work environment, though often during working hours. These techniques might include lectures, conferences, case studies, role playing, simulations, film or television presentations, programmed instruction, or special study.

On-the-job training tends to be the responsibility of supervisors, human resources professionals, or more experienced co-workers. Consequently, it is important for small businesses to educate their seasoned employees in training techniques. In contrast, off-the-job tends to be handled by outside instructors or sources, such as consultants, chambers of commerce, technical and vocational schools, or continuing education programs. Although outside sources are usually better informed as to effective training techniques than company supervisors, they may have a limited knowledge of the company's products and competitive situation. Another drawback to off-the-job training programs is their cost. These programs can run into the multi thousand dollar per participant level, a cost that may make them prohibitive for many small businesses.

Actual administration of the training program involves choosing an appropriate location, providing necessary equipment, and arranging a convenient time. Such operational details, while seemingly minor components of an overall training effort, can have a significant effect on the success of a program. In addition, the training program should be evaluated at regular intervals while it is going on. Employees' skills should be compared to the predetermined goals or milestones of the training program, and any necessary adjustments should be made immediately. This ongoing evaluation process will help ensure that the training program successfully meets its expectations.

COMMON TRAINING METHODS

While new techniques are under continuous development, several common training methods have proven highly effective. Good continuous learning and development initiatives often feature a combination of several different methods that, blended together, produce one effective training program.

Orientations Orientation training is vital in ensuring the success of new employees. Whether the training is conducted through an employee handbook, a lecture, or a one-on-one meeting with a supervisor, newcomers should receive information on the company's history and strategic position, the key people in authority at the company, the structure of their department and how it contributes to the mission of the company, and the company's employment policies, rules, and regulations.

Lectures A verbal method of presenting information, lectures are particularly useful in situations when the goal is to impart the same information to a large number of people at one time. Since they eliminate the need for individual training, lectures are among the most cost-effective training methods. But the lecture method does have some drawbacks. Since lectures primarily involve one-way communication, they may not provide the most interesting or effective training. In addition, it may be difficult for the trainer to gauge the level of understanding of the material within a large group.

Case Study The case method is a non-directed method of study whereby students are provided with practical case reports to analyze. The case report includes a thorough description of a simulated or real-life situation. By analyzing the problems presented in the case report and developing possible solutions, students can be encouraged to think independently as opposed to relying upon the direction of an instructor. Independent case analysis can be supplemented with open discussion with a group. The main benefit of the case method is its use of real-life situations. The multiplicity of problems and possible solutions provide the student with a practical learning experience rather than a collection of abstract knowledge and theories that may be difficult to apply to practical situations.

Role Playing In role playing, students assume a role outside of themselves and play out that role within a group. A facilitator creates a scenario that is to be acted out by the participants under the guidance of the facilitator. While the situation might be contrived, the interpersonal relations are genuine. Furthermore, participants receive immediate feedback from the facilitator and the scenario itself, allowing better understanding of their own behavior. This training method is cost effective and is often applied to marketing and management training.

Simulations Games and simulations are structured competitions and operational models that emulate real-life scenarios. The benefits of games and simulations include the improvement of problem-solving and decision-making sskills, a greater understanding of the organizational whole, the ability to study actual problems, and the power to capture the student's interest.

Computer-Based Training Computer-based training (CBT) involves the use of computers and computer-based instructional materials as the primary medium of instruction. Computer-based training programs are designed to structure and present instructional materials and to facilitate the learning process for the student. A main benefit of CBT is that it allows employees to learn at their own pace, during convenient times. Primary uses of CBT include instruction in computer hardware, software, and operational equipment. The last is of particular importance because CBT can provide the student with a simulated experience of operating a particular piece of equipment or machinery while eliminating the risk of damage to costly equipment by a trainee or even a novice user. At the same time, the actual equipment's operational use is maximized because it need not be utilized as a training tool. The use of computer-based training enables a small business to reduce training costs while improving the effectiveness of the training. Costs are reduced through a reduction in travel, training time, downtime for operational hardware, equipment damage, and instructors. Effectiveness is improved through standardization and individualization.

Web-based training (WBT) is an increasingly popular form of CBT. The greatly expanding number of organizations with Internet access through high-speed connections has made this form of CBT possible. By providing the training material on a Web page that is accessible through any Internet browser, CBT is within reach of any company with access to the Web. The terms "online courses" and "web-based instruction" are sometimes used interchangeably with WBT.

Self-Instruction Self-instruction describes a training method in which the students assume primary responsibility for their own learning. Unlike instructor- or facilitator-led instruction, students retain a greater degree of control regarding topics, the sequence of learning, and the pace of learning. Depending on the structure of the instructional materials, students can achieve a higher degree of customized learning. Forms of self-instruction include programmed learning, individualized instruction, personalized systems of instruction, learner-controlled instruction, and correspondence study. Benefits include a strong support system, immediate feedback, and systematization.

Audiovisual Training Audiovisual training methods include television, films, and videotapes. Like case studies, role playing, and simulations, they can be used to expose employees to "real world" situations in a time- and cost-effective manner. The main drawback of audiovisual training methods is that they cannot be customized for a particular audience, and they do not allow participants to ask questions or interact during the presentation of material.

Team-Building Exercises Team building is the active creation and maintenance of effective work groups with similar goals and objectives. Not to be confused with the informal, ad-hoc formation and use of teams in the workplace, team building is a formal process of building work teams and formulating their objectives and goals, usually facilitated by a third-party consultant. Team building is commonly initiated to combat poor group dynamics, labor-management relations, quality, or productivity. By recognizing the problems and difficulties associated with the creation and development of work teams, team building provides a structured, guided process whose benefits include a greater ability to manage complex projects and processes, flexibility to respond to changing situations, and greater motivation among team members. Team building may include a broad range of different training methods, from outdoor immersion exercises to brainstorming sessions. The main drawback to formal team building is the cost of using outside experts and taking a group of people away from their work during the training program.

Apprenticeships and Internships Apprenticeships are a form of on-the-job training in which the trainee works with a more experienced employee for a period of time, learning a group of related skills that will eventually qualify the trainee to perform a new job or function. Apprenticeships are often used in production-oriented positions. Internships are a form of apprenticeship that combines on-the-job training under a more experienced employee with classroom learning.

Job Rotation Another type of experience-based training is job rotation, in which employees move through a series of jobs in order to gain a broad understanding of the requirements of each. Job rotation may be particularly useful in small businesses, which may feature less role specialization than is typically seen in larger organizations.

APPLICATIONS OF TRAINING PROGRAMS

While the applications of training and development are as various as the functions and skills required by an organization, several common training applications can be distinguished, including technical training, sales training, clerical training, computer training, communications training, organizational development, career development, supervisory development, and management development.

Technical training describes a broad range of training programs varying greatly in application and difficulty. Technical training utilizes common training methods for instruction of technical concepts, factual information, and procedures, as well as technical processes and principles.

Sales training concentrates on the education and training of individuals to communicate with customers in a persuasive manner. Sales training can enhance the employee's knowledge of the organization's products, improve his or her selling skills, instill positive attitudes, and increase the employee's self-confidence. Employees are taught to distinguish the needs and wants of the customer, and to persuasively communicate the message that the company's products or services can effectively satisfy them.

Clerical training concentrates on the training of clerical and administrative support staffs, which have taken on an expanded role in recent years. With the increasing reliance on computers and computer applications, clerical training must be careful to distinguish basic skills from the ever-changing computer applications used to support these skills. Clerical training increasingly must instill improved decision-making skills in these employees as they take on expanded roles and responsibilities.

Computer training teaches the effective use of the computer and its software applications, and often must address the basic fear of technology that most employees face and identify and minimize any resistance to change that might emerge. Furthermore, computer training must anticipate and overcome the long and steep learning curves that many employees will experience. To do so, such training is usually offered in longer, uninterrupted modules to allow for greater concentration, and structured training is supplemented by hands-on practice. This area of training is commonly cited as vital to the fortunes of most companies, large and small, operating in today's technologically advanced economy.

Communications training concentrates on the improvement of interpersonal communication skills, including writing, oral presentation, listening, and reading. In order to be successful, any form of communications training should be focused on the basic improvement of skills and not just on stylistic considerations. Furthermore, the training should serve to build on present skills rather than rebuilding from the ground up. Communications training can be taught separately or can be effectively integrated into other types of training, since it is fundamentally related to other disciplines.

Organizational development (OD) refers to the use of knowledge and techniques from the behavioral sciences to analyze an existing organizational structure and implement changes in order to improve organizational effectiveness. OD is useful in such varied areas as the alignment of employee goals with those of the organization, communications, team functioning, and decision making. In short, it is a development process with an organizational focus to achieve the same goals as other training and development activities aimed at individuals.

OD practitioners commonly practice what has been termed "action research" to effect an orderly change which has been carefully planned to minimize the occurrence of unpredicted or unforeseen events. Action research refers to a systematic analysis of an organization to acquire a better understanding of the nature of problems and forces within it.

Career development refers to the formal progression of an employee's position within an organization by providing a long-term development strategy and designing training programs to achieve this strategy as well as individual goals. Career development represents a growing concern for employee welfare and their long-term needs. For the individual, it involves the description of career goals, the assessment of necessary action, and the choice and implementation of necessary steps. For the organization, career development represents the systematic development and improvement of employees. To remain effective, career development programs must allow individuals to articulate their desires. At the same time, the organization strives to meet those stated needs as much as possible by consistently following through on commitments and meeting the employee expectations raised by the program.

Management and supervisory development involves the training of managers and supervisors in basic leadership skills, enabling them to effectively function in their positions. For managers, training initiatives are focused on providing them with the tools to balance the effective management of their employee resources with the strategies and goals of the organization. Managers learn to develop their employees effectively by helping employees learn and change, as well as by identifying and preparing them for future responsibilities. Management development may also include programs for developing decision-making skills, creating and managing successful work teams, allocating resources effectively, budgeting, business planning, and goal setting.

BIBLIOGRAPHY

Jacob, Ronal L. *Structured On-The-Job Training*. Berrett-Koehler Publishers, March 2003.

Kim, Nancy J. "Continuing Education is No Longer an Option." *Puget Sound Business Journal*. 15 August 1997.

Solomon, Charlene Marmer. "Continual Learning: Racing Just to Keep Up." *Workforce*. April 1999.

U.S. Small Business Administration. Roberts, Gary, Gary Seldon, and Carlotta Roberts. *Human Resources Management*. n.d.

Hillstrom, Northern Lights
updated by Magee, ECDI

TRANSACTION PROCESSING

Transaction process is a term that refers to the adding, changing, deleting, or looking up of a record in a data file or database by entering the data at a terminal or workstation. Most transaction processing systems also include a method of ensuring that all the information entered as a transaction is simultaneously saved. When a large number of transactions are taken and then stored to be dealt with at a later time, the process is known as batch processing. Different examples of transaction processing include automated teller machines, credit card authorizations, online bill payments, self-checkout stations at grocery stores, the trading of stocks over the Internet, and various other forms of electronic commerce.

At the center of most commercial interactions is a transaction so, every business has to deal with its commercial transactions in some form. How a company decides to manage these transactions can be an important factor in its success. As a business grows, the number of transactions it must manage usually grows as well. Careful planning must be done in order to ensure that transaction management does not become too complex. Transaction processing is a tool that can help growing businesses deal with their increasing number of transactions.

TRANSACTION PROCESSING AND THE INTERNET

One place where transaction processing has made a big splash is on the Internet. The advent of online technology has made the international distribution of goods and information a quick and often simple process. Customers have grown accustomed to placing orders online. The emergence of features like secure servers, one-click shopping, and tracking of packages over the Internet have helped make them feel more at ease with the process.

Transaction processing on the Internet includes several options for those who want to use a credit card or a checking account to pay for goods that do not originate from a typical e-business site, almost as if it is digital cash. One example of this type of service is PayPal, (www.paypal.com) the world's first, successful, instant and secure online payment service. With PayPal, anyone can register to send and receive payments through the Internet. This service has gained most of its popularity on auction sites like eBay, but can also be used for simple transactions between any two people in the world that have access to the Internet. Users have found this to be a safe, fast, easy, convenient, and inexpensive way to distribute money in the digital world. PayPal's service is free to most consumers, although there can be small service fees to businesses that decide to use it for a large number of transactions. PayPal only requires that users have either a valid credit card or active checking account.

Retailers have also enjoyed the benefits of jumping on the Internet bandwagon to help with the processing of their transactions. A company can set up a web site through which its customers can purchase merchandise and the order can be taken, fulfilled, and processed by a subcontractor. Yahoo, for example, handles the distribution of products for many online companies. If a business decides to go this route, it should investigate thoroughly the shipping charges that a particular firm will charge to send its goods. Many times, the shipping charges for products purchased over the Internet become inflated, causing consumers to become annoyed and even angry, feeling as if the shipping charges are a hidden extra fee. Any business must work to avoid losing a customer due to the poor service provided by a subcontractor. Other possible problems that often plague the online world—such as computer system outages, slow servers, and security issues—should also be considered.

THE TRANSACTION PROCESSING PERFORMANCE COUNCIL

The Transaction Processing Performance Council (TPC) is a non-profit corporation that defines transaction processing and provides database benchmarks which it shares with the industry. The TPC emerged in the early 1980s just as ATMs, self-service, self-pay gasoline pumps, and other electronic payment devices began to gain in popularity. The industry has grown since then and now the online transaction processing industry registers billions of dollars in yearly sales transactions. The TPC also monitors and measures transaction processing and database performance in terms of how many transactions a system can perform in a given amount of time. Many businesses can benefit from the work of the TPC, including retail stores, online businesses, electronic stock brokers, and travel agencies. Their dedication will only ensure that the quality of conducting transactions remains at the highest possible level. For more information on what they do, visit http://www.tpc.org.

SMALL BUSINESSES AND TRANSACTION PROCESSING

The growth in the transaction processing industry portends good things for small businesses. A company that distributes and manages coin operated video games and vending machines, for example, can expand its business by teaming up with a transaction processing firm that will help allow the machines to accept credit cards. A small antique store can increase business by marketing its goods over the Internet and then accepting payments through PayPal or another similar service. As is the case

with most sound business decisions, managers should acquire proper education and knowledge about transaction processing before committing to it. It is, after all, just a new way to manage commercial transactions.

SEE ALSO *Internet Payment Systems*

BIBLIOGRAPHY
Epper Hoffman, Karen. "The Changing Face of EBPP: As Electronic Billing Becomes a Maturing Market, New Players are Waiting in the Wings to Make Their Mark." *Bank Technology News.* December 2001.

Gomolski, Barbara. "Automated Billing: Have We Gone Too Far?" *Computerworld.* 20 March 2006.

Hapgood, Fred. "Online Transaction Processing Takes a Bow." *CIO.* 15 February 2001.

Hunt, Clair. "In the Blink of an Eye." *Computer Weekly.* 31 March 1994.

Overton, Rick. "Signed, Sealed, Delivered … Online." *PC World.* November 1999.

Hillstrom, Northern Lights
updated by Magee, ECDI

TRANSPORTATION

Transportation concerns the movement of products from a source—such as a plant, factory, or workshop—to a destination—such as a warehouse, customer, or retail store. Transportation may take place by air, water, rail, road, pipeline, or cable routes, using planes, boats, trains, trucks, and telecommunications equipment as the means of transportation. The goal for any business owner is to minimize transportation costs while also meeting demand for products. Transportation costs generally depend upon the distance between the source and the destination, the means of transportation chosen, and the size and quantity of the product to be shipped. In many cases, there are several sources and many destinations for the same product, which adds a significant level of complexity to the problem of minimizing transportation costs. Indeed, the United States boasts the world's largest and most complex transportation system, with four million miles' worth of roads, a railroad network that could circle the earth almost seven times if laid out in a straight line, and enough oil and gas lines to circle the globe 56 times.

The decisions a business owner must make regarding transportation of products are closely related to a number of other distribution issues. For example, the accessibility of suitable means of transportation factors into decisions regarding where best to locate a business or facility. The means of transportation chosen will also affect decisions regarding the form of packing used for products and the size or frequency of shipments made. Although transportation costs may be reduced by sending larger shipments less frequently, it is also necessary to consider the costs of holding extra inventory. The interrelationship of these decisions means that successful planning and scheduling can help business owners to save on transportation costs.

BASIC MEANS OF TRANSPORTATION

Transportation is divided into modes based on the type of transportation used—waterborne, rail, road-based, air, and pipeline. In turn "single-mode" and "multiple-mode" materials movements are recorded, the latter type sometimes referred to as "intermodal transport." This mixed mode of transport involves two or more modes to make a shipment. An example is oil transport to a port facility by tanker followed by pipeline transport of the crude to a refinery. In the Age of Information, as we like to call our times, we also transport data using wire or wireless methods; but while "data deliveries" are essentially equivalent in some businesses to "shipments," as yet data transfer is not routinely considered to be transportation.

Water, rail, and truck transportation modes are each capable of transporting anything moving in commerce *physically,* but these modes have different levels of access to customers, different speeds, and thus carry different types of cargo. Barges very rarely carry packaged-good shipments and trucks almost never move bulk commodities except over very short distances. Air transport is limited in transporting very bulky and very heavy objects, but air transport is ideal for light packages and for items that must be transported rapidly; pipelines move liquids and gases or other substances that behave in an analogous way but cannot be used in other applications.

Air Transport Air transportation offers the advantage of speed and can be used for long-distance transport. However, air is also the most expensive means of transportation; it is generally used only for smaller items of relatively high value—such as electronic equipment—and items for which the speed of arrival is important—such as perishable goods. Air transport is centralized at airports; the lack of landing sites, even for helicopters, makes air transport a hub-to-hub method. The U.S. Department of Transportation (DOT) therefore considers ancillary transportation associated with air shipments part of air shipments, such as truck or rail delivery of goods to and from airports to final destinations. Despite what has been said about limitations on weight and size,

as these relate to air transportation, an astonishing variety of goods have been flown occasionally under certain circumstances, including very big and heavy equipment—disassembled into appropriate and transportable sub-groupings.

Railways The rail transportation network in the United States included 121,400 major rail lines in the mid-2000s. Trains are ideally suited for shipping bulk products and can be adapted to meet specific product needs through the use of specialized cars—i.e., tankers for liquids, refrigerated cars for perishables, and cars fitted with ramps for automobiles. Roughly two-thirds of all freight moved by rail consists of coal shipments in dedicated trains that run from points of coal mining to electric utilities that burn the coal.

Rail transportation is typically used for long-distance shipping. Less expensive than air transportation, it offers about the same delivery speed as trucks over long distances and exceeds transport speeds via marine waterways. In fact, deregulation and the introduction of freight cars with larger carrying capacities has enabled rail carriers to make inroads in several areas previously dominated by motor carriers. But access to the rail network remains a problem for many businesses.

Motor Carriers Unless a business is located directly at a sea or river port or is served by a railroad siding, it is going to receive its inputs, and ship its products, using truck transportation over the highway network. Transport systems designed around trucks are the most flexible—because a mix of small and large equipment can be readily assembled and deployed and because all points are accessible to trucks. For this reason, by the last quarter of the 20th century, trucking became the dominant mode of transportation. The chief limitations of transport by motor carrier is that large bulk shipments of commodities are expensive to move because, in effect, each railcar equivalent of load requires its own engine and driver. Commodity movements by truck are therefore very limited.

Water Transport Water transportation is the least expensive and slowest mode of freight transport. It is generally used to transport heavy products over long distances when speed is not an issue. Although accessibility is a problem with ships—because they are necessarily limited to coastal area or major inland waterways—piggybacking is possible using either trucks or rail cars. However, industry observers note that port terminal accessibility to land-based modes of transportations is lacking in many regions. The main advantage of water transportation is that it can move products all over the world.

Pipelines Pipelines are used predominantly to transport natural gas and oil. To move such materials long distances in pipes, booster stations must be built at intervals which receive the gas, recompress it, and push it back into the pipeline or receive the liquid and pump it on its way under higher pressure. Chemicals and slurries (e.g., powdered coal in water) can also be transported in pipelines. The most extensive network consists of natural gas pipelines, comprising around 276,000 miles of transmission lines from which around 920,000 miles of distribution lines carry gas to users. In its overall freight statistics, the DOT includes only petroleum shipments by pipeline.

FREIGHT VALUES AND MODAL SHARES

In its most recent (2006) comprehensive report on transportation modes, the Department of Transportation showed data for the year 2002. The value of all freight shipped that year was $13,052 billion, amounted to 19,487 million tons, and the total movement was 4,409 billion ton-miles. A ton-mile is 1 ton of freight moved 1 mile.

Using ton-miles as the overall measurement, 92.4 percent of all freight moved by single modes, 5.3 percent moved by two or more modes (intermodally), and 2.3 percent of freight moved by modes the DOT could not determine. In order of rank, the known modes had the following shares of total transportation as measured by ton-mile: truck (34.4 percent), rail (31.1), pipeline carrying oil (15.6 percent), water (11.0), mixed combinations (3.7), truck and rail combined (1.1), parcel, postal, or courier (0.5), and air transport (0.3) percent.

SEE ALSO *Physical Distribution*

BIBLIOGRAPHY
"Class I Railroad Statistics." Association of American Railroads. Available from http://www.aar.org/PubCommon/ Documents.AboutTheIndustry/Statistics.pdf. Retrieved on 30 April 2006.

U.S. Department of Transportation. *Freight in America.* 2006.

Hillstrom, Northern Lights
updated by Magee, ECDI

TRANSPORTATION OF EXPORTS

An important part of the international trade process for exporters of any size is ensuring that the goods that are shipped reach their destinations intact and in a timely fashion. Appropriate packaging and proper documentation are essential in meeting these goals.

INTERNATIONAL FREIGHT TRANSPORTATION OPTIONS

The exporter's options for transporting goods are dictated in large measure by their final destination. American exporters preparing goods for shipment to Mexico or Canada, for instance, will often make arrangements to transport their merchandise over land routes via truck or rail, while exports that are headed for destinations unreachable via land routes have to be transported by air or water.

Exporters who are faced with the choice of air or water modes of transport need to be cognizant of the advantages and disadvantages of those two options. While shipping by water is generally less expensive than transporting by air, the difference in cost is narrowed somewhat by ancillary costs associated with sea transport, such as the cost of transporting goods to the dock. Merchandise shipped over water also takes longer to reach its ultimate destination, and since some export transactions do not require the importer to pay until they are in possession of the goods, exporters in immediate need of cash infusions will need to weigh this factor carefully.

Of course, the sheer size and tonnage of some export shipments render air transportation impractical.

EXPORT PACKAGING

Consultants to companies who engage in exporting note that the merchandise they ship will generally be subject to more handling and potentially damaging forces during transport than will goods headed for domestic destinations. Intelligent packaging, then, is a key component of the exporting process. Ideally, exporters should use a packaging approach that minimizes the cost of transportation while simultaneously ensuring that the goods reach their destination intact. Many small exporting companies that do not have the financial or operating resources to take care of packaging themselves utilize firms that specialize in providing such services.

Exporting firms need to keep abreast of labeling and marking requirements on goods intended for international destinations as well. Pharmaceutical products, for instance, require special labeling that varies from country to country. In addition, many countries enforce regulations requiring that imported goods bear the name of the country of origin on the outside of their packaging. Packaging containing merchandise intended for foreign ports also typically includes markings indicating the height and weight of the packages, as well as any additional handling instructions.

NECESSARY EXPORT DOCUMENTS

The documentation required for international trade is quite extensive (and potentially confusing), but exporters need to make certain that they have their papers in proper order if they wish to avoid potentially damaging delays in shipment. Documents required for the export of goods include the following:

Export License. While most merchandise can be shipped to overseas customers without benefit of an actual license, some goods are subject to additional regulations and require an Individually Validated Export License (IVL). "Should your particular export be subject to export controls," explained the Small Business Administration, "then a 'validated' license must be obtained. In general, your export would require a 'validated' license if export of the goods would: threaten United States national security; affect certain foreign policies of the United States; or create short supply in domestic markets."

Shipper's Export Declaration (SED). This important document is required for mail shipments of $500 or more, all shipments of more than $2,500 value, and any shipment that is covered by an IVL. SEDs are utilized by the U.S. Bureau of the Census to track export trends in the United States.

Commercial Invoice. The commercial invoice is used by both exporters and importers. Exporters use the document as proof of ownership and an aid in securing payment for goods delivered, while importers use it to confirm that the merchandise they have received matches what they ordered. Commercial invoices are also used by Customs officers to figure the correct duty on the goods being imported, so U.S. exporters generally provide translated copies of the invoice when shipping goods to destinations for which English is not the primary language spoken.

Consular Invoice. This kind of invoice serves the same general purpose as the commercial invoice, but it must be worded in the language of the nation for which the goods are intended. Consular invoices are so named because they can be obtained from the destination country's consulate.

Bill of Lading. This document serves as evidence of ownership of the goods being exported, and also specifies the responsibilities of the transporting company. Two types of ocean bills of lading can be used. The first, known as the straight bill of lading, provides for delivery of merchandise *only* to the person named in the bill of lading. Under the second bill of lading option, called the shipper's order, goods can be delivered not only to the person named in the bill but also to other designated people. Under the latter option, financing institutions are empowered to take possession of the goods being exported if the buyer defaults; they retain title on the merchandise until all payments and conditions of sale have been fulfilled. For exports that are transported by air, documents known as air waybills serve the same general purpose.

Certificate of Origin. Some countries require shipments of goods from foreign ports to include certificates that indicate where the merchandise originated. In instances wherein the importing country has trade agreements in place with the country that is doing the exporting, lower tariffs on those goods can sometimes be imposed.

Export Packing List. This highly involved document provides a detailed description of the contents being shipped. It covers the material in each individual package, providing information such as individual net, legal, tare and gross weights and measurements for each package. These data are typically presented in both metric and U.S. measurement figures. Export packing lists are used by the shipper (or the freight forwarder) to confirm the shipment's contents and figure the total weight and volume of the shipment.

Inspection Certificate. This documentation is bestowed by independent inspection firms, whose services are required when foreign purchasers ask for independent corroboration that the goods meet agreed-upon specifications.

Insurance Certificate. Some international transactions require the exporting firm to provide insurance on the shipment. The insurance certificate describes the type and amount of merchandise contained in the shipment, and confirms that the shipment has been insured.

Inland Bill of Lading. These documents—known as "waybills on rail" in the railroad industry and "pro-forma" bills within the trucking industry—provide information on the inland transportation of goods and the port that will eventually send the exporter's goods on their way.

Dock Receipt. This paper is the international carrier's acknowledgment that goods have been received. It serves to transfer responsibility for those goods from the domestic to the international carrier.

Shipper's Instructions. This document serves to provide transporters of exports with any other information necessary to ensure the effective movement of goods to their final destination.

THE FREIGHT FORWARDER

International freight forwarders are important players in the exporting process for American firms. Knowledgeable about all aspects of international trade—including international and U.S. regulations, import and export rules, and shipping options—freight forwarders serve as agents for exporting businesses, overseeing the transportation of their cargo to overseas destinations.

As the Small Business Administration noted in its *Breaking into the Trade Game,* many freight forwarders provide services at the very beginning of the exporting process by advising exporting firms about freight costs, port charges, insurance costs, consular fees, handling fees, and other expenses. They can also advise small exporters about packaging options, and in some cases can make arrangements to have goods containerized or packed at the port. Freight forwarders have the power to reserve space on freighters and other ocean vessels in accordance with client specifications.

In order to represent their exporting clients as effectively as possible, freight forwarders may review the wide array of documentation necessary for international business transactions, including letters of credit, commercial invoices, and packing lists. Exporters can also ask freight forwarders to prepare necessary documentation for the exporting process, including bills of lading. Once this documentation has been taken care of, they can be forwarded as needed. Finally, the exporter can also ask the freight forwarder to make arrangements with the customs broker to ensure that their merchandise is in compliance with customs export documentation regulations. Given the wide array of services that they provide, and the importance of those services to the exporting process, trade experts view freight forwarders as an extremely valuable resource for small exporting firms. "The cost for their services," contended the Small Business Administration (SBA), "is a legitimate export cost that should be figured into the price charged to the customer."

SEE ALSO *Exporting*

BIBLIOGRAPHY

Cook, Thomas A. *Mastering Import and Export Management.* AMACOM, 2004.

Sowinski, Lara L. "Going Global in a Flash: Numerous Resources Await U.S. Companies Ready to Break into the Global Market." *World Trade.* August 2005.

U.S. Small Business Administration. *Breaking into the Trade Game: A Small Business Guide.* 5 July 2001.

Wiley Spiers, John. *How Small Business Trades Worldwide.* Writer's Showcase Press, 2001.

Hillstrom, Northern Lights
updated by Magee, ECDI

TUITION ASSISTANCE PROGRAMS

Tuition assistance programs are a type of employee benefit in which an employer reimburses employees for the costs associated with continuing education. Assistance usually comes in the form of reimbursements for tuition, fees, and books. Many progressive companies pay for an unlimited number of courses that may or may not be directly related to an employee's current job. In fact, a 2005 survey conducted by the Society for Human Resource Management and reported on in an *HR Magazine* article found that 60 percent of corporations offer some form of tuition assistance. These companies reason that today's rapidly changing work environment requires employees to possess a wide variety of skills, and that education provides a way for them to improve their skills and adapt to the new realities of the business world. Other companies adopt tuition assistance programs on a smaller scale, providing partial reimbursement of certain costs associated with job-related courses.

Although tuition assistance programs can be costly for businesses, there are a number of proven strategies that can be applied to help keep costs down. In addition, tuition assistance programs offer companies a number of important benefits. For example, companies that provide their employees with tuition assistance are building a more educated work force by encouraging workers to pursue higher education. Tuition assistance programs can also provide companies with an effective recruiting tool, and enabling them to attract highly motivated people. Finally, tuition assistance can lead to reduced employee turnover and increased loyalty to the company.

COMMON CONCERNS ABOUT TUITION ASSISTANCE

High Costs Many companies resist instituting tuition assistance programs because of the cost involved. In fact, poorly planned tuition assistance programs do waste money. But as Heather Kirkwood observed in *Kansas City Business Journal,* "experts say a well-designed tuition reimbursement program can turn what seems like a cash-sucking recruiting tool into a revenue-increasing program that creates loyal employees."

There are a number of different strategies that businesses can take to limit the expense of tuition assistance programs. The first step is to determine the specific educational goals of employees in order to better focus their course selections. Outside educational advisory services can help employees understand their goals and thus decrease the chance that they will begin one course of study only to quit and start another. Similarly, specialists within the company can be made available to advise employees about their educational options, rather than simply explaining the features of the tuition assistance program to them. These individuals can help guide employees in educational directions that will benefit both themselves and the company for which they work.

Experts also recommend that employers reimburse fees as well as tuition in order to reduce costs. State-supported universities tend to charge lower tuition rates but higher additional fees than private colleges, which might cause some employees to choose to attend the more expensive private colleges in order to save on out-of-pocket expenses. Another way companies can save money in their tuition assistance programs is to investigate negotiating discounts with the schools. Larger companies or even smaller ones with specific educational needs may be able to save money by providing a certain number of students for a course. If, for example, a dozen employees from one company need to take a basic class, that company may be able to arrange a reduced rate or even a special class just for employees. Employers may also find it beneficial to arrange to pay certain local colleges and universities directly in order to reduce paperwork and other hassles for their employees.

Another way for companies to save money, as well as make the idea of continuing education more attractive to employees, is to provide nontraditional education options, such as correspondence, television, videotape, or Internet classes. Thousands of accredited courses are available through these alternative means, which allow busy employees with family responsibilities to fulfill course requirements on their own time without having to sit in a formal classroom. Collectively known as "distance learning," these options offer employees a great deal of flexibility. However, it is important to make sure that such programs are regionally accredited so any credits earned will transfer to traditional schools if necessary.

Employers can also save money on tuition assistance programs by helping employees receive college credit for skills and knowledge they may already possess. For example, about 600 colleges offer students the opportunity to demonstrate their knowledge of various subjects through a life-experience portfolio. When employees have mastered the content of a course through work experience, they may be able to obtain college credit without actually having to spend time or money on a class. This option might, for instance, enable a person employed as a bookkeeper to pass out of an intermediate accounting course.

Assessment tests, offered by college testing services, provide a similar, relatively inexpensive, option. Such testing enables some employees to reduce the amount of formal education they need to obtain a degree, which also reduces the time and cost involved in their education. In addition, gaining credit for skills and knowledge can enhance employees' self-esteem and bring them recognition for their skills at work.

Will Employees Apply Themselves? Some firms worry that offering a liberal tuition reimbursement policy will not be fully taken advantage of if participants do not invest the effort required to earn passing grades. These firms will often include guidelines and restrictions in their tuition reimbursement policies that attempt to guard against this

possibility. For instance, companies can tie reimbursement to grades—a certain percentage for an A, a B, a C and so on. Employers can also avoid this potential problem by requiring students who fail a course to either repeat it or pay back the company for related tuition and fees.

Employees May Take the Education and Then Leave the Company Many businesses providing tuition assistance to employees fear that the worker will depart for greener pastures after taking advantage of the program. In order to reduce the likelihood of losing newly educated employees, some companies require participants in their tuition assistance programs to remain at the company for a certain length of time or else reimburse the company for part of the tuition paid on their behalf. Many businesses also limit enrollment in such programs to individuals who have already been with the company for a certain amount of time (typically six months to one year). Other companies take the more positive step of rewarding employees who earn their degrees with a gift of company stock. The stock can be set up to mature over a few years, thus giving the employee added incentive to remain at the company.

Complex Tax Implications Finally, some companies are reluctant to establish tuition assistance programs for their employees because of the paperwork related to tax compliance. Some forms of tuition assistance to workers are tax-deductible especially if the coursework is necessary to maintain professional licenses or otherwise ensure that the employee in question can adequately fulfill his/her workplace obligations and responsibilities. Businesses interested in establishing tuition assistance programs for their employees should first consult with an accounting/tax professional to discuss these and other potential factors.

SEE ALSO *Employee Benefits; Training and Development*

BIBLIOGRAPHY
Bolch, Matt. "Bearing Fruit: Usage rates for traditional tuition assistance programs are low, so employers are tempting employees with free tuition and bonuses." *HR Magazine.* March 2006.

Burzawa, Sue. "Employers Can Use State Programs to Help Employees Save for College Education." *Employee Benefit Plan Review.* December 2000.

Kirkwood, Heather. "Education Perks Benefit Employers, Too." *Kansas City Business Journal.* 14 January 2000.

U.S. Small Business Administration. Roberts, Gary, Gary Seldon, and Carlotta Roberts. *Human Resources Management.* n.d.

Hillstrom, Northern Lights
updated by Magee, ECDI

U

UNDERCAPITALIZATION

Undercapitalization is a situation in which a business has insufficient funding, or capital, to support its operations. Although undercapitalization can affect any business, it is particularly common and problematic for small businesses. In fact, undercapitalization is one of the warning signs of major financial trouble for small businesses, as well as a significant cause of small business failure. Undercapitalization also acts to limit the growth of many small businesses, because without sufficient capital they cannot afford to make the investments necessary for expansion. In this way, undercapitalization can pose a problem even for profitable small businesses. "What separates the successful entrepreneur from the unsuccessful? In many cases, it seems to be whether the prospective business owner has access to sufficient funds," Brian Hamilton wrote in the Small Business Administration publication *Financing for the Small Business*. Without sufficient capitalization, companies are unprepared to ride out slow periods in the business cycle, or to fend off a new competitor, or to work through any number of shocks that buffet all businesses from time to time.

There are a number of factors that determine how much capitalization any small business needs. Businesses that offer a service usually require fewer funds than those that manufacture a product. Similarly, businesses in which the owners perform most of the work tend to need less up-front capital than businesses with employees. A company's initial capitalization also depends on the entrepreneur's ability to invest personal funds and institute a sound business plan.

In order to avoid future problems with undercapitalization, entrepreneurs need to perform a realistic assessment of their expenses and financial needs. Some of the major expenses facing a new business include facility rental; salaries and wages; equipment and tools; supplies, utilities; insurance; advertising; and business licenses. Based upon this information, the entrepreneur should prepare a cash flow projection on a monthly basis for the first year. The difference between the funds the entrepreneur is able to contribute, the amount of income the business is expected to generate, and expenses the business is projected to incur provides a rough estimate of the business's financial needs. Ideally, an entrepreneur will secure the necessary equity from various sources to make up the difference and provide the business with sufficient capitalization.

CASH MANAGEMENT AND PLANNING

Managing cash flows is an important aspect of staying ahead of the capital needs that a growing company may have. The goal of cash management is to manage the cash balances of an enterprise in such a way as to maximize the availability of cash not invested in fixed assets or inventories and to do so in such a way as to avoid the risk of insolvency. Factors monitored as a part of cash management include a company's level of liquidity, its management of cash balances, and its short-term investment strategies.

Cash is the lifeblood of a business. Managing it efficiently is essential for success.

In some ways, managing cash flow is the most important job of business managers. If at any time a company fails to pay an obligation when it is due because of the lack of cash, the company is insolvent. Insolvency is the primary reason firms go bankrupt. Obviously, the prospect of such a dire consequence should compel companies to manage their cash with care. Moreover, efficient cash management means more than just preventing bankruptcy. It improves the profitability and reduces the risk to which the firm is exposed.

Cash management is particularly important for new and growing businesses. Cash flow can be a problem even when a small business has numerous clients, offers a product superior to that offered by its competitors, and enjoys a sterling reputation in its industry. Companies suffering from cash flow problems have no margin of safety in case of unanticipated expenses. They also may experience trouble in finding the funds for innovation or expansion. It is, somewhat ironically, easier to borrow money when you have money. For this reason, planning ahead is essential. Knowing when new funds will be necessary and securing those funds ahead of the need is far easier than approaching a bank once there is a funding crunch in the business.

UNDERCAPITALIZATION AND CORPORATE LIABILITY

A little-known problem associated with undercapitalization is that it can increase the likelihood of the owners of a corporation being held personally liable for business-related matters. One of the main reasons that entrepreneurs choose the corporate form of business organization is to protect themselves against personal liability for business debts and court judgments. Incorporation does not afford automatic protection, however. Corporate owners can be held personally liable in a number of situations, including cases where personal and corporate assets are commingled, the corporation does not keep adequate records, or corporate owners intentionally defraud their creditors.

But perhaps the most critical factor in determining whether there should be personal liability for corporate debts is whether the owners provided sufficient capitalization for the business. The ultimate test is whether there are enough corporate assets to satisfy corporate obligations. For example, an entrepreneur could not contribute only $500 to start a new business, knowing that it actually required an initial capital outlay of $10,000, and expect his or her personal assets to be protected in case the business became insolvent. In this instance, a court would be likely to rule that the extreme undercapitalization of the corporation made the owner personally liable for its debts.

SEE ALSO *Banks and Banking; Capital Structure; Cash Management; Debt Financing; Equity Financing; Finance and Financial Management*

BIBLIOGRAPHY

Baldwin, John R. *Innovation Strategies and Performance in Small Firms.* Edward Elgar Publishing, February 2004.

Cannella, Cara. "Where Seed Money Really Comes From." *Inc.* 1 April 2003.

Detamore-Rodman, Crystal. "Going Somewhere? Keeping Financial Road Map in Your Company's Back Pocket is Always a Capital Idea." *Entrepreneur.* December 2002.

Ellison, Mitch, and Neil E. Seitz. *Capital Budgeting and Long-Term Financing Decisions.* HBJ, 1999.

Gage, Jack. "Living Within Your Means." *Forbes.* 26 December 2005.

Hommel, Ulrich, and Michael Frenkel, Markus Rudolf, eds. *Risk Management.* Springer, 2005.

Hosford, Christopher. "Selling Strategies for Small Businesses: Small businesses can struggle from undercapitalization, lack of sales savvy, even not being taken seriously." *Sales & Marketing Management.* April 2006.

Kono, Clyde. "Bank on It: Managing Your Cash Flow." *Hawaii Business.* August 2004.

U.S. Small Business Administration. Hamilton, Brian. *Financing for the Small Business.* 1990.

Hillstrom, Northern Lights
updated by Magee, ECDI

UNDERWRITERS LABORATORIES (UL)

Underwriters Laboratories (UL) is the largest and best known independent, not-for-profit testing laboratory in the world. Based in Northwood, Illinois, UL conducts safety and quality tests on a broad range of products, from fire doors to CCTV cameras. The laboratory provides a full spectrum of conformity and quality assessment services to manufacturers and other organizations. It also assists jurisdictional and provincial authorities, offers educational materials to consumers, and works to strengthen safety systems around the world.

UL provides comprehensive diagnostic testing services in the following areas: fire testing; medical device testing; EPH services (food service equipment, drinking water certification, plumbing equipment); audio/video; home electronics; Source Verification and Inspection Services (SVIS); electric vehicle components and systems; EMC testing and certification; information technology equipment (ITE) industry services; and telecom industry services. It conducts tests on products in these areas to see whether they meet standards set by UL engineers in conjunction with input from manufacturers and product users, but it will also test products to see whether they meet standards set by outside entities, such as a city (in the case of building codes, for instance). In 2005, UL conducted 97,915 product evaluations in 62 laboratory facilities that it operated around the world. As of 2005, there are 20 billion products that carry the UL Mark.

In addition to its work in the U.S. market, Underwriters Laboratories maintains services for companies looking to test products for international markets. This division of UL studies international product certification standards, assists clients with the application process, helps with correspondence and translation, and can coordinate the exchange and review of test data. In order to increase its efficiency in these international realms, Underwriters Laboratories has also launched a sustained effort to establish common standards for safety requirements, testing protocols, and certifications around the world. The impetus for this effort, according to UL, is a recognition that companies seeking to establish a presence in multiple overseas markets sometimes need as many as 20 separate safety certifications for a single product, a requirement that "can cost as much as $8,000 per safety mark per product. Many companies have annual certification budgets of $5 million or more." UL hopes to first establish common standards between the United States and Canada, then turn its attention to other markets.

UL Designations "Underwriters Laboratories, which has been in existence for more than 100 years, is very sensitive to the prevalent but mistaken belief that it approves products," wrote Robert C. Cook in *Security Management*. "The only entity that can actually approve or reject a product is a federal, state, or local government agency—known generally as the 'Authority Having Jurisdiction' or AHJ." However, an AHJ—whether it is a local health code inspection department or the federal Occupational Safety and Health Administration—often requires products to be tested by Underwriters Laboratories or another lab before the agency will approve its use.

UL hands out one of three different designations to products that pass its tests: UL listed, UL recognized, or UL certified. Businesses should note that there is no such designation as "UL approved"; companies that mistakenly tout their products with such a designation will arouse the ire of Underwriters Laboratories, which will insist that the company clarify the matter immediately.

UL Listed. This designation means that the tested product meets the laboratory's standards and can be used by itself.

UL Recognized. This designation is granted to equipment components that are used in combination with other pieces of equipment to create a finished product.

UL Certified. This designation is used by UL when it has been successfully tested to the standards of an outside authority, such as a city's building code requirements.

In 2000 UL announced its intention to transition to usage of Standard Technical Panels (STPs) in its development of diagnostic processes. The STPs will include representatives from consumer protection organizations (such as the National Consumer League), manufacturers, industry trade associations (like the Association of Home Appliance Manufacturers), and regulatory authorities (including government agencies like the Consumer Product Safety Commission). According to UL, these forums will work together to establish consensus opinions on diagnostic standards and will vote on proposed standards before they are adopted.

Businesses considering enlisting the services of Underwriters Laboratories (or similar labs) should be aware that testing can be both expensive and time-consuming. Bills of several thousand dollars per product tested are not unusual in many industry sectors, and the testing procedures usually take about six months to complete, with some tests extending well beyond that time frame. But the importance of UL acknowledgment is very significant to marketplace image in many industries.

BIBLIOGRAPHY
Cook, Robert C. "A Tale of UL Testing." *Security Management.* July 1995.

Jancsurak, Joe. "New Standards for Standards." *Appliance Manufacturer.* August 2000.

Strom, Shelly. "Underwriters Laboratories Gives Seal of Approval." *Business Journal-Portland.* 4 August 2000.

"The Underwriters Labs' Faster Seal of Approval." *Business Week.* 20 December 1993.

"Underwriters Labs Pursues Single Worldwide Standard." *Manufacturing News.* 25 August 2000.

Wingo, Walter S. "A Boom Time for Product Testing." *Design News.* 9 March 1992.

Hillstrom, Northern Lights
updated by Magee, ECDI

UNIFORM COMMERCIAL CODE (UCC)

The Uniform Commercial Code (UCC) is a collection of modernized, codified, and standardized laws that apply to all commercial transactions with the exception of real property. Developed under the direction of the National Conference of Commissioners on Uniform State Laws, the American Law Institute, and the American Bar Association (ABA), it first became U.S. law in 1972.

Since that time, it has undergone a process of constant revision.

The Uniform Commercial Code arose out of the need to address two growing problems in American business: 1) the increasingly cumbersome legal and contractual requirements of doing business, and 2) differences in state laws that made it difficult for companies located in different states to do business with one another. Businesspeople and legislators recognized that some measures needed to be taken to ease interstate business transactions and curb the trend toward exhaustively detailed contracts. They subsequently voiced support for the implementation of a set of standardized laws that would serve as the legal cornerstone for all exchanges of goods and services. These laws—the Uniform Commercial Code—could then be referred to when discrepancies in state laws arose, and freed companies from painstakingly including every conceivable business detail in all of their contractual agreements.

DEVELOPMENT OF THE UNIFORM COMMERCIAL CODE

Work on the UCC began in earnest in 1945. Seven years later, a draft of the code was approved by the National Conference of Commissioners on Uniform State Laws, the American Law Institute, and the American Bar Association. Pennsylvania became the first state to enact the UCC, and it became law there on July 1, 1954. The UCC editorial board issued a new code in 1957 in response to comments from various states and a special report by the Law Revision Commission of New York State. By 1966 48 states had enacted the code. Currently, all 50 states, the District of Columbia, and the U.S. Virgin Islands have adopted the UCC as state law, although some have not adopted every single provision contained within the code.

BUSINESS ISSUES ADDRESSED IN THE UCC

Many important aspects of business are covered within the UCC, and several of them are of particular import to entrepreneurs and small business owners. The Code provides detailed information on such diverse business aspects as: breach of contract (and the options of both buyers and sellers when confronted with a breach); circumstances under which buyers can reject goods; risk allocation during transportation of goods; letters of credit and their importance; legal methods of payment for goods and services; and myriad other subjects.

Articles The UCC consists of ten articles. Article 1, titled General Provisions, details principles of interpretation and general definitions that apply throughout the UCC.

Article 2 covers such areas as sales contracts, performance, creditors, good faith purchasers, and legal remedies for breach of contract; given its concern with the always important issue of contracts, small business owners should be thoroughly acquainted with this section. Article 3, which replaced the Uniform Negotiable Instruments Law, covers transfer and negotiation, rights of a holder, and liability of parties, among other areas. Article 4 covers such areas as collections, deposits, and customer relations; it incorporated much of the Bank Collection Code developed by the American Bankers Association.

Article 5 of the Uniform Commercial Code is devoted to letters of credit, while Article 6 covers bulk transfers. Article 7 covers warehouse receipts, bills of lading, and other documents of title. Article 8, meanwhile, is concerned with the issuance, purchase, and registration of investment securities; it replaced the Uniform Stock Transfer Act. Article 9 is another provision that is particularly important to small business owners. Devoted to secured transactions, sales of accounts, and chattel paper, it supplanted a number of earlier laws, including the Uniform Trust Receipts Act, the Uniform Conditional Sales Act, and the Uniform Chattel Mortgage Act.

Finally, Article 10 provides for states to set the effective date of enactment of the code and lists specific state laws should be repealed once the UCC has been enacted (Uniform Negotiable Instruments Act, Uniform Warehouse Receipts Act, Uniform Sales Act, Uniform Bills of Lading Act, Uniform Stock Transfer Act, Uniform Conditional Sales Act, and Uniform Trust Receipts Act). In addition, Article 10 recommends that states repeal any acts regulating bank collections, bulk sales, chattel mortgages, conditional sales, factor's lien acts, farm storage of grain and similar acts, and assignment of accounts receivable, for all of these areas are covered in the UCC. Individual states may also add to the list of repealed acts at their own discretion.

The UCC has a permanent editorial board, and amendments to the UCC are added to cover new developments in commerce, such as electronic funds transfers and the leasing of personal property. Individual states then have the option of adopting the amendments and revisions to the UCC as state law. For current information on changes within and interpretations of the Uniform Commercial Code, consult the *Business Lawyer's* "Uniform Commercial Code Annual Survey." Also of use is a Web site made available by Cornell Law School which offers the entire text of the UCC in an easily searchable format, located at http://www.law.cornell.edu/ucc/ucc.table.html.

BIBLIOGRAPHY
Stone, Bradford. *The Uniform Commercial Code in a Nutshell.* West, 1995.

"UCC: Uniform Commercial Code." Cornell Las School. Legal Information Institute. Available from http://www.law.cornell.edu/ucc/. 11 March 2005.

White, James J., and Robert Summers. *Uniform Commercial Code.* West/Wadsworth, 1999.

Hillstrom, Northern Lights
updated by Magee, ECDI

U.S. CHAMBER OF COMMERCE

The U.S. Chamber of Commerce is a national not-for-profit business federation devoted to promoting business interests in the United States and around the globe. Founded as a national federation in 1912 and headquartered in Washington, D.C., the U.S. Chamber of Commerce has long championed the cause of large and small businesses alike. Primary areas of activity by the Chamber include efforts to: ease perceived over-regulation of business activities; cut taxes on businesses; strengthen trade relations with other nations; improve labor relations; increase productivity and innovation in all industry areas; develop new markets; study major business policy issues; improve socioeconomic conditions in communities; and reduce business-related litigation.

In 2005, the membership of the U.S. Chamber of Commerce included 830 business associations, approximately 3,000 local and state chambers of commerce; 87 American chambers of commerce based in foreign markets; and 3 million individual business enterprises. Of the latter members, the Chamber counts most of the United States' largest corporations. But according to Chamber of Commerce data, more than 96 percent of the federation's members are small businesses with 100 or fewer employees.

In addition to its intensive lobbying activities on behalf of its membership, the U.S. Chamber of Commerce boasts several affiliated organizations engaged in policy areas of interest to small and large businesses alike. The National Chamber Foundation (NCF), for instance, is a public and business policy research institution dedicated to exploring issues and solving problems found in the modern business world. The Chamber also supports two organizations devoted to legal issues. Its National Chamber Litigation center (NCLC) represents businesses in legal proceedings, while the Institute for Legal Reform (ILR) is dedicated to tort reform and other pro-business changes to the U.S. legal system. Other

foundations associated with and supported by the Chamber include the Center for International Private Enterprise (CIPE), which promotes business development in Third World countries, and the Center for Workforce Preparation (CWP), which endeavors to boost workforce education and training initiatives in all industries. In 2000 the Chamber also announced its intention to establish a humanitarian aid foundation called the Center for Corporate Citizenship Foundation. This organization's mandate will be to channel corporate donations to victims of natural disasters and other groups and individuals in need.

The national offices of the U.S. Chamber of Commerce are located at 1615 H. Street NW, Washington, DC 20062-2000, (800) 638-6582. The Chamber also maintains an Internet presence at http://www.uschamber.com/home.htm.

SEE ALSO *Chambers of Commerce*

BIBLIOGRAPHY
Mack, Charles S. *Business, Politics, and the Practice of Government Relations.* Quorum, September 1997.

U.S. Chamber of Commerce. Small Business Center. Available from http://www.uschamber.com/sb/default.htm?n=rn Retrieved on 15 May 2006.

Hillstrom, Northern Lights
updated by Magee, ECDI

U.S. DEPARTMENT OF COMMERCE

The Department of Commerce, which was established in 1903, is one of the main government agencies intended to assist businesses—large and small—and represent their interests domestically and abroad. The agency states that its broad range of responsibilities include expanding U.S. exports, developing and promoting innovative technologies, gathering and disseminating statistical data and other important economic information, measuring economic growth, granting patents, promoting minority entrepreneurship, and providing stewardship. The department promotes these goals by encouraging job creation and economic growth through exports, free and fair trade, technology and innovation, entrepreneurship, deregulation, and sustainable development.

One of the key offices within the Department of Commerce is the Office of Business Liaison. That office serves as the intermediary between the business community and the agency. Its objectives include:

- To be pro-active in its dealings with the business community and to be responsive and effective in its outreach efforts.

- To keep the current administration aware of problems and issues facing the business community.

- To keep the business community abreast of key administration decisions and policies.

- To regularly meet with members of the business community.

- To help businesses navigate their way through all the federal agencies and regulations through its Business Assistance Program. In addition to producing a wide variety of published materials, the Assistance Program also provides specialists who are available to answer specific questions on government policies, programs, and services.

Another office that is of interest to small business owners is the Office of Small and Disadvantaged Utilization. This office is responsible for ensuring that the department purchases goods and services from small businesses. It helps small businesses identify with which bureaus small businesses should pursue potential buyers, clarifies who the key individuals at that bureau are, and provides small businesses with basic information on the procurement process. The Office of Small and Disadvantaged Utilization also helps businesses develop marketing strategies.

Following is a list of other key offices, departments, and programs at the Department of Commerce that are also of interest to small business owners:

- Bureau of the Census—every 10 years, performs a full census of the U.S. population, collecting a wide variety of information, as well as sorting and analyzing it. The bureau makes this information publicly available, and business owners often use the information for demographic or marketing purposes.

- Bureau of Economic Analysis—promotes a better understanding of the U.S. economy by providing the most timely, relevant, and accurate economic accounts data in an objective and cost-effective manner.

- Economic Development Administration—responsible for creating new jobs, retaining existing jobs, and stimulating industrial and commercial growth in economically challenged areas of the United States.

- International Trade Administration—helps U.S. businesses compete in the global market by assisting exporters, helping businesses gain equal access to foreign markets, and making it easier to compete against unfairly traded imports. Includes separate units for trade development and import administration.

- Minority Business Development Agency—devoted to fostering the creation, growth, and expansion of minority businesses in the United States.

- Office of Consumer Affairs—exists to bridge the gap between businesses and consumers, to help businesses improve the quality of the services they offer consumers, to educate consumers, and to speak for the consumer in regards to each administration's economic policy development. The Office also works with American businesses to help them become more competitive in the global marketplace.

- Patent and Trademark Office—protects innovation in the marketplace by providing inventors and authors with exclusive rights to their creations.

- National Institute of Standards and Technology—promotes economic growth by working with businesses to develop and apply technology, measurements, and standards. Of growing interest to U.S. businesses because of the growing influence of the International Standards Organization (ISO) and international emphasis on quality standards.

- National Trade Data Bank—provides the public with access, including electronic access, to export and international economic information.

- Trade Compliance Center—monitors foreign compliance with trade agreements and provides businesses with information about their rights and obligations under existing trade agreements with other nations.

Extensive information on the Department and its various bureaus and programs is available on the Web site that it maintains, located at http://www.doc.gov.

BIBLIOGRAPHY
U.S. Department of Commerce. "Commerce Organization." Available from http://www.commerce.gov/organization.html. Retrieved on 9 May 2006.

Hillstrom, Northern Lights
updated by Magee, ECDI

U.S. SMALL BUSINESS ADMINISTRATION GUARANTEED LOANS

The U.S. Small Business Administration (SBA) is a major source of financing for small businesses in the United

States. The SBA's various loan programs have provided needed funding for thousands of small enterprises who were unable to secure loans from lending institutions on their own; indeed, businesses cannot solicit loans from the SBA unless they are unable to get funding independently.

Some of today's most successful businesses, including Intel, Apple, and Federal Express, were each given a much needed boost in their early days by SBA loans. This record of success, coupled with the trend toward small-business start-ups and entrepreneurship in America, has encouraged both the SBA and its lending partners to continue to expand its loan programs. The SBA has subsequently set new records in various loan guarantee categories since the mid-1990s. In fiscal year 2005 the SBA made or guaranteed $19 billion worth of loans to small businesses, the most in its history. Loans were provided to more than 80,000 small companies, 28,000 of them were start-ups.

TYPES OF SBA GUARANTEED LOANS

The SBA's 7(a) Loan Program is the most popular of the agency's programs (more than 88,000 of these loans totaling almost $14 billion were bestowed upon small businesses in fiscal year 2005). Under this program, the SBA does not actually make direct loans to small businesses. Instead, it assures the institution that is making the business loan—usually a bank—that it will make payment on the loan if the business defaults on it. Since the SBA is taking responsibility for the loan, it is usually the final arbiter of whether a loan application will be approved or not.

The 7(a) Loan Program was formed to meet the long-term financing needs of small businesses. The primary advantage of 7(a) loans is that business enterprises are able to repay the loan over a very long period of time. Ten-year maturities are available for loans for equipment and working capital (though seven-year terms are more commonplace), and loans for real estate and major equipment purchases can be paid back over as long as 25 years. The SBA can guarantee 75 percent of loans up to $750,000, and 80 percent of loans of less than $100,000. The interest rate of 7(a) loans does not exceed 2.75 over the prime lending rate.

The SBA maintains several individual loan programs under the 7(a) umbrella. These include CAPLines, LowDoc, SBAExpress, EWCP, DELTA, and an assortment of other lending initiatives targeted at specific sectors of the small business world.

CAPLines Limited to $750,000, CAPLines loans are given to small businesses with short-term working capital needs. "Under CAPLines," notes the SBA, "there are five distinct short-term working capital loans: the Seasonal, Contract, Builder's, Standard Asset-Based, and Small Asset-Based lines. For the most part, the SBA regulations governing the 7(a) Program also govern this program."

LowDoc The Low Documentation Loan (LowDoc) Program is a simplified version of the 7(a) loan for businesses with strong credit histories seeking less than $150,000. It combines a streamlined application process (for many loan requests, the application is only one page long) with the elimination of several bureaucratic steps to improve response time to requests. Any small business that posted average annual sales over the previous three years of $5 million or less and employs 100 or few individuals (including all owners, partners, and principals) is eligible to apply for a Low Documentation Loan. Since its inception, the LowDoc Program has proven enormously popular with small business owners and entrepreneurs.

SBAExpress This relatively new pilot program is only available through selected lending institutions. It makes loans of up to $150,000 to qualified businesses.

EWCP The Export Working Capital Program (EWCP) guarantees loans for qualified small businesses engaged in export transactions. It replaced another SBA program known as the Export Revolving Line of Credit Program. Most of the SBA regulations governing the 7(a) Program also govern this program. Loan maturities, however, may be for up to three years, with an option for annual renewals. EWCP loans can be extended for either single or multiple export sales.

DELTA The Defense Loan and Technical Assistance (DELTA) Program was implemented to help ease the impact of national defense cuts on defense-dependent small businesses. According to the SBA, DELTA loans of up to $1.25 million must be used to retain jobs of defense workers, create new jobs in impacted communities, or to make operating changes with the aim of remaining in the "national technical and industrial base." While listed under the 7(a) umbrella of loan programs, DELTA actually uses the 504 CDC program as well, discussed further below.

MicroLoans SBA MicroLoans are short-term loans of up to $35,000. In fiscal year 2005 the SBA provided $20 million worth of MicroLoans, disseminated through non-profit groups, these loans are intended for the purchase of machinery and other equipment, office furniture, inventory, supplies, and working capital. The typical MicroLoan size was $10,500 in 2005.

International Trade Loan (ITL) The ITL provides long-term financing assistance to small businesses who are involved in international trade or who have been hurt by imports. Under this program, the SBA guarantees loans for up to $1.25 million for a combination of fixed-asset financing and working capital needs (though the working capital portion of the guarantee is limited to $750,000).

Pollution Control Program This program extends loans to small businesses engaged in the planning, design, or installation of pollution control facilities.

504 Loans The Small Business Administration's other major loan program is the 504 CDC (Certified Development Companies) Program. CDCs are nonprofit corporations established to aid communities in their economic development efforts. The 504 CDC Program is designed to provide growing businesses with long-range, fixed-rate financing (up to $1 million for qualified applicants) for major expansion expenditures in the realm of fixed-asset projects. These include: real estate purchases and improvements, including existing buildings, grading, street improvements, parking lots and landscaping, and utilities; long-term machinery and equipment; renovation of existing facilities; and building construction. Monies from the 504 CDC Program cannot be used for refinancing, working capital or inventory, or consolidating or repaying debt.

The SBA describes the program thusly: "Typically, a 504 project includes a loan secured with a senior lien from a private-sector lender covering up to 50 percent of the project cost, a loan secured with a junior lien from the CDC (a 100 percent SBA-guaranteed debenture) covering up to 40 percent of the cost, and a contribution of at least 10 percent equity from the small business being helped. The maximum SBA debenture generally is $750,000 (up to $1 million in some cases).... The CDC's portfolio must create or retain one job from every $35,000 provided by the SBA."

Disaster Assistance Loans Finally, the SBA offers these loans to businesses that have been victimized by various natural disasters (fires, floods, hurricanes, earthquakes, etc.). These loans, limited to $1.5 million and not available to firms that were insured for their losses, are available to businesses of any size that need to repair or replace facilities to "pre-disaster" condition. Economic Injury Disaster Loans are also made available to companies that suffered severe economic damage as a result of a given disaster. These loans, which are capped at $1.5 million, are meant to help businesses cover ordinary operating expenses "which would have been payable barring disaster," according to the SBA. It is worth noting that businesses can apply for either type of disaster loan assistance, but they can be awarded no more than a total of $1.5 million from the two programs unless they qualify as a major source of employment for the region in which they operate.

INTEREST RATES ON SBA LOANS

The interest rates on SBA-guaranteed loans are negotiated between the borrowing business and the lending institution, but they are subject to SBA-imposed rate ceilings, which are linked to the prime rate. Interest rates on SBA loans can be either fixed or variable.

According to the SBA, fixed rate loans are not allowed to exceed the prime rate plus 2.25 percent if the loan matures in less than seven years. If the maturity of the loan is seven years or more, however, the rate can be boosted to the prime rate plus 2.75 percent. For SBA loans totaling less than $25,000, the maximum interest rate cannot exceed the prime rate plus 4.25 percent for loans with a maturity of less than seven years (for loans that mature after seven years, the interest rate can be as much as the prime rate plus 4.75 percent). For SBA loans between $25,000 and $50,000, maximum rates are not permitted to exceed 3.25 percent (for loans that mature in less than seven years) and 3.75 percent (for loans with longer terms of maturity).

Variable rate loans, notes the SBA, may be pegged to either the SBA optional peg rate or the lowest prime rate (the optional peg rate is a weighed average of rates that the federal government pays for loans with maturities similar to the average SBA loan). Under variable rate loan plans, the lender and borrower negotiate the amount of the spread to be added to the base interest rate. Such agreements also provide for regular adjustment periods wherein the note rate can be changed as needed. Some agreements call for monthly adjustment periods, while others provide for quarterly, semiannual, or annual adjustments.

ELIGIBILITY ISSUES

The Small Business Administration defines businesses eligible for SBA loans as those that: operate for profit; are engaged in, or propose to do business in, the United States or its possessions; have reasonable owner equity to invest; and use alternative financial resources (such as personal assets) first. In addition, to secure SBA assistance, a company must qualify as a "small business" under the terms of the Small Business Act. That legislation defined an eligible small business as one that is independently owned and operated and not dominant in its industry.

Since the passage of the Small Business Act, the SBA has developed size standards for every industry to gauge whether a company qualifies as a "small business" or not. Size standards are arranged by Standard Industrial Classification (SIC) code, but in general, the following guidelines apply for major industry groups:

- Manufacturing—A key criteria for manufacturing establishments is the size of their work force. Generally, 1,500 employees is the cut-off point for SBA consideration, but even establishments that have between 500 and 1,500 employees may not qualify as small businesses; in such instances the SBA bases its determination on a size standard for the specific industry in which the business under consideration operates.

- Wholesaling—Generally, wholesale establishments seeking SBA financial assistance should not have more than 100 employees.

- Retail and Service—Financial information is the key consideration here; ideally, retail and service industry businesses seeking SBA assistance should not have more than $3.5 million in annual receipts, although the requests of larger establishments are considered (depending on the industry). Establishments engaged in construction or agriculture industries are also evaluated on the basis of their financial reports.

The Small Business Administration also considers other factors in determining whether an establishment qualifies as a small business. For example, if a business is affiliated with another company, the owners must determine the primary business activity of both the affiliated group and the applicant business before submitting a request for SBA assistance. If the applicant business and the affiliated group do not both meet the SBA's size standards for their primary business activities, then the loan request will not be considered.

The SBA also has a number of eligibility rules that apply to specific kinds of businesses. Franchisees, for example, are often favored by the SBA because their businesses enjoy a higher success rate than do other businesses. Nonetheless, SBA officials will examine a franchisee's franchise agreement closely before extending any loan guarantees to him or her. If the officials decide that the franchisor wields so much control over the franchise's operations that the franchisee is basically an employee, then the SBA will turn down the request. Other types of businesses, such as those in agriculture or the fishing industry, are free to apply for SBA assistance, but they are directed to first look to government agencies that deal directly with their industries. Farmers, for example, are supposed to first explore loan programs available through the Farmers Home Administration

(FHA), while some members of the fishing industry—depending on the nature of their need—should first consult with the National Marine Fisheries Service (NMFS). The SBA also notes that some businesses are disqualified from consideration from the outset by the industry in which they operate. Businesses that operate in gambling, investment, or media-related fields, for example, are all ineligible for SBA loans.

Finally, the SBA notes that loans that they guarantee are only to be used for specific business purposes, including "the purchase of real estate to house the business operations; construction, renovation, or leasehold improvements; acquisition of furniture, fixtures, machinery, and equipment; purchase of inventory; and working capital." Using the money for other purposes—payment of delinquent withholding taxes, acquisition of another business, refinancing of debt, and a whole host of other actions—is not allowed.

APPLYING FOR AN SBA LOAN

The chief challenge of any business seeking to secure a loan from the Small Business Administration is to convince the SBA that it has the ability to be successful in its chosen field. To do so, the small business owner should be equipped with a complete understanding of his or her operation (whether existing or proposed) and the benefits that a loan, if granted, will bring to the business. Of course, it is also necessary to effectively articulate this information to the SBA. Business owners disseminate this data through a variety of documents.

Principal documents that should be submitted by the entrepreneur who hopes to start a new business include: resume (and resumes of any other key people involved in the proposed enterprise); current financial statement of all personal assets and liabilities; summary of collateral; proposed operating plan; and statement detailing revenue projections. Perhaps the most important document, however, is the loan request statement itself, for it is this document that should detail all aspects of the proposed business. For established business owners seeking an SBA loan, the most important documents—besides the loan application—are the company balance sheet, personal financial statements, and business income statements. Consultants urge small business owners to be both careful and realistic in preparing these records. They also caution entrepreneurs and small business owners not to distort figures or facts in their presentation. The SBA does not look kindly on misrepresentations in financial statements or any other part of the loan application.

The Loan Application The SBA loan application form serves to summarize much of the information detailed elsewhere in the total application package. Applicants are directed to furnish basic information about themselves and their businesses, including personal information (full legal name, street address); basic business information (employer ID number, type of business, number of employees, banking institution used); names and addresses of management personnel; estimated business expenditures and costs (including details on the SBA loan request); summary of collateral; summary of previous government financing; and listing of debts.

The SBA loan application form also provides a complete listing of the various other items of information that must be provided for a business's application to be considered. These include a personal history statement; personal and business financial statements; business description; listing of management personnel; equipment list; cosigners; summary of bankruptcies, insolvencies, and lawsuits (if any); listing of any familial relationships with SBA employees; subsidiaries, either proposed or in existence; franchise agreements; and statements of financial interest in any establishments with which applicant business does business, if applicable.

SEE ALSO *8(A) Loan Program; HUBZone Employment Contracting Program*

BIBLIOGRAPHY

Cohen, William. *The Entrepreneur and Small Business Problem Solver.* Second Edition. Wiley, 1990.

O'Hara, Patrick D. *SBA Loans: A Step-by-Step Guide.* Wiley, May 2002.

"SBA Loan Approvals on Record Pace." *Mississippi Business Journal.* 25 April 2005.

U.S. Department of Homeland Security. "Emergencies and Disasters: Hurricane Katrina, What Government is Doing." Available from http://www.dhs.gov/interweb/assetlibrary/katrina.htm. Retrieved on 8 May 2006

U.S. Small Business Administration. *SBA's 2005 Performance and Accountability Report.* Available from http://www.sba.gov/2005PAR.pdf/. Retrieved on 8 May 2006.

Hillstrom, Northern Lights
updated by Magee, ECDI

V

VALUATION

Valuation is the process of putting a price on a piece of property. The value of businesses, personal property, intellectual property (such as patents, trademarks, and copyrights), and real estate are all commonly determined through the practice of valuation. Businesses are valued for many tax, legal, and business reasons but selling the business is the usual motive. Determining the value of a business is simple yet complex. The value is what a knowledgeable buyer is willing to pay for it. And what price should a buyer be willing to pay? Here things become complicated. More than one valuation method exists but each one must take future earnings into account if continued operations are planned.

Theory recognizes three approaches to business valuation: the income-based approach, asset-based approach, and the market approach. The income approach is the most commonly used and is based on an entity's estimated future income stream. The asset-based approach is based on a straight forward determination of the collective value of an entity's assets. The market approach is a hybrid form of the earlier two. Using the market approach usually involves utilizing some market multiple of assets and income.

Putting a value on a small company is much more difficult than establishing the value of a large, publicly traded company. Publicly traded companies have a known value on any given day—the value of their outstanding stock. The value of small companies is much harder to establish, especially family-owned or closely held companies, companies that are unique in the marketplace, or companies built by creative entrepreneurs who will not be running the companies in the future. The valuation of a small company is usually best accomplished by using more than one method and melding the results of various assessments in a way that best reflects the individual business.

APPROACHES TO VALUATION

Of the many methods used in determining the value of a business, some are better suited to certain business types than others. Finance companies tend to value a business at what the assets will bring at a liquidation auction. Investment bankers and venture capitalists, on the other hand, tend to be interested in rapid appreciation and high return on investment and, thus value a business on a discounted future cash flow basis. Statisticians tend to use complex deviation curves based on historical performance to project future earnings when doing a business valuation. Corporate America looks to the prevailing profit-to-earnings (P/E) ratios, unless the market is depressed, in which case they use book value.

Rules of Thumb Because the cost of having a formal appraisal performed may be prohibitive for small businesses, owners will frequently turn to their accountants for assistance with a business valuation. Accountants faced with this task often revert to what are known as business valuation rules of thumb to try and determine a range of values for their clients.

Rules of thumb are standards established for businesses in the same industry. Brokers and financial intermediaries involved in mergers and acquisitions observe how certain types of businesses are valued and sold and over time patterns emerge. Based upon these empirical data they derive and publish rules of thumb to guide the valuation of businesses by industry and type. Examples of such rules of thumb are: dry cleaning businesses sell from 75 percent to 90 percent of gross revenues; property and casualty insurance businesses sell for 1.2 to 1.6 times book value, dental practices sell for 50 percent to 60 percent of gross revenues, optometrist practices sell for the value of their net fixed assets plus the most recent year's net income, etc. Many books and professional journals provide information about these rules of thumb. One of the largest collections of such rules is available in the book *Handbook of Small Business Valuation Formulas and Rules of Thumb,* by authors Glenn Desmond and John A. Marcell. Trade associations are another source of information about industry-specific, business valuation rules of thumb.

Income Statement Methods of Valuation The two related valuation methods listed below are by far the most frequently used means of assessing the value of a small business.

- Historical Cash Flow Approach—This is the most commonly used of all valuation methods. Many buyers view this method as the most relevant of all valuation approaches for it tells them what the business has historically provided to its owners in terms of cash. Lawrence Tuller noted in *The Small Business Valuation Book,* "the value of assets might be interesting to know, but hardly anyone buys a business only for its balance sheet assets. The whole purpose is to make money, and most buyers feel that they should be able to generate at least as much cash in the future as the business yielded in the past." This method typically takes financial data from the company's previous three years in drawing its conclusions.

- Discounted Future Cash Flow (DCF) Approach— This method uses projections of future cash flows from operating the business to determine what a company is worth today. The DCF approach requires detailed assumptions about future operations, including volumes, pricing, costs, and other factors. DCF usually starts with forecast income, adding back non-cash expenses, deducting capital expenditures, and adjusting for working capital changes to arrive at expected cash flows. The future cash flow method also is notable for its recognition of industry reputation, popularity with customers, and other "goodwill" factors in its assessment of company value. Once the value of the business's assets has been settled upon, the appropriate discount rate must be determined and used to bring the future cash flows back to their present day value. DCF in its single-period form is known as capitalization of earnings, which usually involves "normalizing" a recent measure of income or cash flow to reflect a steady-state or going-forward amount that can be capitalized at the appropriate multiple.

Balance Sheet Methods of Valuation These methods of valuation are most often employed when the business under examination generates most of its earnings from its assets rather than from the contributions of its employees. These methods are also used, wrote John A. Johansen in *How to Buy or Sell a Business,* "when the cost of starting a business and getting revenues past the break-even point doesn't greatly exceed the value of the business's assets."

- Liquidation Approach—This method assesses the value of a business by gauging its value if it were to cease operations and sell its individual assets. Under this approach, the business owner would receive no compensation for business "goodwill"—nontangible assets such as the company's name, location, customer base, or accumulated experience. This method is further divided into forced liquidations (as in bankruptcies) and orderly liquidations. Values are typically figured higher in the latter instances. Asset-based lenders and banks tend to favor this method, because they view the liquidation value of a company's tangible assets to be the only valuable collateral to the loan. But it is unpopular with most business owners because of the lack of consideration given to goodwill and other intangible assets.

- Asset Value Approach—This approach begins by examining the company's book value. Under this method, items listed on a business's balance sheet (at historical cost levels) are adjusted to bring them in line with current market values. In essence, this method calls for the adjustment of an asset's book value to equal the cost of replacing that asset in its current condition. This method is most often used to determine the value of companies which feature a large percentage of commodity-type assets. The net asset value method, also referred to as net worth or owner's equity, is one of the more commonly employed of all valuation approaches. While flawed in some respects, the net asset value method is popular because this approach can be easily figured from existing financial records.

Valuing Personal Service Businesses The valuation of a personal service business, like a medical practice, is often approached somewhat differently. While equipment, supplies, real estate and other assets that are typically included in assessing the value of companies are also included in assessing personal service business values, they are often of little consequence to potential buyers of the business in question. After all, a buyer may have an entirely new location in mind for the business, and costs associated with leases, utilities, and taxes often change dramatically with relocation. Instead, wrote Tuller, the most important consideration in valuing any personal service business "is how much gross billings can be generated from the customer/client base, not what profits have been recorded or how much cash [the owner has] taken out.... A key consideration to keep in mind if you are selling a professional practice is that the goodwill you have built up over the years is really what you are selling. Sometimes, it is called customer or client lists, or client files, but it is really just goodwill."

VALUATION ISSUES AND STANDARDS

It is important to recognize and deal properly with certain subtleties and standards in the field of valuation. Issues and standards to keep in mind include:

Treatment of Debt If the method used to determine company value uses a pre-debt-service income measure, then debt must usually be subtracted from the resulting figure.

Control Premiums If the valuation methodology used is based on price-earnings ratios of comparable public companies and the interest being valued is the entirety of a company, a control premium may be imposed.

Discount for Lack of Marketability This discount, also known as the liquidity discount, comes into play in situations where the business owner's ability to readily sell his or her business is questionable. For example, publicly traded companies are highly marketable, and their shares can be quickly turned into cash. Closely held companies, however, are sometimes far more difficult to sell. Depending on the valuation, it may be necessary to subtract a discount for lack of marketability, or add a premium for the presence of marketability.

Standard of Value When determining valuation of a company, the standard of value must be clearly defined. That is, it must be clear whether the valuation is based on book value, fair market value, liquidating versus going-concern value, investment value, or some other definition of value. Defining the standard of value is important because of adjustments that are necessary under some, but not all, of these standards.

"As-Of" Dates Valuation methods determine the value of a company at a given point in time. Thus, businesses that undergo a valuation process are said to be worth X dollars "as of" a certain date. Values of businesses inevitably change over time, so it is critical to state the date for any valuation. In addition, the information used by the appraiser should be limited to that which would have been available at the as-of date.

Form of Organization The legal definition of the organization under examination is an important factor in any valuation. Different legal forms of entity—corporations, S corporations, partnerships, and sole proprietorships—are all subject to different tax rules, rules which impact the value of the enterprise being appraised.

Focus of Valuation The focus of the valuation must be clearly identified. The portion of the business enterprise being acquired, the type(s) of securities involved, the nature of the purchase (asset purchase or stock purchase), and possible impact of the transaction on existing relationships (such as related party transfers) can all affect the value of the entity under examination.

Going through a business valuation exercise is useful for any business owner. He or she will learn a lot about the business by applying any one or several of the valuation methods discussed here. In the end, however, the true value of a business is, much like beauty, in the eye of the beholder. Or, in the case of a business owner who wishes to sell, it is the price another is willing to pay for the business.

SEE ALSO *Discounted Cash Flow; Mergers and Acquisitions; Selling a Business*

BIBLIOGRAPHY

Brickey, Honer. "Pricing A Small Business A Delicate Balancing Act, Ohio Experts Say." *Blade (Toledo, Ohio).* 23 February 2004.

Buchanan, Doug. "Business Valuators Must 'Dig Behind the Hype.'" *Washington Business Journal.* 15 September 2000.

Desmond, Glenn, and John A. Marcell. *Handbook of Small Business Valuation Formulas and Rules of Thumb.* Third Edition. Valuation Press, 1993.

Harrison, David S. "Business Valuation Made Simple: It's all about cash." *Strategic Finance.* February 2003.

Jenkins, David S. "The Benefits of Hybrid Valuation Models." *CPA Journal.* January 2006.

Robbins, Stever. "How Much Is This Business Worth?" *Entrepreneur.com.* 12 January 2004.

Sliwoski, Leonard J. "Alternatives to Business Valuation Rules of Thumb for Small Businesses." *The National Public Accountant.* March-April 1999.

Steingold, Fred S. *The Complete Guide to Selling a Business.* Nolo, 2005.

Tuller, Lawrence W. *The Small Business Valuation Book.* Adams Media, 1998.

U.S. Small Business Administration. Johansen, John A. *How to Buy or Sell a Business.* n.d.

"Why Every Company Needs to Have an Up-to-Date Business Valuation." *PR Newswire.* 20 April 2006.

Hillstrom, Northern Lights
updated by Magee, ECDI

VALUE-ADDED TAX

A value-added tax (VAT) is a fee that is assessed against businesses by a government at various points in the production of goods or services—usually any time a product is resold or value is added to it. In many countries this tax is referred to as a Goods and Services Tax (GST). Value is added to a product or service whenever the value increases as a result of the application of a company's factors of production, such as labor and equipment. VAT must be paid by every company that handles a product during its transition from raw materials to finished goods. For example, tax is charged when a manufacturer sells to a wholesaler and again when a wholesaler sells to a retailer.

In calculating the VAT, the taxable amount is based on the value added at each stage of the process of producing goods and bringing them to market. As an example, say that a company that makes socks buys cotton yarn for $1,000; adds $500 to its value in terms of labor, depreciation of knitting machines, and profits; then sells the completed socks for $1,500. VAT would be calculated as a percentage of the $500 value added by turning cotton yarn into socks. Of course, the sock company would also get credit for the amount of VAT it paid on the purchase of inputs, like cotton yarn.

In general, the total VAT accrued during the production of goods is reflected in the price of items sold to final consumers, because each reseller along the way usually passes along its VAT costs. In this way, VAT is somewhat similar to a national sales tax, and the two forms of taxation are often compared by governments. Experts claim that VAT entails higher administrative costs but is easier to enforce than a national sales tax.

The concept of VAT was first adopted by France in 1954. By 2005, there were more than 130 countries around the world that had implemented a VAT or GST. In most cases, the percentage of tax charged varies based on the necessity of the particular product, so the tax on food would generally be less than the tax on luxury items like boats. The United States is the only member country of the Organization for Economic Co-operation and Development (OECD) that does not have a value-added tax. According to the OECD, countries with a VAT collect on average one-fifth of their total tax revenue through this tax.

In recent years, VAT has been proposed for use in the United States as a way to simplify business and personal income tax laws. Proponents claim that VAT would replace other forms of taxation and reduce the costs of tax compliance. In fact, some people say that adopting VAT would eliminate tax returns for individuals and make the Internal Revenue Service obsolete. On the other hand, opponents argue that VAT would be more complicated to implement than other tax-reform options, such as a national sales tax. They also worry that it would increase the cost of food, medicine, and other necessities, which would hurt the poor.

VAT AND E-COMMERCE

VAT is a common form of taxation in the European Union (EU). In fact, VAT rates are as high as 25 percent in some EU countries. In 2000, a group of these countries proposed implementing a VAT for online businesses. The proposed tax would cover all digital products including software, videos, and music downloaded over the Internet in member countries. Since the products of electronic retailers were not previously subject to VAT, EU leaders felt that these businesses gained an unfair advantage over domestic, brick-and-mortar retailers. In addition, they argued that the EU nations were being deprived of tax income on goods sold in their countries by what were essentially foreign corporations.

As E-commerce expands in popularity, it may create hardships for some traditional retailers. As these brick-and-mortar businesses earn lower profits and hire fewer employees, they are likely to generate less tax revenue for their governments. If the new Internet competitors were based in the same country, then the tax situation would likely balance out. But the nature of online businesses often means that they can locate anywhere with sufficient technology and telecommunications capacity. Experts predict that increasing numbers of Internet businesses will base their operations in countries where taxes are low. Some low-tax jurisdictions, like Bermuda, have begun to enact favorable laws to attract such businesses. "Thus governments have to face the prospect of permanent flows of taxable profits out of their jurisdictions," Christine Sanderson wrote in *International Tax Review.* "Taking a European view, there is clearly a potential issue for tax authorities, since E-commerce and Internet development is likely to mean a flow of tax profits away from Europe."

The basic problem facing EU leaders is to determine how to apply VAT laws—which were developed with physical products and traditional retail markets in mind—to new types of goods and services delivered over the Internet. In 2000, representatives of 29 countries convened to develop the Ottawa Framework for dealing with these issues. Although the guidelines have not been finalized, they are expected to bring a higher level of certainty and consistency to the tax situation for E-commerce.

BIBLIOGRAPHY

"EU to Consider Internet Tax." *eWeek.* 23 October 2000.

"International VAT/GST Guidelines." Organization for Economic Co-operation and Development. Available from http://www.oecd.org/LongAbstract/0,2546,en_2649_201185_36177872_119820_1_1_1,00.html. Retrieved on 2 May 2006.

Sanderson, Christine. "EU Forges Ahead on E-Commerce." *International Tax Review.* September 2000.

Tagliabue, John. "From Europe, Creative Taxation." *New York Times.* 28 September 2000.

Hillstrom, Northern Lights
updated by Magee, ECDI

VARIABLE PAY

Variable pay programs are an increasingly popular mode of compensation in today's business world. These programs, which are also sometimes referred to as "pay-for-performance" or "at-risk" pay plans, provide some or all of a workforce's compensation based on employee performance or on the performance of a team. Variable pay proponents contend that providing tangible rewards for superior performance encourages hard work and efficiency and serves as an effective deterrent to mediocre or otherwise uninspired work performance.

Variable pay programs are made up of a variety of different compensation methods. In the broadest sense, variable pay programs include annual incentives or bonus payments; individual incentive plans; lump-sum payments; technical achievement awards; cash profit-sharing plans; small group incentives; gainsharing; and payments for newly acquired skill and knowledge. Some analysts argue that variable pay programs should be defined far more restrictively, but most agree that all of the above share a common emphasis on recognizing achievement, which is the ultimate goal of variable pay plans.

VARIABLE PAY AND THE MODERN BUSINESS ENVIRONMENT

The growing prevalence of variable pay alternatives in business compensation strategies has been attributed in part to a couple of other business trends. Rapidly changing technologies have had an impact on the ways in which we do work in the 21st century. Along with these changes have come rapidly changing job descriptions and a need for people with flexible skill sets to man these positions. At the same time, business observers point out that increased emphasis on quick reactions to changing competitive conditions have triggered a growth in movement toward employee empowerment. And as employees become more empowered, employers have had to find new ways to compensate them for their contributions to the overall enterprise.

Other analysts frame the issue of variable pay in terms of return on investment (ROI). To minimize today's heightened business risk, businesses must reduce their investment in fixed costs and maximize the use of variable costs, which they incur only if they achieve certain results. Nowhere is this situation seen more clearly than in the balance between fixed and variable pay, since employee compensation in many industries is a company's single largest expense.

ADVANTAGES AND DRAWBACKS OF VARIABLE PAY

Most criticisms of variable pay can be traced to concerns about the nature, implementation, and execution of such programs rather than the theories upon which they are based. In practice, many companies fail to make variable pay programs meaningful to individual employees, which in turn robs the program of much of its power to facilitate increased productivity.

In a report published by the Institute of Management & Administration entitled *Companies Are Not Getting Full Value from Variable Pay Programs,* the findings showed, as the title implies, that companies report very mixed results from variable pay programs. The survey reported on in the Institute of Management & Administration article was carried out by the firm Hewitt Associates. The Hewitt data showed that about half of companies with single-digit revenue growth believed that the cost of their variable pay programs outweighed the benefit. Companies with double-digit revenue growth, however, almost all reported positive outcomes from their variable pay programs. "The fact that many companies don't benefit from variable pay plans is a significant issue, as they're spending more than $54 million a year on this type of pay. We've found that companies achieving high-revenue growth have successful programs because they provide the appropriate amount of administrative, communication, and monetary support. These organizations know that if this type of pay plan is implemented correctly, it will reinforce a performance culture."

One of the key differentials between companies with a positive and those with a negative experience with variable pay programs was the selection of appropriate performance measures. Those measures are the primary motivation for employees and they communicate to employees what the objectives of the company are. Companies that focused variable pay measures on the ability to reduce costs reported less satisfaction with the programs than those companies using increases in sales as the measure upon which variable pay was linked. According to Paul Shafer, a manager with Hewitt Associates, "If a company wants growth, it can't reward for cutting costs. Cost reduction and growth can be competing, rather than complementary, goals, so by blending the two, companies run the risk of confusing employees and, in all likelihood, accomplishing neither."

Despite these mixed results, business consultants agree that well-designed variable pay programs that truly reward individual performance can be helpful. The purpose of a good bonus program should be to make the company stronger, more competitive, able to react quickly to change and prosper through growth. A good bonus program draws people into that process. It drives the value of the company by educating people, not with formalized training sessions but through the work they do every day. It provides employees with the support and tools they need to make wise decisions. It provides them with business knowledge they can use to enhance the prospects of the company as a whole as well as their own professional lives.

ESTABLISHING A VARIABLE PAY SYSTEM

Proponents of variable pay programs contend that implementation of such a system is far more likely to be successful if the following conditions are met:

- Employees must have control over their performance. If employees are overly dependent on the actions and output of other employees or processes, they may have little control over their own performance. Variable pay programs that are not based on principles of employee empowerment are almost certainly doomed to fail.

- Differences in performance must mean something to the business. Employees must see that mediocre and high-quality performances are not rewarded equally, and that results count.

- Business goals must be clearly defined and adequately disseminated to employees, and they should be arrived at with their assistance.

- Performance must be measured regularly and reliably. A clear system of performance appraisal and feedback must be put in place, with regularly scheduled meetings as one component.

- Employers should use variable pay as a tool in reaching ambitious business goals. The targets should be set high so that extra effort is needed to reach them.

- Businesses should make sure that their variable pay plans reward employees for actions or skills that actually further the aims of the company.

SEE ALSO *Employee Benefits; Employee Compensation; Human Resource Policies*

BIBLIOGRAPHY

Ang, James S., An-Sing Chen, and James Wu Lin. "Ascertaining the Effects of Employee Bonus Plans." *Applied Economics.* 10 July 2005.

"Companies are Not Getting Full Value from Variable Pay Programs." *Report on Salary Survey.* Institute of Management & Administration. July 2004.

Dietderich, Andrew. "Survey: Pay Based on Performance Gains Ground." *Crain's Detroit Business.* 3 April 2006.

U.S. Department of Labor. Bureau of Labor Statistics. Morton, John D. "Variable Pay in the BLS National Compensation Survey." 30 January 2003.

"Variable Pay Rising in Manufacturing." *Financial Express.* 22 March 2006.

Williams, Valerie L., and Stephen E. Grimaldi. "A Quick Breakdown of Strategic Pay." *Workforce.* December 1999.

Hillstrom, Northern Lights
updated by Magee, ECDI

VARIANCE

A variance has several meanings in business. In an accounting sense, a variance is the difference between an actual amount and a pre-determined standard amount or the amount budgeted. In a statistical sense, a variance is a measure of the amount of spread in a distribution. It is computed as the average squared deviation of each number from its mean. Finally, variance has a meaning related to land use called a zoning variance. A zoning variance is an administrative exception to land use regulations.

ACCOUNTING VARIANCES

In accounting, a variance could be a cost variance, where actual costs may be different from the estimated standards for costs. Variances can be favorable or unfavorable. A variance from standard cost is considered favorable if the actual cost is less than the standard or budgeted cost, and it is considered unfavorable if the actual cost is more than was budgeted. It is also possible to break down the cost variance into the factors that may have caused it to occur—such as a quantity variance, or the difference between the actual quantity and the standard quantity; and a price variance, or the difference between the actual price and the standard price.

When a variance occurs, like the cost variance in this example, top management should examine the circumstances to determine the factors that created it. By doing so, management should be able to identify who or what was responsible for the variance and take steps to correct the problem. For example, assume that the standard material cost for producing 1,000 units of a product is $8,000, but that materials costing $10,000 were actually used. The $2,000 unfavorable variance may have resulted from paying a price for the material that was higher than the standard price. Alternatively, the process may have used a greater quantity of material than standard. Or, there may have been some combination of these factors.

The purchasing department is usually responsible for the price paid for materials. Therefore, if the variance was caused by a price higher than standard, responsibility for explaining the problem rests with the purchasing manager. On the other hand, the production department is usually responsible for the amount of material used. Thus, the production department manager is responsible for explaining the problem if the process used more than the standard amount of materials. However, the production department may have used more than the standard amount of material because its quality did not meet specifications, with the result that more waste was created. Then the purchasing manager is responsible for explaining why the inferior materials were acquired. On the other hand, the production manager is responsible for explaining what happened if the analysis shows that the waste was caused by inefficiencies.

Thus variances—like the cost variance in the example above—trigger questions to be answered within the organization. These questions call for answers that, in turn, should lead to changes designed to correct the problem and minimize or eliminate the variances for the next reporting period. In studying variances in expenditures, a company may find that the assumptions upon which its budgets were made were in error. These too should be corrected so that the budget will more accurately reflects the likely outcome in the next period.

A performance report may identify the existence of the problem, but it can do no more than point the direction for further investigation of what can be done to improve future results. Other common variances in accounting include overhead rate and usage variances.

STATISTICAL VARIANCES

In statistics, a variance is also called the mean squared error. The variance is one of several measures that statisticians use to characterize the dispersion among the measures in a given population. To calculate the variance, it is necessary to first calculate the mean or average of the scores. The next step is to measure the amount that each individual score deviates or is different from the mean. Finally, you square that deviation by multiplying the number by itself. Numerically the variance equals the average of the squared deviations from the mean.

BIBLIOGRAPHY
Hunter, Katharine. "Variances: The Three-Step Method." *Accountancy.* January 1995.

Larson, K. D. *Fundamental Accounting Principles.* Sixteenth Edition. McGraw-Hill, 2004.

Wolinski, John. "John Wolinski Considers the Use of Budgeting in a Business and How Variances Can Be Analyzed." *Business Review.* November 2004.

Hillstrom, Northern Lights
updated by Magee, ECDI

VENTURE CAPITAL

Venture capital is a type of equity investment usually made in rapidly growing companies that require a lot of capital or start-up companies that can show they have a strong business plan. Venture capital may be provided by wealthy individual investors, professionally managed investment funds, government-backed Small Business Investment Corporations (SBICs), or subsidiaries of investment banking firms, insurance companies, or corporations. Such venture capital organizations generally invest in private startup companies with a high profit potential. In exchange for their funds, venture capital organizations usually require a percentage of equity ownership of the company (between 25 to 55 percent), some measure of control over its strategic planning, and payment of assorted fees. Due to the highly speculative nature of their investments, venture capital organizations expect a high rate of return. In addition, they often wish to obtain this return over a relatively short period of time, usually within three to seven years. After this time, the equity is either sold back to the client-company or offered on a public stock exchange.

Venture capital is more difficult for a small business to obtain than other sources of financing, such as bank loans and supplier credit. Before providing venture capital to a new or growing business, venture capital organizations require a formal proposal and conduct a thorough evaluation. Even then, they tend to approve only a small percentage of the proposals they receive. An entrepreneur with a small start-up should not consider venture capital if, for example, her objective is to grow her fledgling graphic design service into a middle-size regional greeting card business. This profile does not fit with the venture capitalists' objectives. Venture capital firms usually look for investment opportunities with firms that offer rapid growth as well as something new: a new technology or technology application, a new chemical compound, a new process for the manufacture of a product, etc. Once an entrepreneur's venture has been determined to be of a kind that may interest venture capitalists, the next move is to start planning. The most important thing an entrepreneur can do to increase his or her chances of obtaining venture capital is to plan ahead.

Venture capital offers several advantages to small businesses, including management assistance and lower costs over the short term. The disadvantages associated with venture capital include the possible loss of effective control over the business and relatively high costs over the long term. Overall, experts suggest that entrepreneurs should consider venture capital to be one financing strategy among many, and should seek to combine it with debt financing if possible.

THE EVALUATION PROCESS

Since it is often difficult to evaluate the earnings potential of new business ideas or very young companies, and investments in such companies are unprotected against business failures, venture capital is a highly risky industry. As a result, venture capital firms set rigorous policies and requirements for the types of proposals they will even consider. Some venture capitalists specialize in certain technologies, industries, or geographic areas, for example, while others require a certain size of investment. The maturity of the company may also be a factor. While most venture capital firms require their client companies to have some operating history, a very small number handle startup financing for businesses that have a well-considered plan, something "new," and an experienced management group.

In general, venture capitalists are most interested in supporting companies with low current valuations, but with good opportunities to achieve future profits in the range of 30 percent annually. Most attractive are innovative companies in rapidly accelerating industries with few competitors. Ideally, the company and its product or service will have some unique, marketable feature to distinguish it from imitators. Most venture capital firms look for investment opportunities in the $250,000 to $2 million range. Since venture capitalists become part owners of the companies in which they invest, they tend to

look for businesses that can increase sales and generate strong profits with the help of a capital infusion. Because of the risk involved, they hope to obtain a return of three to five times their initial investment within five years.

Venture capital organizations typically reject the vast majority—90 percent or more—of proposals quickly because they are deemed a poor fit with the firm's priorities and policies. They then investigate the remaining 10 percent of the proposals very carefully, and at considerable expense. Whereas banks tend to focus on companies' past performance when evaluating them for loans, venture capital firms tend to focus instead on their future potential. As a result, venture capital organizations will examine the features of a small business's product, the size of its markets, and its projected earnings.

As part of the detailed investigation, a venture capital organization may hire consultants to evaluate highly technical products. They also may contact a company's customers and suppliers in order to obtain information about the market size and the company's competitive position. Many venture capitalists will also hire an auditor to confirm the financial position of the company, and an attorney to check the legal form and registration of the business. Perhaps the most important factor in a venture capital organization's evaluation of a small business as a potential investment is the background and competence of the small business's management. For many venture capital firms the most important factor in their assessment is determining the capabilities of the management team, and not the potential product. Since the abilities of management are often difficult to assess, it is likely that a representative of the venture capital organization would spend a week or two at the company. Ideally, venture capitalists like to see a committed management team with experience in the industry. Another plus is a complete management group with clearly defined responsibilities in specific functional areas, such as product design, marketing, and finance.

VENTURE CAPITAL PROPOSALS

In order to best ensure that a proposal will be seriously considered by venture capital organizations, an entrepreneur should furnish several basic elements. After beginning with a statement of purpose and objectives, the proposal should outline the financing arrangements requested, i.e., how much money the small business needs, how the money will be used, and how the financing will be structured. The next section should feature the small business's marketing plans, from the characteristics of the market and the competition to specific plans for getting and keeping market share.

A good venture capital proposal will also include a history of the company, its major products and services, its banking relationships and financial milestones, and its hiring practices and employee relations. In addition, the proposal should include complete financial statements for the previous few years, as well as pro-forma projections for the next three to five years. The financial information should detail the small business's capitalization—i.e., provide a list of shareholders and bank loans—and show the effect of the proposed project on its capital structure. The proposal should also include biographies of the key players involved with the small business, as well as contact information for its principal suppliers and customers. Finally, the entrepreneur should outline the advantages of the proposal—including any special and unique features it may offer—as well as any problems that are anticipated.

If, after careful investigation and analysis, a venture capital organization should decide to invest in a small business, it then prepares its own proposal. The venture capital firm's proposal would detail how much money it would provide, the amount of stock it would expect the small business to surrender in exchange, and the protective covenants it would require as part of the agreement. The venture capital organization's proposal is presented to the management of the small business, and then a final agreement is negotiated between the two parties. Principal areas of negotiation include valuation, ownership, control, annual charges, and final objectives.

The valuation of the small business and the entrepreneur's stake in it are very important, as they determine the amount of equity that is required in exchange for the venture capital. When the present financial value of the entrepreneur's contribution is relatively low compared to that made by the venture capitalists—for example, when it consists only of an idea for a new product—then a large percentage of equity is generally required. On the other hand, when the valuation of a small business is relatively high—for example, when it is already a successful company—then a small percentage of equity is generally required. It is quite normal for venture capital firms to value a company at below the valuation the company has for itself. It is best if the small business looking for venture capital prepare for such an outcome.

The percentage of equity ownership required by a venture capital firm can range from 10 percent to 80 percent, depending on the amount of capital provided and the anticipated return. But most venture capital organizations want to secure equity in the 30-50 percent range so that the small business owners still have an incentive to grow the business. Since venture capital is in effect an investment in a small business's management team, the venture capitalists usually want to leave management with some control. In general, venture capital organizations have little or no interest in assuming

day-to-day operational control of the small businesses in which they invest. They have neither the technical expertise or managerial personnel to do so. But venture capitalists usually do want to place a representative on each small business's board of directors in order to participate in strategic decision-making.

Many venture capital agreements include an annual charge, typically 2-3 percent of the amount of capital provided, although some firms instead opt to take a cut of profits above a certain level. Venture capital organizations also frequently include protective covenants in their agreements. These covenants usually give the venture capitalists the ability to appoint new officers and assume control of the small business in case of severe financial, operating, or marketing problems. Such control is intended to enable the venture capital organization to recover some of its investment if the small business should fail.

The final objectives of a venture capital agreement relate to the means and time frame in which the venture capitalists will earn a return on their investment. In most cases, the return takes the form of capital gains earned when the venture capital organization sells its equity holdings back to the small business or on a public stock exchange. Another option is for the venture capital firm to arrange for the small business to merge with a larger company. The majority of venture capital arrangements include an equity position, along with a final objective that involves the venture capitalist selling that position. For this reason, entrepreneurs considering using venture capital as a source of financing need to consider the impact a future stock sale will have on their own holdings and their personal ambition to run the company. Ideally, the entrepreneur and the venture capital organization can reach an agreement that will help the small business grow enough to provide the venture capitalists with a good return on their investment as well as to overcome the owner's loss of equity.

THE IMPORTANCE OF PLANNING

Although there is no way for a small business to guarantee that it will be able to obtain venture capital, sound planning can at least improve the chances that its proposal will receive due consideration from a venture capital organization. Such planning should begin at least a year before the entrepreneur first seeks financing. At this point, it is important to do market research to determine the need for its new business concept or product idea and establish patent or trade secret protection, if possible. In addition, the entrepreneur should take steps to form a business around the product or concept, enlisting the assistance of third-party professionals like attorneys, accountants, and financial advisors as needed.

Six months prior to seeking venture capital, the entrepreneur should prepare a detailed business plan, complete with financial projections, and begin working on a formal request for funds. Three months in advance, the entrepreneur should investigate venture capital organizations to identify those that are most likely to be interested in the proposal and to provide a suitable venture capital agreement. The best investor candidates will closely match the company's development stage, size, industry, and financing needs. It is also important to gather information about a venture capitalist's reputation, track record in the industry, and liquidity to ensure a productive working relationship.

One of the more important steps in the planning process is preparing detailed financial plans. Strong financial planning demonstrates managerial competence and suggests an advantage to potential investors. A financial plan should include cash budgets—prepared monthly and projected for a year ahead—that enable the company to anticipate fluctuations in short-term cash levels and the need for short-term borrowing. A financial plan should also include pro-forma income statements and balance sheets projected for up to three years ahead. By showing expected sales revenues and expenses, assets and liabilities, these statements help the company to anticipate financial results and plan for intermediate-term financing needs. Finally, the financial plan should include an analysis of capital investments made by the company in products, processes, or markets, along with a study of the company's sources of capital. These plans, prepared for five years ahead, assist the company in anticipating the financial consequences of strategic shifts and in planning for long-term financing needs.

Overall, experts warn that it takes time and persistence for entrepreneurs to obtain venture capital. In the best of economic times, venture capital is difficult to secure. In slower economic times it becomes ever harder. It is not unusual to work on obtaining venture capital for years before an agreement is met, according to Brian Brus who studied the subject for his article "Starting a Business is Harder then Ever in the 21st Century." The hardest thing to communicate to enthusiastic entrepreneurs who come to venture capital firms looking for help, explains Brus, is that they can't just get started making their new product or service. Venture capitalists may be risk takers but for those lucky few with whom they invest, it may not feel that way once all the paper work is done and an agreement is in place.

SEE ALSO *Angel Investors; Financial Planning; Loans; Seed Money*

BIBLIOGRAPHY

Bartlett, Joseph W. *Fundamentals of Venture Capital.* Madison, 1999.

Braunschweiger, Carolina. "Fundraising for Private Equity Hearty in First Quarter." *Investment Management Weekly.* 1 May 2006.

Clark, Scott. "Business Plan Basics: Why Most New Ventures Fail to Raise Capital." *Houston Business Journal.* 17 March 2000.

Davoudi, Salamander, Lina Seigol, and Peter Smith. "Why Private Equity Companies are Piling into Healthcare. Strong Cash Flows, Property and Demographics are Drawing them In." *The Finanical Times.* 26 April 2006.

Gimbel, Florian. "Venture Capitalists Shift Focus to India Technology." *The Financial Times.* 2 May 2006.

Gompers, Paul, and Josh Lerner. *The Venture Capital Cycle.* The MIT Press, 1999.

La Beau, Christina. "Growing in Size But Not in Equity: Women Businesses Still Lag in Venture Capital." *Crain's Chicago Business.* 13 December 2004.

National Venture Capital Association. "The Venture Capital Industry—An Overview." Available from http://www.nvca.org/def.html. Retrieved on 3 May 2006.

Parmar, Simon, J. Kevin Bright, and E.F. Peter Newson. "Building a Winning E-Business." *Ivey Business Journal.* November 2000.

Hillstrom, Northern Lights
updated by Magee, ECDI

VENTURE CAPITAL NETWORKS

Venture capital networks, or clubs, are groups of individual and institutional investors that provide financing to risky, unproven business ventures. Like other providers of venture capital—which may include professionally managed investment funds, government-backed Small Business Investment Corporations (SBICs), or subsidiaries of investment banking firms, insurance companies, and corporations—members of these networks generally invest in private startup companies with a high profit potential. In exchange for their funds, the venture capitalists usually require a percentage of equity ownership of the company, some measure of control over its strategic planning, and payment of assorted fees. Due to the highly speculative nature of their investments, venture capitalists hope to achieve a high rate of return over a relatively short period of time.

The main difference between venture capital networks and other venture capital providers is their degree of formality. Venture capital networks are informal organizations that exist to help entrepreneurs and small businesses connect with potential investors. Before the advent of networks, it was extremely difficult for entrepreneurs to gain access to wealthy private investors, also known as "angels" or "adventure capitalists." The networks—which may take the form of computer databases or document clearinghouses—basically provide "matchmaking" services between people with good business ideas and people with money to invest. In contrast, formal venture capital firms are professionally managed organizations that exist to earn a high return on funds by investing in new and growing companies. These firms are typically highly selective about the companies in which they invest, meaning that venture capital from these sources is not available to the vast majority of startup businesses.

According to *Nation's Business,* wealthy private investors provided American small businesses with $10 to $20 billion annually during the mid-1990s. In the early 2000s the venture capital market slowed dramatically. However, according to Second Venture Corporation, a venture capital network dedicated to helping entrepreneurs find funding with which to start businesses, "The current venture capital market [in early 2006] is rebounding nicely, from the past setbacks of the dot com bubble. Venture capital remains a viable source of funding for startups, which are able to deliver the necessary growth that investors are looking for. Past events should certainly not discourage entrepreneurs who have genuine winning ideas and business plans from looking for funds."

The membership of venture capital networks consists primarily of wealthy entrepreneurs who recognize both the financial potential of new businesses and the importance of capital in the early stages of a business's life. In many cases, these investors wind up sitting on the boards of the companies they fund, where they can provide valuable, firsthand management advice based on their own experiences.

HOW NETWORKS WORK

In the past, it was extremely difficult for entrepreneurs to find and make contact with private investors. In response to this problem, many business groups and universities created networks to help entrepreneurs gain access to interested investors. One of the earliest such efforts was the Venture Capital Network, a computer database that was established by a professor at the University of New Hampshire. This and other computerized networks are similar to computer matchmaking services. Each entrepreneur posts a business plan and a set of financial projections on the network, while each investor submits information describing his or her interests and investment criteria. Due to their previous business experience, different investors may be most interested in investing in companies of a certain size, in a certain industry, or with certain capital requirements. The computer then provides participants with a list of possible matches. Interested

parties are left to make contact with one another and try to reach an agreement.

Non-computerized venture capital networks operate in basically the same way. A central clearinghouse solicits business plans from companies seeking capital, then distributes profiles of the companies to private investors who belong to the network. If a certain investor wants to know more about a particular company, he or she might arrange for a formal presentation. In many cases, both business and investor profiles are distributed anonymously—without names attached—until both parties express an interest in proceeding further. Another similar type of arrangement can be found in a private investment club. These are community-based organizations in which several individuals pool their resources to invest in new and existing businesses on a local level. Such clubs generally solicit business plans and then distribute them to members, but then invest as a group.

The financing provided through venture capital networks can range dramatically in size from investments of $25,000 to more than $1 million (the majority of financing deals are under $100,000). Entrepreneurs searching for venture capital assistance usually pay a small fee to participate in a network—typically less than $500 annually—and institutional investors may pay a somewhat higher fee. Although venture capital networks are usually better sources of funding for startup companies than formal venture capital firms, merely joining a network does not guarantee that a small business will obtain financing. There are usually at least two companies for every one investor listed in databases. In addition, even if a match is made, the entrepreneur still must sell the investor on the proposal and negotiate a mutually beneficial agreement.

SEE ALSO *Angel Investors; Financial Planning; Loans; Seed Money*

BIBLIOGRAPHY
Bartlett, Joseph W. *Fundamentals of Venture Capital.* Madison, 1999.

La Beau, Christina. "Growing in Size But Not in Equity: Women Businesses Still Lag in Venture Capital." *Crain's Chicago Business.* 13 December 2004.

"Raising Venture Capital? Looking for Angel Investors?" Second Venture Corporation. Available from http://www.ventureworthy.com/. Retrieved on 2 May 2006.

"Venture Capital Clubs or Groups." Venture Associates. Available from http://www.venturea.com/clubs2.htm. Retrieved on 2 May 2006.

Hillstrom, Northern Lights
updated by Magee, ECDI

VERTICAL MARKETING SYSTEM

A vertical marketing system (VMS) is one in which the main members of a distribution channel—producer, wholesaler, and retailer—work together as a unified group in order to meet consumer needs. In conventional marketing systems, producers, wholesalers, and retailers are separate businesses that are all trying to maximize their profits. When the effort of one channel member to maximize profits comes at the expense of other members, conflicts can arise that reduce profits for the entire channel. To address this problem, more and more companies are forming vertical marketing systems.

Vertical marketing systems can take several forms. In a corporate VMS, one member of the distribution channel owns the other members. Although they are owned jointly, each company in the chain continues to perform a separate task. In an administered VMS, one member of the channel is large and powerful enough to coordinate the activities of the other members without an ownership stake. Finally, a contractual VMS consists of independent firms joined together by contract for their mutual benefit. One type of contractual VMS is a retailer cooperative, in which a group of retailers buy from a jointly owned wholesaler. Another type of contractual VMS is a franchise organization, in which a producer licenses a wholesaler to distribute its products.

The concept behind vertical marketing systems is similar to vertical integration. In vertical integration, a company expands its operations by assuming the activities of the next link in the chain of distribution. For example, an auto parts supplier might practice forward integration by purchasing a retail outlet to sell its products. Similarly, the auto parts supplier might practice backward integration by purchasing a steel plant to obtain the raw materials needed to manufacture its products. Vertical marketing should not be confused with horizontal marketing, in which members at the same level in a channel of distribution band together in strategic alliances or joint ventures to exploit a new marketing opportunity.

As Tom Egelhoff wrote in an online article entitled "How to Use Vertical Marketing Systems," a VMS can hold both advantages and disadvantages for small businesses. "The main advantage of VMS is that your company can control all of the elements of producing and selling a product. In this way, you are able to see the whole picture, anticipate problems, make changes as they become necessary, and thus increase your efficiency. However, being involved in all stages of distribution can make it difficult for a small business owner to keep track of what is happening. In addition, the arrangement can fail if the personalities managing of the different areas do not fit together well."

For small business owners interested in forming a VMS, Egelhoff recommended starting out by developing close relationships with suppliers and distributors. "What suppliers or distributors would you buy if you had the money? These are the ones to work with and form a strong relationship," he stated. "Vertical marketing can give many companies a major advantage over their competitors."

SEE ALSO *Cooperative; Marketing*

BIBLIOGRAPHY
Baker, Sunny, and Kim Baker. "Going Up! Vertical Marketing on the Web." *Journal of Business Strategy.* May 2000.

Baldwin, Lawrence, Steve Hoffman, and David Miller. *OpenVMS System Management Guide.* October 2003.

Bloom, Paul N., and Venessa G. Perry. "Retailer Power and Supplier Welfare: The Case of Wal-Mart." *Journal of Retailing.* Fall 2001.

Boone, Louis E., and David L. Kurtz. *Contemporary Marketing 2005/With Infotrac.* Thomson South-Western, February 2004.

Egelhoff, Tom. "How to Use Vertical Marketing Systems." Available from http://www.smalltownmarketing.com. Retrieved on 2 May 2006.

Hillstrom, Northern Lights
updated by Magee, ECDI

VIRTUAL PRIVATE NETWORKS

Virtual private networks (VPNs) are systems that use public networks to carry private information and maintain privacy through the use of a tunneling protocol and security procedures. By using the shared public infrastructure, these *virtual* private networks are far more cost effective than were early *real* private networks which companies built using costly private lines and systems. In a VPN some of the parts of the network are connected using the Internet (the public infrastructure). Data that travel over the Internet are encrypted, so the entire network is "virtually" private. This allows users to share private information over a public infrastructure. A typical VPN application would be one created by a company with offices in different cities. By setting up a VPN the company uses the Internet as the connector between the networks in its two offices effectively merging their networks into one. Encryption is used on all transmissions within the network that use the Internet link, making it a private network.

The public infrastructure that provides the backbone for most VPN systems is the Internet. VPNs can connect remote users and other off-site users (such as vendors or customers) to a larger centralized network. Before the Internet, and the easy availability of high-speed or broadband connections to the Internet, a private network required that a company install proprietary and very expensive communication lines. The expense of such an investment put private networks out of the reach of most mid- to small-size firms. This is no longer the case. This fact, along with the universal appeal of the Internet, has enabled the rapid spread of VPN technology. The result is remote access that is quicker, more secure, and wider in scope.

STRUCTURAL OVERVIEW OF VPN SYSTEMS

In the most basic terms, a computer network is a group of computers that are connected with cable. Usually, one or more computers acts as a server within the group. A network may also be formed with computers that communicate through wireless connections but the wireless signal must be caught and transmitted by hardware that is located reasonably near both the sending and receiving machines.

Companies have long networked computers. Until the advent of the Internet, however, the entire infrastructure of these networks had to be built by the companies themselves. They had to purchase and lay cables to connect their computers. They had to purchase and install boosters or repeaters to augment the signals transmitted through cables when large distances were involved. They had to lease high-capacity, dedicated phone lines in order to connect computers or networks in remote locations. They had to build or lease transmission towers in order to send wireless signals long distances and they had to purchase and install the systems used to send and receive these signals. Not surprisingly, most companies did not go far beyond networking computers in a single building since the cost of the infrastructure requirements for anything larger were prohibitive.

With the advent of the Internet and the growth in availability of high speed, broadband communication lines, new technologies were developed to use the Internet as the conduit through which to connect remote computers or networks. A company no longer had to absorb the full cost of building the infrastructure needed for wide area networks (WANs).

The communications protocols that regulate and make the Internet possible are also the basis for the protocols necessary to operate virtual private networks. The underlying collection of protocols is called transmission control protocol/Internet protocol or TCP/IP for short. The protocols for VPNs are called IPSec.

A virtual private network is, basically, a network in which some of its components are connected to one another through the Internet. Software written to use IPSec is used to establish these Internet connections. The connections created in this way are called tunnels, through which all transactions between the two authenticated computers on either end of the tunnel may transmit privately across the public Internet.

Client-to-Network A VPN can be set up to connect single-client PCs with a company's local-area network (LAN) This sort of VPN is usually called a client-to-LAN VPN. This enables companies that have employees who travel extensively or work remotely to equip those employees with a computer that uses the VPN to access the company network and work on it like any other employee from just about anywhere, as long as they have access to the Internet. Small companies may set up a client-to-LAN VPN through which all the employees access a central server from their home offices.

LAN-to-LAN A LAN-to-LAN VPN is one that connects two networks together instead of individual client computers being connected to a single LAN. The mechanisms behind these two types of VPN is the same. A LAN-to-LAN system is useful for connecting a branch office network to a corporate headquarters network, or a warehouse network to a supplier's network. The options are many.

THE COST OF VIRTUAL PRIVATE NETWORKS

The costs of implementing a virtual private network are reasonable for any company that already has a network and high-speed access to the Internet. The two biggest components of a VPN, for those with networks in place, are the software and set-up of the same, and the need in many cases to upgrade the Internet connection service. Because a VPN uses the Internet address of the network server as the access for those logging on the system through the Internet, a company must have a static IP address. Internet Service Providers usually charge slightly more for a service that holds the IP address static.

The software needed to manage a VPN is commonly sold as a part of many network operating systems. Setting up this software takes networking knowledge but can be done by any competent network administrator or network outsourcing supplier.

When a business decides to use an outside provider, it is immediately eliminating any costs for purchasing and maintaining the necessary equipment. The most the business will have to do is maintain security measures (usually a firewall) as well as provide the servers that will help authenticate users. Of course, this too can be done by an outside provider for an additional price. Outsourcing also cuts down on the number of employees that would be required to manage and maintain the virtual private network.

For a firm that does not already have a computer network with Internet access, the task of setting up a VPN is a much larger undertaking.

VIRTUAL PRIVATE NETWORKS AND SECURITY

Virtual private network systems are constantly evolving and becoming more secure through four main features: tunneling, authentication, encryption, and access control. These features work separately, but combine to deliver a higher level of security while at the same time allowing all users (including those from remote locations) to access the VPN more easily.

Tunneling creates the connection between a user (either from a remote location or separate office) to the main LAN. This connection is called a tunnel and is essentially the circuit-like path that transfers encrypted private information through the Internet. This requires an IP address which is an Internet address to which the client PC can direct itself, a pointer to the company network. Unlike other IP addresses, this one is not open to the public but is rather a gateway through which VPN users may enter, and after authentication and logging on, have access to the network.

To avoid crowded connections, a tunneling feature called "switching" was developed. This feature helps differentiate between direct and remote users to determine which connections should receive the highest priority. The switching can either be programmed directly into the virtual private network or upgraded so that the hardware recognizes each connection on an individual basis.

Incoming callers to the virtual private network are identified and approved for access through features called authentication and access control. These features are usually set up by the IT manager who enters a user's individual identification code or password into the main server, which cuts down on the chances that the network can be manipulated from outside the company. Authentication also offers the chance to regulate access to the material on the LAN so that users can be provided access to specific information only.

Encryption is the security measure that allows information on virtual private networks to be scrambled so that it becomes meaningless to unauthorized users. Encrypted data is eventually unscrambled at the end of the tunnel by a user with the proper authorization. This process is usually done via a private IP address that encrypts the information before it leaves the LAN or a remote location.

Despite these precautions, some companies are still hesitant to transfer highly sensitive and private information over the Internet via a virtual private network and still resort to tried-and-true methods of communication for such data.

THE PERFORMANCE OF VIRTUAL PRIVATE NETWORKS

The latest wave of virtual private networks features self-contained hardware solutions (whereas previously they were little more than software solutions and upgrades to existing LAN equipment). Since they are now self-contained, this VPN hardware does not require an additional connection to a network and therefore cuts down on the use of a file server and LAN, which makes everything run a bit more smoothly. These new VPNs are small and easy to set up and use, but still contain all of the necessary security and performance features.

In order for a virtual private network to perform properly, the server must have enough bandwidth to accommodate the number of users active at any one time. The number of remote users can also affect a VPN's performance. In addition, new technology that requires more bandwidth is bound to come out from time to time, and this should be planned for in advance to avoid a potential disruption in performance.

High volumes of traffic are also known to adversely affect the performance of a virtual private network, as is encrypted data. Since encryption technology is often added on via software, this may cause the network to slow down, hindering performance. A more desirable solution is to incorporate encryption technology that uses hardware solutions to keep the network running at the proper speed. New technologies are also constantly emerging that help to decide just how sensitive certain material is (and therefore how intensive the encryption needs to be).

THE FUTURE OF VIRTUAL PRIVATE NETWORKS

As virtual private networks continue to evolve, so do the number of outlets that can host them. Several providers have experimented with running VPNs over cable television networks. This solution offers high bandwidth and low costs, but less security. Other experts see wireless technology as the future of virtual private networks.

A new protocol for VPN systems has emerged in recent years and shows promise for enhancing the flexibility of VPNs. The traditional VPN system was based on Internet protocol security. The new protocol is based on Secure Sockets Layer or SSL. According to an article in *Network World,* "The biggest difference between SSL VPNs and traditional IP Security VPNs is that the IP

Security standard requires installation of client code on the end user's system, while SSL VPNs focus on making applications available through any Web browser."

The popularity of VPNs continues to grow and evolve, providing companies of all sizes a means with which to leverage the Internet to reduce the costs of communication.

SEE ALSO *Communication Systems; Local Area Networks; Mobile Office; Wide Area Networks*

BIBLIOGRAPHY

Administrator's Guide to TCP/IP. Second Edition. Tech Republic, June 2003.

Binsacca, Rich. "Virtual Private Networks." *Builder.* June 2000.

Goldberger, Henry. "The Migration from Frame Relay to IP VPN and VPLS Services." *In-Stat Alerts.* 2 February 2006.

Hayes, Jim. "Managed Data Services." *Communicate.* July 2000.

Schnider, Joel. "SSL VPN Gateways." *Network World.* 12 January 2004.

Winther, Mark. "Avoiding the Challenges of Do-it-Yourself Broadband VPNs." *Business Communications Review.* February 2006.

Hillstrom, Northern Lights
updated by Magee, ECDI

VIRUS

A virus is a program designed to infect and potentially damage files on a computer that receives it. The code for a virus is hidden within a file or program—such as a text document or a spreadsheet program—and when the file is opened or the program is launched, the virus inserts copies of itself, infecting the computer on which these files are opened. Because of this ability to reproduce itself, a virus can quickly spread to other programs, including the computer's operating system. A virus may reside on a computer system for some time before taking any action detectable to the user. Other viruses may cause trouble immediately. Some viruses cause little or no damage. For example, a virus may manifest itself as nothing more than a message that appears on the screen at certain intervals. Other viruses are much more destructive and can result in lost or corrupted files and data. Viruses may render a computer unusable, necessitating the reinstallation of the operating system and applications. Viruses can even be written to imbed some small miscalculation into, for example, a spreadsheet program. This sort of hidden problem may jeopardize the accuracy of **all** the work done with the infected program for a long time before it is even detected.

Viruses are written to target program files and macros, or a computer's boot sector, which is the portion of the hard drive that executes the steps necessary to start the hardware and software. Program viruses attach themselves to the executable files associated with software programs, and can then attack any file that is used to launch an application, usually files ending with the "exe" or "com" extensions. Macro viruses infect program templates that are used to create documents or spreadsheets. Once infected, every document or spreadsheet opened with the infected program becomes corrupted. Boot sector viruses attack the computer's hard drive and launch themselves each time the user boots, or starts, the computer. Viruses are often classified as Trojan Horses or Worms. A Trojan Horse virus is one that appears harmless on the surface but, in reality, destroys files or programs. A Worm attacks the computer's operating system and replicates itself again and again, until the system eventually crashes.

Another line of viruses is referred to as Malware, or, more generically as Spyware. These are viruses that are imbedded in files downloaded onto an unsuspecting computer while the user is browsing the Internet. Spyware programs, once on a computer, allow the creator of the virus to snoop on or monitor the infected computer's browser activities. A spyware virus usually implants "pop-up" ads that will appear on a user's screen periodically. These programs can down a computer, cause it to crash, and in some cases can even record for the sender the recipient's credit card numbers if it is used to purchase items while online. Spyware is usually a nuisance-level virus but in some cases can pose a more serious threat.

VIRUSES AND THE INTERNET

The Internet, with its global reach and rapid delivery times, provides the ideal breeding ground for viruses. Typically, someone who wants to spread a virus does so by sending out an e-mail message containing an infected attachment. The subject line on such a message sounds innocuous, so unsuspecting recipients open the message, unwittingly infecting their computers. More insidious yet, many viruses infect the recipient and then launch e-mail messages using the recipient's e-mail system address book and send themselves out to all of the recipient's list of colleagues, clients, vendors, friends, and family for whom an e-mail is found.

VIRUS PROTECTION

With new computer viruses appearing daily, keeping a computer or network of computers free of viruses is a daunting task. If, however, one views the proper use and maintenance of anti-virus software as a necessary part of running computers, the task becomes just another in the list of things one must do to maintain computers. The following are steps every computer user should follow to protect his or her computer from viruses.

1. Install an anti-virus software program to identify and remove viruses before they can cause any damage. These programs scan, or review, files that may come from floppy diskettes, the Internet, e-mail attachments, or networks, looking for patterns of code that match patterns in the anti-virus software vendor's database of known viruses. Once detected, the software isolates and removes the virus before it can be activated.

2. Update the anti-virus software weekly. Because the number of viruses is increasing all the time, it is important to keep anti-virus software up-to-date with information on newly identified viruses. Anti-virus software vendors are constantly updating their databases of information on viruses and making this information available to their customers via their Web sites or by e-mail.

3. Maintain a regular back-up procedure for all computers. This procedure may be as simple as keeping copies of important files on diskettes or CD-ROMs (in which case original software should be kept with these diskettes or CDs) and it may be as elaborate as a system designed to produce a mirror copy of a system, updating this copy every few minutes. For a small business, the most prudent level of back-up probably falls somewhere between these two extremes. Whatever the schedule is, it should include regular and periodic backing up of all computer systems and the remote storage of the backups' media in case of fire, flood, etc.

4. Do not open e-mail from unknown recipients or messages that contain unexpected attachments. A user should delete these types of messages. As a general rule, a user should scan every e-mail attachment for viruses before opening it—even an expected attachment—as the sender may have unknowingly sent an infected file.

NOTEWORTHY VIRUSES

One of the most costly and memorable viruses was the Love Bug virus of 2000. This virus targeted users of Microsoft's Outlook e-mail program. Originating in the Philippines, the subject line on the Love Bug message was the inviting "ILOVEYOU." If a user opened the attachment to this message, the virus quickly began to destroy files, targeting digital pictures and music files. The Love Bug virus also perpetuated itself by forwarding the original message to all e-mail addresses listed in the current recipient's Outlook address book. In this way, the virus was able to circle the globe in just two hours. The virus brought businesses to a standstill as companies, large and small, were forced to shut off incoming Internet e-mail messages and repair infected systems. In all, the Love Bug virus is estimated to have cost up to $10 billion in lost work hours.

Another record-setting virus, the fastest spreading e-mail worm ever, is MyDoom. This ominously named virus is a computer worm affecting Microsoft Windows. It was first sighted on January 2004 and was designed to send junk e-mail through infected computers. Early speculation about MyDoom held that the sole purpose of the worm was to perpetrate a distributed "denial-of-service attack" against the SCO Group. A denial of service attack is one in which a company Web site is flooded with e-mail causing it to overload, or shut down, and damaging any sales generated through the site, or services provided on the site.

Most viruses do not reach the level of fame that these two achieved, either because they are programmed to change as they spread, making them harder to identify and stop, or because they attack a niche sector of the computer-using market. Nonetheless, the damage that such viruses, even seemingly innocuous ones, can have on a company are great. Lost computer processing power equals slower-functioning computers, a lost of time and productivity. Lost files take time to retrieve from backup systems, assuming good backups exist. And rebuilding a computer that has been damaged by a virus is time-consuming for both the technician and the user.

Protection is the best way to save time, money, and the wear and tear that computer problems can have on all the people involved.

SEE ALSO *Internet Security*

BIBLIOGRAPHY

"Attack of the Love Bug." *Time.* 15 May 2000.

Evers, Joris. "Computer Crime Costs $67 Billion, FBI Says." *C/Net News.com.* 20 January 2006.

Roberts, Paul. "Antivirus Companies Target Spyware, Worms." *PC World.* 25 August 2003.

Szor, Peter. *The Art of Computer Virus Research and Defense.* Addison-Wesley Professional, February 2005.

"The State of Internet Security." Symantec Corporation. Available from http://www.symantec.com/small_business/library/index.html. Retrieved on 13 April 2006.

Hillstrom, Northern Lights
updated by Magee, ECDI

W

WARRANTIES

A product or service warranty (also known as guarantee) is a promise, from a manufacturer or seller, to stand behind the product or service. It is a statement about the integrity of the product and about the seller's commitment to correct problems should the product or service fail. Product and service warranties have become standard practice in most U.S. industries, although opinions vary somewhat regarding their impact on sales. But misleading language in these guarantees has the capacity to spark significant legal troubles for small businesses that run afoul, however inadvertently, of legal guidelines. Consumers can ask the courts to enforce warranties, whether they are express, implied, written, verbal, or given in any other way. Federal, state, and local government entities establish the regulatory basis upon which warranties are judged. The Federal Trade Commission (FTC) is the ultimate arbiter of warranty law in the United States. The FTC's primary tool in monitoring product and service guarantees is the Magnuson-Moss Consumer Warranty Act.

EXPRESS AND IMPLIED WARRANTIES

The law recognizes two basic kinds of warranties—implied warranties and express warranties.

Implied Warranties Implied warranties are unspoken, unwritten promises, created by state law, that go from the seller or merchant to the customers. Implied warranties are based upon the common law principle of "fair value for money spent." The Uniform Commercial Code (UCC) provides for two basic types of implied warranties that occur in consumer product transactions. They are the implied warranty of merchantability and the implied warranty of fitness for a particular purpose. The "implied warranty of merchantability" is a seller's basic promise that the goods sold will do what they are supposed to do and that there is nothing significantly wrong with them. In other words, it is an implied promise that the goods are fit to be sold. According to the law, merchants make this promise automatically every time they sell a product they are in business to sell. By contrast, the implied warranty of "fitness for a particular purpose" is a promise that a seller makes when the customer relies on the advice that a product can be used for some specific purpose. For example, suppose a woman comes to an office supply store and asks for a printer that is able to print 1,000 sheets of paper per hour. If the office supply company recommends a particular model, and the customer buys that model on the strength of this recommendation, the law says that the office supply company has made a warranty of fitness for a particular purpose. If the printer recommended proves unable to produce 1,000 pages per hour, even though it may effectively print 800 pages an hour, the implied warranty of fitness for a particular purpose is breached.

Express Warranty Unlike implied warranties, express warranties are not automatically a part of the sales contract based on state law; rather, they are explicitly offered warranties. They are promises and statements, made voluntarily by the seller or manufacturer, about a product or service and about the commitment to remedy defects and/or malfunctions that the customer may experience.

Express warranties can take a variety of forms, ranging from advertising claims to formal certificates. An express warranty can be made either orally or in writing. While oral warranties are important, only written warranties on consumer products are covered by the Magnuson-Moss Warranty Act.

ELEMENTS OF A WARRANTY

The Federal Trade Commission requires that written warranties bestowed in connection with the sale of a product or service explicitly detail the following information:

- Who is covered by the warranty

- Length of warranty

- Description of the products, parts, properties, or characteristics covered by or excluded from the warranty

- Steps for customer in the event that warranty coverage comes into play

- Warrantor's response when confronted with product/service malfunctions, defects, or failures

- Any exclusions of or limitations on relief such as incidental or consequential damages

- Statement that indicates that some states do not allow such exclusions or limitations

- Statement of consumer legal rights

- Any limitations on the length of implied warranties, if possible

FULL AND LIMITED WARRANTIES

The Magnuson-Moss Act does not require businesses to provide warranties to customers. Indeed, some business owners decide that written warranties are not even necessary to enjoy success in their chosen field of endeavor. But other manufacturers and retailers are convinced that warranties help sell their products, pointing to the popularity of service contracts and the like.

Businesses that choose to provide written warranties may choose from two types: full and limited. FTC regulations concerning full warranties are considerably more stringent than those that apply to limited warranties. According to the Magnuson-Moss Act, "fully guaranteed" products or services must meet the following five criteria:

- Customer receives full money back or replacement or repair of any defective part of product in the event of a complaint

- Prompt and free repairs

- If repairs are not fully satisfactory to the buyer, a prompt refund is available

- Customer has no responsibility beyond reporting the defect to the company

- Acknowledgment of all implied warranties

Limited warranties, which must be prominently labeled as such, limit the liability of the manufacturer or service provider. A limited warranty may offer to replace defective parts free, but only do so for a limited length of time, or require that the consumer ship the product to a manufacturer-approved service center. The distinctions between full and limited warranties and the obligations of manufacturers to honor them vary from state to state, so it is up to the consumer to carefully read the literature and understand what is covered before the purchase.

Disclaimers Vulnerability to express and/or implied warranties can be reduced somewhat through the use of disclaimers. A disclaimer is a means of denying that you are making one or more express or implied warranties. In the absence of a disclaimer, a breach of warranty will often give the purchaser of the faulty item the right to recover the cost of the item as well as additional damages caused by that breach of warranty.

Small business consultants note that warranties—both express and implied—can be negotiated with buyers, but they urge business owners to use specific language when adding such disclaimers to a sales contract. The term "exclusive remedy," for instance, can give a seller of products or services significant legal protection when it is used to explicitly limit a buyer's legal options in the event of complaints about product defects or workmanship. If, however, the customer is left without a working product, the seller may be sued no matter what agreement was signed, on the grounds that it's a remedy that "fails of its essential purpose." Obviously, the obligations imposed by law in the areas of warranty are extensive, so small business owners should make sure that they consult a legal expert so that they can develop the most effective disclaimer possible.

EXTENDED WARRANTIES

Extended warranties are somewhat controversial, but often profitable, warranty packages offered by manufacturers and service providers. Manufacturers sell these warranties, which are basically extensions of basic warranty packages, in hopes that the extended warranty will not be needed or used, thereby resulting in profits. Consumers buy them for peace of mind, reasoning that they are protecting their initial outlay of money. The controversy revolves around what the warranties cover.

Some extended warranties are actually service agreements, resulting in higher charges than might be expected under a warranty. In other cases the fine print in the warranties exclude the very things that the consumer assumes would be covered.

BIBLIOGRAPHY

Pratt, Eddy. "Will the Digital Surge Bring Happier Times for Extended Warranties?" *ERMagazine.* August 2000.

Roberts, Barry S., and Richard A Mann. *Smith and Roberson's Business Law.* Thomson West, March 2005.

Twomey, David P. *Anderson's Business Law and the Legal Environment.* Thomson West, May 2004.

U.S. Department of Commerce. Federal Trade Commission. "A Businessperson's Guide to Federal Warranty Law." Available from http://www.ftc.gov/bcp/conline/pubs/buspubs/warranty.htm. Retrieved on 8 May 2006.

Hillstrom, Northern Lights
updated by Magee, ECDI

WEB SITE DESIGN

Web site design is the process of creating a site on the Internet. Internet users view Web sites with a software program known as a Web browser. Each Web site has a unique address usually referred to as a unique resource locator or URL. Web sites can consist of text, graphics, audio files, video files, and animation. For many businesses, a Web site can be a virtual "storefront" that enables the company to sell products and services to customers and clients around the world at a relatively small price.

The most common way that small companies establish a presence on the Internet is by setting up a simple homepage that provides potential customers with information on the company and its products. The essentially limitless storage space of the computer network means that businesses are free to post as much information as they wish about themselves—computerized versions of brochures and press releases; product catalogs, complete with photos; a company overview; news and notes related to the industry the company serves; and contact and technical support information. This makes it easy for consumers to locate information about the company 24 hours a day.

Business Web sites also provide visitors with the means to order goods and services electronically. With direct online purchasing, customers identify an item they wish to purchase from the company, fill out an order form and provide their credit card number, and then transmit that information electronically to the company. The product is then shipped directly to the customer. The advantages to this method of selling are obvious. Instead of being restricted to a local market, even the smallest company can now reach users around the world. Customers can locate information about the company or order a product 24 hours a day. Customers with questions can now find very specific information about a company's products or services.

HOW TO DESIGN A WEB PAGE
When designing a Web page, certain information should always be included:

- Basic Company Information—This can include vision or mission statements, a history of the business, a summary of business philosophy, etc. The key is to sell the customer on the company.

- Product Line Information—Commercial Web pages should include photos and text descriptions outlining the benefits of the products. Features, applications, and examples can also be highlighted. Consultants often recommend that businesses establish separate pages or sections for each major product line—connected, of course, to the main company Web site.

- Technical support—Frequently asked questions, parts information, product diagrams, and technical specifications are just some of the ways a company can provide support from its Web site.

- Ordering information—Companies should include an electronic mail or hardcopy form with instructions on how to order a product.

- Service section—Free information that is of interest to potential customers, designed to keep them coming back to the site. Industry news and trends are good examples of this kind of information, which is a feature of increasing numbers of business-oriented sites.

- "What's New"—This section is essentially intended to inform visitors of new initiatives, products, etc., that are covered on the Web site.

Once you decide what to put on your homepage, it is time to actually create the site. Web pages are written using a language called the Hypertext Mark-up Language. HTML, as it is more commonly known, is a series of tags and codes that instruct a Web browser on how the text on that page should be displayed. Once a page has been written using HTML, the page must be placed on the host computer, or server, of an Internet provider. HTML can be created using any common word processing package or via any one of the proliferating

HTML editor software packages available in the marketplace.

One of the more important features of HTML is the "hypertext" feature. This means that text can be highlighted on a Web page so that when a customer clicks on a word or an image, a link to a new page on that site (or even another site altogether) is called up on the computer screen. This allows customers to move freely on a site and allows for design creativity and flexibility.

Learning the basics of HTML coding is not difficult, and an ambitious business owner who has the time and the initiative may create his or her own homepage from scratch. However, as the Web has continued to grow, pages have become far more sophisticated in appearance, convincing some businesses to outsource the design and creation of the site to firms that specialize in providing such services.

Having a Web site does not, of course, guarantee visitors. As the Internet has grown it has become much more like any other established marketplace. To attract visitors and attention requires a great deal of marketing work. One would not, for example, tape a small 8-inch by 12-inch promotional sign onto the wall inside of a major shopping mall and expect that the sign alone would generate business. Posting a basic Web site on the Internet is, in many ways, a similar act. Web design firms can be very helpful in establishing a marketing program designed to promote a new Web site. By advertising it in other Internet locations and by registering the site with the dozens of Internet directory services that exist, new site exposure can be increased dramatically.

Flaws in a Web site have a way of causing a disproportionately large negative impact. Company e-sites with errors in content, structure, or navigation have the capacity to plunge businesses far behind their competitors and obliterate painstaking calculations of return on investment. Such flaws can be avoided by proper testing and design from the beginning. The use of a prototype site—a scaled-down working model of the finished product—for pre-launch testing is always a good idea. A prototype lets you get a first look at what users will see as they click through your site, and it can expose unforeseen flaws in your structure and navigation.

Whether you choose to create your company's Web site yourself or outsource the project, the expense of creating a basic informational site is relatively modest. Small business owners should also keep several other cost factors in mind when weighing an entrance onto the Web. For instance, businesses who do not serve as their own Web server are required to pay a monthly charge to a professional Internet hosting firm. Some companies choose to serve as their own host for control and security reasons, but others prefer to enlist a professional hosting firm, which can provide technical support and e-commerce experience at a relatively modest price (hosting fees vary from $10 to $100 a month).

Once the site is on a host computer, users from around the world can then access the homepage, which is given an address that is unique to the entire Web. That address is one part of naming your site. The chosen name can be secured through a domain provider, if the company chooses to go the in-house route. Otherwise, the contracted outside server will purchase the domain name.

POSITIONING AND MAINTAINING A BUSINESS HOMEPAGE

Sites can be freestanding, or they can be a part of a larger online "mall." Hundreds of retail malls have opened on the Web, some more successful than others. Before choosing an Internet provider to store your homepage, do some research on popular online malls and see where your company might best fit in. Visit the sites yourself, and see what you like and do not like. This research step can be an essential component of Internet success for companies, because location can be just as important on the Web as it is in real life.

Even after your Web site has been successfully launched and is up and running, the work does not end. The site needs to be updated on a regular basis to ensure continued content integrity. Areas to monitor include:

- Price changes
- Product changes
- Adding pages to describe other parts of your business
- Adding new links and eliminating obsolete links
- Updating images
- Overhauling the entire site when it becomes tired looking

Once again, you will have to decide if you want to undertake the updating yourself or if you want to hire a firm to handle the work for you.

SEE ALSO *Advertising Media—Internet; HTML; Internet Domain Name; Search Engine*

BIBLIOGRAPHY
"How to Build Your Firm's Web Site." *Baltimore Business Journal.* 23 March 2001.

MacDonald, Matthew. *Creating Web Sites: The Missing Manual.* O'Reilly, October 2005.

McCarthy, Paul. "Small Firms Can Succeed in the E-Business Game." *Computer Weekly.* 30 November 2000.

Morain, Erin. "Web Sites Jockey for Search Engine Optimization: Optimization strategies allow businesses to break through online clutter and stay ahead of improving search engines." *Business Record (Des Moines).* 17 April 2006.

Reynolds, Janice, and Roya Mofazali. *The Complete E-Commerce Book: Design, Build and Maintain a Successful Web-Based Business.* CMP Books, 2000.

Schmeiser, Lisa. "Test Drive Your Web Site." *Macworld.* May 2001.

Thurow, Shari. *Search Engine Visibility.* New Riders, December 2002.

Hillstrom, Northern Lights
updated by Magee, ECDI

WHOLESALING

Wholesalers are "middlemen." Wholesaling is the selling of merchandise to anyone—person or organization—other than the end consumer of that merchandise. Wholesalers represent one of the links in the chain along which most goods pass on their way to the marketplace. As intermediaries between producers and consumers of goods, wholesalers facilitate the transport, preparation of quantity, storage, and sale of articles ultimately destined for customers.

The U.S. Department of Labor describes the important role that wholesalers play in our national economy in a report on the trade simply titled "Wholesale Trade." The report summarizes the wholesalers' role within the economy this way: "They provide businesses a nearby source of goods made by many different manufacturers; they provide manufacturers with a manageable number of customers, while allowing their products to reach a large number of users; and they allow manufacturers, businesses, institutions, and governments to devote minimal time and resources to transactions by taking on some sales and marketing functions—such as customer service, sales contact, order processing, and technical support—that manufacturers otherwise would have to perform."

For the most part, wholesale businesses are small businesses. According to the U.S. Bureau of Labor Statistics, in 2004, fewer than 1.5 percent of wholesale businesses in the United States employed 100 or more people, and 90 percent of wholesale businesses employed fewer than 20 people.

Wholesalers are successful only if they are able to serve the needs of their customers, who may be retailers or other wholesalers. Some of the marketing functions provided by wholesalers to their buyers include:

- Offering the goods of a producer to resellers in appropriate quantities.

- Providing wider geographical access and diversity in obtaining goods.

- Ensuring and maintaining quality verification with the goods that are being obtained and resold.

- Providing cost-effectiveness by reducing the number of producer contacts needed.

- Offering ready access to a supply of goods.

- Assembling and arranging goods of a compatible nature from a number of producers for resale.

- Minimizing buyer transportation costs by buying goods in larger quantities and distributing them in smaller amounts for resale.

- Working with producers to understand and appreciate consumerism in their production process.

TYPES OF WHOLESALERS

There are a number of ways to classify wholesalers. The categories used by the U.S. Department of Commerce in preparing its various Economic Census Reports are the ones used most often. The three categories used in the Census of Wholesale Trade are: 1) merchant wholesalers; 2) agents, brokers, and commission merchants; and 3) manufacturers' sales branches and offices.

Merchant Wholesalers Merchant wholesalers are firms engaged primarily in buying, taking title to, storing, and physically handling products in relatively large quantities and reselling the products in smaller quantities to retailers; industrial, commercial, or institutional concerns; and other wholesalers. These types of wholesaling agents are known by several different names, depending on the services that they provide. These merchant wholesaler names include, jobber, distributor, industrial distributor, supply house, assembler, importer, exporter, or simply, wholesaler.

The merchant wholesaling category can be further broken down. There are two basic kinds of merchant wholesalers: 1) service (sometimes referred to as full-service wholesalers) and 2) limited-function or limited-service wholesalers. Businesses in the latter category, which itself is often divided up into little niches, offer varying levels of service in such areas as product delivery, credit bestowal, inventory management, provision of market or advisory information, and sales.

Agents, Brokers, and Commission Merchants Agents, brokers, and commission merchants are also independent middlemen who usually do not take title to the goods in which they deal, but instead are actively involved in negotiating and other functions of buying and selling while acting on behalf of their clients. Commission merchants typically deal with agricultural goods and commodities like cement, steel, or coal and the like. These types of wholesalers are usually compensated in the form of commissions on sales or purchases. Agents, brokers, and commission merchants usually represent the non-competing products of a number of manufacturers to several retailers. This category of wholesaler is particularly popular with producers with limited capital who can not afford to maintain their own sales forces.

Manufacturers' Sales Branches and Offices Manufacturers' sales branches and offices are owned and operated by manufacturers but are physically separated from manufacturing plants. They are used primarily for the purpose of distributing the manufacturers' own products at the wholesale level. Some have warehousing facilities where inventories are maintained, while others are merely sales offices. Some of them also wholesale allied and supplementary products purchased from other manufacturers.

THE CHANGING LANDSCAPE OF WHOLESALING

Two factors appear to be influencing the wholesale trade industry in the first decade of the 21st Century, consolidation within the trade and the spread of new technology. The trend that has emerged in recent years, towards consolidation of wholesale trade firms into fewer and larger companies, is likely to remain strong. The U.S. Bureau of Labor Statistics describes the trend as follows: "Globalization and cost pressures are likely to continue to force wholesale distributors to merge with other firms or to acquire smaller firms. As retail firms grow, the demand for large, national wholesale distributors to supply them will increase. The differences between large and small firms will become more pronounced as they compete less for the same customers, and instead emphasize their area of expertise. The resulting consolidation of wholesale trade into fewer, larger firms will reduce demand for some workers, especially office and administrative support workers, as merged companies eliminate redundant staff."

The other factor that is causing a great deal of change within the wholesale trading industry is the spread of new technologies. The use of new technologies is helping wholesalers to better serve their customers and in many cases develop systems that interact automatically with those clients.

Inventory management is one area in which wholesalers may be able to offer added value to their clients on both ends of the relationship, their suppliers and their customers.

The newest trend in the area of inventory control and management are vendor-managed inventory (VMI) systems and agreements. One way in which a wholesaler can participate in a VMI system is by agreeing to take over the inventory management for its customers. Based on daily reports sent automatically from the customer to the wholesaler or distributor, the wholesaler replenishes the customers' stocks as needed. The wholesaler sees what is selling in the customers' place of business and makes all necessary arrangements to send the customer new products or parts automatically. No phone calls or paperwork are necessary allowing the supply chain process to remain uninterrupted.

The benefits that can accrue to both parties in a VMI arrangement are noteworthy. Both parties should experience a savings of time and labor. The customer is able to maintain fewer items in stock and can rely upon a steady flow of products or parts. The wholesaler benefits in two ways. First, the wholesaler is able to better anticipate the customers' requirements. Second, the wholesaler benefits from a strong relationship with the customer, one that is more difficult to alter than would be a vendor-customer relationship in which such automated systems did not exist.

New radio frequency identification (RFID) technology has the potential to streamline the inventory and ordering process further and replace the need for manual barcode scans and eliminate most counting and packing errors. As RFID spreads it may lessen demand for administrative workers, particularly order, stock, and shipping, receiving, and traffic clerks. Not all wholesalers will implement this technology though, as it may not be cost-effective for some firms, and workers will still be needed to maintain these new systems.

The 21st century supply chain will create a strong demand for computer specialists in the wholesale trade industry. They will be needed in order to manage ever-more complex and automated inventory systems when dealing with both their suppliers and their customers. Knowledge of information technologies will also be required by wholesalers in order to most effectively leverage the benefits of e-commerce and manage electronic data interchanges (EDI) systems. If the wholesalers do not keep up with these changes in the tools of the trade, they run the risk of being bypassed by technically savvy manufacturers who wish to deal directly with retailers. Wholesalers planning for the future should stay abreast of all the ways in which they can add services to their mix of offerings, to customers on both ends of their business, those from whom they buy and those to whom they sell.

SEE ALSO *Distribution Channels; Inventory Management*

BIBLIOGRAPHY

Hegarty, Ronan. "Retailers Feel Pinch of Rising Wholesaler Costs." *Grocer.* 24 September 2005.

U.S. Department of Commerce. Bureau of the Census. "Monthly Wholesale Trade." Available from http://www.census.gov/svsd/www/mwts.html. 7 April 2006.

U.S. Department of Labor. Bureau of Labor Statistics. "Wholesale Trade." Available from http://stats.bls.gov/oco/cg/cgs026.htm. Retrieved on 8 May 2006.

"Wholesaling." *Do-It-Yourself Retailing.* November 2000.

Hillstrom, Northern Lights
updated by Magee, ECDI

WIDE AREA NETWORKS (WANS)

A wide area network (WAN) is a data network, usually used for connecting computers, that spans a wide geographical area. WANs can be used to connect cities, states, or even countries. WANs are often used by larger corporations or organizations to facilitate the exchange of data, and in a wide variety of industries corporations with facilities at multiple locations have embraced WANs. Increasingly, however, even small businesses are utilizing WANs as a way of increasing their communications capabilities.

Although WANs serve a purpose similar to that of local area networks (LANs), WANs are structured and operated quite differently. The user of a WAN usually does not own the communications lines that connect the remote computer systems; instead, the user subscribes to a service through a telecommunications provider. Unlike LANs, WANs typically do not link individual computers, but rather are used to link LANs. WANs also transmit data at slower speeds than LANs. WANs are also structurally similar to metropolitan area networks (MANs), but provide communications links for distances greater than 50 kilometers.

WANs have existed for decades, but new technologies, services, and applications have developed over the years to dramatically increase their efficacy for business. WANs were originally developed for digital leased-line services carrying only voice, rather than data. As such, they connected the private branch exchanges (PBXs) of remote offices of the same company. WANs are still used for voice services, but today they are used more frequently for data and image transmission (such as video conferencing). These added applications have spurred significant growth in WAN usage, primarily because of the surge in LAN connections to the wider networks.

HOW WANS WORK

WANs are either point-to-point, involving a direct connection between two sites, or operate across packet-switched networks, in which data are transmitted in packets over shared circuits. Point-to-point WAN service may involve either analog dial-up lines, in which a modem is used to connect the computer to the telephone line, or dedicated leased digital telephone lines, also known as "private lines." Analog lines, which may be either part of a public-switched telephone network or leased lines, are suitable for batch data transmissions, such as nonurgent order entry and point-of-sale transactions. Dedicated digital phone lines permit uninterrupted, secure data transmission at fixed costs.

Point-to-point WAN service providers include both local telephone companies and long-distance carriers. Packet-switched network services are typically chosen by organizations which have low volumes of data or numerous sites, for which multiple dedicated lines would be too expensive.

Depending on the service, WANs can be used for almost any data-sharing purpose for which LANs can be used. Slower transmission speeds, however, may make some applications less practical for WANs. The most basic uses of WANs are for electronic mail and file transfer, but WANs can also permit users at remote sites to access and enter data on a central site's database, such as instantaneously updating accounting records. New types of network-based software that facilitate productivity and production tracking, such as groupware and work-flow automation software, can also be used over WANs. Using groupware, workers at dispersed locations can more easily collaborate on projects. WANs also give remote offices access to a central office's other data communications services, including the Internet.

SEE ALSO *Communication Systems; Local Area Networks; Mobile Office; Virtual Private Networks*

BIBLIOGRAPHY

Goldberger, Henry. "The Migration from Frame Relay to IP VPN and VPLS Services." *In-Stat Alerts.* 2 February 2006.

Hayes, Jim. "Managed Data Services." *Communicate.* July 2000.

Schnider, Joel. "SSL VPN Gateways." *Network World.* 12 January 2004.

Symoens, Jeff. "Preparing Exchange for High Availability–You can increase uptime and decrease costs by building a redundant groupware configuration." *InfoWorld.* 10 April 2000.

Winther, Mark. "Avoiding the Challenges of Do-it-Yourself Broadband VPNs." *Business Communications Review.* February 2006.

Hillstrom, Northern Lights
updated by Magee, ECDI

WOMEN ENTREPRENEURS

As of 2002, there were 6.5 million majority women-owned businesses in the United States, employing 7.1 million people according to the U.S. Bureau of the Census. The number of privately held women-owned businesses in U.S. exceeds 10 million if one counts partially women-owned businesses as well. According to a *Business Week Online* article, "between 1997 and 2004 the number of women-owned companies grew 28.1 percent—nearly three times the rate of all privately held businesses." These statistics reflect a sea change in American conceptions of gender roles and abilities over the past half-century.

Women have owned and operated businesses for decades, but they were not always recognized or given credit for their efforts. Often women entrepreneurs were "invisible" as they worked side by side with their husbands, and many only stepped into visible leadership positions when their husbands died. But a variety of factors have combined in recent years to contribute to the visibility and number of women who start their own businesses. According to U.S. Department of Labor statistics, female participation in the workforce was less than 40 percent in 1960 but is predicted to reach 62 percent by the year 2015. As women enter the workforce in ever-greater numbers, they gain professional experience, and managerial skills, both necessary to be successful entrepreneurs. Flexibility is also a factor in many women's decision to start a business. Entrepreneurship is often seen as an ideal way to juggle the competing demands of career and family. Finally, the disparity in the salaries and wages that women earn as compared to men on average has been a factor in motivating some women to decide to establish their own businesses.

Although the small businesses owned by women have traditionally been in the service sector, in recent years women entrepreneurs have been moving rapidly into manufacturing, construction, and other industrial fields. Women business owners still face greater difficulties in gaining access to commercial credit and bidding on government contracts than do their male colleagues, and pockets of resistance to women entrepreneurs remain strong in some industries and geographic regions. But millions of successful businesses launched and managed by women now dot America's business landscape, each a testament to the legitimacy of the aspirations and talents of the woman entrepreneur.

REASONS WOMEN BECOME ENTREPRENEURS

Many studies indicate that women start businesses for fundamentally different reasons than their male counterparts. While men start businesses primarily for growth opportunities and profit potential, women most often found businesses in order to meet personal goals, such as gaining feelings of achievement and accomplishment. In many instances, women consider financial success as an external confirmation of their ability rather than as a primary goal or motivation to start a business, although millions of women entrepreneurs will grant that financial profitability is important in its own right.

Women also tend to start businesses about ten years later then men, on average. Motherhood, lack of management experience, and traditional socialization have all been cited as reasons for delayed entry into entrepreneurial careers. Many women start a business due to some traumatic event, such as divorce, discrimination due to pregnancy or the corporate glass ceiling, the health of a family member, or economic reasons such as a layoff. But a new talent pool of women entrepreneurs is forming today, as more women opt to leave corporate America to chart their own destinies. These women have developed financial expertise and bring experience in manufacturing or nontraditional fields. As a result, the concentration of women business owners in the retail and service sectors—and in traditional industries such as cosmetics, food, fashion, and personal care—is slowly changing.

PROBLEMS FACED BY WOMEN ENTREPRENEURS

One of the main problems facing women entrepreneurs is obtaining financing. In the early 1990s, study after study confirmed that women business owners did not receive equal treatment at financial institutions. Over one half of women business owners believed that they faced gender discrimination when dealing with a loan officer. And for women, venture capital firms appear to show the same favoritism towards men that banks do. According to Sona Wang, quoted in a *Crain's Chicago Business* article and general partner of Inroads Capital Partners, an Evanston venture capital firm that specializes in backing women and minorities, the venture capital business "clearly relies heavily on the old-boy network." Only 5 percent of the companies that received venture capital funding in 2004 had a female CEO, according to the *Crain's Chicago Business* article, a trend that has not changed since researchers started tracking these numbers in 1997.

In an effort to bring more equity into the capital acquisitions area, the Small Business Administration's Women's Prequalification Pilot Loan Program was developed. Introduced in 1994 and expanded nationwide in 1997, the program helps women seeking loans of under $250,000 to complete their loan applications, and also provides an SBA guarantee for repayment of their loans.

Women are prequalified based on their character, credit rating, and ability to repay the loan from future business earnings, rather than on collateral. The prequalification statement from the SBA enables the women to obtain funding much more readily.

Another area in which women business owners have been historically shortchanged is procurement, or the selling of their goods and services to city, state, and federal governments. In the past, fewer than 5 percent of the women-owned firms in the United States were certified to do business with their state government and only 1.5 percent of the billions of dollars in federal contracts went to women-owned firms. Some efforts have been undertaken to rectify this situation. If a company is 51 percent owned and controlled by a woman, it can obtain certification and bid on government contracts. In addition, many government agencies at the state and federal levels have created set-aside programs that specifically help women-owned businesses in the bidding process. Nonetheless, the percentage of government contracts going to women-owned firms remained a meager 3 percent as recently as 2002.

RESOURCES

A number of resources now exist to support women entrepreneurs. In 1988, Congress authorized the Small Business Administration Office of Women's Business Ownership, which created a "Low-Doc" loan program which makes it easier for women entrepreneurs to obtain SBA financing. The SBA also has established a Women's Network for Entrepreneurial Training (WNET) which links women mentors with protegees. Small Business Development Centers (SBDC) are also co-sponsored by the SBA and operate in every state. They offer free and confidential counseling to anyone interested in starting a small business. In addition, many states now have a Women's Business Advocate to promote women entrepreneurs within the state. These advocates are represented by an organization, the National Association of Women Business Advocates.

A number of trade associations also represent women entrepreneurs. The National Association of Women Business Owners is the largest group throughout the country. There are also some smaller regional groups, which can be located through the Yellow Pages or local chambers of commerce. The American Business Women's Association provides leadership, networking, and educational support. The National Association of Female Executives makes women aware of the need to plan for career and financial success. As women-owned businesses continue to create jobs and become an increasingly important factor in the American economy, the resources to support them will continue to grow as well.

SEE ALSO *8(a) Program; Minority-Owned Businesses; National Association of Women Business Owners*

BIBLIOGRAPHY

"About NAWBO." National Association of Women Business Owners. Available from http://www.nawbo.org/about/index.php. Retrieved on 17 April 2006.

Fisher, Anne. "Which Women Get Big? When it comes to building large businesses, women lag far behind men—but that's changing fast." *Fortune Small Business.* 1 April 2006.

Gee, Sharon. "NAWBO Getting Serious About Women's Business." *Birmingham Business Journal.* 11 August 2000.

La Beau, Christina. "Growing in Size But Not in Equity: Women Businesses Still Lag in Venture Capital." *Crain's Chicago Business.* 13 December 2004.

"Taking the Pulse of Women Entrepreneurs; The manager of Wells Fargo's lending program targeted at women-owned businesses talks about the latest trends." *Business Week Online.* 1 May 2006.

U. S. Bureau of the Census. *Survey of Business Owners – Women-Owned Firms: 2002.* Available from http://www.census.gov/csd/sbo/. 26 January 2006.

U.S. Department of Labor. Fullerton Jr., Howard N. "Labor Force Participation: 75 Years of Change, 1950–98 and 1998–2025." *Monthly Labor Review.* December 1999.

Vestil, Donna. "Businesses Owned by Women Fuel National Growth." *Kansas City Star.* 28 June 2005.

Hillstrom, Northern Lights
updated by Magee, ECDI

WORK FOR HIRE

A 'work for hire' is an exception to the general rule that the person who creates a work is the author of that work and holds all rights to the work product. This is a concept of intellectual property protection outlined in Section 101 of the 1976 Copyright Act. In most cases, the person who creates a copyrightable work—such as a story, poem, song, essay, sculpture, graphic design, or computer program—holds the copyright for that work. A copyright is a form of legal protection which gives the holder sole rights to exploit the work for financial gain for a certain period of time, usually 35 years. In contrast, the copyright for a work for hire is owned by the company that hires the person to create the work or pays for the development of the work. The creator holds no rights to a work for hire under the law. Instead, the employer is solely entitled to exploit the work and profit from it. The concept of work for hire is different from the creator transferring ownership of a copyrightable work, because the latter arrangement allows the creator to reacquire rights to the work after the copyright period expires.

There are two main categories of copyrightable materials that can be considered works for hire. One category encompasses works that are prepared by employees within the scope of their employment. For example, if a software engineer employed by Microsoft writes a computer program, it is considered a work for hire and the company owns the program. The second category includes works created by independent contractors that are specially commissioned by a company. In order to be considered works for hire, such works must fall into a category specifically covered by the law, and the two parties must expressly agree in a contract that it is a work made for hire.

"If you show up to a job where somebody tells you what to do and when to do it, and for that you're rewarded with a paycheck, then your work product is classified as a work for hire and you don't own the copyright on it. Instead, it automatically becomes copyrighted in the name of the company," Michael Bertin explained in the *Austin Chronicle*. In the situation of independent contractors, he added, "There are two criteria for works for hire. It has to fit into one of nine specific categories, and there has to be a contract stipulating that it's a 'work for hire.' If one of those two elements is missing, then the work in question is not, repeat not, a work for hire."

The nine categories of materials eligible to be considered works for hire, as outlined in the Copyright Act, include: works commissioned for use as:

1. A contribution to a collective work

2. A part of a motion picture or other audiovisual work or sound recording

3. A translation

4. A supplementary work

5. A compilation

6. An instructional text

7. A test

8. The answer material for a test

9. An atlas

Work-for-hire arrangements affect small businesses in a variety of ways. For example, a small business that hires a Web page design firm to create a company site must make certain that the contract stipulates that the design is a work made for hire. Otherwise, the company may find that it does not hold copyright to various elements of its own Web page, and the design firm may decide to use those elements in pages created for other clients. On the other hand, entrepreneurs who do occasional work for large companies as independent contractors will want to be careful signing work-for-hire

contracts. A consultant who develops a framework for problem solving under contract with one client may be unable to use that framework with any other clients if it was developed under a work-for-hire arrangement.

SEE ALSO *Copyrights; Intellectual Property*

BIBLIOGRAPHY

Bertin, Michael. "Mastering Intellectual Property Rights: Work for Hire." *Austin Chronicle.* 25 August 2000.

Fishman, Stephen. *The Copyright Handbook: How to Protect and Use Written Works.* Nolo Press, 2000.

Lang, Daryl. "Less Money for Photographers as Stock Production Becomes Work-for-Hire: To please investors, big stock agencies are trying to own more of their images." *Photo District News.* April 2006.

Roberts, Barry S., and Richard A. Mann. *Business Law and the Regulation of Business.* Thomson West, February 2005.

"Work for Hire Exception Under Copyright Law." *Internet Law – Business – Web Design.* 1 May 2005.

Hillstrom, Northern Lights
updated by Magee, ECDI

WORKERS' COMPENSATION

Workers' compensation is a mandatory type of business insurance that provides employees who become injured or ill while on the job with medical coverage and income replacement. It also protects companies from being sued by employees for the workplace conditions that caused such an injury or illness.

Businesses are required by law in all fifty states to pay for the medical treatment and lost wages of employees who suffer job-related injuries or illnesses. In order to avoid crippling expenses in this regard, companies purchase workers' compensation insurance policies of one kind or another. Most states give businesses the choice of buying workers' compensation policies either directly from the state or from a private insurer. Each state determines its own system's payment schedules, employee eligibility requirements, and rehabilitation procedures. Although provisions of each state's laws differ greatly, the underlying principle is the same—that employers should assume the costs of injuries, illnesses, and deaths that occur on the job, without regard to fault, and partially replace wage income lost. While income replacement under workers' compensation is usually a percentage of the actual wage, it is counted as a transfer payment and thus is not subject to federal income tax for the employer or employee. Some state laws exempt certain categories of employees from coverage. Those most likely to be excluded are domestics, agricultural workers, and manual laborers.

Given the mandatory nature of workers' compensation coverage and the potential expense involved, the cost of workers' compensation insurance policies is a considerable concern for small business owners. In fact, workers' compensation premiums stand as most companies' second-largest operating expense, after payroll. These rates are based on the employer's total payroll, the classification of the employees, and the employer's accident record. The wages paid each employee are assigned a rate based on the occupational classification in which that employee works. For example, an employee who does office work will be assigned a rate that is lower than one who works re-roofing. The employer's cost of workers' compensation for the office worker will likely be in the range of 0.25 to 1.0 percent of wages earned while the employee who works on roofing projects will cost the company as much as 10 to 15 percent of that employee's gross wages.

Small business owners have less control over the cost of workers' compensation coverage than they do over health insurance costs. State legislatures set the level of benefits and employers pay the full cost, so medical cost-containment strategies like co-payments do not apply. Some insurers avoid handling workers' compensation policies for small businesses because they feel that smaller companies lack the funds to provide a safe working environment. In general, the rates depend upon the type of business, number of employees, and company safety record.

Penalties for failing to carry workers' comp insurance policies can be severe. In general, business owners who are neglectful in this manner can be held liable for the medical expenses incurred by the worker in their employ. Nonetheless, many businesses engage in what is known as "premium fraud," in which they either do not carry insurance as required or lower the costs of their policy premiums through fraudulent record keeping. Methods used to fraudulently reduce insurance premiums include underreporting of employee count or the wages they are paid, paying workers under the table in order to falsify the number of employees, misclassifying the kind of work engaged in by employees in order to reduce premiums through a misclassification of their occupation, etc. However, momentum is building to beef up penalties for these kinds of fraudulent actions, which injure insurers and honest employers alike. Honest employers end up with higher insurance premiums as a result of these sorts of fraud. Law-abiding employers may suffer as a result of fraud in another way as well. Construction companies, for example, may lose out on projects to bidders whose lower bids are made possible because they are absorbing lower overhead costs through intentional workers' compensation fraud.

TYPES OF COVERAGE AVAILABLE

There are three basic methods available for employers to obtain the required workers' compensation protection: state insurance funds, private insurance, and self-insurance through insurance pools. The latter option—which involves setting aside funds in anticipation of workers' compensation claims, rather than purchasing insurance—is seen as a cost-saving method for safety-oriented firms. In the states that permit it, many large employers now self-insure, and many small businesses form groups to insure themselves and decrease the risks.

Group self-insurance plans are worth consideration for small businesses with better-than-average workplace safety records. Such plans work best when the companies involved are in the same or similar industries, so that their level of risk is roughly equivalent. The companies can then join together to purchase stop-loss coverage to protect themselves against claims over a certain amount. Though self-insurance can be less expensive than private workers' compensation policies, small businesses should make sure that they have the financial resources to withstand potential losses.

MANAGING WORKERS' COMP CLAIMS AND COSTS

Small businesses can explore a variety of other measures to reduce their workers' compensation premiums as well. These include:

First and foremost, make the workplace as safe as possible. Companies can reduce premiums by minimizing the number of claims made by their workforce. This requires the implementation of safety programs in such areas as materials handling and ergonomics.

Select the right insurer. Business owners seeking workers' comp insurance policies should seek out insurers with proactive claims adjusting policies. In addition, *Occupational Hazards* contributor Shawn Adams counsels companies to give preference to insurers who assign specific adjusters for accounts. "[When] claims are... handled on a file basis... your account is handled by whatever adjuster happens to be assigned the file for your claim. An assigned adjuster is one who can take responsibility for your account, as opposed to having different adjusters handle different claims against your policy but not coordinating the claims in a comprehensive manner."

Pay attention to your own claims trends. Businesses should take steps to monitor all aspects of their work safety record and insurance coverage, and ensure that all subcontractors carry workers' comp coverage.

BIBLIOGRAPHY

Adams, Shawn. "Risk Management Methods to Reduce Your Workers' Compensation Rates." *Occupational Hazards.* March 2001.

Priz, Edward J. *Ultimate Guide to Workers' Compensation Insurance.* Entrepreneur Press, 2005.

Washington, Corey. "Insurance Bite Still Painful for Employers." *Business Press (San Bernardino, CA).* 10 April 2006.

Hillstrom, Northern Lights
updated by Magee, ECDI

WORKPLACE ANGER

Workplace anger and hostility often manifest in ways that have received a great deal of attention from business owners, researchers, legislators, and members of the business press in recent years. Workplace violence and sexual harassment are probably the two most commonly written about forms of workplace anger and hostility. But anger and hostility can manifest themselves in other, less dramatic ways, that can nonetheless have a tremendously negative impact on a business by producing an environment marked by poor or nonexistent communication, sagging morale, excessive employee absenteeism or turnover, and a host of other undesired conditions. Business owners, managers, and employees who are unable to control their own anger or effectively respond to the angry outbursts of others will likely find that their business and/or career suffers as a result. Organizations that fail to recognize and deal effectively with the problem of workplace anger may end up with even more serious problems with which to deal. Inappropriate displays of anger can lead to all sorts of undesirable outcomes and, in the most serious cases, a company may even be legally liable if they allow a hostile environment to persist.

Of course, many small businesses will never be confronted with the challenge of addressing and correcting problem workers who behave in an angry or hostile manner toward coworkers or customers. This may be because very small firms may not have employees at all. But, even firms with employees often feature a positive work environment and employ staff that enjoy their jobs and relate to one another in a professional manner. But most small business owners that have a payroll will eventually encounter someone who exhibits angry or hostile behavior and looms as a potential threat to the financial and/or spiritual health of the organization.

The problem of angry outbursts is a growing problem in society generally. Robert D. Ramsey writes about the seemingly epidemic levels to which anger in our society has grown in recent years in an article that appeared in the magazine *Supervision*. He put it this way. "It's a modern day epidemic. Rage rules. On the road. In the airways. At sports events. And increasingly, on the job as well.... Anger is a dictator that can control lives and drive behavior. It blots out reason and blurs good judgment. Worst of all, it can lead to dangerous outbursts of violence or other destructive behaviors. Obviously, anger has no legitimate place in any business, office, shop or factory. When it occurs, someone has to see that it doesn't take root or take over the workplace. If managers don't do it, who will?"

Entrepreneurs, like all business leaders, need to prepare themselves for the day when an employee's actions or words seem to be based on feelings of anger or hostility. Some small business owners underestimate the impact that workplace anger and hostility can have on their business and on their staff, and they do so at their peril. One employee who lashes out inappropriately can cause a decline in a company's general morale, can cause friction with colleagues, can cause enough distraction that productivity declines and may even be distracting enough to pose a safety hazard.

Small business owners should be aware that failure to address workplace hostilities can also open them up to legal liability. Moreover, the person who engages in hostile workplace behavior does not have to be an owner or supervisor for the business owner to be vulnerable to charges concerning that person's behavior, because in the eyes of the law, business owners have the power and obligation to control their employees.

CAUSES OF WORKPLACE ANGER AND HOSTILITY

Workplace hostility can often be traced to attitudes that have little to do with the current employment situation in which workers find themselves. Deep-seated feelings of hostility toward other people because of their gender, skin color, sexual orientation, political beliefs, or other factors are often firmly in place long before the person begins working at your company. Often, the small business owner faced with such an employee will have limited options available to deal with such problems; instead, he or she will concentrate efforts on making sure that those undesired attitudes do not disrupt the workplace.

Factors that cause workplace anger, on the other hand, can sometimes be addressed directly. While workplace anger sometimes can be traced back to prejudices that are at the root of deep-seated hostility, on many other occasions, work-oriented factors serve as the primary catalysts. Common causes of workplace anger include:

- General harassment, whether sexual or some other form.
- Favoritism of one employee over another.
- Rejection (whether arbitrary or for good reason) of a proposal or project in which an employee has a significant emotional investment.
- Insensitivity by owners or managers.
- Criticisms of employees in front of staff or clients.
- Depersonalized workplace environment.
- Unfair (or tardy) performance appraisals or criticism.
- Lack of resources for the employee to meet his/her objectives.
- Inadequate training.
- Lack of teamwork.
- Withdrawal of earned benefits.
- Betrayal of trust extended to manager or owner.
- Unreasonable demands on employees.
- Downsizing.
- Lack of flexibility on part of owner or manager.
- Poor communication.
- Feedback is wholly or primarily negative in tone.
- Absentee leadership (such as instances wherein needed disciplinary action is absent).
- Micromanagerial environment in which staff decisionmaking opportunities are limited.

Of course, sometimes a distinction must be made between legitimate and illegitimate catalysts of workplace anger. For example, an employee may express great anger over a negative performance review even though the appraisal was conducted fairly and honestly. Small business owners and managers cannot jettison basic principles of management simply to avoid making one of their employees angry.

Warning Signs Workplace anger is often sublimated by employees until they reach a point where they suddenly burst. This "bursting" point may manifest itself in a variety of ways. One employee may just yell at his manager, while another may impetuously decide to quit. Still others may resort to workplace violence or vandalism. Small business owners and managers should acquaint themselves with the warning signs of hidden anger so that they can address the causes for that anger and hopefully head off an incident before it occurs. Other employees, meanwhile, may exhibit behavior that is more obviously troubling. Following are a range of behaviors that may signal a need for intervention:

- Sarcastic, irritable, or moody behavior
- Apathetic and/or inconsistent work performance
- Prone to making direct or veiled threats
- Aggressive and antisocial behavior
- Overreaction to company policies or performance appraisals
- Touchy relationships with other workers
- Obsessive involvement and/or emotional attachment to job

"Bullying" Explicit workplace violence, sexual harassment, and episodes of discrimination garner the most headlines and receive the bulk of attention from consultants because of their potential legal impact on business enterprises. But researchers contend that simple bullying behavior may be as great a threat to business health and productivity as are any of the above-mentioned problems. Sometimes bullying takes place between employees, but it often is most evident in supervisor-worker relationships, in which one person is perceived to wield greater power. Bullying is not just the problem of an individual, however, but must be seen as a problem of the organization and its culture as a whole. Bullying can take many forms, from persistent, low-key intimidation to devious efforts to make a colleague appear professionally incompetent. These menacing tactics can be difficult to identify and bring to light. It is very important, therefore, to have an avenue through which people feel free and safe to air their concerns about coworkers, supervisors and subordinates. Patterns may emerge which make it more apparent where serious problem lie as long as communications flow reasonably freely. There are always those who will put forward the argument that the making of snide remarks or jokes at another's expense is part of social interaction. However, office banter which is not really designed to offend is recognizably different to the persistent downgrading or undermining of a person by another, particularly if the other is in a position of relative power within the hierarchy.

Confronting bullies about their behavior is often difficult. Where bullying exists the only way to address the matter is through addressing it with the bully and prevailing upon him or her to change. But, since the bully is very likely to see the situation in the same way as the victim(s) of his or her aggression, the first challenge will be to establish that change is needed. Like all human resource problems, the challenge is great. Small business owners and managers, however, should stand fast. Bullying behavior generally does not take place in a vacuum; other employees are usually aware of the situation, and they should be consulted. Finally, owners seeking to eliminate bullying behavior need to make it clear that anyone who is the victim of bullying tactics will receive their full support.

Peer Conflict Another common cause of workplace anger and hostility is peer conflict. Unlike instances of bullying, wherein one employee makes a conscious decision to engage in behavior that is hurtful or uncomfortable for another employee, peer conflict is characterized by mutual feelings of animosity toward the other individual. Peer conflicts are usually caused by differences in personality or perception, moodiness, insensitivity, impatience, or sensitive emotional states such as jealousy, annoyance, and embarrassment. When these rivalries evolve into skirmishes or outbursts, conflict may erupt causing damage to those involved as well as others in the vicinity. Since work relies heavily on the ability of people to interact in a cooperative and harmonious fashion, conflict between employees represents a serious breakdown of the effective working relationship.

According to management theorist Peter Drucker, managers can pursue one of the following routes when attempting to resolve peer conflicts:

1. Convince both workers to accept a mutually agreeable view or agreement about the issue that was the cause of the conflict.

2. Support the position of one employee and reject the position of the other.

3. Make your own decision about the issue and force both people to comply with your perception.

What is important for the manager to keep in perspective is the fact that the problem belongs to those in conflict and only they can resolve it. However, when that problem affects the company then it is the manager's job to insist upon and facilitate a resolution.

Small business owners who find themselves mediating a peer conflict should avoid taking sides (especially if both workers' views have merit), provide an objective viewpoint, keep the discussion from bogging down in tangents or name-calling, and help each worker to understand the perspective of the other. Finally, the small business owner's overriding concern should be to explicitly restate his or her expectations of staff performance, including the ways in which staff members should behave toward one another.

KEYS TO STOPPING OR PREVENTING EXPRESSIONS OF WORKPLACE HOSTILITY AND ANGER

Attempts to address inappropriate workplace behavior through negotiation and mediation are not always effective. In some instances, an employee's conduct and/or performance will leave the small business owner with no

alternative but to resort to disciplinary action. This discipline can take a variety of forms, from suspension to negative comments in the employee's personnel file to yanking the worker off a plum project. Reports on the effectiveness of such steps vary considerably. Some firms contend that such measures inform the employee that his or her problematic behavior will not be tolerated and can be an effective tool in triggering behavioral reforms, especially if the punishment has a financial dimension. But others insist that such measures—especially if used without first pursuing other options—may only deepen feelings of animosity and hostility.

No two small business enterprises or employees are alike. Researchers agree, however, that there are a number of steps that employers can take to address the issues of workplace anger and hostility before they erupt into full-blown crises.

1. Explicitly state your absolute opposition to inappropriate behavior in writing. This can often be included as part of a new hire's employee guidelines package, but small business owners should also consider displaying such "zero tolerance" statements in public areas. Such statements should also clearly delineate which types of comments and actions are regarded as offensive.

2. Encourage an environment that values diversity.

3. Recognize that incidents of workplace hostility tend to get worse over time if they are not addressed. For example, remarks that might at first seem to be merely in mildly bad taste can eventually escalate into full-fledged racist, sexist, or otherwise mean-spirited harassment. Learning to deal with workplace anger issues is critical to creating a workplace that is comfortable—and therefore productive—for employees. Instead, business owners should respond to incidents of workplace anger or hostility promptly and decisively. The whole workforce will likely be watching, looking for some signal about whether management takes such transgressions seriously, or whether it implicitly gives the green light to further incidents.

4. Learn to recognize the symptoms of workplace anger, and try to provide employees with constructive avenues to express frustrations and/or concerns.

5. Monitor workplace culture to ensure that it does not provide fertile ground for unwanted behavior.

6. Make sure you have all the facts before confronting an employee with a charge of workplace discrimination or otherwise unprofessional behavior. This is especially true if the identity of the transgressor is in any doubt.

7. Make sure that your own actions and deeds are a good model for your employees.

8. Recognize that your primary imperative is not to change an employee's mindset about minorities, women, or other co-workers, but rather to ensure that the employee does not engage in offensive behavior in his or her interactions with co-workers or customers. An employer will not likely change the attitudes of employees in these matters, but behavior is something that is within the employer's purview and behavior should be managed.

WHEN THE SMALL BUSINESS OWNER IS ANGRY

Small business owners should also be aware of the challenges of managing their own anger in the workplace. Entrepreneurship brings with it a host of responsibilities and pressures that can make it difficult for them to manage strong emotions such as anger. But it is important for small business owners to handle their anger in an effective manner. Expressing anger can be constructive when the true intent is to maintain, reestablish, or restore a positive relationship with the person who has caused offense. When handled professionally, constructive confrontations assure future harmony, better performance, and improved productivity. The key, of course, is to express anger professionally and as calmly as possible. It helps to be as specific as possible. State the problem as clearly as possible and then give the other party a chance to express his or her side. Listen, and try to understand what caused the conflict. Whenever possible, emphasize that it is the behavior, not the person, that is in question or needs to change.

SEE ALSO *Human Resource Management; Workplace Violence*

BIBLIOGRAPHY
Hall, John R. "Seminar Provides Tips on Hiring Practices." *Air Conditioning, Heating & Refrigeration News.* 20 June 2005.

Meyer, Pat. "Preventing Workplace Violence Starts with Recognizing Warning Signs and Taking Action." *Nation's Restaurant News.* 28 February 2000.

Nay, W. Robert. *Taking Charge of Anger: How to Resolve Conflict, Sustain Relationships, and Express Yourself without Losing Control.* The Guilford Press, 2003

Neville, Haig. "Workplace Violence Prevention Strategies." *Memphis Business Journal.* 8 September 2000.

Ramsey, Robert D. "Managing Workplace Anger: Your Employees', Your Customers' and Your Own." *Supervision.* February 2004.

"Two Million People, Many of them Managers, Bullied at Work." Management-Issues, LTD. Available from http://www.management-issues.com/display_page.asp?section=research&id=2746. 7 November 2005.

Hillstrom, Northern Lights
updated by Magee, ECDI

WORKPLACE SAFETY

Workplace safety refers to the working environment at a company and encompasses all factors that impact the safety, health, and well-being of employees. This can include environmental hazards, unsafe working conditions or processes, drug and alcohol abuse, and workplace violence. Workplace safety is monitored at the national level by the Occupational Safety and Health Administration (OSHA). OSHA has three stated goals that serve as the cornerstones of its policies and regulations: 1) Improve the safety and health for all workers, as evidenced by fewer hazards, reduced exposures, and fewer injuries, illnesses, and fatalities; 2) Change workplace culture to increase employer and worker awareness of, commitment to, and involvement in safety and health; 3) Secure public confidence through excellence in the development and delivery of OSHA's programs and services. The federal guidelines imposed by this agency are complemented by state regulations that are often tougher than those proposed by OSHA.

NATIONAL WORKPLACE INJURY AND ILLNESS DATA

Every year the Department of Labor, through its Bureau of Labor Statistics, publishes the workplace injury and illness data that it gathers and compiles. In 2004, 5,764 people lost their lives while on the job in the United States. These fatalities were caused, primarily, to traffic-related incidents (45 percent), followed by assaults and violent acts (18 percent), falls (15 percent), contact with objects and equipment (14 percent), and finally, exposure to harmful substances.

The nonfatal injuries and illnesses reported in 2004, serious enough to require time-away from work, numbered 1.27 million, a rate of injury equivalent to 141.3 per 100,000 full-time workers. These data include all work-related injuries and illnesses that resulted in time-away from work beyond the day on which the injury occurred. The median number of days away from work per incident in 2004 was 7 days. By category of injury, the national data break down as follows: Sprains and strains (41.7 percent), bruises and contusions (9.1 percent), cuts and lacerations (7.8 percent), fractures (7.5 percent), heat burns and carpal tunnel syndrome (1.5 percent each), and other injuries and illnesses make up the remaining 5.8 percent of workplace injuries. The goods-producing industries have a higher rate of on-the-job injury than do the service industries with one exception. Businesses in the transportation sector are part of the service industry but they have a very high rate of on-the-job injuries.

IMPROVING WORKPLACE SAFETY AT A SMALL BUSINESS

Most small business owners take steps to try and assure that their place of work is a safe one because it is the right thing to do. Beyond being the right thing to do, smaller companies usually recognize that the benefits to be gained by a safe work environment are many. Attention to safety issues can not only help businesses avoid legal penalties, but also improves employee morale, productivity, and retention. Moreover, effective workplace safety programs often have a tremendous impact on a company's bottom-line financial performance. In addition to the hidden benefits in retention and productivity that go hand-in-hand with such programs, businesses armed with solid workplace safety policies and records realize enormous benefits in the realm of insurance. An employer's workers' compensation premium is based on several factors. These include payroll, a classification of employees by occupational type, and the company's accident history. No factor has more control over insurance premiums or is less understood by policy holders than the experience modification or 'mod.' The mod is an indicator of how an individual operation's accident rate compares to other businesses within its industry. Three consecutive years of actual workers' compensation claims provide the statistical basis for an employer's mod. Under this system, companies that are deemed to have a higher accident rate (as determined by workers' compensation claims over a three-year period) than the industry average pay higher premiums. Conversely, companies that boast a claim rate lower than the industry average will benefit by paying less expensive premiums.

Workplace safety programs can take many forms and cover many potential areas of concern. The sorts of actions taken by companies to maximize the safety of the work environment that they create are varied and include:

- Providing for personal safety equipment

- Installing equipment controls

- Creating and disseminating operational manuals

- Establishing and enforcing hazardous materials handling policies

- Adopting a drug and alcohol testing program

- Offering employee counseling services

- Implementing safety training programs.

Following are several avenues that small firms can pursue when implementing or updating a workplace safety program.

Safety Managers and Committees One method that many firms have had success with is to appoint one person in the organization as the safety coordinator. The ideal candidate has a background in safety, but if no one fits that profile, then choose the candidate who best relates to workers and management, has strong communication skills, and has an interest in and commitment to safety. A common title for this person is "safety manager."

For the safety manager to do his or her job, he or she must have direct access to the top manager in the company. Without management buy-in, safety initiatives will not last long. The manager must also have access to every department and work area, and must be able to question people freely for the purpose of gathering information. Regular status reports should be prepared that update management on current safety initiatives and identify areas that still need improvement. Ideally, the safety manager's role will remain an advisory one: responsibility for implementing the manager's suggestions should fall to upper management and the individuals or teams that are singled out by the safety manager. The safety's manager's mandate is to facilitate change, not implement it.

Many analysts believe that businesses should make certain that safety managers are adequately educated on workplace safety issues as well. Business owners are thus often encouraged to send managers to training and education seminars or classes as part of an overall policy of ongoing education. Additionally, management should encourage the manager to seek out safety professionals at other companies to help him or her build a network of contacts and information. Upper management is also responsible for ensuring that safety performance is made a part of every employee's job responsibility and performance reviews. Only when every employee is held accountable for safety will it become a part of a company's culture.

The best starting point for a new safety manager is often to review company records of past safety problems. By drawing up a list of areas that are known problems, the manager can identify the best place to begin implementation of new safety measures. Of course, it is also important that the manager immediately follow up on any disquieting patterns or dangerous situations that are discovered and implement action steps to correct the problems. Unfortunately, in some instances safety managers will find that workplace safety reports are scant or nonexistent. In such instances, the manager should start from ground zero and establish a formal accident/safety reporting system to gather data.

Documentation and record keeping serve two additional purposes—they provide written evidence that the new safety program is providing positive results and they can be used to protect the firm in the event that a lawsuit is filed or safety inquiry launched. Documentation of employee training sessions is especially important, including the topics covered, the date and time at which the sessions were held, and any test scores earned by employees at the sessions. Consultants cite testing as a potentially valuable way of determining employee retention of safety information.

The safety manager should seek to involve all employees and managers in safety initiatives. Inspections should be conducted by the personnel of each department, not the safety manager. In fact, the manager should let each department handle most of its own safety problems—if proper training has been given to all employees, the safety manager should only have to address serious problems that require his or her knowledge and authority.

Studies have shown that safety committees can be valuable tools in implementing and maintaining safety programs as well. Safety committees, which typically feature representation from all operational areas, have been shown to reduce the injury rate at companies, which in turn can boost morale and efficiency. Companies that use committees have also reported some unexpected benefits, including an increased sense of teamwork, better sharing of information, and a drop in absenteeism, discrimination claims, grievances, and sick days. Not all small business enterprises reach a size that warrant creation of such committees. But for growing businesses with a significant payroll, safety and health committees can provide important benefits. The committees, which ideally will include a cross-section of employees, should serve as a central gathering and dissemination point for all information related to safety.

Outside Safety Analysis Another potentially useful option for entrepreneurs interested in determining workplace safety is to have an outside firm conduct a safety analysis. These firms specialize in safety and hazardous materials and can offer many suggestions on how to improve safety. Analysts note that reports submitted by these organizations often range from warnings of regulatory breaches to suggestions on alternative production methods, etc. Not all safety improvement suggestions are implemented, of course. Some courses of action may be deemed excessively expensive, while others are dismissed because of employee resistance or skepticism about their ultimate impact on workplace safety.

Safety Incentives Business owners and consultants alike agree that safety managers and consultants will likely not have a meaningful impact on a company's safety records if the employees are not willing to do their part to help make things better. One of the best ways to ensure employee cooperation is to offer incentives tied to improvements in safety, although observers are quick to add that safety incentives are not an adequate substitute for a strong safety program. In fact, only companies that have a strong program already in place should even think of using incentives. Cash and non-cash awards should only be used to motivate employees to practice what the already-in-place program preaches, which reinforces behavior and encourages participation.

Incentives should reward behaviors that prevent injury by eliminating unsafe work practices. Reward employees who achieve "zero accidents," but be sure to use a broad definition of accident (such as one that would cause an employee to miss time on the job) so that employees do not try to cover up minor injuries in order to keep their zero accident rating. Once the behaviors to be rewarded are identified, then determine allocation of awards (individual, department, or company-wide).

To make an incentive program really work, several things must be done. First, the incentives must be an ongoing element of the workplace. One-time incentive programs tend to get employees interested for a short time, then cause them to lose interest and fall back into bad habits once the period has passed. Second, meaningful incentives should be chosen. Many experts believe that non-cash incentives can be most effective, warning that under cash-based reward systems, employees too often pocket the cash and forget about the ongoing message. Some companies do believe that cash works best, while others feel using cash sends people the wrong message by paying them extra for practices that they should already be doing. Good examples of non-cash incentives include recognition awards, token gifts that build morale, customized items (clothing, for example), and, most effective of all, professional advancement. Finally, goals and results must be clearly communicated to employees at every step of the process.

Small business owners should not be scared of the costs associated with running an incentive program. Even if the program costs several thousand dollars annually, many economists and business experts contend that the expense is insignificant compared to the productivity lost as a result of poor safety practices.

WORKPLACE VIOLENCE AS A SAFETY ISSUE

Every act of workplace violence leaves scars on every person in the organization. One act of violence can change an entire company permanently. The working environment can become so toxic that no work gets done—all employees can think about is what happened.

From the company perspective, violence also leaves the company exposed to lawsuits and liability that can cost millions of dollars.

There are steps that can be taken to prevent or at least minimize the chances of workplace violence. The most important step is for the company's leadership to communicate a zero-tolerance policy for workplace violence and behaviors (bullying, harassment, defiance of management, etc.) that can lead to such events. At the same time, businesses should display a corresponding determination to create and maintain a safe workplace for employees by examining their existing security, hiring, and performance appraisal policies.

In a recent *Risk Management* article the moderator of the round table discussion presented in the piece posed this question: If you could boil down the essence of a successful workplace safety program to a single principle, what would that principle be and why? In response, one of the managers partaking in the discussion offered this summary thought, "For us, the cardinal virtue of workplace safety is visibility. If safety is not a visible, hands-on, personal thing, then it has no impact for the organization."

SEE ALSO *Ergonomics; Industrial Safety; Occupational Safety and Health Administration*

BIBLIOGRAPHY
Huelk, Ernie. "Get the Most Out of Personal Protective Equipment." *Industrial Safety & Hygiene News.* March 2006.

Milam-Perez, Lisa A. *HR How-To: Workplace Safety, Everything You Need to Know to Ensure a Safe and Healthy Workplace.* CCH Incorporated, 2003.

"Off-the-Job Injuries Outpace Gain in Workplace Safety." *Plant Engineering.* April 2006.

"Risk Management Magazine Workplace Safety Round Table." *Risk Management.* November 2005.

U.S. Department of Labor. Bureau of Labor Statistics. "Lost-Worktime Injuries and Illnesses, Characteristics and Resulting Time Away from Work." News Press Release. 13 December 2005.

U.S. Department of Labor. Bureau of Labor Statistics. Wiatrowski, William J. "Occupational Safety and Health Statistics, Data for a New Century." *Monthly Labor Review.* October 2005.

U.S. Department of Labor Occupational Safety and Health Administration. *Computer Workstations Checklist.* Available from http://www.osha.gov/SLTC/etools/computerworkstations/checklist.html. Retrieved on 11 May 2006.

Hillstrom, Northern Lights
updated by Magee, ECDI

WORKPLACE VIOLENCE

Workplace violence is an act of aggression, physical assault, or threatening behavior that occurs in a work setting and causes physical or emotional harm to customers, coworkers, or managers. Broad definitions of workplace violence also often include acts of sabotage on work-site property.

Workplace violence has emerged as a subject of considerable interest to both small and large businesses in recent years. Some small business owners deny that this grim issue is a concern for them, but in reality, workplace violence can strike even tiny start-up firms. And as many analysts and business owners have charged, even the threat of violence can have a dreadful impact on the culture and productivity of a small business. Whereas employees of larger firms generally have more avoidance options to choose from when forced to share workspace with a volatile employee, the more modest facilities and resources of smaller businesses do not provide the same level of protection.

Workplace violence is an issue of which all businesses should be aware. An average of 16 people per day died while at work during 2004. Of these fatalities, 2.2 per day were the victims of homicide. The annual workplace safety data published by the U.S. Department of Labor indicated that 809 workplace homicides took place across America in 2004. Occupational Health and Safety Administration (OSHA) reports that on average they estimate that 2 million employees are victimized annually while at work. When it comes to specific statistics, the most recent data from the U.S. Bureau of Justice Statistics on violent crimes other than homicide are for the year 2003. In that year, 728,000 instances of violent crime were reportedly perpetrated on victims while they were on the job. These crimes include simple assault, aggravated assault, robbery, and rape/sexual assault. Although these crime statistics show a decline over recent years, they also highlight the need for business owners to take precautions and proactive measures to protect employees and coworkers and reduce the likelihood of an incident of violent crime.

ADDRESSING WORKPLACE VIOLENCE BEFORE IT ERUPTS

Small business owners can take several steps to address the specter of workplace violence. Hiring and interviewing practices should reflect the company's desire to establish and maintain a good workforce, and the owner should do his or her best to establish a company culture that does not tolerate non-violent forms of intimidation. After all, insulting and intimidating behavior—which may lead to physically violent behavior if left unchecked—can wreak significant mental harm on its victims, and may even provoke a violent response by victims who feel that they have no other recourse. Indeed, some studies have indicated that victims of harassment actually become less productive than employees who suffer from physical assaults.

Many human resource specialists recommend written violence-prevention policies and regular training sessions to inform employees about what to watch for. According to Paul Viollis, president of the company Risk Control Strategies, writing in *Business Insurance,* "The vast majority of incidents of workplace violence are completely preventable if employees know what to look for and how to report it. While younger individuals and females have increasingly emerged as workplace violence offenders in the past several years—possibly a spillover from school violence—the demographic and behavioral characteristics of the individuals who typically perpetrate acts of violence have, for the most part, remained the same. Such individuals are predominately male, between 25 and 40 years of age, do not handle stress well and are chronic complainers, manipulative and socially withdrawn, among other characteristics."

Other actions that a company may take to minimize the likelihood of workplace violence, albeit unpleasant to contemplate, include boosting security precautions by adding security personnel or installing metal detectors. Some security consultants urge their clients to make it clear that employee desks and lockers are company property that can be looked through at any time, and they should be encouraged to report all violent acts to legal authorities. Finally, business consultants and security experts counsel small business owners to recognize that workplace violence frequently stems from external sources. Indeed, the majority of homicides that take place in workplace settings are actually perpetrated by non-employees (angry customers, robbers, irate spouses or romantic partners).

STOPPING WORKPLACE VIOLENCE

Experts believe that businesses can take a number of steps to dramatically reduce their likelihood of an employee carrying out an act of workplace violence. Many of these are proactive in nature, designed to minimize the business's exposure to violent acts by employees:

Maintain and disseminate detailed policies on workplace behavior. Adopt a zero-tolerance policy that addresses signs of potential violence. Such a policy should clearly state that threats, intimidation, destruction of company property, and violence in any form will not be tolerated. It should also spell out clearly the disciplinary action that will be taken in response to any of these unacceptable actions, providing guidelines that clearly delineate violations that may result in discharge or other disciplinary action so that workers are cognizant of behavioral boundaries. In addition, these policies should explicitly state the company's determination to protect victims and/or informants of violent acts against any form of retaliation.

Maintain and disseminate workplace violence prevention programs. This plan should cover everything from investigatory steps to take when an employee exhibits questionable behavior to the manner in which problem employees are dismissed. "These training programs should focus on teaching employees how to recognize and report suspicious activity and should provide written information on whom to contact in an emergency," wrote Gillian Flynn in *Workforce.* This aspect of the program needs to be addressed with particular care, for staff participation will only occur if they can express concerns about coworkers in a safe and confidential way. Other elements of these programs typically include disciplinary training for managers, security plans, pre-employment screening, and media relations if an incident of workplace violence does take place.

Screen applicants. Every company's workplace violence prevention program should include a thorough investigation of applicants' backgrounds (including employment history and possible criminal record) and qualifications for the job opening. Many experts believe that incidents of workplace violence are more likely to occur when an employee is struggling with his/her responsibilities, so ability to fulfill the responsibilities of the position in question is a particularly relevant consideration. In addition, interviews should include questions that can help identify potential risky hires. According to Michael A. Gips, writing for *Security Management,* such questions include: "What would you do if a fellow employee called you a bad name? Embarrassed you in front of others? What did your previous boss do that made you mad? Tell me about a past supervisor you admired. It is a clear warning sign that a person has problems getting along with others if he can not identify a single past supervisor he liked." In addition to the above background and interviewing techniques, many companies have also adopted drug and alcohol testing, aptitude testing, and honesty testing as part of their overall interviewing process.

Recognize warning signs. Law enforcement and security experts agree that employees who engage in violent acts often—though not always—exhibit behaviors that serve as "red flags" indicating potential problems. These include: engaging in direct or veiled threats against coworkers, paranoid behavior, unreciprocated romantic interest in a coworker, obsession with weapons, pronounced mood swings, excessive anger over company policies or decisions, decreased productivity, and deteriorating relations with fellow staff, customers, or vendors.

Be cognizant of potential "trigger" events. Business owners should remember that workplace violence does not erupt for no reason, and that if it takes place within the walls of the company, the chances are pretty good that it was triggered by a workplace issue or event. Demotions, critical performance appraisals, layoffs, disciplinary actions, and other professional disappointments can all trigger violent behavior.

Counseling. Employee assistance programs can be very valuable to workers who are struggling with stress at home and/or in the office. When confronted with a volatile employee, a company's natural tendency may be to fire the troublemaker. In some cases, however, this action may exacerbates the situation and can even provoke a violent episode. The better approach is to suggest the troubled employee get professional counseling. Paying for it out of your own pocket, if necessary, is worth it, if it will avert a disaster. In addition, some employers have instituted policies designed to give employees an outlet to relate their grievances and concerns. These avenues range from regular meetings with managers to comment boxes or surveys.

Terminate with dignity. Employers can reduce their exposure to workplace violence by instituting and carrying out policies that treat terminated employees with respect. In addition, some consultants encourage companies to offer outplacement counseling for ex-employees as part of their severance packages. Before doing so, however, business owners and managers should discuss possible legal ramifications with a qualified attorney.

Address ex-employees who pose a potential threat. Many businesses erroneously believe that once an employee has been discharged and is no longer in the workplace, the worker no longer poses a threat. But this is not necessarily the case. A study by Northwestern National Life Insurance, for example, stated that 3 percent of the total number of reported incidents of workplace violence were perpetrated by ex-employees. Restraining orders, password changes, and other special security measures may be necessary in some situations.

PROVIDING REFERENCES FOR EX-EMPLOYEES

"The mere act of helping a violent or potentially violent ex-employee gain new employment raises problems, according to legal experts," wrote Gips. He noted that according to legal consultants, "there is no legal duty to warn a prospective employer of another company's experiences with an employee. But if the company purports to say something positive about the employee without revealing negative information, [it] might be interpreted as an endorsement of that employee, which could trigger the duty to tell the whole truth—including the violence or threatened violence." Other potential legal pitfalls await business owners who are asked to comment on ex-employees who engaged in questionable behavior that nonetheless never became violent in nature. Business owners and managers can not simply speculate that an ex-employee *might* be a violence risk, if there is no confirmed behavior upon which to base that opinion. Statutes governing defamation liability in this area vary considerably from state to state, so business owners who are asked about ex-employees who are seen as security risks should seek legal advice before responding.

SEE ALSO *Workplace Anger*

BIBLIOGRAPHY

Flynn, Gillian. "Employers Can't Look Away from Workplace Violence." *Workforce.* July 2000.

Fogleman, Dannie B. "Minimizing the Risk of Violence in the Workplace." *Employment Relations Today.* Spring 2000.

Gips, Michael A. "Transitioning Problem Employees." *Security Management.* November 2000.

Gurchiek, Kathy. "Workplace Violence on the Upswing." *HR Magazine.* July 2005.

Johnson, Kari R. "Workplace Violence: Is Your Business at Risk?" *Business North Carolina.* September 2000.

McDonald, Jane. "Murder at Work." *Risk Management.* March 2001.

Meyer, Pat. "Preventing Workplace Violence Starts with Recognizing Warning Signs and Taking Action." *Nation's Restaurant News.* 28 February 2000.

Neville, Haig. "Workplace Violence Prevention Strategies." *Memphis Business Journal.* 8 September 2000.

U.S. Department of Justice. Bureau of Justice Statistics. "Crime and Victims Statistics." Available from http://www.ojp.usdoj.gov/bjs/cvict.htm. Retrieved on 11 May 2006.

U.S. Department of Labor. Bureau of Labor Statistics. "Lost-Worktime Injuries and Illnesses, Characteristics and Resulting Time Away from Work." News Press Release. 13 December 2005.

Viollis, Paul. "Most Workplace Violence Avoidable." *Business Insurance.* 11 April 2005.

Hillstrom, Northern Lights
updated by Magee, ECDI

WORKSTATION

The term "workstation" is used to describe many different things. The broadest definition of workstation is the entire area accessed by a worker when performing a specific task or job cycle. A somewhat more restrictive definition of "workstation," and one that has gained usage in the last twenty years is; a terminal or personal computer (PC), usually connected to a mainframe or to a network of computers. This definition grew out of the concept of the workstation as the station at which computer work is done while the work product may be stored, and usually is, on a central mainframe system or on a network server. In colloquial usage the term workstation has evolved to mean any computer or terminal where work is performed.

The computers that are referred to as workstations span a broad range of computer power. They include systems that vary from sophisticated, high-powered computer used for computer-aided design (CAD), computer-aid engineering (CAE), graphics, and simulations, all the way to simple data entry terminals with no independent central processing unit (CPU). A workstation typically includes a mouse, keyboard, monitor, and often, though not always, a CPU. It may also include peripheral devices such as a modem, digital camera, scanner, or printer.

COMPUTER WORKSTATIONS AND THE POTENTIAL FOR INJURY

PCs are a fixture in any business, large or small, and are used for word processing, data entry, and other functions. PCs bring with them the expected potential for improved productivity and efficiency. But what most people have discovered over time is that working on PCs for many hours a day can lead to injuries that can be quite severe. In a work setting this can lead to lost productivity, a reduction in morale, and increased costs for health care and workers compensation premiums.

The largest category of injury suffered by heavy computer users are musculoskeletal disorders. According to the U.S. Occupational Safety and Health Administration (OSHA) nearly two million people suffer work-related musculoskeletal disorders, including repetitive strain injury caused by computer use, every year. In the case of computer related musculoskeletal disorders, the most common are the result of repetitive stress. Many of these are called cumulative trauma disorders (CTDs). Injuries of this type are disorders of the musculo-nervous system that involve nerve compression and wear and tear on muscles and tendons. The U.S. Department of Labor reports that all CTDs—not just those related to computer use—account for 32 percent of occupational illness cases.

Repetitive stress injuries generally can be by far the most serious injuries suffered by computer users. Perhaps the best-known type of repetitive-stress injury is carpal-tunnel syndrome, which is usually related to keyboard use. The syndrome is the result of putting pressure on the nerves that run from the hand to the arm and is characterized by pain and weakness in the hand, arm, and even the shoulder.

Another common problem associated with computer use is eyestrain. James Sheedy of the University of California—Berkeley estimates that ten million cases of eyestrain are reported each year. As Don Sellers noted in *Zap!: How Your Computer Can Hurt You and What You Can Do About It,* "The computer is a much more visually demanding environment than people think." To reduce employee eyestrain, employers should adjust lighting to reduce glare on computer screens and encourage workers to take regular breaks to look away from the screen and refocus on a distant object. Employees, particularly those who already wear bifocals, may also want to invest in eyeglasses designed specifically to be worn while working with a computer.

AN EMPLOYEE-FRIENDLY WORKSTATION AND ENVIRONMENT

Dr. Bruce Bernard of the U.S. National Institute of Occupational Safety and Health encourages employers to evaluate the nature and extent of keyboard use. "Generally," he says, "carpal tunnel syndrome is not found in the workplace unless tendonitis appears there first. You don't want to wait until tendonitis presents itself. You really need to take seriously employee complaints of discomfort." Sellers echoes this approach, urging employers "to examine the workstation environment. Just simply look at how a person is using a workstation: Is he or she comfortable?"

To ensure a comfortable workstation, employers need to be aware of workplace ergonomics, which is the effective and safe interaction between people and things. When reviewing the current work environment, employers should look to see if employees have already made their own adjustments to improve comfort. For example, has an employee placed his monitor on a stack of books, added a cushion to his chair, or placed the legs of his desk on blocks? If so, then clearly the original workstation configuration is not effective. Employers may then consider investing in ergonomically designed furniture and computer accessories that can be adjusted to meet the needs of an individual employee.

Employers should also encourage employees who work extensively with computers to take regular breaks. Marvin Dainoff, director of the Center for Ergonomics Research at Miami University of Ohio, urges employers to "remember that people are not machines." Dainoff also recommends stretching as a means of eliminating musculoskeletal problems. Finally, Bernard and other experts urge employers to create an environment where employees feel they can speak up when they are experiencing any pain or discomfort. The sooner a problem is identified, the greater the employer's chance of controlling related costs.

For a thorough checklist of the things that an employer should consider when setting up or retrofitting a workstation for maximum ergonomic efficiency, OSHA provides a web site. The checklist provided there covers how best to set-up the monitor, keyboard, work surface, chair, mouse, document holder, wrist rest, telephone, and desk light. The OSHA checklist may be found at http://www.osha.gov/SLTC/etools/computer-workstations/checklist.html.

SEE ALSO *Ergonomics; Hoteling*

BIBLIOGRAPHY

Cady, Eric. "Is Your Workplace a Trauma Center?" *Small Business Reports.* October 1994.

Freedman, Alan. *Computer Desktop Encyclopedia.* The Computer Language Company Inc., 1996.

Lewin, David L. "Preventive Medicine at Work." *Nation's Business.* March 1995.

Sellers, Don. *Zap! How Your Computer Can Hurt You and What You Can Do About It* Addison-Wesley, 1994.

U.S. Department of Labor Occupational Safety and Health Administration. *Computer Workstations Checklist.* Available from http://www.osha.gov/SLTC/etools/computerworkstations/checklist.html. Retrieved on 11 May 2006.

Hillstrom, Northern Lights
updated by Magee, ECDI

WRITTEN COMMUNICATION

Written communication involves any type of interaction that makes use of the written word. Communication is a key to any endeavor involving more than one person. Communicating through writing is essential in the modern world and is becoming ever more so as we participate in what is now commonly called the information age. In fact, written communication is the most common form of business communication. It is essential for small business owners and managers to develop effective written communication skills and to encourage the same in all employees. The information age has altered the ways in which we communicate and placed an increasing emphasis on written versus oral communications.

The ever-increasing use of computers and computer networks to organize and transmit information means the need for competent writing skills is rising. Dr. Craig Hogan, a former university professor who now heads an online school for business writing, receives hundreds of inquiries each month from managers and executives requesting help with improving their own and their employees' writing skills. Dr. Hogan explains, in an article entitled "What Corporate America Can't Build: A Sentence," that millions of people previously not required to do a lot of writing on the job are now expected to write frequently and rapidly. According to Dr. Hogan, many of them are not up to the task. "E-mail is a party to which English teachers have not been invited. It has companies tearing their hair out." Survey results from The National Commission on Writing study back up this assessment. They found that a third of employees in the nation's "blue chip" companies write poorly and are in need of remedial writing instruction.

The need to develop good writing skills is only highlighted by the fact that in the information age, it is not uncommon to have business relationships with customers and suppliers that are established and maintained exclusively through the use of written communications. In this environment, "the words we write are very real representations of our companies and ourselves. We must be sure that our e-mail messages are sending the right messages about us," explained Janis Fisher Chan, author of *E-Mail: A Write It Well Guide-How to Write and Manage E-Mail in the Workplace,* in an article appearing in *Broker Magazine.* The key to communication, of course, is to convey meaning in as accurate and concise a manner as possible. People do not read business memoranda for the pleasure of reading. They do so in order to receive instructions or information upon which to base decisions or take action. Therefore, highly literary prose is not desirable in business writing. Overly formal prose may also be counterproductive by seeming stand-offish or simply wordy. A style of writing that is too informal can also convey an unintended message, namely that the subject matter is not serious or not taken seriously by the sender. A straightforward, courteous tone is usually the best choice but one that may not come naturally without practice.

THE COMMUNICATION PROCESS

The basic process of communication begins when a fact or idea is observed by one person. That person (the sender) may decide to translate the observation into a message, and then transmit the message through some communication medium to another person (the receiver). The receiver then must interpret the message and provide feedback to the sender indicating that the message has been understood and appropriate action taken.

As Herta A. Murphy and Herbert W. Hildebrandt observed in *Effective Business Communications,* good communication should be complete, concise, clear, concrete, correct, considerate, and courteous. More specifically, this means that communication should: answer basic questions like who, what, when, where; be relevant and not overly wordy; focus on the receiver and his or her interests; use specific facts and figures and active verbs; use a conversational tone for readability; include examples and visual aids when needed; be tactful and good-natured; and be accurate and nondiscriminatory. Unclear, inaccurate, or inconsiderate business communication can waste valuable time, alienate employees or customers, and destroy goodwill toward management or the overall business.

ADVANTAGES AND DISADVANTAGES OF WRITTEN COMMUNICATION

One advantage to using written forms of communication is that written messages do not have to be delivered on the spur of the moment; instead, they can be edited and revised several times before they are sent so that the content can be shaped to maximum effect. Another advantage is that written communication provides a permanent record of the messages and can be saved for later study. Since they are permanent, written forms of communication also enable recipients to take more time in reviewing the message and providing appropriate feedback. For these reasons, written forms of communication are often considered more appropriate for complex business messages that include important facts and figures. Other benefits commonly associated with good writing skills include increased customer/client satisfaction; improved inter-organizational efficiency; and enhanced image in the community and industry.

There are also several potential pitfalls associated with written communication, however. For instance, unlike oral communication, wherein impressions and reactions are exchanged instantaneously, the sender of written communication does not generally receive immediate feedback to his or her message. This can be a source of frustration and uncertainty in business situations in which a swift response is desired. In addition, written messages often take more time to compose, both because of their information-packed nature and the difficulty that many individuals have in composing such correspondence. Many companies, however, have taken a proactive stance in addressing the latter issue. Mindful of the large number of workers who struggle with their writing abilities, some firms have begun to offer on-site writing courses or enrolled employees in business writing workshops offered by professional training organizations, colleges, and community education programs.

E-MAIL COMMUNICATIONS

Electronic mail has emerged as a highly popular business communication tool in recent years. Indeed, its capacity to convey important corporate communications swiftly and easily has transformed it into a communications workhorse for business enterprises of all sizes and orientations. But many users of e-mail technology pay little attention to basic rules of grammar and format when composing their letters, even when they are penning business correspondence addressed to clients, customers, vendors, business partners, or internal colleagues. This sloppy correspondence style reflects a lack of professionalism and may communicate to the recipient a view of the company behind the message as equally unprofessional. The ease and informality of the medium should not be confused with the writing necessary to use it properly.

Given this unfortunate trend, many business experts counsel companies to install firm guidelines on tone, content, and shape of e-mail correspondence. These guidelines should make it clear that all employees are expected to adhere to the same standards of professionalism that (presumably) remain in place for traditional postal correspondence. Proper spelling and grammar and the ability to frame correspondence in suitably diplomatic language should be hallmarks of electronic mail as well as regular mail, especially if the communication is directed at a person or persons outside the company.

SEE ALSO *Communication Systems*

BIBLIOGRAPHY

Bonner, William H., and Lillian H. Chaney. *Communicating Effectively in an Information Age.* Second Edition, Dame Publishing, 2003.

Dillon, Sam. "What Corporate America Can't Build: A Sentence." *The New York Times.* 7 December 2004.

"E-mail That Doesn't Break Your Career." *Broker Magazine.* April-May 2006.

Holz, Shel. "Establishing Connections: Today's Communications Technologies Have Shifted the Dynamic." *Communication World.* May-June 2005.

Murphy, Herta A., and Herbert W. Hildebrandt. *Effective Business Communications.* Seventh Edition. McGraw-Hill, 1997.

Reynolds, Sana. "Composing Effective E-Mail Messages." *Communication World.* 15 July 1997.

Ross-Larson, Bruce. *Writing for the Information Age.* W.W. Norton & Company, 2002.

Schafer, Sarah. "Office E-Mail: It's Fast, Easy and All Too Often Misunderstood." *International Herald Tribune.* 1 November 2000.

Staples, Brent. "The Fine Art of Getting It Down on Paper, Fast." *The New York Times.* 15 May 2005.

Writing: A Ticket to Work... Or a Ticket Out. National Commission on Writing, The College Board. September 2004.

Hillstrom, Northern Lights
updated by Magee, ECDI

Y

YOUNG ENTREPRENEURS' ORGANIZATION (YEO)

The Young Entrepreneurs' Organization (YEO) is perhaps the best known of several groups that emerged during the 1990s to offer educational opportunities and other kinds of support to young business owners. Membership in such groups has increased dramatically in recent years, as more and more young people have abandoned traditional corporate career paths in favor of the increased autonomy and financial rewards that are possible through entrepreneurship. "Times have changed, and today entrepreneurship has become a key career choice for young Americans," wrote Tariq K. Muhammad in *Black Enterprise*. "Highly publicized corporate downsizings have cast a pall over the traditional path to success, and fueled a general perception that well-paying jobs with room for advancement are scarce. The days when professionals could expect to stay with the same company for a lifetime are long gone. Human resources professionals estimate that today's worker will have an average of five to ten career changes in their lifetime. As a result, interest in entrepreneurship has grown."

YEO was founded in 1987 by a group of five successful young entrepreneurs, including the founders of I Can't Believe It's Not Yogurt, the California Closet Company, and Redgate Communications Corporation. The organization later shortened its name to Entrepreneur's Organization or EO. In early 2006, the group included 6,000 business founders based in 40 countries around the world. EO member companies represented more than $81 billion in revenues in 2005. The EO is managed by an international board of directors that oversees the organization's local community chapters.

The mission of EO is to provide its members with mentoring, peer networking, and educational opportunities. Membership is open to individuals who are under the age of 40 and are the founders, co-founders, or majority shareholders of companies grossing over $1 million annually (special exceptions also exist for venture-backed firms). Annual membership fees are $1,300. Local chapters hold monthly meetings and sponsor regular educational events or presentations. In addition, the national organization regularly sponsors tours of other countries to study new business strategies, methods, and innovations. Many chapters also feature "self-help" forums where groups of 10 to 12 entrepreneurs from noncompeting industries get together to work on common problems faced by small business owners, such as hiring good employees or international expansion. Personal issues are also sometimes explored in these private, confidential settings, which are facilitated by trained moderators.

Another popular EO program is its so-called Inventory of Skills (IOS), in which members can turn to fellow members to solve business problems or garner information on business issues they are facing. "YEO lets me benefit from the experience of my peers, who are also entrepreneurs and have already gone through situations I may be going through," one entrepreneur told *Black Enterprise*. "When I'm looking to enter new markets, I already have a contact in any part of the world because of my affiliation with EO." The EO can be contacted via its web site at www.eonetwork.org.

SEE ALSO *Entrepreneurial Networks*

BIBLIOGRAPHY

Applegate, Jane. "Entrepreneurs Have Support of Peer Groups." *Triangle Business Journal.* 30 April, 1999.

Henderson, Barry. "Join the Club." *Kansas City Business Journal.* 26 May 1995.

Mitseas, Catherine. *Organization Focuses on Young Leaders.* 21 January 2000.

Muhammad, Tariq K. "From Buppie to Biz-Wiz: Forget Corporate America—Generation X Is Choosing the Entrepreneurial Path to Success." *Black Enterprise.* January 1997.

Hillstrom, Northern Lights
updated by Magee, ECDI

Z

ZONING ORDINANCES

Zoning ordinances are local or municipal laws that establishing building codes and land usage regulations for properties in a specified area. Most cities and towns are composed of regions that are zoned for residential, commercial, or industrial development, and often these zones are subdivided by additional use restrictions (type of business permitted, etc.). Zoning laws and ordinances may affect such varied issues as parking for customers, setbacks, access for deliveries, the number and types of employees permitted, and the use of signs or other forms of advertising. These ordinances have to be considered by entrepreneurs/business owners wishing to set up, expand, or relocate business establishments. They should check with their city's zoning office and licensing board for restrictions that may apply within the city. Even particular neighborhoods may have land use regulations that should be researched prior to finalizing any business plan.

Zoning and Commercial Businesses Review of zoning ordinances for areas designated for commercial and/or industrial use is a standard procedure for entrepreneurs seeking to establish a business in such places. In most cases, establishing a business in a building that was previously used for commercial purposes will not run afoul of zoning ordinances for the area. Experts warn, however, that businesses seeking to construct a new facility, acquire an existing building for a new use, or launch extensive remodeling efforts should closely examine local zoning and building codes. In instances where local zoning laws present a problem, the business owner has the option of filing for a zone variance, a conditional-use permit, or a zone change. All three of these options have their drawbacks.

A zone change amounts to a permanent change in the zoning classification of the property. There are cases in which this is desirable, but the procedure to successfully trigger such a change is generally a cumbersome one that goes through City Hall. After all, bids for reclassification are based on claims that current zoning is in error or no longer reflects the character of the neighborhood. Many municipalities are reluctant to accept such arguments. Variances and conditional-use permits, meanwhile, are in essence requests for special permission to use the property for a purpose other than for which it was zoned. Such permits are often expensive to obtain, and can take two to four months to go through if they are even approved. But they are usually easier to obtain that outright zoning changes.

Zoning and Home Businesses Checking into local zoning ordinances is a step often overlooked by owners of home-based businesses as well. Such neglect can prove troublesome down the line, for as Janet Attard noted in *The Home Office and Small Business Answer Book,* "zoning laws are established locally, often at the township, city, or village level. Furthermore, each town or village decides for itself what types of home businesses it will allow. Thus in one community you might be able to run a home business that has up to two employees while in another community the same business might be restricted from having any employees. In still another community you might be able to have a home-based business if you are a fisherman or carpenter but not if you are a real estate agent or insurance broker."

Most zoning ordinances restricting home offices in residential neighborhoods were originally designed to protect residential neighborhoods from becoming cluttered with commercial activity and thus maintain the family-friendly flavor and atmosphere of the area. In the past, these laws often were strictly interpreted to keep residents from conducting any sort of business from their home, even if it did not have a visible impact on the rest of the neighborhood. Today, the explosion in home-based business start-ups has sparked a reevaluation of zoning laws in residential areas, but many of the old zoning laws remain on the books.

It is widely recognized that millions of home-based businesses operate for years in violation of zoning laws, and that many of those businesses prosper without ever running into problems. Indeed, many communities simply ignore violations unless a neighborhood resident or someone else complains. These complaints may be triggered by utterly trivial factors—unhappiness with the frequency with which you mow your lawn, for instance, or anger about some real or imagined social slight—but in the eyes of the law, the motivations behind the complaint will generally be of little consequence. "You cannot assume ... that it is OK for you to disregard local law because *some* town boards don't enforce regulations and *some* people get away with operating on the sly," said Attard. "If there are laws prohibiting your type of home business, it will only take one complaint to plunge you into a pot of legal hot water."

SEE ALSO *Environmental Audit*

BIBLIOGRAPHY

Attard, Janet. *The Home Office and Small Business Answer Book.* Henry Holt, 1993.

Barhight, G. Scott, Jennifer R. Busse, and David K. Gildea. "Get the Lay of the Land Before Buying Property." *Baltimore Business Journal.* 8 December 2000.

Barlas, Stephen. "Zone Defense." *Entrepreneur.* February 1998.

Hardin, Pamala M. "Keep Your Firm from Zoning Out: Running Your Business from Your Basement May Get You Zapped with Hefty Fines." *Black Enterprise.* March 1996.

Shilling, Joseph. "Land Use, Zoning, Growth Management, and Planning Law." *Journal of the American Planning Association.* Winter 2006.

Hillstrom, Northern Lights
updated by Magee, ECDI

Index

A

Abbott, Bragdon v. (1998), 1:37
ABC accounting method. *See* Activity-based costing
Absent income, paying taxes on, 2:986
Absenteeism, 1:1–2
    See also Sick leave and personal days
Accelerated Cost Recovery Systems, 1:3–4
    See also Depreciation
Acceptance (contracts), 1:238
Access-control systems, 2:812
Accountants, 1:6, 7
    See also Certified public accountants (CPAs)
Accounting, 1:4–8
Accounting changes, 1:586
Accounting methods, 1:8–9
    See also Tax planning
Accounting Principles Board, 1:4
Accounting systems, 1:5–6
Accounting variances, 2:1146–1147
Accounts payable, 1:9–11, 167
    See also Cash management
Accounts receivable, 1:11–12, 60, 167, 196–197
    See also Cash management
Accounts receivable financing, 1:12
Accounts receivable turnover ratio, 1:503
Accrual basis accounting method, 1:8–9, 587, 2:772, 1093
Acid test. *See* Quick ratio
Acquired immune deficiency syndrome (AIDS). *See* AIDS in the workplace

Acquisitions. *See* Mergers and acquisitions
Action research, 2:831
Active records, 2:935
Activity-based costing, 1:12–14, 2:890
    See also Overhead expenses; Product costing
Activity-based management, 1:13
Adaptability, diversification and, 1:351
Administrative business expenses, 2:1090–1091
Administrative services outsourcing, 1:392
Adobe Systems, 1:316
ADSL (Asymmetric Digital Subscriber Lines), 2:751
Adverse opinions (auditing), 1:507
Advertising
    allowances, 2:1000
    for business-to-business marketing, 1:147
    corporate sponsorship as, 1:252–254, 2:998
    franchising and, 1:527
    via spam, 2:1063
    when selling a business, 2:1021
    See also specific advertising media
Advertising, evaluation of results, 1:20–22
Advertising agencies, 1:14–17
Advertising-based models, 1:149
Advertising budgets, 1:16, 17–20
    See also specific advertising media
Advertising media. *See* Infomercials; Internet advertising; Print

advertising; Radio advertising; Video advertising
Advertising strategy, 1:28–29
    See also Target markets
Advocacy organizations, 2:781
Affirmative action, 1:29–32, 2:747–748, 931
    See also Racial discrimination
Affordable budgeting method, 1:19
African-American-owned businesses, 2:745–746
After-tax income. *See* Net income
Age-based profit sharing plans, 2:962
Age discrimination, 1:32–35
Age Discrimination in Employment Act (1967), 1:33–34, 35–37, 583
Agenda setting, in decision making, 1:303–304
Agendas, 2:732–733
Agents (wholesalers), 2:1161–1162
Aggregate demand, 1:114
AICPA (American Institute of Certified Public Accountants), 1:6, 63, 64, 176
AIDS in the workplace, 1:37–38
Air gapping, 1:508
Air pollution. *See* Clean Air Act (1970); Environmental law and business
Air quality. *See* Clean Air Act (1970); Environmental law and business
Air transportation (distribution), 2:866, 1126
Air travel, 1:142
Alarm systems, 2:812–813
Alien employees, 1:38–41

All available funds budgeting method, 1:19

The Alternative Board®, 1:443–444

Alternative Depreciation System, 1:3

Alternative dispute resolution, 1:**41–43**

Alternative officing, 1:573

Alternative work schedules. *See* Flextime

AM radio, 1:22–23

Ambush marketing, 1:254

American Association of Advertising Agencies, 1:17

American Business Women's Association, 2:1165

American culture, alien employees and, 1:40–41

American Depository Receipt, 2:1071

American Institute of Certified Public Accountants (AICPA), 1:6, 63, 64, 176

American Inventors Protection Act (1999), 1:636–637

American Jobs Creation Act (2004), 2:792–793

American National Standards Institute (ANSI), 1:375

American Society of Composers, Authors, and Publishers (ASCAP), 2:980

American Trucking Associations, Browner v. (2001), 1:188

Americans with Disabilities Act (1990), 1:37, **43–46**, 333–334, 2:951

Amortization, 1:46–47

Anderson, Chris, 1:354

Angel Capital Association, 1:47

Angel investors, 1:47–48, 2:1013
    See also Seed money; Venture capital; Venture capital networks

Annual basis (interest rates), 1:612

Annual inventory turnover ratio, 1:503

Annual percentage rate (APR), 1:**48–49**

Annual plans, 1:137

Annual reports, 1:49–52, 2:1009

Annual Retail Theft Survey, 1:422

Annual Statement of Taxes Withheld. *See* Form W-2 (IRS)

Annuities, 1:**52–55**

ANSI (American National Standards Institute), 1:375

Anti-dating policies. *See* Office romance; Sexual harassment

Anti-spam services, 2:1063–1064

Anti-virus software, 2:1156

Antonio, Wards Cove Packing Company v. (1989), 1:31

Apple Computers, 1:316, 446

Application service providers, 1:55–56

Applied research, 2:953

Appraisers. *See* Business appraisers

Apprenticeship programs, 1:**56–57**, 2:664, 1123

APR (Annual percentage rate), 1:48–49

Arbitration, 1:41–42, 92, 552, 2:1057
    See also Mediation

Arbitration associations, 1:41

Archival records, 2:935

Area locals (unions), 2:665

Armed Service Procurement Act (1947), 1:543

Aronoff, Craig E., 2:771

Articles of incorporation, 1:57–58

Articles of organization, 2:688–689

As-of dates, 2:1143

ASCAP (American Society of Composers, Authors, and Publishers), 2:980

Asian-owned businesses, 2:746

Assembly line methods, 1:**58–59**, 2:976

Assessment tests, 2:1130

Asset-backed bonds. *See* Bonds

Asset-based approach valuation, 2:1141

Asset utilization ratios, 1:60–61

Asset value approach valuation, 2:1142

Assets, 1:**59–61**
    on balance sheets, 1:78
    capital assets, 1:160
    credit securitization and, 1:267–268
    definition, 1:5
    on financial statements, 1:505
    as nontraditional funding source, 2:794
    preferred stock claim on, 2:1070
    purchase of, via credit, 1:264
    sale of, 2:1019
    valuation of, 1:262
    See also Liabilities; Return on assets (ROA)

Assets ranking (Fortune 500), 1:523

Associated Credit Bureaus, Inc., 1:268

Assumptions, 1:**61–62**

Asymmetric Digital Subscriber Lines (ADSL), 2:751

Attendance. *See* Absenteeism

Audience research, 2:720

Audiovisual training, 2:1122

Audit reports, 1:63–64

Auditing, by Internal Revenue Service, 1:614, **646–647**

Auditing opinions, 1:407

Audits, external, 1:**62–65**, 68–69

Audits, internal, 1:**65–70**

Authentication (Internet security), 2:1154

Authority, conceptions of, 1:281

Automated guided vehicles, 1:70–71

Automated storage and retrieval systems, 1:71–72
    See also Inventory control systems

Automation, 1:**72–75**
    See also Management information systems (MIS); Robotics

Automobile emissions, 1:188

Automobile expenses, 2:1091

Automobile leasing, 1:75–76

Automobile manufacturing cluster (MI), 1:192

"Avoid error" (Poka-yoke), 2:927

B

B2B. *See* Business-to-business commerce

B2C. *See* Business-to-consumer commerce

Baby bonds, 1:77–78

Back door software testing, 1:621

Bakers' Strike (1741), 2:666

Bakke, Regents of the University of California v. (1978), 1:31

Balance sheets, 1:78–79
    definition, 1:6
    depreciation, 1:314
    financial analysis, 1:497
    valuation methods, 2:1142

Banker's acceptances, 2:753

Banking. *See* Banks and banking

Bankruptcy, 1:79–82

Bankruptcy Abuse and Consumer Protection Act (2005), 1:80

Banks and banking, 1:82–84

Banner advertisements, 1:25, **84–86**

Bar coding, 1:86–87

Barlow, Marshall v. (1978), 2:804

Barrier removal from facilities, 1:334

Barriers to market entry, 1:87–88

Barter discounts, 1:20

Bartering, 1:88–89

Baseband transmission, 2:697

Basic ESOPs. *See* Employee stock ownership plans

Basic research, 2:953

Basu, Ron, 2:925

Behavioral interviewing, 1:428

Behavioral sciences, 2:829

Benchmarking, 1:**89–90**, 137
    See also Best practices

Benefits. *See* Employee benefits

Benna, Ted, 1:524

Berg, Gabriel, 2:657

Berne Convention for the Protection of Literary and Artistic Works, 1:246

Berners-Lee, Tim, 1:574

Best Manufacturing Practices web site, 1:91

Best practices, 1:**90–92**

Best value evaluations (contracting), 1:545

Better business bureaus, 1:**92–93**

Beyond Budgeting Round Table, 1:109, 139

Bid lists, 2:952

Bidding. *See* Competitive bids

Biggins, Hazen Paper Co. v. (1993), 1:34

Bilateral contracts, 1:238

Bills of lading, 2:1128

Bills of materials, 2:728

Binary notation, data encryption and, 1:291

Biometrics, 1:**93–95**

Bioterrorism Act (2002), 1:376

Blogs and newsgroups, 2:776–778

Blue chip stocks, 1:**95–96**
    See also Fortune 500

Blue sky amount, 1:542

Boards of directors, 1:**96–98**, 591, 2:1068

Boca Raton, Faragher v. (1998). *See* Faragher/Ellerth

Body language, 2:795

Bollinger, Graz v. (2003), 1:32

Bollinger, Gruttter v. (2003), 1:32

Bona fide occupation qualification, 1:33, 36

Bond ratings, 1:99

Bonding (marketing). *See* Database marketing

Bonds, 1:**98–99**, 265, 2:694, 942, 974

Bonus packs, 2:997

Bonuses, 1:408–409

Bookkeeping, 1:**99–100**
    See also Accounting

Boomerang employees, 1:404–405

Boundaryless (organizations), 1:**100–101**

Bragdon v. Abbott (1998), 1:37

Brainstorming, 1:**101–102**

Branching tree networks, 2:697

Brand analysis, 2:720

Brand equity, 1:**102–103**

Brands and brand names, 1:**103–105**

See also Private labeling; Trademarks

Breadboard prototypes, 2:912–913

Break-even analysis, 1:**105–106**, 511

Break-even quantity, 1:105

Brennan, Corning Glass Works v. (1974), 1:534–535

Bretton Woods Accord, 1:615

Briggs, Katharine Cook, 2:759

Brim, Rodney, 2:701–710

British East India Company, 1:537

Broadband transmission, 2:697

Brochures (direct mail), 1:324, 326

Brokerage process. *See* Business brokers

Brokers (wholesalers), 2:1161–1162

Browner v. American Trucking Associations (2001), 1:188

Bucket shops, 1:296

Budget deficit, 1:**106–107**

Budget surplus, 1:**107–108**

Budgets and budgeting, 1:**108–110**
    advertising, 1:16, 17–20
    automation, 1:74
    business plans and, 1:136
    capital budgeting, 1:259
    corporate logos, 1:251–252
    cost accounting and, 1:262

Building contractors, 1:225–226

Bulk packaging, 2:846

Bulletin boards. *See* Electronic bulletin boards

Bullying, 2:1169–1170

Bureau of Competition, 1:492

Bureau of Consumer Protection, 1:491–492

Bureau of Economic Analysis, 2:1025, 1136

Bureau of Economics, 1:492

Bureau of Labor Statistics
    census data and, 1:173–174
    Consumer Price Index, 1:235
    on employee benefits, 1:384
    on family leave, 1:484
    on minimum wage, 2:743–744
    on part-time employees, 2:854
    on productivity, 2:900, 901
    on profit sharing, 2:907–908
    Wages by Area and Occupation Program, 1:388
    on wholesalers, 2:1162
    on workplace injury, 2:1171

Bureau of the Census, 2:1136

Burlington Industries, Inc. v. Ellerth. See Faragher/Ellerth

Bus networks, 2:697

Bush, George W., 1:39

Business appraisers, 1:**110–111**

Business associations, 1:**111–112**

Business brokers, 1:**112–114**

Business casual. *See* Casual business attire

Business closures. *See* Business failure and dissolution

Business contacts, as reference sources, 1:129

Business continuity planning. *See* Disaster planning

Business cycles, 1:**114–117**
    See also Organizational life cycle; Product life cycle

Business descriptions, for loan proposals, 2:692

Business Development Mentor-Protégé Program, 1:369

Business dissolution. *See* Business failure and dissolution

Business education, 1:**117–118**

Business entity changes, pro forma statements and, 2:887

Business ethics, 1:**118–120**
    See also Codes of ethics

Business expansion, 1:**120–122**

Business failure and dissolution, 1:**122–124**, 441–442, 2:657
    See also Bankruptcy; Liquidation; Liquidation and liquidation values

Business format franchises, 1:527

Business hours, 1:**124–125**

Business incubators, 1:**125–127**

Business information sources, 1:**127–129**, 207, 2:1045

Business insurance, 1:**129–133**
    See also Risk management; Worker's compensation

Business interruption insurance, 1:132, **133–134**

Business names, 1:**134–135**

Business opportunity plans, 1:132

Business planning, 1:**137–139**, 486–487, 2:885–886
    See also Strategy

Business plans, 1:**135–137**
    See also Investor presentations

Business processes, human resources and, 1:578–579

Business proposals, 1:**139–141**, 233

Business Responds to AIDS program, 1:37, 38

Business resumption. *See* Disaster planning

Business-to-business catalogs, 2:704

Business-to-business commerce, 1:**143–145**, 2:863

Business-to-business marketing, 1:**145–148**

Business-to-consumer commerce, 1:143, 144, **148–150**

Business travel, 1:**141–143**
  See also Standard mileage rate

Business unions, 2:662

Buy-sell agreements, 1:131, 191, 2:851

Buyers, competitive bids and, 1:208

Buyers, industry analysis and, 1:597

Buyers' cooperatives, 1:242

Buying allowances, 2:1000

Buying an existing business, 1:**150–153**
  See also Selling a business

Buying-selling, psychological aspects of, 2:864

C

C corporations, 1:**155–158**, 355, 356, 589–590, 2:1095
  See also Incorporation; S corporations

Cable modems, 2:751

Cable television advertising, 1:27–28

CAD/CAM, 1:**217–219**

Cafeteria plans (flexible benefit plans), 1:511–512

CAIP (U.S. Community Adjustment Investment Program), 2:1042

Caldwell Legal, U.S.A., 2:675–676

California
  employment-at-will doctrine, 1:419
  insurance pooling, 1:607
  Proposition 209 (1996), 1:30, 32

Call provisions, 2:942

CAN-SPAM Act (2003), 1:215, 377, 2:703, 1063

Canadian small business category, 2:1039

Capital, 1:**158–160**
  access to, business incubation and, 1:125–126
  cost of, 1:262
  partnerships' acquisition of, 2:849
  raising, for sole proprietorships, 2:1061
  raising, when incorporating, 1:155, 588

Capital assets, 1:160, 313–314

Capital budgeting, 1:259

Capital expenditures, cash flow statements and, 1:169

Capital gains, 1:**160–161**

Capital leases. *See* Long-term leases

Capital losses, 1:**160–161**

Capital stock depreciation, 2:907

Capital structure, 1:**161–162**
  See also Undercapitalization

Capitalization ranking (Fortune 500), 1:523

CAPLines Program, 2:1042, 1137

Car rental, business travel and, 1:142

Career academies, 1:118

Career and family, 1:**162–165**

Career development, 1:577, 2:1124

Career planning and changing, 1:**165–167**

Carpal tunnel syndrome, 2:1177

CASE (Computer-aided software engineering), 1:219

Case studies, training through, 2:1122

Cash, as current asset, 1:59–60

Cash, liquidation and, 2:689

Cash balances, 1:171

Cash basis accounting method, 1:8–9, 586–587, 2:1093

Cash collection systems, 1:170–171

Cash conversion cycle, 1:**167–168**

Cash flow
  depreciation and, 1:314
  increases through Accelerated Cost Recovery System, 1:3
  leveraged buyout financing and, 2:679
  loan repayment and, 2:695
  statements of, 1:6
  See also Discounted cash flow

Cash flow statements, 1:**168–170**, 497–498
  See also Financial statements

Cash flow to debt ratio, 1:301

Cash-for-stock, 2:739

Cash management, 1:**170–171**, 2:1131–1132
  See also Accounts payable; Accounts receivable

Cash to total assets ratio, 1:502

Cash turnover ratio, 1:502–503

Casual business attire, 1:**171–173**

Catalog businesses. *See* Mail-order businesses

Catalog showrooms, 2:705

Catalogs, 1:324, 2:704–705

CCC (Copyright Clearance Center, Inc.), 2:980–981

CD-ROM reference sources, 1:129

CDC (Centers for Disease Control), 1:37, 38, 2:1058

CDs. *See* Certificates of Deposit (CDs)

CE Mark, 2:1109

Celebrity endorsements, 1:435–437

Cell manufacturing, 1:59

Cellular technology, 1:201

Census data, 1:173–174

Centers for Disease Control (CDC), 1:37, 38, 2:1058

Central processing units, 1:219–220

CERCLA (Comprehensive Environmental Response Cleanup and Liability Act) (1980), 1:**209–211**, 447

Certificates of Deposit (CDs), 2:753

Certificates of origin, 2:1128

Certification, definition, 2:682

Certification of testing laboratories, 2:1109

Certified Development Companies Program. *See* 504 CDC Program

Certified Lender Program, 1:175

Certified lenders, 1:175

Certified public accountants (CPAs), 1:6, **175–177**

CFTs (Cross-functional teams), 1:**281–285**, 2:919–920, 1113–1114

Chambers of commerce, 1:**177–178**, 443
  See also U.S. Chamber of Commerce

Channel specialists, 1:146

Chapter 7 bankruptcy, 1:80, 123, 2:690

Chapter 11 bankruptcy, 1:80–81, 123, 2:1012

Chapter 13 bankruptcy, 1:80, 123

Chargebacks, 1:618

Charitable foundations, 1:179–180, 2:781

Charitable giving, 1:**178–180**

Chat rooms, 1:630

Chattanooga (TN) cluster analysis, 1:193

Chattel mortgage. *See* Purchase money security interest

Chemical information lists, 2:970

Cherry picking (pricing), 2:699

Chief executive officers, fiduciary duty of, 1:494

Child care, 1:**180–183**

Child care cooperatives, 1:242

Child care industry growth, 2:1055

Child labor. *See* Employment of minors

Children's Online Privacy Protection Act (COPPA) (1998), 1:**183–185**, 491

Choosing a small business, 1:185–187

CIS (U.S. Citizenship and Immigration Services), 1:404

City of Jackson, Mississippi, Smith v. (2005), 1:34–35

Civil Rights Act (1964), 1:30, 2:667

Civil Rights Act (1991), 1:31, 2:930

Clean Air Act (1970), 1:**187–189**

Clean Air Act Amendments (1990), 1:188

Clean Water Act (1972), 1:**189–190**

Clear Skies Act (2003), 1:188

Clerical training, 2:1123

Click through rate media buying, 1:15, 84

Client-to-LAN connections, 2:1153

Closed-circuit surveillance systems, 2:812

Closed-end investment companies, 1:457

Closed-end leases, 1:75–76

Closed shops, 2:663

Closely held corporations, 1:**190–191**

Clusters, 1:**191–194**

Co-ops (education), 1:117

Co-sourcing internal audits, 1:68

Coaxial cable, 2:696

COBRA (Consolidated Omnibus Budget Reconciliation) (1983), 1:**222–225**, 407

Codes of ethics, 1:**194–196**

Collateral, 1:**196–197**, 265, 2:693

Collecting. *See* Accounts receivable

Collection. *See* Debt collection

Collection agencies industry growth, 2:1055

Collection period ratio, 1:503

Collectives, 1:241

Collegiate entrepreneurial organizations, 1:**197–198**

Combined statistical areas, 2:741

Command and control regulations, 2:805

Commercial banks, 1:82–83, 302

Commercial invoices, 2:1128

Commercial paper, 1:266, 2:753

Commercial paper interest rate, 1:611

Commission earnings, 1:386

Commission for Environmental Cooperation, 2:797

Commission merchants, 2:1161–1162

Common stock, 2:1067–1069, 1071

Communication. *See* Communication systems; Intercultural communication; International/cross-cultural communication; Interpersonal communication; Nonverbal communication; Oral communication; Written communication

Communication media, 1:399
See also specific advertising media

Communication systems, 1:**198–202**, 642
See also Interpersonal communication

Communications during crises, 1:276, 277–278

Communications training, 2:1123

Community-based models, 1:149

Community development corporations, 1:**202–203**

Community relations, 1:51, **203–205**, 253, 2:916–917
See also Public relations

Community support of minority businesses, 2:747

Comp time, 1:**205–206**

Company vehicles, business insurance and, 1:131

Comparable profits method (royalty rates), 2:980

Comparable uncontrolled transaction method (royalty rates), 2:979–980

Comparative financial statements, 1:505

Compatibility, between large and small businesses, 2:1053

Compensation. *See* Employee compensation

Competition
business ethics and, 1:119
business hours and, 1:124
industry analysis and, 1:597–598
between large and small businesses, 2:1052
market share and, 2:718–719

Competition in Contracting Act (1984), 1:544

Competitive analysis, 1:**206–207**

Competitive bids, 1:**207–209**, 2:656
See also Requests for proposals (RFPs)

Competitive parity budgeting method, 1:18

Competitive pricing, 2:878

Compiled mailing lists, 2:702
See also Direct marketing lists and databases

Compliance audits, 1:69

Component parts manufacturing, 2:838

Compounding interest, 1:612

Comprehensive Environmental Response Cleanup and Liability Act (CERCLA) (1980), 1:**209–211**, 447

Comprehensive health insurance, 1:559

Comprehensive income, 1:5, 505

Comprehensive interventions, 2:832

Compressed work weeks, 1:515

Computer-aided design (CAD), 1:**217–219**

Computer-aided manufacturing (CAM), 1:73, **217–219**

Computer-aided software engineering (CASE), 1:219

Computer applications, 1:**211–213**

Computer-based training, 2:1122

Computer crimes, 1:**214–217**, 422, 620, 2:814

Computer forums. *See* Electronic bulletin boards

Computer-integrated manufacturing, 1:73

Computer training, 2:1123

Computerized inventory control systems. *See* Inventory control systems

Computers and computer systems, 1:211–212, **219–222**

Concentration (diversification), 1:350–351

Confidentiality, 1:67–68, 448–449
See also Employee privacy

Confidentiality agreements. *See* Non-competition agreements

Conflict resolution
on cross-functional teams, 1:283–284
in employment contracts, 1:426
grievance procedures, 1:551–552
See also Alternative dispute resolution

Conglomerative acquisitions, 2:739

Consideration (contracts), 1:238

Consistency, in advertising, 1:21

Consolidated Omnibus Budget Reconciliation Act (COBRA) (1983), 1:**222–225**, 407

Consortia, child care, 1:182–183

Consortia, small business, 2:**1045–1046**

Construction, 1:**225–226**

Constructive discharge, 1:**226–228**
See also Layoffs, downsizing, and outsourcing

Consular invoices, 2:1128

Consultants, 1:**228–230**, 229–232

Consulting, 1:**231–234**
  accounting, 1:6–7
  business incubation and, 1:125–126
  external audits, 1:65
  from OSHA, 2:807
Consumer advocacy, 1:**234–235**
Consumer catalogs, 2:704–705
Consumer education, 2:917
Consumer endorsements, 1:436
Consumer Federation of America, 1:234
Consumer Price Index (CPI), 1:**235–236**, 2:879
Consumer Product Safety Commission (CPSC), 1:234, **236–237**
Consumer safety legislation, 1:236–237
Consumer surveys and products research, 2:719
Consumers' cooperatives, 1:241–242
Contact scanners. *See* Scanners (bar coding)
Container ships, 2:866
Contests and sweepstakes, 2:997–998
Contingency planning. *See* Disaster planning
Contingent liabilities, 2:681
Continuance of existence, 1:156
Continuity, of sole proprietorships, 2:1061
Continuity assumptions, 1:61
Continuity media buying, 1:15–16
Continuity media scheduling, 1:19
Continuity planning (crisis management), 1:276–277
Continuity plans (succession). *See* Succession plans
Continuity programs (business interruption), 1:134
Continuity programs (sales promotions), 2:998
Continuous review inventory systems, 1:637
Contract facility management, 1:477
Contraction. *See* Economic decline
Contracts, 1:233, **237–239**, 2:677–678, 989–990
  See also Employment contracts; Licensing agreements; Non-competition agreements
Contribution margin, 1:105
Control cultures, 1:280
Control premiums, valuation of, 2:1143
Control reports, 1:255
Controllable costs, 1:261

Controller-based point-of-sale systems, 2:867–868
Controlling communication style, 1:628
Controlling the Assault of Non-Solicited Pornography and Marketing Act (2003). *See* CAN-SPAM Act (2003)
Conventions, business-to-business marketing and, 1:147
Cooperative advertising, 1:**239–241**
Cooperatives, 1:**241–243**
  See also Small business consortia
COPPA (Children's Online Privacy Protection Act) (1998), 1:**183–185**, 491
Copyright, 1:**243–247**, 357, 2:685
  See also Image licensing; Intellectual property; Inventions and patents; Trademarks; Work for hire
Copyright Acts. *See* Copyright
Copyright Clearance Center, Inc. (CCC), 2:980–981
Copyright ineligibility, 1:243
Copyright infringement, 1:105, 635
Copyright notice requirements, 1:244, 245
Copyright registration, 1:245–246
Copyrightable materials, 2:1166
Core-based statistical areas, 2:741
Corning Glass Works v. Brennan (1974), 1:534–535
Corporate acceptance of minority businesses, 2:747
Corporate bond interest rate, 1:611
Corporate bylaws, 1:590–591
Corporate control, 1:591
Corporate culture, 1:40–41, **247–249**, 2:651–652, 829–830, 1101
  See also Business ethics; Corporate image; Small business culture
Corporate giving, 2:783
Corporate image, 1:**249–251**
Corporate logos, 1:**251–252**
  See also Trademarks
Corporate-owned life insurance, 2:792
Corporate ownership, 1:591
Corporate planning. *See* Business planning
Corporate procurement cards. *See* Purchasing cards
Corporate refinancing, 2:942
Corporate response to environmentalism, 1:549–550
Corporate sabotage, 2:814

Corporate sponsorship, 1:**252–254**, 2:998
Corporation names, 1:590, 2:850
Corporation structure, 1:156
Cost accounting, 1:262
Cost-based method (royalty rates), 2:979
Cost basis, 1:161
Cost-benefit analysis, 1:**258–260**
Cost centers, 1:255, 2:904
Cost control and reduction, 1:**254–256**
Cost discounts, 1:20
Cost of goods sold, 1:261–262
Cost-of-living adjustment, 1:235
Cost-of-living index. *See* Consumer Price Index (CPI)
Cost of sales to payables ratio, 1:502
Cost per click media buying, 1:15
Cost per thousand media buying, 1:15
Cost-plus pricing, 2:878
Cost reduction. *See* Cost control and reduction
Cost sharing, 1:**257–258**
  See also Shared services
Cost standards, 1:262
Costs, 1:**260–263**
Council of Better Business Bureaus. *See* Better business bureaus
Counseling, through SBA programs, 2:1044
County Business Patterns census data, 1:174
County of Erie, Erie County Retirees Association v., 1:34
Coupon mailers, 1:263
Coupons, 1:21, **263–264**, 2:997
  See also Rebates
CPAs (Certified public accountants), 1:6, **175–177**
CPI (Consumer Price Index), 1:**235–236**, 2:879
CPSC (Consumer Product Safety Commission), 1:234, **236–237**
Craft unions, 2:662, 664–665
CRC (Cyclic redundancy check), 1:618
Creative services, from advertising agencies, 1:14–15
Creativity, employee motivation and, 1:396
Credit, 1:11, **264–268**
  See also Interest rates; Loans
Credit approval. *See* Credit evaluation and approval
Credit bureaus, 1:268–270
Credit card financing, 1:**270–271**

Credit card use, 1:271, 273

Credit checks, employee screening and, 1:413

Credit contracts, 1:264–265

Credit evaluation and approval, 1:**271–274**

Credit history, 1:**274–275**

Credit policies, development of, 1:272–273

Credit reports. *See* Credit bureaus; Credit history

Credit risk, 1:267

Credit securitization, 1:267–268

Credit terms, 1:265

Credit unions, 1:242
    See also Thrift institutions

Credit worthiness, 1:266, 272

Creditors, partial payments to, 1:10

Criminal liability. *See* Legal liability

Criminal records, employee screening and, 1:413

Crisis communications, 2:917

Crisis management, 1:**275–278**
    See also Business insurance; Disaster planning

Cross-cultural/international communication, 1:**278–281**
    See also Intercultural communication

Cross-functional teams (CFTs), 1:**281–285**, 2:919–920, 1113–1114

Cross-purchase agreements, 1:191

Cross-training, 1:**285–287**

Cryptography, 1:291, 618

CSI/FBI Computer Crime and Security Survey (2005), 1:215

Cultural differences. *See* Cross-cultural/international communication

Currency exchange rate. *See* International exchange rate

Currency risk, 1:267

Currency value factors, 1:615

Current assets, 1:59–60, 78, 639

Current assumption life insurance, 2:686

Current liabilities, 1:79, 2:681

Current ratio, 1:498, 502

Customer databases. *See* Database marketing

Customer loyalty, 1:289

Customer relations, annual reports and, 1:50–51

Customer retention, 1:**287–288**

Customer segments. *See* Market segmentation

Customer service, 1:**288–290**, 649, 2:965–966, 1104

Customer surveys, 1:21

Customers
    corporate logo's impact on, 1:252
    cost sharing with, 1:258
    credit programs for, 1:272–274
    cutting ties with, 1:290
    difficult customers, 1:318–319
    disabled customers, 1:333–335
    distribution differentiation by, 1:346
    retention of, 1:287–288
    smoke free environments for, 2:1059–1060
    as stakeholders, 1:283

Cybercrime. *See* Computer crimes

Cycle stocks (inventory), 1:637

Cyclic redundancy check (CRC), 1:618

D

Dalton (GA) carpet manufacturing cluster, 1:192–193

Daly, Wadman, 2:674

Data encryption, 1:**291–293**, 618–619, 2:1154
    See also Internet security

Data Encryption Standard, 1:292

Data exchange automation, 2:808

Data format standards, 1:375

Data management automation, 2:809

Data marts, 1:295

Data mining, 1:295, 2:720

Data warehouses, 1:295

Database administration, 1:**293–296**

Database management software, 1:294

Database marketing, 1:328

Database research. *See* Data mining

Date of record, 2:1067

Davis-Bacon Act (1931), 1:582

Day trading, 1:**296–298**

Days' receivables ratio, 1:502

Deal loaders, 2:999

Dealers. *See* Distributorships and dealerships

Dealerships. *See* Distributorships and dealerships

Debentures, 1:265
    See also Promissory notes

Debt, 1:156–157, 161–162, 169, 2:1143

Debt burden, 1:272

Debt capital, 1:159

Debt collection, 1:**298–300**

Debt financing, 1:162, **300–303**, 455, 612–613, 2:1049
    See also Equity financing; Mezzanine financing; Royalty financing

Debt ratio, 1:503

Debt retirement, 1:265–266

Debt to capital ratio, 2:680

Debt to equity ratio, 1:301, 456–457, 499, 503, 2:693, 695

Decision avoidance psychosis, 1:305

Decision coercion. *See* Groupthink

Decision drift, 1:305

Decision making, 1:**303–306**, 370, 2:828

Decision support systems, 1:**306–308**

Decline (industrial life cycle), 1:600

Decline (product life cycle), 2:898

Declining-balance depreciation, 1:315

Default judgments, small claims court, 2:1057

Defendants, small claims court, 2:1057

Defense Loan and Technical Assistance (DELTA) Program, 2:1042, 1137

Deferred annuities, 1:53

Deferred profit-sharing plans, 2:908

Deferred savings plans, 2:792–793

Defined benefit plans, 2:860–861, 959, 960

Defined contribution plans, 2:860, 960

Delaware, incorporation in, 1:591

Delegation, 1:**308–311**
    See also Span of control

Delivery services, 1:**311–312**

Delphi forecasting method, 1:522

DELTA (Defense Loan and Technical Assistance) Program, 2:1042, 1137

Demand elasticity. *See* Elasticity

Demanufacturing, 2:948

Deming, W. Edwards, 2:923–927, 1112–1113

Demographics, 1:**312–313**
    See also Market segmentation

Demography, 1:312

Demonstrations, in presentations, 1:643

Department stores, 2:958

Dependent care reimbursement plans, 1:512

Depreciation, 1:**313–315**
    amortization and, 1:46
    of automobiles, 1:75
    of capital stock, 2:907
    costs and, 1:261–262
    IRS on, 2:1091
    of property, 1:3

Deregulation, 2:883
Design for Manufacturing and Assembly model, 2:819–820
Design patents, 1:634
Desktop publishing, 1:**315–318**, 2:808
Development. *See* Research and development
Development stage companies, 1:506
DHL (delivery company), 1:311
Difficult customers, 1:**318–319**
    See also Customer retention; Customer service
Difficult employees, 1:**320–322**
Digital Millennium Copyright Act (1998), 1:244
Digital Rights Management, 1:246
Digital Subscriber Lines (DSL), 2:751
Direct competition, 1:206
Direct costs, 1:260–261
Direct exporting, 1:458
Direct mail, 1:**322–325**, 326
    See also Mailing lists
Direct mail advertising, 1:26
Direct mail packages, 1:324
Direct marketing, 1:**325–329**
Direct marketing lists and databases, 1:327–328
Direct method (cash flow), 1:169
Direct premiums, 2:998
Direct public offerings, 1:**329–331**, 2:943
    See also Initial public offerings
Direct response TV. *See* Infomercials
Direct sellers (business-to-consumer commerce), 1:149
Directors of corporations, 1:156
Disability income insurance. *See* Disability insurance
Disability insurance, 1:134, **331–333**
Disability insurance pools, 1:607
Disabled customers, 1:**333–335**
    See also Americans with Disabilities Act (1990)
Disaster assistance loans, 1:**335–337**, 2:1138
Disaster planning, 1:**337–339**
    See also Crisis management
Disciplining employees, 1:2, 320–321
Disclaimers, 2:1158
Disclaimers of opinion (auditing), 1:507
Discontinued operations, 1:586
Discount interest rate, 1:611, 612
Discount pricing, 2:880
Discount sales, 1:**339–342**

See also Rebates
Discount stores, 2:959
Discounted cash flow, 1:**342–344**, 2:739
Discounted future cash flow approach valuation, 2:1142
Discounts for lack of marketability, 2:1143
Discounts on advertising, 1:19–20
Discretionary income, 1:**344–345**
Discrimination
    downloaded offensive material and, 1:357–358
    employee termination and, 1:419
    against employees with AIDS, 1:37
    See also Affirmative action; Age discrimination; Employee rights; Gender discrimination; Pregnancy in the workplace
Disparate impact, 1:31, 34–35
Display merchandise borrowing, 1:196
Disposable income, 1:344
Distance learning, 2:1130
Distributed denial of service attacks, 1:214
Distribution channels, 1:**345–347**
    See also Physical distribution; Wholesaling
Distribution of annuity funds, 1:54–55
Distribution of coupons, 1:263–264
Distribution to owners, 1:5, 505
Distributors. *See* Distribution channels; Distributorships and dealerships
Distributorships and dealerships, 1:**347–350**
Diversification, 1:40–41, **350–352**, 610
    See also Affirmative action; Multicultural work force
Dividend-payout ratio, 2:1083
Dividends, 1:**352–353**
    cash flow statements and, 1:169
    from common stock, 2:1067–1068
    distribution of, 1:156
    from preferred stock, 2:1069–1070
Division of labor, 2:828
Divorce, family limited partnerships and, 1:481–482
Do-Not-Call Registry Act (2003), 1:491, 2:1103
Dock receipts, 2:1128
Documentary Collection, 1:470
DOL. *See* U.S. Department of Labor (DOL)
Domestic outsourcing, 2:839–841
Donating excess inventory, 1:640

Door opener premiums, 2:998
DOT. *See* U.S. Department of Transportation (DOT)
Dot-coms, 1:330, **353–355**, 426, 604–605
    See also New economy
Double-declining balance depreciation. *See* Declining-balance depreciation
Double-net leases, 2:672
Double taxation, 1:155, 156, **355–356**, 589, 2:687
Downloading issues, 1:**356–359**
    See also Internet security
Downsizing. *See* Layoffs, downsizing, and outsourcing
Downturn. *See* Economic decline
Draft. *See* Documentary Collection
Dress codes, 1:172
Dreyfus, Joel, 1:213
Drinking water standards, 1:451
Driverless vehicles. *See* Automated guided vehicles
Drucker, Peter, 1:445, 2:785–788
Drug Free Workplace Act (1998), 1:360
Drug testing, 1:**359–360**, 401, 413, 2:1076
    See also Substance abuse
DSL (Digital Subscriber Lines), 2:751
Due diligence, 1:**361–362**
Duke Power Co., Griggs v. (1971), 1:31
Dun and Bradstreet Corporation, 1:268
Dutch East India Company, 1:537
Dynamic communication style, 1:628

E
E-commerce
    electronic retail, 1:148
    electronic services, 1:149
    insurance, 1:132
    Internet bartering, 1:88–89
    Internet payment systems, 1:617–620
    merchandise returns, 2:966
    private labels, 2:881
    reciprocal marketing, 2:933
    sales growth, 1:354
    scalability, 2:1003
    transferring brand equity online, 1:103
    value-added tax, 2:1144–1145
    See also Business-to-business commerce; Business-to-business marketing; Business-to-consumer commerce; Online auctions

E-forms, 1:629–630
E-mail, 1:**376–378**, 2:808
   advertising via, 1:25
   groupware and, 1:554–555
   intranets and, 1:629
   sending résumés via, 2:957
   writing skills and, 2:1179
   See also Spam; Viruses
E-retail. *See* E-commerce
E-ticketing, 1:142
E-zines. *See* Online magazines
Early-payment discounts, 1:342
Earn-outs, 2:1021–1022
Earned discounts, 1:342
Earnings before interest, taxes,
   depreciation, and amortization
   (EBITDA), 2:679
Earnings per share, 1:586
Earnings per share ratio, 1:502
Earnings ranking (Fortune 500), 1:523
Ease of entry (industry analysis), 1:597
eBay, 2:816–818
EC (European Commission), 1:462
Eco-labeling, 1:548
Eco-sponsoring, 1:548
Economic decline, as part of business
   cycle, 1:114
Economic Development
   Administration, 2:1136
Economic Development Commission,
   1:303
Economic development initiatives,
   1:203
Economic Espionage Act (1996), 2:911
Economic growth
   choosing not to grow, 1:122
   as part of business cycle, 1:114
   unexpected growth, 1:121–123
Economic Growth and Tax Relief
   Reconciliation Act (2001),
   1:460–461, 480–481, 525
Economic injury disaster loans, 1:336,
   2:1043
Economic order interval systems. *See*
   Periodic review inventory systems
Economic Order Quantity, 1:**363–364**
Economic order quantity systems. *See*
   Continuous review inventory systems
Economic Recovery Tax Act (1981),
   1:525
Economies of scale, 1:**364–366**, 511
   See also Optimal firm size
Economies of scope, 1:**366–367**
ECSC (European Coal and Steel
   Community), 1:463
Education privatization, 2:884

Educational co-ops, 1:117
EEC (European Economic
   Community), 1:463
EEOC. *See* Equal Employment
   Opportunity Commission (EEOC)
Efficiency ratios, 1:503
Egalitarian communication style, 1:628
EGTRRA. *See* Economic Growth and
   Tax Relief Reconciliation Act (2001)
8(A) Program, 1:**367–369**, 544, 2:1044
Elasticity, 1:**370**, 2:859, 1082
   See also Pricing
Eldercare, 1:**371–373**
   See also Career and family
Elective nonqualified deferred com-
   pensation plans, 2:791–792, 861
Electronic bill presentment and pay-
   ment, 1:300
Electronic bulletin boards, 1:**373–374**,
   2:957–958
   See also Newsgroups and blogs
Electronic cash registers, 2:867
Electronic communication networks
   (day trading), 1:297
Electronic data backups, 1:276
Electronic data interchange, 1:**374–
376**
Electronic day trading, 1:297–298
Electronic funds transfer systems, 1:83
Electronic mail. *See* E-mail
Electronic publishing, 1:629
Electronic résumés, 2:957
Electronic retail. *See* E-commerce,
   electronic retail
Electronic services. *See* E-commerce,
   electronic services
Electronic tax filing, 1:**378–379**
   See also Tax preparation software
Elk Clone virus, 1:214
Ellerth, Burlington Industries, Inc. v. See
   Faragher/Ellerth
Emergency preparedness. *See* Disaster
   planning
Emergency procedures, 1:275–276
Emergency supplies, 1:276
Emerging industries and minority
   businesses, 2:747
Emerging markets, 1:**379–380**
Employee assistance programs,
   1:**381–384**, 2:1076–1077, 1176
Employee attendance.
   See Absenteeism
Employee behavior, as grounds for
   termination, 1:419–420
Employee benefits, 1:**384–386**
   child care, 1:180–183

   nonprofit status of, 2:781
   as part of compensation package,
    1:386
   tax deductions on, 1:155–156,
    2:1092
   tax planning and, 2:1094
   taxation on, 2:986
   tuition assistance programs,
    2:1129–1130
   See also Employee reward and
    recognition systems; Flexible
    spending accounts; Health
    insurance; Insurance pooling;
    Keogh plans; Nonqualified
    deferred compensation plans;
    Pension plans; Portability of
    benefits; Sick leave and personal
    days
Employee communications, annual
   reports and, 1:50
Employee compensation, 1:**386–388**
   for cross-functional teams, 1:284
   for family members, 1:485–486,
    2:1094
   hiring and, 1:388–389
   at nonprofit organizations,
    2:787–788, 793
   pay increases and promotions,
    1:398–399
   productivity and, 2:901–902
   sales commissions, 2:987–989
   sales management, 2:994–995
   for telemarketers, 2:1105
   variable pay, 2:1145–1146
   See also Employee benefits;
    Employee motivation; Employee
    reward and recognition systems;
    Nonqualified deferred compen-
    sation plans
Employee compensation legislation,
   1:387
Employee development. *See* Training
   and development
Employee hiring, 1:248, **388–391**,
   2:1076
   See also Employee references;
    Employee reinstatement;
    Employment applications;
    Employment interviews; Job
    descriptions; Probationary
    employment periods;
    Recruiting; Résumés
Employee-initiated reviews, 1:399
Employee leasing programs,
   1:**392–393**
   See also Temporary employment
    services
Employee manuals, 1:**394–395**

Employee motivation, 1:**395–397**
  See also Employee benefits;
    Employee compensation
Employee orientation, 1:390–391,
  2:786–787
Employee performance appraisals,
  1:**397–400**, 407–408, 578, 2:652,
  787
Employee privacy, 1:**400–402**, 2:810
  See also Downloading issues;
    Employee rights; Office romance
Employee references, 1:**402–403**, 413,
  2:1176
  See also Employee hiring
Employee registration procedures,
  1:390–391, **403–404**
Employee reinstatement, 1:**404–405**
  See also Employee hiring
Employee retention, 1:**405–406**, 515
Employee Retirement Income Security
  Act (1974), 1:**406–407**, 494, 525,
  2:757, 853, 960
Employee reward and recognition
  systems, 1:**407–410**, 418, 578
Employee rights, 1:**410–412**, 2:1027
  See also Drug testing; Employee
    privacy
Employee rights legislation, 1:411
Employee screening programs,
  1:**412–413**, 2:1076, 1175
Employee stock ownership plans,
  1:**413–415**, 457–458, 2:1077–1078
Employee strikes, 1:**415–417**
  See also Labor unions; Labor unions
    and small business
Employee suggestion systems,
  1:**417–419**
Employee termination, 1:**419–421**,
  2:652–653
  See also Constructive discharge;
    Layoffs, downsizing, and
    outsourcing
Employee theft, 1:**422–423**
Employee training. *See* Training and
  development
Employees
  abusing sick leave and personal
    days, 2:1033–1034
  contractors *vs.,* 2:1074
  corporate culture and, 1:248
  cost sharing with, 1:258
  customer service and, 1:288–289
  difficult customers and, 1:319
  difficult employees, 1:320–322
  distinguishing interns from,
    1:626–627
  drug testing of, 1:359–360

eldercare impact on, 1:371
exempt status, 1:205, 386, 387,
  2:652, 667, 842
job sharing by, 2:654–655
in job shops, 2:655–656
leaving after company-sponsored
  training, 2:1130
monitoring computer activity of,
  1:357, 401
morale of, 1:309, 2:1101
motivation of, 1:395–397
newly hired, 2:889
non-exempt status, 1:205, 386,
  387, 2:652, 667, 842
of nonprofit organizations,
  2:785–788
office security and, 2:811–814
opinion on overtime, 2:843
part-time, 2:853–855
public relations with, 2:915
resistance to change, 2:712
at seasonal businesses, 2:1007–
  1008
seniority of, 2:1022–1024
smoke free environments for,
  2:1058–1059
substances abuse by, 2:1075–1077
values of, 1:119–120
Employee's Withholding Allowance
  Certificate. *See* Form W-4 (IRS)
Employer benefits, from child care,
  1:181–182
Employer benefits, from eldercare,
  1:371–372
Employer identification numbers,
  1:**423–424**
Employer's Quarterly Federal Tax
  Return, 2:857
Employment applications, 1:**424–425**,
  2:936–937
  See also Employee hiring
Employment-at-will-doctrine, 1:419
Employment contracts, 1:**425–427**
  See also Non-competition
    agreements
Employment Eligibility Verification
  Form. *See* Form I-9 (CIS)
Employment interviews, 1:389–390,
  427–429, 2:786, 937
  See also Employee hiring
Employment of minors, 1:**429–432**
Employment practices liability insur-
  ance, 1:**432–433**, 536
Employment qualifications of family
  members, 1:485
Employment visas, 1:38, 39
Empowerment, employee motivation
  and, 1:396

Empowerment zones, 1:**433–435**
Encryption. *See* Data encryption
Endorsements and testimonials,
  1:**435–437**, 2:706
Endorser collateral, 1:196
Energy use, recycling and, 1:550, 2:940
Engineered standards. *See* Cost
  standards
Engler, John, 2:869
Enron Corporation scandal (2001),
  2:1000
  See also Sarbanes-Oxley Act (2002)
Enterprise resource planning,
  1:**437–440**
Enterprise risk management,
  2:972–973
Enterprise value to sales ratio, 2:739
Entertainment expenses, 2:1091
Enthusiast angels, 1:47–48
Entrepreneurial angels, 1:47
Entrepreneurial couples, 1:**440–442**
Entrepreneurial networks, 1:**442–444**
  See also Mentoring; Networking;
    Young Entrepreneurs'
    Organization (YEO)
Entrepreneur's Organization (EO),
  2:1181
Entrepreneurship, 1:**444–447**
  See also Intrapreneurship
Environment, cross-cultural communi-
  cation and, 1:280
Environmental assessments, 1:136
Environmental audit, 1:**447–449**
Environmental cleanup. *See* CERCLA
  (Comprehensive Environmental
  Response Cleanup and Liability Act)
  (1980)
Environmental influences on organiza-
  tions, 2:827–828
Environmental law and business,
  1:**449–451**
  See also CERCLA (Comprehensive
    Environmental Response
    Cleanup and Liability Act)
    (1980); Clean Air Act (1970);
    Clean Water Act (1972)
Environmental legislation, EPA-admi-
  nistered, 1:449
Environmental Protection Agency
  (EPA), 1:187–190, 447–448,
  451–453
Environmental site assessments, 1:210,
  447
Environmentalism, history of, 1:549
Environmentally responsible market-
  ing. *See* Green marketing

Environmentally responsible production. *See* Green production

EO (Entrepreneur's Organization), 2:1181

Equal Employment Opportunity Act (1972), 1:31

Equal Employment Opportunity Commission (EEOC), 1:**453–454**
on affirmative action, 1:30
on age discrimination, 1:35–36
Americans with Disabilities Act and, 1:43, 45
creation of, 1:535
on racial discrimination, 2:930
on sexual harrassment, 2:1027

Equal opportunity in the workplace. *See* Affirmative action

Equal Pay Act (1963), 1:386, 534–535

Equifax, 1:269

Equipment leasing, 1:**454–456**

Equity
capital structure and, 1:161–162
definition, 1:5
on financial statements, 1:505
incorporation and, 1:156–157
leveraged buyouts and, 2:678–679
replacement of, via credit, 1:264
See also Equity financing; Owners' equity

Equity capital, 1:159

Equity financing, 1:162, 455, **456–458**, 2:1012–1013
See also Debt financing; Mezzanine financing; Royalty financing

Ergonomics, 1:**458–460**
See also Workplace safety; Workstations

Erie County Retirees Association v. County of Erie, 1:34

ERISA (Employee Retirement Income Security Act) (1974), 1:**406–407**, 494, 525, 2:757, 853, 960

Escrow agents, 2:1022

Estate freeze, 1:487

Estate planning, 1:480, 487–488

Estate taxes, 1:**460–462**, 480–481
See also Succession plans

Estimates (business proposals), 1:140

Ethical practices audits, 1:69

Ethnic differences in earnings, 1:387

Ethnocentrism, 1:279

EU (European Union), 1:**462–464**, 2:1109, 1144–1145

European Atomic Energy Community (EURATOM), 1:463

European Coal and Steel Community (ECSC), 1:463

European Commission (EC), 1:462

European Economic Community (EEC), 1:463

European small business category, 2:1039

European Union (EU), 1:**462–464**, 2:1109, 1144–1145

EUROTOM (European Atomic Energy Community), 1:463

Evaluation, when buying a business, 1:151–152

Event-based businesses. *See* Seasonal businesses

Event-triggered inventory systems. *See* Continuous review inventory systems

Exchanges (charitable giving), 1:178–179

Exclusivity clauses, 2:673

Executive Order 8802, 1:453

Executive Order 10582, 2:661

Executive Order 10925, 1:30

Executive Order 12073, 2:661

Executive Order 12866, 2:945

Exempt status of employees, 1:205, 386, 2:652, 667, 842

Exhibits (trade shows), 2:1115–1116

Expanded leave, 1:515

Expected purchases sales forecasting, 2:992

Expedited arbitration, 1:42

Expense accounts, 1:**464–465**
See also Per diem allowances

Expense allowances. *See* Expense accounts

Expenses
definition, 1:5
on financial statements, 1:505
fixed expenses, 1:510–511
on income statement, 1:585–586
per diem allowances, 2:862–863
tax deductible business expenses, 2:1089–1092
variable expenses, 1:510–511

Experian, 1:269

Expert endorsements, 1:436

Expert systems (decision support), 1:307

Export Credit Insurance Program, 1:466

Export documents, 2:1127–1128

Export fluctuations, 1:116

Export-Import Bank, 1:**465–467**

Export Legal Assistance Network, 2:1043

Export licenses, 2:1128

Export packaging, 2:112

Export packing lists, 2:1128

Export Working Capital Program, 2:1042, 1043, 1137

Exporting, 1:**467–470**
See also Export-Import Bank; Exporting financing and pricing; Tariffs; Transportation of exports

Exporting financing and pricing, 1:**470–472**

Express contracts, 1:237

Express Mail Service (USPS), 2:870

Express warranties, 2:1157–1158

Extended-term loans, 1:613

Extended warranties, 2:1158–1159

External audits, 1:**62–65**, 68–69

External communications, 1:201

External databases. *See* Database marketing

External lists. *See* Mailing lists

External research and development, 2:954

External threats to computer systems, 1:216–217

Extra expense insurance, 1:134

Extraction (green production), 1:550

Extranets, 1:629

Extraordinary gains and losses, 1:586

Eyeballing indirect forces sales forecasting, 2:992

Eyestrain, 2:1177

F

Facility layout and design, 1:**473–475**, 2:820

Facility location. *See* Relocation; Site selection

Facility management, 1:**475–478**

Facility ownership *vs.* leasing, 2:1037–1038

Factoring, 1:**478–480**

Fair and Accurate Credit Transactions Act (2003), 1:269, 491

Fair Credit Reporting Act (1970), 1:274, 491

Fair Debt Collection and Practices Act, 1:300

Fair Disclosure Regulation (2000), 1:645

Fair Labor Standards Act (1938), 1:205, 386, 583, 2:667, 743, 853

Fair Packaging and Labeling Act (1966), 1:490, 2:847

Fair use, 1:244–245

Family and career, 1:**162–165**

Family and Medical Leave Act (1993), 1:163–164, **483–485**, 583, 2:871
 See also Employee benefits; Pregnancy in the workplace
Family limited partnerships, 1:**480–483**
 See also Estate planning; Succession plans; Tax planning
"Family Medical Leave: Evidence from the 2000 survey" (Bureau of Labor Statistics), 1:484
Family-owned businesses, 1:**485–489**, 2:734–735
 See also Closely held corporations; Family limited partnerships; Nepotism; Succession plans
Faragher/Ellerth, 1:227, 535
Faragher v. Boca Raton (1998). *See* Faragher/Ellerth
Fayol, Henri, 2:826
FCC (Federal Communications Commission), 1:31–32, 2:1110
Feasibility studies, 1:**489–490**
The Fed. *See* U.S. Federal Reserve
Federal Acquisition Regulation, 1:543–544
Federal Acquisitions Reform Act (1995), 1:544
Federal agency bonds. *See* Bonds
Federal agency notes, 2:752
Federal Cigarette Labeling and Advertising Act (1965), 1:236
Federal Communications Commission (FCC), 1:31–32, 2:1110
Federal Do-Not-Call List. *See* Do-Not-Call Registry Act (2003)
Federal drug testing. *See* Drug testing
Federal Express, 1:311
Federal Food and Drugs Act (1906), 1:236
Federal Insurance Contribution Act (1937). *See* FICA taxes
Federal Property and Administrative Services Act (1949), 1:543
Federal Tax Withholding Form. *See* Form W-4 (IRS)
Federal Trade Commission (FTC), 1:**490–492**
 on children's Internet privacy, 1:183–185
 on Do-Not-Call Registry Act (2003), 2:1103
 on endorsements and testimonials, 1:436
 on franchising, 1:528–530
 on green marketing, 1:548
 on mail-order businesses, 2:705–706
 on obtaining loans, 1:272
 on warranties, 2:1158
Federal Trade Commission Act (1914), 1:490
Federal Trade Commission Act amendments, 1:490–491
Federal Trade Commission Franchise Rule (1979), 1:491
Federal Unemployment Tax, 2:857
Federations (unions), 2:666
FedEx. *See* Federal Express
Fee-based models, 1:149
Fee-for-service insurance plans, 1:132, 558–559, 561, 562
Feedforward and feedback, 1:255
Fees
 business brokers, 2:1021
 consulting, 1:230, 232
 copyright, 1:247
 filing for limited liability companies, 2:689
 patent application, 1:636
Les Femmes Chefs d'Entreprises Mondiales (FCEM). *See* The World Association of Women Entrepreneurs
FICA taxes, 1:**492–493**, 2:857, 1018, 1094, 1099–1100
 See also Payroll taxes; Tax withholding
Fiduciary duty, 1:**493–495**
File servers, 2:697–698
Final offer selection arbitration, 1:42
Finance and financial management, 1:**496**
 See also Undercapitalization
Finance companies, 1:**495–496**
Financial accounting, 1:4, 261–262
Financial Accounting Foundation, 1:5
Financial Accounting Standards Board
 on cash flow statements, 1:169
 financial statement elements definitions, 1:505–506
 income statement elements definitions, 1:585–586
 on pro forma statements, 2:886–887
 revenue recognition principle, 1:587
 See also Generally accepted accounting principles
Financial analysis, 1:**497–499**, 528–529
 See also Balance sheets; Cash flow statements; Income statements
Financial audits, 1:69
Financial intermediation, 1:267
Financial leases. *See* Long-term leases
Financial management. *See* Finance and financial management
Financial modeling, 2:886
Financial planners, 1:**499–501**
Financial public relations, 2:916
Financial ratios, 1:498–499, **501–504**
 See also Profit margin; Return on investment (ROI)
Financial statements, 1:6, **504–507**, 2:692, 1020
 See also Annual reports; Audits, external; Balance sheets; Cash flow statements; Income statements
Financial status audits, 1:647
Financing. *See* Loans; *specific lending programs*
Fingers (Internet utility), 2:777
Firewalls, 1:**507–509**, 621
 See also Internet security
Firing. *See* Employee termination
First-Class Mail (USPS), 2:870
First-in, first-out inventory accounting, 1:639, 2:1094
Fiscal year, 1:**509–510**
Fisher, Roger, 2:769–770
504 CDC Program, 2:1042, 1138
Fixed assets, 1:60, 78–79, 314
Fixed costs, 1:105–106, 260, 261, 364–365, 510
Fixed expenses, 1:**510–511**
Fixed order interval systems. *See* Periodic review inventory systems
Fixed order size systems. *See* Continuous review inventory systems
Fixed price-per-unit royalty agreements, 2:978
Fixed rate loans (SBA), 2:1138
Fixed to worth ratio, 1:503
Flammable Fabrics Act (1953), 1:236
Flat organizations, 2:828
Flexible benefit plans, 1:**511–512**
 See also Employee benefits
Flexible manufacturing systems, 1:70, 73, 366
Flexible spending accounts, 1:224, 512, **513–514**
Flexible work arrangements, 1:164, 514–517, 2:755, 1033–1034
 See also Comp time; Job sharing; Telecommuting
Flexplace, 1:515

Flextime, 1:2, 125, 372, 398, 514–515

Flighting media scheduling, 1:19

Float periods, 1:170

Floating-rate interest. *See* Variable-rate interest

Flood insurance, 1:336

Floor planning. *See* Display merchandise borrowing

Florida Board of Regents, Kimmel v., 1:34

Flow charts, 1:**517–518**

FM radio. *See* Radio advertising

Focus groups, 1:**518–521,** 2:720

Food, Drug, and Cosmetic Act (1938), 1:236

Forecasting, 1:109, 139, **521–523,** 2:820, 991–993
  See also Business planning; Sales forecasts

Foreign exchange rate. *See* International exchange rate

Foreign investment, 2:687–688, 1070–1071

Foreign stock, 2:1070–1071

Form 3 (SEC), 2:1010

Form 4 (SEC), 2:1010

Form 8A (SEC), 1:645

Form 8K (SEC), 1:645

Form 10K (SEC), 1:645

Form 10Q (SEC), 1:645

Form 941 (IRS), 2:1098

Form 1040 ES (IRS), 2:1098

Form 1065 (IRS), 2:1098

Form 1096 (IRS), 2:1098

Form 1099 (IRS), 2:1098

Form 1120 (IRS), 2:1098

Form 1120A (IRS), 2:1098

Form 5500 (IRS), 2:960

Form I-9 (CIS), 1:404

Form of organization, valuation and, 2:1143

Form W-2 (IRS), 2:857, 1098

Form W-3 (IRS), 2:857, 1098

Form W-4 (IRS), 1:404

Formal order acknowledgements, 2:989

Formal organizations, 2:828

Fort Worth Bank and Trust, Watson v. (1988), 1:31

Fortune 500, 1:**523–524**

Found-space displays, 2:737

Four-fifths rule (hiring), 1:31

401(k) plans, 1:**524–526**
  annuities and, 1:53

employee stock ownership plans, similarity to, 1:413
  profit sharing and, 2:908, 962
  safe-harbor formulas for, 2:1050
  See also Employee benefits; Retirement planning

Four Ps (Product, place, promotion, and price), 2:725

Franchising, 1:347–349, **526–530**
  See also Buying an existing business

Franchising and Business Opportunity Ventures Trade Regulation Rules and Subsequent Guidelines (FTC), 1:530

Franchising laws, 1:529–530

Franchisor's disclosure statements, 1:529

Fraud
  alerts from credit bureaus, 1:269
  detection through external audits, 1:64–65
  detection through internal audits, 1:69
  in financial reporting, 1:506–507
  Internet payment systems, 1:617
  tax fraud, 1:647
  workers' compensation, 2:1167
  See also Sarbanes-Oxley Act (2002)

Freelance employment, 1:**531–532**

Freight forwarders, 2:1128–1129

Frequency discounts, 1:20

Frequency media buying, 1:15

Fringe benefits. *See* Employee benefits

FTC. *See* Federal Trade Commission (FTC)

Full disclosure references, 1:402–403

Full payout leases. *See* Long-term leases

Full service leases, 1:455, 2:672

Full-time *vs.* part-time businesses, 2:852–853

Fundraising, 2:783

G

Gains, 1:5, 505, 586

Gambling, day trading as, 1:297

GAO (Government Accountability Office), 1:435

Garbage Can Model of Organizational Choice, 1:305

Garner, Rochelle, 1:103

Gateways (computer networks), 2:698

GATT. *See* General Agreement on Tariffs and Trade (GATT)

Gender discrimination, 1:**533–536**

See also Equal Employment Opportunity Commission (EEOC); Sexual harassment

General Agreement on Tariffs and Trade (GATT), 1:608, 636

General business expenses, 2:1090

General Depreciation System, 1:3

General liability, 1:130

General Motors Corporation
  dealerships, 1:349
  Goodwrench parts, 2:838
  Sloan, Alfred P. and, 2:1072

General partnerships, 2:848

General unions, 2:663

Generally accepted accounting principles
  on accrual basis accounting method, 2:1093
  creation of, 1:4–5
  depreciation, 1:314
  on earnings per share, 1:586
  See also Financial Accounting Standards Board; Sarbanes-Oxley Act (2002)

Generics, 2:880–881

Georgia carpet manufacturing cluster, 1:192–193

Global business, 1:**536–539,** 2:663
  See also Globalization

Globalization, 1:379–380, 537, **539–542,** 579, 2:901–902
  See also Tariffs

Going concern assumptions. *See* Continuity assumptions

Going public. *See* Initial public offerings

Goodwill, 1:**542–543**

Google AdWords, 1:24

Google search engine, 2:1004, 1005

Gordon, Kim T., 1:19

Gould, Myron, 1:257

Government Accountability Office (GAO), 1:435

Government licensing, 2:682–683

Government procurement, 1:**543–546,** 2:1043–1044, 1165
  See also 8(A) Program

Government refinancing, 2:942

Government relations, 2:917

Government spending fluctuations, 1:115

Graphical user interface (GUI), 1:546

Graz v. Bollinger (2003), 1:32

Green marketing, 1:**546–549**

Green office supplies, 2:815

Green production, 1:**549–551**

Grievance mediation, 1:42
Grievance procedures, 1:**551–552**
     See also Alternative dispute resolu-
          tion; Labor unions; Labor unions
          and small business
Griggs v. Duke Power Co. (1971), 1:31
Gross leases, 2:672
Gross profitability ratio, 1:501
Group-based reward systems,
     1:409–410
Group health insurance coverage, 1:484
Group interventions, 2:831–832
Group life insurance, 1:131
Group long-term disability insurance,
     1:332
Group self-insurance plans, 2:1167
Groupthink, 1:305, **552–554**
Groupware, 1:**554–555**, 2:808
Growth (industrial life cycle), 1:599,
     2:833–834
Growth (product life cycle), 2:897
Growth phases, 2:835–836
Grutter v. Bollinger (2003), 1:32
GUI (Graphical user interface), 1:**546**
*Guidelines on Discrimination Because of
     Sex* (Code of Federal Regulations),
     1:411

H

Hackers, 1:214, 508
Halt (organization), 2:1056
Handshaking (Internet protocol),
     1:618, 2:751
Hard assets. *See* Fixed assets
Hardware theft, 1:217
Harmonization cultures, 1:280
Hawken, Paul, 1:445
Hawkins, Charlie, 2:724, 732
Hawthorn Studies, 2:827
Hazard communication programs,
     2:970
Hazard Communication Standard,
     2:805
Hazardous waste handling, 1:451
Hazen Paper Co. v. Biggins (1993), 1:34
Health care industry, biometrics use in,
     1:94
Health insurance, 1:**557–560**
     age discrimination and, 1:36
     business insurance and, 1:131–132
     COBRA, 1:222–225, 407
     economies of scale and, 1:365
     Medicare and Medicaid, 2:730–
          732

Medicare Supplemental Insurance,
     2:731
     tax deductions for, 2:1092
     See also Health maintenance orga-
          nizations (HMOs); Insurance
          pooling; Point-of-service plans
          (PPOs)
Health insurance pools, 1:606–607
Health Insurance Portability and
     Accountability Act (1996), 1:407
Health insurance purchasing co-ops.
     See Health insurance pools
Health maintenance organizations
     (HMOs), 1:558, 559–560, **561–563**
Health promotion programs,
     1:**563–564**
Health savings accounts, 1:560
Hedge funds, 2:974
Help if necessary discounts, 1:20
Hi-speed communications, 1:201
Hicks, Douglas T., 1:13
Hierarchy of human needs, 2:827
High-tech businesses, 1:**564–565**
Hippocratic Oath, 1:194
Hiring employees. *See* Employee hiring
Hiring legislation, 1:391
Hiring quotas, 1:30–31
Hispanic-owned businesses, 2:746
Historical cash flow approach valuation,
     2:1142
Historically Underutilized Business
     Zones. *See* HubZone Empowerment
     Contracting Program
HIV (Human immuno-deficiency
     virus). *See* AIDS in the workplace
HMOs (Health maintenance organiza-
     tions), 1:558, 559–560, **561–563**
Holiday-based businesses. *See* Seasonal
     businesses
Home-based businesses, 1:132,
     164–165, **569–572**, 2:1183–1184
     See also Home offices;
          Telecommuting
Home office tax deductions,
     2:1090–1091
Home offices, 1:**566–569**
Home sales, as capital gains, 1:160–161
Homeowner's insurance, 1:132
Hopkins, Bruce R., 2:788–791
Horizontal acquisitions, 2:739
Hostile takeovers, 1:3, 2:738, 739
Hoteling, 1:**572–573**
     See also Flexible work arrange-
          ments; Mobile offices;
          Telecommuting; Workstations
Hotels, business travel and, 1:141–142

Housebrokers, 1:601
Household budget, 1:107
HTML (Hypertext Markup Language),
     1:**573–575**, 2:1159–1160
     See also Web site design
HubZone Empowerment Contracting
     Program, 1:209, **575–576**
HUD. *See* U.S. Department of
     Housing and Urban Development
     (HUD)
Hudson Bay Company, 1:537
Human immuno-deficiency virus
     (HIV). *See* AIDS in the workplace
Human resources management,
     1:**576–580**
     See also Job descriptions;
          Workplace anger
Human resources management laws,
     1:**582–583**
Human resources policies, 1:**580–582**
     See also Office romance
Hurricane damage (2005), 1:336
Hybrid comparable profits method
     (royalty rates), 2:980
Hybrids (distribution), 1:345
Hypertext Markup Language (HTML),
     1:**573–575**, 2:1159–1160
     See also Web site design

I

IBM racial discrimination policy, 2:931
ICANN (Internet Corporation for
     Assigned Names and Numbers),
     1:617
Identification, biometrics and, 1:93–94
Identification tag systems, 2:812
Identity theft, 1:269
Illegal aliens. *See* Alien employees
Illegal Immigration Reform and
     Immigrant Responsibility Act
     (1996), 1:40
ILOVEYOU virus, 2:1156
Image licensing, 2:683
IMF (International Monetary Fund),
     1:539
Immediate annuities, 1:53
Immigrant visas, 1:39
Immigration law. *See* Alien employees
Impairment of capital rule, 1:352
Implementation (operations manage-
     ment), 2:820
Implied contract violations, as grounds
     for termination, 1:420
Implied contracts, 1:237
Implied licenses (Internet), 1:357

Implied warranties, 2:1157

Import fluctuations, 1:116

Imputed costs, 1:261

In-house advertising agencies, 1:20

In-house lists. *See* Mailing lists

In-house telemarketing operations, 2:1105

In re Sterling Corset Co. (1938), 1:226

In-transit stocks (inventory), 1:637

Inbound telemarketing, 1:326, 2:1102

Incentive pay, 1:285, 397

Income annuities. *See* Immediate annuities

Income-based approach valuation, 2:1141

Income before extraordinary items, 2:772

Income protection, 1:134

Income statement (cash flow). *See* Direct method (cash flow)

Income statements, 1:**585–588**
  cash flow statements and, 1:168
  definition, 1:6
  financial analysis, 1:497
  net income, 2:772
  overhead expenses on, 2:841
  pro forma, 2:888
  valuation methods, 2:1142
  See also Annual reports; Balance sheets; Cash flow statements; Financial statements

Income tax
  double taxation, 1:355, 356
  electronic tax filing, 1:378–379
  payroll taxes and, 2:857
  See also Internal Revenue Service (IRS); Tax returns

Income tax withholding, 2:1099

Incorporation, 1:**588–592**, 2:887–888, 1015–1016
  See also Articles of incorporation; C corporations; Limited liability companies; S corporations; Sole proprietorships

Incremental costs, 1:261

Indentures (bonds), 1:265, 2:694

Independent contractors, 1:**531–532**, 2:858, 1015
  See also Manufacturers' agents; Subcontracting

Independent information specialists. *See* Information brokers

Index to the U.S. Patent Classification System, 1:634

Indirect competition, 1:206

Indirect costs, 1:261

Indirect exporting, 1:468–469

Indirect method (cash flow), 1:169

Individual management, 1:577

Individual retirement accounts (IRAs), 1:53, **592–594**
  See also 401(k) plans; Retirement planning; Simplified employee pension plans

Industrial classification. *See* NAICS (North American Industry Classification System); SIC (Standard Industrial Classification System)

Industrial hazards, 1:595

Industrial recycling, 2:939–940

Industrial safety, 1:**594–596**

Industrial solvents hazards, 1:595

Industrial unions, 2:662–663

Industry analysis, 1:**596–598**

Industry attractiveness, 1:598

Industry life cycle, 1:**598–600**
  See also Organizational life cycle; Product life cycle

Industry specialists (business-to-business commerce), 1:146

Inflation, 1:235, 267

Infomercials, 1:**23**, 327

Informal communications, 1:201–202

Informal organizations, 2:828

Information brokers, 1:**600–601**

Information storage automation, 2:807–808

Information systems audits, 1:69

Information technology, automation and, 1:73

Initial public offerings, 1:329–330, **601–605**, 644–645, 2:943
  See also Direct public offerings; Private placement of securities; Private placement of stock

Inland bills of lading, 2:1128

Innovation, 1:396, **605–606**, 2:967–968
  See also Intrapreneurship; Technological innovations

INS. *See* U.S. Immigration and Naturalization Service (INS)

Inside directors. *See* Boards of directors

Inside sales, 2:864–865

Inspection certificates, 2:1128

Installation, automated storage and retrieval systems, 1:72

Installment plans, 1:273–274

Installment sales, 2:1022

Institute of Internal Auditors, 1:66, 67

Institutional generalists (business-to-business commerce), 1:146

Instructional systems design, 2:1121

Insurance
  business insurance, 1:129–133
  business interruption insurance, 1:132, 133–134
  corporate-owned life insurance, 2:792
  disability insurance, 1:134, 331–333
  employment practices liability insurance, 1:432–433, 536
  extra expense insurance, 1:134
  flood insurance, 1:336
  group life insurance, 1:131
  homeowner's insurance, 1:132
  for leasing property, 2:673–674
  life insurance, 2:685–687
  partnership insurance, 1:131
  riders, 2:686
  See also Health insurance

Insurance agents, 1:129–133

Insurance certificates, 2:1128

Insurance pooling, 1:**606–607**, 2:1167

Insurance purchasing alliances. *See* Health insurance pools

Insurance riders, 2:686

Intangible assets. *See* Intellectual property

Integrated disclosure system. *See* SEC disclosure obligations

Integrated Services Digital Networks (ISDNs), 2:751

Integrators (distribution). *See* Value-added resellers

Intellectual property, 1:**608–609**, 2:979
  See also Inventions and patents; Work for hire

Inter-company directories, 1:630

Inter-group interventions, 2:832

Intercultural communication, 1:**609–611**

Interest arbitration, 1:42

Interest coverage ratio, 1:503

Interest rates, 1:**611–613**
  on baby bonds, 1:77
  definition, 1:265
  on estate tax, 1:461–462
  factors influencing, 1:611–612
  on physical disaster business loans, 1:335–336
  risk and, 1:266–267
  on SBA loans, 2:1138
  See also Annual percentage rate (APR)

Intergenerational care, 1:181, 372

Interim financial statements, 1:505

Interim OSHA standards, 2:803

Intermediaries (business-to-consumer commerce), 1:149

Intermediate-term loans, 2:694

Intermodal transportation, 2:866, 1126

Internal audits, 1:**65–70**

Internal business buyers, 2:1021

Internal communications, 1:201

Internal incubators, 1:632

Internal Revenue Code. *See* Internal Revenue Service (IRS)

Internal Revenue Service (IRS), 1:**613–614**
  approval of accounting method changes, 1:9
  business tax forms, 2:1098
  COBRA revisions, 1:224
  on cost sharing, 1:257–258
  on electronic tax filing, 1:378, 379
  on employer identification numbers, 1:424
  on equipment tax deductions, 2:1094
  on expense accounts, 1:464–465
  on family limited partnerships, 1:482
  on FICA taxes, 1:492, 493
  on flexible benefit plans, 1:512
  on flexible spending accounts, 1:513–514
  on 401(k) plans, 1:524, 526
  on freelance employment, 1:531–532
  on home offices, 1:566, 571–572
  on independent contractors, 2:715, 1015
  on intellectual property, 2:979
  on IRAs, 1:592–593
  on Multiple Employer Trusts, 2:758
  on nonprofit organizations, 2:781, 789–791
  on payroll taxes, 2:857, 858–859
  on per diem allowances, 2:862
  on professional corporations, 2:902
  on profit sharing, 2:908–909
  on quarterly taxes, 2:1095
  on record retention, 2:925, 934
  on S corporations, 2:985–986
  on self-employment, 2:1018
  on simplified employee pension plans, 2:1035
  software tax forms accepted by, 2:1096–1097
  on standard mileage rate, 2:1066

on tax deductible expenses, 2:1089–1091
  See also Income tax; Tax returns

Internal threats to computer systems, 1:216

Internalized business incubators, 1:127

International Chamber of Commerce, 1:177–178

International communication. *See* Cross-cultural/international communication

International Convention for the Protection of Industrial Property (1883). *See* Paris Convention (1883)

International copyright protection, 1:246

International/cross-cultural communication, 1:**278–281**
  See also Intercultural communication

International exchange rate, 1:**615–616**

International freight transportation. *See* Transportation of exports

International Monetary Fund (IMF), 1:539

International Organization for Standards (ISO), 1:648

International Organization of Consumers Unions, 1:234

International trade. *See* Exporting; General Agreement on Tariffs and Trade (GATT); North American Free Trade Agreement (NAFTA); Tariffs; World Trade Organization (WTO)

International Trade Administration, 2:1136

International Trade Initiative, 2:744–745

International Trade Loan Program, 2:1042, 1043, 1138

Internet
  business communications via, 1:212–213
  business reference sources, 1:128–129
  children's privacy and, 1:183–185
  consumer advocacy, 1:234
  copyright law, 1:246–247
  coupon distribution via, 1:264
  credit reporting via, 1:269–270
  database management, 1:295–296
  distributorships and dealerships on, 1:349–350
  economies of scale and, 1:365
  electronic data interchange via, 1:374

electronic tax filing, 1:378–379, 2:1097
  enterprise resource planning and, 1:438–439
  loan application via, 2:695
  marketing, 2:726
  markup languages, 1:573–575
  new economy and, 2:775–776
  online auctions, 2:815–819
  online focus groups, 1:520–521
  online sources for marketing data, 1:323
  proxy statements via, 2:914
  risk management and, 2:972
  rural businesses and, 2:983
  search engines, 1:25, 2:1004–1006
  service agreements, 1:624–625
  social and business networking on, 2:774
  as source for legal advice, 2:676–677
  virtual private networks, 2:1152–1155
  web-based training, 2:1122
  Web consultants, 1:230
  See also Dot-coms; Modems; Web site design

Internet access issues. *See* Downloading issues

Internet advertising, 1:**24–25**
  ad tracking, 1:21–22
  banner advertisements, 1:84–86
  click through rates, 1:15, 84
  cost per click rates, 1:15
  online classified advertising, 2:818–819
  streaming video, 1:28
  video viability and, 1:27
  See also Web site design

Internet business. *See* E-commerce

Internet Corporation for Assigned Names and Numbers (ICANN), 1:617

Internet domain names, 1:**616–617**

Internet incubators, 1:126–127

Internet payment systems, 1:**617–620**, 619, 2:1124–1125
  See also Online auctions; Transaction processing

Internet protocols, 1:618, 2:751, 1153

Internet security, 1:618–619, **620–622**, 2:1154
  See also Computer crimes; Data encryption; Downloading issues; Firewalls; Spam; Viruses

Internet Service Providers (ISPs), 1:85, 617, **622–625**

Internet vulnerability. *See* Internet security

Internships, 1:118, **625–627**, 2:1123

Interpersonal communication, 1:**627–629**
  delegation and, 1:310
  between human resources and employees, 1:581
  ISO 9000 and, 1:649
  during performance appraisals, 1:399
  during presentations, 1:643–644
  via Internet, 1:212–213
  See also Intercultural communication; International/cross-cultural communication; Nonverbal communication; Oral communication; Written communication

Interpersonal interventions, 2:831

Interviewing. *See* Employment interviews

Intranets, 1:295–296, **629–632**

Intrapreneurship, 1:**632–633**

Introduction (industrial life cycle), 1:599

Introduction (product life cycle), 2:897

Inventions and patents, 1:**633–637**

Inventory, 1:**637–640**
  cash conversion cycle and, 1:167
  as collateral, 1:196
  as current asset, 1:60
  Economic Order Quantity and, 1:363
  right-to-know laws and, 2:969–970
  variations in, business cycles and, 1:115
  See also Inventory control systems

Inventory accounting, 1:639–640

Inventory control systems, 1:**640–642**, 2:1162
  See also Material requirements planning (MRP)

Inventory holding ratio, 1:503

Inventory partitioning. *See* Inventory segmenting

Inventory records files, 2:729

Inventory segmenting, 1:638

Inventory to assets ratio, 1:503

Inventory valuation methods, 2:1093–1094

Investment, through SBA, 2:1053

Investment Advisers Act (1940), 2:1012

Investment Company Act (1940), 2:1012

Investment property, 1:160

Investment ratio, 1:502

Investment spending, volatility of, 1:114–115

Investments by owners, 1:505

Investor presentations, 1:**642–644**

Investor relations and reporting, 1:**644–646**
  See also Financial statements; SEC disclosure laws and regulations

Involuntary liquidation, 2:690–691

IQ tests, 1:413

IRAs (Individual retirement accounts), 1:53, **592–594**
  See also 401(k) plans; Retirement planning; Simplified employee pension plans

IRS. *See* Internal Revenue Service (IRS)

IRS audits, 1:**646–647**

ISDNs (Integrated Services Digital Networks), 2:751

ISO (International Organization for Standards), 1:648

ISO 9000, 1:**647–650**, 2:927
  See also Total quality management

ISO 9001:2000, 1:648

Isolation
  at home-based businesses, 1:571
  telecommuting and, 2:1101

iSold It franchises, 2:818

ISPs (Internet Service Providers), 1:85, 617, **622–625**

J

Japan
  employee seniority, 2:1023–1024
  management techniques, 2:709
  quality circles, 2:923–927
  total quality management, 2:1112–1113

Jaycees, 1:178

Job analysis, 1:577–578

Job costing, 1:262

Job descriptions, 1:389, 2:**651–653**, 936

Job interviews. *See* Employment interviews

Job offers, 1:390

Job rotation, 2:1123

Job satisfaction, 1:406

Job sharing, 1:515, 2:**653–655**

Job shops, 2:**655–656**

Jobless recovery, 1:116

Jobs, Steve, 1:446

Joint Application Development, 1:59

Joint research and development, 2:954

Joint ventures, 2:**656–658**, 833

Journal entries, 1:100

Junior chambers of commerce. *See* Jaycees

Junk e-mail. *See* Spam

Just-in-time inventory control, 1:638

Just-in-time manufacturing, 1:58

Just-in-time purchasing, 2:920, 927

K

Kaizen, 1:89

Kaplan, Robert S., 1:12–14

Kennedy, Larry W., 2:786, 787

Keogh plans, 2:**659–660**, 960

Key person insurance policies, 1:131, 2:686

Key person loss, 1:131

Kimmel v. Florida Board of Regents, 1:34

Know-how licensing, 2:683

L

Labeling
  eco-labeling, 1:548
  Fair Packaging and Labeling Act (1966), 1:490, 2:847
  Federal Cigarette Labeling and Advertising Act (1965), 1:236
  Nutrition Labeling and Education Act (1990), 2:847
  organic labeling, 1:548
  packing requirements, 2:846–847
  private labeling, 2:880–881
  right-to-know-laws and, 2:970
  Wool Products Labeling Act (1939), 1:490

Labor Certification Applications, 1:40

Labor Condition Applications, 1:40

Labor costs, distribution and, 2:866–867

Labor laws, 2:667

Labor Management Relations Act (1947), 1:583, 2:667

Labor-Management Reporting and Disclosure Act (1959), 1:583, 2:667

Labor productivity index, 2:901

Labor strikes. *See* Employee strikes

Labor surplus areas, 2:**661–662**

Labor unions, 1:198–199, 2:**662–666**
  See also National Labor Relations Board (NLRB)

Labor unions and small business, 2:**666–669**

LAN-to-LAN connection, 2:1153

Landrum-Griffin Act (1959). *See* Labor-Management Reporting and Disclosure Act (1959)

Language, intercultural communication and, 1:279–280, 609–610

Lanham Trademark Act (1946), 1:490

LANs (Local area networks), 1:221, 2:**696–698**, 1163
  See also WANs (Wide area networks)

Laptops. *See* Portable computers

Large business as customers, 2:1053

Large business/small business relationships, 2:**1051–1053**

Large ticket leases, 1:455

Last-in, first-out inventory accounting, 1:639–640, 2:1094

Layoffs, downsizing, and outsourcing, 1:412, 2:**669–671**

Leadership. *See* Succession plans

Lean manufacturing, 2:927

Learning, employee motivation and, 1:396

Learning curves, 2:**671–672**

Leasehold improvements, 2:673

Leasing. *See* Automobile leasing; Equipment leasing

Leasing property, 2:**672–675**

Lectures, training through, 2:1122

Ledgers, 1:100

Legal information, selling a business and, 2:1020

Legal liability
  business insurance and, 1:130–131
  downloading issues and, 1:357
  employee references and, 1:402–403
  employee termination and, 1:420
  in employment interviews, 1:429
  environmental cleanup, 1:210–211
  incorporation advantages and, 1:588–589
  limiting when incorporating, 1:155
  nonprofits' immunity from, 2:782
  product liability, 2:894–896
  for sexual harrassment, 2:1028
  telecommuting and, 2:1101
  undercapitalization and, 2:1132
  unlimited liability, 2:849
  See also Employment practices liability insurance

Legal services, 2:**675–677**

Letter shops, 2:703

Letters of credit, 1:266, 470

Letters of intent, 2:**677–678**

Leverage, 1:79, 498

Leverage ratios, 1:503

Leveraged buyouts, 2:**678–681**, 1022
  See also Mergers and acquisitions

Leveraged ESOPs. *See* Employee stock ownership plans

Leveraged leases, 1:455

Liabilities, 1:5, 79, 505, 2:**681–682**
  See also Assets

Liability. *See* Legal liability

Licensing, 2:**682–684**, 833
  See also Inventions and patents; Licensing agreements; Royalties

Licensing agreements, 2:**684–685**

Licensing in, licensing out, 2:683

Life insurance, 1:52, 2:**685–687**, 757–758, 861
  See also Multiple Employer Trusts

Lift letters, 1:324

Limited liability companies, 1:588, 2:**687–689**, 848, 903

Limited liability partnerships, 2:903

Limited partnerships, 2:848

Linked supply chains, 1:366–367

Liquid assets. *See* Current assets

Liquidation, 1:81–82

Liquidation and liquidation values, 2:**689–691**
  See also Bankruptcy; Business failure and dissolution; Selling a business

Liquidation approach valuation, 2:1142

Liquidation bankruptcy. *See* Chapter 7 bankruptcy

Liquidation value, 2:773

Liquidity, 1:498

Liquidity ratios, 1:502–503

List enhancement, 1:323–324

Listening skills, 1:200, 628

Living trusts, 1:487

Loan applications (SBA), 2:1139–1140

Loan descriptions, 2:692

Loan origination software, 2:695

Loan proposals, 2:**691–693**

Loan qualification, 2:694–695

Loans, 2:**693–695**
  amortization of, 1:46–47
  credit card use *vs.*, 1:271
  as debt capital, 1:159
  size of, 1:272
  from Small Business Investment Companies, 2:1049
  to sole proprietorships, 2:1061
  syndicated loans, 2:1084–1086
  See also Interest rates; Promissory notes; *specific loan programs*

Local advertising, 1:240

Local area networks (LANs), 1:221, 2:**696–698**, 1153, 1163
  See also Wide area networks (WANs)

Local payroll taxes, 2:857

Local unions, 2:664–665

Location, convenience and, 2:967

Logic bombs, 1:214

Logistics (distribution), 2:865–866

Long-range planning. *See* Business planning

Long Tail theory, 1:354

Long-term disability insurance, 1:331

Long-term leases, 1:455

Long-term liabilities, 2:681

Long-term loans, 2:694

Long-term remedial action, 1:211

Loss leader pricing, 2:**699**
  See also Penetration pricing

Losses, 1:6, 506, 586

Low bid contracts, 1:545

LowDoc loan program, 2:1042, 1137

Lund, Bonnie, 2:751–752

Lynn, Jacquelyn, 1:290

M

Machinery, hazards of, 1:595

Macrocontext. *See* Problem context

Macromarketing, 2:742

Magalogs, 1:324

Magazine advertising, 1:26

Magazine direct marketing, 1:327

Magnuson-Moss Warranty-Federal Trade Commission Improvement Act (1975), 1:491, 2:1157, 1158

Mail list brokers, 2:702

Mail list compilers, 2:702

Mail list managers, 2:702–703

Mail list owners, 2:702

Mail-order businesses, 1:322, 2:**703–706**, 959

Mail order discounts, 1:20

Mail premiums, 2:998

Mail service bureaus, 2:703

Mailing lists, 1:323, 2:**701–703**

Maintenance strategies. *See* Total preventive maintenance

Malcolm Baldridge National Quality Award, 1:91

Malware. *See* Spyware

Managed care insurance plans. *See* Fee-for-service insurance plans

Management
  automation and, 1:74
  diversification and, 1:350

of intranets, 1:631

of a multicultural workforce, 2:754–755

organizational development and change, 2:831

quality circles and, 2:923–925

sponsorship for code of ethics, 1:194

supervisory development and, 2:1124

support of employee suggestion systems, 1:417

by walking around, 1:199

See also Delegation; Span of control

Management accounting. *See* Cost accounting

Management buyouts, 2:1021

Management by objectives, 2:708–710

Management information systems (MIS), 2:706–708

See also Accounting systems

Management ratio. *See* Span of control

Manager recruitment, 2:710–711

See also Span of control

Managerial accounting, 2:890

Managing organizational change, 2:711–713

Mandatory overtime, 2:843

Manufacturer discounts, 1:340

Manufacturer distribution tiers, 1:348

Manufacturers' agents, 2:713–715

Manufacturers' sales branches and offices, 2:1162

Manufacturers' sales representatives, 2:865

Manufacturer's suggested retail price, 2:878

Manufacturing businesses site selection, 2:1036

Manufacturing resources planning (MRP II), 2:728, 729–730

Marital deduction trusts, 1:487

Markdowns. *See* Discount

Market analysis, 2:715–716

Market approach valuation, 2:1141

Market contraction, 1:206

Market entry, barriers to, 1:87–88

Market makers, 1:345

Market questionnaires, 2:716–717

Market research, 2:717–720

See also Market analysis; Target markets

Market Segment Specialization Program, 1:614, 647

Market segmentation, 2:720–722, 899, 1087

See also Target markets

Market share, 2:718–719, **723**

Market share budgeting method, 1:18–19

Market size and structure, 2:718

Market strategies, sales management and, 2:995

Market value, 2:773

Marketing, 1:232–233, 2:**723–727**, 1020

See also Multilevel marketing; Telemarketing; Vertical marketing systems

Marketing, reciprocal, 2:**933–934**

Markup, 2:**727–728**

Markup languages, 1:316

Mars rovers, 1:71

Marshall v. Barlow (1978), 2:804

Maslow, Abraham, 2:827

Mass marketing, 2:721

Massed media scheduling, 1:19

Master of Business Administration (MBA), 1:118

Master schedules, 2:728–729

Matching principle, 1:587

Material requirements planning (MRP), 2:**728–730**

See also Enterprise resource planning

Material Safety Data Sheet (MSDS), 2:805, 969, 970

Maternity leave. *See* Pregnancy in the workplace

Maturity (industrial life cycle), 1:599–600

Maturity (product life cycle), 2:897–898

MBA (Master of Business Administration), 1:118

MBDA (Minority Business Development Agency), 2:744–745

MBTI System (Meyers-Briggs Type Indicator), 2:**759–760**

McDonald's, 1:446

McGrath, Michael, 2:891–892

McGregor, Douglas, 2:827

Meat Inspection Act (1907), 1:236

Media buying, 1:15–16

Media scheduling, 1:19

Mediation, 1:42

See also Arbitration

Medicare and Medicaid, 2:**730–732**

Medicare Prescription Drug Improvement and Modernization Act (2003), 1:560

Medicare Supplemental Insurance, 2:731

Medigap coverage. *See* Medicare Supplemental Insurance

Medium ticket leases, 1:455

Meeting facilitators, 2:733–735

Meetings, 2:**732–735**

Membership, in better business bureaus, 1:92–93

Membership groups, nonprofit, 2:781

Membership mailing lists, 2:702

Mentally disabled employees, 1:44–45

Mentor/protégé relationships. *See* Mentoring

Mentoring, 2:735–737

Merchandise displays, 2:737–738

Merchant wholesalers, 2:1161

Mergers and acquisitions, 1:224, 361, 366, 2:**738–740**

See also Leveraged buyouts

Merit pay, 1:407–408

Mesocontext. *See* Problem context

Message boards. *See* Electronic bulletin boards

Message threads, 1:373

Metacrawlers, 2:1005

Metropolitan divisions (statistical areas), 2:741

Metropolitan Statistical Areas (MSAs), 2:740–741

Mexico, NAFTA and, 2:796–797

Meyers, Isabel Briggs, 2:759

Meyers-Briggs Type Indicator (MBTI system), 2:**759–760**

Mezzanine financing, 2:679, 741–743

Michigan

automobile manufacturing cluster in, 1:192

Civil Rights Initiative in, 1:30

portability of benefits in, 2:869

Microcomputers, 1:220

Microcontext. *See* Problem context

MicroLoans, 2:1137

Micromanagement, 1:309

Micromarketing, 2:726, 742

Micropolitan statistical areas, 2:741

Micros. *See* Nonemployer businesses

Microsoft Access, 1:294

Minimum wage, 1:387, 2:743–744

Minority assistance, through SBA, 2:1044

Minority Business Development Agency (MBDA), 2:744–745, 1136

Minority business organizations, 2:748

Minority-owned businesses, 2:745–748

Minors, employment of, 1:429–432

Minty, Gordon, 2:730

Mintzberg, Henry, 1:137, 138

MIS (Management information systems), 2:**706–708**

Mission statements, 2:652, 748–749

Mobile businesses, 2:750

Mobile offices, 2:749–750
    See also Telecommuting

Modems, 2:751–752

Moderated newsgroups, 2:776

Moderators (focus groups), 1:519, 520

Modern Organization Theory (Haire), 2:835

Modes of transportation (distribution), 2:866

Modified Accelerated Cost Recovery System, 1:3

Modular assembly, 1:58–59

Momentum, 1:115

Monetary damages, discrimination suits, 2:930

Monetary damages, small claims court, 2:1057–1058

Monetary policies, business cycles and, 1:116

Money market bonds. *See* Bonds

Money market instruments, 2:752–753

Money purchase pension plans, 2:962

Mortgage bonds. *See* Bonds

Mortgage refinancing, 2:943

Mortgages, 1:266, 2:694

Most admired companies (Fortune 500), 1:523

Most favored nation status, 1:541

Motivation for self-employment, 2:1016

Motivation of employees. *See* Employee motivation

Motor carriers, 2:866, 1126

Movie industry, seasonal aspect of, 2:1007

Moving. *See* Relocation

MRP (Material requirements planning), 2:**728–730**
    See also Enterprise resource planning

MRP II (Manufacturing resources planning), 2:728, 729–730

MRP reports, 2:729

MSAs (Metropolitan Statistical Areas), 2:**740–741**

MSDS (Material Safety Data Sheet), 2:805, 969, 970

Multi-buy promotions, 1:342

Multicultural work force, 2:753–756

Multiculturalism. *See* Multicultural work force

Multifactor productivity, 2:901

Multilevel marketing, 2:756–757

Multinational companies, 1:537–538

Multiple Employer Trusts, 2:757–758

Multiple Employer Welfare Arrangements, 2:757

Multiple pricing, 2:878

Multiple-step income statements, 1:587

Multitasking, 2:758–759

Municipal bonds. *See* Bonds

Municipal services privatization, 2:884

Municipal solid waste recycling, 2:938–939

Musculoskeletal disorders, 2:1177

MyDoom virus, 2:1156

Mystery shopping, 2:760–761

N

Nader, Ralph, 1:234

NAFTA (North American Free Trade Agreement), 1:380, 2:795–798, 1042

NAICS (North American Industry Classification System), 2:798–802, 1024, 1039

Nanomanagement. *See* Micromanagement

NASBIC (National Association of Small Business Investment Companies), 2:**763–764**

National advertising, 1:240

National Association of Small Business Investment Companies (NASBIC), 2:**763–764**

National Association of Women Business Owners (NAWBO), 2:764–765, 1165

National Association of Women Business Owners Institute for Entrepreneurial Development (NAWBO IED), 2:765

National Business Incubation Association (NBIA), 1:125, 2:765–766

National Commission on Product Safety, 1:236–237

National Foundation for Women Business Owners (NFWBO), 2:765

National goods status, 2:796

National Institute of Occupational Safety and Health, 2:804

National Institute of Standards and Technology (NIST), 1:620–621, 2:1136

National Labor Relations Act (1935), 2:663, 667, 766

National Labor Relations Board (NLRB), 1:415–416, 2:766–767, 924
    See also Labor unions and small business

National Pollutant Discharge Elimination System, 1:189

National Trade Data Bank, 2:1136

National Traffic and Motor Vehicle Safety Act (1962), 1:236

National unions, 2:665–666

National Venture Capital Association (NVCA), 2:**767–768**

Negligence (product liability), 2:895–896

Negligent hiring, 1:412

Negotiation, 1:19–20, 2:768–770

Nepotism, 1:280, 2:770–772

Net earnings, 2:961

Net gains, 1:161

Net income, 1:586, 2:772–773

Net leases, 1:455, 2:672

Net losses, 1:161

Net profitability ratio, 1:501

Net worth, 2:739, 773

Network cards, 2:696

Network point-of-sale systems, 2:867

Network Solutions Inc., 1:617

Network television advertising, 1:27

Networking (business contacts), 2:747, 773–775, 1016

Networking (computers), 1:220–221

Neutral evaluations (dispute resolution), 1:43

Nevada, incorporation in, 1:591

New economy, 2:775–776

New markets, growth and, 2:833–834

New product development, growth and, 2:834

New securities, registration of, 2:1009–1010

News releases. *See* Press releases

Newsgroups and blogs, 2:776–778

Newspaper advertising, 1:26

Newspapers direct marketing, 1:327

Newsreader software, 2:777

NFWBO (National Foundation for Women Business Owners), 2:765

Nierenberg, Gerard I., 2:769, 770

9/11 terrorist attacks (2001), 1:336

NIST (National Institute of Standards and Technology), 2:1136

NLRB (National Labor Relations Board), 1:415–416, 2:766–767

No comment references, 1:402

No-layoff policies, 2:670

Nodes (warehouses), 2:866

Nominal interest rate, 1:611

Nominal price, 2:879

Non-cancelable leases. *See* Long-term leases

Non-competition agreements, 2:**778–780**

Non-elective nonqualified deferred compensation plans, 2:791–792, 861

Non-exempt status of employees, 1:205, 386, 2:652, 667, 743, 842

Non-tariff barriers, 2:1089

Non-traditional lifestyles, 1:124

Noncontact scanners. *See* Scanners (bar coding)

Noncurrent liabilities. *See* Long-term liabilities

Nondisclosure agreements. *See* Non-competition agreements

Nondiscrimination tests (benefits), 1:525

Nonemployer businesses, 2:1016, 1040

Nonimmigrant visas, 1:39

Nonprofit organizations, 2:780–784

Nonprofit organizations and human resources management, 2:785–788

Nonprofit organizations and taxes, 2:788–791

Nonqualified deferred compensation plans, 2:791–793, 861, 962

Nonrecourse financing, 1:478

Nonsmoking policies. *See* Smoke free environments

Nontraditional financing sources, 2:793–794

Nonverbal communication, 1:200, 281, 2:795, 824
  See also Written communication

Norris-Laguardia Act (1932), 1:582

North American Free Trade Agreement (NAFTA), 1:380, 2:795–798, 1042

North American Industry Classification System (NAICS), 2:798–802, 1024, 1039

North Carolina, reported racial discrimination in, 2:931

Northwestern Mutual Life, 1:282, 283

Note taking, during interviews, 1:428

Notebooks. *See* Portable computers

Numerically controlled machines, 1:73

Nutrition Labeling and Education Act (1990), 2:847

NVCA (National Venture Capital Association), 2:767–768

O

Object and task budgeting method, 1:18

Object-oriented database management systems, 1:293

Object-relational database management systems, 1:293

Objectives, business plans and, 1:136

Objectivity, of testing laboratories, 2:1108

O'Brien, Raymond, 1:477

Occupational Safety and Health Act (1970), 1:583, 594, 2:667, 803

Occupational Safety and Health Administration (OSHA), 2:**803–807**
  on AIDS in the workplace, 1:37
  on ergonomics, 1:458–459
  on industrial safety, 1:594–596
  reforms, 2:805–806
  right-to-know laws, 2:969
  on workstations, 2:1177
  See also Workplace safety

Occupational training programs. *See* Apprenticeship programs

Odd pricing, 2:879

Off-the-job training techniques, 2:1121

Offers (contracts), 1:238

Office applications software, 1:212

Office automation, 2:**807–809**

Office hoteling. *See* Hoteling

Office of Advocacy (SBA), 2:1041–1042

Office of Business Liaison, 2:1135–1136

Office of Consumer Affairs, 1:234, 2:1136

Office of Economic Outreach (SBA), 2:1041

Office of Federal Procurement Policy Act Amendments (1979), 1:543

Office of Field Operations (SBA), 2:1041

Office of Information (SBA), 2:1041

Office of Intragency Affairs (SBA), 2:1041

Office of Management and Budget, 2:740, 799

Office of Small and Disadvantaged Utilization, 2:1136

Office of the United States Trade Representative, 1:540

Office of Women's Business Ownership, 2:1165

Office romance, 2:**809–811**

Office security, 2:**811–814**

Office supplies, 2:**815**

Officers of corporations, 1:156

Offshoring. *See* Overseas outsourcing

Old Age Survivors and Disability Insurance. *See* FICA taxes

Older Workers Benefit Protection Act (1990), 1:33–34

Ombuds, 1:42–43

Omnibus Transportation Employee Testing Act (1991), 1:359

On-site child care facilities, 1:182

On-the-job injuries. *See* Occupational Safety and Health Administration (OSHA); Workplace safety

On-the-job training techniques, 2:1121

On-the-job-work experience, 1:56–57

One-stop capital shops, 2:1044–1045

One-way interpersonal communication, 1:627–628

Online affiliate programs, 2:818

Online analytical processing, 1:296

Online auctions, 2:**815–819**

Online classified advertising, 2:818–819

Online focus groups, 1:520–521

Online magazines, banner advertisements and, 1:85

Online reference sources, 1:128–129

Open computer systems, 1:220

Open-ended incentive programs, 2:988

Open shops, 2:663

Open systems theory, 2:827–828

Operating agreements, 2:689

Operating cash flow ratio, 1:168

Operating costs, 1:12, 125–126

Operating income, 2:772

Operating leases, 1:455

Operating system software, 1:212

Operation SOS, 1:237

Operational audits, 1:69

Operational flexibility, 2:821

Operations, cash from, 1:168–169

Operations information, selling a business and, 2:1020

Operations management, 2:**819–821**

Opportunity costs, 1:261, 266–267, 2:**821–822**

Optical Character Recognition, 1:86–87

Optical fiber cable, 2:697

Optimal firm size, 2:**822–823**

Oral communication, 1:200, 2:**823–824**

Oral presentations, 2:823–824

Organic labeling, 1:548

Organization charts, 1:630, 2:**824–826**

Organization theory, 2:**826–829**

Organizational behavior, 2:**829–830**

Organizational characteristics, 2:828

Organizational development, 1:577, 2:**830–833**, 1123–1124

Organizational endorsements, 1:436

Organizational growth, 2:**833–834**
  See also Managing organizational change

Organizational life cycle, 2:**834–836**

Organizational structure, 2:**836–838**
  See also Sole proprietorships

Orientation training, 2:1121–1122

Original equipment manufacturers, 2:**838–839**

OSHA. *See* Occupational Safety and Health Administration (OSHA)

Out-of-pocket costs, 1:261

Outbound telemarketing, 1:326–327, 2:1102

Outdoor advertising, 1:26

Outside directors. *See* Boards of directors

Outside financing, growth and, 2:834

Outside safety analysis, 2:1173

Outside sales, 2:864–865

Outsourcing, 2:**839–841**, 905
  See also Layoffs, downsizing, and outsourcing

Overhead absorption, 2:841

Overhead expenses, 2:**841**

Overnight funds, 1:265

Overseas outsourcing, 2:839–841

Overtime, 2:652, **842–843**

Own occupation insurance policies, 1:331–332

Owners' equity, 1:79

Ownership transfer, 1:588, 2:849

Ozone emissions, 1:188

P

Packaging, 2:**845–847**

Packaging exports, 2:112

Paid search terms, 1:24–25

Paid time off, 2:1033

Paris Convention (1883), 1:608

Parking lot strategy (meetings), 2:734

Part-time businesses, 2:**851–853**

Part-time employees, 2:**853–855**
  See also Temporary employment services

Partial payments to creditors, 1:10

Participative management, 2:1113

Partnership agreements, 2:850, **850–851**

Partnership insurance, 1:131

Partnerships, 2:**847–850**
  definition, 1:588
  between large and small businesses, 2:1051–1052
  pro forma statements, 2:887–888
  selling, 2:1019
  with suppliers, 2:1079–1080
  tax planning and, 2:1094–1095
  See also Limited liability companies

Passwords, 1:93–94, 622

Past sales forecasting, 2:991–992

Patent and Trademark Office, 2:**855–856**, 980, 1136
  See also Inventions and patents

Patent application, 1:635–636

Patent attorneys, 1:635

Patent classification and filling, 1:624, 637

Patent drawings, 1:635

Patent searching, 1:634–635

Patents and inventions, 1:**633–637**

Pay for Applied Services, 1:284

Pay-for-performance. *See* Variable pay

Pay *vs.* profit sharing, 2:986

PayPal accounts, 2:816–817, 1124–1125

Payroll records, retention of, 2:934

Payroll tax exceptions, 2:858

Payroll taxes, 2:**856–859**, 1098
  See also FICA taxes; Tax withholding

Peer conflict, 2:1170

Pegging initial public offerings, 1:604

Penetration pricing, 2:**859–860**

Pennsylvania State Police v. Suders (2004), 1:227

Pension plans, 2:**860–862**, 1092
  See also Simplified employee pension plans

Pensions, 1:61–62

People changes, management of, 2:712

Pepperidge Farm, Inc., 1:446

Per Diem, Travel and Transportation Allowance Committee, 2:863

Per diem allowances, 2:**862–863**

Per inquiry deal discounts, 1:20

Percentage leases, 2:672–673

Percentage of sales budgeting method, 1:18

Percentage points (credit), 1:265

Percentage royalty agreements, 2:978

Performance-based evaluations (contracting), 1:545

Performance budgeting, 1:109

Performance reviews. *See* Employee performance appraisals

Period costs. *See* Fixed costs

Periodic review inventory systems, 1:637

Permanent OSHA standards, 2:803–804

Permits, definition, 2:682

Perpetual existence, 2:903

Personal computers, 1:220, 2:696

Personal days. *See* Sick leave and personal days

Personal financial statements, 1:506

Personal income, 1:344

Personal property loans, 1:336

Personal savings, 1:344

Personal savings rate, 1:107

Personal selling, 2:**863–865**
  See also Sales commissions; Sales force

Personal service business valuation, 2:1142–1143

Personality tests, 1:413, 2:**759–760**

PERT (Program Evaluation and Review Technique), 2:**909–910**

Petty cash, 1:60

Philanthropic Advisory Service, 1:93

Philanthropy. *See* Charitable giving

Physical disaster business loans, 1:335–336, 2:1043

Physical distribution, 2:**865–867**
  See also Transportation

Pick-and-place operations, 2:976

Piercing the corporate veil, 1:589

Piggyback exporting, 1:469

PIMS (Profit Impact of Market Strategies), 2:**905–906**

PIMS database, 2:905–906

Pipeline transportation, 2:1127

Plaintiffs, small claims court, 2:1056–1057

Plan files, 2:777

Planned building leasing, 2:674

Planned expansion, 1:120–121

Planning. *See* Business planning; Career planning and changing; Crisis management; Disaster planning; Enterprise resource planning; Material requirements planning (MRP); Retirement planning; Tax planning

Plant locals (unions), 2:665

Plant patents, 1:634

Plastics, in packaging, 2:845–846

Plowback ratio, 2:1083

Point-of-purchase displays, 2:999

Point-of-sale systems (POS), 1:86, 2:**867–868**

Point-of-service plans (PPOs), 1:559, 560, **561–563**

Poison Prevention Packaging Act (1970), 1:236

Poka-yoke ("Avoid error"), 2:927

Political relations. *See* Government relations

Political unions, 2:662

Politics, business cycles and, 1:115–116

Pollution control. *See* Environmental law and business; *specific laws*

Pollution Control Program, 2:1042, 1138

Portability of benefits, 2:**868–869**

Portable computers, 1:220

Porter, Michael E., 1:191–193, 596–597

Portion packaging, 2:846

POS (Point-of-sale systems), 1:86, 2:**867–868**

Positioning statements, advertising, 1:28–29

Post-consumer surveys, 2:720

Postage meters, 2:870

Postal costs, 2:781–782, **869–870**

Potentially responsible parties, 1:210

PPOs (Point-of-service plans), 1:559, 560, **561–563**

Pre-incorporation agreements, 1:590

Pre-paid legal services, 2:675–676

Pre-Paid Legal Services (company), 2:676

Pre-production prototypes, 2:913

Preemptive right, 2:1069

Preferred stock, 2:1069–1070

Pregnancy Discrimination Act (1978), 2:871

Pregnancy in the workplace, 2:**871–873**

Premium-only plans, 1:512

Premiums (sales promotions), 2:998

Prepaid health insurance plans. *See* Fee-for-service insurance plans

Prepayment risk, 1:267

Preschool cooperatives, 1:242

Prescription drug program, 2:731

Present value, 2:**873–874**

Presentation prototypes, 2:913

Press kits, 2:**874–875**

Press releases, 2:**875–876**

Pretax income, 2:772

Prevailing wage structures, 1:40

Preventive mediation, 1:42

Price, Steven M., 1:476–477

Price bundling, 2:878

Price discounts, 2:997

Price-earnings ratio, 2:739, 772–773, **876–877**

Price lining, 2:879

Price per unit, 1:105

Pricing, 2:**877–880**
    above competition, 2:878–879
    below competition, 2:879
    brand and, 1:104
    costs and, 1:262
    equating customer service with, 1:290
    for foreign markets, 1:471–472
    loss leader pricing, 2:699
    penetration pricing, 2:859–860
    supply and demand and, 2:1082
    target marketing and, 2:725–726
    See also Markup

Primary earnings per share, 1:586

Prime interest rate, 1:611

Print advertising, 1:**25–27**

Print reference sources, 1:128

Printers (computer), 1:316–317

Priority Mail (USPS), 2:870

Privacy, 1:313, 400–402

Private investors, 1:458

Private key encryption. *See* Single key encryption

Private labeling, 2:**880–881**

Private leveraged buyouts, 2:679

Private placement equity financing, 1:159

Private placement memorandum, 2:883

Private placement of securities, 2:**882–883**

Private placement of stock, 1:458

Private privatization, 2:884–885

Privatization, 2:**883–885**

Pro forma invoices, 2:989

Pro forma statements, 2:**885–888**

Probationary employment periods, 2:889

Problem context, 1:303

Problem finding, 1:303–304

Problem management. *See* Problem solving

Problem solving, 1:304–305

Process costing, 1:262

Process design, 2:820

Producers' cooperatives, 1:242

Product, place, promotion, and price (Four Ps), 2:725

Product concept, 1:28–29

Product costing, 2:**890–891**

Product costs, 1:261

Product design, 2:819–820, 897

Product development, 1:282, 2:819, **891–894**
    See also Prototypes

Product launching, 2:893

Product liability, 1:130, 2:**894–896**

Product life cycle, 2:**896–898**
    See also Organizational life cycle

Product life cycle analysis, 1:547–548

Product packaging, 2:846

Product positioning, 1:253, 2:**898–900**

Product protection, 2:846

Product public relations, 2:**915–916**

Product research, 2:720

Product tests, 2:720

Product warranties. *See* Warranties

Productivity, 2:**900–902**

Products research and consumer surveys, 2:719

Professional corporations, 2:**902–904**

Professional employer organizations, 1:392

Professional software, 1:212

Professional unions, 2:662

Profit. *See* Net income

Profit centers, 1:255, 2:**904–905**

Profit Impact of Market Strategies (PIMS), 2:**905–906**

Profit margin, 2:**906–907**

Profit ratio, 2:772

Profit sharing, 1:409, 2:**907–909**

Profit sharing plans, 2:961–962

Profit sharing *vs.* pay, 2:986

Profit split method (royalty rates), 2:980

Profitability, 1:498, 2:789

Profitability ratios, 1:501–502

Program audits, 1:69

Program Evaluation and Review Technique (PERT), 2:**909–910**

Project evaluation, research and development, 2:955

Project management, research and development, 2:955

Project selection, research and development, 2:955

Project termination, research and development, 2:955

Projection, budgets and, 1:108, 109

Promissory estoppel, 1:239

Promissory notes, 1:265, 2:**910–911**

Promotions, job. *See* Employee compensation

Promotions, sales. *See* Sales promotions

Property leasing, 2:**672–675**

Property leasing businesses, 2:674–675

Property losses, business insurance and, 1:130

Proposition 209 (CA, 1996), 1:30, 32

Proprietary information, 2:**911–912**, 953

Prospective buyers of a businesses, 2:1020–1021

ProStores, 2:818

Protected classes, 1:411

Prototypes, 2:897, **912–913**

Proxy servers, 1:508

Proxy statements, 2:**914**

Psychological profiling, 2:720

Public Company Accounting Reform and Investor Protection Act. *See* Sarbanes-Oxley Act (2002)

Public domain, 1:244

Public Health Security and Bioterrorism Preparedness and Response Act (2002). *See* Bioterrorism Act (2002)

Public interest relations, 2:917

Public key encryption, 1:291–292, 618–619

Public policy violations, as grounds for termination, 1:420

Public relations, 1:178, 277–278, 2:**914–918**
   See also Community relations; Press kits; Press releases

Public stock offerings, 1:159, 458

Public to private leveraged buyouts, 2:679

Public Utility Holding Company Act (1935), 2:1011

Purchase money security interest, 1:196

Purchasing, 2:**918–921**

Purchasing cards, 2:920

Purchasing context, 2:968

Push money, 2:999

Q

Qualified opinions (auditing), 1:507

Qualified Replacement Property, 1:414, 2:1078

Qualitative forecasting, 1:521–522

Quality circles, 2:**923–925**, 927
   See also Total quality management

Quality control, 2:684–685, **925–928**
   See also ISO 9000; Quality circles; Total quality management

Quality control testing by laboratories, 2:1109

Quality Functional Deployment model, 2:820

Quality of life, 1:396

Quantitative forecasting, 1:521–522

Quasi-contracts, 1:237

Quick ratio, 1:499, 502

Quicken Legal Business Pro 2006 (CD-ROM), 2:676

R

Racial differences in earnings, 1:387

Racial discrimination, 2:**929–932**

Radiation Control for Health and Safety Act (1968), 1:236

Radio, as a reference source, 1:128

Radio advertising, 1:**22–23**

Radio frequency identification, 2:1162

Rail transportation (distribution), 2:866, 1126

Raising prices, 2:879–880

Rapid prototyping, 2:913

Rate of profit, 2:907

Rate of return. *See* Rate of profit

Rayns, John K., Jr., 1:203

Reach media buying, 1:15

Reagan, Ronald, 1:31, 524

Real estate, as collateral, 1:196

Real interest rate, 1:611

Real price, 2:879

Real property loans, 1:336

Rebates, 2:**932–933**, 997

Recession, as part of business cycle, 1:114

Reciprocal linking. *See* Reciprocal marketing

Reciprocal marketing, 2:**933–934**
   See also Banner advertisements

Recognition programs. *See* Employee reward and recognition systems

Record retention, 2:**934–936**
   See also IRS audits; Sarbanes-Oxley Act (2002)

Recourse financing, 1:478

Recoverable materials, 2:938–939

Recovery, as part of business cycle, 1:114

Recovery, from business failure, 1:123–124

Recovery planning. *See* Disaster planning

Recruiting, 2:**936–937**, 994
   See also Manager recruitment; Résumés

Recruitment, 1:389, 2:785–786

Recycling, 1:550, 2:**938–940**
   See also Green production; Remanufacturing

Redemption agreements, 1:191

Reductions in force. *See* Layoffs, downsizing, and outsourcing

Reengineering, 2:**940–942**

Reeves v. Sanderson Plumbing Products, Inc. (2000), 1:34

Reference materials. *See* Business information sources

References, employee. *See* Employee references

References, for loan proposals, 2:692

Referrals, for child care, 1:183

Refinancing, 2:**942–943**

Refrigerator Safety Act (1956), 1:236

Refunds, 2:997
   See also Rebates

Regents of the University of California v. Bakke (1978), 1:31

Registration of employees. *See* Employee registration procedures

Regular corporation. *See* C corporations

Regulation D (SEC), 2:882–883, **943–944**

Regulatory Flexibility Act (1980), 2:**944–946**

Reimbursement plans, for child care, 1:183

Related diversification, 1:366

Related parties (exports), 1:539

Relational database management systems, 1:293

Relationship marketing. *See* Database marketing

Relevance marketing. *See* Database marketing

Relinquishing communication style, 1:628

Relocation, 2:**946–948**
   See also Site selection

Remanufacturing, 2:**948–950**

Remedial investigation and feasibility studies, 1:211

Remnants and regional editions discounts, 1:20

Removal action. *See* Short-term removal

Renovation, 2:**950–951**

Renting. *See* Leasing property

Reorganization, human resources changes and, 1:579

Reorganization, under Chapter 11 bankruptcy, 1:80–81

Repayment risk. *See* Credit risk

Repayment schedules, 1:265, 2:693

Repeaters (computer networks), 2:698

Repetitive strain injuries, 1:458–459, 2:1177

Repurchase agreements, 2:753

Requests for proposals (RFPs), 1:544, 2:**951–952**
   See also Business proposals; Competitive bids

Requests for quotes (RFQs). *See* Competitive bids

Research and development, 1:14, 527, 2:**953–956**, 977

Resellers, distribution and, 1:345

Residential care industry growth, 2:1055

Residual market value method (royalty rates), 2:980

Residual ownership of common stock, 2:1068–1069

Resistance to change, 2:712

Response devices, 1:324, 326

Response lists. *See* Direct marketing lists and databases

Response mailing lists, 2:702

Responsibility centers, 1:255

Resting bills, 1:10

Résumés, 2:**956–958**, 1014

Retail businesses site selection, 2:1036

Retail trade, 2:**958–959**
   See also Dot-coms

Retained earnings, 1:6, 2:773

Retirement planning, 2:**959–963**
   See also 401(k) plans; Keogh plans; Nonqualified deferred compensation plans; Pension plans; Simplified employee pension plans; Individual retirement accounts (IRAs)

Retrieval systems. *See* Automated storage and retrieval systems

Return management solutions, 2:966

Return on assets (ROA), 2:**963–964**

Return on assets ratio, 1:502

Return on equity ratio, 1:499, 2:1083

Return on investment (ROI), 1:631, 2:**964–965**

Return on investment ratio 1, 1:502

Return on investment ratio 2, 1:502

Return on sales ratio. *See* Profit ratio

Return policies, 2:**965–966**

Reuse and recycling, 1:550

Revenue Act (1916), 1:460

Revenue recognition principle, 1:587

Revenue streams, 2:**967–968**

Revenues, 1:6, 506

Reverse discrimination, 1:32, 2:931

Reverse sexual discrimination, 1:536

Revolving credit, 1:265, 2:693

RFPs (Requests for proposals), 1:544, 2:**951–952**
   See also Business proposals; Competitive bids

RFQs (Requests for quotes). *See* Competitive bids

Rhode Island, licensing in, 2:682

Right-sizing. *See* Layoffs, downsizing, and outsourcing

Right-to-know laws, 2:**968–971**

Right-to-know movement, 2:969

Ring networks, 2:697

Risk, in research and development, 2:953–954

Risk and return, 2:**973–975**

Risk assessment, 1:186–187, 275

Risk management, 2:**971–973**

Risk purchasing groups. *See* Disability insurance pools

Risk Retention Act (1986), 1:607

Riskless assets, 1:60

Risky assets, 1:60

Risky stocks, 2:1071

ROA (Return on assets), 2:**963–964**

Robinson-Patman Act (1936), 1:490, 2:995–996

Robinson v. Shell Oil Co., 1:34

Robotics, 1:73, 2:**975–977**

Robots. *See* Robotics

Rochdale Principles, 1:241

ROI (Return on investment), 1:631, 2:**964–965**

Role analysis technique, 2:832

Role playing, training through, 2:1122

Rollover contribution accounts, 1:593

Roth IRAs, 1:593

Routers, 1:508, 2:698

Royalties, 2:**977–981**

Royalty financing, 2:**981–982**

RSA data encryption program, 1:292

Rudkin, Margaret, 1:446

Rule 504. *See* Regulation D (SEC)

Rule 505. *See* Regulation D (SEC)

Rule 506. *See* Regulation D (SEC)

Rules, as organizational characteristic, 2:828

Rules of conduct, 1:195

Rules of thumb (valuation), 2:1141–1142

Rural business enterprise grants, 2:983

Rural businesses, 2:**982–983**

S

S corporations, 1:356, 589–590, 2:687, 888, **985–987**, 1095–1096
   See also C corporations; Subchapter S corporations

Safety incentives, 2:1172

Safety managers and committees, 2:1172–1173

Safety stocks (inventory), 1:637

Safety testing by laboratories, 2:1108

Salaries. *See* Employee compensation

Salary plus commission, 2:988

Salary reduction, child care and, 1:183

Sales, retail. *See* Discount sales

Sales commissions, 2:**987–989**

Sales contracts, 2:**989–990**

Sales force, 2:**990–991**

Sales forecasts, 2:**991–993**

Sales growth ranking (Fortune 500), 1:523

Sales letters, 1:324, 326

Sales management, 2:**993–996**

Sales monitoring, 1:21

Sales per employee ratio, 1:502

Sales promotions, 2:**996–1000**

Sales representatives, 1:340–341, 2:864–865

Sales territories, 2:995

Sales to receivables ratio, 1:502

Sales training, 2:1123

Salesmanship characteristics, 2:864

Sampling (sales promotions), 2:998–999

Sanderson Plumbing Products, Inc., Reeves v. (2000), 1:34

SARA. *See* Superfund Amendments and Reauthorization Act (1986)

Sarbanes-Oxley Act (2002), 2:934–935, **1000–1003**, 1009, 1012
   on codes of ethics, 1:194
   on expense accounts, 1:465
   on external audits, 1:63

Sarbanes-Oxley Act (2002), *continued*
  financial reporting requirements,
    1:506–507
  on generally accepted accounting
    principles, 1:5
  internal auditing, 1:66–67
  on public board audits, 1:98
  record keeping and e-mail, 1:377,
    400, 401
  Section 404, 1:645
Satellite nonprofit organizations, 2:781
Satellite television advertising, 1:27–28
Savings and loan associations. *See* Thrift
  institutions
Savings banks. *See* Thrift institutions
Savings bonds. *See* Baby bonds
SBA. *See* Small Business
  Administration (SBA)
SBA MicroLoans, 2:1042
SBAExpress Loan Program, 2:1042,
  1137
SBDCs (Small Business Development
  Centers), 2:**1046**, 1165
SBICs (Small Business Investment
  Companies), 1:303, 2:763–764,
  1048–1049
SBIR (Small Business Innovation
  Research Program), 2:1044,
  1046–1047, 1053–1054
SBTC (Small Business Technology
  Coalition), 2:765
Scalability, 2:**1003–1004**
Scanner research, 2:720
Scanners (bar coding), 1:86
Scenario writing forecasting, 1:522
School-to-Work Opportunities Act
  (1994), 1:57
School-to-work programs, 1:118
Schultz v. Wheaton Glass Co. (1970),
  1:534–535
SCOR (Small Corporate Offering
  Registration), 1:330, 2:943–944
SCORE (Service Corps of Retired
  Executives), 2:748, **1026**
Search Engine Watch, 2:1005
Search engines, 1:25, 2:**1004–1006**
Searches and seizures in the workplace,
  1:400–401
Sears, Richard, 1:445–446
Sears, Roebuck, 1:445–446
Seasonal businesses, 1:124, 2:854,
  1006–1008
Seasonal discounts, 1:20
Seasonal employees, 2:1007–1008
SEC. *See* Securities and Exchange
  Commission (SEC)

SEC disclosure laws and regulations,
  2:**1008–1010**
    See also Sarbanes-Oxley Act (2002)
SEC disclosure obligations,
  2:1009–1010
SECA (Self-employment
  Contributions Act) (1954),
  2:**1017–1019**
Second mortgages, 2:794
Secret key encryption. *See* Single key
  encryption
Section 4(2) (SEC), 2:882–883
Secure electronic transport (SET),
  1:619
Secure socket layer (SSL), 1:618,
  2:1154–1155
Securities. *See* Baby bonds
Securities Act (1933), 1:603, 2:1011
Securities and Exchange Act (1934),
  1:66, 68, 603, 2:1011
Securities and Exchange Commission
  (SEC), 2:**1011–1012**
  on annual reports, 1:49, 52
  on boards of directors, 1:97
  on day trading, 1:296
  on direct public offerings, 1:329,
    330
  on generally accepted accounting
    principles, 1:5
  on initial public offerings, 1:602,
    603–604
  on internal auditing, 1:66
  on investor relations and reporting,
    1:645
  on private placement of securities,
    2:882–883
  on pro forma statements, 2:886,
    887
  on proxy statements, 2:914
Securities industry regulations, 2:1010
Security guards, 2:813
Security measures. *See* Internet security;
  Office security; Workplace safety;
  Workplace violence
Seed money, 2:**1012–1014**
    See also Angel investors; Venture
    capital; Venture capital networks
Self-appraisal. *See* Self-assessment
Self-assessment, 1:399, 2:**1014–1015**
Self-employment, 2:**1015–1017**, 1030
    See also Independent contractors
Self-employment Contributions Act
  (SECA) (1954), 2:**1017–1019**
Self-instruction training, 2:1122
Self-policing environmental audits,
  1:447–448

Self-regulation, of nonprofit organiza-
  tions, 2:784
Sellers, 1:208, 345
Selling, via telemarketing,
  2:1103–1104
Selling a business, 2:**1019–1022**
Semi-structured decisions, 1:307
Seniority, 1:33, 2:**1022–1024**
Separate-entity assumptions, 1:61
September 11, 2001 terrorist attacks.
  See 9/11 terrorist attacks (2001)
Service bureaus, telemarketing and,
  2:1104–1105
Service businesses, 2:**1024–1025**
Service businesses site selection, 2:1036
Service Corps of Retired Executives
  (SCORE), 2:748, **1026**
Service guarantees. *See* Warranties
Service level agreements, 1:55–56
Service warranties. *See* Warranties
Services buying, economies of scale and,
  1:365
SET (Secure electronic transport),
  1:619
Set-aside programs, 2:747–748
Settlements, small claims court, 2:1057
7(a) Loan Program, 2:1042, 1127
7-Eleven, 2:1072
Sexual discrimination. *See* Gender
  discrimination
Sexual harassment, 2:**1026–1030**
  constructive discharge and,
    1:226–228
  downloading offensive material
    and, 1:357–358
  gender discrimination and, 1:533,
    535
  office romance and, 2:810, 811
SGML (Standard Generalized Markup
  Language), 1:315
Shanklin, William M., 1:203
Shared services, 2:**1030–1031**
Shareholder agreements. *See* Buy-sell
  agreements
Shareholders, 1:156, 591
Shell Oil Co., Robinson v., 1:34
Sherman Antitrust Act, 2:996
Shewhart, Walter A., 2:1112
Shipper's export declaration, 2:1128
Shipper's instructions, 2:1128
Shoplifting, 2:**1031–1032**
Short-term disability insurance, 1:331
Short-term loans, 2:694
Short-term removal, 1:211

Short-Term Single Buyer Program, 1:466–467

Short-term tax exempts, 2:752–753

Showcase displays, 2:737

SIC (Standard Industrial Classification System), 2:798–799, 801, 1024

Sick leave and personal days, 1:2, 2:**1032–1034**

Signature files, 2:777

Silent partners. *See* Limited partnerships

SIMPLE 401(k) plans, 1:526, 593, 2:961

Simple interest, 1:612

SIMPLE IRA plans, 2:961, 1035, 1050

Simplified employee pension plans, 1:593, 2:961, **1034–1036**

Simulations training, 2:1122

Single key encryption, 1:291

Single-step income statements, 1:587

Sinking funds, 2:792

Site selection, 2:820, **1036–1038**
    See also Relocation

Six sigma, 2:927

60-day preference rule, 1:81

Skill clusters, 2:968

Skimming, 2:859–860

Sloan, Alfred P., 2:1072

Slotting allowances, 2:1000

Small business, 2:**1038–1041**

Small Business Administration (SBA), 2:**1041–1045**
    on bad résumés, 2:937
    Business Development Mentor-Protégé Program, 1:369
    on competitive analysis, 1:206–207
    on costs of complying, 2:944
    on customer service, 1:288
    debt financing by, 1:302–303
    disaster assistance loans, 1:335, 336
    8(A) Program, 1:367–369, 544
    on equity financing, 1:457, 458
    on exporting, 1:468, 469, 471
    on fastest-growing industries, 2:1054–1055
    on Federal Procurement, 1:209
    on freight forwarders, 2:1128–1129
    HubZone Empowerment Contracting Program, 1:209, 575–576
    on incorporation, 1:590
    on leasing property, 2:673
    lending programs, 2:1042–1043
    minority programs, 2:748
    on obtaining loans, 1:272

on pricing for foreign markets, 1:472
    programs for women entrepreneurs, 2:1164–1165
    small business definition, 2:1038–1039
    on training and development, 2:1120

Small business consortia, 2:**1045–1046**

Small business culture, 2:1040–1041

Small Business Development Centers (SBDCs), 2:**1046**, 1165

Small business-dominated industries, 2:**1054–1056**

Small Business Innovation Research Program (SBIR), 2:1044, **1046–1047**, 1053–1054

Small Business Insurance Policy Program, 1:466

Small Business Investment Companies (SBICs), 1:303, 2:763–764, **1048–1049**

Small Business Job Protection Act (1996), 2:743, **1050–1051**

Small business/large business relationships, 2:**1051–1053**

Small Business Lawyer (CD-ROM), 2:676

Small Business Liability Reform Act (2001), 2:895

Small Business Regulatory Enforcement Fairness Act (1996), 2:944, 945

Small business set-asides, 1:209

Small Business Technology Coalition (SBTC), 2:765

Small Business Technology Transfer Program (STTR), 2:1044, **1053–1054**

Small claims court, 2:**1056–1058**

Small Corporate Offering Registration (SCOR), 1:330, 2:943–944

Small denomination municipal bonds. *See* Baby bonds

Small-Order Execution System, 1:297

Small ticket leases, 1:455

Smith v. City of Jackson, Mississippi (2005), 1:34–35

Smoke free environments, 2:**1058–1060**

Sniffers (viruses), 1:214

Social networking, 2:774

Social organization, cultural determination of, 1:280–281

Social/recreational organizations, 2:781

Social responsibility, business ethics and, 1:119

Social Security
    disability insurance, 1:331
    Medicare funding, 2:730
    self-employment and, 2:1018
    See also FICA taxes

Social Security Act (1935), 1:582–583

Social Security Act (1965), 2:731

Sociolinguistics, 1:279–280

Sociotechnical system design interventions, 2:832

Soft assets. *See* Current assets

Software
    anti-virus protection, 2:1156
    back door testing of, 1:621
    for database management, 1:294
    e-mail, 1:376
    for electronic data interchange translation, 1:375
    groupware, 1:554–555
    for legal advice, 2:676
    management information systems, 2:708
    modems and, 2;751
    newsreaders, 2:777
    office applications, 1:212, 2:808
    operating systems, 1:212
    professional software, 1:212
    spam filtering, 2:1064
    for tax preparation, 2:1096–1097
    web browsers, 1:85
    for Web monitoring, 1:358

Sole proprietorships, 1:588, 2:985, 1019, **1060–1062**, 1094–1095
    See also Professional corporations

Soliciting funds for nonprofits, 2:781, 783

Solid waste disposal, 1:451

Source tags, 2:1032

SOX. *See* Sarbanes-Oxley Act (2002)

Spam, 1:214, 215, 377, 2:703, **1062–1064**
    See also CAN-SPAM Act (2003)

Spam filtering software, 2:1064

Span of control, 2:**1064–1066**

Special Small Business Investment Companies (SSBICs), 2:763, 1048

Specialty stores, 2:958

Specific Identification Method, 1:639

Speed-to-market, 2:893–894

SpeedNetworkingTM, 1:444

SPI (Strategic Planning Institute), 2:905

Spin-offs (leveraged buyouts), 2:679

Spohn, Gustav, 1:202, 203

Spot and electric arc welding, 2:976

Spousal IRAs, 1:593

Spray finishing operations, 2:976

Spread discounts, 1:20

Spyware, 2:1155

SSBICs (Special Small Business Investment Companies), 2:763, 1048

SSL (Secure socket layer), 1:618, 2:1154–1155

Staffing levels, absenteeism and, 1:1

Stagflation, 1:116

Stakeholders, on cross-functional teams, 1:283

Stand-by rate discounts, 1:20

Standard Generalized Markup Language (SGML), 1:315

Standard Industrial Classification System (SIC), 2:798–799, 801, 1024

Standard Mail (A) (USPS), 2:870

Standard mileage rate, 2:**1066**

Standard of value, 2:1143

Star networks, 2:697

State of the art defense, 2:896

State OSHA standards, 2:804–805

State unemployment taxes, 2:857

Stateful inspection firewalls, 1:508

Statistical quality control, 2:926, 1112, 1113

Steel recycling, 2:940

Stock equity, 1:158

Stock exchanges, 2:1022

Stock-for-stock, 2:739

Stock issuance, cash flow statements and, 1:169

Stock options, 1:409, 2:843

Stock purchases, cash flow statements and, 1:169

Stock sales, 2:1019

Stockholders
    acquisition and mergers and, 2:738, 740
    control and voting by, 2:1068, 1070
    as corporate board members, 1:97

Stockholders' equity, statements of, 1:6

Stocks, 2:974, **1067–1071**
    See also Blue chip stocks

Storage systems. *See* Automated storage and retrieval systems

Store brands. *See* Private labeling

Storefront window displays, 2:737

Storymercials, 1:23

Straight commission, 2:987

Straight-line depreciation, 1:315

Straight salary, 2:987–988

Strategic changes, management of, 2:711

Strategic planning. *See* Business planning

Strategic Planning Institute (SPI), 2:905

Strategic sourcing, 2:918–919

Strategy, 2:726, **1071–1073**

Strict product liability, 2:896

Structural changes, management of, 2:712

Structured decisions, 1:306

Structuring communication style, 1:628

STTR (Small Business Technology Transfer Program), 2:1044, **1053–1054**

Subchapter S corporations, 2:1050

Subcontracting, 2:**1073–1075**

Subjective approach forecasting method, 1:522

Subjugation cultures, 1:280

Subscription materials, for private placement of securities, 2:883

Subsequent events, 1:506

Substance abuse, 2:**1075–1077**

Substitutes, industry analysis and, 1:597

Succession plans, 1:486, 487, 2:**1077–1079**

Suders, Pennsylvania State Police v. (2004), 1:227

Sum-of-the-years-digits depreciation, 1:315

Summary annual reports, 1:52

Sunk costs, 1:261

Superfund. *See* CERCLA (Comprehensive Environmental Response Cleanup and Liability Act) (1980)

Superfund Amendments and Reauthorization Act (1986), 1:209

Supermarkets, 2:958–959

Supervisory and management development, 2:1124

Supplemental executive retirement plans, 2:792

Supplemental health insurance, 1:559

Supplier relations, 1:51, 597, 2:**1079–1081**

Supply and demand, 2:**1082–1083**

Surety bonds, 2:1043

Surplus labor. *See* Layoffs, downsizing, and outsourcing

Surveillance and investigation of employees, 1:401

Survey feedback, 2:832

Sustainable growth, 2:**1083–1084**

Sweepstakes and contests, 2:997–998

Sweethearting, 1:422, 2:814

Swipe cards, 2:812

Switching (Internet security), 2:1154

Symmetric encryption. *See* Single key encryption

Syndicate formation, 2:1085–1086

Syndicated loans, 2:**1084–1086**

System audits, 1:69

T

T-bills. *See* Treasury bills

Taft-Hartley Act (1947). *See* Labor Management Relations Act (1947)

Tall organizations, 2:828

Target consumers, 1:29

Target markets, 2:720, 724–725, **1087–1088**
    See also Market segmentation

Tariff Act (1894), 2:789

Tariffs, 2:796, **1088–1089**

Tax Acts (2003, 2004), 1:356

Tax benefits, automobile leasing, 1:76

Tax credit, empowerment zones and, 1:434–435

Tax deductible business expenses, 2:**1089–1092**
    charitable giving, 1:178
    depreciation, 2:1091
    employee benefits, 1:155–156, 2:1092
    equipment purchases, 2:1094
    home offices, 1:571–572, 2:1090–1091
    interest paid on debt financing, 1:612–613
    travel expenses, 1:142–143
    tuition assistance programs, 2:1130

Tax-deferred savings plans
    flexible spending accounts, 1:512, 513–514
    401(k) plans, 1:524
    IRAs (Individual retirement accounts), 1:592–594
    Keogh plans, 2:659–660

Tax-exempt status, 2:788–791, 793

Tax fraud, 1:647

Tax identification numbers. *See* Employer identification numbers

Tax liability, depreciation and, 1:314

Tax liability, estate tax and, 1:462

Tax planning, 2:**1093–1096**

Tax preparation software, 2:**1096–1097**

Tax Reform Act (1986), 1:3

Tax returns, 2:**1097–1098**
  See also IRS audits

Tax withholding, 2:**1099–1100**
  See also FICA taxes; Payroll taxes

Tax withholding form. *See* Form W-4 (IRS)

Taxation
  on absent income, 2:986
  advantages of incorporation, 1:588
  on C corporations, 1:157
  of corporate dividends, 1:352–353
  on employee benefits, 2:986
  on IRAs, 1:592–593
  of nonprofit organizations, 2:788–791
  of part-time businesses, 2:853
  on partnerships, 2:848
  payroll taxes, 2:856–859
  on professional corporations, 2:902–903
  research and development credits, 2:955–956
  on S corporations, 2:985
  self-employment and, 2:1017–1019
  See also Income tax; Tariffs

Taylor, Frederick W., 2:826–827

Team-building exercises, 2:1122–1123

Team interviewing, 1:428–429

Team production (manufacturing), 1:59

Tech-prep programs, 1:117

Technical training, 2:1123

Technological innovations
  business cycles and, 1:115
  business hours and, 1:124
  communications and, 1:200–201
  cross-cultural communication and, 1:280
  inventory control and, 1:641
  management information systems and, 2:707
  managing change, 2:711–712
  multitasking and, 2:758–759
  revenue streams and, 2:968
  wholesaling and, 2:1162
  See also Inventions and patents

Technology, distribution differentiation by, 1:346

Technology licensing. *See* Know-how licensing

Telecommuting, 2:**1100–1102**

Telemarketers, public opinion of, 2:1105

Telemarketing, 1:226–327, 2:**1102–1105**

Telemarketing and Consumer Fraud and Abuse Prevention Act (1994), 1:491

Telephone-based direct marketing. *See* Telemarketing

Teleservicing. *See* Inbound telemarketing

Television, as a reference source, 1:128

Television advertising, 1:27–28

Television direct marketing, 1:327

Temporary emergency OSHA standards, 2:803

Temporary employment services, 2:**1106–1107**

Temporary workers *vs.* overtime, 2:834

Term life insurance, 2:685

Term loans, 1:266, 2:693

Testimonials and endorsements, 1:**435–437**, 2:706

Testing, before hiring employees, 1:412, 413

Testing, direct mail, 1:324–326

Testing laboratories, 2:**1107–1110**
  See also Underwriters Laboratories (UL)

Theft, by employees, 1:422–423, 2:1032

Theft, of computer hardware, 1:217

Theory X, 2:827

Theory Y, 2:827

Theory Z, 2:828–829

Third party debt collection, 1:300

Third party sponsored IRAs, 1:593

360-Degree feedback, 1:399, 2:1014

Thrift institutions, 1:83

Tier ratings (ISPs), 1:624

Tiers (distribution), 1:346, 348

Time-triggered systems. *See* Periodic review inventory systems

Timing, in research and development, 2:953–954

Title I (Americans with Disabilities Act), 1:44

Title I (Sarbanes-Oxley Act), 2:1001

Title II (Americans with Disabilities Act), 1:44

Title II (Sarbanes-Oxley Act), 2:1001

Title III (Americans with Disabilities Act), 1:44, 333

Title III (Sarbanes-Oxley Act), 2:1001

Title IV (Americans with Disabilities Act), 1:44

Title IV (Sarbanes-Oxley Act), 2:1001–1002

Title V (Americans with Disabilities Act), 1:44

Title V (Sarbanes-Oxley Act), 2:1002

Title VI (Sarbanes-Oxley Act), 2:1002

Title VII (Civil Rights Act)
  on affirmative action, 1:30, 31
  on age discrimination, 1:35
  on employee rights, 1:411
  on gender discrimination, 1:533–534, 536
  on human resources responsibilities, 1:582
  on pregnancy discrimination, 2:871
  on racial discrimination, 2:929–930
  See also Equal Employment Opportunity Commission (EEOC)

Title VII (Housing and Community Development Act), 1:434

Title VII (Sarbanes-Oxley Act), 2:1002

Title VIII (Sarbanes-Oxley Act), 2:1002

Title IX (Sarbanes-Oxley Act), 2:1002

Title X (Sarbanes-Oxley Act), 2:1002

Title XI (Sarbanes-Oxley Act), 2:1002

Toll-free telephone numbers, 2:**1110–1111**

Top heavy rules, 1:525

Top-level Internet domains, 1:616

Total cost of ownership, 1:222, 2:918

Total market sales forecasting, 2:992

Total Maximum Daily Load, 1:189–190

Total preventive maintenance, 2:**1111–1112**

Total quality control, 2:924

Total quality management, 2:832, 927, **1112–1114**
  See also ISO 9000

Toxic waste handling, 1:451

Toxins, hazards of, 1:595

Toyota Motor North America, Inc., image of, 1:250

Trade associations, 1:469

Trade Compliance Center, 2:1136

Trade credit, 1:265, 302, 2:694

Trade deals (sales promotions), 2:999–1000

Trade Expansion Act (1962), 1:540

Trade financing, 1:470–471

Trade journals, 1:128

Trade promotions, 2:999–1000

Trade secrets. *See* Proprietary information

Trade show attendance, 2:1115, 1117
Trade shows, 1:147, 2:999, **1114–1117**
Trademarks, 1:104–105, 2:683, **1117–1120**
Trading credits, 1:88
Trading exchanges. *See* Bartering
Traditional budgeting, 1:109
Traffic, convenience and, 2:967–968
Traffic builder premiums, 2:998
Training and development, 2:**1120–1124**
    for automated systems, 1:74
    for customer service, 1:288–289
    delegation and, 1:310
    flexible work arrangements and, 1:516–517
    hiring and, 1:391
    as human resources duty, 1:578, 580
    in a multicultural workforce, 2:755
    for office automation, 2:809
    right-to-know laws and, 2:970–971
    by sales managers, 2:994
    through Small Business Association, 2:1044
    See also Internships; Tuition assistance programs
Trans Union, 1:269
Transaction processing, 2:**1124–1125**
Transaction Processing Performance Council, 2:1125
Transactional databases, 1:293
Transferability, of sole proprietorships, 2:1061
Transportation, 2:**1125–1127**
    See also Physical distribution
Transportation of exports, 2:**1127–1129**
Transporters (distribution), 1:345
Travel agencies industry growth, 2:1055–1056
Travel agents, 1:142
Travel deductions, 1:142–143
Travel expenses, 2:1091
Treasury bill interest rate, 1:611
Treasury bills, 1:266, 2:752
Treasury bond interest rate, 1:611
Treasury bonds. *See* Bonds
Treaty of Maastricht (1992), 1:463
Treaty of Nice (2003), 1:463
Trial balances, 1:100
Trial periods, for employees. *See* Probationary employment periods
Trials, small claims court, 2:1057
Tripartite arbitration, 1:42
Triple-net leases, 2:672

Trojan horses, 1:214
Troughs. *See* Recession
Trucking (distribution). *See* Motor carriers
Trust Fund Recovery Penalty, 2:856, 858–859
Trust Indenture Act (1939), 2:1011–1012
Truth in Lending Act (1969), 1:490
Tuition assistance programs, 2:**1129–1130**
Tunneling (Internet security), 2:1154
Turnover ratio. *See* Sales to receivables ratio
Twisted wire pair networks, 2:696–697
2005 FBI Computer Crime Survey, 1:215
2005 National Business Ethics Survey, 1:119–120
2-2-2 rule, 2:943
Two-way interpersonal communication, 1:627–628
Typesetting, 1:315–316

U

U-shaped assembly lines, 1:59
UAW (United Automobile Workers), 2:662–663
UCC (Uniform Commercial Code), 2:989, **1133–1135**
UL Certified designation, 2:1133
UL Listed designation, 2:1133
UL Recognized designation, 2:1133
Uncertainty
    budgets and, 1:109
    business planning and, 1:137
    in decision support systems, 1:307–308
Uncontrollable costs, 1:261
Undercapitalization, 2:**1131–1132**
Underwriters Laboratories (UL), 2:**1132–1133**
Underwriting, on initial public offerings, 1:603
Unemployment
    of disabled people, 1:45
    Federal and state unemployment tax, 2:857
    in labor surplus areas, 2:661–662
    See also Layoffs, downsizing, and outsourcing
Unfair labor practices, 2:767
Uniform Commercial Code (UCC), 2:989, **1133–1135**
Uniform Franchise Offering Circular, 1:529

Uniform Partnership Act, 2:848–850
Uniform Product Liability Act, 2:895
Uniform Resource Locators (URLs), 1:616
Unilateral contracts, 1:238
Union membership, 1:415, 2:663, 667
Union presence, 2:664
Union stewards, 2:665
Unit-of-measure assumptions, 1:61
Unit-of-production depreciation, 1:315
Unit sales budgeting method, 1:19
United Automobile Workers (UAW), 2:662–663
United Kingdom
    baby bonds, 1:77–78
    empowerment zones, 1:434
    small business category, 2:1039
United Parcel Service (UPS), 1:311, 2:966
U.S. budget deficit, 1:106–107
U.S. budget surplus, 1:107
U.S. Census, 1:312
U.S. Computer Emergency Readiness Team (U-CERT), 1:217
U.S. Constitution, on copyright, 1:243
U.S. Postal Service (USPS), 1:311, 2:966
    See also Postal costs
U.S. Small Business Administration guaranteed loans, 2:**1136–1140**
U.S. top trading partners, 1:538
U.S. trade treaties, 1:540–541
U.S. Chamber of Commerce, 2:1135
U.S. Citizenship and Immigration Services (CIS), 1:404
U.S. Community Adjustment Investment Program (CAIP), 2:1042
U.S. Copyright Office, 1:243–247, 2:980
U.S. Corporate Income Tax Return. *See* Form 1120 (IRS); Form 1120A (IRS)
U.S. Department of Commerce, 2:**1135–1136**
U.S. Department of Homeland Security, 1:275, 276
U.S. Department of Housing and Urban Development (HUD), 1:434, 435
U.S. Department of Labor (DOL)
    on child care reform, 1:180
    COBRA revised rules, 1:224–225
    on employment of minors, 1:430–431

hiring practices evaluation, 1:30–31
on labor surplus areas, 2:662
on layoffs, 2:669
new exemptions regulations, 2:842
on part-time employees, 2:853–854
on wholesaling, 2:1161
U.S. Department of Transportation (DOT), 1:359, 2:1127
U.S. Export Assistance Centers (USEACs), 2:1043
U.S. Federal Reserve, 1:82, 611, 612
U.S. Immigration and Naturalization Service (INS), 1:39–40
See also U.S. Citizenship and Immigration Services (CIS)
Units. *See* Break-even quantity
Universal Copyright Convention, 1:246
Universal life insurance, 2:686
Universal Product Code (UPC). *See* Bar coding
University of Michigan Law School admissions policy, 1:32
Unlimited liability, 2:849
Unmoderated newsgroups, 2:776
Unqualified opinions (auditing), 1:507
Unreimbursed medical expense plans, 1:512
Unrelated business income, 2:791
Unsolicited e-mail. *See* Spam
Unstructured decisions, 1:306–307
UPC (Universal Product Code). *See* Bar coding
UPS (United Parcel Service), 1:311, 2:966
Urban revitalization and minority businesses, 2:747
URLs (Uniform Resource Locators), 1:616
Ury, William, 2:769–770
US-CERT (United States Computer Emergency Readiness Team), 1:217
Use it or lose it policy, 1:2
Use of premises (leasing), 2:674
USEACs (U.S. Export Assistance Centers), 2:1043
Usenet, 2:776
USPS (U.S. Postal Service), 1:311, 2:966
See also Postal costs
Utility cooperatives, 1:242
Utility patents, 1:633–634

V

Valid contracts, 1:237
Valuation, 2:**1141–1144**

of closely held corporations, 1:190–191
of common stock, 2:1069
mergers and acquisitions and, 2:739–740
of preferred stock, 2:1070
venture capital and, 2:1149
Value-added networks, 1:375
Value-added resellers, 1:346
Value-added tax, 2:**1144–1145**
Variable costs, 1:105, 106, 260
Variable expenses, 1:**510–511**
Variable life insurance, 2:861
Variable pay, 1:408, 2:**1145–1146**
Variable-rate interest, 1:612, 2:693, 1138
Variance, 2:**1146–1147**
Vehicle checks, employee screening and, 1:413
Vendor-managed inventory, 2:1162
Venture capital, 2:768, **1147–1150**
See also National Venture Capital Association (NVCA); Seed money
Venture capital firms, 1:457
Venture Capital Network database, 2:1151
Venture capital networks, 2:**1150–1151**
Venture capital proposals, 2:1148–1149
Vertical acquisitions, 2:739
Vertical integration, 1:350–351
Vertical marketing systems, 2:**1152**
Veterans' assistance, through SBA, 2:1044
Video advertising, 1:27–**28**
Virtual private networks, 2:**1152–1155**
Virus protection, 2:**1155–1156**
Viruses, 1:214, 620, 621, 2:**1155–1156**
Visual aids, for presentations, 1:643, 2:823–824
Void contracts, 1:237
Voidable contracts, 1:237
Voluntary liquidation, 2:690–691
Volunteers and volunteerism, 2:783–784, 786, 787, 1026

W

W-2 Form. *See* Form W-2 (IRS)
W-3 Form. *See* Form W-3 (IRS)
W-4 Form. *See* Form W-4 (IRS)
Wage-Hour Act (1938). *See* Fair Labor Standards Act (1938)
Wages. *See* Employee compensation

Wages by Area and Occupation Program, 1:388
Wagner Act (1935), 1:419, 582
Walsh-Healy Public Contracts Act (1936), 1:583
WANs (Wide area networks), 1:221, 2:**1163**
Ward, John L., 2:771
Wards Cove Packing Company v. Antonio (1989), 1:31
Warehouse databases, 1:293–294, 641
Warehouse operations, 1:641–642
Warehouse receipts, as collateral, 1:196
Warehouses (nodes), 2:866
Warranties, 2:**1157–1159**
Waste handling (green production), 1:550
Waste-to-energy conversion, 2:939
Water pollution. *See* Environmental law and business
Water transportation, 2:1126
Watson v. Fort Worth Bank and Trust (1988), 1:31
WBOC (Women Business Owners Corporation), 2:765
Web-based training, 2:1122
Web browser software, 1:85
Web consultants, 1:230
Web crawlers, 1:144, 355
Web site advertising, 1:24, 84–86
Web site design, 2:**1159–1161**
Web stocks, 1:95
Webb-Pomerene Export Trade Act (1918), 1:490
Weber, Max, 2:826
Weblogs. *See* Newsgroups and blogs
Welch, Jack, 1:100–101
Wellness programs. *See* Health promotion programs
Wheaton Glass Co., Schultz v. (1970), 1:534–535
Whole life insurance, 2:686, 794
Wholesale businesses site selection, 2:1036
Wholesaling, 2:**1161–1163**
Wide area networks (WANs), 1:221, 2:**1163**
Wiley Pure Food and Drug Act. *See* Federal Food and Drugs Act (1906)
Wills, 1:487
Wireless communications, 1:201, 2:696, 697
Withdrawal communication style, 1:628

WNET (Women's Network for Entrepreneurial Training), 2:1044, 1165

Women
businesses owned by, 2:746
equal pay for, 1:387
in nonprofit organizations, 2:784
pregnant employees, 2:871–873
as shoppers, 1:354
SBA business owner programs for, 2:1044

Women Business Owners Corporation (WBOC), 2:765

Women entrepreneurs, 2:**1164–1165**

Women's Demonstration Program, 2:1044

Women's Network for Entrepreneurial Training (WNET), 2:1044, 1165

Women's Prequalification Pilot Loan Program, 2:1164–1165

Wool Products Labeling Act (1939), 1:490

Work for hire, 1:245, 2:**1165–1166**

Work force reductions. *See* Layoffs, downsizing, and outsourcing

Work schedules for home-based businesses, 1:570–571

Work sharing, 1:515

Worker Economic Opportunity Act (1999), 2:843

Workers' compensation, 1:131, 331, 2:**1166–1168**

Workers' cooperatives, 1:242–243

Workforce expansion *vs.* overtime, 2:834

Working Capital Guarantee Program, 1:466

Workplace anger, 2:**1168–1171**
See also Workplace violence

Workplace privacy. *See* Employee privacy

Workplace safety, 2:**1171–1174**
See also Ergonomics; Office security

Workplace violence, 2:1173–1174, **1174–1176**

Workstations, 2:**1176–1178**
See also Ergonomics

The World Association of Women Entrepreneurs, 2:765

World Trade Organization (WTO), 1:540, 608

Worms (viruses), 1:214

Wright, J. Nevan, 2:925

Writing skills, need for, 1:199, 2:1178

Written communication, 1:199–200, 2:**1178–1179**

WTO (World Trade Organization), 1:540, 608

Y

Yellow Pages advertising, 1:26

Yield, of bonds, 1:99

Young Entrepreneurs' Organization (YEO), 2:**1181–1182**

Z

Zero-based budgeting, 1:109

Zoning ordinances, 1:567, 2:**1183–1184**
See also Relocation